A painting from the series A Tale of Pistils and Stamens by Franz Kupka; oil on canvas; 85×73cm (33×29in); 1919
Musée National d'Art Moderne, Paris (see page 869)

A HISTORY OF ART

General Editor

Sir Lawrence Gowing

Grange
BOOKS

Project Editor Valerie Mendes
Picture Research Christine Forth, Diana Morris,
    Jo Rapley
Additional Research Mel Cooper
Production Clive Sparling
Design Sarah Tyzack, Trevor Vincent
Art Editor Jerry Burman
Text Editors Robert Peberdy, Chris Murray
Index Sandra Raphael

AN ANDROMEDA BOOK

Planned and produced by
Andromeda Oxford Limited
11–13 The Vineyard, Abingdon
Oxfordshire, England OX14 3PX

Published by Grange Books
An Imprint of Grange Books PLC
Kingsnorth Industrial Estate
Hoo
Nr Rochester
Kent ME3 9ND

Revised edition published 1995, Reprinted 2000

ISBN 1-85627-758-5

Printed in Spain by BookPrint S.L., Barcelona

10 9 8 7 6 5 4 3 2

Andromeda wishes to thank the following individuals and institutions for their
help in the preparation of this work:

INDIVIDUALS: Margaret Amosu, Professor Manolis Andronikos, Janet
Backhouse, Claudia Bismarck, John Boardman, His Grace the Duke of
Buccleugh, Richard Calvocoressi, Lord Clark, Curt and Maria Clay, James
Collins, Bryan Cranstone, Mrs E.A. Cubitt, Mary Doherty, Judith Dronkhurst,
Rosemary Eakins, Mark Evans, Claude Fessaguet, Joel Fisher, Jean-Jacques
Gabas, Dr Oscar Ghez, Paul Goldman, G. St G.M. Gompertz, Zoë Goodwin,
Toni Greatrex, A.V. Griffiths, Victor Harris, Barbara Harvey, Maurice
Howard, A.D. Hyder, Jane Jakeman, Peg Katritzky, Moira Klingman, Andrew
Lawson, Betty Yao Lin, Christopher Lloyd, Jean Lodge, Richard Long, Lorna
McEchern, Eunice Martin, Shameem Melluish, Jennifer Montagu, Sir Henry
Moore, Richard Morphet, Elspeth O'Neill, Alan Peebles, Professor Dr Chr.
Pescheck, Pam Porter, Professor P.H. Pott, Alison Renney, Steve Richard,
Andrew Sherratt, Richard Shone, Lawrence Smith, Don Sparling, Graham and
Jennifer Speake, Annamaria Petrioli Tofani, Mary Tregear, the late Jim Tudge,
Betty Tyers, Ivan Vomáčka, Tom Wesselmann.

INSTITUTIONS: Ashmolean Museum, Oxford; Bibliothèque Nationale, Paris;
Bodleian Library, Oxford; British Library, London; British Museum, London;
Courtauld Institute of Art, London; Gulbenkian Foundation, Lisbon; Louvre,
Paris; Merseyside County Museums, Liverpool; Metropolitan Museum, New
York; Museum of Modern Art, New York; Museum of Modern Art, Oxford;
Oriental Institute, Oxford; Oxford City Library; Petit Palais, Geneva; Phaidon
Press, Oxford; Pitt Rivers Museum, Oxford; Sainsbury Centre for the Visual
Arts, Norwich; Sotheby Parke Bernet & Co., London; Tate Gallery, London;
Victoria and Albert Museum, London; Warburg Institute, London.

Andromeda wishes to thank the numerous individuals, agencies, museums,
galleries, and other institutions who kindly supplied the illustrations for this
book.

Andromeda also wishes to acknowledge the important contributions of Judith
Brundin, Ann Currah, Bernard Dod, Herman and Polly Friedhoff, the late
Juliet Grindle, Jonathan Lamède, Giles Lewis, Andrew McNeillie, Penelope
Marcus and Louise Pengelley.

Contents

A wooden Dan mask of the African Poro society; height 21cm (8in). Private collection (see page 514)

The structure of the elements of this volume is based on the belief that one of the best ways of learning about the origins and content of visual art is by changing the context within which art is seen, from general views to specific ones.

The chronological table on pages xiv–xv shows the temporal relationships between the cultures that have given the world its heritage of visual art. Within the bands denoting the activities of the major cultures smaller bands show important historical periods.

The arts of the cultures are treated at greater length in the 54 chapters that make up the major part of the volume. Each is the work of a specialist writer, but all have concerns in common—to show how art emerged within contexts molded by beliefs, aims, ideals, patronage, and more general social and economic factors. The major creative individuals are located similarly within the contexts of their times and their personal contacts.

Special features, of two kinds, set within the chapters at appropriate points, provide further shifts of outlook, narrowing and deepening the reader's attention.

"Gallery Studies" take a broader view, comparing and contrasting works of art to explore, for example, the variety of work created within a genre (e.g. Paleolithic Venuses, pp 6–7; Chinese Landscape Painting, pp 320–1; Romantic Landscape Painting, pp 748–9), the development of a genre as artists struggle to accommodate new influences within their own traditions (e.g. Mughal Painting, pp 262–3), or to show the social context within which works were created (e.g. the Impressionists' Paintings of La Grenouillère, pp 798–9).

In the "Close Studies" we are brought face to face with individual works, as varied as the Strettweg Cult-wagon (pp 90–1), Bernward's Column (pp 556–7), and Jackson Pollock's *Cathedral* (pp 926–7). Through them the reader can learn about the problems involved in trying to find the historical context of an undated work of art (e.g. The Gundestrup Caldron, pp 214–15; The Antioch Chalice, pp 364–5), about the conventions of a culture as witnessed in methods of composition (e.g. The Stela of Mentuhotep, pp 26–7), about the schemes of symbols to be found active within individual works (e.g. The Neak Pean Shrine, Angkor, pp 284–5; *Arnolfini Wedding* by Jan van Eyck, pp 666–7), and about how with a particular work an artist broke away from conventions, and established new ones (e.g. *Assumption of the Virgin* by Titian, pp 688–9; *Vision after the Sermon* by Gauguin, pp 810–11).

Technical matter in the contributions and captions has been edited according to the following conventions. Titles of works are given in English, except where a title in another language is more familiar. Wherever possible the locations of works are provided, by reference to the full name of an institution and to the town or city in which it stands. Names of institutions in English, French, German, and Italian are normally given in their original forms. Others have been translated except where an original name is familiar or because an idiomatic translation is not possible. The names of some major institutions have been abbreviated. A statement of location does not necessarily imply a statement about ownership.

The Bibliographies usually specify latest editions. Where possible, details of publication in both the United Kingdom and the United States of America are given.

In the captions dimensions are given in the order height × width (× depth in the case of sculpture). Measurements for most works are given to the nearest centimeter with, in parentheses, an imperial equivalent to the nearest inch. Where possible, the media of works are also given, but for many works, especially those from the period of European painting when tempera and oils were both in common use, media have not been specified in full because the binders and pigments of such works have not been analyzed.

R.P.

PREFACE

A team of authorities as distinguished as those whom I am privileged to introduce does not often come together to work on a book like this. The publishers and I felt proud to have them with us and now the book is finished our feeling seems justified.

In this connected *History of Art*, as one specialist after another takes up the more or less continuous story, even readers who already know something about a culture or period are likely to join the rest of us in discovering a little more. We find ourselves closer to actual objects—sometimes spotlit in special features—than most histories attempt to bring us. Yet reading the book, none of us doubts that what is of most value in its subject is precisely that which is in some sense unknowable, something beyond the reach of words, however well-informed and perceptive. The essence of art, which gives purpose to a survey like this, is notoriously variable. The altering character and changing focus, which makes art as elusive as it is entrancing, also makes it harder to read about sometimes than need be: we hope and believe that no more thoroughly approachable or more delightful history of art than this exists. Yet if the going is not uniformly easy, I counsel persistence, in the confidence that the rewards are certain. In one respect writers and readers are fortunate that the mental climate in which we write has peculiar advantages. We all mistrust generalization; the most significant thing we know about the faculty of art is that even in the most distant periods and places in this History, nothing human was foreign to it.

If we are discouraged to learn, what history teaches, that the essence which we extract from art is perennially the creation of the culture that extracts it— is in fact itself a part of history—we can take courage. Knowledge of art is without doubt not only a luxury, a self-indulgence, and an unfailing joy— though it is all these things—it is knowledge, and very likely our deepest, most unguarded knowledge, of humankind.

LAWRENCE GOWING
(1918–91)

◄ Apostles surrounding the Baptism of Christ, the dome of the Arian baptistery, Ravenna; c500 (see page 367)

DAWN ADES
Lecturer, Department of Art, University of Essex; author of *Dada and Surrealism*, etc

GEOFFREY ASHTON
Authority on Baroque and Rococo architecture

ROBIN BARBER
Head of Department of Classical Archaeology, University of Edinburgh

ELIZABETH P. BENSON
Former Curator of the Pre-Columbian art collection, Dumbarton Oaks Research Library and Collections, Washington, D.C.; author of *A Man and a Feline in Mochica Art*, *The Mochica: a Culture of Peru*, etc

A.D.H. BIVAR
Lecturer in Central Asian Art and Archaeology, School of Oriental and African Studies, London

ESMÉ BERMAN
Author of *Art and Artists of South Africa*, *The Story of South African Painting*, etc

JOHN BOARDMAN
Former Lincoln Professor of Classical Archaeology and Art, University of Oxford, and Curator of the Cast Gallery, Ashmolean Museum, Oxford; author of *Greek Art*, *The Greeks Overseas*, etc

ALAN BOWNESS
Director, Tate Gallery, London; author of *Modern European Art*, etc

ROBERT BRAIN
Author of *Friends and Lovers*, *The Tribal Impulse*, *The Decorated Body*, etc

ANTHONY CHRISTIE
Senior Lecturer in the Art and Archaeology of South East Asia, School of Oriental and African Studies, London; author of *Chinese Mythology*, etc

ROBERT JUDSON CLARK
Department of Art and Archaeology, University of Princeton

ROBIN CORMACK
Reader in the History of Art, Courtauld Institute of Art, London

ELIZABETH COWLING
Lecturer, Department of Fine Art, University of Edinburgh

FREDERICK J. DOCKSTADER
Author of *Indian Art in America*, *Indian Art in Middle America*, *South American Indian Art*, etc

DOROTHY DOWNES
Former Assistant Keeper, Merseyside County Museums, Liverpool

MARK EVANS
Assistant Keeper of Foreign Art, Walker Art Gallery, Liverpool

BRIONY FER
Lecturer in the History of Art, Open University

VALERIE FRASER
Lecturer, Department of Art, University of Essex

PETER GATHERCOLE
Curator, University Museum of Archaeology and Ethnology, Cambridge

JANE GEDDES
Inspector of Ancient Monuments, Ancient Monuments Division, Department of the Environment, London

BASIL GRAY
Former Keeper of Oriental Antiquities (retired), British Museum, London; editor of *The Arts of India*, etc

NICOLETTE GRAY
Author of *Lettering as Drawing*, etc

MICHAEL GREENHALGH
Senior Lecturer in the History of Art, University of Leicester; author of *The Classical Tradition in Art*, etc

ALASTAIR GRIEVE
Senior Lecturer, School of Fine Arts and Music, University of East Anglia

DOUGLAS HALL
Keeper of the Scottish National Gallery of Modern Art, Edinburgh; author of *Klee*, *Modigliani*, etc

MARTIN HENIG
Editor of *A Handbook of Roman Art*

T.A. HESLOP
Lecturer, School of Fine Arts and Music, University of East Anglia

JOHN HOUSE
Lecturer in the History of Art, Courtauld Institute of Art, London; author of *Monet*

MAURICE HOWARD
Lecturer in the History of Art, University of Sussex

PETER HUMPHREY
Lecturer in the History of Art, University of St Andrews

SAM HUNTER
Department of Art and Archaeology, University of Princeton; author of *American Art of the Twentieth Century*, etc

CHRISTOPHER JOHNSTONE
Curator of Education and Information, National Gallery of Scotland, Edinburgh; author of *John Martin*

HELEN LANGDON
Author of *The Mitchell Beazley Pocket Art Gallery Guide*, *Holbein*, and *Everyday Life Painting*

PETER LASKO
Director, Courtauld Institute of Art, London; author of *Ars Sacra 800–1200*, etc

NORBERT LYNTON
Emeritus Professor of History of Art, University of Sussex; author of *The Story of Modern Art*, etc

ELLEN MACNAMARA
Author of *Everyday Life of the Etruscans*

ANDREW MARTINDALE
Professor of Visual Arts, School of Fine Arts and Music, University of East Anglia; author of *Gothic Art*, *The Rise of the Artist in the Middle Ages and Early Renaissance*, etc

JOHN MILNER
Senior Lecturer, Department of Fine Art, University of Newcastle-upon-Tyne; author of *Symbolists and Decadents*

LYNNE MITCHELL
Research Student, Courtauld Institute of Art, London

PARTHA MITTER
Lecturer in South Asian History, University of Sussex; author of *Much Maligned Monsters: History of European Reactions to Indian Art*

E.J. PELTENBURG
Lecturer in Archaeology, Department of Extra Mural and Adult Education, University of Glasgow

†E.D. PHILLIPS
Formerly Professor of Greek, The Queen's University of Belfast

RONALD PICKVANCE
Richmond Professor of Fine Arts, Department of Fine Arts, University of Glasgow; author of *Degas '79*, etc

A.J.N.W. PRAG
Keeper of Archaeology, The Manchester Museum, University of Manchester

N.K. SANDARS
Author of *Prehistoric Art in Europe*, *The Sea Peoples*, etc

ANDREW SHERRATT
Assistant Keeper, Department of Antiquities, Ashmolean Museum, Oxford; editor of *The Cambridge Encyclopedia of Archaeology*

ANN SIEVEKING
Author of *The Cave Artists*, etc

LAWRENCE SMITH
Keeper of Oriental Antiquities, British Museum, London

JOHN STEER
Head of Department of History of Art, Birkbeck College, University of London; author of *A Concise History of Venetian Painting*, etc

SARAH SYMMONS
Lecturer, Department of Art, University of Essex; author of *Goya*

DANIEL THOMAS
Senior Curator of Australian Art, Australian National Gallery, Canberra

KATHRYN THOMPKINS
Lecturer in the School of Classical Studies, University of Manchester

MARY TREGEAR
Keeper of Eastern Art, Ashmolean Museum, Oxford; author of *Chinese Art*, etc

WILLIAM VAUGHAN
Reader in the History of Art, University College, London; author of *Romantic Art*, *German Romanticism and English Art*, etc

PETER VERGO
Lecturer, Department of Art, University of Essex; author of *Art in Vienna 1898–1918*, etc

NICHOLAS WADLEY
Head of Department of Art History and Complementary Studies, Chelsea School of Art, London; author of *Cubism*, *Cézanne and his Art*, etc

GEORGE ZARNECKI
Emeritus Professor of History of Art, Courtauld Institute of Art, London; author of *Romanesque Art*, *Studies in Romanesque Sculpture*, etc

CHRONOLOGY OF ART HISTORY

	30,000 BC	25,000 BC	20,000 BC
EUROPE		Upper Paleolithic	
ASIA			
AMERICA north			
south			
AFRICA			

Queen Mai, a detail of a relief in the tomb of the vizier Ramose at Thebes, Egypt; c1400 BC

Deidameia, from the Temple of Zeus at Olympia; mid 5th century BC. Archaeological Museum, Olympia

Christ, a detail of the relief *Christ in Majesty* attributed to Bernard Gilduin; late 11th century. St Sernin, Toulouse

A mask used in Japanese *No* drama. British Museum, London

	1000 BC	900	800	700	600	500	400	300	200	100	0	100	200
EUROPE				N. Italy Etruscan		Central Europe Celtic				Roman period			
		Greece Archaic				Gr. Classical							
						East Mediterranean Hellenistic							
ASIA Middle East/Iran									Parthian				
Eurasian Steppes							Steppe Animal style						
India													
China		Bronze							Han				
Japan				Preliterate									
AMERICA north													
south				Preclassic									

1 Western Europe Carolingian   2 Germany Ottonian   3 Mannerism   4 Rococo   5 Neoclassicism   6 Romanticism
7 Realism   8 Impressionism   9 Post-Impressionism   10 Symbolism and Art Nouveau   11 modern movements
12 Five dynasties   13 Westernized industrial culture

15,000 BC   10,000 BC   5,000 BC   0   AD 1000

Neolithic

Bronze and Iron

Aegean

Neolithic Iran   Neo. India

Neolithic China

Neolithic Japan

native arts

Preclassic

Ancient Egypt

Sahara Cattle period

A bronze head from the kingdom of Benin (Nigeria); 14th century. National Museum, Lagos

The head of the figure of *Dawn* by Michelangelo; c1526. New Sacristy, S. Lorenzo, Florence

A detail of a bust of *Madame de Sérilly* by Jean-Antoine Houdon; 1782. Wallace Collection, London

Head 1955 by William Turnbull; bronze. Collection of Mr D. Blinken, New York

400   500   600   700   800   900   1000   1100   1200   1300   1400   1500   1600   1700   1800   1900

Scandinavia Viking   Gothic outside Italy   3   8

Med. Early Christian   England Anglo-Saxon   Romanesque   Italian Renaissance   Baroque 4   5   9

1   2   Gothic Italy   N. Renaissance   6   10

East Mediterranean Byzantine   7

11

Sassanian   Islamic

Buddhist   Indo-Islamic   Mughal   Westernization

Hindu

Northern and Southern   Tang   12   Sung   Yuan   Ming   Ch'ing

Early Buddhist and Courtly Culture   Later Buddhist and Feudal Culture   Secular Urban Culture   13

native arts

Classic   Postclassic   Colonial   Postcolonial

PICTURE ACKNOWLEDGMENTS

Abrams Inc., New York: 925 (c ADAGP Paris and DACS London 1995). Acquavella Galleries Inc., New York: 853 (c DACS 1995). Akademische Druck-und Verlagsanstalt, Graz: 470t, 471tl, 471tr. Albright-Knox Art Gallery, Buffalo: 812. Alinari, Florence: 168 (photo Anderson), 198 (photo Anderson), 588, 631, 634tl, 639tl, 646, 649, 654, 687, 698t, 698b, 837bl. Andromeda Picture Archive: 125, 188tr, br and bl, 189tl, cr and br, 234r, 347, 634bl, 666, 666tl, 669, 670, 678l, 684, 686, 692b, 699, 706, 710, 711, 713, 714, 718, 752, 754, 761, 776r, 777, 779, 780, 781, 787, 788, 794,795, 799bl, 800, 809, 811, 823 (c The Munch Museum/The Munch-Ellingsen Group/DACS 1995), 836bl, 842br (c ADAGP Paris and DACS London 1995), 843tl, 844 (c DACS 1995), 845t and b, 849r (c DACS 1995), 849l (c ADAGP Paris and DACS London 1995), 859 (c ADAGP Paris and DACS London 1995), 862, 866 (c ADAGP Paris and DACS London 1995), 872c (c ADAGP Paris and DACS London 1995), 872bl (c ADAGP Paris and DACS London 1995), 873 (c ADAGP Paris and DACS London 1995), 879t (c ADAGP Paris and DACS London 1995), 880, 884t (c SPADEM/ADAGP Paris and DACS London 1995), 885b (c ADAGP Paris and DACS London 1995), 892bl, 893b and t, 939, 954t, 957b. Archaeological Museum, Madrid: 93br, 582. Architectural Association, London: 920b. Archives of American Art, Washington: 931t (c Estate of David Smith/DACS London/VAGA New York 1995). Art Gallery of New South Wales, Sydney: 964, 965, 967, 968. Art Institute of Chicago: 481bl, 485l, 803, 850. The Art Museum, Princeton University: 583tl (private collection). Arts Council of Great Britain, London: 931b (Professor W Rubin Collection, c Estate of David Smith/DACS London/VAGA New York 1995). Ashmolean Museum, Oxford: 11, 15bl, 16, 17bl, 28l, 34c, 35bl, 57r, 89, 177, 187, 193, 202, 209l and r, 219, 295, 297, 298l, 308, 311b, 329, 892. James Austin, Cambridge: 576tl and tr, 577t and b, 598l and r. Australian National Gallery, Canberra: 961, 962, 963, 966, 967, 968, 969. Barnaby's Picture Library, London: 530. Barnes Foundation, Merion, Pa.: 837br. Bauhaus Archive, Germany: 891l and r, 894. Bayerisches National Museum, Munich: 421. Bayerische Staatsbibliothek, Munich: 539r, 543r, 551bl, 553. Bibliotheque d'Assemble Nationale, Palais Bourbon, Paris: 472b. Bibliotheque Municipale, Dijon: 572 (photo Minirel Creation). Bibliotheque Nationale, Paris: 384l and r, 385l and r, 533, 536, 538bl and br, 543l, 606, 634tr, 741b. Bildarchiv Foto Marburg: 535, 540, 547, 556t, 556bl and br, 557l, 559, 566b, 576bl, 583b, 599tr and br, 602, 727l. Bildarchiv Preussischer Kulturbesitz, Germany: 51t and b, 200b, 216b, 481br, 482b, 537, 616b, 635tc, 689tr. A D H Bivar, London: 223b. Bodleian Library, Oxford: 256, 395l, 538tr. Lee Boltin, New York: 232b, 234l. Boymans-van Beuningen Museum, Rotterdam: 824 (Michael Perinet Collection, Paris). Bridgeman Art Library, London: 237, 267b, 423, 624, 824tr, 833 (c DACS London 1995), 836–7 (c DACS London 1995). British Library, London: 263r, 271, 394l, 402, 403, 405, 410br and tr, 411tl, 411br and bl, 412, 413, 454, 608tr, 608bl and br, 609bl, 609tl and tr. British Museum, London: 5, 21, 40, 48, 60c, 61t and br, 67, 69, 73b, 118, 144bl and br, 146t, 147t, 149, 158, 185tr, 186, 211, 217t, 224tl, 225tl, 227b, 229, 269, 298b, 333, 345, 350t and b, 353, 354, 399, 401, 450, 471b, 510, 526, 655, 672, 748tr. The Duke of Buccleugh: 461c (photo Beedle & Cooper). Bulloz, Paris: 720. Burrell Collection, Glasgow: 792b, 796. Caisse Nationale des Monuments Historiques et des Sites, Paris: 1, 595b. Capilla Real, Granada: 669. Leo Castelli Gallery, New York: 934 (Mr and Mrs Leo Castelli Collection c Jasper Johns/DACS London/VAGA New York 1995), 935 (Mr and Mrs Leo Castelli Collection c Robert Rauschenberg/DACS London/VAGA New York 1995), 937. Castle Museum, Nottingham: 731. Central Museum, Northampton: 28r. Centre National d'Art et de Culture Georges Pompidou, Paris: 863t (Nina Kandinsky Collection, c ADAGP Paris and DACS London 1995), 863b (c ADAGP Paris and DACS London 1995). Chartreuse de Champmol, Dijon: 617. Anthony Christie, London: 284tl and bl, 289. City and County Museum, Kingston-upon-Hull: 87r. City Museum, Bristol: 511br. Cleveland Museum of Art, Ohio: 225r (Leonard C Hanna Jr. bequest), 317 (John L Severance Fund), 351 (John L Severance Fund), 360 (John L Severance Fund). Collections Baur, Geneva: 310br (photo P A Ferrazzini). Elizabeth Cowling, Edinburgh: 885tl. Corpus Christi College Library, Cambridge: 571. Courtauld Institute, London: 735 (Witt Library). Cyprus Museum, Nicosia: 81b. Dallas Museum of Fine Arts: 926, 927. Dominique Darr, Paris: 908, 912. Percival David Foundation of Chinese Art, London University: 310t and bl, 311t, 312, 324. Dayton Art Institute: 480bl. Dean and Chapter, Durham Cathedral: 410l. Dean and Chapter, Westminster Abbey: 607. Delaware Art Museum, Wilmington: 784. Department of the Environment, London: 207bl. Des Moines Art Center, Iowa: 930r (gift of the Gardener Cowles Foundation in memory of Mrs Florence Call Cowles, c Estate of David Smith/DACS London/VAGA New York 1995). Deutsche Fotothek, Dresden: 725. Deutsches Archaologisches Institut, Athens: 115. Deutsches Archaologisches Institut, Rome: 192. Douglas Dickins, London: 244, 246, 248, 252br, 253t, 255, 259, 267t, 275, 291t and b, 346t, 348l, 485r. Domschatz- kammer, Aachen: 551t; (photo Ann Munchow) Domschatzkammer, Cologne: 394tr. Domschatzkammer, Essen: 55r, 558. Dumbarton Oaks Research Library and Collection, Washington: 365tl, 479. Ecole Francaise d'Extreme Orient, Paris: 284br, 285, 286, 287. Egyptian Expedition, Metropolitan Museum, New York: 34t, 35tl. Ekdotike Athenon, Athens: 13, 97, 99, 100tr and br, 101bl, 103, 105, 106t, cl, cr and b, 107tr, cr and bl, 108, 109, 110, 131, 138r, 139, 146b, 157r, 159, 162, 163t, 194. Elsevier, Amsterdam: 102b. Ethnographic Museum, Leiden: 281l, 293. Mary Evans Picture Library, London: 774. Fitzwilliam Museum, Cambridge: 748br. William Hayes Fogg Art Museum, Cambridge, Mass.: 262br, 814, 824br. Werner Forman Archive, London: 39b, 44tr, 86, 232t, 247, 277, 279, 281r, 303, 415, 417, 418br and bl, 419br and b, 467, 476, 487, 488, 490l and r, 492, 494, 495, 498, 501tl, 503, 505, 506, 507, 509, 512, 513, 514, 516, 517, 524, 852br and tr. Fotostudio Otto, Vienna: 17tr, 215br. Fototeca Internacional, Madrid: 668. Alain Fournier, Paris: 9b and t. Alison Frantz, Princeton, NJ; 134, 135. Freer Gallery of Art, Smithsonian Institution, Washington: 266r, 300t and br, 301, 430, 448, 821. M Gimbutas, Los Angeles: 14tr and bl, 15br. Giraudon, Paris: 6bc, 53, 70, 77, 81t, 550l, 601, 671, 739, 856 (c DACS 1995). G St G M Gompertz, Reading: 309 (photo E Hare). Basil Gray, Abingdon: 457. Nicolette Gray, Abingdon: 443, 446bl, 447tr, 452.The Green Studio, Dublin: 393b, 396. Gulbenkian Foundation, Lisbon: 760. Egon Guenther Gallery, Johannesburg: 975. Solomon R Guggenheim Museum, New York: 865 (c ADAGP Paris and DACS London 1995), 873b (c ADAGP Paris and DACS London 1995), 945 (c ADAGP Paris and DACS London 1995). Haags Gemeentesmuseum, The Hague: 875. Sonia Halliday Photographs, Weston Turville: 373, 375, 376, 378, 379l, 381, 56, 458, 561, 585, 590, 591. Hamburger Kunsthalle, Hamburg: 783. Hannibal, Athens: 131b. Robert Harding Picture Library, London: 44br, 56, 95 (photo Harissiadis/Rainbird), 100tl and bl, 101tr, 104b (photo Harissiadis/Rainbird), 335, 380, 389, 432, 437, 439, 442, 463, 493, 496, 501tr, 504, 675. D Harissiadis, Athens: 101tl. G Herrmann, Oxford: 223t. Lucien Herve, Paris: 896, 897, 898t and b. Hessische Landes-und Hochschulbibliothek, Darmstadt: 548, 549. A A M Van der Heyden, Amsterdam: 23t, 45, 477. G F Hill *A Corpus of Italian Medals of the Renaissance before Cellini*, London, 1930, vol 1: 626 (photo J R Freeman). John Hillelson, London: 50 (photo Brian Brake). Hirmer Fotoarchiv, Munich: 17br, 33, 42, 43, 59l, 60bl, 62, 63l and r, 72, 73t, 75, 102t, 104t, 111, 113, 129t and b, 136t, 143br, tr, bl, cr and tl, 152, 172r, 173t, 359, 361, 362, 366, 369, 372, 375b, 382l. Joseph Hirschhorn Museum, Washington: 923, 929. Michael Holford, Essex: 4, 36r, 39t, 44tl, 59r, 60tl, 132t and b, 175, 201br, 339, 474, 515, 566, 579, 587, 736tr, 811tr (c DACS 1995). Holle Verlag, Baden-Baden: 7tc, 23b, 61, 116, 233, 235, 345t, 354, 440, 483, 583t, 630b, 717, 726bl, 772, 901t. Honolulu Academy of Arts: 327. Angelo Hornak, London: 427, 431, 434. Hutchison Library, London: 518–9. Jacqueline Hyde, Paris: 852bl. India Office Library, London: 240, 258.Iran Bastan Museum, Tehran: 222. Iraq Museum, Baghdad: 221l. Isle of Man Museum, Douglas: 420. Johannesburg Art Gallery: 973. Judges Limited, Sussex: 208, 406. Jusautor, Sofia: 14 (except sculpture), 15t. Kaiser Wilhelm Museum, Krefeld: 951r (c ADAGP Paris and DACS London 1995). Keir Collection, Surrey: 460b (phoo A C Cooper). A F Kersting, London: 407, 408, 595t, 597b, 723, 724, 726br, 727r, 740, 741t, 767. Kroller-Muller Museum, Otterlo: 815, 822, 824tl, 827 (c DACS 1995). Kunstmuseum, Dusseldorf: 861 (c ADAGP Paris and DACS London 1995). Kunstsammlung Nordrhein-Westfalen, Dusseldorf: 838 (c ADAGP Paris and DACS London 1995), 839 (c DACS 1995), 854 (c ADAGP Paris and DACS London 1995). Landesmuseum Joanneum, Graz, Abteilung fur Vorund Fruhgeschichte im Schloss Eggenberg: 90tr, br and l, 91t (all photo Hoftstetter-Dia). Andrew Lawson, Oxford/Dr J Waechter: 3, 7tl and br. Lehtikuva Oy, Helsinki: 889 (photo Ensio Ilmonen), 902 (photo Ensio Ilmonen). Library of Congress, Washington: 907, 909. Lucy Lim, New York: 299. Linden-Museum, Stuttgart: 480 (photo Ursula Didoni), 511tr. Lesley A Ling, Stockport: 136b. Los Angeles County Museum of Art: 866b, 915. Mansell Collection, London: 382r (photo Alinari), 557r, 626tl (photo Anderson), 733. J H Marshall, *Monuments of Sanchi*, Calcutta 1913–4, vol ll: 242, 243 (all photo E Hare). Pierre Matisse Gallery, New York: 952 (c ADAGP Paris and DACS London 1995). Leonard von Matt, Buochs: 172l, 189bl, 203, 564, 574, 578. MEPhA, London: 426, 428, 429, 446tr and br, 447br and bl. Merseyside County Museums, Liverpool: 26, 27, 29r, 32l and r, 34b (on loan from School of Archaeology and Oriental Studies, Liverpool University), 36l, 38, 41 542. Metropolitan Museum, New York: 44bl, 46 (gift of Edward S Harkness), 117 (gift J Pierpont Morgan), 121 (Fletcher Fund), 126tl and tr, 127t, 127bl (bequest of Joseph H Durkee, gift of Darius Ogden Mills and C Ruxton Love, by exchange), 181 (Rogers Fund), 224br (Fletcher Fund), 226, 263l (Kevorkian Foundation supplementing the Rogers Fund), 364 (Cloisters Collection), 365br, 365bl (Fletcher Fund), 462, 481r (gift of Nathan Cummings), 482t (gift of Mrs Harold L Bache), 554 (gift of George Blumenthal), 662 (Cloisters Collection), 715, 793, 799tl, 805, 919b, 924 (on loan from the Art Commission of the City of New York c Estate of Stuart Davis/DACS London, VAGA New York 1995). Minneapolis Institute of Arts: 215tr, 736tl (William Hood Dunwoody Fund), 807. Partha Mitter, Brighton: 274t. Modern Museum (National Museum), Stockholm: 874r, 881 (c DACS 1995), 950 (c ADAGP Paris and DACS London 1995). Henry Moore Foundation, Much Hadham: 941. Moravian Museum, Brno: 7bc. Julian Munby, Oxford: 204. Musee Borely, Marseilles: 217b. Musee Cernuschi, Paris: 300l (photo Luc Joubert). Musee de l'Ecole de Nancy, Nancy: 829 (photo Gilbert Mangin). Musee de l'Homme, Paris: 529, 852tl. Musee de Peinture et de Sculpture, Grenoble: 837tl (photo Ifot). Musee des Arts Decoratifs, Paris: 227t. Musee d'Unterlinden, Colmar: 673. Musee Fabre, Montpellier: 769, 774r, 775b (all photo Studio O'Sughrue). Musee Gustav Moreau, Paris: 817, 825l. Musee Jacquemart-Andre, Paris: 661. Musee Nationale d'Art Moderne, Paris: 867 (c ADAGP/SPADEM Paris and DACS London 1995), 869 (c ADAGP Paris and DACS London 1995), 870t (c ADAGP Paris and DACS London 1995), 872tr (c ADAGP Paris and DACS London 1995), 872br (c ADAGP Paris and DACS London 1995), 886r (c DACS 1995), 943 (c ADAGP Paris and DACS London 1995). Musee National du Bardo, Tunis: 157l. Museum der Bildenden Kunste, Leipzig: 825r. Museum of Fine Arts, Boston: 128t, 776l. Museum fur Ostasiatische Kunst, Cologne: 353. Museum of Far Eastern Antiquities, Stockholm: 300tr. Museum of Fine Arts, Ghent: 756. Museum of Modern Art, New York: 84l, 847 (c DACS 1995), 868, 870b, 883 (c SPADEM/ADAGP Paris and DACS London 1995), 884b (c ADAGP Paris and DACS London 1995), 886l (c ADAGP Paris and DACS London 1995), 919t (c Man Ray Trust/ADAGP PAris and DACS London 1995), 922, 951l (c ADAGP Paris and DACS London 1995), 957t. Museum Volkwang, Essen: 795. National Anthropology Museum, Mexico City: 475. National Gallery, London: 652bl, 656bl, 667, 695, 701, 711t, 748bl, 758, 763, 791, 798, 814l. National Gallery of Scotland, Edinburgh: 810, 811tl. National Gallery of Victoria, Melbourne: 954b. National Gallery of Art, Washington: 828 (Chester Dale Collection). National Museum, Copenhagen: 83, 185br, 214br, bl and t, 215bl. National Museum, Dublin: 87l, 391, 393t. National Museum, Lagos: 511tl. National Museum of Korea, Seoul: 305t, 324l. National Museum, Stockholm: 799tr. National Palace Museum, Taipei: 307, 313b, 314, 315, 316, 318, 320r and l, 321l, 323, 330. National Portrait Gallery, London: 461tl. The National Trust, London: 461b. Naturhistorisches Museum, Vienna: 6tr, 85. William Rockhill Nelson Gallery of Art, Kansas City: 305b, 313. Neue Pinakothek, Munich: 819. Ny Carlsberg Glyptothek, Copenhagen: 201bl. Offentliche Kunstsammlung, Kunstsmuseum Basel: 849l. Oriental Institute, University of Chicago: 78. Osterreichische Gallerie, Vienna: 845t. Osterreichische Nationalbibliothek, Vienna: 451 (photo Lichtbildwerkstatte "Alpenland"). Pace Gallery, New York: 933. E J Peltenburg, Edinburgh: 80. C Pescheck, Munich: 91b. Philadelphia Museum of Art: 851 (c DACS 1995). Photoresources, Dover: 93bl, 233b, 274b. Pierpont Morgan Library, New York: 538tl, 539l, 573. Pitt Rivers Museum, Oxford: 521, 527, 528t and b, 531. Josephine Powell, Rome: 231, 371, 383, 388. Pretoria Art Museum: 971, 974. Mauro Pucciarelli, Rome: 122, 124, 147b, 165, 169, 170, 196, 201tl, 635bl. Quiriconi-Tropea, Chicago: 877 (ADAGP/SPADEM Paris and DACS London 1995), 879b (c Man Ray Trust/ADAGP Paris and DACS London 1995), 938 (c Richard Estes/DACS London/VAGA New York 1995). Rapho, Paris: 708, 709. Rheinisches Landesmuseum, Bonn: 216. D Rice, Oxford: 343. F Robicsek, Charlotte, NC.: 473. Roger-Viollet, Paris: 719, 712t and b, 726tr. Romermuseum, Augst: 205 (photo: T. Schneider). Romer-Pelizaeus Museum, Hildesheim: 241. Royal Academy of Art, London: 785. Royal Commission on Historic Monuments (England), London: 206b, 207t, 743. Royal Library, Stockholm: 395r. Royal Ontario Museum, Toronto: 465. Royal Scottish Museum, Edinburgh: 200t, 511bl. John Rylands Library, Manchester: 639br. Scala, Florence: 35tr and br, 47, 57l, 58, 60br, 64, 88l, 123, 131t, 151, 163b, 171, 173b, 174b, 182t and b, 184, 190, 191, 199, 206t, 207br, 221l, 357, 363, 367, 387, 565, 566t, 568, 569, 570, 594, 597t, 599bl, 604, 605, 611, 612, 613, 614, 621, 622, 623, 625, 626br, 627t, 629, 630t, 632, 634br and bl, 635tr and br, 636, 638, 641, 643, 644, 645, 647, 648, 650t and b, 652tr, 657, 659, 664, 665, 677, 678r, 682, 684l, 685, 688t and b, 689l and br, 690, 691, 692t, 693, 697, 700, 702, 703l and t, 705, 826, 857. Schloss Charlottenburg, Berlin: 761. R V Schoder, Chicago: 119r, 137, 144l. Murray Schoonraad, Pretoria: 972. Scottish National Gallery of Modern Art, Edinburgh: 944 (c ADAGP Paris and DACS London 1995). Service de Documentation de la Reunion des Musees Nationaux, Paris: 30, 49, 61bl and c, 66, 71, 126br, 128b, 555l, 635tl and cl, 736bl, 737, 742, 745, 747, 749b, 755, 757, 766t and b, 775t, 789, 790, 792t, 836. Ronald Sheridan, Middlesex: 101c, 107tl. R W Skelton, Surrey: 264, 266l. Ya I Smirnov, *Vostochne Serebro*, St Petersburg, 1909: 224bl, 225bl (both photo E Hare). Olive Smith, Saffron Walden: (photo Edwin Smith): 88r. Sotheby Parke Bernet and Co., London: 205. Staatliche Antikensammlungen und Glyptothek, Munich: 119l (photo Kruger Moessner), 138l (photo Studio Kopperman), 140 (photo C Moessner. Staatsbib- liothek, Bamberg: 552. Staatliche Museen zu Berlin: 154, 155, 156. Staats- galerie, Stuttgart: 874l. Stadelsches Kunstsinstitut, Frankfurt: 615. Stadtbibliothek, Trier: 550t, 551br and tr (all photo Tomassin). Stadtische Galerie im Lenbachhaus, Munich: 842bl (c ADAGP Paris and DACS London 1995), 842tr (c ADAGP Paris and DACS London 1995). Stadtische Kunsthalle, Mannheim: 844. State Art Museum, Copenhagen: 653tr, 836br. State Historical Museum, Stockholm: 92. Stedelijk Museum, Amsterdam: 871. Sterling and Francine Clark Art Institute, Williamstown: 262t. Andrew and Marilyn Strathern, Cambridge: 523. Tate Gallery, London: 748tl, 749t, 751, 764, 835 (c ADAGP Paris and DACS London 1995), 930l (c Estate of David Smith/DACS London/VAGA New York 1995), 932 (c ARS New York and DACS London 1995), 946t and b, 953 (c Richard Hamilton 1995 All rights reserved DACS), 955, 958t and b. E Teitelman, Camdn, NJ: 900, 901r, 920t, 921tr, br and l. Telegraph Colour Library, London: 252bl, 253b, 501b. Textile Museum, Washington (Mr and Mrs Marshall Wolf Collection): 461tr, 484. Tokugawa Reimikai Foundation, Tokyo: 343. Topham Picturepoint, Kent: 8t, 65, 167. Trinity College, Cambridge: 411tr. Trinity College, Dublin: 397. Estate of Spyros Tsardavoglou, Athens: 160, 161. Universitatsbibliothek, Wurzburg: 556cb. University Library, Utrecht: 541r. University Museum of Northern Antiquities, Oslo: 418tl, 419tl and tr. University Museum, University of Pennsylvania, Philadelphia: 480br. University of California Art Museum, Berkeley: 949. Vautier Phototheque, Paris: 282t and b, 288, 337, 340, 341, 346b, 905, 911t, 913l. Jean Vertut, Issy-les-Moulineaux: 6bl, 7tr, 8b. Victoria and Albert Museum, London: 260, 261, 268, 272, 460, 765. Edoardo Villa: 975. Walker Art Center, Minneapolis: 936. Walker Art Gallery, Liverpool: 956. Wallace Collection, London: 652tl, 653br, b and c. Walters Art Gallery, Baltimore: 262bl, 365cl. Warburg Institute, University of London: 404. Weltliche und Geistliche Schatzkammer, Vienna: 545. Wan-go H C Weng, Lyme, NH.: 321r. Whitney Museum of American Art, New York: 917. Whitworth Gallery, Manchester: 948 (c ADAGP Paris and DACS London 1995). Robert Wilkins, Oxford: 120, 142tl, cl, br, cr and bl. Roger Wood, Kent: 19, 24r, 25. Wurttembergisches Landesmuseum, Stuttgart: 213. Yale University Art Gallery, New Haven: 221r. Zaucho Press, Tokyo: 326, 349, 355. Zefa Picture Library, London: 31, 599tl, 728, 729, 913r. B E H Zimmerman *Vorkarolingische Miniaturen* Berlin, 1916: 394br (photo John Webb).

Private Collections: 843 (ADAGP Paris and DACS London 1995), 855tr (c ADAGP Paris and DACS London 1995), 887 (c ADAGP Paris and DACS London 1995)

Works by the following artists are still in copyright:

Joseph Albers, Alexander Archipenko, Augustin Arman, Kenneth Armitage, Keith Arnatt, Conrad Atkinson, Frank Auerbach, Francis Bacon, Giacomo Balla, Ernst Barlach, George Bellows, Charles Biederman, Peter Blake, David Bomberg, Fernando Botero, Edward Burra, Alberto Burri, Reg Butler, Anthony Caro, Lynn Chadwick, Christo, Bernard Cohen, James Collins, Stuart Davis, Charles Demuth, Robyn Denny, Jim Dine, Otto Dix, Jacob Epstein, Richard Estes, Alexander Exter, Michael ffolkes, Dan Flavin, Sam Francis, Helen Frankenthaler, Roger Fry, Naum Gabo, Eric Gill, Fritz Glarner, Arshile Gorky, Adolf Gottlieb, Duncan Grant, Walter Gropius, Philip Guston, Richard Hamilton, Duane Hanson, Barbara Hepworth, Patrick Heron, Roger Hilton, Ivon Hitchens, David Hockney, Hans Hofmann, Edward Hopper, John Hoyland, Robert Indiana, Augustus John, Jasper Johns, Allen Jones, Donald Judd, Ellsworth Kelly, Philip King, Ernst Ludwig Kirchner, R B Kitaj, Franz Kline, Willem de Kooning, Gaston Lachaise, Peter Lanyon, John Latham, Wilhelm Lehmbruck, Wyndham Lewis, Sol Le Witt, Max Liebermann, Richard Lindner, Jakoff Lipchitz, El Lissitzky, Richard Long, Morris Louis, L S Lowry, Stanton Macdonald-Wright, F E McWilliam, Kasimir Malevich, Marino Marini, Kenneth Martin, Laszlo Moholy-Nagy, Henry Moore, Giorgio Morandi, Robert Motherwell, Edvard Munch, Elie Nadelman, Louise Nevelson, Barnett Newman, Ben Nicholson, Isamu Noguchi, Sidney Nolan, Georgia O'Keeffe, Claes Oldenburg, Orozco, Eduardo Paolozzi, Victor Pasmore, Tom Phillips, Jackson Pollock, Jose Posada, Maurice Prendergast, Ceri Richards, Bridget Riley, Diego Rivera, Alexander Rodchenko, Mies van der Rohe, Mark Rothko, Oskar Schlemmer, Charles Sheeler, Walter Sickert, Matthew Smith, Richard Smith, Tony Smith, Robert Smithson, Stanley Spencer, Philip Wilson Steer, Saul Steinberg, Frank Stella, Clyfford Still, Vladimir Tatlin, Pavel Tchelitchew, Jean Tinguely, Carl Tubby, William Turnbull, Frank Lloyd Wright, Andrew Wyeth, Jack Yeats

PALEOLITHIC ART

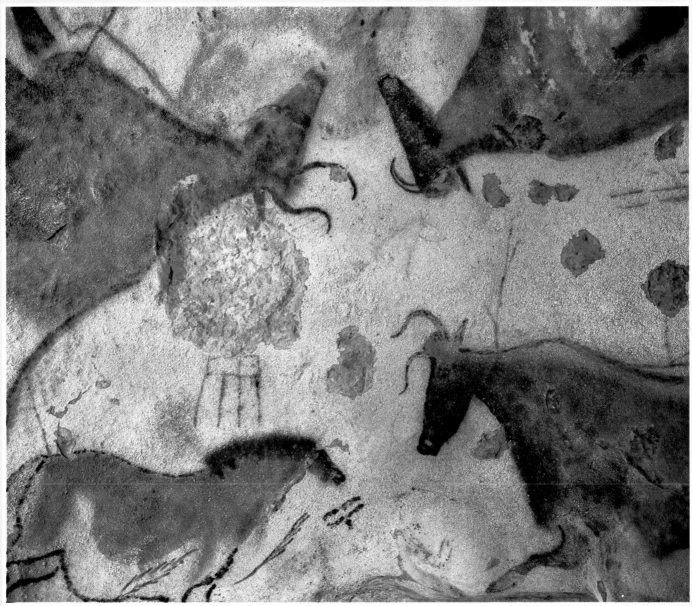

A horse and three cows painted on a gallery ceiling at Lascaux; the total length
of the figure at bottom right is 200cm (79in) (see page 8)

PALEOLITHIC is the name given to that period of man's history before he invented agriculture, domesticated animals, or discovered the use of metals. For his subsistence he depended on hunting and gathering, a way of life that sufficed for more than two million years. Art, however, had not so long a development, and is known only from the latest, or Upper, stage of the Paleolithic, a period we recognize by technological changes in bone- and flint-tool production that took place *c*40,000 years ago.

Such art as remains from this period is of two forms: either small objects found among the debris left by Paleolithic hunters in their camps, or murals in rock-shelters and deep caves. The first group is described in French as *Art Mobilier* and both the terms "mobiliary" and "portable" are used in English, but "miniature art" is a preferable description. The size of these pieces is a clear reflection of the nomadic economy of their makers, for to a nomad all sizable possessions are a burden.

Miniature art consists of three-dimensional figurines of animals and women, of pieces of bone, ivory, or stone with naturalistic or schematic engravings cut upon them, and a number of carefully ornamented tools. Obviously only objects made of the most durable materials have lasted: originally

there were perhaps many decorated objects made of wood or leather, but they have not survived.

Mural art is represented in daylit rock-shelters by low-relief carving and, in some cases, engraving, and in more sheltered deep caves by engraving and painting. The pigments used are manganese, carbon, and ochers with a color range of black, red, brown, yellow, and, very rarely, purple. Both naturalistic and schematic motifs are used in mural art, the naturalistic consisting almost exclusively of animals, principally the large herbivores such as horses, bison, and mammoths, and the schematic element of signs. Much of the painting is beautiful and highly accomplished. In 1995 a new cave complex, decorated with sensational mural art, was discovered at Vallon-Pont-d'Arc in the Ardèche, France.

Paleolithic art has a time span of more than 20,000 years, lasting from approximately 30,000 to 9,500 years ago. The first datable art objects that we have are ascribed to the Aurignacian Culture (an early geographical variant within the Upper Paleolithic) and were found at Vogelherd, in Germany, in a level dated to more than 30,000 years BC. One of the characteristics of Paleolithic art is its homogeneity and its adherence to formulas. The drawings in caves, for example,

Distribution map of main Paleolithic art sites in Western and Central Europe

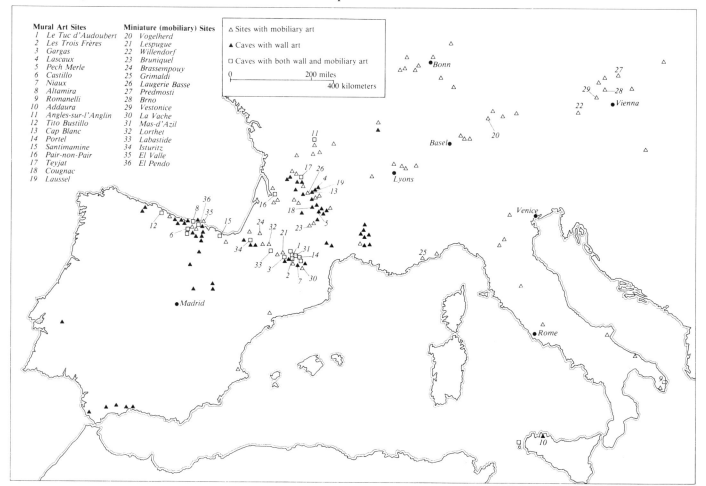

Mural Art Sites	Miniature (mobiliary) Sites
1 Le Tuc d'Audoubert	20 Vogelherd
2 Les Trois Frères	21 Lespugue
3 Gargas	22 Willendorf
4 Lascaux	23 Bruniquel
5 Pech Merle	24 Brassempouy
6 Castillo	25 Grimaldi
7 Niaux	26 Laugerie Basse
8 Altamira	27 Predmosti
9 Romanelli	28 Brno
10 Addaura	29 Vestonice
11 Angles-sur-l'Anglin	30 La Vache
12 Tito Bustillo	31 Mas-d'Azil
13 Cap Blanc	32 Lorthet
14 Portel	33 Labastide
15 Santimamine	34 Isturitz
16 Pair-non-Pair	35 El Valle
17 Teyjat	36 El Pendo
18 Cougnac	
19 Laussel	

△ Sites with mobiliary art

▲ Caves with wall art

□ Caves with both wall and mobiliary art

0   200 miles

400 kilometers

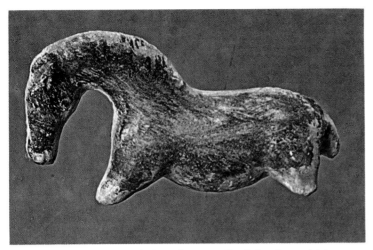

A small ivory carving of a horse from Vogelherd; length 5cm (2in)

subscribe to a particular inventory and this persisted with little change throughout the period in which caves were decorated. Such continuity over so great a period of time is unique in the history of art and the only explanation for it is that it reflects the social stability we postulate for its creators.

Beyond the fact that they were all members of the genus *Homo sapiens* (that is, modern man) we do not know who these men were and so in the absence of almost any skeletal material are forced to group them by their tool types. Equally, it is virtually impossible to identify the artists, although we could speak of "the Painter of the Altamira ceiling" and we can recognize certain objects as made by the same hand (two spear-throwers, for example, from Bruniquel in the Tarn-et-Garonne and Laugerie Basse in the Dordogne, France). It is quite probable, however, that each, or many, Upper Paleolithic tribes supported a specialist. Australian Aborigines living in a much poorer environment than prevailed in the Upper Paleolithic are known to have had enough surplus to support one man whose only occupation was making and repairing their tools. On this analogy an Upper Paleolithic group could have supported a tool-maker and decorator, whose work perhaps included painting a nearby cave or carving the rock-shelter wall.

Paleolithic art is in itself the beginning of art, although the earliest surviving pieces are not necessarily man's first artistic efforts. The Vogelherd figures, for example, are already so accomplished that we should perhaps regard them as the earliest surviving objects made of durable material, in this case mammoth ivory, which were originally preceded by an experimental series in wood. Within the span of 20,000 years all techniques are found at all periods, that is, sculpture does not precede two-dimensional work, nor engraving painting. In western Europe the latest periods are the richest, however, principally those that are associated with the middle and late stages of the Magdalenian (another industrial variant of the Upper Paleolithic, taking its name, as do the majority of these designations, from a type site in France). As it has no precursors, so Paleolithic art has no direct descendants—the Mesolithic cultures that followed the Paleolithic in Europe produced little art and that of a simple and rudimentary type. With the exception of the narrative rock-shelter painting of the Spanish Levant, which has only tentative links with

Paleolithic art, the naturalistic tradition died out completely at the end of the last Ice Age.

As the content of Paleolithic art is constant, so its distribution is limited. It is confined to the northern hemisphere of the Old World and to certain regions within this area, although the products of Upper Paleolithic industries with which it is associated have a much wider distribution. Miniature art is found in Spain, principally in the Cantabric region; in France, principally in Aquitaine and the Pyrenees; in Italy; in central and eastern Europe in the Ukraine and the Don Valley; and in Siberia, near Lake Baikal. Culturally this distribution forms two major groups: the western group including Spain, France, and Switzerland; the eastern, Italy, central Europe, European Russia, and Siberia. The arts of these two groups show great similarity, their principal difference being that in the East art is only known in its miniature form and is mainly three dimensional, while in the West the existence of mural art strengthens the two-dimensional factor, and enriches the total.

Mural art, by its nature, demands a location in caves or rock-shelters, but in fact the occurrence of karst formation limestone does not determine the distribution of this art form, which is concentrated in the Dordogne, the French Pyrenees, and the Basque provinces of Spain. Suitable caves exist elsewhere, in Moravia for example, but with the exception of Krapova in the Urals no painting is known outside France and Spain and very little engraving. There is a group of engraved caves in South Italy and Sicily, the most famous being the Grotta Romanelli near Otranto and Addaura near Palermo, but in style they are closer to the eastern cultural group than to the western. That the earliest examples of art, either miniature or mural, are widely scattered gives further support to the idea, put forward above, that the earliest pieces of art we have do not represent the first made.

The first pieces of Paleolithic art to be recognized as such were excavated in France in the middle years of the 19th century. After Darwin had established the antiquity of man, the search for human remains moved from the gravel pits of the Somme to the rock-shelters of the Perigord, rich in Upper Paleolithic deposits. By 1878 enough miniature art pieces had been retrieved to fill a case at the Exposition Universelle in Paris: they attracted great interest. In the 1890s Piette and others extended the search to the Pyrenees. We have a large corpus of art objects from these 19th-century excavations, although due to poor early methods of excavation we possess little scientific data about them.

Miniature art in the East is a much more recent discovery: with the exception of Predmosti in Moravia; which was first dug in 1880, the major sites have all been explored in this century and, in comparison to the West, are still few in number.

In France miniature art was accepted without question as the work of "early cave man" but mural art, interestingly, was at first firmly rejected. It is true that its date can seldom be established except by comparative means, that is, miniature art is found in the accumulated layers of domestic rubbish

A bison on the ceiling of the Altamira cave; length of figure 195cm (77in)

while mural art stands clear on the wall of a cave or shelter, except in a few instances where rubbish has accumulated against a wall, giving a terminal date. However, such proofs exist and, since the drawings on miniature-art pieces are similar to those in caves, it is hard to see why 19th-century scholars, having accepted the first, repudiated the second.

The story of the discovery of Altamira, in northern Spain, is well known. A famous ceiling there shows bison and other animals, painted with a marvelous utilization of the natural bosses on the stone roof. The accidental shapes suggested to the Paleolithic artist that he should depict a number of bison lying down and use the stone projections to add to the illusion of relief in each painting. They are painted in polychrome and are perhaps some of the most sophisticated and elegant work known from the Paleolithic. Their modern discoverer, the Marquis de Sautuola, believed in their authenticity and Paleolithic origin but could convince no one else of these. Indeed, he died without vindicating his opinions, although further discoveries made after his death have forced archaeologists to accept that Altamira and other similar caves are both genuine and of great antiquity. Perhaps it was the actual

quality of Altamira that made it unacceptable as the work of primitive man, or perhaps it was that this form of painting, which is almost idiomatic and is easily understood in the 20th century, after the impact of Matisse, for example, was quite alien to 19th-century eyes. Whatever the reason Altamira, one of the most beautiful of Paleolithic caves, was not unanimously accepted as such until 1902, 23 years after its discovery.

Having briefly considered the modern history of Paleolithic art, let us look at the present state of knowledge. In eastern, central, and western Europe there are respectively 14, 18, and 71 sites that contain miniature art pieces in significant quantities, while in western Europe there are more than 80 decorated caves of major importance and as many again of minor. From this evidence, although it is still extremely inadequate, we may attempt some analysis of styles and chronology.

Miniature art is found in both eastern and western cultural provinces. The sites in central Europe and European Russia, though few, are often very rich and the Venuses are probably the most famous series of objects known from them. They are naked female figurines, usually less than 3 in (8 cm) in height, made of stone or ivory, in which certain features are much exaggerated at the expense of others. Breasts, buttocks, and stomach are usually voluminous, while hands, feet, and facial features are not represented at all. Their appearance is of age, rather than youth, and although so fat, few can be described as pregnant. The Venus of Willendorf in Austria is typical of them, and there are notable series from Kostienki on the Don (Russia) and two sites nearby (Avdeevo and Gagarino), as well as from Dolni Vestonice in the Czech Republic. Not all Venuses are fat, nor are all figurines feminine; for example, an ivory male figure was found in the grave of an adult man at Brno, Czech Republic. All figures are associated with settlements, however, and because of their placing in the houses, very often near the hearths, or grouped at one side, it is considered that they are perhaps house guardians whose importance is domestic rather than erotic.

Most Venuses are very naturalistic, even if exaggerated in form, but with time very schematic and stylized syntheses of these figures were developed. At Mezin in the Ukraine such stylized figures were covered with decorative patterns of chevrons and "Greek key" designs. These geometric patterns were used in the East for the decoration of ornaments, such as the ivory bracelets from Mezin, and even for tools. The designs are often elaborate and beautifully executed, being cut with a sharp flint point on ivory or bone. A few engravings of animals on such material are also known and a number of animal statuettes, usually of marl. Often only fragments survive, as at Kostienki (Russia), but at Dolni Vestonice (Czech Republic), where they are very numerous, some complete figures have been found. Here they were made of a mud compound, and baked in a kiln.

Venuses are both more numerous and of greater variety in the East, suggesting that this was the cult's area of origin, but they occur in western Europe and appear at a similar date, that is early in the Upper Paleolithic, between approximately 26,000 and 24,000 years BC. As in the East it is common to find a group of Venuses at one location, and such groups have been found at Grimaldi, on the Côte d'Azur, and at Brassempouy in the Landes (France) but there are a number of single finds also. the very stylized Venus from Lespugue (Haute Garonne, France) is one example. The western Venuses are similar to the eastern and follow the same later pattern of stylization, finally making a transition to mural art, as at Angles sur-l'Anglin in Vienne (France) where, on the frieze, three half-figures are carved in low relief among the animals.

Schematic decoration is used on tools and ornaments in western Europe, but it is here that the naturalistic tradition has its greatest development and this is reflected in both miniature and mural art. Engravings of animals occur on non-manufactured pieces and on bone and antler tools, and low- and full-relief carving are used. Decorated pieces are known from all Upper Paleolithic stages in France and Spain but more than 80 percent of such work, as well as that of greatest quality, belongs to the middle and late stages of the Magdalenian, that is from c13,000 to 8,000 years BC. Much of the most beautiful work is found on antler tools, tools that a man would retain, such as spear-throwers, or thong-softeners, rather than on expendable objects such as javelin points. For example, spear-throwers are weighted with three-dimensionally carved animals, thong-softeners are decorated with engraved head and forequarters, and rib bones are made into spatulas, decorated with animal heads or fish.

Magdalenian IV is a particularly rich period, not only are a number of objects and techniques peculiar to this stage, but the way in which animals are drawn is both elaborate and stylized, with much shading and infilling. After this stage, although its inventory is much reduced, miniature art develops a freer and more lifelike style, with occasional narrative scenes, unrealistic combinations, and some essays in perspective. Many of the richest miniature-art sites are in the foothills of the French Pyrenees, for example La Vache, Mas-d'Azil, Lorthet, and Labastide, while Isturitz is farther west in the Pays Basque. Two sites farther north, Laugerie Basse and Bruniquel, are closely allied to the Pyrenean group, and there are two rich sites in northern Spain, El Valle and El Pendo near Santander.

Miniature art is found only in daylit habitation sites, mural art, however, although sometimes also found there, was mainly used to create sanctuaries in deep caves. Some of these painted or engraved panels are in extinct subterranean rivers that are difficult to reach and in positions that are awkward to see. At no time were such caves inhabited and they were probably little frequented. Nevertheless, many of the most beautiful decorated caves, such as Lascaux (Dordogne, France), and Niaux (Ariège, France), belong to this group.

Two reindeer carved on a reindeer antler; from Bruniquel, France; length 21cm (8in). British Museum, London

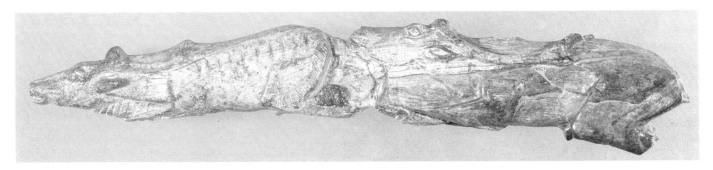

Paleolithic Venuses

The greatest achievements in naturalistic representation in the Upper Paleolithic period (whether in two dimensions or three), with one very important exception, were made at a late stage. This exception is the group of miniature sculptured female figures, described as "Venuses", that were found between Europe's Atlantic coast and Siberia and were made at an early stage of the Upper Paleolithic, a period described variously as the Upper Perigordian or Gravettian, which dates from *c*26,000 to 24,000 BC.

If, at first sight, it seems inappropriate to describe figures that are usually neither young nor slender as Venuses, it may be justified by their beauty of form, for the balance of mass and the symmetrical positioning of shapes achieved in these figures is remarkable. While hands, feet, and facial features are almost always omitted, and certain sexual characteristics, such as the pubic triangle, are on occasion represented, or on occasion also omitted, it is the essentially feminine forms of buttock, breast, and stomach that are emphasized. Viewed objectively, the Venus of Lespugue has pendant breasts, a protruding stomach, and fat buttocks, all developed to the point of distortion; but viewed aesthetically, the incline of her breasts and the curve of her buttocks are beautiful and each shape complements the other.

▼ The Venus of Lespugue, front view; height 15cm (6in). Musée de l'Homme, Paris

▼ The Venus of Lespugue, back view. Musée de l'Homme, Paris

Many of these little ivory or stone figurines have a high polish, which suggests they were much handled and carried about; they are often found in groups and are habitually associated with living sites, whether these were constructed huts, as were made in eastern Europe, or rock shelters, as were used in the west. The individual appearance of the Venuses suggests they are figures of fecundity, made to endow or ensure plenty in some form, rather than to be erotic symbols, and the context in which they are found endorses a domestic importance: beyond this one can offer little explanation of their purpose. As a group (a group which to date numbers nearly 150 examples) they show great uniformity and with time the basic figure is adapted and simplified into schematized forms of considerable sophistication. The Venuses of Vestonice, Balzi Rossi, and Lespugue are typical examples of the basic naturalistic shape; the Venuses from Kostienki in Russia, from Gagarino, or the remainder of the group from Balzi Rossi all fall into this type, as does the Venus of Willendorf and the figure from Brassempouy in France, though this statuette has an atypical, more natural beauty, as though a portrayal from life had interfered with the formalized concept. The Venus of Laussel, unusual in that it is carved in low relief on a freestanding stone block, is also atypical; in this case, although the detail is executed carefully, the general ungainly shape suggests a lack of conceptual ability.

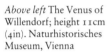

Above left The Venus of Willendorf; height 11cm (4in). Naturhistorisches Museum, Vienna

▲ A Venus from Dolni Vestonice, Czech Republic (a cast of the original); height 11cm (4in). Moravian Museum, Brno.

▲ The Venus of Laussel, France, holding a bison horn; height 42cm (16½in). Musée d'Aquitaine, Bordeaux

◄ Schematic figures from Vestonice: *above* fork-shaped, emphasizing the hips; height 8cm (3in); *below* straight, emphasizing the breasts; height 8.5cm (3½in). Both Moravian Museum, Brno

► The ivory head of a young girl, from Brassempouy, France; height 3.8cm (1½in). A cast. The original is in the Musée des Antiquités Nationales, St-Germain-en-Laye

With time the Venus figures become diversified, some hermaphroditic forms occur, and the naturalistic female figures are superseded by more schematic forms; in eastern Europe two such variants appear, one based upon the hips, the other upon the breasts of the basic female figure, while in western Europe it is the raised seat profile, a form of the second variant, that is predominant. The profile shape finds its ultimate reduction in the claviform signs that are drawn in caves in the Magdalenian era; and it is interesting that this final simplification of the Venus figure is not only the last expression of the cult, but here has found a change in location: claviforms are generally part of the decoration of deep, uninhabited caves.

ANN SIEVEKING

Further reading. Abramova, Z.A. "Palaeolithic Art in the U.S.S.R.", *Arctic Anthropology* IV no. 2, (1967) pp1–179. Delporte, H. *L'Image de la Femme dans l'Art Préhistorique*, Paris (1979). Hancar, F. *Problem der Venusstatuetten im Eurasiatischen Jungpaläolithikum*, Berlin (1940). Leroi-Gourhan, A. *The Art of Prehistoric Man in Western Europe*, London (1968). Passemard, L. *Les Statuettes Féminines Paléolithiques dites Venus Stéatopyges*, Nîmes (1938). Saccasyn della Santa, E. *Les Figures Humaines du Paléolithique Supérieur*, Anvers (1947).

The head of a horse engraved on the wall in Lascaux; the complete figure is 60cm (24in) long

It is probable that, originally, every Paleolithic shelter habitation had a painted or engraved overhang, but apart from a few fragments that have been preserved by falling on to the ground below, no painting now remains, with the exception of the newly found cave of Tito Bustillo at Ribadasella (Spain) where a rockfall sealed off the habitation area and its painted overhang. There are a number of rock-cut, low-relief friezes, the most beautiful perhaps being that at Angles-sur-l'Anglin in Vienne (France) or the horses at Cap Blanc in the Dordogne. The work required to create these, cutting limestone with flint picks, must have been tremendous. It could not have been attempted in deep caves, but from these sculpture is not entirely absent. In the Tuc d'Audoubert (central Pyrenees, France) there are two beautiful bison modeled in mud that was collected from the cave floor nearby.

When people speak of Paleolithic art they are usually referring to the painted caves, and most probably they consider Lascaux, in the Dordogne, as typical: but the most striking aspect of Lascaux, the fact that the cave is decorated as a single unit, is an almost unique feature. In most caves the paintings are not displayed in this way; only certain, often inconspicuous parts of the cave are decorated; the drawing of one animal is not placed in relation to another with any regard for size or availability of space so that they are often superimposed, even jumbled together; some are unfinished and some may be upside down.

Of the animal species drawn, horses are much the most numerous, followed by bison, oxen, mammoth, deer, ibex, anthropomorphic figures, and carnivores; fish are rare, birds almost unknown. A few caves have a series of hand prints. Gargas, in the Pyrenees, is famous for these, and in certain areas, or at certain periods, signs are abundant. These signs are schematic: they may be quadrangular, brace-shaped, or composed of groups of dots or lines, and they give some indication of local grouping in cave art. Certain quadrangular signs, for example, are restricted to the Dordogne area while club-shaped signs are found at a later date in the Pyrenees and Spain.

Schematic signs in Castillo; the sign second from right is 63cm (25in) high

It is not easy to establish a chronology for cave art; style is probably the safest guide. The large-bodied, small-headed animals of Pech Merle (Lot, France) and Lascaux, for example, are early and have affinities to the low-relief friezes, while the very tautly drawn black outline figures of Niaux and Portel (Ariège, France) or Santimamine (Spain) are of characteristic Middle Magdalenian style. Fifty years ago the Abbé Breuil attempted a detailed classification of cave art based upon style and superpositions and concluded that there were two cycles in its development, but this is no longer accepted: as in miniature art one cycle seems adequate here.

There are decorated caves of an early date but present evidence suggests that the use of deep caves was short lived. The decorated rock-shelters and shallow daylit caves are mainly of early or late date, such as, respectively, Pair-non-Pair (Gironde, France) or La Mairie at Teyjat (Dordogne, France), while in the Middle Magdalenian period (from approximately 15,000 to 14,000 BC) there was a fashion for decorating caves progressively deeper and where access was more difficult. Lascaux, which has a date of 15,000 years ago, Pech Merle or

A horse in the cave of Niaux; length of figure 30cm (12in)

An ox and a mammoth from Pech Merle; the mammoth is 140cm (55in) long

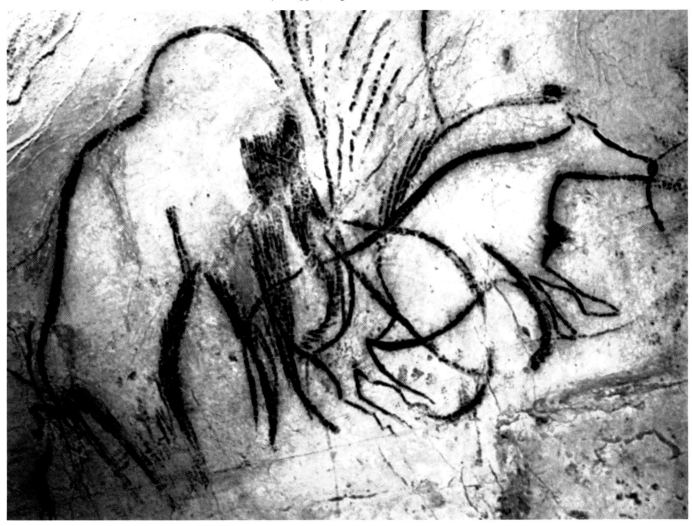

Cougnac (Lot, France) are among the earliest of these deep sanctuaries while Niaux, Le Portel, and the Volp caverns (Les Trois Frères, Le Tuc d'Audoubert), in the French Pyrenees and the Spanish group in Monte Castillo near Santander (Castillo, Monedas, Pasiega, Chimeneas) are among the later, as is Altamira. Some caves are clearly one period in style, such as Niaux; others, such as Castillo, had a long use and show a succession of styles. The majority are difficult to reach and cannot have had an everyday use and, although miniature art may have filled that requirement, the deep caves were apparently abandoned in the Late Magdalenian in favor of open-air sanctuaries once more, formed by groups of engraved plaquettes or wall engravings.

Breuil and his contemporaries were interested in the content and style of mural art but could see no meaningful design in its layout. They concluded that it was the creation of each individual drawing that was important and the animal species shown, mostly edible animals, suggested that this art was a form of sympathetic magic for hunting; a view endorsed by the occurrence of arrows drawn on the flanks of some animals. For a time such an explanation seemed adequate but the recent work of Leroi-Gourhan and others has called it into question. Leroi-Gourhan has studied specifically the layout of cave paintings and concludes that this is far from haphazard: in fact he considers that it follows a formula. Certain animals, horses and bovines, are of primary importance and are given central positions. Others, such as ibex and mammoth, are peripheral and of secondary importance; superpositions, unfinished outlines, signs of various forms all have their place and the formula may be repeated, at intervals, a number of times in one cave. The virtue of his interpretation is that it takes account of elements such as superpositioning, human figures, and signs for which sympathetic magic could offer no explanation. Certain signs may indeed be interpreted as traps, clubs, or even houses, but such an explanation does not invalidate Leroi-Gourhan's conclusions. There are further objections to the theory of sympathetic magic. Firstly, archaeological evidence shows that reindeer was the principal game of Upper Paleolithic hunters, but it is little represented in the art. Secondly, although climate and the available animal species varied greatly throughout the Upper Paleolithic, the inventory of animals in the art is remarkably constant. And finally, current ethnographic research suggests, by analogy, that the Upper Paleolithic was a period of considerable plenty.

We know that, although the climate was periodically severe, vegetation and large animals were very abundant and we should realize that, far from being threatened by starvation, Paleolithic man had no need to supplicate for food to be provided. The creation of cave sanctuaries suggests Paleolithic art had a magical or religious importance, while its quality, its homogeneity, and its duration demand a social sanction of great strength. We may conclude that it was not simply decorative, but had a great and continuing social importance. It may be assumed that miniature art is an expression in different media and locations of the same beliefs as mural art; tools, for example, may be invested with some added power by decoration.

Ethnographic parallels are of little value in explaining Paleolithic art, beyond the fact that Australian aboriginal art, for example, suggests that its meaning may be very complex. Leroi-Gourhan thinks that the limited and repeated number of animals in mural art constitutes a mythogram and that what one sees may only represent a vehicle for a meaning that one can only guess at; in his opinion, a synthesis of the universe, perhaps.

The Paleolithic is a period for which we have no social history; rather we look to the art to give us some insight into the mentality of its creators. In so doing we see the work of artists who could perfectly conceptualize and execute a formula, who had mastered all the problems of rendering three dimensions in two, and who could instantly create an image by an ideogram. Further, from the development and duration of the art we can deduce a considerable degree of social harmony. Paleolithic art represents an unbroken religious and artistic tradition lasting for 20,000 years, a phenomenon that has not been repeated.

ANN SIEVEKING

Bibliography. Abramova, Z.A. "Palaeolithic Art in the U.S.S.R.", *Arctic Anthropology* IV no. 2, (1967) pp1–179. Breuil, H. *Four Hundred Centuries of Cave Art*, Montignac (1952). Giedion, S. *The Eternal Present: the Beginning of Art*, New York and London (1962). Graziosi, P. *Palaeolithic Art*, London (1960). Leroi-Gourhan, A. *The Art of Prehistoric Man in Western Europe*, London (1968). Marshack, A. *The Roots of Civilization*, London (1972). Naber, F., Berenger, D.J., and Zalles-Flossbach, C. *L'Art Parietal Paléolithique en Europe Romane* Parts 1 and 2 (3 vols), Bonner Hefte zur Vorgeschichte nos. 14–16, Bonn (1976). Sieveking, A. *The Cave Artists*, London (1979). Ucko, P. and Rosenfeld, A. *Palaeolithic Cave Art*, London (1967).

2

NEOLITHIC ART

A human skull from Jericho, its features molded in plaster and cowrie shells inset for eyes;
7th millennium BC. Ashmolean Museum, Oxford (see page 12)

THE Neolithic period is the earliest phase of agricultural society, before cities and before the widespread use of metal for tools and weapons. After the end of the last Ice Age some 10,000 years ago, new climatic conditions brought woodland once again into Europe and the tribes o reindeer-hunters who had created the remarkable cave art of France and Spain (see Paleolithic Art) were no longer able to exist in their accustomed way. Small groups of hunters remained in the woodlands or on the coasts, but after 5000 BC these were increasingly absorbed or displaced by the colonizing activity of farmers, spreading with their flocks and cultivated grains from a homeland in the Near East, and settling in villages on the more fertile soils. Cutting down the forests for fields and pastures, these peoples used the new and effective polished-stone ax—hence the archaeologists' term "Neolithic", or New Stone Age. This period began c8000 BC in Iran, but only c4000 BC in the British Isles. It lasted down to 3500 BC in the Near East, and nearer 2000 BC in Europe.

The way of life of these peoples, and hence the character of their art, was in great contrast to that of the hunting groups they replaced. They lived, for example, in solid-built houses rather than the caves or makeshift shelters of their often nomadic predecessors. They developed, and brought with them to Europe, the technique of making pottery. They lived in larger communities and therefore developed more organized forms of religion and public ritual. And they probably had to work harder to make a living than their predecessors, for, contrary to popular belief, the development of agriculture was not "emancipation from the food quest"; it probably created less spare time than hunting. The achievements of Neolithic artists were not, therefore, simply the result of sufficient leisure to devote to creative pursuits, but arose from the nature of their society, their technology, and their mythological beliefs, and from the increasing number of their material possessions, mostly still produced on a domestic or village scale. The achievements of Neolithic art are thus mainly in the areas of domestic design and decoration.

Distribution of main Neolithic sites

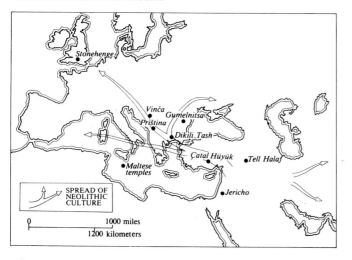

In discussing the various media used by Neolithic man, it must be remembered that we know practically nothing of his output in organic materials—textiles, woodcarving, featherwork, leather objects, or painted decoration on perishable materials. Enough survives in fragments to hint at the importance of all these, but it is impossible to recapture the vividness and color of the originals. Nor is the significance that these objects once had to their makers clear or easy to reconstruct. There are, of course, no written texts from this period, and there is very little realistic representational art before the coming of cities. What representations there are show single figures: there are very few groups, or figures that are part of a wider scene. Portrayal is often schematic and detail ambiguous. While it is likely that figures and motifs had a mythical or religious significance, attempts to reconstruct beliefs are pure speculation.

The mudbrick villages of the earliest farmers spread gradually across Iran and Turkey and into Europe through Greece and the Balkans. Most of these were small communities, though in the richer lowlands some larger sites not only grew to the size of small towns but also served as craft and religious centers.

Two examples of these (dating from c7000 and 6000 BC) are the original settlement at Jericho, and the site of Çatal Hüyük in southern Turkey. At the latter, an impressive shrine has been excavated, with the skulls of long-horned wild cattle (aurochs) covered in mud plaster and set into the wall of the sanctuary. The smoothed wall surfaces of nearby buildings were painted in red ocher with representations of hunting scenes, showing men surrounding the bull. Other scenes in the sanctuary depict large birds pecking at what are probably human corpses—strongly suggesting that bodies were exposed before burial. At Jericho, a similar concern with the body after death is shown by skulls with plastered faces and cowrie shells set in the eye sockets.

More widespread than these practices associated with central cult areas was the manufacture of small figurines for domestic ritual. The slightly later site of Hacilar (in western Turkey) has provided a great diversity of these objects, many of which have been copied by forgers and ultimately sold to museums. They are usually female, and in some cases show birth scenes or groups of a mother and child. The corpulent mothers are unclothed, but the rounded bodies are schematically treated and often covered in painted decoration. Anthropomorphic vessels were also made, with obsidian inlay used for eyes.

In addition to the production of small sculpture, a variety of utilitarian and decorative crafts were widely practiced in these earliest villages in Turkey. The pottery was fired at low temperatures, but effectively decorated by slips and painted areas of white, iron-free clay on red iron-bearing clay oxidized to a fine red color. These were evenly burnished before firing in the same manner as the figurines. Woodworking and basketry are sparsely preserved—the former as carbonized fragments and the latter as mat-impressions—but the designs of woven fab-

A clay model of a house, from Greece; 5th millennium BC. Archaeological Museum, Volos

rics with their strong geometric emphasis are reflected in the repetitive zigzag and rectilinear ornament of the painted pottery.

Personal ornaments made use of a variety of decorative stones obtained through long-distance trade. Beads were bored from steatite, turquoise, carnelian, onyx, and malachite, which later became an extensively used ore of copper. Indeed, even at this time some small ornaments may have been made by hammering small nuggets of naturally occurring pure copper. Shells were another commodity widely in demand for use as ornaments. These were carved into simple shapes as beads or bangles.

In southeast Europe, including Greece, no sites of the size and importance of Çatal Hüyük have yet been discovered, but from the 6th millennium BC onwards the same crafts were practiced, and the pottery shows a similar kind of design with "step" and "flame" motifs clearly relating to woven textiles. Figurines are similarly common, and again show local styles.

Thessaly, in particular, produced a wide range of forms, but further north the types are more standardized. Especially characteristic of Macedonia are the so-called "rod-head" statuettes with an exaggerated head and neck, the lines of which are broken only by applied pellets of clay forming "coffee-bean" eyes. This style is important in demonstrating the links between communities on the north Aegean coast and those further north in Yugoslavia. The religious area of Çatal Hüyük has its counterparts, on a smaller scale, in cult-houses, differing from ordinary dwellings in their size and painted-plaster ornamentation. The designs (as at the Bulgarian site of Karanovo) are purely geometric—often spirals and meander motifs—and the only representational designs besides anthropomorphic figurines are a few schematic "stick-figures" made of applied strips of clay on coarse pottery. When they have any specific identity, they are most often of animals such as deer.

As Neolithic groups moved further north into Europe in the 5th millennium BC, fine-painted pottery became increasingly rare and the surviving assemblage appears artistically impoverished in comparison with contemporary products in the eastern Mediterranean. We lack objects made of organic materials, however, and in consequence our impression of artistic poverty may be wholly false: a vast artistic and cultural legacy may have perished with the materials in which it was fashioned. Certainly, wood was a much more important raw material than clay or stone for many purposes in northern Europe. Large areas of heavy woodland had to be cleared for settlement, and for building houses timber was more appropriate than mudbrick in northern climates. Drinking vessels and tableware were probably increasingly the products of woodcarvers rather than potters, though pottery remained important for storage and cooking vessels. Until the later part of the 3rd millennium BC, fine pottery was a regional speciality rather than a universal commodity in northern Europe. Cult-houses were still built in each village, but the earliest farmers of central Europe did not produce figurines like those so characteristic of southeast Europe. Fine craftsmanship continues to appear in the stonework, however. Axes were naturally essential working tools, but finely polished examples in attractive and widely traded hard stone were also significant as indicators of status and power. Along with imported shell ornaments, they were placed in the graves of the older male members of the community.

In the far west and north of Europe, along the Atlantic seaboard and in the north European plain, the introduction of agriculture in the 4th and 3rd millennia BC involved the clearance of huge stones from fields. Now not only timber dwelling-houses but also large monumental tombs of undressed blocks were built, serving as cult-centers, and also as territorial markers among the more scattered hamlets of these areas. The earliest monumental architecture in stone used two techniques: in one, vast unhewn blocks were lined up or piled up one on top of another to provide burial chambers, and in the other, drystone construction techniques were used either to fill in the gaps between these blocks or to roof over a chamber by corbeling. Some of the most impressive of these tribal mortuary shrines occur in Brittany, Ireland, and the Orkney islands. Maes Howe in Orkney, for instance, has three side-chambers under a covering cairn.

A particularly well-preserved group of prehistoric monuments of this type was built in the Maltese islands, where the soft and easily worked limestone hardens on exposure to give an enduring record of the kinds of carving that may well have been made in wood further north. The temples were modified and enlarged over the centuries, as the cathedrals of the Middle Ages were to be, over four millennia later. Besides spiral and scroll ornament on lintels and altars, gigantic statues—somewhat reminiscent of the east Mediterranean terracotta figurines—were erected in the temples. Laboriously pecked ornament of spirals and concentric circles was also used on a smaller scale, for instance to adorn megalithic struc-

Gumelnitsa and Vinča Ceramics

The style of pottery making and modeling that characterized the Neolithic and Copper Age communities of southeast Europe in the 4th millennium BC is one of the high-water marks of prehistoric European art. The culture of this period represents the culmination of 2,000 years of indigenous development in this area, when the traditions established by the earliest farmers reached their peak.

The artistic achievements of this period are most notably expressed in pottery and terracotta figurines, painted or incised in a characteristic decorative style which ultimately reflects designs used on textiles and basketry. The sites that have produced examples of this style of art are the mounds (formed by the remains of successive prehistoric villages) that occur in lowland areas of northern Greece, Yugoslavia, Bulgaria, Rumania, and Hungary. Excavations at Gumelnitsa near Bucharest and Vinča near Belgrade have given their names to local groups within this cultural province. These well-preserved settlements of mud-and-timber huts, grouped in small village communities, contain plentiful remains of decorated ceramic objects; while their nearby cemeteries may yield examples of rarer metal (copper or gold) ornaments, which were placed as offerings in graves.

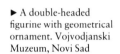
► A double-headed figurine with geometrical ornament. Vojvodjanski Muzeum, Novi Sad

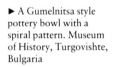
◄ A Vinča figurine from Selevac, central Yugoslavia

► A Gumelnitsa style pottery bowl with a spiral pattern. Museum of History, Turgovishte, Bulgaria

► A Gumelnitsa style painted pottery bowl, its incised decoration filled with white paste. Museum of History, Turgovishte, Bulgaria

► A Gumelnitsa style painted pottery bowl of more complex shape. Museum of History, Turgovishte, Bulgaria

The decorative art of this period was closely related to domestic ritual and cult. Similar types of decorative patterns and representational elements appear on fine pottery, models, and on certain parts of the houses themselves. These categories thus overlap one another: "cult-vessels" such as triangular pottery lamps were decorated with modeled animal heads, while domestic fittings used for cult purposes, like ceramic pillars and offering-tables, were painted in the same way as fine pottery. The concentration of these elaborately decorated features in specific houses and rooms suggests they were cult objects used by particular members of certain families.

The style of decoration contains both abstract and representational elements, though the latter are always strongly schematized and often themselves bear geometrical ornament. This ornamentation takes two basic forms: a flowing meander or spiral pattern, and a more rigid, rectilinear version resembling woven matting. These were not mutually exclusive, and were sometimes combined on the same object. In the west (Yugoslavia) the figurines are more elaborate, though the pottery bears less decoration: in the east (Bulgaria) the figurines are often fairly schematic, while the pottery has a profusion of painted ornament.

▲ Human figures and furniture: the cult scene from Ovcharevo. Museum of History, Turgovishte, Bulgaria

The fully developed Gumelnitsa style of painted pottery emerged in the later 5th millennium BC from earlier traditions based on repetitive geometrical motifs executed as incisions filled with white paste. The vessel shapes became more complex, while the ornament—now usually painted—often took the form of freely swinging curves and spirals. At about the same time, more developed forms of terracotta models came into use. These included not only human figures but also items of furniture, as in a famous "cult scene" from Ovcharevo in northeast Bulgaria.

The most elaborate examples of such figurines come from the Vinča group in Yugoslavia. These are characterized by three-dimensional "mask" faces with protruding, almond-shaped eyes and sharp noses, sometimes depicted as seated on chairs or stools. Some show suggestions of dress and *coiffure*, and ornaments such as bracelets or pendants. Occasionally a more naturalistic rendering of the head was attempted, as in the attractive example from Dikili Tash in Greek Thrace, ornamented with graphite paint.

The production of these types of object came to an end in the 3rd millennium BC, when economic and social changes cut across established traditions in religion and art, and the beginnings of bronzeworking introduced a new medium for ornament and display.

ANDREW SHERRATT

Further reading. Gimbutas, M. *The Gods and Goddesses of Old Europe*, London (1974). Sandars, N.K. *Prehistoric Art in Europe*, Harmondsworth (1968). Todorova, H. *The Eneolithic Period in Bulgaria in the Fifth Millennium BC*, Oxford (1978).

◄ A head of a man from Dikili Tash in Greek Thrace. Ashmolean Museum, Oxford

▼ A head from Predionica, southern Yugoslavia; height 18cm (7in). Kosova Museum, Pristina

4th millennium biconical vessels of the Tripole group, found in the Ukraine. Ashmolean Museum, Oxford

tures in Ireland and Scotland. It has often been suggested that these are the results of contact with the west Mediterranean, or even ultimately from the Aegean—perhaps involving some kind of missionary activity. Modern methods of dating, however, have shown such influence to have been unlikely; similarities in social structure and local raw materials seem to be a more probable explanation for these resemblances.

While the megalithic style of architecture was developing in the north and west, the prosperous communities of southeast Europe began a period of economic expansion that ensured the continuation of their way of life and allowed them to develop new techniques.

The growth of trade meant that desirable materials traveled over long distances. Experimentation with new substances for use as paints, and more complex firing procedures, resulted in more elaborate multicolored pottery in a variety of blacks, reds, and browns and also a silvery color obtained from graphite. This was especially effective because of the deep black color that could now be produced in the pottery fabric by controlled firing in a reducing atmosphere. It could also be enhanced by the addition of powdered manganese minerals such as pyrolusite, lumps of which have been found in graves. Interestingly, there were mines for cinnabarite, which produces a bright vermilion tint not found on the pottery; we may

take this as an indication that striking colors were also used on organic materials.

Some of the most attractive surviving artistic products of the 4th millennium BC are the ceramics of the Gumelnitsa and Salcutsa groups in Bulgaria, and the related Cucuteni and Tripole groups of Rumania and the Ukraine. Their pottery shapes make use of elegantly opposed curves, especially carinated forms with a convex profile above and a concave one beneath. The elegance of shape was complemented by painted ornament of geometric intricacy. In the early phases of the style the paint was mainly applied in narrow multiple lines, making a repetitive succession of motifs. With time, the linear style gave way to a block-painted style in which larger areas were covered with paint, and the motifs themselves became bolder and simpler. Individual panels of ornament gained an organic relationship with one another, with bold curves balanced on opposite sides of the vessel. Finally, the continuity of decorative elements was broken and individual motifs occurred in isolation—circles or squares rather than spirals—sparsely distributed around the surface of the vessel. This cycle of development—emergence, florescence, and decline into incoherence—is a characteristic feature of the evolution of particular styles in decorative systems over long periods of time.

The figurines of the Gumelnitsa and related groups were in general flat and highly schematized, but in other contemporary contexts, and especially that named after the site of Vinča near Belgrade in Yugoslavia, more three-dimensional work was attempted. The Vinča figurines are characterized by their exaggerated triangular faces with staring almond-shaped eyes. As these statuettes are quite detailed (showing, for example, hands and feet with fingers and toes) and as there are contemporary examples with naturalistic faces, their schematized faces may represent masks. Rows of perforations around the rim of the mask may have held feathers or tufts of straw. Some sites in the Pristina area of southern Yugoslavia have produced larger, life-sized versions of these figurines. More naturalistic modeling of the facial features is a characteristic of southern Thrace, and the site of Dikili Tash in northern Greece has yielded attractive "portrait" faces as well as the more schematic types.

Evidence about these figurines is relatively substantial because they derive from a large number of excavated sites belonging to the same period. They are commonly found in houses, often in very large numbers. It has been claimed that one such house (at the site of Sabatinovka in southern Russia) with 32 figurines, was a special shrine, but the presence of ordinary domestic fittings makes this unlikely; this discovery

An anthropomorphic jug from northwest Bulgaria, c6000 BC; height 25cm (10in). Vratsa Regional Museum

Vinča pottery representation of a seated figure.
Ashmolean Museum, Oxford

A Halaf polychrome bowl from northern Iraq. Iraq Museum, Baghdad

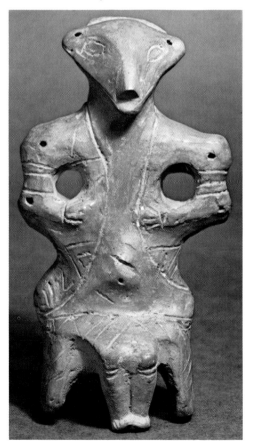

seems rather to indicate that these terracottas were extremely common objects.

A significant technical development of the period was the discovery of copper smelting. (Because of this the mature Neolithic period is also termed the Eneolithic or Copper Age; but metal had little economic significance.) Copper was cast in open molds; it was used mainly for heavy, flat axes, but also for small personal ornaments such as pins with double spiral heads, or flat, hammered disks pierced to be sewn on to clothing. Gold was also used, on a smaller scale, especially in the regions in contact with Transylvania. It was beaten into small pendants and larger pectoral ornaments (up to 12 in, 30 cm, in diameter), sometimes decorated with rows of repoussé dots.

Whereas in Europe urban life only began in the 2nd millenium BC and only became widespread in the 1st, in the Near East there were large cities as early as the 3rd millennium BC, which followed a long period of proto-urban development. Copperworking, too, had a long history, and the term "Neolithic" has a somewhat different meaning than in the European context. Nevertheless, there are many points of similarity between the southeast European Neolithic groups and corresponding early village communities further east; and it is the ceramics that dominate the surviving art objects.

Before the colonization of the Mesopotamian plain and the growth of irrigation-based towns and temple centers in the lowlands, the cultural focus of the Near East in the 5th millennium BC lay in the villages of the arc formed by the flanks of the Taurus mountains to the north, connecting northern Syria with northern Iraq along the upper reaches of the Tigris, the Euphrates, and their tributaries. The relatively open character of the country promoted wider contact than was possible in the forested regions of Europe, and not only raw materials such as fine stone but also finished pottery was traded over long distances. This resulted in a uniform culture which allows us to speak of the whole area from the Mediterranean to the Tigris as a single cultural entity. It has been called the Halaf culture after the German-excavated site of Tell Halaf in Syria.

The pottery of the Halaf culture was produced by similar techniques to those used in the Copper Age of southeast Europe (though fired at higher temperatures) but stylistically there is little in common between the two. The flowing curves of the Balkan products have no equivalent in Halaf. Instead, rectilinear panels packed with lines, dots, crosses, and rosettes are the basis of ornament, sometimes mixed with naturalistic motifs of animal, bird, or human figures. Bulls' heads and deer are common images, but always as small, repetitive elements in a closely packed design. Early pieces were executed in single-colored paint on a slipped background, but in the later phases of the style several colors of paint were combined, as in the magnificent polychrome plate from Arpachiyah in north Iraq.

It would be hard to claim that these decorative styles or the representational techniques of the terracottas made any lasting contribution to the art of succeeding cultures. New cultural needs and technical possiblities altered both the style of art and the materials that were employed. Only in our own day, with a wide familiarity with primitive and tribal art, can Neolithic art be appreciated for what it is.

ANDREW SHERRATT

Bibliography. Gimbutas, M. *The Gods and Goddesses of Old Europe*, London (1974). Mellaart, J. *The Earliest Civilizations of the Near East*, London (1965). Sandars, N.K. *Prehistoric Art in Europe*, Harmondsworth (1968). Sherratt, A.G. *Animals in Early Art*, Oxford (1978). Torbrügge, W. *Prehistoric European Art*, London and New York (1968).

3

EGYPTIAN ART

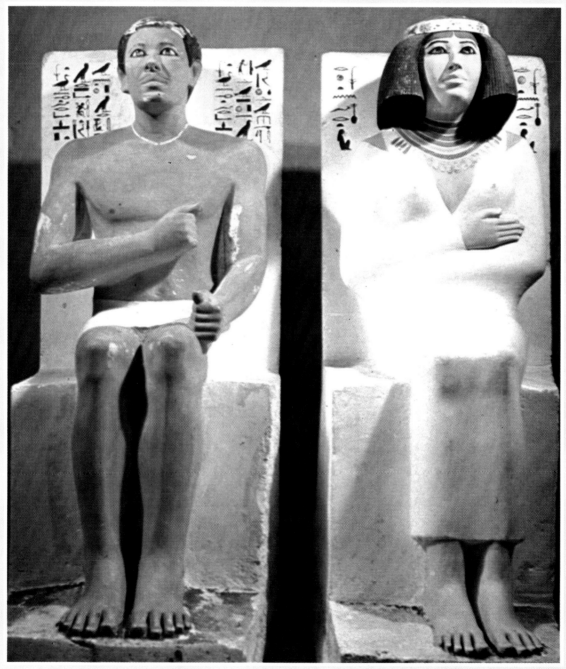

Old Kingdom sculpture: Prince Rehotep and his wife Nefert; c2620 BC. Egyptian Museum, Cairo (see page 25)

ART to the people of ancient Egypt was not an abstract concept. The works of Egyptian artists and sculptors served a practical purpose; they were not simply the tangible expressions of inspiration and imagination. If an object, a person, or even an occasion was represented in art—in sculpture, relief, painting, or as a model—and the right religious formula was inscribed on it, or even just recited, it would continue to exist forever. Therefore objects or scenes in tombs could be made "real" to equip the dead person for his existence in the afterlife. Every aspect of public and private life was involved with the pattern of religious belief and practice. The statues and reliefs that decorated the temples were not intended to be admired from a distance, to be awe-inspiring and remote. They linked the people with their gods through the person of the living god, and the king of Upper and Lower Egypt.

Distribution map of the main centers of Egyptian civilization

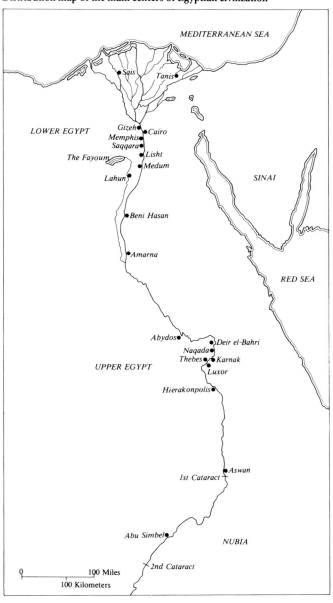

The traditions followed by the artists and craftsmen of ancient Egypt were established at an early date. The result was a sense of unity in art that persisted until Egypt became a province of the Roman Empire. In fact about 3,000 years elapsed between the establishment of the kingdoms of Upper and Lower Egypt and the death of Cleopatra, the last of the Ptolemies. During this time techniques developed, fashions changed, and variations did occur, but in general the basic patterns were faithfully reproduced by generations of Egyptian craftsmen. It is possible to look at a statue or a piece of jewelry and to be certain it was made in ancient Egypt, even though its exact date may not be at once apparent.

Geographical background. In Egyptian art nearly everything had a specific or indirect religious significance, and illustrated the special response of the people of the Nile Valley to their environment. They called their country *kemt*, the Black Land. The fertile valley running almost exactly north and south is an anomaly in the desert latitudes of North Africa. The civilization of ancient Egypt could not have occurred without the river, which created cultivable land in the middle of a desert to produce enough wealth to support not only farmers but craftsmen. The cultivable area, only a mile wide in some places, broadens out into the flat lands of the Delta in the north. The dark, rich color of the soil is in sharp contrast to the parched country to east and west, the Arabian and Libyan deserts.

The White Nile rises south of the Equator and flows north towards the Mediterranean Sea. Its chief tributary is the Blue Nile, which in spring is swollen by the melting snows from the mountains of Ethiopia. The floodwaters carry rich silt which is eventually deposited in a fertile layer over the alluvial plain to the north of Egypt.

To the people of ancient Egypt rising waters signaled the beginning of another agricultural year. A "good Nile" promised a successful harvest and a year of plenty. The floods moved steadily northwards; by the end of July the season of Inundation had begun at Memphis, the ancient capital of Egypt south of the Delta, and by early September the waters were at their height. After they had subsided, sowing could begin, the growing crops almost taking care of themselves in the fertile soil. With irrigation channels the floodwaters could be carried further, and otherwise-barren land could be brought under cultivation.

The Nile not only gave life to Egypt but united it in a very practical way. The Delta coast was 600 miles (965 km) north of the first cataract at Aswan and the southern boundary, but river traffic kept the capital in close touch with the provinces. Agricultural produce of all kinds was carried by water, and raw materials could be taken swiftly to the places where they were needed. Gold and ivory from Nubia, granite and sandstone from the quarries near Aswan, and fine limestone from Tura, near Memphis, were easily transported on the river. Indeed, much labor could be avoided in the construction of great royal monuments such as the pyramids at Gizeh. During the Inundation huge blocks of stone could be floated right to the edge of the floodplain, close to the sites where they were to be used, so they only needed to be dragged on rollers for comparatively short distances.

For sculptors and other craftsmen, Egypt was rich in stone of all kinds. Fine sandstone, granite, dolerite, and serpentine were quarried in the south, and limestone of all qualities was readily available. The finest, from Tura, was used to carve reliefs of exquisite detail, although rougher stone was, of course, cheaper. Calcite, commonly called Egyptian alabaster, the stone most often used from earliest times to make vessels, was utilized for its lovely banded markings. In the deserts to east and west semiprecious stones were found, the most common of which were pebbles of garnet, carnelian, and amethyst. For metal, the ancient Egyptians exploited the copper mines of Sinai, and imported gold from Nubia. Fine wood, such as cedar, also had to be imported. The knotted native woods, such as acacia, had to be jointed to produce pieces of useful size; the joins in coffins and furniture were disguised by surface decoration.

Historical background. In prehistoric times the alluvial plain was marshy and teeming with wildlife, while the edges of the Nile Valley were still covered with enough vegetation to support large numbers of wild animals. Both areas provided rich hunting-grounds for a basically nomadic population. However, until it became possible to begin to coordinate efforts to cultivate the land, the valley itself was almost uninhabitable. Drainage and irrigation systems were essential for productive agriculture, and they had to be organized and constructed by people working together. The first settlements were situated on spurs of land above flood-level, and have been found round the lake in the Fayoum Depression west of the Nile, and on the edges of the valley itself further south. By c3600 BC the hunting-and-collecting economy of the earliest inhabitants had developed into a settled agricultural system. At settlement sites, evidence has been found of progress in social organization, with communal granaries for storing wheat and barley, and shrines for the local gods.

Succeeding prehistoric cultures not only developed and improved techniques of cultivation, but also of pottery making, which in this early period constituted a major element of their creative art. Even as early as 4000 BC, the people of Badari in Upper Egypt had been making black-rimmed pottery vessels with thin walls and a highly polished surface. Slightly later, other groups began to produce jars and bowls with combed or white-slip decoration, while from c3600 BC the characteristic painted pottery of the later prehistoric period is found in large numbers in the great cemeteries of Naqada and other sites in Upper Egypt.

This was the time when the potter's art flourished, more than at any other period in ancient Egypt. Vessels were made in a great variety of forms, decorated mostly in red on a buff ground with a wealth of patterns. These range from spirals and dots imitating contemporary stone vessels to stylized landscapes with water, hills, birds, and animals covering the

A painted pottery box from the late prehistoric period, height 8cm (3in). British Museum, London

surfaces. Most elaborate of all were the scenes showing ships with many oars, carrying the standards of local deities.

Fine stone vessels were also produced, the earliest examples of one of the most characteristic products of ancient-Egyptian craftsmen and later to claim more attention than the pottery. Tools and weapons of stone and flint were also skilfully made; and objects of luxury and personal adornment included beads, ivory combs, and stone cosmetic palettes often carved in the form of fish, antelopes, hippopotamuses, and other animals. The earliest inhabitants of the Nile Valley were already showing their delight in the natural forms that were such a familiar part of their daily life. In prehistoric times, too, the first stylized figurines in human form were made of clay, ivory, or bone, and are sometimes found with offerings in graves.

Gradually the districts of the Valley in the south and of the Delta in the North were banded together under the strongest of the local chieftains until two separate kingdoms were formed: Upper Egypt with its capital near Naqada in the south, and Lower Egypt with its capital at Buto in the Delta. About 3200 BC the king of Upper Egypt, known to us as Narmer-Menes, completed the unification of the Two Lands, and established some kind of centralized government.

Little is known about the so-called Archaic period that followed, but the tombs of kings and courtiers found at Saqqara, Abydos, and elsewhere, and the desert graves of poorer people, have yielded objects of all kinds demonstrating that the craftsmen of Egypt were able to flourish and to improve their skills under a stable government.

Written records soon began to be kept, and from surviving fragments the history of Egypt can be pieced together. The names of kings are known, and often the numbers of years they reigned. The main periods of Egyptian history can be divided into Dynasties of rulers, each Dynasty usually spanning the period of time in which one family was in power.

During the Old Kingdom, the period when Egypt was ruled by the kings of the 3rd to 6th Dynasties, strong central government meant that artists and craftsmen were drawn to the court to work under the patronage of the king and his great nobles. Techniques of working in stone, wood, and metal made tremendous progress, demonstrated by surviving large-scale monuments, such as the pyramids of the 4th Dynasty and the sun temples built by 5th-Dynasty kings. These monuments celebrated the divinity of the kings of Egypt, linking the people with the great gods of earth and sky who controlled the welfare of the land.

This was a time when trade and the economy flourished. Craftsmen worked in the finest materials which were often brought great distances, and were able to experiment with recalcitrant stones as well as new techniques of metalworking. This enabled them by the 6th Dynasty to produce large metal figures. The earliest that survive are the copper statues of Pepi I and his son, found at Hierakonpolis. Made c2330 BC they are badly corroded but still impressive in their stiffly formal poses. The eyes are inlaid, and the crown and kilt of the king, now missing, were probably originally made of gilded plaster.

The Old Kingdom ended with the reigns of weak kings and the disintegration of the centralized government that Egypt needed to enable the economy to flourish. The so-called First Intermediate Period, c2160–2000 BC, was a time of relative chaos, of petty kingdoms and the breakdown of the bureaucratic system. Artists and craftsmen who depended on national prosperity for their livelihood were the first to suffer, and few monuments of any consequence survive.

The prosperous period known as the Middle Kingdom really began with the reunification of the country started by Mentuhotep of Thebes c2050 BC. His successors, the strong kings of the 12th Dynasty, moved their capital from Thebes in the south to Lisht near Memphis, a more convenient administrative center. Under their rule Egypt flourished and looked once more beyond the boundaries of the Nile Valley. Lower Nubia was annexed to Egypt, and the copper mines of Sinai were exploited. Egyptian influence was strong in the states of Syria and Palestine, and was also felt in Cyprus. Fortresses were built to defend the southern and eastern borders, and within Egypt itself the administration was reorganized and new areas of land brought under cultivation. For two centuries Egypt enjoyed the benefits of peace under a capable government, and craftsmen achieved new levels of excellence. Very little architecture remains—many royal monuments were robbed for their stone in later periods—but what has survived shows great simplicity and refinement. The quality of royal statues was never surpassed, nor was the jewelry found in the tombs of royal ladies of the 12th Dynasty, although it may not be as famous as the treasures of Tutankhamun made over 400 years later.

The stability of the Middle Kingdom, like that of the Old Kingdom, disintegrated into a period of chaos called the Second Intermediate Period. Once again Egypt became a prey to civil strife, and the way was opened for foreign invaders.

Nomads from Asia infiltrated the Delta, and finally ruled Lower and Middle Egypt until they were driven out by Ahmose of Thebes who founded the 18th Dynasty c1550 BC. Egyptian propaganda later represented the Hyksos, as these nomads were known, as cruel persecutors. In fact, although surviving works of art are comparatively rare, these rulers seem to have adopted Egyptian traditions and to have encouraged native artists and craftsmen.

The establishment of the 18th Dynasty marked the beginning of the New Kingdom and a new blossoming of the arts and crafts of ancient Egypt. Under warlike kings such as Tuthmosis III and Ramesses II the boundaries of Egypt were extended far to the north and east, and trade flourished as never before. Craftsmen benefited from wider contact with other civilizations, such as those of Crete and Mesopotamia, and were also able to work with imported raw materials.

The kings gave encouragement to artists and craftsmen of all kinds by ordering great temples and palaces to be built throughout Egypt. The temple walls were covered with reliefs celebrating the achievements of the kings and the powers of the gods, and the courtyards and inner sanctuaries were enriched with statuary. The formal traditions of earlier periods were followed, though it is possible to detect a certain softening of line and pose even in the statuary intended to decorate the temples. The so-called heretic king, Akhenaten, 1363–1346 BC, actively encouraged a break with tradition. In his city at Tell el-Amarna, a more naturalistic style was developed which became extreme in its exaggeration of the human form. After his death the earlier traditions were resumed, but works of art now lacked something of the obvious strength and vigor of those of the Old and Middle Kingdoms.

In applied art new techniques included glassmaking, which began after the conquests of Tuthmosis III had opened up contacts with the glass industry already established in Syria and Mesopotamia. As always the Egyptian craftsman showed his ability to excel in the handling of materials, and to master new skills if encouraged to do so.

The New Kingdom lasted for about 500 years, and was the last lengthy period of stability and prosperity enjoyed by the ancient Egyptians. A succession of short-lived dynasties followed, and at times Egypt was again divided into several kingdoms. During the Late Period, 715–330 BC, Egypt prospered again but some of the ruling dynasties came from outside the Nile Valley. In the Saite period, the 26th Dynasty, 664–525 BC, a conscious effort was made to recapture the artistic styles and techniques of earlier times when Egypt had been so great. This was an attempt to give the people a renewed pride in past achievements, and a sense of unity at a time when they were threatened. In 525 BC, however, Cambyses of Persia invaded Egypt and annexed it to the Achaemenid Empire. Later, for a brief period, Egypt was ruled by native kings, but a second Persian domination was followed in 332 BC by the conquest of Alexander the Great; Egypt was no longer an independent country.

After the death of Alexander, Egypt was ruled by the de-

Relief sculpture showing Ramesses III striking his enemies, on his mortuary temple at Medinet Habu

scendants of his general, who became Ptolemy I. The administration of the kingdom was reorganized, and Alexandria became an intellectual center and great commercial city of the eastern Mediterranean. The Ptolemies encouraged the ancient traditions of Egypt. Many great Egyptian sanctuaries were reconstructed on a larger scale, or rebuilt, and decorated with reliefs in traditional style as if to underline the claims of the kings to rule the country and to show their awareness of its past greatness.

The gateway of the Ptolemaic temple of Horus at Edfu

The purpose of art in Egypt. The magical reasons for the work of the Egyptian craftsmen have already been mentioned. The vital aim of a statue was to ensure the survival of the person represented for the rest of eternity. By being inscribed with his name and titles, it became magically endowed with his personality, and would provide an eternal dwelling place for his spirit after his death. The correct religious formulas would likewise make a statue fit to house the presence of a god. Such statues might have beauty, but even the roughest would fulfil its purpose if it was correctly inscribed. Many indeed were never intended to be seen by the living; once buried with their owners in tombs, they belonged to the spirit world of eternity.

Any representation, whether sculpture in the round, relief, or painting, was therefore intended to be timeless. To produce a portrait of a person was not the aim; instead the human form was idealized, so that men were shown in the prime of life and women in the gracefulness of youth. There were exceptions, however. Some men who held particularly high offices are shown as they must have appeared in later life. The seated limestone statue of the Prince and Vizier Hemon, for instance, c2550 BC (Römer- und Pelizaeus-Museum, Hildesheim), found in his tomb at Gizeh, is an imposing realistic example, showing this son of King Snefru in formal pose as a heavy, corpulent, but majestic figure.

Other rare realistic portrayals, mostly dating from the Old Kingdom, include statues of more ordinary people. There are famous limestone statues of scribes sitting cross-legged, each with a papyrus roll across his knees, as well as the famous

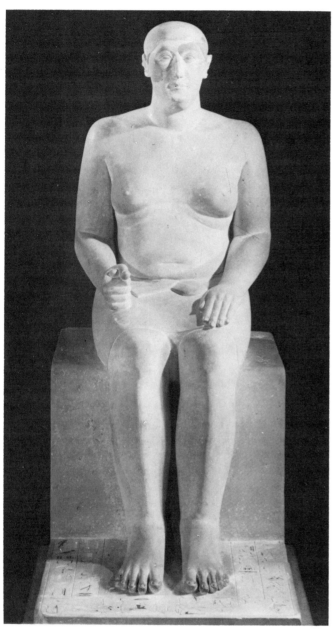

Limestone statue of Prince and Vizier Hemon, c2550 BC. Römer- und Pelizaeus Museum, Hildesheim

wooden figure called the Sheikh el-Beled, or village headman (Egyptian Museum, Cairo). It was made for Ka-aper, a priest and high official, c2400 BC, and shows him in prosperous middle age. A thin layer of painted stucco originally disguised the joints in the wood, and the lifelike appearance was enhanced by eyes made of quartz and crystal inserted in a copper mount. It was found in his tomb at Saqqara.

Several striking figures and groups show individuals with congenital deformities. The court dwarf Seneb, who owed his obvious success and wealth to his physique, is shown realisti-

Right: A wooden figure called the Sheikh el-Beled made for Ka-aper; height 109cm (43in); c2400 BC. Egyptian Museum, Cairo

cally in a small limestone funerary group, c2350 BC, sitting cross-legged next to his wife (Egyptian Museum, Cairo). The sculptor has treated him sympathetically. His deformity is not over-emphasized, and the group, completed by his son and daughter in the traditional pose of childhood, conveys the impression of a family closely united for the rest of eternity.

Traditional conventions. Most figures of individuals follow accepted conventions, and statues of kings and the gods in particular do achieve a timeless ideal. Treatments of the human figure in the round and in relief consistently draw on the same formal traditions. Men are usually shown striding forward on to the left foot, their hands at their sides, while women stand with their feet together or slightly apart.

Ancient traditions were also followed in coloring statues and reliefs fashioned in wood and limestone, which were usually brightly painted in their finished states. The skin of men, who spent much of their time out-of-doors, was always painted brown or reddish-brown, in sharp contrast to the creamy yellow or light pink tints used for the skin of royal and noble ladies who were expected to remain secluded from the harmful rays of the sun.

The two seated statues portraying the Prince Rehotep and his wife Nefert, c2620 BC, are remarkably well-preserved (Egyptian Museum, Cairo). Found in their 4th-Dynasty tomb at Medum they were probably carved by the same craftsman. In spite of the somewhat conventional and even sketchy treatment of the bodies, particularly the feet, the effect of the painting and the inlaid eyes is startlingly lifelike. The brown skin of Rehotep contrasts with the brilliant white of his short linen kilt and the white paint covering his chair which provides a background for the inscription. His wife is enveloped in a tightly-fitting white mantle. The hair of both is black, and fine detail such as the prince's moustache and the decoration on Nefert's headband have been left entirely to the painter.

By the mid 18th Dynasty, both men and women were often painted in the same reddish-brown, especially in tomb paintings, which often show large numbers of human figures outdoors in the marshes or indoors attending formal banquets. But with the elaboration of the dress of the late New Kingdom a different convention appears. The nobleman Menna is shown in two scenes in his tomb at Thebes, c1400 BC, in one fishing with a harpoon, in the other hunting wildfowl with a hunting stick. He wears a long sleeved garment of transparent linen over his short kilt. His face, forearms, and feet are painted the usual red-brown, but his legs and chest, outlined beneath the transparent robe, are colored creamy yellow. The effect, rather as if he was wearing dark gloves and socks, is quite common during the 18th and 19th Dynasties.

The convention of relative size was also followed from the earliest times: the most important figure in any scene was always shown larger than the rest. Thus the power and divinity of the king is at once apparent in his domination of any scene. The earliest surviving royal monuments, the ceremonial maces and palettes of c3000 BC, show that this convention

The court dwarf Seneb and his wife, limestone; height 33cm (13in); c2350. Egyptian Museum, Cairo

was already well established at the time of the union of Upper and Lower Egypt. The slate palette of Narmer, which presumably was made in celebration of his victories, depicts the king twice (Egyptian Museum, Cairo). On one side, wearing the Red Crown of Lower Egypt, he proceeds to inspect rows of corpses, perhaps of Lower Egyptian rebels. His figure is twice as large as those of his priest and sandal-bearer, who in turn are larger than the four standard-bearers who precede them. On the other side the king wears the White Crown of Upper Egypt, and is shown in the act of smiting an enemy. He appears to tower over his captive, though the contrast is achieved here by the kneeling posture of the latter who is in fact drawn to the same scale as the king. The sandal-bearer, however, is again much smaller than his lord.

The limestone Scorpion mace-head, which may have belonged to Narmer's immediate predecessor in the southern kingdom, was found at Hierakonpolis (Ashmolean Museum, Oxford). Again the king is at least twice as large as his followers and attendants, and is shown carrying out one of the most important functions of an Egyptian king: the first rite of the agricultural year, to ensure successful cultivation and a good harvest, performed as soon as the floodwaters had receded. The king's divinity enabled him to overcome his enemies, but his chief responsibility was for the welfare of the land of Egypt and its agricultural prosperity.

The Stela of Mentuhotep

Monumental stelae were first made c2850 BC and were set up to perpetuate the name of an Egyptian noble or official at the site of his tomb. The best are carved slabs of limestone or granite, and although their details vary according to the fashion of the time, they conform to a relatively standard pattern. The dead person is shown seated in front of an offering table, with inscriptions recording his name and titles. A ritual prayer formula, usually inscribed at the top of the stela, was meant to ensure that offerings would continue to be made to him throughout eternity.

The stela of Mentuhotep is a fine example of the small painted limestone stelae made during the Middle Kingdom, c2050–1750 BC. Mentuhotep, an official, sits at his offering table which is heaped with loaves, a calf's head, the foreleg of an ox, and a bundle of onions. Underneath the table are two pottery wine jars on ring stands: the seal of one is intact, but the other has been opened, ready to refill the cup on a tall stand at Mentuhotep's side. The dead man has the shaven head of a priest, and is prepared as if for an earthly feast, wearing a fine linen kilt, a broad necklace, anklets, and bracelets, and holding a lotus flower.

Stelae made during the Old Kingdom (c2680–c2180 BC) usually represent only the deceased, but here, at a later date, several members of Mentuhotep's family are also depicted on the lower part of the stela sharing his feast, although Mentuhotep himself is given due prominence. Their names and relationships are inscribed beside them, and, in fact, three generations of his family benefit from the magical power of the stela. In the register below his large figure, Mentuhotep appears again, this time on the right, facing his father of the same name. The bottom register includes three figures: on the right stands Renefseneb, a priest and probably Mentuhotep's brother, who faces a woman named in the register above as Henut, Mentuhotep's mother, seated next to her father, Kemmu, another priest.

The figures and offerings are carved in "incised" or "sunk" relief, which means that the outlines are cut deeply into the smooth prepared stone so that even modeled details with a raised and rounded form, such as the pots, never rise above the level background surface. The inscriptions consist of neat, precise hieroglyphs incised in two main lines at the top of the stela, while smaller signs are used for the individual names. The final details were painted on the carved surface so they stood out clearly against the honey color of the fine limestone background. Traces of the colors can still be seen; the red-brown used for the skin of the male figures, the pottery vessels, and the table supports has survived the best. The skin of the Lady Henut was yellow, the hieroglyphs blue, and the conventional border of rectangles between incised parallel lines was originally black, red, blue, yellow, and white. The red and yellow pigments were obtained from natural ochers, white from gypsum and black from soot, while blue was prepared from frit, a crystalline compound of silica, copper, and calcium. All the pigments were finely ground and mixed with water, and bound with either a gum or white of egg. The brushes used for small detailed work were rushes with frayed ends.

The carving of the human figures is stylized in the usual manner, with the head and legs in profile and the upper part of the body and the eye shown as from the front, which the Egyptians believed gave a perfect representation of the human form on a flat surface. The brother Renefseneb is the only standing figure, and his left leg is placed in the traditional way. They are all shown in the prime of life—how they wished to appear for the rest of eternity.

Certain features, such as the slightly elongated head and the prominent ears, help to date the stela to the early part of the Middle Kingdom, and this is supported by other details, including the personal names. The name Mentuhotep, for instance, was borne by four kings of the 11th Dynasty before 1190 BC, and it was always fashionable in Egypt to name a child in honor of the king reigning at the time of his birth. These kings had their capital at Thebes in the south, and it is possible that this stela was originally found in one of the Theban cemeteries.

The composition of the funerary formula and the way in which the hieroglyphs are carved are also characteristic of the Middle Kingdom. Beneath the two stylized eyes of the falcon sky-god Horus at the top of the stela, the formula, or prayer for offerings, is incised in two well-spaced lines. It is read from right to left, towards the animal and bird signs:

> A gift which the king gives to Osiris, lord of life of the Two Lands, that he may give invocation offerings of bread and beer, cattle and birds, linen and alabaster, incense and *merhet* oil to the *ka* [spirit] of the revered Mentuhotep, justified [before Osiris], born of Henut, justified [before Osiris].

Funerary stelae continued to be made in Egypt for nearly 2,000 years after this one. The prayers and formulae changed as time passed; later the deceased are shown praising the gods rather than sitting at their own funerary feast. But whether they are made of stone or cheaper, painted wood, the basic purpose remains the same: to preserve the identity of the dead for ever.

DOROTHY DOWNES

Further reading. James, T.G.H. *An Introduction to Ancient Egypt*, Oxford (1979).

Far right The funerary Stela of Mentuhotep; 51×38cm (20×15in). Merseyside County Museums, Liverpool

▶ A detail of the main register: Mentuhotep and a lotus flower

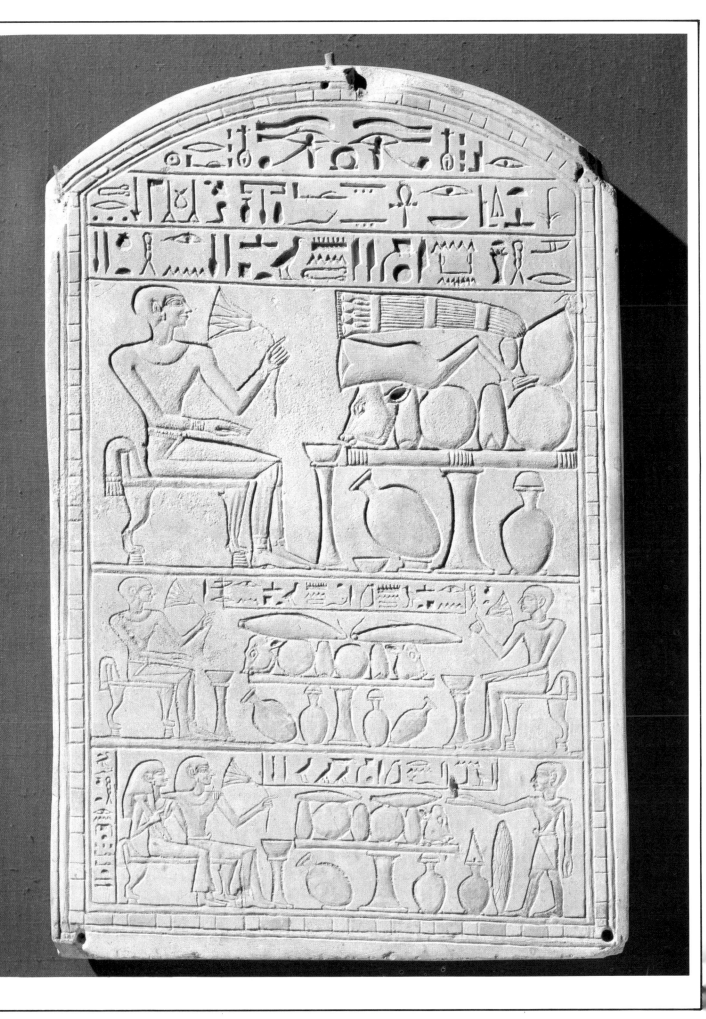

Limestone Scorpion mace-head from Hierakonpolis height 23cm (9in).
Ashmolean Museum, Oxford

Ceremonial reliefs of the Old and Middle Kingdoms, though rare and fragmentary, show that the traditions of relative size were consistently followed. In the New Kingdom the emphasis was on the king as a victorious leader of armies or as a mighty hunter. Great scenes in relief on the gates and walls of temples show him in his chariot galloping across mounds of the bodies of his enemies, or leading his personal guard to hunt in the desert. Similar scenes on a smaller scale appear as decorations on the painted casket found in the tomb of Tutankhamun, c1340 BC (Egyptian Museum, Cairo).

Members of the king's family, and later other nobles and officials, gradually adopted customs and rituals that had originally been the prerogative of the king. By the end of the 5th Dynasty the walls of tombs of nobles of the Old Kingdom at Saqqara, Gizeh, and elsewhere were covered with scenes depicting life on their estates, with the magical aim of ensuring it would go on forever. The lord—hunting, fishing, or presiding at the counting of cattle and supervising work in the fields—was shown, like the king, as larger than any of his servants or the rest of his family.

This tradition of differentiation by size was often followed by sculptors portraying husbands and wives. Whether standing or seated, quite ordinary officials were shown up to three times as large as their wives. The limestone statuette of Sekhem-ka, c2400 BC (Central Museum, Northampton), shows him seated with his wife beside him, her legs tucked

gracefully beneath her. She touches his right leg in a gesture of affection, but her head only just reaches the level of his knee. The offering-bearers carved in relief on the sides of the block seat are even smaller.

Egyptian artists and craftsmen. The men who carved sculptures and reliefs and painted the walls of rock-cut tombs were not artists in the modern sense in which an artist is supposed to be a creative individual. The approach of the ancient Egyptians was essentially practical, and their art was rather the work of paid artisans who were trained and who then worked

Limestone statuette of Sekhem-ka; height 75cm (30in); c2400 BC.
Central Museum, Northampton

as part of a team. The master craftsman might be very versatile, and capable of working in many branches of art, but his part in the production of a statue or the decoration of a tomb was anonymous. He would certainly guide his assistants as they worked, and help to train beginners, but his personal contribution cannot be assessed.

Men at all stages of their craft worked together. The initial outline drawing would be executed by one or more, who would then be followed by others carving the intermediate and final stages. Painters would follow in the same manner. Where scenes have been left unfinished it is possible to see the corrections made to the work of less-skilled hands by more practised craftsmen.

Many master craftsmen reached positions of influence and social importance, as we know from their own funerary monuments. Imhotep, the architect who built the Step Pyramid complex for King Zoser, 2660–2590 BC, was so highly revered in later times that he was deified. The credit for any work of art, however, was believed to belong to the patron who had commissioned it.

Carving in relief and painting. Carving in relief and painting may be considered together as the conventions followed by craftsmen of one or the other were, at least in the initial stages of a work, very similar, and most reliefs were intended to be completed by the addition of color.

The earliest incised figures and scenes in relief date from prehistoric times when slate cosmetic palettes and combs of wood, bone, and ivory were buried in the graves of their owners. These were carved in the simple, effective outlines of species familiar to the people of the Nile Valley—antelopes, ibex, fish, and birds. More elaborate ivory combs and the ivory handles of flint knives which probably had some ceremonial purpose were carved in relief, the scene standing out from its background.

On the so-called Carnarvon knife handle, *c*3400 BC (Metropolitan Museum, New York), 10 species of wild animals are grouped around a boss, decorated with a rosette, in a way that suggests the representation of a naturalistic desert scene. On other fragments where animals occur they are arranged more formally in rows. Sometimes unusual themes occur, such as the hero figure shown between two lions on the Gebel el-Arak knife handle, of similar date, which seems to indicate Mesopotamian influence (Louvre, Paris).

By the end of the prehistoric period the distinctive Egyptian style is unmistakable. So far there were no great architectural monuments on which the skill of the sculptors could be displayed. From the meager evidence of a few carvings on fragments of bone and ivory we know that the gods were worshiped in shrines constructed of bundles of reeds. The chieftains of prehistoric Egypt probably lived in similar structures, very like the *mudhifs* still found in the marshes of South Arabia.

The work of sculptors was displayed in the production of ceremonial mace-heads and palettes, carved to commemorate

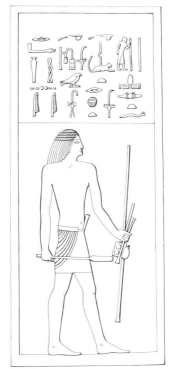

The relief decoration on a panel from the tomb of Hesire at Saqqara

An ivory fragment showing a prehistoric shrine. Merseyside County Museums, Liverpool

victories and other important events and dedicated to the gods. They show that the distinctive sculptural style, echoed in all later periods of Egyptian history, had already emerged, and the convention of showing the human figure partly in profile and partly in frontal view was well-established. The significance of many details cannot yet be fully explained, but representations of the king as a powerful lion or a strong bull are often repeated in Dynastic times.

Early royal reliefs, showing the king smiting his enemies or striding forward in ritual pose, are somewhat stiff and stilted, but by the 3rd Dynasty techniques were already very advanced. Most surviving examples are in stone, but the 11 wooden panels found in the tomb of Hesire at Saqqara, 2660–2590 BC, show the excellence achieved by master craftsmen (Egyptian Museum, Cairo). These figures, standing and seated, carved according to the conventions of Egyptian ideals of manhood, emphasized in different ways the different elements of the human form. The head, chest, and legs are shown in profile, but the visible eye and the shoulders are depicted as if seen from the front, and the waist and hips are in three-quarter view. However, this artificial pose does not look awkward because of the preservation of natural proportion. The excellence of the technique, shown in the fine modeling of the muscles of face and body, bestows a grace upon what might otherwise seem rigid and severe.

Hesire, carrying the staff and scepter of his rank and the palette and pen case symbolizing his office of royal scribe, gazes proudly and confidently into eternity. The care of the craftsman does not stop with the figure of his patron, for the hieroglyphs making up the inscription giving the name and titles of the deceased are also carved with delicacy and assurance, and are fine representations in miniature of the animals, birds, and objects used in ancient Egyptian writing. The animals and birds used as hieroglyphs are shown in true profile.

The great cemeteries of Gizeh and Saqqara in which the nobles and court officials were buried near their kings provide many examples of the skill of the craftsmen of the 4th, 5th, and 6th Dynasties, a skill rarely equaled in later periods. The focus of the early tombs was a slab of stone carved with a representation of the deceased sitting in front of a table of offerings. These funerary stelae were usually placed above the false door, through which the spirit of the dead person, called the *ka*, might continue to enter and leave the tomb. The idea behind this was that the magical representation of offerings on the stelae, activated by the correct religious formulas, would exist for the rest of eternity, together with the *ka* of the person to whom they were made.

The stela of the Princess Nefertiabtet, *c*2550 BC (Louvre, Paris), from her 4th-Dynasty tomb at Gizeh, is not, perhaps, technically as fine a piece of carving as the panels of Hesire. The original color, however, is excellently preserved, and shows how these stelae were intended to appear, with the carving providing a raised foundation for the brightness of the painted detail that brings the stone to life. The king's daughter is seated on a chair with bulls' legs in front of her offering table. Her simple, closely fitting garment is of leopard skin, and she has ornamental bands at throat, wrists, and ankles. Her name is inscribed above her head, and the hieroglyphs listing the items of food, drink, oils, and linen needed for eternity are delicately outlined, spaced, and colored, while the whole scene is neatly enclosed within a painted border. As in the scenes arranged on the walls of Old Kingdom tombs, and all tomb and temple scenes of later periods, the Egyptian artist kept his characters inside the framework designed for them.

In single scenes, or in registers filling a wall from ceiling to floor, every figure had its proper place and was not permitted to overflow its allotted space. One of the most notable achievements of Egyptian craftsmen was the way they filled the space available in a natural, balanced way, so that scenes full of life never seem to be cramped or overcrowded.

The horizontal sequences or registers of scenes arranged on either side of the funerary stelae and false doors in 5th- and 6th-Dynasty tombs are full of lively and natural detail. Here

The Stela of the Princess Nefertiabtet from her 4th-Dynasty tomb at Gizeh; *c*2550 BC. Louvre, Paris

the daily life of peasant and noble was caught for eternity by the craftsman—the action of herdsman and fisherman frozen in mid-step, so that the owner of the tomb would always be surrounded by the daily bustle of his estate. The subjects were intended to be typical of normal events, familiar scenes rather than special occasions.

Egyptian craftsmen did not employ perspective to suggest depth and distance, but they did establish a convention whereby several registers, each with its own base line, could be used to depict a crowd of people. Those in the lowest register were understood to be nearest to the viewer, those in the highest furthest away. A number of these scenes occur in the Old Kingdom: many offering-bearers bring the produce of their estates to a deceased noble at his funerary table, for instance, or troops of men are shown hauling a great statue. Statues represented in reliefs, like the hieroglyphs, are shown in true profile, in contrast to the figures of the men hauling them. Perhaps the best-known scenes showing nearness and distance, however, are the painted banqueting scenes of the New Kingdom, where the numerous guests, dressed in their finest clothes, sit in serried ranks in front of their hosts.

The registers could also be used to present various stages in a developing sequence of action, rather like the frames of a strip cartoon. In the Old Kingdom, the important events of the agricultural year follow each other across the walls of many tombs: plowing, sowing, harvesting, and threshing the grain are all faithfully represented. The herdsmen are shown at work in the pastures caring for the cattle so prized by the ancient Egyptians, while other scenes depict the trapping of waterfowl in the Nile marshes and fishing in the river itself. Other domestic activities, such as baking and brewing, also vital to the eternal existence of the dead noble are represented; other scenes show carpenters, potters, and jewelers at work.

It was in these scenes of everyday life that the sculptor was able to use his initiative, and free himself to some extent from the ties of convention. The dead man and his family had to be presented in ritual poses as described—larger than life, strictly proportioned, and always calm and somewhat aloof. The workers on the estates, however, could be shown at their daily tasks in a more relaxed manner, capturing something of the liveliness and energy that must have characterized the ancient Egyptians. While the offering-bearers, symbolizing the funerary gifts from the estates to their lord, are depicted moving towards him in formal and stately procession, the peasants at work in the fields seem both sturdy and vigorous. They lean to the plough and beat the asses, tend the cattle and carry small calves on their shoulders clear of the danger of crocodiles lurking in the marshes. Boatmen fight in sport among themselves, as in the tomb of Ptah-hotep, c2400 BC. Many scenes have titles in well-carved hieroglyphs that are an integral part of the action, and the comments of the workers themselves, not always polite, are also inscribed above them.

There are some excellent scenes showing work in the fields in the tomb of Mereruka, c2350 BC, who is depicted watching the harvesting of flax and corn (in situ; copies in Oriental

Scenes in the 5th-Dynasty tomb of Ti at Saqqara, 2470–2320 BC

Museum, Chicago). The sheaves are being loaded into panniers carried by asses, while on the threshing floor the corn is tossed by men with pitchforks, and trodden out by groups of goats, asses, and oxen. Comments such as "Hurry up" and "The barley is very fine" are included.

The decoration of many tombs survives in fragmentary condition, but some, like the tomb of Mereruka, are famous for the quality and quantity of the scenes that remain. Another fine example is the 5th-Dynasty tomb of Ti, 2470–2320 BC, also at Saqqara. The marsh scenes in this tomb are among the most vivid of all Egyptian reliefs. The herdsmen are shown urging their cattle through the water. One cow bends her neck to taste a clump of grass, while another raises her head to call to a calf, carried by a herdsman, which turns to look at her. The men themselves are not quite so successfully carved. The right shoulder of one, towards the viewer, supposed to be bent with the effort of carrying a water bottle on a staff, appears hunched and unnatural because the sculptor has not kept to the traditional frontal view of the shoulders. The man carrying the calf, however, is well done. He bends forward under the weight, and his receding hair shows he is old. Further naturalism is added by the clever combination of carved relief and painting. The carving of the legs stops at the surface of the water which is indicated by vertical zigzags, and the effect of the legs of men and animals being visible under water is achieved by painting them across the ripples.

The natural details used to fill odd corners in these tomb scenes show how much pleasure the ancient Egyptian craftsmen took in observing their environment. Birds, insects, and clumps of plants were all used to balance and complete the picture. The results of sharp-eyed observation can be seen in the details that distinguish the species of birds and fish thronging the reeds and shallow water of the marshes.

Little survives of the reliefs that decorated the royal temples of the early 5th Dynasty, but from the funerary temple of the first king, Userkaf, c2460 BC, comes a fragment from a scene of hunting in the marshes (Egyptian Museum, Cairo). The air above the graceful heads of the papyrus reeds is alive with birds, and the delicate carving makes them easily distinguishable even without the addition of color. A hoopoe, ibis, kingfisher, and heron are unmistakable, and a large butterfly hovering above provides the final touch.

From fragments it has been possible to reconstruct the great hunting scene carved on the wall of the sun temple built by Userkaf's successor Sahure at Abusir. This scene is particularly interesting because for once the sculptors did not keep to the convention of parallel registers. The base lines are there, but they undulate and give an impression of desert landscape. Hunting dogs pursue many different species of antelope and gazelle, or wait to seize newly born antelope. The larger animals are beautifully outlined, but the smaller animals again provide the finishing touches: hedgehogs, jerboas, and desert hares crouch among the tussocks of grass, or scuttle across the open areas of sand.

The tradition of finely detailed decoration in low relief, the figures standing out slightly above the background, continued through the 6th Dynasty and into the Middle Kingdom, when it was particularly used for royal monuments. Few fragments of these remain, but the hieroglyphs carved on the little chapel of Sesostris I, now reconstructed at Karnak, show the sure and delicate touch of master craftsmen.

During the late Old Kingdom, low relief was combined with other techniques such as incision, in which lines were

Stela of Hotep; height 95cm (37in); 2000–1800 BC. Merseyside County Museums, Liverpool

Limestone funerary Stela of Ne-ankhteti; 84×66cm (33×26in); c2250 BC. Merseyside County Museums, Liverpool

simply cut into the stone, especially in non-royal monuments, and the result is often artistically very pleasing. The limestone funerary stela of Ne-ankhteti, c2250 BC, is a fine example (Merseyside County Museums, Liverpool). The major part of the stela, the figure and the horizontal inscription above it, is in low relief, but an incised vertical panel of hieroglyphs repeats his name with another title, and the symbol for scribe, the palette and pen, needed for the beginning of both lines, is used only once, at the point at which the lines intersect. The result is a perfectly balanced design, and a welcome variation in the types of stelae carved during the Old Kingdom.

A further development is shown in the stela of Hotep, carved during the Middle Kingdom, 2000–1800 BC (Merseyside County Museums, Liverpool). The figures of three standing officials and the hieroglyphic signs have been crisply incised into the hard red granite. Originally the signs and figures would have been filled with blue pigment, to contrast sharply with the polished red surface of the stone. (Incidentally, the inscription is an excellent example of the standard prayer for funerary offerings, the *hotep-di-nsw* formula, in its classic Middle Kingdom form. Hieroglyphs are read towards the front of the animal and bird signs, here from right to left, and this inscription begins: "A gift which the King gives to Osiris, Lord of Busiris, the good god, Lord of Abydos, that he may give invocation offerings of bread and beer, oxen and fowl, alabaster and clothing, and every good and pure thing on which a god lives, to the revered superintendant of the palace, Hotep, born of the Lady Khnumhotep", and more genealogy follows. In this inscription the hieroglyphs are in outline, and are not shown in the exact detail of some of the inscriptions already mentioned, but here again the sense of space and balance that seems to have been so natural to the ancient Egyptians is very much in evidence.)

During the Middle Kingdom the use of sunk relief came into fashion, and in the 18th and early 19th Dynasties it was employed to great effect. The background was not cut away as in low relief to leave the figures standing above the level of the rest of the surface. Instead the relief design was cut down into the smoothed surface of the stone. In the strong Egyptian sunlight the carved detail would stand out well, but the sunk relief was better protected from the weather and was therefore more durable.

Some of the finest 18th-Dynasty scenes in low relief decorate the mortuary temple of Queen Hatshepsut, 1490–1470 BC, at Deir el-Bahri, where the delicate carving is complemented by the colors that give light and beauty to the elaborate scenes. Hatshepsut, needing to underline her claim to the Egyptian throne, had the traditional scenes of daily life supplemented for the first time in Egyptian history by scenes depicting actual events. On the north side of the central terrace is the divine conception and birth of the queen, while the south side is devoted to the story of the expedition that she

Queen Hatshepsut drinks from the udder of the cow goddess Hathor in her mortuary temple at Deir el-Bahri

sent to fetch incense trees from the land of Punt. The ships commissioned by the queen are carved with loving care, while the artists surpassed themselves in the details of Punt itself. Native huts, various species of plants and animals, and the people themselves, are all represented with great accuracy, particularly the Princess of Punt with her lined face and bulky body.

Similar delight in natural detail is shown in the scenes carved in a room of the temple of Tuthmosis III at Karnak, c1470–1450 BC. Here the animals and plants brought back to Egypt after the king's campaign are depicted, and the result is gay and joyful. In the more public halls of this and other great temples scenes showing the successful campaigns of victorious New Kingdom rulers were designed as propaganda, with the aim of emphasizing the all-powerful nature of the kings of Egypt. Delicacy frequently gives way to the need for bold, eye-catching detail, especially during the 19th Dynasty. Later, however, many Ptolemaic reliefs are characterized by the subtle modeling of the rather fleshy features of royalty and gods alike.

Painting in ancient Egypt followed a similar pattern to the development of scenes in carved relief, and the two techniques were often combined. The first examples of painting occur in the prehistoric period, in the patterns and scenes on pottery already mentioned. We depend very much for our evidence on what has survived, and fragments are necessarily few because of the fragile nature of the medium. Parts of two scenes depicting figures and boats are known, one on linen and one on a tomb wall. Panels of brightly colored patterns survive on the walls of royal tombs of the 1st Dynasty, the patterns representing the mats and woven hangings that decorated the walls of large houses. These patterns occur again and again throughout Egyptian history in many different ways. Some of the finest may be seen on the sides of the rectangular wooden coffins found in the tombs of Middle Kingdom nobles at Beni Hasan and elsewhere, c2000–1800 BC.

The earliest representational paintings in the unmistakable traditional Egyptian style date from the 3rd and 4th Dynasties. The most famous are probably the fragments from the tomb of Itet at Medum, c2725 BC, showing groups of geese which formed part of a large scene of fowling in the marshes (Egyptian Museum, Cairo). The geese, of several different species, stand rather stiffly among clumps of stylized vegetation, but the markings are carefully picked out, and the colors are natural and subtle.

Throughout the Old Kingdom, paint was used to decorate and finish limestone reliefs, but during the 6th Dynasty painted scenes began to supersede relief in private tombs for economic reasons. It was less expensive to commission scenes painted directly on walls of tombs, although their magic was just as effective.

During the First Intermediate Period and the Middle Kingdom, the rectangular wooden coffins of nobles were often painted with elaborate care, turning them into real houses for the spirits of the dead. Their exteriors bore inscriptions giving

Wooden Models from the Tombs

The tombs of Egyptian nobles and officials have yielded a rich variety of objects, but none more valuable to the archaeologist than the small, wooden models showing scenes of daily life which were packed into the tomb chamber around the coffin. Most of these were made between 2000 and 1750 BC for the magical purpose of ensuring that life after death would incorporate all earthly necessities and comforts. So the models depict every aspect of life on the great man's estates.

In general they do not exhibit a high degree of skill in carving and construction, the average model consisting of painted peg-doll figures (parts of which are often missing) crudely mounted on a wooden base about 16 in (40 cm) square. However, this very roughness contributes to an impression of vitality, and many people find them charming and attractive. Traditional artistic conventions are respected as far as possible, the men-servants painted reddish-brown, the women yellow or cream, all with exaggeratedly large eyes. A tendency towards realism is shown in such details as the wisps of actual linen tied over the painted garments, and it is this quality of verisimilitude that makes them so fascinating. Through them we can build up a detailed picture of daily life in Egypt 4,000 years ago.

A particularly fine example is a model from the Theban tomb of the Chancellor Meket-Re showing the annual cattle census. The noble sits under a shady canopy with his sons, while scribes record the count as herdsmen drive the beasts past. Scribes also feature in the granaries, which are a favorite subject of the model-makers, and are shown recording the number of sacks carried up by laborers to be emptied into the grain bins. Other models represent the work done in the fields, with men hoeing and teams of oxen plowing.

▲ A sailing boat from Beni Hasan. Ashmolean Museum, Oxford

◄ A baker and a butcher. Merseyside County Museums, Liverpool

But the whole range of jobs involved in the running of a busy estate is depicted in three-dimensional fullness. Kitchen models show women engaged in all stages of bread-making, grinding, kneading, and baking, side by side with men making beer, straining the mash from fermented barley bread into beer vats, while trussed oxen lie ready at the butchers' feet. Great quantities of linen were required by a large household, and we can watch some women spinning and winding the thread, while others weave cloth on horizontal looms. Sometimes these are merely painted on the base of the scene, but sometimes the looms and all their fittings have been carefully modeled. Other sources may tell us that the estate carpenters were highly skilled men who furnished the noble's house on earth and provided much of his funerary equipment, including the all-important coffin to house him for eternity, but the models give us an insight into how they worked: sawing planks from logs lashed to vertical posts, and wielding their mallets and chisels and adzes.

Boat models emphasize, by the frequency of their occurrence, the importance of the Nile in Egyptian life, and illustrate the different types of craft: large cargo boats with oars for rowing downstream, and detachable masts which were erected for sailing upstream; passenger boats with hide-covered cabins for important passengers and kitchen boats following to supply creature comforts; lighter vessels made of bundles of papyrus reeds lashed together. These included the craft the nobles used for pleasure—pleasure which was continued after death by the inclusion of the models in the tombs.

For all these models were made for the benefit of great men who dominated their fellows during earthly life, and who dominate our view of their civilization because of the attention paid to their afterlives in the form of funerary furnishings. Not the least value of the wooden models is the glimpses they give of the everyday existence of ordinary laborers and artisans in ancient Egypt.

DOROTHY DOWNES

Further reading. James, T.G.H. *The Archaeology of Ancient Egypt*, London (1972). Jordan, P. *Egypt, the Black Land*, Oxford (1976). Winlock, H.E. *Models of Daily Life in Ancient Egypt*, Cambridge, Mass. (1955).

▶ A private boat showing rowers and the owner from Deir el-Bahri. Egyptian Museum, Cairo

▼ Estate Carpenters from the tomb of Meket-Re. Egyptian Museum, Cairo

Below left A granary. Ashmolean Museum, Oxford

▼ Nubian soldiers march to war. Egyptian Museum, Cairo

the names and titles of their owners, and invoking the protection of various gods. The remaining surface areas were covered with brightly painted panels imitating the walls of houses hung with woven mats, and incorporating windows and doors in complicated geometric patterns. Great attention was paid to the "false door" situated at the head end of the coffin through which the *ka* would be able to enter and leave as it pleased. This panel always included the two sacred eyes of the falcon sky-god Horus, which would enable the dead to look out into the living world.

The interior surfaces of the coffins were sometimes painted with the offerings made to the dead, ensuring that these would continue in the afterlife. An offering table piled with bread, meat, and vegetables was the central feature. A list of ritual offerings was also important, and personal possessions such as weapons, staffs of office, pottery and stone vessels, and items of clothing were all shown in detail. Headcloths were painted at the head end, and spare pairs of sandals at the feet.

These coffins were placed in the small rock-cut chambers of Upper Egyptian tombs, where the stone is often too rough or crumbly to provide a good surface for painting. Fragments of painted murals do survive, however, and some tombs have lively scenes of hunting in the desert or of agricultural work. Acute observation also produced unusual subjects such as men wrestling or boys playing games, shown in sequence like a series of stills from a moving film. Others are painted with outstanding skill. Part of a marsh scene in a tomb at Beni Hasan, *c*1800 BC, shows a group of birds in an acacia tree. The frond-like leaves of the tree are delicately painted, and the birds, three shrikes, a hoopoe, and a redstart, are easily identifiable.

Tomb painting really came into its own, however, during the New Kingdom, particularly in the tombs of the great necropolis at Thebes. Here the limestone was generally too poor and flaky for relief carving, but the surface could be plastered to provide a ground for the painter. As always, the traditional

The "false door" at the head end of the coffin of Keki. Merseyside County Museums, Liverpool

A banquet scene from the tomb of Nebamun; *c*1400 BC. British Museum, London

conventions were observed, particularly in the formal scenes depicting the dead man where he appears larger than his family and companions. Like the men who carved the Old Kingdom reliefs, however, the painters could use their imaginations for the minor details that filled in the larger scenes. Birds and animals in the marshes, usually depicted in profile, have their markings carefully hatched in, giving an impression of real fur and feathers; and their actions are sometimes very realistic. In the tomb of Nebamun, *c*1400 BC, a hunting cat,

already grasping birds in its claws, leaps to seize a duck in its mouth.

Fragments illustrating a banquet from the same tomb give the impression that the painter not only had outstanding skill but a particular delight in experimenting with unusual detail. The noble guests sit in formal rows, but the servants and entertainers were not so important and did not have to conform in the same way. Groups of female musicians kneel gracefully on the floor, the soles of their feet turned towards the viewer, while two in one group are shown almost full-face, which is very rare. The lightness and gaiety of the music is conveyed by their inclined heads and the apparent movement of the tiny braids of their elaborately plaited hair. Lively movement continues with the pair of young dancers, shown in profile, whose clapping hands and flying feet are depicted with great sensitivity. A further unusual feature is the shading of the soles of the musicians' feet and pleated robes.

Painting not only decorated the walls of New Kingdom

tombs, but gave great beauty to the houses and palaces of the living. Frescoes of reeds, water, birds, and animals enhanced the walls, ceilings, and floors of the palaces of Amarna and elsewhere; but after the 19th Dynasty there was a steady decline in the quality of such painting. On a smaller scale, painting on papyrus, furniture, and wooden coffins continued to be skillful until the latest periods of Egyptian history, though there was also much poor-quality mass-produced work.

Techniques of relief and painting. Before any carving in relief or painting could be done the ground, whether stone or wood, had to be prepared. If the surface was good, smoothing was often enough, but any flaws had to be masked with plaster. During the New Kingdom, whole walls were plastered, and sometimes reliefs of exquisite detail were carved in the plaster itself. Usually mud plaster was used, coated with a thin layer of fine gypsum.

The next stage was the drafting, and the scenes were sketched in, often in red, using a brush or a scribe's reed pen. This phase was important, particularly when a complicated scene with many figures was planned, or when a whole wall was to be covered with scenes arranged in horizontal registers. Some craftsmen were confident enough to be able to use freehand, but more often intersecting horizontal and vertical lines were used as a guide. These could be ruled, or made by tightly holding the ends of a string dipped in pigment, and twanging it across the surface. Quite early in Egyptian history the proportions of the grid were fixed to ensure that human figures were drawn according to the fixed canon. Since the decoration in some tombs was never finished, the grid lines

A limestone fragment with a figure of Tuthmosis I; height 36cm (14in); 1530–1520 BC. Merseyside County Museums, Liverpool

and sketches can be clearly seen, together with corrections made by master craftsmen.

The next stage in producing a relief was to chisel round the correct outlines and reduce the surrounding level, until the scene consisted of a series of flat shapes standing against the background in low relief. Then the final details could be carved and the surface smoothed ready for painting. Any corrections and alterations made to the carving could be hidden beneath a coat of plaster before the paint was applied. A limestone fragment with a figure of Tuthmosis I, 1530–1520 BC, now bare of plaster and paint, shows a change in the position of the arms which would not have been visible when the relief was finished (Merseyside County Museums, Liverpool).

A number of finely decorated tombs were left with the carving finished but unpainted on the death of the owner. Scenes in the tomb of Ramose at Thebes, c1400 BC, show the guests at his banquet, seated in pairs in front of their host. The painting of the scene never progressed beyond the eyes, and the skilful modeling of the elaborately plaited wigs and finely pleated linen robes can be examined in detail. The carving is sophisticated and beautifully finished, although the warmth and vigor evident in Old Kingdom reliefs seem to be missing.

The painter working directly to a draft on a flat surface, or coloring a relief, began with the background. This was filled in with one color, gray, white, or yellow, using a brush made of a straight twig or reed with the fibers teased out. The larger areas of human figures were painted next, the skin color applied, and the linen garments painted. Precise details, such as the markings of animals and birds or the petalled tiers of an ornamental collar, were finished with a finer brush or a pen.

The pigments were prepared from natural substances such as red and yellow ocher, powdered malachite, carbon black, and gypsum. From about six basic colors it was possible to mix many intermediate shades. The medium was water to which gum was sometimes added, and the paint was applied in areas of flat color. During the New Kingdom delicate effects were achieved by using tiny strokes of the brush or pen to pick out animal fur or the fluffy heads of papyrus reeds. Shading was rarely used until the mid 18th Dynasty, when it was employed, particularly in crowd scenes, to suggest the fine pleating of linen garments. The figure of Nefertari, Queen of Ramesses II, 1301–1235 BC, in her tomb at Thebes, is carved in plaster. The relief is most delicately painted, the face in an unusual shade of light pink. The subtlety of the painting is enhanced by shading, particularly on the face and neck.

The comparative freedom felt by painters when dealing with subsidiary figures has already been mentioned. Close examination of groups of figures, particularly in tomb scenes, is often rewarding because tiny details are not always easy to see. Figures in a group may at first appear to be exactly alike, but slight variations in the positions of arms and head give individuality to each, while the faces of female mourners, for instance, are finished with the marks of tears.

Sketches made by painters on flakes of limestone, mostly dating from the New Kingdom, show that when they drew for

In the tomb of Ramose at Thebes: Ramose with his wife (left); c 1400 BC

their own pleasure they were unfettered by convention. Some are painted and finely finished, such as the figure of an acrobatic dancing girl bending backwards with her hair trailing on the floor (Museo Egizio, Turin). Others are simply quick sketches catching their subjects in the middle of an action; a girl painting her lips or a man riding.

Sculpture in the round. Egyptian craftsmen were producing a wide variety of small figures in clay, bone, and ivory, well before the emergence of a formal style of sculpture at the time of the unification of the Two Lands of Egypt. A few, fragile figurines have been found in prehistoric graves. The tradition

Right: A New Kingdom sketch of an acrobatic dancing girl.
Museo Egizio, Turin

of making such objects survived right down to the New Kingdom. Bone and ivory were used to make stylized female figures of elaborate workmanship between 4000 and 3000 BC. Clay, which was easier to shape, was molded into representations of many species of animals, easy to identify because their characteristics have been captured by acute observation.

By c3000 BC ivory statuettes were being carved in a more naturalistic style, and many fragments have survived. One of the finest and most complete was found at Abydos, representing an unknown king, depicted in ceremonial costume (British Museum, London). He is wearing the tall White Crown of Upper Egypt and the short cloak associated with the *heb sed* or Jubilee ceremonies, here patterned with lozenges. He strides confidently forward in the pose used for all male standing statues in Dynastic times, left foot in front of right. The quality of the carving is shown in the way in which the robe is wrapped tightly across the rounded shoulders, and the head is thrust forward with determination and strength of purpose.

From this period, just preceding the 1st Dynasty, there is evidence that sculptors were making great advances, and were using wood, and stone of various kinds. This development continued through the Archaic Period, when the first larger royal statues were made. Work in metal also made progress; miniature copper statuettes and gold amulets have been found in tombs, while an inscription of the 2nd Dynasty records the making of a royal statue in copper.

Much more evidence, of course, survives to show the development of sculpture in stone. It was in the late 2nd and early 3rd Dynasties, from about 2700 BC, that what could be termed the characteristic ancient-Egyptian style of sculpture in stone was established, a style transmitted through some 2,500 years to the Ptolemaic period with only minor exceptions and modifications. The predominant features of this style are the regularity and symmetry of the figures, solid and four-square whether standing or seated. Michelangelo is reputed to have believed that a block of stone contained a sculpture, as it were in embryo, which it was the artist's task to reveal. The typical ancient-Egyptian completed figure gives a strong impression of the block of stone from which it was carved. The artists removed an absolute minimum of raw stone, commonly leaving the legs fused in a solid mass to a back pillar, the arms attached to the sides of the body, while seated figures were welded to their chairs. Not that these sculptures seem clumsy or crude; they convey an impression of severe elegance, a purity of line that suggests by its tautness a restrained energy.

The first stages in the making of a statue, as with relief and painting, involved the drafting of a preliminary sketch. A block of stone was roughly shaped, and the figure to be carved was drawn on at least two sides to give the front and side views. Guidelines, and, later, a squared grid ensured that the proportions of the statue would be made exactly according to the rules fixed early in Dynastic times. Master-drawings, some of which have survived, were available for reference. A wooden drawing board with a coat of gesso, now in the British Museum, London, is a good example. A seated figure of Tuthmosis III, 1504–1450 BC, first sketched in red and then outlined in black, has been drawn across a grid of finely ruled small squares. Master craftsmen after years of practice would be able to work instinctively, but inexperienced sculptors would keep such drawings at hand for easy reference.

The actual carving of a statue involved the sheer hard work of pounding and chipping the block on all sides until the rough outline of the figure was complete. New guidelines were drawn in, when it became necessary to keep the implements cutting squarely into the block from all sides. The harder stones, such as granite and diorite, were worked by bruising and pounding with hard hammer-stones, thus gradually abrading the parent block. Cutting by means of metal saws and drills, helped by the addition of an abrasive such as quartz sand, was used to work the awkward angles between the arms and the body, or between the lower legs. Each stage was long and tedious, and the copper and, later, bronze tools had to be resharpened constantly. Polishing removed most of the toolmarks, but on some statues, particularly the really large ones such as the huge figures of Ramesses II at the temple of Abu Simbel, traces of the marks made by tubular drills can still be seen. For a colossal statue, scaffolding was erected round a figure, enabling many men to work on it at once. Limestone, of course, was softer, and therefore easier to work with chisels and drills.

An ivory statuette of an unknown king, found at Abydos; ivory; height 9cm (3½in). British Museum, London

Unfinished statues provide useful evidence of the processes involved. Most of them showed that work proceeded evenly from all sides, thus maintaining the balance of the figure. A quartzite head, possibly of Queen Nefertiti, found in a workshop at Amarna, *c*1360 BC, is obviously near to completion (Egyptian Museum, Cairo). It was probably intended to be part of a composite statue, and the top of the head has been shaped and left rough to take a crown or wig of another material. The surface of the face appears to be ready for the final smoothing and painting, but the guidelines are still there to indicate the line of the hair and the median plane of the face. Rather thicker lines marking the outline of the eyes and the eyebrows make it look as if further work was planned, to cut these out to enable them to be inlaid with other stones so that the head would be really lifelike when it was finished.

Egyptian statuary was made to be placed in tombs or temples and was usually intended to be seen from the front. It was important that the face should look straight ahead, into eternity, and that the body viewed from the front should be vertical and rigid, with all the planes intersecting at right angles. Sometimes variations do occur; large statues for instance were made to look slightly downwards towards the spectator, but examples where the body is made to bend or the head to turn are very rare in formal sculpture. The four little goddesses who protect the canopic chest of Tutankhamun with outstretched arms, their heads slightly turned to the left, are among the most delightful of such exceptions.

It is usually accepted that the finest craftsmen worked for the king, and set the patterns followed by others who produced sculpture in stone, wood, and metal for his subjects throughout Egypt. The Old and Middle Kingdoms in particular saw the production of many statues and small figures that were placed in the tombs of quite ordinary people to act as substitutes for the body if it should be destroyed, to provide an eternal abode for the *ka*. Quality was desirable, but was not particularly important, for as long as the statue was inscribed with the name of the dead person it was identified with him. In fact it was possible to take over a statue by simply altering the inscription and substituting another name. This was done even at the highest level, and kings often usurped statues commissioned by earlier rulers. It was also believed to be possible to destroy the memory of a hated or feared predecessor by hacking the names and titles from his monuments. This happened to many of the statues of Akhenaten, and the names of Hatshepsut were erased by Tuthmosis III.

Most of the *ka* statues found in the tombs of nobles of the Old Kingdom follow royal precedent. Royal tombs at Gizeh and Saqqara were surrounded by cities of the dead, as the officials sought to be buried near their king and to pass into eternity with him. Gradually the beliefs once associated with the king or his immediate family were adopted by his nobles, and then by less important people, until everybody at their death hoped to become identified with Osiris, the dead king; but the quality, size, and material of the *ka* statue buried in a tomb depended upon the prosperity and means of its owner.

A wooden statuette of a servant carrying a lotus jar; height 21cm (8in); *c*1350 BC. Merseyside County Museums, Liverpool

The earlier private sculptures, like the royal ones they imitated, were very much in the ritual tradition. In later periods craftsmen, particularly those working in wood, often produced small figures of great charm when they did not feel themselves bound by magico-religious convention. Such small statuettes were often made to serve a practical purpose and carried containers which held cosmetic substances; later they were buried among the personal possessions of their owners. A fine example in dark wood is the figure of a servant carrying a lotus jar, *c*1350 BC, which he supports with one hand while his back bends beneath its weight (Merseyside County Museums, Liverpool). Another of about the same period, now at Durham (Gulbenkian Museum) depicts a young maidservant with her body curved sideways to counterbalance the heavy cosmetic jar which she carries on her left hip.

Life-size limestone statue of King Zoser; c2660–2590 BC. Egyptian Museum, Cairo

It is the sequence of formal royal sculpture, however, that most clearly shows the changes in detail and attitude that occurred during the many centuries of Egyptian history. Unfortunately very little royal sculpture has survived from the earliest periods, but one of the oldest examples is also one of the most impressive. This is the life-size limestone statue of King Zoser, c2660–2590 BC, found in a small chamber in the temple complex of the Step Pyramid, which was planned by the Vizier Imhotep (Egyptian Museum, Cairo). Once in place, the statue would never again be seen by the eyes of the living. It was made to provide a dwelling place for the *ka* of the king after his death, and was walled up in a niche. Two holes were left opposite the eyes so that it could look out into the adjacent chapel where daily offerings were to be made. The king, seated on a square throne, is wrapped in a mantle. The face, framed by a full wig, is impassive and full of brooding majesty, conveyed in spite of the damage caused by thieves who gouged out the inlaid eyes. Smaller statues of nobles from the first three Dynasties, seated in the same position with the right hand across the breast, convey a strong impression of the density of the stone from which they were carved.

The magnificent diorite statue of Khephren, c2500 BC (Egyptian Museum, Cairo), builder of the second pyramid of Gizeh, once stood with 22 others in the long hall of the Valley Temple there. The posture of the king has changed a little from that of the statue of Zoser, and both hands now rest on the knees. The detail of the body, no longer enveloped in a mantle, is superbly executed. Protected by the falcon of the god Horus, the king sits alone with the calm assurance of his divinity. This statue was intended to be seen in the temple, and the power of the king is underlined by the design carved on the sides of the throne which symbolized the union of the Kingdoms of Upper and Lower Egypt with a knot of papyrus and lotus plants.

The sculptures preserved from the funerary temple of another 4th-Dynasty king, Mycerinus, at Gizeh, dating from c2480 BC, are still full of the concept of divine majesty, but depict the king with more humanity than his predecessors. The statue groups are cut from schist, showing traces of painting; one portrays the king with his queen; the others are triads where he is shown with gods of the provinces of Egypt. The double statue, nearly 5 ft (1.5 m) high, was never quite completed. The legs and base were not given their final polishing, and the statue is uninscribed. The powerful figure of the king is supported with affection and dignity by the figure of the queen who stands slightly behind his left shoulder, gazing directly ahead, with her right arm round his waist and her left hand touching his left arm. There is similar contact between the figures in the triads, also of schist, which are slightly smaller. The hands of goddesses, placed delicately on the arms of the king, promise divine support to the ruler. As is usual in ancient Egypt the goddesses are represented with the features of the queen.

Few fragments of royal sculpture in stone survive from the remaining period of the Old Kingdom. A granite head of Userkaf, c2470 BC, three times lifesize, provides the first evidence for colossal statuary in Egypt and is clearly by the hand of a master craftsman. A diorite dyad showing King Sahure with the god of the Coptos district, however, although carved in the tradition of the magnificent sculpture of the 4th Dynasty from Gizeh, does not show the same mastery in its proportions or the same skill of workmanship and finish, although the feeling of majesty remains.

The sculptors represented the rulers of the Old Kingdom as gods on earth. During the Middle Kingdom the surviving fragments of royal statues show a line of rulers who had achieved their divinity by their own power and strength of personality. The aloof and solitary nature of kingship appears in their portraits, but it is combined with an awareness of a human personality beneath the trappings of royalty. The heads and statues of these Middle Kingdom rulers give the impression of being real portraits, carved by craftsmen of consummate skill.

In some ways the sculpture recalls earlier royal statuary. A portrayal of Amenemhat III, c1840 BC, as a sphinx shows a face strongly reminiscent of the statue of Zoser, carved nearly 1,000 years earlier, in the cast of its eyes and mouth, the large

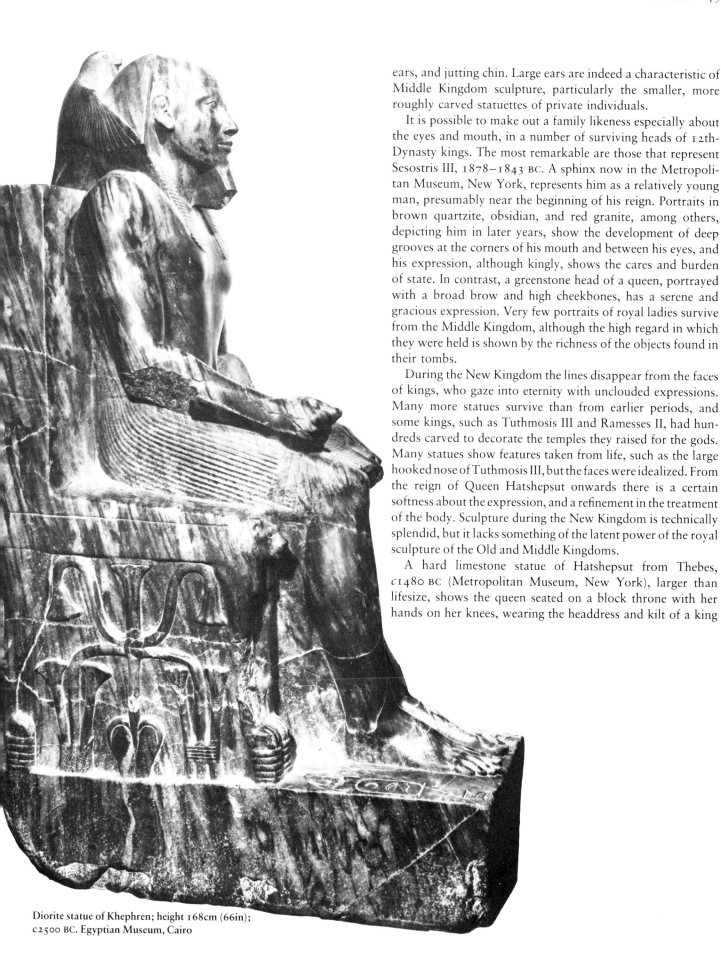

Diorite statue of Khephren; height 168cm (66in);
c2500 BC. Egyptian Museum, Cairo

ears, and jutting chin. Large ears are indeed a characteristic of Middle Kingdom sculpture, particularly the smaller, more roughly carved statuettes of private individuals.

It is possible to make out a family likeness especially about the eyes and mouth, in a number of surviving heads of 12th-Dynasty kings. The most remarkable are those that represent Sesostris III, 1878–1843 BC. A sphinx now in the Metropolitan Museum, New York, represents him as a relatively young man, presumably near the beginning of his reign. Portraits in brown quartzite, obsidian, and red granite, among others, depicting him in later years, show the development of deep grooves at the corners of his mouth and between his eyes, and his expression, although kingly, shows the cares and burden of state. In contrast, a greenstone head of a queen, portrayed with a broad brow and high cheekbones, has a serene and gracious expression. Very few portraits of royal ladies survive from the Middle Kingdom, although the high regard in which they were held is shown by the richness of the objects found in their tombs.

During the New Kingdom the lines disappear from the faces of kings, who gaze into eternity with unclouded expressions. Many more statues survive than from earlier periods, and some kings, such as Tuthmosis III and Ramesses II, had hundreds carved to decorate the temples they raised for the gods. Many statues show features taken from life, such as the large hooked nose of Tuthmosis III, but the faces were idealized. From the reign of Queen Hatshepsut onwards there is a certain softness about the expression, and a refinement in the treatment of the body. Sculpture during the New Kingdom is technically splendid, but it lacks something of the latent power of the royal sculpture of the Old and Middle Kingdoms.

A hard limestone statue of Hatshepsut from Thebes, c1480 BC (Metropolitan Museum, New York), larger than lifesize, shows the queen seated on a block throne with her hands on her knees, wearing the headdress and kilt of a king

The Sphinx in Ancient Egypt

From the 15th century AD European travelers carried home tales of the mysterious and amazing remains of the civilization of Egypt. One of its most remarkable monuments, which still evokes this sense of awe and might, is the Great Sphinx of Gizeh, the oldest surviving sphinx, dating from *c*2550 BC, carved from a natural outcrop of rock. The body is 240 ft (73 m) long and the face is over 13 ft (4 m) wide.

Sphinx is a Greek word, but is probably derived from *shesep ankh*, "living image", and the true Egyptian sphinx, unlike the Greek version in the story of Oedipus, was a male creature, depicted with the crouching body of a lion and a human face. It portrays the king, usually wearing the striped *nemes* headdress with the royal uraeus above the forehead, and a ceremonial beard. The head-dress actually helps to disguise the join between the animal body and the human head and neck.

The concept of the king as a powerful lion goes back into prehistoric times, and several

▲ The Great Sphinx of Gizeh

▲ Limestone sphinx from Queen Hatshepsut's temple, Deir el-Bahri. Metropolitan Museum, New York

▲ Head of a sphinx from Tanis, *c*1800 BC

▶ Sphinx of Ramesses II, Memphis

▼ A sphinx of the Ptolemaic era, Alexandria

ceremonial objects have survived which depict him in this guise, overthrowing his enemies. The sphinx was, therefore, a natural development, personifying the divine power of the king as a force protecting his land and repelling the power of evil. The human head was the means of individualizing the sculpture, so that the Great Sphinx probably bears the idealized features of Khephren whose pyramid is nearby. A colossal red granite head of King Userkaf, c2400 BC, may have been part of a sphinx, but there is little other evidence of sphinxes in the Old Kingdom (c2680–2180 BC), although there surely was a tradition: relatively little royal sculpture of any kind has survived from this early period.

The Middle Kingdom (c2050–1750 BC) yields an interesting variation on the established convention in the shape of four gray granite sphinxes dated to the reign of Amenemhat III, c1840 BC, which were found at Tanis in the Delta. In these the king's face is framed not by the *nemes* headdress but by a stylized form of lion's ruff, mane, and ears. The effect is rather to emphasize the majesty and realism of the human features, contributing to the brooding power of the statues. This type of "lionized" head reappears in two small, painted limestone sphinxes from Queen Hatshepsut's temple at Deir el-Bahri, these dated some 300 years later in the New Kingdom. However, the temple also contained six larger, red granite sphinxes which wear the *nemes* headdress, and are notable for the sensitive portrayal of the face and the skillful modeling of the heavy muscles of the lion's body.

The alabaster sphinx of Ramesses II, which still stands among the ruins of Memphis, was carved c1250 BC, and seems initially more impressive than Hatshepsut's sphinxes through sheer size, being more than twice as large at 26 ft (8 m) long, 14 ft (4.2 m) high and weighing about 80 tons (81 tonnes). Although the carving is skillful enough, however, it does not convey such an impression of vitality and character as the earlier ones. As time passed, sphinxes continued to be made as royal monuments, but technique had so taken over that the latest sphinxes, of the Ptolemaic era, 332–30 BC, are bland imitations of their powerful precursors.

The Great Sphinx is one of the most distinctive and dominant of all the images of ancient Egypt, which is perhaps the source of the misconception that sphinxes are of central importance in Egyptian culture and proliferate throughout its history. However, those that have survived are among the most impressive as well as intriguing examples of Egyptian sculpture.

DOROTHY DOWNES

of Egypt in support of her claim to rule. The body is set squarely in the ancient tradition and the eyes are steadfast, but the chin is pointed and delicate and the effect is feminine. When Tuthmosis III succeeded in replacing her on the throne of Egypt, the sculptors knew what was expected of them and produced statuary that celebrated the power of a capable, warlike king, a confident link between his people and the gods.

Royal sculpture from Tell el-Amarna. When Amenophis IV broke with the old traditions he moved his capital to the city he built in the desert at Tell el-Amarna, which he called the Horizon of Aten. He changed his name to Akhenaten and worshipped the Aten, the lifegiving force of the sun, in light and airy temples decorated with statues and reliefs. Encouraged by the king, craftsmen between 1363 and 1346 BC produced scenes and sculptures characterized by a new informality that had begun to appear during the reign of Amenophis III. Members of the royal family were shown taking part in ceremonies, as before, but the artists also went behind the palace facade, as it were, to depict more domestic scenes. The king, his queen Nefertiti, and their daughters are portrayed relaxing in their private apartments, and although ritual is observed in the way that the hands of the Aten rays reach down to protect the family, the princesses scramble upon their parents' knees or play beside their chairs. Hands touch not merely in the ancient gesture of protection but in genuine affection, and the princesses may be said to smile.

During the early part of Akhenaten's reign, and probably at his own instigation as a rebellion against the idealism and decorum of earlier times, many royal statues appear to show the human form exaggerated to the point of caricature. Some are even repellent. All the physical peculiarities of the king, his long head and pointed chin, sunken chest, protruding stomach and large thighs, are shown in detail, and some of the colossal statues are quite overpowering in their effect. This distortion, particularly in official statues, must be the result of the king's own wish to display, rather than conceal, what was probably a pathological condition. In spite of this, the sculptors still manage to communicate a god-like quality to the larger statues of the ruler.

Later in the reign, the trend to naturalism asserted itself. Surviving fragments show that the ideal female form was young and lithe with gently swelling belly and thighs. The body was shown naked or covered with light garments of clinging linen. Studies of the heads of the princesses have been found, and these, together with the quartzite head of Nefertiti already mentioned, and the beautiful painted limestone bust of the queen now in Berlin (Staatliche Museen), are outstanding in their delicacy and charm. The painted head, found at Amarna in a sculptor's workshop, was a master-portrait used as a model for other studies, some of which have been found. The face and neck are finely modeled, and are painted in most natural colors. The left eye was never inserted, but the right is effectively inlaid in rock crystal with a black pupil.

Above: Seated statue of Ramesses II; c1290 BC. Museo Egizio, Turin

Left: Fragment of a red quartzite head of Sesostris III. Metropolitan Museum, New York

After the death of Akhenaten his successors returned to Thebes, and government and religion resumed their traditional courses. The influence of the Amarna style lingered, however, in a soft delicacy of touch which is shown in the best of later New Kingdom art. In formal sculpture the rulers of the 19th Dynasty were represented in statues which in style recall those of the early 18th Dynasty. Sometimes, however, they were represented in contemporary dress and not always in the simple traditional garment of the king. A beautifully finished, black granite, seated statue of Ramesses II, c1290 BC, in the Turin Museum, portrays the king wearing the helmet-shaped Blue Crown, and long, finely pleated linen robes. Traditional detail is supplied by a figure of the queen, standing by his left leg but not even as tall as his knee. His reign became the great period of colossal sculpture, and among many huge figures of Ramesses II that survive, the seated statues at the temple of Abu Simbel and those showing the king as Osiris in his mortuary temple at Thebes are among the most famous.

Smaller statues from his mortuary temple, the Ramesseum, include figures of royal ladies in painted limestone. The carving is very fine, particularly the details of the wigs, collars, and ornaments, and the faces are idealized and serene. These statues have their parallels in the funerary figures placed in the tombs of nobles and officials. Many of these are carved with meticulous care by sculptors trained in the royal traditions.

Statues of private individuals were also dedicated in the temples, and here, with the development of the block statue, there is a trend towards compactness and simplicity. The figure, squatting with its knees drawn up towards the chin and enveloped in a mantle, is reduced almost to a block from which only the head protrudes. The heads of many block statues are well-carved, but the stylized body was intended to be as simple as possible in order to provide the ground for the inscription, often covering the entire surface and including the name and titles of the votary. This type first appeared during the Middle Kingdom, and gradually became more common during the New Kingdom. The climax of its popularity occurred during the 19th Dynasty.

In later periods, royal sculptors, although very competent, produced statues very much in the traditions of earlier Dynasties, and mostly of a smaller size. In c660 BC, however, Montuemhat, who was High Steward of the Divine Consort of Amun at Thebes, gave great patronage and encouragement to a new movement in art. This drew its inspiration from past glories, setting out to reestablish national pride at a time when foreign powers were threatening Egypt. For a time there was a new flowering of technical brilliance, particularly in the treatment of hard stones; and several outstanding pieces of sculpture survive. A remarkable dark granite statue of Montuemhat himself, found at Karnak, is an exciting amalgam of the traditions of 2,000 years of art. The pose and dress conform to the traditions established early in the Old Kingdom, and the wig is in the fashion of the New Kingdom; but the face is a portrait of real character, carved with a sensitivity worthy of the great craftsmen of the Middle Kingdom.

Block statue of Amenophis, steward of Memphis; height 74cm (29in). British Museum, London

Sculpture in wood and metal. Although the very nature of stone imparts a certain stiffness to statuary, this same rigidity tends to be repeated in other materials such as wood or metal where greater freedom is in fact possible. The innate conservatism of the Egyptians meant that craftsmen kept to the established artistic conventions, mainly for magical or religious reasons, though certain differences do appear in lighter materials. Plinths and back pillars can be abandoned when their support is no longer needed, and legs and arms can be separated from the body, giving a lighter effect. These figures, however, seldom survive in perfect condition. Metal corrodes, and wood rots if damp, and is susceptible to the ravages of ants and other pests. Copper was precious so many statues were probably melted down and the metal reused.

From inscriptions we know that royal statues of copper had been made as early as the 2nd Dynasty, but the 6th-Dynasty statues of Pepi I and his son are the earliest that survive. From that time onwards metal figures occur in a wide range of sizes. One of the most notable is the tiny gold figure of Amenophis III, 2 in (5 cm) high, found in a miniature coffin in the tomb of Tutankhamun, c1340 BC. This was probably cast in a mold by the *cire perdue* method.

The bronze statuette of Queen Karomama of the 22nd Dynasty, *c*825 BC, is one of the most sophisticated surviving examples of sculpture in metal (Louvre, Paris). Nearly 2 ft (61 cm) in height, it was made for her chapel at Karnak, and shows the queen with her arms extended before her. The hands originally held scepters or an offering, but, like the crown and plumes that must have adorned her head, these were probably of gold and have long since disappeared. The details of her elaborately patterned dress and collar were originally inlaid with gold, silver, and electrum, and the face, arms, and feet were gilded. Much of this is now lost, but the queenly and womanly beauty of the figure and the open expression of her face are very striking. Other fine bronze statuettes of about this period show the skill of workers in metal. They include figures of other royal ladies, and one of the god Amun.

Royal statues made of wood survive in relatively large numbers. The most impressive are those placed in the tombs of kings after playing an important part in the funerary ritual, representing them as they would have appeared during their coronation ceremonies and on other important ritual occasions. A figure of Sesostris I, 1971–1930 BC (Egyptian Museum, Cairo), found at Lisht, is one of the earliest and best preserved. Finely carved in cedar wood and wearing the high White Crown of Upper Egypt, the king strides forward on his left foot, holding a long crook in his left hand. The right hand would have held the other royal symbol, the so-called flail. The crown and kilt are white with a layer of gesso, and the body and eyes are painted with natural colors.

A series of statuettes (Egyptian Museum, Cairo), each under 3 ft (1 m) high, found in the tomb of Tutankhamun, *c*1340 BC, a young and relatively unimportant ruler, shows that such figures were an essential part of royal funerary equipment. It was believed that after death the king would continue to perform ritual acts on behalf of his people. Similar figures must have been placed in other royal tombs, but most were looted by tomb robbers. One statuette represents Tutankhamun, wearing the Red Crown of Lower Egypt. He is in the same pose as Sesostris I 600 years earlier, and paces forward holding crook and flail, solemn and intent. The effect of the realism of the Amarna period is shown in the relaxed, slightly drooping shoulders, which contrast with the straight and powerful shoulders of Sesostris. The most graceful statuette of the group shows Tutankhamun like the god Horus, poised effortlessly on a small papyrus skiff, about to cast the harpoon that would kill Seth, the enemy of his father Osiris, transformed into a hippopotamus.

Besides a number of beautifully carved wooden *ushabtis*, or figurines of funerary servants, also found in his tomb, the splendor of the burial of Tutankhamun is underlined by the two life-size statues found guarding the walled-up entrance to the funerary chamber itself (Egyptian Museum, Cairo). They represent the king as Osiris, not mummiform but with the face, body, and legs coated with shining black resin. Against this the gilding of the garments, and the gold eyes and eyebrows stand out with startling effect.

The bronze statuette of Queen Karomama; height 61cm (24in); c825 BC. Louvre, Paris

Gold inlaid back of a throne found in Tutankhamun's tomb. Egyptian Museum, Cairo

One of the most striking of royal portraits carved in wood is a small ebony head of Queen Tiye, wife of Amenophis III, *c*1360 BC (Staatliche Museen, Berlin). It was intended, presumably, to form part of a composite statue. The wig is covered with painted plaster, and the earrings and eyes are inlaid. The sculptor, working with great skill in the hard wood, has managed to convey the impression of an acute and perhaps ruthless personality in portraying a commoner who became the Great Royal Wife of a king of Egypt.

Applied art. The craftsmen who produced the fine furniture, beautiful jewelry and small personal possessions which were obviously so beloved by the people of ancient Egypt, were not limited in the same way as sculptors who were normally expected to conform with religous tradition. It is quite clear that they appreciated the beauty of natural things, and delighted in their ability to reproduce them in stone, fine wood, ivory, and precious metal. Few of these objects had the magical purpose of the statues and reliefs, but were buried with their owners as cherished, familiar things. Craftsmen could let their imaginations run freely in the decoration of utilitarian objects, many of which are ingenious as well as beautiful.

From the earliest times jewelry was made of gold and semiprecious stones. Prehistoric beads of garnet, amethyst, haematite, and carnelian, laboriously ground and polished by hand, are found in the most ordinary of graves. Later, four bracelets (now in the Egyptian Museum, Cairo) found on a linen-wrapped arm cast aside by tomb robbers in a royal tomb at Abydos, c3000 BC, show that the Egyptian love of brightly colored beads, strung together in elaborate patterns, was already well established, and during the Old Kingdom some exquisite pieces of jewelry were made. Outstanding among these are the bracelets found in the tomb of Queen Hetepheres, c2600 BC, some produced specifically for funerary use (Egyptian Museum, Cairo). Made of beaten sheet silver, they are decorated with delicate butterfly patterns inlaid with turquoise, jasper, lapis lazuli, and carnelian.

The jewelry buried with the princesses Khnumet, Sithathor-yunet, and Mererit at Lahun, c1900 BC, shows that the craftsmen of the Middle Kingdom were never surpassed as designers. Inlaid diadems, ceremonial pendants, bracelets, and filigree wreaths of gold and semiprecious stones are richly decorated, elegant, and beautiful. Technically the craftsmanship of the New Kingdom was more polished, but although many pieces are more splendid, the effect can sometimes be gaudy and unrestrained. The best known are the sumptuous pendants, diadems, earrings, and finger rings found in the tomb of Tutankhamun, c1340 BC (Egyptian Museum, Cairo).

The techniques used to produce vessels and other objects of precious and base metal apart from personal jewelry were very accomplished. A gold falcon's head from Hierakonpolis, c2330 BC, is one of the finest examples of goldsmiths' work of the Old Kingdom (Egyptian Museum, Cairo). Eyes of polished obsidian give a lifelike appearance to the head, crowned with a gold uraeus and tall plumes, that must have formed part of a composite statue. The copper nails that fixed it to a body, probably made of wood sheathed in copper, are still in place.

Extensive use was made of precious metal in the furnishing of royal burials, and the few that have escaped the attention of plunderers show how splendid and magnificent the others must have been. Within a series of wooden coffins sheathed in gold, and inlaid with glass and semiprecious stones, the funerary mask of Tutankhamun (Egyptian Museum, Cairo) was of solid gold, and the rich equipment found in the tomb of Psusennes at Tanis, c1050 BC, included fine silver coffins and gold funerary masks.

Gold inlay was used to pick out the details on wooden statuary, and to decorate the bronze statuettes made in increasing numbers from c1000 BC. Many of these figures represented various gods shown in characteristic attitudes, and were probably for household shrines. The great gods of earth and sky are among them, but there are also many figures, often roughly made and finished, of the familiar, domestic gods worshiped by ordinary people.

Ebony head of Queen Tiye; c1360 BC. Staatliche Museen, Berlin

Head of a priest from the Ptolemaic era. Staatliche Museen, Berlin

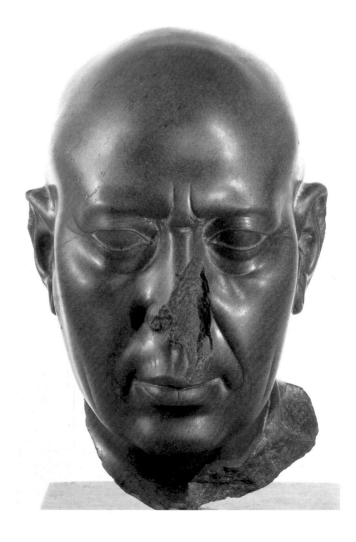

Precious metal was also widely used by the makers of fine furniture, and in cases where the wood has rotted away it has been possible to reconstitute items of furniture from the gold mountings that have survived. Supplies of good timber were always scarce and usually had to be imported, but Egyptian carpenters were adept at disguising joins and flaws in the poor native wood with layers of plaster and paint. Chairs, beds, and chests of the highest quality were covered with thin sheet gold, and this could be enhanced by inlaid decoration of ivory, ebony, and semiprecious stones. The work of the cabinetmakers had already reached a high degree of excellence early in the Old Kingdom, when the magnificent pieces of furniture found in the tomb of Queen Hetepheres, c2600 BC, were made (Egyptian Museum, Cairo). These have been reconstructed using the gold mountings, and the sheets of gold that covered the poles of the canopy, and the chairs, chests, and bed reveal an austere beauty of design and a wonderful quality of workmanship, delicately underlined here and there by inlaid panels of ebony set with tiny gold hieroglyphs.

Some of the chairs of state of New Kingdom date, those found in the tomb of Tutankhamun for instance (Egyptian Museum, Cairo), are wonderfully decorated with colored inlay. On the gilded back of one, an elaborate scene in silver, glass, and faience inlay represents the young king seated, with his wife standing in front of him anointing his ceremonial collar. Sometimes the effect of such craftsmanship is almost too exuberant, but small chests, jewel boxes, and gaming boards of cedar wood and ebony, minutely inlaid and painted, are often more tasteful and elegantly made.

Egyptian faience or glazed composition was often used for inlay. It consists of a core of ground quartz coated with an alkaline glaze, and was made from prehistoric times onwards. The colors vary, but the most characteristic are blues and greens produced by adding copper compounds in the required proportions to a glaze made by heating sand and natron. A brilliant clear blue glaze, mainly typical of the New Kingdom, was the most admired. Faience was used as a substitute for semiprecious stones, as well as in its own right in the making of beads, scarabs, and inlay. In the New Kingdom finely decorated bowls and chalices of faience were made, together with thousands of funerary figures or *ushabtis* which are to be found in many Egyptian graves.

Real glass was not made regularly in Egypt until the conquests of Tuthmosis III in the 18th Dynasty opened up contacts with the glass industries already established in Syria and Mesopotamia. The finest Egyptian glass, in the form of small vessels and colored inlay, was made during, and just after, the Amarna period, c1350 BC.

Although the majority of the ordinary people of Egypt could not afford objects of the artistic quality that characterized the funerary furnishings of the tombs of their nobles and kings, a great deal of evidence can be gathered from the modest equipment found in humble graves. Copies in wood and poorer stone reflect the work and style of more skillful craftsmen, and nearly every burial includes a treasure of some kind, such as a tiny cosmetic holder made of polished stone. Every object helps to fill in a detailed picture of the civilization of ancient Egypt, which owed so much to the resources of the Nile Valley and its people, and so little to external influences.

Foreign emissaries brought tribute to Egyptian rulers, and the trade in fine wood, metal, and other commodities scarce in Egypt meant that officials were in regular contact with the peoples of Africa to the south, and of the East Mediterranean and Mesopotamia to the north and east. But very little outside influence is to be detected in the work of Egyptian craftsmen. Imported objects were regarded more as valuable curiosities than as sources of inspiration to Egyptian artists, who were required to work by method and ritual.

Even dynasties of foreign rulers adopted the ancient traditions, rather than trying to impose new ideas, because they realized that they were then more likely to be accepted by the majority of the people. Artists flourished under the rule of the Ptolemies, but they were employed to rebuild and decorate temples in the ancient Egyptian manner. Even the influence of Greek sculpture made very little immediate impact, and a tendency towards more rounded, realistic forms becomes apparent only gradually. The faces of statues were quite often lively and expressive, but the bodies remained unbending and traditional until Roman times.

It is only relatively recently that the work of ancient Egyptian craftsmen and artists has begun to be appreciated in its own right. The forms and traditions they followed are foreign to the artistic heritage of the west, rooted as it is in the Classical tradition. Napoleon's expedition to Egypt in 1798, and the discovery of the Rosetta stone, led to a great vogue for Egyptian antiquities, but they were regarded more as curiosities than as works of art. Many great collections were founded in the early 19th century, but it was not until towards the end of the 19th century when the decipherment of hieroglyphic writing and the development of systematic archaeology had begun to reveal the complexities of the civilization of the Nile Valley, that the work of ancient-Egyptian craftsmen really began to be appreciated. It could then be seen that forms of art, which had seemed primitive in design and limited in achievement, were rather the products of an alien and highly sophisticated culture, embodying the response of the people of the Nile valley to their environment.

DOROTHY DOWNES

Bibliography. Bourrian, J. *Pharaohs and Mortals: Egyptian Art in the Middle Kingdom*, London (1988). Hayes, W.C. *The Scepter of Egypt*, New York, Part One (1959) Part Two (1960). Posener, G. (ed.) *A Dictionary of Egyptian Civilization*, London (1962). Robins, G. *Proportion and Style in Ancient Egyptian Art*, London (1994). Wilkinson, R.H. *Reading Egyptian Art: A Hieroglyphic Guide to Ancient Egyptian Painting and Sculpture*, London (1992).

4

ANCIENT NEAR EASTERN ART

A mural relief figure of a royal guardsman at Susa, the capital of Achaemenid Persia
c404–358 BC. Louvre, Paris (see page 78)

EARLY Mesopotamia. The setting for the development of one of the first literate civilizations, that of the Sumerians (c3500–2000 BC), was the land enclosed by the two rivers, the Tigris and the Euphrates. In the lower reaches of these silt-depositing rivers (in modern Iraq), in the dangerous and inhospitable oval of marsh and desert between Baghdad and the Shatt al-Arab waterway, primitive society overcame formidable challenges and succeeded in wresting economic surpluses from well-tended alluvial soils and in establishing urban communities. Partly as a consequence of such achievements monumental art made its first appearance, as an element in buildings used for religious observance. Its abiding themes were man's relationship with the deities and with the forces of nature that surrounded him, which were usually considered malevolent.

Modern knowledge of the Sumerians was slow to materialize because their monuments, built of poor stone since good-quality material was unavailable in Sumer, disappeared long ago, and because of the scarcity of historical records.

In 1850 Edward Hincks suggested that there were older, non-Semitic elements in the known Akkadian language that had been used by the Assyrians and the Babylonians. They were identified as Sumerian a few years later. In 1877 Ernest de Sarzec, a French Consul, began at Tello the first major series of archaeological investigations at a Sumerian site. Others followed, Americans at the larger mound of Nippur, Germans at Uruk (biblical Erech, the city of the hero of *The Epic of Gilgamesh*), the British at the sites of Kish and Ur. But these are only a few of the many Sumerian cities and villages that remain to be investigated in this 10,000 sq mile (25,900 sq km) area, so our understanding of these people and their art remains extremely patchy.

The influence of the Sumerians extended well beyond the frontiers of their homeland. In order to obtain minerals and timber for building, for example, they traded over enormous distances, with Syria, Anatolia, and beyond the Persian Gulf, thereby spreading artistic influence through exported works. In return the Sumerians were influenced by materials they imported. At times there were also foreign craftsmen employed in Sumer.

Although we speak of "Sumerian civilization" we in fact refer to an amalgam of several peoples. The cuneiform or wedge-shaped writings demonstrate the coexistence of at least two languages (the non-Semitic Sumerian and the Semitic Akkadian) whilst a third group of inhabitants, probably indigenous, is indicated by the names of the main rivers, principal

The Ancient Near East showing main sites

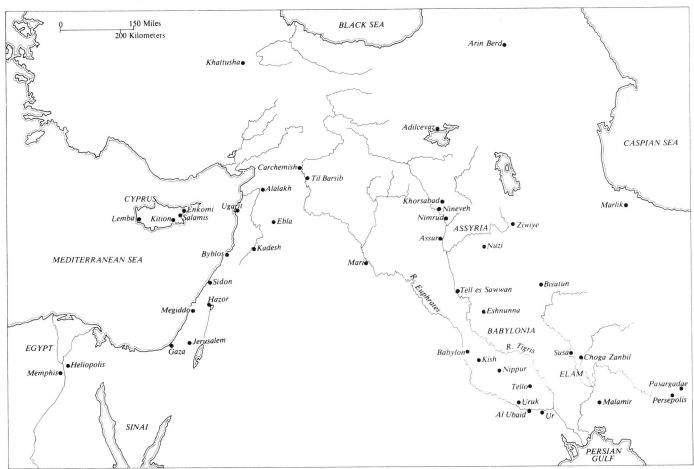

cities, and native crafts which are in a third language. So we must imagine Sumerian society to consist of a basic Sumerian element which was ineluctably overwhelmed by the constant renewal of Semitic stock from the deserts to the west.

The elements of this society cannot be distinguished in its works of art until certain trends within its development are transformed by an interlude of Semitic political control. But before this, in the most ancient protohistorical periods, the distinctive Sumerian contribution can be most readily identified.

The prehistoric periods (c6000–3500 BC). Sedentary communities are found first in northern Mesopotamia where rainfall was sufficient for many types of edible crops to be grown without the irrigation necessary in the south. At Umm Dabaghiyah, a settlement in marginal terrain, there are wall-paintings that probably depict onager hunts. But they mark the end of a great Paleolithic tradition rather than the beginning of a new form. In fact for centuries afterwards painting was only employed in the decoration of pottery and some of the first attempts in this novel genre, mere blobs and squiggles, were made at this site.

The pottery of two northern cultures subsequently reached great heights of excellence; firstly Samarra pottery, which incorporated swirling figures on the bases of dishes, and secondly Halaf pottery which, while including abbreviated motifs such as *bucrania* is perhaps most noteworthy for the intricacy of its polychrome floral decoration. Although both styles were ultimately replaced, the symbolism inherent in the stylization of some Halaf designs was a forerunner of the earliest Sumerian writing, which was based on pictograms, and the bitumen hairdresses and inlaid eyes, features of alabaster statuettes from Tell es Sawwan near Samarra (Iraq Museum, Baghdad), recur in Sumerian statuary.

By the late 5th millennium BC the inhabitants of southern Mesopotamia had made such advances that the initiative in artistic development had passed to them. So little is known about this change that we can only guess that the fertile soils of the area were being better exploited. The decoration of pots changed, from all-over textured patterns to carelessly applied dabs of paint. And this in turn was abandoned in favor of monochrome washes. The making of statuettes continued, usually of female figures, the normal shape evolving into a slender, columnar figure with broad shoulders and a pinched face resembling that of a lizard.

Even towards the end of the prehistoric period we can discern the beginnings of Sumerian civilization. The beginning of wealth accumulation, and external contacts, is suggested by a strip of gold from Ur. And also dating from this period are large temples at Eridu, the first cult-center to receive kingship according to the Sumerian king-list. They are built in a form that heralds the classic early Sumerian tripartite shape. Similar and better preserved examples have been found in the north, their walls tinted in red, black, ocher, and vermilion. At this same site, Tepe Gawra near Khorsabad, a series of stamp seals has been found (now in the University Museum,

Philadelphia). Believed to possess amuletic properties, they were used to mark individual property and offer us an important insight into the development of figurative art during this period. In the earliest examples men and animals appear randomly deployed in free-field compositions. But towards the end of the period the figures become more corporeal and the scenes more orderly, often arranged in rotation form or around a vertical axis. Such scenes were probably derived from ritual.

The Early Sumerian Period (c3500–3000 BC). It is fair to conclude that the culture of this period revealed by finds from the site of Uruk is Sumerian on account of its continuity into later times, and also from Sumerian language texts of slightly later date whose signs are directly evolved from those on tablets found at Uruk.

Some scholars have suggested that Sumerian newcomers were responsible for the many innovations that now took place in southern Mesopotamia. But, as we have seen, there were indigenous antecedents for some of the developments and furthermore a similar pattern of development occurred in neighboring Elam. Perhaps a change in the nature of trading patterns and a collateral increase in wealth may be the causes we are seeking. This is certainly suggested by the recent discovery of early Sumerian sites along the bend of the Euphrates, 500 miles (800 km) upstream in northern Syria, at a crucial junction on the route to timber and mineral resources in the northwest. It may be that archaeological finds will demonstrate that the suddenness of these changes in Mesopotamia is more apparent than real, but we should not underestimate the importance and extent of this sudden burst of artistic and other activities.

In the city of Uruk the most outstanding features of the period were two sacred complexes. The first, Eanna, the House of Heaven, was probably dedicated to the goddess Inanna, the other to Anu. Both were rebuilt during the Early Sumerian Period apparently without any change of character, but the Sumerians' practice of reconstructing their temples on the bases of their predecessors' (as also happened at Eridu) eventually led to the appearance of ziggurats.

The ground plan of the monumental temples of Eanna was rectangular though the walls were deeply recessed to provide niches. Within, the predominant feature was a long, narrow, axial court, sometimes opening out into transept-like rooms in front of a rear chamber. We have not been able to discover their purpose from contemporary documents (the pictograph inscriptions of the period have not yet been deciphered) but later buildings of similar form were undoubtedly temples, though they often featured a niche for a cult-statue in the *cella* or rear chamber. No example of this has been found at Uruk, nor have the ancillary rooms and courts that usually indicate a cult bureaucracy.

Within one of these buildings there was a decorated hall or court, capable of holding a large number of people. At one end stood two rows of six massive mud-brick columns. They occupy a raised area which was reached by a central staircase leading up from the court. The walls, staircase parapet, and columns were all inlaid with baked clay cones—thousands of them, set contiguously so that their protruding painted heads formed colorful linear patterns. Similar cones were also driven into the exterior walls of other buildings in Eanna to provide both decoration and protection (as suggested by copper-sheathed cones found at Eridu).

The impulse to embellish by such laborious means must have lain deep in the Sumerian psyche. Its expression is unmistakable—a true myriad of parts creating a unified entity. Evidence of its influence can be found in a temple in North Syria where the altar bears a frieze of gold and bicolored limestone and the walls are decorated with mosaics of colored cones and rosettes of black, white, and red stone petals. Only occasionally were the walls of buildings painted, one of the few examples being the terraced temple at Uqair, just north of Kish, where there are representations of animals and humans, the latter perhaps offering-bearers, similar to those depicted on a ritual vase from Uruk.

Three-dimensional and relief sculpture flourished in this period, presumably for religious purposes since most surviving examples come from the sacred precincts at Uruk. In its substantial forms and figurative quality Sumerian sculpture surpassed earlier work and indeed the work of this period

The near-life-size female head from Uruk; height 20cm (8in); c3200 BC. Iraq Museum, Baghdad

manifests a solid confidence that later Sumerian society rarely achieved.

The statuettes of the period were executed in stone, replacing the earlier medium of clay. They display a fresh massiveness, emphasized by the sculptors' reluctance to free figures from their matrices. Legs appear almost as thick as hips—only a shallow incised line separates them. On one exceptional example the muscles of the chest and forearms are cursorily rendered (Iraq Museum, Baghdad). Attention was normally directed to the face which, in the case of male figures, features a prominent nose framed by a large beard, and a cap with a thick rolled edge. One example of particularly sensitive facial modeling is a near-life-size female appliqué head found in the precinct of Eanna. Faint depressions around the thin-lipped mouth heighten the individuality of the work whose eyes are naturalistically oval rather than stylized as in later products. The pupils themselves are lost, but like the brows and hair were probably made of bitumen, shell, and precious blue lapis lazuli from Afghanistan. Originally such composite works were gaudy in appearance; otherwise harmonious surface planes were broken up by the insertion of alien materials—a practice similar to the method of architectural decoration just described. Bull figurines treated in this manner display an unearthly might.

The artistic endeavor directed into reliefs sought to represent the experience of religious observation. This purpose is implicit even in apparently secular reliefs, in which, for example, a man slays lions with a spear and arrows. There can be no doubt, however, about the contents of the three relief bands on a tall alabaster vase from Uruk (Iraq Museum, Baghdad). Below the lowest frieze are two incised wavy lines representing water. Moving upwards, there are then cereal crops and caprids—a progression from basic water through the plant and animal kingdoms which are represented by the species most important to the Sumerian economy and therefore most beneficial to man. In the next frieze upwards men are shown bearing gifts. Whilst above, in the top frieze, a procession of animals and men faces a woman, wearing a long robe, who stands before two tied bundles of reeds, symbols of the goddess Inanna. It is not certain whether the figure is the goddess herself or a priestess. This scene includes cult paraphernalia and should probably be interpreted as showing the property of the goddess stored in her temple treasury. The formal planning in the order of friezes suggests that the artist is seeking to do more than just depict Sumerian ritual. For here he has surely transcended the dictates of mere representation to represent as ritual a total view of Sumerian society. Such preoccupying depth of thought implies that Sumerian society was now served by specialist, full-time artists.

The flat relief carving, used on the alabaster vase just described, was later abandoned in favor of high relief in which, for example, rows of animals become almost detached from vases. Many cult vessels decorated in this heavier, later style feature lions attacking domestic bulls: an epitome of the perpetual conflict in nature. The marauding lions that infested the dense marshscapes of Sumeria in the 4th millennium caused immense human fear—vividly evoked in the writings of Austin Henry Layard and other 19th-century investigators. A bearded protector figure, with arms draped over the bulls, was sometimes introduced into high-relief works. He is the "tamer of animals", a significant theme in the religious thought of many ancient societies. It was taken up by Egyptian iconography *c*3000 BC, demonstrating the existence of contacts between Sumeria and Egypt and, indeed, the preeminence of the former.

The cylinder seal was another invention of this period. It was usually made of stone and carved with intaglio designs so that it left impressions when rolled along a plastic surface. The effect it created—the endless repetition of stock motifs—influenced other forms of art, for example vase decoration. On the other hand, engravers borrowed subjects from larger works of art, adapting scenes showing ritual boating, architecture, construction, and antithetic compositions, many ill-suited to the new miniature form.

Both seals and impressions were sufficiently varied and numerous to provide us with an unmatched source of infor-

A cylinder seal from Uruk; *c*3000–2750 BC. **Ashmolean Museum, Oxford**

An alabaster vase from Uruk; height 92cm (36in); *c*3200 BC.
Iraq Museum, Baghdad

mation about life at that time. A familiar figure in them is the distinctive Uruk Man who, with his cap roll, beard, and kilt, is often much taller than other humans. In one scene of surpassing mastery he is shown feeding leaping goats, heraldically arranged.

The period of the early city-states (c3000–2371 BC). The causes and indeed the events of the breakdown of the old Sumerian order are not known. Perhaps one important contributory factor was the increased flooding of settlements, accounts of which were later condensed into the Sumerian and biblical flood stories. The period's change of character, the replacement of confidence by tension and timidity, is well demonstrated, however, by its surviving works of art.

Seals provide a particularly good thread of evidence across the void linking the two periods. Human forms became less frequent, their place taken by exploded, stylized animals arranged in brocade-like patterns. They in turn were replaced by attenuated semihuman and animal figures locked in mortal

Brocade-like patterns (left) produced from early cylinder seals

combat. Similar development is seen in statuary where roundly modeled bodies gave way to geometric, abstract conceptions whose production sprang from utterly different motives.

The period of the early city-states saw a growth in population and a proliferation of urban centers. Towards its conclusion there was armed conflict between cities and the beginning of historical writing. Each city was held to be the property of a deity, and the leader of each cult-center to be the divine steward or bailiff. But as strife (often caused by disputes over water rights) became endemic, religious leaders became military leaders and the period developed into an age of heroes. Gilgamesh, hero of *The Epic of Gilgamesh*, lived in this age. But as the claims of rulers escalated little room was left for independent cities.

Such developments are well represented in temple architecture and objects. The worshiper was increasingly distanced from his deity and stores, priestly living quarters, and courtyards were interposed before the *cella*. At the holy city of Nippur a dual shrine lay beyond no less than three courtyards, one of which had columns. To overcome the resulting separation of the deity statues of worshipers were made to stand before him in continual prayer.

With the emergence of secular power during this period there appeared secular architecture. At Mari and Kish where, according to the Sumerian king-list, kingship first descended from heaven after the flood, complex structures that were probably palaces have been discovered. Further remains of this phase are the objects found in the mass burials at Ur, excavated by Sir Leonard Woolley. Their variety is bewildering; they show a delight in gold, silver, lapis lazuli, and carnelian—all deservedly worked to the highest standards of native craftsmanship.

As an introduction to the stiff and severe plastic statuary of the period we can consider the group of statues from the Abu Temple at Eshnunna (Iraq Museum, Baghdad). The largest wears a typical plain skirt with tufted hem on a stylized torso. The hair is corrugated and the beard stained with bitumen. Its impression of geometric immobility, however, is belied by the folded hands around the cup and the enlarged eyes which express the internal tension between the man, peering after the unattainable, and his god. Compositions too reflect a similar state. Indeed the consciousness of a breach is made salient by the rarity of representations of men and gods together.

Local schools of sculptors were well established in this period. At Mari, for example, fine work was produced for the temples in a style in which appeared complacent, smiling figures wearing richly flounced skirts, standing one foot in front of the other, with delineated strands of hair and their names inscribed on their torsos (National Museum of Aleppo). It is not know whether the style began here or elsewhere but it certainly became universally popular and used for metalwork as well as stone sculpture, as shown by a metal figure of a scribe who dedicates himself to the goddess Ningal, the Great Lady.

At the same time as statuary reappeared so also did relief

works. The most popular form was a square tablet with a central hole to secure it, perhaps to the wall of a building. The pattern of division into registers, seen on the Uruk vase of the Early Sumerian Period, was maintained but new subjects including boating, wrestling, and, above all, feasting to the accompaniment of music were introduced.

This important new theme, the "banquet scene" (which occurred throughout southern Mesopotamia) was also executed in mosaic-like inlaid panels composed of several precious materials. Such was the Sumerians' love of this form of decoration that, in spite of the inherent limitations of working with fragile and intractable shell, narrow friezes were inlaid high on temple walls. One such frieze, at Ninhursag's temple at Al Ubaid near Ur, shows sacred herds of cows being milked to produce cheese. The medium is white shell against a slate background.

Another prevalent motif was that of an eagle with spread wings and a leonine head resting its talons on the rumps of stags whose heads, in the round, are turned outwards in traditional manner. One of the finest renderings of this also comes from Ninhursag's temple at Al Ubaid, again a relief, but of copper sheet.

The apogee of inlaid decoration can be seen in finds from the cemetery of Ur, especially on vases and the sound boxes of harps. A harp appears in the top register of the Standard of Ur (British Museum, London) which also shows a banquet in white and red tinted shell, surrounded by irregular lapis lazuli chips inlaid in bitumen on wood. The other side of the standard shows a battle involving infantry and heavy, four-wheeled chariots: the scene presumably explains the feasting on the other side.

The same medley of materials plus gold and silver was used

A rampant goat from a tomb at Ur; c2600–2500 BC.
British Museum, London

The largest statue from the Abu Temple at Eshnunna; height 72cm (28in); c2700 BC. Iraq Museum, Baghdad.

The Royal Standard of Ur

Reconstructed from numerous fragments of lapis lazuli, shell, and reddened limestone, the Ur "Standard" is still the most colorful treatment of two perennial themes of the Sumerian Heroic Age, that of the Victorious Battle and the Banquet or Symposium Scene. It lay "war" side upwards in a corner of the back room of a plundered tomb in the "Royal" Cemetery at Ur beside a man wearing a cap woven with thousands of lapis lazuli beads. Sir Leonard Woolley's masterful recovery is an assurance that the present arrangment of the mosaic is correct.

Each flat, sloped side has three registers divided by narrow bands of lapis and red limestone squares. These tesserae and the shell were fixed to a wood base by bitumen. The lapis was ultimately derived from sources in distant Afghanistan, but was obviously cut to shape locally, probably at Ur itself. The figures of contrasting white native shell were executed in silhouette form; engravers, however, were also capable of producing more sophisticated relief work.

On the "war" side are wagons and infantry in battle, while in the top register a central leader, much larger than the other figures, receives bound-and-yoked prisoners. The military engagement is stylized, for the vanquished are already without armor or clothes, but the victors are represented with attention to detail. Particularly notable are the high-fronted wagons, each with driver and, standing behind him on a projecting platform, an ax- or spearman. They are early forms of wheeled transport with fixed front axles, so they could not maneuver like chariots. Two-part solid wheels like those depicted have been found in excavations, as have the double-looped rein rings. A silver example from another Ur grave is surmounted by a bull mascot and indeed oxen rather than the onagers or wild asses of the Standard were used to draw similar wagons into adjacent tombs and death pits, probably for practical and ceremonial reasons.

The onagers link the two sides, since they recur, without wagons, on the "peace" panel in a procession of variously dressed persons leading other animals and carrying fish, a lamb, baskets, and sacks. These probably represent the spoils of the victory being celebrated by an assembly of seated figures, about to drink, to the accompaniment of a lyre and singer or dancer. Again, a larger man is shown in this top register, attired in a fleeced skirt rather than the plain ones of the six who face him beyond two attendants. The reality of detail is once more confirmed by the discovery of identical bull-fronted lyres from the same cemetery. Moreover, statues of figures holding cups, as here, are also known from Sumer, and the long hair that distinguishes the person on the far right also adorns a roughly contemporary statue of Urnanshe, who is identified as a singer.

Whatever the function of this object—perhaps the sound box of a harp—the com-

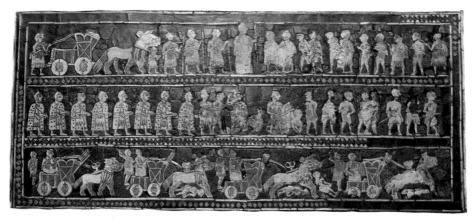

▲ The Royal Standard of Ur: the "war" panel. British Museum, London

▼ Urnanshe, the singer, from Mari. National Museum, Damascus

▲ The Royal Standard: an end panel. British Museum, London

▶ The golden lyre from the Royal Cemetery, Ur. Iraq Museum, Baghdad

▲ The Royal Standard of Ur; the "peace" panel. 20×48cm (8×19in); mid 3rd millennium BC. British Museum, London

▶ An inlaid wooden portable panel from Mari. Louvre, Paris

position belongs to a genre well established in Sumer. It is found on wall plaques and, in fragmentary form, on other wooden portable panels, almost all from temples. The latter show variations in costume and motifs, like some cylinder seals from the site of Mari in Syria, but usually the Banquet Scene involves a female dignitary. This has led to suggestions that a Sacred Marriage or New Year's Festival is represented. At the top left of the "peace" panel is another large but destroyed figure with what could originally have been a flail or leaf like that held by the female on a Nippur plaque.

It would be important to know who is represented at the top left since the presence of a female, as well as the existence of the explicitly religious and mythological content of the side-panels, would make the Standard much more comparable with the wall-plaques. Her position, however, would be unusual and without her the feast in this case lacks clear religious symbolism when compared with other Banquet Scenes of the age, and looks more like a general and his officers in congratulatory poses. It is therefore an exceptional variation of an established theme and this military aspect may have to do with the status of the occupant of the tomb in which Woolley found it. Unfortunately, the tomb when found was thoroughly disturbed and yielded only one name, that of a man, Ezi, and, apart from odd finds and traces of a few more bodies, five spear-bearers at its entrance.

E.J. PELTENBURG

▼ A clay model of a chariot from Tello. Louvre, Paris

▶ An engraved shell plaque from the Royal Cemetery at Ur. British Museum, London

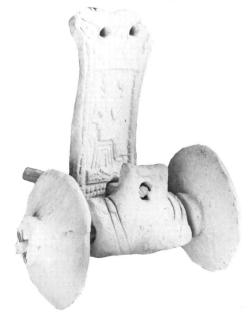

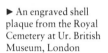

Further reading. Amiet, P. *La Glyptique Mésopotamienne Archaïque*, Paris (1961). Boese, J. *Altmesopotamische Weihplatten*, Berlin (1971). Moorey, P.R.S. "Some Aspects of Incised Drawing and Mosaic in the Early Dynastic Period", *Iraq* vol. XXIX (1967) pp97–116. Moorey, P.R.S. "What do We Know about the People Buried in the Royal Cemetery?", *Expedition* (Fall, 1977) pp24–40.

in an enigmatic object, from a tomb at Ur, showing a rampant goat peering through shrubbery (British Museum, London). Its significance is difficult to understand—it seems to be more than just a picture of a goat. At the least it reflects the Sumerians' strong belief that divine power resided in animals.

In the last century of the period of the early city-states the stela—a large decorated slab that stood in public—was introduced (c2400 BC). Its purpose was to act as a public record of an historical event and to this end combined equally both inscriptions and scenes with figures. A particularly fine example is the stela of Eannatum of Lagash, "the Stela of the Vultures" (Louvre, Paris). On one side Ningirsu, the tutelary deity of Lagash, defeats his enemies by capturing them in a net. On the other, Eannatum, riding in his chariot at the head of a phalanx of infantry, achieves his destiny. In Sumerian minds the two actions were indissolubly bound: the former realized the latter. And so we see another Sumerian pictorial affirmation of their belief that harmony between the gods and men is the basis of peace in human society.

The stela also shows how the visual arts were employed to convey the content of Sumerian epics and poetic literature, since the sequence showing Ningirsu clubbing his enemy is known from the *Epic of Creation*. This scene also demonstrates how the Sumerians have begun to represent their deities—in human form. But numinous qualities are not portrayed by facial distinctions; details of attire and divine attributes such as bulls' horns are preferred.

The Stela of Eannatum of Lagash; height 180cm (71in); c2500 BC. Louvre, Paris

The period of the Akkadian Empire (c2371–2230 BC). This was the period of the first Semitic Empire and it takes its name from the new city of Agade, built perhaps near Kish by the first king of an upstart dynasty. The name is also used for the Semitic language which now began to supplant Sumerian.

The change involved an internal shift of power—not an invasion (our information about a major change is available from written sources for the first time). Political organization, cultural attitudes, religious outlooks, and art differed considerably from the time of the proto-imperial city-states, but many changes were crystallizations of previous trends, now with Semitic dimensions.

Two major developments were the broadening of areas of political and military interest and an intense centralization of power into the hands of one king. Into the orbit of Akkadian power came the areas covered by modern Turkey, Syria, and Iran. Boats from Dilmun (modern Bahrain) and far beyond tied up at the quaysides of Agade. The importance of Sumer was diminished and indeed it was treated as one unit in "Sumer and Akkad", the new official title for South Mesopotamia. In place of kings in this area governors were appointed—often relatives of the king of Sumer and Akkad.

The position of the king was now akin to that of a lordly sheikh—he was no longer just a humble servant of the gods. To ensure a loyal personal following it was necessary to foster charisma. In the case of the founder Sargon (his throne name, meaning "real" or "true king") this was so strong that he was celebrated in epics and omens for several centuries after his death. The inevitable outcome of developing a cult of the king was reached within a few generations: the king came to be regarded as a god.

These traumatic historical changes were reflected in the statuary of the period. Both subject matter and the spirit that pervades it are new. Statuettes of worshipers became extremely rare. Instead, imposing life-size statues of kings were carved. Their drapery ripples with a sense of life never even attempted before, and underneath there was organic musculature in place of the earlier flat planes and angles. We have reached a major turning point in Mesopotamian art. Henceforth it is often concerned with the royal personage. So unambiguous was the change that a famous, uninscribed bronze head from Nineveh (Iraq Museum, Baghdad) with portrait-like qualities can, without any hesitation, be claimed as a portrait of Sargon or one of his successors.

The movement away from Sumerian abstract and geometric forms to Akkadian animation and grandeur can be traced in several stelae, for Sargon retained both the use of such monuments for recording historical incidents and similar arrangements and styles on them. However, a harder diorite became the favored medium and there were stylistic developments: more pointed beards and, of more importance, space between individual figures where previously there had been clusters of manikins. Advantage of this change was taken later to present tense scenes of combat between individuals. Such scenes and files of warriors and naked prisoners were the main subjects of

A bronze head from Nineveh; height 37cm (15in); c2371–2230 BC. Iraq Museum, Baghdad

The Victory Stela of Naram-Sin; height 200cm (79in); c2291–2255 BC. Louvre, Paris

reliefs, usually drawn from particular incidents and underlined with inscriptions such as that of Sargon who "fought with Lugalzaggesi, the King of Erech, took him prisoner, and brought him in a neck-stock to the gate of Enlil".

The zenith of Akkadian art was reached in the Victory Stela of Naram-Sin (Louvre, Paris), the third ruler after Sargon. It is a dramatic paean to the might of the deified king who is shown wearing the symbol of divinity—a horned headdress. Gone is the rigid stela shape, the constricting register divisions, and the set battle pieces. Instead the monument is nearly conical in form, which stresses the upward movement of the soldiers it depicts climbing in wooded mountains. Their gazes lead the observer's eye upwards to the archetype of invincibility. Contorted postures heighten the drama; see the two crossed foes trampled underfoot by the King and the kneeling trumpeter (also a defeated enemy) whose back is arched.

The Stela of Naram-Sin displays a change of content that may imply a change in purpose. The battle concerned is over, victory assured; by suggestion it is futile to resist. The triumphal pose of Naram-Sin on the stela was subsequently adopted for use on rock reliefs that were cut in enemy territories during this period. They served as much to warn as to celebrate. Yet in spite of ubiquitously displayed confidence the dynasty was to last only approximately 64 more years. It then fell, at the hands of barbarians.

During the period of the city-states, seal-engravers almost exclusively carved bands of fighting figures—animals, demigods, and humans, usually upright, often crossed and compressed in furious biting and stabbing. Banqueting and other scenes sometimes featured as did myths during the proto-imperial period. But most figures were schematic, lifeless, staring: the products of poor workmanship.

The popularity of myths and legends during the Akkadian period opened up a new and seemingly inexhaustible fund of themes for glyptic art. The struggling figures were not forgotten—some produced during this period stand as examples of the finest glyptic art ever. For by choosing to present contests between individuals rather than crowd scenes, against an empty background (compare the development of relief composition in this period) individuals are deeply modeled, tense, and life-breathing warriors. Scenes in which a human is presented to a deity were also finely composed with realistic figures. The Sun God, fertility deities, and others frequently appear on surviving examples, but rarely can scenes be assigned to any particular legend. On some seals a man shown sitting on an eagle can be identified as Etana, who was taken to heaven on an eagle he had rescued from a pit, in order to secure the plant of birth (examples in the Pierpont Morgan Library, New York and Vorderasiatisches Museum, Berlin). The legend (of which we do not know the end) is familiar only from later sources, but was probably current at this time.

The Neo-Sumerian period (*c2113–2006* BC). According to Sumerian documents, the Dynasty of Agade was doomed and Sumer laid waste because Naram-Sin wantonly destroyed the Ekur, the sanctuary of the god Enlil in Nippur. The instrument of Enlil's vengeance was the Guti, a barbarous horde perhaps from the mountains to the east, who brought chaos and anarchy to Sumer.

From the ashes of the catastrophe came a revival of former artistic traditions but in forms heavily indebted to Akkadian advances. In the Guti period the *ensis* or steward-rulers of Lagash seem to have been particularly important as patrons. They certainly had command over some of the finest artists in the land and were able to obtain materials from abroad. The results were magnificent buildings containing statues, stelae, votive tablets, and basins.

The statuary of the period radiates a chastised, pious, and yet complacent strength—perhaps the hallmark of the age. The figures possess an inner life of their own. On their lower portions are inscriptions which chronicle the construction of holy places and canals and also dedicate the work, using the first person. For example, the inscription on a statue of Gudea I (Louvre, Paris) reads, "I am the shepherd loved by my king [the god Ningirsu]: may my life be prolonged."

Statues of the Neo-Sumerian period retain the felicitous rendering of the naked human figure and the folds of garments (though the cloth now represented is heavy and tends to conceal the human form with its stiffness) which developed during the previous Akkadian period. New details appear; a wide-band headdress, shaven head, stylized conjoined eyebrows, and elongated fingers.

The many surviving fragments of relief work demonstrate clearly the conservatism of the period and its deliberate at-

A statue of Gudea I; c2200 BC. Louvre, Paris

tempt to revive the "good old days" of the past. An imposing example of this is the 10 ft (3 m) high stela of Ur-Nammu (the founder of the last Sumerian dynasty; University Museum, Philadelphia) which reverts to the shape and register divisions of the stela of Eannatum. A memorial to the king's service to the gods, it also displays the same tranquility as the sculpture in the round of this period.

In the stela's top register Ur-Nammu, dominated by two divine symbols, makes a sacrifice to a horned deity. In the one below he stands before two seated deities, probably Nanna and Ningal, whose positions are determined by a peculiar foldout perspective. Behind Ur-Nammu is a minor interceding deity whose pose is repeated with monotonous regularity on seals of the period depicting similar scenes. For access to the great gods could seldom be direct and was usually facilitated by the intercession of a personal, guardian deity of minor status. For such deities household shrines proliferated in this period and the tedious reiteration of rituals became a stock theme of Mesopotamian art. So too did vases with flowing water, reflecting cult practice. This can also be seen in Ur-Nammu's stela, in the top right where a hovering deity pours life-giving water over the major scene.

The purpose of Ur-Nammu's stela was to embody divine justification and indeed encouragement for a building project. This is symbolized in the middle register where Ur-Nammu is seen receiving a rod and line; he is also shown realizing his project as he shoulders mason's tools. He was in fact a prodigious builder and was responsible for, among other works, the famous ziggurat or stepped tower to the moon god Nanna at Ur, ziggurats in other cities of his empire, the enormous complex for the goddess Ningal in which her statue is placed so as to be visible along an axis passing through several doorways, a palace, and his vaulted royal tomb.

Building activity on such a widespread scale has resulted in the preservation of many of the copper figures that were sealed under the walls and thresholds of buildings to provide magical protection. They were mass produced, and the figure of the king, carrying a basket, perfunctorily rendered. The last specimens of a type that began as part man, part nail in the period of the early city states, they disappeared along with many other Sumerian conventions in the cultural disintegration following the arrival of more waves of Semites in southern Mesopotamia.

The Old Babylonian period (c1890–1600 BC). The demise of Sumerian civilization at the beginning of this period took place at the same time as a complete rearrangement of the props and actors on the ancient Near Eastern stage. The Amorites established themselves in the south. Assyrian power grew in the north. Hurrians moved from east to west across the northern Mesopotamian marches. The Hittites assumed political control in Anatolia.

In Sumer and Akkad there was strife, until Hammurabi, the sixth king of the First Dynasty of Babylon (1792–1750 BC) welded together a precarious empire. Its formation required

Upper part of a statue of a water goddess from Mari; height of statue 140cm (55in); c1900–1760 BC. National Museum of Aleppo

the destruction of several cities, including Mari. It is this city, rather than the later rebuilt Babylon, that has yielded the most information about this phase of Mesopotamian history.

Mari was both renowned and rich. Kings from places as far away as Ugarit on the Mediterranean coast requested permission to visit the city's 200-room palace. From its control of trade Mari derived its wealth, even from abroad. Texts of the period mention a dagger from Kaptara or Minoan Crete. The products of its artists, however, were infused with Amorite spirit.

In one of the courts of the palace stood a near life-size statue of a water goddess holding a jar similar to the one on the stela of Ur-Nammu (now in the National Museum of Aleppo). This one actually dispensed water since the vase was connected by a pipe through the body to a hidden basin. Through its stream onlookers were able to discern fish. These were lightly incised on the goddess's robe, which was flounced—a Sumerian practice. New interpretations are to be seen, however, in the rendering of the shoulder straps, the tabbed hems, and the massive yet crisply modeled head.

Similar water goddesses appear in the lower panel of the central structure of the *Investiture of Zimrilim*, a wall-painting from a court of the palace of Mari (Louvre, Paris). It is difficult to interpret the whole composition because its iconographical concepts and painters' conventions are not understood. Parts are more easily comprehended. The upper panel of the middle box may show a cult scene inside a temple, surrounded by the sacred trees and guardian figures that would have stood outside the building.

The painting's "investiture" scene derives from the earlier "introduction" theme; so do the postures of the individuals. But against this religious and cultural continuity stand novel aspects in dress and perspective. The king wears a fringed garment and a tall headdress. There are composite monster-griffins. An attempt is made to render the divine horns in profile perspective. And the goddess Ishtar, holding out rod and line, adopts a new stance by placing one foot on a lion (her attribute)—a pose ultimately derived from Naram-Sin's. She also holds an eye-ax which was the forerunner of a scimitar.

The last important monument that survives from the Old Babylonian period before the destruction of Babylon by a Hittite army (c1600 BC) is the diorite stela of Hammurabi inscribed with his law code (Louvre, Paris). Shamash, the sun god (identified by the rays emanating from his shoulders) hands a rod and line to Hammurabi—perhaps the tokens of divine authority for the king's dispensation of justice. Although Hammurabi's heavy dress, beard, and headgear seem to muffle his body, the folds of the cloth and the muscles of his forearm are carved and polished with greater accuracy than ever before.

A detail from the Stela of Hammurabi; basalt; height of scene 71cm (28in); c1792–1750 BC. Louvre, Paris

Assyria and Babylonia. Our information on Mesopotamian art for several centuries effectively ceases with the destruction of Mari by Hammurabi (c1760 BC). A few cylinder seals from the time of Hammurabi's five successors are known, but they do not reveal any important artistic developments. Nor is much known about the art of the Old Assyrian Empire which flourished just before the time of Hammurabi.

The main reason for the dearth of artistic effort in Mesopotamia was the enfeeblement of the established kingdoms in the wake of newcomers. Two groups, the Kassites and the Hurri-Mitanni, became politically important in the Near East, but the extent of their independent contributions to the culture of the area has yet to be assessed.

The Kassites (c1550–1157 BC). The origins and affinities of the Kassites, who wrested control of Babylonia after the Hittite raid mentioned above, are unknown. Their language and customs were certainly alien to the lowland plains of the south. But their arrival in Babylonia is recorded by one of the few breaks in the archaeological record—a major turning point in a historical sequence of cultures generally noted for their impressive continuity.

The earliest Kassite remains date from the time just prior to the international epoch known as the Amarna period (corresponding to the reign of the Egyptian pharaoh Akhenaten (1363–1346 BC) in whose palace at Amarna diplomatic correspondence from the whole of southwest Asia has been found). Molded clay bricks have been found at Ur, Susa, and other cities. Those found at Uruk have been reconstructed to produce the decorated, recessed facade of the temple of Inanna (Iraq Museum, Baghdad). Both the facade and the layout of the temple are in new idioms. The scheme of decoration had been first seen c2000 BC, but the Kassites must be credited with the responsibility for its inclusion in the artistic repertory. The form culminated in the Ishtar Gate of Nebuchadnezzar at Babylon.

In the recesses of the facade stand gods and goddesses, each holding a vase of flowing water above their elongated trunks. The streams of water link the deities in a manner similar to that on the painting from Mari discussed earlier, suggesting that many older traditions were preserved in spite of the new rulers. This is indeed confirmed by the archaic features and contents of writing from this period. This architectural use of sculpture was in fact similar to the Hittites' practice in Anatolia—a hint of the many international artistic similarities that were to follow. Palace walls were now painted, with rows of heavily robed courtiers. The walls of other buildings were enriched with glass.

The most distinctive artistic form in this period and the one slightly later was the *kudurru*, a stone boundary marker erected to confirm the royal grant of land to an individual—an entirely new concept in the organization of society. The sanctity and therefore permanent nature of the grant was usually expressed by reliefs containing a plethora of divine symbols. Actual representations of divinities were now being replaced by monstrous creatures and symbols derived mainly from the Old Babylonian period. The change reflects a profound alteration in the religious outlook of Babylonia and elsewhere. Similar creatures also appeared on cylinder seals but in fact columns of inscriptions came to replace figures almost completely.

The Hurri-Mitanni (c1700–1350 BC). During this period of the 2nd millennium two disparate peoples infiltrated northern Mesopotamia (into the area between the Zagros mountains of Iran and the Mediterranean Sea). The first group, the Hurrians, of northeastern origin, were populous but completely lacking in political cohesiveness and the artistic display of higher civilizations. The second, slightly later intruders, the Indo-European Mitanni, worshiped Indra, Mitra, and Varuna. In spite of being fewer in number they formed a ruling caste vigorous enough to bring tenuous political unity to the area. It lasted until c1375 BC, managing for a time even to eclipse Assyria to become one of the strongest empires in the Near East.

It is still a matter for debate whether the Hurri-Mitanni produced any original art. No distinctive large sculptures or paintings survive from the area's central region, only a few ivories which were inspired by, if not actually imported from, the Levant. But then the Empire's capital city has yet to be found.

Two peripheral sites have been excavated. Nuzi, in the eastern sphere of the Empire, contained two temples and a building that was perhaps an administrative center. The latter contains a fragment of wall-painting, an empaneled series of stylized trees, bulls' heads, and female heads that were obviously copied from the Egyptian Hathor heads in the Levant.

Alalakh, in the west on the bend of the River Orontes, hovered between independence and vassalage to the Mitanni and other powerful states. At the time when an important statue and palace were erected its population was largely, though by no means entirely, Hurrian. The most impressive feature of the half-timbered palace was its double-columned entrance portico which formed the main part of the complex later imitated by the Assyrians. There is no proof, however, that this was a specifically Hurrian concept—indeed, an earlier palace with an internal columned entrance has been found there, suggesting a native origin for the feature.

The statue of King Idri-mi, the putative builder of the palace (British Museum, London), has a receding chin, an unbroken line from brow to nose tip, and large eyes. All these may be recognized as traits of Hurrian art, for the statue-heads of his predecessors are differently rendered. Similar features are to be found on several bronze figurines from Ugarit, where there was also a large Hurrian element (Louvre, Paris). Idri-mi's robe has a rolled border, a North Syrian feature adopted by Mitannian kings, and is covered with his autobiographical inscription. It tells of his rejection, exile, and triumph through his acceptance by the Mitanni: "our word seemed good to the kings of the warriors of the Hurri-land".

The statue of King Idri-mi; height 104cm (41in); c1500 BC. British Museum, London

Present evidence suggests that this group rejected monumental artistic expression in favor of small works sometimes produced by new techniques in new media. This may reflect the more mobile life of this society, for now appeared the horse and chariot and the charioteer *maryannu* warriors as the society's knights. One such heroic charioteer, with reins tied round his waist to free his hands for firing arrows at fleeing animals, may be the figure on a gold bowl from Ugarit (Louvre, Paris) but such scenes and figures had now become widespread motifs. If the work shows any particularly Hurrian element it is the exclusion of landscape, which was usually included in outdoor scenes on other works, for example on another gold bowl found alongside the one mentioned above (National Museum of Aleppo).

On the seals of the period free-field composition also produces an image of timelessness. Heterogeneous yet recognizable motifs from Babylon, Syria, and Egypt are mixed, combined, and modified, but the result is an undisciplined *mélange*. Another, more restrained type shows worshipers or animals beside a sacred, artificial tree. They are mass produced in faience, a medium which, together with glass, is now of some importance.

The art of the Hurrian craftsmen-artists was essentially derivative. They showed themselves most successful in the production and decoration of small objects, such as the iron dagger that was sent to Egypt. Their independent position in northern Mesopotamia did not outlast the destruction of the kingdom, but some Hurrians continued for several centuries to live independently in the highland fastness of northwest Iran.

Middle-Assyrian art (*c*1500–1045 BC). An internal resurgence enabled Assyria to take advantage of declining Mitannian power and rise from servitude to independence and great statehood. The Mitanni's position in the political context of the Near East was also assumed—correspondence began with Egypt, the Hittites were threatened, and Babylonia was first checked and then conquered. In the new expanded state the principal influences came from the Hurri-Mitanni and Babylonia—the latter was especially influential in literature, learning, and religion. In the reigns of Eriba—Adad I and Ashuruballit I (1392–1330 BC)—a renaissance occurred: from this time a new burst of creativity can be traced.

Cylinder seals provide the best guide to stylistic development, for several are attested by impressions on datable tablets thereby providing a chronological framework. On the earliest ones (for example, those in the Pierpont Morgan Library, New York) are griffins and other monsters, fewer in number than before and spread across the complete width of the cylinder surface. Although the seals' motifs are often Hurrian, the style's monumentality, plasticity, and sense of orderliness is distinctly Assyrian. Landscape appeared in seal designs towards the end of the 14th century BC, passed to Assyria from Minoan Crete by way of Syria's cosmopolitan workshops, but was only used with diffidence.

During the 13th century BC a restrained mastery was achieved in glyptic art by using empty space and isocephaly to highlight intricately observed combats between a single pair of figures. New monsters, such as the centaur and "Pegasus", were unleashed into this fanciful, magico-religious iconography. One convention typical of the period was the mannered treatment of the kicking hind leg. Such work may have influenced late Kassite glyptic art. In tone and execution it is reminiscent of Akkadian verve.

Few large works of art survive from this period. One that does, from a site near Ashur (whence "Assyria"), is a paneled arrangement like the Nuzi painting showing opposed gazelles on either side of a sacred tree. The medium is painted stucco, the finishing colors red, white, black, and blue. Linked palmettes and lotus plants form a border that foreshadows later Assyrian patterns. So too did the stone pedestal reliefs of King Tukulti-Ninurta I (1244–1208 BC), which were in effect small prototypes of the great flat reliefs of the palaces.

Although the few surviving objects demonstrate that a vigorous and original Assyrian style had evolved well before the end of the 2nd millennium BC, scholars still ask themselves to what extent the foundations had been laid for the art of the later famous palaces. Tukulti-Ninurta's reliefs are the first Middle Assyrian attempt known at such a form, but they did not constitute murals. But two obelisks, which seem to belong to a transitional period, are known (British Museum, London). The pillar-like stones are stepped at the top with bands of reliefs on the sides. Their rendering is inept, but within their designs the ideas of narrative pictorial art and the appropriateness of hunting, besieging, and tribute-giving scenes are quite implicit.

Further evidence is provided by inscriptions that mention the existence in the late Middle Assyrian Period of many features that were typical of the one following. For example, in speaking of his father's palace, King Tiglath-Pileser I (1115–1077 BC) says:

> I heightened its walls and gate-towers, I surrounded it as in an enclosure with tiles of *surru* stone, lapis stone, alabaster, and marble. Pictures of date trees of *surru* stone I placed on the gate-towers, bronze nails with round heads I put round about. I attached tall doors of pinewood, with bronze sheet did I encase them and placed them in the gate.

Even if our knowledge of the styles mentioned is imprecise, the tone of the language used, the concentration on grandiose, decorated architecture, and the individual elements mentioned prefigure a Neo-Assyrian outlook.

The Assyrian palaces and their reliefs (*c*890–610 BC). Travelers to the Near East had often reported the existence of great mounds near Mosul. Although Claudius Rich, the British Resident at Baghdad, made a famous map and description of Nineveh in 1820, it was not until M. Emil Botta, the French Consul in Mosul, switched his attention in 1843 from Nineveh to Khorsabad, the Fort of Sargon, that the first sculp-

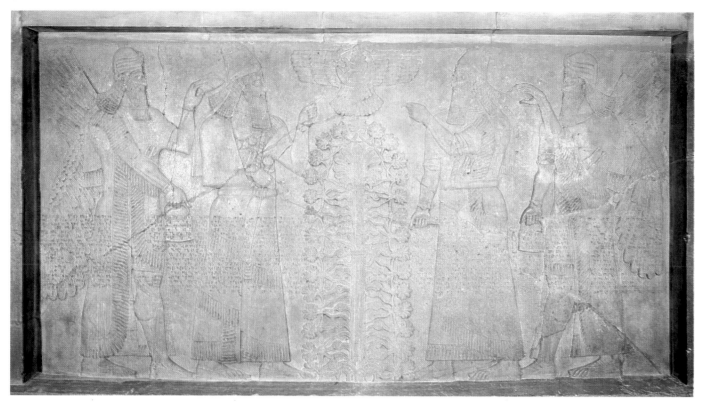

A relief from the reign of Ashurnasirpal II; height 193cm (76in); 883–859 BC. British Museum, London

tured slabs were found *in situ*—a frontage no less than half a mile (0.8 km) in length.

At this point the field of investigation was entered by Austin Henry Layard, a gifted observer and draughtsman who was to make astounding discoveries at Nimrud (biblical Kalah) and Nineveh. By 1851, as a result of fearless courage and persistence in undertaking excavations in trying conditions, Layard had discovered eight palaces and established the discipline of Assyriology. Excavations, though on a smaller scale, have intermittently continued on these mounds ever since. The most recent, by Iraqi archaeologists, have revealed traces of paint, noted also by Layard, but subject to fading.

News of the discovery of the Assyrian palaces came like a revelation to western Europe, hitherto steeped in Greco-Roman Antiquity. It stimulated an interest in corroboratory biblical research in an intellectual world that was being attuned to new perspectives following the Great Exhibition of 1851 and the publication of Darwin's *Origin of Species* in 1859. It led to the present rich collections of Assyrian murals, especially those in the Louvre, Paris and the British Museum, London.

In origin Assyria was a small state with its original capital at Ashur, beside the Tigris, about three days' ride from the top of the triangle in which most of the important cities clustered. When it expanded to form the first world empire (even taking in part of Egypt) it was forced to organize under its tutelage a mass of peoples with radically different cultures. Ultimately it failed: its capital, Nineveh, was destroyed. But the means whereby control of such an enormous area was attempted are of abiding interest, and it is in this light that painting and wall-paintings assume importance for they buttressed the crucial characters and functions of Assyrian kings. For each ruler a new style was inaugurated.

Assyria's king was the chosen warrior of the state god, Ashur. He was also the repository of the society's fortunes. Both themes were depicted in the decoration of the earliest palaces, but by the 7th century BC the secular, warlike aspect was most emphasized.

The shift probably paralleled changes in the nature of kingship and the purpose of the reliefs. In the early reliefs from the reign of Ashurnasirpal II are compositions showing rituals, in which the king achieves supernatural status, larger and in greater number than scenes of war (British Museum, London). And even the latter are imbued with spiritual significance by the presence of Ashur winging his way above the chariots' teams of horses or crouching inside a battering ram. The reliefs of the later empire make quite a contrast. Here there is no transcendence: ritual scenes are shunned, the army marches without its god. Instead of depicting the point of a battle when victory is in the balance, even if eventually assured, a narrative demonstrating the king's invincible, earthly might is shown—a tedious parade of slaughter, tribute-taking, and deportation, seen for example in the reliefs of the Elamite campaigns. In fact, gods are represented mainly by their symbols in Assyrian palace art. As the Empire grew in size the king assumed more supernatural powers though he never claimed to be divine. On the bronze door reliefs of the New Year's shrine at Ashur "the figure of Ashur going to do battle against Tiamat is that of Sinnacherib".

During the 9th century BC an unprecedented geographical expansion of Assyria took place and reliefs were carved to chronicle the king's deeds and commemorate his heroic actions. Then followed a phase of weakness succeeded by a time when new confidence is reflected in a greater number of reliefs. When illiterate kings, princes, and messengers came to Assyria, and beheld the miles of pictures in the Babylonian,

Arab, and Susiana rooms at Nineveh, they must surely have been inpressed by the might of Assyria, the hopelessness of resistance, and the futility of rebellion.

Slab after slab, room after room, the message recurred. Reliefs provided intense propaganda immediately relevant to the political context of palace life. They proved that once the Assyrian army was mobilized the result of battle was a foregone conclusion, so foreign kings under diplomatic pressure (for example Hezekiah at Jerusalem, mentioned in 2 Kings 18: 17f.) were wise to submit before the ultimate resort of war.

Such reliefs were only one element of palace decoration, the lowest on walls that had aesthetically unrelated, colorful, painted and glazed adornment higher up. The palaces themselves were composed of several courtyards, which were divided into public and private sectors by the long, narrow throne room with its great buttressed elevation and sumptuous relief decoration. In the citadel of a city founded by Sargon, Khorsabad, several temples and a ziggurat were closely linked with the palace, a conjunction reflecting and stressing the dual political and religious importance of the king.

The Assyrians produced artistic work in forms other than

A mural relief from Sargon's Khorsabad: shooting fowl in a grove; height 127cm (50in); 721–705 BC. Louvre, Paris

reliefs, and did not necessarily hold the latter in higher esteem than the former. This is borne out by Sinnacherib's description of his rebuilding of Nineveh. The earlier palace there was "not artistic" so he had a new one constructed with cypress doors "bound with a band of shining copper", cedar and copper pillars on bases in the forms of two lions or two mountain sheep, the "protecting deities", and limestone reliefs that were "dragged" in by the conquered. Elsewhere Sinnacherib introduced portals "patterned after a Hittite palace"; "female colossi of marble and ivory ... pegs of silver and copper"; pillars with capitals of lead; beams sheathed in silver; lion, bull, and cow colossi over posts and crossbars. He was particularly pleased to find new veins of raw materials and to have metals carted down from the mountains so that sculptors could pour the molten material into clay casts for bronze images in Assyria itself. Such was Sinnacherib's close interest in artistic work that he called himself "wise in all craftsmanship".

Layard excavated a small part of Sinnacherib's palace and reports that "seventy-one halls, chambers and passages whose walls ... had been panelled with slabs of sculptured alabaster ... nearly two miles of bas-reliefs, with twenty-seven portals formed by colossal winged bulls and lion-sphinxes were uncovered".

Assyrian art: the early phase (883–824 BC). The minimal standards for the art and architecture of the Assyrian Empire were set by Ashurnasirpal II (883–859 BC) in his new eight-winged palace at Nimrud, opened in the presence of 69,000 inhabitants from his newly conquered territories. Although certain sculptured and architectural prototypes existed in Assyria and Syria, and there were already walls with attached relief orthostats in northern Syria, an area that helped to populate the rising metropolis of Nimrud, Ashurnasirpal II was no mere copyist. He did not simply draw together preexisting traditions and employ them for work of larger proportions, but contributed something original and enduring in the form of narrative, pictorial art.

The annalistic depiction of Ashurnasirpal II's deeds—besieging cities, taking tribute, hunting lions and bulls—displays the systematic planning of several slabs to create a consecutive unified world of action. The earlier individual slabs of northern Syria accommodated only a handful of figures. Another development was the introduction of a horizontal division to produce two bands of equal height which were then carved separately. The division took the form of inscriptions although they did not yet serve as captions. Each slab was tentatively linked to its neighbor by the structure of the events and sometimes by the original and important feature of an overlapping minor detail. The reason for the division is not known; perhaps simply to provide more space for the portrayal of more deeds at greater length, or to avoid problems of

Right: A winged bull-god from Sargon's palace at Khorsabad; height 396cm (156in); 721–705 BC. Louvre, Paris

Taureau ailé à face humaine
Gardait l'entrée d'une porte du palais de SARGON (VIIIe s. av.)

⑫

perspective presented by the idea of carving the previous large surface.

The problems of composition seemed to have loomed larger in the minds of artists than the problems of modeling. In fact, for the rest of the Neo-Assyrian period figures remained flat, drawn, and incised, rather than sculpted. This suggests the influence of paintings or tapestries, either direct or indirect by way of the glazed orthostats of Ashurnasirpal II's predecessor.

In contrast to the alabaster murals, giant winged bull-gods were integrated into the walls in an architectonic manner. Within them dwells a timeless quality that is absent from the historical episodes. Their enduring character derives from myth and ritual and stands in opposition to the time-bound deeds of the king. A similar character is found, however, in murals that deal with traditional Mesopotamian rituals centered on the tree of life.

Various features of the reliefs indicate the work of apprentices following the limited repertoire of a master's copybook, for example heads awkwardly placed on bodies, bodies fixed at different angles, and repeated scenes. But in spite of these observations the workmen created "a strongly accented sequence by means of a rising and falling flow of figures into an organized rhythm related to the picture's meaning", to quote a modern commentator, Moortgat, who compares these relief compositions to music and poetry.

The reliefs are, of course, packed with historical information, often so accurate that we can only assume that "war artists" attended campaigns. On the Black Obelisk of the reign of Shalmaneser III (858–824 BC) appears the only representation of an Israelite monarch, Jehu. Also from Shalmaneser's reign comes the most complete example of bronze sheeting, originally part of the gates at Balawat near Nimrud. Showing 24 strips of battles and rituals from Urartu to Tyre, the bisected band system of Shalmaneser's predecessor is retained, but the whole reveals a real decline into mediocre, conventional narrative.

Assyrian Art: the late phase (744–627 BC). The work prompted by Sargon (721–705 BC) at Khorsabad is distinguished by attempts to attain a new monumentality. The complete heights of the slabs were employed for figures that were modeled in higher relief than before. But figures were still not freed from two dimensions, as shown by the provision of five legs for a *lamassu* (winged lion) which was intended to be recognized as complete whether viewed from the front or the side. It highlights a new concern, however: the striving to render impressions of spatial depth which was to concern Assyrian designers for the rest of this period.

Two other notable developments occurred in this period. The first was the growth of concern to introduce sufficient

On the Black Obelisk of Shalmaneser III: Jehu of Israel pays tribute to the King; 858–824 BC. British Museum, London

detail to heighten a picture's historical reality—hence captions appear and also landscape to give an action geographical context. The second was the introduction of courtly leisure in the parks as an acceptable subject for representation—both reflecting the mood of secularization and a landmark in the subject matter of the art of western Asia.

Unfortunately we know many of Sargon's reliefs only from drawings—the originals sank on a raft in the River Tigris. But of approximately the same period are some of the wall-paintings from Til Barsib, once a provincial Assyrian center in northern Syria (now in the Louvre, Paris and the National Museum of Aleppo). They are in fact of greater interest than subsidiary paintings from Assyria itself since they duplicate the subject matter of reliefs and provide us with evidence of painting's separate existence as a major art form. They are also evidence of the original polychrome appearance of the reliefs.

In the reliefs carved in the reign of Sinnacherib (704–681 BC) and in the early years of the reign of Ashurbanipal (668–627 BC) the love of detail of location reaches its most intense expression (British Museum, London). Multitudes of people are packed in to create confusing tumults which are shown to be representations of specific scenes by the accompanying legends. Just above the beheading episode on one relief the inscription reads:

> Te-umman, the King of Elam, who was wounded in a violent battle, and Tamaritu, his eldest son, grasping his hand, fled to save their lives and hid themselves in a thicket. With the help of Ashur and Ishtar, I killed and beheaded them.

On the same slab the section showing the battle of the River Ulai discloses the uneasy compromise reached by designers trying to retain their traditional sense of perspective in settings that have broadened beyond the rigid narrow friezes of earlier times. Above, files of prisoners are marched along the bands in the old fashion, though natural features such as streams are often used to separate these files. Below, on the left, register base lines remain visible, but on the right where the intention was to produce an open field, the registers were artificially continued in the guise of dead and dying bodies, and, in one case, a horse.

Similar divisions of the field can be seen in the reliefs of Sinnacherib's marsh battles and in the siege of Lachish where the drama is focused in the apex of a triangle in order to break up the picture of a single, wide siege ramp. By this arrangement movement was unintentionally introduced, but in the last phase of Assyrian relief sculpture it was deliberately employed in order to unite the narrow registers to which the art had returned, as seen for example in a relief of the Arab Wars.

Ashurbanipal's Great Lion Hunt may be considered the apogee and finale of Assyrian relief sculpture (British Museum, London). Artists show themselves now to be once again preoccupied with the problems of composition rather than landscape—the wheel has come full circle. With their accumulated skills experienced artists now had the scope to

A detail of a wall-painting from Til Barsib; height 76cm (30in); c744–705 BC. National Museum of Aleppo

Assyrian relief sculpture: Ashurbanipal's Great Lion Hunt; 668–627 BC. British Museum, London

convert minor subjects into accurately observed studies, such as those of dying animals, though the contrast with stiffly carved human figures remains. The new style probably sprang from the wishes of Ashurbanipal himself.

In the garden scene he returns to the old Sumerian conventional banquet scene as originally shown on the "Royal Standard" from Ur. The war trophy in this case is Teuman's head, attached to the second tree from the left. But the style was prevented from developing by the upheavals that preceded the overthrow of Assyrian power.

The Neo-Babylonian period (625–539 BC). The state that succeeded Assyria has become more famous through the Bible and the writings of Herodotus than from surviving monuments. *Entemenaki*, the Tower of Babel, is known from its ground plan, whilst we have insufficient knowledge to be able to reconstruct the appearance of Nebuchadnezzar's Hanging Gardens.

The main reason for this scarcity of evidence of Babylonian art is simple. Although Babylon was the center of a world empire, and of paramount influence in Near Eastern art of this period, most of her buildings were constructed in the traditional southern Mesopotamian medium of perishable mud-brick—indeed, Babylon was so renowned for her work in the medium that Babylonian craftsmen were assigned the task of molding bricks for a palace built for Darius (522–486 BC). Thus no reliefs survive that are in any way comparable to those from the Assyrian palaces.

The principal influences in Babylonia were not Assyrian, however, but Sumero-Akkadian and Old Babylonian. Late-Kassite *kudurru* stones returned to favor; presentation scenes were modeled with greater plasticity; the rod and line motif reappeared; temples were laid out along earlier lines. It is unlikely that the Neo-Babylonian concept of kingship even produced reliefs to chronicle the deeds of kings.

Other features of this period's art are consistent with this independently archaic attitude. Glazed, polychrome bricks were used to coat the walls of palaces, the Processional Way, and the Ishtar Gate at Babylon. On the latter Sumerian dragons alternate with bulls, symbols respectively of the underworld and life. Such symbolism must have been a predominant feature of Babylonian monumental art.

The Hittites and Anatolia. In the centuries around the beginning of the 2nd millennium there was wholesale and repeated destruction of thriving settlements in Anatolia. Later references indicate that this was the first outburst in a prolonged struggle for dominance in the central region. Indeed, it was not until the reign of Hattusilis I in the 17th century BC (c1650–1620 BC) that Hattusas, modern Bogazkoy, was selected as the capital of the Hittite Old Kingdom, thereby indicating the establishment of stability.

The Hittites entered a country whose indigenous rulers wrote a different language from their own Indo-European one. The terrain was mountainous and literally interlaced with a Mesopotamian presence. Assyrian mercantile colonies or *karums* were to be found at most of the large cities; they were linked to each other and to Ashur by trade routes. Mesopotamia, the native Hattians, and to a much lesser extent the Levant were to exercise a predominant influence on the artistic expression of the newcomers; indeed the originality and distinctiveness of Hittite art have been questioned.

During the period of the Old Kingdom (c1740–1460 BC) the Hittites managed to consolidate their domestic position, at least by the time of Labarnas I (1680–1650 BC), in spite of being a minority ruling class. Under his two successors spectacular foreign victories were won in Syria and Babylonia. But these proved ephemeral, causing internal dissension and instability and provoking raids that threatened the capital Hattusas itself. The paucity of archaeological remains found during excavations at its site as well as elsewhere has confirmed the documents' picture of a basically weak state.

The Hittites reached the height of their power during the succeeding Empire period (c1460–1190 BC) in the reign of Suppiluliumas (c1380–1340 BC). They managed to sweep aside their traditional foes, the Hurri-Mitanni of northern Mesopotamia, and even challenge Egypt for the supremacy of the Levant. Most Hittite monuments belong to this century and the following one, surely a reflection of the Hittites' increased wealth and power and their unerring confidence in central government.

After the destruction of the Empire a host of Neo-Hittite successor states were founded within the territory by Cilician and northern Syrian peoples. Although they wielded little power, they have bequeathed a staggering number of bas-reliefs, statues, and minor objects, out of all proportion to their importance in other cultural activities. It must be noted, however, that these works may have no connection with the true Hittites; they are known by this same name because it was used by the Assyrians, but their societies were in fact mixtures of northern Syrians, Aramaeans, and people from other stocks.

The art of the Empire period (c1460–1190 BC). The amount of surviving Hittite art is small compared with the products of the Egyptian and Mesopotamian civilizations; its variety even more limited; and its derivative elements even more obvious. Political and religious themes predominate and correspond with the outstanding caliber of Hittite ritual prayers and diplomatic acumen revealed in their texts. Their state religion was intensely nationalistic with the king having responsibility for both kingly and priestly duties, usually intimately interconnected. This is deftly pointed by the following extract from the autobiography of Hattusilis III (c1275–1250 BC):

> The goddess, my lady, always held me by the hand; and since I was a divinely favored man, and walked in the favor of the gods, I never committed the evil deeds of mankind.

On many royal stamp seals, which must figure among the most distinctive Hittite works of art, the king is shown be-

A momentous meeting of the gods: the rock relief at Yazilikaya; c1450–1200 BC.

neath the borrowed winged sun disk, guided under the protecting arm of his tutelary deity. The motif occurs elsewhere, perhaps at its most magnificent in the smaller of two natural chambers of the open-air sanctuary at Yazilikaya where Tudhaliyas IV (1250–1220 BC), dressed in characteristic trailing robe and shoes with curled toes, carrying a long crook, is embraced by the youthful god Sharruma. On the end wall of the other chamber the main scene depicts, as the culmination of a procession realized in unmatched scale, a momentous meeting of the gods. On the left is Teshub, the Hurrian weather god, supported by two mountain deities. Facing him is Hebat followed by Sharruma. The divinities are named by hieroglyphs, and the inclusion of Teshub emphasizes the Hurrian influence in Hittite religion.

The work at Yazilikaya near Khattusha (Bogazkoy) represents the mature Hittite relief style of the Metropolis, and contrasts sharply with the flat reliefs of the provinces or later work such as the libation offering of King Shulumeli at Malatya (Archaeological Museum, Ankara). Another example of the Metropolitan style is the figure of the powerful god who protectively flanks the King's Gate at Bogazkoy (Archaeological Museum, Ankara). Its apparent simplicity masks the skill of a master sculptor who has created an embodiment of massive strength (6 ft, 1.8 m high) in three-quarter relief against a starkly plain background. Its stance is purposeful, and detail in the kilt and chest hair carefully incised. An inscription claims that the local artists had been trained by Babylonian master sculptors; if so, this relief demonstrates that the Hittites were quick to develop an unfettered stylistic independence.

Little survives of the minor arts that carry perhaps their most distinctive work. We have a few examples of their red pottery libation vessels, with their exaggerated spouts and sharply defined lines. From their texts we know, however, that animal vases were particularly popular:

> cups, and *rhyta*, silver, gold and [precious] stones thou [the god Telipinus] has in the Hatti land ... reverence is paid to thy temple, thy *rhyta* [thy cups] [and] thy utensils.

The Hittite artists' most successful medium were metals, often with various inlays, shown for example in a silver stag *rhyton* (Norbert Schimmel Collection). The relief band near the rim shows three offering-bearers before a god on a stag and a seated deity, as well as a slain stag beside a stylized tree.

The Neo-Hittite period (c1150–750 BC). Wall reliefs were the outstanding form of Neo-Hittite art. Many survive, often roughly and even incompetently worked, and contain motifs and themes from various sources reflecting the active competition between petty states. It is a sterile activity to search for a predominant pure Hittite influence.

Whenever they could afford it, kings had orthostats with reliefs set up along the bases of external walls of processional ways, courts, and, especially, around gates and porticoes which were also enriched with impressive columns set on lion bases. Subject matter ranged, according to taste, from intimate family scenes, to ranks of soldiers, tribute bearers, banquets with musicians, warfare, hunting, myths, and demons. The variety of content is as wide as that of the Hittite Empire was restricted, although the Hittite rock relief genre persisted, as shown, for example, at Ivriz near Konya.

There is substantial evidence to demonstrate that the Hittite element of this society was significant, for example the use of Hittite hieroglyphs—especially on the reliefs at Carchemish, the administrative center of the Empire in Syria whose importance continued beyond the destruction of the Empire—and the Hittite names of kings. But the history of art shows the workings of other influences. At first Hittite and Aramaean impulses combined, but they were gradually eclipsed by the power of Assyria which first caused stylistic and thematic changes before removing the political independence from which Neo-Hittite art had sprung.

The monuments of this period have an importance for the history of art by demonstrating the extraordinary wealth of Oriental imagery current in northern Syria at a time when the Greeks were both venturing into this area and at that crucial stage of their own artistic development known as Orientalizing.

Urartu. In the 8th century BC the kingdom of Urartu became the most powerful state in western Asia. It lay to the east of the center of the Hittite Empire, around the area of Lake Van, and until recently was only sketchily known from stray finds, some early work at Toprak Kale, historical references, and a relief of Sargon II of Assyria which focused on the sack of the important temple of Khaldi, one of Urartu's chief gods. But recently the excavation of several standardized temples has revealed fine drystone masonry and surrounding colonnades—the main features of flat-roofed buildings. The decorations (Archaeological Museum, Ankara) included caldrons in stands, cows with suckling calves, guardian humans at doors, large spears and spearheads, and, attached to the walls, shields with lion protomes.

The palaces of the mountain kingdom of Urartu were located in strongly fortified citadels. Like the temples they were richly adorned. At the palace of Arin-Berd, for example, the following decorations have been found: polychrome wall-paintings with protective genii, crenellation patterns, and bulls and lions placed antithetically beside concave-sided squares (State Historical Museum, Erevan). All these motifs, as well as the compositions, were borrowed from Assyria, which influenced Urartian culture in many ways.

At Nor-Aresh near Arin-Berd an example of bronze strips showing narrative scenes, worked with engraving and repoussé yet reminiscent of Assyrian murals, has come to light. It shows hunters, infantry, and cavalry. In another example, from Keyalidere, lions attack chariots, each with helmeted driver and two huntsmen. Its free-field design is reminiscent of the seals of the Hurri-Mitanni. Indeed, some scholars relate the Urartians to the Hurrians. The relief sculpture of Urartu is, however, unlike contemporary Neo-Assyrian relief by virtue of its concern with religious motifs, such as the representation of Khaldi standing on a bull at Adilcevaz.

There are indications of Urartian links with the Aramaean kingdoms and perhaps even Phoenicia, in unworked ivory

from workshops. But in the case of a gilded ivory seated lion (Archaeological Museum, Ankara), the treatment is distinctively Urartian: slender body, bulbous wrinkled muscles, snarling angular mouth, small circular eyes, sharply incised mane, with projecting ruff and long tail.

The most outstanding accomplishments of Urartian artists were executed in bronzework, the copper for which was plentiful in this region. Although large-scale sculptures were made, most surviving works are small pieces such as figures, shields, caldrons, strips, candelabra, and parts of a throne. The products of this bronzeworking center were distributed over an extremely wide area and with them their Oriental iconography. So figurines from Karmir Blur in the northeast display the Mesopotamian horns of divinity. To the east many Urartian features recur in early Scythian art, as in the Kelermes kurgan for example. To the west, in Greece and Etruria, Urartian or Syrian caldrons with griffin and bull protomes were imported and imitated in bronze and other media.

The Persians and Iran. The best-known forms of art from the Persian Achaemenid Empire are firstly the architectural decorations of monumental buildings and secondly small, luxury objects such as vessels and jewelry chased and embossed in precious metals. The roots of the architectural decoration are to be found in the manner in which the Persians, a migratory tribal group, came to terms with their role as a world power. It developed into an original form of expression. The small luxury objects or toreutics were derived from the artisanry of peoples and places in the Zagros mountains with whom the Persians came into contact before settling at the southern end of the chain.

The influence of the Medes was especially important. The 1st-century BC Greek historian Strabo reported that:

> the "Persian" stole, as it is now called and their [the Medes'] zeal for archery and horsemanship, the service they render their kings, their ornaments, ... came to the Persians from the Medes.

He continued by stating that their dress was adopted from conquered peoples, namely the Elamites. So were other features of their way of life. The arts of the Persians were undeniably eclectic in origin and development, but from the various sources they were capable of producing independent forms.

The Elamites. The Elamites dwelt in the lowland extension of the southern Mesopotamian plain through which the Kerkha and Karun rivers flow. From c3500 BC to c650 BC their civilization was distinctive. It was destroyed by the Assyrian army which created a vacuum, filled by their successors: the Persians.

Although the Elamites frequently imitated Mesopotamian art they often produced works of outstanding individuality. The Elamite ziggurat at Susa, decorated in blue-glazed bricks and crowned with brilliant copper horns, so moved Ashurbanipal, the conqueror of the Elamites, that he described and illustrated it. The Elamite tradition of monumental and highly

From the Elamite Golden Age, the bronze statue of Queen Napir-Asu from Susa; height 129cm (51in); c1250 BC. Louvre, Paris

ornamental building in fact stems from the earliest days of Elamite civilization. Some of the earliest constructions are depicted on contemporary cylinder seals (c3300 BC; Louvre, Paris) whilst one of its most outstanding examples was the sacred complex at Choga Zanbil (c1250–1230 BC).

The earliest seals (for example, those in the Louvre, Paris) were intimately connected with those from early Uruk, but in their representations of vases, animals, and figures engaged in hunting, fighting, and building they display a radical departure from previous conventions. The latter had demanded gracefully stylized figures which, when painted on pots, produced tectonic designs that emphasize or contrast with the shape of a vase.

Throughout the 3rd millennium Elamite art was almost completely indebted to Sumer. The Elamites' own creations consisted of representation of small, lively figures of animals and kneeling humans and polychrome-painted jars and metalwork. At an even later date dependence can still be traced as, for example, in the archaic dress and the symbols of divinity on a gold and bronze standing deity. But even this figure displays typically Elamite features, in the sharp nose and the stereotyped thick-lipped V-shaped mouth, often with a moustache.

During the so-called Elamite Golden Age (c1350–1000 BC) Elamite arts began to display increasingly independent characteristics. A burst of great building and artistic activity occurred: at least this is suggested by stone and metal statuary, relief stelae, rock reliefs, and small objects of faience.

Typical of the three-dimensional figures engaged in ritual that were produced at this time is a bronze statue of Queen Napir-Asu (c1250–1230 BC; Louvre, Paris). It is a work of studied elegance—she stands with her hands crossed over her waist, her dress splayed—and of great technical achievement. Unfortunately the head is missing.

Many graves of the period have produced bronze and faience figures. During the period they display a development towards realism which culminates in a series of female terracotta heads which, except for the eyebrows, are astonishingly free of stylization. They may well, indeed, be attempts at portraiture.

The Elamites at times in their independent history benefited from contacts with the highlands. The link is indicated by the 8th-century BC rock sculptures at Malamir. They were executed in flat relief and although they have been defaced by Sassanian reliefs and badly weathered, monotonously multiplied figures usually arranged in horizontal registers can be seen. This device in fact heightens the themes of paying homage to kings and making sacrifice; it is Elamite in origin and may well have been copied and exploited on a larger scale by the Persians.

In the later 3rd millennium BC the mountains to the north of Elam became a major center of bronzeworking in the Near East, although scholars have sometimes been too eager to attribute the works of Hurrian, Kassite, Median, and Cimmerian metalsmiths to it. Recent studies and excavations have shown that the greatest number of figurative works were produced between c1200 and 600 BC, and that the arrival of a nomadic steppe people stimulated the Elamite- and Babylonian-influenced native craftsmen into utilizing the animal style and religious iconography.

Within the smiths' repertoire two classes of objects were dominant: firstly the horsebits, harness mounts, rein rings, and axes of the hunter-warrior; secondly votive pins shaped like hand mirrors and the standards of shrines. A standard usually consisted of a long tube incorporating animal haunches and human heads below a female who grasps rearing felines along an arc. It is in fact a fantastic version of the traditional Mesopotamian "tamer of animals" motif in which adequate scope has been given for the imagination and religious beliefs of mountain dwellers.

This period saw several peoples on the move in the Zagros

Relief carvings on a staircase of the Palace of Darius at Persepolis: servants carry dishes and young animals; 518–428 BC

mountains. The fluidity of the times is reflected in the works of ivoryworkers, metalsmiths, and glaziers contained in the so-called Treasure of Ziwiye (c750–650 BC). Hundreds of precious objects were found, many of them in a bronze tub incised with a scene showing an Assyrian dignitary receiving tribute from Iranians. Perhaps it was a hoard of Scythian loot? One piece is an Urartian type of crescentic gold pectoral or gorget which exemplifies the iconographic mixture on work of the period (Iran Bastan Museum, Teheran). In the center are Urartian palmette trees. Flanking them, arranged in two registers, are repoussé mythical animals—a winged Assyrian bull, a human-headed winged bull in Atlas pose, either Assyrian or Neo-Hittite, Syro-Phoenician griffins, and crouching bears and hares in Scythian style.

Marlik. An impressive degree of Mesopotamian influence and local originality is displayed in the works from a late-2nd-millennium cemetery at Marlik, near the Caspian Sea and once astride several migratory routes from the north and east into Iran. Local originality is mainly seen in the smooth outlines of stags, bulls, and humans on vessels and as figurines. The animal style displayed is akin to the one known in the Caucasus rather than the style of the northern steppes. Subsequently bracelets with lion-headed finials became popular in Iran. Where vases found in the cemetery display lowland motifs in their decoration these have been handled with expertise and confidence, especially the use of body stippling and the balance of composition both rendered in an eloquent native style.

Achaemenid Persia (559–330 BC). The Persian Empire was established in 539 BC as the result of Cyrus the Great's victories over the Medes, Lydians, and Babylonians. The victor built a residence for himself at Pasargadae which at once typifies and distinguishes the architecture of the Achaemenids. Its character was summed up by the Greeks' description: the "camping ground of the Persians". It contained three monumental buildings, well spaced from each other, built on large platforms. The Audience Hall is known to have contained a central rectangular colonnaded room and to have been surrounded by porches of columns half the height of the internal hall. The prolific use of columns, large blocks of stone, and contrasting black and white colors, may have come ultimately from Urartu. And the winged bulls echo Assyrian reliefs. But the diffused arrangement of the buildings is a novel principle.

Although Susa was the capital of Persia it is Persepolis that survives in best condition. It was built as a national sanctuary hard against the mountains in an area that contains several royal tombs. Its construction began in the reign of Darius I, in 518 BC, and it came to consist of several groups of buildings on an immense platform which, together with its enclosing wall reached a height of approximately 85 ft (26 m). Its main architectural features were the gates and grand staircases that led up to the square *Apadana* and Hall of a Hundred Columns. The stone columns of the latter are a peculiar mixture of foreign elements and are often surmounted by double bull capitals. It is likely that foreign craftsmen were employed in the construction of Persepolis, as we know they were at Susa, and their influence accounts for many foreign traits. But the majestic synthesis of Persepolis is a crowning Persian achievement.

The gates, door-jambs, and staircases of Persepolis are adorned with painted and gilded reliefs which may have been the work of Ionian stone-cutters. They show the king receiving reports, or seated on a throne supported by representative members of his Empire, or processions of offering-bearers, or the king decoratively stabbing a lion—themes that proclaim the unity of the Persian Empire. Thus they lack the historical and narrative interest of Assyrian reliefs. However, the figures project from the background surface in high relief and the folds of their drapery are now accurately represented. They possess an organic life which was absent from most earlier Near Eastern representational art. It demonstrates the influence of late-6th-century Greece.

Other reliefs were carved on natural rock faces, such as the one at Bisutun where Darius is shown receiving the submission of rebels who had supported the Magian Gaumata in his bid for the throne, and the relief on the facade of Darius' tomb at Naqsh-i Rustem near Persepolis. Later reliefs at Susa, showing Babylonian-type monsters and royal guardsmen, are made of polychrome glazed bricks.

In the decorative arts the Persians achieved a greater sense of balance and mastery of materials than in the reliefs. Especially worthy of note are their drinking vessels, which terminated with animal forequarters or had two animal handles; their bracelets and pectorals with animal finials; and their circular bracteates in which animals are used to create a pattern on the inside.

Persian craftsmen favored lions, ibexes, and bulls as subjects for decorative work but treated even them in a contrived way; winged beasts, for example, were shown with their heads turned back. And from groups of animals ornamental and balanced patterns were created. Perhaps it was inevitable that in becoming sedentary the Achaemenid goldsmiths lost the sort of spontaneity that marks the animal styles of the Scythians and Marlik culture. But what they forfeited in vigor they gained in technical excellence.

The arts of Phoenicia and Israel. The modern lands of Cyprus, Syria, Lebanon, Israel, and Jordan stand on a crossroads. In ancient times they were the main area of contact between the cultures of the ancient Aegean and the Near East, between Europe and the Orient, between city-dwellers along the Mediterranean littoral and nomads of the deserts. The area produced some of mankind's most outstanding literature, and saw the birth of two of the world's major religions. But the region's visual arts, after the prehistoric Natufian and Chalcolithic periods in which individual styles flourished, as seen in a female figure from Lemba, Cyprus (Cyprus Museum, Nicosia), could hardly rise above the imitative, derivative, and syncretic to produce a distinctive expression.

Art that served royalty tended to be derived from the models of powerful neighbors. Religious art concerned itself with fertility cults. There was little freedom for artistic production to surpass technical sophistication. These shackles were further compounded by the political and cultural fragmentation of the Levant which prevented the emergence of a major political power and a new seminal art.

The Levantine petty states lacked the cultural continuity and inclination necessary for the production of monumental works—in marked contrast to Egypt. According to sources ranging from Homer to the Assyrian annals Levantine craftsmen excelled in the production of small metalwork objects that were often inlaid with gold or silver, jewelry, dyed cloths, woodwork (especially furniture), and perhaps above all, ivorywork. The jewelry and ivorywork are, of course, epitomized in the Bible's descriptions of the caldrons, pillars, and "cherubs" and floral appliqués of Solomon's temple in Jerusalem and Ahab's House of Ivory in Samaria. But in both instances the work was that of Phoenician, not Israelite craftsmen. Israel and Jordan produced little of artistic merit. Their topography was full of divisions; they were constantly subject to nomadic incursions and invasions by neighbors such as the Egyptians. Their most notable achievements were in the fields of pottery making—their pots are amongst the most balanced and aesthetically pleasing of all produced in the Levant.

The Levant's cultural dependence on its neighbors was evident by at least the 3rd millennium BC when the production of cylinder seals began in north Syria. Not only the idea but also the designs were derived from Mesopotamia. Similarly sculpture produced in the Syrian hinterland, such as the statues found at Tell Chuera, can be considered as merely provincial renderings of Sumerian forms of the early city-state period. The custom of erecting such statues in Syrian shrines presumably implies that the inhabitants of the area were alive to Sumerian religious thought.

The strength of Mesopotamian influence increased during the Ur III-Mari age (c2113–1750 BC) when several Syrian cities became important in the new context resulting from Amorite expansion. A clear source of evidence of this is provided by a large stone basin found at the already important city of Ebla, just south of Aleppo (National Museum of Aleppo). The upper of its two registers shows figures dressed in the developed Sumerian flounced robe and the plain cloak with tabbed hem which is familiar from the Mari paintings, crowned with Ur III hairstyles. The basin also features a nude Sumerian hero with projecting hair and beard curled at the tips who enjoyed a revival in Mesopotamian iconography during the Old Babylonian period. Here he is shown grasping the tail of a winged beast which first became popular on Neo-Sumerian seals.

The decoration of the basin includes some details of local origin but it was principally in metalwork that the inklings of an independent artistic spirit began to show themselves. This is demonstrated, for example, by a group of nude bronze figures from Judeidah (Oriental Institute Museum, Chicago). Some of them have arms extended forward in a manner similar to that of a figure imported into Mari.

For most of the 2nd millennium BC the Semites of

Mesopotamia called the greater part of the Levant Canaan, a name derived from the purple dye that was obtained from the murex shell from the waters along its coast, and the period is also known by this name. It witnessed Egyptian influence in Canaan which profoundly affected the native visual arts.

From the reign of Sesostris I to Amenemhat III (1971–1797 BC) the Egyptians sent numerous objects to Byblos, a coastal city nestling under Lebanon's cedar mountains. Its kings were so impressed with all they saw and heard of Egypt that they styled themselves with Egyptian titles and instructed their artists to copy Egyptian work in stone, faience, and metal. They adapted with varying success. A gold Horus-hawk collar, for example, faithfully reproduces its model, whereas an elliptical jewel with a gold filigree hawk inlaid with semi-precious stones, bearing hieroglyphs spelling the local name Ypshemu-abi, cannot be considered more than a

A prehistoric female figure from Cyprus known as the Lemba Lady; height 36cm (14in); c3000 BC. Cyprus Museum, Nicosia

clumsy effort (now in the National Museum, Beirut). However, the ivory handle of a dagger covered in gold foil bears a figure wearing a pharaonic kilt and "White Crown" adapted to a native design.

Egyptian influence affected other cities less strongly. Often it was Egyptian symbols that found ready acceptance. *Ankh* signs, for example, appear on Syrian-style seals found at Alalakh (British Museum, London), and a *waz* scepter and Egyptian royal crook feature on stelae at Ugarit (National Museum of Aleppo; Louvre, Paris). The way in which Egyptian trappings were incorporated into native works suggests that their meanings were known and appreciated, but they had little effect on compositions into which they were incorporated.

In the period of its history known as the New Kingdom (c1580–1200 BC) Egypt extended its kingdom into the Levant. Borrowing from Egyptian art increased and now affected style as well as subject matter. The influence of the Egyptian Amarna style is seen, for example, in the portrayal of royal figures on an ivory bed panel from Ugarit, one of the wealthiest cities in the period. An Egyptian princess is actually depicted on a marriage vase in attendance on one of the kings of Ugarit.

Egyptian scenes of feasting, chariot battles, and marsh-scapes, and motifs such as sphinxes, flowers, Bes and Hathor figures are all found, in fact, on other works, but they are rarely slavish copies. Syrians actually settled in Egypt at times and produced an Egyptian style that included other influences of international origin. A typical example of this is a polychrome *rhyton* from Kition in Cyprus which is Aegean in shape, Egyptian in technique, and predominantly Syrian in the style of its figures, though even in these Aegean and Egyptian elements can be noticed (Cyprus Museum, Nicosia).

A major feature of art produced during the late Canaanite era was the influence of the Aegean. In the earlier period some Minoan items had been imported into prosperous Byblos but they were considered too exotic to be serious models, unless some silver bowls with swirling patterns from Tod in Egypt are Levantine imitations rather than originals (examples in the Louvre, Paris). Contacts with the Aegean only reached a point of strength in the 14th and 13th centuries when they provoked a vogue for adapting aspects of Aegean work. Ultimately from Minoan Crete come the goat and cow shown on a gold bowl from Ugarit. Their pose is a slightly contorted flying gallop. An ivory lid from its port shows a seated goddess feeding goats: the theme is Aegean, the rendering Syrian (Louvre, Paris).

With the arrival of numerous Aegeans in Cyprus and Philistia in the 12th century BC the Aegean-influenced native style, which had hitherto remained a mixture, fused into a lively, original entity. A type of bichrome pottery was the special product of Philistia; in Cyprus remarkable ivories and metal figures whose oriental iconography is injected with vigor by the modeling were produced. A good idea of the contrast between the new style and its predecessor can be obtained by

A Byblos copy of an Egyptian Horus-hawk collar; c1840–1785 BC. Louvre, Paris

Phoenician ivory work: a gilded panel found at Salamis; height 7cm (2¾in); c800–700. Cyprus Museum, Nicosia

comparing the Horned God of Enkomi (Cyprus Museum, Nicosia) with earlier similar objects from the mainland (for example, those in the Louvre, Paris).

Although most artistic works of the Levant produced during the Canaanite era were hybrids of local and foreign styles, some works survive—a few masterpieces—of undoubted indigenous origin, untainted by the desire or attempt to emulate the works of foreigners. However, they are isolated works, difficult to locate in a detailed historical sequence.

In a 17th-century BC head from Alalakh, sculpture reached a poise and balance that it can surely have rarely reached in Syria (Antakya Museum). The rendering is completely natural and antedates a tendency to geometric abstraction. The development is seen in the statue of Idri-Mi (British Museum, London), in a group of pillar-shaped figures from which only limbs, face and sometimes genitalia emerge (Antakya Museum), and in the lion orthostats from Alalakh and Hazor (Israel Museum, Jerusalem).

A similar attenuated rigidity is also a common feature of various standing bronze figures. Examples from Byblos (National Museum, Beirut) are often of plaque-like slenderness. Others from elsewhere wear horns of divinity and brandish spears; many of them are also plated with gold. They probably represent Baal, the god with the most powerful and widespread cult of the western Semitic pantheon.

Occasionally items of late-Canaanite ivorywork show independent artistic attitudes, for example several items found in a hoard from Megiddo (Oriental Institute Museum, Chicago), and, from Ugarit, an ivory head in the round (National Museum, Damascus) and an ivory tusk modeled in high relief with a fertility goddess. Her head is aligned with the point and her body is flanked by sphinxes in shallow relief.

Phoenician art. This term is used to describe the artistic works made by Phoenician craftsmen anywhere in the Near East and sometimes in the western Mediterranean in the period of the late 1st and early 2nd millennia. Perhaps best described as artisans, the Phoenician craftsmen ranged beyond the frontiers of Tyre and Sidon (where later disturbances have obliterated traces of them) to the Jordan Valley in order to produce the bronzework required for Solomon's temple. They journeyed to Kara Tepe to help carve "Neo-Hittite" reliefs. They sailed to Cyprus, where many Phoenicians eventually sought refuge from the Assyrians. Their work is characterized by the blatant misuse of Egyptian motifs.

Their gaudy works could be heartily welcomed abroad—such is the suggestion of Homer's reference to a Sidonian bowl used at Patroclos' funeral games. Phoenician figured metal bowls, which have been found in places as far apart as Nimrud and Etruria, continued a tradition well known at earlier Ugarit (examples in the British Museum, London). They are usually embellished with three friezes containing an assortment of embossed Egyptian and Assyrian motifs and themes. The meaningless pastiche suggests that purchasers

wanted them for their ornamental value rather than their imagery.

In Cyprus, on the other hand, there arose a vigorous, independent, and vivacious pottery style. For this the Cypriots developed a style of free-field composition for application especially to jugs. The use of figures could be either extravagant or restrained, but never without freshness and confidence attuned to produce the balance demanded by the vessel's shape.

The other medium especially worked by the Phoenicians was ivory. Numerous carved pieces have been found at Salamis in Cyprus, many with their gilding intact (Cyprus Museum, Nicosia). They are small objects, mainly from the 9th and 8th centuries BC, intricately worked in the round, ajouré, and relief. They were often intended to decorate furniture, for example a throne. The most abundant deposit of such articles, however, was found at Nimrud: Assyrian loot from the west. From examples contained in the hoard (British Museum, London) a north Syrian style can be recognized, but it is clumsy and ill-proportioned. The main motifs used by the Phoenicians in their ivories were sphinxes, griffins, "women at the window", Egyptian deities, winged goats (disposed symmetrically, often with ornate foliage), and a griffin-slayer which harks back to the Enkomi mirrors and became a Near Eastern legacy to later Europe finding renewed expression in the story of St George and the Dragon.

E.J. PELTENBURG

Bibliography. MESOPOTAMIA: Frankfort, H. *The Art and Architecture of the Ancient Orient*, London (1970). Mallowan, M.E.L. *Early Mesopotamia and Iran*, London (1965). Moortgat, A. *The Art of Ancient Mesopotamia*, London (1969). Parrot, A. *Sumer*, London (1960). Strommenger, E. and Hirmer, M. *The Art of Mesopotamia*, London (1964). ASSYRIA AND BABYLONIA: Barnett, R.D. *Assyrian Palace Reliefs*, London (1960). Frankfort, H. *The Art and Architecture of the Ancient Orient*, London (1970). Gadd, C.J. *The Stones of Assyria*, London (1936). Koldewey, R. *The Excavations at Babylon*, London (1914). Moortgat, A. *The Art of Ancient Mesopotamia*, London (1969). Parrot, A. *Nineveh and Babylon*, London (1961). Strommenger, E. and Hirmer, M. *The Art of Mesopotamia*, London (1964). THE HITTITES AND ANATOLIA: Akurgal, E. *The Art of the Hittites*, London (1962). Bittel, K. *Die Felsbilder von Yazilikaya*, Istanbul (1934). Bossert, H.T. *Altanatolien*, Berlin (1942). van Loon, M.N. *Urartian Art*, Istanbul (1966). Vieyra, M. *Hittite Art*, London (1955). THE PERSIANS AND IRAN: Amiet, P. *Elam*, Auvers-sur-Oise (1966). Ghirshman, R. *The Arts of Ancient Iran, from its Origins to the Time of Alexander the Great*, New York (1964). Godard, A. *L'Art de l'Iran*, Paris (1962). Pope, A.U. (ed.) *A Survey of Persian Art from Prehistoric Times to the Present*, vols. I and IV, London (1938). Porada, E. *Ancient Iran*, London (1965). PHOENICIA AND ISRAEL: Barnett, R.D. *A Catalogue of the Nimrud Ivories ... in the British Museum*, London (1957). Frankfort, H. *The Art and Architecture of the Ancient Orient*, London (1970). Harden, D.B. *The Phoenicians*, Harmondsworth (1971). Karageorghis, V. *Cyprus*, Geneva (1968). Mallowan, M.E.L. *Nimrud and its Remains* vol. II, London (1966). Pritchard, J.B. *The Ancient Near East in Pictures Relating to the Old Testament*, Princeton (1969).

5

BRONZE AND IRON AGE ART

The Trundholm horse and sun-disk; bronze and laminated gold; length 60cm (24in)
14th century BC. National Museum, Copenhagen (see page 86)

THE arts of the 2nd and early 1st millennia BC in Europe are very different from the Neolithic arts that preceded them (see Neolithic Art). Some fine pottery was still made, but on the whole Bronze Age arts are of bronze or gold, or, more rarely, silver: the work of the smith rather than the potter and modeler. Even pots now imitate the suave lines and restrained ornament of metal tableware. Modeling in clay practically ceases, and where it does appear it is quite altered and, lacking in plastic sensuous qualities, has become a vehicle for imparting iconographic information. On the other hand, figure castings in the round appear, especially towards the end of the Bronze Age, and there are also the beginnings of narrative representation, on sheet metal in the south, and on rocks in the Scandinavian north—a return to a sort of art that had not been seen since the Mesolithic. Contact with more advanced societies outside Europe increased with the centuries, bringing new techniques and new orthodoxies. But it is still the craftsman metalworker who dominates this world.

There is no clear demarcation between Neolithic and Bronze Age Europe; all that can be said is that throughout the 3rd millennium BC the use of metals and their alloys was growing commoner and society was changing. Two opposing tendencies can be seen: one towards the seminomadic pastoral life, without fixed village settlements, whose focus appears in collections of stately burials under barrows. This was a warlike, hierarchical society whose leaders, by whatever name one calls them—tribal chief or king—enjoyed the display of weapons and ornaments, things portable and personal. On the other hand, on the plains of eastern Europe, and the European shores of the Mediterranean, there were settled societies whose villages and strongholds still survive, the former as tells, mounds of debris from fallen houses and walls, sited generally not far from some great river, and the latter as defended hills or cliff castles and townships from which the countryside was cultivated and boats put out on various ventures. By the mid 2nd millennium, within the Carpathian ring and on the Hungarian plain, we find material remains of what can reasonably be called an heroic society very much as Homer has described it, and it is here we might start with a review of some of its more durable remains.

The discovery of a large cemetery at Varna near the Black Sea coast of Bulgaria has put southeast Europe in the forefront of early metallurgical technology, especially goldsmithing. The date of the cemetery is probably 4th millennium BC. One grave alone contained 2.3 lb (1.05 kg) worth of gold objects, as rich an assemblage of gold as may be found anywhere at

Important places mentioned in the text

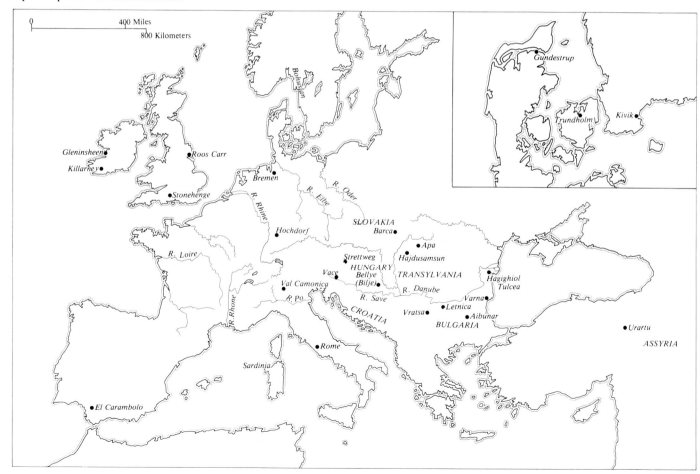

this early date. There are scepter-mounts, gold pectorals, animal profiles, plaques beaten out (none of the gold is cast), and in one almost royal grave features were modeled in clay with a beaten gold diadem and mouth-cover lying on them. Recent discoveries have also revealed very early mining for copper ores in Yugoslavia and Bulgaria. The mines at Aibunar in southern Bulgaria seem to have been contemporary with Varna.

In the mid 2nd millennium precious metals as well as copper and tin were readily available. A large amount of serviceable bronze weaponry was produced, but also luxury and symbolic objects such as solid gold swords, and silver and gold axes. These were a form of wealth valued not so much for the cost of the metal as for its incorruptibility.

The metallurgists must not be underestimated. As much skill and artistry are needed to carve the complex and beautiful molds that were used for casting axes and bracelets as to carve an animal in the round. Techniques of casting and chasing call for the dexterity of bone-carver, wood-carver, and engraver, as well as some knowledge of the chemistry of metals. For the rigid categories of "art", "design", "industry", "science", and "alchemy" were still closely linked, merging into each other, and the artist as smith and draftsman might be united in one individual or one family working under one roof.

The spheres of certain workshops, or groups of workshops, are recognized by the distribution of their products. One of these was active during much of the 2nd millennium BC in Transylvania, Hungary, and Slovakia. Its hallmark was a very beautiful curvilinear traced decoration applied to heavy cast axes of bronze, to swords and daggers whose blades, as well as hilts, were covered with running curvilinear patterns, and to bracelets like the gold one from Bellye (Bilje), northern Yugoslavia (Naturhistorisches Museum, Vienna), and occasionally to a gold cup or bowl. The decoration was "drawn" with a sharp tracer and hammer. It took great skill to produce the spiral and other curvilinear designs. Compasses were not used by this school, though they were used on bone objects of about the same date in Hungary, Slovakia, and Croatia, and possibly on small gold sheet ornaments with more geometric repoussé designs, concentric circles, and "pulley-patterns".

With very few exceptions the chased designs are non-representational; but within certain limits they show much freedom in adapting to the shapes of ax-butt and blade. At Hajdusamsun in northeastern Hungary and at Apa in northwestern Rumania fine axes and swords decorated in the same style were found. The Bellye bracelet shows exceptionally skillful casting, and the chased lines of the decoration have been deepened by tiny toothmarks, perhaps with a different sort of tracer. A Mycenaean Greek source has sometimes been suggested for this decoration, but in fact the styles are very different. Although spaced dots were used in setting out the designs, the spirals and sprays are neither geometric nor symmetric but seem to flow along the surfaces sprouting subsidi-

Gold bracelet from Bellye, Yugoslavia. Naturhistorisches Museum, Vienna

ary spirals in a way that foreshadows much later Celtic art. Dating is difficult, but probably some time after the middle of the 2nd millennium BC the designs begin to fall apart into isolated geometric motifs: circles, arcs, and multiple lines, while the center of gravity moves away to the north where a geometric and rectilinear phase of ornamentation suddenly changes and multiple lines, dotted fringes, and flowing tendrils reappear, though it soon relapses into compositions put together from isolated motifs.

The decoration of gold and bronze has a counterpart within the Carpathian ring, and to some extent throughout the whole of eastern Europe, in the decoration of pots, either in high relief—linked spirals surround molded bosses as on a mug from Barca in Slovakia (Archaeological Institute of the Academy of Sciences, Nitra); or else are incised, or stamped, or both as in Rumania and Bulgaria. Shapes keep the metallic profile introduced with the plain burnished pottery of the 4th millennium BC (Baden culture). A few small cult-figures were modeled and covered with symbolic patterns; some are mounted on miniature wheeled carriages, for cult purposes.

The practice of wearing personal wealth, and of being buried with it—men with their war-gear, women wearing their heavy bangles—and the rites of burial in closed single graves, have meant that much has survived in Scandinavia and the Baltic which may have been lost in regions where other rites prevailed. Also in the north, since remote Mesolithic days, treasure was dedicated to the gods and exposed beside lakes on the moors, or thrown into meres. These, becoming peat-bogs have preserved the treasure along with the men and women who were sometimes buried or immolated in the same way, so that human flesh, hair, and the tartan thread of clothing has survived, as well as gold and bronze ornaments and weapons and wooden coffins.

The northern metalworkers like those of central and eastern Europe preferred casting to forging when making swords, axes, and bangles. They had mastered the *cire perdue* method of casting and used it with skill and sophistication. It was used to cast the famous bronze horse drawing a bronze and gold "sun-disk" found in a bog at Trundholm, Odsherred, Denmark (National Museum, Copenhagen). The two faces of the disk have different patterns of concentric circles, running spirals, loops, and zigzags; but one face also has a thin gold sheet pressed onto it so that it takes the pattern. Horse and disk were mounted on wheels for the purpose of enacting the movement of the sun across the heavens in the cosmic drama of day and night, the whirling, spiraling patterns representing the sun in splendor.

A little later than the Trundholm group a huge tomb for the burial of a chieftain was constructed of stone slabs covered by a barrow at Kivik in southern Sweden. The slabs inside the chamber of the tomb were carved with symbolic and narrative scenes in a manner unique for the north, and more at home in the Mediterranean world. On the six surviving slabs subjects are arranged in horizontal registers; horses, boats, and axes are shown, while two stones have scenes of ceremony. On one a man drives a two-wheeled chariot (the earliest depicted north of the Alps), among long-robed, hooded figures, and armed men in procession; and next to it in a more complicated scene the same hooded figures stand on either side of an altar (Historical Museum of the University of Lund). Compared to the highly professional gold and bronzeworking, the artistic level, is not very high, though neither naive nor tentative. The gestures are not the less expressive for being conventional and hieratic.

Rock-engraving in a different style, that is, nearer to the old Mesolithic tradition of Scandinavian rock-carving, had a remarkable renaissance in the early 1st millennium. Dating is uncertain and it may have started a little earlier than this. It is found on natural rocks, occasionally in Denmark and much more often in Sweden and Norway. The method is the usual shallow pecking with a hammer. Boats are a favorite subject, as are two-wheeled carts, all very schematic. In Bohuslan in southwest Sweden, near the Norwegian border, there is a different style again, of greater variety and with magical and mysterious subjects: masked men blowing horns, ithyphallic dancers, and longhaired women. In the Val Camonica in the Italian Alps, rocks are engraved with very schematic agricultural and hunting scenes.

From around the 12th century BC the northern smiths, particularly in Denmark and North Germany, were making bronze razors with long sub-triangular blades, the blade at first undecorated, ending in a naturalistic man's or animal's head cast in the round. Later, in the first centuries of the 1st millennium BC, the holding end became a snake's head coil of

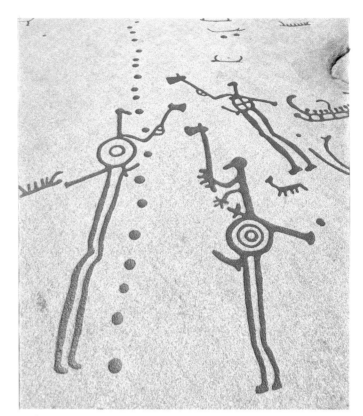

Rock carvings of ithyphallic figures at Bohuslän, Sweden

metal, and the surface of the blade was chased with pictorial scenes. Often a boat was the subject, as on the rocks; or there are boats within boats like Chinese puzzles; or, more interestingly, there is a tableau staged on a boat, like a miniature picture within a frame limiting both space and time. The group on a razor from Bremen, West Germany, may copy a Phoenician jewel left in southern Spain (Zentral Museum, Mainz); but the boat is the northern war-canoe with animal prow and stern and a ram. On these small bronzes, spirals take possession of kneeling gesticulating figures. This style could have evolved out of the Apa-Hajdusámsun decoration of Hungary and Transylvania, but the spirals and sprays are no longer abstract; they have become organic, sprouting heads of horses and elk, and tumbling like waves.

In the British Isles there was an early and independent school of metallurgy which reached great heights of skill. In Ireland in the early 2nd millennium a gold rod was beaten out very thin into the crescent shape of a "lunula" neck ornament; it was then given a simple incised rectilinear ornament of great delicacy which may be derived from "beaker" pottery. The "lunula" from Killarney is a good example of this work (National Museum, Dublin). Some centuries later gold rods were twisted into handsome arm and neck ornaments, but there was no continuous tradition of metalworking, no long-lived school of decoration as in central or northern Europe, and the remarkable renaissance of gold-working in the 8th and following centuries, though still based on the supply of Irish gold, was probably due to fresh stimulus from European workshops, especially those of Denmark and the north. The gold "gorget" of the later period from Gleninsheen has superb repoussé and chased decoration (National Museum, Dublin).

Compared to the Continent, the British Isles were undistinguished in their arts until they adopted the La Tène Celtic style in the last two to three centuries BC. But there is one important exception. Stonehenge in Wiltshire really is a unique monument, setting aside the controversy over its purpose. It was the focus for pastoral people whose burials under round barrows are scattered over the surrounding chalk downlands. The huge sarsen stones, most of which have stood till today, were brought from the Marlborough Downs and set up, probably in the early 2nd millennium.

But the site was already sanctified by earlier structures, perhaps of wood, inside an earthwork. There were a number of reconstructions, mostly affecting the smaller "blue stone" circle; but it is the tall sarsen circle with its once continuous lintels, and the setting of five pairs of uprights, each with its own lintel, in a horseshoe inside the circle, that makes the unique teasing monument we see today.

Apart from sheer size—the uprights average 13 ft 6 in (4.1 m) in height and the largest stone weighs 50 tons (50.8 tonnes)—the technical feat is the most astonishing part of Stonehenge. Huge stones were moved by Neolithic tomb builders, but here the accuracy and sophistication of the

The Killarney lunula. National Museum, Dublin

Warrior figures found at Roos Carr in Yorkshire, England; length of boat 51cm (20in). City and County Museum, Kingston-upon-Hull

work—dressing the stones, levelling the lintels, fitting tenon and mortice, and above all the cunning of entasis by which the taper of the uprights is given a convex curve so that there is an optical illusion of straightness, while the lintels are inclined inwards toward the bottom—this is something so wholly unexpected that some scholars have looked for master builders from the eastern Mediterranean.

It is impossible to say how much wood carving was done in Europe because so little has survived. An idea of its primitive quality can be had from the few carvings that have been found; these owe their survival to the acid bogs in which they lay, scattered from Ireland to the Urals. Most are rough images of male virility, like the four gaunt warriors with staring pebble eyes that stand in an animal-prowed boat found at Roos Carr in Yorkshire, England (City and County Museum, Kingston-upon-Hull). Some wooden figures are no more than slightly improved branches or trunks of saplings that may have been ritually dressed and undressed, like the goddess Nerthus of Tacitus' *Germania*.

The arts so far described have followed an indigenous European course, for the most part isolated from centers of civilization beyond the Mediterranean and the Bosphorus. But from time to time these "frontiers" became channels for closer contacts and the transmission of new skills, new needs, and new fashions; as was the case in the first half of the 1st millennium.

Some time before this a new impetus was given to the techniques of forging. Large objects of sheet metal, hammered and riveted with embossed decoration, began to appear. The method was more economical of labor and material than casting and chasing. It may have been introduced from the Aegean in the late 13th or 12th centuries and it made possible a new range of products: buckets, basins, cups, as well as shields, helmets, and corselets. Some of these found their way to the north, and gradually the old workshops were superseded there, as they had been further south.

There was also a strong school producing embossed bronzework in Italy. It required no less skill to manufacture these handsome objects than to cast in molds. Although coarser than the work of the older tradition a rich appearance could be

A "four-eyed" bronze warrior figure from Sardinia.
Museo Archeologico, Cagliari

these evidently kept their contacts open with their oriental homeland, for the most likely source of the Sardinian bronze sculpture of the 8th to 6th centuries is Cyprus and the Phoenician cities of the Levant.

Sardinia has a lot of drystone buildings dating back to the 2nd millennium that were still used by the people who made bronze sculptures. Buildings were sometimes clustered into compact villages with labyrinthine curvilinear walls, round towers, and encircling walls. The number of these *nuraghi* that still dominate much of the Sardinian landscape suggests a fairly dense population. More than 400 small bronze figures have been found; one or two come from 8th-century Etruscan tombs in Italy, but generally in Sardinia they are found heaped together in hoards of votive gifts in houses and sanctuaries. The *cire perdue* method of casting was used; and the style—or rather styles, for there are at least two—is quite individual and a long way removed from that of both Greek and Oriental bronzes, though closer to the latter. Some male figures, like the oriental "divine warrior", are armed with sword and shield and wear a helmet with bull's horns; but there are also archers with arrows at the ready, and a patriarchal cloaked figure with a staff. Some figures are undoubtedly gods with duplicated eyes, arms, and shields. They are solemn, hieratic, and have been called "Geometric" or "Formal". Another group is full of action and expression and has been called "Barbaric" or "Informal"; there are pipers and bowmen, a mother-and-child, wrestlers, and some people who simply appear to be talking. With rare exceptions there is no interest

A Sardinian bronze "mother-and-child". Museo Archeologico, Cagliari

achieved exploiting light and shade, and changes in texture.

Iron technology was gradually introduced into Europe during the early part of the 1st millennium from the eastern and the Mediterranean corridors. New orientalizing arts came the same way giving rise to a school of bronze sculpture in Sardinia, of sheet bronze with narrative repoussé pictures in Italy and the east Alpine valleys, and jewelry, vase-painting, and monumental carving in Iberia, and something of all these in southeast Europe.

In the early 1st millennium BC the Mediterranean was full of pirates, and of bands of colonists and merchants hardly distinguishable from pirates. In the 9th and 8th centuries some of these found Sardinia, an island rich in copper deposits, where some of the inhabitants were probably descended from other settlers of the 12th century or earlier still. Unlike the waves of colonists in the Neolithic and Early Bronze Age,

A situla found in a grave at Vace, Yugoslavia; bronze; height about 30cm (12in); late 6th–early 5th century BC. Ashmolean Museum, Oxford

in bodies, which are treated as clothes-racks and coat hangers for cloaks and weapons. It is an art of expressive silhouette, of hands and gestures caught in movement or the full flood of argument, a small-scale art, very anticlassical and far more alive than its Cypriot and Levantine forerunners.

A combination of Greek, Oriental, and Etruscan contacts south of the Alps led to a new naturalistic taste in the decoration of bronze buckets, belts, and bowls, but especially buckets. Plain versions of these "situlae" had been made in 12th-century central European workshops. Because of the number and grandeur of their decoration, this style has been called "Situla Art".

The Strettweg Cult-wagon

A unique religious scenario from the European Early Iron Age (7th century BC) has been preserved at Strettweg near Judenberg in the Austrian Alps. This is a four-wheeled bronze conveyance on which are a number of figures, human and animal. It was found in a rich cremation grave under a tumulus, along with bronze vessels, horse-harness, bronze and iron weapons, and implements, all of which, apart from the "cult-wagon" can be matched at the eponymous cemetery of the Hallstatt culture some 31 miles (50 km) to the west in the Salzkammergut, which dates from the 7th to the 5th centuries BC. Hallstatt depended on the local salt deposits for its wealth, but at Strettweg the accessibility of ores in the Styrian mountains probably accounts for the richness of the find.

The scene is a tableau arranged symmetrically around a central figure of the "goddess", who stands on an 11-spoked wheel cut in the floor of the carriage. Her divinity is shown by her size (9 in, 22.6 cm), twice the height of the other figures. She is naked except for a girdle, and both hands are lifted to support a shallow bowl resting on a cushion on her head. The bowl is also supported by four struts of twisted bronze and must have been intended to carry a certain weight. Four mounted warriors with oval shields, javelins, and conical helmets flank the goddess in front and behind. Between them stands a man brandishing an ax and a woman with hands held in a gesture of supplication, while at front and rear two sexless figures grasp the massive antlers of a stag. All the figures are naked, and the platform, where it is attached to the axles, ends in four bovine heads. Surprisingly no birds are featured.

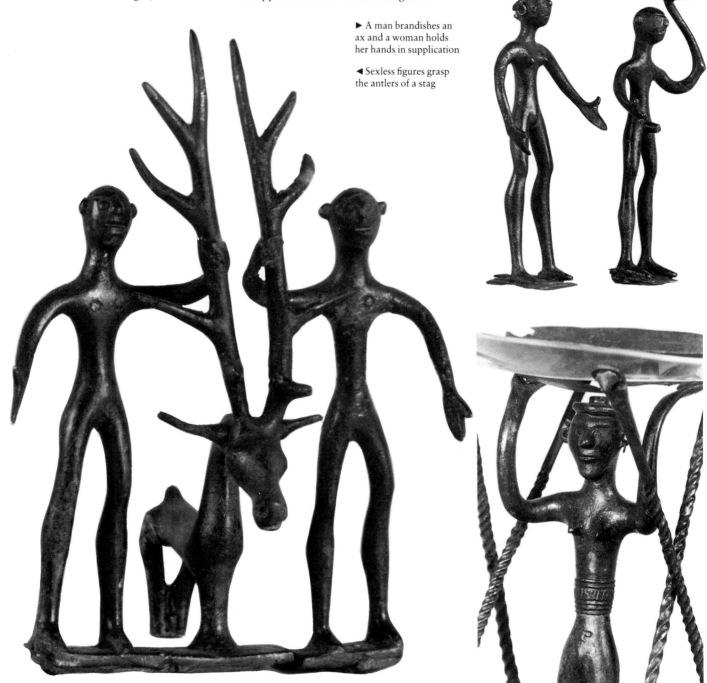

▶ A man brandishes an ax and a woman holds her hands in supplication

◀ Sexless figures grasp the antlers of a stag

Although the Strettweg tableau is unique, bronze vessels mounted on wheels and attended by figures, usually birds, are known from earlier in the Late Bronze Age, from Denmark to Bohemia. There is a small example in a cremation grave at Acholshausen, north Bavaria. In the Hallstatt Iron Age small bovines, horses, birds, and men (not women) were occasionally attached to bronze vessels, but there is nothing to compare with the technical and iconographic complexity of Strettweg.

▲ The Strettweg Cult-Wagon; bronze; base 35×18cm (14×7in). Landesmuseum Joanneum (Abteilung für Vor- und Frühgeschichte im Schloss Eggenberg), Graz, Austria

▶ The bronze caldron wagon from Acholshausen, Bavaria

◀ The central figure of the goddess; height 23cm (9in)

In Italy small bronze figures were attached to tripods and other furniture but none were like the "goddess". This tall, slender figure must owe her proportions and style to a group of warriors, or early Zeus figures, best known at Olympia where a "Zeus" of the early 7th century BC is remarkably similar. The Strettweg horses may owe something to Greek Late Geometric workshops, for this was a time when craftsmen were very mobile.

The same *dramatis personae* appear modeled in clay attached to handsome pots in a 7th century BC chieftain's grave at Gemeinlebarn, lower Austria.

The Strettweg scene is neither a hunt nor a sacrifice, but rather an apotheosis of the "goddess with the vase" or cornucopia. The later Celts of nearby Salzbach worshiped Aeracura, a goddess who had a horn of plenty or basket of fruit and was associated with a god wielding a mallet. It is not possible to make any further interpretations but the date can be fairly confidently placed in the early 7th century.

N.K. SANDARS

It had just begun before 600 BC though most work was done in the later 6th and 5th centuries. The earliest examples came from Italy (Bologna and Este) but the liveliest work was done in east Alpine centers, with one group in Slovenia. Here situlae were sometimes used as urns holding cremated ashes and buried in groups of round barrows. The repoussé ornament, hammered on the inside, was finished with chasing on the outside, and details were added with the tracer. The area to be decorated was divided into horizontal zones, and the subjects are, for the most part, already familiar in the art of the eastern Mediterranean. There are files of animals—wild, domestic, and fantastic; carts and chariots, horse and footmen; there are banquets, musicians, boxing contests, farming and erotic scenes. All the figures are in profile and although the style of representation varies, they were the work of probably only a few artists.

The situla from a large flat grave at Vace not far from Ljubljana in Slovenia (Archaeological Museum, Ljubljana) shows both the weakness and the vitality of Situla Art. Some of the subjects may have come from copying Greek 7th- and 6th-century vase-painters and metalworkers, others from as far as Urartu in eastern Anatolia and from Assyria; but here they are transformed into genial bucolic celebrations which are technically quite accomplished, but which nevertheless betray the gaucherie of the artist working in a style that is uncongenial and outside his artistic experience. The results are neither civilized, nor strongly barbarian, but provincial. In this they are inferior to the highly professional and quite unclassical work of the northern workshops that produce "pictorial razors", or the embossed decorative bronzes of central European workshops.

In Situla Art and in a lot of the later "Hallstatt" work in Europe, we find signs of a loss of direction and an uncertainty which seems to result from an introduction to really first-class Greek and eastern Mediterranean work now occasionally imported or captured. It was evidently highly prized, for it was buried (after some lapse of time) in the graves of local potentates. There was a positive attempt to adapt and master the humanistic arts of Greece but they were too alien; and in fact the future for Europe lay in a quite different direction, as emerged in the course of the 5th century BC.

"Hallstatt" is the name given by archaeologists to the centuries immediately preceding the appearance of Celtic La Tène

Human and animal heads on a pin-head from Rovalls, Sweden. State Historical Museum, Stockholm

art in the mid 5th century BC, that is to say in the early mid 1st millennium BC north of the Alps. The name comes from a salt-mining center in the Austrian Alps. While society was evolving rapidly, with some accessions from the east—new wheel-wrighting techniques, ironworking, and perhaps fighting on horseback with long swords—native chieftains were buried on fine hearses wearing gold diadems and surrounded by masterpieces from southern workshops. At Hochdorf near Stuttgart, Germany, in a very recent find, the body of a man lay on a bronze couch supported by eight bronze figures with raised arms, each standing on a single wheel. The find also included much gold work with repoussé designs. All the work appears to be local apart from three Greek lions. The well-preserved textiles with colored patterns include silk thread.

The local decorative bronzework was for the most part dull and repetitive, beating and stamping out geometric patterns on belts, or covering them with a carpet of tiny figures repeated like noughts and crosses. Geometric patterns on pots, sometimes in graphite paint on a red slip, are more successful.

In Yugoslavia and the Balkans an orientalizing influence was felt, rather different from the one that reached Italy and Sardinia. It had started, perhaps, from further east on the borders of Persia and the Caucasus, and it stimulated bronzesmiths in eastern Europe to cast small animals in a much freer style than was done in western Hallstatt centers, and indeed at Hallstatt itself. This so-called "Hallstatt Orientalizing" work traveled north to Scandinavia, as had the linear decorative style in the 2nd millennium. In Sweden and Denmark human and animal figures appear as knife-handles and heads of pins, or as scepter-ornaments, some of them having an odd likeness to the bronzes from Luristan (Persia), though no direct connection is possible.

The most ambitious Hallstatt bronze is a sacred tableau on wheels which owes most to Greek bronzes of the 7th century. This is the "cult-wagon" from Strettweg in Austria (Landesmuseum Joanneum, Graz). The central figure is a goddess who stands on an 11-spoked wheel, cut out of the floor of the "carriage", and supports on her head the bottom of some sort of bowl. This is the figure that owes most to Greek Geometric bronze warriors. Identical mounted armed men are placed before and behind the goddess, and two pairs of ambiguous figures, perhaps young girls, touch the antlers of a huge stag. The whole scene is quite static; it is not a hunting scene but rather an epiphany of the goddess and her attendants, meant, no doubt, like the Trundholm horse, to be pulled forward on its wheels in the performance of the ceremonies.

The Bosphorus and the Hellespont had never been a barrier between Europe and Asia, and this is particularly true in the first half of the 1st millennium BC. There was then a loosely linked continuity of settled communities between the Taurus and the Carpathians, whose members came to be known by such names as "Phrygians", "Thracians", "Getae", "Dacians". There was interchange and crossing and recrossing, so that the same names occur in Asia Minor and in the Balkans. From early in the 1st millennium eastern Europe was moving

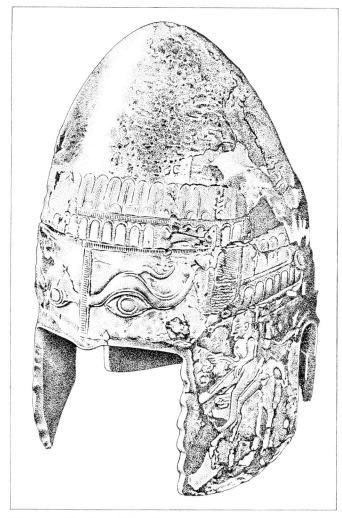

Helmet from Hagighiol, Tulcea, Rumania. National Museum, Bucharest

into an iron-based economy with iron technology learnt from western Asia. Phrygian arts have an echo in late-Hallstatt painted pottery and in bronze bowls (*phiale*), caldrons, and their handles. None of these owe anything to those Scythians who had reached northern Rumania, and who, having left the Caucasus and the Ukraine at the end of the 7th century, had reached northern Rumania, and who introduced their own style of animal art to the Hungarian plain. The fast potter's wheel made its appearance in eastern Europe, probably from Greek colonies on the Black Sea, in the 6th century BC, well before the west had it from Massilia (Marseilles) and the Rhône Valley.

In the late 6th century, still more in the 5th, a new school of decorative metalworkers in Rumania and Bulgaria began to turn out all sorts of ornamental silver and goldwork, including helmets or tiaras, with a very individual style of decoration. The partially gilt silver helmet from a tumulus burial at Hagighiol, Tulcea, in Rumania of *c*400 BC (National Museum Bucharest) shows the barbaric grandeur combined with naiveté that is characteristic of "Thraco-Getic" art. This art attempts to imitate motifs from the Greek Black Sea and Asiatic colonies, and others from oriental (Phrygian and Persian) sources. The Greco-Persian wars introduced a confusion of races and tribes to the borders of Europe, but the connection of this particular branch of decorative art is not with Achaemenian metropolitan workshops but, through that common substratum of loosely related societies, across

Detail of the above: a warrior on horseback

The lady of Elche; height 56cm (22in). Prado, Madrid

Anatolia from the Balkans to the more advanced workshops of northern Persia. This connection accounts for the strange simiiarity with much earlier work at Marlik in the Elburz. It is a popular art that, to a great extent, bypassed the "official art" of Susa and Persepolis; though the latter did curiously leapfrog into central Europe to be grasped at by Celtic La Tène craftsmen (see Celtic Art). A silver plaque from Letnica near Lovec in Bulgaria (Archaeological Musuem, Lovec), Thracian work of the early 4th century, shows a mounted hunter wearing greaves with human-faced kneecaps, full-size examples of which, in repoussé silver, have been found in Bulgaria in the Mosilanska mound at Vratsa and in Rumania at Hagighiol.

This style had great powers of survival, outlasting the impact of Greeks and Persians—it was still being produced in the 1st century AD. But probably the masterpiece of this school was found not in the Balkans at all, but in Denmark. The silver (once gilt) caldron from Gundestrup (National Museum, Copenhagen) like so much of the wealth from ancient Denmark was dug up in a bog. When found it was dismantled, its seven (originally eight) outer panels, and five inner panels piled on the base medallion. All are ornamented. Some interpretations of the iconography of the panels—the squatting antlered god of one, and the shields and animal-headed war-trumpets (the Celtic carnyx) of another—have claimed it as a La Tène work of art, but that it most certainly is not. Most authorities now agree it was made not far from the Black Sea, within the orbit of those Thracian and Dacian workshops that seem to have had large supplies of silver at their disposal. This would have been probably at the turn of the 2nd and 1st centuries BC, by which time Celtic tribes were well-spread throughout the Carpathian-Danubian basin (and even established in Asia Minor), an area as Professor T.G.E. Powell has written "where Thracian versions of ancient Orientalizing art were still executed by craftsmen who were perhaps not exclusively Thracian or Celtic". The repoussé work is in rather high relief and the surface is heavily chased, giving an overall effect of the texture of pelts and clothes. The work of at least three different craftsmen has been detected. The outer panels with the busts of gods flanked by attendant minor gods and creatures have severe idealized features. The narrative scenes on the interior are in a different, more agitated style, full of movement, much of it circular. The arrangement here is not in horizontal zones but continuous. There are many oriental features, from elephants to winged monsters, while the style of these panels is closest to that of Hagighiol and Letnica.

The medallion that forms the base is the work of an altogether more sophisticated artist. A bull in high relief, its head completely in the round with sockets for horns of some other material, is a powerful adaptation of a classical subject. Its connections are with a series of bronze medallions, perhaps phalerae from the harness of horses, which have been found from the Black Sea to the Channel Islands, and all of which show variations of the same triad of late Greek, Oriental, and native influences.

There is an odd pendant to this eastern European Orientalizing style in the Iberian art of the far west, and for rather similar reasons. The oriental sources in this case were the Phoenician and Carthaginian colonies in southern and south-eastern Spain. Before the colonies were established, perhaps in the 8th, certainly by the 6th century BC, Phoenician traders had opened up the west, Greeks joining in not much later and providing a counter attraction, less strong than in the Balkans but distinct. There is an Iberian counterpart to Hallstatt Geometric art, though with a strong Phoenician flavor, that can be seen in the sumptuous gold jewelry from El Carambolo (Archaeological Museum, Seville), with "breastplates" in the shape of ox-hides, bracelets, and plaques, all probably 6th century BC. Contact with Greek Classical and Oriental traditions also led to the rise of a native school of monumental stone-carving, in the 5th and 4th centuries, of which the so-called "Lady of Elche" (possibly as late as the 3rd century; Prado, Madrid) is exceptional for the calmness and refinement of the expression that transcends the heavy jewelry and grand but stuffy clothing. Originally the stone was painted but, fortunately, little color remains, for the effect would have been altogether too rich. The Iberians painted their pots in a crowded lively style in which hunting, fighting, and all kinds of occupations were depicted and which has odd reminiscences of the 12th-century Aegean and Levant.

N.K. SANDARS

Bibliography. Condurachi, E. and Daicovicin, C. *Romania*, London (1971). Kimmig, W. and Hell, H. *Vorzeit an Rhein und Donau*, Lindau-Constance (1958). Piggott, S. and Daniel, G.E. *A Picture Book of Early British Art*, Cambridge (1951). Poulík, J. and Forman, B. *Prehistoric Art*, Prague and London (1956). Powell, T.G.E. *Prehistoric Art*, London (1966). Sandars, N.K. *Prehistoric Art in Europe*, Harmondsworth (1968).

6

AEGEAN ART

A gold mask from Mycenae; height 31cm (12in); c1550–1500 BC
National Museum, Athens (see page 112)

THE term "Aegean" is conventionally used to describe the art of the civilizations that flourished in the Aegean area in the Bronze Age (c3000–1100 BC). The Aegean Sea is that part of the Mediterranean between mainland Greece and Asia Minor (modern Turkey), limited on the south by the large island of Crete. Stretching southeast from the Greek mainland is a group of islands known as the Cyclades.

In the course of the period, the major source of creative energy, both artistic and political, seems to have shifted gradually from one part of the area to another. In the Early Bronze Age (c3000–2000 BC) the Cyclades were dominant. In the Middle Bronze Age (c2000–1600 BC) it was the turn of Crete, whose culture is called Minoan after the island's legendary king, Minos. After a transitional period at the beginning of the Late Bronze Age (c1600–1100 BC) when Crete maintained her position, her power was eclipsed by the Mycenaeans of mainland Greece. Their civilization takes its name from the mainland site of Mycenae, which seems to have been the center of power. According to a Greek legend Agamemnon, the leader of the Greek expedition against Troy, was King of Mycenae.

The Cyclades and the Early Bronze Age (c3000–2000 BC). Village settlements of stone and mudbrick are known in the Early Bronze Age. The houses were simple and rectangular, frequently formed into blocks by the use of common walls. Modern villages, particularly in the islands, are basically similar. In the Early Bronze Age this simple form of social organization was standard over the entire area, although each region had its own distinctive variations in material culture. Communal activities probably took place on a village scale and the degree of artistic sophistication corresponded to this. Most of

Distribution of the main centers of Aegean civilization

the Cyclades are small but would have been self-sufficient, and although only a limited standard of living could be achieved, the small communities on them prospered.

The islands, however, certainly had political and trading connections with each other and beyond. The islands of Melos and Yiali possessed the only sources of obsidian in the Aegean. Obsidian, a kind of volcanic glass, is used, like flint, to produce cutting edges on tools and weapons. In a period when metal was rare there was considerable demand for this material, and its exploitation was a source of profitable external contacts and experiences. Marble too was a traded commodity, largely within the islands but sometimes also beyond. Objects of Cycladic origin have been found in Early Bronze Age contexts on Crete, the Greek mainland, and the Aegean coast of Turkey.

This was the setting in which the Cyclades were prominent. But before the end of the Early Bronze Age, a series of disturbances in and around the Aegean broke up the established patterns of existence. Many sites were destroyed and migrants probably entered the area from Asia Minor and the northeast, overrunning by force settlements that lay in their paths.

Towards the end of the Early Bronze Age there was a striking reduction in the number of separate communities in the Cyclades. The entire populations of all but the largest seem to have become concentrated into individual large settlements, more easily defensible. Several are known to have been fortified.

Crete and the Middle Bronze Age (c2000–1600 BC). From the beginning of this period Crete, whose earlier artistic achievements were by no means negligible, assumed the role of pacemaker. The Cretan palaces were constructed, of which that at Knossos is the prime example. They represent a revolution in both architectural and social terms.

A single huge complex presumably housed a supreme ruler and his retinue. It was also the religious center of the community where rites were conducted and ritual games held. But the Cretan palace was even more than this. It was the administrative center of a wide area to which the more remote farms and villages sent their produce to be accounted and redistributed. Such a center could also equip and operate workshops (for example in metals) of a sophistication that no smaller community could possibly have afforded.

Not only was Crete larger and more fertile than any single Cycladic island but also the scene of that critical economic and political transition from local (village) to regional organization. Thus living standards were raised and the central authority became strong enough to influence events beyond the shores of Crete. Prosperity stimulated rapid technical and artistic developments. As in other communities at other times, much of this increasing artistic sophistication was closely connected with religious life.

Minoan palace civilization did not, of course, develop overnight. The crucial social changes took place and the characteristic palace layout developed late in the 3rd millennium BC.

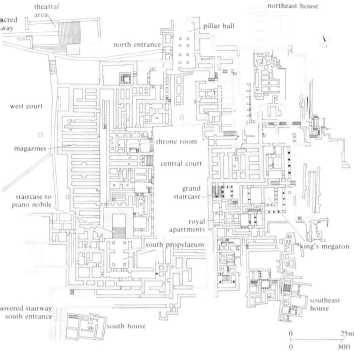

Plan of the Palace of Minos at Knossos; *c* 1400 BC

palaces, were built before 2000 BC. There is another palace at Zakro in the extreme east of the island on a slightly smaller scale, and almost certainly a fifth under the modern town of Chania in the west. Their creation belongs to a period of major social change in which Crete was organized into regions, each having a palace as its administrative center. There is a tendency to assume that Knossos was the ultimate capital but there is no real proof that it was more than one among equals.

The remains visible today are mainly those of the extensive rebuildings that took place after major earthquake destructions *c* 1700 BC. But parts are later still. The basic layout seems to have remained unchanged. A large open rectangular court was surrounded by buildings of two or more stories. All the palaces share this design but differ in the details. Rooms of private, state, ritual, technical, and domestic function have all been identified. It is significant that cult-rooms regularly have direct access to the central courts. The bull-leaping sport depicted in various artistic media must have been a ritual activity and may have taken place in the latter.

Apart from their complexity of plan (Knossos contains the labyrinth of the Theseus and Ariadne legend), striking constructional features are the use of large, finely worked blocks of masonry and of columns that taper characteristically down-

But these centers continued paramount well into the Late Bronze Age (until *c* 1450–1400 BC) and it is from this Later Palace Period that much of our knowledge comes.

Knossos, Phaestos, and Mallia, the three great Cretan

The throne and part of the throne room of the Palace at Knossos; *c* 1400 BC

wards. The stone walls were reinforced with inset wooden beams to give some flexibility in the face of earthquakes. Light wells were used to help with illumination.

Throughout most of the life of the Cretan palaces there seems to have been nothing on the mainland or in the Cyclades to compare with them. There were indeed substantial structures outside Crete, but lacking refinements in design and construction.

In the later 16th century BC, impressive buildings, whose construction must have been influenced by Cretan models even if they were not actually built by Cretans, are found in the Akrotiri settlement on the island of Thera. Here the Cretan techniques were applied to the construction of a town rather than a palace (at least no palace has yet been discovered) and some features more appropriate to a monumental complex are not found. Slightly later, there are signs of Cretan influence on mainland construction, though the plan of the Cretan palace was never adopted there.

Late Bronze Age I (1600–1450 BC): Crete and Mycenae.

In the preceding period neither the islands nor the mainland had been able to match the authority or the artistic sophistication of Crete. Cycladic insularity, both geographical and political, was now more of a bar to advancement than an aid. The island centers continued to flourish, and developed individual art styles and traded abroad (particularly with Crete). But they were not in a position to exert unified political strength.

On the mainland, there was no sign of the social revolution that had taken place in Crete and, until late in the period, artistic products are few and have neither the sophistication of Cretan nor the spontaneous freshness of some Cycladic work. But before the end of the Middle Bronze Age, in the earlier of the two grave circles at Mycenae, there are finds that point to greater wealth and sophistication and imply some form of social change.

The later and more famous grave circle, discovered in the 19th century by Heinrich Schliemann and with burials continuing well into the Late Bronze Age, spectacularly confirms these trends. The objects found in the graves of what can only be a warrior dynasty are of an amazing profusion and wealth. The array of weaponry proves that these people were far more warlike than the Minoans. The imposition (or perhaps evolution) of this warrior caste in Mycenaean society is undocumented in detail but nevertheless a fact.

A second event, this time natural, is crucial to our understanding of this period of change. The island of Thera lies in the southern Cyclades, only about 60 miles (97 km) from the north coast of Crete. The core of the island was a volcano which, early in the 15th century BC, first erupted and finally exploded. The whole crater of the volcano collapsed and the tidal waves generated must have had a disastrous effect on coastal sites in their path, particularly those in Crete.

The settlement at Akrotiri on Thera, submerged in ash and pumice from the eruption, and thus remarkably well preserved, illustrates the extent to which the power of Crete was dominant at that time. Almost the whole local artistic produce of Akrotiri is derived from Crete and many objects actually imported. We have already noted Minoan influence on the architecture of the site. Cretan taste and authority had not only permeated the islands—on the mainland too, in this period of transition, we find Cretan objects and inspiration.

Late Bronze Age II (1450–1100 BC): The Mycenaean Empire.

The emergence of warlike Mycenaeans together with the consequences of the explosion of Thera led to the downfall of Cretan power. By the time Thera exploded, the Mycenaeans were strong enough to take advantage.

Many Cretan sites were destroyed in the 15th century. Some of the coastal settlements may have suffered from the side effects of the Theran disaster, some were probably destroyed by invading Mycenaeans. Mycenaean objects appear in Crete in the later 15th century, and shortly afterwards a palace of characteristically Mycenaean type was built at the important site of Phylakopi on the island of Melos, clearly demonstrating that Mycenaean authority was replacing Minoan.

The Cretan palaces were all destroyed about this time and the Mycenaeans concurrently developed their own palace-centered civilization. Some of the methods of organization seem to be derived from Crete, including the script in which administrative records were kept. But the Mycenaean palace itself was quite different in plan from the Cretan and reflects a different social emphasis. The similarity with the Cretan system lies in the use of the palace as an economic and political coordination center for a large area. The central unit is the so-called "megaron", long and rectangular with a main room, antechamber, and porch. The main room, lavishly decorated, had a ceremonial hearth in the center and a throne against a sidewall. Secondary rooms surrounded the megaron, though not necessarily with direct access to it: living quarters, storerooms, workshops and administrative archives. It is not easy to tell how early this form of Mycenaean palace developed. It may have originated in the 15th century or a little earlier, but only developed fully after 1400 when the Mycenaeans had gained control in the Aegean.

Massive fortifications, nonexistent in Crete, are found at many of the major Mycenaean centers. They are built with enormous unshaped blocks of stone in a style called "Cyclopean". The wall-circuit at Mycenae is entered through the monumental Lion Gate, so called from the two lions, set heraldically either side of a central pillar, carved above the lintel.

At Tiryns, where the entrance is defended by massive gateways, the Cyclopean walls contain vaulted galleries within their breadth. The Acropolis at Athens also had Mycenaean fortifications, though little now remains.

Also peculiarly Mycenaean are the "tholos" or beehive tombs which were the burial places of the mainland kings, successors to those interred in the shaft graves. Each of these tombs, cut into a hillside near the settlement with which the

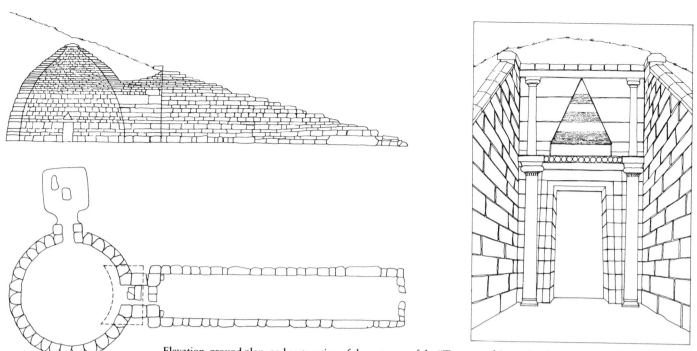

Elevation, ground plan, and restoration of the entrance of the "Treasury of Atreus" at Mycenae, the finest tholos tomb; 14th century BC

king was associated, had a long unroofed approach passage (stone-lined in the more sophisticated examples), an elaborate entrance, and a round chamber, often with side-rooms opening off it. The vault is corbeled and curves upwards to a narrow opening which was crowned with an external capstone.

These tombs may have been derived from the much cruder circular built tombs of Early and Middle Bronze Age Crete. The earliest are from southern Greece which was particularly open to Minoan influence in the transitional period.

In the generations following 1400 BC Mycenaean influence spread throughout the Aegean and beyond, and such is the degree of cultural unity that we can now speak of a Mycenaean "empire". During the 13th century, however, this empire encountered problems, either internal or external or perhaps both. Symptomatic of these are the erection of the great defence walls, and destructions at Mycenaean sites, which are widespread c1200 BC. At this point the empire broke up, the former centers of power declined, and cultural unity disintegrated. New regional centers in more remote positions developed with their own distinctive tastes. In the 12th century these in turn declined and the area entered a period of low living standards and artistic poverty.

The radical differences between Cretan and Mycenaean art will become apparent in the following pages. Mycenaean art has tendencies towards the extravagant, the formal, and, in subject matter, the violent, none of which are particularly characteristic of Minoan. The society that Mycenaean art represents was authoritarian and warlike, and probably lacked the intellectual sophistication of earlier Crete. Differences in religious tradition may have had much to do with this.

Pottery. In the earlier part of the period vases are mostly made by hand without the aid of a potter's wheel. This was introduced, in a crude form, before the end of the Early Bronze Age and its increasing use led to greater regularity and symmetry in vase shapes.

All but the most ordinary domestic pottery had some form of surface treatment. This might be simple smoothing or more elaborate burnishing (polishing) with a tool whose marks can often be seen. A slip of dilute clay was frequently painted on to the surface, especially if decoration was then to be applied. Sometimes slipping and burnishing were employed together to produce an exceptionally deep and lustrous finish.

The use of burnishing as a primary decorative technique is most common in the Early and Middle Bronze Age. Incised patterns are early and Cycladic. The incised lines are sometimes filled with a white substance. Until the Cretan palaces were well established, most painted decoration was simple linear. After this, in Crete and subsequently on the mainland, it became increasingly complex and naturalistic motifs were adopted. In the course of time these often became stylized and their origin would be quite obscure were it not possible to

An example of incised decoration: a Cycladic pyxis; height 11cm (4in); early 3rd millennium BC

Mycenaean Metalwork

Mycenaean craftsmen worked both ordinary and precious metals, producing weapons, armor, tools, utility objects, and luxury goods. Only weapons and armor (mainly in bronze) and luxury goods (often in gold or silver) concern us here. Sometimes they overlap—when weapons themselves are *objets d'art*.

The Mycenaeans seem to have learnt more sophisticated metallurgical techniques from the Minoans during the period of close contact between the two civilizations which began about the time of the Shaft Graves. The style and/or subject matter of some pieces found on the mainland is so Cretan that they must have been made by men trained in a Cretan school. Especially striking are the Vaphio cups, worked in repoussé. The subject of one is the capture of bulls, a theme particularly appropriate to Minoan ritual practices. The fluid "torsional" and very naturalistic style is thoroughly in accordance with the general principles of Minoan art and at variance with the more formal qualities of Mycenaean taste. Another gold vessel, from a tomb at Dendra, not far from Mycenae, is also distinctly Minoan, both in style and in its use of marine motifs.

In contrast to the pieces just mentioned, a gold box cover from Mycenae has mainland characteristics. The lion, stag, bull's head, and floral motifs are formally assembled without any real attention to a naturalistic relationship and the elements are all somewhat stylized.

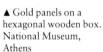 ▲ Gold panels on a hexagonal wooden box. National Museum, Athens

▼ Mycenaean jewelry: a necklace of rosette gold beads from Dendra. National Museum, Athens

 ▼ A battle scene, in relief, on the Siege *rhyton*, c1550 BC. National Museum, Athens

▲ A gold Vaphio cup; height 8cm (3in); 1500–1450 BC. National Museum, Athens

Fragments of a badly preserved silver vessel, the so-called Siege *Rhyton*, were found in Shaft Grave IV at Mycenae. The vase carries scenes of a sea-borne attack on a city, a "genre" subject also mentioned in discussion of the Thera Frescoes. A long time before the Thera scene was discovered, it had been suggested that the picture on the *rhyton* was probably based on a larger scale painting.

Metal vases are quite common in the early Mycenaean period. Many are of bronze, fine and elaborate, though less costly than gold. Another gold example from the Shaft Graves is the Cup of Nestor, named thus because its characteristics resemble those of a vessel, belonging to King Nestor of Pylos, described in Homer's *Iliad*.

◀ The so-called Cup of Nestor, with two birds on the lip; height 14cm (5½in). National Museum, Athens

▶ A gold tiara from a woman's grave. National Museum, Athens

▼ Sword blade with inlaid scene of a lion hunt; bronze inlaid with silver; width about 6cm (2in); c1500 BC. National Museum, Athens

▼ A gold covered sword hilt from Skopelos; c1550-1450 BC. National Museum, Athens

Among the gold riches from the Shaft Graves were a number of unusual masks which were laid on the faces of the dead.

Mycenaean tombs of all periods often contain pieces of personal jewelry or minor ornaments which were buried with the dead, for example necklaces, headbands, and cut-out ornaments, the latter sometimes pierced for attaching to garments. These have in-cised, repoussé, even granulated decoration. Finger- and earrings are also found, some of the former with very elaborate scenes in intaglio.

Weapons are prominent in the Mycenaean repertoire from the beginning. Many are entirely functional, but some swords are highly decorated, with gold-covered hilts and/or rivets and complex scenes inlaid in the blades. The technique in which these scenes were produced has been called "metal painting" and it required the use of gold, silver, and a black compound called niello. The technique is known earlier in the eastern Mediterranean and was probably learned from there by the Mycenaeans. Several ex-amples survive, one or two with marine motifs in a seemingly Minoan style. On

others the thematic and stylistic elements are mixed. The hunting scenes and heavily ar-mored figures are Mycenaean; but some of the bird and animal subjects are almost Egyptian—an influence already noted in some fresco scenes from Thera, which may have been channeled via Crete.

Among the relatively few surviving pieces of Mycenaean body armor, pride of place goes to a fine bronze corselet from a tomb at Dendra. It consists of 15 different parts—front and back body shells, adjustable rings to guard the lower body, shoulder pieces and arm guards, a collar, and a chest piece. Otherwise, fragments of scale armor, greaves, and helmets all testify to the range and skills of Mycenaean armorers.

R.L.N. BARBER

Further reading. Hood, S. *The Arts in Prehistoric Greece*, London (1978).

A "sauceboat" from Spedos on the island of Naxos; length 28cm (11in); mid 3rd millennium BC. National Museum, Athens

An example of Kamares style pottery: a clay pithos from Phaestos; height 51cm (20in); c1700 BC. Heraklion Museum

trace the history of the motifs from source. Such stylization is particularly characteristic of the later part of our period. Figured scenes occur but are not common.

In the Early Bronze Age the simpler forms of decoration mentioned above—burnishing, incision, linear painted patterns—predominate. In Crete a special firing technique was invented which produced a mottled red and black effect. Shapes also tend to be simple. Some are particularly characteristic of certain areas—the Cretan chalice, "teapot", and jug, the Cycladic suspension vases and *kernos* (a sort of multiple candlestick), and the mainland "sauceboat".

The pottery of the first Cretan palaces in the Middle Bronze Age is decorated in a "light-on-dark" style—lighter colors on a dark slipped vase surface. Simple white painted patterns had been used earlier. Red paint was later employed in addition to the white, and then other shades and colors. Patterns became more complex with the adoption of spiral and curvilinear elements. There were also floral motifs.

The most sophisticated Cretan pottery is the so-called eggshell ware decorated in the Kamares style. Kamares ware is polychrome on a black background, and is named after the cave in Crete in which examples were first found. There are delicate cups with very thin walls, their shapes often angular in imitation of metal vessels. The basic dark surfaces are lustrous. Larger vases too were decorated in the same style. Some vessels have plastic additions. Later vases of this kind have a smaller range of patterns executed in a cruder style and with fewer colors.

Contemporary pottery from mainland Greece and the Cyclades has little, if anything, in common with that of Early

Palatial Crete. The two most common varieties of mainland pottery at this time are called Gray Minyan (after Minyas, the legendary king of Orchomenos, at which site this type of pottery was first identified) and Mat-painted ware respectively.

Gray Minyan is always distinctive since it is a uniform dark gray color, and smooth and soapy to the touch. In its early and cruder form it belongs to the end of the Early Bronze Age but the classic shapes, which have sharp contours and seem to imitate metal prototypes, are later.

Mat-painted ware, as the name suggests, has patterns in (usually) dark mat paint on a light ground and seems to have originated in the Cyclades, but the development of the style took different courses in the two areas. Some of the shapes are similar to those of Gray Minyan ware. Polychrome designs occur at a late stage.

Barrel jars and beaked jugs are common in the Cycladic Mat-painted style, from which the mainland pottery is derived. Patterns are initially strictly rectilinear, though the rigidity is later broken up by the use of curvilinear elements.

At a developed stage of the style, the shapes are better proportioned and the vases usually made (at least on Melos from which most of our knowledge of this pottery comes) of a distinctive white fabric, often of fine quality. The decorative motifs are more ambitious and, though unsophisticated, have much freshness and spontaneity.

Popular throughout this period in the islands was dark slipped pottery with surfaces burnished to a high luster, often in red but also other shades through brown to black. Plain bowls with incurved rims and sometimes loop handles are common. Sometimes Gray Minyan shapes are imitated in these local burnished wares. True Gray Minyan is found in the Cyclades but was clearly imported. A fair proportion of the burnished wares are decorated with white patterns.

A most attractive bichrome style which combines features of Mat-painted and burnished pottery was introduced on Melos towards the end of the Middle Bronze Age. This consisted of decorative motifs whose red elements (usually circles) were burnished, the remainder being painted in the normal mat black. Birds are frequently portrayed on these vases.

We have already described the striking community of taste between Crete and the mainland in the earlier part of the Late Bronze Age. It is sometimes impossible to decide in which of the two regions a vase was made. The inspiration was clearly still from Crete whose palaces, rebuilt after the 18th-century destructions, continued to flourish. Many of the finer objects found at this time on the mainland were certainly made either in Crete or by Cretan craftsmen working abroad.

Apart from the introduction of new shapes, several of which appear before the end of the preceding period, Late Bronze Age Cretan pottery is particularly distinguished from earlier styles by the use of a radically different decorative technique. Instead of the light-on-dark system, designs are now painted in dark paint on a light-colored vase surface. Although the mainland had a light-on-dark decorative tradition (the Mat-painted style), new stylistic developments

Gray Minyan ware: a ring-stemmed goblet; c 1700 BC

there are clearly more closely associated with contemporary Crete. In the Cyclades the trend was now away from local innovation and towards a copying of Cretan models.

Many of the patterns used are abstract—the spiral, sometimes elaborated with dots and/or white paint, is particularly popular. Apart from these more conventional designs, there are two trends in Cretan decoration. The first and earlier involves the use of plants, flowers, leaves, and grasses as decorative elements. The second depends on motifs from marine life—octopus, sea urchins, nautili. Such types also reached the mainland, where formal patterns were more in evidence.

Towards the end of the 15th century these motifs became more and more stylized. This tendency is particularly clear on the large "Palace style" jars from both Crete and the mainland. Since the trend coincides with the critical years of the transition of power from Minoans to Mycenaeans we may see in it evidence of the subjection of Cretan energy and naturalism to the heavier formalism of the mainland.

In the islands, Thera (destroyed before the introduction of the Marine and Palace styles) has an exceptionally large number of Cretan imports. The local pottery from the site is heavily dependent on Cretan shapes and decorative motifs, especially spiral and floral. These patterns were also much imitated on Melos. Imported Cretan pottery is found too on other islands, Paros and Kea for example.

Both the high technical quality and the dark-on-light decorative system flourished on the mainland and in Crete during the years of the Mycenaean empire. Only at the end of this period did the quality of the ware deteriorate and the decoration become careless and imprecise.

It is now Mycenaean pottery that sets the standards and Cretan products follow it in shape and ornamentation. Many Mycenaean decorative elements represent stylizations of earlier, more naturalistic motifs, often derived from Crete. They

A "Marine style" jar decorated with nautili from Zakro; height 28cm (11in); c1500–1450 BC. Heraklion Museum

A stirrup-jar from a tomb at Makresia near Olympia; 13th-century BC

are most commonly set in zones or panels.

In the Cyclades, from the beginning of the Empire period, the local decorated pottery is entirely Mycenaean in character and most of it probably imported. Analysis may show, however, that methods of refining the usually coarse Cycladic clays had been discovered to enable local production of "Mycenaean" vases.

One of the most typical Mycenaean shapes is the *kylix* or stemmed goblet. Many examples, both plain and decorated, come from sites of this period. The stirrup-jar, although originally Cretan, becomes a standard Mycenaean shape. Such vases, which have one spout on the shoulder and a false spout incorporated in the handle on top, were easily sealed. Some have spikes projecting from the true spout to facilitate the fixing of some form of stopper. They were probably used for transporting liquids.

Vases with figure decoration are not common but there is one striking group of *kraters* (large bowls). More of these have been found in Cyprus than in Greece but clay analysis shows that they were made in Greece. Scenes connected with warfare—warriors, horses, and chariots—are particularly

prominent, revealing one of the chief preoccupations of the people for whom they were made.

The pottery of the final stages of the Mycenaean period should be considered in close conjunction with contemporary history. We have already seen how, even before 1200 BC, some Mycenaean sites had built or strengthened their defence systems. At the end of the 13th century most sites were destroyed or abandoned and only a few reoccupied. We still do not know exactly what happened, whether there was a massive invasion, a civil war, or a major climatic change which ruined the food supply, causing some to starve and others to turn against their own in a desperate fight for survival.

Whatever happened, the Empire as a centralized authority was broken, but the wealth, technical and artistic skills that had flourished within it were not entirely dissipated. Refugees from the former centers of power established themselves elsewhere—in the more remote parts of Greece and even in Cyprus. High-quality vases were produced, for example on Naxos and in the southeastern Aegean. The mainland "close" style, which has some parallel in Crete, stands firmly in the inherited tradition. However, marked regional variations appear, and there is an even greater tendency to formalism.

The more sophisticated post-Imperial styles did not survive to the end of the Bronze Age. The latest vases (appropriately called sub-Mycenaean and sub-Minoan) have a restricted range of basic shapes and ornaments. Their technical quality is poor and the contours of the vases sag and are markedly less vital. These inhabitants of the Aegean obviously lost heart and initiative in the adverse conditions which prevailed, a fact clearly reflected in the quality of their pottery.

The contrast between these gloomy products of a dying civilization and the new vitality of the subsequent Protogeometric revival is the more marked because the two styles, so totally different in feeling, share similar shapes and motifs. (*See* Archaic Greek Art.)

Frescoes. The Cretan palaces were built on a scale that left large areas of wall space free for embellishment and thus it was that the art of fresco painting developed. In the earlier palaces it was mostly limited to plain colors and simple linear patterns on the plastered walls. Later, figured and naturalistic scenes were common and many motifs can be related to those found on contemporary pottery.

Most of the advanced figured scenes belong to the later palaces. The lily fresco from Amnisos (Heraklion Museum), a villa on the north coast of Crete, is transitional. It has the characteristic red background and some of the linear patterning of the earlier style but the lilies themselves represent a more elaborate composition. The flowers also indicate the concern with plants and wildlife which were important sources of subject matter in later frescoes and vase-painting.

There are frequent ceremonial scenes, perhaps both religious and secular. An elegant lady, dubbed "La Parisienne", is from one of these. Others show figures in procession or watching events. A bull-leaping scene must have a significance

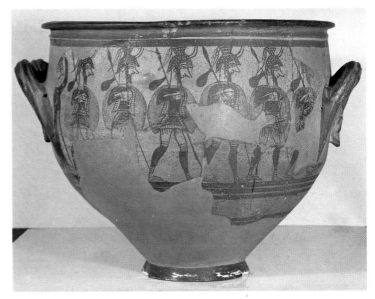

A krater from Mycenae: the "Warrior" vase; height 41cm (16in); c1200–1150 BC. National Museum, Athens

that is lost to us. This dangerous sport seems to have played an important part in Minoan religion. Analysis of the architecture of the palace at Mallia has led to the suggestion that it took place in the central court, which was closed off for the purpose with temporary barriers to protect the spectators.

Outside Crete, there are frescoes from sites in the Cyclades. A piece from Melos showing flying fish (National Museum, Athens) clearly relates to Cretan work in choice of subject matter, but is somewhat cruder and fresher in style. Extensive fresco scenes, spectacular both for their subject matter and state of preservation, have recently been discovered beneath the volcanic debris on Thera. They too in many cases have this distinctively Cycladic feeling, though there is no doubt that the technical foundation is Cretan. Again there are many scenes from nature—flowers, birds, and animals.

The most interesting fresco so far found on Thera, particularly from a historical point of view, is in miniature. It shows a landscape with towns and figures. Before one of the towns a naval battle is taking place. Features of the landscape have much in common with Cretan work but the remaining elements are most unusual. The only real parallel for the subject matter in Aegean art is the silver Siege *rhyton* from Mycenae (see page 100).

Although the style of the frescoes is vigorous and conveys a strong impression of naturalism, perspective is barely observed and gestures and features are conventionalized. Eyes are frontal and heads in profile. The Theran battle scene demonstrates the inability of the artist to show a body falling naturally.

There are no frescoes from the mainland contemporary with those on Crete and in the Cyclades, since the architectural form to accommodate them had not yet been developed. But the palaces of the Empire period were extensively decorated in this way. While the basic technique is the same as the one developed earlier on Crete, the surviving scenes create a very different impression, perhaps best illustrated by a restoration of the scene from the throne room of the Palace of Nestor at Pylos in the far southwest of mainland Greece. The naturalism typical of Crete has gone. Plant and animal life is

The Thera Frescoes

▲ The Ship Fresco; height 40cm (16in). National Museum, Athens

► The Ikria Fresco. National Museum, Athens

The frescoes at the Akrotiri settlement on the island of Thera belong to the late 16th century BC. They owe their remarkable state of preservation to the volcanic debris under which they were buried and have added immeasurably to our knowledge of prehistoric Aegean painting. Perhaps their most striking feature is the successful combination of high decorative quality with significant narrative or symbolic content.

The ships in the Ship Fresco are beautifully adorned with devices, flags, and bunting. The landscapes are rendered in bold colors thought to represent the variegated volcanic rocks of Thera itself. The essential theme, however, is a formal one, possibly a festival to celebrate the Annual Resumption of Navigation—clearly a key event in a maritime community.

The Ikria Fresco, so-called because its motif, repeated eight times, is the *ikria* or stern cabin seen on the flagship in the Ship Fresco, displays a similar union of the decorative and the symbolic. The *ikria* is a gay, attractive object. Placed so prominently in the decoration of a finely appointed town house in Akrotiri, as well as on the flagship, it surely indicates the status of the occupant of the house—Admiral of the Fleet.

In the same room as the Ship Fresco and also of miniature size (approx. 16 in, 40 cm high), are scenes of a sea battle set against a town and a tropical landscape. The former seems to have been a standard subject in Late Bronze Age art in the eastern Mediterranean; the latter reflects an interest in nature evident in both Cretan and Theran paintings which sometimes, as here, shows signs of Egyptian influence, probably absorbed through Crete.

◄ The Priestess. National Museum, Athens

▲ The Spring Fresco. National Museum, Athens

Before the discovery of the Thera frescoes, knowledge of Bronze Age wall-painting was fragmentary, derived from finds on Crete, Mainland Greece, and (to a lesser extent) two other Cycladic islands. The Thera pictures are most closely related to those from Crete. There are a number of similarities in subject and style (compare, for example, the Cretan "La Parisienne" with the Theran lady in the Crocus Gatherers Fresco). Technical analysis has shown that the pigments used and the methods of painting employed were virtually identical in the two places.

In spite of this, there is a strong and very attractive local Cycladic quality in the Thera painting—a quality that can also be discerned in the arts of other islands. This is manifest in a confident simplicity of line and a real, if somewhat rustic, charm. A number of the subjects and motifs are not found in Crete; there is no Minoan parallel for the Ship Fresco for example.

▲ The Lady of the North Wall. National Museum, Athens

▼ The Boxing Children. National Museum, Athens

▲ Scenes from the Ship Fresco: *above* a sea battle; height 40cm (16in). National Museum, Athens

▲ *Below* a tropical landscape; height 40cm (16in). National Museum, Athens

The use of natural themes at its most purely decorative is to be found in the flowers, rockwork, and swallows (a distinctively Theran subject) of the Spring Fresco. Floral motifs also form the central elements in other scenes and, in one case, were used to adorn a window recess.

An attractive treatment of the natural location can also be seen in the Crocus Gatherers Fresco, where the rocks, clumps of flowers, and grasses are charmingly rendered. The same delicacy can be seen in the figures, who wear fine dresses and jewelry. Some carry baskets; one picks a thorn from her foot. The dresses and hair styles are clearly Cretan. The theme of crocus picking is found also on Crete, but the participants there, as in another Theran fresco, are monkeys!

This scene too probably had special significance. The flowers may have been gathered for some ritual purpose, possibly the making of saffron offering-cakes which the "Priestess" of another picture may be carrying.

The "Priestess" is an impressive, interesting figure, striking for her unusual formality in the general context of these frescoes. The only comparable figures are the so-called Boxing Children, engaged in an activity we cannot readily interpret.

Another figured scene with ladies displays something of the solemnity of the "Priestess", although the figures are more in the style of those in the Crocus Gatherers Fresco. The background is plain but the border strongly patterned—a reminder that border patterns are common, and unfigured designs consisting solely of patterns are also found.

Although technically primitive by more sophisticated standards—in anatomical naturalism, composition, the rendering of spatial relations—the Thera frescoes are remarkably effective, colorful and appealing pictures. We may assume their very existence to be proof of the success of their formal role.

R.L.N. BARBER

Further reading. Hood, S. *The Arts in Prehistoric Greece*, London (1978). Morgan Brown, L. "The Ship Procession in the Miniature Fresco" in Doumas, C. (ed.) *Thera and the Aegean World I*, London (1978). Warren, P.M. "The Miniature Fresco from the West House at Akrotiri, Thera, and its Aegean Setting", *Journal of Hellenic Studies* vol. 99, (1979) pp115–29.

"La Parisienne", a fresco figure from Knossos; height of figure 20cm (8in); c1400 BC. Heraklion Museum

form a vase interior. Hollow reeds may have been initially, again with an abrasive. Later the raw stone itself was rotated under a fixed drill. The people of the Cyclades, with their extensive marble beds, were early masters of stoneworking and achieved a remarkable degree of sophistication.

Marble figurines of schematic, though recognizably human form are regularly found in Cycladic graves of the Early Bronze Age. They vary in height from a few inches to several feet. We have no means of telling exactly what role they played in funerary practices but they must have been primarily associated with these as they are found much less often in settlements. The islands richest in marble, Paros and Naxos, probably found in these figurines and other marble products a profitable trading commodity, which may partly explain their prosperity early in the Bronze Age.

Most of the figures are standing, their arms usually crossed over their bodies. Their faces are long, oval, and backward-sloping, their noses being the only worked features. Earlier figurines are less naturalistic and reduce the human form to the shape of a violin. The "folded-arm" category includes some more complex types. Arms are set in different poses and there are some seated figures. Prominent amongst these are two musicians, one playing a harp and the other a flute. These figures have an intrinsic abstract appeal. Their firm, simple lines are certainly at home among the sharp light and fierce colors of the Aegean world.

Many vases were manufactured in stone, and most of the Cycladic stone shapes are also found in terracotta. There are simple, flattish open bowls and dishes, as well as more complex vessels. Suspension vases, with wide bodies and narrow necks and feet, had side perforations by which they could be hung.

Crete, too, was a center of stoneworking from early times and became more important than the Cyclades in this respect. The Cretans used a much greater variety of stones. Characteristic is the "Bird's Nest" Bowl, but more elaborate shapes were attempted, even at this early period.

From the later palaces come several stone vases with decoration in relief. The "Harvesters" Vase from Ayia Triadha near Phaestos shows a harvest procession, the figures carrying appropriate equipment (Heraklion Museum). It is made of black steatite and, in common with other such vases, was originally covered with gold leaf.

The palace at Zakro has been a particularly rich source of stone vases. Many of them seem to show ritual scenes and several are of the *rhyton* shape. This type of vase is especially associated with religious activity. One Zakro example shows a worshiper at a hilltop sanctuary. Other *rhyta* were made in the form of animals' heads.

There are also many undecorated vases, their appeal stemming from elegance of shape and the varying characteristics of the stone used.

stylized; poses are formal and rigid; the composition is heavy and forbidding; and figures are vast and undynamic. There is a new emphasis on scenes of combat.

Stone objects. Early stoneworking must have been a laborious process. Objects were roughly shaped with chisels and then smoothed and polished with an abrasive. Emery is found in the Cyclades (mainly on Naxos) and is ideal for this purpose.

Before the end of the Early Bronze Age in Crete, a form of drill was invented to extract the core from a block of stone, to

Right: A marble harpist from the island of Keros (Cyclades); height 23cm (9in); mid 2nd millennium BC. National Museum, Athens

A suit of armor with boars' tusk helmet found at Dendra, near Mycenae;
1450–1400 BC. Argos Museum

Some attractive vases were also made from rock crystal. A *rhyton*, again from Zakro, is of this material (Heraklion Museum), as is a bowl with a handle in the form of a duck's head from the earlier Grave Circle at Mycenae (National Museum, Athens). This is one of the many Cretan objects from the Mycenae graves.

Relief sculpture is practically unknown in Bronze Age Greece. But crudely sculpted grave-markers are found in the Mycenae Grave Circles (National Museum, Athens). The scenes are typically Mycenaean – the battle and the hunt.

Sealstones. Large numbers of seals, and sometimes fragments of clay bearing their impressions, have been found on Aegean Bronze Age sites, particularly in Crete. They are found early in the period but at that time they were mostly made of more easily worked materials—wood or bone. Later they were made in a variety of different stones and often most delicately and skillfully engraved.

Such objects were used to impress signs of ownership, as genuine seals in the manner of signet rings, and as amulets. They were probably also treated as a form of jewelry and were highly prized as personal possessions, often being buried with the dead.

Basic stylistic developments match those already observed in other art forms. Apart from the early examples which mainly have linear decoration, seals tend to be decorated with figured scenes—animal, human, or divine. These seals were often transmitted from one generation to another. In later times (*c*700 BC) the discovery of prehistoric seals was to inspire a new school of gem-cutting.

Metal objects. Prehistoric societies have traditionally been described according to the materials on which they depended for basic tools and implements, hence the terms Stone, Bronze, and Iron Ages. Early in our period bronze was relatively rare and obsidian still widely used for tools and weapons. Bronze, however, gradually became the main material from which such objects were manufactured and, with increasing availability and more sophisticated working methods, was also used for nonessential luxury objects. Other metals, especially precious ones like gold and silver, were used exclusively for the latter.

Crucibles and molds (usually of clay or stone) for making metal objects have been found on Aegean sites. Initially the molds were mostly simple and open. Later they were more often closed. Larger objects, for example armor, were made by hammering out sheets of metal and riveting them if necessary.

The weapons of war which show a steady technical development throughout our period cannot often be classed as works of art. But some of them bore additional decoration which made them fit for princes and qualifies them for this category.

During the Middle Bronze Age the long sword came into its own. One such sword from Mallia (probably a ceremonial

Detail of the painted limestone sarcophagus from Ayia Triadha, Crete; left, the pouring of libations, right, offerings at the tomb; length of sarcophagus 137cm (54in); c1400 BC. Heraklion Museum

object since it seems too large to have been effectively used in battle; Heraklion Museum) had a gold covering to its pommel. Round the circular field an acrobat is stretched, his head touching his feet.

The Mycenae Shaft Graves bristled with weapons. Among them were daggers whose blades were inlaid with scenes in gold, silver, electrum, and niello—a technique that came to Greece from the eastern Mediterranean. The subjects include hunting scenes, plants, and wildlife, as well as simple recurring motifs. They have a strange mixture of themes, from nature as found in Minoan frescoes, to more violent scenes perhaps closer to Mycenaean taste. The fluidity and delicacy of the execution points very definitely to Cretan workmanship. Other weapons carry incised patterns.

Body armor has rarely survived the ravages of time but from a later tomb at Dendra, not far from Mycenae, came a complete suit (Argos Museum). It consists of two separate shells, covering the chest and back, with extra attachments to guard the neck, shoulders, and lower body. This panoply included greaves or leg-guards, also known from a few other Mycenaean sites. The head was protected by a helmet of pieces of boar's tusk sewn on to a leather cap.

Such armor and, most strikingly, the helmet are described in the Homeric epic poems as worn by the legendary heroes of the Trojan war. If this war were a historical event—something that can neither be proved nor disproved—it should have taken place during the Mycenaean period. Certain objects de-scribed in the Homeric poems actually correspond with objects discovered in Mycenaean contexts.

These and other Mycenaean weapons, together with scenes of battle portrayed in various artistic media, combine to produce a picture of a distinctly warlike people. The Minoans were not lacking in weapons but the decorative attention paid to them in Mycenaean society and the prominence with which they are portrayed suggest that, whether because of circumstances or natural tendency, the Mycenaeans lived violent lives.

Gold and silver objects are found in the Early Bronze Age, though they are not common. There is a gold version of the mainland "sauceboat" shape (Louvre, Paris), and silver vessels have been found on Amorgos in the Cyclades. From Early Palatial Crete comes a gold pendant with two wasps heraldically opposed over a granulated circle. Fine techniques for gold-working, specifically filigree and granulation, must have reached the Aegean via contacts with Syria and lands further east.

Distinctively Minoan in feeling, though found on the mainland in the earlier part of the Late Bronze Age, are some gold cups. From a *tholos* tomb at Vaphio, near Sparta, are two cups decorated with scenes of the hunting and capture of bulls (National Museum, Athens). The fluidity and naturalism of the composition as well as the subject matter (bulls being caught for the ritual games?) leave their Minoan origin in no doubt. Clay vases of similar shape are commonly found and are called *Vaphio* cups. Another Minoan gold cup, from Dendra, has a wider, flatter shape and is decorated in "marine" style with octopus, fishes, and sea life (National Museum, Athens).

Rather earlier than these cups, in the Mycenae Shaft Graves, we find an astonishing richness of gold objects. Their significance lies not only in the quantity, which is considerable, but also in the fact that there is no tradition of the possession or working of gold objects on the mainland.

Some of the objects, like the cups described above, are certainly Cretan in inspiration and, presumably, workmanship. Others, although perhaps made by Cretan craftsmen, have scenes or compositions that are more characteristic of Mycenaean taste. The gold masks are not only unique, as objects, to the mainland but are distinctly un-Cretan in feature compared with figures from Minoan art.

In addition to the masks and gems, there are a variety of gold vessels from the Mycenae graves as well as a wealth of personal ornaments (gold leaf headbands with engraved patterns) and smaller pieces which may have been sewn on to garments. A remarkable silver object—a fragment of a *rhyton* (National Museum, Athens)—has part of a scene showing the siege of a city, a similar theme to that on the miniature fresco from Thera.

Other materials. Art objects in a variety of other materials have come down to us from the Aegean Bronze Age—bone and ivory, faience (an artificial compound covered with a vitreous glaze), as well as terracotta objects distinct from pottery. Simple clay figurines were offered in religious sanctuaries from early times but the more sophisticated, and indeed most of the minor objects considered here, come from contexts not earlier than 1700 BC.

Common in Mycenaean times are small schematic figurines named after the Greek letters Φ, Ψ, and Τ which they roughly resemble. In recent years a small shrine has been excavated at Mycenae with fresco decoration on the walls (Nauplia Museum). It contains a variety of cult-statues 15 in (40 cm) or more in height. There are male and female types and others in the form of snakes. The dresses of some of the figures bear motifs also found on pottery. Figures of a markedly different type with hands raised in a ritual gesture, come from 13th-century Crete.

Both Crete and the mainland produced *larnakes* or coffins in the Late Bronze Age. These usually carry some form of painted decoration which can often be related to contemporary pottery or fresco painting. The most impressive example, of limestone, was found at Ayia Triadha in Crete and its four sides have detailed scenes of preparations for the sacrifice of a bull and of people bringing offerings to the tomb of the dead man. The priestess on the *larnax* resembles, at least in costume, a female faience statuette found at Knossos at the end of the Early Palace period (both in the Heraklion Museum). The snakes she holds are certain indications that she was a cult-figure.

Also in faience are some pieces of the "town mosaic", perhaps originally inlaid into another material. The surviving elements represent buildings, presumably parts of an integrated design (Heraklion Museum).

Bone was worked from the Early Bronze Age for tools and simple ornaments. Ivory figures in the round and plaques for inlay are fairly common in later times. A group of two women and a child from Mycenae is likely to be Cretan while the sphinx on a plaque from Spata in Attica is in Mycenaean style (both in the National Museum, Athens).

Conclusion. Many times in the preceding pages the essential stylistic and thematic characteristics of the art of the Cyclades, Crete, and the Greek mainland have been emphasized: the open, unsophisticated freshness of Cycladic taste, the subtler fluidity of Minoan art and its concentration on subjects from nature and religion, the formality, insensitivity, and violent preoccupations of the Mycenaeans.

These are the characteristics of the different areas at the periods of their greatest achievement. At other times the characteristics may still exist but their natural development is suppressed by other factors. The Cyclades—it is easier for islands to preserve their independence—retained much of their early individuality into the 2nd millennium BC until subordinated to Cretan and then Mycenaean power. Palatial Crete developed unhindered her free and vital art until the eruption of Thera and Mycenaean invasions curtailed liberty and stifled artistic progress. The Mycenaean Empire arose after violent clashes with Crete and her allies and faded in violence. Small wonder that its art reflects this and mirrors the preoccupations of men who valued victory and brash riches above the subtler charms of an artistic delicacy which might have developed in a different social setting.

R.L.N. BARBER

Bibliography. Higgins, R. *Minoan and Mycenaean Art*, London (1967). Hood, S. *The Arts in Prehistoric Greece*, London (1978). Hood, S. *The Minoans*, London (1971). Vermeule, E. *Greece in the Bronze Age*, Chicago (1964). Zervos, C. *L'Art des Cyclades du Début à la Fin de l'Age du Bronze*, Paris (1957).

7

ARCHAIC GREEK ART

A water-jar from Caere in Etruria showing King Eurystheus, Cerberus, and Herakles
height 43cm (17in); c530–525 BC. Louvre, Paris (see page 122)

I N its broadest sense the term "Archaic" can be applied to all forms of Greek art from the collapse of the Bronze Age cultures of Mycenae and Knossos at the end of the 12th century BC (*see* Aegean Art) down to the Persian invasions of 480–479 BC. During these six centuries artistic techniques and conventions developed steadily and objectives changed; a number of phases with markedly different characteristics can be distinguished. What unites them, and marks them off from the much shorter Classical period that followed (*c*480–330 BC) is a difference of attitude. Where the Archaic artists were outward-looking—striving after a complete understanding of the forms they were endeavoring to represent (in particular the human form) and also after a technical understanding of the materials they employed, assimilating new ideas and methods from outside—the art of the Classical period had absorbed all it needed and is introspective and self-sufficient.

The advance in bronzeworking is typical of technical progress during the Archaic period. From the early 8th century the first figurines appeared, generally solid-cast but sometimes still made up of beaten sections, of which the best-known examples are the group of standing male figures from Dreros in Crete (now in the Heraklion Museum). By the end of the 6th century the Greeks had learnt to cast hollow statues in life size or larger by the *cire perdue* process. In carved sculpture there was progress from the small limestone figures of the 7th century, which still readily betray their wooden forebears, to the monumental statues or *kouroi* (youths) and *korai* (maidens) carved in hard marble during the 6th century and later. The initial stimulus was provided by contact with Egypt,

but subsequent development was rapid and is easily charted by the art historian because sculptors advanced by stages, never relinquishing the knowledge they had acquired. In vase-painting the period opened with a tradition of pattern-work only; the first Geometric figures in the 8th century were schematic and stylized. By 500 BC, with the advent of the red-figure technique, even three-quarter views were understood, and the way lay open for complete solution of the draftsman's problems. For this was the period during which were developed the techniques and traditions fundamental to Classical Greek art, and thus to the arts of all later periods that draw on it.

It is probably the pervading element of exploration and progress that has made Archaic Greek art so appealing to modern eyes. For Archaic art reflects a world of enormous political and social change. At first, however, it was an illiterate world—the writing techniques of the Mycenaeans had been forgotten and the alphabet was formed only in the 8th century. The poems of Homer were composed in an oral tradition, in which images of the poet's own Archaic world were overlaid on folk-memories of the Bronze Age, producing a picture in need of careful analysis before it can be treated as historical evidence. The first proper histories to survive are those of Herodotus and Thucydides, written in the second half of the 5th century. Both provide useful information about the earlier period, and the dates given by Thucydides provide an essential chronological framework for the 7th and 6th centuries. The art objects of the Archaic period are also evidence for the archaeologist and historian. In themselves they can be

The Archaic Greek world

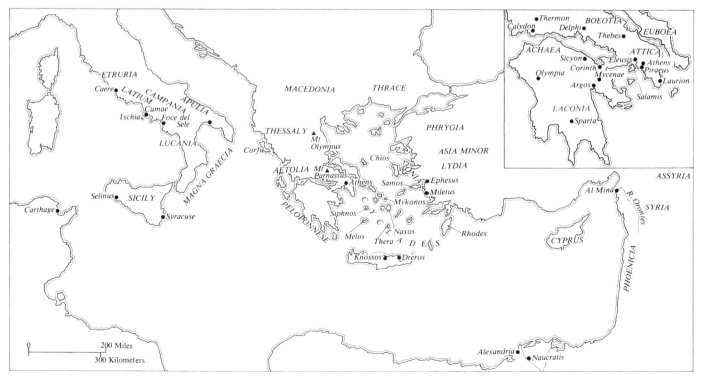

indicators of stylistic, social, and commercial contacts and development, while their decoration provides illustrations of the Greeks at their daily business, and of their myths and legends.

However, because knowledge of Archaic Greek art depends on the chances of archaeological survival it has some serious omissions. Wood and ivory have rarely survived, textiles hardly at all; very few bronzes remain, having been melted for scrap, while marbles have always been fodder for the limekiln. Very few free paintings survive (except insofar as vases reflect them) since most were murals painted on buildings now destroyed. Fortunately, during the Archaic period the Greeks developed vase-painting to an art in its own right, for the pottery vase, apart from being broken into pieces, is almost indestructible, and served for most of the purposes for which metal, plastic, and cardboard containers are used today.

Forerunners: Sub-Mycenaean and Protogeometric styles. In the Dark Age that followed the destruction of the wealthy palace-oriented and highly organized society of the Bronze Age, the Greek communities became divided into isolated and virtually autonomous villages, with neither place nor economic scope for the richer arts of the goldsmith, bronzeworker, or sculptor. Apparently only the potter's craft continued. Mycenaean shapes and decoration survived, for the Dorian invaders had no artistic tradition of their own, but the underlying principles of design were forgotten.

This Sub-Mycenaean ware endured for a century and a half, but c1050 BC there was a dramatic change. The slack and ill-organized shapes were replaced by tauter forms—developments of the old ones but conceived in a new way. There was enormous technical improvement, of which the introduction of the fast potter's wheel was a symptom rather than a cause. Shapes became more precise, and the decoration corresponded, generally being applied while the vase was turned slowly on the wheel. The repertoire consisted largely of horizontal bands and lines, often in groups of two or three, and concentric circles or semi-circles applied with compasses and a multiple brush. These simple patterns led to the more varied designs of the ensuing Geometric style, so this period is usually called Protogeometric.

The patterns themselves were found all over Iron Age Europe, but their organization on the vase was peculiar to Greek art. Perhaps for the first time the decoration complemented and articulated the shape, for the pattern-bands seem particularly placed to draw attention to the most prominent part of the vase. This feeling for harmony and form was fundamental to Greek art. Crediting its discovery to the Protogeometric potters and painters—probably at Athens, hitherto a relatively insignificant city—is to acknowledge their true position at the head of a major tradition in European art.

Geometric style. Around 900 BC another great step forward occurred, into the Geometric style proper. Some of the old motifs, concentric circles for example, were dropped, but

An Attic Protogeometric amphora; height 52cm (20in); c950 BC. Kerameikos Museum, Athens

others such as zigzags and triangles were elaborated. New elements were introduced, including meanders, swastikas, and a variety of linear and essentially Geometric designs. Two basic methods of decoration were established early: the repetition of a single motif to create a continuous frieze round the vase, organized so as to articulate its shape, and, in the 8th century BC, friezes of panels, narrow and wide, in which an elaborated design such as a swastika or rosette could serve as a vertical element to accentuate particular areas.

Around 800 BC the first figures were introduced: horses, then goats and deer, birds, dogs, lions, and finally human beings. Drawings were in silhouette, and remained schematic. The artist drew what he knew to exist, rather than what he saw, thereby illustrating the most cogent elements of each figure. Men were shown with their muscular legs in profile, their broad chests frontal, and their heads again in profile. Female breasts were drawn as short strokes; a warrior's helmet-crest became a wavy line. Figures were not necessarily shown clothed, but an awesome impression of a rank of soldiers was conveyed by allowing their bodies to be entirely obscured by their spears and shields.

At first the figures were used in exactly the same way as the linear designs. With a tradition of abstract art already three centuries old this was no more surprising than that the first conventions of figure drawing should be rather stylized. As confidence later grew the figures became less stiff, so that by c700 BC their bodies were more rounded and lifelike, with a greater feeling for individual movement.

Attic Geometric art is important because it was the first consistent tradition of figured drawing since the end of the Mycenaean world, and thus stands at the head of a continuous development in western art. About 750 BC it first becomes possible to distinguish different internal trends: within the *Kerameikos*, the potters' quarter in Athens, the styles and the products of individual painters and their workshops can be distinguished. Since we cannot know their names, they are called after their outstanding pieces, favourite themes, or

An Attic Geometric grave-amphora by the Dipylon Master; height 150cm (59in). National Museum, Athens

quirks of style. Perhaps the most outstanding and influential was the Dipylon Master, named after a vase found in the cemetery by the Dipylon Gate in Athens (now in the National Museum, Athens).

The most popular shapes were large *amphorae* (storage jars), *kraters* (mixing-bowls for wine), jugs, and two-handled cups and bowls. The potting was of an extremely high standard, and often displayed an exuberance that matched the decoration: small vases were modeled in the shape of baskets or granaries; *pyxides* (toilet boxes) have lids with a whole team of horses for the handle. There was now a lively tradition of modeling terracotta figures of humans and animals, to be used as votive offerings in sanctuaries, as ornaments, and even as toys.

It was matched by the appearance throughout Greece during the 8th century BC of cast bronze figurines. Like the vases, they at first depicted animals and warriors, but scenes of daily life and mythology crept in—a hero fighting a centaur, a helmet-maker, a hunter and a lion. The bronzesmiths too represented what they knew rather than what they actually saw, and so even those compositions that appear to be groups, like the centaur-fight, are in fact made up of a series of two-dimensional views.

Other minor arts reappeared during the 8th century. The rising standard of living created a demand for bronze *fibulae* (safety pins), and in Athens and Boeotia we see their catchplates decorated with incised patterns or figured scenes, while gold bands with similar ornamentation have been found in the graves of the rich. Engraved seals apparently reappeared in Greece as early as the 9th century BC, though they were rare before the 8th. The most common type was a square limestone block, once probably set in a wooden handle; the decoration was most commonly a linear pattern, but figured scenes had appeared by 700 BC. Although the stimulus may have come from the eastern Mediterranean civilizations, the style was pure Greek Geometric.

The new style has certain implications about 8th-century society. If the Protogeometric style was now too austere for contemporary taste it suggests a way of life that could look beyond bare necessities. This is borne out in several ways: by the reappearance of gold ornaments, and of seals (which implies the existence of property worth marking and thus of a property-owning class), and by the functions of vases (for example, mixing wine) and their decorative motifs: by the 6th century BC ownership of a horse had become an official criterion of status, and we can fairly assume that in the 8th century it gave even more distinction, and therefore the possession of a vase decorated with horses or chariots reflected the aspirations if not the actual standing of their purchasers. There was still relatively little competition from metal wares, so these vases represented the best that could be obtained. Vase-painting was still the major pictorial art of the Greeks. Despite their growing prosperity, architecture remained unpretentious: small houses, rectangular or apsidal with at best a two-columned porch, not providing contexts for mural paint-

A hero fighting a centaur; cast bronze; height 11cm (4in); c750 BC.
Metropolitan Museum, New York

ing. Since there were no sculptures larger than the small bronzes and terracottas in the Geometric world either, these vases also fulfilled that role. Many of the large *kraters* and *amphorae* served as grave-markers. Because of their small-scale decoration it is not easy to convey the size of these vases, some of which stood over 5 ft (1.5 m) high. Although the painters could not yet conceive a drawing higher than a few inches, the design as a whole was conceived with a monumentality that was typically Greek. It was found on the mainland in the art of the Mycenaeans in the Bronze Age, but was totally absent from Minoan art.

The depiction of funerals, or files of warriors or chariots, on grave vases probably indicated the vases' functions or the social standing of the deceased. A number of the smaller Late Geometric vases, and the bronzes and seals, show scenes of activity that are clearly narrative. Some are probably pure fantasy, such as the figure fighting a centaur, but several seem to illustrate incidents than can already be related to Greek legends. Thus a picture of a man beset by a flock of birds may be Herakles fighting the Stymphalian birds, while the sailor who has saved himself on the upturned hull of his ship while his companions drown among the fish could be Odysseus: such epic poems as the *Odyssey* and the *Iliad* were now being composed in the form in which we know them.

Increasing stability and prosperity in Greece led to increasing trade. An important indication of this was the establishment—probably under Euboean leadership—c800 BC of a trading settlement at Al Mina at the mouth of the Orontes. It was one of the most important of such settlements in the 8th

and again in the 7th centuries. Thanks to Woolley's excavations its history can easily be reconstructed. Through such entrepôts came both raw materials and finished objects—metals such as bronze and iron, and, increasingly, gold (though Greece always had an adequate supply of silver from sites such as Laurion in eastern Attica), ivory and amber, and foodstuffs and textiles about which we can do little more than guess. The finished objects have left their mark more clearly. Ivory figures made before 700 BC have been discovered on the islands of Samos, Crete, and Rhodes, and in Athens itself, and others, made a little later, in the Peloponnese as well. Some figures of north Syrian and Phoenician origin have also been found. Bronzes occasionally came through from Cyprus to Crete and Athens as early as the 9th century, but most bronzes reaching Greece originated in Phoenicia and North Syria and, from the 7th century onwards, in Assyria, Phrygia, and Phoenicia. Finds of stands, bowls, and caldrons (especially caldron-attachments) have been made at most of the major Greek sanctuaries.

Foreign objects themselves influenced Greek artists, both in choice of subjects, such as the animal friezes with lions and hybrid monsters or floral decoration, and in their treatment of them. A grave of 750–725 BC in Athens contained five nude female ivory figures of eastern "Astarte" type, carved in an eastern technique but by an Athenian with a Geometric sense of form. The Oriental bronze caldron-attachments were soon imitated by Greek craftsmen. In many cases there are signs that they were taught by foreigners resident in Greece, and there is good evidence that a workshop was established in the 8th century in Crete by eastern bronzesmiths. There is a third possibility, that some elements may have survived from the extensive contact between Greece and the East during the Bronze Age.

Increasing prosperity resulted in increasing population. In a poor country like Greece with few natural resources the only solution was to found colonies abroad. The first such settlement was made from Euboea to the island of Ischia c750 BC, but shortly afterwards the colonists moved across to Cumae on the Italian mainland. Around 734 BC Syracuse was founded, one of the first Greek colonies on Sicily, and in 706 Taras (Taranto) on the south Italian mainland. So many other settlements followed in the 7th century that this area was called Magna Graecia, or Great Greece. The generally accepted dates of foundations are those given by Thucydides. Since the founding colonists presumably took with them the pottery fashionable in their home cities, these dates are very important for establishing the chronology of the pottery styles of the end of the Geometric and the ensuing Orientalizing period.

For the earlier period the stylistic development of the pottery itself, aided by a few chance finds of exports outside the Greek world, provides the only yardstick for measuring time in the Geometric world. Studies have tended to concentrate on Attic Geometric, largely because of its undoubted quality and its accessibility, but Coldstream, Schweitzer, and others have distinguished a number of other flourishing traditions, notably those of Corinth, Argos, the Cyclades, and Boeotia, while Crete continued to maintain a vigorous tradition, though it soon became merely provincial. Contrasted with the uniformity of the Mycenaean IIIb style half a millennium earlier this proliferation of local styles is remarkable. It can no longer be explained in terms of an unsettled world where trade was impossible (as the founding of the Olympic Games in 776 BC shows); it provides a very sensitive index of influence and contact for the archaeologist, while also supplying a key to the most important political development of the early Archaic period, the rise of the independent and autonomous city-state, which was to dominate Greek history until at least the rule of Alexander.

Orientalizing style (c725–590 BC). During the 7th century BC the tendency to break down Geometric rigidity intensified. Greater population pressure and prosperity led to the opening up of new areas by the Greeks. The Sicilian colonies were enlarged and multiplied. In the East, the Ionian cities, led by Miletus, expanded into the northern Aegean and thence into the Black Sea. Commercial contact was established with peoples such as the Phrygians of Anatolia, and, by 650, with the Assyrians.

There were internal changes too, typified by events at Al Mina. The predominant type of Greek pottery passing through this port was now Corinthian, and East Greek from the Aegean Islands and the Ionian settlements in Asia Minor. This suggests that these were now the major Greek trading powers, probably with the Aeginetans and, later, Athens in close competition. Meanwhile the old kingdoms were being replaced by oligarchies of landowners, merchants, and soldiers. The first proper stamped coins appeared c650 BC (though the exact date and circumstances of their introduction are disputed). All this can hardly have failed to affect the arts.

The influence of the eastern cultures on the Greeks extended well beyond the visual arts and crafts, and was not restricted to an intellectual level, but it is through the arts that we can trace it most easily, even in mythology. To the native Greek centaur was added a whole range of monsters—Gorgons, Chimaeras, griffins, Harpies—but each of them was Hellenized, made elegant and comprehensible, and thereby less terrifying.

The Greeks' reaction to the Oriental stimulus was essentially selective, but two broad trends can be distinguished: first that of Corinth and most of the rich Dorian cities of the Peloponnese, and second that of Athens, the Ionian cities of Asia Minor, and Dorian Crete, Rhodes, and Argos. The Geometric Corinthian artists had not developed a strong figured tradition, though they excelled at fine linear decoration, particularly of smaller vases, and thus they were more receptive to the imported arts of the Near East and developed their own Protocorinthian style with remarkable rapidity and confidence.

In the period of assimilation, Early Protocorinthian (c725–700 BC), Geometric patterns still appear alongside the new

A miniature scent-vase by the Macmillan Painter, found at Thebes; Middle Protocorinthian; height 7cm (2¾in). British Museum, London

motifs: a few animals and birds, flamboyant rosettes, cable-patterns, and great curling plants that recall the Oriental Tree of Life. The preference for small vases persisted, and in the Middle Protocorinthian (c700–650 BC) the vase-painters adapted the Oriental metal-engraver's method of incision to create the black-figure technique. Details were incised with a point into figures drawn in silhouette in black "glaze" (in fact, black glossy slip), so that the pale background showed through.

In a tradition that gave no scope for shading this technique allowed the artists to show considerable detail. It was a wholly artificial, draftsman's technique, very limited in expression and subtlety, but accepted throughout the Archaic Greek world. It lent itself admirably to the miniaturist style of the Corinthians. Their favorite shape was the *aryballos* (miniature scent-vase) which developed from round (Early Protocorinthian) through ovoid (Middle Protocorinthian) to pointed (Late Protocorinthian), finally reverting to a globular shape in Ripe Corinthian. It was rarely more than 4 in (10 cm) tall, and the main figure-zone was often only 1 in (2.5 cm) high. The Macmillan Vase (British Museum, London) demonstrates the elegant vigor and passion to which Protocorinthian could rise.

However, these narrative scenes were the exception. The staple subjects of Protocorinthian art were the friezes of animals and monsters, interspersed with floral decoration, deriving directly from Oriental sources. Corinthian vases had gained enormous popularity after 700 BC, but the standard could not be maintained. In Late Protocorinthian (c650–640 BC) the decline set in, accelerating during the Transitional and Ripe Corinthian periods (640–550 BC) as the files of animals became steadily larger, more banal, and more crowded. In contrast to the miniaturists stands the more conservative, more monumental, and ultimately more successful tradition, headed by Athens but including the Ionian cities and Dorian Crete, Rhodes, and even Argos. The initial effect of the new influences on the strongly ordered Geometric styles of this area was slow. In contrast to Corinth, it is possible to see their impact on individual Athenian artists, so that it appears more violent, and the new Protoattic style (c710–600 BC) is permeated by unexpectedness and exuberance that amaze and delight.

The father of the Early Protoattic (c710–680 BC) was the Analatos Painter. During a long career, his style grew out of his training in a progressive Late Geometric workshop into a massive confidence whose occasional crudeness is irrelevant. In his work outline drawing replaced silhouette; there was more detail and much more movement in the figures. Within a superficially traditional framework almost everything about the filling ornament was new—its nature (monstrous vegetables and rosettes), and its placing (crowding rays at the foot).

Three painters stood out in the next generation (Middle

Odysseus blinds Polyphemus: a detail of a Protoattic grave-amphora by the Menelas Painter; height of panel 43cm (17in); c670–650 BC. Eleusis Museum, Greece

A Protoattic krater by the Analatos Painter; height 38cm (15in); c690 BC. Staatliche Antikensammlungen, Munich

Protoattic, including the Black and White style, c680–650 BC): the Painter of the New York Nessos amphora, the Ram Jug Painter, and the Menelas Painter. The innnovations were now accepted with restrained confidence, but the spirit of adventure persisted. The neck-panel of a grave-amphora by the Menelas Painter (c670–650 BC) shows this well (Eleusis Museum). The scene is the blinding of Polyphemus by Odysseus and his companions—story-telling was something that the Athenians loved above all.

During the Late Protoattic (c650–620 BC) consolidation continued, until the Athenians had fully adopted the Corinthians' black-figure technique, but without losing their own humor and spontaneity, or their feeling of monumentality (for example the name-vase of the Nessos Painter, in the National Museum, Athens, c615 BC).

Local styles still persisted all over Greece. The reason must lie in part at least not in the difficult terrain, but in the exuberant and individualist spirit of the time. Notable schools were those of Laconia with its idiosyncratic shapes recalling metalwork; the Cyclades, especially Melos, Thera, and Naxos; and the East Greek states, of which the Wild Goat style of Rhodes and Chios was the most widespread. Most lasted into the 6th century, but they were decorative rather than artistically influential styles.

Incision was also employed on other fabrics. During the 7th

century Boeotia and a number of the Cyclades developed a significant minor tradition of narrative scenes on large coarse-ware vases with details incised on relief decoration. A striking *amphora* showing the Trojan Horse was found in 1963 on Mykonos.

Painted vases like the Corinthian Macmillan *aryballos*, occasionally also had parts added in the round, in the tradition of modeling and sculpture. The Greek terracotta industry underwent a fundamental revolution soon after 700 BC with the introduction of the mold from Syria or Cyprus. This made standardization and high-quality mass-production possible. Immigrant craftsmen who had established workshops in Greek lands probably initiated the change, but imported plaques of the goddess Astarte must themselves have influenced Greek coroplasts.

These plaques were made in relief, and were frontal in conception, laying particular emphasis on the head. The Greeks soon combined this notion with their own earlier method of modeling in the round, into the "Daedalic" tradition. Its most distinctive feature was a triangular face with a pointed chin, thick wig-like hair framing the face, large eyes, and a prominent nose. Between c680 and 610 BC it evolved from an angular, geometric type into a chubbier, trapezoidal shape. It was universally applied to clay figures, jewelry, bronzes, and to sculpture.

Pausanias and other ancient writers mention wooden cult-images which were supposed to date from the 7th century and before. None survive, but they appear to have been formless planks or pillars, rather than carved figures. In the 7th century Daedalic conventions were applied to sculpture in limestone, and presumably in wood as well. Both are soft materials, and could be carved with a knife. It is probably significant that only statuettes no more than 2 ft (61 cm) high are known.

However, during the 7th century the Greeks were making contact with Egypt and soon after 650 BC 12 Greek cities, mostly East Greek, founded a trading settlement at Naucratis. Egyptian art and architecture made a deep impression on them. They found here, for instance, statues of life size and larger, carved in hard stone. Significantly, the first Greek attempts at large-scale sculpture were made in the Islands, and then Athens—both areas that had preserved the true Greek monumental spirit in their vases. Possibly the moment of intensive contact was psychologically opportune, coming when the artistic dominance of the Corinthian miniaturist style was on the wane.

The oldest surviving complete "monumental" statue is that of a woman, dedicated on Delos by Nikandre of Naxos (c625 BC). Nikandre's sculptor has used the superficial conventions of the Daedalic because for the female figure he knew no others.

For the male figure, the Egyptian standing type with one leg forward and hands clenched at the sides provided a suitable model. It was used by the Greek bronzesmiths from the early 7th century. Fragments of over-life-size marble figures of c640 BC survive on Delos, but the earliest complete *kouroi*

Left: Daedalic statue of a woman (the Auxerre kore); height 63cm (25in). Right: The statue of a woman dedicated on Delos by Nikandre of Naxos; height 175cm (69in). Casts in the Ashmolean Museum, Oxford

(youths) are an outstanding group from Attica (c610–590 BC). Unlike the earlier figures, and the Egyptian ones, these are nude: an important change, because it presented a greater technical challenge to the sculptor, and also because it was the form of the human body that especially interested the Greeks. The first *kouroi* followed the Egyptian canon of proportions, while the bodily features were rendered as beautiful patterns. Within a generation this canon was abandoned, and the four-square appearance caused by carving the statue out of a rectangular block gave way to a real feeling of form as the sculptors came to understand the working of the body beneath the skin. The development of the *kouros* from a type that the Egyptians had used almost unchanged for two millennia into a figure capable of movement and expression belongs to the High Archaic period. It is the story of the beginning of the European sculptural tradition.

From the Egyptians the Greeks also derived the notion of monumental architecture, at first using wood and then limestone and marble. The first "peripteral" temple, using basically the classic plan with an external row of pillars around the *cella* or sanctuary, was constructed on Samos *c*640 BC.

The beginning of monumental architecture had important effects on painting. Greek sculptures and buildings had been embellished with paint, but substantial buildings now gave scope for "free" painting, and at this stage the metopes on Doric buildings were sometimes decorated with painted scenes. Surviving examples such as those at Thermon and Calydon in Aetolia (*c*640–625 BC) are very rare, but further evidence is provided by the Polychrome style of some Middle Protocorinthian vases (*c*680–650 BC), for example the Macmillan *aryballos* (British Museum, London) or the Chigi Vase in Rome (Villa Giulia). The free painter had a much greater range of colors than the vase-painter, and could conceive his pictures more grandly, with landscape backgrounds, but the basic principles of composition and drawing were common to both.

One further source of inspiration came from the Bronze Age. Miniature decorative work, whether gold, silver, or bronze jewelry (such as pendants, Daedalic plaques, earrings), or carvings in ivory and even amber, had received considerable impetus from demand caused by the new prosperity and from the Oriental stimulus. Series of ivory disk-seals were carved in Corinth, Argos, and Sparta with Orientalizing figures on shapes that recall Geometric stone seals. Around 670 BC begins the series of "Island Gems", carved probably on Melos in local limestone or serpentine. These copy two distinctive Bronze Age seal shapes, the lentoid and the amygdaloid (almond shape), and some Minoan motifs not found in Near Eastern art, such as griffins and twisted animals. Nevertheless, these seals, which were produced for about a century, imply neither continuity nor a throwback to Bronze Age culture. Melos had been rich and influential in the Bronze Age, and we can easily imagine that finds made by chance digging or through deliberate tomb-robbing stimulated gem-engravers at a time when they were seeking new ideas. For the art historian the Island Gems are interesting because they are the direct forerunners of later Greek and thus Roman gem-engraving.

The High Archaic period (*c*590–530 BC). The High Archaic period was the age of the Tyrants, benevolent despots, who generally rose to power as the champions of the merchant and artisan against the landowning aristocracy—Periander at Corinth (*c*625–585 BC), Pisistratus (560–527 BC) and his sons (527–510 BC) at Athens, Polycrates at Samos (*c*540–*c*522 BC) for instance. Many of these men encouraged circles of artists and poets at their courts.

Right: An Athenian kouros of the late 7th century BC; height 184cm (72in). Metropolitan Museum, New York

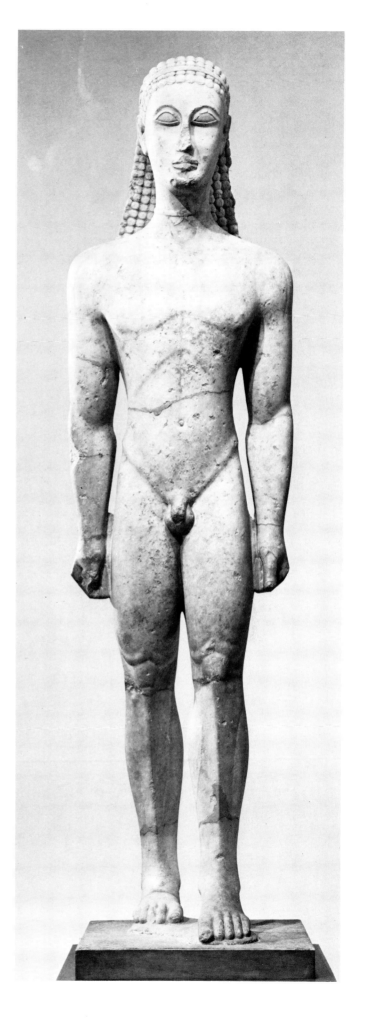

Myths became more popular as subjects in art, while the scope of figured decoration widened, running hand in hand with the growing appeal of epic and lyric poetry. This occasionally led to the political use of certain myths, sometimes in very general terms—the fight against the Centaurs as a triumph for Greek civilization, for example—but occasionally also rather more specifically. Herakles features frequently on Athenian vases made during Pisistratus' period of power, but at the end of the 6th century, when Cleisthenes' democratic reforms drove his family out, it was the truly Athenian hero Theseus who took over.

Trade expanded greatly during the 6th century BC and both artists and their products traveled throughout the Mediterranean. Trading settlements like the one at Naucratis flourished, while the arts of the Scythians on the Black Sea and the Etruscans in the west now showed strong Greek influence for the first time. In all these places the Ionians were most in evidence. After a period of high prosperity the Greek cities of Asia Minor were threatened first by Lydia under Croesus (after 561 BC), and again c547 BC by the victorious Persians. It was natural that they should seek refuge with their kinsmen, either in Attica where Ionian influence may be seen in architecture and sculpture, or in places where Ionian settlements already existed, like the Black Sea and Italy.

These movements suggest that a feeling of common race pervaded the Greek world, but local styles continued to flourish. The Spartans, renowned for their austere life-style, had a distinguished tradition of bronzeworking and during the 6th century developed a highly individual black-figure style, painted over a creamish slip and enlivened with purple. Their most characteristic shape is the cup on a high foot, but other shapes, particularly large pots, were also popular. Three workshops led from c580 to 510 BC: those of the Arkesilas Painter and his pupils, the Naucratis and Hunt Painters.

A wedding procession on a Corinthian krater; c570–560 BC. Vatican Museums, Rome

Many of the Ionian migrants carried with them the traditions of their native city. Most idiosyncratic was the Phocaean whose workshop at Caere in Etruria produced the series of Caeretan *hydriae* (water-jars) (c530–510 BC). In their polychromy and their attention to landscape these black-figure vases must recall wall-paintings. The rounded Ionian features of the figures and the zest and gaiety of the mythical scenes which the painter loves are quite unmistakable—see for example his version of King Eurystheus hiding from a lively and highly-colored Cerberus, led by Herakles in a very natty lion-skin (Louvre, Paris).

Another distinctive fabric was the "Chalcidian", probably manufactured in southern Italy by settlers from Euboea between 550 and 510 BC. It too favored large vases liberally decorated with purple and white paint, but its black-figure tradition is much closer to that of Athens.

The Corinthian Ripe style had been very popular but now declined: the Animal style was effectively dead by 550 BC, though the Human Figure style fared rather better. Padded dancers and riders were popular, but so were mythical scenes. The pale Corinthian clay favored the use of added color in the black-figure technique, but by c575 the painters were meeting Attic competition with the Red-Ground style: large areas of background were now covered with a reddish slip, to emulate Attic, but the Corinthian love of color meant that it had none of the Attic somberness. For all its brilliance and variety of subjects this final Corinthian phase did not last beyond the mid-century. It had started as a miniaturist style, and its potential was exhausted.

Attic clay, ideally suited for the new black-figure technique with its rich red and superb black glaze, coupled with Athenian skill and inventiveness, helped the Athenian vase-painters to capture completely the rising market for fine table vases by the end of the century, and to retain it for 200 years. At first they imitated the Corinthian Animal-Frieze style, but by 570 BC typically Attic scenes of myth and daily life abounded.

During the 6th century Attic vases were sometimes signed by the potter or painter (who could have been the same), or by both separately. Their personalities and influences are more easily distinguished now, and the picture of the close-knit community of the *Kerameikos* and also of its customers becomes clearer. Many vases bear the word *kalos* (beautiful) following the name of a young man, presumably the fashionable darling, and we may assume that the vase-painter was working with his circle in mind.

The Corinthianizing group was, perhaps surprisingly, led by such men as the Gorgon Painter and Sophilos (*fl.* c580–570 BC), who had been brought up in the Protoattic tradition. Their drawing was miniaturist, and scenes were arranged in friezes, particularly on large vases. Perhaps the most outstanding surviving example is the François Vase of c570 BC, a volute-*krater* signed by Ergotimos as potter and Kleitias as painter, standing 26 in (66 cm) high and decorated with six friezes showing several mythological themes but concentrating on the story of Achilles (Museo Archeologico, Florence). Its exquisite liveli-

The François Vase; height 66cm (30in); c570 BC. Museo Archeologico, Florence

ness and wealth of invention, and its sheer technical dexterity, stand in pointed contrast to the rival Corinthian *kraters*.

This school really excelled as cup-painters. The development of the Attic cup progressed steadily from c580 BC: first the Comast cup, decorated with padded dancers, copying a Corinthian shape; then the sharply profiled Siana cups, and c550 "Little Master" cups, with delightful miniature figures on the lip or in a band at the handle-zone.

The alternative Athenian tradition inherited the native monumentality of Protoattic. Prominent in it were men like the Painter of Acropolis 606 and Nearchos, their figures more massive and serious, lacking the refined elegance of the Corinthianizers. Artists like Lydos (*fl.* c560–540 BC) and his contemporary the Amasis Painter could introduce a note of lively gaiety with paintings of Dionysus and his satyrs. His rival

Exekias (*fl.* c545–530 BC) combined outstanding technical skill with unequaled depth of feeling; indeed, he probably took black-figure to its limits of expression. It was essentially a highly formalized engraver's technique, though it could be used in hack workshops to provide quick lively results, for example the Tyrrhenian *amphorae*, produced for the Etruscan market in the 560s and 550s.

Shapes now covered the full repertoire, including after 550 the *kylix* (one-piece cup) which by 500 had developed into its classic shallow form. Panathenaic *amphorae* deserve special mention: these were awarded as prizes at the Panathenaic Games from 566 onwards; they were always decorated with a panel-picture of the city's goddess, Athena, and on the other side with the event in which they were won. They could be painted by leading artists and because they were at times in-

Pollux and his mother Leda: a detail of an amphora painted by Exekias; height 23cm (9in); c540–530 BC. Vatican Museums, Rome

scribed with the archon's (magistrate's) names they provide important absolute dating evidence in a field that otherwise relies largely on stylistic evidence.

In free-standing sculpture the steady development of the *kouros* from a four-square to a more naturalistically treated figure is our clearest guide to the growing confidence and ability of the sculptor and now the bronzeworker too. The Tenea (*c*565) and Anavyssos (*c*530) *kouroi* demonstrate the advance most vividly (Glyptothek, Munich and National Museum, Athens respectively). Men were seen naked in the *palaestra* and gymnasium; Athenian women normally remained decently clothed, in life and in Archaic art. The sculptor treated them partly as a vehicle for drapery patterns (for instance, the curious *Standing Goddess* in Berlin, Staatliche Museen, *c*575 BC), although one of the earliest of the series of *korai* (maidens) from the Athenian Acropolis wears a plain woolen *peplos* (tunic) through whose subtle folds the artist has suggested the taut body beneath. Neither *kouroi* nor *korai* are portrait statues: most are dedications to a deity, some are grave-markers heralding, and from the mid-century running parallel with, the fine grave stelae carved in relief with an idealized figure of the dead. Other free-standing types were evolved, on low bases or none at all, like the riders in Athens (Acropolis Museum), or on columns, such as the sphinxes erected by the Naxians at Delphi and Delos (Delphi Museum;

Delos Museum). All these were dedications to the gods: the same purpose lay behind most architectural sculpture which until late Classical times was normally restricted to buildings with religious functions. During the 6th century the two chief orders of Greek architecture were developed fully: the Doric, with cushion-capitals, popular in the western colonies and at first in Old Greece; and the Ionic, whose columns had volute-capitals like ram's horns and stood on bases, and which originated in Asia Minor and the Islands but later found favor on the mainland. To break up the essential verticals and horizontals of Greek buildings decoration was added at certain places. Acroteria (ornamental statues) might be placed on the roof-peaks and gable-ends; the triangular pediment was filled with figures in very high relief or in the round; on Doric buildings the metopes (spaces between the beam-ends) were filled with relief panels; in Ionic this was replaced by a continuous frieze.

The earliest substantial survivors are the fine pediments from the Temple of Artemis at Corcyra (modern Corfu; *c*590 BC). The sculptor has solved the problem of filling the triangular pediment satisfactorily by varying the scale of the figures, by using animals to fill the slope, and by placing sitting and reclining bodies in the corners. These devices continued in use for at least a century, though later they were more subtly applied through groups of fighting animals, monsters, and wrestling scenes (as on the Archaic temples on the Athenian Acropolis). Because the interplay of lines they provided contrasted with the straight lines of the architecture, combat-scenes often featured on metopes too, along with other stories from myth (for example, the *Heraion* at Foce del Sele in southwest Italy, the Sicyonian treasury at Delphi, and the temples at Selinus in Sicily).

Terracotta was occasionally used for decorating buildings and for reliefs, particularly in Cyprus, Italy, and Sicily, where marble was scarce, but its chief use was for figurines. From *c*550 onwards, into the next century, the number of types became fewer, but style and expression improved. Their chief functions as votive offerings, toys, or ornaments are reflected in their findspots and in the commoner types—jointed dolls, animals, seated women, often holding an offering or child. Perfume vases modeled as women or youths, animals or even feet and helmeted heads became popular, just as bronze figurines of men and women, animals and monsters, were designed not only as figures but also as handles and other ornaments for mirrors and vases, like the enormous Lakonian *krater* found at Vix on the Seine (now in the Musée Archéologique, Châtillon-sur-Seine).

In general the "minor arts" followed the same trends as vase-painting and sculpture during the 6th century, developing from patterned and angular stylization to rounded naturalistic forms. The quality of work produced, especially by the engravers of gems and coin-dies, could be equally high.

Under eastern influence gems were now being cut with a

Right: The Anavyssos kouros; height 194cm (76in); c530 BC. National Museum, Athens

A Red-figure Vase by Euphronios

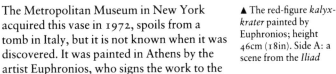

The Metropolitan Museum in New York acquired this vase in 1972, spoils from a tomb in Italy, but it is not known when it was discovered. It was painted in Athens by the artist Euphronios, who signs the work to the right of the head of the central figure, Hermes, on the front; to the left of the head another inscription praises the beauty of the Athenian youth Leagros, a topical compliment often met on vases of this period; and behind Sleep, left of Hermes, the potter Euxitheos signs too. We call the shape a *kalyx-krater*, not knowing its ancient name. It was a comparatively recent invention and its tall, straight walls appealed to the better artists since the fine drawing of their figures suffered less distortion. It was used in feasts for the mixing of wine and water, and we know this speciment was prized because it had been broken in Antiquity and mended with lead clamps, the holes for which can be seen on the reverse.

Euphronios was a leader of the so-called Pioneer Group of red-figure artists who worked *c*520–500 BC and who were the first to realize the full potential of the new, reserving, "red-figure" technique which had been invented some 25 years before this vase was made. Predecessors had experimented with mixed techniques while retaining something of the color range of the older, black-figure style, but the Pioneers preferred the more austere black-and-red and used added color sparingly. Euphronios was a masterly draftsman and his eye for pattern, in dress and wings, can be well appreciated here. But this is a period in which the pattern of anatomy was also the artist's delight, partly

▲ The red-figure *kalyx-krater* painted by Euphronios; height 46cm (18in). Side A: a scene from the *Iliad*

▲ Side B: five men arm themselves for battle

▼ Detail of a *kalyx-krater* by Euphronios: Herakles wrestles with the giant Antaios. Louvre, Paris

► A detail of side A: Sleep and Death carry dead Sarpedon from the battlefield with Hermes

derived from observation of the body but still mainly dictated by considerations of design. Thus, eyes are still set frontal in profile heads, and details like ears and pubic hair are stylized into patterns, but the anatomical patterning of the body lifted by the two winged figures on the front of the vase shows at least a moderate understanding of superficial abdominal musculature. The rest of the poses are still strictly frontal or profile with no real three-quarter views of foreshortening,

but the contrast of profile and frontal (as in the dead man's legs—and notice the top view of a foot) is moving towards this, and the next generation achieved these breakthroughs in two-dimensional naturalism for the first time in the history of art. Compare the yet finer display of anatomical understanding and pattern displayed by Euphronios on another *kalyx-krater*, less well preserved, in the Louvre, Paris, showing Herakles wrestling with the giant Antaios. Here the

opaque gloss paint is neatly contrasted with the thinned paint used for the hair of the two struggling figures, and this contrast in intensity of line and mass is exploited well by the Pioneers in lieu of less subtle color contrasts. This is a draftsman's art rather than a painter's, at least in the sense of "painting" as understood in later Greek and European art.

Though many of the Athenian vases were exported to the west, to lie eventually in Etruscan tombs, the subject matter of the scenes on them reflect current life or episodes of Greek myth, and sometimes the myth can be used to comment upon contemporary events in the way more familiar to us from the works of Greek poets and playwrights. On the front of our vase is an episode from Homer's *Iliad*. Dead Sarpedon is carried from the battlefield by Sleep and Death, winged warriors, with Hermes, escort of souls, beyond them. Two comrades watch. Sarpedon was a Lycian prince, fighting on the Trojan side, but it is not uncommon for

Greek artists and poets to treat sympathetically the distress of their adversaries of myth—indeed, they seem to make a point of it. Notice the attention to detail—the pads at the bottom of the greaves to stop them chafing ankles, minutiae of armor and weapons, on the reverse the strange shield blazons: a scorpion and a crab playing pipes! These may be heroes but their dress is that of 6th-century Athenians, and we learn much of contemporary life and manners from scenes of myth. On side B of the vase five men arm themselves. Inscriptions praise Leagros again, and name the men. Two bear the names of the two earliest archons (leading magistrates) of Athens and it has been suggested that these arming Athenians of the "good old days" are an allusion to recent restrictions on citizens carrying arms made by the tyrant rulers of Athens. This is attractive, but the other three names are not Athenian, and three of the five names are also carried by heroes fighting at Troy, for the Trojans, so any contemporary allusion there may be is perhaps more subtle than we can readily understand.

JOHN BOARDMAN

Further Reading. von Bothmer, D. "Greek Vase Painting: an Introduction", *The Metropolitan Museum of Art Bulletin* vol. 31 Part 1, (1972) p2, pp34–9. von Bothmer, D. "Der Euphronioskrater in New York", *Archäologischer Anzeiger*, Berlin (1976) pp484–512.

▼ A detail of side B

A youth restrains a horse: a chalcedony scaraboid by Epimenes; length 1.7cm (⁶⁄₁₀in); c500 BC. Museum of Fine Arts, Boston

The sack of Troy on a red-figure cup by the Brygos Painter; diameter 33cm (13in); c490 BC. Louvre, Paris

wheel from harder stones, such as carnelian, agate, and chalcedony, into new shapes like the Egyptian scarab and then the scaraboid with plain back, showing new themes. The result is seen well on the groups of Greco-Phoenician gems (from 550 BC onwards), where Greek engravers transformed and Hellenized eastern themes. Soon local schools can be distinguished all over Greece, and individual engravers like Epimenes stand out.

The same is true of the coins, in scope, tradition, and quality. By 500 the major cities except Sparta were issuing their own silver coins, stamped on both sides and marked with their own devices. While three main artistic divisions can be distinguished—Ionia, Old Greece, and Magna Graecia—coin types, especially those of the commerically more influential cities, changed more slowly than other art forms because of natural conservatism. In this way alone do they stand slightly aside from the steady development of the Archaic tradition.

The Late Archaic period (*c*530–480 BC). The years 530–480 BC saw considerable changes in Greece as the tyrants were replaced by democracies and Persian expansion was only checked at the battles of Marathon (490) and Salamis and Plataea (480–479 BC), but in the world of art this Late Archaic period merely showed a continuation of the trends of the previous half century, in style, technique, and subject matter, though because of particular advances sculpture and vase-painting merit special examination.

By the end of the 6th century most provincial schools had succumbed to the overwhelming popularity of Athenian vase-painting. After Exekias at least one further generation of artists worked in black-figure, improving drawing and making composition fuller and better related. The Leagros Group (named after their favorite *kalos*-name) produced the last flowering of the stronger tradition with a series of heroic and domestic scenes (*c*510–500 BC). Black-figure continued to be used for hackwork in the 5th century, and for the Panathenaic *amphorae* into the 2nd, but after *c*530 BC the more adventurous painters worked in red-figure.

This was the earlier technique in reverse: the body of the vase was covered with black "glaze" and the decorated parts left reserved in the natural color of the clay, details being added in a distinctive relief line, and sometimes in white and purple paint. Although more difficult, it presented much greater scope for expression and emotion even if still typically mannered. This is clearly reflected in the composition, drawing, and gestures of early red-figure painters as they groped after the full potential of the new technique.

In the next half century the painters made great strides in mastering technical problems such as foreshortening and the three-quarter view. Many potters were also painters, and in-

Right: A kore wearing a chiton and a himation; c525 BC.
Acropolis Museum, Athens

The battle of the Gods and Giants on the Treasury of the Siphnians at Delphi; height of frieze 66cm (26in)

stances of cooperation and of changing partnerships were common. Influential artists stand out—Euthymides (*fl. c*520–500 BC), Euphronios (*fl. c*520–465 BC), and Phintias among the late-6th-century "Pioneers". Their often massive figures look best on large vases such as *amphorae*, *kraters*, and *hydriae*. There were also excellent cup-painters, like the neater, prolific Epiktetos (*fl. c*490–420 BC or later) and Oltos (*fl. c*525–500 BC).

These men exemplify the tendency towards specialization, and shapes like the elegant, high-stemmed *kylix*, created *c*500 BC, required special skills in potting and painting. Among the outstanding cup-painters of the early 5th century were the Panaitios Painter, the Brygos Painter, and Makron and Douris, who combined powerful, lively composition with delicate draftsmanship and considerable feeling. Their vase-pictures can have a surprisingly monumental quality (perhaps recalling wall-paintings) which is even more striking in works of such men as the Kleophrades Painter (*fl. c*500–470 and later) who specialized in large vases showing complex mythological scenes. On the other hand the Berlin Painter (*fl. c*505–460 BC) achieved an equally compelling effect through simple, spacious groupings that foreshadow the Classical period.

A similar trend ran through Late Archaic sculpture. *Kouroi* and especially *korai* of the last quarter of the 6th century have a mannered, confident grace about them, perhaps—because it undoubtedly reflects a trend in dress fashions—best illustrated in the *korai*, who now wear a fine linen *chiton* (sleeved tunic or dress) under a woolen *himata* (cloak). The sculptor makes much of the contrast; the latest figures in the series, *c*480, are also endowed with expression, and with the first intimations of movement. This is clearer on the nude *kouroi*. The anatomy was now fully understood, and the body given a twist and a tilt that corresponded to the distribution of weight, clearly seen on the *Critian Boy* (Acropolis Museum, Athens). Free-standing sculpture was about to move into the Classical period.

The new dress fashions of the *korai* show growing Ionian influence, and in architecture the elaborate Ionic order appeared in mainland Greece. A fine example is the Treasury of the Siphnians at Delphi (*c*525 BC), with a frieze depicting the battle of the Gods and Giants and scenes from the story of Troy. Pedimental sculptures were now produced to a single scale, the gable-ends filled with crouching or falling figures. Fights were popular themes, as on the temple of Athena Aphaia on Aegina, *c*500 BC.

One can rarely pinpoint the precise moment when a style changes, but from our standpoint the defeats of the Persians in 480–479 BC seem to have coincided with the moment when the Greek artists had reached a full understanding of the human body, of their own techniques, and when their mood became more introverted. The change cannot have been a sudden one, but it must have been accelerated by the upheavals of the war years.

A.J.N.W. PRAG

Bibliography. Arias, P.E., Hirmer, M., and Shefton, B.B. *A History of Greek Vase-Painting*, London (1968). Boardman, J. *Athenian Black-Figure Vases: a Handbook*, London (1974). Boardman, J. *Athenian Red-Figure Vases: the Archaic Period*, London (1974). Boardman, J. *Greek Art*, London (1973). Boardman, J. *Greek Sculpture: the Archaic Period*, London (1978). Boardman, J. *Pre-Classical: from Crete to Archaic Greece*, Harmondsworth (1967). Cook, R.M. *Greek Painted Pottery*, London (1972). Homann-Wedeking, A. *Archaic Greece*, London (1968). Richter, G.M.A. *A Handbook of Greek Art*, Oxford (1974). Richter, G.M.A. *The Sculpture and Sculptors of the Greeks*, New Haven (1970). Robertson, C.M. *A History of Greek Art* (chapters 1–4), Cambridge (1975).

8

CLASSICAL GREEK ART

The bronze Zeus from Artemisium; height 209cm (82in); c460 BC.
National Museum, Athens (see page 133)

CLASSICAL Greek art spans the period from the defeat of the invading Persian armies (480–479 BC) to the ascendancy of Alexander the Great (336 BC). It is traditionally more familiar than Archaic, but the problems presented by the survival of the evidence are much the same: virtually no organic material remains, little bronze, and not much original marble sculpture. Most public and many private buildings were now of stone, while because of the Roman passion for things classical, more sculpture survives in the form of Roman copies. With the decline of vase-painting as a major art after the 5th century we lose close contact with developments in Greek painting, for little survives except through the adaptations of the vase-painters and the Roman artists.

There is, however, a "complete change in spirit between archaic and classical art ..., in part a change from interest in doing to interest in being" (C.M. Robertson), for which the evacuation and sack of Athens in the Persian War of 480 was surely the catalyst. Because of the Greeks' oath not to rebuild the temples destroyed by the Persians, and Athens' slow recovery, the first postwar temple was that of Zeus at Olympia

(c470–456 BC). When the Athenian program of rebuilding began under Pericles and Pheidias after 450 BC it was a deliberate political step towards turning the old voluntary Delian League into the Athenian Empire.

The serene confidence of High Classical art of the mid-century turned to flamboyance and prettiness as the Peloponnesian War (432/1–405/4 BC) became more wearing and demoralizing, turning again to a brooding introspectiveness after Athens' final defeat by Sparta. The 4th century saw further political and social change, with the decline of the city-state, the resurgence of Persia, and finally the Panhellenic vision of Alexander the Great (336–323 BC). Partly under the influence of such poets as Euripides and such philosophers as Socrates, his enemies the Sophists, and Plato and Aristotle, the individual became more important, which led to a softening and humanizing of form, style, and subject in the arts. The use of myths became much rarer, and domestic scenes gained ground, though frequently given a mythological label.

"Classical art" usually refers to Athenian art, except perhaps in sculpture; but the Greco-Persian gems of the 4th century BC are one example of how the tide of artistic in-

The Classical Greek world: sites mentioned in the text

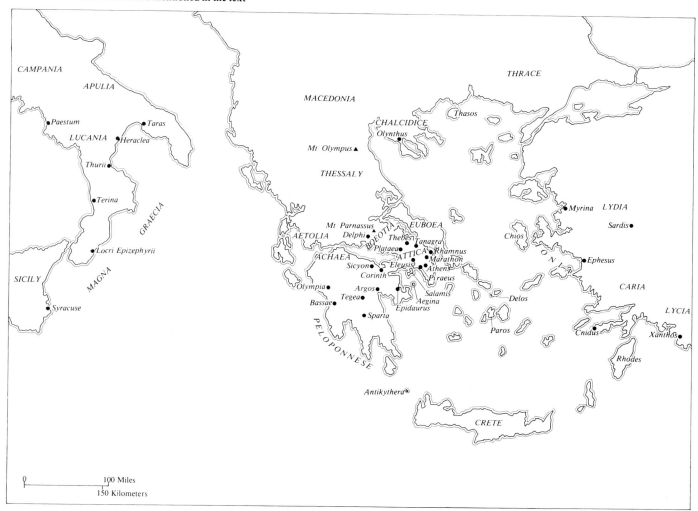

fluence began to turn from Athens. Most provincial styles declined, but with the rise in the 5th century of the powerful tyrants of the colonies in Sicily and southern Italy this area became artistically important, particularly for architecture. Because of the lack of good marble there, little sculpture was made, but vase-painting so flourished that by the 4th century South Italian vase-painting schools (notably the Apulian and Lucanian), originally inspired by the Panhellenic colony of Thurii on the Gulf of Taranto, founded in 443 BC by, among others, Athenians, had completely overtaken the Athenian workshops.

Sculpture. The sculptors of the early Classical period (c480–450 BC) made full use of the knowledge of the human body attained by the late Archaic artists. The result was well summarized by the carvings on the temple of Zeus at Olympia (constructed c470–456 BC). On the west pediment, the fight between the Centaurs and Lapiths was shown: frenzied, often savage action, but broken down by the designer into comprehensible groups. On the east end, where the worshiper entered the temple, the moment before the chariot-race of Pelops was depicted. Here the figures stand still, but the emotion is much tenser. Feeling and individuality are, characteristically for the period, conveyed through pose and gesture rather than facial expression—compare the bronze charioteer from Delphi (Delphi Museum). The calm, commanding figure of Apollo in the center of the west pediment typifies this aspect, and demonstrates the new, easy stance with the weight on one leg. The triangular shape of the pediment was now used to advantage, to draw attention to the central figures and to show the effect of the main action on those others who sit or crouch in the corners. Only the six metopes at either end were decorated at Olympia, with the 12 labors of Herakles. These too are confidently and sensitively composed within the square frame, even though little of the fine detail would have been seen from the ground.

The only other major architectural sculptures from this quarter-century are the metopes from Selinus (Temple E) in Sicily (Museo Nazionale, Palermo; c470–460 BC)—significantly also away from the area affected by the Persian invasion —but there are numerous smaller reliefs. From Athens there are only votive and record reliefs at this time (for example the so-called *Mourning Athena* from the Acropolis, c460 BC; Acropolis Museum, Athens), but in the Islands and the Greek colonies the series of tall grave-stelae surmounted by a palmette continued. Like the Archaic ones, they normally showed the dead person standing quietly, and it is interesting to see how fashion has changed again and the women now wear only the plain woolen *peplos* (dress). To this period also belong the problematical three-sided reliefs from southern Italy known as the Boston and Ludovisi "thrones" (Museum of Fine Arts, Boston, and Terme Museum, Rome).

For the 5th and 4th centuries our knowledge of sculpture in the round suffers particularly from the lack of original evidence, because so few examples survive. However, the de-

scriptions of such ancient authors as Pausanias, Pliny, and Lucian can now be supplemented by Roman copies, though often carved in different materials. We know the names of several major sculptors, such as Kritios and Nesiotes, Pythagoras, Calamis and Myron, and it is clear that all were experimenting with the new anatomical and technical achievements. The *Omphalos Apollo* (a copy of a work of c460–450 BC, now in the National Museum, Athens), a study of the way slight asymmetry of pose goes with perfect balance, has been attributed both to Calamis and to Pythagoras—an example of the problem of attribution, for ancient descriptions are usually too imprecise to link these Roman copies with named originals.

With Kritios and Nesiotes we are on slightly surer ground. They made the statues of the *Tyrannicides Harmodius and Aristogeiton*, erected in 477/6, which have been identified in several copies that show a vigorous composition of two striding, threatening figures with powerfully modeled musculature. The famous bronze Zeus, poised to throw his thunderbolt, found in the sea off Artemisium (National Museum, Athens), is an original of the same type, some 15 years younger. All are shown at that self-contained moment of balance, just before an action, in which the sculptors of the Transitional period were particularly interested, and which was developed to its limits c460–450 BC by Myron of Eleutherae with his *Discobolus* and his *Athena and Marsyas* (copies in Museo Nazionale, Rome; Städtische Galerie, Frankfurt am Main; and Lateran Museum, Rome, respectively).

These Transitional compositions followed logically from the Archaic, but they manifest an inherent and unsatisfying restlessness which is the rider to the experimental approach of the artists. Their successors after 450 BC overcame this. Several names are known to us, like those of Strongylion, who followed the traditions of Myron, and Cresilas (*fl.* 450–425 BC), a rather severe sculptor whose portrait of Pericles is typical of the idealizing portrait figures now becoming popular. But it is the name of Pheidias that stands out.

We get a good idea of his style through the sculptures of the Parthenon at Athens (constructed 449–432 BC), over whose design he had general control. At least here we can examine original 5th-century work, whereas most of his other statues are only known to us from copies, often on a small scale. Although there is plenty of life and movement about his compositions on the Parthenon, his style is a quiet, idealizing one, and the figures are self-contained and inward-looking.

The Parthenon contained many sculptural innovations, such as the presence of the frieze on an otherwise Doric building, and the fact that the themes of pediments, frieze, and metopes were all linked with Athena and Athens. The design of the pediments now showed complete confidence: foreshortening is fully understood, and even the shallow frieze is conceived with a proper sense of depth. Two drapery styles are evident on the building, demonstrating how many hands were involved: a plainer one, where the heavy cloth only hints at the body underneath, and an ornate style, emphasizing the

The Pediments of the Temple of Zeus at Olympia

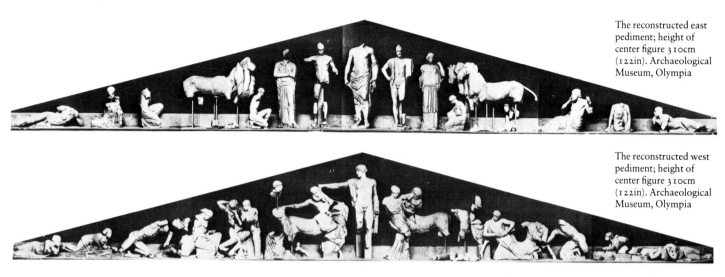

The reconstructed east pediment; height of center figure 310cm (122in). Archaeological Museum, Olympia

The reconstructed west pediment; height of center figure 310cm (122in). Archaeological Museum, Olympia

The Temple of Zeus suffered several accidents and repairs from as early as the 4th century BC and the corner figure of the west pediment had to be replaced in Antiquity. In AD 426 it was burnt and in the 6th century overwhelmed by an earthquake and subsequently covered with up to 16 ft (5 m) of alluvial sand. This accounts for the good preservation of the sculptures, some of which had also been built into the walls of a Byzantine village.

The subject matter of the architectural sculpture of a Greek temple is not always readily related to the deity and cult. In the east pediment, over the temple entrance, we see the god of the temple, Zeus, presiding over the ceremonies before the chariot race between King Oinomaos of Pisa (who stands at one side with his wife Sterope) and the younger Pelops (who stands at the other with

the king's daughter Hippodameia, whom he will win). Their chariots, attendants, and seers wait. It was said in Antiquity that Pelops' success was achieved by bribing the kings charioteer, but an alternative version simply gave Pelops divine horses. The subject reflected on both the importance of chariot races at Olympia and on Pisa's recent removal from control of the Games by the Eleans. The west pediment shows the young god Apollo, Zeus' son, as arbiter in the drunken brawl between centaurs and the Lapiths, whose king Pirithoos' wedding feast had been broken up by their animal behavior. The theme was popular in Greek art and, in the 5th century, might be taken symbolically as a demonstration of Greek superiority over the uncivilized and barbarian—a reflection on the role of the northern Greeks (the home of the centaurs) in the recent invasions of the

Above On the west pediment: *left* a Centaur, *center* a Lapith boy

▲ On the west pediment: the head of Apollo

Persians in Greece which had been repelled. For a different deity to the occupant of the temple to be honored in the secondary pediment is not without parallel.

The composition of the east pediment is static and strictly symmetrical, dominated by the figure of Zeus, who is slightly taller than the protagonists in the race. The effect is dignified and has an architectonic quality well suited to the decoration of the principal gable of the temple and impressive even from a distance—remember that the floor of the pediment was 52 ft (16 m) above the ground level before the temple. By contrast, the west

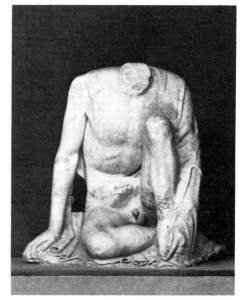

◄ A Lapith girl on the
west pediment

▲ The seated boy on the
east pediment

▼ The old seer on the
east pediment

pediment presents groups of two and three
struggling figures, some half animal. Although the groups are distinct and the general composition symmetrical, the overall impression is one of restless movement; the
designer must have been more concerned to
demonstrate the confusion of the fight and its
narrative detail.

There is an overall unity of style which
indicates the hand of a master designer who
provided models for his studio to execute.
The figures offer our best examples of the
early Classical or Severe style. The standing
males adopt the new, relaxed pose with the
weight of the body shifted on to one leg and
the resultant effect on posture properly observed. The women wear the heavy *peplos*
(dress) whose austere lines contrast so
strongly with the fuss of pattern and pleats
favored by the sculptors of Archaic Greece.
Command of anatomy is advanced but not as

yet complete, and the pattern of the composition determines pose as much as considerations of naturalism. The dress too is still
conceived as pattern and can in places be
shown falling illogically over the limbs of
figures which, though executed in the round,
were designed to be seen from the front only.
There are, however, surprisingly advanced
examples of accurate observation of both
expression and anatomy in a period of Greek
art in which such naturalism had been barely
tried. The head of the old seer clearly shows
his dismay and foreknowledge of his patron's
doom, and his body is a masterly study of
slack senility. Contrast the slight modeling of
the boy and his unaffected posture, playing
with his toes while he waits for the action.
There is contrast too in the physique of the
mother and daughter in the east pediment,
and in the soft form, almost puppy fat, of one
of the Lapith girls. Stronger emotions are

variously portrayed in the grimacing centaurs, stubborn resistance in a Lapith, Olympian dignity in the Apollo. This new freedom
of sculptural expression is barely caught
again in the succeeding idealizing styles
which we judge best in Classical Athens on
the Parthenon, but the genius of the Olympia
Master reawakens to inform the development of later classical sculpture in the 4th
century.

JOHN BOARDMAN

Further reading. Ashmole B. and Yalouris N. *Olympia*, London (1967).

Three goddesses from the east pediment of the Parthenon; height of figure on the left 134cm (53in); c449–432 BC. British Museum, London

contrasts between the folds of fine material and the flesh that is allowed to show through. The fine style became very popular in the late 5th century: for example, the frieze of the Temple of Apollo at Bassae (c425–420 BC; British Museum, London), the Nike by Paeonius in Olympia (c420–410 BC), and the parapets of the Temple of Athena Nike at Athens (c410 BC). By then technical confidence was such that even in the plain style folds were carved very deep, allowing a double contrast with smooth material and with the flesh: for example, the curious Caryatids from the Erechtheum on the Athenian Acropolis (c420–413 BC; Acropolis Museum, Athens, and British Museum, London).

Other buildings with sculptural decoration were erected in Athens during this half-century, mostly as part of the Periclean program (for example the Hephaisteion, c450–440), and elsewhere in Greece (for example the Temple of Nemesis at Rhamnus in Attica, c436–421 BC, and the new Heraion near Argos, started in 423 BC) and the Greek world (for example the Heroön at Gjolbaschi, c420–410 BC, and the Nereid Monument at Xanthos, c400 BC, both in Asia Minor).

Sculptured gravestones reappeared in Attica—people could now afford them again, and after the enormous building program sculptors were available. The artistic standard was often exceptionally high, and many reflect the style of the Parthenon very closely. The slabs are squatter than those of the Archaic period, admitting more figures, but except where the inscription remains, as on the stela of Hegeso from the Dipylon cemetery (c400 BC; National Museum, Athens) it is often difficult to distinguish the dead person.

The development of votive and record reliefs ran parallel

Left: The Stela of Hegeso; height 149cm (59in); c400 BC. National Museum, Athens

with the gravestones (like, for example, the one showing Demeter, Persephone, and Triptolemos from Eleusis, *c*440 BC, National Museum, Athens), and provides important dating evidence for stylistic changes. These traditions of relief-carving also continued in other parts of the Greek world, not only the Islands, Ionia, and Magna Graecia but regions like northern Greece and Boeotia that had no major sculptural traditions of their own. However, Athens now became the chief center, having herself apparently relied heavily on Island carvers at the time of Pericles' revival after 450 BC.

However, the Peloponnese, particularly Argos, maintained its own tradition, with broader, rather heavier figures. Its best-known exponent was Phidias' contemporary Polycleitos. His style is best deduced from copies of his *Diadoumenos* (*c*440–430 BC) and the *Doryphoros* (*c*450–440 BC) which illustrated his lost book on ideal human proportion, the *Canon*. In place of the surface patterns of archaic sculpture he apparently aimed at a full depth and full naturalism of both individual parts and the whole body. Thanks partly to his interest in *chiasmus* (the tension and corresponding relaxation of limbs and muscles on opposite parts of the body) he achieved a harmonious design which, unlike the single-aspect compositions of the Transitional sculptors, was satisfying when seen from any angle.

Polycleitos' statues have, like Pheidias', a certain austerity that recalls the previous generation. We know Polycleitos had followers, but only their names survive, such as Patrocles, Naucydes, Daedalus, and the younger Polycleitos. However, just as the Phidian tradition relaxed with the developing drapery styles and more sensual forms, so these men evidently softened the square, heavy-muscled Polycleitan types into more slender and flowing figures like the bronze *Idolino* (Museo Archeologico, Florence), a Roman copy of a late-5th-century original which for once copies the material in which most Polycleitan statues were made (though like most Greek sculptors he worked in stone, wood and fine metal and ivory too).

Among Pheidias' pupils a few names stand out: Alcamenes, who seems to have inherited the majesty of his teacher's style; Agoracritus from Paros, a fragment of whose *Nemesis* made for the Rhamnus temple survives in the British Museum, London; and Callimachus, whose reputation for too finicky attention to detail accords well with the final stages of the transparent drapery style at the very end of the 5th century.

The sculptors of the early 4th century continued the traditions of the later 5th, with balanced poses, transparent or heavy drapery, and serene, rather remote expressions—for instance, the sculptures from the temple of Asclepius at Epidaurus, ascribed to Hectoridas, Timotheos, and Thrasymedes (*c*400–380 BC; now National Museum, Athens) are younger brothers of those on the parapet of the Athena Nike temple.

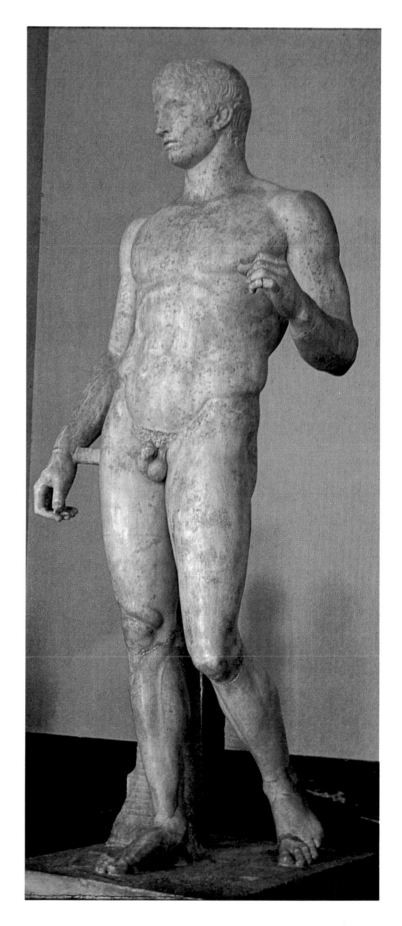

A Roman marble copy of Polycleitos' bronze spear-carrier (Doryphoros); height 199cm (78in). Museo Archeologico Nazionale, Naples

Hermes and the child Dionysos, by Praxiteles; height 215cm (85in). Archaeological Museum, Olympia

Within 20 years a humanizing, more personal element appeared. Poses became more flowing, faces softer and more emotional; technical dexterity was less flamboyantly and more subtly expressed. Cephisodotus' *Peace holding the infant Wealth* illustrates this well (best copy in the Glyptothek, Munich). Though at first sight its design resembles Phidian statues, its spirit is utterly different. There is a tenderness and an intimacy between mother and child that is alien to the 5th century; the spectator is now excluded because they are absorbed in each other, no longer because of any remote serenity. It is a statue that points the way sculpture would go. The massive drapery with its deep-cut folds recalls the Erechtheum Caryatids, but there is a new feeling for texture, for the intervening layers of cloth as well as for the flesh under them.

The first half of the 4th century was another period of

Left: A copy of Peace holding the infant Wealth, by Cephisodotus; height 199cm (78in). Glyptothek, Munich

restless transition, between the confident, introspective High Classical and the baroque freedom of the Hellenistic. The next step is seen in the work of men like Praxiteles (fl. c370–330 BC), Cephisodotus' son (?) and artistic heir. He was a prolific and influential sculptor, and many Roman copies have been linked with him. The descent of his *Hermes* at Olympia from the *Peace* is clear, but the pose is more sinuous and relaxed, the relationship between the two figures less remote and more subtly shown, and the features more limpidly modeled. At last the sculptor seems aware of the flesh and bones beneath the skin. Praxiteles' most influential statue, the *Aphrodite of Cnidus* (known only in copies), was shown naked (a 4th-century innovation). She was set up to be visible from all sides—much attention was now being devoted to the third dimension, and compositions encouraged the spectator to move round the statue, giving a feeling of restlessness, particularly in scenes of violent emotion.

The trend towards greater depth is also evident in the Athenian gravestones, whose volume of production now reached its height. The basic design remained the same, but everything was underlined, as it were: figures were carved almost in the round, domestic scenes were virtually heroized, and a Hellenistic emotionalism began to appear. It was achieved by the disposition of the figures, and by such traits as making their eyes deep-set and thoughtful.

This particular mannerism first appeared on the sculptures of the Temple of Athena Alea at Tegea (c370–350 BC; National Museum, Athens), where it has been attributed (on slender evidence) to Praxiteles' contemporary Scopas of Paros. It became fairly general, even on otherwise placid figures like the seated Demeter of Cnidus (c350 BC; British Museum, London). The tendency towards depicting emotion encouraged individual portraiture in the 4th century, though the figures, often great men of the past, were still idealized conceptions.

Many of the trends of the earlier 4th century were only fully realized in the Hellenistic period: the Praxitelean soft modeling bore fruit in the "Alexandrian" style; Praxiteles' figures were made to a new set of proportions which were fully worked out by his slightly younger contemporary Lysippos; the emotionalism linked with Scopas found full expression in the gravestones, portraits, and action scenes of the late 4th and following centuries.

Terracottas. The term 'minor art' is perhaps applied more aptly to terracotta figures than to any other Greek art form, for here sculpture is often brought down to a domestic level. Large figures in clay became rare after the early 5th century, though they had a longer life—especially as acroteria (on the corners of temple roofs) and in similar architectural contexts—in places like Cyprus, Sicily, and Italy, where good marble was uncommon. One of the most imposing is the half-life-size Zeus and Ganymede at Olympia, which still has many late Archaic features, such as the smile and general exuberance, but which as a composition fits better with the

An Athenian marble grave-stela: a young man with his father, a dog, and a child; height 168cm (66in). National Museum, Athens

Transitional marbles and bronzes.

This time-lag was even more marked in figurines. The years c480–475 were much less revolutionary for coroplasts (modelers) than sculptors. The first quarter-century had seen a general improvement in terracotta manufacture in mainland Greece, apparently after the East Greek supply dried up following the Ionian Revolt (499 BC). Most terracottas were now mold-made and hollow, with handmade backs, though some solid handmade types persisted, for instance at Corinth. The change to early Classical came gradually, but by 450 BC it was most noticeable in the simplification of drapery styles. For example, the "standing woman" figures from Attica can be divided into a "first type" (c475–450 BC), where the pose and the stylized folds are typically late Archaic, but otherwise the strong horizontal-vertical accent of the *peplos* (not the late Archaic *chiton*) is a concession to Classical austerity, and a "second type" (from c450 to at least 400 BC), which carries this to its logical conclusion—the hands at her sides emphasize the horizontal-vertical accent, and the whole recalls the style of the Olympia sculptures.

By the later 5th century the influence of the Parthenon could be seen in showy drapery effects. The large number of figurines from the earlier 4th century tend to reflect Praxitelean forms, reusing traditional types while generally raising standards, especially in Attica. Despite these overall trends and the obvious commercial intercourse of the Classical Greek world, local peculiarities and styles persisted in terracottas as in virtually no other form of Greek art. Athens was an important center, but so were Boeotia and Corinth, Rhodes and Halicarnassus, and in the West, Sicily, Locri, Taras (Taranto)—almost every city seems to have harbored some production of its own.

The general conservatism is to be explained by the rather domestic purposes for which terracottas were made: as votive offerings, as decorations for the home, and as toys. The votives represented the deity or the worshiper, and much the most common type in the 5th century was still the standing or seated female figure, frequently holding an offering or attribute. Hollow masks and busts have also been found, especially from Locri and Taranto. In vase-paintings they are shown hanging on walls, presumably to seek divine protection. Those classified as toys include animals and jointed dolls, but it can be difficult to draw the line: many figurines may simply have been household ornaments. Alongside these, more original studies from mythology and daily life began to appear, and by the late 5th and the 4th centuries the range include many subjects which, paradoxically, large-scale sculpture ignored until the Hellenistic period, such as actors (especially comic actors), and genre figures of dancers and women gossiping or about their business—types that look forward to the Tanagra and Myrina figures of the Hellenistic period.

A distinctive type of votive terracotta are the relief plaques made at Locri in southern Italy between c480 and 450 BC. Nearly all illustrate scenes from the story of Persephone, Queen of the Underworld, and were presumably intended as offerings to her. As is to be expected, there is still an Archaic flavor though Classical elements appear. A much duller 4th-century series from Taranto is mainly concerned with the heroized dead. The relief tradition of Melos (c465–435 BC) is more interesting, including scenes of mythology and daily life: these reliefs were high-fired to resist wear, and were presumably intended to decorate chests and other furniture, or to be hung up in houses. Later, terracotta—often gilded as well as painted—was used for other forms of appliqué work for furniture too, as well as for buttons and medallions.

In the 5th and 4th centuries coroplasts occasionally worked for Athenian and South Italian vase-painters to make "plastic", that is, modeled vases, generally cups or *rhyta* in the form of animal or human heads recalling a metal prototype, but sometimes also more complicated groups. Terrracotta was often used as a substitute for more precious substances, particularly metal, and thus provides important archaeological source-material for the life-style of less wealthy Greeks. But

here again the very bright colors—reds and pinks, blues, yellows, whites, and gold—which survive on many clay figures remind us of how they were intended to look.

Bronzes. Bronze statues were made throughout the Classical period. Larger works were hollow-cast by the *cire perdue* process, their eyes added in glass and eyelashes in silver. The Delphi Charioteer is an outstanding example from the beginning of the period (Delphi Museum), while the Athena excavated in the Piraeus in 1959, and the two youths from the sea off Anticythera and Marathon show the softening that was typical by the third quarter of the 4th century (National Museum, Athens). More expensive small-scale work was made of ivory (now mostly lost) or bronze, generally solid-cast but following the conventions of major sculpture. Such works often give the impression of being large statues reproduced at domestic scale simply to provide human pleasure.

Figurines were also used as accessories on the rims and handles of bronze vessels, particularly *kraters, hydriae*, and *oinochoae* (mixing-bowls and jugs), and large basins. The tradition had continued from the late Archaic period, but the range of subjects was now more limited. In the 4th century genre scenes became more popular. For decorating belts, helmets, cuirasses, and similar items cast reliefs were used, often depicting mythological figures; details were incised, and sometimes inlays of precious metals added. When new these bronzes had a warm golden tone against which incision would stand out darkly—quite unlike the patinated or over-restored articles in many museums.

Among the most common decorated bronzes were mirrors, of several distinct types. The late Archaic model continued until *c*450 BC. Here the handle was formed by a figure (generally female) cast in the round and usually standing on a support. Their rather elaborate and fussy details contrast with modern notions of "Classical simplicity", and are perhaps survivals of late Archaic mannerism. Around 450 BC a new type appeared, without a handle but with a hinged cover, normally ornamented in repoussé relief with a female head, mythological scene, or palmette. The underside of the cover was often incised with a similar scene, of the kind thought appropriate for women's rooms; an important class has only this incised decoration. The simplest type had a plain handle and simple palmette decoration.

Gold and silver plate and jewelry. After the Persian Wars the production of gold- and silverware increased considerably, though these metals were not used for mirrors or small toilet-vases. Until *c*450 BC the most popular shapes were the traditional ritual vessels, such as the *phiale mesomphalos*, a shallow libation-dish with a boss let into the center of the base for the fingers. Before the end of the 5th century almost all plate in Greece was dedicated in sanctuaries and temple treasuries, where it has not survived, either because it was regarded as bullion or else because it disappeared with pagan religion. Thus most of what remains comes from the graves of barbarian chieftains in the surrounding lands, most notably the Thracians in Bulgaria and the Scythians in south Russia and the Crimea. It is clear that these people appreciated Greek silver and gold from the quantities that have been found there; in the late 5th and 4th centuries Greco-Scythian metalwork was produced for their benefit, and imitated locally.

From *c*450 BC the repertoire of shapes expanded under Achaemenid influence to include, for instance, the animal-head *rhyton*, though the *phiale* always retained its popularity. Also *c*450 engraved silver vessels came into vogue, the expensive counterparts of red-figure vases. Towards the end of the century gold- and silverware became more common in private houses, and the simpler shapes are often reflected on a humbler scale in the plain black-glazed pottery of Athens. The great revival of repoussé work around this time apparently killed the engraving technique, and the 4th century saw some superbly elaborate designs incorporating vegetable and floral patterns, and the repeated figures or heads of animals, humans, and monsters.

The jeweler's art was developed fully during the Classical period, and the techniques of filigree and granulation were mastered. Our chief sources are again on the fringes of the Greek world. Among the most popular items were earrings in great variety, wreaths, necklaces—many with pendants—and bracelets, small embossed plaques to be attached to drapery, and rings.

Gems and finger-rings. Plain rings existed at all times, but the Classical period was marked by the growing popularity of rings with metal or inset stone bezels, similar to the modern signet ring. Some fine examples are known, particularly from the 4th century: for example, Cassandra on a gold ring (Metropolitan Museum, New York). They served the same function as the Archaic type with a carved gem set on a swivel, which continued to be the most common form, even though relatively speaking fewer have survived. They were still the preserve of the rich but during the 5th and 4th centuries the wearing and using of seals spread to the whole Greek world. The find-spots range from Italy and Sicily to the Persian Empire and south Russia. More Classical than Archaic gems have been found in controlled excavations, but because of their long life as heirlooms this helps little in dating, and although gem-engraving spread to new centers (probably including southern Italy) their styles hardly differed, with the exception of the Greco-Persian stones and those carved by the Etruscans for their own use. Artists' signatures were fewer, but more significant, for example Sosias (*fl.* 450–420), Onatas (*fl.* 1st half of 4th century), and Athenades (*fl.* 425–400), but the outstanding figure is Dexamenos of Chios, who signed four scaraboids datable to the third quarter of the 5th century—a fine sensitive "portrait", elegant water-birds, and a woman at her toilet.

Left: A hollow-cast bronze statuette of a naked girl; height 25cm (10in); c430–400 BC. Glyptothek, Munich

Engraved Gems and Classical Coins

▲ A lion and a stag. Rock crystal scaraboid; height 2cm ($\frac{4}{5}$in); c450 BC. British Museum, London

▼ A satyr toiling under the weight of a wineskin. Carnelian scaraboid; height 1.7cm ($\frac{3}{4}$in); c480 BC. British Museum, London

A characteristic of Classical Greek art is its unity of style regardless of scale and material. In the miniaturist arts of the engraving of gems and of coin dies, the monumental quality of the major works of sculpture is somehow miraculously caught. The two genres are related. Coin-dies are of metal, the device cut in intaglio to strike the coins which, in their varying states of wear or preservation, are our only evidence for the original work. The gems were cut like the dies, intaglio in the stone, but in this case we have the originals, not the impressions. Both arts were relatively new to Greece since, before the 6th century BC, the Greek world had known no coins, and its artists had forgotten the arts of cutting hard stones for gems since the Bronze Age.

Gemstones were not, in the Classical period, prized for their intrinsic value or even, so far as we can judge, for their color, but as a medium for intaglio engraving which enabled them to be used for sealing, identification, sometimes simply for decoration. The stones are generally quartzes—carnelian, chalcedony, jaspers—semiprecious to us but rarer in Antiquity. The earlier engraved gems had been small and usually of the scarab shape, about 6/10th in (15 mm) long, but in the 5th and 4th centuries BC they are larger, about 1 in (25 mm) long, and simpler in shape (scaraboid), designed to be set in pendants rather than on finger-rings. With the 4th century similar stones are more often set immobile in rings in the manner familiar to us today. The cutting was done without the aid of a magnifying lens, probably on a fixed lathe worked by a bow drill, and despite the difficulty of the technique extreme finesse of detail was achieved. We know that major artists and sculptors also cut gems (compare the achievements of Cellini much later) and in some of these miniature masterpieces we surely have originals from masters whose larger works we can know only from copies of later periods.

The range of subjects for the stones is restricted only by their size and, naturally, multi-figure myth scenes are usually avoided. Head studies are less common than we might expect, though more frequent towards the end of the Classical period when portraiture begins to be developed. One carnelian scaraboid has the old, Archaic subject of a satyr toiling under the weight of a full wineskin, and an agate "sliced barrel" shows an unusual study of the statue of a boy boxer, almost certainly the work of the master Dexamenos (unfortunately there are few signatures on gems). The animal studies are among the most ambitious and successful in Greek art and, from the later 5th century, there are more studies of women and Aphrodites. The half-naked Victory (Nike) building a trophy is among the finest of all ancient gems; it must be from the hand of a great artist whose name survives among the many recorded by later writers but is unretrievable because his signed and identifiable work eludes us.

▼ A Victory erecting a trophy. Chalcedony scaraboid; height 3.5cm ($1\frac{3}{8}$in); c350 BC. British Museum, London

Above left A woman playing a harp. Rock crystal scaraboid; height 3.5cm ($1\frac{2}{3}$in); c420 BC. British Museum, London

◄ A boy boxer. Agate sliced barrel; height 2.5cm (1in); c450 BC. British Museum, London

▼ A head of Helios (the Sun) on a coin from Camirus (Rhodes); diameter 2.5cm (1in); c375–350 BC

◄ Eagles with a hare and a locust from Acragas, Sicily; diameter 4cm (1½in); c412 BC

▼ Herakles and the lion, from Heraclea in southern Italy; diameter 2.5cm (1in); c350–330 BC

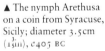

◄ A satyr on a coin from Naxos, Sicily; diameter 2.5cm (1in); c460 BC.

▲ The nymph Arethusa on a coin from Syracuse, Sicily; diameter 3.5cm (1⅜in), c405 BC

Most Classical Greek coins were struck in silver: gold or electrum coins are rare and confined to special mints or occasions, and bronze coins were only beginning to be used for smaller denominations. Coins at first served only local needs but were soon carried further, virtually as bullion, for interstate trade (a bewildering variety of weight standards was employed). They are thicker than modern coins, the devices often rendered in high relief—often too high to ensure the survival of higher areas of the design after handling, which is why frontal heads or similar ambitious subjects were rarely attempted. There was a natural tendency for the larger mints to be conservative in their choice of devices and it was often the less prominent

states that issued the greater variety of devices and even with artistically superior designs. But a traditional device can be reinterpreted in successive issues, and at Syracuse, where the coins carry the head of the nymph Arethusa, first-rate artists designed a series of masterly dies, some of which they signed (and signatures are as rare on coins as on gems). One of them is by Kimon. The Greek colonies of south Italy and Sicily produced some of the finest Classical coins. One coin of c460 BC still retains something of the Archaic in its bold anatomical study of the squatting satyr. Animal subjects are as common as they are on gems and there are rather more mythological figures or even action scenes since the need may have been felt to allude to

local cults. Although the coins were mass-produced it is only the accidents of wear and burial that stand between us and a full appreciation of the quality of the original die. The cutting on the metal die is generally less meticulous than in the stone gem-intaglio but comparable considerations of design apply for the oval and the circular fields, and probably the same artists were employed.

JOHN BOARDMAN

Further reading. Boardman, J. Greek Gems and Finger Rings, London (1970). Kraay, C.M. and Hirmer, M. Greek Coins, London (1966).

A scaraboid gem by Dexamenos of Chios; width 1.7cm (⁶⁄₁₀in).
Museum of Fine Arts, Boston

The scarab shape lost ground to the simplified and generally larger scaraboid. Other shapes included lions, sliced cylinders and barrels, and tabloids. The most popular stone was chalcedony, followed by carnelian; jasper, agate, rock crystal, and glass were also used. Subjects were more limited than in the Archaic period: myths were rarer, but domestic scenes and naturalistic studies of animals and even insects were in demand. The old encircling border lost favor, sometimes being replaced by a groundline, but the tendency was towards spaciousness, particularly among the Ionians.

The one "regional" style that is readily distinguishable is the Greco-Persian, made in the Persian Empire for about 200 years from the late Archaic period. The exact circumstances in which this very large and widespread group of pieces were carved are still debated, but it seems highly probable that at first and in the western empire Ionian Greek engravers were involved. The formal Persian style was broken down by a new and un-Oriental intimacy and informality, as typically Greek animals and domestic scenes were introduced and groups reduced to single figures without extraneous ornament. However, Greco-Persian gems differed from purely Greek ones in subject matter (showing, for example, Persians, such animals as the antelope and bear, and animals at "flying gallop") and,

most noticeably, in technique, because where the Greeks concealed their technique these engravers even exploited the marks of cutting and drilling. Eastern shapes like the prismatic and conoid stamp seals survived, but high-domed Ionian scaraboids, especially of blue chalcedony, became the most popular form.

In the Archaic period, artistic influence had passed from east to west: Greco-Persian gems show a reversal of direction. An interesting instance is the animal fight, an old eastern motif now reintroduced in the Greek manner; while the fact that a number of Greco-Persian stones have apparently been found in Sparta tallies with the historical picture of close Spartan contact with Persia in the late 5th and 4th centuries.

Coins. It is not surprising that the same artists sometimes carved both coin-dies and gems. Stylistic links between them are often difficult to deduce, but occasionally artists signed both forms, as in the case of Phrygillos (one gem, and coin-dies for Syracuse, Thurii, and Terina) which also demonstrates how widely engravers traveled. The broad stylistic divisions of Ionia, mainland Greece, and the West persisted, but while the major commercial states like Athens and Corinth only changed their coin-types slowly because familiar coins encouraged confidence in trade, the cities of north and east Greece and in particular southern Italy and Sicily issued series of different and often flamboyant devices. Most cities identified their coins with inscriptions as well as their own deity and symbol: for example the beautiful dekadrachm of Syracuse, 405 BC, signed by Cimon, which carries the Syracusan dolphin and nymph Arethusa, and on the reverse a

The dekadrachm of Syracuse by Cimon. British Museum, London

chariot. The Arethusa series illustrates changes of hair and jewelry styles throughout the 5th century, and demonstrates, in the three-quarter view of the chariot and in the sensuous profile head, how well coin-engravers kept pace with contemporary developments in painting and sculpture. This issue is now connected with the Syracusan victory over Carthage, but such historical cross-references are rare.

Architecture. The architectural traditions of the Archaic period were continued in the Classical, with a general trend towards greater elegance and refinement of details, such as the curve of the stylobate and of the columns (entasis). The Greek temple plan allowed great scope for variety of dimension and spatial organization, as study of any of the numerous temples erected during the 5th and 4th centuries shows, from large complex Doric buildings like the Parthenon (447–438 BC) to small, elegant Ionic structures such as the Temple of Athena Nike (427–424 BC), both on the Athenian Acropolis. The Doric order reached its climax in the Parthenon, while some grandiose Ionic temples were erected in Asia Minor in the later 4th century, such as those of Artemis at Ephesus (c355–330 BC) and Sardis (c350–300 BC). The ornate Corinthian capital of acanthus leaves first appeared on the Temple of Apollo at Bassae (after 430 BC), and was occasionally used thereafter (for example at Tegea, c370–350 BC). It only became popular in Hellenistic and Roman times.

Marble was the normal material in mainland and east Greece, but in Italy, Sicily, and occasionally on the mainland, limestone covered with stucco was used. Details such as capitals were colored, and temples were generally decorated with sculptures, as in the Archaic period.

Similar decoration could be applied to other public buildings, such as monumental altars, treasuries, and *tholoi* (circular buildings), while on the fringes of the Greek world there were elaborate tomb structures. Theaters were now built of stone for the first time. Other monumental buildings included *odeia* (music-halls), *stoai* (colonnades), council buildings, fountains, and even hotels. Private houses remained simple, but from an early date the Greeks (especially the Ionian colonists) had been interested in town-planning—Aristotle credits Hippodamus of Miletus, planner of the Piraeus c450 BC, with the invention of the grid-plan.

Painting and mosaics. With the exception of a few painted tombstones, often now reduced to mere sketch-lines, virtually no free painting from before 350 BC survives, but it is clear from its influence on vase-painting (especially white-ground vases) and mosaics, and on copies made for Roman taste (and thus unreliable as sources), and from the enthusiasm of writers of the Roman period such as Pausanias, Lucian, and the elder Pliny, that the importance of free painting in the Classical period was out of all proportion to the meager archaeological record: most paintings were murals, done on wooden panels or sometimes plaster, and have been lost with the buildings they adorned.

Like the sculptors (but unlike, for instance, vase-painters) free painters were held in high esteem, and the names of influential artists survive. Polygnotus of Thasos (fl. c475–447 BC) was regarded as the "inventor" of painting. He decorated several buildings at Athens, sometimes collaborating with the Athenian Mikon, but his most famous works were *Troy Taken* and *The Underworld* in the *lesche* (clubhouse) of the Cnidians at Delphi. His characters were noble, showing emotion on their faces, in their pose and in their gesture. He was also a skillful delineator of character. This implies a great change from the action scenes of the Archaic period, set on the

surface of the picture and not needing this third dimension to make them interesting. Not surprisingly, portraiture in sculpture now emerged, at a time when vases also briefly displayed an interest in the old, ugly, or alien personage.

The preoccupation of early Classical painters with spatial construction apparently led Agatharchos of Samos to attempt perspective representation in the second half of the 5th century. Vitruvius' account of this is confused, and vase-paintings shed little light on contemporary developments since vase-painters were always more concerned with the surface of the pots. Agatharchos probably established the principle of the vanishing point, but rather than organizing the whole picture around a single one, he allowed different vanishing points for each object or area.

In the late 5th century painters returned to the problem of shading. The Athenian Apollodorus (fl. c430–400 BC) was nicknamed "the shadow painter" because he "mimicked form through shading and color" (Hesychius). He was probably the first to use mixed colors—Polygnotus' palette had consisted only of black, white, red, and brown—and so gave his figures "the appearance of reality". Of his younger contemporaries Zeuxis of Heraclea (fl. c430–395 BC) took these discoveries further, while Parrhasios of Ephesus (fl. late 5th century) produced his effects of volume by subtlety of line; his figures were praised for their inner life and passive suffering, in the tradition of Polygnotus.

The 4th-century artists, men like Pausias of Sicyon (who invented the encaustic technique; fl. mid 4th century) and Nikias of Athens (fl. c340–300 BC) continued this pursuit of realism into the Hellenistic period. The *trompe l'oeil* effects they desired are known to us only from anecdotes and Roman derivatives like the "unswept floor" at Pompeii. It was achieved by bold foreshortening and partial perspective, but though the figures were shaded to stand out from the background, it was not until the Renaissance that they were shown as lit from a single source. Classical paintings had no spatial unity.

Mosaics of the late 5th and the 4th centuries are found in considerable numbers in houses at Olynthus and in places like Olympia and Alexandria, and in Macedonia. They were made with natural pebbles, black, white, and multicolored. The cube technique (and with it shading) was only introduced after Alexander's conquests, and thus Classical mosaics have a stark linear effect akin to vase-painting. The subjects are those of the other arts.

Vase-painting. The evacuation and Persian sack of Athens in 480 BC had remarkably little effect on potters and vase-painters, and early Classical vases show an unbroken continuation of the trends of the late Archaic, having undoubtedly been produced by the same artists.

The black-figure technique, used by hack workshops until c450 BC, was employed for the Panathenaic prize-*amphorae* into the 2nd century, surviving all other painted wares. For a time in the 4th century these vases carried the archon's (magistrate's) names and so provide important absolute dating evidence.

In the red-figure technique there were technical advances; for example, the profile eye was now shown correctly, and the fussy, precise zigzag pleats and hems of Archaic drapery yielded to a freer rendering of interrupted lines and hooks. The Archaic continuity of line was breaking up; under the influence of free painting the use of dilute glaze for details increased and in the 4th century the relief line was abandoned.

Red-figure was essentially an Archaic technique in which the figures stood out as surface designs against an unmodulated background. The new interests demanded the sort of spatial concepts being evolved by Polygnotus and Mikon. Some vase-painters reacted with a spirit of experimentation, exemplified by daring foreshortening and ambitious composition, but after c450 BC they could no longer compete, and vase-painting declined to the position of a minor art. The great painters made their advances in free painting, to which the vase-painters approached most closely with the white-ground technique.

In the early Free style (c475–450 BC) several new trends can be distinguished. The Mannerists harked back to the preceding decades, combining Archaic conventions with new freer renderings. Their leader, the Pan Painter, "is that rare thing, a backward-looking genius", but his followers lacked his inspiration. In contrast stood the large vases with spacious compositions on several levels that reflected Polygnotan murals, with statuesque figures and contorted poses recalling contemporary Transitional sculpture. Prominent artists were the Altamura Painter and the Niobid Painter. Another group preferred quieter, more delicate designs that looked forward to the classicism that followed, men like the Villa Giulia Painter and his pupil the Chicago Painter, the Penthesilea Painter (a more ambitious man who could overreach himself under free painting influence, as on his namepiece in Munich (Antikensammlung) and the Pistoxenos Painter, whose cup in London (British Museum) showing Aphrodite riding on a goose perhaps embodies this quiet ideal. This was painted in the white-ground technique, used in late black-figure but exploited more fully in the 5th century. It recalls closely the white plaster of wall-paintings. At first dilute glaze was used for outlines, and the use of color masses—reds, browns, greens, and blues—restricted. But this attempt to emulate free painting was unsuccessful—even though after 450 the best vase-painting was in the white-ground technique—partly because the vase-painters were too deeply entrenched in the "silhouette" principle, and partly because the result was not durable. White-ground therefore remained a sideline of red-figure, and in the second half of the 5th century was restricted to lekythoi (oil-flasks) intended as grave offerings.

The outstanding artist of the Free style (c450–420 BC) was the Achilles Painter, notable especially for his white lekythoi, on which more color and mat-painted outlines were now used. His style has a quiet Periclean grandeur, into which his pupil the Phiale Painter introduced a domestic liveliness. The

Aphrodite on her goose: a cup by the Pistoxenos Painter; diameter 24cm (9in); c470 BC. British Museum, London

A white-ground lekythos of Group R; height 48cm (19in).

Eretria Painter exemplifies a tradition of fine draftsmanship, continued by the Meidias Painter whose clinging draperies recall later 5th-century sculptures. The Kleophon Painter and his less solemn pupil, the Dinos Painter, illustrate the later Polygnotan tradition on vases: round fleshy forms, loose draperies, and a good spatial and emotional sense. The end of the century saw the latest white-ground *lekythos* workshops (the Woman Painter, Group R, the Reed Painter, etc): solemn, brooding figures, reflecting the bitter disillusion of the final humiliating years of the Peloponnesian War.

Two distinct trends can be detected in the 4th-century red-figure: the Ornate style, growing from the florid traditions of artists like the Meidias Painter, which favored thick lines and heavily patterned drapery (presumably reflecting current dress fashions) with copious added white and yellow. Three-quarter views were much used and tiered compositions were again

A detail from the name-vase of the Darius Painter; c340–330 BC. Museo Archeologico Nazionale, Naples

Pelike by the Marsyas Painter: Peleus wrestles with Thetis; height 42cm (17in). British Museum, London

popular with men like the Talos, Pronomos, and Suessula Painters. During the century more added color, gilding, and even relief details were used, until finally whole figures and scenes were applied to the surface in relief, sometimes completely in the round. In opposition to this last attempt to compete with free-painting stood the Jena Painter and other exponents of the Plain style, following in the Dinos Painter's tradition. At their best they were skilled and restrained draftsmen who used little accessory color, and reverted to profile figures emphasizing the surface of the pot.

From c350 BC a few artists managed to combine the best of both traditions in the "Kerch" style. The *pelike* by the Marsyas Painter (British Museum, London), illustrates this well: restrained but rather sketchy drawing of details and folds; deliberate use of white to emphasize prominent figures; a tiered, rather emotional composition, but one where the turning figures (especially the nymph on the right) subtly underline the form of the vase without competing against it. None of these outlived the decade 330–320 BC, leaving the field in Athens open to plain "black-glazed" ware and to "West Slope" vases. Presumably the best painters were working elsewhere, and tastes in tableware had changed.

Outside Athens there was little painted pottery, though the Corinthians and Boeotians imitated Attic wares. The latter possessed a strong black-figure tradition which continued into the 4th century, to culminate in a lively, crude series of parody vases from the Cabirion sanctuary near Thebes.

The only fabric to rival Attic was South Italian, produced from c440 BC onwards and throughout the 4th century to satisfy the needs of the Greek colonists in the West. South Italian glaze tended to be less lustrous than Attic and the vase shapes more varied, if less precise. Particular interest lies in their depiction of rare myths and scenes from lost plays.

Two styles springing from Attic traditions can be distinguished by 430–420 BC, one based on Taras (Taranto) which developed into Apulian, the other, leading to Lucanian, which is known by the recent discoveries of pottery-kilns to have been centered on Heraclea (Policoro). Apulian was the more monumental, with a fondness for large *kraters* (mixing-bowls) with elaborate compositions, often in several registers. But although individual groups and figures could show drama and emotion, the composition as a whole was often static and uninspired. Apulian did not lose contact with Attic, and never became provincial or barbarous like most other late Italiote. In the 5th century BC the leading artist was the Sisyphus Painter, who stood behind the two 4th-century traditions: the Plain style, typified by the Tarporley Painter and his school, which lasted until the end of the century, its quality declining as quantity increased; and the Ornate, whose apogee was in the school of the Darius Painter (c350–325 BC) who produced huge, elaborate vases with much added color, especially white, yellow, and red. Out of this the Gnathian style evolved

at Taranto from c360 onwards, using only added colors and no longer any reserved red-figure. Perhaps of all the vase-painting styles this one most reflected free painting developments.

Lucanian, the product of the prolific workshops of the Pisticci and Amykos Painters (*fl. c*440–410 BC), was generally monotonous. In the 4th century Lucanian was influenced by both Apulian trends, but because of its isolation even better artists like the "ornate" Primato Painter could lapse into provincialism, and late-century vases were so bad that it may be asked if Greeks painted them at all.

The three far-western styles only began in the 4th century. Paestan (at Paestum, Greek Posidonia) grew out of Lucanian from 375 onwards, and was dominated by Asteas' and Python's workshops, whose best pieces are the *phlyax* vases, in the middle and later century, showing burlesque stage scenes. Campanian and Sicilian were always closely related, though the former showed more variety. There were several Campanian workshops, of which the Cumae Group was the most important, using much added yellow and white, as well as green, red, and blue. Sicilian, descended from this, more original in choice of subject and, particularly late in the century, more lavish in its use of color on a pale clay, was very different from the restrained, stylish work of early Classical Athens.

Conclusion. The convenient date for the "end of Classical art" is the accession of Alexander of Macedon in 336 BC, but art did not actually come to an end then, as the ancients liked to think. Rather, it had reached that point of complete technical confidence which opened the way for the experiments in human proportion of sculptors like Lysippos, and the corresponding baroque fancies of Hellenistic sculpture and architecture. With the decline of the city-state, the individual became more important, as is reflected in the rise of real portraiture and the corollary, grotesques and caricatures, in a more "humanized" artistic context. In painting this is shown in the decline of vase-painting in the face of free painting which could render emotion and characterization, and on the other hand of the silver and gold vases, and jewelry, demanded by the ostentatious and wealthy, which the potters could only imitate on a more humble level in plain black-glazed wares. Typically, Greek art was ready to adapt and use the new concepts brought by Alexander's conquests.

A.J.N.W. PRAG

Bibliography. Arias, P.E., Hirmer, M., and Shefton, B.B. *A History of Greek Vase-Painting*, London (1968). Boardman, J. *Greek Art*, London (1973). Cook, R.M. *Greek Painted Pottery*, London (1972). Richter, G.M.A. *A Handbook of Greek Art*, Oxford (1974). Richter, G.M.A. *The Sculpture and Sculptors of the Greeks*, New Haven (1970). Robertson, C.M. *A History of Greek Art*, Cambridge (1975).

9
HELLENISTIC ART

A section of the east frieze from the Mausoleum at Halicarnassus: Amazons fight the Greeks
height 39cm (15in); c350 BC. British Museum, London (see page 150)

HELLENISTIC is a chronological term applied to art produced in the Greek world from the second half of the 4th century BC until probably the 1st century BC. To define it more precisely is extremely difficult, though the historical events that mark its beginning and end are plain enough.

In 336 BC Alexander the Great became King of Macedonia. In his brief, brilliant career, Greek influence was extended far beyond its previous limits, as far east as the Indus and from the Crimea to Egypt. Over this wide area trade and cultural interchange thrived, stimulating fresh artistic inspiration. When Alexander died in 323 BC he left no strong successor, so his Empire was torn apart by jealous rivalries. From c306 BC separate kingdoms grew up under new dynasties: the four main ones were Macedonia itself, under the Antigonids; Syria under the Seleucids; Egypt under the Ptolemies; and Pergamum under the Attalids. These new rulers had both resources and inclination to support the arts, and especially in the 3rd and 2nd centuries BC their courts commissioned craftsmen from far and wide.

Southern Italy was the other major center of Greek art during the period. Most Greek colonies in this area enjoyed some prosperity, especially Syracuse and Tarentum, despite the struggle with Carthage and the growing threat of Rome. Rome was the force that finally put an end to Hellenistic art, as Roman dominion extended to southern Italy in the late 3rd century and then to Greece and beyond. By 146 BC Greece was a Roman province. In 133 BC Attalus III, the last King of Pergamum, died, leaving his kingdom to Rome. Syria was taken over in the 1st century, and Egypt annexed after the death of Cleopatra VII in 31 BC. So perhaps 27 BC, the year in which the entire Greek world first became subject to the rule of imperial government centered on Rome, is the neatest date with which to conclude the period.

The Romans played a vitally important part in the dissemination and preservation of Hellenistic art. Their tastes developed from the stimulus of enormous quantities of booty, brought to Italy from the 3rd century BC onwards. They became great patrons and collectors of art, wealthy men building up extensive collections of Greek masterpieces—several temples in Rome even became art galleries. If original works were not available, copies were quite acceptable, as they had been earlier especially to the kings of Pergamum. Such copies—most mere hackwork, lacking subtlety and indeed accuracy—together with coins, scraps of comparative evidence, and a few inadequate descriptions in ancient authors, are often the only evidence we have for the work of major artists of the Hellenistic period. Most originals are in the minor arts, and are often hard to date.

Sculpture. As early as 350 BC distinctively new ideas can be detected in the tomb built for Mausolus, ruler of Caria, at Halicarnassus, the original Mausoleum. This flamboyant building, a great pyramid-like structure, was lavishly adorned with freestanding and relief sculpture, the work of four sculptors, Scopas, Timotheos, Leochares, and Bryaxis, and two architects, Pythios and Satyros. Though there is much dispute about delegation of responsibility and details of reconstruc-

The Greek world, late 4th–1st century BC

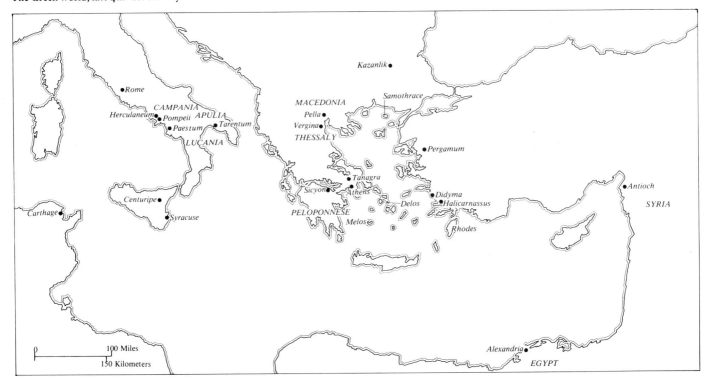

tion, Scopas was probably the dominant artist. Trained in the Peloponnese before 360 BC in the tradition of Polycleitos, his enthusiasm was channeled into dramatic, emotional figures with intense facial expressions, as in the east frieze of the Mausoleum (British Museum, London). This depicts the battle between Greeks and Amazons, with strong diagonal lines to emphasize motion and effort, and deeply drilled, swirling drapery.

One of the freestanding pieces from the Mausoleum a tall, well-dressed man, possibly a member of Mausolus' family (British Museum, London), was a forerunner of another major development of the Hellenistic period—portraiture. Here is a careful likeness of an individual with a heavy face, somewhat arrogant since his full lips curve disdainfully. At about the same time realistic portraits were being produced elsewhere, of which the most famous is perhaps a bronze showing the grim face of a victorious boxer at Olympia (c335 BC; National Museum, Athens), often attributed to Silanion. From Alexander's lifetime onwards portraiture became very popular, his fame stimulating the demand for likenesses of living people. The foremost artist in this development was Lysippos, who had been entrusted with the official portrait sculptures of Alexander. Unfortunately none of his original works survive, so it is impossible to assess accurately the quality of the idealism with which he may have endowed his work. Coming from Sicyon in the Peloponnese, he claimed to be self-taught, though he acknowledged the influence of Polycleitos, and enjoyed a long career of about 50 years beginning c360 BC, profoundly influencing later artists. He is credited with many inventions, though surviving copies do not illuminate these. He appears to have favored the tall, slender, narrow-hipped figure, with the head smaller in proportion to the body than before. More important was the new three-dimensional quality he added to his works. In his *Apoxyomenos* (copy in the Vatican Museums, Rome) we see an athlete scraping himself with a strigil. The pose is momentary, with arms raised in a direction different from that of the body, the left arm obscuring the chest. The figure is intended to be seen from any angle, a feature of Lysippos' other works.

The works of two of Lysippos' pupils demonstrate clearly how sculpture was used for propaganda purposes. Eutychides of Sicyon made a statue of Tyche, Good Fortune, commissioned c300 BC by Seleucus I to symbolize Antioch as the capital of the new kingdom of Syria. The surviving miniature replicas (Louvre, Paris; Vatican Museum, Rome) enable us to assess the lively symbolism. The regal goddess, wearing a turreted crown, sits on a rock, her foot on the shoulder of a swimming personification of the Orontes, the river of Antioch. Particularly noticeable is the three-dimensional composition, emphasized by the strong diagonal drapery and contrasting positions of the figures. About the same time Chares of Lindos, Lysippos' favorite pupil, designed for Rhodes its

A copy of Lysippos' Apoxyomenos; marble; height 205cm (81in); original c320 BC. Vatican Museums, Rome

A battle between Greeks and Persians: a section of a side-panel on the Alexander Sarcophagus; height of frieze 59cm (23in); the figure on the extreme left in a lion-skin helmet may be Alexander. Istanbul Archaeological Museum

Colossus—an enormous bronze effigy of the Sun, a symbol of the city's pride in its freedom.

An interesting original sculpture of the last third of the 4th century BC, also made with political purpose, is the so-called Alexander Sarcophagus, a rectangular chest with relief sculpture on all four sides (Archaeological Museum, Istanbul). Perhaps commissioned by Abdalonymus whom Alexander installed as King of Sidon, it commemorates Alexander's military victory over Persia and the reconciliation between conqueror and conquered. On one long and one short side spirited battle scenes are carved, including perhaps Alexander himself conspicuous in a lion-skin, on a rearing horse, hurling his spear at a Persian. On the other sides are hunting scenes in which Macedonians come to the aid of a Persian whose horse is being attacked by a lion.

In the 3rd century portraiture continued its development towards realism, though our knowledge is distorted because Roman taste has chiefly preserved philosophers and literary celebrities. A climax was reached c210 BC in the eloquent portrait of Chrysippos by Euboulides (Louvre, Paris); the simple cloak of the philosopher hangs over his bent, emaciated form, his face hollow, his beard ill-trimmed. For portraits of kings, coins are the best source. A fine example is the forceful portrait on the obverse of the rare silver octadrachms of Ptolemy I, King of Alexandria 305–282 BC (Museum of Fine Arts, Boston). Studies of anonymous individuals and children became popular too. The life-size *Antium Girl* (c250–225 BC; Terme Museum, Rome) shows a young woman in a momentary pause while walking, turning to her left, her attention concentrated on the religious objects she is carrying. A study of a different type is the so-called *Barberini Faun* (Glyptothek, Munich), a sleeping satyr, a remarkable rendering of the total relaxation of sleep. Such realism was based on a more exact knowledge of anatomy, sustained by a growing interest in science. At the beginning of the 3rd century Lysistrates, brother of Lysippos, started taking casts from the human face, while a little later doctors in Alexandria were conducting dissections.

From 250 BC one city emerged as the chief and most influential center for sculpture: Pergamum. The court attracted artists of many different origins and traditions, and it stimulated them to produce dynastic propaganda in a remarkably homogeneous style. After 228 BC Antigonos from Greece and Epigonos of Pergamum were requested to celebrate the victory of Attalus I (reigned 241–197 BC) over an invasion of Gauls, or Galatians as they came to be called. The resulting monument was a large round base on which a Galatian who had killed his wife was about to kill himself to avoid capture (Terme Museum, Rome). Round it were four dying Galatians, their slanting bodies leading the eye to the central group. In this dramatic, three-dimensional composition the artist's object was realism. The limp dejection of the dead woman, the blood spurting from wounds, bulging muscles, shaggy hair, deep, savage eyes, even ethnic characteristics such as moustache, torque, and trumpet, combine to convey the splendor of victory through the pride and courage of the foe.

Eumenes II (reigned 197–160 BC) enthusiastically continued his predecessor's policy of making Pergamum a great cultural center. To preside over Attalus' new library a copy of Pheidias' Athena Parthenos, smaller than half size, was commissioned in Athenian marble. In the same room stood statues of the great traditional figures of Greek literature to link the new firmly with the old. Athens had its Parthenon, so Pergamum should have an equivalent—the Great Altar of Zeus and Athena (Pergamon Museum, Berlin), probably but not certainly built by artists of several nationalities for Eumenes between 180 and 160. The Altar recalls the temple not only in the use of sculpture to illustrate national events but also in details. The figure of Athena on the east frieze of the Altar, for example, is similar to the one that was on the west pediment of the Parthenon.

The Altar itself stood on a high platform approached by steps from the west and surrounded on three sides by a wall and a colonnade which projected in spurs on either side of the steps. There were two friezes, the main one on the outer faces of the platform and flanking the steps, the other on the inner side of the wall round the Altar. The Great Frieze on the outside shows the battle between gods and giants, a mythological parallel for the conflict between Pergamum and the Galatians. On the longest east side we have Zeus and Athena towards the northern end where they would be immediately visible to visitors entering the Altar precinct by the main gate from the city, together with other gods, each fighting one or more giants. On the south side there are deities of light and sky, on the north chiefly those of night, and on the west the sea gods and Dionysos. Everywhere there is movement—in the repeated rhythms of individual combats, the changing diagonals, sweeping gestures, and swirling drapery—and constant variety in a wide range of poses. Beside the entrance the figures leave the frame and support themselves on the steps. There is no less variety in the picturesque details, which pay meticulous attention to traditional mythology—a giant with a lion's head, with wings of leaves, or serpent-footed; or the gods with their accompanying beasts; or triple-bodied Hecate or Poseidon's chariot drawn by sea-horses.

The inner frieze, which survives in a very fragmentary condition (Pergamon Museum, Berlin), was smaller. It told the story of the life of Telephos (Herakles' son, whose mother, Auge, was believed to have brought the cult of Athena to Pergamum and from whom the Attalids claimed descent) by means of a novel episodic narrative in which scenes were separated by trees, columns, or back-to-back figures. The arrangement of the figures was also an original feature—they were placed arbitrarily on two or three levels, none using more than two-thirds of the vertical height of the frieze.

A little earlier than the Great Altar is a fine dramatic piece, the *Winged Victory* (Louvre, Paris), now sadly incomplete but probably of Pergamene origin, originally set up on the island of Samothrace c190 BC to commemorate a naval victory. The over-life-sized female figure alights on a ship's prow, her feet firmly planted against the rushing wind. Movement is emphasized by the curving wings and the drapery blown back against the body to reveal its shape, an elaborate, careful treatment of clothing which became fashionable. A portrait statue of Cleopatra, for instance, still in her house on Delos (138–137 BC) shows her wearing a light shawl of fine material over her dress.

Other sculptures are narrative. The group showing the death of Laocoön and his sons, the work of three Rhodian sculptors, Hagesandros, Polydoros, and Athanodoros, probably dates from c100 BC (Vatican Museums, Rome). The terrifying situation as the three figures wrestle with the monstrous snakes sent by Apollo to destroy them is emphasized by their twisted, agonized bodies. The group clearly owes much to the Great Altar and, like a piece of relief sculpture, is designed to be viewed from one point only. Comparable with it is a tremendously powerful, pyramidal group, known only from a florid copy of the early 3rd century AD (Museo Nazionale, Naples) which shows Dirke being tied to a bull and about to be torn to pieces. According to literary sources the group was set up on Rhodes but the artists were Apollonius and Tauriskus of Tralles in Asia Minor, the adopted sons of Menekrates of Rhodes, a sculptor who was probably the designer of the Great Altar at Pergamum. Such interchange of ideas and personnel makes it hard for us to trace and identify regional schools or individual styles with any precision.

From the 2nd century onwards an especially popular class of sculpture was the female nude or seminude, presumably Aphrodite with slim, sloping shoulders, small breasts, and broad hips. The Aphrodite from Melos (Louvre, Paris) is one of the most famous examples, a standing figure over 6½ ft (2 m) high. Her body has a complicated twist as the upper part turns to the left and the hips to the right, which is emphasized by the cloak round her legs. Other completely naked figures crouch, as does a Rhodian statuette (100 BC; Archaeological Museum, Rhodes) based on a type perhaps originated by Doidalsas of Bithynia (fl. c250). The goddess's plump, sensuous body has a three-dimensional twist as she kneels on an ointment box, lifting up her hair with both hands.

Studies of individuals continue. A fine example is the bronze boxer (c50 BC; Terme Museum, Rome). A stocky, muscle-bound figure, he turns his dull, ill-humored face to the right, as he rests wearily, forearms on knees, hands stiff and awkward in their protective strapping. His right shoulder and elbow are gashed; his nose broken; his ears cut and swollen. Physical abnormalities and monsters (especially centaurs in the 1st century BC) became popular subjects with sculptors, presumably because of their customers' tastes. There were also excellent portraits, the bronze head of a man from Delos (c100 BC; National Museum, Athens), for example, or the head of Homer (Museum of Fine Arts, Boston), probably slightly earlier, with its realistic rendering of blindness—wasted eye sockets, thin lids, and wrinkled brows.

In the 2nd century, however, there were signs of a reaction against exaggerated realism. The statue usually identified as Demetrius I of Syria (reigned 162–150 BC; Terme Museum, Rome) with its godlike nudity shows an idealized picture of statesmanship and intellect. His body is massive and haughty,

The Great Altar at Pergamum

The reconstruction of the west facade shows part of the Great Frieze, which has been rescued from Byzantine fortifications and 19th-century limekilns. To aid comprehension of the uniquely extended battle the figures were named, giants usually below the frieze and gods above.

The figures of the Great Frieze, taller than life size (height 7 ft 5 in, 2.3 m), are carved in extremely high relief, casting strong, dramatic shadows. In the chief group mighty Zeus lunges, his aegis round his left arm, and originally a thunderbolt in his right hand. Serpent-footed Porphyrion struggles, his muscular back contrasting with the frontal view of the young giant next to Zeus, who sinks, clutching his wounded right shoulder, the veins of his arm cording in agony.

To Zeus' right another giant has fallen, his thigh pierced by a thunderbolt. The anguish of his profile face is echoed in the full countenance of winged Alcyoneus, with its deep-set eyes, furrowed brow, and open mouth. Athena, crowned by hovering Victory, lifts him by his hair to drag him away from his mother Ge, Earth, who rises pleading pitiably, entreaty in her every line.

Attention to detail contributes greatly to the sculpture's narrative force. Artemis in the short tunic of a huntress strides forward, one of her beautifully booted feet on a dead giant. Her dog bites a snaky-tailed giant, well-endowed with body hair, who retaliates by gouging out the animal's eye. To exaggerate the power and strength of the bite, the dog's muzzle is elongated and the giant's hair mingles with its mane. Even the interiors of shields are carefully decorated, while the moon goddess, Selene, rides on a shaggy saddle cloth, interestingly different from the smooth hide of her mount.

Above The Great Altar at Pergamum as reconstructed in the Pergamon Museum, Berlin

▲ Detail of the east frieze: *from left to right* a wounded giant, Zeus, a young giant, and Porphyrion

Above right On the south frieze: the moon goddess Selene

▶ Detail of the east frieze: the winged Alcyoneus is lifted by his hair

◄ On the north frieze:
Nyx, the goddess of the
night

▼ On the east frieze:
Otus and Artemis

Below A scene on the
inner frieze: building the
boat for Auge

The treatment of drapery clearly illustrates
stylistic differences among the sculptors of
the frieze. Clothes billow and surge to emphasize the movement of Zeus and Athena,
or in a more traditional manner complement
the tall figure of Apollo as he towers over his
fallen opponent. Selene wears a soft dress, its
delicate folds highlighting the fine skin of her
back and contrasting with the heavier cloak
round her legs. As Nyx, the goddess of the
night, strides forward hurling a serpent-
wreathed vessel at a giant, her heavy robes
sweep back, the thin veil fluttering behind.
Her dress shows a new fashion in drapery:
double lines of creases, or perhaps embroidery, which run across the main folds.

The later inner frieze, only 5 ft (1.5 m)
high, placed at eye level, is of a different
genre, analogous to painting, though probably never painted in its unfinished state. In
the scene showing the construction of the
boat in which Auge, daughter of the king of
Arcadia, is to be set adrift, disgraced by the
birth of Telephos, four carpenters work dili-
gently, presumably supervised by the male
figure on the left. The grief-stricken Auge
with two servants is above, smaller in scale
because further away. On the right, at the
foot of a rocky knoll on which a nymph is
sitting, a girl tends a fire under a caldron of
pitch for caulking the boat. Meanwhile
Herakles finds his son being suckled by a
lioness in a rocky landscape. He watches,
club and lion skin by his side, his back to the
plane tree that marks the beginning of this
episode.

K.B. THOMPKINS

Further reading. Bieber, M. *The Sculpture of the
Hellenistic Age*, New York (1961). Hansen, E.V. *The
Attalids of Pergamon*, New York and London (1971).
Robertson, M. *A History of Greek Art*, Cambridge
(1975). Schmidt, E. *The Great Altar of Pergamon*,
Leipzig (1962).

his brow deeply furrowed, his expression contemptuous—all to emphasize his kingly aloofness. Other works too show a return to the less realistic treatment of earlier centuries, sometimes even imitating the style of the Archaic period. An exponent of this kind of work was Damophon (*fl.* mid 2nd century) who made several cult-statues for sanctuaries in Greece, and was much influenced by Pheidias whose statue of Zeus at Olympia he restored. In the 1st century Arkesilaos was a versatile imitator. He carved a Venus for the temple in Rome dedicated by Julius Caesar in 46 BC, in the manner of a 5th-century statue.

Terracotta figurines. The manufacturers of terracotta figurines benefited greatly from increased personal wealth and enthusiasm for decorative pieces in the Hellenistic period. Their products were small, sharing many characteristics of large-scale sculpture.

The first type, Tanagra figurines, taking their name from the cemeteries in Boeotia where they were found in enormous numbers, were favorite offerings to the dead. Made in Athens and in many other centers in Italy, Asia Minor, and elsewhere, they were extremely popular throughout the Greek world from *c*340 until 200 BC. Tanagra figurines were chiefly female, fully clad, and represented scenes of daily life, though occasionally one may be interpreted as a goddess, a Muse (perhaps with a musical instrument), or Aphrodite half-naked. Women and girls stand, dance, or sit, sometimes playing knucklebones. Occasionally young men and boys—seated or standing—are the subjects, or chubby, babyish Erotes, usually in flight. There are also a few grotesque figures, probably in part influenced by contemporary comedies—ugly old nurses, for example, or enormously fat women. Naturalism was the aim, with relaxed poses and familiar dress to give the figures a human quality which helps to explain their popular appeal.

The manufacturing technique was an advance on previous practice, using molds of several pieces to achieve a greater variety of shapes. Often the body and arms were made from one mold, and the head from another, while attributes such as hats, fans, or wreaths were added, enabling an enormous variety of figures to be produced from a small set of molds. The figurines were colored in the traditional manner. White slip was first applied and then, after firing, bright colors, including a large range of reds, blues, and yellows.

After 200 BC the terracotta industry fragmented, different centers concentrating on certain subjects. One particularly important group is called Myrina, after the small town near Pergamum whose cemeteries yielded large numbers of figurines. Tanagra types, in bigger, more varied, and more elaborate forms, continued until *c*130 BC as production and repertoire gradually increased. Mythological subjects featured frequently and comic actors too, many of whom are very fine, though the style in general finally degenerated into grotesque coarseness.

Left: A terracotta figurine of a young woman from Tanagra; height 33cm (13in). Staatliche Museen, Berlin

Bronze statuettes. Bronze statuettes were very popular, whether copies of major sculptures simply for decoration, or portraits of poets and philosophers for their admirers or of rulers as neat compliments. The old schools of mainland Greece were halfhearted and lost their reputation to new centers, Pergamum, Alexandria, or Delos. Although much was cheap and vulgar, made in large quantities for an undiscerning public, a few pieces were really fine. As in major sculpture vitality was all important with new, sensational dramatic poses. The *Loeb Poseidon* (Staatliche Antikensammlungen, Munich), for example, shows the god in a restless, rather theatrical pose, the proportions of the figure very much recalling the work of Lysippos. The *Baker Dancer* (Walter Baker Collection, New York) too, an Alexandrian piece of *c*230 BC, with its composition of triangles in different planes, owes much to Lysippos and his pupils, while its treatment of clothes, rolled and stretched tight, typifies the new attitudes.

Realism was especially characteristic of some bronzes made in Alexandria where the cosmopolitan population provided a rich source of subject matter. Negroes were common, as were native Egyptians such as priests with shaved heads and enveloping mantles. Hard-featured peasants were shown, so too were children, and characterizations of the sick; an extremely emaciated, seated man (1st century BC; Dunbarton Oaks Foundation, Washington), for example, or a humpbacked beggar with a humble, yet resentful expression (Staatliche Museen, Berlin). Dwarfs were also popular, as were hunchbacks, though many of these pieces are poor quality and hard to date.

A bronze statuette of a dancing dwarf from Mahdia, Tunisia; height 30cm (12in). Musée National du Bardo, Tunis

The Derveni krater; bronze; height 91cm (36in); late 4th century BC. Archaeological Museum, Thessalonica

Metalwork. Utilitarian bronze objects also reveal the high living standard of the Hellenistic period. Furniture which had highly ornamented parts made of bronze, was popular, as were bronze vessels, pails, mirrors, and other utensils—especially *kraters* for mixing wine and water. The only manufacturing center known for certain was southern Italy, especially Tarentum, which exported very widely though articles must also have been made elsewhere. One of the finest examples of all is the *krater* used as an ash container in a grave at Derveni in Macedonia (probably late 4th century BC; Archaeological Museum, Thessalonica). The handles and the figures on the shoulders are cast, a technique much favored in southern Italy at the time; the rest is repoussé, with some added silver detail. The subject matter is Dionysos who sits with his leg in the lap of his bride, Ariadne, surrounded by whirling maenads and satyrs. He reappears in solid bronze on the shoulder with two maenads and a sad satyr mourning the dead.

Much more gold and silver plate was manufactured during the Hellenistic period, not only for the proverbially rich rulers, but also for wealthy private individuals who found it a useful investment. More metal became available as the resources revealed by Alexander's conquests were exploited. The repertoire of gold- and silversmiths increased as they produced many more objects for domestic use, with varying decoration—sometimes floral patterns, sometimes human or animal heads, sometimes mythological scenes—though once again the freedom with which artists traveled makes it difficult to isolate the products of any particular place from the limited surviving material.

Jewelry. Jewelry also flourished in the prosperity of the period, encouraged by the increased availability of raw materials. Most of our examples come from tombs where the custom of burying whole sets of jewelry with the dead bears witness to the wealth of the time. As with other metalwork, jewelry was made in many places and though we cannot isolate individual styles two centers seem to have been important: Alexandria and Antioch.

Many of the basic designs—diadems, naturalistic wreaths of leaves, some of extreme delicacy, ear- and finger-rings, or bracelets—continued virtually unchanged, as did the old techniques of filigree, enameling, and granulation. Egyptian motifs became popular, however, especially an old protective device, the Knot of Herakles, favored as a centerpiece for diadems and bracelets for 200 years after 300 BC. The crescent from western Asia was also much used as a pendant on necklaces. Of the traditional Greek designs Eros was most popular, though other mythological characters appeared, while a new animal- or human-headed hoop earring was fashionable from *c*330 BC, an innovation probably from northern Greece. Most important of all was the exploitation of a previously rare technique: the attachment of stones and colored glass to give a

Hellenistic jewelry: a necklace and crescent, part of a diadem, and a hoop earring. British Museum, London

bright, polychrome effect. At first chalcedony, carnelian, and especially garnet were popular; later a wider range of stones and also pearls were used.

Gem-cutting for rings became an important art, and oval garnets and amethysts were particularly popular. Portraits were quite common and more ambitious scenes show the influence of contemporary sculpture for mythological themes or more everyday topics. The cameo in layered stones, especially sardonyx, was invented and used extensively, not only for jewelry but also for larger toilet articles, cups, and bowls. A rare survival from Alexandria is the Farnese Cup (probably 2nd century BC; Museo Nazionale, Naples), clearly a piece of visual propaganda, extolling the benefits obtained from the Nile floods, though its precise interpretation is a matter of great controversy.

Architecture. The eclecticism that informed Hellenistic jewelry was equally characteristic of architecture. The old orders disintegrated, their parts being treated as interchangeable, while Ionic and Corinthian developed at the expense of the less decorative Doric. Flamboyance was the fashion, and nowhere more so than in the Ionic temple of Apollo, Didyma (from 300 BC) with its deliberate diversity of column bases and capitals, richly decorated with mythological, abstract, animal, and plant designs. The Corinthian capital also readily lent itself to magnificent display, with many leaves in two high crowns, and luscious volutes and flowers, as the temple of Zeus in Athens (after 175 BC) clearly shows.

Major architectural work naturally focused on the centers of prosperity. The long years of civil war in the 4th century had left Greece too poor to initiate much, though gifts of buildings were gratefully received by cities and sanctuaries. The wealthy courts and rich mercantile classes of the Hellenistic kingdoms stimulated not only religious and civic architecture but also the building of palaces and opulent private houses set in streets made fine by colonnades and fountains. Evidence for palaces is scanty, but adequate to convey an impression of great magnificence. Pella, Alexander's capital, and Delos contain fine examples of private houses, with floors and walls richly decorated and an abundance of sculpture.

No less indicative of the individualism and opulence of the age were the monumental tombs. The historian Diodorus (*fl.* 60–30 BC) describes the tomb set up for Alexander's favorite, Hephaistion, an enormous stepped pyramid lavishly decorated with statues; and there are many parallels for such mausoleums, notably at Halicarnassus. They were particularly popular in Asia Minor, and perhaps owed their origin to the tombs of native kings. Another type, more popular in Macedonia, was the elaborate chambered tomb, mostly below ground, comprising a room and an antechamber with a decorative facade, approached by a passage. The most lavish tombs of all, like houses but wholly underground and heavily decorated, were in the necropolis at Alexandria.

Wall-painting. Surviving examples of Hellenistic wall-painting are provincial and inferior. For first-rate works we are dependent on Roman copies and adaptations, chiefly from Pompeii and Herculaneum, where much of the work is mediocre, probably produced, under contract, from rough copy books. Sometimes there are several versions of one theme, suggesting derivation from some earlier work, or a distinctively Hellenistic topic, such as the recurring story of Telephos. Dionysos and Ariadne in the famous paintings from the Villa of the Mysteries, Pompeii (*in situ*), are remarkably similar to a terracotta group from Myrina (Louvre, Paris); perhaps both are based on Pergamene paintings.

Hellenistic tombs and private houses had stuccoed, painted walls. At first the effect was simple; a wall was divided into three major zones, the lowest painted white, the main field red, and the cornice yellow. Later the plaster was sometimes modeled to imitate wall courses and a projecting cornice, and the paint mottled like colored marbles. As the decoration became more elaborate, the architectural effects were heightened by illusionist painting, the first example being on Delos *c*100 BC (House of Dionysos; Delos Museum) where modeled pilasters and entablature frame a painting of a foreshortened coffered ceiling, to give an impression of space between the columns.

Such house walls were a natural setting for compositions with figures, probably painted mainly on wooden panels. Of the specialist artists who made these paintings we know only a little more than their names, chiefly from the Roman writer Pliny the Elder (AD 23/4–79). For the third quarter of the 4th century BC we hear of Pausias of Sicyon who specialized in flowers, the widespread influence of which can be traced in mosaics and metalwork as far apart as Thessaly or Italy. Or there was Nikias of Athens with his large, solemn, cleverly shaded figures (a new technique) gazing at the spectator, or Apelles, Alexander's official portrait painter whose style may be reflected in some Roman paintings.

From a careful study of the copies some development can be traced, especially an increasing ability to depict three-dimensional scenes by means of highlighting, shading, and foreshortening. Valuable confirmation comes from original Hellenistic tomb paintings, occasionally very elaborate such as the facade of a tomb at Lefkadia in Macedonia with its painted imitations of sculpture (*in situ*), usually simpler with a decoration of domestic objects and wreaths. At Kazanlik in Bulgaria is an elaborate tomb (*c*300 BC; *in situ*), with particularly fine paintings on walls and ceiling, including a frieze centering on the dead man and his wife, who are receiving offerings.

As composition techniques in painting gradually improved, the physical setting of the figures, interior or exterior, became more important. Gravestones, especially from Thessaly, provide a little contemporary evidence for the styles of the mid 3rd century BC, though because the encaustic technique was used, much of the quality of the color has disappeared. The dead person is often shown seated with a servant and appropriate furniture; a particularly ambitious example shows

A reconstruction of the facade of a tomb at Lefkadia, Macedonia

Hediste who died in childbirth, with an open door behind her revealing more of the house (Archaeological Museum, Volos).

For the final phase of Hellenistic painting there is only one good example and a little literary evidence, supported by copies, which names Timomachos of Byzantium as the last great easel painter—his works were bought by Julius Caesar at enormous cost. In a house on the Esquiline Hill in Rome (*c*50 BC) a damaged series of scenes closely based on Homer's *Odyssey* has been found (Vatican Museums, Rome). Odysseus' wanderings are given an elaborate and realistically accurate setting of landscape, sea, and architecture, though the figures remain of paramount importance.

Mosaics. The art of the mosaicist thrived and became more ambitious. For evidence of the work of the late 4th and 3rd centuries the houses at Pella in Macedonia, with their well-preserved pebble mosaics, are our chief source, the best dating from the 3rd century. Big pebbles were used in simple geometric designs that covered large areas of floor, mainly in white, gray, and green, similar to the simple patterned floors in some Macedonian tombs. Smaller pebbles were used at Pella in figured scenes for which hunting was a popular subject. The *Stag Hunt* (*in situ*) is signed by Gnosis, apparently an artist of considerable ability, versatile in his modeling of the hunters and their cloaks, and skillful in his composition not only of the main scene but also of the fine floral border. His success was the more remarkable because he used natural colored pebbles and lead strips to outline the figures.

After *c*250 BC pebble mosaics were no longer made. Their place was taken by tessellated work which in its most developed form used tiny squarish pieces of naturally colored stones and later glass, set in a bed of cement and ground smooth. The origins of the technique are uncertain but by the 2nd century Pergamum seems to have become a center for the

The Tomb of Philip

The partially excavated east front of this tomb (*in situ* at Vergina; 350–325 BC) has a finely painted frieze above its brightly colored Doric facade. Hunters armed with spears, some on horseback, pursue wild animals through a winter landscape suggested by leafless trees, recalling the work of Philoxenos of Eretria (*see* Hellenistic Art, p163). The main room of the vaulted tomb is entered from the spacious antechamber by a marble door. Perhaps because Philip's assassination in 336 BC cut short the work, the walls of the inner chamber are unfinished, though the antechamber has high quality plaster, and a nearby tomb has three fine murals, additional evidence of unprecedented value for 4th-century BC painting.

Near the center of the back wall of the inner chamber stood a marble sarcophagus, containing a gold casket whose weight including contents was almost 24 lb (11 kg). Delicate leaf and flower patterns enhanced by applied rosettes, some inlaid with blue glass paste, decorate the casket's front and sides. Its legs are shaped like lion's paws and on the lid is a multi-rayed star: the emblem of the Macedonian royal family. Inside were the cremated bones of a man in his forties, covered with a gold oak wreath. Philip II, father of Alexander the Great, was 46 when he was killed.

A similar but smaller, more simply decorated casket, the only other one known, stood in a marble sarcophagus in the antechamber.

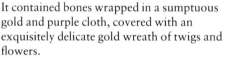

▲ The ivory portrait head; possibly of Alexander (actual size)

▲ The ivory portrait head identified as Philip (actual size)

▲ The east front of the tomb

It contained bones wrapped in a sumptuous gold and purple cloth, covered with an exquisitely delicate gold wreath of twigs and flowers.

Offerings to the dead were found in the southwest corner of the main chamber. A perforated bronze lantern decorated with a fine gold head, and other vessels, chiefly of bronze, together with a still pliable sponge, surrounded the large circular cover of a now disintegrated leather ceremonial shield—ornamented with ivory, colored glass, gold and silver—on a wooden frame. Beside it were two pairs of greaves and between them the first Macedonian iron helmet ever found. To the right was a circular, adjustable diadem of gold-plated silver, often seen on portraits of kings of Macedon.

In the antechamber was a pair of gilded bronze greaves whose uneven length and different modeling should perhaps be associated with Philip's lameness. The relief decoration on the gilded silver quiver shows the sack of a town with scenes of furious attack and desperate defence. The elegantly simple jug, found with other silver vessels of comparable workmanship by the north wall of the main chamber, is excellently executed,

especially the small repoussé head added at the base of its handle.

In the main room were fragments of ivory, including heads, hands and feet from five figures, perhaps originally decorations of now decomposed wooden furniture. One portrait head identified as Philip (who was partially blinded in battle) shows a mature, bearded man with a deep scar over his right eye. Another, a youthful face with upward gaze is sometimes identified as the only extant contemporary portrait of Alexander. A third could be his mother, Olympias. Perhaps the others are Philip's parents, and the whole series a miniature copy of the ivory and gold statues of the royal family commissioned from Leochares in 338 BC for dedication at Olympia.

K.B. THOMPKINS

Further reading. Andronicos, M. "The Royal Tomb of Philip II, an Unlooted Macedonian Grave at Vergina", *Archaeology* (Archaeological Institute of America) Vol. 31, Sept/Oct 1978. Hammond, N.G.L. and Griffith, G.T. *A History of Macedonia, Vol. II, 550–336 BC*, Oxford (1979). Kurtz, D.C. and Boardman, J. *Greek Burial Customs*, London (1971). Ninos, K. (ed.) *Treasures of Ancient Macedonia*, Athens (1978).

◄ A silver jug; height 25cm (10in)

▲ Offerings to the dead found in the southwest corner of the main chamber

▼ The gold casket; height without legs 17cm (7in), length 40cm (16in)

► A gilded silver quiver, and gilded bronze greaves of uneven length found by the door of the antechamber. Length: *left* 38cm (15in) *right* 41cm (16in)

ΓΝΩΣΙΣ ΕΠΟΗΣΕΝ

production of mosaics, which rapidly increased in finesse. Sosos of Pergamum (*fl. c*170 BC) was ranked as an old master by the Romans chiefly for two works known from Roman copies: his *Doves Drinking* (Museo Capitolino, Rome) with its mastery of light and shade on the metal vessel and the reflection of the birds in the water, and his *Unswept Floor*, with its minute attention to details and skillful shading (Lateran Museum, Rome).

The subjects of mosaics were essentially decorative, not pictorial. Their backgrounds were normally plain, a dark greenish-blue, for example, for the solidly modeled *Dionysos Riding a Panther*, from Delos (*c*150 BC; *in situ* in the House of the Masks, Delos). Occasionally, however, the mosaicist copied an important picture. The Alexander Mosaic from Pompeii (*c*150 BC; Museo Nazionale, Naples) may be a fairly careful copy of a work by Philoxenos of Eretria (*fl.* 319–297 BC), slightly coarsened by the change of technique which used almost 1½ million tiny cubes of stone and glass to reproduce Alexander's victory over the king of Persia at the Battle of Issus (333 BC). The strong lighting and bold foreshortening of the dramatic scene as the young, bareheaded Alexander pursues the elaborately robed, fleeing Darius is enhanced by one stark tree and a mass of diagonal spears.

Left: The Stag Hunt, by Gnosis, at Pella in Greece (in situ)

The Alexander Mosaic from Pompeii; c150 BC. Museo Archeologico Nazionale, Naples

A 3rd-century lidded bowl from Catania; height 56cm (22in). Institute of Classical Archaeology, Catania University

Pottery. Because artists had so much scope for other activities, traditional styles of Greek pottery-painting survived into the Hellenistic period only for special objects, for funeral rites, perhaps, or for athletic prizes. Only in southern Italy did red-figure continue for local markets until a little after 300 BC, benefiting from the reduced competition of Athenian imports. There were several regional schools, modifying traditional red-figure and experimenting with new techniques, all influenced by developments in easel painting. Apulian, based probably on Tarentum, was the major style, specializing in large, often excessively decorated funeral vases, frequently with scenes taken from mythology or tragic drama. The pots were much more colorful than Athenian red-figure with considerable use of white, yellow, and deep red. The other schools, Lucanian, Campanian, and Paestan were provincial by comparison, though Lucanian specialized in caricature and they all produced a lively class of vases showing scenes from rustic farces with actors in padded costumes.

The best work of Sicilian potters in the last quarter of the 4th century was executed in a bright polychrome technique which continued after 300 BC when more traditional styles had gone out of production. There was a flourishing industry based on Centuripe, near Catania (280–150 BC), making large, ornamental pots, often bowls or dishes with lids. Women sacrificing or in a religious procession were frequent subjects, set against a rose-pink background, enlivened by careful attention to facial expressions, skillful treatment of near-transparent robes, and subtle coloring and shading.

Another south Italian product, Gnathia Ware, was made for almost 100 years after 350 BC, probably in the same workshops as Apulian. The pots were smaller, made in imitation of metal shapes, painted black with white, red, purple, or yellow designs on top. The decoration was confined to a limited range of leaf patterns with occasional figure scenes. In Greece itself West Slope Ware was similar with a small repertoire of naturalistic and abstract patterns. It lasted probably into the 1st century BC over a wide area of the eastern Mediterranean, being manufactured perhaps in Pergamum and Alexandria, as well as in the cities of mainland Greece.

Hadra Ware, mainly used as ash urns in the cemeteries of Alexandria and probably made in that city in the second half of the 3rd century, demonstrates a different effect: decoration in color on the white or pale surface of the pot. Stylized foliage, wreaths, fantastic animals, and abstract patterns are most common, arranged sparingly in bands chiefly on the neck, shoulder, or upper belly.

Another method of decorating pottery gained some popularity as a cheap imitation of metalwork: the addition of molded ornament. Sometimes it was simple (a laurel wreath round the neck of a pot, for example) but occasionally it was used for an entire figure scene. In the 3rd and 2nd centuries Megarian bowls were important, made, despite their name, in many places. They were black or brown, with decoration in relief, either molded with the pot or stamped out and separately attached. In addition to plant motifs and patterns there were elaborate figure compositions, including an interesting series in the 2nd century illustrating stories from literature.

Conclusion. Over a wide area the Hellenistic period was a time of change. Artists and craftsmen lived and worked in a world of new political organizations, new cultural contacts, and new economic opportunities, a world that inevitably conditioned their products from the most elaborate and costly to the smallest and most humble. The individual was now all-important; monarchs required material manifestations of their power, while all classes strove to improve their living standards, not least wealthy merchants who wished to live with every luxury their money could buy. Everywhere people displayed a fresh, enthusiastic interest in human life, particularly in its more picturesque aspects; even traditional religious ideas and mythological themes were reinterpreted in personal terms. Such an approach far outlasted the chronological limits of the Hellenistic period; its influence on subsequent art, especially Roman was both extensive and profound.

K.B. THOMPKINS

Bibliography. Charbonneaux, J. *Hellenistic Art*, London (1973). Havelock, C.M. *Hellenistic Art*, London (1971). Tarn, W. and Griffith, G.T. *Hellenistic Civilisation*, London (1966). Webster, T.B.L. *Hellenistic Art*, London (1967).

10

ETRUSCAN ART

Amazons fight a Greek warrior: a painted scene on an Etruscan stone sarcophagus from Tarquinia
Museo Archeologico, Florence (see page 174)

THE Etruscans inhabited the region of Italy bounded to the north by the valley of the Arno, to the east and south by the Tiber, and on the west by the Tyrrhenian Sea. In Antiquity it was called Etruria and contained great forests and rich potential for agriculture and mining. The ethnic and linguistic affinities of the Etruscans are not clear. According to a tradition well known in Antiquity they migrated from western Asia Minor around the 12th century BC. To date no firm archaeological evidence supports this story but Etruscan is similar to a dialect once spoken on the Aegean island of Lemnos. Both languages may be survivals of an ancient Mediterranean tongue, or the Etruscans may have brought their language to Italy at an early date.

Archaeologists call the Iron Age culture of ancient Etruria "Villanovan", reserving the name "Etruscan" for the period after *c*700 BC. This nomenclature stresses a theory, still upheld by some scholars, that the Etruscans only arrived in Italy at this time. But a strong continuity links the 8th and 7th centuries in the region and the Villanovan culture is now generally regarded as the true precursor of Etruscan civilization, though a profound change did occur in Etruria during this time.

Distribution of sites mentioned in the text

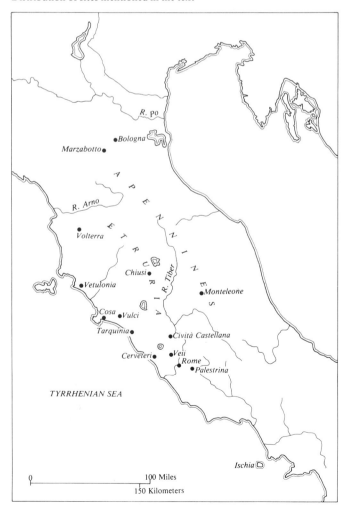

Phoenician and Greek merchants and colonists became active in the western Mediterranean in the Geometric period (*see* Archaic Greek Art) and had made contact with Villanovan villagers by *c*800 BC. Thereafter the Villanovans and their successors, the Etruscans, were gradually drawn into the mainstream of Mediterranean culture. The Greeks founded their first colony in Italy on the island of Ischia before 750 BC, and by 600 BC a chain of Greek colonies ran along the shore of southern Italy from Naples to Taranto and round the eastern coasts of Sicily. The Phoenicians held the western tip of the island, opposite Carthage in Africa, and had colonies on Sardinia.

Greek and Roman authors mention some early events in central Italy but the Etruscans only emerge into history during the 6th century BC. By then, the political system of city-states, with a social and religious structure familiar in later centuries, had crystallized. Etruscan kings ruled Rome; the Etruscans had established colonies in Campania, the lower Po Valley, and Corsica. It was the period of their greatest power, but during the late 6th and early 5th centuries they were expelled from Rome and defeated at sea and on land by their Greek neighbors.

During the 5th and 4th centuries BC Greek fleets occasionally plundered Etruscan coastal sites. To the south of Etruria the young Roman Republic was growing in strength, while to the north the Gauls had settled in the Po Valley and periodically raided south of the Apennines. Surrounded by these dangers, the Etruscan city-states failed to unite effectively. Veii and other cities fought intermittent but fierce wars with Rome and by 280 BC they were probably all subject-allies of the Republic.

Afterwards, the Etruscans continued to enjoy some local self-government but gradually they were assimilated into the Roman world. In 89 BC they were granted Roman citizenship. By the end of the 1st century BC their language was obsolete and their culture had merged with that of Imperial Rome.

Traditionally 12 in number, the Etruscan city-states were autonomous. They formed a loose confederation, united by their common language and religion (always a profound influence in Etruria) but often following their own interests. In early times the cities were ruled by kings but by the 5th century BC power had passed to the wealthy and exclusive class of nobles.

This political and social structure had a deep effect upon the development of art in Etruria and upon the type of surviving evidence. The individuality of the city-states generated a fascinating divergence of local art forms. The nobles were gifted patrons of the arts and custom dictated that men and women of great families should be placed in fine tombs, surrounded by prized possessions, some of which have come down to us.

Etruscan artistic styles. The Villanovans were capable craftsmen, decorating their pottery and bronzes with geometric designs and occasionally with primitive representational scenes. During the 8th century BC they began to copy goods obtained from Phoenician and Greek merchants, but traditional Italic forms remained dominant until c700 BC.

In the next 100 years the Etruscans achieved a new prosperity, based upon the export of metal ore. Since Greek art was under the influence of the high cultures of the eastern Mediterranean, Greek goods in the Orientalizing style reached Etruria together with exotic objects from Asia Minor, the Phoenician cities, Cyprus, and Egypt. These imports were imitated in Etruria, the craftsmen excelling in the production of decorative objects in the Orientalizing style (c700–600 BC) for their princely patrons.

Greek inspiration prevailed in Etruria during the period of the Archaic style (c600–475 BC); Corinthian, Ionian, and Attic styles in turn dominated the taste of the Etruscan city-states, where local artistic styles were now very individual. Town-planning was introduced, monumental architecture and large-scale sculpture and painting became firmly established as major art forms. The exuberance of the Archaic style reflects the self-confidence felt by the Etruscans, now at the height of their power.

As the Greeks emerged victorious from the Persian War, the Classical style appeared in Greece. By this time, Etruscan civilization had already begun to decline; there was a recession of trade with Greece and the Etruscans were slow to accept the Classical style (c475–300 BC). Archaic forms survived and Etruscan artists were reserved in adopting the severe, idealizing style of Greek early Classical art. The Etruscans responded more fully to the less austere manner of the late Classical style and there was a sporadic revival in Etruria during the 4th century BC.

After the death of Alexander (323 BC) the Greek world expanded around the eastern Mediterranean and developed the elegant Hellenistic style (c300–1st century BC), which strove to express emotion and emphasized dramatic moment. Rome became the capital of the Mediterranean world and increasingly contributed to Hellenistic culture. The Etruscans, no longer politically independent, adopted the style but maintained some regional characteristics.

Throughout the seven centuries of their individual artistic expression the Etruscans were dependent upon foreign inspiration, principally that of the Greeks. Thus the major styles of Etruria are called by the same names as those of Greece. But whereas the Greek styles grew organically, reflecting their historical, social, and intellectual background, the Etruscans accepted outward forms without always assimilating inner content. It is hard to find a parallel in the history of art for the Etruscans' consistent borrowing of Greek styles, yet they were not shallow imitators. They were sensitive to the beauty of Greek visual arts and proved themselves most able craftsmen. They used Greek art forms, styles, themes, and even details, but were always selective, adapting them to Etruscan conventions to express Etruscan taste, often in the idiom of a single city-state.

Architecture. The Etruscans adopted the grid street-plan used at Greek colonial sites in Italy, but ideal town-planning was difficult to impose on the older cities of Etruria, which had grown from Villanovan villages. An example of an ideal plan is the colonial site of Marzabotto, near Bologna, founded towards the end of the 6th century BC. A main street ran due north and south and was crossed at right angles by three streets of similar width, all flanked by drains. A grid of smaller streets divided the rest of the town. Buildings for religious observance crowned the nearby hilltop and cemeteries lay outside the habitation area, an Etruscan custom.

Throughout their history the Etruscans were deeply concerned with the afterlife. Many of their cemeteries were veritable cities of the dead—their sites remain evocative. The tombs differ from place to place and from century to century, much depending on whether inhumation or cremation prevailed as the local funerary rite. Some tombs are rock-cut chambers, approached by steps from ground level or entered by a doorway with an architectural facade carved in the cliff face. Others were constructed of stone blocks, either standing above ground or partially buried, like the great *tumuli* whose molded drums were cut from the rock and had masonry additions. Masonry was used in early times for false vaults, false arches, and false domes, while true barrel vaults were built in the Hellenistic period.

Earlier masonry city walls had squared blocks which were set in regular courses; later walls were constructed in the polygonal manner. Hellenistic reliefs show city walls with turrets, castellations, and arched gateways. Such gateways, which are occasionally decorated with human heads carved in relief, and stretches of great city walls are very often the most imposing monuments at Etruscan sites.

An Etruscan gateway: the Porta all'Arco, Volterra

A reconstruction of an Etruscan temple from Alatri. Garden of the Villa Giulia, Rome

Little is known about the external elevations of houses, though tomb facades and representations, especially on cinerary chests, presumably reflect their appearances. Examples show facades each with a porch and columns, and indicate an upper story. A cinerary chest in the Museo Archeologico, Florence, represents a stone house with fine masonry and arched doorways, flanked by pilasters.

More is known of the ground plans of Etruscan houses. The Villanovans had lived in huts, often oval in layout. At Marzabotto houses were arranged on a rectilinear pattern but had no uniform plan, though several had rooms grouped around a central courtyard with a passage leading in from the street. Contemporary 6th-century tombs echo a more complex house plan with an entrance corridor flanked by a chamber on either side, and a central hall which opened into three back rooms. Later tombs sometimes have rooms on either side of the hall, an arrangement similar to houses at Pompeii. There is also evidence that the hall or *atrium* on occasion had an opening to the sky, a development known in the Hellenistic period and associated with the Etruscans in Antiquity.

Many internal domestic features are represented in the tombs, which are often painted in gay colors. Beams are supported by columns with capitals in Doric or sometimes Aeolic style, and some ceilings are coffered. Doorways have heavy lintels and inclining jambs, some doors have strong frames with metal studs and handles, and windows are rectangular or arched.

Etruscan temple architecture was allied to Greek forms, which the Etruscans modified, principally in their use of materials and the ground plan, to suit their own religious needs. The Etruscans characteristically only used stone for the base or *podium* of a temple. The walls were of unfired brick, covered with plaster, and the columns and beams of timber—plentiful in Etruria. The exposed wooden elements of the superstructure were protected by terracotta plaques. Together with the stone substructure, the temple terracottas often survive as our best evidence for the original appearance of Etruscan buildings.

Unlike Greek forms the *podium* of an ideal Etruscan temple was almost square and approached by a flight of steps from the front alone. The front half of the temple was a deep porch with two lines of four columns. At the back, there were three rooms or *cellae*, their doors opening onto the spaces between the columns. An alternative arrangement had one *cella* between two wings, open at the front. The columns were traditionally made of wood, without flutes; the capitals had round cushions and square abaci, resembling the Doric order.

The great wooden beams and overhanging eaves gave Tuscan temples a top-heavy appearance. This was emphasized by their brightly painted terracotta decorations. The horizontal beams were covered in terracotta slabs, often with repeating patterns in bas-relief, while the ends of the ridgepole and roof beams were capped by plaques, sometimes decorated in high relief. The roof was tiled and where the tiles overlapped at the eaves the joints were masked by decorated antefixes. Statues or acroteria might be set upon the gable or along the ridgepole but unlike the Greeks the Etruscans left the pediment open, not filling it with sculpture until Hellenistic times.

The Etruscans also built temples with one *cella* and two columns; models and tomb facades demonstrate that fluted columns and Ionic capitals were used. Little is yet known of other public buildings in Etruria, though there are extant examples of stone platforms with fine moldings, probably for taking the auspices, and models of arcades and freestanding towers. Early bridges were constructed of wood, set upon stone foundations, while arched stone bridges were built in Hellenistic times.

Sculpture. The Villanovans made models of familiar objects and primitive statuettes from clay and bronze. Their human figures have large heads with ill-defined features and thin, straddling limbs, while their lively animals sometimes recall Greek Geometric types.

During the Orientalizing period objects of faience, ivory, precious metals, bronze, and pottery from the eastern Mediterranean and Greece reached Etruria. Some of these imports were carved or modeled in the round, others were decorated in bas-relief. Etruscan craftsmen enthusiastically imitated them, making lavishly embellished objects for personal and household use. They portrayed monsters, strange men, and draped female figures, usually presented in compact volume and often with carefully noted details. Foreign repertoires were mingled and Italic themes occasionally added to produce an eclectic Etruscan Orientalizing style.

At Chiusi, a contemporary sculptural form probably had local inspiration. The ashes of the dead were often placed in vessels with lids fashioned as schematic human heads, though some examples seek to convey individuality.

Towards the end of the period, large-scale sculpture appears. Seated figures from Cerveteri, delicately modeled in terracotta, are some 20 in (50 cm) in height (Palazzo dei Conservatori, Museo Capitolino, Rome; British Museum, London). Stone statues from Vetulonia, crudely carved in the round, reach life-size (Museo Archeologico, Florence). Stone funerary stelae have figures in bas-relief or incised, one accompanied by an inscription in Greek letters, adapted for the Etruscan language.

It is important to note the conventional Etruscan choice of materials for sculpture. In contrast to Greek tradition, they usually reserved stone for funerary monuments, mainly using the local stone. Bronze was appreciated and employed for offerings dedicated to the gods, for household goods and personal possessions, which often attain a high artistic standard. Terracotta served for architectural decorations, for sarcophagi, cinerary urns, and votive offerings.

New sculptural forms reached Etruria during the Archaic period and the ability of sculptors developed rapidly. They followed Hellenic styles but local idioms occur. At Tarquinia stone slabs were carved in bas-relief, sometimes illustrating narrative themes. At Vulci and other centers, stone statues of monsters, animals, and humans were set up outside tombs as guardians. A fine example represents a centaur (Villa Giulia, Rome). The nude male form, derived from the early Archaic style of Greece, has a large head, staring eyes and sturdy limbs, held in motionless frontal pose.

At first Archaic bronze figures were somewhat rigid, with stress on vertical lines but they soon acquired new characterization and vitality. Cast statuettes of recognizable gods appear, and to decorate the increasing number of household bronzes warriors, athletes, dancers, and other types are often shown in vigorous action. The emphasis on expressive detail, such as the head or hands, is characteristic of the Etruscans,

A stone statue of a centaur from Vulci; volcanic stone; height 76cm (30in); early 6th century BC. Villa Giulia, Rome

while the flowing lines, long heads, and plump bodies indicate Ionian taste.

Sheet bronze was worked in repoussé to decorate furniture and wooden objects, for example the magnificent chariot found at Monteleone (Metropolitan Museum, New York). Large works were fired in terracotta—outstanding examples are the sarcophagi from Cerveteri, shaped like couches with smiling married couples reclining upon the lids (Villa Giulia, Rome; Louvre, Paris).

Simple temple decorations in terracotta occur about the middle of the Archaic period. Subsequently antefixes of various designs were made in molds; some have heads surrounded by a shell motif, others depict complete figures. The bas-relief friezes repeat groups of gods or men and some lively horsemen. Most celebrated, however, are the compositions in high relief and statues, modeled in the round, which were set upon the roof. The sculptors, inspired by the achievements of the Greek late Archaic style, created naturalistic figures capable of expressing both movement and emotion. Energy is implicit in fighting warriors, their details picked out in color, from Cività Castellana, and there is latent menace in the striding Apollo from Veii (both in the Villa Giulia, Rome). The sculpture of Veii was famous in Antiquity and the Romans recalled that Vulca of Veii, the only Etruscan artist known by name, decorated a temple in Rome towards the end of the 6th century BC.

Works in the Archaic manner were produced at some Etruscan centers well into the 5th century BC. This is apparent in bas-reliefs on sarcophagi, cinerary chests, and other monuments from the region of Chiusi, or from the stelae of Bologna (Museo Archeologico, Chiusi; Museo Archeologico, Bologna). Their style is lively, their design simple, and they often depict aspects of ordinary life.

The severe style of early Greek Classical sculpture was not so fully assimilated by the Etruscans, though they became more interested in representing human anatomy and accepted a trend towards idealization. A head, which forms the lid of a cinerary urn, demonstrates such impersonal presentation, an example of the association of Greek style with a local art form (Museo Archeologico, Florence). The development of the Classical style in Etruria is shown in a series of votive statuettes in terracotta and bronze. The men are either nude or when clothed they sometimes wear an Etruscan cloak or military equipment, while the dignified women are finely dressed. The Mars of Todi, one of the few surviving large-scale bronze statues, illustrates the later Classical style of Etruria. It is a graceful study of a pensive young soldier, standing in a well-balanced pose with the weight upon one leg (Vatican Museums, Rome). Many contemporary household bronzes are of outstanding quality with their cast components, for example the handles or feet, formed of well-composed groups of figures.

In Hellenistic times there was a revival of temple decoration. The most important feature now was the sculpture filling the pediment. Moments of high tension were illustrated and supple figures shown dramatically posed. The bronzes include strange, elongated statuettes, often of priests, muscular males, and elegant women. Some wear fashionable clothes and jewelry but others are nude, their small heads with elaborately dressed hair set upon slender bodies.

Stone sarcophagi were still carved in the region around Tarquinia; the production of cinerary chests was maintained at Chiusi; and at Volterra the local alabaster was used for fine cinerary chests (now in the Museo "Guarnacci", Volterra). On many are reliefs showing episodes, often violent, from Greek mythology, or scenes of farewell—the dead setting out on their journey to the underworld. Figures reclining upon lids were sometimes shown with exaggerated features, in the spirit of caricature. Frequently, however, they are genuine portraits, with inscriptions recording the name, family, age, and offices held by Etruscan nobles.

Painting. Almost all large-scale Greek paintings have perished but we can trace the development of their drawing from painted pottery styles. Greek graphic art had a profound influence upon Etruscan polychrome wall-paintings, which form the most numerous group of murals to survive from the pre-Roman Classical world. The Etruscan wall-paintings have come down to us because underground tombs at some Etruscan centers were decorated in fresco. This art form probably had a religious purpose: to perpetuate the efficacy of funerary rites and to recreate the familiar surroundings of life in the dwellings of the dead.

The oldest known painted tomb in Etruria is the Tomb of

A terracotta fighting group from Cività Castellana. Villa Giulia, Rome

The bronze Mars of Todi; height 142cm (56in); c400–350 BC.
Vatican Museums, Rome

Of mid-6th-century date, the five Boccanera slabs show the influence of Corinthian vase-painting. They depict seated sphinxes and figures, standing stiffly, linked only by their gestures (British Museum, London). The more flowing lines of the Campana plaques (Louvre, Paris) suggest Ionian taste. Movement is introduced and figures carefully interrelated. Whether the figures represent gods or men, details of dress and symbolism are Etruscan.

From mid Archaic to Hellenistic times Tarquinia was the greatest center of tomb-painting. The fresco technique was generally used—walls of rock-cut tombs were thinly covered in plaster, the outlines of the picture sketched or incised, and the painting filled in while the plaster remained damp. Some of the paintings can be seen in the tombs; others are in the Museo Nazionale, Tarquinia.

The Archaic paintings have a two-dimensional plane, their designs based upon the relationship of figures and colors employed. Heads are drawn in profile, shoulders are frequently full-view, and legs are again in profile. Artists filled in these outlines with a uniform wash, adding some internal details. Blue and green were added to the palette and differing shades of color were used.

The Etruscans' paintings abound with exuberant life, fully reflecting their confidence at this time. Funerary themes, such as banquets and athletic games, are repeated but other aspects of life appear. Only the back wall of the Tomb of the Bulls, dated 540–530 BC, is fully decorated. Its principal scene illustrates a Greek epic story but erotic subjects are also shown. On all four walls of the Tomb of the Augurs are themes of funerary ritual and sports, some figures recalling the contemporary style of black-figure vase painting. The Tomb of Hunting and Fishing has carefree outdoor scenes whilst the main person in the Tomb of the Jugglers watches a display in his honor. The Tomb of the Baron illustrates a tranquil moment of worship or greeting.

Some late Archaic and early Classical tombs have banqueting scenes on the end wall, while on the sidewalls accompanying musicians and dancers are shown, representing the performing arts for which the Etruscans were famous in Antiquity. In the Tomb of the Leopards, two figures recline on each of the three couches and naked boys serve wine. The sidewalls of the beautiful Tomb of the Triclinium, c470 BC, have fine compositions with a lyre-player, flautist, and energetic dancers, their draperies emphasizing movement. The drawing displays a new competence, familiar from Attic red-figure pottery at the beginning of the Classical period.

At this time the custom of tomb-painting had spread inland to Chiusi and other centers. At Tarquinia there are fewer tombs painted in the Classical period but, by the 4th century BC decisive developments had taken place in the graphic arts. The drawing style of the painted pottery and engraved bronzes evokes three-dimensional space, in which overlapping figures are presented in integral groups, their heads and bodies sometimes shown in three-quarter poses and with foreshortening. These techniques were also used in large-scale paint-

the Ducks at Veii. On the walls are plain red and yellow zones, divided by horizontal bands of red, yellow, and black, upon which struts a row of birds. The colors and drawing recall 7th-century pottery in the Subgeometric style. Painted scenes flank an inner doorway of the Campana Tomb, also at Veii; here natural colors and proportions are disregarded and every available space filled with animal or floral motifs.

There were early painted tombs at Cerveteri and painted terracotta plaques have been found in both the necropolis and the living area, demonstrating that buildings, like tombs, had wall-paintings. Two series are outstanding, both painted in black, white, brown, and red/purple on a light background.

The Tomb of the Augurs

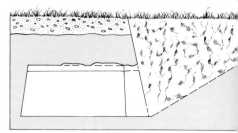

▶ Section and plan of the Tomb of the Augurs

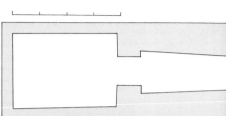

Near the ancient city of Tarquinia lies the Colle dei Monterozzi, the site of a great Etruscan cemetery. An occasional mound or tumulus, surrounded by cut-stone walling, might still be seen in the 19th century and some earthen mounds survive today. These tumuli crowned Etruscan tombs; the tombs were entered by a rock-cut stairway, leading from the open air down into the dark, cool chambers below. A few of the tombs were decorated with wall-paintings.

The Tomb of the Augurs is a small, rectangular chamber, cut from the soft rock, with the ceiling shaped to resemble a gabled room. The walls and ceiling were smoothed, plastered, and painted in fresco and the surviving paintings retain a fresh coloring with bright reds predominating. The architectural features of the ceiling are emphasized by color, the central beam in red and the sloping sides in white; the pediment space of the back wall (opposite the entrance) was filled with two feline animals attacking a deer, a scene now much damaged. Below this there is a horizontal band composed of black, red, white, and green stripes, and then the principal figurative frieze which has a white background. A red stripe forms the ground upon which the figures stand; below is a white stripe and a black dado reaching down to the floor. These elements continue around the whole chamber and serve to unite the figurative scenes of the frieze.

As in other Archaic wall-paintings, the artist first incised or outlined the forms in black, also sometimes dividing the areas of differing colors, and then filled them in with a uniform wash, adding some internal details. The figures and objects are drawn with little realization of three-dimensional space but the artist has striven to present a material realism and to note significant details. The delightful effect is achieved by the confident drawing of the lines, the interrelation of the figures together with a desire to fill the adjacent spaces, the bright colors, and the vitality of the scenes.

A fine doorway is shown at the center of the back wall—the lintel, jambs, and door frame are in contrasting reds, with the nail-heads picked out in white—and may symbolize an entrance into the afterlife: on either side stand men in attitudes of mourning and farewell. They wear white tunics and short black and red cloaks and boots. The adjacent spaces are filled with growing plants and a bird.

▼ The final figure on the left wall: a masked man in precipitous flight

Below right On the right wall: a boy carries a folding stool towards a man. A small mourning figure crouches between them

Three groups of figures, each forming a separate scene but all taking part in funerary games or ritual, appear on the right wall. On the left is a boy, dressed in a white tunic covered with black dots, carrying a folding stool towards a bearded man wearing a loosely draped, red cloak and boots, who gazes back over his shoulder. These figures are related by their gestures; between their feet, a small figure is crouched in an attitude of deep dejection, a black garment pulled over the head. To the right of this group stands a bearded man, bare-footed and wearing a black and red cloak over his tunic, who holds a curved stick or *lituus* in his right hand. Once he was considered to be an augur, or soothsayer, a theory that gave rise to the accepted name of the tomb, but this figure represents an umpire: he faces and gestures towards two burly wrestlers, the central figures of this wall. The wrestlers' attitude is tense and vigorous; they lean towards each other, their heads almost touching, their wrists clasped, as if to test each other's strength. The prizes, a pile of bronze bowls, are set between them; flowers

and flying birds fill the adjacent spaces. A second pair of combatants is shown on the right; a masked man, the word *Phersu* written beside his head and dressed in a short black tunic and red loincloth, holds a vicious dog on a leash; the dog is attacking a man who is blindfold and armed with a huge club. This scene, together with much of those painted on the entrance wall and the left wall, is sadly destroyed but the final figure on the left wall survives and shows a masked man in precipitous flight. Here, the artist has achieved a fine feeling of movement and filled the spaces between the limbs with plants and birds.

The Tomb of the Augurs is dated *c*530 BC, when the custom of decorating some tombs with wall-paintings was becoming well established at Tarquinia and the artists were capable of responding in a mature Archaic style, reflecting Greek black-figure vase-painting and closely allied to contemporary Etruscan ceramic art. At this time, Etruscan art was especially influenced by East Greek or Ionian taste and it is known that Ionian artists settled and worked in Etruria. A

▲ The back wall of the Tomb of the Augurs: the doorway with mourning men on either side

▼ On the right wall: an umpire, two burly wrestlers, and a masked man

familiarity and delight in Ionian style is shown in the flowing lines and corpulent figures of the paintings of the Tomb of the Augurs; the artist might have been of Ionian origin. These Ionian elements are mingled, however, both with subject matter and details often of purely local significance: the

figures wear Etruscan clothes; folding stools with ivory appliqué were much used in Etruria; and the *lituus* was an Etruscan symbol of authority. The games, held in honor of the dead, include wrestling, a sport adopted from the Greeks by the Archaic period, but also a more bloodthirsty ritual, described above. Though analogies are rare in Etruscan art, this must represent an Etruscan form of ritual or enactment of a myth. The words, written beside some figures, are descriptions in the Etruscan language; the

word *Phersu*, set beside a masked man, is found in Latin as *persona* meaning a mask, actor, or the part he played and hence has passed into several European languages, including English.

It is never simple to rationalize either religious beliefs concerning the afterlife or the manner in which they may have affected the construction or decoration of tombs. We do not know why some wealthy Etruscan families decided to decorate their tombs with wall-paintings, yet some idea that the dwellings of the dead should resemble the familiar homes of the living is inherent in the custom of carving a room from the living rock and of emphasizing its architectural features. The themes selected for presentation in the tomb paintings include scenes of earthly pleasures, perhaps in some sense expressing a hope of continued enjoyment after death. But often they also record the funerary games and rites held in remembrance of the dead and sometimes scenes of mourning, as do those of the Tomb of the Augurs.

ELLEN MACNAMARA

Bucchero jugs with modeled, impressed, and molded decoration

ings in polychrome, in which shading and highlights were added to express volume: the artists were also concerned to contrast light and dark areas. The scene of a Greek fighting Amazons, on a sarcophagus from Tarquinia (Museo Archeologico, Florence), illustrates late Classical handling of perspective and color tones. It may have been painted by a Greek artist working in Etruria.

As in other Etruscan art forms, a mood of despondency and a preoccupation with death are shown in Hellenistic tomb-paintings. Dreadful demons appear, often escorting the dead to the underworld and an idea of judgment is evident. Strong family feeling prevails, however, in paintings like those in the Tomb of the Shields at Tarquinia, in which successive generations are shown banqueting. The artist has attempted to express individuality and names are written beside the portraits. Occasionally civic pride appears, as in the illustration of the rescue of some famous Etruscan prisoners and the murder of

their captors, or a full-length portrait of a nobleman in ceremonial robes from the François Tomb at Vulci (Museo Torlonia, Rome). Such scenes remind us of the Etruscans' own recollections of their glorious past and of their contribution to Roman ritual.

Minor arts. In the absence of fine objects of wood, leather, textiles, or other perishable materials, the minor arts of the Etruscans must be judged mainly from their pottery and metalwork. Since both personal possessions and household objects were placed in tombs, they survive in some quantity and provide an eloquent commentary on the major arts.

Traditional Villanovan pottery had forms characteristic of the Italic Iron Age—fired, brown/black, with incised decoration. During the 8th century BC they also began to copy the shapes, light-colored fabric, and designs painted in red/brown, of Greek Geometric imports. By 700 BC, local potters were imitating yellow/buff Corinthian ware, decorating it in dark paint, sometimes depicting monsters, animals, or men from the Orientalizing repertoire.

The principal ceramic contribution of the Etruscans is a black, glossy ware called *bucchero*, which appears before the middle of the 7th century BC. Sometimes Villanovan forms with incised decoration were followed, but Greek pottery shapes became increasingly copied. Modeled embellishments were added, especially on vases imitating metalwork or carved ivory, and repeating patterns were impressed with a roller stamp. In the Archaic period, *bucchero* became heavy and over-decorated and, during the 5th century BC, production ceased.

Until *c*550 BC, Corinthian black-figure imports continued

Gold clasp from the Barberini Tomb, Palestrina; 7th-century BC. Villa Giulia, Rome

An earring and a ring decorated with granulation; 7th–6th century BC. British Museum, London

to dominate the Etruscan markets. Subsequently Ionian influence is evident and Ionian craftsmen even worked in Etruria. Their most outstanding products are the Caeretan *hydriae*, a series of water-jars made at Cerveteri. Athenian potters manufactured special exports for Etruria and, as their superb black-figure and red-figure pottery increased in popularity, they monopolized the trade. Meanwhile Etruscan potters produced black-figure vases with Greek forms. The painting is seldom elegant, but is usually bold, with lively figures.

The Etruscans were slow to adopt the true red-figure technique. At first they painted figures in red over a black ground, though they were aware of the development in drawing technique in the early Classical period. By the end of the 5th century BC fine red-figure vases, closely following Attic style, were being made, mainly at Vulci and at Cività Castellana. The south Italian schools also influenced Etruscan pottery of the 4th century BC, when northern cities, including Volterra, were producing red-figure ware. Black-glaze pottery became popular and, during the Hellenistic period sophisticated vase forms, silvered to imitate metal, were manufactured in central Etruria.

The Greeks praised Etruscan metalwork, particularly their goldwork and bronzes. Bronze was used for a very wide variety of goods, from jewelry to armor, from horse-gear to household furniture. Bronze was hammered, worked in repoussé, cast and engraved, the craftsmen following contemporary technical developments and artistic styles.

Pottery forms, especially those used for serving wine, were reproduced in bronze. Ladles, strainers, candelabra, incense-burners, braziers with their equipment, and other types of household goods were made of bronze and often finely decorated. Personal possessions include men's helmets, shields, armor, and beautiful toilet articles for women. Among these are caskets, in which combs, carved powder boxes, delicate perfume bottles, and the accompanying perfume pins and oil flasks were kept, and the wonderful series of hand mirrors with mythological and genre scenes engraved upon the backs.

Among luxury goods, amber and ivory were carved, the former used mainly for jewelry and the latter for chalices, combs, and boxes. Multicolored glass served for beads, brooches, and perfume-bottles. Semiprecious stones were cut and employed in rings and other jewelry. Gold and silver were used for cups and jugs and, above all, for jewelry.

Etruscan jewelry is celebrated for its craftsmanship, particularly for goldwork using the technique of granulation. In the 7th century BC Italic forms and Orientalizing designs were mingled in Etruscan jewelry but later Hellenic taste was followed. Brooches, pins, finger-rings, bracelets, earrings, hairbands, buckles, and other pieces were exquisitely worked in the contemporary artistic style, a reminder of both the good taste and the ostentation of Etruscan nobles in the centuries of their prosperity.

Conclusion. Modern art historians have reached different conclusions about the achievements of the Etruscans in the visual arts. Some have considered them mere plagiarists, adopting Greek forms with little originality and indifferent ability. Others, noting how the Etruscans educated their Italic neighbors, have credited them with exceptional sensibility and craftsmanship.

Some truth lies at both extremes. Without a substantial Italic tradition in the visual arts, the Etruscans were inspired by Hellenic styles in all seven centuries of their independent artistic development. Yet lacking the historic and intellectual background of Greek art, Etruscan artists sometimes failed to respond to Greek ideals and were capable of producing poor-quality work unacceptable in the Greek world. Etruscan art cannot claim to rank with that of Greece but its merit distinguishes it from contemporary Italic cultures and requires that

it be judged by Greek standards. The Etruscans were always selective in their choice of Greek artistic precedents but, when their artists carefully followed them, they came close to the Hellenic models. When they took Greek forms and styles but adapted them to Etruscan conventions and taste, they subtly transformed them into their own, and even contributed new art forms.

The Etruscans must also take their place in the history of the visual arts as vital intermediaries between the Greeks and Romans. Profiting from the rich resources of their homeland, the Etruscans welcomed the civilization of their Greek contemporaries. During Rome's early development the neighboring Etruscans were an acknowledged source of culture, and introduced many Hellenic forms to Rome.

ELLEN MACNAMARA

Bibliography. Boëthius, A. *Etruscan and Early Roman Architecture*, Harmondsworth (1979). Coarelli, F. (ed.) *Etruscan Cities*, London (1975). Haynes, S. *Etruscan Sculpture*, London (1971). Heurgon, J. *Daily Life of the Etruscans*, London (1964). Moretti, M. and Maetzke, G. *The Art of the Etruscans*, London (1970). Pallottino, M. *Etruscan Painting*, New York (1952). Pallottino, M. *The Art of the Etruscans*, London (1955). Pallottino, M. *The Etruscans*, London (1975). Richardson, E. *Etruscan Sculptures*, London (1966). Richardson, E. *The Etruscans, their Art and Civilization*, Chicago (1964). Sprenger, M. and Bartoloni, G. *Die Etrusker: Kunst und Geschichte*, Munich (1977).

11

ROMAN ART

**A bronze statuette of a household god, adapted from a Hellenistic prototype
c31 BC–AD 14. Ashmolean Museum, Oxford (see page 178)**

ROMAN Art—strictly speaking—is the art of the city of Rome, or at least art executed by or for Romans. Such a definition is, however, too narrow and ignores the great cultural achievements of the *pax romana*. Between the 1st century BC and the 4th century AD diverse traditions, Hellenistic, Italic, Celtic, Berber, Levantine, and Egyptian interacted and acquired a distinctively Roman stamp, at once diverse and unified. In the later Empire, contemporaries did not find it incongruous that the Empire was ruled from Trier, Milan, Nicomedia, or Constantinople. In a famous encomium, Rutilius Namatianus an early 5th-century aristocrat from Gaul, wrote that "because Rome has given the conquered equal rights under her Law she has made a City out of what was once a world".

The character of Rome's cultural achievement is often misunderstood. To some extent this is a legacy of the Roman literary tradition. Cicero (106–44 BC) in his prosecution of Gaius Verres, Governor of Sicily (and notorious art-thief), in 73–70 BC contrasted the Greek love of statues and painting with the near indifference of the average Roman. Yet Cicero was a noted connoisseur and Philhellene, whose passion for art was no doubt equal to that of his Greek clients. Virgil (70–19 BC) writing a Latin epic, the *Aeneid*, to rival Homer,

conceded Greek supremacy in the arts; the Roman mission was "to impose the way of peace, to spare the conquered and crush the proud". If the popular image of Roman civilization lays emphasis on the might of her legions, the cruelty of her rulers, and the vulgarity and decadence of her arts and morals, this reputation stems from such persuasive (and biased) writers as Petronius, critic and satirist (*fl.* mid 1st century AD), Seneca, moralist and embittered poet (*c*4 BC–AD 65), Tacitus, historian and enemy to the pretensions of the Julio-Claudian and Flavian dynasties (*c* AD 56–*c* AD 115).

Of course some truth lies in their perception, if the population of the empire is to be rigidly divided into "conquerors" and "conquered" and the name "Roman" taken in the narrowest of all senses. But such over simplification ignores the Roman army's part in bringing and encouraging Mediterranean art styles in distant corners of the Empire. Consider, for example, the delightful Antonine reliefs set up by the legions of Britain in southern Scotland to mark the completion of a new frontier (*c* AD 143), or the distinctive tombstones carved in military workshops around all the borders of the Empire. It ignores the restraint of so much Roman architecture—the Market at Leptis, the little round temple at Tivoli, and even the Imperial fora at Rome—whose effectiveness derives more

The Roman Empire with some places mentioned in the text

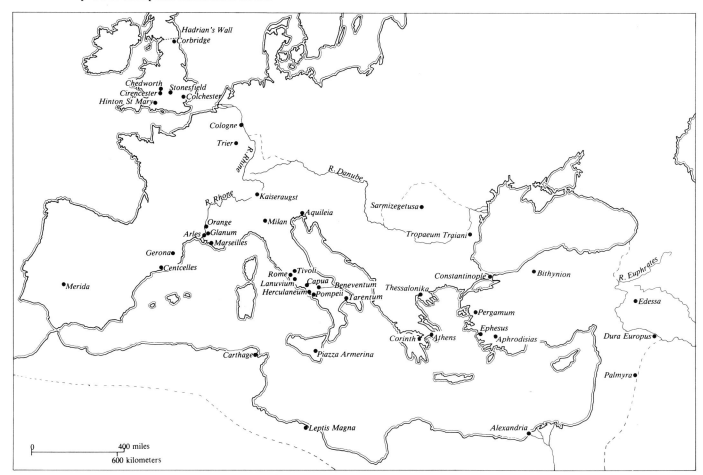

from skillful planning, from the positioning of buildings in organic relationships to others, and from the natural environment, than simply from sheer size. Even if Trimalchio in the *Satyricon* misused refinement, it certainly exists in the chastity of the best sculpture, painting, silverware, gems, and glassware. Any prolonged study of Roman art must emphasize the links with Classical and Hellenistic Greece, with a culture manifestly living and vital.

A second difficulty in assessing Roman art arises from the nature of classicism itself. Sculptors and painters of the 5th and 4th centuries BC are known to us by name, and their individual innovations were recorded at some length by such writers of the Roman age as the Elder Pliny (AD 23–79) and Pausanias (*fl.* mid 2nd century AD). Unfortunately our sources look backwards in their attitudes—Pliny dismisses the creative High Hellenistic Age (296–156 BC) in one short sentence: "Then Art stopped." Judged by such standards, copying and pastiche were the only respectable approaches, and although Pasiteles in the 1st century BC achieved some fame as a classicizer in both sculpture and toreutics, it must have been hard for artists to achieve distinction. The ways of representing the human body, its musculature and gestures had been learned. All that was left was to combine figures in a meaningful way, symmetrically, as in the *nymphaeum* of Herodes Atticus at Olympia (mid 2nd century AD), or dramatically, as in the grotto at Sperlonga (1st century AD). What had been perfected by the masters could not be improved. Copying was a craft, like milling or shoemaking, and like them its products were seldom signed.

Fortunately the artists came from different backgrounds, and so did not treat the Classical heritage in the same way. They were challenged by new political ideologies—and produced a fine tradition of Imperial State relief; by new techniques—and developed the crafts of the mosaicist and stuccoist; by new religious ideas—and created the symbolism of the various mystery cults.

Roman art was both varied and constantly changing. Who could deduce the hieratic symbolism of the base of the obelisk of Theodosius (AD 390) at Constantinople from the tree-figure groups of *Ara Pacis*, so obviously modeled on the Parthenon frieze? And do the little niche mosaics at Herculaneum (1st century AD) give any real premonition of the great 4th-century vault at Centcelles near Tarragona, perhaps the mausoleum of the Emperor Constans who died in AD 350? How free the painting of the Villa of the Mysteries, Pompeii (1st century BC) seems alongside the formal row of Orantes from the Lullingstone house-church (British Museum, London; 4th century AD). The art of the Roman period not only bridged Antiquity and the Middle Ages but was an era of staggering achievement in its own right.

The Republic (*c*500–31 BC). Early Republican art was basically Etruscan. Latium lay between the important centers of northern and southern "Etruria" and was influenced by both. In the early 5th century BC Vulca, the great sculptor in ter-

racotta from Veii, was summoned to make the cult-image of Jupiter for the temple on the Capitoline Hill. The southern Etruscan enclave around Praeneste was noted for its bronze-work; a fine engraved casket, the Cista Ficoroni (4th century BC; Villa Giulia, Rome), carries a Latin inscription on its handle: "Novios Plautios made me in Rome; Dindia Macolnia gave me to her daughter."

Before Rome became a Mediterranean power early in the 2nd century BC, Greek influence was experienced largely at second hand via Etruria. This did not imply indifference to the arts: Fabius Pictor, from the renowned *gens* of the Fabii and, as his name implies, a painter, decorated the temple of Salus (Health) in 304 BC. A painting of battle and treaty scenes from a tomb on the Esquiline may give some idea of his somewhat archaic style (*c*200 BC; Museo Capitolino, Rome).

Art was, no doubt, largely practical. A famous passage in Polybios (*c*200–*post* 118 BC) describes Roman funerary rites:

> they place a portrait of the deceased in the most prominent part of the house, enclosing it in a small wooden aedicular shrine. The portrait is a mask which is wrought with the utmost attention being paid to preserving a likeness in regard to shape and contour ... When a prominent member of the family dies, they carry them in the funeral procession, putting them on those who seem most like the deceased in size and build.

This attention to the features of the dead is typically Etruscan, suggesting that Roman attachment to *verismo* portraiture and the idea of the portrait bust itself must be of Italian origin, however much their forms were transformed by new materials and techniques from the Hellenistic east.

A relief in the Museo Capitolino from Rome is carved in the coarse local travertine. It shows the busts of Blaesius and his wife Blaesia within a rectangular frame. No attempt has been made to model the upper parts of their bodies, and their heads are frontal, icon-like masks similar to those on the reclining figures of Etruscan sarcophagi. We observe the same rounded faces, prominent lips, and (in the case of Blaesius) large ears. The relief dates from *c*75 BC. Similar in general design, but probably about 30 years later, the tombstone of L. Ampudius Philomusus, his wife and daughter, now in the British Museum, London, marked a considerable advance in technique. The wrinkles on Philomusus' face bring to mind a bust in the Museo Torlonia, Rome, which depicts an old man, as well as the portraits on coins of C. Antius Restio (*c*46 BC).

The more integrated structure of these heads springs from contact with the Greek world, demonstrated by the head of a priest from the Athenian Agora, where the marks of age are treated with the same simple dignity as on the Museo Torlonia Bust. Indeed, many late Republican portraits from Italy were doubtless the works of immigrant sculptors. Instead of low quality travertine they used marble, which allowed sculptors to model with greater precision than had previously been possible. Native traditions were never forgotten—a marble statue of Augustan date in the Museo Capitolino, Rome, depicts a Roman with the busts of two ancestors, as though he were a participant in the funerary ceremony described by

Polybios. It is easy to see strong Hellenistic influence in the drapery and in the figure's head, but the subject is undeniably Roman.

Two reliefs, possibly from the same monument (the Altar of Domitius Ahenobarbus) but certainly of the same date, show that at least two styles of relief were current in mid-1st-century Italy. The relief in Munich (Staatliche Antikensammlungen) shows the marriage of Peleus and Thetis in a marine *thiasos*—reminiscent of work from western Asia Minor. The other slab, in the Louvre, Paris, depicts a Roman official taking a census and a state sacrifice, in the prosaic "matter-of-fact" manner of the Esquiline painting. If the gestures of the figures—magistrates, soldiers, and priests—appear somewhat stiff, it is because they were the first step towards mastering historical relief, achieved barely half a century later in the *Ara Pacis*.

The art of painting was well established in Etruria as well as among the Greek cities of Magna Graecia. Despite the existence of a local tradition epitomized by the Esquiline tomb-painting and inferred from the literary descriptions of tableaux displayed at military triumphs, the main line of development in the late Republic came from the Hellenistic world.

As early as the 4th century BC, plaster relief based on architectural forms, such as cornices or wall-facings imitative of marble, were employed at Athens and Olynthos. The Masonry style became common throughout the Hellenistic world, for example at Pergamum, Delos, and the cities of southern Italy. In Campania, where elaborate architectural compositions are to be found in the House of the Faun, Pompeii, and in the Samnite House, Herculaneum, it is frequently called the First Pompeian style.

The decorative potential of such walls was, of course, limited and attention was frequently centered on elaborate polychrome floor mosaics. These again emphasize the Greek origins of Romano-Campanian decoration, whether in the case of the great Battle of Issus pavement from the House of the Faun (Museo Archeologico, Naples) based on a painting by Philoxenos of Eretria (*fl.* end of 4th century BC) or in that of a winged Dionysos seated upon the back of a snarling tiger, an *emblema* in the House of Dionysos, Delos. One of the most famous mosaics from Pompeii (Museo Archeologico, Naples) depicts a group of wandering musicians and exploits the late Hellenistic skill in genre scenes. It is signed by Dioskourides of Samos (*fl.* early 1st century BC) and is thus certainly of eastern inspiration whether Dioskourides was resident in Italy or exporting small, fully-assembled pavements from the Greek Islands.

From *c*70 BC a major change in interior design becomes evident, but because of lack of evidence outside Italy it is not possible to know whether the Second style originated in Italy or resulted from outside impetus. As Rome was now the major center of artistic patronage in the Ancient world there is much to be said in favor of the first possibility, although many of the artists involved were doubtless Greek.

The Second style was a logical extension of the First. In-stead of the room being enclosed by blocks of imitation stone, a skillful use of perspective produced a world of receding vistas, which allowed full play to the imagination. In the House of the Labyrinth at Pompeii, a *tholos* (circular pavilion) is glimpsed just beyond the garden wall. Similar *tholoi* are shown in the *triclinium* of a recently excavated villa at Oplontis and in the *cubiculum* of the villa of Publius Fannius Synistor, Boscoreale (paintings now in the Metropolitan Museum, New York). They probably had a funerary significance and can be compared with such monuments as the Mausoleum of the Julii at Glanum in Provence or the mausoleum called *La Conocchia* (the distaff) at Santa Maria Capua Vetera. At Boscoreale the wall of the room includes fanciful representations of buildings as well as landscapes and garden scenes which introduce a sense of space. However, the presence of the so-called "Adonis gardens", broken pots from which herbs are growing, suggests that the owner had a special interest in the Adonis myth and in the ideas of rebirth connected with it.

This theme is developed in a cult-room containing paintings, some of which are now in New York (Metropolitan Museum) and some in Naples (Museo Archeologico). The figures boldly painted on a red ground almost certainly contain representations of Adonis and Aphrodite (Venus), but some details, including a Macedonian shield, suggest that the fresco was adapted from a Hellenistic original.

The Villa of the Mysteries, just outside Pompeii, also has a cult-room similar in general conception and probably of the same date (*c*40 BC). Round the room, as though on a stage, preparations are being made for an initiation; it ends in a marvelous detail of Ignorance attempting to whip the neophyte. She, however, is protected by Initiation and beyond her we observe a Maenad dancing in ecstasy, symbolizing the successful accomplishment of the ordeal. Dionysos and Ariadne preside over the ceremony. The cult of Dionysos (Bacchus) had achieved certain notoriety earlier in the Republic (*c*186 BC) but came to be an accepted part of Roman religion, bringing as it did the promise of salvation.

Not all Second style painting is strictly religious. A frieze in the Vatican Museums, Rome, from a house in Rome shows scenes from the *Odyssey*. Individual figures are identified by name (in Greek characters); it is possible that the artist based his work on an illustrated scroll of the work. There is nothing small scale, however, in the rocky landscapes of the country of the Lestrygonians, the mysterious house of the enchantress Circe, or the almost medieval horror of the tribulations of the damned in Tartarus.

Perhaps the most successful surviving painting in the Second style is the luxuriant wild garden depicted in an underground room of a villa at Prima Porta near Rome (paintings now in the Terme Museum, Rome). The house was built in the third quarter of the 1st century BC for Livia, wife of Octavian (who was later known as Augustus) and the painting can

Right: Panel II from the cubiculum of the villa of Publius Fannius Sinistor, Boscoreale; height 244cm (96in). Metropolitan Museum, New York

A luxuriant wild garden: a Second style painting from Livia's villa at Prima Porta; height 300cm (118in). Terme Museum, Rome

probably be dated to *c*25 BC. In place of the somewhat stylized vistas of the Boscoreale bedroom we seem to have unimpeded access to a garden in which all manner of trees, shrubs, and flowering plants—laurels, oleanders, cypresses, quinces, roses, periwinkles, poppies—grow in luxuriant profusion. Beautiful birds fly amongst the foliage adding to the general impression of peace and harmony. Actual gardens which may have approximated to the Prima Porta "ordered wilderness" have been revealed by excavation (for example at the Palace of Fishbourne, Sussex, England, from the late 1st century AD, perhaps the residence of a local client king called Cogidubnus). The virtuosity of this painting is matched by that of the

A still-life composition from the house of Julia Felix, Pompeii. Museo Archeologico Nazionale, Naples

marvelous still-life compositions showing bowls of fruit, eggs, thrushes, silver vessels, and pieces of textile in the House of Julia Felix, at Pompeii (Museo Archeologico, Naples). Like the Prima Porta fresco, which reveals a truly Roman taste for nature, they provide rare examples of Roman inventiveness which does not seem to look back to Greek precedents.

The molded elements of First style walls were forced upwards in the decorative schema of Second style rooms, and in late Republican lunettes and vaults achieved a high level of accomplishment. In the House of the Griffins, Rome (*c*70 BC), a pair of spirited confronted Griffins fill one lunette and a plant motif the other. The style of these devices is reminiscent of decorative sculpture used widely at this time for garden furniture. Greater originality is shown in the vaults of the House of the Cryptoporticus, Pompeii (*c*40 BC), which are enriched with coffers containing devices in relief: plants, items of armor, objects connected with Bacchus. In these ceilings the use of color was avoided (as, indeed, on contemporary floors with their monochrome mosaics), so that attention might be focused on the walls.

Although the Second style displayed an orderly and consistent strength in planning it soon gave way to a more truly decorative fashion. In the vault in one room of the House of the Cryptoporticus there are fanciful pairs of animals confronting each other. Similar conceits are found on the walls of Livia's villa in Rome, the Farnesina House, which can be very little later than the Prima Porta house. The organic unity of the walls was finally broken. Small panel pictures were divided from each other by purely decorative elements which do not betray any idea of function. The design of the vaults followed the same scheme: panels between fanciful ornament.

Vitruvius, a contemporary writer on architecture (*fl.* late 1st century BC) complained that

> those subjects which were copied from actual realities are scorned in these days of bad taste. We now have fresco paintings of monstrosities, rather than truthful representations of definite things. For instance, reeds are put in place of columns, fluted appendages with curly leaves and volutes, instead of pediments, candelabra supporting representations of shrines, and on top of their pediments numerous tender stalks and volutes growing up from the roots and having human figures senselessly seated upon them; sometimes stalks having only half-length figures; some with human heads, others with the heads of animals. Such things do not exist and cannot exist and never have existed ... For how is it possible that a reed should really support a roof, or a candelabrum a pediment with its ornaments, or that such a slender, flexible thing as a stalk should support a figure perched upon it, or that roots and stalks should produce now flowers and now half-length figures? (*Vitruvius, the Ten Books on Architecture*, trans. Morgan, H.M., Harvard University Press, 1914.)

The most delightful examples of this style of elegant conceit may be seen in Naples and New York. They come from the Villa of Agrippa Postumus (12 BC–AD 14) at Boscotrecase. Here we find floral motifs reminiscent of those on the *Ara Pacis* and light architectural frames which merely serve to emphasize the solidity of the walls. However, the sense of illusion so prominent in the great Second style cycles of painting is not absent. Mythological and sacro-idyllic landscapes encapsulate the natural world in the same small-scale ways as do the watercolors of early-19th-century landscape artists. Pliny mentions a painter, probably named Ludius or Studius (the text is corrupt)

> active during the time of the Divine Augustus ... who first instituted that most delightful technique of painting walls with representations of villas, porticoes and landscape gardens, woods, groves, hills, pools, channels, rivers, coastlines.

However artificial works of the Third style are in general effect, individual elements were well observed. Thus the swags in a room of the Farnesina House, Rome, contain a profusion of different sorts of fruit recalling the swags carved on the inner screen wall of the *Ara Pacis*, the unique Caffarelli Sarcophagus (Staatliche Museen, Berlin) and numerous altars and ash-chests of the time.

These normally portray garlands suspended from *bucrania* (bulls' skulls) by ribbons, which billow out in accordance with the demands of symmetry, not the wind. On the four sides of the ash-chest of Aelia Postumia (Fitzwilliam Museum, Cambridge) a pair of birds is shown beneath each swag and either a bird or a Gorgoneion above. An altar from the theatre at Arles (Arles Museum) depicts swans holding garlands in their beaks. Delightful as such artifice certainly is, Vitruvius could not have approved. Yet the sculptors of the late 1st century BC and the early 1st century AD were capable of such *tours de force* as Livia's garden room at Prima Porta. An altar in the

Terme Museum, Rome, has a couple of crossed plane branches portrayed on its front face. The curl of the leaves and the perceptible variety in their shapes suggest that they were sculpted from nature, although the arrangement of the composition as a whole remains artificial.

The early Empire (31 BC–AD 193). The reign of Augustus (31 BC–AD 14) does not mark a watershed; so it is not very helpful to contrast the late Republic with the Augustan Age. Only in the sphere of propaganda and state art can a new sense of purpose be discerned.

> We have reached the last era of Sibylline Song. Time has conceived and the great sequence of the Ages starts afresh. Justice, the Virgin, comes back to dwell with us, and the rule of Saturn is restored (trans. E.V. Rieu).

So wrote Virgil in his famous fourth Ecologue.

Graphic expression is given to these lofty thoughts by the *Ara Pacis*—the Altar of Peace—which is both the culmination of Republican Hellenism and the masterpiece of Augustan art. It was erected, according to its own propaganda, to celebrate the major achievement of the regime: the restoration of peace to the Roman world after more than a generation of violence and civil war. The site was consecrated in 13 BC and the structure finished in 9 BC.

The altar itself is ornamented with a very small frieze which recalls a similar frieze in the temple of Apollo Sosianus (*c*20 BC). Here we observe the Suevotaurilia (sacrifice of bull, ram, and pig), and a number of priests and vestal virgins who await Augustus as the officiating magistrate. All the awkwardness of the Altar of Domitius Ahenobarbus has gone; instead we discern a minute gem-like precision which suggests the influence of cameo-carving, which had achieved a peak of technical virtuosity. The famous *Gemma Augustea* belongs to the early 1st century AD (Kunsthistorisches Museum, Vienna), but other masterpieces of glyptic art are known to have originated in court studios at an even earlier date.

At the corners, decorative griffins and sprays of acanthus recall the ornamental garden furniture of the late Republic, perhaps carved by artists from Asia Minor (from Pergamum?). We have noted similar motifs on stucco in the House of the Griffins, Rome.

The long sides of the outer screen walls are divided into two registers. (Inside, the hanging swags and *bucrania* already mentioned recall the original ceremony on the site in 13 BC when a temporary fence was erected to shield the officiating priests from sights of ill-omen.) The lower, an intricate conceit of acanthus combined with other plants and flowers and inhabited by birds and small creatures, closely recalls the Third style in painting. The swans, which perch on tendrils too slender for them, bring to mind one of the motifs on the Farnesina stucco, as well as the device on the Arles altar. They allude to Augustus' veneration for the god Apollo, to whom swans were sacred. Above this decorative band is a procession led by Augustus himself, doubtless inspired by the Parthenon frieze but modified according to the factual character of Roman

On the Ara Pacis (Altar of Peace), erected to celebrate peace in the Roman world: Italy, or Mother Earth, between personifications of air and water

historical relief. As in actual life, not everyone is intent on the ceremony. For example, the children of members of the Imperial family are more concerned about not getting lost and grasp the garments or hands of their parents; Augustus' sister Octavia has to rebuke her daughter Antonia who is talking to her husband Lucius Domitius Ahenobarbus as the sacred rites are about to begin.

A different treatment is accorded to the end walls which contain the entrances. Above the acanthus register are carefully chosen neo-Attic reliefs, which recall the private commissions rich people in the late Republic kept in their houses (for example, Dionysos visiting a poet who reclines on his couch in front of a rich architectural background, on a slab in the British Museum, London). The only difference here is that the devices chosen serve the ends of State propaganda. The best preserved of these reliefs are the Sacrifice of Aeneas in front of a temple of the Penates at Lanuvium, and Italy (or Mother Earth) between personifications of air and water. The latter figure can be compared with Tellus as portrayed on the breastplate of the Prima Porta Statue of Augustus, certainly of eastern origin, and based on clear Hellenistic precedents.

Few compositions so clearly challenge us with the basic problems of Roman art as the *Ara Pacis*. It is supremely harmonious, and marries baroque and classicizing tendencies with great skill. It is the consummate expression of the Roman mission, "to spare the conquered and put down the proud". The historical context of its erection is known. Yet, for all that, it is the work of Greeks and *unknown* Greeks at that.

Gems and silver plate also frequently carry propaganda devices. They are often of high quality and engraved gemstones are often signed by the artists responsible. The compliments paid to the Emperor and his family are extremely fulsome and recall the adulation bestowed on Hellenistic kings. Of course this was only possible because they were intended for courtiers who were not hostile to the frankly monarchic ambitions of the Caesars.

An intaglio (now in the Museum of Fine Arts, Boston) depicts Octavian (Augustus) as Neptune driving a chariot pulled by sea horses. It presumably refers to his victory over Marcus Antonius and Cleopatra at Actium (31 BC). A pair of gems show the Emperor in the persona of the god Mercury (private collection, London), and Octavia his sister, as the goddess Diana (British Museum, London). The style in each of these cases matches the signed work of the gem-cutter Solon in its baroque intensity.

One of Augustus' signet rings, mentioned by both the Elder Pliny and by Suetonius, carried his own portrait and was cut by a certain Dioskourides (not, of course, the mosaicist mentioned above). This gem does not survive but several others by Dioskourides are extant. The best is perhaps the one at Chatsworth, Derbyshire, England, which shows Diomedes stealing the Palladium from Troy, a popular theme also tackled by other gem-cutters such as Gnaios (Chatsworth) and Felix (Ashmolean Museum, Oxford). An intaglio by Dioskourides, in Naples (Museo Archeologico), depicts Achilles wearing the armor of Thetis. The neoclassicism of these gems recalls the

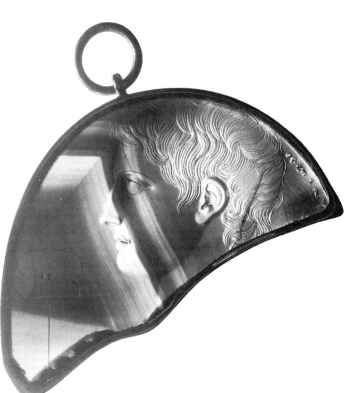

The Emperor Augustus as Mercury: an agate intaglio; mount modern. Private collection

Octavia as Diana: an agate intaglio. British Museum, London

work of the sculptor Pasiteles, and gives us considerable insight into Augustus' own tastes. The Achilles gem in particular may have been intended to compliment the Emperor's supposed heroic qualities. It is noteworthy that we are told that prior to using his own portrait he employed a signet depicting Alexander the Great, a known admirer of Achilles.

Certainly a silver cup from a chieftain's grave at Hoby, Denmark (National Museum, Copenhagen) depicts Achilles, with the features of Augustus, confronting a submissive Priam. The artist, a certain Cheirisophos, was making a subtle allusion to Rome's magnanimity to the barbarian world, specifically to Parthia in the east. The cup should be compared with one of a pair found at Boscoreale, dating from the reign of Tiberius (AD 14–37; Rothschild Collection, France) which depicts Augustus receiving the submission of a native chieftain. It is executed in the same matter-of-fact style as most Roman state reliefs but the relative positions of the two key figures (Emperor and barbarian) are the same as on the Hoby cup.

The most famous Roman cameo is probably the *Gemma Augustea* (Kunsthistorisches Museum, Vienna). It dates from the end of Augustus' reign (*c*AD 12) when Tiberius had been adopted as heir. Augustus is shown as if still in the prime of youth. A Capricorn, his birth-sign, above his head, the goddess Roma seated beside him, and other features identify the Emperor as no ordinary mortal but the beloved companion of the gods. Tiberius, however, steps naturally enough from his triumphal chariot in order to pay his respects. The everyday world intrudes—it is the *numen* (spiritual power) of Augustus, not his body, that is incorruptible; the Imperial power not the Emperor's that is continuous and eternal.

This use of allegory is derived from Hellenistic art and may be seen on the *Tazza Farnese* (Museo Archeologico, Naples). Though it has been variously explained, J. Charbonneaux suggested that it glorifies Cleopatra I (Regent 181–176 BC) in the persona of Euthenia-Isis, wife of the Nile, and that the youthful figure beside her is her son, Ptolemy VI, as Harpokrates. It is possible that this fine cameo was brought to Italy as a spoil of war after the Battle of Actium (31 BC). A piece of silver plate, found at Aquileia (Kunsthistorisches Museum, Vienna) might be dated to just before the battle if the key figures represented are Marcus Antonius as Triptolemos and Cleopatra as Demeter. As on the *Tazza Farnese*, the seasons are personified and the earth goddess, Tellus, also appears.

The silver cup from Hoby. National Museum, Copenhagen

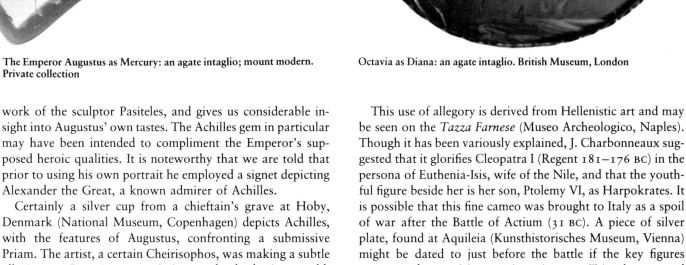

Some scholars assign the work to the reign of Claudius, but his features are not resembled by those of Triptolemos.

Political and eschatological allegory have much in common. The Portland Vase, a blown glass vessel in two layers cut as a cameo, now one of the treasures of the British Museum, London, has been interpreted as portraying Augustus as Peleus and Livia as Thetis, though there are simpler, perhaps more cogent, explanations. Certainly, both Peleus and Thetis are shown on the vase and also, to follow Professor Ashmole's explanation, Achilles and Helen of Troy resting after death on the White Island in the Euxine Sea. The meaning of both scenes is that heroic souls achieve felicity after death. A vase in Naples, produced by the same method, portrays cupids gathering grapes and again alludes to the idea of resurrection within the context of generalized Dionysiac belief. Fallen capitals shown on both the Portland Vase and the Blue Vase have counterparts in the discarded drinking vessels below a pair of centaurs playing musical instruments on the funerary altar of the Imperial freedman Amemptus dating from the reign of Tiberius (AD 14–37; Louvre, Paris). The meaning is surely

The Portland Vase; height 25cm (10in); 1st century AD.
British Museum, London

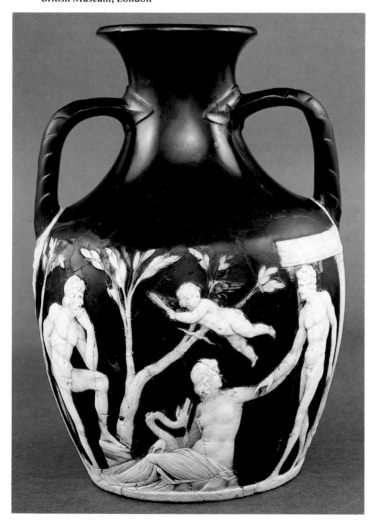

connected with the discarding of earthly things in favor of the joys of the other world.

The art of the Julio-Claudian period (AD 14–68), at least until c AD 60, continued to be fashioned in the same Augustan mold. Thus the portraits of Tiberius (AD 14–37), Gaius (AD 37–41), Claudius (AD 41–54), and other members of the *Domus Divina* (including a formidable company of Imperial women such as Livia and Agrippina I) are shown with much the same features as those of Augustus and his contemporaries. In general their traits are idealizing but individual. See, for example, the details of coiffure or prominence of jaw or nose. The portraits are Greek in conception and some of the best examples come from the East (for example, the veiled head of a Julio-Claudian prince, dated c AD 29, in the site Museum, Corinth).

The Prima Porta statue of Augustus from Livia's suburban villa (Vatican Museum, Rome), is a posthumous work as the bare feet common to gods and deified mortals testify. It combines a typical Julio-Claudian portrait with a body taken from the famous Doryphoros of Polykleitos. However, what might have been incompetent pastiche is given vibrancy and power by an adaptation of the gesture so that the right arm is held out in an attitude of command; by the adoption of the dress of a Roman general; and even by the support—a cupid on a dolphin which provides a reference to the descent of the Julii from Venus Genetrix. Most fascinating of all is the breastplate which is reminiscent of the art of state cameos and silver plate as well as of the *Ara Pacis*. The central motif is the return of a Roman Eagle captured from Crassus by the Parthians. Other figures represent conquered provinces, one of which is Gaul, and we also observe personifications of Earth and Sky.

An altar similar to the *Ara Pacis*, the *Ara Pietatis*, was begun in AD 22. Two of its scenes survive showing figures standing in front of buildings (Villa Medici, Rome). Although the groupings are somewhat mannered, the introduction of architecture as an important element in the background of Roman reliefs was an advance, and looks forward to the complex scenes of Trajan's Column. One of a pair of silver cups from Boscoreale showing state scenes has been mentioned; the other portrays Tiberius in a triumphal chariot and the sacrifice of a bull, very similar to the sacrifice on one of the *Ara Pietatis* slabs. Continuity with the past is also reinforced by a state cameo, almost as famous as the *Gemma Augustea*, the *Grand Camée de France* (Cabinet des Médailles, Paris). Tiberius now occupies the dominant position, seated in majesty as the "earthly Jupiter". Beside him is his mother, Livia, and in front of them stands Germanicus, returned from campaigning on the northern frontier and about to depart for the east (AD 17). Above the mortal members of the Imperial house are the deceased members who have become gods (*divi*), foremost among them Augustus, holding his scepter. Both the *Gemma Augustea* and the *Grand Camée* show representations of conquered barbarians in a subsidiary lower register. The flowing hair of the unfortunate captives and the sense of rhythmic order are in the High Hellenistic manner, which flourished in the Greek world during the 2nd century BC, and it is very clear that this style still had its admirers.

The most interesting and, perhaps, significant development of these years (at least in the Roman west) occurred in southern Gaul. It would be hard to credit the fact that the Arch at Orange was erected and carved in the same decade as *Ara Pietatis* if epigraphic evidence had not fixed its dedication to AD 26. Above the side passages is an assortment of Celtic arms which seems highly appropriate in a structure marking the refoundation of a colony of legionary veterans. Names of Gaulish origin appear on the shields, either as a record of the conquered chieftains or, more probably, as signatures of the artists who carved these impressive panoplies. It has been suggested that the words "Voillus/avot" on one shield mean "Voillus fecit"—"Voillus made it" (although both "Voillus" and "Avot" could be different names). If so, the arch gives valuable testimony to the existence of skilled artists who were not Greeks. In the light of this, it is all the more of a shock to realize that the brilliant illusionism of the relief derives from such compositions as the balustrade of the temple of Athena Nikophoros at Pergamum and not from a study of contemporary Gaulish ethnography. A similar antiquarianism is to be seen in the panels of naval spoils above them. They are shown because it was appropriate that a victory monument in the Pergamene tradition should contain such allusions. Ever since the Battle of Actium Rome had been undisputed mistress of the seas.

The reliefs in the attic of the arch were quite unlike anything in Rome at the time: magnificent battle scenes involving a grand melée, clearly related to the sort of composition found on the frieze of the temple of Artemis, Magnesia (in Asia Minor) in the 2nd century BC (Louvre, Paris). But they are not unique because similar battle scenes concerned with events from Greek mythology ornament the base of the mausoleum of the Julii at Glanum, a work dating from the late 1st century BC, mentioned above in connection with *tholoi* in Second style frescoes. Here, and in other major sculptural groups from southern Gaul, such as the trophy of Saint Bertrand-de-Comminges, there existed a full-blooded version of High Hellenistic art which had not been watered down by the classicizing tendencies of the Pasiteleans. It must be remembered that Marseilles (Massilia) was still Greek in culture and had strong links with Magna Graecia as well as with areas even further to the east.

In the reign of Nero (AD 54–68) and to an even greater extent in Flavian times (AD 69–96), these baroque tendencies manifested themselves in Italy. The change can be seen first in painting where the Third style gave way to the Fourth, which was illusionistic and, like the Second style, aimed to open out the wall. However, unlike these earlier paintings the vistas do not allow any true escape from the room but merely present a progression of theatrical *scaenae*. Although the idea of the style came from Greece, it was championed by Emperor Nero whose court artist Famulus is one of the few Roman as opposed to Greek artists whose names have come down to us.

A coin of Nero

Pliny tells us that

> he was grave and severe in his person, while his painting was rich and vivid ... He painted for a few hours only in the day, and treated his art seriously, always wearing the toga, even when mounted on scaffolding. The Golden House [Nero's palace] was the prison of his art, and hence not many examples of it are known.

Although buried beneath later structures, some of the rooms in Nero's Golden House have survived. Others were preserved until the time of the Renaissance, when the fanciful paintings from underground grottoes gave rise to the word "grotesque".

The reopening out of the wall reached its apogee at Pompeii in decoration executed after the earthquake of AD 62. The scenes of Atys amongst the nymphs and of Iphigenia in Tauris in the House of the Gem-engraver Pinarius Cerialis present tableaux taken direct from the theater. A series of paintings from the basilica at Herculaneum (Museo Archeologico, Naples) depicts mythological episodes with an educational theme, again with a *trompe l'oeil* setting. A vivid portrayal shows Theseus after he has slain the minotaur receiving the salutations of the children he has rescued. The difference between the hero and his companions is emphasized by the contrast in their ages, in the great difference of size between Theseus and the boys, in his much darker coloring, and in his bold "heroic" gesture. Theseus as Savior-hero (*Soter*) has little to do with ordinary humanity, but the work tells us a great deal about how the later Greeks regarded their gods, their heroes—and their rulers.

The work is a masterpiece, as are others in the Basilica such as the centaur Chiron teaching Achilles the lyre, copied from a Hellenistic sculpture (the type is also known on engraved gem stones). The originality of the composition springs from the accurate portrayal of nuances of gesture and expression, and from an extraordinary sense of depth, making the most of what was then known about perspective. Another picture based on an earlier prototype is that showing Hercules finding Telephus suckled by a hind in Arcadia. Arcadia is shown as a female personification, reminiscent of a Roman portrayal of a province such as Britannia, or Hispania. The same subject can be seen on the Telephos frieze of the Great Altar of Zeus from Pergamum; although there Telephos is suckled by a lioness. The Herculaneum picture seems to be a free adaptation of the Pergamene work.

Of course the means by which such baroque devices in painting reached Italy are not altogether clear. A marble pilaster from the Aventine (now in the Uffizi, Florence) and considered to be of Domitianic date (AD 81–96) is covered with

The House of the Menander

The terrible eruption of Vesuvius in AD 79, which destroyed the cities of Pompeii and Herculaneum, has enabled antiquaries from the 18th century onwards to recover many details of the daily life and and artistic tastes of men and women of all classes living in Campania during the last century of the Republic and the first century of the Empire. The House of the Menander, so named from a painting of this great Greek writer of comedies (who worked in the 4th and 3rd centuries BC) in an *exedra* (recess) opening off from the peristyle (garden colonnade), belonged to a member of the local gentry called Quintus Poppaeus. The family achieved considerable eminence during the reign of Nero (AD 54–68) whose second wife was the notorious Poppaea Sabina.

Although the house was originally fairly small, with the main rooms grouped around the *atrium* (hall), it was enlarged and replanned in the middle of the 1st century BC when the great peristyle was constructed, with luxurious rooms painted in the naturalistic Second style opening off it. A fine example is to be seen in an *exedra*, whose walls seem to be pierced by ovoid windows, giving us a view of plants and birds beyond. The decorative scheme recalls that of the "garden room" in the house of Augustus' wife Livia at Prima Porta near Rome. Another room has a fine mosaic pavement showing pygmies in boats

in a landscape of the Nile, a theme found on a much larger scale in the temple of Fortuna at Praeneste (Palestrina) which must have originated in Hellenistic Alexandria.

Most of this decoration was swept away after an earthquake, which struck Pompeii in AD 62, damaged the house. The new, Fourth style paintings are arranged more formally as panels. Apart from the fresco of Menander holding a scroll, they include a series of scenes connected with the fall of Troy, in a room off the *atrium*, all painted with considerable verve. Especially dramatic is the moment when the unwitting Trojans drag the wooden horse into their city.

Most owners of houses in Pompeii had had time to remove their valuables when the eruption of 79 began; but the House of the Menander was still being renovated when disaster struck. The slave or freedman steward called Eros, who felt he lacked the authority to remove the family's silver and jewelry and was unwilling to abandon his responsibilities, died in his room. The valuables lay undisturbed in a cellar until this century.

▲ The recess painted in the naturalistic Second style

▼ The mosaic pavement of pygmies in boats on the Nile

▶ A dramatic Fourth style panel-painting in the House of the Menander: the unwitting Trojans drag the wooden horse into their city

◀ A silver mirror with a bust, possibly of the goddess Diana, chased in relief on its back

The silver plate consisted of 118 items and included a mirror with a bust, probably of a woman (the goddess Diana?) chased in relief on its back, as well as a number of drinking cups including two showing the Labors of Hercules, for example the hero taming the horses of Diomedes and plucking apples from a tree guarded by a serpent in the garden of the Hesperides.

Amongst the jewelry were a number of gold rings in the beautiful and simple form current through the 1st century AD. The wearing of gold rings was limited to members of the aristocratic senatorial and equestrian orders, additional confirmation, if any were needed, of the high social rank of the owners of the property. The rings are set with engraved gemstones cut in intaglio for use as signets. These miniature masterpieces of the jeweler's art would have been more highly prized than the frescoes on the wall or even than the family's silver. The best is a garnet cut with a representation of a charioteer watering his horses. Another gem, a green jasper, portrays a herdsman with his goat. Like almost all the treasures found in this house, they reveal a sense of taste and style far removed from the vulgarity which, rather unjustly, in the minds of many people, is the hallmark of Roman art.

MARTIN HENIG

Further reading. Maiuri, A. *La Casa del Menandro e il suo Tesoro di Argenteria*, Rome (1933).

◀ A Fourth style portrait of Menander holding a scroll

▼ A scene on a drinking cup: Hercules fighting a centaur

Below A gold ring set with a garnet shows a charioteer watering his horses

Theseus after slaying the Minotaur, from Pompeii; 1st century AD. Museo Archeologico Nazionale, Naples

arms and armor that resemble those carved on the Orange Arch and thus provide one piece of evidence linking the Flavian baroque with the Hellenism of southern Gaul. There are hints of late-1st-century chiaroscuro in the reliefs of a lioness and her cubs and of sheep in a rocky landscape (now in the Kunsthistorisches Museum, Vienna) which can probably be ascribed to the late Julio-Claudian period. What is certain is that by the reign of Domitian (and probably earlier) the new pictorialism had become widely disseminated. The fine sphinx carved in local stone, from a cremation cemetery in Colchester

(Colchester and Essex Museum, Colchester), has wings comparable with those of a Domitianic winged Minerva (or Minerva conflated with Victory) from a gate in Ostia, or the more famous Victory of Brescia (Museo Romano, Brescia). The rich detail of reliefs from the tomb of the Haterii (Lateran Museum, Rome) with its graphic portrayal of a crane worked by a treadmill and of a richly ornamented temple tomb employs the same essentially Hellenistic techniques, although many details—especially the ceremonies connected with the deceased and the little busts in their niches—bespeak a strong

Italian influence, which is perhaps to be ascribed to the wishes of the patron.

The most famous Flavian reliefs are those carved on the Arch of Titus, erected by Domitian (AD 81–96) in memory of his brother. The display is much simpler and more restrained than the decoration on the Orange Arch, and the main sculptures are confined to the single passageway. In Antiquity the Arch of Titus was hemmed in by the Porticus of Nero and the Temple of Jupiter Stator; and despite the conventional but finely detailed little frieze around the entablature and the spirited victories in the spandrels, the traveler passing through the arch was not prepared for the rich effect of the passageway. The veristic illusion produced by an imaginative treatment of light and shadow allowed genuine participation in Titus' achievement in quelling the Jewish revolt in Palestine (AD 66–70). On the south side we see the spoils from the temple of Jerusalem in a tableau that gives life to Josephus' description of the triumph. Josephus mentions

> a gold table weighing many talents, and a lampstand, also made of gold, which was made in a form different from that which we usually employ. There was a central shaft fastened to the base; then arms extended from this ... and on the end of each of these a lamp was forged. There were seven of these, emphasizing the honour accorded to the number seven among the Jews.

On the north side Titus is shown in his triumphal chariot, accompanied by a Victory, his horses guided forward by the goddess Roma. Above the two reliefs and linking them is a fine coffered vault with a small relief in the soffit of Titus being carried up to the heavens by an eagle. Such a scene involving a viewpoint from an unusual angle was well suited to Flavian baroque art. We may compare the stucco rendering of the *Rape of Ganymede*, in the underground basilica by the Porta Maggiore, Rome. The purposeful flight of the winged genius (who here replaces the usual eagle) is contrasted with the relaxed, passive body of the shepherd boy surrendering himself to his fate as the cupbearer of Jupiter (Zeus). Such a comparison of active and relaxed forms was a favorite subject of Pergamene sculpture in the 2nd century BC. However, other scenes which treat themes from Greco-Roman legend as well as those portraying life in school and gymnasium are more restrained in their classicism.

There were, of course, many links between Julio-Claudian and Flavian art, for many artists continued to work in their accustomed manner. When a pair of reliefs were found in the area of the papal Palazzo della Cancelleria (Vatican Museums), one of which clearly portrays Vespasian and his younger son, the other Domitian setting out to campaign in Germany, the restrained, classicizing style came as a great

A scene on the Arch of Titus: Titus in his triumphal chariot, Rome

surprise to scholars who regarded the Arch of Titus as the typical Flavian monument. But Rome was conservative so it is not so puzzling to find the art style of *Ara Pietatis* still in vogue in the Rome of the 80s. In any case, although the illusionistic shadows and highlights are missing, the subject matter—especially of the *profectio* (departure) of Domitian— marks a definite change of emphasis. Gods and personifications appear alongside the Emperor as they do indeed on the Arch of Titus (and on Julio-Claudian cameos) but they imply a concept of Empire to which Augustus and Tiberius would hardly have risked giving public expression. Under a thin veil of the Republican decencies we breathe the heady air of oriental monarchy.

The Cancelleria Reliefs are of considerable interest in illustrating the factors that governed a commission. Most surviving state sculptures come from monuments that were both completed and successfully served a purpose. But here the artist was engaged on an important work at the time an unpopular Emperor was assassinated and thus faced a problem. On the *profectio* relief, instead of Domitian setting out to campaign in Germany we see the aged Nerva who succeeded him: but Nerva (AD 96–8) never went on such an expedition during his brief tenure of the Imperial throne and even a cursory glance at the relief shows that the head is in fact a recarved head of Domitian. In the event, both pieces were considered unsatisfactory and unsuitable as state propaganda. So the artist put them aside for the future in his mason's yard where they became covered with earth and rubbish, lost and forgotten for 1,800 years. They were rediscovered just before the Second World War.

A true fusion between classical and baroque tendencies was not achieved until the erection of Trajan's Column a century and a half after the Altar of Domitius Ahenobarbus. Under Trajan's successor, Hadrian (AD 117–38), this conscious classicism, combined with a baroque freedom in the portrayal of emotion or scenes of violent action, continued to hold sway. Then, in the Age of the Antonines, there was a decisive return to Flavian illusionism, and a decline in classical influence.

The second century AD marked the acme of Roman Civilization:

If a man were called to fix the period in the history of the world during which the condition of the human race was most happy and prosperous, he would without hesitation, name that which elapsed from the death of Domitian to the accession of Commodus.

Edward Gibbon was not thinking here especially of the visual arts, but in them it is possible to sense a creativeness in counterpart to soaring optimism and general confidence in the Empire. In part it reflected a more cosmopolitan attitude. The Greeks were accepted into partnership in the Empire in quite a new way or, in other words, the Roman Empire assumed most of the characteristics of a commonwealth. Aelius Aristides (*fl.* 2nd century AD) wrote the most fulsome defence of the Roman Empire; Marcus Aurelius, the Emperor (reigned AD 161–80), composed a volume of philosophical ideas in

Greek. Nor must we forget the satirist Lucian (*fl.* 2nd century AD), a sculptor manqué who put in the form of a dream the rival attractions of sculpture and literary culture, so telling us how an educated man regarded the arts. Sculpture, which could almost be an hereditary craft, promised fame and moderate wealth without wandering abroad while Literature counters with the gibe that a sculptor would always rank as a common craftsman. Greek and Roman attitudes to such things were in truth very much the same. Hadrian, the greatest of Rome's philhellene Emperors, must take much of the credit for creating the 2nd-century Empire, both politically and culturally, but the roots of the new polity lie further back, with Trajan (AD 98–117).

A number of important state monuments can be associated with Trajan, but whilst the *Tropaeum Traiani* at Adamklissi (Rumania) is incompetent provincial work the Great Trajanic Frieze, largely incorporated in the Arch of Constantine at Rome and the Arch of Trajan at Beneventum, are in large part (if not entirely) Hadrianic. The column in Trajan's Forum and the architectural works surrounding it are his finest memorial. The column, which dates from AD 113, is a hollow shaft of Parian marble, about 100 ft (30 m) high, standing on a plinth. A continuous spiral scroll, carved with scenes from the Dacian Wars of AD 101–2 and 105–6 winds up it, in a band about 3 ft (1 m) in width. Like Trajan's market and the forum it was doubtless planned by the architect Apollodorus of Damascus (*fl.* late 1st/early 2nd century AD). On the base are Dacian arms disposed in a manner already familiar to us from the Arch at Orange although some of the details no doubt come

Trajan's Column: part of the battle, Rome

from actual observation of Dacian arms and armor which were probably new to Roman artistic tradition.

In the frieze, scene succeeds scene in a manner reminiscent of the Vatican *Odyssey* landscapes although here the hero is not a mythological figure but Trajan, the *Optimus Princeps*, shown with his companions—both generals and soldiers. Indeed, it was important that the Emperor was not shown as a figure different *in kind* from his comrades either in size or in the character of his uniform. As in Julio-Claudian art, the gods hardly appear. However, when battle scenes are shown, Roman achievement called for the sort of artistic response found in the attics of the Orange Arch and common to the baroque tradition. So the accurate representation of men and buildings coexisted with a more heightened and poetic approach.

The story begins at the bottom with the watchtowers of the Roman *limes* and a personification of the Danube (apart from Jupiter Tonans helping the Romans in a battle, the moon goddess Luna informing us that a battle was taking place at night, and a Victory with a shield, the only non-human figure in the composition). It proceeds to the Emperor's council of war, a religious ceremony, and Trajan's harangue to the troops, and then onwards through the events of the first war. The successful conclusion of that campaign is shown by the victory mentioned above, an adaptation of the Flavian "Victory of Brescia" type. The renewed outbreak of hostilities and the campaign leading to the assault on Sarmizegetusa are graphically shown. The culminating point is a great set piece, the death of Decebalus, where the baroque language of the Hellenistic battle scene (celtomachy or gigantomachy) is combined with the matter-of-fact observations of the Roman war artists with such skill that an original masterpiece was created. This can now be shown thanks to the recent discovery, near Philippi in northern Greece, of the tombstone of Tiberius Claudius Maximus (*ob.* AD 116) who came upon Decebalus at the moment he was committing suicide and carried his head to the Emperor. He had the earlier episode carved as his own memorial (Archeological Museum, Kavalla). As a work of art it is poor, but is surely a more reliable record of the event than the dramatic, heroic posing of Decebalus and his Roman enemies on the column.

The sympathy shown for Decebalus, which is also to be found in some freestanding statues of Dacians, such as the so-called *Thusnalda* (in the Loggia dei Lanzi, Florence), is no doubt, in part, a response to the vaunted "spirit of the age" found, for example, in the letters of the younger Pliny, but it also springs from the admiration of the noble savage (usually a Celt) already seen in Pergamene art.

Another important early-2nd-century monument is the Arch of Trajan at Beneventum. This was voted by the Senate before Trajan departed to campaign in Parthia (AD 114) but references to Hadrian's sensible, but inglorious, retrenchment in the east show that it was not finished until the reign of his successor. Its debt to the Arch of Titus is obvious, especially in the use of passageway reliefs and the richly coffered vault,

again with a figural device in the soffit (Victory crowning the Emperor with a wreath). However, the main faces of the Beneventum arch are carved with reliefs as well, their theme being the benefits Trajan conferred on the Empire. As on the Cancelleria Reliefs, the world of the gods and of men is made to seem close and friendly but, in this instance, without the pedantry and overglorification of the Emperor which disfigures the Flavian sculpture. Trajan talks to a recruit, to foreign embassies, founds colonies, fosters trade. In the passageway he inaugurates a new road and distributes bread to needy families. Only the little entablature frieze is strictly triumphal; it shows a procession of captive Dacians and the treasure of Decebalus.

The emphasis on public works rather than warfare upon the arch is Hadrianic: where Trajan was a great soldier and conqueror, Hadrian was a consolidator, with a strictly practical approach to the management of the legions. In his frontier policy he can be likened to Augustus in the latter part of his reign. He believed that the boundaries of the Empire were finite and, in consequence, that within them Romanization should be vigorously pursued. He was greatly interested in architecture (he is said to have quarreled with his architect, Apollodorus of Damascus) and may have been personally responsible for the rebuilt Pantheon with its fine dome. In Athens he completed the great temple of Olympian Zeus and built a library; and at Tivoli he planned and built an extensive country palace.

A gold coin of Hadrian

Much the most famous type in Hadrianic art is that of Antinous, although unfortunately—in common with most of the works of the Roman period—we do not know who created it. Hadrian met Antinous during a visit to Bithynia in Asia Minor, perhaps in AD 124, and thereafter the young provincial was accepted as a member of the Imperial entourage. Although much salacious gossip has accrued to the nature of the relationship between the Emperor and his young favorite none of it is contemporary. But it is reasonable to guess that Hadrian, himself the son of a minor aristocrat from a western city (Italica in Spain), was attempting to honor a member of that same curial class from an eastern town and perhaps even toying with the idea of involving someone of Greek birth in the succession, and ending the political monopoly of the Latin-speaking West in the government of the Empire.

Unfortunately Antinous was drowned in the Nile in AD 130 and Hadrian's grief—widely shared in the eastern provinces—resulted in the growth of a new hero-cult. Statues of Antinous equate him with Apollo, Dionysos, Hermes, Asklepios, and Silvanus—savior gods or vegetation deities. Pausanias tells us there were fine paintings of Antinous as Dionysos at Mantineia, the mother city to his native Bithynion. The type of Antinous with its cascading hair, delicate features, and expression of brooding melancholy is unforgettable, blending the Classical ideal with something more individual and particular. A large number of the extant statues and reliefs are works of very high quality. The Antinous Farnese in Naples is carved in Greek marble and presents the subject as Hermes, guide of souls. Here the contours of the face are particularly well modeled and the curls of hair formed into an especially pleasing pattern. The face evokes great intensity of feeling, partly through the device of outlining the pupils of the eyes—a practice beginning to enter portraiture at this time. The colossal head in the Louvre, Paris, the Antinous Mondragone, combines the physiognomy of the young Bithynian with the general form taken from a 5th-century Apollo. Winckelmann called it "the glory and crown of sculpture in this age as well as in all others". A relief found near Lanuvium and now in the Instituto dei Fondi Rustici, Rome, depicts Antinous in the persona of Silvanus. It is signed by Antonianos of Aphrodisias, and is carved in the richly pictorial style so characteristic of Asia Minor. Antinous stands in relaxed pose under a spreading vine and in front of an altar. His hound stands beside him. The skill manifest in this relief, which recalls earlier Greek tombstones, was to find a ready outlet in the carved sarcophagi which appeared from this time onwards.

Hadrian wrote a poem to a departing soul, usually taken to be his own, though he may have been addressing Antinous. This more personal sense of individual identity may have been a leading factor in the reemergence of inhumation as a burial rite and of the sarcophagus as an art form, although no fundamental religious change can be discerned. Many of the ash-chests and grave-altars of the 1st century AD manifest a strong belief in the afterlife.

In the east, sarcophagi stood in the open or in the center of open tomb-chambers and are carved on all four sides; but in the west where they were placed against the walls of the tombs, the back was left uncarved. In some respects it is valid to talk of "Eastern" and "Western" sarcophagi, but it must be remembered that in all instances the artists were of Greek origin.

The early (Hadrianic) sarcophagi were designed with a strong sense of form and proportion. Overcrowding was avoided and individual figures never allowed to dominate the total impression by such over-dramatic devices as standing too far in front of the background. Details were skillfully carved—the sculptor had not yet adopted the bad habit of rendering details by means of a host of drill-made borings. During the 2nd century the freshness of these Hadrianic sarcophagi was lost. We should compare the Pashley Sarcophagus from Crete (Fitzwilliam Museum, Cambridge), which shows the triumph of Bacchus, with a sarcophagus depicting

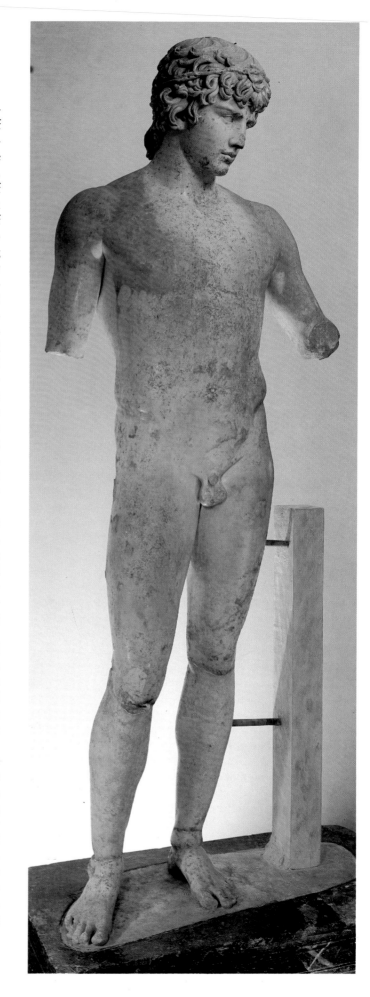

A statue of Antinous as Apollo. Delphi Museum

the same subject, carved a century later, now in the Metropolitan Museum, New York. In the former, the cortege of the god has power, life, and dignity. Figures are disposed along its length singly or in natural groups, moving forward in a real procession. In the early-3rd-century example, the carving is awkward and the figures bunched together in order to create a textured screen of highlight and shadow.

Some sarcophagi show scenes from classical mythology—gigantomachies; Orestes revenging himself on Clytaemnestra and Aegisthus; the destruction of Niobe and her children by Apollo and Artemis. Others, following the tradition of the ash-chests (and of the unique, Augustan, Caffarelli Sarcophagus, Staatliche Museen, Berlin) have decorative garlands held by putti, satyrs, or some other figures, though the space above the garland sometimes contains a scene such as the myth of Actaeon or Diomedes seizing the Palladium from Troy, the former recalling the ravening power of death and the latter expressing the ancient ideal of heroism as the true purpose of human endeavor.

A very attractive group of "Eastern" sarcophagi show full size amorini (cupids) representing the happy immortality of the soul in paradise. They no longer support garlands but play musical instruments, dance, and generally behave as young children. The majority have been found in Greece and, indeed, Athens, may have been the center of production.

Amorini are also figured on the highly ornate and accomplished pilasters from the Baths of Aphrodisias (Istanbul Museum) where they inhabit well-cut, fleshy acanthus scrolls together with Herakles and members of the Dionysiac *thiasos*. Other reliefs from the building include a frieze with a city goddess (Tyche) and a male equivalent (perhaps the *demos*) reclining and holding horns of plenty. Female torsos, springing from acanthus are, appropriately enough, closely paralleled in a relief above the entrance to the *cella* in the Temple of Hadrian, Ephesus, carved by artists of the same school. They are immediately reminiscent of figures from a frieze in the Temple of Venus Genetrix, Rome (similarly combined with vegetal elements) but the tradition can be taken back to the eccentricities of the early Third style as well as forward to Severan works at Leptis Magna and from Torre Annunziata (Museum of Fine Arts, Boston).

Hadrian's Palace at Tivoli gave full scope to the Emperor's aesthetic tastes. Buildings of complex plan, displaying idiosyncracies of design, from different parts of the Empire, housed a varied art collection. The sculpture galleries of the world are full of works said to have been unearthed on the site. Many are reproductions of such Greek statues as the Erechtheion Caryatids, happily *in situ* as part of the surround of an ornamental pool, the *Canopus*. Here they demonstrate the way in which the Romans could find new uses for well-known types and dispose them in different relationships to each other. In the case of the Caryatids it may be noted that Augustus had previously used copies to ornament his forum. Other sculptures from Tivoli are more baroque in tradition, such as the pair of centaurs, copies by Aristeas and Papias of Aphrodisias,

based on Pergamene or Rhodian work of *c*150 BC (Museo Capitolino, Rome). It should also be noted that ten representations of Antinous have been found in the Palace. In addition to the sculptures, there are a number of mosaics including án *emblema* of doves drinking from a bowl, based on a work by Sosos of Pergamum (*fl.* 2nd century BC) and a more violent composition of a male centaur revenging himself on wild beasts who have killed his wife (Museo Capitolino, Rome).

The Hadrianic achievement is summarized by the coin series that shows personifications of the varied provinces of the Empire. The effect recalls the arch at Beneventum, with its stress on the Emperor as restorer and benefactor. It was appropriate that Hadrian's successor, Antoninus Pius, should place idealized sculptures of the provinces in the Temple of Divus Hadrianus in Rome (*c* AD 145). Here the Roman world appears as a voluntary federation of cities and provinces, partaking of a common culture. The classicizing mode of representation, calm and urbane, reinforces this happy theme to which Aelius Aristides gave voice, in a panegyric at about the same time.

> You have made the word "Roman" apply not to a city but to a universal people. You no longer classify peoples as Greek or barbarian ...there are many people in each city who are no less fellow citizens of yours than of those of their own stock, though some of them have never seen this city ...The whole world, as if on holiday has turned to finery and all festivities without restraint. All other competition between cities has ceased, but a single rivalry obsesses every one of them—to appear as beautiful and attractive as possible.

In the light of these words, it is fitting that the best series of state reliefs of the reign of Antoninus Pius should be not from Rome but from Asia Minor, at Ephesus. The altar with its reliefs (now mainly in the Kunsthistorisches Museum, Vienna) was set up *c* AD 140 and depicts the adoption of Antoninus Pius and Marcus Aurelius in AD 138. In general design the altar owes a great deal to the Great Altar of Zeus at Pergamum, though it is less complex. Reliefs were set up around three sides of the monument. On the right there were generalized scenes of combat, in style similar to the Great Trajanic Frieze (incorporated in the Arch of Constantine) or the battle scene on the strongly Hellenistic Amendola Sarcophagus from the Via Appia outside Rome (AD 150; Museo Capitolino). On the left side this is balanced by goddesses, including an Apotheosis of Diva Plotina, through whose agency Hadrian was helped to the succession. The longest and most important side was set between them and shows a personification of Ephesus (perhaps also a personification of Alexandria); a cuirassed emperor, presumably Trajan, mounting a chariot accompanied by Nike (Victory), Virtus, and Helios. Then the great scene of sacrifice attended by the Antonines and Hadrian, presents the monument's *raison d'être*. An intriguing possibility is that a youth in the background with long curling hair is indeed Antinous. His presence here, neither as a *divus* nor as a mortal (for he had been dead eight years), would have served to remind the population of Asia

Minor that the Empire (and its ruler) was not interested in the west alone. In the event the younger of the two adopted Antonines, Marcus Aurelius, was to become very much of a Greek both in his thought and in his writings.

The impact of the east is very marked on the base of the Column of Antoninus Pius (AD 138–61) which was set up in his memory by Marcus Aurelius (AD 161–80) on a site in the Campus Martius (Vatican Museum). The great Apotheosis relief shows the same subtle blend of historical and allegorical as the Altar of Ephesus, and epitomizes the hold Hellenistic tradition had by now achieved in Rome. The illusionistic tendencies begun in Rome under the Flavians had triumphed and would last for as long as a healthy organic development continued in Roman art, that is until the late 3rd century AD.

There had been earlier scenes of Apotheosis (including one on the *Grand Camée de France*, and another on the Arch of Titus, mentioned above), but for our purpose the closest parallel is a Hadrianic relief from the demolished *Arco di Porto-gallo* showing a winged female figure (*Aeternitas*) carrying Sabina, Hadrian's wife, up to the heavens while Hadrian looks on (Palazzo dei Conservatori, Rome). In the Antonine relief, the general composition is similar to the one on the Hadrianic Apotheosis, and was probably inspired by it. A male figure reclines on the left, personifying the Campus Martius. On the right, occupying the same position as Hadrian in the Conservatori relief, sits the goddess Roma. The surprise comes with the flying figure, which has been turned into a youth with long hair and majestic pinions which sweep the heavens while his feet almost touch the body of Campus Martius or the Egyptian obelisk (the so-called *Gnomon* of Augustus) which he is carrying and which indeed stood in the Campus Martius. The identity of the figure is established by the globe set with crescent and stars and the serpent he holds. He is *Saeculum Aureum*, the Golden Age, and represents renewal and eternity. Above him Antoninus Pius and Faustina are enthroned as Jupiter and Juno, looking down on the hap-

The Apotheosis relief on the base of the Column of Antoninus Pius. Vatican Museums, Rome

piness of a world that was fostered by them and will be maintained by their successors. Few reliefs in Roman baroque style ever managed to rival this in power of execution or majesty of design.

The other carved side of the base is a relief showing a funerary *decursio* of the praetorian guard and various members of the Roman nobility. The figures are seen in what may be termed bird's eye perspective, with more distant figures raised above those in front. This device was not new in the 160s (it is found on Trajan's Column), but it was to become much more common in late Antonine and Severan times. The somewhat stumpy little figures mark a regression from the careful rendering of anatomy in the Apotheosis, but the relief appeals to those who admire the primitive in art.

The Arch built to commemorate Marcus Aurelius' wars on the Danube (AD 168–76) no longer exists, but 11 sculptures from this period survive, eight in the attic of the Arch of Constantine and three in the Palazzo dei Conservatori, Rome. The use of large reliefs is reminiscent of Trajanic and Hadrianic work at Beneventum. As might be expected, the cutting is rich and deep; figures tend to stand clear of their background which is generally carved with architectural details. Thus events and ceremonies are each shown in a definite setting.

In a scene of triumph, Marcus stands within his triumphal chariot, which is about to swing round through an arch (as on the famous processional scene in the Arch of Titus, although *there* the chariot itself lacks this focus: it was left to Marcus' sculptors to combine the chief elements of the two scenes). Other episodes include a sacrifice, a *durbar* at which captives are pardoned, the giving of a new king to the Quadi, and the donation of a largesse to the citizens. The general impression is of dignity and a lack of conflict, even when the theme is a military one.

However, the wars of Marcus Aurelius' time ended the calm order of Antonine civilization and the column (which was begun in his own reign but finished during that of his unworthy son Commodus (AD 180–92) makes the point unconsciously, but all the more poignantly, by being closely modeled in its external features on Trajan's Column. But whereas, on the latter, soldiers go about their tasks with order and decorum, here both Romans and barbarians display emotional instability. The figures, smaller and more contorted (resembling those on the base of the column of Antoninus Pius), are frequently disposed in tight little bunches. They reflect perfectly the beginning of what Professor Dodds has called an "Age of Anxiety". One scene is especially moving. The rain is succouring Roman troops and throwing their enemies into confusion, but instead of a straightforward portrayal of this "miracle", the sculptor has introduced a strange, dominating being, partially composed of long streaming hairs (of rain). The British reader is reminded of the water-deity whose head appears in the center of the temple pediment at Bath (Bath Museum), instead of a Gorgoneion. In both cases we perceive one of those glimpses, alas all too rare, of daring originality in Roman art.

Sculpture was produced for private patrons throughout the 2nd century. The fountain building or *nymphaeum* erected by Herodes Atticus at Olympia, built in the form of a hemicycle, and set with statues of members of the donor's family as well as with Imperial images, continued the tradition of arranging sculpture in symmetrical relationships which may be observed at Tivoli and in the Pantheon (whose niches originally contained statues of the gods). Portrait sculpture also demonstrates a certain conservatism. The Italic features of the Flavian portrait and the high "pompadour" *coiffures* of the ladies gave way to a more restrained style under Hadrian. Female heads could almost be confused with portraits of Julio-Claudian date but those of their husbands are universally distinguishable by virtue of their "philosophers'" beards—a fashion that must have owed much to Hadrian. At first they were short and fairly closely clipped but under Antoninus Pius and even more under Aurelius the beards became both long and straggly.

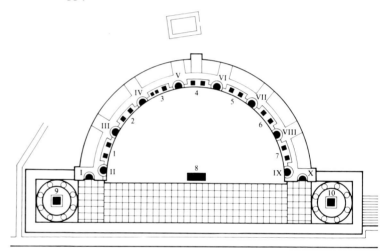

II	Sabina	5	Son/Son-in-law of Herodes
I	Nerva (?)		and Regilla
1	Grandfathers of Regilla	VII	Lucius Verus
III	Hadrian	6	Mother/Father of Herodes
2	Mother/Father of Regilla	VIII	Faustina the Elder
IV	Children of Marcus Aurelius	7	Grandfather/Granddaughter
3	Youngest Children/Daughters of		of Herodes
	Herodes and Regilla	IX	Antoninus Pius
V	Faustina the Younger	X	Trajan (?)
4	Regilla/Herodes	8	Bull
VI	Marcus Aurelius	9	Hera (?)
		10	Zeus (?)

The fountain building of Herodes Atticus at Olympia

Such beards were, of course, worn by men portrayed on Antonine sarcophagi. More important changes made were an ever increasing depth in relief, the employment of the drill to give the effect of detail, and a more mannered approach to composition. These features can be observed in the Medea Sarcophagus in the Terme Museum, Rome, where three scenes of increasing dramatic impact (showing first Medea contemplating the children she is about to murder, then the deed itself, and finally her escape in a chariot drawn by dragons)

Detail of the corner of a vault in the tomb of the Pancratii, Rome

establish a continuous style which is nevertheless far less visually satisfactory than the integrated design of a generation earlier. The fussy elaboration of some of the detail makes for heaviness. A similar criticism could be made of the Casali Sarcophagus in Copenhagen (National Museum) where various deities gather on either side of Bacchus and Ariadnĕ. The most successful Antonine sarcophagi, at least those of "Western" type, display battle scenes. Although the Via Tiburtina Sarcophagus in the Terme Museum, Rome, is so full of figures that individual identities are submerged, the piece is essentially honest in its approach to a battle and indeed it follows on from the tradition of Hellenistic battle scenes. Sarcophagi of "Eastern" type frequently show statuesque figures set against a background of columns and niches. Outstanding amongst these are the Melfi Sarcophagus (c AD 170; Palazzo Pubblico, Melfi), and the even more elaborate one in Velletri (late Antonine; Antiquarium, Velletri). The design of these works was influenced by temples, nymphaea, and theaters—especially those of the Greek east—in which sculpture was integrated with an architectural setting.

A similar effect was sought by stuccoists, who took their art to a very high level of achievement in Antonine times. The Tomb of the Valerii under St Peter's depicts various deities and members of the owner's family as well as figures from the Bacchic thiasos. Polychrome (including gilding) is used in place of the plain white stuccos of earlier times. In the Tomb of the Pancratii in the Via Latina, mythological episodes, for example, the seizure of the Palladium, Priam before Achilles, the Judgment of Paris, all executed in stucco, alternate with paintings. Here the decoration continues over the entire vault, creating an amazingly lavish impression on the visitor. Even when ceilings were decorated with simple, nonfigurative stucco, as in the Tomb of the Ax under S. Sebastiano with its rosettes within roundels, a very beautiful effect was obtained, remarkably like that achieved by some 17th-century ceilings in England.

Unfortunately the Antonine achievement in painting is less impressive. After Pompeii and Herculaneum had been overwhelmed by Vesuvius in AD 79, it becomes harder to pursue the development of painting in detail. Though it is clear from examples in Italy, such as the figures shown against colored backgrounds in a house in the Via dei Dipinti, Ostia and the Toilet of Venus in the Baths of the Seven Sages in the same city, as well as from others in the provinces, such as figures and decorative details in Leicester and Verulamium (St Albans), England, that the use of perspective, so outstandingly good in the Herculaneum basilica, had been in large measure abandoned. Few Antonine paintings of high quality are known. There are exceptions, for example the Mithraeum at Capua where the emotional intensity of the best Antonine sculpture was transferred to painting. In the center of the composition we observe the elemental struggle between Mithras and the bull on which the eyes of the sun, moon, earth, and ocean, shown in human guise, are fixed. The sun and moon are especially fine. The former appears in the persona of a charioteer wearing a red cloak fastened over his shoulder by means of a gold brooch. His hair is wild and wind-swept, his eyes stare with vivid intensity at the central action. There is more than a reminiscence of Alexander the Great as he appears on the mosaic from the House of the Faun. Luna (the moon) is almost equally compelling, recalling the figure of Arcadia in the Pergamene-inspired "finding of Telephos" fresco from the Herculaneum basilica.

The importance of eyes in middle- and late-imperial art cannot be overstressed. They were regarded in Neoplatonic theory as the link between the outward body and the inner mind of man. Panel-paintings on wood or linen, both in encaustic—a wax-based paint rather like oils—and in tempera have been found attached to mummies in Roman-period cemeteries in the Fayum, Egypt; for example at Hawara. They provide graphic instances of this. Although there was considerable stylistic development here between the 1st and 4th centuries, almost all these portraits were designed frontally and fix their eyes firmly on the onlooker. (Note the fine examples in the British Museum, London; the Royal Scottish Museum, Edinburgh; and Fogg Art Museum, Cambridge, Mass.)

The elemental struggle of Mithras and the bull in the Mithraeum at Capua

The Later Empire. Under the Severan dynasty (AD 193–235) emotion—the hallmark of Antonine art—appears to have given way to formalization. In the case of state art, this meant the expression of a more hierarchical relationship between the ruler and the inhabitants of the Empire. In sarcophagi the gods confront mortals across a similar divide; even the Christian frescoes in the Roman catacombs were not untouched by the new hieraticism (witness the "Orans" figure in the cemetery of Priscilla, Rome).

A painting in tempera executed upon a wooden panel from Egypt (now in Staatliche Museen, Berlin), provides a good introduction to early-3rd-century art. It represents Septimius Severus (193–211), his wife Julia Domna, and his sons Caracalla and Geta. They wear special clothes, and jeweled diadems which mark them out as distinctive. They stare outwards, as though interrogating the onlooker. It is true there is much individual characterization—even Severus with his forked beard looks vaguely Antonine, but he could not be mistaken for Marcus Aurelius. Here is no kindly philosopher but a stern and absolute ruler.

Severus and his wife are also depicted on the Arch of the Argentarii in the Forum Boarium, Rome. Once again they seem to be distant and "posed". The ornamental surround to the scene is reminiscent of the intricate detail found on Flavian tomb-altars (not the only case of Severan sculptors in Italy harking back to work of a century earlier). The Arch of Severus (AD 203) which dominates the Forum is a sad disappointment, as the sculptures are so battered, but it is clear that the style of composition with its little groups of stunted figures has much in common with the Column of Marcus Aurelius. Certainly the large panoramic scenes with their out-of-scale figures present an alarming contrast to relief sculpture of the 2nd century, but part of this divergence is simply that the Arch of Severus in Rome is rather badly carved. Septimius Severus lavished his greatest care on his home town Leptis Magna, and it is there that the best and most typical sculptures of his reign can be found. The attics of the contemporary triumphal arch at Leptis contain a magnificent scene of triumph in which the Emperor stands facing the spectator from the platform of his chariot. The other figures around him are rigidly frontal as on the scene of sacrifice. An almost Byzantine aesthetic prevails here, accentuated by the deeply carved folds of the drapery. Earlier emperors had built Imperial fora at Rome; characteristically Severus built his great basilica and public square at

A 2nd-century panel portrait of a woman. Royal Scottish Museum, Edinburgh

Leptis, and brought in Aphrodisian sculptors to decorate it. The pilasters at the entrance to the basilica with their inhabited scrolls recall earlier Hadrianic prototypes in Asia Minor.

The increasingly "Royal" style of the emperor and his family opened up opportunities of patronage for gem-engravers and other craftsmen. A cameo in the British Museum, London, conflates Julia Domna with Juno Caelestis and shows her riding in a chariot drawn by two bulls, while another in Kassel (Staatliche Kunstsammlungen) gives her the attributes of Victory. An intaglio from Castlesteads, Cumberland (now lost), depicted Severus as the Egyptian god Serapis. All the members of the Imperial family (Septimius Severus, Julia Domna, Caracalla, and Geta) appear on a fine cameo in Paris (Cabinet des Médailles). Other gems, such as the Bear Cameo from South Shields (Newcastle Museum) carved on Indian sardonyx, make no direct reference to state propaganda, but were possibly the products of state workshops. Presumably only the very wealthy or influential would wear such jeweled settings in their brooches. All these gems are distinguished by the same rather two-dimensional carving as we find in sculpture on a larger scale.

Linearity and frontality were just two aspects of the provincial art in the eastern provinces of the Empire which came to influence Roman sculpture and painting as a whole. The deities carved on stone beams from the temple of Bel, Palmyra, exemplify this to a marked degree as early as AD 32 (site museum). The idea was apparently to bring the gods into a closer relationship with living men, rather than to stress the divide between the two worlds, as the Romans were later to do. A similar notion was responsible for the practice of employing frontally disposed portraits to seal ossuaries in tombs. These display strong Greco-Roman influence in the modelings of their features, and yet they could not be confused with western sculpture. In the case of female portraits, such as the masterpiece in Copenhagen (Ny Carlsberg Glyptotek) called *The Beauty of Palmyra* (early 3rd century AD) this is partly a matter of the lavish use of jewelry but in all cases, not only at Palmyra but also at Hatra beyond the Imperial frontiers, and at many lesser centers, line and pattern were more important than volume.

An interesting example of how Palmyrene art reached the west is presented by two tombstones from South Shields (site museum) carved by a Palmyrene, in one case for a Palmyrene patron called Barates who was burying his British-born wife Regina, and in the other for Victor, a Moor from north Africa. The movement of artists even on a small scale in the Empire would have been sufficient to spread various modes of representation. At the end of the 3rd century tetrarchic sculpture seems to reflect the workshop traditions of the north Balkans, unfortunately less refined than those of Asia Minor or of Syria.

Painting and mosaic were increasingly subject to local in-

Left: Septimius Severus and his family, a painted panel; early 3rd century. Antikenabteilung, Berlin

A decorated pilaster on the basilica of Severus at Leptis Magna

A stone bust of a roman from Palmyra. Ny Carlsberg Glyptothek, Copenhagen

fluences. Many of the finest mosaic pavements of the middle Empire are to be seen in north Africa, especially in Tunisia where the use of bold, contrasting colors set against simple, generally white, grounds together with developed intricate decorative borders produced an unusually lively response to the problems of two-dimensional design. A floor from La Chebba (Musée National, Tunis) has, as its centerpiece, a roundel showing Neptune rising from the sea in a chariot drawn by sea horses. Around this *emblema* are delicate personifications of the seasons as young women holding appropriate attributes, each enclosed in a light vegetal frame, and vignettes of men pursuing various seasonal activities. Equally attractive is a floor from Oudna, also in Tunis, with a central scene of Bacchus giving the vine to Icarius in Attica, and a surround comprising a luxuriant vine in the midst of which cupids are gathering grapes. A pavement found at Acholla (Musée National, Tunis) presents a Marine *thiasos* with nereids seated on dolphins and sea creatures of various kinds, as well as vegetal motifs, combined with human figures. The centerpiece is a "Triumph of Bacchus" which alludes to the salvation of the soul from the powers of death, presumably in the Islands of the Blessed on the other side of Ocean, through the lifegiving beneficence of the god of wine. The mosaic of Rural Labors at Cherchel (site museum) presents an overall carpet design in rich polychrome, with men amongst vines which are neither in the foreground nor the background but act as rhythmic interruptions of the human activity. As at Leptis pattern was more important than naturalism.

The frontally disposed formal group of soldiers in a fresco showing a scene of sacrifice in the temple of the Palmyrene

A mosaic floor from La Chebba. Musée National du Bardo, Tunis

gods at Dura Europus (Yale University Art Gallery, New Haven) is, however, closer to the Leptis Arch in feeling and cannot be many decades later in date. Instead of a presiding emperor, the chief figure here is the tribune of the local garrison, Julius Terentius, who is pouring a libation on the altar.

The most remarkable paintings from Dura are the biblical scenes adorning the synagogue (National Museum, Damascus) which must have been executed prior to AD 245 as the building was destroyed at that time by fortifications hurriedly erected against the Persians. Samuel, depicted on a larger scale than other Israelites, anoints David who stares passively in front of him in the company of a group of men who stand as rigid as statues. To take another example, in the *Vision of Ezekiel*, the *manus dei* descends from the heavens (an anticipation of Byzantine iconography) and seems to manipulate the strange trousered men below, whose faces are equally blank and impassive. At their feet lie the little doll-like bodies and parts of bodies belonging to those yet to be resurrected. This scattering of objects in the field is also seen in the synagogue in the shattered paraphernalia from the Shrine of Dagon and, of course, goes back to a Hellenistic pavement by Sosos. But many of the other details, such as the dress and the frontal rigidity of the figures, are certainly Oriental. A fine series of mosaics ornamenting the floors of tombs at Edessa date to a period shortly after the Romans had established control (late 2nd/early 3rd century AD). They depict local notables with their families, in a style very close to the Dura paintings. Various groups of trousered men and long-robed women are disposed in fixed frontal attitudes, with their heads and arms as formally posed as in Victorian photographs, and provide further striking confirmation that the tendencies which are—in the west—first made manifest in the Marcus column had their source along the eastern borders of the Empire.

The apparent prosperity of the Empire under Severus and even his immediate successors gave no hint of the turmoil of the 3rd century which in many areas (including Rome) had serious repercussions on the arts. The production of state reliefs, so important in the previous age, almost ceased, for rulers had neither time nor money for expensive monuments. In order to obtain a consistent picture of 3rd-century propaganda we must turn to coins, struck in large numbers and debased metal (as well as in gold, although gold coins are admittedly very rare). Every new claimant to the Imperial throne hoped he would fare better than his predecessors and avoid being killed either by the Persians or in civil war, and realized that it was vital that the populace of the Empire should be able to recognize him and accept his propaganda. Thus the quality of portraiture was never higher: in their coins we see the taut, worried features of the Emperors, for example Macrinus (217–18), Decius (249–51), and the stylish Gallienus (253–68), his hair and beard carefully combed; the good-natured Postumus (259–68), a Gaulish usurper whose portrait is deliberately reminiscent of the Antonines; the rugged head of Carausius (287–93) with his thick bull neck

whose image gives the appearance of energy, and the mask-like features of the joint-Augusti Diocletian (284–305) and Maximian (285–305) which are in line with the general later Roman tendency of stressing the divide between Emperors and their subjects.

A coin of Carausius

The failure of the Empire in foreign wars was eloquently expressed by reliefs set up by Persian monarchs to show their victories over Severus Alexander (AD 232), Philip the Arab (AD 244), and Valerian (AD 260). In choice of setting—the sides of rocky gorges—the reliefs harked back to much earlier Achaemenid prototypes, and this is especially notable in the highly formalized composition from Darabgird showing Ardashir (224–41) accepting a Roman submission in the 230s (?232). This style was nevertheless sometimes influenced by art from the west, notably in a relief at Bishapur, dated to *c* AD 260 and possibly the work of Roman prisoners settled in Iran, which depicts Shapur (AD 242–72) triumphing over the Roman Emperors, one of whom is certainly Valerian who was actually captured by the Persians. The faces and equipment of the defeated Roman troops are considerably more naturalistic than was normally the case in Persian art, and the Roman Emperor, humbled and kneeling, is a figure of sympathy.

To see an emperor in triumph we must turn to a private work—a sarcophagus showing a Roman general on horseback riding forth from a melee of writhing figures. The general has been identified as the Emperor Hostilian who reigned, briefly, in AD 251 and this is presumably his coffin (Terme Museum, Rome). We may note the persistent use of the drill, making for an interesting trellis-like pattern, though the carving of individual figures is rather mechanical.

The Hellenistic tradition of Antonine days flowered again in the cultivated court of Gallienus, which also provided a home for philosophers, for example Plotinus (AD 205–70). Indeed, to judge from the persistence of certain types of sarcophagi showing philosophers and the "Gallienic" style of the rival "Gallic" Emperor Postumus, the "Gallienic Renaissance" was fairly widespread. The term "Renaissance" is something of a misnomer as the artists did not have to learn their craft anew, but the revival of patronage was a significant milestone in 3rd-century art.

A baroque head from the Theater of Dionysos, Athens, has long curling locks which cascade down the nape of the neck, somewhat like the hair of Antinous. The carefully trimmed beard seems to be consciously modeled on Hadrian's. It is not surprising that some scholars have dated this piece and others like it (such as a head in Dresden) to late Hadrianic or Antonine times. However, the eyes have strongly outlined pupils, appearing to gaze into the distance, and the expression is far

The triumphant Hostilian: a scene from the Ludovisi Sarcophagus; marble; height 145cm (57in); mid 3rd century. Terme Museum, Rome

less calm than any Antonine portrait. It is exactly matched on another splendid head in the Terme Museum at Rome which has much shorter hair and can be compared very closely with Gallienus' coin portraits. The Athens head bears some likeness to the head of Alexander the Great found at Pergamum (Istanbul Museum) and dated to the 2nd century BC; it may represent Gallienus in the guise of Alexander. If so, the comparison was hardly a happy one as Gallienus, whatever his other qualities, lacked military success. The reference to Hadrian was both apt and deliberate, no doubt to draw attention to the fact that like his forebear he was a hellenizer and philosopher.

The Sidamara Sarcophagus (Istanbul Museum) was carved in Asia Minor at about this time and has reliefs on all four sides. The most striking of these is an enthroned philosopher in profile, reading from a scroll. Beside him is his wife and they are accompanied by Artemis and the Dioscouri. In the background is a rich architectural framework but, as opposed to earlier "Eastern" sarcophagi, the figures are far more dominant. A similar and equally fine philosopher sarcophagus may be seen in Rome (Lateran Museum).

Gallienic in style, although conceivably later in date, are the reliefs from the *Arcus Novus* which seem to belong to the 260s rather than to the 280s (tetrarchic period). Most of them are now in the Boboli Gardens, Florence, but an important fragment is in the Villa Medici, Rome, showing a Victory inscribing vows for the emperor's safety on a circular shield. The subject matter of the pedestals in Florence is traditional— captive barbarians, Victories, and the Dioscuri. But the bold cutting, high relief, rich plastic textures of the Victories' hair and draperies, and the fine proportions of all the figures take us back to the High Antonine style of the Arch of Marcus Aurelius. The conscious pursuit of beauty is, indeed, very ap-

parent and is matched exactly in the Athens Gallienus. It is not surprising that these reliefs were copied in the reign of Constantine although the result, to be seen on Constantine's Arch, was of very low quality.

The only public sculpture of the tetrarchic age of much merit when judged by the standards of the Greco-Roman past is the Arch of Galerius at Thessalonica whose original form was that of a quadrifons (four-way arch). Only two of the original four piers survive, each with four superimposed layers of relief, which were in part derived from the designs on sarcophagi. The scenes of battle are fairly effective from a distance, and the thin bands of vegetal ornament separating the various zones were cut with the panache we have come to expect from the sculptural school of Aphrodisias in Asia Minor.

Scenes of Imperial audiences, with the Emperor frontally seated and quite immobile amongst his equally impassive subjects, mark further acceptance of an Oriental aesthetic since the time of Severus, but one by no means unexpected to anyone who has looked at art from Palmyra or Dura Europus. The most famous sculpture from the tetrarchy is the portrait group of the complete college of four emperors, now in St Mark's Square, Venice (AD 285–305), but once in Constantinople. The work was carved in Egyptian porphyry, a purple stone used only for sculptures of members of the Imperial family. Each emperor is indistinguishable from his fellows; they have identical mask-like faces, jeweled daggers and diadems. Their personal characteristics are not of interest; all that matters is their status (and so, their large eyes proclaim, they are less human than forces of mediation between the gods and men). Similar porphyry sculptures, for example the figures of Diocletian and Maximian in the Vatican, the head of Constantius I (?) in the British Museum, London, and the bust of Licinius (from Athribis) in Cairo, are equally harsh, equally untouched by ordinary emotion. The humanistic traditions of the Greco-Roman portrait here gave way to the all-seeing eye of the Imperial icon.

To understand the origins of late Roman or Byzantine art we must consider the Roman attitude to the gods and the supernatural. The forms of state art did not, and were not meant to, fulfil an emotional need though it was widely believed that it was both wise and well-mannered to observe *Pax Deorum*. The army regularly initiated official acts of worship and it is not surprising to find that the late Roman fort at Luxor in Egypt contained a shrine and magnificent paintings of emperors and their bodyguards, now unfortunately lost—destroyed by Egyptologists in their scramble for pharaonic reliefs below. Here the *numen*, the divine spirit as opposed to the earthly body, of the emperor and the gods of the Roman state were venerated with fitting pomp.

For private worship men turned to whichever deities most attracted them: Aelius Aristides, the apologist of the 2nd-century Empire to Asklepios; Apuleius (*c* AD 123–late 2nd century) to Isis; and presumably the owners of the great Dionysiac (Bacchic) pavement in Cologne to Dionysos (late 2nd century). Sometimes the cults were relatively new importations, such as Mithraism, but by no means always. Worshipers at the temple of Mithras in London venerated the Iranian god, but the best sculpture from it is a head of the Egyptian Serapis of late Antonine date, while a small votive group of Dionysos and his *thiasos* offers "life to wandering men" in an accompanying inscription. This is unlikely to antedate the 3rd century. As in the Hellenistic world, people expected their gods to be saviors, and it is in this capacity that Dionysos and Hermes are shown on sarcophagi.

Emperors who brought security, for example Diocletian and Maximian, were hailed as having "Jovian" or "Herculean" characteristics; from here is was a short step to regarding them as different from the rest of humanity. It might have been thought that Christianity, which became the religion of the Roman state under Constantine, would have abolished such pretensions. Instead, it further established them by attributing to the Emperor the function of God's deputy on earth. The enormous marble head of Constantine, now in the Palazzo dei Conservatori in Rome, is impressive and mask-like, scanning the world through great drilled eyes in approximation to the divine ruler of the universe (*Cosmocrator*). A parallel may indeed be noted in the Christ painted in the Catacomb of Commodilla in Rome.

The old human values had not been forgotten; at its lowest level the reuse of pillaged Hadrianic and Antonine sculpture in the Arch of Constantine (and the inept Victories, river gods, and captives of contemporary date) display an awareness of earlier traditions. A ceiling painting from the Imperial Palace at Trier (Bischöfliches Museum, Trier) shows female members of the Imperial family, which are highly accomplished portraits in their own right, and a cameo in the Hague portrays

Head of the Egyptian deity Serapis. Museum of London

Constantine, his mother Helena, his wife Fausta, and his son Crispus in a chariot pulled by centaurs. The workmanship, if a little heavy, is classical enough to have led the great German scholar Adolf Furtwängler to suggest that it was a Julio-Claudian work showing the British triumph of Claudius. In some measure, of course, it *is* based on a 1st-century state cameo just as some of Constantine's coins attempt to suggest that he was the new Augustus Caesar.

To a greater extent than before, Roman art in the 4th century was eclectic. For the most part, though not exclusively, the freer, classicizing works are associated with paganism and the hieratic formalism of the Conservatori head or the little friezes on the Arch of Constantine (showing the Emperor elevated and separated from his subjects) with Christianity and the Imperial Court.

Aristocratic patronage is well represented in the many examples of 4th-century silver frequently unearthed in hoards. Silver plate tends to be very conservative in appearance, and the range of pagan subject matter suggests a far from moribund interest in the old cults. A picture-dish from Ballana, Nubia, probably looted from Roman Egypt (Egyptian Museum, Cairo) shows a deity who combines the attributes of

Apollo with those of Hermes, Dionysos, and other deities such as Ares and Hephaestos. The plate illustrates the tendency to "syncretize" the gods and to see them all as the manifestation of a greater whole.

The great Oceanus Dish in the Mildenhall Treasure (British Museum, London) depicts Dionysos with his *thiasos*, satyrs, maenads, Pan, and Hercules, dancing around an inner register of nereids and tritons. At the center is the mask of a sea-god which has given the dish its name. Although found in Britain with several other splendid pieces of silver it was not manufactured there, but imported from the Mediterranean area. Another British find, from Corbridge (Alnwick Castle Collection) is a *lanx* (rectangular dish) which depicts a group of deities, notably Apollo, worshiped on Delos. It was probably made to celebrate the emperor Julian's visit there in AD 363. Julian was a convert from Christianity to the old religion and his "apostasy" may have given considerable encouragement to pagans, even after his untimely death fighting against the Persians (later that year). The hope of a future pagan revival lingered at least until the end of the century.

Instead of the saints of Christianity, the pagans venerated their heroes, especially Achilles. The Achilles dish from Kaiseraugst (Römermuseum, Augst) has a central *emblema* which portrays the hero disguised amongst the daughters of Lycomedes, and, on the rim, a number of other scenes from the early life and education of the hero. It is certainly 4th century in date, and the didacticism of the piece can be regarded as a deliberate counterblast to the teaching aspects of Christian art, for example the silver flask found at Traprain Law near Edinburgh (Museum of National Antiquities of Scotland, Edinburgh) or sarcophagi from the Les Aliscamps Cemetery, Arles, or the Church of S. Felix, Gerona, with scenes from the Old and New Testaments.

Similar aristocratic patronage may have been responsible for the "Rothschild-Lycurgus" cup in the British Museum, London, which belongs to the type of glass vessel known as *diatreton*. These were beakers, laboriously cut out in two layers; essentially a cameo-cutting technique used on the Portland Vase, though no doubt it required even greater technical expertise virtually to separate the two strata. The Rothschild cup depicts Lycurgus, one of the enemies of Dionysos, being strangled by the nymph Ambrosia, whom he had been pursuing and who had conveniently been metamorphosed into a vine. Other *diatreta* were purely decorative and were cut in such a way that the outer layers present a trellis of geometric forms. Magnificent examples have been found both at Cologne and Trier.

An art that made considerable headway in the 4th century was that of the mosaicist. Hitherto his form of decoration had been principally confined to floors, but now it invaded vaults as well. The church of S. Constanza was built as a mausoleum for Constantina, Constantine's eldest daughter (*ob.* mid 4th century AD). As yet there was nothing specifically Christian about its mosaics, indeed the art was studiously neutral. The various emblems of immortality were scattered around the

The Achilles dish from Kaiseraugst; 4th century. Römermuseum, Augst

annular vault as on Sosos' "unswept floor" mosaic (of which a copy from the Aventine is to be seen in the Vatican). Here are shells, peacocks, and pomegranates which most directly bring to mind the voyage of the soul over the sea to the islands of the blessed, the journey of the soul to the sky and immortality, and the Persephone myth with its promise of future resurrection. Another vault mosaic depicts amorini treading grapes and vintaging, a reference to Dionysos. No doubt a Christian could have accepted these symbols indeed, vintaging cupids are shown on a porphyry sarcophagus from the church (Vatican Museums, Rome), presumably Constantina's. Another contemporary mausoleum, perhaps that of Constans, one of Constantine's sons, at Centcelles near Tarragona in Spain, had a complex vault decoration which is admittedly Christian in part but also has some lively hunting scenes which are reminiscent of hunt mosaics from Utica and Carthage (British

A diatreton (cage cup); c 300 AD

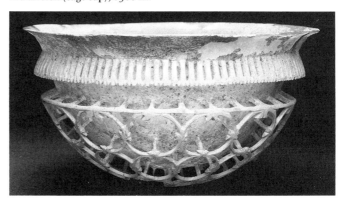

The Hinton St Mary Mosaic

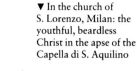

▼ In the church of S. Lorenzo, Milan: the youthful, beardless Christ in the apse of the Capella di S. Aquilino

► From the Hinton St Mary Mosaic: the Head of Christ. The pomegranates on either side are symbols of immortality. British Museum, London

The mosaic discovered at Hinton St Mary, Dorset, England, in 1963, and now in the British Museum, London, measures 28 ft 4 in by 19 ft 6 in (8.6 m by 6 m). It covered the floor of a square room with its vestibule which comprised part of a country house dating from the early 4th century AD.

Dominating the room is a roundel containing the bust of a man, clean-shaven and endowed with large, staring eyes. On either side is a pomegranate, symbol of immortality, and behind his head the sacred Christian monogram, the *Chi-Rho*, composed of the first two letters of Christ's name in Greek. There is little doubt that the figure is Our Lord although the placing of *signum Salvatoris Christi* on floors was specifically forbidden by an imperial decree of AD 427, which perhaps implies that such an abuse was known earlier. It is probable that the design of the pavement was originally intended for a mosaic vault of a type found surviving in late Roman churches of the Mediterranean area, for example the one in the apse of the Cappella di S. Aquilino in the church of S. Lorenzo, Milan, which also portrays a youthful Christ. Certainly the scenes in the lunettes, three of which show hounds chasing deer and a fourth, the Tree of Life, as well as busts occupying the corners of the panel (and presumably derived from wind deities or seasons although they have been bereft of pagan attributes and might now symbolize the Evangelists), could only all be viewed the right way up at the same time if the vault explanation for the composition is adopted.

The central motif in the vestibule is a roundel showing the hero, Bellerophon, mounted upon the winged horse Pegasus, holding a spear in his right hand with which to pierce the monstrous Chimaera. Unfortunately the figure of Bellerophon was damaged and patched in the later 4th century, and the mosaicist has shown the Chimaera as a gamboling feline with a rather lifeless goat-head emerging from its back and an equally unconvincing serpent as a tail. Nevertheless, the composition is relieved by a bold linear sense and an attractive control of color. The legend is fairly common in ancient art, and indeed was the motif on a Greek pebble-mosaic from Olynthos dated to the 4th century BC. In late Antiquity it assumed a Christian significance as the victorious struggle of Good against the powers of Evil. It was found on a mosaic at the nearby villa at Frampton (which incidentally also had a *Chi-Rho* device) as well as at Lullingstone in Kent, a villa with a Christian painted chapel. A fragment of bronze sheeting in the Historisches Museum der Pfalz, Speyer, displays the motif in relief alongside another roundel containing portraits of the family of Constantine, the first Christian Emperor, while a signet ring found at Havering-atte-Bower, Essex, which also shows Bellerophon and the Chimaera, is certainly of late Roman date, when Christianity was the official religion of the Empire.

▼ From the Hinton St Mary Mosaic: Bellerophon on his winged horse Pegasus slays the monstrous Chimaera. British Museum, London

On either side of this scene is a rectangular panel which, like the three lunettes already mentioned, show hounds and deer. They may be interpreted either as continuations of the Bellerophon theme, the struggles of the Christian life, or as symbolizing the joys of Paradise. Similar hunting scenes are recorded elsewhere in Christian contexts—for instance in the Basilica of Cresconius, Djemila—although once again the theme was adapted from the common repertory of secular art (for instance, the *Little Hunt* at Piazza Armerina).

The style of the mosaic is almost identical with that found in other mosaics from the same area and especially the example from Frampton already mentioned. It was laid by a highly original school of mosaicists which almost certainly had its headquarters at the nearby town of Dorchester (*Durnovaria*). Clearly this was no ordinary villa dining room but must have been a small chapel with a narthex containing the Bellerophon scene, symbolizing the Christian's struggles against the evil of the world, and the cult-room itself, dominated by the sublime figure of Christ as *Cosmocrator*—Ruler of the Universe.

MARTIN HENIG

Further reading. Painter, K.S. "The Design of the Roman Mosaic at Hinton St Mary", *Antiquaries Journal* vol. LVI, (1976) pp49–54. Toynbee, J.M.C. "A New Roman Mosaic Pavement found in Dorset", *Journal of Roman Studies* vol. LIV, (1964) pp7–14.

◄ From the villa at Lullingstone, Kent: another example of Bellerophon and the Chimaera (*in situ*)

▼ The Little Hunt at Piazza Armerina. Villa Romana del Casale, Sicily

Museum, London) and of the Little Hunt floor mosaic at Piazza Armerina in Sicily.

Hunting was an activity that cut across religious differences. At Piazza Armerina we see not only the normal activities of the chase where the quarry was boar or deer, but also a great mosaic which shows ferocious lions, leopards, and other exotic fauna being captured alive for exhibition in the Roman arena. The presiding magistrate in his rich robes has been identified as the Emperor Maximian, but it is possible that the floor was laid at a later date, perhaps the mid 4th century. Obviously, the owner of the great country estate centered on Piazza Armerina was immensely rich, but so were several members of the late Roman aristocracy, such as Q. Aurelius Symmachus, who was known to have had specific responsibility to put on shows for the Roman people. The pagan nature of other floors at Piazza Armerina depicting Hercules, the myths of Lycurgus and Ambrosia, and of Ulysses blinding Polyphemus, is not in doubt.

As in the case of silver plate much valuable evidence comes from Britain—in the 4th century a land with many large villas, some no doubt owned by members of the native aristocracy and others by men whose fathers and grandfathers had fled Gaul in the civil unrest and invasions of the 3rd century. Of course silver plate could be imported, but mosaics had to be laid on the spot. Firms of mosaicists thus grew up in the towns of the province. At Cirencester there was a workshop with a particularly robust sense of color, line, and pattern. Indeed, one example of a Corinian pavement has been found at the capital city of Trier. An especially notable floor depicting Orpheus and the beasts was laid at the palatial residence at Woodchester—did it belong to the governor of Britannia Prima? Orpheus occupies a central roundel, which is encircled by an inner register of birds and an outer one of quadrupeds. A similar but simpler mosaic was laid in the villa at Barton Farm, just outside the walls of Cirencester (Corinium Museum). Mosaics from Chedworth, Gloucestershire, and Stonesfield, Oxfordshire, portrayed Dionysos. The latter, known only from an engraving, showed the god with his panther in a circular medallion surrounded by a rich border (incorporating a running scroll which appears to issue from the head of Neptune). The Chedworth mosaic can be presumed to have been the centerpiece of a floor which retains part of its octagonal, segmented surround containing vigorous portrayals of nymphs and satyrs. All these mosaics have decorative motifs in common, for example the Stonesfield scroll is also found at Chedworth and Woodchester.

The Corinium mosaics display a well-mannered paganism, which, as in S. Constanza, would not have been obnoxious to Christians. Indeed Christian and pagan motifs are combined in mosaics from Frampton (no longer extant) and Hinton St Mary (British Museum, London), both laid by the firm of mosaicists from Dorchester, Dorset. Both depict the Christian *Chi-Rho* and the latter the head of Christ as well; but they also portray Bellerophon on Pegasus slaying the Chimaera, and at Frampton the head of Neptune, and figures of Bacchus

The Hare mosaic from a house in Cirencester. Corinium Museum, Cirencester.

and Venus and Adonis are shown as well.

Some of the best Romano-British mosaics depict genre scenes like the chariot race at Horkstow, Lincolnshire (British Museum, London), the leopard leaping on to a gazelle from the villa at Dewlish in Dorset, which demonstrates an interest in wild animals similar to the Piazza Armerina mosaic, and the hare mosaic from Cirencester, showing a much quieter approach to nature.

The late Roman aristocracy had scholarly pretensions and in Taunton Museum, a mosaic from Low Ham, Somerset, England, shows episodes from the *Aeneid* dealing with the wanderings of Aeneas and his sojourn at Carthage. It is probable that this floor was actually copied from an illuminated manuscript such as the *Vergilius Romanus* in the Vatican Library, which with its bold, linear outlines and rich colors seems to belong to a Romano-British or Romano-Gaulish milieu. More conventionally Classical in feeling, but less imaginatively drawn, the *Vergilius Vaticanus* (also in the Vatican Library) shows how the neoclassical style could survive in the minor arts through the medium of copying. A translation into ivory of a couple of pictures of priestesses pouring libations (Victoria and Albert Museum, London; Musée Cluny, Paris) demonstrates that a real understanding of Classical canons of beauty could be kept alive by craftsmen in the circle of wealthy aristocrats, like Quintus Aurelius Symmachus and Nichomachus Flavianus who commissioned the ivory diptych cited above to celebrate their children's wedding in AD 393/4.

A remarkable late Roman pagan shrine in the Via Livenza,

Rome, has a fine fresco portraying the goddess Diana hunting in a woodland setting, and a mosaic floor discovered in the Kornmarkt at Trier seems to come from a room of similar function as Jupiter and Leda with their offspring, Castor, Pollux, and Helen of Troy, appear together with a number of votaries of a cult (Landesmuseum, Trier). For the most part the religion of the last pagans was a private and small-scale affair. The philosopher Proclus in Athens (AD 411–85) who dreamed that the goddess Athena had asked him to give her sanctuary as she had been ejected from her home in the Parthenon, is a good example of late Antique piety and of the essentially quietist nature of the faith of the last champions of the Greek and Roman gods.

Unlike the dividing point between "Greece" and "Rome" (the occurrence of which is a matter for debate since in the east there was complete cultural continuity) the religious and social fabric of life was now threatened. The public celebration of cult acts was forbidden by Theodosius (AD 391) and temples were pillaged throughout the Empire by undisciplined mobs. It is a mistake to think of the "barbarians" merely as an external threat when temples and the academies of classical learning were under attack from illiterate peasants such as the *Circumcelliones* in north Africa. Nor did it make any difference that this "vandalism" was perpetrated in the name of a Christian emperor.

The old cults had dwindling numbers of adherents in the towns—few people could match up to the bravery of Hypatia, martyred by a rabble of monks in Alexandria (AD 415). Insofar as it survived under the protection of rich senators or eminent philosophers, the Hellenic faith belonged to the sort of coterie we glimpse in Macrobius' *Saturnalia*. Elsewhere worship of the gods lingered in the countryside which was less touched by Christianity than the towns. In Britain there are examples of rural shrines at Lydney in Gloucestershire (which even had a fine mosaic commissioned by an official of the temple) and at Maiden Castle near Dorchester, Dorset. Thus, the ancient cults of whatever origin became known to posterity as "Paganism", the religion of the *pagani*—countrymen.

The art of the court which we contrasted with that of the aristocracy continued to follow in the formal, nonclassical traditions of the Arch of Constantine and the Conservatori head. The bronze head of Constantius II in the Capitoline reminds us of the historian Ammianus Marcellinus' description of that Emperor seated immobile on his horse and looking neither right nor left. The style became even more rigid and a head found at Constantinople showing the Emperor Arcadius portrayed even the hair as a kind of extension to the diadem. Empresses followed suit, as we may see on the Rothschild Cameo (Rothschild Collection, France) with its portraits of Honorius and his wife Maria (although other identifications have been proposed; not surprisingly for it is almost impossible to tell 4th-century emperors apart). In the whole parade of 4th-century portraits it is only with those of the Pagan Julian (and on coins, Procopius his kinsman and Eugenius who was trying to take power at the end of the century with pagan support) that we find any real individuality. Here an attempt was made to return to Antonine prototypes but the sculptors and die-engravers were not sure how to give life to the face and injected rather too much of 4th-century stiffness and formalism into their basic designs. The cleanly "chiseled" beard on Julian's portraits and his philosophic mien, however, add variety to what is otherwise the depressing end of one of Rome's greatest art forms.

A coin of Constantius II   A coin of Julian

The Emperor Constantine built a new Imperial Capital on the Bosphorus. Although there had been a Greek city—Byzantium—on the site, the massive scale of the new works made Constantinople a place unencumbered by the trammels of pagan tradition. Here was a "New Rome" in every sense.

A number of works of art were gathered from sites where they had been venerated for ages and here set up as mere secular embellishments to the city. The bronze tripod from Delphi standing on a base of three entwined snakes was thus reerected in the hippodrome where part of the base survives. Rather different was the case of the Column of Arcadius which set out to imitate the forms of Trajan's Column and the Column of Marcus Aurelius. Only a small fragment remains, but fortunately some fine drawings of it were executed in the 16th century. Here the past was being manipulated to serve the turn of imperial propaganda. The ruler sits in state and is adored by his subjects. He does not *lead* his soldiers into battle as their comrade and friend, like Trajan or Marcus, but rather *presides* over the exploits of his army.

An Egyptian obelisk brought, like the tripod, to the hippodrome from elsewhere stands on a sculptured base that depicts Theodosius presiding at the horse races. He stands in a special box, a head taller than his companions, other members of the Imperial family. Outside the box we see his entourage and bodyguard. Below are the Roman people ranked in monotonous and unvarying frontality. Again, one feels, the Roman tradition of state relief has nothing left to say. Byzantine sculpture—screens, pulpits, sarcophagi, columns—can be charming but it is for the most part purely decorative.

Mosaic did not lapse into triviality, but had to find a new iconography, except where, for example, classical personifications could be useful. Victories became angels, and river-gods could represent the Jordan in baptisteries. In the Mausoleum of Galla Placidia in Ravenna we can still discern a link between Christ the Good Shepherd amongst his flock and the old Greco-Roman pastoral.

There are admittedly certain surprising survivals even in court circles, such as the 5th- or 6th-century floor mosaics in the Great Palace at Constantinople, showing men at their rural labors, and various animals and birds. Greco-Roman secular art struggled on, but without the beliefs that gave it sustenance. Compromise was impossible between the ever stricter Christian beliefs of the emperors and the ethos of the last pagans—"Not by one path alone can man attain so great a mystery" proclaimed the great Symmachus (AD 382) in trying to persuade Emperor Valentinian II to give the Altar of Victory back to the Senate.

A large silver plate found near Merida in Spain was evidently a costly gift celebrating the 10th anniversary of the reign of Theodosius (AD 388; Archaeological Museum, Madrid). It shows the earth goddess disporting herself with three amorini. She is similarly placed to the goddess on the Aquileia patera of early Imperial times, and even recalls Tellus on the *Ara Pacis*. However, above her there is no enactment of the Demeter myth nor affirmation of public missions; instead we see Theodosius enthroned between his sons, Valentinian II and Arcadius, within the confines of a shrine-cum-palace. They appear unapproachable, "like lizards" in the apt metaphor of Hypatia's pupil, Synesius (AD 370–413). Beside them are their bodyguard, of whom the same author writes

> their faces and foreheads are bathed in sweet perfume; they carry golden shields and golden spears. Their presence announces the appearance of the prince, just as the first, faint morning light heralds the rising of the sun.

The Roman achievement and its legacy. The Roman achievement was vast, but it depended less on individual artists and movements than in the fact that Greek and Hellenistic art did not perish, as have so many traditions of the human past, but were taken—by Rome—to distant corners of Europe and the Levant where they struck deep roots. Romanesque art was heavily influenced by the surviving monuments of the Empire and International Gothic saw the emergence of a classical style (at Chartres, Reims, and elsewhere) under the chisels of men who could never have looked upon a Greek statue. In the east, Byzantine art—different as it is from what went before—showed a constant awareness of its origins.

The similarity in the linear design of a tombstone from Murrell Hill, Cumberland, England (Tullie House Museum, Carlisle) and the figures of the Evangelists in the Lindesfarne Gospels (British Museum, London) has been pointed out by George Henderson. The portraits of Virgil in the *Vergilius Romanus* (Vatican Library, Rome) are even closer, and perhaps all three works of art taken together show how a local style in one province could effectively survive the Dark Ages.

But even beyond the possibilities of immediate survival, Roman art was one of the sources of direct inspiration to the Renaissance. Instead of copying and adapting the work of the Middle Ages, there were Roman statues to emulate and adapt. Donatello created his David in the image of Antinous, a cupid was closely based on an ancient bronze of Atys (such as the fine figurine that is one of the treasures of Trier Museum). The Laocoön, a rather overblown work of late Hellenistic times, apparently the statue praised by Pliny as "a work to be preferred to all that the arts of painting and sculpture have produced" turned up in Rome in 1506 and helped to mold the art of Michelangelo and his contemporaries. From statues it was but a short step to rediscovering the human body and its true proportions.

In the past century and half, enthusiasm for Rome has declined before new knowledge of Greek art in all its phases, and some well-known writers on art are extremely harsh in their judgment on Rome's achievement. Perhaps we are now beginning to see that this is unfair, and while some Roman sculptures and paintings are indifferent copies of Classical masterpieces commissioned by people with more money than taste, others are highly refined and subtle attempts to build on the labors of the Greek past. In particular we may single out the great sculpture workshops of Asia Minor and the inventors of Roman illusionistic painting. It should always be remembered that when Petronius wrote of Trimalchio's vulgarity and lack of taste, he was not describing a typical "Roman" but inviting us to laugh, with him, at the follies of the parvenu outsider.

MARTIN HENIG

Bibliography. Boëthius, A. *Etruscan and Early Roman Architecture*, Harmondsworth (1979). Boëthius, A. and Ward-Perkins, J.B. *Etruscan and Roman Architecture*, Harmondsworth (1970). Brown, P. *The World of Late Antiquity*, London (1971). Painter, K.S. *The Wealth of the Roman World*, London (1977). Pollitt, J.J. *The Art of Rome* c *753* BC–AD *337*, New Jersey (1966). Strong, D. *Greek and Roman Gold and Silver Plate*, London (1966). Strong, D. *Roman Art*, Harmondsworth (1976). Toynbee, J.M.C. *Death and Burial in the Roman World*, London (1971). Vermeule, C. *Roman Imperial Art in Greece and Asia Minor*, Cambridge, Mass. (1968).

12

CELTIC ART

Celtic bronze flagons with coral and enamel inlay found at Basse Yutz
height 39cm (15in). British Museum, London (see page 216)

I N the eyes of the ancient world the Celts were a nation, though a nation made up of many tribes loosely grouped together, and always liable to break up into smaller bands. When and how the Celtic language arose is not known, but the archaeology of 2nd-millennium Europe gives some hints as to how this particular "nation" was consolidated. In the later 2nd millennium we find in much of central and western Europe an amalgamation of pastoralists and settled agriculturists. The pastoralist tradition brought with it the custom of burying the chieftain in isolated splendor with his weapons and other finery, and sometimes with his slaves and womenfolk. The other tradition appears more egalitarian, with large cemeteries of urn-burials, all much on a level of wealth. There may also have been small groups of warlike conquerors from further east who welded the older inhabitants into wellorganized aggressive tribes. The pattern of barrow-burials, grouped around a defended hill site, found on the upper Danube, the middle Rhine, and in Bohemia, suggests the tribal center of a chieftain or even a minor king commanding a fixed territory.

A rather similar dichotomy existed during the 5th and early 4th centuries BC when the first truly Celtic art appeared. There was one zone of rich burials, known as the Zone of Chieftains' Graves, which spread in an arc from the eastern Alps through the middle Rhine and Moselle into Champagne, with extensions into southwest Bohemia and to the Loire. The burials were generally under tumuli and often held imported treasures, as well as fine work from local craftsmen. Beside this, and only slightly later in its beginnings, lies a second zone characterized by cemeteries, some very large, of flat inhumation graves, which probably started in central Switzerland, with a minor extension into Burgundy in the west and a major extension eastwards through southwestern Germany to north Bohemia, Moravia, and the borders of Hungary. In Champagne the zones overlap. It is from this Flat-grave Zone with its poorer burials and more uniform social structure that the main Celtic expansion took its greatest impetus. A historical watershed comes c400 BC. By then some bands of Celts had already crossed the Alps into Italy, but the great expansion followed around, or soon after, 400 BC, taking one band to sack Rome in 379 BC and others a little later into Transylvania and the Balkans, till about 100 years later still Celts were looting Delphi and crossing the Hellespont into Anatolia.

The society that had grown up in the Celtic heartland, mainly the Chieftains' Graves Zone, by the 6th century BC, just before the appearance of La Tène art, was tribal, aristocratic, bellicose, and prosperous. This is seen especially in the richest burials, made in wood- or stone-lined chambers, usu-

Distribution of main sites mentioned

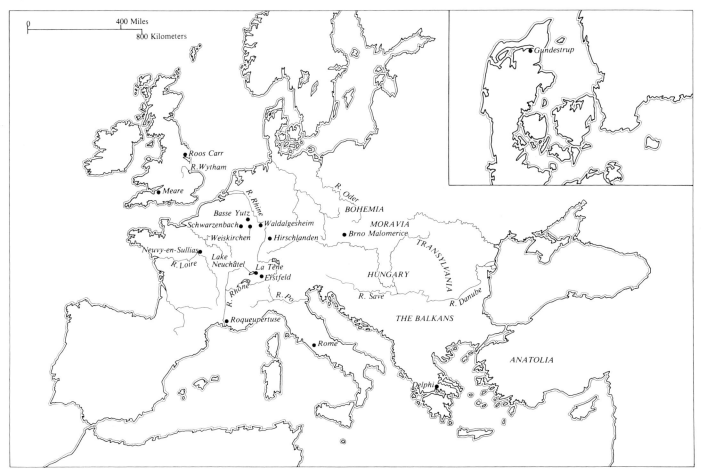

ally under round barrows. The cart, hearse, or later two-wheeled chariot, in which the dead were carried to the grave, was buried too, and the body was accompanied by weapons, ornaments, and other prized possessions, all of which were richly ornamented. The graves were grouped round fortified hill sites, and on top of one, at Hirschlanden in Württemberg, there stood for a few years an almost life-size, naked stone warrior (Württembergisches Landesmuseum, Stuttgart).

The rich gear placed in the graves included bronze tableware, Etruscan flagons, Greek vases, and even ivories from the Levant and silk from the Far East. Through these exotic imports Celtic craftsmen were first brought into touch with the products of Classical Mediterranean workshops, which they were to transform and make their own. The presence of these well-dated imported objects helps to date the beginning of early La Tène art. The new style appeared in the first half of the 5th century BC, but for a little while it ran parallel with the outgoing "Hallstatt" tradition. This aristocratic element, with its improved tribal organization, added to a heavier agricultural use of the land and, in a few places, overpopulation also contributed to the Celtic expansion at the end of the 5th century.

La Tène art. It is arguable that Celtic La Tène art was the first authentic art style to have arisen in Europe since the Upper Paleolithic. It is named after an underwater site on Lake Neuchâtel in Switzerland from which a quantity of bronze, iron, and other weapons were dredged, many decorated in a new, flowing linear style, unlike the earlier arts of Europe and equally alien to the Classical styles of the Mediterranean. La Tène now usually means the art produced by the Celts while they were still independent of Roman and other conquerors. It is generally speaking a small-scale art created for a warrior aristocracy that, in Stuart Piggott's words, "demanded flamboyant display from its head-hunting, charioteering chieftains and their petty courts; or somber trappings and imagery in the forest sanctuaries of a religion in which human sacrifice and the cult of the severed head played an important part. It is strange and unfamiliar to us as it was to the Greeks and Romans. So much of the finest work comprises small, intense and exquisite pieces of intricate workmanship in gold, silver or bronze, which capture and concentrate preciousness, virtuosity, symbolism and beauty". It was among the 6th- and early 5th-century BC Celtic-speaking inhabitants of the land lying northward of the Alps that this art was invented, for invention it was. There is no single source, native or foreign, and no gradual unfolding. In fact it is rare to find an art style so different from anything that went before, whose archaeological setting can be studied and understood, yet which itself remains profoundly elusive and unpredictable.

In describing La Tène art it is still best to use the system of styles and names worked out by Paul Jacobsthal in 1944, in spite of his Western bias, which excluded some important Hallstatt-based geometric material from the more easterly branch of the Chieftains' Zone, for Early style is in fact the art

The sandstone statue from Hirschlanden; height without feet 150cm (59in). Württembergisches Landesmuseum, Stuttgart

of the Chieftains' Graves. It was the suddenness of the appearance of this art that led Jacobsthal to formulate his three roots: the Classical art of the Mediterranean, received generally through Etruscan intermediaries; Oriental art, principally Scythian and Persian; and a native root, from the Hallstatt style of geometric decoration. In Early style the sources can still be discerned without much difficulty, but it was followed in the 4th century BC by a second or Waldalgesheim style which, though still receiving inspiration from Classical and Etruscan decorative motifs, is far more radical in its transformations. This in turn was followed by a heavier, three-dimensional, Plastic style; and running partly parallel with it, a more linear Sword style. British insular art began later than continental La Tène, but had a not dissimilar development.

The Classical root of the First or Early style has been studied more closely than the others. Palmettes, lotus buds, and

The Gundestrup Caldron

From the end of the last Ice Age votive offerings were made in the Danish bogs and meres. The most extraordinary is probably the silver caldron found in 1891 at Gundestrup near Børremose, Jutland. As discovered it was dismantled and has been reconstructed with the help of small portions of rim and an iron hoop. The sides are formed by seven outer panels placed back to back with five larger inner panels. They do not make a good fit and one outer panel may be missing. There is also a roundel at the base. All are decorated in high relief, hammered from below and chased above. The outer panels and base were originally covered with thin gold foil. At least three different artists worked on the panels and the author of the base was the most sophisticated.

Ever since its discovery there has been controversy over this magnificent vessel. It has been claimed as Celtic work on the strength of the iconography, and as Thracian or Dacian on style and technique; but there is some agreement on its date. The busts of the outer panels appear to represent male and female gods surrounded by their emblems, attributes, and elements of myth. They are dignified, formal, and static, their features tending to abstract pattern but in a manner not specifically Celtic. An exception is an uncomfortable female with attendants. The inner panels are alive with circular movement. An antlered god squats between a stag and a wolf, holding a "torque" and a horned serpent, and has been claimed to be a Celtic god; elephants, winged griffins, the combat of man and lion, and a person astride a dolphin (or more probably a Black Sea sturgeon) are ultimately Oriental or Hellenistic.

Another scene shows a tree of life, dividing spurred and helmeted horsemen from foot-soldiers, with three trumpeters blowing in-

◄ The silver Gundestrup Caldron, reconstructed; height 42cm (17in); diameter 69cm (27in). National Museum, Copenhagen

Below left An inner panel of the Caldron; 20×42cm (8×17in)

▼ An outer panel of the Caldron; 20×25cm (8×10in)

struments that ancient authors called *carnyx*. The Celts are known to have terrified their enemies with the hoarse sounds reverberating from their animal mouthpieces, and this *carnyx*, which was used by the Galatians in Asia Minor as well as by the western Celts, is the only exclusively Celtic object represented. The towering figure at the other end of the panel may be performing a sacrifice or else dipping a dead warrior in the caldron of revivification known in Irish legends.

The search for the stylistic ancestry of the Gundestrup Caldron begins near the Caspian in northern Persia where a wealth of gold and silver work was produced, especially in "Amlash" and at Marlik in the 12th century BC, in a peculiar "Animal style" which is a provincial version of Babylonian and Assyrian art. This style, which is quite unlike Scythian, can be followed westwards to the kingdom of Urartu in eastern Anatolia, to the Phrygians of the central plateau, and finally to the Thracian population of the Balkans. The lopsided drawing of antlers and the "hanging feet" of animals on gold work that is Urartian, though found in a 6th-century Scythian tomb at Kelermes in the Kuban, are conventions followed by Gundestrup, while in 4th-century Thrace, still independent though under strong Greek influence, the

local Thracian style of beaten goldwork looks even more like Gundestrup. Since this was the art of provincials its divergence from Greek and Persian-Achaemenian court art is explained. Certain medallions or horse *phalerae* found from south Russia to the Channel Islands show the style surviving into the 1st century AD.

Considerations of style and technique lead us to look for the Gundestrup workshop in a place where Thracian versions of ancient Orientalizing art were still executed, and where silver was readily available, which narrows the field to the Carpatho-Danubian region and the Transylvanian and Balkan silver mines. If the stylistic argument is preferred to more subjective interpretations of iconography, there is still the problem of

how the caldron reached the Baltic, and how it acquired its Celtic characteristics. There was a long tradition of northern contact with central Europe which continued through the last centuries BC. From c218 BC a Celtic kingdom existed in Bulgaria, but from this advanced position the Celts were soon driven back to their central European homeland, so that refugee metalwork found its way to the north as well as to western Europe. However, a western origin for the caldron still has its advocates.

N.K. SANDARS

► Animals on the gold sheathing of a battle ax handle from a 6th-century Scythian tomb at Kelermes in the Kuban. Hermitage Museum, Leningrad

Far right A stylistic ancestor of the Gundestrup Caldron: a silver beaker, probably from Marlik, Persia. Minneapolis Institute of Arts

▼ The base roundel of the Caldron; diameter 24cm (9in). The bull's horns are lost

► 4th-century Thracian metalwork: the top of a silver-gilt greave from Vratsa, Bulgaria; height 46cm (18in). National Museum, Sofia

tendrils, the stock-in-trade of the Classical repertoire, were taken to pieces by Celtic craftsmen and reassembled into still coherent but quite unclassical patterns. The gold openwork bowl from a grave at Schwarzenbach in the Hunsrück, Germany, is a good example (Staatliche Museen, Berlin). The eastern root is more elusive, for though objects in the Scythian style have been found in Hungary and even further west, the orientalizing root of La Tène art is more indebted to Persian (Achaemenid) objects which did not get further into Europe than Bulgaria. For some scholars all these oriental elements were filtered through Etruscan intermediaries, but they could have come by way of the Persian occupation of Thrace between 513 and 479 BC. This orientalizing takes the form of fine decorated drinking horns (never popular in the Classical world), in a taste for monsters, and for backward-looking heraldic pairs like those on a belt-clasp from Weiskirchen, Saarland (Rheinisches Landesmuseum, Bonn). The native (Hallstatt) root was probably a good deal stronger than used to be thought. Its importance appears in the Early style of the eastern Chieftains' Graves Zone with stamped decoration, and compass-based geometric motifs that take the place of the flowing designs of the west, though both are based on a Classical floral motif. Intersecting arcs and circles are built up into patterns that certainly owe something to the Hallstatt tradition. But there were some less rigid native arts surviving from an earlier phase of the late Bronze Age which may also have had a part in the genesis of Celtic art. In an astonishingly short time the diverse elements—floral, geometric, orientalizing, and classical—were fused together into a consistent style which is unlike any one of them alone.

The gold openwork bowl from Schwarzenbach; diameter 13cm (5in). Antikenabteilung, Staatliche Museen, Berlin

Gold ornaments from the chieftain's grave at Waldalgesheim. Rheinisches Landesmuseum, Bonn

La Tène art, especially in its early phase, was the art of a warrior society. The styles were used in the decoration of weapons, parts of war chariots, and all the bowls and flagons necessary for serving wine in Barbarian versions of the symposium, adopted, along with the wine itself, from Mediterranean lands; as well as on personal ornaments: torques, bracelets, and belt-clasps. Celtic artists made their own version of the Etruscan and Oriental beaten bronze flagons with animal-shaped handles. Perhaps the most accomplished, as well as the most oriental, are the pair found at Basse Yutz in Lorraine, France (British Museum, London). The handle and rim animals, with their characteristic spiral motif for ears and joints, have their nearest relatives in the Urals where we find both at Pazaryryk, which is broadly contemporary, while earlier eastern examples are known in wood and bone. Technically these flagons with their enamel inlay are as fine as anything produced in Classical or Oriental workshops. A chance find of gold neck-rings and bracelets from Erstfeld, Canton. Uri, in Switzerland, though certainly of Celtic workmanship, contains four neck-rings in the most Oriental style of any yet found, with intertwining animal, human, and floral subjects. They may be allied to some of the more orientalizing ornament in Rhenish Chieftains' Graves, but they are quite unlike Etruscan work and their origin remains a problem.

The second style of La Tène art has been named after one of the last of the great Rhenish princely chariot burials found at Waldalgesheim, Kreuznach, Germany. It is probably early to mid 4th century BC, and so a generation later than the majority of the Chieftains' Graves. Like many rich Celtic burials it held the body of a princess, with her gold bangles and finely decorated bronze chariot fittings, and also an imported Italian bronze situla. The decoration of this was used by the native craftsman who worked with a new freedom, and an audacious, rather wayward attitude towards design which is also new. This second style appeared almost as suddenly as the first. There was no gradual transition, except perhaps on the Marne, France. It is markedly absent from the Zone of Chieftains' Graves and belongs to that of the Flat Graves in Switzerland, southwest Germany, and eastern France. This was the style that the Celts who had gone down into Italy, adopted in the early to mid 4th century BC, and which was also carried eastwards into Transylvania and to the Balkans. Throughout this vast region there was contact and exchange between workshops. One characteristic of the style, which was carried over into much later work, is a particular sleight of hand, by means of which designs that appear asymmetric in fact depend on the reversing and transposing of symmetric elements, to form a whole which partakes of both. The subtlety with which compass-work is disguised, and the linear twinings and convolutions that are made to appear organic and floral, but which turn out when examined to be abstract and inorganic, all belong to a peculiarly Celtic species of ambiguity.

Plastic style, which developed in the late 4th century BC, owes almost as much to the Early style as to the Waldalgesheim, a feature made possible by the chronological overlap between the two. It inherited from Early style the transformations of men and monsters and the visual punning. But there was a new treatment of man and animal in which mass and contour, body and limb became three-dimensional patterns with their own inner coherence, which is not that of the natural creature. The simplified swirl of contour is shown admirably on bronze openwork fittings of unknown function that were found at Brno Malomerice in Moravia, Czechoslovakia (Moravian Museum, Brno). There is also an abstract version of Plastic work which was used on bracelets and bangles from the Pyrenees to Bulgaria.

Sword style, or sometimes Hungarian Sword style, is so called because it was first recognized on scabbards and iron swords of the 3rd century BC, in Hungary and Switzerland. It shows a tendency, exactly opposite to that of Plastic style, towards flat, linear, often asymmetric designs of great elegance and sophistication. It had a very wide currency, and its source lies in the convoluted Waldalgesheim tendril and other abstract, sometimes asymmetric, motifs. The delight of the Hungarian swordsmiths in transverse patterns and in sym-

Limestone Janus heads from Roquepertuse; height 22cm (9in). Musée Borely, Marseilles

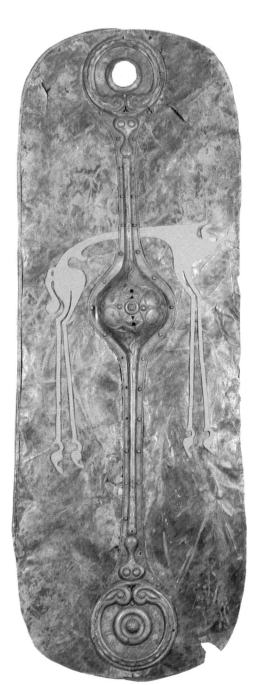

Bronze shield found in the River Witham; diameter of inlaid center roundel 15cm (6in). British Museum, London

metric, as well as asymmetric, designs owes most to an eastern Danubian Waldalgesheim, but the equally popular motif of a lyre in the guise of confronted dragon pairs with spiral twisted tails may have a western origin and was much used on Swiss swords. Tendril interlace seems to be a new development in this style, which also appears on spears and other metalwork.

Celtic religion did not require natural representations of the gods, or of the otherworld and its supernatural beings. This does not mean that religious ideas are not expressed in abstract and decorative designs. The large number of votive offerings found in sanctuaries, rivers, and meres suggests that they were. In monumental carving in stone and wood the religious dimension became explicit. Here again there are opposing tendencies, towards both the abstract and the natural, and there is a concentration on the head, severed or attached, as there is in Celtic literature and legend. A group of life-size and larger-than-life stone heads and figures from the Rhineland and Württemberg probably stood on the tops of mound graves. In a sanctuary at Roquepertuse in Provence, France, there are Janus heads with a characteristically sardonic physiognomy (Musée Borely, Marseilles); also friezes and seated figures, in which classical models can be recognized. Bronzesmiths also occasionally worked on a monumental scale, and one of their masterpieces is the boar, 1.26 m (4 ft 2 in) long, found in a sanctuary at Neuvy-en-Sullias on the Loire, and probably of the 1st century BC (Musée Historique et Archéologique de l'Orléanais, Orléans). Figures like this (especially boars) were carried as standards. Bronze caldrons were also beaten out with ornamental panels, though the most spectacular, a silver caldron found at Gundestrup in Denmark, owes virtually nothing to La Tène art.

La Tène art reached the British Isles at a late date and was in great part due to the arrival of the Belgae from northern Gaul. Before this time there was virtually nothing that could be called art in the British Isles, neither in domestic pottery nor metalwork, though there was a high level of technical accomplishment in the making of weapons and in the ornaments made by Irish goldsmiths; the work of the wood-carver is virtually unknown apart from the Roos Carr figures from Holderness, Yorkshire. But when the La Tène style of art did at last arrive it enjoyed an extraordinarily prolonged life. A few continental objects may have come independently of any settlement as early as the 5th century BC. Early style stamp-decorated pottery, and a little corresponding metalwork, was the immediate inspiration of the British Iron Age pottery found at sites like Meare in Somerset, and also for some of the decoration on the earliest British La Tène bronzework. There cannot have been any great interval between this and the continental models. Such comparisons give the needed link between the rich, inventive, continental workshops of the early 4th century BC (not all of them in the west), and insular art of the 3rd and 2nd centuries BC.

As on the continent, the finest workmanship was lavished on the warrior's panoply, and especially on shields, helmets, and horsebits, as well as the more usual swords, sheaths, spears, and bangles. The shield boss from the River Wytham is one of the finest (British Museum, London). Then, quite late, at the turn of the 1st century BC, mirror-backs were decorated with compass-based designs of great intricacy. An insular version of the Plastic style, using animal and human heads and animal handles, was developed, and there is abstract plastic ornamentation on heavy gold bangles. Many designs show an obsessional preoccupation with birds seen in profile, dismembered, or disjointed. There also grew up a deliberate use of the voids within a design for decorative purposes, which was developed to such a degree that negative and positive have equal weight. Basketry, sometimes done with a rocked graver, was preferred as a filling motif to continental pouncing; and a crinkly line was reproduced by tapping along a ridge in place of filigree or beading. In Ireland this art survived during the Roman occupation of Britain where, as all over the continent, it was driven underground, only to reemerge in the rich aftermath of early Christian Celtic art, when many of the same designs reappeared and underwent yet another transformation.

From the 2nd, and still more the 1st, century BC onwards, Celtic tribes minted their own coins, based on the Macedonian gold *stater*. But the Celtic delight in misreading Classical subjects and employing them decoratively, became a vice and, by distorting naturalistic motifs, led to confusion and anarchy.

La Tène craftsmen inherited from Late Bronze Age metal-work-shops a superlative technique: great precision, control, and clean design. What had been lacking was breadth of treatment and subject matter, invention and variety. This deficiency was made good by the new artists who were masters of all the goldsmith's techniques except granulation. The use of the compass in the layout of designs was sophisticated and subtle, from 5th-century-BC Early style to masterpieces of ambiguity like the British mirror-backs of the turn of the 1st century, where an extraordinarily complicated deployment of the geometry of compass-arcs gives an illusion of flowing freehand draftsmanship.

In potting, the fast wheel was new to western Europe beyond the classical world, while some of the painted designs belong to the same decorative schools as the metalwork. Success in monumental sculpture shows that its rarity, and the concentration on small ornaments and personal gear, came from social causes, not lack of skill. Some have seen the hands of individual artists, but the point is hard to prove; certainly workshops had their individual styles. It is above all the peculiar sort of ambiguity of subject, the delicacy of techniques, the equilibrium and consistency, and its professionalism which ensure La Tène art a unique place among the art styles of the world. It possessed moreover a toughness which allowed it to dominate over much of Europe during four centuries, and to survive another four underground and on the peripheries (such as Ireland) until its second flowering in the early Middle Ages.

N.K. SANDARS

Bibliography. Cunliffe, B. *The Celtic World*, London (1979). Duval, P.-M. *Celtic Art in Ancient Europe*, London (1976). Duval, P.-M. *Les Celtes*, Paris (1977). Filip, J. *Celtic Civilization and its Heritage*, Wellingborough (1977). Hatt, J.-J. *Celts and Gallo-Romans*, London (1970). Jacobsthal, P. *Early Celtic Art*, Oxford (1944). Megaw, J.V.S. *Art of the European Iron Age*, Bath (1970). Powell, T.G.E. *The Celts*, London (1980).

13

PARTHIAN AND SASSANIAN ART

An Indo-Parthian bronze rhyton from the Indus region; height 25cm (10in)
Ashmolean Museum, Oxford (see page 220)

THE Parthians. Towards 238 BC the nomad chief Arsaces and his successors, founders of the Arsacid dynasty of Parthia, at the head of their followers, the tribes of the Parni and Dahae, entered northeastern Iran from the Caspian steppes. By 148 BC under Mithradates I, they had wrested most of the Iranian Plateau from the hands of the Seleucids, the Macedonian successors of Alexander the Great. Arts and technology of Greek derivation, mixed no doubt with recollections of the Achaemenid past, must at this time have been widely diffused in the urban centers. Naturally Seleucid art reflected the well-known forms of Classical Greece and the familiar deities of Classical mythology, represented according to the anthropomorphic conventions of the Greeks. The enormous wealth obtained by the Macedonians from captured Achaemenid treasures, or accumulated from later tribute, will have made possible the creation of noteworthy monuments, of which literary sources give hints, but of which next to nothing survives.

Such antecedents are reflected in the earliest Parthian constructions and artifacts. This first phase is represented, in particular, by finds from Soviet excavations at Nisa in Turkmenistan. The large number of ivory drinking-horns (*rhyta*) recovered from this site reflect Hellenistic influences in their decoration, though the form and origin of such vessels is Iranian, together with certain religious nuances.

In architecture, easily obtainable mudbrick was preferred as a building material, rather than stone. The peristyles of stone columns traditional in Greek, and in modified form in Achaemenid architecture, gave way to compound piers of mudbrick masonry, or to engaged piers attached to the wall face. In the latter arrangement, further visual relief was provided by alternating niches. The decorative details of the facades were rendered no longer in marble but in carved gypsum plaster, a medium capable of most ornate effects. The trabeate roof elements of earlier periods were replaced by the architectural arch, a major innovation, which had probably evolved at Babylon soon after Alexander. The Parthian arch, like the Roman, was semicircular. Its introduction was followed by the barrel vault, which effectively consisted of a series of juxtaposed arches, and took the place of timber roofing.

The development of the barrel vault in turn led to that of the *aivan*, a barrel-vaulted portico open to the front, which usefully provided shelter from the high midday sun, yet relieved the winter chill by admitting the slanting rays of morning, or of midwinter. A favorite ground plan of Parthian times, and constantly influential in succeeding centuries, was the rectangular enclosure with four interior *aivans*, one serving also as the entrance passage. By the close of the 1st century AD the mudbrick dome made its appearance for roofing a square chamber. The underlying square was accommodated to the circular dome by the bridging of its corners with arches to form a squinch. That this innovation was of Parthian date is confirmed by its appearance at Ribat-i Safid in Khurasan, where a fire temple of the subsequently classical "quadruple-arch" design is dated to the 2nd century AD on the evidence of associated structures. The palace of the Sassanian, Ardashir I, at Firuzabad, near Shiraz (c AD 224) used several domes, and though the work of the succeeding dynasty, must have been started under Parthian rule.

In sculpture, Hellenizing subjects progressively gave way (towards AD 50, a trend that has been associated with the

Distribution of important centers

Statue of Sanatruq, lord of Hatra; height 220cm (87in); 1st–2nd century AD. Iraq Museum, Baghdad

Detail of a fresco from the Mithraeum at Dura Europus showing, possibly, Zoroaster. Yale University Art Gallery, New Haven

prolonged revolt from the empire of the Hellenized city of Seleucia-on-the-Tigris) to a new insistence on themes that emphasized Iranian life and customs: equestrian feats, archery and hunting, with the typical Iranian costume of overshirt and baggy trousers, the latter essential for a life on horseback. In scenes of court life the garments were splendidly jeweled and brocaded. Princely figures wore a decorated "tiara" or an exotic crown. Already in Hellenistic art, profile representation had been increasingly replaced by three-quarter renderings made possible by the artists' increasing command of perspective. By the 1st century AD, a mechanical frontality became typical of provincial Parthian schools of sculpture, such as those of Bard-i Nishande in Elymais, or at Dura Europus and Palmyra. This was partly the consequence of technical developments; partly desired in the context of religious sculpture to focus the attention of the worshiper; and eventually a mere

fashion of the period, by which Parthian work and Parthian personalities are instantly recognizable. On Arsacid coinage, where legitimate successors followed the precedent of the founder, Arsaces, and placed their portrait to the left, the facing bust was usually an indication of rebellion.

The supreme medium of Parthian art was originally painting, but of the numerous illuminated manuscripts and frescoes that must have existed relatively few remain. The paintings of Kuh-i Khwaja (in Sistan), and of Miran in eastern Turkestan (the last more specifically Kushan, but showing details in Parthian style) give an indication of its quality. The Old Testament frescoes of the Synagogue at Dura Europus show Jewish subjects, but many figures are in Parthian costume. In the *Mithraeum* at Dura, the hunting fresco shows a typical Parthian scene. There are also many vividly sketched graffiti of Parthians sacrificing at an incense altar, hunting on horseback, or riding in cavalry armor. The Greek philosopher Philostratus in his *Life of Apollonius* describes palace frescoes at Babylon under Vardanes (AD 42). The heresiarch Mani (AD 215–73), the founder of Manichaeism, whose syncretic doctrines reflect the Parthian culture in which he was born, is said to have been greatly skilled at manuscript illumination, a craft pursued with devotion by his medieval followers.

The great Parthian rock sculptures at Bisitun, Sar-i Pul (Hulwan), and at Shimbar, Izeh, and Tang-i Sarvak in Elymais, employed flattish, low relief, with surface textures ren-

The life-size bronze statue of a Parthian chief from Shami, near Bard-i Nishande. Iran Bastan Museum, Teheran

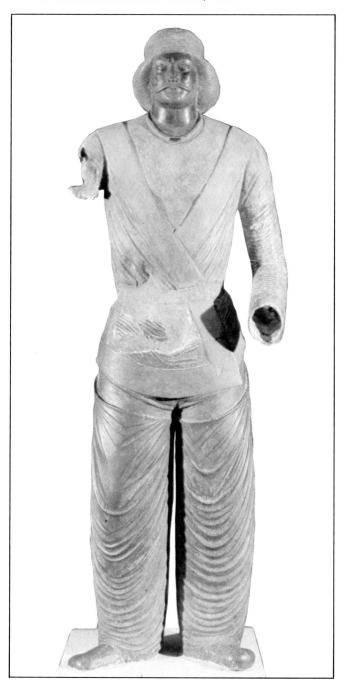

dered in hatching—techniques borrowed from the draftsman and the painter, rather than typical of the sculptor. There were few sculptures in the round, although there is a marble head of a Parthian queen from Susa and a magnificent life-size bronze of a Parthian chief found at Shami. Especially splendid were the 2nd-century AD statues of princes at Hatra.

In the minor arts, marked differences prevailed between the various regional styles, for example between those of Babylonia and the Iranian Plateau. In the former district, pottery with greenish glaze is found in the shape of *amphorae*, and the typical "slipper-sarcophagi". Further east there are reddish, unglazed wares of well-fired clay. Spouted jugs, pilgrim flasks, vessels with zoomorphic handles and even a spouted *rhyton-amphora* were found at Shahr-i Qumis. Other sites of the period are barely investigated: but hemispherical drinking bowls of hard red pottery ("clinky" or cinnamon ware) with parallel forms in metal, have occasionally been reported, and may have evolved from the Hellenistic "Megarian bowls". In the Indo-Parthian region (Afghanistan, Punjab) pedestal cups are typical, usually in yellowish ware with horizontal burnishings. At Taxila and elsewhere, related forms in silver, horizontally fluted, prove the introduction of the metalworker's lathe. In glass, the typical form is again a hemispherical bowl (mold-blown), with wheel-cut facets.

Few textiles of Parthian date have been recovered (but notably at Germi in Persian Gilan, decorated with key, swastika, and chequer patterns). Arsacid coinage, in silver and copper, has somewhat stereotyped themes, with the recurrent reverse type of the Royal Archer. It is, however, of great historical interest, since the large silver issues are often dated not only to the year, but also to the month. Parthian seal-engraving, unlike that of other Iranian dynasties, is sparse and obscure, but a number of clay impressions are known from Nisa and Shahr-i Qumis.

An art style derived from that of Parthia prevailed also in the Arsacid "frontier kingdoms", where feudatory rulers maintained local courts (Elymais, Characene, Persis, Hatra, Adiabene, and Iberia/Georgia, besides Armenia, which, nominally a condominium, was subject to frequent and forceful Roman interference). Also Parthian in culture though politically independent was the kingdom of the Indo-Parthians (AD 25–60), whose Emperor Gondophares is said to have entertained the Christian Apostle Thomas. Here Iranian, Indian, and Classical influences were intermingled. After AD 60 the region was overrun by the Central Asian Kushans, under whose rule the "Greco-Buddhist" art of Gandhara made its appearance (*see* Indian Art).

The Sassanians. Towards AD 224 the dynasty of the Arsacids was overthrown by the Sassanian family, originating from the southern province of Fars (Persis). Though the capital of the new empire, like that of its predecessor, was soon established at Ctesiphon on the Tigris in Babylonia, the new rulers lavished special attention on their home province. The founder, Ardashir I (ruled AD 224–41) built there the circular city of

Ardashir I: part of a relief at Firuzabad; length 18m (59ft)

Gur, later known as Firuzabad. His son, Shapur I (ruled AD 240–72), founded Bishapur, further to the north. The greatest Sassanian city of the province, Istakhr, had long stood close to the ruins of Achaemenid Persepolis. All three cities are the sites of notable rock sculptures, some of the best-known monuments of Sassanian art. Those at Firuzabad immortalize the victory and coronation of Ardashir. The first, a scene of equestrian combat, in particular, employs the flat relief reminiscent of Parthian times.

The reign of Shapur I was celebrated for the overthrow of three separate Roman emperors: Gordian III (AD 238–44) slain on the Euphrates, Philip I ("the Arab") forced to sue for peace soon afterwards, and Valerian (AD 253–9) captured and carried away to Persia. In art, Sassanian kings are easily distinguished by their tall and bulbous individual crowns, which also appear on coinage. Roman emperors are generically recognizable by their gilded wreaths, but the identification of individuals is less certain. Panels showing the overthrow of one, two, or three Emperors by Shapur I may be seen at Naqsh-i Rustam (near Istakhr), at Bishapur, and also at Darabgird, south of Shiraz.

Bahram II (AD 276–93) and his chief priest Kardeir are prominent in sculptures at Naqsh-i Rustam (acclamation, equestrian combats); also at Sar Mashhad where a magnificent composition of a lion-hunt stands, no doubt with allegorical reference to their Roman antagonist Carus (AD 282–3). At Bishapur, Bahram's triumph over the Arabs is represented; at Naqsh-i Bahram, an enthronement scene. On the most probable interpretation, the newly discovered sculpture at

Tang-i Qandil, near Bishapur, depicts the same ruler's betrothal while still a prince, possibly to Shapurdukhtak, granddaughter of Shapur I. A similar subject appears at Barm-i Dilak near Shiraz. An equestrian combat sculpture of Bahram II at Rayy near Tehran is known to have been destroyed during the 19th century.

Later sculptures at Naqsh-i Rustam are an investiture attributed to Narseh (AD 292–302), an equestrian combat of Hormizd II (AD 302–9) with an unknown opponent; and perhaps Shapur II (AD 309–79) overthrowing the Roman Julian the

Bahram II (center) hunting lions: part of an allegorical relief sculpture at Sar Mashhad

Sassanian Silverware

Magnificent silverware was especially typical of the Sassanian period, and was much in demand for the banquets of the court, in particular the great festival of Mithra, the Mihrgan. On some occasions the plate may have subsequently been presented to the guests, especially to foreign envoys or influential tribal chiefs. During the 3rd and 4th centuries AD the prevalent shape was the *calotte*, a shallow segment of a sphere, standing on a foot-ring. The usual method of manufacture for the body of the bowl was by spinning on a lathe, a process often revealed by traces of horizontal striations. On the grandest examples the decorative figures were in high relief, shaped separately by the repoussé method, and attached to the interior of the vessel. Often, there was a separate inner shell which carried the figures. On simpler pieces, ornament was limited to incised decoration. Highlights of the relief were frequently gilded by the use of mercury

◄ A 4th-century silver bowl with high-relief decoration of the goddess Nana sitting on a lion. British Museum, London

Below left On a *c* AD 360 plate: Varahran II Kushanshah hunts boars; diameter 28cm (11in). Hermitage Museum, St Petersburg

▼ On a 5th-century AD Sassanian silver bowl: Peroz hunts gazelles; diameter 22cm (9in). Metropolitan Museum, New York

malgam. Later, during the 5th and 6th centuries AD, more varied shapes are attested. They include drinking-horns (*rhyta*) adorned with human busts or the foreparts of animals, plain elliptical bowls, lobed dishes, jug-like ewers, and flasks.

There are two main groups of decorative subjects. The first consists of representations of the Sassanian kings, either enthroned, or more frequently engaged in their favorite sport of hunting, usually on horseback. The individual personal crowns of the kings can in some cases be recognized from their coinage, as can those of one of the governors of Bactria (northern Afghanistan), princes who bore the title of Kushanshah. Several other unrecognized crowns may be those of unrecorded princes. The characteristic Sassanian dress consisted of long shirt and full trousers, with the streaming ribbons from neck and ankles that were indicative of royalty. Unlike the cavalry of the Middle Ages, the Sassanians rode without the use of stirrups, and their composite bow was drawn with the fingers, the arrow laid on the left side of the bow as in European archery. On the earliest group of pieces (4th century AD) the hunter-prince engages two formidable creatures, lions or wild boar. During the 5th and 6th centuries, the commonest quarry is a larger flock of innocuous herbivores, *mouflons*, or gazelles. The second main group of subjects consists of stylistically modified copies of the inconography of classical silverware. Dionysiac themes are prevalent, with frequent emphasis on the whirling forms of the maenads, female devotees of the god. It is likely that booty from Roman temples came to be dedicated in the Zoroastrian sanctuaries of the Sassanians, and later copied, with such modifications as a Zoroastrian interpretation of the figures might suggest.

The vast prestige attaching to the Sassanian court silverware led to the production of imitations in provincial centers, notably on the Caspian coast; and, with recognizable modifications of style, in most of the adjoining states, particularly in Sogdia beyond the Oxus and among the Kidarite Huns who occupied Afghanistan after *c* AD 380. Despite their religious inhibitions, the Muslim Arabs who conquered Sassanian Iran after AD 651 accumulated huge quantities of silverware, and their triumphant paladins occasionally indulged in banquets and wassail in the Sassanian manner. There are even a few bowls that can be dated on internal evidence to the period of Arab ascendancy, and others showing that the tradition was revived under Muslim Iranian princes, such as Adud al-daula, Prince of Shiraz (AD 949–83), the Samanids of Bukhara, and the Seljuk Turks. Inevitably, the appearance of antiquarian forgeries has been suspected in recent times, but their detection has depended in the main on stylistic judgment. Problems of authenticity have evoked a lively discussion in cases where a well-established provenance was lacking.

A.D.H. BIVAR

Further reading. Carter, M. and Grabar, O. *Sasanian Silver*, Ann Arbor (University of Michigan) (1967). Erdmann, K. "Zur Chronologie der Sassanidischen Jagdschalen", *Zeitschrift der Deutschen Morganländischen Gesellschaft* Vol. XCVII, 2, (1943) pp239–83. Ettinghausen, R. *From Byzantium to Sasanian Iran and the Islamic World*, Leiden (1972). Porada, E. *Ancient Iran*, London (1965).

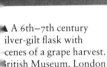

▲ A 6th–7th century silver-gilt flask with scenes of a grape harvest. British Museum, London

Above right A female head and buffalo head decorating a 5th- or 6th-century *rhyton*. Cleveland Museum of Art

► On a Sassanian-style bowl produced under Muslim rule: an Islamic hunter; 8th century AD. Hermitage Museum, St Petersburg

Apostate (AD 355–63). At Taq-i Bustan, near Kirmanshah, in northwest Iran, was a game park, pool, and grottoes decorated with sculptures of Shapur II (309–79) and Shapur III (AD 383–8), Ardashir II (AD 379–83), and Khosrau II (AD 591–628), all in investiture scenes. The last is rendered in high relief, with all the details of his splendid costume; and again below on his charger in full armor, perhaps on the eve of his invasion of the Byzantine Empire. This whole corpus of sculptures provides a notable record of the ideology, costume, and history of this dynasty, whose full significance is only gradually emerging.

Sassanian architecture developed logically from the forms which had been brought into being under the Parthians. Arch, barrel vault, *aivan*, and dome were established from the beginning in the palace of Ardashir at Firuzabad. However, the characteristic profile of all these forms was no longer semicircular, but elongated into an ellipse. Greater height and flexibility were made possible by the modification. Materials used in monumental structures included sun-dried brick, baked brick (appearing on the Plateau only towards AD 540, but earlier in Babylonia), or pebbles and rubble set in gypsum mortar. Squared (ashlar) masonry was used only in the most formal structures. Characteristic Sassanian building plans included the "quadruple-arched" fire temple, which was a square chamber, roofed with a dome on squinches, with open archways in each of the four walls. More elaborate fire temples were provided with a square (or cruciform) sanctuary, domed, and often opening into a large *aivan*, and thence to the courtyard. This plan had a notable influence on the evolution of the Persian mosque. An elaborate complex of Sassanian religious buildings, representing the fire temple of Adhurgushnasp, has been excavated at Takht-i Sulaiman in Azarbaijan. Structures at Firuzabad in Fars are still under investigation.

Caravanserais and forts were generally rectangular enclosures, with circular towers at the corners, and occasionally in

A leaping bear: a stucco panel from Ctesiphon

the middle of each wall. These towers were characteristically of "stilted" plan, so as to increase the projection of the tower from the wall line, and achieve more effective flanking fire. Occasionally, for example at Turang Tepe, the towers were given an elliptical plan, resembling the profile of the arches. Their lower stories were regularly built solid, for defence.

The most celebrated of Sassanian palaces is the Taq-i Kisra, at Ctesiphon, near Baghdad. The ruins of this complex, ascribed by some to Shapur I though traditionally the work of Khosrau I are said to cover 29 acres (11.7 ha). Its main surviving feature is the elliptical *aivan* vault, 84 ft (25.6 m) in span. Exterior walls are varied with engaged columns and niches. Other surfaces were richly ornamented with molded and carved stucco, which (here and at other Sassanian sites) employed geometrical motifs, hunting scenes, royal portraits, and heraldic "devices" in great profusion. Smaller palaces near Veramin, and at Damghan, probably of the early 5th century AD, possessed especially fine stuccos. Other palace complexes existed at Qasr-i Shirin, near the Persian border with Iraq, and at Dastagerd on the Iraq side of that frontier.

Another important vehicle of Sassanian art was luxury silverware, required for the exuberant banquets that were a feature of the period. The impression made by these magnificent vessels was often stressed in later Arabic and Persian literature. The open bowls were usually manufactured by turning on the lathe. Decorations were made separately by the repoussé method, and later slotted and soldered into place. The finest pieces often employed very high relief. Simpler works were merely incised or inlaid, and during the 3rd century the use of niello is found. Finished work was enhanced by gilding, which also served to cover joins resulting from the first method.

Such silverware was so greatly admired by later generations that more or less convincing imitations have been produced in every succeeding period. Products of the Islamic Middle Ages are usually recognized by anachronisms of technical detail and social custom, costume, and equipment. The characteristic crowns are inaccurately rendered on "post-Sassanian" works, or adopt the devolved forms perpetuated by certain Muslim rulers (the Buyids, Samanids etc). There is no reliable rule of thumb to distinguish modern antiquarian forgeries, though laboratory tests have provided some indications.

The most important early class of Sassanian silverware was the circular bowls depicting Sassanian kings (and several princes) hunting. Two groups have been distinguished, on the grounds of composition: in the earlier the king vanquishes two ferocious creatures and in the later the quarry is a whole flock of timid herbivores. There is literary evidence that silver bowls (especially no doubt of these kinds) were used by rulers and princes as diplomatic presents. Their manufacture may have been a monopoly of special court workshops. Less strictly ceremonial are a class of bowls, flasks, and ewers bearing subjects which allude to viticulture or revelry, and reflect the Dionysiac motifs of the classical world. These were no doubt appropriate for convivial occasions. Several other pieces display adaptations of subjects from Greco-Roman mythology, for example the girl carried off by the eagle on the bowl from Tcherdin in the USSR, originally inspired by the classical myth of Zeus and Aegina. Or the bowl in the Metropolitan Museum (New York) depicting two youths with winged horses, a subject variously interpreted as derived either from the Dioscuri, or from Belerophon with Pegasus. A later phase is exemplified by the numerous flasks with dancing or standing female figures, musicians, or the heraldic *senmurv* (griffon), a subject also carved on the robes of Khosrau II at Taq-i Bustan, and considered almost as an official badge of his kingdom. Many of these themes were echoed in various styles under the medieval Muslim rulers of Iran, for whom the prestige of the Sassanian tradition, and the appeal of its courtly splendor, outweighed the Islamic prohibition on figured representation.

Among textiles of the Sassanian period, it is above all the magnificent silk brocades that have survived, or have been perpetuated through the decorative tradition of later schools from Byzantium to Japan. Iran occupied a strategic position between China and the Roman world, and was thus able to capture the supplies of silken yarn, or to control the flow of silk thread, and of fabrics made from it, to the Mediterranean world. By the mid 4th century, important silk-weaving establishments had been founded in Iran, especially in the province of Khuzistan, and their ornate fabrics of highly characteristic designs were winning worldwide celebrity. Most typical was the use of animal and bird forms, within circular medallions, surrounded by borders of white bezants representing pearls. Several examples have been preserved with relics in the cathedral treasuries of Europe; others, now at the Louvre, Paris, or in Lyons, were recovered from a graveyard at Antinoe in Egypt. Typical motifs are the boar's head, Pegasus, the diademed ram, and the *senmurv*—all significant for Sassanian iconography. Hunting scenes are not attested in the surviving work; but imitations in the later derivative styles of medieval Iran suggest that hunting scenes must also have been used in Sassanian textile factories. The weave used in textiles of the Sassanian period is the "compound twill" technique. It is only in the ornate derivatives of Sassanian figured silks manufactured under the later Islamic dynasties in Iran that the more elaborate "lampas" weaves were introduced. The Sassanian figured textiles with their circular "medallions", followed by these later imitations, were imported to Byzantium, and also influenced the development of textile design in Europe.

Two lesser arts which attained distinction under the Sassanians were coinage and seal-engraving. The obverse type of the coins was throughout the bust of the reigning king, distinguished by his individual crown. The details of dress and ornament are rendered with meticulous care. On the reverse, with very few exceptions, the fire altar appears, symbolizing the Zoroastrian religion of the dynasty. Because of the fine style, issues from the first century of the dynasty have the greatest aesthetic appeal. Those of its last century (AD 551–651) on the other hand, offer the greater historical value, since they are inscribed with both date and mint-abbreviation. Silver

A fragment of silk decorated with a senmurv, a fabulous winged creature; height of roundel 36cm (14in); 6th or 7th century.
Musée des Arts Décoratifs, Paris

A silver drachm of Shapur I. British Museum, London

pieces, of thin, spread fabric, constitute the bulk of the coinage. Gold was struck only for rare presentation pieces, probably used at coronations. Sporadic issues are known in billon, bronze, and even lead. The east of the empire, in central Asia and Afghanistan, was ruled until AD 360 by viceroys of the Sassanian family, who issued separate coinage. Their distinctive crowns differ in construction from those of the suzerain rulers. In the east gold coinage circulated widely, as it had under the previous dynasty in that region, that of the Kushans. It was only in the reign of Khosrau I Anushirvan (AD 531–79) that really large volumes of silver coinage came into circulation in Iran, and rural economy passed on to a cash basis. For this reason, coins of the later reigns are relatively common.

Seal-engraving attained a high standard under the Sassanians, and output was copious—evidence no doubt that seals were required everywhere for legal and official transactions. Engraved gems are almost indestructible, and have therefore preserved a larger and more representative range of motifs than any other medium. The portrait bust is the most common subject, with headgear appropriate to the owner's rank— magus, scribe, official, or prince. The domed tiara was typical of the nobles, sometimes distinguished by a linear "device". Such marks originated as cattle brands, but were used to designate high office and membership of the chief aristocratic families. Human or divine figures are often found, singly or in groups. Gems showing a couple holding a ring between them are usually thought to come from wedding rings.

In the huge variety of other subjects, animal forms are numerous. Lions, camels, bulls, and stags are typical, but the wolf suckling twins is evidently reminiscent of the "Romulus and Remus" theme popular in Roman art, here probably reinterpreted as a reference to Zoroastrianism. Particularly attractive is the wide range of fabulous creatures—Pegasus, sphinx, and griffon. Birds, of good omen in Zoroastrianism, are common, and there are also flowers and plants, and religious scenes showing fire altars and priests. Sometimes a seal was engraved with a "device" alone, and most of the finer specimens bear the name and title of the owner, carefully engraved in Pahlavi script. There is evidence that the Sassanian lapidaries were able to engrave on hard stones such as emerald and sapphire; even, it is alleged, on diamond. The majority of surviving pieces are on colored quartzes such as cornelian and onyx. After AD 500 jasper, rock crystal, and garnet become popular. Many of the stones were shaped as ring-bezels, some of remarkable size. Separate stones had the form of ellipsoids, and later, domes. In some cases an entire ring is carved out of a large block of quartz. More bizarre in style are the medical and magical amulets, recognizable by their subjects and the fact that the inscriptions are not reversed to read correctly from an impression.

A.D.H. BIVAR

Bibliography. Bivar, A.D.H. *Catalogue of W. Asiatic Seals in the British Museum, Stamp Seals II, the Sassanian Dynasty*, London (1969). Colledge, M.A.R. *Parthian Art*, London (1977). Ghirshman, R. *Iran: Parthians and Sassanians*, London (1967). Godard, A. *The Art of Iran*, London (1962). Harper, P.O. *The Royal Hunter: Art of the Sasanian Empire*, New York (1978). Herrmann, G. *The Iranian Revival*, London (1977). Herzfeld, E. *Archaeological History of Iran*, London (1934). Pope, A.U. *A Survey of Persian Art* vol. 1, Oxford (1938). Sellwood, D. *An Introduction to the Coinage of Parthia*, London (1971).

14

STEPPE ART

A bronze stag pole-top from the Ordos Desert; Han period
206 BC–AD 221. British Museum, London (see page 235)

THE term Steppe Art has come to be used for a certain group of interrelated styles illustrated by finds made mainly from the 18th century onwards in the excavation of tombs on the Eurasian steppe or near it. Some of the finds are of metal, bone, or wood, though not of stone. They served as ornaments, badges, or symbols on the clothing and equipment of mounted nomad warriors on the Eurasian steppes from Hungary to Manchuria. But sometimes figures in the same style occur on larger surfaces, such as textile fabrics, or on pieces of worked-and-dyed leather. These must have decorated the tents of nomads during their lifetimes, but they have been preserved for centuries afterwards by the accidental effects of the climates to which they were exposed in certain regions. Not all the materials mentioned were represented in any one place, but it is reasonable to assume that in most of the best-equipped burials all of them existed together before natural decay destroyed some or plunderers removed others.

The styles are thought to have prevailed during a period which began shortly after 700 BC and lasted into the early centuries of the Christian era, for different lengths of time in different places. In spite of their variety, they have a common feeling which is not that of civilized art, and a common origin among nomad peoples living beyond the steppes; but in their later phases they were subject to various outside influences.

The most characteristic manifestation of Steppe art is the well-known Animal style, as M. Rostovtzev first called it. Originally established c500 BC, the style represents animals, birds of prey, and certain monsters—particularly griffins—in a distinctive way. Remoter foreign influences also appear in the introduction of animals unknown on the steppes, such as lions and large serpents. But the tame animals on which the nomads lived are absent from the Animal style, except that it is not always clear whether horses found fairly frequently are tame or wild. There must have been a pervasive reason behind this preference for wild animals. The same nomads from time to time represented the human forms of warriors and hunters, and even of goddesses, but these are rare. Vegetation is found as a background in some pieces, mostly in ones known from the eastern steppes which seem to represent scenes from well-known legends. These pieces may be regarded as marginal to nomad art.

Though other peoples have created styles representing animals, these nomad styles are distinctive. The Animal style appearing in them was created by the white nomads—Indo-Europeans of the Iranian branch, who inhabited the western half of the steppes, extending from the Danube basin and south Russia in the west to Zungaria and the Pamir in the east. Tribal migrations also carried forms of it further eastward to regions within the range of Chinese influence. In its earliest and undeveloped form it is represented by small carvings in bone of the 8th and 7th centuries BC as at Zabotin in south Russia; the material limited both size and shape, and made necessary a certain degree of contortion. But the tradition that arose continued in such things as the metal plaques of the developed style.

The main development evidently resulted from contacts, peaceful or warlike, in the 7th century BC with the civilized peoples of the Near East, but it still resulted in a barbarian art. The effects of these contacts were spread far and wide, as if over an inland sea. The strongest influence in development beyond the earliest stage appears to have come from Iran, which, as R. Ghirshman argues, had such strong links with the steppes that these should be named "Outer Iran", particularly as before the Turkish expansion from Mongolia kindred languages were spoken in both regions. Iranian culture, apart from its own character, received much influence from Assyria

The Eurasian steppes

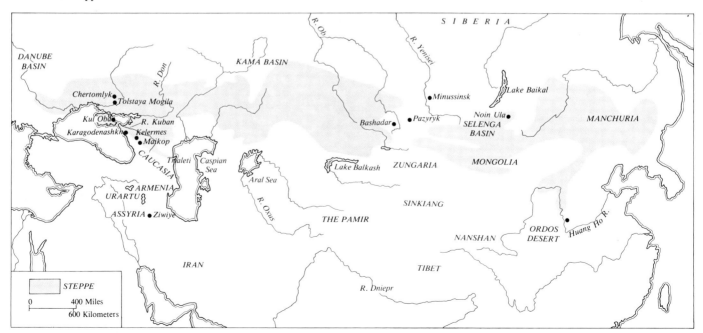

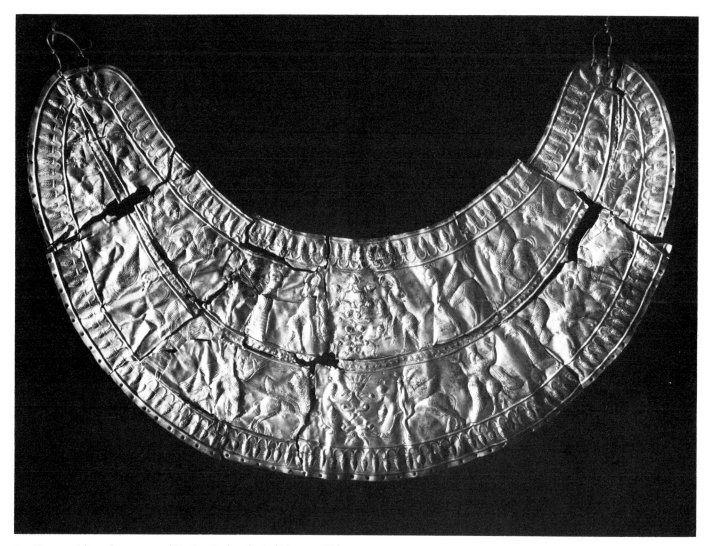

A gold pectoral from the treasure of Ziwiye. Archaeological Museum, Teheran

and from the ancient kingdom of Urartu in Armenia. The nomads were affected by both these older cultures whether by direct contact or by mediation through Iran. Direct contact often took the form of raiding and the carrying off of civilized craftsmen to work for nomad masters.

The spread of styles and techniques would still have been furthered by the perpetual movements of peoples on the steppes, particularly in times of disturbance. These movements could cross and intermingle and sometimes be reversed, making new patterns as currents in an estuary do at change of tide.

It is time to describe the various styles, region by region. The best known, and perhaps the oldest in its full development, is the Scythian style of the Pontic Steppe in south Russia. A Near Eastern prelude to this style is apparent in the treasure of Ziwiye in Kurdistan, a hoard of goldwork and other objects perhaps collected by a Scythian chief during the Scythian invasion (Iran Bastan Museum, Teheran). Two objects from this may be picked out. One is a lunate sheet of gold probably once worn as a pectoral ornament by the chief. It shows in two registers symmetrical processions of Phoenician and Assyrian monsters converging on a Tree of Life, in each case a small feline beast of prey of purely Scythian style bringing up the rear. The other is a piece of beaten gold plate bearing a repetitive design, in the manner of modern wall-

paper, in which stags and ibexes are represented entirely in the Scythian manner, each animal enclosed in a network of branches. The vegetation in both pieces is in Urartian style.

Scythian metalwork of just this kind, with features added from Urartu, was found in the great Scythian kurgans of the Kuban and the Dniepr. The stag with thrown-back antlers and drawn-up legs, prominent here, was a widespread emblem of Scythian origin, used on plaques decorating shields, bowcases, ax handles, and pole-tops used as standards. A common feature, as in Siberia, is the beveled junction of two slanting surfaces, used to represent the rounded body or haunches of an animal. It is likely that this originated in woodcarving.

One southern animal subject was the lion, not a native of south Russia or Caucasia. It is a sign of Near Eastern influence. This influence appears again in such a creature as the panther figured on a gold plaque from Kelermes in the Kuban Basin (Hermitage Museum, Leningrad). It has hollows in its ears and paws which must once have been filled with cloisonné inlay, a feature of polychrome style as continued later in a Sarmatian work of an Asiatic tradition. From the illustrations it will be seen how vivid and lifelike the Animal style can be, careless though it often was of proportion and natural posture.

Among human figures, where they appear, the commonest are those of the Great Goddess, as found at Karagodenashkh

Goldwork from the Kuban: a panther-shaped blazon of a shield.
Hermitage Museum, St Petersburg

in the Kuban, attended by her priests, and those of warriors carrying the severed heads of enemies.

Some of the goldwork from the Kuban and the Dniepr shows Greek influence from the Pontic colonies. Some later examples, such as the plaque and ornaments from Kul Oba in the Crimea, and a silver gilt vase from the rich burial of Chertomlyk on the lower Dniepr, are actually Greek work (both in the Hermitage Museum, St Petersburg). Most striking of the

Greek work carried out for Scythian masters is a gold pectoral ornament from Tolstaya Mogila in the Ukraine (Hermitage Museum, St Petersburg). Its outer rim shows a lion and a griffin attacking horses, and a lion attacking a boar, while its inner rim shows among other things a cow suckling a calf, two Scythian bondmen milking a ewe, and two other Scythians mending a shirt. All these representations are entirely Greek in style. Greek influence indeed contributed sometimes so powerfully to the native art as to destroy its original Scythian quality either in style or even in theme.

At the eastern end of Iran nomad presence during the same period may be assumed but actual evidence only emerges a little later, after the Median Empire had fallen to the kindred Persians. It is contained in the Oxus treasure, a large collection of goldwork of various dates, the earliest belonging to the height of the Achaemenid Empire or even a little earlier (British Museum, London). While many of the objects are in Persian style, some are so close to nomad styles that they may

Two griffins attack a horse on a gold pectoral from Tolstaya Mogila. Hermitage Museum, St Petersburg

be taken to be the work of the Sakas of central Asia. Other specimens of Saka styles so far discovered are comparatively few and not striking. Large tombs discovered in this part of central Asia have proved to be empty. Otherwise we should have better examples of the styles of the Massagetae, the Saka people against whom Cyrus the Great fell fighting after he had conquered the rest of his empire.

Another, remoter link with Achaemenid Persia has been found north of the Saka territory in the frozen tombs of Pazyryk in the High Altai (5th century BC), which are also crucial for the understanding of nomad art in eastern Asia. A Persian tapestry from the fifth tomb, the oldest tapestry known, shows embroidered figures of women apparently performing a sacrifice. From their attire these should be Persian royal ladies. The same tomb contained the oldest known Persian carpet bordered with a procession of stags, and outside this another of walking grooms and mounted horsemen in Achaemenid style.

These imported textiles are of great interest as signs of contact with the Persian Empire, but they are not nomad art any more than the Greek and oriental metalwork earlier described. More remarkable and characteristic of the steppes is a felt hanging from the fifth tomb, decorated with appliqué felt in bright colors, showing a horseman in tight trousers and a short cloak riding up to a seated figure who holds in one hand something that may be a Tree of Life (Hermitage Museum, St Petersburg). The seated figure appears to be female but completely bald under a heavy fur cap, while her chair is of Assyrian pattern. The figure is likely to be a local form of the Great Goddess. A strange monster in colored appliqué felt which appears on another hanging from this tomb is a human-headed sphinx with an animal body, wings, and apparently horns. The Near Eastern influence still seems to be present, but these hangings are unique.

The Animal style in appliqué felt and also in wood carving has a close resemblance to the Scythian, but the suggestion of formal monumentality which hangs over the Scythian figures is gone. Illustrations of these finds from the Altai show wilder and more bounding animals for the most part, sometimes with twisted bodies possible in a cat or weasel, but not in horses as represented. The style was making new departures. A wavy and rippling character is particularly noticeable in a relief on the side of a coffin at Bashadar in the central Altai (6th century BC)—the animal figures are tigers carrying prey. This quality appears even more in some Sarmatian work from the steppe region north of the Black Sea (Hermitage Museum, St Petersburg).

In the fifth tomb of Pazyryk further links with civilization are shown in a canopy decorated with figures of swans very much in Chinese style. The canopy once belonged to a carriage of Chinese form also found there. At this date the Persians of the Achaemenid period were not acquainted with the Chinese, but these nomads seem to have been in contact with both. Indeed, from a far earlier period, the Karasuk culture of Minussinsk (12th century BC) which had connections with

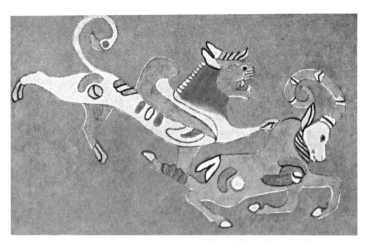

A winged lion attacks an ibex: an appliqué felt saddle-cloth decoration from Pazyryk. Hermitage Museum, St Petersburg

A tiger carved on a cedarwood coffin from Bashadar. Hermitage Museum, St Petersburg.

Shang China, is regarded by some scholars as having contributed to the Animal style, after the advent of nomadism (8th–7th centuries BC).

Much longer known than the art of the Altai, but equally striking, are the gold plaques collected from tombs in southern Siberia in the 17th century by Russian prospectors and settlers on the initiative of Peter the Great and carefully preserved by his order. The actual sites from which these pieces came are not known though they came from the region of Kazakhstan, so that nothing can be said about the other contents of the tombs. Nor were the rich sources of gold in Siberia used in ancient times by civilized peoples ever traced. The subjects of Peter were interested only in amassing the gold, which they had intended to melt down. It was Peter himself who had sufficient appreciation of the art of these Scythian pieces to forbid the melting.

Like the art of the Altai, that of these south Siberian plaques was more full of life than the art of the Pontic Steppes and more varied in its choice of subject. The figures seem to mirror the outward life of the nomads and beyond that their imaginations and beliefs. Pieces with imaginative content show ferocious combats of wild beasts and monsters. There are also other kinds of plaque which have been called anecdotal because they seem to represent particular episodes in legend and story. In technique there is much use of hollows, as in some of the Scythian pieces. These contained brightly colored stones, and show affinities with pieces from the Oxus treasure which were probably made by the Sakas (British Museum, London). There are also affinities with Chinese art. Another eastern feature is the openwork form in which many of them are cast.

A good example of animal combat in this west Siberian style, dated to the 4th century BC, shows a lion-griffin, with small wings indicated on its shoulders, biting through the neck of a collapsing horse (Hermitage Museum, St Petersburg). Like other animal victims of beasts or monsters, as sometimes also in the Altai, the horse is so twisted that its hind legs reach upwards and its forelegs and muzzle downwards. This twist is hardly found in Scythian work. Another plaque shows a more or less equal battle between a tiger and a griffin, in which both creatures seem likely to be mauled to death. Some of these animal figures reappear further east in the art of the Ordos Desert (3rd century BC), but in bronze, even if cast in copies of the same molds that had been used for the gold. The relation of these pieces and those of the Ordos shows the wide diffusion of this Steppe culture. The style is so intensely dramatic, that some powerful myth may be supposed to underlie it.

The anecdotal pieces again seem to be a new departure, representing episodes in the life of some nomad hero. Figures of ordinary mortals do appear in Scythian art, carrying the heads of enemies, but these human figures are different and far more interesting. One for instance represents a hunter on the forested edge of the Siberian steppe with drawn bow pursuing a powerful boar from which another rider has taken refuge by climbing a tree, while his horse seems to be trying to climb after him. A more mysterious piece likewise shows a forested scene, where a warrior lies with his head on the lap of a woman squatting on the ground and wearing a headdress like a Turkish *tarbush*, while a groom squats near them holding the reins of two horses. Such narrative scenes seem to be exclusive to the Sarmatian style in Siberia; they have not yet been found among Sarmatian remains further west in south Russia or the Danube Valley. The figures of two wrestlers that appear in this art are known also in Scythian art. This seems to show that the Turkish and Mongol love of wrestling had a long ancestry among nomads. One apparently Far Eastern theme was the curled animal with mouth to tail, found from the Pontic Steppe to the Ordos Desert.

The Ordos Desert, in fact, is the next important region to consider. Though it lies on the southern side of the great bend of the Huang Ho and has usually been reckoned part of China, its people usually belonged with the nomads to the east and north of them beyond the Great Wall. Its style of nomad art was mostly an eastern continuation of the Sarmatian, but showed in many places a strong influence from China. The Chinese influence blended much more easily with the recipient nomad art here than did the Greek with Scythian art at the other end of the steppe. Indeed, further inside China pieces have been discovered in which Chinese and nomad characters are inseparably blended like the colors on shot silk. This is the so-called Huai style of Chinese art, just south of the basin of the Huang Ho. This shading of Chinese art into nomad might be better compared to the shading of Persian into Saka art which is seen in the Oxus treasure.

The Ordos bronzes are often difficult both to date and classify for Chinese and western scholars alike, since, as with the Sarmatian goldwork, their places of origin are not exactly known. But they cover the period when the Indo-European tide moving eastward across the northern steppes was halted and reversed by the Altaic current which is much better known in history. The critical moment in this process was c160 BC, when Giyu, ruler of the Hsiung Nu confederacy inflicted a crushing defeat on the rival confederacy of the Yueh Chih under its Iranian rulers, and drove them westward from their pastures by the Nan Shan into Zungaria and Sinkiang.

A forest scene with men and horses, in gold. Hermitage Museum, St Petersburg

A gold curled panther from western Siberia; 6th century BC. Hermitage Museum, St Petersburg

This appears to have happened during the period of the Ordos bronzes, which perpetuated an originally Iranian tradition under new masters, the Hsiung Nu. Like the Yueh Chih, the Hsiung Nu were a variegated confederacy, and it has been remarked that many of their tribes were white. It was perhaps these white tribes, probably speaking a Turkic language, who carried on the western tradition of nomad style in altered circumstances, and under some influence from the Chinese.

The pieces from the Ordos are plaques, belt-ornaments, belt-clasps, pole-tops, knives, daggers, and axes with some ornamentation, and occasionally human figures, even mounted ones. The Scytho-Sarmatian ancestry of the animal figures is clear to see both in style and in some cases in the suggestion of ruthless ferocity. But some figures, animal and human, are playful or grotesque in a manner not known elsewhere on the steppes; this is perhaps part of the Chinese influence. Within their sequence an earlier group is attributed to a time before the rise of the Han power in China in the 3rd century BC, and a later one to the period of continual warfare between the Han and the Hsiung Nu.

In the intervals of warfare the Hsiung Nu not only plundered northern China in an irregular fashion, but also traded with the Chinese. Traces of both kinds of contact are clearly seen among the contents of the tombs of Noin Ula in the Selenga basin south of Lake Baikal and east of the Altai, where Chinese goods, particularly textiles, are found along with specimens of nomad art (Hermitage Museum, St Petersburg). There are also suggestions of another style of nomad art distinct from the Sarmatian. The name Noin Ula in Mongol means "Lords' Hill" and was doubtless given because the Mongols saw that many chiefs of peoples who had held power earlier than themselves were buried in this valley. Modern scholars are content to link the excavated tombs with the Hsiung Nu at the time of their greatest power and widest contacts. The chiefs were buried in strong coffins placed within timber chambers, very much in the Scythian manner. Two hundred and twelve were located in P.K. Kozlov's expedition, but less than 20 have been excavated. If the remainder are eventually excavated, there will be great gains for the history of the Hsiung Nu and later nomads of this region.

As the contents of the Pazyryk graves were preserved in ice, so the finds of Noin Ula were kept intact by water which had soaked through the ground and prevented alternation of drying and wetting. This was particularly advantageous because so many of them were rugs and carpets and other textiles, often Chinese, such as women's cloaks and bonnets. There were also some metal pieces similar to those from the Ordos. On one carpet a winged monster like a wolverine is shown attacking a bellowing elk; on another, less well executed, a yak faces a monster hard to identify (Hermitage Museum, St Petersburg). The yak sometimes appears in Sarmatian metalwork further west, but was evidently an important animal for the makers of this art, for a silver plaque shows a yak with characteristic horns, and hair on its belly (Hermitage

A silver plate from Noin Ula decorated with a yak. Hermitage Museum, St Petersburg

Museum, St Petersburg). The head is shown frontally, not in profile as in Sarmatian pieces, and the feet of the animal show little relation to the rocks on which it stands against a background of trees. This piece seems to be of native inspiration, not in the Sarmatian manner.

More remarkable so far eastward is a tapestry showing two moustached faces of central Asian Turkic type, perhaps south Russians. Purely Chinese on the other hand is a tapestry representing turtles swimming among water plants (both in the Hermitage Museum, St Petersburg). The stages in the decay of the Animal style in Mongolia may be further documented when more of the tombs of Noin Ula have been opened.

Our survey has carried us right across the northern steppes, where mounted nomads, at first all of them Indo-Europeans, practised the Animal style and others connected with it even in some parts east of Zungaria after 700 BC. Certain earlier traditions of art appearing, for instance, in the gold and silver figures of bulls from Maikop in the northern Caucasus and in the embossed vessels of Trialeti in Transcaucasia, were indeed continued in some of the regions included, but have been passed over because of their early date before the rise of mounted nomadism. But it is worth noting that the art of Maikop was deeply indebted to the arts of early Iran and Mesopotamia, and that of Trialeti to some traditions in Anatolia, before in each case links with the southern civilizations were broken off. Scythian art shows a revival of these southern links in new circumstances.

During the Scythian period the arts of Ananyino in the Kama basin and of Tagar in the Minussinsk basin of Siberia were strongly influenced by the animal art and weapons of the nomads but were not practised by nomads.

In south Russia the Scythians were succeeded in the 3rd century BC by the Sarmatians, whose art as known from Siberia has been described. In present usage the name of Sarmatian is used for Iranian nomads scattered over an immense area east of south Russia as far as the borders of China. In ancient usage the nomads of south Russia and the Danube Valley were sometimes called Sarmatians, but the name has no wider connotations. The Sarmatian nomads of eastern Europe fell under the rule of the Huns, who appear not to have used any form of the Animal style in the west, even if their ancestors had done so in eastern Asia. Under the next domination of the Danube Valley, that of the Avars, there appears to have been a certain revival of the Animal style during the late Avar period from AD 670 onwards, when the Avars were less influenced by Byzantine art than they had been in the first generations after their arrival. Their belt-plaques and belt-clasps, and the pieces of metal hanging from their belts to indicate rank, show a crude form of the Animal style, particularly in the figures of griffins, which it is natural to attribute to a revival of Sarmatian tradition, whether of local origin or carried westward from Asia. This tradition faded out early in the Middle Ages.

The Turks of Mongolia and central Asia did not, so far as is known, use art of the Scythian and Sarmatian traditions during their great age of expansion when they ruled most of the remaining Indo-European nomads. Elsewhere in Asia the Animal style survived for a time in northern Tibet, but is not otherwise known. In Europe the art of the Germanic tribes for some centuries contained traces of the Animal style, as might be expected from the several centuries of close contact between Germans and Sarmatians.

It remains to offer a few remarks on the significance of the Animal style. This element in nomad art may be regarded as aristocratic, for it has only been found in the graves of chieftains and important warriors. It may be compared to the coats of arms adopted much later in medieval Europe, which were likewise the marks of a warrior caste. As in the Middle Ages armorial bearings were of more than local significance, so in nomad society plaques, badges, and pole-tops in the Animal style are likely to have been symbols of warrior bands made up from the chieftain's families of various tribes who might join in common enterprises of migration or war. The ferocity that appears so often in the animal figures could symbolize the spirit of these bands. The content of the scenes of animal combat, ultimately of Assyrian origin but which had traveled to the east, has been variously interpreted. That they symbolize struggles between light and darkness or good and evil seems unlikely, for which animal is which of these? It is more probable that the animals are tribal totems in conflict: animals akin to the tribe and never killed or eaten by its members except in special circumstances. But totemism seems a shade more primitive than this nomad art. To take another age, we do not regard the fighting lion and unicorn or other heraldic animals of the Middle Ages as totems. However, there is an analogy between these animal figures and the wolf, and the doe inherited from a remoter past and regarded as ancestors in Turkish and Mongol belief. Other writers regard the animals as protective spirits taking animal form, such as appear in shamanistic belief as guides to the shamans or others on visits to the world of spirits, or as a development of hunting magic, such as inspired the paleolithic cave-painters. It cannot be said that we fully understand the significance of nomad art.

The beauty of some of these figures is surely incidental to their main purpose, if that was magic or shamanistic cult. Their quality, especially when grouped in scenes, is entirely barbaric, in spite of influences from the southern civilizations. This was not civilized art, but represented a special world and a special cast of mind, inimical to civilization, as Herodotus saw. An analogy can be seen in the different but equally distinctive art of the Celtic peoples of the same centuries (*see* Celtic Art), most strikingly illustrated in such work as the decoration of the celebrated caldron from the bog of Gundestrup in Denmark dated *c*100 BC (National Museum, Copenhagen) with its human and animal figures of unapproachable wildness.

†E.D. PHILLIPS

Bibliography. *Frozen Tombs: the Culture and Art of Ancient Tribes of Siberia*, (British Museum) London (1978). Jettmar, K. *The Art of the Steppes*, New York (1969). Minns, E.H. "The Art of the Northern Nomads", *Proceedings of the British Academy*, London (1942). Minns, E.H. *Scythians and Greeks in South Russia*, Cambridge (1913). *Or des Scythes: Trésors des Musées Soviétiques*, Paris (1975). Rice, T.T. *The Scythians*, London (1957). Rudenko, S.I. (trans. Thompson, M.W.) *Frozen Tombs in Siberia: the Pazyryk Burials of Iron Age Horsemen*, London (1970).

15

INDIAN ART

Radha and Krishna in a Grove, a Kangra school painting; 27×18cm (11×7in); c1820–5
Victoria and Albert Museum, London (see page 272)

INDIAN Art can be understood in a restricted or a wider sense: it can refer to the art produced in the South Asian subcontinent—comprising the present Republics of India, Pakistan, and Bangladesh—or it can also be taken to include the spheres of Indian cultural influence—Kashmir, Nepal, Tibet, and Sri Lanka. The development of art in the South Asian subcontinent may be conveniently divided into three periods: the first—the Buddhist, Jain, and Hindu art of the ancient period—came to an end in the north with the Muslim conquest of India in 1210, although it continued in the south until the 20th century. The second, the Indo-Islamic period, lasted until 1757 when British power was established in India. From that time until now is the third period of the westernization of India.

The civilization of the Indus Valley (*c*2500–1500 BC). The earliest evidence of Indian art and architecture is found in the two ancient cities of Mahenjo-daro and Harappa (*c*2500–1500 BC) in the Indus Valley in the northwest. Apart from the material remains very little is known about the inhabitants, because their script remains undeciphered even today. Their remarkable achievements were the two cities, based on precise grid plans and served by an advanced drainage system, unrivaled in the ancient world until the Romans' 2,000 years later.

In India, cities based on grid plans and oriented strictly in the four cardinal directions have a continuous tradition, at-

Important centers mentioned in the text

tested by architectural manuals as well as by the Hindu city of Jaipur. Unlike Egyptians and Sumerians, with whom they traded, Indus people had no taste for monumental sculpture: they preferred small-scale sculptures, human and animal. The famous torso (National Museum of India, New Delhi), whose antecedents are unknown, shows not only a mastery of the human form but foreshadows later sculpture in the loving treatment of soft, warm flesh. Entirely different in style is the aborigine girl (National Museum of India, New Delhi) treated with verve and spirit, whose anklets and bangles remind us of rich personal ornaments depicted by later Indian sculptors. No less impressive are the animal reliefs on seals, especially the naturalistic bull with its exquisitely carved dewlaps (National Museum of India, New Delhi)—yet again a reminder of the achievements of the later period.

When the two flourishing cities fell before the advancing Aryans from the north, art disappeared for over a millennium (1550–300 BC). No art from the Vedic period (1500–1000 BC) has been discovered; possible exceptions are literary references to sacrificial altars which may be regarded as early exercises in the art of design and building. We may ask why Vedic mythology, whose gods have similarities with Greek gods, did not encourage a similar development of narrative art. It was much later that *Puranic* gods provided inspiration for narrative art. One reason offered is that Vedic elemental gods like Fire or Wind did not lend themselves easily to visual representation. An alternative explanation may be that the Vedic sacrificer's contractual relation with divinity did not require an elaborate pantheon. Nor did worshipers concern themselves with images except for their limited use in Vedic ritual. Admittedly the pastoral Aryans were socially less complex than the urban Indus people, but their literature shows a deep love of nature eloquently expressed in lyric hymns of great beauty and feeling.

Buddhist art from *c*3rd century BC to *c*12th century AD. Indian society had evolved from tribal societies into republics and kingdoms with flourishing cities as their capitals by about the 5th century BC—a period famous for intense intellectual activity, above all debates on metaphysical questions. The Buddha (*c*563–483 BC) founded the first great world religion, soon to spread all over Asia. His message was attractively simple and directed to the average householder; it demanded neither costly Vedic sacrifices nor painful austerities but urged him to lead a moderate, virtuous life. The message was powerful enough to draw many people; it also provided the first major impulse for art in the historic period. Grateful for showing them the moderate eightfold path, wealthy merchants of ancient cities like Vidisha or Kashi flocked to him; it was they who searched for appropriate monuments to venerate his sacred memory.

As in many other religions, existing popular objects of worship were taken over by the Buddhists and invested with sacred meaning. *Yakshas* and *Yakshis*, popular semidivine beings, who still figure in folklore, were made to serve the religion of the Buddha. Age-old worship of the tree enclosed by a fence now came to be a reminder of the great Teacher's attainment of enlightenment under the Bodhi tree. Thus the *stupa*, originally a tumulus placed over burial ashes of a monarch or other important person, emerged as the first Buddhist sacred architecture. Relics of the Buddha were generally placed in *stupas*. We know that a battle between different tribes took place over Buddha's mortal remains. The great Emperor Ashoka is said to have built many *stupas*; the ones that remain intact or even in fragments from the early period are Bharhut, Sanchi, Bodh Gaya, Amaravati, Jaggayapeta, Manikyala, and Butkara (Swat).

The most impressive as well as the best preserved of the early *stupas* is the great *stupa* at Sanchi, which allows us to study its form in some detail. The fact that Sanchi was an important religious center for both Buddhists and Hindus is borne out by archaeological evidence covering a millennium. Its special importance must be explained partly by its close proximity to Vidisha, a major ancient city. It also lay at the meeting point of arterial trade routes. The great *stupa* was not conceived as a single unified piece of architecture but grew in stages over centuries, attaining its final form in the 1st century BC. The original modest hemispherical solid mound of earth covered by bricks, dating from Ashoka's reign, was enlarged to twice its size and enclosed in dressed ashlar masonry.

As it stands today it consists of several parts. The main hemispherical part, called the *anda* (egg) and embodying the universal symbolism of the cosmic egg, rests on a very high base (*medhi*). The swastika-shaped ground plan suggests its origin in a solar cult, similar to common stone cist-graves in India, as in Brahmagiri. Buddhists, who compared the Buddha with the sun, reinterpreted the original circular plan as the Buddhist "wheel of doctrine", but the worshiper was still required to conform to the solar cult and to go around the shrine in a clockwise direction. The whole *stupa* was surrounded by a stone railing of massive proportions and marked by four elaborate and beautiful gateways. In keeping with solar symbolism there are precisely 120 uprights. On top of the hemispherical dome was the sacred relic, once again guarded by a stone fence. The shaft that pierces the dome in the center right down to the ground is crowned with three stone umbrellas celebrating the Buddha as the universal emperor of the spiritual world. In contrast to the deliberate simplicity of the main dome, the four gateways are richly adorned with narrative sculpture.

When the *stupa* was one of the great centers of Buddhist religion it left an impression far removed from the one created by its present ruined state. It was painted a brilliant white and decorated with gay festoons and banners on festival days. In Amaravati, on the Kistna in south India, we can gather from the remaining fragments and from the replica left to us that the idea of a white *stupa* was brilliantly realized through the use of limestone to cover the drum of the *stupa*.

The second type of Buddhist architecture was the rock-cut *chaitya*, which, unlike the *stupa*, could accommodate people inside and thus met the need for a meeting place for the congregation. Since it is the earliest surviving form of building or shelter, properly speaking, it gives us an idea about ancient Indian architectural practice. From the Greek ambassador Megasthenes' account we know that Ashoka's grandfather Chandragupta Maurya had built a splendid three-storied, pillared hall of wood and stone, whose foundations have recently been discovered. From this evidence we can certainly guess that wooden architecture was advanced in this period. But we still do not know how the buildings were constructed.

The *chaitya* form arose in order to house *stupas*. When Buddhist *stupas*, most of which were small and quite unlike Sanchi in scale, began to be covered with roofs, so that the faithful could circumambulate them in all weathers, the choice of the material—stone—was as simple as it was ingenious. Unlike wood or even brick, stone was durable and abundant. This solution may have taken some time to reach, for early *chaityas* were close copies of wooden buildings. But in matters of religion, convenience can never be the only criterion, and we are in danger of oversimplifying faith if we overlook symbolic associations of carving the temple of god out of the very heart of the living rock.

The *chaitya* was generally part of a whole complex of buildings forming a Buddhist monastery. The monks and nuns, who needed shelter in the rainy season when they were in retreat, lived in *viharas* or pillared halls with living cells all around them. It was they as well as the laity who paid their respects to the *stupa*, the most important symbol of the faith. The rock-hewn *chaitya* or a simple covered hall with a *stupa* at one end thus arose to cater for their needs. The earliest ones are in the Barabar caves in Bihar, but the rock-cut *stupa* form developed here spread to other parts of India. They are however mostly concentrated in the Western-Ghat mountains near Bombay, notably in Bhaja, Kondivte, Kondane, Nasik, Bedsa, Pitalkhora, Aurangabad, Ajanta, Kanheri, and Karle.

The Lomash Rishi is an early *chaitya* and displays a brilliant finish on the stone, a characteristic feature of the Maurya period *c* 2nd century BC. Although it is not a Buddhist cave, we can clearly see the basic *chaitya* plan set out here. The long hall is separated from the circular room, which contains the *stupa*, by a wall with a door in the middle. The roof of the circular room is hemispherical to accommodate the *stupa*, while the ceiling of the hall is in the form of a barrel vault. The shape of the ceiling is echoed outside in the horseshoe-shaped facade of Lomash Rishi, a feature that was to become universal in *chaityas*. The striking feature of Lomash Rishi is that although it is a stone building it reproduces rafters, laminated planks, tie rods, and other elements from wooden buildings—not only on the exterior but in the interior as well. As the *chaitya* form evolved, increasing use was made of stone, but in many cases actual wood was used along with stone, and wood continued to be used in late examples.

The climax in *chaitya* building was reached in Karle, not the latest but the grandest in conception, rivaling some of the greatest Hindu temples of the later period. Therefore in Karle

The chaitya at Karle, 2nd century AD; a side view of the entrance

we can study the main architectural features of the early *chaitya* quite well. Built in the 2nd century AD, it was an ambitious project in which the whole community took part—we even know the name of one donor, Bhutapala. Karle is in the form of a main hall with a lofty ceiling, flanked by two narrower halls with lower ceilings on either side. The main hall is separated from the two smaller ones by means of rows of robust columns, whose capitals contain human and animal sculptures. The entrance to the rock-cut hall is through three doors in the profusely sculptured facade set in a recess cut out of the surrounding virgin rock. The horseshoe-shaped window, which cleverly solves the problem of illuminating the interior with natural light, dominates the whole facade by its design and size. The shape of the horseshoe window is carried on in the interior ceiling, undoubtedly the most spectacular feature of this monument. The closely packed wooden arches, which give the vault the shape of an inverted boat, rise slightly above the two massive rows of columns. The way they are cunningly placed, slightly back from the pillars, creates the impression that they are floating in space. This, together with the unusual height of the ceiling and the slight outward curve of the supporting arches, produces the impression of the lofty vault of heaven, a boldness of architectural vision quite un-rivaled in this period. A close scrutiny of Karle will reveal that the actual height of the ceiling is only 45 ft (13.7 m)—certainly less than that of Notre Dame of Paris. The sense of height and elegance of Karle owes a great deal more to the careful proportions of the different parts skillfully deployed than to its actual dimensions. At the farthest end of the *chaitya* is the *stupa*; the columns that separate the main hall from the aisles continue around the *stupa*, but behind it they become undeco-

rated octagonal ones. A further elaboration of Karle from earlier prototypes is the intermediate area between the front entrance and the main hall, which helps us to adjust our vision from the bright sunlight outside to the quiet grandeur of the interior. *Chaityas* continued to be built; cave XIX at Ajanta belongs to the 5th century. The decoration has become richer and the sun-window turns into a perfect circle, but the bold-ness and the impetus of Karle is absent.

As in architecture, the most powerful impulse to sculpture came from Buddhism and the earliest examples are from the reign of the great Buddhist Emperor, Ashoka (c269–232 BC). The aftermath of the bloody Kalinga war led to his conversion to nonviolence and subsequent resolution to conquer nations by moral persuasion instead of war. There already existed in India the tradition of freestanding pillars representing the *axis mundi* or marking royal graves, a tradition common to the whole of the ancient world. Ashoka turned them into power-ful instruments for disseminating his humanitarian ideas all over his Empire, so that today they are invariably associated with him. These freestanding pillars, whose lower parts are buried deep into the ground, rise generally to a height of 40 to 50 ft (12 to 15 m) terminating in a bell-shaped capital.

An especially fine example is the Rampurva Bull capital, whose abacus is decorated with the honeysuckle and palmette motif derived from western Asia (Presidential Palace, New Delhi); other capitals often show animal and bird motifs alter-nating with symbolic wheels. These capitals were surmounted by animals and crowned with large representations of the Buddhist Wheel of Law. The Rampurva Bull shows the re-assertion of Indian mastery of the animal form, last seen in the Indus. The most important reason why these pillars were iden-tified as Ashokan was the Emperor's use of the pillar surface to inscribe his spiritual message, a practice also extended to rock surfaces. This feature, together with other western motifs, and the knowledge of Persian and Greek expansion into the northwestern frontiers of India led scholars to attri-bute Persian and Classical origins to Ashokan art. In fact India borrowed motifs such as honeysuckle or the heraldic lion from the common cultural pool of western Asia in the same way as Persians and Greeks did, long before the actual Persian invasion of India. Trade links which went back to the Indus civilization probably encouraged a continuous flow of artistic motifs to India. A striking feature of animal sculpture from Ashoka's times is the high mirror-like finish which seemed to disappear with the Mauryas.

Actual Buddhist narrative art appeared after Ashoka on the surface of the Sanchi gateways and in Bharhut and Bodhgaya. The *Jatakas*, popular stories, taken over by Buddhists as vehicles of instruction because of their powerful hold over ordinary people, are to be found depicted at Sanchi in places where they could be prominently seen. In the days of restricted literacy, the narrative friezes, whether in medieval Europe or in ancient India, were the chief means of reminding the faithful of the basic tenets of their faith. Sanchi also celebrates the personal spiritual triumph of the Buddha by depicting the various stages of his life that could remind his followers of his great achievement and message. But because the Buddha discouraged the worship of his person, which would have distorted his precept of personal moral responsibility, his followers carefully avoided representing him in human form. Instead he is symbolized by an empty throne, a tree, or a *stupa*.

A typical example of Sanchi sculpture is the north gateway in three tiers, each containing in the central parts continuous narratives derived from Buddha's life as well as from the *Jatakas*. The most impressive are the wide range of animals and birds decorating the gateway. The representation of these different subjects shows the considerable skill of the sculptors in telling stories that involve the use of many figures. The depiction of distance is avoided in the reliefs: the areas between figures are filled with huts, houses, and trees. The narrative art in Sanchi received further elaboration in Amaravati, where the figures show greater movement, grace, flexibility, and expression, partly because of the use of limestone. In general the sculptures of Sanchi and Amaravati tell us a lot about contemporary secular life including some depiction of the prevalent wooden architecture, little of which has survived.

In the early centuries of the Christian era Buddhist art began to seek different subjects, as Buddhism itself was moving away from the earlier *Hinayana* form into the *Mahayana* order which looked upon the Buddha as a divine, savior figure to be actively worshiped. This new attitude encouraged the need for a sacred image of the great teacher. In fact the emerging *Bhakti* movement, which sought a transcendent god to whom the worshiper was bound by personal devotion, was not confined to Buddhism alone. In the 2nd century Krishna emerged as the great transcendent god of the Hindus in the mystical poem *Bhagavad Gita*, where he appears as a god who demands absolute devotion. If we look to the Classical world a little earlier, transcendental deities in various mystery religions, notably the god Dionysos, had come to dominate the spiritual life of the period. In the West the different syncretic faiths eventually coalesced within Christianity, the most powerful religion to emerge in this period.

The human form of the Buddha, created partly under the influence of *Mahayana* Buddhism, evolved in two centers of the Kushan Empire, Gandhara and Mathura. The Kushans, originally from central Asia, set up an eclectic empire based on Classical and Indian civilizations and became the most important patrons of Buddhism since the days of Ashoka. Gandhara, lying in the northwest corner of India with its capital Takshashila (Greek: Taxila), came under successive Persian and Greek influence, especially after Alexander's incursions into these parts. Fragments of the Corinthian order, Greco-Roman sculptural pieces and coins have been discovered here which suggest the presence of artists and craftsmen from the west. It is significant that when the need arose for the sacred image of the savior, in both Christianity and *Mahayana* Buddhism in Gandhara, the sculptors naturally turned to an artistic tradition prevalent in the Roman Empire. It is thus evident that

craftsmen serving both religions had been trained in the watered-down version of Roman art, suggesting a remote connection with the metropolitan center. Both Christ and the Buddha were presented wearing the *pallium*, the robe worn by ancient Greek philosophers, because of their role as great spiritual teachers. The Roman derivation of Gandharan art may also be seen in the narrative cycles of the life of the Buddha which are similar to Roman reliefs and unlike the Sanchi reliefs. In Gandhara the episodes are broken up on the panel, unlike the Sanchi treatment of the stories in the form of a continuous narrative. Although Gandhara Buddhas have been rightly criticized for being crude, provincial Roman works which failed to capture the serene spiritual triumph of the great master, the finest examples certainly combine the best of the two worlds—the vivid naturalism of the Classical and the idealized beauty of the Indian.

In Mathura, the other center of the Kushan Empire, the more robust type of the standing and seated Buddha figures drew inspiration from the indigenous tradition of the colossal *Yakshas*. The enormous Bodhisattva from the 2nd century AD,

A painted Buddha at Gandhara

Relief Sculptures at Sanchi

The relief sculptures on the great *stupa* at Sanchi represent the first important period in the history of Indian narrative art. The didactic requirements of Buddhism, the world's first major evangelical faith, gave rise to these dramatic reliefs. The faithful, already familiar with stories from the Buddha's life and preaching, were meant to "read" them when they visited the *stupa* to pay homage to the great teacher. Although the early *stupas* at Bharhut and Bodh Gaya represented Buddhist scenes, it was in the Sanchi great *stupa* that a project was undertaken on an unprecedented scale in the 1st centuries BC and AD, based on subscriptions raised from the community, as attested by inscriptions on the *stupa*. The *stupa* itself remained unadorned until the very end: but decorative ornaments of beautiful women; animals, floral, foliate, and geometrical motifs; and series of narrative sculptures in relief celebrating the life and spiritual achievements of the Buddha cover the curved architraves and pillars of the gateways.

Significantly, this great Buddhist cycle only show Buddha through symbols recalling his

◄ Narrative sculpture on the north gateway at Sanchi

▼ Flowing narrative on the bottom architrave of the north gateway

piritual progress. Some 60 themes were reated here and repeated according to their mportance; their arrangement on the four ateways in the four cardinal directions suggests that the most "meaningful" stories aced the faithful as they approached the ateways. In contrast to earlier, flat treatment of reliefs, including deeper undercutting o convey distance, Sanchi sculptors use a "pictorial" convention, showing recession by educing the size of distant figures. Instead of harhut's bare background, we have here

clearly depicted forests and towns, with their recognizable balconies and vaulted roofs, surrounded by moats; and unlike earlier, stiff, frontal poses we now have animated figures in many poses. The sculptors adopt two narrative conventions: the first is a continuously flowing narrative, as seen in the *Vessantara Jataka* (north gate, bottom architrave, front and back), a story dealing with the Buddhist doctrine of *dana* (charity), a story so familiar that the faithful had no difficulty in following its course along the

architrave, from the front through to the back. The second convention is seen in the *Battle for the Relics of the Buddha* (south gate, back, middle architrave), one of the most dramatic scenes in Sanchi. The central panel depicts the great tumult of the battle, the town as background, while next to it is the scene showing the victorious kings departing with relic caskets. In other words, scenes representing two successive points of time are here presented simultaneously or synchronically. The most striking feature is the treatment of the crowd by the artists, who subordinate the individual features of figures in favor of capturing the great din and bustle, the general rhythm and movement of the crowd. We also see the range of expressions, from the beautiful *Yakshis* to the exploration of the grotesque and humorous in the representations of the demon hosts of Mara who tempt the Buddha. No less impressive is the treatment of animals, notably elephants and water buffaloes, confirming the Buddhist view of the unity of all living creatures.

PARTHA MITTER

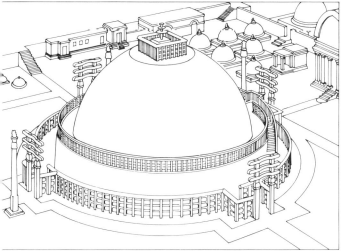

◀ The great *stupa* at Sanchi, showing the positions of the gateways

Below Adjacent successive scenes, as used on the middle architrave on the back of the south gateway at Sanchi

Bottom The middle section of the lowest architrave on the back of the north gateway at Sanchi

Further reading. Marshall, J.H. *The Monuments of Sanchi* (3 vols.), Calcutta (1913–14).

dedicated by the monk Bala (Sarnath Museum), is an impressive example of the style and may be contrasted with Gandhara Buddha. Both scale and gesture are heroic and the expression is full of latent energy. The close-fitting robe which leaves the right shoulder bare reveals rather than conceals the powerful frame. The serene beauty of the Gandhara Buddha is not aimed at; instead the sculptor chooses to represent him as the great spiritual conqueror. The seated Buddhas too have an air of immediacy about them and a scorn for physical beauty. When Jains, the other great dissident sect, fashioned the sacred image of their leader, they naturally turned for inspiration to Buddhist art, and there is no stylistic difference between the image of the Buddha and Jina. The Jains, however, differed from Buddhists with regard to iconography. The Jain ideal of the teacher who had conquered all worldly cravings, including sexual, was realized in the fully naked Jaina images—the only totally nude figures in Indian art.

The ideal form of the Buddha, which partially emerged in the formative phase of the Gandhara and Mathura schools, attained technical perfection and conceptual maturity in the Gupta period (AD 320–540). When the physical beauty of Gandhara and the spiritual strength of Mathura came together to produce the finest Buddha images—images that provided the iconographic and aesthetic norm for Buddhist art all over Asia, right up to Japan. The Gupta period, named after the Imperial family, which ruled most parts of India in this age, represents the supreme cultural achievement of ancient India, made largely possible by political unity.

With the Guptas is associated ancient India's greatest poet, Kalidasa (c 5th century AD). Rules about good living were formulated and standards of criticism set. The early-5th-century Chinese traveler Fa Hsien has left us a vivid account of his own impressions of great peace and security in India under the Guptas. The sculptors of this age, who were given the task of presenting the spiritual triumph of the Buddha over worldly cravings, chose to represent this through a new type of physical beauty. The Sarnath Buddha (Sarnath Museum), one of the great examples of this style, expresses in his gently enigmatic smile the serene, inner confidence that denies the anguish of worldly existence. The power of this beautiful image can be seen all over Asia for it soon became the great ideal for all Buddhists to emulate. The Indian norms of beauty—perfect oval face, lotus eyes, and lion-like torso—as well as iconographic rules such as the third eye, top knot, webbed fingers, and the nimbus became well-established. The nimbus which appeared behind Gupta Buddhas was delicately carved with decorative motifs.

This period also witnessed the supreme achievement in the field of painting in ancient times. The spirit of the Gupta age informs much of the Buddhist paintings in the *chaityas* and *viharas* of Ajanta, although the actual area was outside the immediate sphere of Imperial hegemony. We know very little about the origins of this tradition apart from the information available from early-1st-century caves (IX, X). But most of the important paintings belong to the 5th century and deal with

A Gupta-style Buddha at Sarnath; sandstone; height 160cm (63in); 5th century AD

stories from Buddha's life and Buddhist legends. Although the context is religious, the world revealed before us is the secular, vivacious one of 5th-century India, so memorably described by the poet Kalidasa.

The particular approach chosen by the artists was naturalistic, and even trivial everyday subjects came under their close scrutiny—beggar with bowl and stick, hunter with dog, cook preparing meal, seafaring ships, and other themes of human interest are constantly interwoven with the major religious stories from *Jatakas*. Everything from internal and external architecture, indigenous and foreign people and their different costumes, and patterns of textiles, flora, and fauna, are all captured in warm, glowing colors which have until recently resisted the ravages of time. Foliate, floral, animal, and geometrical decorative patterns are to be seen in great profusion, especially on ceilings.

Ajanta artists used colors based on organic substances which were mixed with water and gum and applied on a treated, plastered surface. Two of the best-preserved and most famous subjects are the Bodhisattvas or Buddhist saviors from Cave I, resplendent in their bejeweled, princely costumes, epitomizing earthly beauty. The face of the Bodhisattva, who holds the lotus, represents the traditional Indian ideal of beauty with the lotus eyes and perfect oval face seen in the sculpture of the Gupta Buddha. Here the painter sought to convey the sense of solidity by the use of highlights and shading, reinforced by means of a dark brown outline.

Form in Ajanta is defined more by light and shadow than line, however, and the pictorial surface is dominated by a series of closely related tones of grays and browns that avoid pure colors. The Ajanta artists loved to use many figures which they arranged in complex patterns in a continuous narrative all around the walls. Another famous subject in Cave I, the renunciation of his Kingdom by Mahajanaka, related in the *Jataka*, is a typical example of their approach. Here the painter has chosen the moment when, according to ancient custom, he was ritually washed with water before leaving his kingdom. Mahajanaka, who in his renunciation was seen as prefiguring the Buddha, is shown here seated in a similar pose. The whole scene taking place in his palace shows careful observation of contemporary interior architecture and other details, such as the deer throne, the servants, and the women who surround him.

The important achievement of Ajanta was not allowed to be forgotten; all over Asia up to China and Japan, Buddhists took Ajanta to be their ideal and modified, elaborated, and interpreted Ajanta art in the light of their own experience. In India, paintings slightly later and similar to Ajanta were produced in Bagh and Ellora, fragments of which remain. Wall-paintings were continued in the south, and as late as 1540 we find an impressive series of paintings in the Lepakshi temple in the Vijayanagar, the last great Hindu kingdom, notably the famous boar hunt.

Hindu art from *c* 5th century AD to *c* 17th century AD. In the reign of the Guptas in the 5th century, Buddhist art reached great heights both in sculpture and painting. This was also the first great age of Hindu art, exemplified by the evolution of the temple. In the Hindu temple, architecture and sculpture are related by a common principle; but for the sake of convenience they will be treated separately here. The same spirit of *Bhakti* which led to the development of the image of the Buddha also brought about changes in Hinduism. In the period of the Vedic sacrifice temples were unnecessary. Their rise followed the establishment of the two important groups within Hinduism, the worshipers of Shiva and Vishnu, who built temples to their own supreme personal gods. When Hindus searched for the appropriate architectural form to adopt they did not have to look far, for they already had important examples before them.

Architects had reached a very high level in the art of building in the Gupta period and they naturally applied their experience in Buddhist buildings to the new requirements of Hindu art. Thus we see in the early Hindu temples clear traces of the *chaitya* form. From the very beginning the requirements of the two faiths were entirely different, and this is seen in the arrangement of the early temples. The Buddhist sacred building, the *chaitya*, was designed to accommodate a large gathering; the Hindu temple was above all the house where the particular god resided. Initially this did not need more than a cell for the sacred image. The basic form was also from the outset profoundly affected by cosmological symbolism, the most important aspect of which was implicit in the word applied to the cell, "garbha griha" (womb-house). Religion also required the temple to be correctly oriented in four cardinal directions and to face the east, a principle generally adhered to except where the geographical peculiarities of the site demanded necessary changes.

Unlike Buddhist architecture, the ideal shape of the temple was the square, the symbol of eternity, standing outside time. This was expressed through the cosmological symbolism of the *mandala*, and even an early temple like the Deogarh (5th century) was based on an elaborate *mandala* ground plan governed by strict geometrical principles. But a layout derived from a strict grid system was not unique to sacred architecture; it determined the plan of secular buildings and, as we have seen, the layout of cities. The sacred geometry had much to do with astronomical considerations.

The earliest Hindu temple is found in Sanchi (Temple 17), a square flat-roofed room with a covered portico supported by columns in front. The shape of the columns was traditional— square with octagonal variations. In India a square was the favored shape for the column; round pillars are very rare. Of the several Gupta temples from this period, namely Bhitargaon, Bhumara, and Deogarh, the last one is by far the most impressive. Built of ashlar masonry and containing a now-ruined, square tower, the most striking features of the Deogarh temple are the typical Gupta doorway framed with beautifully decorated pilasters and the three sculptural reliefs on three sides set in deeply recessed niches, framed, like the doorway, by elegant pilasters. The whole temple was designed to stand on a high plinth to separate it, as it were, from the mundane world, a conception peculiarly Hindu. Another feature that separated this early temple from Buddhist *chaityas* was the absence of great stress on the facade; while the main entrance was to the east, the other three sides were given equal architectural and sculptural importance.

The Gupta temple of Deogarh was a fine but isolated example. For the evolution of two main types of Hindu temples, later to be classed as northern and southern, we must turn to the clusters of temples in the old Chalukyan capitals of Aihole, Badami, and Pattadakal, in Dharwar. They are of great historic importance. Two in Aihole belonging to the 5th century reflect an experimental period when architects were searching for inspiration. The Lad Khan temple, a rectangular building with massive capitals and flat roof covered with stone slabs, was derived from ancient village meeting halls. The Durga temple, on the other hand, sought inspiration in Buddhist *chaityas* and has the unusual feature of a corridor going right around the temple. Its "garbha griha" ends like a *chaitya* in a semicircle. As in Deogarh, a tower marked the shrine; the preceding hall was added in the design to accommodate worshipers.

The Durga temple at Aihole; c500 AD

The Chalukya capital shifted to Badami and finally to Pattadakal where two of the finest early temples are to be found. The Papanatha (Shiva) temple (680) is distinguished by the gently curved tower, known as the northern kind, as distinct from the flat, stepped tiers of southern temples. In the Papanatha, the basic northern form is somewhat modified by tiers, each consisting of *chaitya* and fluted round *amalaka* disc motifs. Another unusual element is its length in relation to its height and width, achieved here by joining two halls together, lending it an elegant appearance. With other Gupta temples it shares an elaborately carved, framed main doorway, while a very important development is the decoration of the sides—carefully worked out and spaced niches formed by pilasters and crowned with pediments. Their decoration consists of geometric, foliate, and mythical animal designs. The Virupaksha (Shiva) temple built in 740 is more elaborate, containing a uniform south-Indian type of tiered tower. The design is more developed and the sculptures, now playing a more important role on the niches, appear at regular intervals, thus anticipating the common arrangement in southern temples of later periods. In their two temples the Buddhist *chaitya* window (horseshoe) motif becomes a common decorative feature.

About the time the Virupaksha was built, the Pallavas (625–800), impressed by the Chalukya achievement, undertook to embellish their own kingdom in the south with splendid temples. On the eastern shores of the Indian Ocean, in Mamallapuram, are to be found the first experiments by designers to discover the appropriate form—the five *rathas* built of solid stone in five different styles including some variations of the *chaitya*. The most successful among them was the Dharmaraja *ratha*—a pyramidal tower made up of diminishing terraces, similar in shape and design to that of Virupaksha. The advantages of this form were its square shape oriented in

four cardinal directions and the incorporation of any number of equal parts which could be varied according to the size of the tower. The individual motifs as well as the crowning solid polygonal dome were derived from the *chaitya*.

When c700 the great Shore Temple at Mamallapuram was built, architects were able to use their experience with Dharmaraja *ratha* profitably. And yet the designers were not entirely bound by tradition. The many unusual features of the Shore Temple follow the peculiar needs of the site. The main shrine surmounted by the pyramidal, terraced *shikhara* faces towards the sea in the east so that the *linga* image could be seen by the passing ships, while a smaller shrine with less lofty *shikhara* was added which could be approached from the town in the west. The main *shikhara* also has a very slender appearance, produced by virtually stretching each tier vertically including its *chaitya* motifs. Because the temple was to serve as a landmark for sailors, its height was of great importance; even today the *shikhara* of the Shore Temple dominates the coast. Much of the temple has fallen down, but the strong enclosing wall surmounted by seated bulls exists as well as pilasters containing springing lions—a southern feature that makes one of its first appearances here. The other great Pallava temple, the Kailasanatha (Shiva) at Kanchipuram, was simply Virupaksha on a grander scale.

A unique development of the southern style took place when the Kailasanatha temple in Ellora was built for the Rashtrakutas (752–83). Made out of a solid block of rock (250 ft, 76 m long, 150 ft, 46 m wide, 100 ft, 30 m deep) separated from its surroundings, it is one of the most imaginative achievements in the history of architecture, and the supreme achievement in the field of rock-temples in India. Instead of the traditional practice of making a tunnel in the rock face, the designers decided to carve a complex two-storied, freestanding temple by working from the top downwards. The enormous range of details, such as single and multiple levels, bridges, halls, richly ornamented columns, and the great variety of fine sculptures required the most rigorous planning, for a single error could have marred the imposing effect. The whole grand impression is further enhanced by the choice of a very high plinth (25 ft, 7.6 m) for the temple.

The final achievement of the southern style was seen c1000, when the powerful Chola rulers built the high Brihadishvara temple in Tanjore. Here the enormously high *shikhara* (190 ft, 58 m) dwarfs the other components of the temple. The impression of great height is produced partly by conceiving the *cella* containing the image in two lofty stories. The niches here, a common southern feature, are deployed harmoniously and contain some very powerful sculptures of Shiva.

The development of southern temples took a new turn after Tanjore. From this time onwards the main shrine and the *shikhara* no longer interest the builders, while great ingenuity and imagination are lavished on the temple gateways which now rise to great heights. The purpose of great height for the

Right: the Shore Temple at Mamallapuram; c700 AD

The Lingaraja temple at Bhubaneswar; c1000 AD

tower gateways (*gopuras*) was to offer symbolic protection to the sacred temple precinct. The 17th-century temples of Madura and Srirangam increasingly resemble fortified cities with their concentric walls and gate-towers, and they were actually fortified against different invaders. Two other southern architectural elements deserve special mention: water tanks and handsome assembly halls standing on sometimes up to a thousand rows of pillars.

In the north, the distinguishing feature, the *shikhara*, followed along the lines seen first in the Papanatha temple in Pattadakal, and this style reached its culmination in two areas, Orissa and Khajuraho, around the 1st millennium. There is yet another important distinction between the north and the south. Although relieved by symmetrically aligned niches with sculptures, the elevations of the southern temples are generally flat; in the north, on the other hand, the elevations are elaborately articulated with alternate projections and recesses, a

principle carried on in the tower over the shrine.

The Orissan style may be best studied in the most complete example, the Lingaraja temple in Bhubaneswar. To the traditional arrangement of the main shrine with high tower, preceded by an assembly hall, were added two further halls. The basic shape of the tower is a tall spire (148 ft, 45 m) which curves slightly inwards at the top and is crowned with a fluted, bulging disk resembling the Indian *amalaka* fruit. On closer inspection we can see that the alternate projections and recesses are intensified by deep incisions of vertical lines right from the *amalaka* down to the base. The further elements are the horizontal ribs as well as the tower (*shikhara*) motifs on various scales punctuating the whole surface of the main tower, as well as sculptures filling the gaps in the recesses. The assembly hall is a square building with a pyramidal roof consisting of two groups of three tiers surmounted by an *amalaka*.

Before leaving Orissa we must mention the magnificent but

unrealized dream, the Sun temple at Konarak, of which only the colossal front hall and the Hall of the Dance remain. Dedicated to the Sun god, the temple is in the form of a handsome, 12-wheeled chariot drawn by seven pairs of horses. From the coherence of the total design to the large sculptures—richly decorated wheels and sculpted erotic couples of various sizes—the immense attention to details, however trivial, is astonishing. Built in the 13th century, it is the last exuberance of the human spirit already threatened with extinction by the invading Muslims.

In the Chandela capital at Khajuraho (950–1050), a variation of the northern style appeared. Impression of lofty heights was created by architects here in a different manner from the Orissans. First, the temple as a sacred precinct was stressed by a very high base which separated it from the surrounding plains. The sense of height is increased by the narrow, high flight of steps leading to the temple entrance. The three main elements, the shrine with its tower, the assembly hall, and the portico are all joined together as one edifice, unlike Orissan temples. A sense of airy space is created by a circumambulatory passage going right around the temple, lit by large, open balconies. The tower of the fine Kandariya Mahedeo (Shiva) temple has repeated on its four sides a number of vertical projections as smaller, variously graded scales. This, along with the deep recesses contrasting with projections, make for an intense play of light and shadow under the Indian sun, and is quite unlike the relatively unbroken surface of the Orissan temples. A further element here is the figure sculpture in several parallel rows over the base and below the tower.

Among important local variations are the temples built for Hoyshala kings in Belur, Halebid, and Somnathpur in the south, famous for their exquisitely detailed sculpture covering the surface and for their star-shaped ground plans. The stellar plan was achieved by a complex geometrical pattern of superimposed squares at angles to each other, forming a succession of related projections and recesses so strictly ordered that a circle may be drawn around them. The form of the towers of these temples is closer to the north. In a very fine example, the Keshava (Vishnu) temple (1268) at Somnathpur, the plan is based on a group of three-star towers. Profusion of delicate carvings on a temple surface is also to be seen in the north in the Jain marble temples of Rajasthan (1032–1232), the Vimala Shah and Tejahpala temples on Mount Abu. Built for affluent merchants, these white marble temples are remarkable for the "crisp, thin, translucent, shell-like treatment" of the delicate marble. The work required such care that ordinary chiseling would have been disastrous. So the carvings were produced by scraping the marble away and "masons were paid by the amount of marble dust so removed" (Zimmer, H. *The Art of Indian Asia*). Finally, another provincial style, the terracotta temples of Bengal (100–1600), has recently rewarded patient study: *see* McCutchion, D.J. *Late Medieval Temples of Bengal* Calcutta (1972).

As in Buddhism, the stress on absolute devotion to a personal savior god partly contributed to the creation of the ideal image of the Buddha and Bodhisattva, so in Hinduism, after the rise of *Bhakti* movements and the emergence of Vishnu and Shiva as the greatest gods, superseding all others, came the creation of permanent images of the two gods. Although literary references to images of gods occur very early, including the description by a foreigner of an androgynous many-limbed symbolic god (Bardesanes' testimony recorded by Porphyry, 3rd century), the earliest extant images of Vishnu and Shiva are in fact from the Gupta period, parallel to the rise of temples. An early Vishnu from the Gupta period looks strikingly like a Bodhisattva because artists applied their experience in Buddhism to the new religious art.

In Hinduism, there are two kinds of images, those worshiped at home and those in temples; we are concerned here with the art of the latter. In the temple the main shrine, over which the tower rises, is windowless, bare, and purposely austere—a repository of inscrutable mystery, darkness, and the numinous. Similarly, the main image installed there is often not primarily aesthetic in its concern. Indeed, in the greatest temples the images are purposely abstract, archaic, primitive, and often bizarre, so that worshipers may respond to them on multiple levels of symbolic meaning. But there is a whole range of sculptures, including images of gods on the outer surface of the temples, usually connected with the mythological cycles related to the particular divinity inhabiting the temple. The range of sculptures on the sides of temples—from the large images of gods and main narrative cycles portraying the *Puranas*, the Hindu sacred mythology, to the detailed geometrical, foliate, and mythical animal decorations—are all strictly ordered within a hierarchy of levels of meaning.

However, some of the greatest artistic treatments of Hindu mythology are to be found in the panels of narrative sculptures on the outer walls of temples, in a spectrum of reliefs ranging in depth from the lowest to the highest relief. In fact the evolution of narrative sculpture from Sanchi to the late Hindu period demonstrates the importance of the actual depth of the reliefs as settings for the dramatic events depicted. As artists learned to represent stories more convincingly they moved away from the early shallow reliefs of Sanchi and Bharhut to greater depth of background. In the finest examples the whole scene is often presented within a deep square niche where some figures are cut in high relief while others half emerge from the rock. These different depths combine to create a dramatic effect of light and shadow, and lead to great expressiveness under the strong, natural Indian light.

The repertory of Hindu temple sculptures is large; only some of the most striking ones may be considered here. From the outset, certain *Puranic* myths, whether they related to Vishnu's or Shiva's exploits, found favor among artists because of their sculptural possibilities. Both gods were responsible for the creation, preservation, and destruction of the universe, while Vishnu had more solar attributes and was generally life-affirming. Shiva, a more complex god embodying contrary elements—namely asceticism and sexuality—was more chthonic by nature. Both their myths relate either their benign act of creation after periodic dissolution of aeons or their fierce aspect of battling with forces of darkness—the demons (*asuras*). But while these gods destroy the evil demons they also hold out to their victims the possibility of redemption, thus indicating that these destructive acts of the god are his cosmic "play". Sculptors, faced with the problem of treating these scenes, presented them as the enactment of divine theater.

In one of the first great pieces of sculpture in the Deogarh Vishnu temple, we see the sleep of Vishnu between the dissolution of the world and its recreation depicted. He is attended by his wife Lakshmi while he sleeps on the serpent embodying time (*shesa*). The creator, Brahma, rests on a lotus springing from his navel. While other gods watch the scene, his weapons, personified here, battle with two demons. Vishnu is also associated with the notion of incarnation (*avatara*) and assumes mortal form to restore righteousness. One of the most powerful images of monumentality is to be seen in Udaigiri (*c*500), where Vishnu as a cosmic boar rescues the goddess earth from under the waters as a multitude of sages (*rishis*) sing his praise.

From a cave in Ellora (*c*600) comes a spirited depiction of Vishnu's man-lion incarnation where he destroys the demon by emerging from inside a pillar. Here the artist has chosen the moment of the fight between the demon and the god, which is treated with a great deal of movement and expression. In Ellora senses of movement and dynamism are the important developments from more static Deogarh sculpture. Other representations of Vishnu include the Krishna incarnation holding a flute, commonly seen in the south, as well as his four-armed frontal image wearing an elaborate crown and holding four attributes—conch, discus, mace, and lotus—in his four hands.

Like Vishnu, Shiva is represented in both his benevolent and fierce aspects, and with him the chthonic aspects are particularly important. Unlike Vishnu who wears a crown Shiva is always shown with the matted hair of the ascetic. His favorite weapon of destruction is the trident. Between the 6th and 8th centuries, sculptors in the area extending from Ellora to Elephanta produced some of the most remarkable groups of Shiva stories, closely related in style and unified by a common iconography. Among them, the sculpture of Shiva destroying the three cities of the demon Tripura in the Kailasa temple, Ellora, is full of movement and energy. The destruction of the demon Andhaka in the Elephanta temple is famed for its power of expression, showing the moment when Shiva pins the demon on his trident with one hand while with another he holds a cup to collect the victim's dripping blood.

At these sites there are also a number of very fine sculptures of the dancing Shiva, whose cosmic acts of creation and destruction are always presented in the form of the dance. In Ellora, the sculptor who depicts Shiva performing the mea-

The three faces of Shiva in the temple at Elephanta; c 8th century AD

sured dance, known as *katisama* in classical dance repertoire, shows him dancing before his family as well as other gods, as if in a theater. In another, Shiva does a more abandoned dance, full of grace and rhythm. In both these sculptures the artists have presented Shiva as a beautiful man and have taken special care in the treatment of his hair and personal ornament. In Elephanta there also exists the sculpture of the great three faces of Shiva: horrific, feminine, and tranquil. This bust, meant to emerge in half light and darkness because of the deeply cut niche that frames it, is possibly the supreme achievement of the period.

Other dancing Shiva figures include the famous Chola Nataraja (King of the Dance) bronzes, many examples of which exist outside India in European museums (for example, Musée Guimet, Paris). The divine dancer with her slender, graceful build and elegant fingers and toes is shown dancing on the little demon, Ignorance, while he is ringed by the conflagration that destroys the cosmos. Shiva is also represented in an androgynous form. In the case of the classical hermaphrodite, the male and female elements are blended in the figure while Indian sculptors chose to emphasize the two contrary principles by dividing the figure equally into male and female.

Among depictions of goddesses, the myth about the destruction of the buffalo demon by Devi, Shiva's wife, is the most popular. Legend has it that when unrighteousness became intolerable each god offered up part of his power to fashion the miraculous goddess who would be greater than all of them, and thus Durga was conceived. Among the several famous scenes depicting her destruction of the Buffalo demon, one at Ellora and several at Mamallapuram are most moving. In Ellora she is shown struggling with the enormously powerful demon with all the weapons presented by gods in her ten hands. The scene is characteristically full of movement and action, a favorite with sculptors here.

But the main problem artists faced was how to show a great, bloody battle in which Devi engaged in order to kill

Mahishasura and yet present her, so literature has it, as a young woman of great beauty and gentleness. In Mamallapuram this is solved, interestingly, by the choice of the moment shown: she is represented as a beautiful young girl standing demurely and the only trace of the great battle is in the severed head of the buffalo lying under her.

Apart from Vaishnava and Shaiva deities, one god dating from the Vedic period continued to draw the allegiance of worshipers. Surya, the Sun god, to whom a number of temples were dedicated from the 5th to the 11th centuries AD, including the great Konarak temple, is recognizable by his high boots and seven horses, as seen in the fine image from Konarak. We may marvel at the achievements of great power and beauty in the major relief cycles about stories of gods, but we cannot neglect more intimate treatments, especially of women, an area very close to the heart of the sculptors from the days of Sanchi. Male figures, apart from the Door Guardians, were generally vehicles of religious symbolism, and while many of these figures are very beautiful we cannot separate the beauty of these divine figures from their symbolic attributes. In other words, even in their beauty they are larger than life and remote from us. Women, on the other hand, were direct, intensely human, and represented as desirable. In Sanchi we encounter the nubile tree-spirits. In Ellora there are several memorable feminine images. Some of the finest, however, come from c10th century, and are full of grace and feeling. The sculptors were particularly adept in bringing out the soft, bare quality of flesh by contrasting it with rich jewelry and exquisite costumes, as in the striking Lady of the Tree (Central Archaeological Museum, Gwalior), a perfect translation of Kalidasa's poetry into stone.

Apart from this universal celebration of the physical beauty

One of the masterpieces of Indian erotic art: sculptured figures on the Sun temple at Konarak; 13th century

Sculpture of Devi at Ellora

The sculpture of Devi or the Goddess slaying Mahisasura, the buffalo demon, in the precinct of the 8th-century Hindu rock-cut temple of Kailasa at Ellora in western India is a truly remarkable piece of work at a site filled with many of the finest achievements of ancient Indian art—Hindu, Buddhist, and Jain. The piece is one of the twin sculptural compositions that adorn the site of the Kailasa temple, belonging to the worshipers of Shiva. The other one depicts Shiva's destruction of Tripura, the demon of the three cities. Both relate stories from the sectarian mythology of the Saivas and both relief panels treat battle scenes in which the deities are engaged in destroying the demon that has upset the cosmic order, so that the order may be restored. Both sculptures, particularly the scene depicting Devi's great battle, represent a high point in the development of Hindu iconography and its treatment in narrative sculpture as well as the treatment of the human figure, and above all in the solving of compositional problems and problems of expression. In short, this compositional piece is one of the most dramatic treatments in the history of Indian monumental sculpture.

The theme of Devi destroying the buffalo demon has been one of the most popular subjects for artists, from the rise of Hindu sculpture to the present. To Hindus it is also one of the most inspiring legends, as seen in the worship of the image in its present form in Bengal. The story of the great goddess,

Devi or Durga, as it occurs in its most complete version in the *Markandeya Purana*, is as follows: the universe is dominated by the eternal struggle between *devas* (gods) and *asuras* (demons or antigods who happen to be half-brothers of gods), in which struggle the world order is periodically upset when the demon king, through sheer willpower, gains ascendancy over the mythological gods. Then it becomes necessary for either of the supreme gods, Vishnu or Shiva, to come to

the rescue of the mythological gods and restore cosmic order by destroying the demon. On this occasion the particular demon, who took the form of a water buffalo, is so powerful that even the two supreme deities are unable to destroy him. So all the gods come together and with their concerted willpower and energy they produce a wonderous woman, the fairest one, the invincible one, more powerful than any of them. Each god gives up part of his power and his favorite weapon, such as the *chakra* of Vishnu or the *trisula* of Shiva, to this deity. Thus armed she goes forth in battle with the

◀ Devi or Durga (left) slaying Mahisasura, the Buffalo demon; in the 8th-century Kailasa temple at Ellora

▼ Shiva destroying Tripura, the demon of the three cities; in the temple of Shiva at Ellora

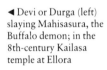

▲ Durga and her companions confront Mahisasura; a relief sculpture at Mamallapuram

▼ A 6th-century figure of Durga in a niche on the veranda of the Durga temple at Aiholi

demon king and his army, riding on her animal, the lion. After a great and bloody battle in which weapons fly in all directions and innumerable demons lie dying and dead, the buffalo demon is at last cornered. When finally he tries to escape from the dying buffalo form in the guise of a man, he is dealt the death blow and perishes.

The legend has been a favorite subject of Indian sculptors because of its dramatic possibilities; and only by a comparison of various versions of the theme can we fully appreciate the achievement of the sculptor at Ellora. The nature of the story offered a number of possibilities to the artist. What proved intriguing to him was the idea that although the goddess was described in the *Puranas* as invincible and even more powerful than the gods, she was nonetheless a beautiful woman in the first bloom of youth; so any suggestion of masculinity had to be avoided, even though she engaged in the most masculine of acts: making war. This contradiction led to the crucial choice of the particular moment to represent in sculpture: whether to show the aftermath of the great battle when the demon lies subdued and no carnage is evident, or whether to depict the actual battle with all its fury and ugliness.

In an early image in the Durga temple at Aiholi the powers of expression are not fully developed, and the sculptor presents a more hieratic image with very little movement as the weapons presented by various gods are placed in a symmetrical manner while the buffalo demon is a diminutive figure—hardly terrifying. It was at the 7th-century

Above The temple of Kailasa at Ellora, a temple of Shiva cut in the rock hillside

Shiva dancing: an example of Shiva in the Kailasa temple, Ellora, contemporaneous with Devi

site in Mamallapuram that artists began to consider the expressive possibilities of the story. In a less-known image from the place, now in the Museum of Fine Arts, Boston, the sculptor has concentrated on the physical charm of the goddess. This sculpture is indeed one of the most beautiful feminine figures in the history of Hindu art. The sculptor ignores the essential tension of the story; the carnage is hinted at by the muted sculptured head of the buffalo. By stressing grace the artist has chosen to sacrifice dramatic tension. In fact there are only two outstanding dramatic treatments of the theme in the early period: the better-known Durga image at Mamallapuram and the great one at Kailasa in Ellora. Their treatment of the theme is similar in some respects and yet different. At Mamallapuram, Durga and her companions confront Mahisasura who is large and menacing, whose powers are still intact, while the gods watch the spectacle. Durga is presented here as a slender, graceful maiden, and even though the sculpture is badly weathered, we can still see traces of her beauty on her face. Although feminine, she is nonetheless presented as an invincible warrior as she wields her bow and a multitude of other weapons. In the horizontal composition there is a great forward thrust from left to right which is suddenly stopped by the massive diagonal of the Mahisasura's defiant form.

This kind of dramatic treatment reaches its climax in Ellora with this wonderful composition. There is hardly any symmetry, and the dead and wounded scatter in great confusion. The sculptor also follows the text carefully by showing the weapons of Durga flying in all directions. The tension is built up by the use of a vertical composition with the gods witnessing the event from above. Here Mahisasura is not a monster but a proud heroic figure: there can be no doubt that this depiction of the buffalo demon is one of the finest in early sculpture. Although today it is difficult to say what Durga's face was like because it is so badly damaged, her striking and unusual seated posture as well as her graceful, slender form is still recognizable. If we are to take other sculptures from the period at Kailasa as an indication then her head must have been very beautiful too. In Kailasa we find some of the most beautiful faces of Shiva. Finally, it is the combination of grace, beauty, power of expression, and complex and dramatic composition that makes the Durga of Ellora a remarkable relief sculpture.

PARTHA MITTER

Further reading. Gopinatha Rao, T.A. *Elements of Hindu Iconography*, Madras (1914). Zimmer, H.R. *The Art of Indian Asia* (2 vols.), New York (1955).

of women, sexual love played a central role in the literature and art of ancient India and there was no hesitation in depicting the beauty of sexual love and amorous couples. Indeed Indian literature is full of praise for the life-affirming power of physical love, and one of the great objective studies of sex was made by the Indian Vatsayana, the celebrated, 5th-century, author of *Karma Sutra*. This attitude in the secular world is mirrored in the sacred. Love plays an important role in it, although there is a dialectical relationship between asceticism and sexuality. If we remember this, it becomes easy to see why there was no hesitation in representing erotic scenes on the temple walls. The connection between religion and the erotic went back to the Kushan period in the 2nd century. However, among the masterpieces of erotic art may be mentioned two scenes showing couples kissing, the first in the Kailasa temple, Ellora, remarkable for its tender elegance, and the second from Konarak Sun temple, equally moving for a subtle presentation of a much-treated theme in India.

Indo-Islamic art under the Delhi sultanate (1210–1526). The arrival of Islam marks the end of the old order in India, at least in the north. From now on the hierarchical order of Indian society was to be deeply affected by the ideas of equality and brotherhood preached by Islam, as well as by its sheer vitality; Islam in its turn was to be affected by the caste system. By AD 712 only a century after Muhammad's death, Arabs had invaded the Indus Valley: it was about the same time as, in the West, they conquered as far as Spain. Unlike Europe, where Arab learning contributed substantially to medieval civilization, it did not leave much trace of its incursion except for an early lively account of Brahmans and their culture by the great encylopedist Al-Biruni. The Arabs did, however, carry the Hindu system of numbers westwards, to be subsequently known as Arab numerals. The Muslim adventurers, such as Mahmud of Ghazni, who followed the Arabs were mainly interested in the gold and precious stones that filled temples like Somnath in western India. It was the decisive victory over a coalition of Hindu powers in 1192 that led to the founding of the first Turkish Sultanate 18 years later. In theory the whole population had to be converted or, if they resisted, put to the sword, and initially many were probably converted. But because of the overwhelming number of the conquered people it was found more convenient to tax them, an expedient adopted in other parts of the Muslim world. Accordingly, the status of *Ah l-iqitab* (people of the book), accorded to Jews and Christians in the Middle East, was, significantly, extended to the Hindus.

The Delhi Sultanate lasted from 1210 to 1526, when it was overthrown by the Mughals. During this period architecture was clearly the most important form of artistic expression; the sultans were prolific builders both in Delhi and in the provinces where further sultanates were set up. Indian architecture underwent a profound transformation because the requirements of the conqueror were very different from those of the native inhabitants. Indeed, someone traveling in this period through both the north and the south, which remained Hindu in essence right down to the 20th century, would have been struck by the great differences between the buildings of the two areas. He would have noticed, for instance, that while on the walls of mosques the only forms of decoration permitted were geometric and abstract patterns, those details were strictly subject to the overall simple, elegant design of the building. In Hindu temples the basic design was governed by precise mathematical rules; at the same time this precision was combined with a rich decorative surface, mostly based on human figures. Even though many temples were of great height the emphasis was horizontal, in the sucessive layers of stone. In the mosques the universal use of arches to span a wide area was the rule.

The design of the mosque is dictated by the need for a prayer area for a large gathering. In its simplest form it is an open quadrangle, surrounded on four sides by pillared cloisters, the west or *qibla* side pointing towards Mecca and containing the *mihrab* or walled recess, often surmounted by a dome. Another essential architectural element is the minaret from the top of which the *muezzin*, or Muslim crier, calls the faithful to prayer. The general plan and design of Indian mosques was to a large extent determined by famous models like the great Mutawakkil mosque in Sammarra (Iraq) and possibly by later examples of the Seljuk madrasahs developed in Persia. But the great strength of Islamic architecture lies in its successful combination of certain universal elements with the regional and national peculiarities of places such as Arabia, Persia, North Africa, and central Asia. India was no exception. Because importing labor on a large scale was very expensive, India's masons and builders were employed almost from the very beginning. Indian builders, whatever their own persuasion, had until then served all traditional Indian religions equally well; with Islam they simply had to adjust their skill according to the task set before them. This led to the development of a mixed style in which the general conception was broadly Islamic while many of the details were of Indian inspiration. The Indian mastery of stone-cutting is also evident in the use of dressed stone rather than brick in the construction of mosques.

In the reign of the first sultan, Qutb ud-din Aibak (1191–1211), the earliest mosques such as the Qutb mosque in Delhi (1195) were hastily built with fragments from the destroyed Hindu temples. The use of columns of different shapes and sizes from different temples give them a most bizarre appearance but in this case faith triumphed over discretion. Nonetheless, the need for a tangible expression of the ideals of Islam remained. Work on an ambitious project was therefore begun only a few years after the hesitant start with the Qutb mosque. This was the Qutb minar, an effort of great architectural importance, built to accompany the first mosque. Ostensibly in the form of a minaret for the purpose of the call to prayer, its

Right: the Qutb minar, Delhi, begun in 1199 (the top two stories were rebuilt at a later date)

scale and grandeur make it an ideal symbol of Islam's victory over unbelievers. The red sandstone tower formerly 238 ft (73 m) high, consists of four diminishing stories with projecting balconies, each differently designed with combinations of circles, flutings, and star-shaped patterns. A particularly noticeable feature of the tower is the calculated use of different textures and shapes for different levels, the bottom level containing abstract patterns, employing Arabic inscriptions of great visual beauty based on quotations from the Koran. Here, unable to use human figures, Indian artists adapted their carving skill for Islamic purposes to brilliant effect.

The succeeding sultans probably felt secure enough not to need such symbols to impress their subjects. Their buildings were conspicuously modest. A new form was introduced, however, by the second sultan, Shams ud-din (1211–36). The mausoleum, the early use of which was by the Muslim sultans of Egypt, was to be raised to supreme heights by the Mughals. Shams ud-din's tomb (1235) is a simple square edifice, three sides of which have three doorways, while the fourth, the western side, repeats the *mihrab* thrice. The deceptively rugged exterior ingeniously conceals the interior with rich decorative effect in red sandstone and white marble, using motifs of koranic inscriptions.

Alauddin Khalji (1296–1316) of the succeeding dynasty had the ambition of building a tower to dwarf the lofty Qutb. While this dream was never fulfilled he has, however, left us an elegant gateway (1305) next to the Qutb which marks the next important advance in Indo-Islamic architecture in a successful blending of Seljuk and Indian elements. The Alai Darwaza (Gateway of Victory) is also the first of the series of elaborate gateways from the Muslim period to be seen in many parts of India. The 60 ft (18 m) high monument has four doorways on four sides in the form of long and elegant arches, repeated on each side by bottom rows of smaller mock arches with perforated stone screens. The doorways lead into four spacious halls and the monument itself is crowned by a low, wide dome giving a general impression of great symmetry. The decoration as usual consists chiefly of abstract patterns, based on the Koranic text, in red sandstone and white marble.

The tomb of Ghias ud-din Tughlaq (1320–5) of the next dynasty uses marble for the first time to cover the whole dome. Apart from this delicacy of treatment the whole monument has a rough simplicity which suggests that this soldier-monarch deliberately rejected anything that hinted at needless pomp and luxury. Situated in the middle of what was once a lake and protected by massive bastions, the tomb has an unmistakable air of a fortress and may have served as such to protect the sultan's treasures from the hostile indigenous population. His grand-nephew Firuz (1351–88), equally austere but a prolific builder, founded Firuz Shah Kotla, a city on the outskirts of Delhi, although strained financial conditions allowed him only rubblework in his buildings. In the tomb of his minister, numerous cupolas appeared on the roof—a new architectural element.

By far the most spectacular architectural achievement of the Sultanate period was the mausoleum (1540) of Sher Shah, the brilliant Afghan general who drove out the Mughal Emperor Humayuan and ruled in Delhi for a brief period and became the last great Sultan (1540–5). The style is of the period of the Lodi sultans of Delhi the successors of the Tughlaqs, but the monument was built in Sher Shah's original home in Sasaram, in Bihar. The architect, Aliwal Khan, conceived it as an enormous and very complex pyramid, consisting of many levels; it rises to a height of 150 ft (48 m) and is 250 ft (76 m) wide. A columned pavilion, resting on a high base, lifts its head up straight from the waters of the artificial lake surrounding the tomb. Above the pavilion is an elaborate octagon which goes up in three diminishing stages and ends in a low, broad white dome. From the distance the mixture of solidity and elegance, the skilful manipulation of different shapes and materials such as Chunar sandstone and glazed tiles, above all the shining white dome make it a truly arresting sight. Many different styles of great originality and power were produced in the courts of local Muslim rulers. From these one example may be chosen for its sheer beauty of detail: the Sidi Sayyid mosque (1516) in Ahmedabad, Gujarat. Its reputation owes a great deal to the ornamental patterns of the perforated stone screen walls, among which the finest is possibly the brilliantly conceived tree motif by an unknown artist.

The history of painting in the Sultanate period is obscure and full of conflicting evidence, and remains so until the arrival of the Mughals. But in order to understand Mughal art it is necessary to make our way through this difficult period. The previously held commonplace belief that the Delhi sultans actively discouraged painting has ceased to convince us after important researches into the literary evidence for painting in the Sultanate, although actual examples of painting have not been positively identified.

Long before the arrival of the Turks, as early as the 10th century, the nature and patronage of painting in India was changing. The great tradition of wall-painting, which went back to Ajanta, was in decline in the north and its place was increasingly taken by small-scale works, mainly book illustrations. The increasing political uncertainties and consequent insecurity of life and wealth must have contributed to the decline in patronage. The center of activity shifted to the east, which was relatively immune from foreign raids.

This was also the age when Buddhism was in retreat all over India except in the great monasteries in the eastern Pala kingdom (c760–1142) which extended its patronage to a new Buddhist movement, the Vehicle of the Thunderbolt (*Vajrayana*). The new sect represented the growing importance of *Tantra* in Buddhism, a mystical cult which sought the highest spiritual truth through the means of the senses and through elaborate sexual rites and esoteric symbolism. The tiny paintings on palm leaves, measuring 22 in by 2 in (59 cm by 5 cm) often accompanying *Vajrayana* texts, reflect the secretive nature of the sect. They were not meant to be openly displayed but were kept carefully wrapped up to preserve their magic and only shown rarely to initiates. An illustration from the 11th-century manuscript *Astasahasrika-Prajnaparamita* (Bodleian Library, Oxford) shows the Pala artist's characteristic treatment of figures with delicate curved lines as well as his use of primary colors and avoidance of tones. Pala painting was to inspire art in Nepal and Tibet, where a complex symbolic language of pure colors was evolved. But even here the colors tend to be emblematic; red, for instance, stands for passion.

It is important to see Pala painting and sculpture together to realize the common ideal of human beauty that both sculptures and painters draw upon. The Pala artists, Dhiman and Bitpala (both *fl. c*900), celebrated in literature, may well have been connected with the cultural center in the great monastery at Nalanda. Both stone and bronze sculptures were executed in the Pala period, but even stonework follows metal in its linear treatment of the figure with emphasis on beautifully elaborate and curvilinear patterns incised on stone. Both kinds of sculpture, however, are distant echoes of Gupta art, al-

A Tantra painting from the 11th-century manuscript *Astasahasrika-Prajnaparamita*. Bodleian Library, Oxford

though they now concentrate on sensuous lines. Similarly, if for a moment we forget the Pala treatment in the above painting and take a close look at the adoring figures around the central Bodhisattva, we see how close in pose and gestures their upturned faces are to Ajanta figures. Here, however, the artist has sacrificed the naturalism and the dramatic narrative character of Ajanta art in favor of a timeless sacred icon.

Pala art provided inspiration for art in Nepal and Tibet in the successive centuries down to the present. It had no further role to play in India. Its contemporary in western India, Jain religious painting, on the other hand, had great importance for the future development of painting in India. Jain painters were provided with a greater scope for development in the 15th century when they changed from palm leaf to paper. As with Pala paintings these works had a specific religious purpose. In earlier times pious Jain merchants had often been able to bear the cost of enormous marble temples in Mount Abu and other places; the presence of Muslim powers in the north increasingly forced them to turn to more modest ways of acquiring merit for it was a pious act to commission the illustration of stories from the *Kalpa sutra* or *Kalakacharya Katha* dealing with the miraculous births of Jain saints and their conversions of unbelievers.

The paintings were modest in scope, the style deliberately rigid as befitting sacred art where any deviation from the original formula may constitute sacrilege. The three-quarter face of the figures often has staring eyes with large pupils, while the farther eye is shown crossing the facial outline. The torso resembles a triangle, while shoulders are broad and the waist extremely narrow, a formula applied equally to both sexes making it difficult for us to distinguish them. There is not the slightest trace of any borrowing from Ajanta; if the painters knew of the achievement of these caves they preferred to ignore them. Within the framework of this rigid style some of the paintings are very expressive in their austere fashion. As the 16th century progressed, the original limited palette of reds, blues, and greens was enriched by gold and ultramarine, while composition became more complex as painters learned to use scroll-like clouds and other decorative motifs from Persian art. Persian merchants, who may have introduced the art of their own country to Jain artists, possibly served as the model for the portrait of the foreign Saka king converted by a Jain teacher in the *Kalpa sutra* dated 1475 (Devansano Pado Bhandar).

The pictorial tradition associated with Jain texts affected the neighboring states of Malwa and Rajasthan, although the subject and spirit of their paintings are entirely different. They are mostly visual representations of romantic poetry; the finest example of the style and also the best known is the *Chaurapanchasika* series illustrating the Kashmiri poet Bilhana's celebrated *Forty Verses of a Thief* (N.C. Mehta Collection, Gujarat Museum, Ahmedabad) dated *c*1500. "Even today do I see the fair arms that encircled my neck, when she clasped me close to her breast, and pressed her face against my own in a kiss, while her playful eyes half closed in ecstasy",

wrote the 12th-century poet Bilhana. The mood of gentle eroticism that informs the work of this poet marks an important development in Indian literature from the 10th century onwards as the formal elegance of classical Sanskrit gives way to the intimate atmosphere of vernacular languages. Romantic love, whether secular or couched in the allegory of Vaishnava mysticism, becomes the vehicle of this new literature, which will be discussed later in connection with Rajput painting.

The *Chaurapanchasika* paintings clearly show that while the artists worked within the Jain pictorial convention the subject of love between a poet and his beloved clearly required a different treatment. The heroine Champavati's features still contain traces of Jain art such as the triangular torso or staring eyes, but the whole spirit of the work is festive, as flowering trees, her gray-blue patterned skirt, the chequered bedspread, and marble architectural detail bring relief to the traditional Jain red background. A new pictorial device introduced here, the division of the picture plane into several parts by means of a columned open pavilion that allows us a glimpse into the interior of the house, was to be used in painting for several centuries by succeeding generations of Rajput artists. The charming gait of Champavati reminds us of Indian classical dance gestures. The reflection of a long and confident Hindu cultural tradition when Hindu powers were in retreat everywhere makes us conclude that the series was executed for the rulers of Mewar, the only Hindu power to recover from Muslim domination and establish its hegemony in Rajasthan in the 16th century.

Similar in style were illustrations to the *Laur Chanda*, a romantic tale about the Hindu aristocracy composed, significantly, by a Muslim poet, Maulana Da'ud. Initially Muslim rulers, who regarded Hindus as unbelievers, made no attempt to establish cultural and social contacts with them. The Hindus on their part considered everyone outside the caste system as being beyond the pale. But as the two communities began to live side by side links were formed. The first to build the bridge were Muslim Sufis, Hindu Yogis, and leaders of the *Bhakti* movement. This common sympathy helped create a new syncretic religion, the traces of which remain in India in the form of shrines attended by both Hindus and Muslims. As the text of *Laur Chanda* embodies this new spirit, so the styles of paintings that illustrate the work represent a mixture of two styles, Gujarati and Persian.

The version in the John Rylands Library, Manchester, is a rich storehouse for the study of contemporary modes and manners, but the paintings in the Prince of Wales Museum, Bombay, are particularly remarkable for their blend of delicate colors, most unusual for the period. If we do not have any Sultanate painting, we have 16th-century paintings done for a Muslim court in western India. Nadir Shah Khalji (1500–10), the Sultan of Malwa, asked his artists to illustrate a cookery book (*Nimat-nama*) for him. The story that he replaced men with women in the kind of jobs usually reserved for men is corroborated by the paintings. The background of these pictures, showing scroll-like clouds and landscape

A scene from the *Nimat-nama*, the cookery book illustrated for Nadir Shah Khalji; c1500. India Office Library, London

dotted with tufts of grass, suggests a knowledge of Persian painting. The trade connections between western India and Persia may well have encouraged painters to seek employment at the Muslim court of Malwa. But what is puzzling is that these paintings also frequently incorporate figures of women derived from Jain art. Were Gujarati painters also employed to collaborate in the work as was to be common in the Mughal period? This curious mixed style is also to be seen in another contemporary (16th-century) text from Malwa, the *Miftah-al Fuzala*. These related western Indian styles from contiguous areas have some important differences but much in common, which lends support to the hypothesis that they all draw upon a common artistic background in western India. This was the general situation of painting in northern India when the Mughals arrived in the country.

Indo-Islamic art under the Mughal dynasty (1526–1757). The founder of the Mughal dynasty, Babur (1526–31), was descended from two world conquerors, Chingiz and Timur, one a Turk, the other Mongol; the culture he adopted was Persian. In 1526 Babur crushed the Delhi Sultan, and the following year the Rana of Mewar suffered the same fate; in both cases gunpowder decided the issue. With the Mughal dynasty a new era begins in India. They were Muslim but very different from the religious, austere Delhi sultans, and were to have great influence on the development of painting and architecture in India. They were intellectually curious, urbane, secular, and highly gifted individuals. Great connoisseurs of beauty, both natural and artificial, they brought a new, heightened sensibility to art and life and introduced clear principles of taste in judging works of art. The court of "The Great Mogul" (Mughal) became synonymous with pomp and circumstance. The Mughals introduced formal gardens, fountains, and the game of polo to India; their courtly etiquette was eagerly

emulated and their sartorial habits assiduously copied in the provinces—their cuisine is remembered even today. The splendor, the courtly etiquette, the wealth, all were faithfully recorded in painting, the most naturalistic in the history of Indian art. It is true that in order to maintain the high cultural standards of the Empire later emperors were forced to levy increasingly oppressive taxes, but at least in the period of the early emperors India enjoyed remarkable peace and prosperity. Babur himself was a curious mixture of blood-thirsty warrior and reflective man of letters; his autobiography is delightful to read. He was steeped in Persian culture and did not know India well enough to care for it. His early death led to a period of chaos in India when his son was driven out to Persia for a number of years.

The great age of the Mughals begins with the accession of Akbar (1556–1605) at the age of 13, destined to become one of the greatest rulers the world has seen. The great Catholic encyclopedist Athanasius Kircher (1602–80) paid a tribute to him when he stated that Akbar was renowned for "la beauté de son esprit". His age breathes such an air of confident optimism and vitality that it brings to mind an earlier one, that of the Guptas. In the 16th century Muslims and Hindus had come closer and yet the latter suffered from certain disadvantages in the Muslim state. Akbar took the decisive step of removing all the marks of inferiority, such as the poll tax, which defined Hindus as the conquered subjects. He also married into Rajput houses and made this powerful political group partners in his Empire. Although his immensely busy life left him little time for a formal education he showed lively intellectual curiosity in many things, above all in the nature of religion. At the end of his life he came to accept that all religions contained something of value, a position that brought him in conflict with the orthodox divines (*ulema*). His reign marks an advance in architecture in the spaciously constructed tomb of his father, which anticipates the style of the Taj Mahal.

But it is the architecture of the city of Fathpur Sikri, abandoned when the water supply ran out, that engages our attention. Wide, spacious terraces and courtyards separate the numerous palaces, pavilions, and shrines in Fathpur which rest on a windswept ridge somewhat elevated from the surrounding plains. The imaginative conception of the architect is brought out with clarity in the two extremes of buildings; the towering Buland Darwaza (Triumphal Gateway) whose overwhelming strength is tempered by a series of kiosks with cupolas that lighten the heaviness of the red sandstone. This gateway may be considered the culmination of the process begun with Alauddin's modest Alai Darwaza. The other extreme is an intimate and delicate little tomb of the saint Salim Chisti, with its perforated stonework of rare delicacy, giving us a foretaste of the Taj Mahal.

When the great Emperor set up his huge artistic establishment he is said to have answered the Muslim argument, that when an artist created images he was usurping God's prerogative to infuse creatures with life, with a counterargument. His

Part of the Panch Mahal, a summer palace in the abandoned city of Fathpur Sikri; second half of the 16th century

answer was calculated to silence the divines but it also indicates his mystical approach to religion. According to his friend and chronicler Abul Fazl, he stated that the very fact the artist could create likenesses of mortal creatures but not give them life made him all the more aware of God's omnipotence.

Akbar's studio was set up under the guidance of two 16th-century Persian artists, Mir Sayyid Ali and Khwaja Abd al-Samad, persuaded by Akbar's father, Humayun, to emigrate to India. This event marked the beginning of a steady flow of Muslim artists from Persia and neighboring countries to the Mughal court where they knew they were welcome. In setting up his studio Akbar naturally chose the Persian school with which he was familiar. Book illustrations, which emerged in the 13th century in Iran, owed many of their motifs, such as cloud forms or rocks and other landscape elements, to the art of China, although Persian artists had reduced the atmospheric idiom of Chinese art to charming patterns of lines and colors. Akbar, who had been taught to paint by Abd al-Samad, personally supervised the painters who were recruited in large numbers to illustrate the enormous collection of manuscripts inherited by the Emperor. There is a touching picture by the Persian master showing young Akbar offering his own work to Humayun.

The first great project was undertaken in the 1580s to relate the romantic tales of Amir Hamza, an uncle of the Prophet, in 1,700 large-sized (at least for Persian book illustration) paintings on cotton. But for a chance discovery, these works of considerable historical importance, some of them masterpieces, would have been irretrievably lost. Today 200 remain in various European museums (two main collections are those of the Österreichisches Museum für Angewandte Kunst, Vienna, and the Victoria and Albert Museum, London). It is hardly surprising that Akbar's ignorance of Indian art made him import Persian style into India; what is astonishing is the rapidity with which Mughal art cut its Persian umbilical cord and stood on its own feet. As with the architects, the majority of the painters were Indian, some definitely known to be Gujarati, who brought their own traditions with them. Indeed the unique feature of Mughal art is the happy confluence of three pictorial traditions, Persian, Indian, and as we shall see later, European.

In the *Hamza-nama* the main compositional elements are Persian, like the so-called aerial perspective, ideally suited for historical and dramatic subjects as it gave a panoramic view of the scene depicted. Another feature is the dazzling combination of pure colors in decorative patterns. These two elements

Gujarati girls drawing water from a well: a detail from a painting in the Hamza-nama; 1580s. Victoria and Albert Museum, London

been alien to the ordered sensibility of the Safavid artist. Significantly, the Indian preference for naturalism was shared by Akbar, who increasingly turned away from the pure Persian idiom because he needed a form of art to record faithfully the immensely eventful life at the court. This preference is revealed in Mughal appreciation of European art as well as in Abul-Fazl's statement that in art "even inanimate objects look as if they had life". Thus in *Hamza* we have dazzling Persian details in tiled architecture or richly patterned carpets set against men and women in violent combat with men or with supernatural beings. The realism and immediacy of the pictures is enhanced by the device of cutting off foreground figures, giving a snapshot impression of the scene. On balance, there is some loss of the abstract charm of Safavid painting; the gain is in terms of powerful drawing, fiery colors, and expressive figures which from now on are to be psychologically related.

A conqueror himself, Akbar took great delight in scenes from epics and histories. He was the first Muslim ruler to take an interest in Hindu literature. What is revealing is that when he had the great epic *Mahabharata* (finally edited in the 2nd century AD) translated into Persian, the title given was *Razm-nama* or the *Book of Wars*; this interest is clear from the 179 paintings, the majority of which deal with scenes of war and other violent activities. The frenzied actions, the great ability to show movement, the violent colors, and very complex compositions in which many figures are engaged in mortal struggle are most compelling in their peculiar expressionist, even obsessive manner. The movement, the violent clash, of colors and feverish activity in paintings of Akbar's reign have often been attributed solely to Akbar's dynamic personality, much as Jahangir's introverted nature has been seen in the restrained, delicate pictures of his period. It is no doubt true that Akbar's close personal scrutiny and active interest had much to do with the rapid progress of Mughal art. Indeed the extraordinary rapport between the emperors and their artists is rare in the history of art. But the important role of the painters and their personalities should not be underestimated, however little we may know of their specific contributions.

Although the *Razm-nama* paintings are collaborations in typical Akbari fashion, the early ones, especially 30 of them, include the signature of a tormented genius, Daswanth (*c*1550–*ob.* by 1584), whose talents were discovered early by Akbar himself. Daswanth became a legendary figure in his lifetime but his melancholic spirit eventually made him take his own life at an early age. His expressionist brush which could not be contained within the bounds of balanced pictorial composition must have had a profound effect on his contemporaries.

With Daswanth's death *c*1584 the Dionysiac element in Mughal painting gave way to the Apollonian, under the influence of the other major painter of the period, Basawan.

seem to have liberated Indian artists from a limited range of colors seen in Gujarati painting, and contributed to the development of a pictorial tradition of epic and historical narratives. But *Hamza* paintings are far removed from the delicate, magic world of decorative patterns in Persian art. The Indian artist's preference for naturalism breaks through in revealing details, like the Gujarati girls drawing water from the well in the top right-hand corner of the painting depicting the giant Zummurad (Victoria and Albert Museum, London).

The Gujarati element may also be seen in an early work of the leading painter Basawan (1556–1605) in the Cleveland *Tuti nama*, dating from this period (Cleveland Museum of Art). Naturalistic details of familiar animals rendered with loving care in *Hamza* are also more characteristically Indian. But above all, there is an important departure from the Persian tradition in the use of many figures engaged in dramatic and violent action, the very actuality of which would have

Right: A scene from the Akbar-nama, a cheetah hunt; 1590.
Victoria and Albert Museum, London

کوی چنکه از زبان هند اوردی گویند بطرز خاص کشیده ند و چند غلاده چیته انجا سکار کرده موکب اقبال بجانب دیدیه

مشرف ساختند اگرچه دربوده علی پیش ازینه بسیار جمع آمده بود اما که نخیته را بحضور اقدس رسیده فرمودند

درین مرتبه روز پازده هم آذر ماه الهی موافق شنبه چهارم شهر جمادی الاول بهضد و هشت مثالی دارالملک دلی

مستقر رایات دولت کشت و اردوی بزرگ مشمول بان ساحت دلکشا نزول سعادت فرمود

سرمایه آسایش جهانیان شده بود

Mughal Painting

The 17th century, or more precisely the period from *c*1600 to *c*1660, covering the reigns of the emperors Jahangir (1605–27) and Shah Jahan (1628–58), represents not only the greatest period of Mughal painting but one of the finest achievements in the history of representational art. Jahangir's reign saw great innovations in naturalism built on foundations laid in the previous period. In Shah Jahan's reign the gains in the mastery of representation were further consolidated but did not lead to any major innovations. Undoubtedly the central period of Mughal painting is Jahangir's reign, reflecting an unusually sympathetic interaction between the Emperor's tastes and the artists' personalities, rarely encountered in art patronage. Active encouragement of painting by Jahangir, who gave it priority over the administration of the state, helped take this art to great heights—a central event in the life of the court was the weekly inspection of completed paintings.

▲ *Officers and Wise Man* by Payag. Sterling and Francine Clark Art Institute, Williamstown

▼ *The Presentation of the Book* by Abul Hasan. The Walters Art Gallery, Baltimore

► *Hindu Holy Men*, a yogi scene by Govardhan; *c*1626–30. Williams Hayes Fogg Art Museum, Cambridge, Mass.

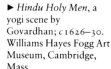

▶ *The Young Hawk and the Hunt:* an illustrated album leaf by Aqa Riza; 23×14cm (9×5½in). British Library, London

◀ *King Vulture and Griffin* by Mansur; color and gilt on paper; 39×26cm (15×10in). Metropolitan Museum, New York

Seventeenth-century Mughal painting is dominated by twin pulls, between the formal color and linear arrangements of Persian art and the new requirements of representational art at the court, whose ultimate source was European prints. The nucleus of Jahangir style is the series done in Allahabad in the 1590s when the rebel prince set up his capital there. The studio was led by Aqa Riza who preferred the Persian idiom, even though interest was shifting to European naturalism and a number of copies of European prints had been produced in this period. European naturalism enabled painters to tell stories more convincingly, introducing, for example, exploration of psychological relationships between figures, as seen in the late Akbar period painting of the dying king, from the *Gulistan* manuscript (The Walters Art Gallery, Baltimore), in which the faces, especially the king's emaciated face, are intensely individual. Secondly, a convincing background is created with natural or architectural details, occasionally ones derived from European prints. Above all, "consistent lighting" is employed, though not always consistently.

The best known Jahangir paintings are portraits, which include some very fine individual portraits as well as group portraits representing court ceremonials, historic and dynastic subjects, and animal studies which often combine acute observation of details and a remarkable perfection of finish, as seen in Mansur's *King Vulture and Griffin*. Less appreciated until recently are the picturesque "genre" scenes, dealing with the life of ordinary people far removed from courtly life, though sometimes scenes from the imperial zenana are also included. Less concerned with high finish, they are in many ways the

most fascinating and rewarding, as they give glimpses of the Mughal artist's powers of observation. Two examples are the detail of a cat from a zenana scene and a striking study of a scribe.

Jahangir's patronage, with his concentration on a limited number of masters, marks a distinct change from the large-scale workshop of Akbar. This led to the abandonment of collaboration among painters and the emergence of individual artists with their specific traits and predilections within a common idiom. One of the finest masters of naturalism is Abul Hasan, who, unlike Manohar with his studied elegance, is keen to explore the effect of light on objects, especially on fabrics. Of special interest is his sympathetic exploration of the individuality of different faces, and the softening of outlines to create more subtle naturalism, as seen in *The Presentation of the Book*. Similar concern is seen in the work of Govardhan, a fascinating and enigmatic personality. His genre scenes, notably with yogis, probe the relationship between lying and seated figures. He is unique in showing a great deal of concern with life outside the court circle. His paintings with their soft modeling of figures

and subtle erotic overtones, reflect a rather unusual sensibility; the subject of naked yogis he was so fond of painting gave him an opportunity to develop the relationship between light and shadow on the surfaces of the figures. Payag, an artist who rose to prominence in the Shah JaNan period, continues this concern for representation in a remarkably ambitious painting, bringing the Mughal art of story-telling to its culmination. In the night scene *Officers and Wise Man*, the figures are seated around a centrally placed candle, cleverly creating a single light source in the picture. His subtle combination of various light and shadow areas in the picture and skilful characterization of figures make him one of the most outstanding artists of Shah Jahan's reign.

PARTHA MITTER

Further reading. Beach, M.C. *The Grand Mogul*, New York (1978). Ettinghausen, R. *Paintings of the Sultans and Emperors of India*, New Delhi (1961). Ettinghausen, R. *Persian and Mughal Art*, London (1976). Ettinghausen, R. *Paintings from the Muslim Courts of India*, London (1976). Welch, S.C. *The Art of Mughal India*, New York (1964).

Abul-Fazl, our invaluable guide in these matters, mentions that some critics preferred him to Daswanth. Basawan was more interested in pictorial composition, in the foreshortening of figures, and in relating several figures to one another as well as to their landscape or architectural setting, such experiments probably prompted by the Mughal discovery of European art. His colors too were subtle and full of tonalities. A court scene from the *Anwar i-Suhayli* (Bharat Kala Bhavan, Benaras) gives us a good idea of the complex arrangement of figures he was particularly fond of. He had a leading role in creating the very fine series of paintings now in the Victoria and Albert Museum, London (*Akbar-nama*); among them "Akbar struggling to contain enraged elephants as courtiers anxiously watch him", captures the scene most vividly. Basawan moved away from the pure color harmonies of the Persian idiom towards consistent chiaroscuro, especially evident in the treatment of the elephants. Yet another style emerges in the work of a different painter, Miskin (late 16th–early 17th centuries), who in his interpretation of the night scene from Jami's *Baharistan* (Bodleian Library, Oxford) has made subtle use of atmospheric light and delicate colors, learnt from European art.

Akbar's concern with accurately documenting the major events in his reign encouraged the growth of the "reporting" style of painting which led to the search for a naturalistic idiom that was new in India; he himself is said to have sat for his likeness. In the 1580s when the Jesuits, keen to convert him, brought presents including Plantin's Polyglot Bible, illustrated with engravings, Akbar and his artists must have eagerly examined the Western prints. Akbar was particularly interested in Christian themes, but his own collection included secular European paintings and engravings, as well as tapestries and even a musical instrument—the organ. Engravings and other forms of art continued to pour in, even during Jahangir's reign (1605–27), notably a miniature by the leading English miniaturist, Isaac Oliver, presented by James I's emissary, Sir Thomas Roe. Dated copies of European works include Kesu's copy of Heemskerck's *St Matthew*, Nadira Banu's copy of Sadeler's *St Jerome*, and the 13-year-old Abul Hasan's fine copy of St John from Dürer's *Crucifixion* (1511). It is difficult to put dates to stages in the absorption of Western pictorial convention; the first period was probably one of wonder and experimentation, leading gradually to more selective borrowings.

European subject matter, motifs, and techniques seem to have appealed to Mughal artists; among these copies two may be chosen for their specially interesting features. A copy of a *Deposition from the Cross* based on a Raimondi print of a lost Raphael, by an unknown artist, is a striking adaptation because of its accomplished handling of colors, close to European Mannerist art. This is probably the work done for Jahangir in 1598 described by the Jesuit Jerome Xavier. A close look at the picture reveals that not only has the artist chosen the tragic theme of Deposition but that he has also filled the background with details from another painting by an

as yet unidentified European painter. In Mughal painting European motifs are often combined in a particular work, sometimes in such a playful manner that to a European it would pose problems of compatibility.

There is another interesting picture showing a mythological figure holding up a dragon-shaped object (formerly S.C. Welch Collection, Cambridge, Mass.); it may well have been based on Botticelli's *Judith with the Head of Holofernes*, only in this case Judith's right arm, instead of holding a sword, is joined to the head on a salver carried by the attendant. These departures do not fail to delight us but the important question is, what permanent gains were made by these artists? Illusionistic art made a deep impression upon them, as it was to do later in Japan. Skilled at the naturalistic rendering of objects, including portraiture, they found European art challenging. The technique of representing consistent lighting through chiaros curo was easily grasped as the Persian mode of formal coloring was gradually abandoned. Foreshortening and the suggestion of distance by making distant objects small compared with the ones in the foreground were also successful adopted. But linear perspective posed the greatest challenge

A Mughal mythological figure that may have been copied from a painting by Botticelli. Location unknown

and continued to do so even in the 18th century. While the quality of Mughal painting was in no way affected by whether perspective was correctly applied or not, it is nonetheless worth pondering why they failed in its application. Although in a number of traditions it was known that distance could be suggested by making distant figures small, linear perspective, specially applied to architecture, based on precise rules governing the recession of objects in space, was a Renaissance invention. Its laws could not be comprehended through copying and Mughal artists had no opportunity to learn the theory behind them.

From the copious documentation of Akbar's reign by Abul Fazl, and because of the importance attached to painters and paintings, we know about the organization of workshops, set up on a large scale with over 100 painters including a woman, Nadira Banu (fl. mid 16th–early 17th century). Three-quarters of the artists were Hindus, who were picked out by Abul-Fazl for special praise. The identification of individual styles in the early period when collaboration was the rule, poses problems for us. Main design, sketch, and later corrections were reserved for major artists. For portraits, thumbnail sketches were kept in stock. Stress was laid on details such as hands, which were drawn with infinite care, an Indian characteristic since the time of Ajanta. Some Mughal painters were born in the royal household and received training at an early age. They were given drawing exercises from pattern books, beginning with simple shapes like spirals and triangles, then graduating to birds, flowers, architectural details, and finally moving on to the human form. Flower drawings were meant to develop their aesthetic sense. The beautiful finish in painting much admired in this period was obtained from careful priming of the paper and smoothing it with agate. Paper, initially imported from Persia, was produced in Sialkot, in Punjab. A drawing was created by transferring to paper a tracing made on deer skin; black chalk was used to correct drawing with red chalk. These stencils, introduced from Persia and imported in fair quantities with color indications, made possible the continued use of Persian design in Mughal art. Brushes were made from the hair of different animals; organic and mineral colors were held together on the paper by means of glue. In the final analysis the quality of work depended a great deal on imagination and talent; a master could transform the mechanical process of tracing into something pulsating with life.

When Jahangir came to the throne (1605) he already possessed a large establishment of painters, including the Persian artist Aqa Riza (fl. late 16th–early 17th centuries); he now inherited Akbar's studio, which consisted of a number of important painters. Basawan trained his son, Manohar (c1565–c1628). Others, like Mansur (fl. late 16th–mid 17th centuries) and Abul Hasan (c1589–c1650), had served their apprenticeships in the Akbar period. From the end of Akbar's reign individual works without accompanying texts, forming parts of albums, began to be assigned to each master. Also noticeable is the quietening down of the bustle and fury of

Hamza and *Razm-nama*; now colors are in low key and related in tonal values. Complex scenes with numerous figures in violent movement are given up in favor of single figures against a plain background.

The major preoccupation of Akbar, epic and history painting, was abandoned; instead, portraits, court scenes, animal and flower paintings were further developed and now became models of ordered simplicity and lyrical understatement. We know artists such as Abul Hasan, Mansur, Bishndas, Manohar, Bichitr, Padarath, and Daulat from their works; we even know what some of them looked like from a sketch by Daulat of five painters, including his self-portrait, and from a self-portrait of Manohar. Jahangir, who was happy to maintain the territorial integrity of the Empire without any further expansion, found particular pleasure in the company of his artists whom he honored in various ways. A man of great culture, learning, and sensibility, a collector and the author of a delightful autobiography, he was above all the foremost creator of the Mughal tradition of connoisseurship and taste for art as well as the criteria for judging styles and the quality of painting. He remarks on his discerning eye in his autobiography:

> my liking for painting and …judging it have arrived at such a point that when any work is brought before me …I say on the spur of the moment that it is the work of such and such a man. And if there be a picture containing many portraits and each be the face of a different master, I can discover which face is the work of each of them.

One of the consequences of the lively appreciation of the Mughal masters by their contemporaries was the rise of the practice of copying well-known masterpieces, which makes the task of distinguishing the real work from the fake rather difficult.

Portrait painting assumed great importance in Jahangir's reign. In the formal portraits of assembled courtiers and the Emperor a curious feature is often noticeable. In a late picture, for example the *Durbar of Jahangir* (c1620; Goloubew Collection, Museum of Fine Arts, Boston), we may find young courtiers mingling happily with ones long since dead. The fact is that these *durbar* scenes were not literal representations of actual events but were meant as records of the personalities of the reign. The likenesses of the subjects, based on stencils kept in stock, are so accurate that we know the rulers and courtiers from the Mughal period very well. But they were considerably stylized, as for instance where Jahangir's dignified mask-like profile is meant to convey the solemnity of the occasion at Diwan-i-Khas in Agra.

Quite opposite in spirit are informal portraits such as the joint portrait by Govardhan of Jahangir and his beloved Nur Jahan, one of the great beauties of the age. One of the finest of this genre is the monarch's son Khuram's portrait in a bright amber dress against a dark emerald background holding a jeweled brooch (Victoria and Albert Museum, London). This is by Jahangir's favorite Abul Hasan who has picked out such details as his personal jewelry and patterns on his scarf and

A durbar scene: Emperor Jahangir (1605–27) receives Prince Parviz.
Victoria and Albert Museum, London

Jahangir Prefers Sufis to Kings by Bichitr; 25 × 18cm (10 × 7in).
Freer Gallery of Art, Washington, D.C.

sash with brilliant effect.

Portraitists served diplomatic purposes as well. Jahangir's second major portrait painter Bishndas was sent with an embassy to depict the likeness of Shah Abbas of Iran and was honored with gifts on his return. Some of the best likenesses of the Persian monarch are by Bishndas in the St Petersburg Album (Hermitage Museum, St Petersburg). Similarly, on receiving from the English ambassador Roe a work by Isaac Oliver, Jahangir presented him with his own portrait by Manohar, which survives only in a print in *Purchas his Pilgrimes*, the famous 17th-century travelogue of the Revd. Samuel Purchas. Jahangir's portraitists such as Abul Hasan developed a special type of symbolic portrait expressing complex iconography and often accompanied with allegorical poems. Of the four in the Freer Gallery of Art, Washington D.C., dealing with Jahangir's imaginary encounters with other rulers, the one by Bichitr called *Jahangir prefers Sufis to Kings* is probably the most striking and complex. Jahangir is shown here sitting on an elaborately carved hourglass with grotesques carved on it symbolizing Time and representing his long life. Little winged cherubs derived from Western art turn away from him in anguish as he spurns worldly kings like the Turkish Sultan and King James I and seeks the company of Sufis or mystics.

Jahangir's autobiography testifies to his great intellectual curiosity. He had agents who scoured home and abroad for exotic people like Siamese twins and bearded ladies. Sometimes his curiosity verged on the bizarre, as when a noble of the realm, Inayat Khan, was dying from an excess of drugs and alcohol—he had a drawing made of the poor emaciated man just before his death. While his caprices need no longer hold our interest, this particular outcome was certainly a hauntingly powerful picture.

Animal painting, begun in the previous period (see the fine works in *Anwar i-Suhayli*, School of Oriental and African Studies, London) now reached new heights. Jahangir's favorite animal recorder, Mansur, made faithful paintings of a large variety of birds and animals, including the exotic zebra and turkey, as well as of hundreds of flowers and plants from Kashmir. Mansur's style is one of studied elegance and great precision, as if he carefully dissected each subject for anatomical accuracy, to be seen for instance in the Chameleon (Royal Library, Windsor) although the Cheer pheasant (Victoria and Albert Museum, London) by him is livelier. Warmth and movement in the depiction of animals is to be seen in a superlative example of Mughal animal art by the portraitist, Abul Hasan. It may seem a paradox that Mansur, famous for his animals, produced the portrait of *The Vina Player* (Edward Croft Murray Collection, London), a very fine ex-

The Taj Mahal at Agra, a mausoleum built by Shah Jahan for his wife. The mausoleum was built between 1632 and 1643 and the surrounding complex finished in 1654

ample of Mughal figure painting, while Abul Hasan, prized by Jahangir for his portraits, produced in the *Squirrels in a Chennar Tree* (India Office Library, London) one of the finest animal paintings, unrivaled except for ones by Chinese artists and Dürer. Another exceptional animal painting is Padarath's *Mountain Sheep* (Chester Beatty Library, Dublin).

Shah Jahan (1628–58), who succeeded Jahangir, is known to us mainly for the Taj Mahal at Agra, built in memory of his wife. His prodigious building activity forms a contrast to Jahangir's almost total indifference to architecture. The personal and intensely passionate intervention of his son is evident in the range and quality of the architecture of the period; the same mastery over architectural material and the art of building is to be seen not only in grand conceptions like the Taj but in exquisite cameos like the Pearl Mosque (Moti Masjid, Agra), with its perfect proportions and refinement of details.

With the Taj Mahal the climax in the art of mausoleum building is reached not only in Mughal architecture but in the whole tradition of Islamic tomb architecture. This mausoleum, consisting of a central structure with a high dome and smaller cupolas and minarets set at the end of ornamental gardens with lotus pools and fountains, is justly famous for its simplicity of conception, symmetry, and lucidity as well as for

From Squirrels in a Chennar Tree by Abul Hasan. India Office Library, London

علی گورهکن

its perfect proportions. Another feature of the Taj, unique and legendary in the history of architecture, is the very special quality of Markrana marble which changes its delicate shades in response to the atmospheric light from the rose of the Indian dawn to the pristine white of a moonlit summer night in Agra. But the Taj is no less exquisite in the details of its perforated screen and *pietra dura* work.

Among small objects of great beauty is the jade winecup belonging to Shah Jahan (1657; Victoria and Albert Museum, London). Painting, however, continued to be important in his reign. History painting was revived, some of the finest examples of which are in the *Shah Jahan-nama* (Royal Library, Windsor). Formal group portraits showing many courtiers increased in number, ranging from stiff, unimaginative hackwork to items of ingenuity and imagination. The main innovation of the period was the equestrian portrait, to be widely adopted by provincial rulers all over India within a short time. The painting by Govardhan of Shah Jahan and his favorite son, Dara, a great patron of Hindu philosophy (Victoria and Albert Museum, London), shows the mastery over line and shading achieved by Mughal artists as well as the subtle range of tones used in the work. Equestrian portraits and other forms of Mughal art of the Jahangir and Shah Jahan periods made their way into Rembrandt's collection. His delicate sketches after Mughal art, which show his own mastery of expression without destroying the essential nature of Indian works, form a fascinating chapter in the history of cultural borrowings.

With the accession of the orthodox Aurangzeb (1658–1707), painting and other arts ceased to be of importance at the court. As tradition has it, his musicians in a symbolic gesture of protest buried their instruments in the earth. This act apparently left the Emperor unmoved. In this atmosphere, painting naturally suffered. After him, increasing disintegration of the Empire led his successors to withdraw into their harems, where they continued to support an intensely romantic and gently erotic school of painting with misty landscapes, atmospheric colors, and pretty women. Gradually artists began to seek employment elsewhere while popular painters began a veritable industry of copying masterpieces.

Schools of painting flourished in the Muslim courts of Ahmadnagar, Golconda, and Bijapur from the 16th century onwards, independent of and parallel to the Mughal atelier, their independence symbolizing the resistance of these courts to the might of the Emperor in the north. The influence of the Safavid School of Persia came through trade contacts and marriage alliances: it can be seen in the landscape in the *Tarif i-Husayn Shahi* album painted for the Ahmadnagar ruler, Husayn Nizam Shah I (Bharata Itihasha Samshodaka Mandala Collection, Poona). The affluence of Golconda, partly owing to the newly discovered diamond mines, is reflected in the lavish jewelry worn by the subjects portrayed as well as in the generous use of gold.

From Golconda comes one of the most remarkable paintings, until recently wrongly identified as Mughal: Muhammad Ali's *The Poet in the Garden* (Museum of Fine Arts, Boston), which shows a great delicacy of drawing and colors. The best-known Deccani paintings are of course the portraits of Bijapur sultans and courtiers with their fully rounded forms and flowing transparent skirts. One of the most striking examples of this style is the portrait of a courtier whose powerful frame and expression is underlined by the deliberately low-key background relieved only by two bright yellow flying birds, a style that makes an interesting contrast with Mughal portraits. These important schools declined *c*1627, partly because the three kingdoms were gradually absorbed in the Mughal Empire.

With the decline of the Mughal Empire the center of gravity for painting shifts to the hills of Rajasthan and Punjab, although inferior works continued to flow from the metropoli-

A Deccan school miniature of a Bijapur courtier. British Museum, London

Left: Shah Jahan and his son Dara by Govardhan.
Victoria and Albert Museum, London

tan centers of Agra and Delhi. The Rajputs, including the fiercely independent rulers of Mewar, the chief of the Rajput clans, had ceased to resist the Mughals during Jahangir's reign. Mewar chiefs built a new capital on the beautiful Pichola lake when Chitor had to be abandoned after its sack by Akbar. The Rajputs who took office under the Mughals were obviously impressed by the naturalistic achievements of the Mughal artists; there exists a picture of the Rana of Mewar with Shah Jahan in Mughal style. From the Mughals these princes learned to appreciate portraits and every Rajput court from the tiniest to the most exalted had its portraitist for whom the rulers eagerly posed. Frequently they are represented on horseback or, for instance, out hunting wild boars in the green Aravalli hills dotted with shrubs, a passion they shared with the Mughal emperors.

As the Mughal tradition receded, however, the portraits increasingly concentrated on formal harmonies of color and line, even though attention continued to be given to the accurate likeness of the sitter. In fact the Mughal formulas of profile portraits were adapted to Rajput purposes. But while Rajput princes happily adopted Mughal costume, etiquette, and pastimes, they nonetheless never forgot they belonged to a very different tradition. Neither had the old tradition of painting exemplified by the *Chaurapanchasika* series been totally forgotten. As we shall see, it makes its appearance again in the 17th century in Mewar.

But to understand the subjects chosen by artists for the Rajput courts we must examine the deep undercurrent of mystical romanticism that flowed through the whole of India from the 10th century onwards, a form of mysticism that refused to draw the line between sacred and profane love and expressed itself through the divine love of Radha and Krishna, the love of God for the human soul. The change is seen clearly in literature: the aristocratic elegance of Kalidasa's Sanskrit was meant for the aristocratic literati, for courtly Sanskrit was not accessible to everyone. The new literature was addressed directly to the common man in the vernacular, the language he could understand. A number of religious leaders like Ramanuja (*ob.* 1137), Ramananda (*c*1370–1440), and Chaitanya (*c*1485–1533) were largely responsible for these changes. From the early centuries of the Christian era older forms of Hinduism had already been challenged by the new *Bhakti* movement, which sought a direct covenant between the devotee and his transcendental God. The Krishna of the *Bhagavad-Gita* was the perfect example of this. *Bhakti* movements swept right across India over a number of centuries and gave rise to major religious leaders and reformers, who sought to reach all people across the caste barriers. There were various different forms of *Bhakti* cults, both Shaiva and Vaishnava, but the most powerful impulse came from the myths relating to Krishna and Radha and their love for each other.

The earliest of the poets to celebrate this love were Jayadeva (12th century), Chandidasa, and Vidyapati (both in the 14th century) in the remote eastern corner of India, but their songs were heard several thousands of miles away in Rajasthan soon

after. Secular literature mirrored this new development in mystical love poetry as well as its creation of literary conventions to describe the different phases of Radha's beauty from youth to maturity and the different states of her emotions on which poets like Chandidasa loved to dwell. These conventions of emotional states crystalized into two main kinds, love in separation and love in union, both providing inspiration for Rajput artists (as well as the literary divisions of heroines and heroes into different kinds according to their emotional state). The intensely romantic Rajput society had parallels with the chivalric tradition of the feudal society of medieval Europe. In a society bound by the rules of fidelity in marriage the extramarital love of the divine pair offered an ideal surrogate. The very ambiguities of a make-believe world in which the ruler and his beloved dressed up as Krishna and Radha with genuine mystical emotion inspired artists to treat the theme on different levels.

Here we must also raise the question why monumental sculpture was replaced in this period by painting. Earlier gods, like Shiva or Vishnu as in the cosmic image of the Boar in Udaygiri, were meant to awe the worshiper with their transcendental quality. The intention of the sculptor was to create a distance between man and god. On the other hand the Krishna of the later *Bhakti* movement was intensely human, a god whose human beauty, colorful dress, and blue-green peacock feathers could only be captured in painting. A further element entered these romantic traditions of painting. To the dictum *ut pictura poesis* should be added music. Paintings based on *ragas* and *raginis* or personifications of modes in Indian music were first seen in Jain texts, and became an important genre of expression in Rajasthan and Hill states, although Ragamala paintings are also to be found in the Deccan. In general certain conventions became popular for depicting the *ragas* and *raginis*; their iconography was, however, by no means fixed. The modes were rather points of departure which the artist used freely to make his own imaginative contribution.

There exists an early painting of the Dipak *raga* (1605) by a Muslim painter Nisaradi from Mewar, whose direct antecedent is the *Chaurapanchasika* style, although here the colors are mellower and the composition more complex. The interesting new element, which suggests Mughal contact, is the arrangement of the bottles in the niches on the wall, a feature first seen in early Mughal works such as the *Tutinama* (Cleveland Museum of Art). On the other hand the men and women here are derived from pre-Mughal western Indian art. The Lalita *ragini* painted by another 17th-century Muslim painter, Sahibdin, in 1628, in the period when the ruler of Mewar had already joined the Mughal court for some years, shows even greater Mughal contact though the picture is conventionally divided into sections by means of an open pavilion. The lover who leaves in disappointment because the lady is offended and feigns sleep is in Mughal costume, with a transparent skirt over his trousers.

Sahibdin, a remarkable artist of the period, illustrated sec-

A forest landscape from the Ramayana illustrated by the school of Sahibdin; late 17th century. British Museum, London

tions of the *Ramayana*, the *Sukar Kshetra Mahatmya*, and *Bhagavata Purana*, dealing with Krishna's life, between 1648 and 1656. These is a striking picture in the British Museum, London, from the *Ramayana* done by the school of Sahibdin which depicts a forest landscape; its most notable feature is the whole range of flowering trees, painted with great care and imagination. For us Mewar is especially interesting because we can trace the evolution of its style on the basis of dated paintings, from the *Chaurapanchasika* type to the ones done under Mughal influence. But in the final analysis it was not so much the Mughal idiom absorbing the local tradition as adding a new dimension to the old themes and manners of painting.

From the many different courts, three may be selected for their special interest. To the state of Bundi is attributed a remarkably delicate *Bhagavata Purana* (1640)—the style is a transition from *Chaurapanchasika* figures to one of graceful naturalism and gentle blend of colors. The story depicted is about the child Krishna who subdues the gigantic serpent Kaliya. Mughal influence is evident in the group of musicians in the Akbari style as well as in the ubiquitous theme of bottles in wall niches. But Bundi is more famous for the so-called "white" paintings, mainly from the 18th century, representing a new ideal of small-breasted feminine beauty, showing women with high foreheads, hair brushed back, reminding us of 15th-century Flemish paintings. It is interesting that during the height of Mughal art neither the nude nor the beauty of women ever constituted an important subject for the artists. In the Rajput courts, however, the perennial Indian concern for feminine beauty returns with renewed vigor and produces several memorable versions of loveliness. A very fine Bundi work is *Lady Yearning for Her Lover* in which the semidraped figure of the woman and her attendant dominate a delicate warm gray, almost totally bare background (John Kenneth Galbraith Collection, Cambridge, Mass.).

The ruler Ummed Singh (1771–1819) of the neighboring state of Kotah was obsessively interested in lion and tiger hunts and his painters recorded this passion with great faithfulness. A fine example is *Raja Guman Chand Shooting Tigers* (Victoria and Albert Museum, London) where the painter has woven a fantasy world bathed in the light of the moon, reflected in the rich growth of shrubs, trees, and smooth rocks—a perfect poetic image of a tropical jungle, not familiar enough to encourage confidence, yet not too strange to be repellent.

In Kishangarh, set in the midst of an idyllic country of mountains and lakes, one of the finest developments of art based on the legend of Krishna and Radha takes place. This happened when Raja Sawant Singh (1748–57) during his brief rule in Kishangarh persuaded a highly gifted artist, Nihal Chand, to work for him. The life of this ruler, himself a gifted poet, painter, and a devotee of Krishna, reads like a romantic story, especially in his love for the musician, Bani Thani. Their love was celebrated in Nihal Chand's works in the 18th century as the earthly form of love of Radha and Krishna. Nihal Chand, whose portrait we possess, introduced a new ideal of a beautiful woman, possibly based on Bani Thani, with curved eyes, arched eyebrows, sharp nose, pointed chin, and enigmatic smile. Paintings of exquisite mannerism and delicate range of colors mark this school.

Painting made further progress in the so-called Hill states (Pahari), lying in the foothills of the Himalayas and deep in the valleys of Jammu, Kangra, and Kulu, some of the most breathtakingly beautiful parts of India. Their very seclusion protected these small princes from the devastations taking place in the north Indian plains and enabled them to create a cloistered, self-contained fairy-tale world in the 17th and 18th centuries—a world where men were eternally elegant and women eternally enchanting, poised, aristocratic, and remote.

Much of the life of these princes and princesses was recaptured in paintings from these areas. Two most important schools are the somewhat earlier Basohli and the later Guler-Kangra. The first phase of Basohli is represented by paintings based on Bhanudatta's *Chittarasamanjari*, a text which deals with various kinds of lovers and different states of love. Produced in Kirpal Pal's reign (1678–95), the unknown artist makes clever use of red and orange and of open pavilions in the *Chaurapanchasika* tradition, but he has also chosen to represent carpets in great detail. There is one among the series called *Secretly Belonging to Another* (Victoria and Albert Museum, London), representing an unfaithful wife who blames her love-bruises on the cat seen on the upper floor. The cat-and-mouse game represented by the artist echoes the dangers she faces in taking a lover. Details in the picture such as the red petticoat under a blue transparent skirt are very carefully drawn. In this period beetle wings were employed to produce certain brilliant greens.

The 18th-century artist Manaku, who did a series of paintings on Jayadeva's poem about the love of Radha and Krishna, belonged to a talented family of artists who were employed in different Pahari courts. His father Pandit Seu, originally from Kashmir, had settled in Guler, which already had a flourishing school of painting. Manaku's early style showed the influence of the Basohli tradition, but it began to change under the influence of his brother Nainsukh (*c*1725–*c*1790), who was undoubtedly one of the finest painters in this period and was responsible for introducing elements from Mughal naturalism in the hills. It is not known how Nainsukh received training in

The miniature from the series Secretly Belonging to Another; late 17th century. Victoria and Albert Museum, London

the Mughal idiom but his accurate portraits, his composition and arrangement of different figures, and his colors and drawing all show an intimate knowledge of the techniques perfected by Mughal artists, especially those associated with the Emperor Muhammad Shah (1719–48). Nainsukh took employment under Balwant Singh, whose career he recorded with great fidelity. His works of this period, including a self-portrait, are characterized by elegant naturalism and penetrating psychological studies of his subjects. While they were affected by Mughal art, their individual style could not for a moment be mistaken for that of Mughal works. After his patron's death he was invited to join the household of the Basohli ruler, Amrit Pal (1757–76), where his brother Manaku was already employed. This important event marks a radical change in the painting of Basohli, from mannered paintings of pure warm colors to a new lyrical and graceful naturalism. Today the painting of the Hill courts is known chiefly for the graceful naturalism whose best-known example is Kangra art.

The Radha-Krishna cult was important not only in the art of the Hills but in its culture, for it was very much a deeply felt, living religious tradition. But as Hindus, whose religious approach was essentially syncretic, the Hill rulers were also worshipers of Shiva and Shakti. These deities are therefore represented in art in great profusion. There is a very powerful picture of Kali with her nocturnal and chthonic attendants from the small state of Chamba.

Pahari rulers, like the Rajputs, sat frequently for their portraits; among a whole variety of portraits, one may be chosen as a particularly fine example of the genre. For sheer formal harmonies the portrait of Raja Ajmat Dev of Mankot (Victoria and Albert Museum, London) is unsurpassed in the careful arrangement and interrelation of each shape and color. At the same time it is not entirely a formal exercise, for the subject is very much a living person who sits smoking his *hookah*. The artist has been able to capture the elegance and culture of these small courts with rare economy.

However interesting these works may be, the major concerns of the painters are still the subjects of love, divine and secular, and beautiful women in various activities and guises. It is in Kangra ruled by Sansar Chand (1775–1823) that we find the last magnificent vision of feminine beauty in Indian art; Kangra comes to mind first when we think of this type of ideal, but it was shared by artists in all the courts in the late 18th and early 19th centuries. Unlike the women of Basohli or even Kishangarh, those of Kangra are a delicate balance between the ideal and the real; their limpid dark eyes, delicate noses, aristocratic features, and elegant figures make them entirely convincing as real, desirable women. They are the result of synthesis between Mughal naturalism and the Indian artist's search for ideal feminine beauty whose roots go back to the *Yakshis* of Sanchi. We do not know who created this image in the Pahari region, but it had a very powerful influence and was so widely copied that today the Kangra type of beauty suffers from overexposure.

Even if today we fail, rightly, to be moved by the unimaginative reproductions of this kind of art, we must not underestimate the value of the original impulse. Sansar Chand's great interest in art and his enormous collection of paintings are mentioned by contemporary European visitors to his court. It was the happy combination of his unusual interest in painting and the presence of a number of talented painters in the region that created the intensely vital art movement in Kangra which lasted until Sansar Chand himself fell from power. Among his artists were the descendants of Nainsukh and Manaku, namely Khusala, Fattu, and Gaudhu (all active in the late 18th and early 19th centuries), suggesting the continued participation of this talented family in the development of Pahari art. To give a final instance of this exceptionally productive period there is a beautiful example of Kangra art dating from the 1780s, *Radha sees Krishna with the Cow-girls* (Bharat Kala Bhavan, Benaras), which epitomizes the whole period in its evocation of spring with red, pink, white, and yellow flowers, birds, mango trees, and above all, in the celebration of the beauty of the two women, Radha and her girl friend.

Westernization. As patronage began to dry up in princely courts because of political upheavals which began to affect even the remote areas, artists faced the problem of making a living; some began to find work elsewhere, especially with the English employees of the East India Company. The centers of what might be called the Company Style were Murshidabad, Patna, and Lucknow; the artists made conscious attempts to modify their own tradition in view of the demand for naturalism by the English and even received suggestions about perspective and other conventions. There are many natural history drawings in the India Office Library done by Indian artists for the English. (An Indian artist did sketches for Sir Charles Malet when he visited Ellora in the late 18th century.) There are instances of artists dealing with scenes from contemporary life, both European and Indian. There was also a very interesting and flourishing tradition of bazaar paintings at Kalighat in Calcutta, which produced some lively and often amusing accounts of daily life among the Sahibs and the natives. This situation continued until the middle of the 19th century when new art movements followed the westernization of the rising elite and the growth of national political consciousness.

The profession of artists in India, as in Europe before the Renaissance, was not a socially exalted one. Therefore the initial impact of Western ideas among the elite was restricted to literature and did not include the visual arts. When Western academic art became the medium of instruction for artists, the traditional artist classes did not have much share in it; from now on art became the prerogative of the educated. Both European architecture and painting had begun to spread in India from the late 18th century. The trend of neoclassical architecture set by the East India Company was taken over by English residents and then by Indians, as country villas of affluent Bengalis with classical facades sprang up everywhere in Bengal. Portraits in oils were commissioned by Indian aristocrats from itinerant European artists.

The first Indian artist who saw great possibilities in using western techniques to represent a realistic scene was Ravi Varma, *fl.* 1874–1905. His fame soon spread all over India, helped by the issue of cheap prints of his oils. Ravi Varma's paintings, based mainly on ancient literature of India, suffered from a self-conscious manner common to 19th-century academic history painting in Europe; his heroines had the air of well-brought-up young ladies taking part in an amateur theatrical production. Actual art schools of the English kind were set up in India in an entirely separate context in the 1850s, to train artisans. Industrial revolution, it was generally recognized, had caused serious damage to traditional industries in India as it had done in the West. The present art schools in Britain owe their origin to the need felt to teach artisans the correct principles of design in the aftermath of the Great Exhibition of 1851. This idea was extended to India but without any significant result.

Meanwhile as the 19th century came to a close, after more than 50 years of westernization which had helped India to enter the modern age, the search for cultural identity began. This was a period of immense intellectual ferment in the major cities, especially Calcutta, epitomized by the universal genius of the poet Rabindranath Tagore (1861–1941), who gathered around him the rising groups of Bengali intellectuals.

The Calcutta Art School, in existence since 1854, had been concerned with imparting English academic art education which included the study of Classical antiques and the nude. At this point a committed artist, E.B. Havell (1861–1934), arrived as the head of the Calcutta Art School. Havell, like several other famous English men and women who had adopted Indian culture as their own, had a crucial role to play in the future development of art in India. A meeting between him and Abanindranath (1871–1951), Tagore's nephew, whom he subsequently inspired, led to the founding of a national style of art, the Bengal School. Discarding drawing from the antique as well as from life in the Western manner, Abanindranath sought to derive his style from a combination of styles that did not imitate nature, notably Mughal and Far Eastern art. The Bengal School represented the reaction to Ravi Varma's westernization and the search for cultural roots, and yet Abanindranath's own work suffered from his early training in Western academic art and excessive eclecticism. But his role was that of teacher and inspirer rather than a major creative force, and he certainly inspired a whole new influential group of painters, soon to spread to different parts of India—notably Nandalal Bose (1882–1966), the Ukil brothers (born c1900), Deviprasad Roychaudhury (1899–1975), and Abdur Rahman Chughtai (born 1899). Deviprasad became a powerful figurative sculptor. Chughtai applied the "archaeological" style of the Bengal School to his own Islamic and Persian heritage and created a mannered style full of erotic overtones and languid Beardsleyesque lines.

Reactions against the Bengal School came with the news of the achievements of modern European artists, who had similarly revolted against Renaissance naturalism. In 1922 an important exhibition of modern artists took place in Calcutta, which included works by Klee and Kandinsky. Even in Abanindranath's family two people disagreed with him. His brother Gaganendranath (1867–1938) found that decorative elements of synthetic Cubism provided him with the means of realizing his own visions of fantasy landscapes and interiors, some of which are delightful in their delicate color combinations. Abanindranath's uncle, the great Tagore, took up painting in 1928 when he was 67 years old. A catalyst in his case was probably Freud, but it was Klee's *jeux d'esprit* that struck a sympathetic chord in Tagore. His art began in the form of doodles and patterns made out of part of the writing he crossed out, and had the character of ink blots used in Rorschach tests.

Another artist, Amrita Sher-Gil (1913–41), who spent her early years in Europe and had been trained in France, evolved a style balanced between formal simplification and naturalistic treatment of figures, reminiscent of Gauguin. The simplicity and dignity of her peasant studies are very moving. George Keyt (born 1901), a Sri Lankan, had close emotional ties with India and translated from Sanskrit poetry. He recaptured the ancient Indian ideals of voluptuous womanhood and tender eroticism, paradoxically through the idiom of Cubism. But it is significant that he chose the decorative qualities of synthetic Cubism rather than the austere fragmentation of the analytical period. In fact the solid volumes of his women are distinctly reminiscent of Léger's tubular women.

The dialectic between tradition and modernity in the form of international contemporary styles is the problem that still faces the Indian painter. It was given the most compelling solution by probably the only genius of this period, Jamini Roy (1887–1974). He went through the usual phases of academic painting in Calcutta Art School as well as a revivalist Bengal School period, but a profound spiritual crisis led him to seek expression in the popular and folk art of Bengal. He created powerful images of the primitive Santals, containing radical simplifications and touches of tender eroticism. His later phase became more austere and included some moving interpretations of the life of Christ—seen as a spiritual hero in the eyes of a Hindu artist. Gradually coming to accept that art should be within the reach of ordinary people, he set up his workshop with pupils and assistants, producing collaborations with his assistants and denying that art should be concerned with individual expression.

Kashmir, Nepal, Tibet, Sri Lanka. Among the immediate neighbors of India belonging within its cultural sphere, Kashmir's greatest period was *c*600 to 1350, when fine works of art and architecture were produced as well as the great historical treatise *Rajatarangini*. In the fluted columns and tympana with triangular pediments enclosing trefoil arches, belonging to the *stupas* of Parihasapura, the echoes of Classical art through the mediation of Gandhara are evident. These elements and other stylistic features from the Gupta period were

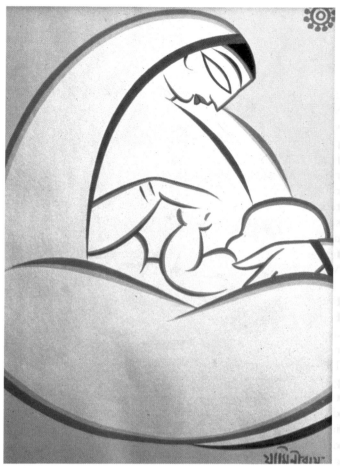

Mother and Child by Jamini Roy (1887–1974)

A Buddhist stupa with added eyes near Katmandu, Nepal

carried over to Hindu temples as exemplified by the famous
Sun temple of Martand, set impressively in the midst of a
valley on a high plinth with double pyramidal roof and with
porticoes that allowed solar rites. The sloping roofs and projecting gables of the small Shiva temple at Pandrenthan, on the
other hand, remind us of European buildings mainly because
of the adaptation of the roof to the cold climate. The "lantern" ceilings of Kashmir temples made up of overlapping
squares are another interesting architectural feature of the
area. Sculpture too shows Gandharan elements; bronze
figures and stone pieces such as the fine tricephalic 9th-century
Vishnu from Avantipura are worthy of note.

Nepalese architecture, which employs much wood and
brick and provides carvings and paintings on its walls, had
been praised by ancient Chinese pilgrims. In Nepal, as in other
areas outside India proper, the umbrellas assumed increasing
architectural importance in the *stupas*. A unique feature in
Nepal was the introduction of two eyes on the *stupa* to suggest that it represented the cosmic man—a feature extended to
the great Hindu temple of Pashupatinatha (Shiva) at Katmandu. The well-known bronze and brass sculpture and the painting tradition of Nepal represent a vigorous and imaginative
development of the style and iconography of Pala Vajrayana
art. In the Museum of Fine Arts, Boston, an early masterpiece
of the 12th century, showing Buddha surrounded by the *mandala* of eight great Bodhisattvas and deities of the Vajrayana
pantheon, is characterized by sensitive drawing and great delicacy of colors. The same Museum contains a gilt copper figure
of a ten-armed cosmic (Vishvarupa) image of Vishnu.

In Tibet, as in Nepal, Buddhism was introduced by monks
from the Pala kingdom but here it was superimposed on existing shamanistic cults. Situated on cultural crossroads, Tibet's
art absorbed elements from two great traditions, Chinese and
Indian. *Stupas* (*chorten*) here take the form of a square base
with bulbous middle part—a form that occurs over an area
extending to Java. The type of architecture, however, that we
immediately associate with Tibet is the fortress-monastery
such as the Potala at Lhasa built of sun-dried bricks, whose
doors and windows become somewhat smaller at upper levels.
Sculptures include gilded bronze figures from the Vajrayana
pantheon. Wall-paintings include the famous 10th-century
works in the Tung Huang area but the best known Tibetan
paintings in the West, for example those in the Victoria and
Albert Museum, London, are the sacred banners (*tankas*)
which represent *tantric* cults through erotic imagery and an
esoteric language of pictorial forms. Elements like landscape
background owe much to China while in general the colors
are pure and glittering in their undiluted brightness.

Sri Lanka's history begins with Ashoka's conversion of King
Tissa (247–207 BC); the history is scarred with successive
Tamil invasions which led to the abandonment of once flour-
ishing capitals, Anuradhapura and Pollonaruva. Sri Lanka

The statue of Parakrama Vahu I wielding the yoke of administration,
at Pollonaruva, Sri Lanka; late 12th century AD.

which remained Theravadin (*Hinayana*), produced some very important examples of Buddhist art. A typical early example of early Buddhist architecture, the well-documented brick-work *dagoba* (*stupa*) of Ruanveli, whose base, drum, and mast are precisely proportioned, lays special importance on the ringed spire of seven umbrellas, an important departure from the early practices in Sanchi and elsewhere. Its impressive height is in accord with the enormous square base with four outer altars. Begun in Dutta Gamani's reign, the relic in this *stupa* rests in a chamber which has access from the outside. While there are a number of striking colossal Buddhas here, it is the great image of Dutta Gamani that impresses us with its austere grandeur. The simplicity and almost archaic power of these colossal figures as well as other sculptures in Sri Lanka owe as much to Theravada doctrine as to the character of the massive boulders from which these images are carved.

It is with the reign of Parakrama Vahu I (AD 1164–97) that we associate the architecture of Pollonaruva. The seven-storied Sat Mahal Pasada, the temple containing the tooth relic with its simple exterior of ashlar masonry broken only by decorative bands, and the famour circular Wata-da-ge shrine with Buddhas facing four directions are the three major buildings. Here the columns used in the Nissanka Lata Mandapeya are designed in the form of lotus with stalk which gives them a most unusual appearance. The colossal sculpture of Parakrama Vahu I wielding the yoke of administration, carved out of a large boulder, is comparable in dignity to the earlier one of Dutta Gamani. The finest wall-paintings in Sri Lanka occur in Sigiriya, the fortress capital of Kassapa I (479–97). The style and treatment of celestial maidens, half-hidden in clouds, owe much to Ajanta but here line takes precedence over tone and color. The composition, colors, and expressive quality of these paintings are also more limited. Examples of South Indian temple tradition and bronze sculpture are associated with the invading Cholas. A fine example of sculpture is the colored brass Pattini Devi (British Museum, London).

Conclusion. The history of Indian art and architecture spans nearly 5,000 years, during which period great and radical changes took place in the form, style, and subject matter of art, and yet there was a coherence and unity underlying these changes, reflecting the specific and recognizable civilization that evolved in this subcontinent. In the ancient period, the mainsprings of art were the two religions, Buddhism and Hinduism, which found dominant expression in sacred monumental architecture and narrative sculpture, notwithstanding the fact that Ajanta represented the highest achievement in painting for the ancient period. In the Islamic period, particularly the Mughal period, the main interest shifted to small-scale paintings, even though there are abundant instances of fine buildings from this age, not to mention the Taj Mahal, acknowledged to be a universal wonder. Interests may change and new forms may replace old ones but there flows through history a clear and unwavering concern with subjects of human interest and a lively curiosity about the minutiae of nature. It is true that Indian interest in nature was never objective to the same extent as Greek empiricism, but it was no less intense. Also, outside the orbit of Greek civilization perhaps no other tradition offered so many variations on the theme of the nude, so many versions of feminine beauty, from the nubile *Yakshis* of Sanchi to the slender princesses of Pahari painting. With the arrival of the British, Indian society underwent a profound change. This also affected art, leading to the spread of a style deriving from European academic art of the 19th century. But even today, when little trace of traditional art remains, the human subject has continued to engage the attention of the artist.

PARTHA MITTER

Bibliography. Archer, W.G. *India and Modern Art*, London (1959). Archer, W.G. *Indian Paintings from the Punjab Hills* (2 vols.), London (1973). Barrett, D. and Gray, B. *Indian Painting*, London (1978). Basham, A.L. *The Wonder that was India*, London (1954). Brown, P. *Indian Architecture*, Bombay (1968). Desai, D. *Erotic Sculpture of India*, New Delhi (1975). Gascoigne, B. *The Great Moghuls*, New York (1971). Getty, A. *The Gods of Northern Buddhism*, Oxford (1914). Hambly, G. *Cities of Mughal India*, New York (1968). Kramrisch, S. *The Art of Nepal*, London (1964). Kramrisch, S. *The Hindu Temple* (2 vols.), Calcutta (1946). O'Flaherty, W.D. *Hindu Myths*, London (1975). Pal, P. *The Arts of Nepal* (pt 1), Leiden (1974). Paranavitana, S. *Art of the Ancient Sinhalese*, Colombo (1971). Parimoo, R. *The Paintings of the Three Tagores*, Baroda (1973). Rao, T.A.G. *Elements of Hindu Iconography* (4 vols.), Delhi (1971). Rowland, B. *The Art and Architecture of India*, London (1953). Singh, M. *Ajanta*, Lausanne (1965). Snelgrove, D. *The Image of the Buddha*, London (1979). Tucci, G. *Tibetan Painted Scrolls* (3 vols.), Rome (1958). Volwahsen, A. *Living Architecture: Indian*, London (1969). Zimmer, H. *The Art of Indian Asia* (2 vols.), Princeton (1955).

16

SOUTHEAST ASIAN ART

A Dong-son lamp-holder from Lach Truong; c 2nd century BC
height 13cm (5in). National Museum, Hanoi (see page 278)

THE countries of Southeast Asia—Vietnam, Laos, Cambodia, Thailand, Burma, Malaysia, Singapore, and the two island republics of Indonesia and the Philippines—have been markedly influenced by their neighboring cultural zones, the Indian subcontinent and China. Yet, to varying degrees, they have also produced their own distinctive art forms, though these have not necessarily been confined within their present political boundaries.

The earliest surviving forms of art, described as Dongsonian after a site in Vietnam, date from the 2nd century BC onwards. Bronze drums, for example, demonstrate something of the nature of one apparently indigenous tradition: a combination of geometric motifs, clearly derived from Eurasiatic connections, and almost naturalistic "drawing". Other items, for example figurines and a 5 in (13 cm) high lamp-holder based on a kneeling figure, from Lach Truong (National Museum, Hanoi), demonstrate an understanding of three-dimensional work.

The typical Dong-son artifact is a single-ended, waisted drum, cast in a bronze alloy with high lead content either in a stone mold or by the *cire perdue* method. On the largest examples the tympanum, usually at least 3 ft (1 m) in diameter,

has concentric rings in linear low relief showing geometric motifs, sequences of birds, animals, or other creatures, and scenes of plumed figures dancing, pounding rice, or playing on mouth organs; others strike gong-chimes or drums of the Dong-son type. The innermost motif is a multi-pointed star which often has stylized faces in the spaces between the points. On the curved section below the tympanum plumed figures, in boats, are often depicted. Similar figures, or dancing warriors, are also to be found in panels on the body. They may carry spears, play musical instruments, or parade with the sort of pediform axes still used in southeast Asia as ritual weapons, especially among the Konyak Naga on the India-Burma border. Some of the drums have three-dimensional frogs mounted on the tympanum. It is suggested in Chinese texts of later date that the drums were used in rainmaking ceremonies.

The Dong-son culture had links with the bronze-using people of Shih-chai-shan, Yunnan. Bronze drums and pediform weapons, as well as certain decorative motifs, are common to both but the Yunnanese sites have yielded much three-dimensional art, including groups of small figures arranged as tableaux on the tympana of the drums. It seems that

The modern countries and main sites of artistic importance of Southeast Asia

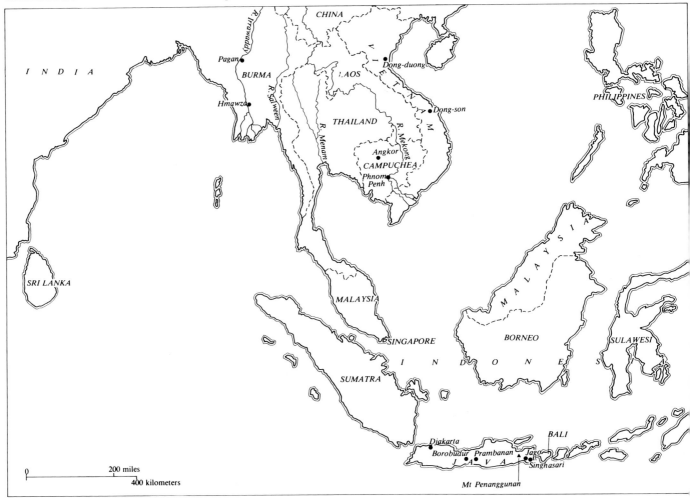

A sacred bronze drum, known as the Moon of Pejeng; height 180cm (71in). Panataran Sasih temple, Pejeng

these contacts date mostly from the Western Han period (206 BC–AD 26) when the Chinese proper were in the process of gaining control of the region.

The Dong-son culture is also found in eastern Southeast Asia, in Malaysia, and in parts of Indonesia, which has produced the largest known bronze drum, the Balinese "Moon of Pejeng" (Pura Panataran Sasih, Pejeng). Six ft (1.8 m) high with a tympanum 5 ft (1.6 m) in diameter, this drum belongs, like other Dong-son drums found in Indonesia, to a late phase of the Dong-son culture, in the early centuries of the Christian era, when traders and pilgrims traveling between the Far East and India began to use maritime routes rather than those by land across central Asia along which journeys were being interrupted by nomadic hordes. From the 1st century AD onwards this seabound traffic led to the development of entrepôts, controlled by local rulers, where Indian goods and, later, Indian ideas began to make an impact upon indigenous cultures.

There is sufficient evidence to prove that goods traveled from one end of Eurasia to the other. A lamp from Pompeii was found at Pong Tuk, Thailand (National Museum, Bangkok). Jewels and amulets from the Roman Orient have been excavated at Go Oc-Eo in the Mekong Delta—a trading complex linked to the interior by a system of canals—and seals and signet rings have also been found there (now in the National Museum, Ho Chi Minh City).

A number of Buddhist images, from the Korat Plateau, the coast of Vietnam, eastern Java, and the island of Sulawesi, have been compared with types from Amaravati in southeast India, Sri Lanka, and Gupta India, but the tendency now is to date them later, after AD 400, though B.-P. Groslier argues for

a considerably earlier date (3rd century AD) for an extremely fine Buddha from Sulawesi (Museum Pusat, Djakarta). Another splendid example comes from Dong-duong in Vietnam, which later became a major Buddhist center (National Museum, Hanoi). Clearly of northern Indian inspiration it may have been the model for images found in the interior of mainland Southeast Asia. Its date is certainly later and it may have been manufactured locally.

But for the most part, all we know of the first stages of Indian influences in Southeast Asia comes from Chinese accounts of the region. They mention the kingdoms of Funan (possibly a version of the modern Khmer *phnom*, "mountain") and Lin-i, in the Mekong Delta and central Vietnam respectively, and another in west Java. The texts also mention temples and images but these have not yet been located.

It is from the final period of Funan (AD 200?–560) and its successor, Chen-la (560–700) that the earliest statuary and shrines come: they are linked with a Vaishnavite ruler, Rudravarman (AD 514–?39). Terracotta heads framed by false windows are known from Nui Sam in Vietnam (National Museum, Ho Chi Minh City) and a group of statues from Phnom Da, near Angkor Borei (National Museum, Phnom Penh) which seems to have been his capital. The group includes two images of Krishna holding up the mountain, one in a manner derived more from the eastern Mediterranean than India, and a Harihara (the gods Shiva and Vishnu combined in a single figure) which may be a little later in date. A great eight-armed image of Vishnu has its hands and their attributes supported on a horseshoe arch, perhaps because the artists were unsure whether the local stone was strong enough for a figure larger than life size.

The skill of local sculptors is shown in a horse-headed deity from Kuk Trap and in two Harihara figures from Prasat Andet and Sambhor Prei Kuk (both in the National Museum, Phnom Penh). A headless female figure from the latter site and a Lakshmi (wife of Vishnu) from Koh Krieng, both with rounded breasts and both in the National Museum, Phnom Penh, suggest the influence of an Indian prototype rather than a local one on which sloping breasts usually featured. An Avalokiteshvara (the compassionate Bodhisattva who has vowed to defer his own attainment of Buddhahood until all sentient beings have attained Nirvana) from Rach-gia (now in the Collection Didelot, Paris, France), who stands with each foot on a lotus, and standing Buddhas from Tuol Prah Theat and Vat Romlok show something of the Sarnath classical manner of Gupta India (AD 320–540), but their faces are Southeast Asian. It may be that we are witnessing in them the beginning of a development by which royalty and Buddhahood became subtly but increasingly identified.

Although images from Phnom Da seem to have been housed in a kind of artificial grotto, the earliest surviving buildings are probably the brick tower at Prah Theat Tuoch and a sandstone structure at Ta Keo, Ashram Maha Rosei, which was probably derived from a Pallavan prototype and which left no Cambodian successor. Both would have been covered in stucco, as were the many buildings of Sambhor Prei Kuk where surviving sandstone lintels give some idea of later Chan-la decoration. They bear garlands of flowers and jeweled swags whose ends are swallowed by *makara* (crocodile-like sea monsters) and sometimes inhabited by dwarfs and deities: they prefigure the lintels of the classical Khmer manner and support the view that the overthrow of Funan by Chen-la (*c* AD 555) was in fact the Khmer breaking free from their possibly Indonesian overlords. The little statuary surviving from the period displays a further evolution from figures in very high relief with a supporting arch, worked from the back as well as from the front but still not truly three-dimensional, towards fully freestanding figures. Female images show increasing stylization, but the number of male images declines, perhaps because of an increase in Shaivism with its aniconic *linga* (a more or less stylized representation of the phallus, usually set on a base, the *yoni*, which symbolizes the vulva), later the specific embodiment of Khmer kingship.

To the northeast of Funan/Chen-la, Lin-i gave way to the kingdom of Champa (*c* AD 400–1640). Several pieces of statuary from the important religious center of Mison show affinities with pieces from Malaysia: with the Buddha found at Dong-duong in central Vietnam these may have led on to later Khmer developments. Elements that were to characterize later Cham art—especially in the adornment of altars—are encapsulated in a pediment with a reclining Vishnu and in a beautiful pedestal for a *linga* which is decorated with relief figures of hermits and of a very lively dancing girl doing the splits (both in the National Museum of Cham Sculpture, Da Nang). The affinities with Malaysia suggest that the arts of both areas shared a common origin in the Indian school from which Pallava art stemmed.

Similar features are also to be seen in the early pieces from Indonesia. Following the collapse of Chen-la, political developments in Indonesia led to the emergence of firstly a new maritime power, Srivijaya, based on Sumatra, and secondly a land-oriented kingdom among the Khmer, with its center around Angkor-Siemreap. At the same time, the Shailendra dynasty, which probably had links with the rulers of Funan, came to power in central Java and initiated the great period of temple building which produced Borobudur, Kalasan, and the Prambanan group.

Apart from isolated Buddha images and crude figures of Vishnu from west Java in "international Pallava" style, the earliest surviving evidence for Indianizing cultures in Indonesia is in the temple groups of Dieng and Ungaran, both volcanic sites with buildings in a simple manner. Their affinities are generally with southern India, though Chandi Bima, Dieng, combines a *shikhara* type superstructure (the towerlike structural form characteristic of northern Indian temple architecture) with *kudu* (horseshoe-shaped niches on the bodies of temples) of south Indian style and human heads, jewels, or vases in the niches. All these buildings, as well as the two earliest from east Java, Badut (now tentatively dated to

the 10th century), and Sanggariti (with a spring-fed well in its *cella*) are Shaivite. Related images of deities have the *vahana* in human form; only the head is the shape of the appropriate animal. (The *vahana* is the animal upon which a Hindu or Buddhist deity is believed to ride. Shiva rides the bull Nandin; Vishnu, the eagle Garuda.)

A fine group of images from Chandi Banon, near Borobudur—of Shiva Mahadeva with Nandi, Ganesha, Mahaguru (the bearded, pot-bellied teacher), Brahma, and Vishnu with Garuda—shows that Javanese sculptors were capable of carving figures larger than life, in stone, with considerable virtuosity: Vishnu is over 6 ft (2 m) tall (Museum Pusat, Djakarta). Evidence of metalworking is provided by a number of Buddhist images (in the Museum Pusat, Djakarta), including a ten-armed Avalokiteshvara in bronze and a curious pair representing Shiva and Paravati, made of gold, found near Dieng. But even the largest surviving metal figure, a silver-plated bronze Avalokiteshvara (33 in, 83 cm high), gives no real idea of the very large works that odd fragments suggest once existed: we must look to stone figures for glimpses of the achievements of Javanese makers of monumental images.

Fine examples of such images can be found in the complex of buildings of which Borobudur is the center. They date from *c* 800. Chandi Mendut and Chandi Pawon, 1.8 miles (3 km) and 1 mile (1.75 km) respectively to the east of Chandi Borobudur, form with it a single, linear complex. They have entrances facing northwest. The Borobudur reliefs show that it was originally approached by the eastern one of its four staircases.

Mendut has a single *cella*, reached by a flight of steps, with small *jataka* panels on the outer walls—stories telling of the Buddha's many previous existences before his final attainment of Enlightenment which marked the end of the necessity for him, in common with all other beings, to undergo reincarnation. On the inner walls of the porch are large panels in low relief showing Hariti (on the entrant's left) and either Panchika or Atavaka on the right (an ogress and an ogre converted by the Buddha from child-eating to child-protection). On the panels of the plinth, decorative patterns alternate with angelic figures who gesture upwards to the body of the temple. Its outer walls portray, in large vertical panels, Lokeshvara and the Eight Mahabodhisattva, a group not otherwise known in Indonesian art. Side-panels show Buddhist female deities. Inside the *cella* are three colossal seated figures, Buddha with Lokeshvara and Vajrapani to his right and left; they form a triad facing the entrance. A pair of niches to either side probably housed figures of Jina-buddhas to form a pentad with the central image. (Jina-buddhas are the five Buddhas associated with the five directions—the cardinal points and the zenith—and who, unlike ordinary Buddhas who strive for Enlightenment through millions of lives, have existed as Buddhas from the beginning. They are a feature of *Mahayana* Buddhism and seem to have been introduced about the middle of the 8th century AD.) The central image is shown in *dharmachak-*

An aerial view of the temple of Borobudur; c800 AD

A relief scene from Borobudur: Queen Maya traveling to the Lumbini grove where the future Buddha will be born

ramudra: on a throne, seated "in the European manner", with two deer and a wheel, the usual indication of the First Sermon.

The *cella* of Pawon is now empty. Its exterior reliefs, however, depict wish-granting and wealth-bestowing trees, money-pots, *kinnara* (a fabulous creature, half man, half bird, who served as a celestial musician), and bearded dwarfs, all of which suggest a connection with Kuvera, god of riches and of the merchant community—a reminder of the capital resources that must have been required for the construction of the main temple, one of Buddhism's greatest shrines.

Borobudur essentially consists of walled galleries, arranged in four tiers of squares with stepped ("redentate") corners, on a base which provides a broad circumambulatory. Above the squares are three circular platforms with 72 small *stupas* in concentric rings round a larger central *stupa* on a circular base. At the center of each side is a stairway which leads to the top, passing through elaborate archways in the gallery walls. The sides of the temple (403 ft, 123 m long at the base) are oriented to the cardinal points.

There is a striking contrast between the square terraces—richly carved on their inner faces with narrative reliefs, their walls crowned with miniature *stupas*, jewels, and niches which house seated Buddha figures—and the bare circular platforms with only the *stupas* housing seated Buddhas. The Buddhas in the niches are appropriate to the quarters. Each is distinguished by its *mudra* (hand gesture): Akshobya, earth-touching, East; Ratnasambhava, gift-bestowing, South; Amitabha, meditation, West; Amoghasiddha, fear-dispelling, North. The niches on top of each side of the fourth terrace have Vairochana (the Illuminator), disputation. The figures under the brick-lattice *stupas* on the circular platforms are in

the preaching *mudra*. The existing circumambulatory was added later to the original structure, as is shown by the fact that it conceals a set of 160 panels carved with reliefs based on the *Karmavibhanga*, a text dealing with rewards and punishments for good or evil actions. Some of the reliefs are incomplete, which suggests that the addition was made while the building was still under construction.

Each of the walled galleries carries reliefs on its inner faces concerned with various aspects of Buddhism and the Buddha. On the inner wall of the first gallery one tier presents the life of Shakya-muni (Prince Siddhartha of the Shakya kingdom) up to the preaching of the First Sermon. Below this, previous lives are depicted, as they are also on the outer wall. Higher galleries show further previous lives and also carry a most important set of reliefs giving an account, based on the *Gandhavyuha* and the *Bhadracari*, of a Mahayanist pilgrim's search for ultimate truth—the symbolic meaning of the central *stupa*. This is the final release from the effects of *karma*—the inexorable law whereby the deeds of beings determine their future incarnations—so vividly portrayed on the concealed reliefs at the foot of the monument.

The 1,200 carved panels constitute a major achievement of pictorial narration, a Javanese invention without parallel in India. It is tempting to speculate on its relationship with the *wayang beber*, a pictorial scroll, held and unrolled by a reciter who tells the story depicted on it by enacting the parts of the various characters. It was first reported in east Java by a 13th-century Chinese traveler; now only one survives in central Java.

The virtuosity of the artists and sculptors who worked on the monument was a worthy match to the ingenuity of those who planned the symbolic layout of this great shrine, a highly sophisticated *mandala* in stone. But there is little agreement as to how it should be interpreted, or about its relation to the dynasty presumably responsible for its erection, the Shailendras, Lords of the Mountain.

Another *mandala* pattern is to be seen at Chandi Sewu, Prambanan, probably a century later in date. The central temple here, based on a cruciform ground plan, evidently housed a Mahayanist pantheon of an Adi-Buddha (a transcendental form epitomizing the concept of Buddhahood) with attendant *dhyani*-Buddhas, Bodhisattvas, and their Taras (savioresses who help beings to cross the Ocean of Existence to Enlightenment). Surrounding the main shrine are 240 minor ones arranged in four rows, each with 13 standing figures in relief on the outer walls. Each housed one or more images: one has niches for 41. The complex covers an area of 607 by 541 ft (185 by 165 m) and is surrounded by a wall with entrances at the cardinal axes guarded by giant *dvarapala* (guardians and gatekeepers). None of the images from the main temple has survived, and the few stone ones from the minor shrines have not yielded their precise functions.

Another variant of the *mandala* is to be seen in the double complex of Chandi Plaosan, near Sewu. On the walls of the main buildings (which seem to have housed Buddhist triads, as at Chandi Sari, accompanied by the eight Mahabodhisattva) are figures of donors. The outer walls were adorned with heavenly figures, again arranged in two series as at Sari. The statuary and reliefs from the complex are characterized by finely cut features and benign expressions. A number of monks' heads in stone have also been found.

The principal Hindu monument of central Java, the Shaivite complex of Lara Jonggrang, Prambanan, probably dates from *c*900. Here three shrines of cruciform ground plan, dedicated to Brahma, Shiva, and Vishnu, from south to north, face east towards three lesser structures which house their *vahana*. A simpler version of the central temple stands at either end of the north–south axis which runs between these two groups. The whole stands in a walled compound 360 ft (110 m) square, with gates at the cardinal points. This in turn is enclosed by another wall, with sides of 728 ft (222 m) with cardinal gates set in projecting salients. Within the space thus created were 224 minor temples, about 46 ft (14 m) high (for comparison, the Shiva temple is 154 ft, 47 m high) arranged in four rows. A third wall lies eccentrically about the temple enclosures which are located in its southwest sector. The gates in the outermost walls lie on the cardinal axes and are therefore set irregularly within it.

The *cella* of the main temple contains a four-armed image of Shiva (9.8 ft, 3 m high). The wall behind the image is carved with a low-relief pattern which probably derives from a Chinese silk hanging. Similar carvings are found at Sewu. The subsidiary *cellae* house Mahaguru, Ganesha, and Durga. The main image is of no great artistic merit, though the carving of the details of dress, jewelry, and attributes is fine. The complex's ritual center is not under this main image as we

The shrine of Shiva in the complex of Lara Jonggrang, Prambanan

A relief scene from the Ramayana, at Lara Jonggrang; c900 AD

would normally expect but in a small shrine set in the angle between the temple body and the south wall of the main access staircase.

The four staircases are topped by towered arches with *stupa*-like finials, behind which is the entrance to the *cella* with a great *kala*-head in relief surmounted by a triple gadrooned *stupa* motif. Similar *stupas* crown the exterior wall of the circumambulatory and the architraves of the six-storied tower above the central body of the temple which is divided horizontally into two zones, with 24 niches in each, which once held statues.

The exterior of the main plinth of the temple is elaborately decorated with niches containing celestial beings in groups of three, alternating with dancers and musicians. Below these are other ornaments, the most important—because peculiar to the site—being a lion, in a niche, flanked by celestial trees, which have pairs of animals, rams, hares, deer, monkeys, geese, peacocks, or *kinnara* at either side of their trunks.

The base of the body of the temple has 24 panels with seated figures who are believed to be the various forms of the regents of the quarters. On the inner wall of the balustrade are relief panels, noticeably different in style from the Borobudur reliefs, illustrating scenes from the *Ramayana*, the story of how the deity Rama and his wife Sita are exiled, how she is carried off to Ceylon by the demon Ravana, and how Rama, accompanied by an army of monkeys, among them Hanuman, defeats the demons and recovers his wife. These panels take the story as far as the arrival of the monkey army on Ceylon. The narrative continues on the balustrade of the Brahma temple. The Vishnu temple has reliefs telling of the youthful adventures of Krishna.

At about the time Borobudur was under construction (at the end of the 8th century) Prince Jayavarman (the second, according to the Khmer king list) went from Java to Cambodia, and set up a new dynasty there with the *linga* as its palladium. (The kings of Champa had earlier instituted such a system, the royal *linga* having a name linked to that of the ruler.) At first this royal symbol seems to have been installed on some natural eminence which was treated as Mount Sumeru, the world axis. But the absence of suitable eminent sites in the central Cambodian region led to the construction of an artificial temple-mountain, to serve as the axis of the kingdom and hence of the world. To construct such a temple and an associated system of waterways, both to portray Ocean (which was believed to surround the world) and to irrigate crops on the plains surrounding the capital, became the prior responsibility of Khmer rulers.

There is evidence to suggest that a temple of the Cham type was the first model, but Khmer builders soon evolved a style of their own. Other influences came from Srivijaya, suzerain over parts of Malaysia, and from the lower Menam Basin which, once part of the maritime kingdom of Funan-Chen-la, now constituted the kingdom of Dvaravati. Here flourished a Buddhist art derived from eastern India which favored the use of stucco and terracotta, and probably a vigorous secular

tradition, suggested by some striking genre heads. Images of Buddha and Bodhisattva in both stone and bronze survive. Of the latter, an Avalokiteshvara from Chaiya, showing him in royal attire, is a major achievement of Mahayanist art. This school provided the basis for Khmer Buddhist art which reached its royal climax in the complex of Angkor Thom and Bayon.

No doubt Jayavarman, the Cambodian ruler from Java, brought ideas with him, and possibly also artisans, for there are demonstrable Javanese elements and motifs in early Khmer art. The preoccupation with mountain shrines also had Indonesian analogs. This influence may explain why, after a series of temporary capitals in the region north of the Tonle Sap, Jayavarman set up the royal shrine on Mount Kulen, about 19 miles (30 km) northeast of Angkor. Called Kruh Prah Aram Rong Chen, in a form reminiscent of a step-pyramid, it is thought to have once housed the palladium. But the site was certainly unsuitable for a capital, and the king returned to Roluos.

From here Jayavarman's second successor, Indravarman (877–89), a scholar-king, was to develop further these hesitant attempts to found a great central and symbolic city. His first act, significantly, was to create a great artificial lake, Indratataka, whose waters filled the moats of the temple of Prah Ko, then those of Bakong, the royal temple-mountain, of Prasat Prei Monti, the palace, and finally, imbued with both divine and royal essence, flowed through the rice fields. At the same time, boats from the great lake were given access to the capital and great quantities of stone for building temples could be easily transported from the quarries in the hills to the north of the complex.

The temple of Prah Ko was dedicated to the royal ancestors in 879. Within its great enclosure two rows of three towers set on a single terrace housed images of Indravarman's precursors, males in the front row, females in the rear. Because he was probably a usurper, his symbolic claim assumed more importance.

The grouped towers were decorated in carved stucco, with branched foliage, monsters supporting rings in which small figures swing, and lotuses. Lower down the wall sandstone slabs are carved in high relief with figures of protective deities whose rich jewelry, like the bristling hair of the male figures, suggests a Javanese origin. Lintels show horsemen among the foliage, surmounted by half-length worshipers; the scenes on the pediments remain unidentified.

As a central mountain to house the royal *linga*, Bakong was dedicated in 881 and set the pattern for subsequent royal foundations at the center of the Cambodian capital. Five superimposed terraces, faced with sandstone, held in place by stone elephants at the corners, represent the layered worlds of the cosmos. Various small towers housed protective deities and possibly the lords of the planets, often portrayed in Khmer sculpture. Subsidiary buildings round the base included one with an image of the king. The topmost *cella*, on a terrace 49 ft (50 m) above the ground, housed the *linga*. The

The Neak Pean Shrine, Angkor

▲ The central pool and the main shrine

Architectural symbolism is of very great significance in Southeast Asia. An example is provided by one of the smaller monuments, Neak Pean, "Entwined Serpents", which was erected by King Jayavarman VII (1181–1219). It is situated on an artificial island with stepped stone embankments and stone elephants at the corners, in the (now dry) great lake he constructed to the east of Prah Khan, a temple housing an image of his father as the Bodhisattva Lokeshvara. An inscription tells us that Lake Jayatataka is "like an auspicious mirror, colored with jewels, gold, and garlands. At its center is a prominent isle, its charm derived from the basins that surround it, cleansing from the mud of sin those who come into contact with it and serving as a boat to cross the ocean of existence".

In the middle of this island is a square basin with stepped stone sides at whose center is a circular islet surmounted by a small sanctuary. Four subsidiary basins are set on the flanks of the main tank, with chapels on the cardinal axes of the shared embankments. The stepped base of the islet is surrounded by a pair of serpents, their entwined tails to the west, their separated,

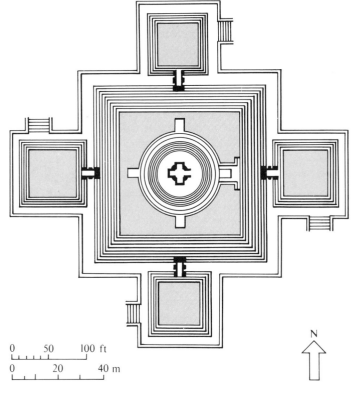

0   50   100 ft

0   20   40 m

N

▲ A ground plan of the artificial island, sanctuary, and main shrine at Neak Pean. The boundary wall of the complex is not shown

▶ The east front of the central sanctuary at Neak Pean and the entrance to the shrine. The panel above the door shows the future Buddha cutting his hair. The approach leads between the heads of entwined snakes

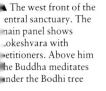

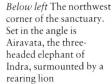

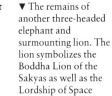

◄ The west front of the central sanctuary. The main panel shows Lokeshvara with petitioners. Above him the Buddha meditates under the Bodhi tree

Above right The north front of the sanctuary. Above the doorway is the Great Departure. Below, Lokeshvara is flanked by seated Bodhisattvas with heavenly figures above and laymen below

Below left The northwest corner of the sanctuary. Set in the angle is Airavata, the three-headed elephant of Indra, surmounted by a rearing lion

▼ The remains of another three-headed elephant and surmounting lion. The lion symbolizes the Boddha Lion of the Sakyas as well as the Lordship of Space

hooded heads to the east: hence the name. A causeway between the heads gives access to the platform, on which a base in the form of the corolla of a 16-petalled lotus supports the sanctuary. The shrine, two-storied with a lotus finial, is cruciform in plan, just a simple *cella*: the image is missing. The entrance is on the east where the doorway is crowned by a tympanum on which Siddhartha is depicted cutting his hair. The false doors have tympana showing the Great Departure (north), the Enlightenment (west); the south tympanum is defaced. The sanctuary was originally open on all four sides, but later panels, showing aspects of the Bodhisattva Lokeshvara, were added to block three of the entrances. At the same time tricephalic elephants, similar to those of Angkor Thom but surmounted by rearing lions instead of human riders, were set in the angles of the building. ▶

The four axial chapels on the main embankment are so set that only the part from the bottom of the tympana upwards is visible. Vaulted structures rising somewhat above the level of the embankment form tunnels into either face of it, their entrances set in flamboyant frames. The sides have carved tympana and stepped-back pediments. The whole structure is crowned by a four-sided pillar, with rounded top, and paneled sides with reliefs of the Bodhisattva. Healing is the motif of all the narrative carvings. In each chapel a pipe within the structure terminates in a lotus basin surmounted by a female bust. The outer end, above a circular lotus platform with a pair of footprints cut on its upper surface, forms a gargoyle. The one to the east is a magnificently carved human head. The others, notably inferior as works of art, are a lion's head (south), a horse's (west), and an elephant's (north). Pilgrims bathed under them to cleanse themselves ritually from physical or spiritual imperfection.

◀ The central pediment of the south outflow shrine. In the lower panel Lokeshvara blesses petitioners

▲ One of the four minor shrines housing the outflow tunnels. They are all covered with figures of Lokeshvara

▼ On the east outflow is this magnificently carved human head

▲ On the platform on the eastern cardinal axis Lokeshvara, as the horse Balaha, rescues the shipwrecked merchants

▼ The complex of Neak Pean is surrounded by a wall. At its northwest corner stands this elephant, another symbol of Space

Four platforms on the cardinal axes within the main basin once supported stone objects. Those on the west and north have disappeared. To the south are the remains of groups of *linga*; the inscription quoted above also speaks of "thousands of *linga*". The eastern platform, facing the entrance to the shrine, supports a colossal horse, made from carved stone blocks, to whose body human figures cling. The group represents a well-known Buddhist story. A party of seafaring merchants is wrecked on an island inhabited by ogresses who take them to husband and then, mantis-like, devour them. The merchant Simhala calls on the compassionate Avalokiteshvara, who protects from every peril: shipwreck is specifically mentioned, a fact suggesting a mercantile cult. The Bodhisattva appears in the form of a flying white horse to carry the survivors to safety, a somewhat curious version of the "boat to cross the ocean of existence". Similarly, King Jayavarman, through his patronage of Buddhism and his self-identification with the Bodhisattva, brings the Khmer people to salvation.

The layout of the monument as a whole is modeled on the Buddhist sacred lake

Anavatapta which is believed to lie high in the Himalayas. There Buddhas, Bodhisattvas, arhats, and ascetics bathe, while from its four banks the four great rivers of the world, including the Ganges, flow through gargoyles, lion, elephant, horse, and bull, to bring the fertilizing waters to mankind, just as the beneficent king provides irrigation for his realm and its inhabitants. The similarity with the royal *tirtha* of Java and Bali is obvious, though there is no exactly parallel shrine. Neak Pean is also, indeed, unique in Cambodia. Common to the two cultures is the concept of the mountain, associated so closely with kingship, as the source for the vivifying waters.

ANTHONY CHRISTIE

Further reading. Coedes, G. *Angkor: an Introduction*, Hong Kong (1963). Christie, A. "Natural Symbols in Java" in Milner, G.B. (ed.) *Natural Symbols in South East Asia*, London (1978). Finot, L. and Goloubew, V. "Le Symbolisme de Nak Pan" *Bull. Ec. Franc. Extr. Orient*, vol. 23 (1925) pp401–5. Glaize, M. "Essai sur la Connnaissance de Nak Pan après Anastylose" *Bull. Ec. France. Extr. Orient*, vol. 40 (1940) pp351–62.

existing structure is of the 12th century, but the decoration is consciously archaizing. There are two enclosure walls and two moats, the latter crossed by east–west causeways to the main gates which show the earliest surviving examples of *naga*-balustrades—a feature of classical Khmer sculpture. The *nagas* (snakes) are being hunted by the freestanding Garudas. The wall of the fifth terrace is carved with scenes which have become too worn for identification but are evidence of an amazing skill in the depiction of movement.

Once again the manner points to Javanese inspiration. Indeed, B.-P. Groslier has even compared Borobudur and Bakong; it is at least tempting to believe that Indravarman wished to build a dynastic temple to rival that of the Shailen-dras from whom Jayavarman had sought to set Cambodia free. The king himself is shown at Bakong, flanked by two of his wives: another innovation of the period, though there are already signs of the standardized formulae that dominate later art. As Groslier writes: "By this time we find the whole Khmer order of society perfected. Under Indravarman, Jayavarman II's work took root; Angkor has been founded and will continue to grow."

Two elements of symbolic art remained to be created: the quincunxial central shrine and the cloisters to house long panels of reliefs, but both are present in embryo.

The central tower on the top terrace was shortly joined by four others to make a five-fold top characteristic of Sumeru. This appeared by 893, at Bakheng, the central temple of In-dravarman's successor Yashovarman. Bakheng is a master-piece of cosmological symbolism on a far greater scale than Bakong, from which it evolved. Yashovarman's lake Yashodharatataka, six times the size of Indratataka, relied on the natural flow of the Siemreap River to fill a system of moats on the periphery of his capital, with its amazingly sophisti-cated cosmic temple on a natural hill at the center. It presents the seven tiers of Mount Meru with its 33 gods (the number of towers visible from the middle of any side). One hundred and eight subsidiary towers—this number being the product of 4 and 27—subsume the four phases of the moon and the 27 lunar mansions; another combination represents the 60-year cycle of Jupiter. It is an astronomical calendar in stone.

Within another 70 years the final element of Khmer archi-tecture was added. At Prei Rup (dedicated in 961) the subsidi-ary terraces had long, stone chambers with tiled roofs on timber frames—the prototypes for the cloister galleries of Angkor Wat. This period also saw further examples of the freestanding images of the kind noted at Bakong, including brilliantly conceived monkey wrestlers, presumably from the *Ramayana*.

To this same period belongs the gem of Khmer architecture, Banteay Srei, dedicated in 967, not by a king but by a royal Brahmin, Yajnavaraha. A Shaivite shrine, it is built on a mini-ature scale: the central one of its three main *cellae* is only 33 ft (10 m) high, but it is richly ornamented, with many elements drawn from earlier phases of Khmer art. Niches set in foliated panels, where dancers and animals flit among the leaves,

A niche figure at Banteay Srei

house exquisite flower-carrying nymphs in deeply cut relief. The tympana display scenes from myths and legends, like the-atrical sets with carefully posed actors. Masques probably formed part of court entertainment at this time, as they did until recently. Statuary of the period shows some return to anatomical reality after a phase of stylization. Freestanding figures of the Bakong-Koh Ker type are found: Shiva seated with his consort Uma or Parvati, his eyes open and sensual, his lips fleshy, seems to preside over a true paradise on earth.

At the beginning of the 11th century, at Ta Keo, the con-tinuous cloister was to be constructed, on the second terrace, which also had an impressive *gopura*-like entrance on the east and lesser gateways on the other three sides (a *gopura* being a gateway surmounted by a towerlike structure). The quincunx was set on the fifth platform somewhat towards the western end of the enclosure. This is the final form of the temple-mountain, a masterpiece, and one of the finest buildings in the Siemreap region.

Of the same period are the remains of a colossal bronze Vishnu: head, shoulders, and two right arms of a reclining figure which must have been about 13 ft (4 m) long. Now in the National Museum, Phnom Penh, its original location was on a plinth, probably in the form of the world serpent Shesha, in a pool in the West Mebon, an island set in the Western Baray, the great reservoir that lies to the west of Angkor Thom. The image was constructed in sections by the *cire perdue* method and was once encrusted with gold, while jewels and enamels were used for the eyes. A Shiva head, also in bronze, gilded, with encrustations of leadglaze, 12½ in (32 cm) high without its chignon, from Por Loboeuk (now in the Angkor Conservation Depot, Siemreap), bears further testimony to the skill and mastery of Khmer metalworkers, so little of whose work has survived.

Stone images were of secondary significance, though from these we are forced to judge Khmer glyptic. Although Khmer sculptors had shown an early interest in producing genuine work-in-the-round, after eliminating various supporting devices they chose to develop the frontal poses of images on thick legs, with little attempt to reproduce natural anatomy.

The Chams, who inhabited the area that now constitutes central and south Vietnam, were more inclined to model poses other than frontal. This was undoubtedly the result of using altars with a reredos and retable, open on three sides, with the main image at the back surrounded by guardian figures, subsidiary divinities, animals, worshipers, and donors. All these faced towards the principal image, forcing the artists to consider non-frontal presentation. The Chams were also most successful in portraying movement, a skill found less often among the Khmer: those responsible for the Khmer reliefs were exceptional.

In architecture, the Chams almost exclusively used brick for their buildings, reserving sandstone for ornamentation in the earliest and, usually, best examples, where it is confined to door-frames, pilasters on the corners of the body, and accent pieces on the superstructure which rose by repetitive and decreasing stories. Blind arches, without the tympanum found on Khmer buildings, project over door or facade: their fronts are carved with foliage and bear a monster head at the peak, curiously reminiscent of central Javanese temples.

The great 9th-century temple complex at Dong-duong is Buddhist, although Champa was generally shaivite and may well have been the source for Khmer Shaivism. Brick *stupas* are of a grooved cylindrical form and seem to be of Chinese origin. The decorative style is complex, but the sculpture's impressive vitality is informed with the illusion of movement. Buildings at Po Nagar and Mi-son, dating from a couple of centuries later, show a renewed interest in discrete ornamentation on elegant structures whose tall silhouettes seem to be outlined by stone flames. The sculpture, in contrast with the almost primitive vitality of that of Dong-duong, is restrained but sensual. Parts of an enormous altar from Tra-kieu (National Museum of Cham Sculpture, Da Nang) on which a frieze of dancers and musicians, cut deeply in blue-gray sandstone, honor the god embodied in the *linga* supported by the altar. On another pedestal the female dancer has become an arabesque in stone. This marks the apogee of Cham art which slowly declined as the Vietnamese, moving inexorably southwards, gradually swamped the small centers of Cham culture. The area as far south as Hue was annexed by 1306, the area to Cap Varella by 1471. The last Cham temple, Po Rome, is usually dated to the mid 17th century, when the last parts of Champa, many of whose inhabitants had adopted Islam, came under Vietnamese rule.

On the other side of the Khmer Empire the Mons of Dvaravati continued to develop various forms of Buddhist art and architecture, some of which found their way into Cambodia from the 11th century onwards. Their relic shrine was a brick cube, surmounted by receding stories with figures set under arches and often with a galleried circumambulatory set on a terrace of Khmer type. With the addition of stucco decoration this became the model for later northern Thai architecture. Two Buddha figures also evolved in Dvaravati: the standing Buddha wearing a single garment with both arms held out symmetrically, and the seated figure, meditating under the hood(s) of a coiled *naga*. When Buddhism became the state religion towards the end of the Khmer Empire (late 12th century) they provided two important icons.

The image with pendent legs did not enter the Khmer repertory, but was favored in central Java, where it may have appeared earlier than it did on the lower Menam.

But above all, it was as a source for *Hinayana* Buddhist art that Dvaravati and the succeeding Thai states were important, once the Khmer had fallen. And to this repertory the Mons of Burma made a major contribution, most significantly after Anawratha (1044–77) had incorporated them into a united Burma with its great Buddhist center at Pagan. Other components came from the Pyu who had long practiced *Mahayana* Buddhism, with some elements from Hinduism.

It was from an amalgam of Pyu, Mon, and Burman that a new art and architecture were to emerge. The Pyu developed tall, cylindrical *stupas* of brick, crowned with a bell-like finial with a central spire. The plinth was shallow, stepped, and circular. A typical example is the Baw-bawgyi at Hmawza, nearly 164 ft (50 m) high.

The Pyu temple was either rectangular in plan, with a single entrance facing an image set against the rear wall, or consisted of a square central block, with relief images on each face

An arabesque-like female dancer and a musician on a Cham pedestal. National Museum of Cham Sculpture, Da Nang

opposite doorways in each of the four walls. At the Pyu site of Hmawza, the Bebe Paya represents the first type while the Lemyethna, which may be of slightly earlier date, represents the second.

The East Zegu at Hmawza, perhaps a little earlier in date, demonstrates the earliest true arch in Southeast Asia. The arch has no place in Khmer or Javanese architecture. But its use by the Pyu in the 8th century undoubtedly made possible the barrel-vaulted, two-storied structures of brick found in Pagan 200 or 300 years later.

From the Pyu period (3rd–9th centuries AD) come a number of stone images of Vishnu and some bronze Bodhisattvas, as well as Buddhas carved in stone relief which seem to belong to the *Theravada* tradition (Hmawza Museum, Hmawza; National Museum, Rangoon). Ashes of the royal dead were housed in fine stone urns; but the people had to rest content with pots. Reliefs reveal that arcaded Buddha figures were set round the drums of *stupas*. Another type of shrine consisted of two slabs with Buddha images in relief set several feet apart at either end of a narrow brick terrace marking a place where Buddhas are said to have "walked and talked".

After Anawratha, King of Pagan (1044–77), captured the capital of the western Mon, Thaton, in the mid 11th century, Mon culture contributed to the development of architecture. In part they transmitted influences from the artistic reservoir of Dvaravati and from Sri Lanka, with which they had direct contact and where *Theravada* Buddhism was already flourishing. The Mon had a tradition of temple shrines, of which the Nan-paya at Pagan is a fine example.

The Burmans probably acquired their Buddhism in large part from the Pyu and the Mon. Their own contribution to the amalgam was the cult of Nats: nature spirits. Once they were innumerable but by the time of King Kyanzittha (1084–1112) the total had stabilized at 37. The Buddha was sometimes treated as their chief. They were often housed in special shrines on pagoda platforms, as at the Shwezigon.

The leaders of the nature spirits, the Mahagiri Nats on Mount Popa in central Burma, were provided with shrines at the Sarabha Gate of Pagan. They show the typical low pilasters and molded architraves of Pagan buildings, almost all of which are brick built with a stucco engobe (embellishment). The Pyu *stupa* was adapted so that the terrace became more important, the body reduced in scale, and the spire greatly elongated and emphasized. Around this structure, which was treated as the core of the Lemyethna, a circumambulatory was created, its doors set at the cardinal points of the outer walls. Entrance corridors were added to these, with richly elaborated frontispieces. The angles of the roofs were accented with spires derived from that of the central mass.

By this process of development the Pagan builders produced their major achievement: the Ananda pagoda. It is still a center of worship, with its great standing Buddhas, its countless small reliefs of *jataka* and other themes—many carrying the inscriptions in the script of the Mon that prove their responsibility for this school of Buddhist architecture.

Most of the thousands of shrines at Pagan and in its neighborhood are variants of the two forms—*stupa* and shrine—with subsidiary buildings which were libraries or monasteries. In 1287, under Mongol attack, the site was abandoned, but Burmese Buddhist art and architecture had been established.

While Anawratha's successors had been filling Pagan with further elaborations of the Burmese style, Khmer art and architecture was approaching its climax under a new dynasty which had come to power in 1080. In 1113 the great-nephew of the founder, Suryavarman II, embarked on a great campaign of military and architectural aggrandizement. There was no space in the existing capital area for a new temple and surrounding enclosure to form a whole new city, but a site was found, on the royal road from Baphuon to the Tonle Sap, for a spectacular temple-mountain: Angkor Wat. Its construction occupied most of Suryavarman's reign (1113–50).

Its main facade faced west, the direction of the setting sun, the region of Death; perhaps symbolic of the temple's role as a shrine for the dead king in his apotheotic form. The enclosure is rectangular, surrounded by a moat more than 195 yds (180 m) wide, fed from the Siemreap River. An embanked road, flanked by *naga* balustrades, crosses the moat to the main gate, which reproduced the facade of the actual temple building. At the end of a paved road is a three-tiered pyramid whose central tower rises to a height of 230 ft (70 m). The three tiers have corner towers and central pavilions preceded by steps. The main tower with the *cella* is linked by pillared galleries to the entrance pavilions of the quincunx. A triple staircase links the western entrance of the first tier to that of the second: these pillared galleries are covered by corbeled vaulting. The whole structure is consciously designed to appear as a pyramid to the approaching worshiper. By means of correctly judged ratios between access and facade, the calculated staggering of the succeeding terraces towards the east, and increases in height, the builders avoided giving any sensation that the structure was falling towards the viewer. All these elements, as well as the layout of the site, had been present at Baphuon: at Angkor Wat they achieve perfection.

The whole of the stone surface is covered with decoration. Storiated pediments, lintels, and doorposts portray gods and heroes: capitals and gallery cornices have lotus friezes; the walls have heavenly dancers in low relief (set against carved panels whose patterns derive from textiles)—almost 2,000 of them and each one different in detail from the others. The gallery linking the entrances and corner towers of the first tier has pillars in place of the outer wall to allow light to fall on the inner wall which has a series of scenes carved in low relief, about 6 ft (2 m) in height and more than 1 mile (1.75 km) in overall length. Apparently these reliefs are meant to be read counterclockwise, a characteristic of funerary rites, supporting the view that Suryavarman intended the temple as his mortuary shrine. One whole panel is dedicated to Yama, ruler of the underworld, judging the dead. Other scenes are based upon Vaishnavite themes: the churning of the ocean, Krishna stories, and episodes from the *Mahabharata* and the *Ramaya-*

Angkor Wat, Suryavarman II's temple-mountain; early 12th century; a view across the moat

na. One panel of great interest shows the king himself, at first seated in his court, and then sitting on a royal elephant leading his army.

The reliefs, which were certainly gilded and possibly colored, are the ultimate fruition of an art that began at Borobudur and was further developed at Banteay Srei and at the temple-mountain of Baphuon. Chinese elements have been detected, but, as P.S. Rawson has pointed out, the mode of expression owes much to the dance. This, in combination with umbrellas, banners, weapons, and scarves, gives an amazing sense of movement. The relief is very shallow, about an inch deep, but complex sequences of overlapping curves create a convincing sensation of depth: in its conception the whole work is painterly. The galleries must be ranked among the greatest examples of relief art in the world.

It was perhaps some realization of his father's achievement that led Jayarvarman VII (1181–1219), towards the end of his reign, to attempt the creation of a Buddhist shrine to rival Angkor Wat and to occupy the center of the royal domain. This was the Bayon. Built on the site of a city founded more than a century earlier by Udayadityavarman II, it was surrounded by a great wall, more than 10 miles (16 km) long, with five gateways and bridges across the moat, more than 110 yds (100 m) wide. The bridges have balustrades of gods and demons holding serpents, a vast representation of the churning of the Ocean with the Bayon as the churnstick. The bridges also represented the rainbow path which links heaven, the royal microcosmic enclosure, and earth, the surrounding kingdom of the Khmer. The gate pavilions were topped with triple towers carved with huge faces, the great artistic innovation of the reign to be repeated on the 54 towers of the central temple. The faces, gazing out to the cardinal points, are those

of the King as the compassionate Bodhisattva Lokeshvara.

His temple-mountain consisted of a galleried structure in the form of a "Greek" cross surrounding a central platform with a circular shrine and 12 subsidiary radiating chapels. The original cross was then modified by the addition of extra galleries to form a rectangle enclosed within another gallery. The subsidiary towers rise over the intersections thus created, des-

Jayarvarman VII's temple at Angkor, the Bayon; carved faces of the King as Lokeshvara

ignating shrines which may have represented the provinces of the Empire. Out of this forest of stone the main tower rises to a height of 140 ft (43 m). The whole structure was, however, subjected to a number of modifications—some seemingly capricious—during the course of its construction, so its meaning cannot be properly analyzed.

Two galleries carry reliefs, showing episodes in the life of the King and the history of his military campaigns: amazingly vivid scenes of everyday life in a profusion that lacks the controlled elegance of reliefs at Angkor Wat. A new element of naturalism is present, and at least one attempt at aerial perspective possibly made under Chinese influence.

But the resources that built the Bayon and a host of other vast buildings diverted labor from the basic economic activities of the state. Jayavarman's desire to glorify the dynasty through Buddhism probably contributed to both the downfall of the dynasty and the replacement of the royal *Mahayana* Buddhism by *Theravada* Buddhism. But Jayavarman's memory is preserved in his inscriptions, which record buildings, roads, and bridges; in buildings themselves; in several splendid stone statues, which include the so-called Leper King (Angkor Thom, Siemreap), the Lokeshvara from Prah Khan, probably a portrait of the King's father (National Museum, Phnom Penh); in a seated Buddha from the shaft under the center of the Bayon; and, above all, in the portrait head of the King himself, a worthy tribute in stone to a ruler who employed so much of that material to the glory of Buddha as king (both in the National Museum, Phnom Penh).

In Java, towards the middle of the 11th century, the seat of power seems to have shifted from the center to the east of the island. Thereafter, no more great unified complexes were to be built, though certain centers were developed, often in the Cham manner as found at Mi-son.

Typical of this tendency are Panataran (the name meaning something like Pantheon) and Mount Penanggunan which has more than 80 shrines, including two constructed round sacred fountains. Jalatunda (977) has a rectangular basin, filled with water from the mountain, is identified with Sumeru, with its multiple peaks. The water gushed from a fountain with one central and eight subsidiary spouts, its base encircled by a serpent, into the main basin through holes in slabs carved with themes from the *Mahabharata*, undoubtedly of dynastic significance. Under the basin lay a burial casket.

At Belahan a similar structure, which was originally part of a larger complex, is believed to be the burial place of King Airlangga who was portrayed there as Vishnu on Garuda (Mojokerto Museum). The monument, dated to 1049, takes the form of a brick basin in the bed of a stream. Set in its back wall are three niches surmounted by heavenly clouds with figures. In the center stood the Vishnu image with the king's principal wives, Shri and Lakshmi, installed on either hand. From a spout in Garuda's left hand, a jar held by the goddess in the southern niche, and the breasts of the northern deity, water falls into the basin and then makes its way down to the fields below.

An analogous shrine lies in front of the famous Goa Gajah cave, with its witch mask over the entrance, near Bedulu in Bali. Here water spouts from the breasts of six female figures. Many other examples of spout-figures are known from Java and Bali.

The small pool in the Panataran enclosure, dated to 1415, has animal panels, though not all can be identified. The complex itself contains buildings dated from 1197 to 1454 and appears to have been dedicated to Shiva as Lord of the Mountain. On the southwest slopes of Mount Kelut there are three successive courtyards with the main shrine nearest the peak—a layout characteristic of temple enclosures in present-day Bali where it is held to be of east Javanese origin. The first enclosure has a ceremonial entrance and a large platform whose walls are decorated with relief panels. Most of the figures are in profile, the style is semi-naturalistic. In the second enclosure is the so-called "Dated Temple" (1369), its *cella* standing on a low plinth with an entrance on the northwest and three false doors. The reconstructed roof is in three receding double tiers surmounted by a cubic top. In the same enclosure is another, roofless, structure, whose *cella*, this time on a high plinth with an ornamented staircase, is decorated below the cornice with the bodies of great serpents supported by nine regally attired figures holding priest's bells.

The main shrine, in the third enclosure, has a projection on the front with two stairways leading to the circumambulatory. The guardian figures, just over 6 ft high (1.9 m) with backs decorated with animal reliefs, are dated to 1347. The walls of the first terrace are divided by pilasters which carry *Ramayana* reliefs, but only the episodes involving Hanuman and the monkey army. They are treated in silhouette and are reminiscent of shadow theater. On the second terrace long panels show scenes from the life of Krishna in a much more naturalistic manner. The third terrace, on which the main *cella* was set, has alternating winged serpents and winged lions. This platform encloses the remains of an earlier brick structure of unknown date. At the corners of the *cella* are male deities; females are in niches on the walls, serpents between: probably another system to indicate Sumeru.

Other temples of similar style are found in east Java, mostly serving as the mortuary shrines of kings and their immediate kin. Among them is Chandi Jago, of the late 13th century, set on two terraces with the *cella* towards the rear of the upper one. Images from this, now in the Museum Pusat, Djakarta, show that it housed a pantheon with an eight-armed Amoghapasha (a form of the Bodhisattva Avalokiteshvara) as the central figure—an interesting feature because no fewer than five bronze plaques, about 8½ in (22 cm) high, dedicated by King Kertanagara, are known, which display the same group of 14 figures (Museum Pusat, Djakarta; Royal Tropical Institute, Amsterdam; Ethnographic Museum, Leiden). So too does a great stone relief, over 5 ft (1.6 m) high, from central Sumatra and now in Djakarta (Museum Pusat). According to an inscription dated 1286, this was brought from Java by a prince who was to marry a Sumatran princess. An enormous stone Bhairava (a horrific deity in the Buddhist tantric tradition) also came to Djakarta from the same site in Sumatra; the image is thought to represent the mid-14th-century King Adityavarman of Sumatra. Indeed, everything points to considerable cultural exchange between Java and Sumatra which appear to have shared a royal tantric cult.

The reliefs of Chandi Jago which, unusually for Java, run counterclockwise, include a Javanese version of the Sanskrit *Panchatantra* animal fables, the story of Kunjarakarna and various adventures of the Pandavas. Native, Buddhist, and Hindu elements were included in the cult which seems to have been strongly salvationist. The temple's statuary, in late Pala manner, differs stylistically from the reliefs. It may belong to a major rededication of the shrine about a century after its original foundation.

The tower type of temple is exemplified by Chandi Kidal, of the mid 13th century, where the story of Garuda's search for nectar to buy his mother's freedom from the *nagas* is depicted: another east Java redemption theme. The *cella* housed a theomorphic image of King Anushapati as Shiva, a typical posthumous royal portrait.

At Singhasari the surviving building was unfinished, though the images for the outer niches were in place, before they were all, except the figure of Mahaguru, removed to Leiden (Ethnographic Museum). The figure of the goddess Durga—a fierce form of Uma, the consort of Shiva—slaying the buffalo-demon is a magnificent piece. The straddled posture, unknown in other Javanese examples and certainly improper in contemporary Javanese behavior, suggests eastern Indian influence, but the technique of carving does not. Uniquely, the *cella* of the temple is located in the plinth; the apparent shrine is an empty cube, without entrances, which is linked to the *cella* and to the superstructure by special openings in its floor and ceiling. The plan is probably of ritual significance in view of the preoccupation with mystery religions which characterized the Singhasari dynasty (1222–92).

Statuary reached new heights during the later East Javanese period. A Chakrachakra (so-called on the rear of the image—a ferocious form of the god Shiva, naked and hung with skulls and severed heads, sitting on a jackal; Ethnographic Museum, Leiden) from Singasari epitomizes another aspect of royal tantrism, while the colossal guardian figures, some 12 ft (3.7 m) high, indicate the confidence with which the sculptors of the period handled great blocks of stone. A beautiful image in very high relief against a background throne, depicts Prajnaparamita, Perfection of Wisdom, meditating with crossed legs and with hands in *dharmachakramudra*, the gesture of setting in motion the Wheel of the Law—that is, of preaching the Buddhist doctrine (Ethnographic Museum, Leiden). To the left of the crowned and bejeweled figure a lotus supports her palm-leaf book: her face portrays the tranquillity brought by transcendental wisdom. It is believed that the image is a portrait statue of Queen Dedes who was concerned in the violence that brought her husband to power and to found the

The goddess Durga slaying the buffalo-demon, from Singhasari, Java; 13th century; height 175 cm (69 in). Ethnographic Museum, Leiden

Singasari dynasty in the first half of the 13th century.

Another genre of sculpture is shown by the remarkable seated Ganesha, originally from Jimbe on the banks of the Brantas River (now in Bara village, near Blitar in east Java): in Java this god often guarded river-crossings. The almost-square figure, dated on the rear of his skull-adorned plinth 1239, is deeply carved so that the shadows emphasize the mass. He is richly bejeweled and crowned: his trunk lifts a sweetmeat from his skull-bowl. On the back of his great head and across his shoulders is a vividly carved *kala* head (the depiction of the face, without its lower jaw, of a mythical monster with apotropaic head): the protector is himself protected.

The royal portraits are generally shown in the guise of Hindu or Buddhist deities, but the human hands are usually without attributes. In the case of King Kertarajasa (1293–1309), founder of the Majapahit dynasty, the main attributes are Vaishnavite, but the upper right hand bears not a conch but a snail emerging from its shell. Some pieces, such as a royal pair from Jebuk, Tulung Agung, Kediri, while clearly deriving from a Shiva-Uma group, achieve a markedly informal air which makes us regret that so little of the most attractive work in terracotta has survived.

Conclusion. The development of art and architecture in Southeast Asia from the Dong-son period to the 14th century reflects the various elements that contributed to it: native,

Indian, and especially in the case of Vietnam, Chinese. Their influences varied over the centuries and so too did the cultural forms in which such influences were manifested. Indian influence was predominant in religious iconography; Chinese influence was central to the development of ceramic art in Vietnam and Thailand; while Chinese export wares were, and still are, in great demand in Southeast Asia, not only among the plains-dwellers but also among the various hill-peoples. Native influences determined the practice of portraying dead rulers and their kin in the guise of Hindu or Buddhist deities, a practice that can be linked with the carving of ritual images in wood among such groups as the Ngaju Dyak of Sulawesi or the people of Nias off the coast of Sumatra.

During the 13th and 14th centuries the cultures of Southeast Asia became increasingly independent of those of their great neighbors while differences between areas of Southeast Asia became more marked, though the influence of one region on another was often of great importance. A clear example of the latter is the influence of the Thai style of Ayudhya upon post-Angkorian Khmer art which resulted from sackings of the Kampuchean capital in 1353, 1393, and finally in 1431, the end of the Angkor period. Sometimes a much older tradition, long encapsulated within strongly Indianizing art and architectural forms, reemerged. The two 15th-century shrines on the slopes of Gunung Lawu in central Java, Candi Sukuh and Candi Ceto, with their terraced layouts and unroofed shrines—in many ways reminiscent of religious structures in the Pacific—represent such a development.

Changes in religious patterns also played their part. The shift from *Mahayana*, court-supported, Buddhism—ostentatious, demanding expensive monuments—to the *Theravada* school with its simpler requirements had a profound effect. The spread of Islam in Indonesia and Malaysia, as well as in parts of Champa, became increasingly significant in the 14th and 15th centuries. Though Islam was unable to repress wholly a vigorous iconic tradition—in Southeast Asia it inherited a culture rather than imposed one—its spread certainly decreased the demand for many artistic skills. An example of Islamic culture based on inherited forms is provided by the typical Southeast Asian mosque, usually without a minaret, which owes much more to the Javano-Balinese multi-roofed temple than to the Middle Eastern domed building. In the wake of Islam, Hinduism almost completely disappeared, save in Bali and Lombok where it can still be observed, though in a highly modified form, and in the royal courts of the Buddhist kingdoms of mainland Southeast Asia, where Brahmins are required to provide rituals, coronations for instance, for which *Theravada* Buddhism makes no provision. But although *Theravada* rejected the conspicuous monumentality of earlier monarchical Buddhism, it still required craftsmen to carve and gild monastery buildings or to adorn them with glazed tiles and complex ceramic finials. Chinese influences

played an important part in the development of later Buddhist architecture. In Vietnam, where *Mahayana* Buddhism continued to flourish, together with Taoism and neo-Confucian cults, the arts of the court were strongly influenced by Ming China. Elaborate royal palaces, tombs, and dynastic temples were constructed, though little has survived the recent years of war.

Throughout Southeast Asia painting appears to have increased in importance, perhaps as the decrease in royal patronage produced a decline in sculpture and statuary. Only the simplest images were required, and these, more often than not, in a consciously archaic style. Narrative art, once in bas-relief, as in the great panels of Borobudur or those in the cloister of Angkor Wat, took the form of mural paintings, especially in the areas of Thai influence. And painting was the art form in which European influences were first experienced in the mid 19th century. At first, individuals such as the Javanese Raden Salah (1814–80) went to study in Europe, but gradually colonial powers instituted art schools under European directors.

Although the intention may have been to develop the native tradition, increasing evidence of western influence can be detected, though this may have been a natural outcome of the search for new idioms to express contempoary ideas. Certainly, there has been a marked swing towards secular subjects to be seen most clearly in the work of those artists in Bali who, between the wars, came under the influence of such Westerners as Rudolf Bonnet (b. 1927), Miguel Covarrubias (1904–57), and Walter Spies (1896–1947). Their pictures show a great simplification of forms and a proliferation of non-mythological themes. Further changes were brought about by the various independence movements, when artists played a part in the anti-colonial struggles. Ideological considerations led to an interest in popular and folk art, as well as in the search for new, non-Western idioms, to express Third World ideas and ideals. There is yet little sign of new art forms for the older Asian religions, but there are some interesting indications that those concerned with Christian art feel free to interpret this in Asian forms rather than in those evolved in Western Europe.

ANTHONY CHRISTIE

Bibliography. Boisselier, J. *La Statuaire du Champa*, Paris, École Française d'Extrême-Orient (1963). Boisselier, J. *Thai Painting*, Tokyo (1976). Boisselier, J. *The Heritage of Thai Sculpture*, New York (1975). Frederic, L. *The Temples and Sculpture of Southeast Asia*, London (1965). Groslier, B.-P. *Angkor: Art and Civilization*, London (1966). Groslier, B.-P. *Indochina: Art in the Melting-pot of Races*, London (1962). Hejzlar, J. *The Art of Vietnam*, London (1973). Holt, C. *Art in Indonesia: Continuity and Change*, Ithaca (1967). Kempers, A.J.B. *Ancient Indonesian Art*, Cambridge, Mass. (1959). Luce, G.H. *Old Burma, Early Pagan*, Locust Valley, N.Y. (1969). Ramseyer, U. *The Art and Culture of Bali*, Oxford (1977). Rawson, P.S. *The Art of Southeast Asia*, London (1967).

17

CHINESE AND KOREAN ART

A Famille Rose decorated plate; 18th century. Ashmolean Museum, Oxford (see page 331)

ALTHOUGH it is often said that China has the longest unbroken cultural tradition in the world, there are evident changes within that culture in the relative values of the visual arts. Chinese art displays no simple evolution from primitive beginnings to a mature artistic tradition. Indeed, there is at least one clear change of direction. In a very simple analysis, we can find a change from an "object oriented" culture of the early ritualistic societies of the Neolithic and Bronze Ages to the "painting and calligraphy honoring" culture from the Han period (*c*200 BC). From then on, although emphases and fashions change the basic evaluation is unchanged and the position of calligraphy and painting as "fine" arts is never questioned. This implies a radical change in cultural outlook just before and during the Han dynasty (206 BC–AD 221) for which there is both literary and archaeological evidence.

Before the Han period, society and its culture had been centered on a ritualism stemming from the ruler which controlled all aspects of life. In the earliest periods of the Neolithic settlement (4th millennium to 18th century BC) aesthetic considerations seem to have been of no great importance except in the making of ceramics, particularly those associated with burial rituals. Funerary pots seem to have been the most important works of art produced by these peoples.

The Bronze Age cult of ruler and state required grand objects and explicit symbolism and the Chinese produced magnificent bronzes which, in their symbolism, come closer to the expressiveness of "fine" art. But as ritual fell away in import-

Important centers mentioned in the text

ance toward the end of the Chou dynasty in the 3rd century BC, the casting of bronzes took its place among other crafts; this change coincided with the development of writing styles and the aesthetic consideration of calligraphy, itself regarded as a parent of the art of painting in China. Almost from the time of its appearance in the last centuries of the Chou dynasty painting was regarded as the one true art, with its close relation calligraphy. The art of painting has many roles, from the recording of likeness in portraiture, the creation of decoration or symbolism in bird and flower painting, to the expression of religious, poetic, or philosophic themes leading almost to abstraction. In China the separation of these roles is quickly marked and classified so that the aristocrat of the painter's world is at the poetic, philosophic abstraction end of the spectrum, and the decorative recording arts of portraiture and flower painting are at the other. This severe classification of subject matter had its basis in literary scholastic judgments, for to the scholarly meritocracy who became China's ruling class these judgments seemed natural.

The concern of scholars with both painting and poetry throws light upon the tradition which evolved, and helps to explain its cohesion. Culture is cumulative and China's emphasis on honoring the great, spread a strong web over the whole culture and kept alive a tradition of painting which in its limitation of materials and techniques might, at first consideration, appear over-restrictive. The wish to stay within the tradition was not a slavish copyist's instinct but a desire to remain in good company. The artist expressed his individuality within the tradition and the great artist enriched that tradition for future painters.

With the notable exception of images for the Buddhist church, sculpture never recommended itself to Chinese artists as a mode of anything but monumental expression. There must be many explanations for this but perhaps the most powerful is that it would be unthinkable that a scholar-artist should work with materials other than ink, paper, and silk. This would preclude the recognized "fine" artist from working in sculpture. As an extension, this same scholarly artist-patron would have no interest in artistic work produced by an artisan—except again in the context of Buddhism. There was indeed in Chinese civic and domestic architectural planning no need of sculpture; the great sculpture of China was produced for a church that has its roots in India, where sculpture was the chief medium of expression. The Chinese sculptor followed a foreign tradition to produce images, but this tradition did not take root in China.

The other applied arts of China, so highly regarded abroad, should be considered as the furnishings and trivia of a highly sophisticated and diverse society. In so far as they satisfy the eye and are made for their looks they can be considered as art but they never, after the inception of expressive painting, play anything but a minor role in China's visual culture.

Pottery of the Neolithic period (4th millennium–18th century BC). The Neolithic peoples of north China took a lively interest in the decoration and shape of pottery. This pottery is the only surviving expression of their artistic style although we know, from fragmentary remains, that they made basketry and wove silk and ramie. These materials do not survive the long time (some 8,000 years) of burial; we have to look to pottery for glimpses of current ideas of beauty and style.

The population of Neolithic China was widespread over the north and east of China. The early center of a culture given the type name of Yang Shao seems to have been in the Wei river valley, and here at the Pan P'o site (Sian) and the nearby settlement at Miao Ti Kou we find the potters already making a range of shapes: simple bowls and pointed based jars, which are of a rough cord-marked ware, and also decorated ware of fine-bodied pottery painted with slip in red, white, and black; the motifs are either of a geometric type or a stylized representation of fish and human faces. Further east, as this people spread along the valley of the Yellow River, we find similar shapes and decorated pots, but in each local area the decoration differs, and flower-derived designs are introduced in a non-repeating elegant design of curving lines and areas of dark and light.

Yet further to the east in the region of present-day Shantung and to the north and south of this region a related Neolithic people, given the type name of Lung Shan, also made distinctive pottery, sometimes also slip-decorated. They greatly enlarged the vocabulary of shapes to include composite forms, which necessitated luting together different parts, and it is clear that during the 4th and 3rd millennia BC the potter's wheel was developed in this eastern area of north China. This innovation made possible the production of very thin-bodied wares which were burnished, fired, and "reduced" to produce a glossy black pottery, only occasionally decorated by the addition of a pastry-type trimming. This very sophisticated pottery was the artistic tradition of the later Neolithic people who seem to have been closely related at least in their craft work to the metalworkers of the succeeding period.

While the metal culture peoples of the central and eastern area were overwhelming the Neolithic peoples of the central Yellow River area, there were many Neolithic settlements in present day Kansu for which the potters made most handsome painted urns and bowls—footed bowls—for their burial pits at the famous sites of Pan Shan, Ma Chia Yao, Hsin Tien, and Ch'i Chia P'ing. These late Neolithic decorated pots are the richest in the painted pottery tradition, the motifs moving from a formalized spiraling movement of Pan Shan to animal designs and even models of human heads in the round forming the cover of the jar. This is a style that died only as the area was eventually overrun by the Han.

The Bronze Age (18th–3rd centuries BC).

The flowering of art more nearly in the sense of an expression of some culturally meaningful ideas in a visually memorable form came with the perfecting of bronze-casting techniques and the elaboration of the ceremonial culture during the Shang dynasty (c1766–1122 BC). The question of the origin of the bronze culture and

A large Neolithic slip-decorated jar from Pan Shan in modern Kansu. Ashmolean Museum, Oxford

the proposition that the apparent absence of copper or tin artifacts may point to the importation of bronzecasting as a technique, is one that awaits further study. But as with the Neolithic peoples it is possible from evidence, particularly of weaponry, to suppose that at least part of the answer to the possible origins lies in the area to the northeast, the Baikalia region. The motifs, decoration, and shapes of the surviving bronze vessels are certainly all "Chinese" in character and were evolved to take part in a very specific cultural ceremonial. At least by the mid Shang period (14th century BC) the state of Shang was "Chinese". There was a written script, part hieroglyphic, part phonetic, which is recognizable as the ancestor of the present-day script; the shapes of the ritual vessels of these early people have in many cases been preserved, in a modified form, in the shapes of the traditional pottery, down to the present day. This was a typical Bronze Age society, with powerful warrior kings, a highly developed ceremonial, which included the sacrifice of humans and animals, particularly dogs, and enormous funeral pomp associated with the royal house. The mass of the population were to all intents still living a Neolithic life.

Thus the art of this society which survives in the durable materials of bronze and jade is exclusively associated with the ruling class and appears to have an overpowering ceremonial significance. With this in mind we can appreciate the exquisite productions found at the capital site of Anyang, especially in the royal tombs at Hsiao T'un. The full vocabulary of vessel shapes cast in bronze had been developed by this Anyang period (14th–12th centuries BC) and indeed some shapes were already on their way out. So this is the classic period of Shang bronze.

The decoration cast into the bronze was of two very different styles: one a simple representational style as seen in the animal masks and human faces, very telling and surprisingly

A bronze tripod caldron (ting) of the mid Shang period, decorated with dragons and a t'ao t'ieh mask. Ashmolean Museum, Oxford

tender; the other a stylized animal forming either a ferocious mask, the *t'ao t'ieh*, or a processional band around the vessel. This last style was the one developed and elaborated during the Shang period. The little one-legged *k'uei* dragon with a snout, horns, and ears seems to be the basic unit of much of this decoration. Confronted, a pair can become a very effective monster mask, albeit without a lower jaw. Although this *t'ao-t'ieh*, as it came to be called, has been interpreted as a symbol of greed, we can only guess the meaning of this motif. During the last two centuries of the Shang period the richness of the relief and surface texture was at its height. The animal character of the decoration was still fierce and the background developed a rich texture of spiral whorls so that even small ritual bronzes have an imposing monumentality and express a period style of solemnity and richness.

In a quite different way jade-carving, the other ceremonial art, bears this same period character. Following the simple style of bronzes, there are large numbers of small realistic representations of animals and birds, usually pierced as though for attachment to a thread or fabric. These are in the form of flat slips of stone cut into a silhouette shape, very simply incised and often called "amulets" for no very firm reason. Alternatively this very precious material was used for the ritual disks, possibly developed from Neolithic rings.

These have been given the general titles of *pi* and *huan* in Chinese and are associated with burial ritual and the ceremonial for the sacrifices to heaven. In the Shang period these ceremonial shapes seem to have been undecorated and to have held a meaning inherent in their shape and material which itself has a special place in Chinese culture.

Probably derived at this time from the Baikal area, the true nephrite jade has never been found within the greater China borders. This perhaps accounts for some of the mystique attached to it. However this may be, the very subtle qualities of toughness and the smooth, lustrous, unglassy surface and coolness to the touch have attracted the Chinese craftsman and connoisseur throughout the ages, and it is significant that jade had already taken this place in the culture of China in the Bronze Age.

Although there is a change in dynasty title with the overthrow of the Shang by the Chou (1111 BC), who would appear to have been their neighbors and possibly even relatives, the early years of the new dynasty saw little change in the general character of the crafts commanding attention. However, with territorial expansion and the enfeoffment of princelings to rule subsidiary states, regional styles emerged presenting a rich picture, still largely concentrated in bronze vessels. The appearance of birds in the decoration lends a lightness to the animal relief, while the dragon evolves to resemble a four-legged lizard or a serpent; the use of either of these variants leads to a totally different surface decoration. The serpentine interlaced dragon of the north, eventually studded with semiprecious stones, makes a rich textural effect in contrast to the elegant lizard dragons of the south, curling their way over a finely cast rhomboid decoration of interlocking square whorls. This introduces one of the favorite juxtapositions of the Chinese designer, sinuous line over an angular geometric motif.

To the south, in the state of Ch'u, was a foreign culture which became increasingly influential. It was strongly animistic, and gave birds, snakes, and antlers a special significance. There must have been for these people a vivid mythology in which real and imagined beings mixed freely, and from the aesthetic viewpoint this was one of the generating areas of the

An incised jade pendant of the Shang period. British Museum, London

visual arts. From this area comes lacquer-painted wood, pottery, and more rarely bronze, in which a poetic vision of life is expressed in terms not entirely allied to ritual. The style is free and elegant with loose, yet controlled lines and brilliant color which is striking and entirely characteristic. This whole culture of the southern state greatly influenced the northerners; and indeed the complex variety of this period, picturesquely known as the Warring States period, is only just now beginning to be understood. For clearly there were also people to the west in Szechwan, partly cut off from the central valley but aware of the crafts of the main culture; there were also very different people further southwest who rose to cultural maturity under the Han. And in the far north and west there were people in close contact with nomads and their crafts.

The Han period (*c*200 BC–AD 221). The 400 years of the Han dynasty, with the important preceding short Ch'in dynasty, saw the establishment of a recognizable nation-state covering an area bearing some relation to the China of today, except that the control of the east coast area was still unsure. The union of the Warring States of the last years of the Chou dynasty was achieved by the Ch'in in 221 BC under the "First Emperor", who called himself just that, Shih Huang-ti. This great administrative genius coordinated a road system, city building, and a defensive wall system in the north. The so-called Great Wall is a complex aggregation of various parts, which had existed in part as interstate boundaries. The arts of the Ch'in dynasty have not yet been fully investigated but the united country embraced a wealth of artistic traditions which began to make themselves felt during the Han period.

The Han dynasty is often referred to by the Chinese as possibly the finest, if not the greatest, of their history. It was certainly one of splendid experiment and achievement in many directions. In the arts, painting became a true means of artistic expression—or perhaps it would be fairer to say it was the first time in which there were ideas and concepts which required painting for their expression. As we have seen, before the Ch'in Han period, the chief cultural requirements had at first been ritual objects which were produced in jade and bronze, and then status objects again of jade, bronze, and lacquer in which were embodied some elements of the cult and ritual of the earlier dynasty.

The Han emperors brought under their control a wide area which included many subcultures, not only the imaginative and poetic culture of the Ch'u people, the myths of Szechwan, and the whole compendium of legends of the center and north, but also the much less understood cultures of the outlying areas of present-day Yunnan in the southwest and of the nomadic far north. Although the central government was at some pains to unify beliefs and to codify "religion" as part of the unification program, the few remains of painting on lacquer or on cloth give clear evidence of a richness of ideas which do not appear in the *Shih Ching*, the official record of the period. Painting became explicitly the prime means for expression of a complex of ideas whose symbolic meaning is

The banner found in the tomb of Lady T'ai; 1st century BC. Changsha Museum

not fully comprehensible today.

However, one can now point to specific examples of quality painting in this period. Firstly in the tombs of the Marquis of Tai, his wife, and son, at Ma Wang Tui, Changsha, Hunan, painted hangings were found draped over the coffins, in fine condition, as was everything in the tomb. A painted cloth has also been found in the same area. The hangings appear to represent the four layers of existence: the heavens, the sun, the moon, and heavenly beings; the mundane world of the dead; limbo; and at the bottom of the banner the netherworld. The whole design is composed with the wreathing lines and dragons of the bronze and jade decoration of previous centuries but with the addition of rich colors and, particularly in the upper portion, a feeling for atmosphere. In the middle portion

Chinese Bronzes

Casting bronze by the piece-mold method was the traditional craft of the Chinese metalworker in the Bronze Age (*c*18th–4th centuries BC). The most beautiful and elaborate objects were the ritual vessels found buried in grand tombs. These vessels, an important element in the rituals of the day, were quickly classified by shape and decoration all of which had names, often recorded in inscriptions. The shapes are associated with the preparation and serving of food and wine, an important part of the ceremonial. The decoration is to be seen as an expression of ideas and beliefs behind that ritual. This is particularly true of the earlier pieces produced before the 11th century BC.

▼ A wine vessel (*yu*) of the Shang period in the shape of a tiger with a human being. Musée Cernuschi, Paris

The metal alloy used is unusual because it contains lead (its constitution: copper, 73 percent; tin, 12 percent; lead, 12 percent). The method of casting bronze by multiple piece molds is complex and requires great skill from the potter, for he must produce an accurately keyed mold which can be assembled, into which the bronze can be poured, and then the mold removed. Neolithic potters achieved considerable expertise and must have been the major craftsmen in the development of the new bronzecasting technology. So accurate was the casting that Chinese metalworkers did not customarily tool their bronzes after casting; all the decoration was cast in the mold.

Above A mirror-back from the Warring States period (481–221 BC); diameter 14cm (5½in). Museum of Far Eastern Antiquities, Stockholm

▲ A wine vessel (*yu*) of the early Chou period, late 12th–11th centuries BC. Height 23cm (9in). Freer Gallery of Art, Washington, D.C.

A shallow bowl (*p'an*) of the Shang period, 13th–12th centuries BC. Diameter of rim 33cm (13in), depth 12cm (5in). Freer Gallery of Art, Washington, D.C.

Below right A vessel for storing liquids (*pien hu*) inlaid with silver; 4th century BC; height 31cm (12in). Freer Gallery of Art, Washington, D.C.

The vessels of the great period, mid to late Shang (14th–12th centuries BC), are elaborately decorated and sturdy in form. Their motifs are exclusively animal ones though they may be real or mythological. The chief animal is the *k'uei*, a little snouted two-legged creature always shown in profile. At an early date it developed ears and horns and a very pronounced eye. The mask, called a *t'ao t'ieh*, also dominates earlier pieces. It may appear as a mask in its own right or as a composite of two *k'uei* placed face to face at a join in the molds. These two motifs are enriched by a surface texture motif, a squared spiral (*lei wen*) and a growing vocabulary of animals: deer, elephant, fish, cicada, and felines. The human face, which gives such a haunting effect to rare bronzes, is perhaps the most vivid example of the power of the mixture of real and mythological in expressive art.

The role of the bronze vessel changes gradually from ritual to status symbol and this is reflected in both motifs and shapes. They become more varied and are freely used. Birds with curving plumes and crests were popular in east China and quadruped feline creatures or serpentine dragons make their appearance in the north and more metropolitan region. Shapes were often exaggerated or became almost domestic. Abstraction from the curving line to a plant scroll completed the change of character. Writhing snakes and bird-head motifs in undercut and cut-through style required the *cire perdue* casting method which Chinese craftsmen adopted and used as it was needed, though the source of their knowledge of this technique is not known. The logical development was to a decorative art in which inlay and gilding played an important role. The fine possible in silver and gold inlay on bronze produced some of the most elegant metalwork ever made in China.

MARY TREGEAR

Further reading. Barnard, N. and Sato, T. *Metallurgical Remains of Ancient China*, Tokyo (1975). Rawson, J. *Ancient China, Art and Archaeology*, London (1980). Watson, W. *Ancient Chinese Bronzes*, London (1962).

of the Lady Tai Banner (Changsha Museum) a skill in portraiture is evident, for the lady shown with her retinue is undoubtedly the lady of the tomb herself. The body in this tomb was so well preserved that we can make this assertion with unusual confidence.

Many of these characteristics of painting style can be seen in the remains of wall-paintings in the brick and stone tombs of the period with their detailed characterization of the figure painting, their lively observation of animals, and their use of sinuous brush strokes. Pictorial composition was still at the experimental stage: the allover placing of the elements of the picture read from bottom to top, to denote foreground to background. Problems of scale are unimportant at this time and where hills and trees are introduced, though beautifully expressed in a formalized style they "read" with no relationship of scale to figures and animals.

The brushwork and the quality of line are free and assured and have a fascinating strength—not surprising, for this is the era of the "draft script", that free but mannered calligraphy, often miscalled "grass script". The invention of the chancery clerks, it was quickly taken up by scholars. Thus during the Han period calligraphy became an "art" form with many well-recognized variants of script, and with it was developed a system of aesthetics which though simple could be sophisticated.

The aesthetics of calligraphy seem to have been expressed in moral rather than artistic terms. The equation of aesthetic quality with moral value is one ever after present within Chinese culture. This is partly due to the critical vocabulary and the literary tradition within which aesthetic writing is framed, but it also reflects the Confucian doctrine that "rightness" is an all-embracing term which can be applied to all judgments. The Chinese also had a penchant for classification which led very early to the naming and defining of the various calligraphic styles: for example, the Seal script (large and small), the Li or formal script, Hsing or running hand, and finally the draft or clerkly script. Each style has its own distinct character and use and the great masters of each style quickly entered the lists of artists.

The applied arts of the Han period begin to represent the paraphernalia of aristocratic life. The needs of ritual were now quite subordinate to the decorativeness and showiness of the object. Made in gilt bronze, or bronze inlaid with decorative stones, vessels are sometimes the traditional ritual shapes but characteristically the more utilitarian *hu* (storage jar) shape and the *tou* (stemmed covered bowl) became popular. The incense burner in the form of a mountain landscape, the *po shan lu*, caught designers' imaginations and was clearly important in the varied new religious rituals now practiced. Buddhism had come to China in the 1st century and at about the same time Taoism became formalized and ritualized, creating a need for objects and regalia to match the fully developed iconography of Buddhism. The consequent multiplication of materials and shapes is evident and the use of showy material is one of the features of the period. The chief materials used were bronze, both gilt and inlaid; lacquer, which is painted in the lively swirling styles originating in the southern states of the Warring States period; and carved jade, which retained throughout the centuries something of the mystique of earlier periods, although its use was increasingly decorative.

Weaving was also important during this period, with silk thread fully developed and indeed exported to the Middle East and very fine fabric woven into gauzes and handsome damask cloth of self-colored pattern. This was sometimes further enhanced with a multicolored silk embroidery in chain stitch in swirling design as a counterpoint to the rhomboid designs of the woven fabric.

The more outlying areas of the Empire brought special flavors to the visual arts. In Yunnan the kingdom of Tien claimed descent from the Han royal house but was clearly a quite different society. It had an obsession with bulls, perhaps to the point of worshiping them as we can see in the marvelous animal bronzes and cowrie containers covered with vivid village scenes. In artistic expression these people owed little to the metropolitan traditions, apart from the technique of fine bronzecasting. To the northwest in western Kansu, at the gateway to the central Asian trade routes, there had always been settlements from Neolithic times, and by the middle Han period this was a cosmopolitan area where some of the earliest Buddhist monastery settlements were to be established at Tun Huang in the 3rd century AD. The Chinese skills of bronzecasting had also traveled to the northwest, for the finds of a cast bronze cavalcade of horses and riders with chariots show a typical Chinese chariot and mounted horsemen, apparently originally silk dressed. This lively portrayal of the large horses from western Asia predates the T'ang ceramic tomb figures by many centuries but is evidence of the Han interest in foreign cavalry horses—and also perhaps further evidence of the Chinese preoccupation with the tribes on the western borders, an ever-present source of both trouble and trade.

In the mountains of Szechwan, now controlled by the metropolitan Chinese government, the expression of ideas in the arts has survived most happily in the carved soft stone and stamped brick panels. These range from fanciful mythological scenes depicting beliefs beyond the canon of "official" stories and beliefs that appear in the written literature of the period, to those showing ordinary scenes of hunting and salt-mining. There are also occasions when the world of mythology meets the everyday world which again seems characteristic of the expressive arts of the time. Contrasting in style are the well-cut and compositionally "tight" stone reliefs of the Shantung area, notably at the Wu Liang Tz'u. Here the traditional stories are told in pictures of bold, flat, low relief and striking silhouette, in compositions constructed, as were the paintings, to be read from bottom to top, showing recession without respect for scale. Chinese influence extended further to the north at this time through Manchuria and into north Korea, as we know from the famous tomb found by the Japanese at Lo Lang. The Han period marks the colonization of this area and the introduction of Chinese customs of burial, architecture, and perhaps of potting.

Architecture, although never regarded as an art in China, was developing in important ways in the Han period. The traditional technique of building, with stone footing, wooden pillar, and beam had developed over many centuries. In the late Chou dynasty the introduction of ceramic tiles and the consequent increased weight of the roof led to the development of the distinctive Chinese bracket taking the load from a wide span on to the columns. By the end of the Han period the engineering of these brackets seems to have been fully explored and the disposition of one-story buildings around courtyards had become established; from then onwards, with elaborations, this was to be the style and the tradition. Also in the Han period fire-baked brick and stone for building and for facing the traditional heavy beaten earth walls were introduced. It seems they were used primarily for tombs, whose barrel vaults were constructed underground, or for defensive walls, either for cities or for the huge and composite Great Wall.

Although there were later technical innovations, the main characteristics of traditional Chinese architecture of all types were established during the Han period, and Chinese settlements of the time must have looked similar to those of the 19th century, if simpler. The requirements of these buildings were the same: there was no great opportunity for interior wall decoration, except in the temples and tombs, and there was little felt need for or use made of sculpture, except the monumental type. The great exception to all these observations was the decoration and furnishing of the Buddhist temples and monasteries which began to be built toward the end of the Han dynasty.

Korea to the far north of China was inhabited by Neolithic peoples until the northern part of the peninsula was conquered by the Chinese during the empire-building period of the Han. A Chinese army of occupation was established at Lo Lang, and for a while at least the Koreans were under the control of Chinese rulers, learning for the first time something of Chinese language and culture. Evidence for this is preserved in the tomb of the period at Lo Lang. The famous painted lacquer basket with its scenes of filial piety found in this tomb is certainly a Chinese object and there is little, as yet, to show a local culture which was surely present as is shown in the early Koguryo tombs of Pyong Yang.

Northern and Southern dynasties (AD 220–581). With the collapse of the Han dynasty China moved into a period known as the Northern and Southern dynasties. As the name suggests

A Han period Chinese painted lacquer basket found in a tomb at Lo Lang in Korea, then under Chinese colonization. National Museum of Korea, Seoul

there were a number of autonomous states, each with its own court and coterie of artists. Very little survives of the painting and calligraphy of this period. However, it is the period of the great Buddhist cave temples, and the lavish sculptures and wall-paintings in them have been preserved. The cave temples are all situated in the northern states and so must represent the arts of the Wei and the Northern Ch'i. The painting and sculpture are, however, iconic in concept; this is new in Chinese art and must be regarded as a foreign inheritance. The sculpture in these caves is an unusually rich production by Chinese artists in this medium.

Although a considerable output was achieved in China in the service of the Buddhist church, little of the style spills over into secular art. In the south, the state of Chin has left us one artist, Ku K'ai-chih, both in the records and perhaps only indirectly represented, but nevertheless characterized, in at least one handscroll. This court artist seems to have been largely concerned, like all his contemporaries, with portrait painting. But it is also clear from their writings that the conception of the possibilities of painting as an expressive art were being explored perhaps more felicitously in theory than in practice and the treatise of Hsieh Ho (*c* AD 500), though terse to the point of obscurity, clearly carries some subtle understanding of the special quality of painting as an art.

Hsieh Ho's *Ku Hua P'in Lu* enumerates the six principles essential to the judgment of great painting:

First, spirit resonance which means vitality; second, bone method which is [a way of] using the brush; third, correspondence to the object which means depicting of the forms; fourth, suitability to type which has to do with the laying on of colors; fifth, division and planning, that is, placing and arrangement; and sixth, transmission by copying, that is to say the copying of models. (Acker, W.R.B. *Some T'ang and Pre-T'ang Texts on Chinese Painting*, Brill (1954) p4.)

These principles were probably based on an earlier set perhaps devised to assess the excellence of calligraphy. This may explain the apparent use of technical terms, now difficult to interpret but probably current at that time. The first principle seems at its simplest to refer to that quality in any painting which we may assert to be "alive" as opposed to "dead"—the quality in fact without which all other excellences are worthless. The second principle refers to the "strength" of brushwork, a quality that has nothing to do with the weight of the brush line but to its tensile quality, the ability of the artist to transmit his nervous and muscular control through the brush and the ink. This is a significant quality in calligraphy but equally in painting in China because of the use of the same media. The brush and the ink must always be the controlling factors and the manner of their use the main medium of expression.

The third and fourth principles seem somewhat mundane and must refer to a need for verisimilitude; remembering that this was a period of portraiture this need is clear. The fifth principle, of the composition of the painting, is interesting for from the few fragments of silk painting and from the wall-paintings of the period, it is clear that ideas of composition were forming. Even the beginnings of the great preoccupation with landscape painting which later formed the main theme of Chinese painting are visible in the surviving stone reliefs and wall paintings. The sixth principle seems to refer to the method of learning from copying models, and the consequent adherence to tradition.

These principles form a brief introduction to a short treatise on the major artists, past and present, arranged by classes of excellence as is the custom in so much Chinese critical writing. Unfortunately none of the work of the artists listed in the first and second classes remains and the critical assessment can give us no clear idea of their style. Ku K'ai-chih appears in the third class.

Perhaps the clearest hint of the style of the figure painters of the period comes through the surviving stone relief carvings. The simplest is a stamped brick wall found in the Yangtse area and preserved in Nanking Museum. It depicts the sages seated under trees. The men each sit under a tree in a mode of "figure and tree" group which survived for a long time. Each unit is slightly different but the treatment of the flowing line and the stylized tree is common and builds a quiet but moving composition which is almost two-dimensional and may have been taken from an ink painting original. The other very striking example is the stone sarcophagus now in the William Rockhill Nelson Gallery in Kansas City. Here the scenes show stories of filial piety with figures now really within a landscape setting, though still very stylized. Here is some indication of a tradition developing to express current poetic mythical themes.

Apart from painting and calligraphy the chief applied art of this period, about which surprisingly little is known, is the pottery of the eastern area, the state of Chin. In the northern part of Chekiang slow but steady progress was made through a succession of kilns in the making and perfecting of the elegant gray stoneware with a green glaze which was to be one of the technical and artistic achievements of the Chinese potter. From the 3rd to the 6th century potters in this area made strong pots in a great variety of shapes for everyday use. They also made a heavy well-potted stoneware for burial furniture, ornately decorated at first, later undecorated but bizarre in shape. These pots, with a gradually developing glaze, were the antecedents of the famous celadon wares of the 12th and 13th centuries.

As little is known of the arts of northern China apart from that produced for and preserved in the Buddhist temples and monasteries, it is hard to trace the links between China and Korea at this time. Indeed the only clear links are those of the Buddhist arts, sculpture, architecture, and bronze images, which occur in Korea apparently in a completely Chinese form. However, it is possible to see some distinctive Korean characteristics in the painting remaining on the tomb walls of the Tomb of the Dancers, at Tung Kou, Manchuria, or the vivid tortoise and snake preserved at the Namdo in Pyong Yang, the capital of Koguryo (37 BC–AD 668). Both these examples reflect a style of painting already seen in China but, particularly in the case of the dancers, there is something new in the color and formal arrangement—a characteristic angularity and sharpness which recur throughout the centuries. The tortoise and snake, a Chinese motif for the Black Warrior symbolizing the north, presents a nice contrast in style and marks another Korean style of sinuous line and delicate drawing which recurs often in decorative arts. While Koguryo is noted for its painting, Paekche is rich in Buddhist remains. The state of Old Silla with its capital at Kyongju was known by the Japanese as the "Land of Gold". Its goldsmiths produced the famous gold crowns found in the Kum Kwan-ch'ong tomb, and other rich gold jewelry. Jade was also a treasured material in Korea and the distinctive comma-shaped pendants, called by the Japanese *Magatama*, appeared at this time. The Japanese were very interested in the southern Korean state and many of the craft styles of Old Silla reappear in Japan.

The T'ang dynasty (618–906). By the 6th century in China the Sui state was subjugating the other kingdoms; ruler Sui

A gold crown from the Kum Kwan-ch'ong tomb; 5th–6th centuries AD. National Museum of Korea, Seoul

A section of the engraved side of a gray, stone sarcophagus; height 61cm (24in); c AD 525. William Rockhill Nelson Gallery, Kansas City

Wen-ti reunified the country and laid the foundations for one of the classic great dynasties of China—the T'ang. Artistically the Sui was a southern dynasty, but foreign motifs flourished and experiments were made particularly in large glazed ceramic figurines. Colored glazes were not yet used but the massive cream and brown guardians excavated at Anyang (Palace Museum, Peking) mark a move toward a tradition which flourished at its most flamboyant in the next 300 years.

The 300 years of the T'ang dynasty are ones of artistic vitality and great innovations, sophistication of patronage, and riches, but are poorly recorded in the arts. We know from literary references that painting became a major art, not only in the metropolitan life of palaces and great houses, but also in the temple building of the period, during which Buddhism was very influential. Great artists are recorded and were clearly treated with respect. Stories are preserved of the uncannily lifelike quality of their work: paintings of horses which galloped away and dragons which flew off into the clouds. Portrait painting was of importance, as one would expect in a time of affluence, and the giants such as Han Kan (*fl.* 742–56), Yen Li-pen (*ob.* 673), and Chou Fang (*fl.* 780–810) have cast their shadows down the ages. It is most unlikely that any of their actual work has survived but no doubt some of the copies of copies preserve something of their style. They show a refined and wiry drawing, and a strength of composition unknown before.

Probably our best clue to the special quality of figure painting at this time is to be gained from wall-paintings in the few tombs of the period that have been carefully excavated. In particular there is the tomb of the Princess Yung T'ai, made in AD 706 to be the burial place of a young girl murdered in a court intrigue and buried in state several years later by her father when he regained the throne. This is therefore an imperial tomb decorated by the court office, whose business this was. The court office was usually headed by a notable artist of the day. Thus the well-preserved wall-paintings in the processional way to the tomb chamber (now in Sian Provincial Museum) have a special interest. Their main subject is an extensive procession of guards (military and civil), servants, and retainers along both walls of the passage leading to the tomb chamber and culminating in a finely drawn group of ladies of the Princess' own household. These paintings show an assured representation of gently moving figures arranged in groups which have a most convincing spatial relationship to each other. The depth of the group is not ambitious and the painting of the figures, as opposed to the drawing, is little more than a "coloring in". However, the strength and confidence of the line remain in the mind's eye and must be regarded as an example of the current style of figure drawing.

We should remember that court tomb decoration at this time reflected the changed status of the emperor, who was now only a member of the aristocracy and not always of the most prestigious family. So although an imperial tomb would be planned with care and skill by the court artist, there was now no theocratic element in the position of the royal family to require a funerary art that differed from the seriously composed art for the living.

In terms of painting this can be demonstrated in the consideration of landscape painting. In the same tomb there are passages of ambitiously planned landscape, palace and hunting scenes carried out in color with some bravura. The piling of mountain on mountain and the placing of animals among trees again show an interest in spatial composition and hint at the solution of many problems which had previously remained unsolved. But a comparison of these landscapes with the famous painting called *The Flight of the Emperor Ming Huang* in the National Palace Museum, Taipei, shows the difference in quality between tomb painting and that of real life. In the Ming Huang painting the composition is ambitious and spatial relationships are worked out with care. The painting is in fresh blues and greens with touches of bright vermilion making a beguiling picture of an idyllic mountain valley. Indeed it has been suggested that far from depicting a desperate flight of an emperor, this is the scene of an aristocrat's pleasure excursion. This ambiguity of subject and mood highlights a later critical view of this type of painting as superficial and decorative.

The 8th century was a period of great artistic vitality which saw two of the very great artists of China, Wu Tao-tzu and Wang Wei. Wu (*c*680–*c*740) was a marvel of his time, a man of great energy and enormous output if we are to believe even some of the stories told about him. He decorated temples and palace buildings with figures, animals, landscapes, and religious scenes, and his vitality of line became a legend. Indeed this is all that is left for no certain paintings survive and only few somewhat crude stone engravings after his style have been preserved in ink rubbings. However, his reputation was such that a school of figure painters long traced their ancestry to him, and he remains the foil to his contemporary, the retiring poetic Wang Wei (699–759). Wang Wei is credited with the foundation of the school of ink landscape painting which was to become the basis of much of the serious painting of China for the next millennium. The discarding of color and the development of the sensitive use of ink on silk or paper marked a decisive change of style which had a lasting influence on Chinese painting and aesthetic ideas.

Apart from these important developments in landscape painting, the earlier half of the dynasty saw a great output of Buddhist art, painting, sculpture, and bronze, to decorate the many temples built on the mountains of China. This is the period of rich patronage of both the Buddhist and the Taoist churches, and the vogue for pilgrimage to the newly designated holy places of China. In many cases these were at places hallowed by time, which had had some special significance to the native animistic religions, but which were now marked by Buddhist and Taoist buildings. Unfortunately for a study of the temple arts, the fierce anti-Buddhist iconoclastic movement of the early 840s has left little of the buildings or their contents. Thus the chief remains are again remote cave temples and again in the north of the country.

青綠關山迴
埒岊道路長
宋人於使長
李自國祥泫
爲名和利邢
霜芳輿忙年
陳失共氏共宗
近季庫
甲午新秋
尚題

The Flight of the Emperor Ming Huang; 8th century; ink and color on silk; height 56cm (22in). National Palace Museum, Taipei

The great capitals at Ch'ang-An and Loyang, planned and built by Sui Wen-ti and his son, became under the T'ang the first splendid cosmopolitan centers of the Far East. Uighur Turks, Sogdians, and foreigners from further west were visitors and traders in the flourishing cities. Cosmopolitan richness is evident in all the applied arts of the time: silver and gold vessels which show a marked Sogdian character and thus preserve the strong tradition of Sassanian art; the use of glass, rare in China and always apparently under foreign influence; and the more traditionally Chinese crafts of silk weaving, lacquer, and pottery in a colorful variety of styles. Recent finds in Turfan of woven brocades and embroidered damasks as shoes and fragments bear witness to a flourishing silk industry which drew its inspiration for design from outside China but produced a style that is readily recognizable as of the 7th and 8th centuries in China.

The lacquer wares of the T'ang dynasty, richly painted or inlaid with a showy mother-of-pearl and amber decoration, aptly show the period style and accords with the general ideas of the court. The collection of lacquer wares preserved in the Shoso-in in Nara gives some indication of the range of possibilities of the medium at this time. The delicately painted landscape on the *pi-pa* (lutes) and the elegantly inlaid furniture contrast with the richly inlaid mirror-backs. The latter are an example of the use of lacquer as a material for inlay on a metal ground. It also appears that carved lacquer was a technique developing during the latter part of the T'ang

dynasty. The earliest example known is the lacquer-painted leather armor from Miran in which disks were cut into the lacquer to show successive layers of different colors. This must be regarded as the forerunner of one of the major lacquer techniques developed by the Chinese.

In ceramics a similar taste for the colorful and lively resulted in the traditional funerary pottery being made of colored glazed earthenware, an idea and probably a technique borrowed from the Middle East but made so completely Chinese that many authorities question its origin. The tomb models of people, animals, and buildings were made for a purpose similar to those of the previous dynasties: representations of the household and equipment to be enjoyed by the dead. But in fashionable metropolitan society they also became status symbols for the living and were paraded before burial as a show of wealth and position. Thus for a few years they became more than funeral objects and although they cannot quite be classed as sculpture, the finest examples do have some quality of modeling and vitality which appeals directly to people of quite another age. By the very nature of their mass production and the reason for their manufacture these tomb models must stand in somewhat the same position to the fine arts as do the tomb wall-paintings.

In the main line of potting in China, that of the high-fired wares, the T'ang period sees the further development in the north from the firing of a white-bodied ware to the production of true porcelain by the 7th century. In the south, in Chekiang, the gray-green stoneware was refined, reaching the elegance of the Yueh ware of Shang Lin Hu by the 9th century. Apart from these are the handsome black-glazed stonewares of the north, sometimes with a striking gray or purple splash, and the start of the long-lasting kilns of Hopei which specialized in slip decoration of a buff-bodied stoneware, known under the generic term of Tzu Chou ware. Pottery is not a localized craft in China, and with the unification of the country and the establishment of an immense consumer market in the two capitals there was a rapid growth in the circulation of all notable wares. In turn this led to the imitation of popular types in all the major kilns; and so diversification became complex and increased from this period onward.

The great richness and inventiveness associated with the T'ang period arts probably more rightly belongs to the mid T'ang and particularly to the reign of the Hsuan Tsung Emperor (847–60). For, with the recurring troubles that followed his reign, the country, and the patronage on which the arts depended, became more unsettled. We know little of the details of late T'ang dynasty art and it would be wrong to assume that quality fell away. It was, rather, that the character changed as once again the country was divided under separate courts during the 10th century.

The Five Dynasties period (907–60). Although no actual scrolls remain from this period it is clear from their persisting reputations that there were great painters during this very influential century. Such giants as Fan K'uan (fl. 990–1030), Li Ch'eng (fl. 940–67), Tung Yuan (fl. 947–70), and Chu Jan (fl. 960–80) have been regarded with awe by painters of later centuries. They were versatile court artists who could be asked to paint portraits, Buddhist paintings, and decorative work, but nevertheless earned their reputation in the exacting art of ink on silk landscape painting. With their contemporaries they developed the magnificent large mountain landscapes which have been given the name of "master mountain" compositions. Their pictures seemed to their contemporaries to embody much of the current thought of the literati concerned with ideas of Taoism and the place of man within the world. These ideas can be dramatically demonstrated by placing man in mountain surroundings; and the magnificent mountains of north and east China, with their cloud-wreathed peaks and streaming waterfalls, became the models for the classical painting of the 10th- and 11th-century painters.

At first these large paintings were grand in scale and concept, whether they were derived from the gaunt northern landscape or the softer southern hills of Kiangsi. Human beings occasionally appear but seem to be ants creeping through an overpowering terrain, not at home in a paradise like their T'ang predecessors. The rocks are huge and usually build up to a towering center block of background, dominating the picture but divided from the nearer scenes by a wreath of cloud, itself creating a sense of mystery and unexplained distance. Incidentally, the cloud perhaps also disguises a change of distance, for the falling eye-level of the composition was

still fairly simply applied and a large step was often hidden by the cloud. The mid-to-foreground of the picture would then be composed in two or three levels but never approaching very close to the viewer. Five Dynasties' pictures, known only from copies, are typically remote in feeling and express the grandeur of nature at its most dramatic and eternal. There is no expression of weather in these paintings, except for the snow of winter and the bare trees of the north, compared with the grassy slopes of the southern artists and the leafy trees of a more hospitable climate. No effects of light and storm are used. This is understandable in an aesthetic concerned with the expression of the eternal reality of nature.

With the brief establishment of regional courts in the 10th century and the southern court at Nanking, the kilns of the Chekiang area came into prominence once more with a very refined production of gray-green high-fired wares at Shang Lin Hu. This considerable group of kilns, at least 25 around the lake, made varied qualities of this gray-green ware, but the best was called Yueh ware. The name derives from the old name of the area, the state of Yueh running down the east coast of China. This lovely pottery has a finely ground gray

A Yueh ware ewer; 10th century; height 20cm (8in). Ashmolean Museum, Oxford

body, strongly but often thinly and elegantly potted, sometimes quite plain but often decorated with a very fine incised line in bird and flower decoration which shows faintly through the thin, blue-green glaze. These wares were very highly valued in their time and praised in the writings on tea which was then becoming popular. The gray-green ware was thought to be the most suitable for tea cups, in contrast to the white wares of the north, which, also of a fine and elegant quality, were valued as wine cups but thought too anemic for the pale, greenish tea.

It is interesting that pottery was from now onward a collector's item and worthy of note by poets and scholars who even graded the wares from the more notable kilns in order of preference. This patronage must have a great deal to do with the variety and quality of pottery production in China. It was paralleled by an interest in all the minor arts which provided objects for the wealthy and cultured man's house: those of the jade-carver, the bamboo-carver, the ink stone maker, and to some extent the metalworker. This seems to be the start of the cult of the scholar's taste which encouraged the elegance and restraint so often associated with Chinese taste in the applied arts, but which is only one of the strands of a much more complex thread. As we have seen in the account of the T'ang period, the wealthy had a taste for the showy and the rich. This taste persisted and is evident in all periods of affluence and was indeed reflected in the peasant arts of all periods, in their love of bright color and ebullient decoration. However, with the establishment of a scholar class, an influential patronage grew for restrained design, elegance of form, and above all for a high-quality technical workmanship. Not for the Chinese scholar the Japanese cult of the faulty or the "simple"; sophistication and perfection seem to guide the eye of the gentleman.

Korea under the Koryo dynasty (918–1392). For Korea this was a period of relaxation in China's influence with the establishment of the Koryo dynasty. The arts of Korea nevertheless still show some family resemblances to those of China. It is, however, noticeable that painting in Korea remained an applied art in the sense that all surviving works are portraits of the most formal kind or specifically Buddhist iconographic subjects. Likewise sculpture, which plays a relatively important role in Buddhist artistic expression, was produced in monumental size in the earlier part of this era. It is in the smaller craft arts of metalwork and ceramics that the style of the period is most clearly seen. This is a style both conservative and experimental, in which we are aware of the precursor but also of the inventiveness and innate lightness of touch of the Korean craftsman. The graceful metal forms inlaid in silver with landscape scenes seem to be specifically Korean in both form and character of decoration; so are the mother-of-pearl inlaid lacquers and perhaps most strongly the celadon glazed ceramic.

Early in the Hu period (993–1150) some of the most elegant green-glazed wares of any part of the Far East were made in

A Korean inlaid celadon bowl; 10th–11th centuries. Collection of G.St.G. Gompertz

the tunnel kilns of Koryo. They are in some way related to the 10th-century Yueh wares of north Chekiang, but the character has been subtly changed; for the Korean celadons have a softness and gracefulness of form combined with a softness of blue-green glaze which sets them apart. In the 12th and 13th centuries the Korean potters evolved a technique of decorative inlay into the leather-hard body of the pot. This involved a fine incising of the decoration which was then inlaid with colored clay, dark gray and white. The whole was then covered with the lustrous blue-green glaze which resulted in a muted three-tone decoration. In the earlier examples this decoration is sparse and graceful, much as was seen in the silver inlaid bronzes. Later the designs became more crowded and clumsier and degenerated into stiff and trivial decorations. The latest move by the Koryo potters (1250–1350) was the introduction of underglaze metallic oxide painted decoration. In Korea this seems to have started with the use of underglaze iron painting which gives a dark brown color, appearing black under the celadon glaze overlying it. Copper and cobalt were quickly added to the repertoire to match but not to imitate the experiments being carried out in China; indeed Korean potters may well have been in the lead in these technical experiments with metallic oxide underglaze painting.

The Sung dynasty (960–1279). The relations between China and her northern and western neighbors in the period of the Sung dynasty is of great importance in political and social terms. In the visual arts this is a period of unrest, division, and ultimate reunification. First the Chin Tartars troubled the north and gradually overran the country north of the **Yangtse**

Sung Ceramics

A highly developed taste for and understanding of pottery is one of the characteristics of Chinese artistic taste. It has had a profound effect on the position of pottery within the culture of the country and indeed upon the status and quality of potting throughout the world, to the extent that in English one of the words for high-quality pottery is "China".

In such a craft, technology and design go hand in hand, for the material and techniques of production largely control the finished results. One of the great contributions of Chinese potters was the development of a high-fired stoneware and matching glaze. Body and glaze both contain a high proportion of some form of alumina and silica which provide the strength and fusibility of the fired clay; the natural melting temperature of such a clay would be far above the reach of a potter's kiln and so a flux of potassium or calcium is added to lower the melting point to within the 1,200–1,350°C level, within the range of a kiln. Even this temperature is difficult to achieve and hold for the required time—a problem that had to be overcome by the kiln builders. At first they developed a simple up-draft pit kiln, which in east China gave way to a more effective single chamber down-draft kiln. By the 13th century this in turn was extended to produce a climbing multichamber kiln, effectively a chain of down-draft kilns, similar to the *noborigama* used in Japan today. The Chinese "dragon" kiln is a tunnel in which successive fires are lit to maintain a strong up-draft on a sloping site.

A whole group of monochrome stonewares all with a gray body and iron-bearing glaze have come from all over China, reaching their greatest quality in the Sung period (11th–13th centuries). The reduction firing, common to all stoneware production in China, has produced all the green, blue, gray, and even dark brown/black colors of the glazes, and also the gray body. These wares share a feeling of great strength on handling and a distinctive smoothness of glaze, not usually shiny but glossy. An affinity with jade in handling quality and even in looks was obviously appreciated, and beautiful simple wheel-made forms were developed to make some of the classics of ceramic art. The two greatest wares are perhaps the Ju ware of the Kaifeng area in the 11th and 12th centuries and the Lung Ch'uan celadons of the 13th and 14th centuries.

◀ A Lung Ch'uan celadon bowl. Diameter 14cm (5½in). Percival David Foundation, London

Below left A Ju ware cup and stand. Diameter 17cm (7in). Percival David Foundation, London

▼ A Ying Ch'ing cup and stand; height 9cm (3½in). Collections Baur, Geneva

The white-bodied wares, developed in parallel but a little later in north China, have their own quality and indeed their own forms. Early in taking their inspiration from imported silver wares, the potters made a thin-walled ware with an elegant finish of the lip and foot which are features of the pre-porcelain white wares. The most elegant among many such white wares is the Ting which has an ivory tinged glaze and a thin but not translucent body. Although translucency had been achieved by the 7th century, it was some time before it was exploited, especially for wine and food vessels. The Ching-te-chen kilns have made porcelain production their speciality from the 11th century until the present day. Here they have made some of the world's finest white porcelain; characteristically it is a pure white body with a pale bluish translucent glaze called Ying Ch'ing. The decoration current in the Sung period (960–1279), of an incised line under the glaze, acquires a special quality when used on this translucent material.

In a country in which pottery was used for all domestic purposes, it is natural there should be a tradition of strong, heavy-grade wares. Notable among "folk" potting are the slip-decorated jars, bowls, and pillows, first made in the north and called Tzu Chou wares and then produced in countless kilns throughout the country. Painting in slip under a transparent glaze produced some of the strongest graphic decoration in the world. This tradition was the basis for the later cobalt oxide underglaze traditions of the famous "blue and white".

Another local potters' tradition is the "tea ware" of Fukien. Coming originally from the Chien Yang area of west Fukien it has a chocolate-colored body and a thick brown glaze in which impurities caused a streaked effect called "hare's fur". The bowls from these kilns were used for tea drinking in the Ch'an (Zen) sect of Buddhism—popular in the Hangchow area temples of the 13th and 14th centuries. The association of the bowls with the ceremony was so strong that the Japanese, who came to China to learn the teaching and traditions of Zen, took the bowls back with them and called them *Temmoku* after the area of the temples (T'ien Mu Shan) in which they had found them. This is the generic term for all imitations of the Fukien wares.

MARY TREGEAR

Further reading. Gompertz, G. St G.M. *Chinese Celadon Wares*, London (1958). Gray, B. *Early Chinese Pottery*, London (1953). Palmgren, N., Steger, W., and Sundius, N. *Sung Sherds*, Stockholm (1958).

Above A Ting ware bowl. Diameter 28cm (11 in). Percival David Foundation, London

▲ A *Temmoku* "hare's fur" bowl; diameter 10cm (4 in). Ashmolean Museum, Oxford

River. In 1124 the Southern Sung court was set up in Hangchow and remained until the late 13th century when the Mongols, under Genghis Khan, conquered both the Chin and the Sung to reunite the country under foreign rule. This makes the assessment of the culture of the country complicated; for example it is difficult to trace the course of the arts of the influential north China area during the Chin occupation.

The applied arts of the Sung dynasty as a whole have acquired a special reputation for superb craftsmanship and elegance of design. This reflects the scholar gentlemen's taste, which was also that of the court in this unusually cultured period. Although present in all aspects of design from architecture to jade-carving, this special taste can be most clearly seen in the ceramics of the period. Although ceramics were a minor art, they represent for us most faithfully the taste of the Sung, for the pots are among the few completely reliable remains from the period.

The scholar taste is typified by the elegant monochrome stonewares and porcelain. First came the northern wares of Ting, Ju, and Chun, to be followed by the southern Lung Ch'uan celadons, Fukien Temmoku ware, and Ching-te-chen Ying-Ch'ing porcelains. The creamy white wares of the Ting Chou kiln area were thinly potted and incised or impressed with a floral or fish motif, then coated with a thin, transparent, ivory-colored glaze and the finished ware was warm-toned and elegant. The finer-quality pieces are translucent.

This was the most favored ware of the 11th century, but it was superseded by Ju ware in the 12th. Made at kilns near the capital at Kaifeng, Ju is a gray stoneware with a green-gray glaze and epitomizes the sober but sensitive taste of the scholar. These highly prized wares were made in shapes either reminiscent of the old ritual bronzes or in simple ceramic bowl forms, their chief beauty being their nicely balanced shape and rich glaze. In Sung times the glaze on a gray stoneware was thickly applied and fired in a way that left many small bubbles suspended in the glaze, thus giving it almost a third dimension, accentuating its thickness as the light is diffused within it. The addition of a crackle for a short time during the mid Sung period seems also to have been a device to accentuate the thickness of the glaze. It had the additional fascination of

A Sung dynasty Ju ware bowl; diameter 17cm (7in). Percival David Foundation, London

similarity to the flawing in jade.

Indeed the quality of texture and translucency of the thick feldspathic glazes of the gray stoneware tradition of the Sung often come very close to the qualities of nephrite. The southern wares came into their own in the late 12th and 13th centuries; Lung Ch'uan, Chekiang celadons, and the frail-looking Ying Ch'ing porcelains of Ching-te-chen are the descendants of their northern counterparts in style and quality. Only the Temmoku wares of Fukien seem to have a new quality to add to the black glazes of the north. These fascinatingly glazed, dark-bodied wares were the local product of a kiln at Chien Yang, central Fukien, which were adopted by the Ch'an (Zen) Buddhist sect temples which flourished in that district in the 13th century. Thus this ware has achieved a reputation as "tea ware" and engendered a whole style of potting associated with tea ceremonies both in China and Japan. The body and glaze are heavily ferruginous and have been fired in an oxidizing atmosphere, but the glaze has impurities in it which can result in lovely "hare's fur" or "oil spot" effects. The popularity of this ware is exemplified by the number of imitations made at other kilns, both in central and northern China; in each case the clay is dissimilar and the resulting ware, though clearly close in spirit, can be distinguished.

The everyday wares of the north, notably the large group known as Tzu Chou, are made of sturdy gray stoneware with ingenious decoration under the glaze involving the use of slip, either as a painting material or as a coating through which the design is incised. These boldly decorated wares with an iron or copper underglaze decoration, which were initiated in the south, reveal the continuing interest in decoration found in the north of China in most periods.

The first century of the Sung dynasty, although politically hazardous, saw particular activity in the sphere of painting. The court at Kaifeng attracted the greatest artists of the period and with Imperial patronage, notably of the Hui Tsung Emperor, an Academy was formed which gave official artists a parity with other academicians and court officials. This recognition brought with it all the benefits of honor and risks of stultification which similar systems have demonstrated throughout the world. At first the great landscape school of the 10th century blossomed with such masters as Kuo Hsi (c1020–90) carrying through the classicism of the earlier masters in a baroque style. His paintings have survived only in copies, but they show a virtuosity which matches his reputation among contemporary critics. This massive style of painting seems to be both the culmination of a century-long tradition and a solution to the problem of creating a landscape "in which one can walk about", the ambition of the scholar-artist-official of the period. It provides, with its complex composition, a variety of experience for the viewer which is almost overwhelming.

It also bears within its enormous richness the seeds of the experiments of the 12th and 13th centuries. Perhaps directly associated with the taste of the academy-court artist the paint-

From a Northern Sung dynasty painting: Fishermen by Hsu Tao-ning. William Rockhill Nelson Gallery, Kansas City

Bamboo Branch by Wen T'ung (fl.1049–79); ink on silk. National Palace Museum, Taipei

ing of the mid 12th century also brought to the fore a style of small-format painting which is so to speak a detail of the previous massive paintings. Here the painter brings all his observation and understanding of the natural world—landscape, birds, flowers, or bamboo—down to the scale of an album leaf or slightly larger, a format that demands a new and special technique of composition. This can be most clearly demonstrated by the bird and flower compositions of the court of the Hui Tsung Emperor. The surface pattern of the composition has now been brought into play and a new dimension is in the hands of the painter. The interplay of space, line, and form becomes the special concern of the bamboo painter and the bird and flower painter. The development of a sophisticated surface composition—the so-called "one corner" arrangement—and the sensitivity to near-balance and off-balance produced some of the most delightful paintings in this category.

Landscape painting seems entirely to change its *raison d'être*. The philosophy of the Taoist-poet is replaced by the more romantic artist creating a world of a specific atmosphere of soft sadness, weeping mists, and evening light. The painters of the Southern Sung court at Hangchow were the heirs to the mid-12th-century Kaifeng court. The link was the artist Li T'ang who, as an old man, was appointed director of the new academy in Hangchow. As a younger man he had developed a new brush style and compositional interest, parts of which influenced other artists. In line with the new self-consciousness of composition came a conscious invention and naming of brush strokes, to such an extent that in Southern Sung court painting the brushwork and ink tone (ink "play") could almost become the subject of the painting. But never wholly, for Chinese painting never takes the full step to abstraction. However, Li Tang's "axe cut" stroke, a chopping harsh brush stroke executed with the side of a brush full or half-charged with ink and swept sharply down, was one of the first of the tradition.

The greatest exponents of this school of painting were Hsia Kuei (1180–1230) and Ma Yuan (1190–1224), contemporaries and shining lights of the later Southern Sung academy. They could handle small or large, and especially horizontal compositions and embody the great aphorism of the period "to represent 1,000 *li* of space in one foot of silk." This expression of space was very influential among the Japanese painters of this and later times. The Chinese artists had such a sureness of touch in the handling of ink tone that it became a very expressive medium, capable of evoking not only space, but also color and texture. Moreover paper was now often the chosen base for painting, offering a wider scope for ink texture than silk.

The elegancies of the court artists of the 13th century were carried further by the great Ch'an (Zen) artists of the period. Both Mu Ch'i (fl. c1269) and Liang K'ai (c1140–1210) appear to have been trained in the academic styles of their day, but their religious experience and motives for painting took them along different paths. In their work, preserved in

Early Spring by Kuo Hsi

This large landscape in the National Palace Museum, Taipei, Taiwan, is painted in ink and slight color on a tea-colored silk. The evocation of a dry, early spring season in the mountains is an elaborate composition of vignettes of life and scenery ranging from fishermen on the river side to a temple half way up the mountain and a far receding valley to the left. It seems to be a composite memory of more than one landscape which has been constructed in the style of the rich post-classical period of painting: Kuo Hsi (c 1020–90) has composed the picture by the traditional means of a series of eye-levels, in this picture not always extending right across the panel so that we view it in a series of steps to either side of the central column. Each scene is actually at eye level, carefully observed and expressed quite directly with a free but well controlled brushwork.

A disjointed effect is avoided by the other traditional tool of the Chinese painter: the surface composition is sensitively balanced by both line and tone. Kuo Hsi likes to use a swirling, curving line which gives this composition a movement swinging our eyes up the picture and carrying them smoothly from one scene to another. The use of tone in such an ink painting—for the color is very slight and in touches of green and brown—serves to compose the surface so our eyes are enticed and held. Quite unlike a European painting in which atmospheric tone is all important, a heavy tone and strong contrasts being reserved for the foreground, accents in Chinese painting are placed at crucial points over the surface of the painting, often in conflict with the requirements of recession. It is in the control of these two modes of composition, the balance of eye-level recession, of linear and surface composition, that the mastery of this style of painting rests. *Early Spring*, masterpiece as it clearly is, is one of the earliest large scroll paintings to survive in the original. This makes it one of the chief touchstones and reference points in the study of Chinese painting.

MARY TREGEAR

◄ Two details from *Early Spring: above* waterfalls and temples among mountains, from the right-hand side; *below* fishermen on the river side, from the bottom left corner

► *Early Spring* by Kuo Hsi; 158×108cm (62×43in), 1072. Painted in ink and light color on a tea-colored silk scroll. National Palace Museum, Taipei

Japan, the marvelous ink and brush control is used to express a vibrant life in all objects, living or inorganic. Mu Ch'i can express the weight, color, texture, and form of persimmons as readily as the extraordinary peace of the Kuanyin in meditation, while Liang K'ai expresses the texture and movement of a monk's robe and a humorous insight into the psychology of the monk himself.

Thus 13th-century south China seems to have produced a school of painters of sensitivity and self-awareness using techniques of a very high order, either in the service of a romantic, elegant sadness or of a lively Buddhist cult. It is not clear what happened in the north after the Chinese court had left. It seems possible that painters continued to work and more than likely that they worked anonymously; several paintings of distinction have been put forward as belonging to the period and they reflect a tradition of minute observation and unselfconscious concern with all aspects of life. They have been classed as genre paintings, but they include landscape painting of a serious kind, not of the grand school but borrowing much of the technique and calmness of those masters.

The Yuan dynasty (1279–1368). It may well be that the fusing of two general lines of painting, the sophisticated and the minutely observed, generated the great art of the 14th century. Much is made, traditionally, of the peculiar position of the official in a highly organized bureaucratic society when that society is controlled by a foreign head of state. The choice facing the Confucian scholar official was either a career in the service of a foreign regime or a self-imposed retirement from the capital to the simple life, probably on the family estate. Such was the position when the Mongols conquered China in 1280 and Kublai Khan set up a capital at Khanbalik, or Peking. The position of the Chinese intelligentsia was given one more complicated twist. The Yuan government now

A detail showing bamboo stems from an album painted by Wu Chen in 1350; National Palace Museum, Taipei

headed a united country, but under the domination of an uncultured but very strong foreign clan. A great number of potential officials decided to retire from service and the painters among this class probably found themselves with time to practice their art. They were in no way restricted and were in contact with each other but living away from the center that would have been their natural milieu in other times.

So the enrichment of the painters' outlook, brought about by the unification of the country and a renewed awareness of the grand traditions of the North, coincided with an unusual isolation of the artists, who at the same time were able to concentrate on their art free from concerns of court or patronage. This is an almost unique set of conditions and one to which the richness of the artistic output of the period is often ascribed. It is certainly true that during the 70 years of the Yuan dynasty some half-dozen great painters were active and produced work that has influenced Chinese artists to the present day.

Chao Meng-fu (1254–1322), a cultured and successful official, calligrapher, and painter, whose wife, Kuan Tao-sheng (1262–c1325), was also an accomplished painter of bamboo, stands out as the scholar artist who did not retire but who fulfilled his career and painted perhaps in the "court" style of the day. There was in fact no academy, but Chao Meng-fu and his son continued the scholarly Northern court tradition of thoughtful landscape painting and quiet observation. Wu Chen (1280–1354) and Li K'an (1245–c1320), individuals of great power in painting, worked in a style of fluent brushwork, both favoring bamboo as a subject although Wu Chen also excelled in marvelously free landscape painting. There is something here of the Southern courtly style in the brushwork and in the nature of the landscape for these artists tended to congregate in the lower Yangtse area—the Nan Chiang area in the south and Anhui in the north. Again and again the landscapes are of low hills, lakes, and rivers painted in the wet, smooth ink tones of Wu Chen or the silvery, dry ink of Ni Tsan (1301–74). This artist was a real eccentric with a restricted but clear-sounding genius. His style, his composition, and indeed the spirit of his uninhabited landscape haunted painters over the centuries, although none have quite matched the necessary asceticism to catch his spirit.

Of the group of great artists Wang Meng (1309–85) was probably the least accessible and so less obviously influential although his work was much admired by 17th- and 18th-century masters. Wang Meng painted bravura compositions, constructed in the classic style but treated in a completely individual style, densely worked and textured to a richness not usually tolerated in China. The absence of sky in some compositions is an experiment not repeated until the 18th century.

Finally we cannot leave this creative half-century without looking to Huang Kung-wang (1269–1354) and his Fu Ch'un mountain handscroll (National Palace Museum, Taipei). This magnificent landscape, the work of a 70-year-old artist, is the apotheosis of his style. With economy of brush but marvelous variety of handling he builds up a landscape immediately at-

A Yuan dynasty porcelain jar; height 39cm (15in). Cleveland Museum of Art

tracting and absorbing. This scroll became the greatest treasure to artists through the centuries and the opportunity to see and study it was a matter of pilgrimage for such varying painters as Shen Chou (1427–1509), Shih T'ao (1630–1707), and Wang Chien (1598–1677). This painting seems to stand as a beacon: it synthesizes the materials and tradition of the classic Northern court style and shines a light over the school of Wu painters who follow, through to the 17th century.

Thus the Yuan dynasty period is astonishingly rich in individual painters. Their work, perhaps in the original in some cases, comes through to the present day with great clarity and has been respected and admired by all artists in the intervening centuries.

The Yuan court of Mongol administrators was uninterested in the literati arts of south China but took a lively interest in the applied arts: jewelry, metalwork, ceramics, and silks. Here it is likely that their knowledge of Middle Eastern art was influential. Portraiture became very important and some Imperial portraits have survived. These have the straightforward boldness of the record of a grandee who requires a likeness of himself and his accoutrements. As always with Chinese portrait painting, however formal, the character of the sitter is there, although there may be little interest in solidity of form or nuance of color.

For the furnishing of aristocratic houses, craftsmen produced metalwork of silver and gold, engraved and inlaid. The use of precious metals in China for bowls and other vessels is often regarded as a foreign-style craft. However, it was a consistent if not very flourishing craft from the T'ang period onward. Chinese metalworkers always tended toward casting as their first choice of technique, using turning and beating only when essential. Consequently their work sometimes has a bizarre appearance, achieved as it is by a combination of techniques. But in the 14th century a love of decoration and richness lent itself to rather heavy pieces which could take encrustation with semiprecious stones. The Mongol rulers were familiar with the metalwork of the Middle Eastern craftsmen and had a taste already formed for this work.

But in the matter of porcelain the rulers were introduced to a new material. The kilns at Ching-te-chen in Kangsi were in strong production by the fall of the Southern Sung and were making high-quality white porcelain and developing techniques of underglaze decoration. Although most ceramic production was for home use, the Chinese increasingly used porcelain in trade. Not all the trade porcelain came from Ching-te-chen, for the ports used were Canton and Ch'uan Chou on the Fukien coast. As there were already kiln areas developed in the south, a certain proportion of the porcelain exported came from the vicinity of the port. However, the products of superior quality were all from Ching-te-chen. This trade went to Japan, the Philippines, Indonesia, Malaya, India, and the Middle East, notably to Hormuz on the Persian Gulf and Cairo in Egypt.

In modern times a considerable quantity of the very best 14th-century blue and white decorated porcelain has been found in Damascus, Syria, and there is some discussion of the route of entry for this. It may be that an overland route was used for special cargo although the Chinese have always preferred water transport for ceramics. This porcelain can be of the most exquisite quality of drawing on a strong, heavy-bodied pot or dish. The control of cobalt is clearly almost complete. The vocabulary of decoration is elaborate and follows a style usually explained as a combination of motifs from Near Eastern and Chinese sources. The Chinese tendency to arrange a design on a vessel in parallel bands is adopted for blue and white decoration, though the zones vary in width. The apparently inconsequential choice of motifs to fill the various bands is a fascinating aspect of Chinese decorators' art. There seems no good reason for the juxtaposition of the complicated motifs on the blue and white vases dated 1351. However, a tradition soon grew up for certain motifs to take certain positions, though these may vary from time to time and be one of the clues to dating.

Coming very close to the underglaze decorated porcelain is the lacquer ware of the Yuan. Most striking are the monochrome, dark brown to black wares in exquisite shapes, which epitomize the work of the lacquer makers of Chekiang, centering around the Shouchou district. Here the beautiful sheen of the material was left to speak for itself, but in this period the *ch'iang-chin* inlay technique was also used in a most striking style.

The Yuan dynasty, though short, was one of great stimulus

Returning Home from a Spring Outing by Tai Chin; ink and light colors on a silk scroll; 170×80cm (67×31in). National Palace Museum, Taipei

not least in the sphere of town building and particularly in palace architecture. The Mongols were interested in city planning and built a capital city at Peking, which they called Khanbalik, and made an imperial palace, a walled city which has been incorporated in the Ming and Ch'ing building now known as the Ku Kung (Old Palace), or Forbidden City. Recent excavations of the northwest corner of the Yuan Palace have uncovered a massive wall and gateway, similar to those gateways in the wall that has been preserved.

The Ming dynasty (1368–1644). It was not long before the Mongol rulers lost their drive and power. Revolts started among the Chinese and eventually a peasant leader was successful and formed a new dynasty to which he gave the name of Ming (bright). To mark the change from a foreign rule and to celebrate the real reunification of China the capital was at first moved to Nanking, literally Southern Capital. Much of the spirit of the new dynasty looked back to the glories of the past, particularly to the Han and T'ang when China had been strong, unified, and a nation. With a largely unlettered court of strong men the country was culturally without a center. Moves were made by the court to entice artists and scholars to serve the emperor. Confucian philosophy regained its vigor, but the attempted academy never was established and indeed those artists who did go to court were regarded with some suspicion and scorn.

Even this very simple estimate of the situation explains a little of the complex positions of the painters at the start of the dynasty. There was a group of artists painting in Chekiang who followed the style of Li K'an, Wu Chen, and the Southern Sung academy painters with an elegant, wet ink style and sweeping compositions. One or two of these, notably Tai Chin (1380–1452) stayed only briefly at court. Realizing that intrigue and courtly pastimes were not for him, Tai Chin returned to his native Chekiang for the last 20 years of his life, creating many fine paintings in the Hsia Kuei-Ma Yuan school but on a large scale which was to become characteristic of early Ming painting. His painting of river boatmen (Freer Gallery of Art, Washington, D.C.) is one of the major works of Chinese painting which has perhaps survived in the original. The fragility of scroll painting and the assiduous copying of all masterpieces has created a problem of connoisseurship in the study of Chinese painting which must always be in mind when considering works of great masters. However, as the period more nearly approaches our own it is at least likely that masterpieces may be judged to be originals and to that extent the whole appreciation of painting takes on a new and more exciting flavor. Tai Chin used color but in the texture of the ink painting of his great works there is a clear indication of the different character that finds its way into most early Ming painting. There is a panache and freedom of brushwork exploiting the larger format, and the self-conscious composition of the Southern Sung artists is loosened.

Closely allied to the Che School and yet worlds away from them were the court artists proper of the early Ming. These were the men who made their entire reputation at court, who painted to the needs of the court and were indeed professional painters. Lu Chi (fl. c1560) is perhaps the greatest exponent of this art; using mostly the bird and flower subject he created magnificent compositions which have much of the meticulous observation evident in the painting of Sung Emperor Hui Tsung (1082–1135), but once again the tight control of the composition has been relaxed and the subject is allowed to dictate the movement. Also it is clear that the birds and flowers are painted in their own surroundings so that the atmosphere is of a wild place rather than the rarified setting of the perfect bird on the perfect branch.

So much of Chinese decorative painting is romantic in style that we must differentiate between the romanticism of the Northern Sung, that of the Southern Sung, and now the broader warmth of the Ming. These court artists are not by any stretch of the term literati painters, but neither are they journeymen decorators of whom there were always a great many in China. But they are serious artists working within a genre which was much admired at this and every other time, except by those whose judgment of art was strictly moralistic.

By contrast and in conflict with the Che School painters were the group who are associated at first with Wu-hsien, present-day Suchow. These were painters consciously in the mold of the classic artists of the Yuan. They knew and respected the older paintings and took seriously the precept that artists should study the masters before branching out on their own. The first great artist of this group, called the Wu School, is Shen Chou (1427–1509). Shen Chou was an eclectic in the best tradition of the literati painters; his earlier work imitates the masters of the Yuan, whose works he would have known, for he lived in the same area where they had worked only a century before. He did, however, develop a strong style of his own which has been regarded as the best of the middle Ming. Shen is one of the dozen or so great painters in China who still have influence, in his case for his effortless, straightforward brushwork and telling compositions in which the human being is often the focus and seems to be the artist himself. This introduction of the painter into his own picture gives it an immediacy which, with the poem often also added by the artist, makes this both a private work and one that speaks directly to the viewer. This directness is a new twist to the literati tradition—the poet-painter is both speaking to the viewer and inviting him into his vision. The small painting of the poet singing on the cliff top (William Rockhill Nelson Gallery, Kansas City) is a marvelously vivid example. The poem says:

White clouds encircle the mountain waist like a sash
Stone steps mount high into the void where the narrow path
   leads far.
Alone, leaning on my rustic staff I gaze idly into the distance.
My longing for the notes of a flute is answered in the murmuring of the gorge.

(Sickman, L. and Soper, A. *The Art and Architecture of China* p177.)

Directly we are there and identify with the figure in the landscape in a way quite different from any other landscape with figures previously produced in China. Another aspect of this use of a figure is shown in his large landscape in the style of Ni Tsan (National Palace Museum, Taipei). Although some of the brush and compositional style of Ni Tsan is echoed, Shen Chou has knitted the landscape together in a solid interrelationship of rock and tree shapes, avoiding the special ascetic sparsity of Ni Tsan and the creation of space and light of

Landscape Painting

There are many strands in the web that unites the varied styles of landscape painting of the scholar class of China across the centuries. These include brushwork—personal ink mannerisms, the ways of painting trees and rocks—but the strongest link is in the use of modes of composition. Early in the development of landscape as a serious subject for the painter a method of composing in depth was evolved and accepted as traditional. This method has been called the "rising eye-level",

a system of successive eye-levels which allowed an expression of depth in a tall format; it is the conventional perspective of Chinese landscape painting.

The surface composition of these paintings, the way in which the composition is tied to the edges and in which it can be read, is something common to all paintings composed within a rectangular frame but which has a special character when the painting is not in color. In surface composition the edges

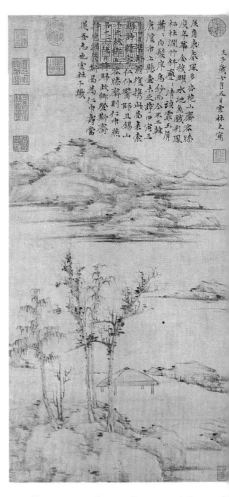

▶ *Jung Hsi Studio* by Ni Tsan; height 74cm (29in). National Palace Museum, Taipei

◀ *Walking in the Mountains* by Shen Chou; 159×72cm (63×28in). National Palace Museum, Taipei.

are all-important but understressed; lines of trees and mountains intersect and touch the edge at carefully devised spots. It is often upon the success of this composition that the feeling of balance within the picture depends. The balance of the surface is worked to a large extent independently of the in-depth composition; in the largely monochrome tradition of China considerations of tonal recession can be ignored in deference to surface balance. The eye is led around the surface of the painting by accent of tone and line.

The balance of surface and depth composition was a major interest for many Chinese painters. From this aspect alone the painting *Walking in the Mountains* (National Palace Museum, Taipei) by Shen Chou (1427–1509) shows a closely knit composition of interlocking spurs of land composed by the rising eye-level method. An overlay of lines from the trees and the figure firmly ties the composition of the surface to produce a sturdy equilibrium characteristic of this artist. He regarded himself as within the tradition of the 10th-century painter Tung Yuan whose landscape *Festival Invoking Rain* (National Palace Museum, Taipei) is organized more loosely on the rising eye-level, interlocking spurs method. In this calm and open composition the trees and bushes

◀ *Festival Invoking Rain* by Tung Yuan; 145×163cm (57×64in). National Palace Museum, Taipei

▼ *Dwelling in Ch'ing Pien Mountains* by Tung Ch'i-ch'ang; height 217cm (85in). Cleveland Museum of Art

re accents and guides to the eye, gently ading the attention over the surface which ere is not governed by a network of lines.

Between the time of Tung Yuan and that of hen Chou many experiments had been made ith techniques of composition. An example at relates the two masters is the *Jung Hsi udio* (National Palace Museum, Taipei) by i Tsan (1301–74). Here the rising eye-level, terlocking spur composition has been stretched" to the point at which the islands most do not interlock. Contact with the dge of the painting is subtle and the judg- ent of the points of contact and the division f the line are carefully made to avoid plitting the composition. Trees in Ni Tsan's ainting are important as elements to direct e eye-lines of the surface and also to act as strong tie to strengthen the surface within e frame. They are indeed controlling the entral part of the picture. Shen Chou ad- ired Ni Tsan's work and borrowed many of is composition techniques, notably the use f trees in the foreground. A simple compari- on of these three artists seems to place Shen hou between the other two. His was not the st word on this interplay of ideas: his pupil Ven Cheng-ming (1470–1559) took up Ni san's composition seemingly in a purely clectic spirit in his *Spring Landscape* in

color. Closeness to the earlier painting is limited to the formal composition, for by the use of full color Wen Cheng-ming here produces a very different painting. The blues and greens of the landscape cancel the tra- ditional tonal composition of the surface. Quite apart from the recession qualities of the color of which the painter was apparently unaware, he is unable in color to use the techniques of accent by tone which ink painters had developed since the time of Tung Yuan.

Tung Ch'i-ch'ang (1555–1636), the great analyst and student of classical painting, makes a clear comment on the aspects of landscape painting under discussion in his landscape *Dwelling in Ch'ing Pien Moun- tains* (1617; Cleveland Museum of Art). This painting, with its interest in painting itself as a subject of painting, summarizes much of the special nature of the Chinese scholar landscape school. For although the evocation of a scene remained a primary reason for painting, Tung saw the reinterpretation of other painters' work as of equal interest for the artist. Here the bones of the painting are evident and the way in which the composi- tion is constructed is as much the subject of the painting as is the representation of a mountain landscape.   MARY TREGEAR

Further reading. Loehr, M. *The Great Painters of China*, Oxford (1980). Sullivan, M. *The Birth of Landscape Painting in China*, London (1962).

the earlier artist. But more outrageously, he has introduced a figure quietly walking through the landscape who becomes the focus of the picture. Comparison with the single figure in landscape of Ma Yuan (National Palace Museum, Taipei) gives us a clue to the special dimension of these Shen Chou figures, which seem to invite the viewer to identify with them and to look at the landscape from inside the picture rather than from a distance.

Wen Cheng-ming (1470–1559) was contemporary with and lived in the same general district as Shen Chou, and they are inevitably associated in the Wu School. However, they were quite different personalities and produced very different work although they were both members of the literati class and worked from an eclectic base. Such was the variety of the 14th-century Old Masters from whom they could claim descent that Wen Cheng-ming, fundamentally a decorative artist interested in color and texture and even light and atmosphere, could fit into this very loosely grouped School. Wen and his large family were the generators of the later (16th and 17th century) Wu School which did move away from the intensity of vision and personal experimentation of Shen Chou into calmer waters and large and impressive landscapes.

Two of the great 16th-century painters were Ch'iu Ying (c1494–c1552) and T'ang Yin (1470–1523). They do not quite fit into the tidy grouping of painters as professional, court or literati artists. Ch'iu Ying was originally a journeyman painter, not an educated man and therefore not easily accepted as a named artist. But he was a great natural artist and so spectacularly beautiful was his painting that he became popular and has been influential ever since. His large oeuvre has been grossly swelled by copyists and imitators but we must believe that he painted a wide variety of subjects. He is best known for his palace genre scenes and his colored landscapes. These last link him to the Wu School in its more decorative aspect.

T'ang Yin was quite a different case. He was a disgraced scholar who seems to have "dropped out" in a very modern fashion but who, in his more sober periods, painted so beautifully, in the traditional literati style with an added personal comment, that he must be accounted a major artist. Chinese aesthetic assessments are apt to see signs of moral lapses revealed in the artists' work. Thus in assessing T'ang Yin it would seem that the natural elegance of the painting has been confused with degeneracy. However this may be, his output was small and his paintings rare.

The recording and preservation of the work of these two nonconforming artists is a small hint of the movement taking place in the art world of China toward the end of the Ming dynasty, a movement to loosen the admittedly not very strong bonds of tradition. No strong academy was formed in the Ming dynasty, the most highly respected artists all lived away from court, so there was in no sense an establishment, other than the Wu School, to which serious artists aspired. The Wu School gradually held under its umbrella a wide variety of artists but the tendency seemed towards a colored decorative

style retaining a Yuan/Northern Sung composition. This tendency was noted and caused disquiet to the scholarly who admired the solemn grandeur of the 12th-century Old Masters and their followers in the 14th century. Tung Ch'i-ch'ang (1555–1636) and his friend, Mo Shih-lung (fl. 1567–1600) were the leaders of the discussion and together they wrote on the theory and philosophy of aesthetics until Mo Shih-lung's death.

Tung Ch'i-ch'ang was a rare and complex artist, an analyst and theoretician. He was interested in the construction of paintings and in the relationship of one painting to another. A Confucian scholar by training and a Ch'an Buddhist by conviction, his treatises on painting are interesting to read. Unfortunately he is best known for his strictures, notably those inherent in his classification of the Northern and Southern Schools. But more fruitful is his idea of transformation, the process by which an artist expresses what he sees in brush stroke and composition. For Tung this came to be the central interest of painting.

The early 15th century was the period of the major building of the Forbidden City—the Imperial Palace—in Peking. The Yung Lo Emperor (1403–25) moved the capital north after a struggle for power with his nephews which left him with a very shaky power base in the Southern capital of Nanking. Having moved to his own fief in the north he planned and started to build the large enclosed palace we know today. This is a rectangular walled compound, enclosing the Yuan palace; the buildings are carefully aligned on a north–south axis and consist of a series of ceremonial halls each approached across an awesome courtyard. To the east and west of these are a series of court offices with the domestic courtyards and living quarters for the Emperor to the west and the women and children of the court to the east. Officials of the court lived outside the walls but close to the palace which was the winter residence of the Emperor. Various princes and other members of the Imperial family had palace residences in Peking and it became the custom to have a summer residence up in the hills out of Peking to escape the dry heat. This Imperial building in the traditional wooden pillar-and-beam style, but with more and more elaborate roof bracketing to take the wide sweeping tiled roofs, is an example of a widespread building activity in China. It is characteristic that neither the style nor the technique and materials of building had changed since the T'ang dynasty.

The interior of the houses of the increasingly wealthy new merchant class and the rich bureaucrats must have become more and more colorful and rich-looking. There is a general heaviness of style, carried through from the Yuan period in which furniture was solidly constructed of dark, polished wood.

Ceramics, always an important minor art, saw a stylization of the underglaze blue of the Yuan period. Imperial patronage

Clearing after Snow in a Mountain Pass by T'ang Yin; scroll, ink and light colors on silk; 71×35cm (28×14in). National Palace Museum, Taipei

畫閣雪霽推入稠輕載驢騾
畫店前山積鐵鏦
油晉昌唐寅仿

of the kiln at Ching-te-chen, where a government office was established to manage the considerable orders required by the palaces alone, led to a more obvious progression of styles of decoration. There was such a strong element of fashion that motifs come and go in succession in the highest quality wares, only to survive and become combined in the provincial wares of south China and Annam. During the Ming dynasty the high quality products of the Ching-te-chen kiln were marked with the reign and dynasty on the base of the piece. Thus a few of the reigns have become noted for the special qualities of the wares produced for them. Probably the Yung Lo reign is the first great period; the pots are close in style to Yuan pieces but still unmarked, and are of very high quality. The floral scrolls are rich and generously drawn, the leaf and flowers dominating the stem. The figure and animal painting of this period can be vigorous and of the highest quality. Pieces tend still to be massive.

The Hsuan Te reign (1426–36) is the next notable porcelain period in which exquisite blue and white porcelain was produced. It was of a more delicate design in which the floral scroll is dominated by the line of the stem; the leaves and flowers were reduced and became accents to the sinuous curve. During this period too, the glaze became finer and less blue, marking a gradual but continuous move toward the perfection of a clear shining glaze through which the intense cobalt blue would shine at its brightest in the 17th and 18th centuries. The Cheng Hua reign (1465–88) is famous for its delicate small pieces, perhaps most notably the *tou-ts'ai* or "fighting color" pieces in which the transparent pale-colored overglaze decoration is superimposed on and completes the underglaze blue decoration. This so-called enamel or overglaze decoration gradually superseded the underglaze blue, but not completely until the 18th century. Throughout the Ming period potters experimented with the rich palette of five colors—red, green, yellow, blue, and purple—which they had at their disposal.

Three other periods need to be mentioned in relation to ceramic wares. The Cheng Te reign (1506–22) saw a vogue for painting in double outline and the decoration often included an inscription of good wishes or an Arabic Koranic quotation. This last reflects the Muslim Eunuch's influence at court for this reign. The Chia Ching period (1522–67) is notable for colored and blue and white pieces; the decoration is now more informal, even light-hearted, probably marking the enlargement of the market for these wares within China. No longer the prerogative of the court and the very wealthy, they must now have been the most common decorative materials.

The overseas trade in porcelain was growing and in the late 16th and 17th centuries considerable quantities were sent to Europe to start a vogue which gathered momentum and became immense in the 18th century. Europeans were partial to blue and white porcelain and this trade supported the production of blue and white in China at a time when Chinese taste was moving toward polychrome decorated porcelain. The Wan Li Emperor (1573–1620) presided over one of the

A bowl of the Cheng Hua period (1465–88) with floral underglaze blue decoration. Percival David Foundation, London

last of the cultured courts of the Ming dynasty. During his reign Ching-te-chen produced some very fine thin and elegant wares presumably for domestic use, in contrast to the heavy, handsome wares exported to Europe.

Lacquer became very popular during the Ming period, particularly carved red or black lacquer. Polished red lacquer has a particularly beautiful voluptuous quality when carved in the generous style of the early Ming. The depth of lacquer and soft richness of carving are unequaled in any other period, and reflect the quality of contemporary aristocratic taste. With rather heavy simple jade carving, rich silks, heavy, dark wood polished furniture, and opulent bird and flower painting, the 15th-century interior could be one of great richness. With the passing years the richness increased as more and more decorative material was produced in cloisonné enamel, painted enamel, carved ivory, amber, jade, hard stones, and such exotics as rhinoceros horn. The decoration tended to become more complex and the scale diminished so that where in the late 14th and early 15th centuries most media show a relatively large design on a simple-shaped object, as time passed this character changed and shapes became more bizarre. Gradually the clutter was enlarged; the amassing of wealth, though halted or redistributed to some extent at the downfall of the dynasty, must be regarded as a continuing movement through to the 18th century. The scholar's taste in the midst of this worldliness was for beautiful, simply-made but elegant material, and so monochrome glazes appear, simpler forms of carving in bamboo, ivory, and rhinoceros horn. This last material was a favorite among the superstitious for not only was it thought to be an aphrodisiac, it was also regarded as a sure indicator of poison. Hence the vogue for cups of this material. This quickly developed into a style of carving in a shape adapted to the short horn of the Java rhinoceros.

Korea in the Choson and Yi periods (1392–1910). Although Korea was invaded from Japan during the Yi period (in 1592) and a specifically Korean script had been invented and adopted (in 1446) Korea remained culturally close to China.

Nowhere is this more evident than in the visual arts.

After the development of plain and inlaid celadons by the Koryo, potters turned their attention to a white-bodied stoneware with underglaze decoration. This closely follows the move in the Chinese pottery trade, but it is thought that the Koreans may have led the way with the use of copper oxide under the glaze, which when satisfactorily fired (reduced) produces a red. However this may be, it is clear that the 14th century saw the initial experimentation and exploitation of the underglaze technique with the three metallic oxides, iron, copper, and cobalt. The Koreans had their own graphic style, closely following the flower painters' style of the period. They tended to use decoration sparingly and to great effect on the full-bodied shapes they were making in heavy white stoneware. The Korean potters always seem to have one eye on the Chinese craftsmen but never became subservient to them in either technique or style.

In the more homely wares of the earlier part of the Yi period the Koreans developed the Pun Ch'ong wares. In many ways these have an affinity with the northern wares of China and Manchuria, the Tzu Chou or Liao type of slip and incised decorated gray stonewares. In Korea the gray body is incised or impressed with simple decoration and the whole is then lightly brushed with white slip. This will effectively inlay the decoration, leaving a distinctive streaky white surface on the warm, gray body, which is then glazed. Pun Ch'ong wares are also more traditionally decorated with slip decoration, both painted and incised and also with iron-painted underglaze decoration. This ware has a great influence on Japanese potting, notably of Karatsu, but the relationship with Japan is that of inspiration or even actual teacher; with China there seems a less obvious but quite persistent link. Likewise with lacquer the Koreans continued the mother-of-pearl inlay techniques of the Chinese, and during the 14th to the 16th centuries produced boxes, trays, and chests of a bold, rich design if not of exquisite workmanship. Another inlay technique which is solely Korean is that of insetting the surface of boxes and small chests with sheets of horn painted with bright colors. The painted side is set inside and the translucency of the horn lends a richness to the coloring. These are truly folk art pieces, but attractive and typical of the Korean genius for unsophisticated, colorful works of art.

During this long period painting emerged as a major art. As in China the Koreans had both professional and literati painters, although they were organized differently. Both schools owed their original character to the Chinese. However, there were very few Imperial patrons of the arts and so painting was not centered around an academy, nor were there the scholar-official schools of the 14th or of the 16th and 17th centuries, so influential in China. In the early centuries of Yi, the Office of Painting, established in the Koryo period, continued and many artists were trained there. The only great Imperial patron was Prince Anp'yong who amassed an important collection including Chinese Sung and Yuan paintings. However, he died young and his collection was dispersed.

The outstanding Korean painters of the earlier period, the 15th and 16th centuries, were professionals. An Kyon (1418–?), a protégé of Prince Anp'yong, was trained in the Northern Sung and Chao Meng-fu styles. His most famous work, *The Fairyland Seen in a Dream* (or *Spring Dream*; private collection), was painted for his patron and shows his academic style. An Kyon was the first master of the Yi period and his work was much admired. Yi Sang-jwa (1465–?), a follower of An and a specialist in the Hsia Kuei, Ma Yuan style, is a typical professional painter of the early Yi. He rose from humble beginnings to become a painter in government employment; his painting is close to Chinese styles. Many painters are recorded, all in this school, specializing in portraiture, bird and flower, bamboo, and most strikingly in Buddhist painting where Zen styles predominated.

The contrast with the later period, the 17th to the 19th centuries, is striking, for at this time the literati painters of Korea came to the fore and painted in the styles of the Chinese Wu School and the Individualists of the 17th and 18th centuries. However, the Korean artists added their own characteristic of a persistent genre setting in any painting containing figures. A certain informality already noted in Korean paintings as compared with their Chinese forerunners is quite clear in the later paintings. There is also a love of grotesquery in the painting of rocks, which become jagged and abrupt, and trees, reduced to dashingly abbreviated symbols.

Chong Son (1676–1769) stands out as one of the great artists in this style. He was a theorist and teacher who produced practical guidebooks to his style. His landscapes depict actual beauty spots in areas around Seoul and particularly in the Diamond Mountains. Later followers of this style are the brothers Kim Tuk-sin (1754–1821) and Kim Sok-sin (1758–?), each painting both landscape and genre scenes with figures reminiscent of the Southern Sung painter, Hsia Kuei (1180–1230).

Korean calligraphy was affected by the introduction of the Korean script Han'gul. However, the educated literati class continued to use the Chinese script in an elegant if somewhat weak style. The Han'gul script, regarded as a plebeian and illiterate mode, was nevertheless developed by the court ladies into a cursive script of some distinction.

Ch'ing dynasty (1644–1911). At the beginning of the 17th century culture in China was at a low ebb as the dynasty fell into disorder and degeneracy, to be overrun by the Manchu rulers from the north who founded the Ch'ing dynasty. Once again a pattern was set of a foreign imperial power, but this time the rulers were uncultured and admired Chinese ways. Chinese bureaucrats and literati were encouraged and indeed the administration of the country was run in tandem. Thus coinage and official seals had Manchu writing on one side and Chinese on the other. All official posts were in duplicate (Manchu and Chinese) and strenuous efforts were made to make official life attractive to the Chinese scholar. Three successive courts under the K'ang Hsi (1662–1723), Yung Cheng

Steep Rock Formation by Chong Son (1676–1769). National Museum of Korea, Seoul

(1723–36), and Ch'ien Lung (1736–96) Emperors fostered good living, serious philosophical thought, and cultural activity.

However, of even greater importance in the consideration of the visual arts is the rapid enlargement of private wealth. Great merchant houses were established based on commodities such as silk and salt. A vivid picture of the gradual demise of one of these large families is drawn in *The Dream of the Red Chamber*, the first modern-style novel written in China in the 18th century. It was therefore a more complex

society within which artists functioned. Firstly there were the artists who retired from official circles for political reasons. Amongst these must be placed two of the great Individualists Chu Ta (Pa Ta Shan-jen) and Shih T'ao (Tao Chi).

Chu Ta (1626–1705), a fine exponent of Ch'an (Zen) painting, was a minor member of the Ming royal family and an eccentric who retired to live in a monastery. In the tradition of Ch'an artists he was a literati-trained painter who used his great skill in the handling of ink and paper in intense paintings of birds, flowers, and landscape. Much has been made of the isolation of Chu Ta, but although he lived a solitary life, he was in touch with such contemporaries as Shih T'ao. The Ch'an tradition has always been a dynamic but limited force in Chinese art. The particular style of composition and concept of brushwork used remained constant. The one unusual aspect of Chu Ta's work is his landscape painting, which curiously shows a clear understanding of and interest in Tung Ch'i-ch'ang's analytical work on the composition of landscape. Chu was one of the very few artists to follow up Tung's experiments with landscape painting and to try to clothe them in the warmth and life of his brushwork.

Shih T'ao (1630–1707) was a quite different personality. Cast in the mold of Shen Chou, he was a dedicated painter and devout Buddhist, with no taste for official life. Shih T'ao was an educated and sophisticated scholar, well acquainted with the Old Masters but with such originality of vision that he very soon imbued everything he painted with his own romantic view of the world. He developed all the classic techniques of *ts'un* and dots but used them in color or on such a scale as to change their character. As a painter Shih T'ao was

Left: Waterfall on Mount Lu by Shih T'ao (1630–1707); hanging scroll, ink and light colors on silk; width 64cm (25in). Tokyo National Museum

A landscape by Chu Ta (1626–1705); 24×28cm (9×11in). Honolulu Academy of Arts

the antithesis of Tung Ch'i-ch'ang whose theorizing he distrusted, for where Tung classified and sought to dissect, Shih saw the unity of painting and relied on nature for his inspiration, the expression of which was his sole objective. Thus he attacked Tung Ch'i-ch'ang's theories of "transformation" and stressed that the only starting point for a painting was the observation of nature.

Although Chu Ta and Shih T'ao were so opposed in outlook it is salutary, from our distance, to see within what a short focus this opposition took place, for both would stand by the literati concept of the artist as based within the tradition of the Old Masters. Each was to some extent eclectic in his method of work, but Shih T'ao represents the greatest liberation in his personal expression of the artist's vision. This is a clear illustration of the narrow scope within which Chinese painters worked. There is never any suggestion that new materials or format should be used, no experimentation with the media such as the Japanese indulged in. So that where we acknowledge an outstanding individual, he is always within the broad framework of the accepted styles and forms of painting established over the previous seven centuries.

Having introduced the 17th century and the new dynasty with two great masters traditionally regarded as of astonishing originality, we must step back to the orthodox school represented again traditionally by the four Wangs. These four artists follow the Wen Cheng-ming school of colored, massive landscapes. The eldest of the Wangs was contemporary with Shih T'ao, with whom he was acquainted and whose work he admired. Although no great innovators themselves these artists at their best seem to embody all that is positive in the theories of Tung Ch'i-ch'ang; they followed the old traditions with sincerity and intelligence but they were also able, within narrow confines, to produce individual work of some power. Indeed Wang Yuan-ch'i (1642–1715) came close to cubist expression. He experimented with ideas of solid form in a way that has never been further explored. This inhibition from development of ideas of an abstract nature—color, form, or line—is one of the striking characteristics in Chinese painting.

A spirit of experiment, however, was alive among the painters in the flourishing cities of Suchow and Yangchow. Here the personal wealth of some of the great families encouraged the collection of all sorts of artifacts including paintings. The patrons were not traditional, well-informed, scholarly gentlemen but successful businessmen with uncultured eyes. They were intrigued by originality, and the "different" quality in works of art fascinated them. In an almost modern situation painters sought to differ from each other and gained the title of Eccentric Groups of loosely connected artists, such as the Eight Eccentrics of Yangchow or the Four Hsinan Masters who seemed the epitome of highly successful fashionable collectors' artists. These men do not fit into the pattern of court, professional, or scholar painter thus far examined. They were men of education and culture, but they painted for a market outside their own circle and were financially successful in their painting.

Thus a new artist entered society in the 18th century and he has been there ever since. Nineteenth-century and especially 20th-century painters are of this type: they paint in much the same way as the European artist, for an unidentified clientele of collectors. The concept of schools and even of the scholar-painter must be reconsidered, for although traditional scholars and painters certainly existed through the 19th century, the mainstream of painting now flowed through the Eccentric or Individualist painters. The differentiation between these two categories is much a matter of degree and standing; the Individualists were all major artists schooled in the classical tradition, each forming a personal style of such power that it could stand alone. The Eccentrics, by comparison, were lesser artists who evolved a completely personal style of expression; but each worked in a limited field so that while their painting is easily identifiable by style, they have not inspired later painters to develop their ideas further. The differentiation amounts to a subjective assessment of the germinal quality of the painting.

There were few great painters in the 19th century. Jen Po-nien (1840–95) was a lively bird and flower painter who used a spiky brushwork and attractive color. He was an influential painter who led the way to a style of painting both decorative in its use of color and capable of expression in the brushwork. Jen Po-nien had contemporaries who painted in a similar style and this became established as one of the major styles of the late 19th and 20th centuries—for bird and flower painting was a popular subject for some of the major artists of this period of change in Chinese society.

A few names stand out amongst the artists working in the first half of the 20th century: Wu Ch'ang-shih (1844–1927) who painted in a strong ink style, often painted bird and flower but also landscape and bamboo; he in turn influenced Ch'i Pai-shih (1851–1957), one of the best-known of 20th-century painters. This long-lived artist was an instinctive painter who often painted brilliantly. He was heir to the Ch'an tradition, but in his art used elements from other old decorative traditions both of meticulous and free painting.

Ch'i was one of the minority of his generation of artists who did not travel abroad. Hsu Pei-hung (1895–1953) went to France as did Lin Feng-mien (1901 or 1906–) and they brought back elements of European art, the concept of "drawing" as then practiced in art schools. This led to the curiously anthropomorphic animals of Hsu and the concept of color of the French Post-Impressionists translated to a delicate freedom when used in the Chinese tradition. Other artists, notably Fu Pao-shih (1904–65), went to Japan and joined the experiments of the Japanese artists with texture and paper. Fu Paoshih appears to paint in the tradition of Shih T'ao but more blandly. He was interested in historical styles and painted figures in a T'ang style, curiously at variance with his romantic landscapes. In this versatility he was matched by Chang Ta-ch'ien who has done much archaistic work but has also painted delightful paintings in his own personal style. Chang was one of the first artists to study and transmit the

Birds and Branches by Jen Po-nien (1840–95); ink and color on paper; 66×46cm (26×18in). Ashmolean Museum, Oxford

great wall-paintings at Tun Huang and introduce his countrymen to the great heritage of the early Buddhist paintings. In this he stepped outside any role of painter yet practiced in China. Indeed the 20th century has seen much change in the role and the production of artists who now seem to occupy a position closer to that of the artist in the West. The work of the traditional painters shows their links with the traditions within which they still work. Contemporary arts present such a wide spectrum that a different criterion is required for their discussion, but Chinese painting as an art form is alive and as expressive as ever of the society of which it is part. As that society evolves, so painting will inevitably change.

As the Ch'ing dynasty ran its course the decoration and furnishing of houses became more and more elaborate. Craftsmen were kept busy producing exquisite toys and decoration for the wealthy. This increase in personal wealth was one of the major influences of the period. Ceramics remained the staple material for all eating vessels and Ching-te-chen the major kiln area for the production of porcelain. The court

reestablished its factories; the government official overseeing Imperial orders became a notable person and his name was recorded. Thus the official in the brilliant K'ang Hsi reign (1661–1720), Tsang Ying-hsuan, fostered the production of brilliant blue and white ware decorated with figure scenes taken from the woodcut book illustrations so popular at this time. These scenes often depict characters from plays such as the *Hsi Hsiang chi*, a Yuan drama. The K'ang Hsi period also saw the finest of the Famille Verte decorated porcelains; the colors in overglaze were of the group called Five Color in the Ming. The tendency was toward the refinement of the colors which became paler as they were applied over the bright transparent white glaze. The potters devised a technique of overglaze decorating on a biscuit fired porcelain which resulted in a richer coloring as the reflection of light through the primary glaze was cut out. The on-the-biscuit Famille Verte represents a class of pottery of the curious style becoming more popular in collectors' circles. For the rich of Soochow by no means restricted their collecting to paintings but amassed extensive holdings of pottery, bronze, jade, lacquer, enamel, and textiles.

Among the visitors to the K'ang Hsi court were foreigners from many countries, and the Jesuits sent their missionaries to court in Peking where they were tolerated as mathematicians. One of the Jesuits, Guiseppe Castiglione (1688–1716), caught Imperial attention as a painter; trained as he had been in the Italian schools, he attempted an amalgamation of styles with the Chinese. He was known in China as Lang Shih-ning and painted in Chinese format with ink and color on silk or paper. His exquisite flower paintings, stiffly organized and entirely un-Chinese in feeling, were appreciated for their "lifelike" drawing as indeed were his paintings of horses and figures. This artist, who worked in the Yung Cheng and early Chien Lung periods, stood at the head of a style of hybrid painting which found favor with the decorators at a time when Europeans were engaged in an extensive trade with China and later with Japan. The trading companies set up by Holland, Spain, Sweden, and Britain maintained a trade through Canton in ceramics, lacquer, and silk, with other commodities such as spices and tea, sufficient to affect the manufacture of these things in China. Chinese craftsmen evolved a style and vocabulary of decoration which they associated with work for foreigners and which they did not employ on objects specifically for their own use. This is one example of an export style of which there are others in China, for they made for the Islamic market in the Far East and Near East as well as for the Europeans. It is therefore understandable that foreign ideas of decoration for each specific market should be regarded as something apart from that used in work for the home market.

During the short Yung Cheng reign (1723–36) the overseer at the Imperial factories of Ching-te-chen, Nien Hsi-yao, ordered the production of a beautiful series of archaistic wares in the style of the Sung court wares of the 12th and 13th centuries. Ju and Kuan type wares were produced and cherished in the early 18th century. The body of these wares

was usually white porcelain which lightens the overall effect of the thick crackled glaze. The similarity with the earlier pieces is striking, and shows a fine understanding of Sung aesthetics. Also in the Yung Cheng period a very delicate "boneless" style of overglaze decoration was introduced using the new palette of Famille Rose. This marked the introduction of a crimson color, derived from colloidal gold, and an opaque white derived from arsenic, both used in low-fired overglaze decoration. Both these colors came from Europe and their use is a rare example of technical innovation being accepted from outside China at this time.

Following this very brief period was the long reign of the Ch'ien Lung Emperor (1736–96). During his era the most notable official at Ching-te-chen was T'ang Ying. The kilns during his term of office reached the technical peak of their production, indulging in the tricks of imitating of other materials in ceramic to such a standard that it is difficult to distinguish even porcelain "brocade-covered books" except on touch. This period of very ornate taste finds its treasures in the elaborate gilded and carved wares, the brilliant technical feats mentioned and, relatively rarely, blue and white or perfect white porcelain faultlessly decorated in tightly designed motifs.

As we have seen at other periods, Chinese taste is not monolithic and so in the 18th century the scholar-gentleman demanded a less showy but nonetheless exquisite ware. To meet this demand came typically the brown basalt-type ware of I Hsing, a fascinating ware of unglazed brown clay which could be carved and modeled. It caught the eye of both the Japanese (Bizen) and English (Wedgwood) potters. In some respects this sophisticated cult of a rough-looking ware has parallels with the Sung cult of tea wares. The Ch'ing scholars also affected carved bamboo on their desks in a similar attempt to attain a simplicity not present in the other rooms of their houses. After this period Ching-te-chen, though still producing fine workmanship, was not such a consistent kiln, and indeed ceramics in general in China seems to have suffered a lack of strong patronage, reflecting the gradual disintegration of society and loss of confidence in artistic judgment which marks the 19th and 20th centuries. In the 20th century good quality porcelains have been and still are made at the great kiln sites, albeit still in the traditional style with little reference to the movements in design originating in Japan and the Scandinavian countries. However, as Chinese technical achievements are still inspiring such potters the wheel still has time to come full circle.

A similar line of technical perfection linked to elaborate decorative taste may be traced in the many applied arts furnishing the great houses of the 18th and 19th centuries. Carved jades and hard stones approximated to jewelry, immense boulders of jade carved as a landscape were treasured by the very rich and intricately carved tinkling hanging rings on ar-

chaistic vases were popular with collectors. The gentleman scholar collected lapidary carved desk screens, water pots, and snuff bottles; the latter, developed from the small medicine bottle of plain porcelain, became a vogue in the 18th century with the introduction of snuff from Europe. Snuff bottles were indeed made in every material and technique in this later period.

The craft of enameling metal, used in the Ming dynasty in the cloisonné enamels, was enriched if stylized in the Ch'ing. The cloisonné enamels, made in the Soochow region of China, became heavy and solid pieces with, at their richest, gold cloisonné and colored enamels. These objects, usually in archaic bronze shapes, reflect in their decoration the motifs used in ceramic Famille Rose wares. The heavy gold outlining of the color gives an added glamor to the Imperial pieces. By contrast the development of the so-called Canton enamel produces a delicate effect. This technique of laying enamel on the surface of a metal vessel and firing the whole to achieve an effect similar to the Famille Rose porcelain of the period was developed in Canton although the metal bodies were made in the Hangchow district of north Chekiang. This very skilled work was developed as a substitute for porcelain, supposedly to be stronger and so to travel more safely. In fact although it does not fracture as porcelain, it is susceptible to stress and chipping and stands wear and tear much less kindly.

Curiosities naturally find a place in the urban society of the 18th and 19th centuries, such as carvings in rhinoceros horn, a rare material which has some of the warmth, lightness, and translucency of amber. Bamboo root carving is a weird affectation of the period, almost an *objet trouvé* cult, but the root is aided by carving and by composition. This same aesthetic is evident in the gardens of the period which were already traditional. Grotesque stones had for many centuries been used to form the focus of a landscape in miniature, and stones were collected from all over the kingdom. Some of the best-preserved of these gardens are now in the palaces of Peking, and in Hangchow and Canton. Here the idea of a garden as a symbolic landscape is carried through in a formalized layout including the rock mountain and possibly water with flowers and plants often provided in containers.

These gardens were furnished with bamboo, lacquered or porcelain furniture in the form of stools, and tables used either as seats or stands. Inside the house the chief furnishing material was still dark wood but this was becoming rarer and its place was taken by rosewood. Southern grandees liked to use marble and mother-of-pearl inlay in furniture and in most areas bamboo chairs and tables became fashionable. The sheer wealth of material to be contained in a house made the construction of shelves and cabinets essential and this is the time of the irregular display shelving associated in Europe with the chinoiserie vogue.

As always the scholar's room was usually different with a restrained use of color and an insistence on exquisite workmanship and materials. Here we find the elegant bookbinding, in silk brocade with ivory or jade fittings, and all the para-

The Monkey of Cochinchina by Lang Shih-ning (1688–1716); color on silk; 190×84cm (75×33in). National Palace Museum, Taipei

phernalia for the viewing of scrolls—the weights for hand-scrolls, the stick to hang the long scroll, the weights to keep it still—all made with minute taste. The Chinese gentleman at this time used a toggle much as the better known netsuke; he carried a fan, often a card case and tobacco and pipe. These could be made in ivory, wood, or any hardstone, for the Chinese love of material for its own character is always present. However, in times of affluence the tendency to torture material is exaggerated. Hence the intricate carving of ivory until it splinters, the use of one material to imitate another noted especially in porcelain, and the minute carving of jade until it is paper thin and loses its weight and sense of strength. This, often regarded as a failure of taste visible in many cultures with the rise of the rich middle class, was the companion to the loss of direction seen in painting of the later 18th and 19th centuries. It seems to mark a loss of judgment in so many directions. The patrons, in this case the rich aristocratic and mercantile upper classes, apparently largely subscribed to a taste insecurely grounded in tradition and governed by a feeling for display. These two sterile qualities do not together give a craftsman enough inspiration or impetus to keep his craft more than technically alive. The admiration for technique, an essential ingredient for the appreciation and patronage of craft, is however not enough. Remembering that no personal reputation was possible, for Chinese craftsmen were normally anonymous, the craftsmen must rely on the interest of the buyer, however remote, to spark their interest in design and help to form a taste even within themselves.

It is possibly this same set of circumstances in different degrees that are at play today. There is no doubt that traditions and techniques are still alive; the interest now lies in the character of patronage. This question, recurrent in most present-day societies, awaits an answer in China where the visual arts still play a very important role in everyday life.

M. TREGEAR

Bibliography. CHINA: Cahill, J. *Chinese Painting*, Geneva (1960). Cahill, J. *Hills beyond a River: Chinese Painting of the Yuan Dynasty*, New York and Tokyo (1976). Cahill, J. *Painting at the Shore: Chinese Painting of the Early and Middle Ming*, New York and Tokyo (1978). Chang, K.C. *Archaeology of Ancient China*, New Haven (1977). Lee, S.E. *A History of Far Eastern Art*, London (1964). Medley, M. *The Chinese Potter*, Oxford and New York (1976). Sickman, L. and Soper, A.C. *The Art and Architecture of China*, Harmondsworth (1971). Siren, O. *Chinese Painting*, (7 vols.) London (1956–8). Sullivan, M. *The Arts of China*, Berkeley (1977). Sullivan, M. *Chinese Art in the 20th Century*, London (1959). Valenstein, S. *A Handbook of Chinese Ceramics*, New York (1975). Watson, W. *Ancient Chinese Bronzes*, London (1977). Watson, W. *Cultural Frontiers in Ancient East Asia*, Edinburgh (1971). KOREA: Chewon, K. and Kim, W.Y. *Arts of Korea*, Seoul (1970). Gompertz, G.St.G.M. *Korean Pottery and Porcelain of the Yi Period*, London (1968). McCune, E. *The Arts of Korea*, Tokyo (1962). Ministry of Culture and Information of South Korea *The Ancient Arts of Korea*, Seoul (1970).

18

JAPANESE ART

Catching Fireflies by Eishosai Choki; c1794. British Museum, London (see page 352)

JAPANESE art is easy to define, being the art produced in the islands that form modern Japan. Until 1945, Japan was never controlled from outside. In the prehistoric period cultural links with East Asia were close, but she never owed practical allegiance to a continental power. In the early historical period we are uncertain in some cases whether artistic monuments are the work of native or East Asian artists (for example, the 8th-century AD frescoes at the Horyuji Temple). Since then, no major work of art produced in Japan is by an immigrant. Examples of important Japanese artists working abroad are equally rare—until the later 19th century AD, Sesshu is the only example and he only for a short time. Japanese art is therefore very self-contained, though ideas usually originated from outside.

Japan's geographical position encouraged both general isolation and dependence on East Asia. Until modern times the only country easily reached was Korea, and that by a stormy sea-crossing of some 120 miles (195 km). So cultural ideas from China and northeast Asia came slowly and often acquired a Korean slant before settling down in semi-isolation. That is why Japanese art, though superficially like Chinese or Korean, usually has a strong character of its own.

This character was influenced partly by the danger and impermanence of life. Most Japanese were threatened by earthquake, landslide, typhoon, tidal wave, or fire. Hard stone for buildings and monuments was largely absent, so culture developed in a setting of wooden, easily replaced buildings, divided inside by light, paper-covered screens. Arts tended to the small, the light, and the replaceable. In no other advanced culture have paper, wood, and lacquer played so important a part.

After the 7th century AD there were no important immigrations into the islands, and the character of the people developed in isolation. A gentle melancholy overlaying a core of tortured violence may derive from their physical situation; a deep love of nature and of the strongly marked seasons is strengthened by their accessibility in semi-openair houses. But their unerring sense of mostly unsymmetrical design seems to be innate, as are their craftsmanship and feeling for materials.

The preliterate period (c10,000 BC–mid 6th century). Japan's preliterate period lasts until the introduction of higher Chinese civilization in the mid 6th century AD—an age without writing or firmly recorded history. The islands formed part of a Northeast Asian cultural area, with advanced pottery, woodwork, textiles, and metalwork, but no higher civilization in the Chinese sense.

The main interest for students of the visual arts is the magnificent *Jomon* pottery, which gives its name to the Japanese neolithic (c10,000–300 BC). It was produced by a culture of gatherers and hunters. Basically a simple earthenware, fired at low temperatures to a dull red or black, a fantastic variety of shapes and decorations were developed, dominated by the cord-impressed pattern (*Jomon*) displaying extraordinary inventiveness, energy, and plastic sense. These qualities were later to be overlaid by Chinese civilization, but they remain under the surface of Japanese art at all periods. *Jomon* figurines of fertility goddesses, with protruding breasts and huge, blind science-fictional eyes, display a barbaric force unsurpassed in Asian plastic art. The great vases with their elaborate openwork superstructures and impressed and incised abstract patterns are monuments of vitality.

Similar power is found in the red pottery *haniwa* figures of the Great Tombs (*Kofun*) period, c AD 250–552. These tombs of the great are proof of a more elaborate social system, able to organize builders and craftsmen in large numbers. The guardian *haniwa* were placed on the outsides of the often huge moated tumuli. Their cut-out eyes give them a deathly quality which recalls some 20th-century Western painting and sculpture. Buddhism introduced in the mid 6th century diverted these plastic qualities into sculpture, and ceramics were thereafter more restrained.

Of early painting, only murals on inner rock walls of 5th- and 6th-century AD tombs survive. They are boldly done with simple pigments, usually red, black, blue, and yellow. But the technique employed was primitive and they are often painted straight on to the rock face. The emphasis is on geometrical patterns, but there are also human figures under parasols, recalling contemporary Chinese and Korean murals but obviously copies at second hand or after verbal descriptions. Simi-

Centers of artistic importance

HOKKAIDO

SEA OF JAPAN

Tokyo (Edo)

Kamakura

Kyoto

Osaka • Nara

SHIKOKU

KYUSHU

PACIFIC OCEAN

0   200 miles

200 kilometers

The inner shrine of the great shrine at Ise, rebuilt every 20 years since at least the 8th century AD

lar patterns and figures, the latter like children's "stick" drawings, are engraved or cast on the bronze bell-like objects called *dotaku* which date from the preceding *Yayoi* period (*c*300 BC–AD 250), when Japan adopted the settled rice-growing life of East Asia, creating conditions for the growth of specialist arts and crafts. (*Yayoi* is the name of a Tokyo archaeological site.)

Aesthetic continuity between the Preliterate Age and successive periods is found in architecture associated with Shintoism, which originated in the *Yayoi* period. Shinto, "the way of the gods", pays respect to "gods" called *kami*, which can represent natural forces like wind, a mountain, or a tree, the personality of any dead person, the spirit of a craft or profession, or the spirit of Japan herself. The *kami* are rarely represented artistically, hence there seems to be little Shinto art. But since the Japanese conceive Shinto more as an expression of their national character and beliefs than as a conventional religion, most Japanese art can in a sense be considered Shinto.

Incised drawings on *dotaku* and *haniwa* models of buildings show that the simple, strong architecture still used today in Shinto shrines began in the ordinary buildings of these early periods. The great shrine at Ise has been ritually rebuilt in its ancient style every 20 years since records began in the 8th century AD. Its simple structure and strong association with the natural woodlands around it are typical of much Japanese architecture in later periods, and seem to have no continental origin. The extended beams of the pitched roof, crossing into

an X-shaped projection, are found now only on Shinto shrines and older rural buildings.

Early Buddhist and courtly culture (552–1192). The Japan into which Buddhism arrived at the beginning of her recorded history, in AD 552, was apparently unified, except for the Ainu in the north, according to the earliest records, and therefore ready to receive a more complex civilization. By the time of the death in AD 621 of the religion's first great patron, the Regent Prince Shotoku, Buddhism was the established religion of Japan, coexisting with the tolerant Shinto worship. With Buddhism came the arts, ceremonies, literature, and philosophy of a great world religion, and inevitably the Chinese system of writing and theories of government. Japanese patrons of the arts were now educated nobles and priests, so a concept of the higher arts began to emerge. This was intensified by the move to the first settled capital, at Nara, in AD 710—modeled on the Chinese capital at Ch'ang-an, and surrounded by the ever more influential Buddhist temples—and taken even further after the founding of the Heian capital (Kyoto) on yet grander lines.

Buddhist sculpture in Japan was for long dependent on Korean and Chinese patterns—the search for a truly national style stretched into the mid Heian period (*c* AD 900). Nevertheless these early centuries produced much of the greatest surviving Far Eastern Buddhist sculpture, movingly innocent at first, later grandly cosmopolitan.

Though sculpture from the 10th century onwards was

almost always in wood, in earlier times bronze, clay, and lacquer were also much used; but suitable stone for carving was almost entirely absent. These materials were painted or gilded, though such decoration rarely survives. To have developed a monumental sculptural tradition without stone was a great achievement.

Early Buddhism in Japan was aristocratic and elitist—the superior man could aspire to Buddhahood through contemplation. The earliest carvings are therefore mainly single figures or triads of Buddhas and Bodhisattvas in contemplative poses, such as the 8th-century gilt-bronze figure of the Bodhisattva Maitreya in the British Museum, London. The half-bare torso, the calm smile, the sweet face, the detached but not forbidding attitude are typical of this time—witnesses

A detail of a wooden Bodhisattva in the Hall of Dreams in the Horyuji Temple, Nara; gilded wood; height of statue 6ft 5in (1.97m); 7th century

of the hope that the new religion brought to the hard realities of life. Bigger examples in wood are the Bodhisattvas in the Koryuji Temple (Kyoto) and the Chuguji nunnery near Nara.

Next to the Chuguji is the Horyuji, the oldest surviving Japanese temple (founded by Prince Shotoku in the early 7th century) and in effect the world's oldest museum. Many of the sculptures of this primitive period were preserved here, including a series of 47 bronze contemplative Bodhisattvas, all different, and the unique standing wooden Bodhisattvas known as the Kudara Kannon and the Kuze Kannon. The exaggerated but graceful proportions and mysterious, inward smiles of these figures must have impressed the early Japanese converts even more than they impress today. There is much of Korean sculpture in them, but only in Japan have such old wooden figures survived to the present.

With the founding of the Nara capital in AD 710, the metropolitan civilization of T'ang China reached Japan. The tableau of clay figures of the Death of the Buddha in the pagoda of the Horyuji (c AD 710) strives to emulate the complex stone groups and rock temples of T'ang China. More ambitious 8th-century clay guardian figures in the Hokkedo hall of the Todaiji Temple have a confident, classical internationalism, unique to that age but nowhere else so well preserved. These athletic figures complemented the increasing grandeur of the great Buddha images, culminating in the 52 ft (16 m) high bronze Vairocana in the Todaiji. This is hardly, in its much repaired state, a beautiful image, but it indicates a high level of metal technology in the mid 8th century.

Sculptural modeling from lacquer was usually done by soaking it into thick cloth over a wooden frame, and then finishing it with more lacquer. The liquid medium gave lightness and an unprecedented refinement of facial expression, at its most moving in the central face of the three-headed, six-armed divinity Ashura in the Kofukuji Temple, Nara (AD 734). The largest lacquer sculpture in Japan is the 12 ft (3.5 m) standing figure of the Bodhisattva Fuku Kenzaku Kannon in the Hokkedo of the Todaiji, a masterpiece of withdrawn compassion. The elaborate halos, scepters, and jewelry are features that came to dominate Buddhist sculpture in later periods when strong religious inspiration had disappeared.

While Buddhist sculpture expressed the higher traditions of Asia, there lingered a more vigorous and barbaric strain from the nomadic peoples of the Steppes, whose culture had entered Japan by way of Korea. The big 8th-century wooden *Gigaku* masks, many of which are preserved in the Horyuji, were used in a dramatic temple dance of burlesque character. The extrovert liveliness of these masks seems secular in spirit. After the Nara period *Gigaku* was replaced by *Bugaku*, a court entertainment. The masks continued the vigorous tradition of the grotesque, but were smaller, more comical, and often had moving parts.

Right: The head of a clay guardian figure in the Todaiji Temple, Nara; 8th century; height of statue 330cm (130in)

Japan's second permanent capital city, called Heian (modern Kyoto), remained the center of politics for almost 400 years (793–1192) and of art for nearly 1,200 years. New sculpture was needed for the many temples that grew up around the city, and to supply images for the new sects imported from China. Of these the *Shingon* (a mystical and esoteric sect) was artistically important. Its concept of a universe populated by countless divinities encouraged a vivid art, depicting them separately or in schematic groups. The latter were better suited to paintings (called *mandalas*) but sculptural schemes exist, notably in the Toji Temple (Kyoto). Here the massive, square-chested central figure of Fudo, the Immovable, sitting on rocks and surrounded by groups of guardians and divinities, is typical of the early Heian monumental style. A technique of carving most of a figure from one great block of wood came to prominence, and the result was often heavy, in the Chinese late T'ang style.

In the 11th century a major innovation in technique combined with deepening confidence in native Japanese taste to usher in the greatest era of Japanese sculpture. The method was the *Yosegi*, by which a figure was built up in small pieces, each carved to suit the grain, then covered with gesso and gilded or painted. Greater expressive flexibility gave even the largest sculptures lightness and movement. The founder of this style was Jocho (*fl.* 1022–57) whose masterpiece is the 10 ft (3 m) high seated figure of the Buddha Amida in the Phoenix Hall of the Byodoin Temple near Kyoto. The cult of Amida, the Merciful, who would lead all believers into his Western Paradise, was becoming the one most congenial to Japanese sentiment. The sweet face carved by Jocho is peaceful and withdrawn, gazing with recognizable humanity at the devotee. The half-relief figures of divine attendants in the Buddha's great halo and the bigger ones round the walls of the hall are by members of Jocho's school: their graceful movement is a new feature in sculpture.

In spite of natural disasters, Japan has preserved the oldest surviving wooden buildings of the Far East. Up to *c* AD 900 buildings reflected Chinese and Korean architectural styles which can no longer be seen in their original countries. Because wood and light plaster were used (the only durable parts being ceramic roof tiles and beam-ends), the grandiose was rarely attempted. The exception is the Main Hall of the Todaiji, Nara, built to house the Great Buddha. The hall, a 17th-century two-thirds-sized rebuilding of the original, is the biggest wooden structure in the world. Its double-roofed style is found in the 7th-century Golden Hall of the Horyuji, which is the oldest building in Japan and reflects contemporary Korean styles, as does the slightly later, irregularly stepped pagoda of the nearby Yakushiji Temple. A quieter, Chinese-derived taste of almost Grecian proportions is preserved in the 8th-century main halls of the Shin Yakushiji and Toshodaiji temples (Nara). The Horyuji's octagonal Hall of Dreams, built in 739, is a perfect and unrepeated achievement.

Direct continental influence diminished after AD 900. A more native style grew up to suit the refined but not austere tastes of the Kyoto aristocracy. Surviving examples include the complex symmetrical pagoda of the Daigoji Temple built in 951, its worldly elegance heightened by the red painted timberwork, and the Phoenix Hall of the Byodoin (Uji), built in 1053 and made to resemble the shape of a phoenix with extended wings. Originally a palace, its galleries connect the wings to the main building, half enclosing a garden and lake, in the secular aristocratic style of the later Heian period. Both buildings use a complicated system of roof-beams and brackets which interlock to form a functional but decorative story above the main pillars and below the roof tiling, a feature much used in later times.

Few paintings have survived from before the mid 11th century, and most are on hard surfaces—walls, wooden doors, pillars, shrines, and even musical instruments. Only a handful of paintings on paper, hemp, and silk remain from these early centuries. But our sketchy knowledge was increased by the discovery, in 1972, of murals in a late-7th-century tomb at Takamatsuzuka in the Asuka area. A non-Buddhist tomb, but decorated well into the Buddhist age, it provides evidence of artistic continuity. On the walls are scenes of attendants in procession, mostly in greens, reds, and yellows with strong black outline, and vigorous portrayals of the animals guarding the four quarters. The mixture of Korean and Chinese styles suggests a typically Japanese synthesis of foreign culture. Mineral pigments, like those on continental murals, and prepared wall-surfaces show that full technical competence had been reached.

The 8th-century Buddhist murals of the Horyuji were almost entirely destroyed by fire in 1949. They depicted four Buddhist paradises peopled by hosts of heavenly beings. They were monuments of the T'ang style, grave, elevated, and graceful, done in clear double outline of red and black, and rich colors dominated by black, purple, dark red, and yellow. Foreign artists may have contributed, but in the Nara period over 100 official painters were maintained, most of whom must have been Japanese. From that time onwards there were nearly always official painters. The pigments of the Horyuji murals were used on wooden panels and pillars in the Daigoji pagoda (951), but elevated gravity was turning to a more Japanese sweetness, and the heavenly beings have considerable humanity. This process had gone further in the paradise scenes, now set in a very Japanese landscape, on the mid-11th-century doors of the Phoenix Hall. These are the last great monuments of wall-painting on solid surfaces. The true Japanese style which emerged was happier, with warmer, lighter pigments on paper or silk.

In the later Heian period better techniques of mounting paper and silk as hanging- or hand-scrolls encouraged the development of more native styles and formats. The period 1050 to 1300 was the great age of Buddhist painting—elevated, sentimental, warmly colorful, sensitive in line.

The esoteric *Shingon* and the popular Amidist sects provided most of the inspiration and subject matter. The numerous divinities—benign, fierce, or mysterious—of the *Shingon*

The octagonal Hall of Dreams in the Horyuji Temple, Nara; built in 739

doctrine were best portrayed in painting, where their complicated iconography could be more subtly expressed and balanced, than in sculpture. The big, mid-11th-century painting of Dai-itoku-myoo (Museum of Fine Arts, Boston) and the famous "blue" Fudo (Shorenin, Kyoto) are splendid examples. The former makes the blue-bodied, three-faced, many-armed-and-legged god, seated on a green bull, into a powerful yet beautiful image. The blood-red fiery halo at once symbolizes energy and provides the perfect decorative pattern for the background. This work shows the new features that give strong flavor to Heian and Kamakura Buddhist painting—supple black line, freely done in a semicalligraphic style, use of eggshell-white under the colors to give them depth, lavish detail in the brocades, and the use of cut gold leaf

(*kirikane*) on the body ornaments, scepters, etc. *Kirikane* laid on in complex patterns became the main element of many paintings by the Kamakura period (1192–1333), transforming them into semi-sculptural golden images.

The comforting Amidist doctrine stated that the Buddha Amida would take all his believers at death to his Paradise of the West. From the 11th century onwards many sumptuous works were commissioned by temples and rich patrons showing the great Buddha, with hosts of divine attendants and musicians, descending to earth to receive the soul of the believer (whose thoughts would be turned to his savior by the unrolling of the hanging scroll before his eyes as he lay dying). The greatest is the 12th-century triptych at the Mount Koya temples (Wakayama Prefecture). The central figure glows with

Buddhist Kamakura Sculpture

Buddhist sculpture in Japan reached the last and greatest of its peaks in the Kamakura period (1192–1333). Supreme technique in wood carving, a vigorous military culture, religious fervor, and a rediscovery of earlier sculptures combined for about 150 years to produce one of the world's great artistic achievements.

As so often in art history, the confidence of a new dominant class combined with rediscovery of long-past ideals to produce originality and vitality. The Kamakura military dictators had destroyed the effete Kyoto aristocracy; hence physical strength displayed in the rippling torsos of ferocious Buddhist figures became aesthetically desirable. The wars they fought destroyed the ancient temples of Nara. Rebuilding and the repairs of 8th-century carvings showed 13th-century sculptors a vigor long forgotten. As the almost dormant court culture was swept away, new, more humane styles from Sung China were imported and copied. The soft, very human figure of Dainichi by Unkei is very close to Sung Buddhist painting. At the same time, new, more popular Buddhist movements rose to replace the rarified aristocratic *Tendai* and *Shingon* sects. An age of

deep faith produced the endless comforting images of the Buddha Amida or the Bodhisattva Kannon, 1,001 images of whom were sculpted for the Hall of the 1,000 Kannons in Kyoto in the 13th century.

In the 11th century, the *yosegi* (multi-block) method of construction was developed in order to make bigger wooden images quickly. Craftsmen produced different parts under the direction of a master carver. But the effect was still refined, aristocratic calm, as in Jocho's 10 ft (3 m) high Amida of AD 1053. The 26 ft (8 m) Kongo Rikishi (AD 1204) of Unkei and Kaikei uses this technique in a new way to extend the physical limits of wood carving and to produce dynamic movement and power. The draperies are released to move where the sculptor wished. An 8th-century figure of Shukongo Shin from the same temple served as inspiration, but there is much less freedom in its body and garments. The vitality of the Kamakura sculptures is further enhanced by the *gyokugan* technique of inlaying eyes in crystal lined with paper on which the pupils were painted. Most pieces were brightly painted and gilt, but only traces of pigment normally remain.

◄ The portrait statue of Uesegi Shigefusa. 13th century; painted wood; height 70cm (28in). Meigetsuin Temple, Kamakura

▲ The humane, aristocratic face of the Amida made by Jocho in 1053. Height of statue 300cm (118in). Byodoin Temple, Uji

Truth to nature is the keynote of the age.
Sculpture was made for new militaristic patrons instead of for the aristocracy, or for
vigorous new sects such as *Jodo* or *Shinran*.
Although they were not strictly speaking
human, every Buddha, divinity, or guardian
was carved with an intense awareness of the
human face or body. Vigor and violence, as
in Jokei's superbly muscular guardian Kongo
Rikishi, was balanced by the sweetness and
humanity of the Buddha Amida, the major
object of worship of the *Jodo* sect. The
terrifying contortions of Koyu's judge of hell,
Shoko-O, have their answer in the truly
monumental calm of the great Buddha of
Kamakura, which was, unusually, cast in
metal sections which are the bronzeworker's
reply to the multi-block technique.

Great sculpture portraits of real people
were also a feature of the age, reflection of a
new humanity. The figure of the formidable
Uesegi Shigefusa is a rare secular example,
but there are many masterly portrayals of
religious figures. Unkei's magnificently
weighty life-size carving of Muchaku combines dignity with a powerful sense of the
real person, while pathos and spirituality are
combined in the portrait of the priest
Chogen.

LAWRENCE SMITH

Further reading. Kuno, T. *A Guide to Japanese
Sculpture*, Tokyo (1963). Mori, H. (trans. Eickmann,
K.) *Sculpture of the Kamakura Period*, London
(1974).

◀ The great Buddha of
Kamakura, cast in 1252
by Ono Goroemon.
Bronze; height including
dais 14.9m (49ft).
Precinct of Kotokuin
Temple, Kamakura

▲ The head of Shoko-O
by Koyu; mid Kamakura
period; painted wood;
height of statue 102cm
(40in). Ennoji Temple,
Kanagawa prefecture

kirikane, while the garments of the attendants are painted in deep, rich colors, their bodies in pink-shaded white. All are unified by the white, swirling clouds on which they descend. This was the compositional prototype for many *Amida Raigo* (Descent of Amida paintings).

The Kamakura period (1192–1333) continues this tradition to *c* AD 1300, after which Buddhist painting slowly loses its conviction and becomes mere image-making. The Kamakura colors are more somber, the compositions more rational, reflecting the serious spirit of the age. A favorite figure of this period was Jizo, saver of souls. He was an aspect of Amida, usually shown as a compassionate shaven-headed monk holding a staff and a sacred jewel. His human face suited the naturalistic tendencies of the age; the use of *kirikane* with somber colors on his robes gave a restrained, introverted richness. The dynamism characteristic of this period was better expressed in sculpture and in the narrative handscroll.

Patronage of the arts in the period 900–1150 was dominated by the Kyoto aristocracy and by the big temples around Kyoto. Lessening Chinese influence after AD 900 encouraged new and more Japanese styles of architecture, sculpture, painting, decorative arts, and literature, patronized by these classes, and especially by the controlling Fujiwara family.

Domestic architecture became intimate; fragile sliding screens covered with paper (*shoji*) and portable folding screens (*byobu*) were used to divide open-plan floors, which were now raised above the ground on low stilts. Literary references mention that these screens were decorated with scenes of the natural world, especially of landscapes in the four seasons and the 12 months, and of views of beauty spots. They were called *Yamatoe*, "Japanese pictures", as opposed to *Kara-e*, "Chinese pictures", most of which must have been grand, imaginary mountain landscapes like the one preserved on the leather of a lute from the mid-8th-century repository called the *Shosoin* at Nara.

Yamatoe depicted the round-hilled, intimate landscape of the Kyoto/Nara area with strong feeling for the changing seasons, humanized by the addition of domestic buildings and people in ordinary occupations. The earliest surviving examples are the Buddhist Paradises set in the four seasons on the doors of the Byodoin. All the features of the style are already present—the viewpoint above the foreground, looking across to the far hills; the simple black outline with clear, mostly unmixed colors; the water, expressed by closely set, black lines representing ripples; the loving detail of the trees, flowers, people, and wild creatures; and the lack of sustained perspective and proportion between parts of the composition. This is an intimate art, the sky almost omitted by the high horizon. It reappears in folding screens of landscapes with religious figures, like the 11th-century ones from the Toji Temple, Kyoto. These were used in Buddhist ordination ceremonies. By this time the Japanese view of nature was thought elevated enough for such purposes, and it forms the basis of all subsequent schools in native taste.

At this period the small-scale *Yamatoe* paintings were illustrating calligraphic albums of poetry, none of which survive. In the 10th century a fully Japanese calligraphy had emerged. Important as calligraphy was in Chinese civilization, the Japanese had never excelled at the square hands which were most to Chinese taste. But with the development, from very simplified forms of characters, of a syllabary called *hiragana* to express Japanese sounds, a very cursive and liquid calligraphic style grew up. Its greatest executants were often Heian court ladies, whose menfolk by convention kept to Chinese. The poetic, feminine nature of this style suited the short nature-dominated poems called *Waka*, which could be written with a few movements of the brush. From the 12th century onwards survive *shikishi*, collage sheets of carefully matched, dyed papers, on each of which a poem was written. These rank among the most elegant productions of Heian court civilization. Such was the status of calligraphy in Japan that these survived where the paintings did not. Album paintings illustrating these sheets survive only from later periods, but their style was certainly the basis for the handscrolls which were the next to develop.

The *Tale of Genji*, written *c* AD 1000 by Lady Murasaki, was the greatest of the prose romances which were copied in *hiragana* in the form of handscrolls from the 10th century onwards. They came to have illustrations attached, one section of writing succeeded by one picture as the scroll unrolled from right to left. These *emakimono* (picture handscrolls) differ technically from the only earlier surviving picture scroll, the 8th-century *Ingakyo* (version in the Jobun Rendaiji Temple, Kyoto). This was a life of the Buddha, in a fairly primitive style; the columns of writing in square characters ran continuously along the bottom of the scroll but the columns were too short to allow the freedom necessary for a good *hiragana* hand.

The earliest remaining *Genji* scroll sections (some are in the Tokugawa Museum, Nagoya) show a fully fledged illustrative style in the early 12th century. The point of view is almost vertically above the buildings, into which we peer as though they were roofless. The beams of the buildings themselves are represented by carefully ruled lines without foreshortening. The story is emotionally and symbolically illustrated, because emotionally subtle situations appealed to the aristocratic readers. The faces are perfunctorily done—two slits for the eyes, a hook for the nose; women's feelings are expressed through the black windings of their long hair. Colors are rich, with purples, dark yellows, oranges, greens, and dark reds—a regal palette which hardly recurs in later Japanese art.

Later Buddhist and feudal culture (1192–1573). The mid-12th-century civil wars of the Taira and Minamoto clans ended in the victory of the latter and the end of the courtly age. Their leader, Yoritomo, was a provincial military man. In 1192 he was appointed *Shogun* (generalissimo) and moved the effective capital to the small eastern town of Kamakura. This government was feudal. In place of governors appointed by a Kyoto bureaucracy, Japan was controlled by local lords loyal to Yoritomo.

Art was never so capital-oriented again. Centers of culture grew up in the provinces, and the arbiters of taste were now the men of action. Art became more naturalistic and energetic, less exquisite, often more concerned with ordinary people. Gradually Zen Buddhism came to dominate other sects intellectually, and the Muromachi period (1392–1573) was the greatest period of Zen art.

The years 1150–1350 saw also the flowering of that most Japanese art form, the narrative or descriptive handscroll. Increasing interest in new things, places, and ideas extended subject matter, and styles became more varied to suit them. Ever-longer continuous sections were painted with masterly organization, while textual sections became smaller. In the 14th century the ability to organize a long composition declined, and the bands of clouds found on earlier works become long, formalized bars linking sections of the narrative in a very arbitrary manner.

The late Heian style, used for courtly novels and collections of poems (c1000–1192) became less distinguished in the Kamakura period (1192–1333), but its spirit continued in the *hakubyo* "white drawing" style, done in thick, lustrous ink, heightened with lacquer, on a pure white paper. This uniquely Japanese manner was almost calligraphic. The sinuous, jet-black strands of the ladies' hair formed the main element of design.

There was little interest in the common people among the aristocratic patrons of Heian art, though recent discoveries of very racy caricatures of artisans under the borders of mounted Buddhist paintings suggest a hidden tradition. This came into

the open during the Civil Wars, notably in the vigorous crowd scenes of the *Story of Ban Dainagon* (Sakai Collection, Tokyo) which, significantly, may have been the work of the court painter Mitsuhiro, c1150. The nervous graphic style of the figures and the individuality of the faces began a tradition which still persists. Other good examples are *The Legends of Mount Shigi* (Choyosonshiji, Nara) from the 12th century, and the 14th century *Fukutomi Zoshi Emaki* (Cleveland Museum of Art).

In illustrating war stories based on the recent civil wars, the pictorial organization needed to handle large crowded scenes of action reached its zenith. The section of the 13th-century *Story of the Heiji Rebellion* (Museum of Fine Arts, Boston) illustrating the burning of the Sanjo Palace in Kyoto is a masterpiece of movement fitted into a narrow format to make a satisfying design. Carefully ruled lines of buildings frame the scene and give it stability. The brown roofs, seen from above, form thick bars unifying the composition. Across the bottom left pour charging horsemen and soldiers, painted with lively detail. The top right is filled with the horrifying flames and smoke of the burning palace, both turned into beautiful patterns of white edged with red. Another monument of this type records the Mongol invasions of 1274 and 1281, and *The Latter Three Years' War* of 1347 is one of the last great handscrolls (Tokyo National Museum).

Much beauty and sheer entertainment was insinuated into Buddhist and Shinto scrolls recording the horrors of hell, histories of saints, and the founding and miracles of temples and shrines. In the latter the *Yamatoe* landscape style reaches its zenith, best of all in the lovingly recorded landscapes of the *Life of the Monk Ippen* by En'i, AD 1299 (Kankikoji, Kyoto).

A detail from an illustrated scroll of the Tales of Genji; 2nd half of the 12th century. Tokugawa Reimeikai Foundation, Tokyo

Unusually on silk, it tells of Ippen's apostolic wanderings over Japan, depicting in lyrical detail the actual landscapes of each area and the lives of the people. There is a touch of Sung Chinese rationality in these scenes, but there is no doubt that the Japanese of this period deeply revered their country's fabric. Such feelings originated in Shinto but it was a new pride in localities and their gods that revitalized religious painting. The *Suijaku* doctrine, that Shinto gods were manifestations of Buddhist divinities, further encouraged it. Apart from handscrolls, there are many hanging scrolls from the Kamakura and Nambokucho periods (1192–1333 and 1333–92) showing shrines and temples set among their native landscape and peopled with large figures of their guardian gods.

The greatest of the Shinto works is the *Kitano Tenjin Engi* (Kitano Shrine, Kyoto). The largest of all the scrolls, over 20 in (50 cm) in height, it records the life of Michizane, the 9th-century scholar who died in exile, and the building of his shrine. Dated to 1219 its main interest is the lively detail of human life and nature, but selection of pictorial material simply for the sake of the composition is beginning to show. People and animals, as well as trees, rocks, and buildings are placed on the page with a monumental certainty which is the mark of Japanese decorative genius. The line tends to become ornamental in itself, and brilliantly warm, unmixed colors are laid on in clearly separated patches. Here are premonitions of the *Rimpa* style of the 17th to 19th centuries. They are seen more strongly in the mid-14th-century *Life of the Monk Honen* (Chion'in, Kyoto); an enormous work in many scrolls. In some sections the *Yamatoe* style of rounded hills is simplified to almost concentric bands of gray ink, blue, green, and gold.

Until the 12th century, brush ink outline in *Yamatoe* and Buddhist painting had been sensitive and supple, but undynamic. During that century there emerged in Kyoto a high level of skill in pure ink sketching of *Shingon* divinities for iconographic purposes, particularly at the Toji, Ninnaji, and Daigoji temples in Kyoto where big collections of such sketches remain. Good as they were, a more dynamic line, influenced from China and Korea, developed at the Kozanji Temple at Takao near Kyoto. The most famous product of this school (the temple was that of the semimystical Kegon sect) is the late-12th-century set of scrolls of animals called the *Choju Giga*, a series of satires on contemporary clerical life. Done in ink without color, the line is freer than ever before, and ink shading is used to suggest volume and movement. The scene of frogs and rabbits wrestling is a representative enthusiastic satire of the world of men. They are attributed to a monk, Toba Sojo, after whom such works are often called *Tobae*.

The possibilities of brushwork are carried further in the slightly later Kozanji scrolls of the lives of the Kegon monks Gisho and Gengyo, romantic tales of adventure and love. The colors are kept deliberately light, so that the emotional and varied pictorial line can be properly seen. Ink wash was also blended with gold, green, and blue to give tonal range, a technique adopted in later painting. Their artist, the monk Enichi-bo-Jonin (*fl. c*1210–30) also did a memorable hanging scroll of the Kozanji patriarch Myoe, seated in meditation among the local woodlands. The thick, expressive line of both trees and rocks gives flowing unity to this mystical vision of man in the natural world.

The Takuma School of Buddhist painters (named from their founder, Takuma Tameuji who worked in the late 10th century) were inspired from the 12th century onwards by influences from Sung China. In place of the simple lines and formal backgrounds of Kamakura Buddhist painting, they employed a nervous line with less decoration and often backgrounds of Chinese-style ink landscape. The panels of 12 divinities attributed to the late-13th-century Takuma Shoga (Toji Temple, Kyoto) are splendid examples of this energetic style. Gnarled portraits of the Buddhist apostles called *Rakan* were supplied by this school and continued as late as the early 15th century by *Mincho*.

The strong individualism of the *Shogun* Yoritomo and his captains favored realistic portraiture. The standard was set by the works of the courtier Fujiwara Takanobu (*ob.* 1205). Of his three large-scale portraits surviving in the Jingoji Temple at Takao near Kyoto, the most famous is of Yoritomo himself: the lean face with its hard steely eyes is unforgettable. The black mass of the formal robes of his seated figure throws more attention on the face. The handscrolls of portraits of previous emperors, courtiers, famous horses, and even prize ritual bulls also express the naturalistic spirit of the age.

Portraiture, both in painting and sculpture, was one of the glories of Kamakura culture. From the 14th century the inspiration and power of Buddhist sculpture and painting declined and some of the native ability to model plastic figures and faces went into masks. A more subtle style was used for the masks of the *No* drama, a restrained, static form of poetic dance-play which developed in the 14th century. Delicate expression was achieved by both refined carving and very sensitive painting over thick gesso. The masks were for stock characters, for example a young woman, and could reflect and project the changing moods of the actor himself.

Zen Buddhism encouraged every man to discover both his own Buddha-nature and the nature of existence through contemplation and action. It appealed in some measure to all the influential classes: the aristocracy for its aesthetics, the priests and scholars for its seriousness (though it was far from solemn), the fighting *samurai* for its sharpening of the intuitive action in martial skills. Zen was thus by accident of the times fitted to achieve cultural dominance in the Muromachi period (1392–1573) when all three classes were powerful.

Zen's most enduring monuments in Japan are its temples and gardens; most of the greatest are in Kyoto. In them, the formality and comparative grandeur of Heian and Kamakura buildings and gardens were forgotten. The large Zen temple was a collection of restrained buildings, never ostentatious even when big, each walled in its own garden, set along tree-lined or walled avenues. The most famous is the Daitokuji,

Portrait of Yoritomo by Fujiwara Takanobu. Jingoji Temple, Takao, near Kyoto

A mask of a young woman used in Nō Drama; c1800. British Museum, London

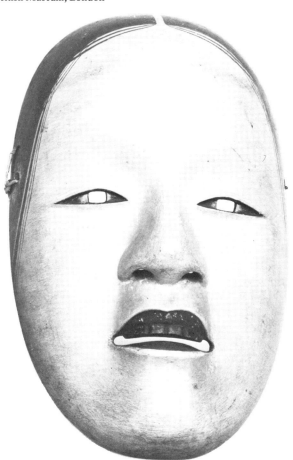

Kyoto, a very large complex of sub-temples and a cradle of Zen arts during the Muromachi period.

The gardens are all designed to help contemplation; none have flowers, so they seem fresh in all seasons. The biggest are the "borrowed landscape" type where the surrounding hills are included in a design of lakes, hillocks, and foliage. The best known are at the Golden Pavilion and the nearby Ryoanji temples. At the latter is also the most famous of the rock gardens, a small enclosed space viewed from a veranda, consisting now of only a few mossy rocks set in a sea of raked pebbles, although it once included a few trees. The importance of the garden reaches its peak in the Kyoto Moss Temple, a landscaped fantasy of mossy undulations set round water under trees, where the buildings are almost unnoticeable.

The Golden Pavilion and the Silver Pavilion, both secular in origin, are the monuments of upper-class domestic architecture of Muromachi Kyoto. The first was the house of the abdicated *Shogun* Yoshimitsu from 1395 to 1408. It has, unusually, three floors instead of one and is, uniquely, covered in gold leaf. From its upper floor the Zen devotee could contemplate, overlooking a lake and "borrowed landscape" of superlative beauty. The Pavilion itself is of the lightest structure and overhangs a still lake on which it appears to float. The Silver Pavilion (Ginkakuji) is associated with another arbiter of taste, the *Shogun* Yoshimasa (in power from 1449 to 1474). Faced in plain wood, it is the epitome of the restrained Zen taste of the period.

In the gardens of the Silver Pavilion was perhaps the first example of a Tea House with a four-and-half-mat floor (approximately 80 sq ft; 7.5 sq m). The Tea Ceremony originated in austere Zen devotions in China, but in Muromachi Kyoto it became a gathering of cultivated friends, in conditions of carefully planned simplicity, to drink tea in a prescribed manner and to discuss the utensils used, the architecture of the house, the flower arrangement, and the painting or calligraphy, usually in ink only, decorating the alcove called the *tokonoma*. Its artistic importance is that it formed the aesthetic framework in which men of taste met and agreed on their tastes. It gave a unifying aesthetic to a number of related arts. Naturally, in this developed form it included much that was not originally Zen.

In the Chinese-dominated artistic milieu of Muromachi Kyoto the ink painting traditions of China inevitably made a rather delayed entry into Japanese art. Ink painting was one way by which a Zen priest could search for reality, and the idealized Chinese landscapes themselves, like the rock gardens, inspired meditation. The existence of new patrons who appreciated Chinese art deeply inspired a flowering of this painting in 15th-century Japan: it was found on the sliding screens of Zen temples, on hanging scrolls hung in the Tea Houses, and handscrolls and albums perused by connoisseurs.

The pioneer attempts at monochrome painting in the late 13th and 14th centuries are unexciting by Chinese standards but by 1415 at least one masterpiece, a hanging scroll on the Zen parable *Catching a Catfish with a Gourd*, had been pro-

Part of the Daitokuji Temple complex in Kyoto

A rock garden, in the Daitokuji Temple complex, Kyoto;
constructed in 1509

duced, by Taiko Josetsu of the Sokokuji Temple, Kyoto, which was an early center of this art (the painting is now in the Myoshinji, Kyoto). It shows already the Japanese fondness for subtly graded ink-and-color washes which are decorative rather than symbolic. This tendency continues in the works (all attributed) of his pupil Tensho Shubun (fl. c1426–65) whose visit to Korea may account for his deep interest in spatial depth and recession. A splendid landscape by his pupil Tenyu Shokei (Tokyo National Museum) has the characteristic division into a foreground of rocky outcrops, pavilions, and trees, a middle ground of water, mist, and dimly seen spits of land, and a far distance of almost vertical mountains, edged in blue wash. Other artists in Shubun's general style are Gakuo (fl. 1504–20), Bunsei (fl. mid 15th century), and Kenko Shokei (fl. c1478–1506).

Misty effects in wash reach their apogee in the sliding screens of Soami (*ob.* 1525) in the Daisen'in, and in another set of about 1491 in the Shinjuan attributed to Jasoku II (both sub-temples in the Daitokuji, Kyoto). The *fusuma* (sliding doors) of this treasure house of ink painting are the earliest surviving of this form, done in continuous compositions across four paper-covered doors. The beginnings of other landscape ink styles are found there too, including the dynamic *haboku* (ink splash) style, which originated in China. A whole landscape is suggested with a few powerful splashes of ink, done in a high moment of Zen-induced concentration.

Haboku was one of the styles mastered by Shubun's pupil, Sesshu Toyo (1420–1506), considered by the Japanese to be their greatest artist. Of all Japanese painters Sesshu was unusually grave and serious. His characteristic line is weighty, his ink shading solid, his landscapes rational and convincing: his study visit to China probably accounts for all this. The famous landscape scroll in the Mori Collection (Mori Museum, Chofu) is a work of a complex unity, equaled only in China. In the magnificent large sketch of the famous scenery of Ama-no-Hashidate (Kyoto National Museum) he transfers his elevated vision from imaginary to real landscape.

In the late Muromachi period the only great Zen ink painter is Sesson Shukei (*c*1509–*post* 1589). Working independently in northeast Japan, consistently inspired by Sesshu's works, his technique is deliberately rough but his works impress by their deep religious sincerity.

In the 15th century two schools were established which were to dominate official painting until the mid 19th century. Members of the *Tosa* School had been artists to the Court for some time (they claimed the School had begun in the 13th century) and were guardians of the *Yamatoe* tradition in landscrolls, albums, and decorative screens. Their best-known member was Tosa Mitsunobu (*ob. c*1521) who in 1502 painted an excellent version of the *Kitano Tenjin Engi*, thus putting himself firmly among the masters of the handscroll tradition.

The *Kano* School begins with Kano Masanobu (1454–90) who became head of the academy of the Ashikaga *Shoguns*. An Amidist, his appointment broke the Zen dominance of ink painting and opened the way for the secular decorative *Kano* manner. His few surviving works are mostly in the Daitokuji temple, which remained a center of *Kano* style for over a century after his death; they show strong contrasts between thickly outlined and hatched rocks and trees and delicately graded mists which are already beginning to take on a significance which is more decorative than representational.

His son Motonobu (1476–1559) developed the style further, decorating whole rooms with large-scale birds, trees, and figures in landscape backgrounds, and fixing the technical repertory of the school. His masterpieces are the sliding doors of the Daisen'in (in the Daitokuji, Kyoto) and of the Reiun'in (in the Myoshinji, Kyoto). Motonobu used more color than earlier ink painters. His marriage with Mitsunobu's daughter marked the partial union of the *Tosa* and *Kano* schools, their

Landscape with a waterfall by Sesshu (1420–1506); ink on paper. Marquis of Hosokawa Collection, Horishige

future cooperation, and the mutual influence of their styles. An important result was the use of gold washes in ink screen compositions, leading to the Momoyama period outburst in this genre.

The age of secular urban culture (1573–1867). The Momoyama period (1573–1615) was one of strife and great vitality. Three unaristocratic leaders, Oda Nobunaga (1534–82), Toyotomi Hideyoshi (1536–98), and Tokugawa Ieyasu (1542–1616) unified the country after the turmoil of the late Muromachi. Nobunaga ended the long stalemate of a century of civil wars by decisively shifting the balance of power toward one dominating alliance of feudal lords loyal to him. Hideyoshi completed the reunification of the country, began a system of fierce central control, and led Japan's first foreign adventure by invading Korea. Ieyasu followed him, destroyed the last resistance to central rule, and laid down an elaborately bureaucratic system of government, controlling almost every facet of life, which lasted until 1867. He also expelled most Europeans, suppressed Christianity, and took the first steps that led Japan into isolation. These men in their castles and palaces became the new art patrons. Hideyoshi's splendid Momoyama Castle gives its name to the period 1573–1615. The arrival of European traders and missionaries, the invasions of Korea (1592 and 1597), and trade with China and southeast Asia temporarily extended the horizons of the Japanese people. From now on the dominant class in the arts were the *samurai* and the great merchants, whose attitudes merged to form a middle class with tastes of unprecedented refinement.

In 1603 Ieyasu founded his Tokugawa Government and moved the capital to Edo (modern Tokyo), leaving a powerless court at Kyoto. The period up to 1867 is called after Edo (or Tokugawa after Ieyasu's family name); in the city itself a modern-style consumer society grew up. Although a vigorous popular culture flourished in Edo, Kyoto remained the center of both traditional and most new schools of art.

In 1639 the Tokugawas banned Christianity and imposed isolation from the outside world. A few licensed Dutch and Chinese traders, restricted to Nagasaki, brought a trickle of books and paintings from their countries which were seized on by Japanese artists as the basis for new schools, but the general mood of the period was inward-looking, with an emphasis on the minor and applied arts—prints, lacquer, metalwork, miniature carving. Higher artistic talent went mostly into painting, and schools proliferated, with complex inter-relationships.

The building of castles was the great architectural development of the Momoyama period, necessitated by perpetual wars in which gunpowder was used for the first time. A castle typically consisted of a huge mound faced by tall walls consisting of great stone blocks. An inner moat surrounded a smaller but similar walled moat on a higher level and this supported the main wooden structure which soared in roofed stories in between, like a broad pagoda. Such were the Momoyama Castle (now Osaka), Nagoya, and Himeji. The prototype was Nobunaga's great Azuchi Castle (built 1576–9) on the east side of Lake Biwa, of which only the foundations now remain.

These spectacular castles inspired an unusually exuberant

art. But with characteristic duality, Japan also saw at this tim the height of the Tea Ceremony, under its greatest Te Master, Rikyu, inspiring temple and domestic architecture o serene quietness. The Katsura Palace in Kyoto, for example, a perfect fusion of restrained building and carefully planne gardens; it was designed by the Tea Master Kobori Ensh (1579–1647). New types of quiet yet forceful pottery we developed at this period for the Tea Ceremony—the Rak ware of Kyoto, the Ignand Shigaraki wares from the east o Kyoto, and the Shino and Oribe wares of Mino province.

The brilliant screen style of painting, which lasted until th late 17th century, was created by Motonobu's grandson Kan Eitoku (1543–90). Used at an early date in the great castle its features are strong line, bold composition (such as a tre spread over the whole of a wall), brilliant colors, and muc use of gold wash and gold leaf as background. Interest focused on the foreground. Such is the cypress tree, of almo brutal power, its great brown trunk set against a gold le background, painted by Eitoku and now in the Tokyo Natior al Museum.

Eitoku's sons Kano Mitsunobu (1565–1608; not to be co fused with Tosa Mitsunobu) and Takanobu (1571–1618) an his pupil Sanraku (1559–1635) continued the decorative tra dition of which the *Kano* School had a monopoly challenge only by Hasegawa Tohaku. After Eitoku's death more en

The moss garden of Katsura Palace, Kyoto, designed by Kobori Enshu (1579–1647)

phasis was placed on the details of foreground objects, and a quieter style developed for domestic and temple apartments, such as Mitsunobu's suite in the Kangakuin (Miidera Temple, Otsu) where the faded gold backgrounds unify the main room with an intimate richness.

In the earlier 17th century *Kano* activities diversified into decorative work, ink painting, and genre. The new generation worked on the great Nijo Palace in Kyoto, and Nagoya and Edo castles. Its members included Kano Koi (*ob.* 1636), Sadanobu (1597–1623), and the brothers Tanyu (1602–74), Naonobu (1607–50), and Yasunobu (1613–85). Tanyu came to lead the school and dominates its later history. He and his brothers produced powerful ink painting for Zen temples, as did Naonobu's son Tsunenobu (1636–1713). They became official painters at Edo, while Sanraku and his pupil Sansetsu (1590–1651) remained at Kyoto where they produced fine decorative work. The painting at Nagoya Castle shows the strains imposed on artistic invention by such vast commissions.

The later history of the *Kano* school is of decline and academic dullness. Many good Edo-period painters trained with them but then founded new schools.

The *Kano* school did not dominate ink painting until the mid 17th century. In the Momoyama period (1573–1615) there were many groups of ink painters retaining a sense of

elevation typical of the Muromachi period, many of them *samurai* devoted to Zen. The most important were Unkoku Togan (1547–1618), in the tradition of Sesshu and founder of the Unkoku School; Soga Chokuan (*ob. c*1610), founder of the new Soga School characterized by vigorous brushwork; Hasegawa Tohaku (1539–1610), possibly the most gifted of Japanese ink painters; and Kaiho Yusho (1533–1615), who displays great intellectual power. Both Tohaku and Yusho produced semidecorative screens using both ink and gold washes with great seriousness; and Tohaku's colored screens at the Chishakuin, Kyoto, are the greatest of the age.

In the next generation two individualists stand out from *Kano* orthodoxy: the swordsman Miyamoto Niten (1584–1645), and the calligrapher Nakamura Shokado (1584–1639). Both emphasized abbreviated dynamic line, though Niten could handle washes with great skill.

The increasing importance of urban dwelling in the great cities of Kyoto, Osaka, and Edo led almost inevitably to an art for ordinary people. During the 16th century the *Yamatoe* style landscape screen with strong bands of gold cloud linking parts of the composition was adapted to include townspeople at work and play; especially in crowds at festivals. The artists were often of the *Kano* or *Tosa* schools. Eitoku himself is credited with panoramas of the sights of Kyoto, each revealed through breaks in gold clouds (this popular type of composi-

Cypress: an eight-fold screen by Kano Eitoku (1543–90); color on gold-leafed paper; 170×460cm (67×181in). Tokyo National Museum

Shino Ware

The appreciation of pottery was the most advanced aesthetic skill acquired by a devotee of the Tea Ceremony. In 16th-century Japan certain styles of pottery were developed in response to the demands of these Tea Masters, and one of the most admired was Shino ware. With whitish glazes, Shino was made in Mino Province (modern Gifu prefecture) in the area round Tajimi and Toki, northeast of Nagoya. The name comes from the great incense connoisseur and Tea Master Shino Soshin (1440–1522). But he lived before the pottery itself was made; the association seems to have been the mistake of a later period.

The aesthetics of the Tea Ceremony were unified by quietness, sobriety, and balance. Depth was sought in unpretentiousness. The ceramic tea-bowls themselves stood at the center of this taste; they were appreciated not only visually, but also through the lips during tea-drinking, and through handling when emptied. Qualities of texture, weight, and balance were therefore much appreciated and were extended from the Shino bowls, such as the famous Deutzia Trellis Bowl (Mitsui Collection), to the other necessary utensils. Of these the most impressive was the water-jar (*mizusashi*) used to carry cold water into the tea-room for transfer to the kettle for heating.

The shape of this jar, like all Shino pieces, was deliberately distorted, away from perfection, on a slow-moving potter's wheel. The indentations and ridges of the body, and the irregularities of the rim, gave the piece a personality different from any other. This was not at all an act of self-expression, like that of a Western art potter, for the Japanese craftsman knew he would always remain anonymous. What was important was that the piece had solidity and coherence as well as variety. Only intense familiarity by a connoisseur would reveal whether those qualities were sufficiently present to maintain interest and admiration over a long period.

The iron-bearing clay of Shino was local and relatively unrefined. It was a natural white, but baked, when unglazed, to a subtle, restrained yet glowing orange-rust color, and parts were usually left unglazed so that this color could be appreciated. In this particular water-jar a triangular patch has been left for that purpose, but the color also shows in much subtler streaks where the glaze has drawn back in firing. To achieve this, the glaze was applied with inspired carelessness. The feldspathic glaze is thick, milky, but slightly translucent. It is soft and varied to the touch and has that "wet" appearance which was so much prized. It seems to grow out of the body, giving a feeling of unity. Any tension between body and glaze would have disturbed the aesthetic calm of the Tea Ceremony.

Shino was fired slowly in cool and technically inefficient kilns. It was therefore not possible to predict the final result exactly, and it individuality was most admired. Even the pinholes in the glaze, regarded as a fault in more polished types of pottery, were regarded as a virtue. Many of these qualities of body and glaze seem to mirror in white the low-fired Black Raku pottery of Kyoto, which at the same period was an even more admired Tea Ceremony ware.

The design was painted with a brush to the body in an iron-bearing slip before glazing. It fired to a restrained bluish-gray, but where the glaze was very thin or not applied at all it burned to mixtures of red, brown, and purple, as seen in the triangular patch on this piece. The design is sketchy and suggestive. To the Japanese it shows clearly reeds crossed by the wind on a riverbank and a man in a boat above them. So the surrounding space is filled with the suggestion of water, and the rim acquires a hint of a distant bank or far hills. Such a design responded to the contemplation it would receive at the Tea Ceremony. In some pieces, the design was applied over the bulk of the piece. It would then fire bluish-gray in color, and this type was called Gray Shino.

LAWRENCE SMITH

Further reading. Fujioka, R. (trans. Morse, S.C.) *Shino and Oribe Ceramics*, Tokyo and New York (1977).

Above left A Black Raku tea bowl decorated with plum blossom; early 19th century; diameter 13cm (5in). British Museum, London

◄ A Shino food bowl decorated with a motif of grass; 18th century; diameter 20cm (8in). British Museum, London

► A Shino water-jar of the Momoyama period (1573–1615); height 18cm (7in). Cleveland Museum of Art. Notice the triangular patch left unglazed

tion was called *Rakuchu-Rakugai* "in and outside the Capital").

Depictions on some screens included Europeans, mostly Portuguese and Spanish missionaries and merchants, evident in Japan after 1549 and a source of curiosity. Paintings of this sort are called *Namban* art (*Namban*, "southern barbarians", means foreigners arriving via the southern sea routes).

The prominence of the standing human figure in Western art probably encouraged the emphasis given to fashionable women in mid-17th-century popular paintings. The most striking are the Matsuura screens in the Yamato Bunkakan Museum, Nara, showing stylishly dressed women, all attention devoted to the details of their dress and to their attractive faces. This world of painting—human, frivolous, joyously sensuous—is called *Ukiyoe*, "pictures of the fleeting world". Born in Kyoto, it moved to Edo in the late 17th century where its highly idealized view of the *demi-monde* inspired the first genuinely original style from the metropolis. *Kano* traditions dwindled, and some *Ukiyoe* artists like Hishikawa Moronobu (*ob.* 1694) and Miyagawa Choshun (1682–1752) signed themselves "*Yamatoe* artist".

The fame of *Ukiyoe* woodblock prints has obscured the excellence of the painting, some by artists such as Choshun and Utagawa Toyohiro (1774–1829) hardly known from prints. These artists excelled in painting beautiful women and their admirers in simple, often indoor settings. The Kabuki theater inspired many great prints but few good paintings. Distinguished work in both prints and paintings was done by members of the Kaigetsudo studio (early 18th century); by Katsukawa Shunsho (1726–92), Hosoda Eishi (1756–1829), and the two semi-*Ukiyoe* individualists Katsushika Hosusai (1760–1849) and Kawanabe Gyosai (1831–89).

In the mid 17th century the publishing industry began to produce single *Ukiyoe* prints and picture books (*ehon*) of the gay world, and a little later of the Kabuki theater and its actors. The new art drew on a 1,000-year-old tradition of textual woodblock printing, until then little used for pictorial purposes. The artists who designed for these works did not cut the blocks or print them. The art resulted from a unique cooperation of artist, craftsman, and publisher.

Early *Ukiyoe* prints were produced in black line only, sometimes hand-colored: they were dominated in the late 17th century by Hishikawa Moronobu and his school (specialists in book illustration), and in the early 18th century by the Torii School who popularized the actor-print, and the Kaigetsudo group, whose large, bold prints seem to have been made as cheap substitutes for their vigorously colorful paintings of beautiful women of the day. In the 1720s pink and green color blocks were first effectively used by Torii Kiyomasu (1706–63) and Okumura Masanobu (1690–1768). In the 1760s the full-color "brocade print" (*nishikie*) developed in the hands of Suzuki Harunobu (1724–70) and Isoda Koryusai (*fl.* c1760–80) to great heights of *faux-naif* erotic fantasy. The late-18th-century works of Torii Kiyonaga (1752–1815), Kitagawa Utamaro (1753–1806), and Hosoda Eishi (1765–1829) are

A Beauty painted by Torii Kiyonaga (1752–1815). British Museum, London

the pinnacles of the form. The actor-prints of Shunsho, Toshusai Sharaku (*fl.* only 1794–5), Utagawa Kunimasa (1773–1810), and the young Utagawa Toyokuni (1769–1825) are outstanding.

The years 1790–1850 saw the production of many deluxe prints called *surimono* illustrating poetic subjects and using very finely graded color blocks, *gauffrage*, and applied gold, silver, and mica, used as greetings cards. They indicate the refined taste of the Edo middle classes. The master designers of *surimono* included Shuniman (1757–1820), Hokusai (1760–1849), Shinsai (1764?–1820), Hokkei (1780–1850), and Gakutei (1786?–1868).

In the early 1830s Hokusai first used European Prussian

Blue in his landscape series *Thirty-six Views of Mount Fuji*. This strong color, previously unavailable, made more varied landscape prints possible. Hokusai, Ando Hiroshige (1797–1858), and Keisai Eisen (1790–1848) all produced landscape prints of great verve and sensitivity. They were widely sold and greatly influenced later landscape painting.

After 1842, prints of heroic and legendary subjects became popular. The leader of this movement was Utagawa Kunyoshi (1797–1861) with his dynamic three-sheet designs.

The *Tosa* School continued to paint in the courtly style and Tosa Mitsuyoshi (1539–1613) in the late 16th century produced traditional works like his *Tale of Genji* album (Kyoto National Museum) in which each page is a masterpiece of detailed, richly colored romanticism. The static atmosphere of these album sheets recalls the miniatures painted for Indian courtly patrons (*see* Indian Art). In the 17th century Tosa Mitsuoki (1617–91) took advantage of the strong nostalgia in Kyoto for its classical past to extend the scope of the school to include bolder decorative screens and bird and flower hanging scrolls of exquisite refinement, but his *Tosa* successors lacked vitality.

One *Tosa* artist, Jokei (1599–1670), formed an Edo branch called *Sumiyoshi*. Its best artist was Sumiyoshi Gukei (1631–1705) whose varied works included elements of the *Tosa*, *Kano*, and *Ukiyoe* styles. Much of his work was done in Kyoto; after his death his school settled in Edo, subdivided, and produced little work of note.

In the early 19th century, an antiquarian spirit and a growing interest in Japan's Imperial past found expression in the *Fukko Yamatoa* (Revival *Yamatoe*) school. Its leading lights were Reizei Tamechika (1823–64), Tanaka Totsugen (1768–1823), and Ukita Ikkei (1795–1859). Tamechika studied and copied ancient handscrolls, but his own work is shot through with contemporary decorative romanticism. This movement contributed to the unified *Nihonga* style after the Imperial Restoration in 1867.

The founder of the style used by the *Rimpa* School was Tawaraya Sotatsu (*ob.* 1643?), though the school's name derives from its greatest member, Ogata Korin (1652–1716). A Kyoto fan painter by trade, Sotatsu was the first artist to accept the native decorative tendency completely; he created a style in perfect accord with Japanese temperament. It was basically *Yamatoe*, but with thicker line or brilliant patches of color without outline. One special technique was to drop a color on to the wet surface of another color, producing a marbled effect. *Rimpa*'s essence was strong composition, best suited to screens, sliding doors, and fans. The prototypes are Sotatsu's screens of the wind and thunder gods, one green and one white, rampaging against a gilt background enlivened by smoke done in a dazzling welter of black, green, and rust inks (Kenninji, Kyoto). Sotatsu and his pupils used the studio name I'nen, which appears on many screens brilliantly decorated with clumps of flowers on a gold-leaf background.

After the deaths of Sotatsu and his pupils most members of the School were individual painters who admired and adopted the style. The greatest was Ogata Korin (1658–1716); his screens of irises in simple blue and green on a plain gold background (Nezu Museum of Art, Tokyo) and of flowering plum trees overhanging a broad blue-and-brown stream flowing out to engulf the viewer (Atami Art Museum), are high points of Japanese decorative style. Other *Rimpa* painters were Watanabe Shiko (1683–1757), Shirai Kagei (*fl.* 1740–50), Sakai Hoitsu (1761–1828), Suzuki Kiitsu (1796–1858), and Nakamura Hochu (*fl. c*1795–1818). Hochu simplified flowers and rocks almost to abstract forms. *Rimpa* declined in the later 19th century but its ideas dominated much 20th-century *Nihonga* work.

Most schools of Japanese painting after Korin degenerated into academicism, but this decline was relieved by individualists such as Ito Jakuchu (1713–1800), Soga Shohaku

Two landscape panels by Yosa Buson (1716–83), a member of the Bunjinga movement. Museum für Ostasiatische Kunst, Cologne

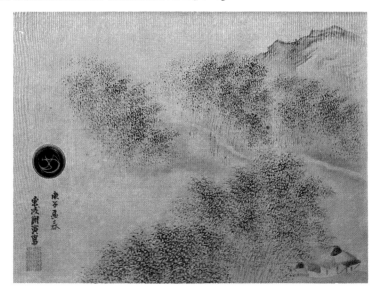

(1730–81), and the Zen painter Hakuin (1685–1758); by the *Nanga* movement; and by the *Maruyama/Shijo* School. They all produced an unexpectedly healthy climate for painting in the later Edo period.

The term *Nanga* ("Southern painting") was used to denote all foreign styles filtering through the licensed port of Nagasaki. Dutch prints, oil paintings, and watercolors had wide influence on spatial composition, but little of importance was produced by those working in Western styles, who were called *Ranga* ("Dutch painters"). The *Obaku* School, on the other hand, consisted mainly of Chinese priests of the neo-Zen *Obaku* sect, who used strong line and simple color with underlying seriousness and pioneered the use of plastic shading. The so-called Nagasaki School itself excelled in the late Ming/early Ch'ing decorative bird and flower style as taught by the Chinese Ch'in Nam-Pin who painted in the city from 1730 to 1733. Kumashiro Yuhi (1712–72), and in Edo, So Shiseki (1712–86) worked in this manner.

Most important was the *Bunjinga* (scholar painting) movement, which attempted to emulate the depth of Chinese landscape and flower and rock painting done by the Confucian scholar class called *Bunjin*. The models for such painting were at first only low-grade works such as the landscapes of the Chinese Nagasaki resident I Hai, and woodblock-printed Chinese albums, especially *The Ten Bamboo Studio* (British Museum, London) and *The Mustard-Seed Garden Manual* (Museum of Fine Arts, Boston). Hence *Bunjinga* lacks the astringent brushwork, subtle washes, spatial depth and complex construction of the Chinese models. Instead, the early

Bunjin such as Gion Nankai (1677–1751), Sakaki Hyakusen (1698–1753) Yanagisawa Kien (1706–58), and Nakayama Koyo (1717–80) developed a sort of abbreviated Chinese landscape with very free line and often patches of arbitrary decorative color. A tendency to paint actual places in Japan produced the glorious fantasy landscapes, part real, part imaginary, which are the great achievement of the school. Masters of this style are Ike no Taiga (1723–76), Yosa Buson (1716–83), Uragami Gyokudo (1745–1821), and Aoki Mokubei (1767–1833). Buson's deep love of nature led him into a more native lyrical style.

In the early 19th century artists like Tanomura Chikuden (1777–1835) and Yamamoto Baiitsu (1783–1856), with access to good Chinese originals, produced distinguished work of a genuinely "scholarly" nature. In Edo, the movement was dominated by Tani Buncho (1764–1841) and Watanabe Kazan (1793–1841), both very eclectic. After 1850 only the great individualist Tomioka Tessai (1836–1924) rescued *Bunjinga* in its turn from academicism.

In the painting of the Edo period one element had been lacking—a sense of the need to paint the natural and human worlds from life. This was provided by Maruyama Okyo (1733–95) who learned from both Western and Chinese models, as well as from the *Kano* School which educated him. Okyo himself achieved most in large-scale screen composition, an art form he revived. His insistence on sketching from life inspired his successors, especially the Mori family animal-painters Sosen (1747–1821), Tessan (1775–1841), and Ippo (1798–1871). Okyo's brilliant brushwork in ink was excelled

Below: A detail of a flower scroll painted by Matsumura Keibun (1779–1843). British Museum, London

Right: Poppies by Kobayashi Kokei (1883–1957), an example of modern, Western-influenced Japanese painting. Hanging scroll; 164×99cm (65×39in). Tokyo National Museum

only by that of his greatest pupil, Nagasawa Rosetsu (1755–99).

A soft, atmospheric style in landscape and bird-and-flower sketching called *Shijo* was introduced by Matsumura Goshun (1752–1811), who joined Okyo in mature years after training with Buson. Followers of Goshun's style were his brother Matsumura Keibun (1779–1843), Okamoto Toyohiko (1773–1845), and Shibata Gido (1780–1819).

At the end of the 19th century the late *Shijo* artists Imao Keinen (1845–1924) and Takeuchi Seiho (1864–1942) contributed major elements to the synthesized *Nihonga* style. The atmospheric washes, free brushwork, and simple sensuousness of the style made it the natural one for 19th-century artists. Other schools gradually adopted it, including *Ukiyoe* artists in their figure work (notably Hokusai, Eishi, and Utamaro), the successors of Kishi Ganku (1749–1838) who originally favored a very chunky line, and the school of Hara Zaichu (1750–1837) who used Okyo's spatial construction.

The great technical skill in woodblock-cutting was put to use for illustrated books from the late 17th century onwards. They included albums of poems interspersed with sumptuous plates like Utamaro's *Ehon Kyogetsubo* (Book of the Moon-Mad Monk; example in the British Museum, London), and books of designs by famous artists, alive or dead, perhaps to be used by students. The designs are usually boldly placed across an opening. Some show great refinement of graded color and extraordinary imitations of actual brush strokes. Among the best are the *Taigado Gafu* after Ike no Taiga, and from the *Maruyama/Shijo* School, *Suiseki Gafu* after Sato Suiseki (*fl. c*1800–30) and *Chinnen Gafu* after Onishi Chinnen (1792–1851); (examples in the British Museum, London).

Westernized industrial culture (1867 to present). The opening of Japan to foreigners in 1853 and the establishment of a Westernizing government in 1867 broke old patterns. Since then the major influences on Japanese art have been Western. In the Meiji period (1867–1912) technical competence in oil painting was certainly achieved but it is doubtful that any work done then is internationally significant, though in Japan the French-inspired paintings of Asai Chu (1856–1906), Kuroda Seiki (1866–1924), Fujishima Takeji (1867–1943), and Aoki Shigeru (1882–1911) are admired. With increasing confidence in the medium, however, artists of real vitality and Japanese inspiration emerged, among them Umehara Ryusaburo (b. 1888) at his best in big, colorful landscapes with thick line, simple color, and powerful design, influenced by Cézanne.

In the early Meiji period, native styles of painting began to decline under the force of the impact of Western methods (with the great exception of Tessai), but a movement soon sprang up to preserve them, culminating in the foundation of the Japan Art Academy in Tokyo in 1898. The Academy's leaders were Yokoyama Taikan (1868–1958), a great virtuoso in ink, inheritor of *Kano* and Chinese techniques, Shimomura Kazan (1878–1930), reviver of ancient *Yamatoe* styles, and Hishida Shunso (1874–1911), a neo-*Shijo* artist. In Kyoto, Takeuchi Seiho (1864–1942) successfully combined *Shijo* with Western elements and from these strands there grew a new style called *Nihonga*, opposed to Western painting (*Yoga*). It flourishes to the present. It is colorful, simple in line, supremely confident in design, subtle in emotional feeling, decorative in intent in the *Rimpa* traditions, and it maintains a high level of native craftsmanship. But its restricted scope suggests that the great painters of the future will be those who achieve a new Japanese synthesis of Western oil painting.

LAWRENCE R. H. SMITH

Bibliography. Akiyama, T. *Japanese Painting*, Lausanne (1961). Doi, T. *Momoyama Decorative Painting*, Tokyo and New York (1976). Hillier, J. *The Uninhibited Brush: the Shijo School*, London (1974). Lane, R. *Masters of the Japanese Print*, New York (1962). Miyagawa, T. *Modern Japanese Painting*, London and Tokyo (1967). Mizuo, H. *Edo Painting: Sotatsu and Korin*, Tokyo and New York (1973). Mizuno, S. *Asuka Buddhist Art: Horyuji*, Tokyo and New York (1975). Mori, H. *Sculpture of the Kamakura Period*, Tokyo and New York (1975). Ooka, M. *Temples of Nara and their Art*, Tokyo and New York (1975). Tanaka, I. *Japanese Ink Painting: Shubun to Sesshu*, Tokyo and New York (1975). Yamane, Y. *Momoyama Genre Painting*, Tokyo and New York (1974). Yonezawa, Y. and Yoshizawa, C. *Japanese Painting in the Literati Style*, Tokyo and New York (1974).

19

EARLY CHRISTIAN ART

The ivory throne of Maximian; 6th century. Museo Arcivescovile, Ravenna (see page 368)

ARLY Christian Art is not a style term, like Baroque, nor the art of an historically identifiable period, like Carolingian Art. The label describes the artistic production of the centuries between Classical Antiquity and the Middle Ages. At first sight it is a fallow period, when Classical forms slid into medieval formulae without any positive gains. Under scrutiny, however, the period emerges as a crucial one in European art, for its historical conditions ensured that Christianity accepted and continued antique cultural values.

By the 3rd century Christians in the Roman Empire had begun to borrow the art forms of their pagan contemporaries for the decoration of meeting-rooms (churches) and tombs. Such patronage of the arts received a great impetus in 312 when Constantine the Great decided to continue the policy of tolerating Christianity rather than trying to destroy the religion by persecution, as had been systematically attempted by the Emperor Diocletian at the end of the 3rd century. This Edict of Milan initiated the erection and decoration of more permanent and magnificent cult-buildings than had previously been possible for a religion illegal and devoid of large numbers of wealthy adherents. Constantine embraced other religions as well as Christianity. His encouragement of Christianity was politically surprising, for Christians must have formed a very small proportion of the Roman population. His decision must therefore have been due to personal conviction.

Christianity did expand quite rapidly during the 4th century, and was declared the official State religion by Theodosius in 392. Yet in this century the Imperial families and aristocracy tended to be eclectic (or opportunist) in religious affiliations and preferred to subscribe to a mixture of cults, committing themselves to baptism only on their death beds. This sort of religious syncretism can explain some of the iconography of 4th-century art and was a disincentive to any radical departure from traditional pagan traditions in style.

After 400, the Church became increasingly institutionalized, and theologians began to define attitudes towards art.

The exuberance of 4th-century art was trimmed, in favor of more dogmatic iconography and a more imposing figure-style. This shift in taste had its social counterpart in the "ascetic movement" and growth of monasticism, and for some art historians marks the end of true Early Christian art. This is probably a too subtle period distinction, but it does have the merit of finding an end for it. As it is, the term overlaps with early Byzantine art in the east Mediterranean and with the Dark Ages in the West. Alternative ends proposed for the period are the accession of Justinian (527) or the coronation of Charlemagne (800).

Not only is the chronological range of the term a matter of disagreement, but the kind of art subsumed within it is ambiguous. The period includes some notable non-Christian masterpieces, such as the Dioscurides manuscript (Nationalbibliothek, Vienna; Cod. med. gr. 1) or the portrait sculpture of Ephesus.

Most Early Christian art has been lost. The fundamental problems of when, where, and how Christian art began can only be explored, not solved. The period can hardly be characterized; it is easier to savor its random survivals.

Few early Christians encouraged artistic production, either through indifference or actual hostility. Their feelings were serious—serious enough for an undercurrent of hostility to persist for the next few centuries and to erupt in the 8th century as Iconoclasm, the attempt to stamp out religious figurative art in Byzantium. Iconoclasm was state policy for over a century. The early Christian opposition had several sources. The Jewish tradition of the Second Commandment against graven images was accepted into Christianity although the Jews themselves in some communities had relaxed the prohibition from the end of the 1st century. Paganism was also a factor, for the Christians were for some centuries a small sect outnumbered by many varieties of pagans who all had in common the worship of a statue or visible cult-object. Some pagans had seen this as a weakness of their religion, and tried to excuse the images on symbolic grounds. The Christians were able to attack these practices as idolatry, and to emphasize the spirituality of their own religion—but only so long as they avoided such representations themselves. Spanish Christians did specifically ban idolatrous art in churches (at the Council of Elvira, c300). Another attitude which discouraged art was the apocalyptic nature of the religion: the world was about to end, and the Gospels preached the need for repentance before the end of the world. What relevance or interest could art have for the committed? Apart from intellectual or emotional considerations, Christians before Constantine did not necessarily belong to a social class that patronized artists; and the various times of intensive persecution must have worked against the production (or survival) of art.

Despite radical opposition to art, the visual arts—a prominent feature of Classical culture—percolated into churches and Christian settings. The earliest firm evidence of Christian art comes from Italy and from the extreme eastern frontier of the Roman Empire in the first half of the 3rd century.

Centers of Early Christian art discussed in the text

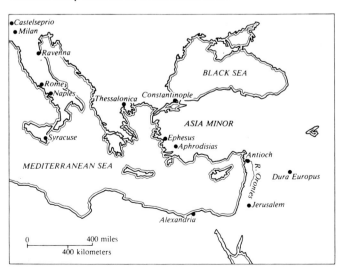

The Roman catacombs. The catacombs supply the greatest area of surviving painting from the period, though no art historian would maintain that Christian art owed its creation to underground communities in them. Certain limitations must be recognized before assessing this evidence.

The catacombs lie outside the walls of Rome, for Roman law required that the burial of the dead should normally take place outside the city. Wealthier families built masonry tombs, as along the Appian Way; presumably these subterranean passages represent the communal burial places of lower social groups. The relatively better-off Christians could afford to buy more space, and to excavate modest family vaults. Instead of using just a grave in a passage (the Latin term was *loculus*), these families could excavate a chamber (*cubiculum*), and could sometimes ornament the tomb with a framed setting (*arcosolium*). It is in these more pretentious *cubicula* that most of the painted decoration occurs.

The ground at Rome was volcanic and easy to tunnel into galleries. The passages were first dug at one level, and later extended by tunneling downwards, sometimes to depths of 30 to 50 ft (9 to 15 m). Bodies were inhumed at each level in boxes in the walls, closed by slabs or bricks, and sometimes accompanied with inscriptions. Such inscriptions are in Latin and Greek, and so indicate a Christian community of mixed nationality. This method of excavation means that the highest *loculi* are the earliest; the most recent graves are at the present floor level. Sometimes several phases of workings can be distinguished, which has been of assistance in dating-studies.

Since the catacombs began as passages, it is clear that their original function was for burials, though possibly the tombs did receive annual commemorative visits. The theory that the catacombs were excavated as churches can be dismissed, since no suitable chambers were ever cut.

The organization of "the cemetery" was attributed to Pope Callixtus (elected *c*218). A date *c*200 for the catacomb of St Callixtus accords well with the archaeological examination by P. Styger. In all, about 40 sets of catacombs were cut around Rome, and catacombs are not limited to Rome but are also known from Naples, Syracuse, and the Roman East. Present opinion on the Roman catacombs sees the first excavations as *c*200, but the earliest paintings not much before *c*250. The catacombs continued in use after the Edict of Toleration, but fell out of favor in the early 5th century, partly from feelings of insecurity outside the walls after the sack of Rome in 410, but also because they had been superseded by large cemetery Basilicas and the use of churches for housing relics.

The evidence from catacomb painting is therefore limited in its chronological range (after *c*250), in its function (as purely sepulchral art), and in its social range (for the lower classes). There was the further limitation that since the cult was illegal, to avoid confrontation with authority, inoffensive and traditional symbols were often used. However, the murals allow some insights. The style of all the paintings is fairly uniform; color and line is used to suggest solid figures in illusionist settings, but the level of execution makes them the im-

The Good Shepherd, a wall-painting in the catacomb of St Callixtus, Rome; c250

poverished successors of 1st-century works of Pompeii and Herculaneum. Catacomb painting does not differ in style from contemporary pagan art, but is limited in quality due to the third-rate artists Christian patrons were only able to afford.

The subject matter of catacomb art was Christian, and so its content was new in the history of art; but the visual language in which its message was encoded took the same form as existing pagan art. Its nuances could therefore only be fully understood by the convert educated in Christian literature and ritual. The basic message conveyed was similar to that of pagan art—the theme of salvation—but, for the new religion, this promise was only made to those who believed in God. Salvation meant escape from death through the promise of an afterlife. The promise was illustrated through a small number of images: by symbols, such as the fish (for Christ) and the orant (probably the praying soul of the departed), or by Old Testament witnesses of the promise of God, such as Jonah, Daniel, Sussanah, Noah, and others, or by a limited repertory of New Testament scenes, mostly concerned with the miracles of Christ, such as the Multiplication of the Loaves and Fishes, the Raising of Lazarus, and others. The same theme of salvation was illustrated in pagan art by a range of mythological stories taken to prove the afterlife, such as those concerned with Achilles, Phaethon, or the daughters of Leucippus.

The early Christian repertory was probably suggested to artists by the examples of salvation featured in Jewish and Christian prayers, notably those used in the office for the burial of the dead. This role for the prayer of the *commendatio animae* is widely accepted by scholars while admitting that their texts were not established before the 9th century.

Jonah under the Gourd Tree, a marble sculpture of c250–75;
31×46×18cm (12×18×7in). Cleveland Museum of Art

The catacomb painters made no attempt to clothe the new iconography in a new artistic form. The shift from pagan to Christian art lay not in appearances but relied on the initiation of the spectator. This conclusion from the evidence of the catacombs seems confirmed from the fragmentary material in other media and in other parts of the Roman Empire. A good case is a recently discovered set of small marble sculptures (Cleveland Museum of Art) which were probably carved in western Asia Minor in the third quarter of the 3rd century. Apart from a set of family portrait busts, there are five symbolic figures, freestanding, and cut in a lively, Hellenistic style. A spectator might identify one figure as a river god, but the Christian would have seen that this reclining man was Jonah under the Gourd Tree and that four of the pieces represent the popular catacomb cycle of the Salvation of Jonah. The sculptures are a symbolic representation of the Fall of Man, his Redemption, and Rewards in Paradise. The fifth figure of the group could be identified by Christians as a Good Shepherd (with reference to John 10: 1–16), whereas the same piece would be quite meaningful to a pagan as a Hermes or as a symbol for Philanthropy.

Analysis of iconography is therefore the best means of discovering the nature of innovation in Early Christian art. It can be stated that if a Christian scene reflected some parallel theme in existing late antique art, then the established form was taken over. Many cases can be adduced: angels derive from Victories; Apostles, Prophets, and some types of Christ derive from standing Pagan Philosophers; Evangelists from Seated Poets; Eve from Venus; Jonah from Endymion; David from Orpheus; the Creation of Man from the myth of Prometheus; and more.

The question to ask is: where and when were these artistic adjustments made? The low-grade artists of the catacombs are not likely to be the actual innovators as these paintings are no more than an accident of survival. The Cleveland sculptures seem closer to a moment of invention. Unfortunately most of the art of the major eastern Mediterranean cities from the 3rd and 4th centuries is lost.

The answer to the question of origins may be different for Old and New Testament subjects. Old Testament illustration could have a long tradition, for the Bible was translated into Greek in Alexandria in the 3rd century BC, and the hellenized Jews of this city might have commissioned illustrated manuscripts of the Septuagint. Book illumination might have been the medium in which the new iconography was generated. There is no straightforward evidence to decide this controversial point, for the earliest surviving Old Testament books with pictures belong to the 5th century, by which time books were in the new codex form (invented c100), and the earlier *rotulus* format was superseded (a format less suitable for painted illustration).

Dura Europus. The evidence from the city of Dura Europus is important here. This was a Hellenistic settlement which became a Roman frontier garrison on the Euphrates. It was partially excavated in the 1930s, and the finds are now shared between the National Museum, Damascus, and Yale University Art Gallery, New Haven. It was found that the citizens abandoned the area around its walls c256 in the face of a threatened Persian invasion. Among the buildings evacuated was a synagogue, and a structure built as a house but which had recently been converted into a church. Both the synagogue and the church are datable to before 256.

The wall-paintings of the synagogue belong to the early 3rd century. The subjects are partly symbolic (like the Temple with the Ark) and partly narrative (like a Moses cycle and other scenes, which are however selected with a purpose in mind, the declaration of the salvation of the Jewish people). Some of these images did enter Christian art, notably the Sacrifice of Isaac, but never in precisely the same form as in the Dura synagogue. It is clear that the Jews of the Diaspora did have a cycle of Old Testament pictures, for Dura Europus cannot be unique. Whether such illustrations were disseminated in monumental or miniature form, and whether they occurred before the 3rd century, is unknown. Christian artists probably made borrowings from the Jewish tradition (whether or not it was older than Christian art), but they did not take over the entire cycle.

The canon of the text of the New Testament was only established in the mid 2nd century, in fact not very long before the catacombs. Catacomb painting already shows a uniformity of treatment and composition—standard formulae such as Daniel between the Lions. The conversion of the house at Dura Europus into a church and the fitting and decoration of one of its rooms as a baptistery dates from the 230s or 240s. The baptistery's paintings are therefore contemporary with the earliest catacomb art. The paintings—such as the Good Shepherd and Adam and Eve above the font, and the Healing of the Paralytic, Peter walking on the Water, and the Three Women at the Sepulcher (?) on the walls—give evidence of a Salvation cycle at the eastern limits of the Roman Empire with some individual scenes treated in the same form as the catacombs. It may be concluded that New Testament illustration was in a state of elaboration in the 3rd century with some consistency throughout the Roman Empire.

The medium in which scenes were developed and disseminated is unknown. It follows that any suggestion about the place or places where Christian art began, or among which social class, must be conjectural. But the simplest solution is to suppose that those classes who had traditionally commissioned funerary monuments or expected to worship in a decorated environment did continue to patronize artists after their conversion. This situation would explain the continuation of traditional patterns of art. Possibly such patrons were the less radical members of the church, selecting their religious beliefs with circumspection and without exclusiveness. A striking case of late Roman religious eclecticism is given by the Emperor Alexander Severus (222–35), who placed in his household oratory (*lararium*) statues of such figures as deified Emperors (only the most noble selected) and other sacred persons including the philosopher Apollonius of Tyana, Christ, Abraham, Orpheus, and Alexander the Great.

Early Christian sculpture. The medium in which the best quality Early Christian art has survived is in marble sculpture, predominantly in sepulchral work. The sequence of datable sarcophagi from Rome gives some picture of the patronage of wealthier Christians during the years when the cult developed from proscription to convention.

A sarcophagus now in the church of S. Maria Antiqua in the Forum at Rome is a fine example of the possible level of achievement of pre-Constantinian art. It was probably made to stand in some grand *cubiculum* in the third quarter of the 3rd century. The relief is deeply cut, and the figures stand against a traditional pastoral background. There are scenes of Jonah and the Baptism of Christ, and figures of the Good Shepherd, an orant woman, and a man seated in the pose of a philosopher. The faces of the latter couple are blocked out; the figures must have been intended for use for donor portraits. One explanation for this lack of finish is that work-

shops kept sarcophagi in stock, to be finished off with the portraits of the purchaser, and that in this case (as in some others) the necessity for a quick burial prevented the final carving. It is not, however, necessary to deduce this pattern of trading; the individual sarcophagus might have been ordered in advance of death, and the portraits left unmade so that a record of the mature donors could be made in due course, or the portraits might be left incomplete for more superstitious motives.

The 4th century saw a substantial increase in the number of Christian sarcophagi; this occurred despite a probable overall decline in marble carving in the period, due to the dislocation of workshop traditions in the political upheavals in Rome in the 3rd century, and perhaps also due to concern about the Second Commandment. The Roman sarcophagi after the Edict of Toleration (312) extend the Christian use of art. In addition to the message of individual salvation, there is the new theme of the triumph of the Christian Church as an institution. In style, these sarcophagi reflect the taste of the Imperial family and the aristocracy.

During the reign of Constantine (*ob.* 337), a number of "frieze" sarcophagi were produced whose style is an incongruous deviation from Hellenistic traditions; the frieze is a row of gesticulating mannequins. Though the iconography is difficult to read, the figures portray a mixture of Old and New Testament scenes, most with a reference to salvation. With their stiff and awkward attitudes, oddly proportioned bodies, and lack of expressions, these figures are inspired by Tetrarchic art, and, more directly, by the new reliefs on the Arch of Constantine (315). The technique is not ineffective in conveying a spiritual message: these are salvation prayers "frozen into stone".

In the second half of the 4th century the more traditional values of the Roman aristocracy reasserted themselves. It is as if artists were required to copy the reused panels on the Arch of Constantine, rather than those of their own time. The grandest production was the sarcophagus of Junius Bassus (Vat-

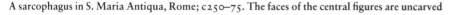

A sarcophagus in S. Maria Antiqua, Rome; c250–75. The faces of the central figures are uncarved

The marble sarcophagus of Junius Bassus; c359. Vatican Museums, Rome

ican Museums, Rome) who died at the age of 42 in 359. The inscription on the lintel records that he was Prefect of the City, and baptized on his deathbed; he is a typical member of the wealthy aristocracy. The front of the sarcophagus is divided into two horizontal registers; each scene is framed by ornamented columns. The central pairs of columns in both registers are decorated with putti climbing vines, a clear reference to the pagan Bacchic paradise. The Biblical scenes have two themes: God's promise of salvation after suffering, and the triumph of Christ and the Apostles after suffering. The message conveyed is of the immortality promised to Christians, and of the triumph of the Church. The sarcophagus is primarily a declaration of Church teaching rather than a memorial to an individual. A later 4th-century sarcophagus, now in S. Ambrogio in Milan, emphasizes even more emphatically the triumph of the established Church.

With the departure of the Christian court patrons from Rome to Milan and then Ravenna at the end of the 4th century, sarcophagus workshops declined due to lack of support. The 4th-century production of high-quality sculpture was not, however, confined to Rome, but is matched in several cities of the eastern Mediterranean, particularly in Asia Minor at Aphrodisias and Ephesus. At Constantinople production is more varied; some sarcophagi worked in limestone are no more than inferior copies of Italian models, but there are outstanding productions, such as a child's sarcophagus in Istanbul Archaeological Museum on which are carved well-modeled

angels in the traditional style of Hellenistic Victories. Theodosius (379–95) and Arcadius (395–408) could find sculptors able to produce cochleate columns to proclaim the importance of New Rome as successor to the Old. Stone and metal sculpture continued in the East to be a major medium to at least the 6th century, when, however, the Marmara and other quarries apparently ceased production.

The religious syncretism of the Junius Bassus sarcophagus is conspicuous on a monumental scale in two mausolea built by the children of Constantine: his own mausoleum, part of the complex of the church of the Holy Apostles in Constantinople, is not preserved. The church of S. Costanza in Rome was erected for Constantina between 337 and 354, and probably decorated with mosaics in the 350s. A second domed, centrally-planned structure at Centcelles, near Tarragona, in Spain, can in all probability be attributed to the mid 4th century as the mausoleum of Constantius (ob. 361). Both monuments have survived, but with no more than fragments of their original magnificent decorations. The dome mosaics of S. Costanza were removed in the 17th century, but had been previously drawn and described. The Centcelles cupola is a wreck, with some discernible elements. Both domes received a mixture of Biblical scenes and pagan funerary elements, such as a river scene with fishermen at Rome and a hunting scene in Spain. The surviving mosaics at S. Costanza, in the ambulatory vaults, have no overt Christian message, and include panels with Bacchic putti. These mausolea with their expensive mosaic vaults (the idea of using mosaic in vaults was a fairly recent innovation in Late Roman art), and marble-clad walls show the ostentatious taste of the new Christian aristocracy. This is the use of pagan art forms in the service of yet another religion.

Early Christian art in the 5th century. The 5th century was a turning point in Early Christian art, perhaps a deliberate reaction to the 4th-century pattern of art. The rise of the ascetics and monks did not prevent the investment of wealth in expensive architecture and fittings, but the Church does seem to have imposed limitations on iconography, and a concern with subject matter probably influenced its stylistic treatment. Stern statements on the Christian use of art were penned by Paulinus of Nola in Italy and Nilus of Ankara in Asia Minor. Nilus condemned the decoration of a church with hunting scenes or fishing scenes and the like as "childish and stupid". Instead he recommends the representation of a cross and pictures of Old and New Testament themes as "the mark of a firm and manly mind". Such theologians began to ask art to perform a serious purpose, such as the instruction of the illiterate in the Bible or the inducement to prayer. Under such thinking the Church began to perfect the use of art as a didactic instrument and as a vehicle for the propagation of the faith.

The new spirit is found in the Papal mosaics in the vast Basilica of S. Maria Maggiore in Rome, decorated by Sixtus III (432–40). The original nave and sanctuary mosaics thus date from the time of the Council of Ephesus (431) at which the status and nature of the Virgin Mary was defined. This issue explains the unusual iconography of the triumphal arch (the lost apse mosaic represented the Virgin); Mary is shown as the Queen of Virgins. The Adoration of the Magi is unique in showing Christ not as usual seated on his mother's lap, but isolated on a throne between two standing figures, Mary (?) and the Church (?). There is no representation at all of the Nativity of Christ. Art here is therefore not employed to tell a narrative, but is used with dogmatic intent. This use of art as theology has influenced the mode in which the subject matter is expressed. The figures are hieratic, set against a gold ground and without an illusionist setting; this marks a new stage of religious art.

The mosaic panels in the nave show Old Testament episodes, and are also selected with some purpose. For example panels near the altar incorporate liturgical elements (such as Abraham meeting Melchizedek). Several other themes are woven into the cycle: the panel of Abraham meeting the Angels has typological references to the Trinity (underlined by the new motive of the mandorla), and to Mary through the antetype of the Annunciation to Sarah. The general sense of the program is as usual Christian salvation and triumph, but perhaps the individual panels were expected to be used by pilgrims as vehicles of their individual prayers, as recommended by Paulinus in his foundation at Nola. The nave panels are not homogenous in style, for some are in the tradition of the late Antique, others more in the hieratic form of

the triumphal arch. This variation is probably due less to the content of the scenes than to the nature of their models. Some compositions may be 5th-century inventions, but others had already gained a conventional appearance after a few centuries of use. S. Maria Maggiore is a key monument for an understanding of the interaction of themes and styles at the point when antique art is becoming medieval. In terms of purely artistic expertise it is less remarkable, since, like S. Costanza, the scenes are too small and too high to be read from the floor.

The problem of scale was treated more satisfactorily in monuments of the mid 5th century in Ravenna and Thessalonica. The interior decoration of the Orthodox baptistery in Ravenna is crowned with a dome composition showing the Apostles around the Baptism within a medallion. It is a scheme probably adapted from a circular pavement composition with personification of the Months known in late Roman floor mosaics, and it is successfully adapted to the size of the building. Even more impressive is the scale of the cupola mosaic of the Rotunda, or church of S. George, Thessalonica. The building was a Tetrarchic mausoleum, built by Galerius *c*300, though not used for his burial, and was converted into a

Abraham meeting Melchizedek, a mosaic panel in S. Maria Maggiore, Rome; c440

The Antioch Chalice

Found accidentally in 1910, buried (reportedly) in the region of Antioch-on-the-Orontes (now Antakya, Turkey), this cup is unique in technique and form among known chalices of the early Church. Soon after its discovery it became the center ot a heated controversy when extravagant claims were made for its origin in the time of Christ (which put it in a category of objects not unlike that of the Turin Shroud).

The Antioch Chalice (Metropolitan Museum, New York) consists of a plain inner silver cup cradled in an openwork silver gilt outer container on which 12 figures are engraved within a trellis of vine scrolls. The first study (by G.A. Eisen) appeared in 1923 with the title: *The Great Chalice of Antioch on which are depicted in sculpture the earliest known portraits of Christ, Apostles, and Evangelists*. The publication, as lavish as its claims, hinted that the inner cup was the Holy Grail and dated the outer cup to *c*50, making it about two centuries earlier than any other known Christian works of art. But while the use of a cup at the Last Supper was sanctioned by the words of Jesus as reported in Mark 14:23, it was believed in the early Church that this was made of onyx and was kept in the church of the Holy Sepulcher in Jerusalem and shown to pilgrims, at least in the 6th century. Also, the legends of the Grail as the cup used at the Last Supper and by Joseph of Arimathea to collect the blood of Jesus belong only to the late Middle Ages. But the most common reaction to the publication of the Chalice's discovery was to condemn the whole cup as a modern fake.

The authenticity of the Chalice was only finally established in 1954 by scientific tests. Its subject matter, date, and place of manufacture still need to be decided. No doubt all of one period, the Chalice has a surface that is worn, broken, and corroded. The central figure on each side must be Jesus. On one side, he is apparently beardless and sits on a chair that encloses his head like a halo; he holds out his right hand in a gesture to indicate that he is speaking, and holds a scroll in his left. He is acclaimed by other seated figures, presumably his Apostles though none of them can be individually identified by attribute or portraiture. The suggestion has been made that this shows Christ giving the keys to Peter and Paul, but there are no keys to be seen. The scene may be Christ teaching his Apostles (perhaps at the time of the Last Supper). The other side may be more specific; again Christ sits among Apostles, but this time he is bearded and has a lamb to his left and below his feet

there is an eagle standing on a basket of grapes. The references are more obviously to the eucharist, to the sacrifice of the Lamb of God, and to the Resurrection. Perhaps this side shows the resurrected Christ in heaven at the time of the Last Judgment. Presumably, the purpose of the decoration was to refer literally to the use of the chalice for holding the wine of the eucharist, and metaphorically to the significance of the rite for the religion.

It was the profile of the Chalice with its low base and deep cup as well as the use of openwork that led to the dating to the 1st

▼ The Antioch Chalice, the side of the beardless Christ; height 19cm (7in); diameter of rim 15cm (6in); diameter of base 8cm (3in). Metropolitan Museum, New York, Cloisters Collection

century, for Roman cups of similar appearance are known. The usual shape of the 6th-century chalice is seen, for example, in another find from the same region now in the Cleveland Museum of Art or as represented on a eucharist bread dish, the Riha paten (Dumbarton Oaks Research Library and Collection, Washington, D.C.): on this, a chalice and a paten together with skins for water and wine are set on the altar used by Christ to give the wine and bread of the eucharist to the Apostles. The Antioch Chalice is, despite its profile, most likely to date from the 6th century. The most similar treatment of figures and vine scrolls are found on the ivory throne of Bishop Maximian of Ravenna of the mid 6th century (Museo Arcivescovile, Ravenna).

The Chalice appears to lack any stamps which would have guaranteed the quality of its silver and possibly have revealed its place

of production. Now damaged after its burial underground, the Chalice was not originally a work of delicacy and refinement. Syria was an active region in the production of art, but it was declining in the 6th century. There is, therefore, a case for supposing that it was a work of the silversmiths of Antioch.

Doubts have been cast on the truth of the find-spot of the Chalice and the accompanying objects. The other pieces are now also in the Metropolitan Museum and appear to be of a 6th-century date: a silver cross, a silver paten, a pair of bookcovers,

and another bookcover. This could well be the church plate of one community, but there is the odd coincidence that in the same region in 1910 another large silver treasure surfaced, the so-called Hama Treasure, much of which is now in the Walters Art Gallery, Baltimore. The suspicion has been voiced that all these silver objects belonged to churches in the Christian cult city of S. Sergios (now called Risafe), and that they were either found there through clandestine diggings or were hidden underground at various spots in the region by Christians fleeing from the advancing Arab army in the 7th century. Whether or not the Chalice was actually found in Antioch, its attribution to the art of the city must be considered seriously. It would then show that important provincial cities like Antioch played some part in the formation of Early Christian art.

R. CORMACK

Above left The Riha paten; diameter 35cm (14in); 6th century. Dumbarton Oaks Research Library and Collection, Washington, D.C.

◄ A silver-gilt chalice showing Apostles, from the Hama Treasure; height 17cm (7in); diameter of rim 14cm (5½in); 6th century. The Walters Art Gallery, Baltimore

▲ A silver-gilt bookcover found with the Antioch Chalice; 28×23cm (11×9in); 6th century. Metropolitan Museum, New York

► The Antioch Chalice, the side of the bearded Christ. To the left stands a lamb and below an eagle on a basket of grapes

Apostles surrounding the Baptism of Christ, the dome of the Orthodox baptistery, Ravenna; c450

church c450. The best preserved register is the lowest zone of the cupola in which are shown groups of standing martyrs (originally these surrounded a medallion of Christ at the apex). The figures are highly modeled but generalized portraits, set against fantastic architecture, and each one was identified by an inscription with his name and month of commemoration. The influence of the liturgy on this program is clear—the mosaics are a visualization of the calendar of the Church year.

It is easier to piece together a "vertical" development of Early Christian art than to understand the "horizontal" situation across the Roman world at any precise point in time. Although Italy, and especially Rome, suffered from a series of political crises and military attacks from the 5th century onwards, causing it to enter a Dark Age, many cities in the eastern Mediterranean enjoyed stable, even prosperous, conditions. The subsequent destruction of nearly all the Early Christian monumental art of Constantinople, Jerusalem, Antioch, and Alexandria (to name only the largest cities) has removed the possibility of assessing the contribution of their artists or even regional traditions to the creation of an international language of Christian art. Yet communications between

cities were good, and the wealthiest patrons could travel and observe church art all around the Christian Roman Empire. Not only emperors traveled; Archbishop Maximiam of Ravenna had seen Alexandria and Constantinople. Any analysis in terms of discrete regional styles or isolated local traditions would therefore be absurd—attempts to confine "illusionistic" style to Alexandria or "frontalism" to Antioch must be rejected. Yet the survivals from two prosperous cities of the period, Ravenna and Thessalonica, intimate that within the international language of art, some local circumstances may cause variations of style, and local themes and interests may emerge in iconography. The development of regional traditions, however subtle, raises the possibility of these influencing other cities. It is unlikely that all innovations should be attributed to artists in one center, for example Constantinople. The course of Christian art was not determined by such polarities as the Orient or Rome; but at present it seems impossible to offer a refined interpretation of the stages through which it developed.

Ravenna at the beginning of the 5th century was a seaport on piles, traversed by canals. It had been designated headquarters of the Roman fleet on the Adriatic by Augustus. Today the sea has receded from the port, then named Classis. When Theodosius died in 395 he left Arcadius to rule the East, and Honorius in Milan to rule the West. Honorius decided c402 to move the court to Ravenna, but developed a site a few miles inland. This "new town" was better placed for contacts with Constantinople than either Milan or Rome.

The monuments of Ravenna belong to three historical stages: in the first the city was developed as an Imperial capital, and the artists and their models must have originated outside, from, for example, Milan, Rome, or Constantinople —the situation might be compared with the building of St Petersburg in the 18th century. As in the new Russian capital, the buildings of the first generation were probably somewhat tentative and modest, and only with the second generation's confidence in survival was Ravenna enriched and ornamented, here too by a female ruler, Galla Placidia, half sister of Honorius (ob. 423) and regent for her son Valentinian III. She died in 450. The process of enrichment is exemplified by the baptistery of the Orthodox cathedral, an insubstantial octagonal building of the beginning of the century which received its new interior decoration of marble, stucco, and mosaic in the middle of the century. The mosaic workshop was probably also employed on the mosaics of the mausoleum of Galla Placidia; its style is so much a development of late antique art in Italy that there is no need to postulate the presence of artists from the Greek East; the artists more probably came direct from one of the extensive mosaic operations underway in Rome.

The second stage of Ravennate art dates from 494, when control of the city fell into the hands of the Goth Theodoric—

Right: Apostles surrounding the Baptism of Christ, the dome of the Arian baptistery, Ravenna; c500

his rule was recognized by Constantinople from 498. Theodoric died in 526, but control of Ravenna was only regained by Constantinople in 540 when Justinian's commander Belisarius entered the city. The rulers of Ravenna from 494 to 540 were Arian Christians. Whereas Orthodox theology stated that the human and divine natures of Christ coexisted, the Arian belief (anathematized in 381) was that the essence of the divine and human parts of Christ were different (so there was a time when Christ was not).

The Arians built a new cathedral and baptistery, and the mosaic decoration of the dome of the latter survives (c500). It copies the Orthodox baptistery directly, but, in contrast, the style is simpler and more linear, and the iconography reduced and simplified. Paradoxically, although the execution of the later mosaic may be less subtle, the differences can be characterized in terms of progress rather than decline. The composition is more literal and empirical, and so gains in clarity and effectiveness. The comparison is an example of the general trend in Early Christian art away from the classical values of plasticity, individual portraiture, and emotional expression, which leads not to loss of expressiveness, but to a new positive medium for the portrayal of Christian dogma and attitudes. The artists of the Arian baptistery and those of the New Testament cycle in the Arian foundation now called the church of S. Apollinare Nuovo but originally dedicated as the Church of Christ, seem closely related to Roman art, almost to the simplicity of catacomb art.

The third stage of the art of Ravenna, the Byzantine period, lasted from 540 to 568, but the city continued as an Exarchate until the Lombards took over in 751. The mosaics of this stage, as for example in S. Vitale, completed c548, show many elements derived from the Greek East, but Italian traditions are not submerged. The panel of Abraham meeting the three angels seems to be a development of and reaction to the similar scene at S. Maria Maggiore. The mosaics of Ravenna develop a distinctive tradition, but are not isolated in their time.

Thessalonica, too, was developed as a luxurious "new town" in the mid 5th century, when the Prefect of Illyricum moved from Sirmium to safer headquarters. The mosaics of the Rotunda were probably executed by a workshop sent by the Emperor from Constantinople. Thereafter local mosaicists of the second half of the 5th century were influenced by its

dome. As a result designs were developed locally out of a work of international status. For example, mosaic panels in the church of S. Demetrius, which show this local cult-saint as the object of citizens' prayers, represent him standing against an architectural setting—the format obviously derives from the martyrs in the Rotunda. Under stylistic comparison the settings for S. Demetrius are seen to be simplified and reduced, but not without new features. The building in front of which he stands is not an idealized church sanctuary, as used in the Rotunda, but a representation of a structure peculiar to Thessalonica, the silver *ciborium* of S. Demetrius, which stood like a tabernacle in the nave of this church. Both Ravenna and Thessalonica did then develop local traditions out of a wider international vocabulary of art, but these did not develop precisely in parallel or at the same rate.

With the accession of Justinian (527) and establishment of Constantinople as the most dominant center of art, the period of experimentation in Early Christian art may be considered to end. In Italy from the mid 6th century down to c800 there were few significant developments, despite major transplants of Byzantine painting, as at various times in S. Maria Antiqua in the Roman Forum and in the church of S. Maria at Castelseprio.

It has to be emphasized that too little art of the period has survived for description and interpretation to be much more than a reflection of modern attitudes and prejudices. While the achievements of the period are seen at their most impressive in monumental painting, mosaic, and sculpture, yet portable objects were produced in expensive materials—gold and silver plate, ivory panels, and illuminated manuscripts. Possibly such glorifications of God were the real purpose of Early Christian art. As it is, Maximian of Ravenna has left no record whether he prized his ivory throne more or less than the mosaics of S. Vitale.

R. CORMACK

Bibliography. Grabar, A. *Christian Iconography: a Study of its Origins*, London (1969). Perkins, A.L. *The Art of Dura-Europos*, Oxford (1973). Volbach, W.F. *Early Christian Art*, London (1961). Wixom, W.D. "Early Christian Sculptures at Cleveland", *Bulletin of the Cleveland Museum of Art*, Cleveland (March 1967).

20

BYZANTINE ART

The reliquary of the True Cross; c945–65. Limburger Domschatz, Limburg (see page 381)

A STRAIGHTFORWARD definition of the material and time span of Byzantine Art does not seem to appeal to art historians. The city now called Istanbul was colonized *c*660 BC by Greeks from Megara, and enters history with a name derived from the mythical founder Byzas. Byzantion was never an important center in the Classical Greek and Roman world. Septimius Severus (*ob.* AD 211) after first destroying the town, did build up its defences and amenities, and renamed it Antonia. Constantine the Great decided to inaugurate a new capital in the Eastern part of the Roman Empire, and after considering several possible sites (for example Nicomedia and Thessalonica) chose this town on the Bosphorus to be his New Rome. *Constantinopolis* was dedicated on 11 May 330, and its inhabitants regarded their city as a Roman capital until it fell to the Turks on 29 May 1453. Although New Rome was not dedicated as a Christian successor to a pagan Rome, the acceptance of Christianity by Constantine, and the imposition of the religion as the official state cult by Theodosius in 392, led to the myth that the city was dedicated to the Virgin, and was a sacred citadel, and a new Jerusalem. The citizens did sometimes call themselves Byzantines and the city Byzantium, but more often they called themselves *Romaioi* or, in the last centuries, *Hellenes*. They spoke and wrote in Greek.

Our term Byzantine certainly refers to the period after 330, and implies a Christian culture, one that developed into the Orthodox community. Byzantine art is the art of this society, but to say that the term describes the art of Constantinople and the regions under its political control between 330 and 1453 is not universally acceptable. In some definitions, Byzantine art really begins only with the reign of Justinian (527–65); but in all it comes to an end in 1453. The problem in defining its geographical extent is only partly connected with political advance and retreat over the period. It is also complicated by the so-called heresies within the eastern Mediterranean Churches. The art of the Monophysite communities is not usually termed Byzantine, though Armenian art, for example, may be seen as influenced by Constantinople or Asia Minor. Coptic art is normally described as distinct, and Syrian art at least partially so.

The definition accepted here is historical (330–1453) and political: the regions that at any one time accepted the Emperor in Constantinople as their supreme constitutional authority. Much of the surviving art is religious art, but a definition in terms of the art of the Orthodox Church must be rejected as too limited. Byzantine art cannot be characterized as a particular style in the history of art, for under analysis the diversity of art produced is found to be immense.

Early Byzantine art. The problem at all periods of Byzantine art is how to reconstruct the production in Constantinople itself, for very little work survives in the city. The corollary problem is how far work in its orbit can be identified as derivative or independent. The evidence is seldom unambiguous enough to allow an objective judgment about the role of Constantinople. The period before Justinian is sometimes treated as Early Christian art, with which it overlaps (*see* Early Christian Art). However, some separate account must be given here, on the grounds that the study of Byzantine art must incorporate a consideration of Constantinople at all periods, and this is not a primary concern in Early Christian art.

Apart from the early-5th-century land walls, the only substantial pre-Justinianic structure to survive in Constantinople is the church of S. John Studios, built *c*453. This large roofless basilica was (or became) the main church of one of the principal monasteries in Byzantine history, but is now no more than an impressive ruin, to be appreciated only for the precise and intricate carving of its capitals, lintels, and cornices. The ornamental vocabulary of this sculptural carving derives from late Roman tradition. Indeed the 5th-century city, from its overall plan down to details of the Studios basilica, proclaims antique urban traditions. It was a city of vast parks and markets, monumental public buildings of prestige materials with marble revetments concealing a brick core in many cases. It had palaces, hippodromes, theaters, baths, fountains, and churches, all laid out in spacious settings, and protected by the massive walls. It was adorned with hundreds of antique statues, removed from the principal cities of the east Mediterranean. Of the size and nature of private dwellings there is little information, beyond the fact that clusters of wooden homes were a frequent fire hazard throughout the period.

The art of Constantinople before Justinian can be only partially characterized. Constantine probably attracted to his new city the kind of itinerant workshops that accompanied

Centers of Byzantine art discussed in the text

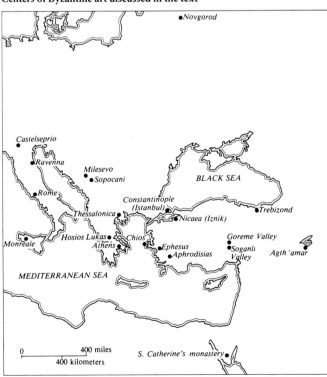

The church of S. John Studios, Constantinople (Istanbul), looking towards the west end; c453

the Tetrarchic Emperors. Some 4th-century sculptures, such as the base of the obelisk of Theodosius I (379–95), still on its original site in the Hippodrome, and the cochleate columns of Theodosius I and Arcadius (395–408), known to us through drawings, suggest that the workshop traditions of Rome were transplanted to the new capital. Late-4th-century sculpture in Rome and Constantinople has been characterized in terms of a "Theodosian Renaissance", but there is no direct imitation of Antiquity in these works. While the figures are softly modeled, their organization into friezes and their stereotyped gestures and frontal poses are indications of the superimposition of Constantinian forms on to Classical traditions. Such late Roman schemes may have entered Byzantium with artists from Italy, but this is not the only feasible source, for Tetrarchic ideas had already been grafted into the East, as for example in the Arch of Galerius at Thessalonica (c300). The ultimate source of some of these ideas may have been the Greek East; they may have developed in such cities as Ephesus, Aphrodisias, Antioch, or others. Marble sent to Italy from the quarries in Asia Minor or from the Marmara may already have had designs blocked out on them before despatch. It is obvious that the new capital was open to influences from the main currents of Mediterranean art; the difficulty is in defining these, and unraveling their sources. The creation of

Byzantine art cannot be explained as the amalgamation of the East and West, since neither polarity is a distinct entity.

Probably mosaicists from Constantinople decorated the Rotunda in Thessalonica when it was converted into a church in the mid 5th century. It was a large round building surmounted by a dome, built c300 as a mausoleum by Galerius. The mosaics portrayed in hierarchical order the Christian community in heaven. Christ was at the apex in a medallion supported by angels. Only the lowest zone is well preserved, a register of martyrs standing in front of fanciful and complex architectural interiors, all set on a gold ground. Despite the resemblances to the theater settings of Pompeiian wall-painting or to the tomb facades of Petra, the settings have been made entirely Christian with a liberal sprinkling of crosses. The frontal, idealized portraits of the martyrs have been made into figures of authority, almost Imperial in their aura. Representations of cool, calm, figures of power are characteristic of this period of Byzantine art, not only in these mosaics but also in sculpture, in marble from Aphrodisias and Ephesus, and in bronze from Constantinople, as probably the enigmatic colossus at Barletta in south Italy. This type of scheme also circulated in a miniature format, in ivory diptychs issued to commemorate the holding of consular office, of which examples are known made in Italy in the 5th century, and in

A sculpture of an official, from Aphrodisias; mid 5th century.
Istanbul Archaeological Museum.

Constantinople in the 6th century until the medium dropped out of use in mid century.

Justinian I (reigned 527–65). Towards the end of his life the Emperor Justinian commissioned the historian Procopius to write a eulogy of his artistic achievements. This book, known as the *De Aedificiis*, and completed *c*562, portrays the patron-age of Justinian as the Emperor wished it to be viewed by later ages (Procopius was quite capable of showing Justinian in a less favorable light, as he did in his *Secret History*). Justinian saw his great achievement as a builder, both of churches and defensive fortifications. He was the patron of great numbers of churches, some of vast dimensions, and he emphasized his personal involvement in their erection, taking credit for the completion of S. Sophia in spite of its daring size and form. Procopius puts it: "We must describe the buildings of this Emperor so that those who see them in future will not refuse because of their great number and magnitude, to believe that they are in truth the work of one man".

In politics, Justinian may be described as "imperialist". His (theoretical) reconquest of Italy, North Africa, and the eastern regions of Asia Minor was celebrated in the traditional Roman manner by artistic commissions to act as the visual witness of a new age of peace. Since Justinian had on his accession inherited a full treasury, his ambitions could be carried out with panache; but by his death in 565, the money had run out, and the Empire was threatened by new invaders— Persians on the East, and hordes of Slavonic raiders on the North and the West. Persia was repulsed in the early 7th century by the Emperor Heraclius (610–41), but only to be succeeded by a more serious threat to Constantinople from the Muslim Arabs. The Slavs and Bulgars soon overran Greece and the Balkans. The reign of Justinian was succeeded by a Dark Age from the 7th to the 9th centuries.

The reign of Justinian was a high-point, in which an enormous amount of artistic activity occurred throughout the Empire, and which arose from the personal aims of one man. This probably encouraged a certain uniformity, and some centralization of artists, though it did not mean the end of stylistic diversity. Justinianic art became a basis from which the medieval art of both East and West Europe developed. So-called periods of "renascence" often seem to depend on inspiration from surviving works of this period. Politically Justinian has been called the last Roman Emperor; his art was the vehicle from which many medieval artists learned the Roman traditions.

The period is best known from three major works: S. Sophia at Istanbul, S. Vitale in Ravenna, and the monastery of S. Catherine on Mt Sinai. S. Sophia (built 532–7) is a building in which all decoration is subordinated to architectural effect; there is no concern to design any subtle exterior articulation; all interest is devoted to the vast interior (as in Imperial Roman architecture). The marble revetment and carving and the nonfigurative mosaic decoration of crosses and vegetal and geometric ornament are integrated into the architectural effects. The church was not actually devoid of figurative art— the screen at least had statues of precious metals—but the architects did not plan for a cycle of mosaic icons. The architects, whose names are recorded—Anthemius of Tralles and Isidorus of Miletus—are known for their works of scholar-

Right: The interior of S. Sophia, Istanbul; built 532–7

ship, but it does not follow that they were merely theoreticians moving into architectural practice for the first time in S. Sophia.

It is not known why Justinian did not insist on figurative mosaics in the Great Church of S. Sophia, but the reason is more likely to be aesthetic or practical than theological. The rich mosaic cycles outside Constantinople should not be interpreted as a provincial phenomenon. The fact that so far only one pre-Iconoclastic figure mosaic has been discovered in Istanbul (a panel of the Presentation of Christ recently uncovered in the mosque called the Kalenderhane Camii), can only be interpreted as the accident of survival. In view of the central place in patronage held by Justinian and his wife Theodora, Constantinople is likely to be source of artists in this age, yet this center can only be approached through the works of its artists whose commissions outside the capital have survived, or alternatively through the works of provincial artists influenced by these metropolitan artists. How far this method is justifiable is open to question.

The most likely product of the artists of Constantinople working outside the capital is the sanctuary mosaic of the Justinianic church in the monastery of S. Catherine on Mt Sinai. The foundation is mentioned in the *De Aedificiis*; this text if combined with inscriptions in the church seems to indicate the precise year of 550/1 for the execution of the mosaic (the Byzantine year began on 1 September and ended on 31 August). The builder of the church was born locally, for his identity is recorded on one of the beams of the roof; he was Stephanus from Aila, the modern Eilat on the Gulf of Aqaba. The structure is built of local stone and materials, and is a basilica with nave and two aisles; there is no hint that Stephanus had come face to face with the new architecture of Constantinople.

The source of the mosaic workshop is more open to uncertainty. One hint of its source is offered by the decoration of the vertical walls below the mosaic, homogenous in date with it. This apse wall is revetted with narrow strips of veined marble, clearly cut in sequence in the quarry. The type of gray-veined marble almost certainly comes from the Marmara islands near Constantinople. The slabs seem more likely to be a specially cut order than a random set chosen from a stockyard in Constantinople or in Jerusalem. If the marble revetment was shipped out specially to Sinai, it is also possible that the cargo was accompanied by mosaicists with their materials. The outstanding quality of the mosaic work may support the hypothesis of a special mission from the capital. It is not sufficient to attribute the workshop to Constantinople on grounds of quality alone, for Antioch or Jerusalem may not have lacked expertise in the medium.

The church was built inside a monastic fortified enclosure and abutted the (supposed) Burning Bush of the story told about Moses in Exodus chapter three. It was dedicated to the Virgin Mary, presumably because theologians explained the Bush as an antetype of Mary. The mosaics decorate the concha of the apse and the triumphal arch above it. The two uppermost panels represent two episodes in the life of Moses connected with the site of the monastery; Moses loosening his sandals, and Moses receiving the tablets of the law. Below the panels of Moses is a composition with five elements; Christ is represented in the form of a lamb which is set against a golden cross. Angels on each side of this central medallion fly towards Christ and offer him the scepter and orb. Two further medallions complete the group; on the left the bust figure is John the Baptist, and on the right the Virgin Mary. These saints were honored as the foremost representatives of the human race in heaven, and so were appropriate for conveying the prayers of mankind to Christ. The Greek word for prayer is often applied by art historians to the grouping of Christ, Mary, and the Baptist, which from the Justinianic period onwards became a standard composition, particularly at the entrance to the sanctuary. This word, *Deesis*, was not used in such an exclusive way in Byzantium.

The concha of the apse held a representation of the Transfiguration of Christ, and is framed by a series of medallion saints, apostles around the concha, and prophets and two monks along the base. The monks have square halos and must have been the living leaders of the community at the time. The six monumental figures in the Transfiguration are stark and impressive, and are deliberately unnaturalistic. The monks and pilgrims who prayed in this church were meant to be awed by the proximity of God, not charmed by art. This work is a masterpiece of Byzantine mosaic, and shows the power of this medium in the 6th century in portraying a vision of the Christian religion.

The Sinai mosaics are in superb condition, recently cleaned, and untouched by restoration. Less overwhelming and more restored are the sanctuary mosaics of the octagonal church of S. Vitale in Ravenna, which were completed c548 under the direction of the Orthodox Archbishop Maximian. The foundation of the church seems not directly due to Justinian, and building was begun in the 530s. The cost of the building was recorded in the epitaph of its donor, a banker (?) called Julianus. His expenditure was 26,000 gold *solidi*.

The mosaic decoration dates from after the recapture of Ravenna from the heretical Goth rulers by the army of Justinian in 540. Like Sinai, the mosaics illustrate several interwoven themes, but the primary aim is to celebrate the return of Orthodoxy to the city. Hence the portraits of the Byzantine rulers Justinian and Theodora, who participate in the divine liturgy (but who never set foot on Italian soil). Higher on the walls Old and New Testament figures proclaim the Redemption of mankind by Christ, as celebrated in the Eucharist. Like Sinai, art is used to express a dogmatic religious message, but the decoration is less single-minded and remote from the antique tradition; the panels and vaults are articulated by a wealth of luxuriant ornament, and the figures are softer and more natural in appearance. This contrast between Sinai and Ravenna cannot be explained as the result of a difference between Eastern and Western Christianity, for the interest in all-over ornament is a feature of S. Sophia, and is found else-

The sacrifices of Abel and Melchizedek, a mosaic in S. Vitale, Ravenna; mid 6th century

where in Constantinople, though in a "secular" context, in the floor mosaics of the Great Palace, possibly a work of the reign of Justinian.

While it may be argued that all Byzantine periods of art are most successful in the monumental decoration of architecture, the sense of monumentality penetrates even small-scale objects. From the 6th century (probably) come a number of illuminated manuscripts; for example three luxurious books with purple-dyed parchment pages, the Book of Genesis in the Nationalbibliothek, Vienna (Cod. theol. gr. 31), a Gospel Book at Rossano in south Italy (Codex purpureus in the Cathedral Treasury), and a Gospel fragment in the Bibliothèque Nationale, Paris (Cod. gr. suppl. 1286). The miniatures in these books are often monumental in effect, and in common with church decorations the Gospel books have an interest in the typological relationships between the Old and New Testaments. Manuscripts may have been one of the important channels through which compositions and figure-style were disseminated between Mediterranean cities; the composition of the Last Supper in the Rossano Gospels is strikingly similar to a mosaic in the church of S. Apollinare Nuovo (c520). Knowledge of art in Constantinople reached the provinces through other media also. An example may be given in the medium of metalwork.

A large silver disk, the Riha paten, now in the Dumbarton Oaks Research Library and Collection, Washington, D.C., seems to have received its decoration of a Communion of Apostles in Constantinople in 577 (when it received a date stamp), and was then sent out as a dedication to a church in Syria (perhaps in the pilgrim city of Sergiopolis). The Stuma paten is a related piece, and its date stamp seems to be from the following year; this paten is in the Istanbul Archaeological Museum. The design of this paten seems to be a direct copy of the earlier piece, and it is somewhat inferior in execution. It may be correct to deduce that the copyist worked in Syria. If so, the comparison documents the transmission of artistic ideas from the capital to the provinces. They would not evidence different styles in the workshops of Constantinople, or different levels of achievement in the capital. Another example

of transmission of objects may be the ivory throne of Archbishop Maximian, now in the Museo Arcivescovile, Ravenna, if it was carved in panels in Constantinople and then despatched for use in, presumably, S. Vitale.

The Dark Ages (late 6th–8th centuries). It is hazardous to explain the artistic developments after Justinian in terms of a response to the historical tensions of the period. Yet the prevalence of fears and superstitions is amply documented in 7th- and 8th-century writings, in which the idolatrous use of icons is reported to be widespread in the Empire. Small panel icons from the period survive in the collection of the monastery of S. Catherine on Mt Sinai (notably encaustic icons of Christ, of St Peter, and of an enthroned Virgin and Child with angels and saints). Monumental mosaic icons were made low down during the redecoration of the church of S. Demetrius in Thessalonica, carried out in the second quarter of the 7th century after a fire. These icons presented the perpetually besieged citizens with accessible saints to whom they could address their prayers for deliverance. Their faith in the supernatural powers of their local cult-saint Demetrius is made clear in the 7th-century compilation recording his miracles. These mosaics, presumably the work of local artists, reduce the saint to a staring, rigid intermediary for prayers to pass from the human to the divine sphere. A similar use of votive panels of saints set low down in a church is found in frescoes in the Greek monastery of S. Maria Antiqua in the Roman Forum. However, there is a great difference of style in the treatment of these figures; unlike the abstract delineation of the human form at Thessalonica, the painting at Rome, which is also the

The Stuma paten; 578(?). **Istanbul Archaeological Museum**

work of Byzantine artists, portrays the figures naturalistically and in atmospheric settings. The treatment of style is not apparently dictated by the purpose of the icons.

Another aspect of Byzantium's struggle for survival is also documented in art: occasions of Imperial success in war. It is to be expected that a Byzantine emperor would celebrate victory with some special commemorative commission. One such trophy can probably be identified in the set of nine silver plates found on Cyprus, now shared between the Metropolitan Museum, New York, and the Cyprus Museum, Nicosia. The plates are stamped in the reign of Heraclius (610–41), and probably belong to c630. The theme of the life of David illustrated on the set is probably a typological reference to victory by the Emperor, presumably in his successful campaigns against the Persians. A further extension of the use of religious icons in Imperial activities occurred when the Emperor Justinian II (685–95 and 705–11) made the innovation of representing a bust image of Christ on his coins.

Iconoclasm (726–843).

A reaction to the growing "abuse" of icons came under the militarily highly successful Iconoclastic Emperors. From the 720s until 843 figurative icons were forbidden in Byzantine churches (there was a brief interlude between 780 and 815, when iconodoules again sat on the throne). Since there had always been a current of opposition to the use of icons in the Christian Church, and since Iconoclasm was contemporary with a rejection of figurative religious art in the Jewish and Muslim worlds, it is reasonable to interpret the ban on images in Byzantium as a genuine religious movement, as a positive attempt to provoke a new Christian nonfigurative art. Byzantine mosaicists who worked for Muslim patrons in Jerusalem (Dome of the Rock, c691) and Damascus (Great Mosque, 705–7) show that they had already experienced composing on a monumental scale without figures.

Artistic production did continue during Iconoclasm but there must have been a diminution in the number of artists to match a reduction in patrons. Texts from the period before Iconoclasm frequently record the patronage of monks like Theodore of Sykeon, who could order expensive church plate for his Anatolian monastery from the workshops of Constantinople. This source of artistic sponsorship was severely reduced by the persecution of monks in the 8th century. However, a number of monuments were built or rebuilt during Iconoclasm, which was an important period for architecture if it is correct to date to it the creation of the small cross-in-square church surmounted by a central cupola, the church plan that became standard from the 9th century.

The Church of S. Eirene in Constantinople was rebuilt, after an earthquake, by Constantine V (741–75), when it received the preserved apse mosaic which features a large plain cross in a gold ground. In Thessalonica, a new cathedral of S. Sophia was built between 780 and 797 under Imperial sponsorship, and it too received a decoration with a large cross in the apse, and more crosses in the sanctuary vault, alternating with a

The church of S. Eirene in Istanbul; mid 8th century

vine leaf ornament (the figurative mosaics in the apse and cupola of the church are a post-Iconoclastic addition to the original scheme). Other Imperial commissions are known from texts to have been executed in Constantinople, but have not survived. An indication of their quality may be offered by some paintings that have survived in western Europe, and which have been attributed to Byzantine artists of the period.

The most striking work is the fresco decoration of the east apse of S. Maria at Castelseprio in north Italy. These (faded) paintings were found in this small, poorly-built chapel (outside the walls of a small medieval settlement) in 1944. The cycle illustrates the Infancy of Christ, and is of outstanding quality, showing a level of achievement in portraying solid figures within a landscape setting unparalleled in medieval monumental art. Their date of execution is controversial, and there are few objective considerations to resolve the controversy (the paintings must be earlier than the graffiti scratched over them; it is agreed that one of these is of the mid 10th century, but a 9th-century attribution of another has been challenged). The problem is whether Castelseprio represents a "renaissance" movement, or alternatively is evidence of a continuation of "perennial Hellenism" into the Middle Ages. The attribution favored here supports the second alternative; it is accepted that these wall-paintings can be attributed to the first half of the 8th century by comparison with frescoes of S. Maria Antiqua in Rome which were commissioned by Pope John VII (705–7). Both groups would be the work of Byzantine artists who had traveled to Italy. The artists of Castelseprio might have been fugitives from Iconoclasm.

Another indication of Greek expertise during Iconoclasm may be given by a group of four Carolingian manuscripts named by Koehler "the Group of the Vienna Coronation Gospels". The problem they present is not the dating of the miniatures (c800), but the actual place of training of artists. The group is exceptional in its Carolingian context for its facility of modeling figures in wet paint. If the artists are correctly identified as Byzantines from Constantinople, it would seem that even during Iconoclasm workshops continued to pass on methods of working derived from the studio practices of Antiquity. Presumably the lost secular art known from texts in the reigns of Constantine V, Theophilus (829–42), and other Emperors, as well as secret iconodoule productions, did supply sufficient figurative works for master–pupil relationships to span the two phases of Iconoclasm. The evidence for an "underground" iconodoule art comes indirectly from the 9th-century Psalters with marginal illustrations, in particular the Chludov Psalter now in the State Historical Museum in Moscow. Its miniatures, though dating after 843, seem in a few cases to reproduce satirical illustrations invented for anti-Iconoclastic pamphlets.

The restoration of Orthodoxy. Iconoclasm was declared a heresy at the Second Council of Nicaea in 787, but it returned as Imperial policy in 815. Orthodoxy was finally restored in 843. This restoration of the icons coincided with an upsurge in the economic and political prosperity of Byzantium, which lasted until the middle of the 11th century. During most of this time Imperial power was in the hands of the "Macedonian" dynasty, established on the throne after the murder of Michael III (842–67) by Basil I (867–86). The Macedonian Emperors had the finance as well as the desire to renovate the churches of the Empire, many of which had received little maintenance since the time of Justinian. After an initial phase of consolidation, they embarked on new building programs and decorations. This period is undoubtedly one of major importance in the history of art, but the context of surviving works is too fragmented for the characterization of the period to be anything but controversial. The enthusiastic statement of Kingsley Porter (*Romanesque Sculpture of the Pilgrimage Roads*, I p19) that "Modern Art may be considered to have begun with the Byzantine Renaissance of the tenth century" is right in spirit, but quite lacking in precision. The concept of a Macedonian Renaissance of Classical Antiquity cannot be justified as long as the "Classical" style on which this interpretation depends is thought to be a perennial element of the art of Constantinople, rather than a rediscovery after the interruption of Iconoclasm.

The biography of Basil I (the *Vita Basilii*) by his grandson, the Emperor Constantine VII Porphyrogenitus (913–59), has for its main theme the idea of restoration of the past, the regeneration of the Empire by an ideal ruler. Although in literary terms this life uses many conventions of classical biography, its account of Basil's artistic patronage cannot be treated as rhetoric, for it does document a real achievement. After 843, the redecoration of public churches was not instant. There was a delay in restoration, which may have been due to political prudence, practical considerations, or a lack of enthusiasm on the part of some theologians. It was over 25 years after Iconoclasm before the large churches of Constantinople such as S. Sophia or the Holy Apostles received with Imperial financial support their mosaic figurative decoration (perhaps in both cases it was the first time they had received such a cycle). The major restorations may have taken place

through the personal initiative and interest of Emperor Basil I and of the Patriarch Photius (who held office 858–67 and 877–86). Photius, who was elevated to the Patriarchal see after an aristocratic secular career, grew up under Iconoclasm and seems to have regarded himself and his family as particular champions of Orthodoxy. Because of his literary achievements and carefully recorded reading of Classical and early Byzantine texts and because of his part in the artistic revival, Photius is one of the few Byzantine intellectuals whose mind can at least be partly entered by modern scholarship.

The restoration of icons began in a fairly literal fashion. Soon after 843, the gold coins of Emperor Michael III changed the Iconoclastic types, and represented on the obverse a bust of Christ. This type of image had only been struck for one previous Emperor, Justinian II, and his innovation may have been a provocation towards Iconoclasm. The coins of Michael III certainly copy this actual pre-Iconoclastic die, for a mistake was made in the early issues which derived from a misreading of this model; Christ's hair trails down oddly in front of the left shoulder, and this mistake occurred because lack of clarity in the casting of the model confused the designer who did not realize that the hair should flow behind.

Another case of a post-Iconoclastic retrogression to the situation before the 720s was exemplified in the sanctuary mosaics of the church of the Koimesis at Nicaea (now Iznik in Turkey): the destruction of this church in 1922 was one of the major 20th-century losses of Byzantine art. The mosaics can only be studied from photographs. At some time after 843, the concha of the apse was redecorated with mosaics of a standing Virgin and Child, and the sanctuary vault in front of the apse with two pairs of angels. These figures replaced an existing Iconoclastic scheme which centered on the representation of a large cross in the concha. However, the evidence of liturgical inscriptions and mosaic surface has revealed that the Iconoclastic work was itself not the original scheme but a substitution. The original phase consisted of a standing Virgin and Child accompanied by angels, as correctly restored after Iconoclasm. It is not known whether the 9th-century planners made the correct deduction from study of the mosaic surface, or had some written records. As well as attempting to replace iconography destroyed by the Iconoclasts, there are indications that 9th-century artists were stimulated by the style of the immediately pre-Iconoclastic period; this might be due to study of any survivals, or because there had been a continuity of style through Iconoclasm.

The most important work of the 9th-century restoration to survive is the mosaic decoration of S. Sophia at Istanbul. The first section of the church to be decorated was the sanctuary vault. These mosaics were inaugurated by a homily delivered on the *ambo* of the Great Church on Holy Saturday, 29 March 867. A recent investigation of the present mosaics in this area revealed that the enthroned Virgin with the Christ Child in the concha of the apse and the Archangel Gabriel and fragment of Michael are without reasonable doubt the original 9th-century works. The apse concha preserves a few letters of its 9th-century inscription (recorded in its entirety in a 10th-century collection of epigrams). It commemorated the restoration with these sentiments: "The images which the imposters [the Iconoclasts] had formerly cast down here, pious Emperors [Michael III and Basil I] have set up again." However, the implication that there were figures in this apse was not supported by the investigation. The figurative decoration of S. Sophia seems to be a 9th-century innovation.

. This new decoration allows some insight into the developing principles of Middle Byzantine church-planning, principles which in course of time became more rigidly applied. The problem in planning a cycle for S. Sophia was that the curved surfaces in the vaults most suitable for the application of mosaic tesserae were so high in the church that only really vast figures would be seen at a reasonable scale to a spectator on the floor. Yet none of the available space could accommodate sufficiently large figures. The largest of the present visible figures, the apse Virgin, looks dwarf-like from the floor. The

Virgin and Child, in the concha of the apse of S. Sophia, Istanbul; late 9th century

visual problems were ignored rather than solved, and the choice of figures made according to theological principles. The highest and most prominent feature of the church, the dome, was chosen for the representation of Christ—the exact form is unknown since the mosaic had to be replaced after 1346 when the dome collapsed. The apse was designated as a suitable place for the Virgin and Child. The huge north and south tympana below the dome held three registers of figures in descending size (and order): from Angels through Prophets to some 14 Church Fathers. The individual choice of the latter depended on some special connection with S. Sophia or its ritual. The vaults of the galleries seem to be part of the 9th-century program; the Biblical scenes here are selected to show occasions of the human vision of God. Another 9th-century mosaic was inserted into the tympanum panel over the "Royal Doors" from the narthex into the center of the nave. In this panel an Emperor prostrates himself in front of an enthroned Christ; the Virgin and an Archangel are also present in medallions. The natural implication of the composition is that it is a representation of the donor of the 9th-century mosaics making his prayer to Holy Wisdom. The full meaning of the panel, and whether the Emperor is Basil I or his son Leo VI (886–912), is still much debated. One further panel may be a part of this plan. This is the panel above the entrance to the narthex from the southwest vestibule on which are represented an enthroned Virgin and Child who accept an offering of the city of Constantinople from Constantine the Great, and the church of S. Sophia from Justinian. The mosaic makes explicit the Byzantine myth, fully developed by the 7th century, that the Imperial capital was under the special protection of the Virgin.

The 9th-century mosaics of S. Sophia reveal several principles of planning: figures are placed hierarchically; figures and scenes were specially selected; and a number of explicit messages were conveyed by them. Unlike the Justinianic decoration, where the presence of God is conveyed symbolically by hundreds of mosaic crosses, each 9th-century unit represents an explicit Christian message. The problem of interpretation for us today is due to the lack of Byzantine statements on art, and our consequent ignorance of how many meanings to expect and how subtle each message was.

The 9th-century program was developed piecemeal but never radically altered. The main additions to S. Sophia were panels in the south gallery; two on the east wall record Imperial donations to the church. The first was put up c1028 by Empress Zoe and her first husband Romanus, but the faces of the Imperial couple and of the enthroned Christ between them were reset c1042 when Zoe married her third husband, Constantine IX Monomachus (1042–54). The second, adjacent, panel represents the gift of money made to the Virgin and Child instead of directly to Christ. The donors recording their generosity to the Great Church are John II Comnenus (1118–43) and his wife Irene, and the panel probably dates from c1118. The portrait of their son, Alexius Comnenus, was probably added to the right of the panel by the same mosaicist

Emperor John II Comnenus, a detail of a mosaic panel in S. Sophia, Istanbul; c1118

Empress Zoe, a detail of a mosaic panel in S. Sophia, Istanbul; c1028, reset c1042

in the year 1122, when he was proclaimed co-Emperor. The position of these commemorative mosaics in the south gallery would have been chosen for the reason that this area was an enclosure set aside for the Imperial attendances at services. At the western end of this enclosure, another panel, the *Deesis*, was set up, probably soon after the end of the Latin occupation of Constantinople (1204–61), during which period S. Sophia served as a Catholic cathedral.

The 9th-century program of S. Sophia is not homogeneous in style, and it may be presumed that the mosaics took several decades to accomplish. The church was shaken by a serious earthquake in 869 and the necessary repairs must have interrupted any decoration planned or in progress. The Virgin and Child and the Archangel Gabriel in the apse were certainly one of the most important commissions of the Middle Ages, and their quality of execution matches their importance. Subtlety and variety in the choice of tesserae achieve a delicate and solid modeling of the flesh of the faces, but the overall effect of the figures is one of intense spirituality, emphasized by their large eyes staring into the distance. The Church Fathers in the north tympanum, though delicate in execution, reveal, like the narthex and vestibule panels, signs of the development towards a more dry and linear modeling.

A linear figure-style of a lively and expressive character is used in the representation of an Ascension of Christ in the cupola of the church of S. Sophia at Thessalonica (datable to

885). The work was commissioned by the Archbishop of the city, Paul, known as a correspondent of Photius, who probably arranged for the workshop to come there from Constantinople. A similar style of bold, rather flat, figures is documented in the capital in a manuscript with illustrations of the *Homilies of Gregory of Nazianzus*, datable from its Imperial portraits to c880 (Bibliothèque Nationale, Paris; Cod. gr. 510). Each Homily in this book is preceded by a full page of pictures carefully selected to illustrate the theological content of the 4th-century text. The intellectual breadth of the planning of the cycle has led to the suggestion that the manuscript was prepared for Basil I by Photius.

Byzantine art in the second half of the 9th century is represented at its highest levels of achievement by a few survivals, and it seems that its character was determined by the Emperor and Patriarch in tandem. Due partly to the organization of education in Byzantium, there was a cultural rift between the aristocracy and the mass of ordinary people. A number of artisans and monks received a primary schooling up to the age of 11, which enabled them to read and write. There are no statistics on the general level of literacy in Byzantium. Only a few children in Constantinople received a secondary or tertiary education—wealthy provincial magnates probably had to send their children to the capital for higher education. Probably at any one time in Constantinople only a few hundred citizens had received a university education. This

The figure of Christ, part of the Deesis in S. Sophia, Istanbul;
2nd half of the 13th century

elite had acquired a philosophical, grammatical, and rhetorical training, and had come into contact with Classical Greek literature at a level well above the "popular" language of Homer. Such aristocrats could, like Photius, write in an artificial "Classical" style, and could appreciate the *ekphrasis*, the rhetorical convention in which to describe works of art, derived from the antique world.

The perpetual emphasis of Classical art criticism had been on the appreciation of the lifelike representation of figures. From this tradition the Byzantine intellectuals were conditioned to use the same concepts and vocabulary when referring to their own art. Photius in his homily inaugurating the apse mosaic of S. Sophia, incredibly to modern eyes, describes the Virgin as "lifelike". Byzantine artists may have continued to work within the conventions and formulae of Classical style, but they should be credited with the transformation of this tradition into a Christian art which rejected illusionism for its own sake and used the human figure to express abstract dogma rather than the purely narrative.

It must be admitted that Byzantine patrons failed to develop any critical language in which to characterize their art. Their unchanging use of Classical terms may have promoted the continual repetition of Classical motives and settings, but since there is a dislocation between the superficial appearance of this art and its underlying purpose, it is difficult to accept the characterization of any period, including that of the Macedonian Emperors, as one of "Renaissance". Unlike Western Europe, Byzantium hardly stood in such a relation to Antiquity that it could rediscover its values after their loss

because of a period of discontinuity. Because of this it might be argued that the history of Byzantine art is one of a decline from the achievements of Greek art. The view accepted here is that it may be interpreted as a positive successor to both Greek and Roman art, and that it was perhaps the most successful religious figurative art at portraying a belief in the overwhelming power of the divine over mankind. The religious content of their art apparently inhibited Byzantine spectators from developing an analytical appreciation of its form.

The 10th century. The great proportion of 10th-century art is lost. What remains from the period shows in particular the gulf in taste and expectations between the educated aristocracy and the lower classes. In parts of the provincial region of Cappadocia in central Anatolia are preserved (in an eroded and battered condition) scores of rock-cut chapels, which date predominantly from the 9th to the 11th centuries, and were served mostly by monks and hermits. The largest of these caves is Tokalı kilise in the Goreme Valley, and this church is characteristic of the Cappadocian development at its highest level of achievement. Its present barrel-vaulted entrance hall was originally a complete single-aisled church, cut and decorated in the first quarter of the 10th century. The vault is arranged in registers in which the life of Christ is portrayed in frieze format. The style of the figures can be recognized as a cruder "provincial" version of the late-9th-century art of Constantinople, as seen in the cupola mosaics of S. Sophia at Thessalonica. The scenes are crammed with stocky, flat, but expressively gesticulating figures. This style appears in a number of other Cappadocian decorations sufficiently frequently to merit a label. G. de Jerphanion, the scholar who published the fundamental study of the region, characterized decorations in this style as the "Archaic Group", and dated them to the late 9th century or first half of the 10th century. A feature of Cappadocian painting is that each chronological group of paintings owes its stylistic stimulation to artists from outside who were in close or even direct contact with currents in Constantinople, yet the new ideas are adapted into a distinctive local form. Cappadocian art is neither a purely regional phenomenon, nor a simple low-level absorption of outside influences.

The present main church of Tokalı kilise has a large transverse nave with three apses. This space was excavated as an extension of the church in the middle of the 10th century. The new paintings also represent the Gospel narrative of the life of Christ, as did the decoration of the entrance hall (or Old Church), but in a totally different style. The figures are elongated, and modeled with care and naturalism. There is a very close parallel for the figure-style and facial rendering, but it is in miniature, not monumental form; this parallel is the Bible made for Leo the Patrician (Vatican Library, Rome; Cod. Reginensis, gr. 1). The donor portraits are the basis for dating the manuscript to the second quarter of the century, and attributing it to Constantinople, though its provenance is not certain. This intrusion of a new style into Cappadocia,

The so-called Large Pigeon House, a rock-cut church in Cavusin,
Cappadocia, Turkey; c963–9

brought no doubt by the artists of Tokalı kilise New Church,
fundamentally affected Cappadocian painting. Tokalı kilise
was imitated in another large rock-cut church in the district,
in the paintings of the so-called Large Pigeon House in the
village of Cavusin; its style is an adaptation of the style of the
"Archaic Group" under the influence of the new current from
the capital. This church is datable from its inclusion of Imperial portraits to the reign of Nicephorus II Phocas (963–9).

These Cappadocian paintings do contain, often at a very
low level of achievement, stylistic features derived from the
aristocratic art of Constantinople. They do therefore help in
reconstructing the art of the capital, though they must distort
its full nature. Certain recurrent features of style and iconography can be isolated as local; and some of the intrusive
elements can be analyzed. The exercise is important, as these
crude cave paintings represent virtually all the known monumental art of the 10th century.

The Cappadocian churches are also informative about the
relation between a society and its church art, for they seem to
survive in something like their original medieval density. Most
of the churches contained burials. Some must represent
cemeteries for the local lay population of this fertile region;
others must have housed the bodies of priests and monks. A
number of inscriptions in the churches suggest that the most
grandiose decorations were made to beautify the mortuary
chapels founded by military officers posted to protect the Byzantine frontier with the Arabs. For these men and their
families, Cappadocia represented the safest haven in Christian
territory. Military commanders are responsible for a number

of dated good-quality decorations in the 11th century, such as
S. Barbara (1006 or 1021) and Karabas kilise (1060/1), both
in the Soganlı Valley. Similar patronage may lie behind the
decoration of three mid-11th-century churches in the Goreme
Valley, Karanlık kilise, Elmalı kilise, and Carıklı kilise. The
development of art in Cappadocia came to an abrupt stop in
the 1070s when the Turks overran the region, and the clergy
and the Byzantine army retreated.

While Cappadocia gives an insight into the nature of monumental art in the service of monastic communities and the
inhabitants of the frontiers of the Empire, the 10th-century
aristocratic art of Constantinople was the interest of a small
group of greater luxury and sophistication. Their manuscripts
abound with ornament which demonstrates that Byzantines
could appreciate the qualities of Islamic calligraphy. Several
luxury media were developed during this period. Enamel
work is an outstanding example of the expertise of Middle
Byzantine art; a datable 10th-century example is the Reliquary of the True Cross, now in the Limburger Domschatz,
Limburg. The prize piece of Byzantine enamel work, incorporating panels from several periods, but arranged in a Western format, is the *Pala d'oro* (altar-piece of gold) in the church
of S. Marco in Venice. Some insight into the connoisseurship
of such aristocratic patrons is also given by the enameled glass
bowl in the Tesoro di S. Marco. Its curved surface is organized
into a series of large and small medallions by ornamental
bands partly derived from Islamic art. Within the medallions
are either profile heads or full-length figures, and these forms
have been interpreted, plausibly, as copies of some rare Byzantine collection of Antique gems.

Tenth-century aristocratic art, like its contemporary literature, achieved a superficially impressive reproduction of
Classical forms. The most famous examples are in manuscript
illumination: the miniatures of the Paris Psalter (Bibliothèque
Nationale, Paris; Cod. gr. 139), and the *Rotulus* frieze illustrating the Book of Joshua (Vatican Library, Rome; Palatina
gr. 431), both attributed to the second half of the 10th century. The difficulty in assessing the achievements of these
miniaturists derives from the medium. Book illustration is frequently a medium of copying from one exemplum to the next
with appropriate additions or subtractions. Without a knowledge of the date and nature of the models used in these works,
the degree of invention or reproduction of the artists cannot
be defined. A crucial work in this controversy is the already
mentioned painting of S. Maria at Castelseprio. Since the
painting in this church is the closest stylistic parallel to the
manuscripts, its dating determines whether they represent the
continuity or rediscovery of Classical art.

The Comnenian Imperial dynasty. Economically, much of the
11th century and the second half of the 12th century were
periods of decline. Under the early Comnenes, however, there
was a substantial recovery (the dynasty was initiated by Alexius I Comnenus, 1081–1118). During these two centuries,
Byzantium lost a substantial area of her territory in Asia

The prayer of Hannah, a painted folio from the Paris Psalter;
mid 10th century. Bibliothèque Nationale, Paris

Minor, and the fatal erosion of her European possessions
under pressure from the Turks and Western European powers
began. Constantinople fell to the armies of the Fourth
Crusade in 1204, and the Byzantine nobility was separated
into enclaves based at Nicaea, Trebizond, and in north
Greece. Loss of possessions was a major factor in the Byzantine economy, for the wealth of the Empire lay in land.

Another social shift occurred in this period, which is directly reflected in art. The wealth of the Church moved from
the secular clergy, that is, from the bishops and the cathedrals,
into the control of the monasteries. The consequences can be
easily exemplified. When the cathedral of S. Sophia in Ohrid
(Yugoslavia) was decorated by the Greek Bishop Leo between
1037 and 1056, the cheaper technique of fresco was employed.
On the other hand, a glance at the most prominent churches
where the expensive medium of mosaic decoration and marble
revetment was executed highlights the wealth of the monasteries: the main church of the pilgrimage monastery of Hosios
Lukas in central Greece (first half of the 11th century), the
New Monastery (Nea Moni) on the island of Chios founded
by Emperor Constantine IX Monomachus in the middle of the
11th century, the church of the Koimesis in Nicaea (a monastery church, renovated after an earthquake in 1065), the
monastery at Daphni, near Athens, rebuilt c1100, and the
monastery of the Pantocrator in Constantinople (now the
Zeyrek Camii), founded between 1118 and 1134 as a
mausoleum for the Comnene dynasty. Other major mosaics

of the period, if not monastic, were frequently financed by
foreign rulers: examples are the church of S. Sophia at Kiev
(1037–1060s), S. Marco at Venice and the church at Torcello,
or in Norman Sicily in the Capella Palatina in Palermo
(1140s), the cathedral at Cefalù (before 1148), in the Mar-
torana at Palermo (1143–51), and in the cathedral at Monreale (1180s), or in the church of the Nativity in Bethlehem
(1168/9). A number of mosaic decorations were, of course,
carried out in the capital, financed by the Imperial family, as,
for example, the Pharos church in the Palace and the redecoration of Holy Apostles celebrated in an *ekphrasis* by Nikolaos
Mesarites; but apart from a fragment of an archangel of the
late 12th century in the Kalenderhane Camii, such mosaics
have not survived.

The mosaics of Hosios Lukas, Chios, and Daphni witness to
the diversity of stylistic treatment in the period. The Hosios
Lukas decoration is the most monumental, setting isolated,
heavy figures against gold grounds. The Chios figures are in a
much more miniature style with compositions less rigidly centralized, and the surface of mosaic very strongly colored. A
parallel for this style is to be found in a manuscript group
associated with a Psalter in the British Library, London (Cod.
add. 19352). This book is dated to 1066, and was illuminated
in the monastery of S. John Studios in Constantinople. Daphni
is the most complicated decoration, probably because several
workshops were employed over a longer period of time. The
earliest work would be that executed in the highest vaults—
this was the normal Byzantine procedure in order to prevent
plaster or paint dripping on to any completed work. The Pantocrator in the cupola and the bust figures of St John the
Baptist and St Nicholas in the side-chapel vaults are distinct
from the rest of the decoration due to their stark and expres-

The Transfiguration of Christ, a mosaic in the church of the monastery
at Daphni, near Athens; c1100

The Lamentation over the body of Christ, a fresco in the church of S. Panteleimon, Nerezi, Macedonia; 1164

sive faces (not too much modified by the late 19th-century restorations which mar the whole church). The lower panels in the naos and the cycle in the narthex represent a softer style, more narrative and decorative in intent. The firm modeling of the flesh and bodies of these lower (and relatively later) figures has been noticed, and the development expressed in terms of a 12th-century "Renaissance". As usual, the term seems acceptable only as a characterization and recognition of a high-quality execution of a mode ultimately deriving from Antiquity. The actual source of inspiration for the artists of Daphni seems to be relatively recent, for a similar treatment of figures can be seen in an early 11th-century manuscript (Vatican Library, Rome; Cod. gr. 1613), the so-called Menologion of Basil II (976–1025). The stylistic evidence of Daphni is to suggest a return to the interests of the period of the "Macedonian Renaissance".

Daphni is not the only work of this period to show how Byzantine art could progress by looking backwards. A related style is found in a group of early-12th-century manuscripts from Constantinople (for example, the two books with the *Homilies of Monk James Kokkinobaphos*, Vatican Library, Rome; Cod. gr. 1162 and Bibliothèque Nationale, Paris; Cod. gr. 1208). The highest achievement of this period is the fresco decoration of the church of S. Panteleimon at Nerezi, near Skopje (Macedonia), which is dated by an inscription to 1164. The workshop, commissioned by a member of the Comnene family, is marked by its interest in narrative. Such scenes as the Deposition of Christ and the Lamentation over the body of Christ succeed in conveying to the spectator a real impression of the emotions of the participants. This is achieved by both composition and the individual expressions of the figures. This 12th-century movement in art cannot be explained simply by postulating a direct study of surviving antique art. It may document both a social change in Byzantine religious experience and also the development of a greater artistic individualism. It is at any rate notable that in the 12th century more Byzantine artists begin to sign their work and to

The Paris Psalter

The 14 full-page miniatures of the Paris Psalter (Bibliothèque Nationale) are masterpieces of Byzantine art. This assessment is not controversial, but those who have studied the cycle have interpreted the achievement of the artist or artists in extremely different ways. The text illustrated by the pictures is that of the Psalms and Odes of the Old Testament in Greek. The Paris Psalter is the grandest of about 60 illuminated Greek Psalters that have survived from the Byzantine period.

Both the qualities and the problems raised by this manuscript can be appreciated in the first miniature of the cycle. Folio 1 is the first of an opening set of seven pictures representing the life of David, the author of the Psalms. The picture is painted within a broad patterned border which frames an almost square composition, slightly higher than

wide. The young David sits on a rock in the center of the scene playing his harp while animals play around him. In the distance to the left is seen the city of Bethlehem, the city of David. A landscape of hills and trees is convincingly portrayed. David is not, however, the only human figure in the scene; there are three others. These three are not, though, real people. The woman who sits beside David and rests her left hand on his shoulder is identified by her inscription. She is called Melodia, and so must represent an abstract personification of David's inspiration. The second female peeping around a column to the right must be the personification of a spring. The man reclining in the lower right corner has the appearance of a river god, but his inscription identifies him (incongruously) as the hill of Bethlehem.

The rest of the miniatures maintain this

special atmosphere of realistic figures within a setting and the intermingling of historical figures and personifications is repeated in most of the scenes. Another good example i a narrative scene is the battle of David and Goliath. David is supported by a female personification called Dynamis (Strength), while Alazoneia (Arrogance) leaves Goliath to his fate.

The style of the Paris Psalter is immediate reminiscent of antique art as known, for example, in the wall-paintings of Pompeii in the 1st century. The use of abstract personifications is reminiscent of antique literature, such as the Homeric legends of Troy, in which the heroes are assisted by gods and goddesses. The creation of the Paris Psalter illuminations must therefore have taken place within an environment where interest in and knowledge of antique art were valued The people involved must have had access to Classical literature and art, either directly or indirectly. The key problem is whether the

The Paris Psalter, folio 1: David and Melodia

The Paris Psalter, folio 4: David and Goliath

pictures were created in the early Christian period at a time fairly close to Classical Antiquity, and so it is the early cycle that was rediscovered in the 10th century by an antiquarian donor and an artist who could copy such a style. Or, as an alternative theory, did the 10th-century artist manage to compose a new cycle in the 10th century by studying whatever antique art had survived to the 10th century and inventing each picture?

Since no early Psalter of this kind has been preserved, the two opposing theories cannot be resolved. In any case a middle course can be taken; that, for example, the artist had some scenes available to him from an earlier work (such as David and Melodia), and that he created new scenes along the same principles of composition.

The date of the miniatures of the Paris Psalter is generally agreed (by stylistic comparisons of the border ornament) as lying in the 10th century (probably in mid century). It must have been executed in the city of Constantinople. Its luxury may point to a provenance in the Imperial court, in which case the scholar and antiquarian Constantine VII Porphyrogenitus (913–59) may have been the patron. Since some of the borders of the pictures have been cut down in the present manuscript and since each picture is on the verso side of a separate sheet, it is widely believed that the pictures are from another book. This issue has not yet been resolved.

At whatever stage in the history of Psalter decoration this cycle was invented, the manuscript shows one kind of art that appeared in Byzantium in the 10th century. It proves that antique style and ideas were still emulated then, and could be recreated.

R. CORMACK

The Paris Psalter, folio 7: the exaltation of David

The Paris Psalter, folio 422: Moses on Mt Sinai

gain some social notoriety.

Hosios Lukas, Chios, and Daphni are also indicative of the consistency of the principles of Byzantine church-planning, and, at the same time, of the possibility, indeed necessity, of the individual flexibility of iconographic choice in each case. Hosios Lukas is conspicuously limited in its selection of Gospel scenes. The distinctive character of its program is given by the representation of dozens of single figures of saints, particularly monastic saints. The choice was clearly made to give visual examples of the ideal ascetic models to be copied by the monks. The pictorial rendering of the virtues of the monastic life is also developed in 11th-century manuscripts when a 7th-century text written by John Climacus of Sinai began to be produced in illustrated editions. Both Chios and Daphni selected far fewer figures of saints, and put more emphasis on the Gospel cycle. It has been suggested that this too has its special significance, by underlining the importance and order of the liturgical year followed by the priests and monks. There is a problem in this interpretation. Except for Hosios Lukas, the selection of the cycles does not seem to distinguish the liturgical functions of monastic and non-monastic churches.

The late 12th century. Eleventh- and early-12th-century art is to a great extent the standardization of the currents of the Macedonian period. The second half of the 12th century was a time of greater ferment and innovation. The dated frescoes of Nerezi are a key point, though no doubt their importance is a little exaggerated through accidents of survival. It is widely accepted that this was a major period of Byzantine influence on Western Europe, but it is more difficult to ascertain if ideas came into Byzantium from the West, although the conditions for such influences were present. For example, Emperor Manuel I Comnenus (1143–80) was married first to a German and next to a French princess, and was interested in Western customs, such as the tournament. He played some part in the international organization of the mosaic redecoration of the Church of the Nativity at Bethlehem, then in the Latin Kingdom of Jerusalem (1168/9). A composite art derived from Byzantine and Western models was developed in the Crusader states, particularly in the media of manuscript illumination, icons, and sculptural ornament. A major production of this environment is the Psalter of Queen Melisende of Jerusalem (British Library, London; Cod. Egerton 1139). This book was illuminated in a scriptorium of the Holy Sepulcher in Jerusalem between 1131 and 1143 by an artist who, despite his Greek-sounding name Basilius, was a Westerner working under strong Byzantine influence.

Emperor Andronicus I Comnenus (1183–5) seems to have been an innovator in art. He patronized a medium not used by Byzantine emperors since the 8th century—portrait sculpture in the round. However, having himself shown in the clothes of a farm laborer instead of in Imperial vestments, he deviates from any Byzantine tradition, and may have been influenced by the West.

The appearance of new ideas in art in the second half of the 12th century, and the documentation of individual artistic personalities does point to the possibility of a positive consciousness of the visual arts by an informed patronage. The 12th-century texts mentioning art, such as the *Description of the Holy Apostles* by Nikolaos Mesarites, may hint at, but do not sufficiently document, a real critical awareness on the part of the Byzantine observer. The texts show that the observer could sometimes describe works of art with accurate perceptions; but a critical judgment which is more than a conventional literary *topos* (a stock rhetorical theme) is difficult, if not impossible, to discover. Perhaps, however, support for the belief in a developing visual awareness in the Byzantine public is offered directly by the art produced. There is a distinctive style found throughout the Byzantine world (and in the West) which is so consciously artificial as to suggest that its popularity was due to public appreciation, rather than its expressiveness. This late-12th-century development is one particularly conspicuous to modern scholarship, in which it is variously described as "the Monreale style", "the Dynamic style", "the Agitated style", "the Storm style", or even as "Byzantine rococo". At its best, as, for example, in the Monreale mosaics of the 1180s, this stylistic mode was effective as a means of expression. The perceptions of the observer were stimulated not only by the garments of the figures drawn with convoluted, fluttering folds, but by the integration of figure groups into a complex mass of overlapping bodies, often placed in a setting in depth suggested by landscape or architecture, though the elements are never aligned from a single viewpoint. Furthermore, the scenes were not always composed as a series of single units, but, when possible, a whole wall was laid out with the various compositions set in harmony or counterpoint.

This style can be recognized at various levels of achievement over a very wide area; for example, in the work of itinerant painters in Russia, as at Nereditsa, near Novgorod, in 1199 (destroyed during the Second World War), in Yugoslavia in the church of S. George at Kurbinovo in Macedonia in 1191, in churches at Kastoria in north Greece, on Cyprus at the Enkleistra of S. Neophytus in the paintings of 1183 by the named artist Theodore Apseudes, and in the church of the Panagia tou Arakou at Lagoudera in 1192, and in a portable painted icon representing the Annunciation, now in the collection of the monastery of S. Catherine on Mt Sinai, a work not dated but generally accepted as a late-12th-century product of an artist in Constantinople. The style certainly appealed to artists, whether or not its wide dissemination was encouraged by patronal taste. Although as an approach to figural composition it sometimes verged on the extreme and became almost caricature, it was a treatment not unprecedented in the Byzantine tradition. It occurs in a more restrained form in the mid-11th-century Cappadocian wall-paintings, and at the same time in S. Sophia at Ohrid. These precedents may suggest that the variations from the calm to the agitated treatment of figures within the tradition are due to artistic interests and

Two mosaic scenes in Monreale Cathedral, Sicily: left, Noah receives the dove, holding an olive twig; right, Noah's servants make the animals climb down from the ark; both c1180

experiment rather than the possible dictates of public taste. However, the speed with which this style became fashionable, and the enormous geographical range over which it appears, does make it a case for the taste of patrons being considered as a conscious factor in the evolution of Byzantine art. A problem in interpreting changes in Byzantine style is that while this art was at no time completely static and fossilized, the rigidity of social organization and the stability of Constantinople enforced a continuity of tradition never experienced elsewhere in Europe, except perhaps in Rome. The effect is that the history of Byzantine art therefore takes on a self-contained aspect, difficult to place in a broader cultural pattern.

Byzantine sculpture. The revival of portrait sculpture by Andronicus I may document some broader activity in this medium. Iconoclasm had finally broken the master–pupil relationship essential for the production of sculpture, though in any case this medium had been already in decline in late Antiquity, and was doomed in Byzantium when the Marmara quarries ceased to be worked in the 6th century. After Justinian, marble sculpture in Byzantium was usually in flat relief on reused material. Most of this work was architectural sculpture, like capitals and cornices, or sanctuary screens. An unusual amount of sculpture is seen in the facades of the Small Metropolis in Athens, a minuscule church of the late 12th century. Most of this exterior decoration is Classical sculpture

reused, rather than new Christian pieces, so perhaps the decoration says more about the taste of the patron than about the sculpture of his time.

If the belief that there was never much sculptural activity in Byzantium is correct, and not a historical distortion as a result of Islamic Turkish depredations, then the appearance in the 10th century of richly carved church exteriors in Armenia and Georgia must be regarded as a local Caucasian phenomenon. The outstanding examples are the church of the Holy Cross at Agth'amar on an island in Lake Van, Turkey, (datable to 915–21), and the church of Osk Vank in Turkish Georgia (datable to 958–66). In the iconography and style of these stone carvings, Byzantium is only one of several influences. Also, outside the orbit of Byzantium, and probably outside that of the Caucasus too, is the series of Russian stone churches with exteriors, in the region of Vladimir-Suzdal. This series developed chronologically with increasing complexity over the period from the church of the Pokrov on the Nerl (c1160) up to the church of S. George at Yuriev-Polski (c1230). The most likely explanation for the group is an initial stimulation from Western sculptors working in a provincial style. The Vladimir churches then seem to have developed as a local tradition fostered by an ambitious and sophisticated Russian court.

There is a case for attributing to Constantinople in the late 12th century the development of the sculptured funerary monument, of which the best examples to have survived belong to a later period. These are the tomb sculptures from the first quarter of the 14th century in Constantinople in the Feneri Isa Camii, the Fethiye Camii, and the Kariye Camii. In these churches, the *arcosolia* which held the tombs of the families of the donors were framed by ornate relief sculptures carved with bust figures of Christ, Archangels, or Apostles. Some idea of the quality of Middle Byzantine sculpture is given by the spoils removed in the 13th century by the Venetians and incorporated into the fabric of S. Marco in Venice.

Late Byzantine art. The sack of Constantinople in 1204 cut short artistic development in the capital. The city never recovered from the depredations of the Latin occupation (1204–61), when churches were stripped of their spiritual protection of relics and physical protection of lead roofing. After the recovery of the city and its rule under the Palaeologan dynasty until its fall to the Turks in 1453, Constantinople inside its walls remained a partial wilderness of ruins and fields. Only a few of its churches were restored in the early 14th century, to act as family mausoleums for a small and inter-related aristocracy, and received an expensive mosaic and marble decoration. After the civil wars of the mid 14th century, further economic decline set in while intellectuals consciously watched the decline and fall of the Empire.

Yet the period of Byzantine painting after 1204 is one of major achievement in the history of European painting. Examples of painting in the "Agitated style" continue to occur in the 13th century, but the best work is painted in a quite different manner, in which the figures are calm, softly modelled, and three dimensional. This manner had probably occurred during the 12th century alongside other currents, for it is one

Detail of an angel guarding Christ's tomb, part of a fresco in the monastery church at Milesevo, Yugoslavia; c1230–9

of several styles found in the frescoes of Nerezi. The patron saint of this church, S. Panteleimon, is distinguished by his rendering in a calm, idealized style. Earlier in the century, this treatment is used for the Virgin and Child of the Vladimir icon, now in the State Tretyakov Gallery in Moscow, and the effect in this scale and medium is almost one of sentimentality. At the end of the century, a fresco decoration in this style is preserved, but in a very fragmentary state, in the church of S. Demetrius at Vladimir in Russia (datable to c1194–7). Sections of the scene of the Last Judgment survive.

This calm and graceful style occurs at a high level of achievement in the first half of the 13th century at S. Sophia at Nicaea (in poor condition), and more extensively at Milesevo in Yugoslavia (1230s). Orthodox Christian courts continued to support art, and in Serbia there was fairly continuous employment to be gained through the century (as at Studenica, Milesevo, Pec, Sopocani, and later in the court of Milutin). The frescoes of S. Sophia at Trebizond (c1260) are also the work of major artists, who show contact with those of Sopocani (1260s). How these apparently itinerant workshops operated is at present obscure, but there is an implication that Byzantine art could flourish without the stable central stimulus of Constantinople. Probably this is because the late 12th century was also a period of decentralization.

Such a situation in art may be inferred in manuscript production. Up to the 12th century, high-quality products seem to come out of the book trade of Constantinople; indeed manuscripts supply a better based and documented context for the art of the capital than monumental painting. In the course of the 12th century, considerable books seem to have been illuminated outside the capital, probably in the rich monasteries around the Empire, from Sinai to Athos. This expansion of production may have caused a fall in standards of execution, and many late-12th-century illustrations are pathetic copies of earlier Comnenian models. An example of this is the group in the style of the Rockefeller-McCormick New Testament (University Library, Chicago; Codex 965), until recently attributed to Nicaea in the 13th century. The place of production of this group outside the capital (or not) is uncertain.

The Byzantine return to Constantinople in 1261 was marked by the use of art to reestablish cultural continuity. This is the context for the setting of the *Deesis* in the south gallery of S. Sophia. The tesserae are set as if to reproduce in mosaic the calm style in painting. The medium is similarly used, with very soft gradations of color, in miniature mosaic icons, a technique originating in the 12th century. Tiny tesserae were set in a wax matrix. The medium reached its height of popularity in the century after 1261; it seems more appropriate to connoisseurship than worship.

Late Byzantine art is best known not from Imperial patronage, but from that of Theodore Metochites, the leading statesman of the reign of Andronicus II Palaeologus (1282–1328). He was a scholar, prolific writer, astronomer, and civil servant, who rose (shadily) to great wealth. During his prosperity, he restored and decorated the monastery of the Chora, be-

The Anastasis, a fresco in the Kariye Camii, Istanbul; c1315–21

tween c1315 and 1321, now the Kariye Camii. The main part of the church received mosaics, probably set by the workshop of the Holy Apostles in Thessalonica (1310–14), and the new south parecclesion (side-church) received frescoes. The mosaics represent the lives of Christ and the Virgin Mary, while the new mortuary chapel had an appropriate salvation cycle and Last Judgment. The cycles are densely illustrated with profuse detail, demanding from the observer a knowledge of both Bible and Apocrypha, and theological commentaries on them. The erudite character of the program must reflect the interests of Metochites, but the proliferation of cycles and the minute treatment of the iconography of each scene is more widely symptomatic of late Byzantine culture. An extreme is reached in the program of Decani in Yugoslavia (1327–35).

The style of the Kariye Camii conforms to Byzantine aristocratic taste. It is a version of the classical tradition with solid figures in a setting which never reaches full spatial illusion. This portrayal of irrational space might be deliberate in By-

zantium at this time when artists must have been aware of Western experiments in spatial composition. On this interpretation, it was the Byzantine enmity towards the Latins, their church, and their culture that provoked the development of an alternative visual aesthetic. The issue depends on whether the artistic representation of space could develop from pragmatic workshop rules of thumb, or whether it required specialized mathematical knowledge. The figure-style of the Palaeologan period is better explained as a reinterpretation of the traditional Middle Byzantine models, rather than as a new period of Renaissance or Humanism.

The distinctive Kariye Camii style of huge, broad, and heavy figures with mannered gestures was developed later in the 14th century into a bizarre and personal form by a named artist, Theophanes the Greek. This painter emigrated from Constantinople to Russia, where he spent his mature years producing icons, manuscripts, and frescoes. His only firmly dated and documented work is the wall-painting of the Church of the Transfiguration in Novgorod (1378), but this is the basis for other attributions. He exaggerated the use of white highlighting as a means of giving character both to garments and faces. The dark flesh of the faces, highlit with energetic white brushstrokes, conveys brooding spirituality beneath an instantly held expression. Another interest of late Byzantine artists was experiment in color, and this may have been stimulated by contacts with the West. Further study of the frescoes of Mystras in south Greece and of the manuscripts is needed before this concern in the late 14th and first half of the 15th century can be documented.

The end of Byzantine art. Byzantine art depended for its existence on a ruling aristocratic Orthodox Christian society. Such an art could not survive the Turkish occupation of Constantinople in 1453. This society had produced an art and a literature of which the prominent feature was in both the continual attempt to present general themes in an elegant language derived from Classical Antiquity. Since the ancient world had no single unified cultural pattern, Byzantine art had considerable variety. The diversity of treatment of the human figure from the carefully observed pose to the abstract vessel for prayer derives from the Classical tradition, and does not need to be explained in terms of Classical or opposing Oriental traditions. The Church did not encourage its artists to seek originality, and consequently it is difficult to identify individual hands in Byzantine art. Even when Georgios Kalliergis de-clared himself in an inscription in the Christos church at Verria in 1315 to be "the best painter in all Thessaly", we cannot distinguish him satisfactorily from contemporary artists in the region.

Since Byzantine art defies attempts to interpret it in terms of individual genius, renaissance, or distinctive regional schools, it is clear that the art historical approach to it must be different from that to most Western European art. This is not to deny the importance of individual artists and patrons in its development, but is to recognize that the opaque quality of this culture was intentional, and needs appreciation. As an art to express Christian dogma in a permanently intelligible form, Byzantine art is unsurpassed. Its importance lies in its positive qualities as religious art. To regard Byzantine art as primarily the carrier of antique art through the Middle Ages would represent a failure to penetrate through its stylistic appearance to its true function as art.

R. CORMACK

Bibliography. Demus, O. *Byzantine Mosaic Decoration*, London (1948). Forsyth, G.H. and Weitzmann, K. *The Monastery of Saint Catherine at Mount Sinai*, Ann Arbor (1974). Kähler, H. and Mango, C. *Hagia Sophia*, London (1967). Lazarev, V.N. *Storia della Pittura Bizantina*, Turin (1967). Mango, C. *The Art of the Byzantine Empire 312–1453*, Englewood Cliffs (1972). Rice, D. Talbot *The Art of Byzantium*, London (1959). Underwood, P.A. *The Kariye Djami*, London (1967).

21

IRISH ART

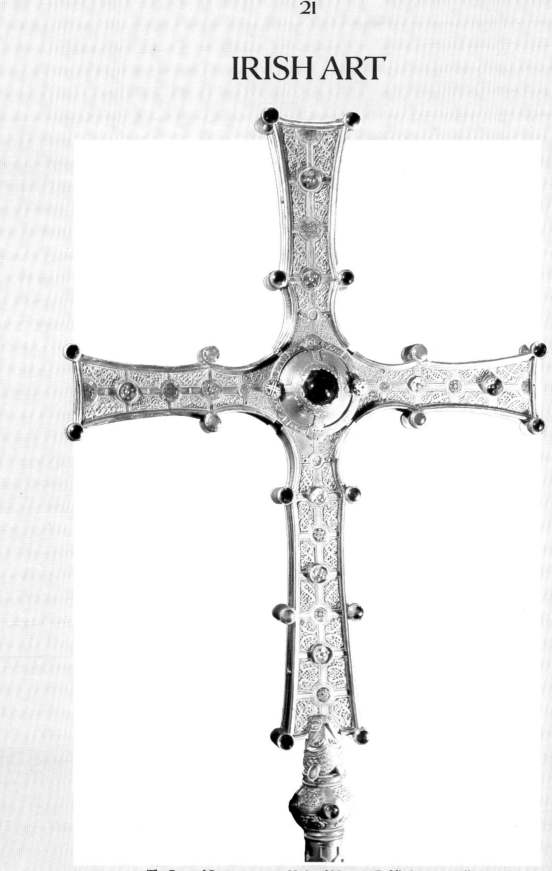

The Cross of Cong; c1122–27, National Museum, Dublin (see page 398)

Two facts of history play vital roles in the development of Irish art throughout the period of the Early Middle Ages. On the one hand Ireland was never part of the Roman Empire, and on the other, Christianity came to Ireland just when the Empire was collapsing, so for several centuries religious links with Rome were quite tenuous. As a result, Ireland lagged behind the rest of Romanized Europe in the development of towns and a monetary economy. Instead, monasteries grew up as the major cultural centers. From an artistic point of view, the prehistoric Celtic art that had existed in Ireland since the 3rd century BC continued unaffected by the naturalistic art of the Classical world.

The Golden Age (c AD 400–800). The Irish were converted to Christianity in the 5th century, notably by St Patrick. Ireland soon adopted a type of ecclesiastical organization different from most others in Europe. Instead of territorial bishoprics, the Irish ecclesiastical unit was the *paruchia*. This was a group of monasteries founded by a saint and responsible to the abbot of the mother-house. The monasteries founded by St Columba (c521–97) and his followers were among those with the greatest cultural influence. They included Derry, Durrow, and later Kells, in Ireland; Iona and then Lindisfarne in Britain (*see* Anglo-Saxon Art). Some early Irish monks lived very ascetic lives, choosing the most rugged and isolated places for their monasteries. For further penance they would break all

Important places mentioned in the text

family ties and leave Ireland as *peregrini*. Some of these self-exiled monks settled in Iceland while others, like St Columbanus (c543–615), founded monasteries all over Europe. Irish continental monasteries, like St Gall, Echternach, Bobbio, and Luxeuil became important centers of cultural interchange between Ireland and the Continent.

Many early buildings in Ireland were made of wood and so no longer survive. Secular buildings consisted of the *rath* or ring fort and the *crannog* or artificial island dwelling. The few surviving religious buildings in stone, on Skellig Michael and the Oratory of Gallerus (Kerry), are beehive huts made of flagstones and shaped like upturned boats. Monasteries like Nendrum (Co. Down) are merely collections of huts surrounded by two or three ring walls. One hut was set apart for the scribes and one for the craftsmen. It is extraordinary that monks could have produced delicate works of art while working under such primitive conditions. However, a description of the church of Kildare, made in the 7th century by Cogitosus, shows that buildings were not as bleak as they now appear. That church's interior was decorated with paintings, ornamented windows, carvings, and jewel-studded monuments.

Around a monastic compound there were usually several large stone crosses. It is possible that services were held in front of such crosses rather than inside the compound's tiny chapel. The earliest crosses, at Aglish, Kilfountain, and Reask (Kerry), are simply slabs of rock with an incised cross design. Later the slabs were slightly trimmed before being incised, for instance those at Falan Mura (Donegal) and Ballyvourney (Cork). Finally, they emerged as freestanding crosses with arms joined by a circle. The most striking 8th-century group is found in southwest Ireland, in the Slievenamon region, with examples at Killamery, Ahenny, Kilrea, Kilkieran, and Kilklispeen. They are characterized by large rectangular bases, a thick cable outline in relief, indented armpits, and large bosses. The latter are placed where the circle joins the arms, where rivets would be expected in wood or metal constructions. Almost the entire surface is covered by a web of spiral whorls and ribbon interlace. The base of the North Cross at Ahenny bears some processional scenes of men, horses, and a funeral.

It is to the fields of metalwork and manuscript illumination that the epithet "Golden Age" truly refers. Ancient Celtic designs deriving from the La Tène period, consisting of abstract whorls and spirals, remained a hallmark of Early Irish art (*see* Celtic Art).

Little is known of the metalwork produced in the 6th and 7th centuries, so the amazing achievements of the Ardagh Chalice and the Tara Brooch (both in the National Museum, Dublin) are hard to place in a chronological context, though they are comparable with each other in technical mastery. For small panels of interlace, exceptionally fine filigree was used and sometimes two wires, one beaded and the other twisted, were soldered over each other. The glinting effects of chip-carved designs were obtained by casting with the *cire perdue*

The Ardagh Chalice, early 8th century. National Museum, Dublin

The Book of Durrow, the first folio of St Mark's Gospel; late 7th century.
Trinity College Library, Dublin

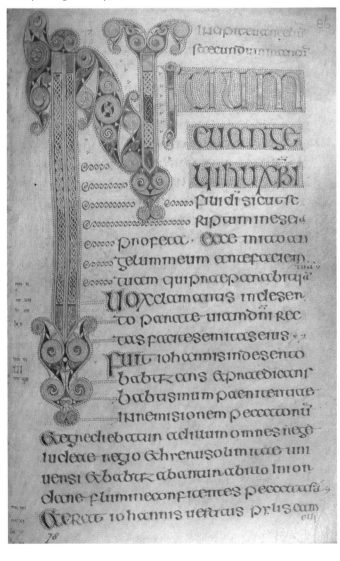

process. Blue, red, yellow, and green enamels were often used, and sometimes subtle effects obtained by alternating opaque enamel with translucent glass in a cloisonné design.

The Ardagh Chalice, made in the early 8th century, was found in 1868. It has been remarkably well preserved. Its design contrasts broad areas of plain silver with concentrations of gold filigree and enamel bosses. The Tara Brooch is more densely covered with ornament. It is made of bronze and divided into tiny panels filled with filigree and niello designs. Many of the finest examples of metalwork from this period, such as the Ekero Crozier (State Historical Museum, Stockholm), the Micklebostad Hanging Bowl (Historical Museum, Bergen), and the Copenhagen Shrine (National Museum, Copenhagen), were looted by the Vikings and thus come to be in Scandinavian museums.

As with metalwork, so many early manuscripts have been lost that little remains to indicate how styles of illumination evolved to the complexity seen in the Book of Durrow. Also, many surviving manuscripts come from the Irish continental monasteries, which escaped the Viking raids, and not from Ireland itself. A controversy has grown up about the scriptoria producing early Insular manuscripts: it is clear that scriptoria were flourishing in both Ireland and Northumbria but from which ones do particular manuscripts come? The *Cathach* of St Columba (Royal Irish Academy, Dublin) produced in the early 6th century, is the earliest Irish manuscript written in Celtic half -uncial letters and initials, decorated with scrolls and dots. In it large initials are followed by gradually diminishing letters. Codex Ambrosianus D23 (Biblioteca Ambrosiana, Milan) contains the earliest "carpet" page, completely covered in abstract designs. The Book of Durrow (Trinity College Library, Dublin), the earliest lavishly illuminated Insular manucript, incorporates a layout that became customary in later gospel books. The four symbols of the Evangelists are given full-page illustrations and are each followed by a carpet page. The book indicates a variety of sources: Ireland, Northumbria, and Coptic Egypt. Experts are undecided whether it was made at Lindisfarne, Iona, or Durrow. Although the Lindisfarne Gospels (British Library, London) were made by the Northumbrian Bishop Eadfrith (698–721), he had certainly been taught in the Irish tradition. Recent investigations have shown that the meticulous interlace of the Lindisfarne Gospels was based on a sketched grid and drawn with compasses. The same methods of marking up were used by Irish metal- and stone-workers.

The Danish invasions (800–1014). In 795 the Vikings raided the island of Lambay in the Irish Sea and a few years later destroyed the monastery of Iona. The monks then abandoned their island and fled to Ireland, founding a new monastery at Kells. Viking raids continued for most of the 9th century and in part were aimed at the wealthy monasteries, including Clonmacnoise, Glendalough, and Bangor. The Irish put up very little resistance and remained absorbed in their interminable tribal bickerings.

Insular Initial Pages

The idea of building letterforms into a whole-page abstract design was invented in the 7th century by the monk-artists of the Celtic tradition, first perhaps in Ireland, and later in monasteries founded by Irish missionaries in Northumbria and on the Continent. Not only was the basic idea new, but the treatment of the letterforms themselves also shows astonishing originality and range of invention.

The germ of the idea appears in the late 7th century in the Book of Durrow (Trinity College Library, Dublin). Each Gospel is prefaced by an Evangelist's symbol, a carpet page of ornament, and an *incipit* page in which the first words of the text are enlarged and elaborated, filling more and more of the page with each successive Gospel. In the next great book, the Lindisfarne Gospels (British Library, London) the idea is fully developed and the whole page has been absorbed. Six pages are so treated, including the words of Matthew 1:18 "XPI AUTEM GENERATIO" and the first words of St Jerome's preface to the Vulgate. The shapes of the first letters dominate the design and give each page its special character: these are created out of great circumscribed ribbons filled with organic patterns, and are balanced by an asymmetrical framework and areas of intricate ornament. The succeeding letters are arranged in bands of differing size, emphasized by outlines and diapers of dots and the filling in of some of the counters with color. The

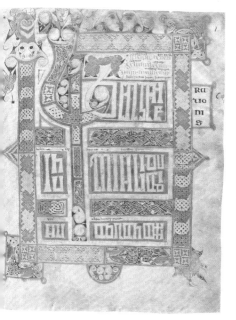

The Macregol ospels, the initial page f St Matthew's Gospel; rly 9th century. odleian Library, Oxford

▶ The initial page of the Codex Aureus, produced in Canterbury; mid 8th century. Royal Library, Stockholm

range letterforms themselves, with their ompressed, angular rhythm, are the final ement in an abstract design of contrasting extures, dynamic movement, and a very arefully balanced complex of linear forms. ut the great power of these pages derives ot just from the artist's mastery of technique nd form, but from his attitude to the text ranscribed. These letters spell out words of ivine power, the Revelation of God, which emands and inspires the artist's supreme esponse.

What earlier sources may have contributed o the evolution of these pages is obscure and ontroversial. At the end of the Roman mpire the form of books was changing, the odex was taking the place of the roll, and he page therefore became the unit of design; ome early pages of decorative designs show-ng the cross are known, and also much xperimental drawing of decorative initial etters. In the same period inscriptions on tone change; classical lettering is replaced by reer more irregular forms which may be nitted into a different sort of unity. Insular rtists possibly took ideas from Coptic and yzantine square-section relief inscriptions Kufic examples are all later) which are lanned in bands, and are monoline, not ominated by the modulated line introduced y the pen. These artists were fascinated by etterforms; they experimented, borrowing rom both Greek and Runic sources, often ntroducing several forms of the same letter n a page and mixing forms of extreme ngularity with swelling curves derived from he Uncial tradition. In the end, they created

something completely new.

The originality of the Insular artists did not come to an end with the Lindisfarne Gospels; experiment and vitality continued.

In one direction artists explored geometric ideas. Here the Gospels of St Chad are transitional: the most remarkable example is the one now in Cologne.

The quality of the line from which letters are made changes. In the Macregol Gospels (Bodleian Library, Oxford) and the St Gall MS.51 there is a positive/negative relation-ship with the background. In the Echternach Gospels (Bibliothèque Nationale, Paris) each letter is dynamic and individual, but this type is more often found in initials and titles than in whole-page designs.

Again there is the organic direction, in which the Book of Kells (Trinity College Library, Dublin) moves beyond the Lindis-farne Gospels in its magnificent *Chi-Rho* page. Now there are eight initial pages, full of

new experiment, though there is a tendency for the pattern and even the figurative ele-ments to take over from pure letter design. Entirely in the lettering medium is the great page from the Leningrad Gospels (Public Library, Leningrad); even more organic are the snake-like intertwining forms of the Barberini manuscript (Vatican Library, Rome).

Standing apart, illustrating the great range of the school, is the page from the Stockholm Codex Aureus (Royal Library) where the influence of the contemporary tradition in metalwork has produced yet another style of design.

NICOLETE GRAY

Further reading. Alexander, J.J.G. *Insular Manu-scripts from the Sixth to the Ninth century*, London (1978). Henry, F. *The Book of Kells*, London (1974). Kendrick, T.D., Brown, T.J. *The Lindisfarne Gospels*, Oltun (1956). Zimmerman, B.E.H. *Vorkarolingische Miniaturen*, Berlin (1916).

Although the Vikings were primarily a destructive force, they also brought Ireland into closer contact with Europe. Heiric of Autun wrote in the 9th century, "Ireland, of which almost the whole people, despising the dangers of the sea, migrate with their crowds of philosophers to our shores". The most notable of these was the Neoplatonist John Scotus Erigena who taught at Laon. Meanwhile, the Vikings established several trading towns, including Dublin, Wexford, and Waterford, and introduced a monetary economy to the country. Their trade brought goods from the north Atlantic and eastern Mediterranean to Ireland. In the 11th century the achievements of the High Kings, like Brian Boru, led to greater political unity among the Irish. However, the cultural and economic influence of the Vikings continued well into the 12th century, in spite of their military defeat at Clontarf in 1014.

The greatest innovation in architecture in this period was the construction of tall round towers near churches. Several survive from the 11th and 12th centuries, but documents indicate that the first ones appeared towards the end of the 9th century. They were primarily used as bell towers: small hand bells were rung from the top of a tower to inform monks working nearby of the passing time. But their construction shows they had secondary functions. They were built up to 100 ft (30.5 m) high with tapering walls and a pointed stone roof. A few narrow windows provided a good commanding view over the surrounding countryside. A door was placed about 8 ft (2.5 m) off the ground and the stories inside were linked by removable ladders. So clearly, they were used as watchtowers and to provide, at least in theory, a safe refuge. Unfortunately, archaeological remains show that several monks and their treasures were burnt by raiders while hiding in the towers. The Irish round towers are related to early specimens found in East Anglia and both probably derive from the detached campanile of north Italy.

The sculptured crosses from this period are somewhat surprising because they are covered with clear iconographic programs derived from the Bible—a great change from the restless spirals and interlace used up to the 9th century and rare in a European context before the Romanesque period. Two transitional groups of crosses combine interlace and biblical scenes. One is found near the monastery of Clonmacnoise, with examples at Gallen, Lorrha, Kinnity, and Bealin (c810). The other group surrounds Kells and includes crosses at Duleek and Termonfechlin. The most common scenes show Adam and Eve, Cain and Abel, Abraham and Isaac, and Daniel in the Den of Lions. Fully developed crosses are found at Monasterboice (West Cross), Kells (Market Cross), Durrow, and Clonmacnoise (Cross of Scriptures and Cross of Muirdach). The latter is dated by an inscription to 923. They usually show the Crucifixion on one side and Christ in Judgment on the other. New Testament scenes are placed below the Crucifixion and their prefigurations in the Old Testament below the Last Judgment.

Compared with the metalwork of the Golden Age, products of this period are an anticlimax; hardly surprising because

The Cross of Muirdach, Clonmacnoise, the west side showing the Crucifixion in the center of the cross

metalworkers were the Vikings' first targets. However, the invaders introduced certain new ideas into the Irish repertoire. For instance, Irish penannular brooches retained their traditional shape with large triangular terminals but the ornament took on a Scandinavian appearance. Instead of continuous ribbon interlace, decorated areas are filled with small, disjointed animals with hatched bodies. Some very striking thistle brooches were made with terminals like prickly thistle heads. The Kells Crozier (British Museum, London) is one of the most ambitious works surviving from this period: a shrine consisting of a yew staff encased in bronze with a decorated crook and four bronze knops. The three lower ones were made in the 10th century and are divided into panels filled with degenerate interlace and small fantastic beasts. The animals are somewhat reminiscent of the Trewhiddle style of south England. By the end of the 10th century designs were becoming very debased and the animals on the Clogan Oir Bell Shrine (National Museum, Dublin) for example, are barely recognizable as such.

In manuscript production there was no sudden break with the past. The traditions established by such books as the Lindisfarne Gospels (British Library, London) and the Lichfield Gospels (Lichfield Cathedral Library) continued in an increasingly lavish manner. The Book of Kells was begun at Iona *c*800 and then taken by the monks, in an unfinished state, to their new home at Kells where additional work was done. Besides the splendid *Chi-Rho* page and the symbols of the Evangelists, the Book of Kells has elaborately decorated canon tables and several full-page illustrations to the text. Even the marginalia and initials are of an exceptionally vigorous type, depicting fabulous beasts and contorted humans. The use of several full-page colored illustrations in one book was unusual at this time. In the Book of Kells they show the Virgin and Child, the Arrest of Christ, the Third Temptation, and a portrait of Christ. Styles in the book show the wide range of sources at the disposal of Irish scriptoria. The canon tables are related to those used by the Carolingian Palace school; some of the animals are Merovingian derivatives; the vine scrolls come from Northumbria; the Black Devil in the Temptation is a Byzantine version; and the iconography of the Virgin and Child comes from Coptic or Armenian prototypes. Some of these ideas probably came from Coptic or Armenian ivories. Irish manuscripts continued to be influential on the Continent. Scholars and scribes who had moved there developed the Franco-Insular school of illumination whose most notable product was the Second Bible of Charles the Bald (Bibliothèque Nationale, Paris).

The Romanesque period (1014–1169).

In the 11th century Irish art experienced a final flourish before losing its identity under English rule. The revival began under Brian Boru who "sent professors and masters to buy books beyond the sea because their writings in every church were burned and thrown into water by the plunderers" The vigor of Irish art in this final phase was partly due to reform within the church and partly to foreign influences assimilated into Irish traditions.

St Malachy (1095–1148), Archbishop of Armagh and papal legate to Ireland, broke the system of hereditary succession in monasteries. He improved spiritual standards in Armagh and Bangor and introduced the Cistercian Order to Ireland. Meanwhile, the anomaly of Irish monasteries without territorial bishoprics had become thought of as an acute problem. The impetus for reorganization came from the Vikings who maintained close contacts with their English confederates. Change began in 1036 when, at the instigation of the inhabitants, Dublin's first Bishop was consecrated by the Archbishop of Canterbury. Soon afterwards bishoprics were established at Waterford, Armagh, and Cashel.

The Book of Kells, a portrait of Christ; c800. Trinity College Library, Dublin

There was also a final wave of Irish activity in Europe. *Schottenkirche* (churches founded by Irish monks in German-speaking lands) were founded in Regensburg (1111–22), Würzburg (1134), Nuremberg (1140), and other places.

In 1169 Ireland was in its usual state of tribal turmoil; High King Rory O'Connor asked Henry II of England to help him put down an insurrection. Instead, the English came in force, subdued the country, and established themselves for good.

Architecture reflects these historical changes closely. In 1134 Cormac Mac Carthy, a supporter of St Malachy, built a church at Cashel in a new style. Instead of the single cell, or nave and chancel plan, Cormac's chapel has a narrow chancel with a rib vault, a barrel-vaulted nave with two flanking towers at the east end, and three deeply recessed sculptured portals. The towers derive from St James, Regensburg, the barrel vault supported by short columns on a cornice is found at St Eutrope, Saintes, and the rib vault is found at Durham Cathedral. The only Irish feature of the church is the chamber between the vault and the stone roof.

Cormac's chapel was more or less copied at Roscrea (Tipperary) and Kilmalkedar (Kerry). The first Cistercian abbey,

Mellifont (consecrated 1157) was built on the usual Cistercian model with nave, aisles, and transepts: a ground plan entirely new in Ireland. The Irish adapted architectural sculpture to their own tastes. Considerable use was made of chevron, dogtooth, and scalloped capitals, adopted from the Anglo-Normans. Often the capitals do not project from their setting: they are simply areas to be covered with interlace or animal heads, without architectural function. This is found in the Nuns' Church at Clonmacnoise. In the same building several rows of voussoirs are decorated with heads or with animals biting a molding. This motif came from the west of France and was probably seen by Irish pilgrims passing through on their way to Compostella in Spain. Elaborate gabled porches are also quite common, the most striking one being at Clonfert. Here rows of heads are arranged in niches, looking more like a Celtic trophy display than a church entrance.

In the 11th and 12th centuries sculptural crosses reappear after a long break in production. Such Romanesque crosses stand at Roscrea, Kilfenora, Aran, Mona Incha, Cashel, and Dysert O'Dea. Carved mainly in high relief, the usual subjects are the Crucifixion, in which Christ wears a long tubular tunic, and a bishop carrying a crozier. Compared with the figures on earlier crosses, such as Muirdach's cross, the Romanesque ones are stiff and solemn. The Cashel Sarcophagus (c1130; at Cashel, Co. Tipperary) is a fine example of how metalwork designs were transposed to stone. Its long side is decorated with symmetrical fighting beasts deeply cut in the Viking Urnes style. Counterparts in metal may be seen in the Cross of Cong (National Museum, Dublin) and in the Lemanaghan shrine in Boher church, Co. Offaly.

Irish metalwork revived in the 11th century, greatly inspired by Viking styles (see Viking Art). Many of the objects produced bear inscriptions which enable precise dating. Two of the finest *cumdachs* or "book shrines" are the Stowe Missal (1032–52) and the Breac Maodhog (c1050; both in the National Museum, Dublin). The former has small panels of narrative scenes including a stag and hounds and a group of fearsome-looking ecclesiastics. The latter is covered with rows of figures whose hair and garments make rhythmic, wavy patterns over the whole surface. Another group of figures can be seen on the Lemanaghan shrine (1126–36; Boher church, Co. Offaly). Designs on their clothes show they are contemporary with the heavy, bossed Greek cross also on the shrine, which is edged by panels of Urnes-style interlace. The Urnes style was readily adopted by the Irish but they modified it. In Irish hands Urnes animals lose their restless asymmetrical quality and become regular and balanced. The Cross of Cong (1122–7) is a magnificent processional cross plated with bronze and covered with gilt openwork panels. Their designs are completely symmetrical. Metalwork declined in quality as monasteries ceased to be the main centers of patronage. In the late 12th century the Irish even resorted to importing mass-produced Limoges ware, such as the Cashel Crozier (National Museum, Dublin).

Manuscripts of the period are more modest than earlier ones. Illumination tends to be confined to initials with very few full-page illustrations. Initials consist of animals and interlace but the lines lack the metallic precision of earlier work and the interlace is less complicated. Colors are more casually applied although very vivid. Scarlet and purple are frequently combined in books like the Liber Hymnorum (Trinity College Library, Dublin) and the Corpus Missal (Corpus Christi College Library, Oxford). After the conquest Irish scriptoria produced little work in their native style. Most liturgical manuscripts were sent from England or copies were made of foreign models in Ireland.

Although Gothic forms eventually prevailed in Ireland, an undercurrent of Celtic taste lingered in folk art. Nonetheless, the survival of Irish churches throughout Europe serves as a reminder of the great role once played by the Irish in the spread of Christian beliefs and learning.

JANE GEDDES

Bibliography. Bieler, L. *Ireland, Harbinger of the Middle Ages*, London (1963). Cone, P. (ed.) *Treasures of Early Irish Art*, New York (1977). Henry, F. *Irish Art* (3 vols.), London (1965, 1967, 1970). Leask, H.G. *Irish Churches and Monastic Buildings* vol. 1, Dundalk (1955). Paor, M. and L. de *Early Christian Ireland*, London (1961). Porter, A.K. *The Crosses and Culture of Ireland*, New Haven (1931).

22

ANGLO-SAXON ART

The Fuller Brooch; nielloed silver; c850. British Museum, London (see page 409)

THE people we call Anglo-Saxons came to Britain from the area now covered by Denmark, northwestern Germany, and northern Holland. The documentary and archaeological evidence suggests that these men were employed as mercenary soldiers, first by the Romans, and later, after the Roman withdrawal in AD 410, by the Romanized British. By the second half of the 5th century, however, the mercenaries had turned against their British employers and were invading and colonizing the country.

The motive for the invasion was primarily the quest for arable land. The Anglo-Saxons were farmers settling a new frontier, and as such their aims and their way of life can be compared with those of settlers in the 19th-century American West. They would have traveled with their weapons, tools, clothes, and jewelry, but probably little else, and as they advanced inland, overcoming the resistance of the local populations, they would have set up farmsteads and small villages. Clearly, their situation was not yet secure enough for organized artistic production. Furthermore, throughout the medieval period Christianity was the major stimulus to art as we know it in western Europe, and at the time of the invasions the Anglo-Saxons were pagans. The arts of painting, building in stone, monumental sculpture, and book production were developed around the Mediterranean and practiced there in late Roman times. Christianity, initially an eastern Mediterranean cult, adopted them, and it was from the Christian Mediterranean, and particularly from Rome itself, that these various art forms spread. At this earliest, pagan stage, there-fore, we must not expect the Anglo-Saxons to have produced painting and sculpture.

The history of Anglo-Saxon art can be divided into four periods. During the first, the period of invasion and settlement, their art was still closely linked in style and purpose to that of their continental homelands. Contact with native Celtic and Romano-British art, and with Christian art at the time of their conversion, effected a change so that by the late 7th century another distinctive phase had begun. This was arguably the most important phase of Anglo-Saxon art, for not only did the new synthesis of styles dominate artistic production in Britain but it was exported to the continent and had a considerable impact on the art of western Europe as a whole. In the third period the Danish invasion disrupted life in Britain, curtailing important artistic enterprise and destroying many existing buildings and artifacts. Furthermore, the Danish conquest of northern England, the eastern Midlands, and East Anglia meant that in its final phase Anglo-Saxon artistic development was largely confined to the south and west.

As always when studying ancient art, the difficulty of understanding it is complicated by chances of survival. For instance, we know from written sources that there were paintings and cult-images, such as gold and silver statues of the Madonna and Child, in Anglo-Saxon churches and yet not one of these has survived. Anglo-Saxon painting is represented only by manuscript illumination and sculpture of any size only by carving in stone. We necessarily have an incomplete picture of that society's range of artistic accomplishment. An additional problem is raised by the fact that many surviving objects are portable, so there is often no indication when or where they were made. Despite these difficulties, however, sufficient evidence exists to give us some idea of the development of Anglo-Saxon art.

The pagan period (c450–c650). The earliest Anglo-Saxon art known to us is nearly all in the form of jewelry and decorated weapons, which have usually been recovered by excavation. The more fragile materials, wood and textiles for instance, have not survived. Consequently our view of the art of the period may be rather one-sided. Of all the hoards of early Anglo-Saxon art so far recovered, the one excavated at Sutton Hoo in Suffolk, England, is by far the most impressive, and can be taken as representative of the art of the pagan period at its most developed. The finds included a wide range of metal objects, many in a marvelous state of preservation, and nearly all show astonishing technical accomplishment and beauty of design. The objects and the ship in which they were buried were almost certainly the possessions of one man, probably a king. The hoard is usually dated, on the evidence of the coins found with it, to around or shortly before the mid 7th century. Its contents are now in the British Museum, London.

Of the domestic, personal, military, and royal objects found with the Sutton Hoo treasure, the personal jewelry is most significant and helpful. Most of this consists of gold inlaid

Anglo-Saxon England

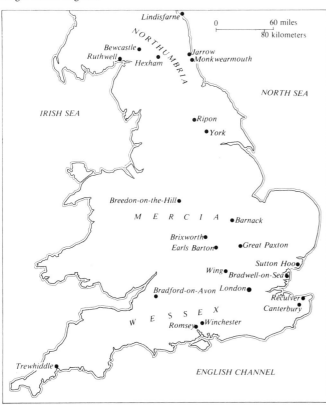

The hinged curved clasps found at Sutton Hoo; mid 7th century. British Museum, London

with intricately cut garnet stones and millefiori glass. Both garnets and glass are set in gold cloisonné cells, and the integration of gold, deep wine red garnets, and white and pale blue glass give a magnificently rich effect. Garnet jewelry seems to have originated with the migrating northern tribes, such as the Longobards, the Franks, and the Anglo-Saxons. In this way it became common throughout western Europe from the 5th century onwards. By the 7th century, regional and to some extent national styles had developed and many of the motifs found at Sutton Hoo were to continue in use in Anglo-Saxon art of the Christian era.

On the curved clasps from Sutton Hoo three particularly important decorative ideas are used together. There are rectangular areas in the centers filled with diagonally disposed garnet and glass inlay with stepped edges. This central area is surrounded by borders of interlaced animals. These have been abstracted and elongated and are only recognized as animals by their heads, which turn back and bite at the mass of intertwining body behind. At the rounded ends of the clasps are two partially superimposed animals, not interlaced as in the borders and of much more naturalistic proportions. Similar animals, birds, biting monsters, and stylized humans are found on the Sutton Hoo purse-lid.

Also from the hoard, and of great importance both in demonstrating the origins and pointing to the future development of art in Britain, are three hanging bowls. The origin of the hanging bowls is disputed, but it is quite clear that the champlevé enamel discs that decorate their rims and centers are Celtic or of Celtic derivation. It is possible that by c600 the Anglo-Saxons had added Celtic spiral patterns to their repertoire, but it is equally likely that they were employing native Celtic craftsmen. "Trumpet" spirals and other spiral and curvilinear patterns had been in use in Britain since before

the Roman conquest, and went on to make their own contribution to the emergence of a remarkable Christian art in the late 7th and 8th centuries.

Christian art in Britain (*c*650–*c*850). Since late Roman times there had been a Christian community in Britain. However, the Celtic Church made little headway in converting the Anglo-Saxon invaders and it was not until 597 with St Augustine's mission to Kent and the roughly contemporary Irish missions to northern England and southern Scotland that the Anglo-Saxons began to take up Christianity. The conversion had enormous artistic significance as well as much wider cultural consequences. It was responsible for introducing books and churches, and hence the arts of writing, painting, and carving and building in stone. Furthermore it broadened the scope of the metalworker because he was now asked to make caskets, shrines, and crosses as well as personal jewelry.

The problems raised by this change in patronage were solved in two ways; firstly by adapting indigenous Anglo-Saxon and Celtic art to a Christian purpose, and secondly by importing Christian art from elsewhere and copying it. It is in manuscript illumination that these developments can best be observed.

The Book of Durrow (Trinity College Library, Dublin), so called because it once belonged to the monastery of Durrow in Ireland, is stylistically the earliest of the surviving decorated books. It contains the four Gospels and was apparently written in Northumbria, although it has been thought to be Irish. Whether English or Irish it may be taken as the starting point of the development of Northumbrian manuscript illumination since the books of Lindisfarne and Echternach, similarly called after their earliest known homes, are clearly in the same tradition.

The Lindisfarne Gospels, the portrait of St Matthew; 698.
British Library, London

The decoration of the Book of Durrow is made up of an Evangelist's symbol, a carpet page, and a set of illuminated initial letters for each of the Gospels, and in addition two extra carpet pages, six decorated canon tables, and a "harmony" page showing the four Evangelists' animals together. The carpet pages are symmetrically patterned with abstract motifs giving an impression rather similar to a carpet or mosaic floor, and are included purely to enrich the manuscript. They owe a great deal in overall design to metalwork such as the Sutton Hoo clasps or the Celtic spiral plaques, and they were doubtless intended to have a similar effect. The individual symbols of the Evangelists—Mark's is the lion, John's the eagle, Luke's the ox, and Matthew's a man—are also given a whole page each. They are abstracted in the same way as the animals and humans on the Sutton Hoo purse-lid, where outlines are simplified and emphasis laid on pattern, especially on the heads and around leg joints. The decoration of the opening words of the Gospels is almost entirely done with Celtic spirals. This method of beginning a text was learned from the Irish missionaries in Northumbria. The diminishing size of the letters in the opening words and the spiral forms can be found in earlier Irish books such as the Psalter called the *Cathach* of St

Columba (Royal Irish Academy, Dublin).

The Lindisfarne Gospels (British Library, London), written and illuminated in 698, is a much richer book. It has many more painted initials and pages of canon tables than Durrow, and includes portraits of the Evangelists, each shown with his symbol. Furthermore, the illuminated opening words of each Gospel are much larger and now take up a whole page. There is also a far greater variety of motif, minuteness of design, and skill in execution than in Durrow. This is particularly noticeable in the carpet pages which have much thinner and more intricate interlace and are painted in a far wider range of colors.

Perhaps the most important aspect of the Lindisfarne Gospels, however, is the evidence they give of artistic contacts with the Mediterranean. This can be seen most clearly in the portraits of the Evangelists. We know from written records that large numbers of Italian books, paintings, and other church furnishings were brought to Northumbria by Benedict Biscop, Abbot Ceolfrith, and St Wilfrid. One of the books acquired by Ceolfrith was the Codex Grandior of Cassiodorus. This was a south Italian Bible written and illuminated in the 6th century. Its decoration was copied in Monkwearmouth or Jarrow, *c*700, in a huge and magnificent Bible known as the Codex Amiatinus (Biblioteca Laurenziana, Florence). One of Cassiodorus' miniatures, the picture of the scribe Ezra, also served as the model for the portrait of the Evangelist Matthew in the Lindisfarne Gospels. Indeed, the whole idea of the author portrait was Mediterranean, and must have been introduced through such Italian books as the Codex Grandior.

Thus by 700 various traditions were available in Northumbria: Irish, Celtic, Anglo-Saxon represented by the books of Durrow and Echternach; the purely Mediterranean tradition by the Codex Amiatinus. The various styles and ideas merged in hybrid manuscripts, such as the Lindisfarne Gospels. Not surprisingly the range of alternatives was very similar in sculpture and metalwork. Like the book, the whole idea of monumental stone sculpture was Mediterranean. However, the main form on which sculpture was used as decoration, the freestanding stone cross, was probably an indigenous development. The two greatest surviving Northumbrian stone crosses, those at Ruthwell and Bewcastle, were probably carved in the last quarter of the 7th century. The Ruthwell Cross is almost complete and stands over 15 ft (4.5 m) high. It is carved on both front and back with figures set in framed panels, and on the sides with an uninterrupted vine-scroll inhabited by birds and animals. It has inscriptions in both Anglo-Saxon runes and Latin. The figure scenes represent a curious selection of subjects. These include the hermit saints, Paul and Anthony, being fed by ravens in the desert, Christ triumphing over the beasts, Mary Magdalene wiping Christ's feet. This iconography seems to extol the virtues of the desert monasticism of the

Right: The Lindisfarne Gospels, a carpet page; 698. British Library, London

The Ruthwell Cross, a panel showing Christ triumphing over the beasts; c675–700. Ruthwell, Dumfries and Galloway

Coptic and Irish Churches; the style, however, is very classical. The beautifully proportioned figures are carved in high relief and clearly reflect Roman or Romano-British sculpture. The vine-scroll too is classical in origin but seems, in this case, to have been influenced by the more stylized plant forms current in Near Eastern art of the 6th and 7th centuries. As with the figure sculpture, it is difficult to find exact parallels, and it is obvious that whoever carved the cross was not making a slavish copy of an antique work but was a creative artist using, but modifying, older ideas. As in so many Anglo-Saxon

works of art, there is here a simplified beauty of outline which gives both grace and strength to the decoration.

The Bewcastle Cross is similar in general layout and style, but figure scenes are limited to the front of the shaft. On the back there is vine-scroll decoration supplemented with interlace on the sides. The carving is in shallower relief yet it still has the grandeur of the Ruthwell Cross. Here we see the fusion of Mediterranean figure-style and Insular interlace so evident in the Lindisfarne Gospels.

However, the most remarkable monument to the interplay of different cultures is the Franks Casket (British Museum, London). A box about 9 in (23 cm) long, it appears, from the evidence of its inscriptions, to have come from northeastern England. It is made of whalebone plaques carved with such diverse subjects as Wayland the Smith murdering King Nithad's son, Titus capturing Jerusalem, and the Adoration of the Magi. Such enthusiastic eclecticism is typical of the Northumbrian Renaissance and is its greatest contribution to the history of European culture, for it preserved for the future so much of the classical past and gave a completely unexpected impetus to Christian art and literature in northern Europe.

Eighth-century art at Canterbury where St Augustine established his archbishopric is represented by two manuscripts, one a Gospel Book now in Stockholm (Royal Library), known as the Codex Aureus, and the other a book of Psalms in the British Library, London, often referred to as the Vespasian Psalter. Their illumination is rather different in style from the Northumbrian examples. David and his musicians in the Vespasian Psalter and the Evangelists in the Codex Aureus are not shown silhouetted against the white of the page but are provided with background colors. These, in two or three broad bands, leave no white page showing and have a rather heavy effect. The figures, especially their draperies, are far more solidly modeled and there is some use of shading. But the modeling is largely achieved by painting the folds and outlines with a thick dark line. This represents the most sculptural figure-style that Anglo-Saxon painting ever attained. In many ways it is rather ponderous, and even the decoration, in the form of the usual Celtic spirals and interlace, is less exciting than earlier northern work. Part of the reason for these differences is to be found in the models available for copying. A Gospel Book now in Cambridge (Corpus Christi College Library) appears to have been given by Pope Gregory to St Augustine for his mission to Kent. It has been shown that this late-6th-century Italian book had a lasting effect on art at Canterbury, and it certainly influenced the layout of the author portraits in the Codex Aureus, where the symbols appear in lunettes over the frontally seated Evangelists. It is also clear from certain palmette and foliage forms that art of ultimately eastern Mediterranean origin was available in Kent.

The Reculver Cross, whose surviving fragments are now in Canterbury Cathedral, is the only outstanding sculpture to survive in southeastern England from this period. Opinions

Right: The Vespasian Psalter, David and his Musicians; c750. British Library, London

about its date vary from the 7th to the 9th century and this may indeed indicate that the pieces are not all from a single object or made at one time. However, the styles are recognizably from the earlier phase of Anglo-Saxon art and show certain similarities with both Mercian and Northumbrian sculptures. Some of the fragments show in modified form the tip-toe stance and bent knees of Mercian sculpture while in others the draperies are far more organized and have the classic solidity of Northumbria.

No doubt some of the splendid decorated books surviving from the period 750–850 are Mercian but unfortunately there are no sure grounds for saying which they are. Consequently it is safest to attempt a definition of Mercian art with reference to sculpture. The largest collection of this is to be found in the church of Breedon-on-the-Hill in Leicestershire, and probably dates from the late 8th or early 9th century, making it about 100 years later than the Northumbrian crosses. The carving is much livelier than the Ruthwell and Bewcastle crosses but has less monumental power and purity of line. There is a great sense of movement particularly on the remains of a small-scale frieze, about 8 in (20 cm) high, where fantastic animals, birds, and humans intertwine with plants and scrollwork. The designs are asymmetrical and have a playful inventiveness quite unlike northern sculpture. In addition to these decorative reliefs there are several panels, at Breedon, and at Fletton and Castor in Northamptonshire, that have standing and half-length figures under arches. In contrast to the restrained figures of Ruthwell these dance on their toes and gesticulate with long thin fingers. They have an air of refinement and mannered elegance which shows that quite new effects were being sought and suggests that a courtly aesthetic was now more appropriate than the heroic grandeur so evident in Northumbria c700.

It is not certain, however, that the characteristics of this sculpture reflect Mercian taste rather than being generally symptomatic of earlier Anglo-Saxon art in its latest phase.

The silver Ormside Bowl, a detail showing the repoussé decoration; c800(?). Yorkshire Museum, York

Thus when confronted with the beautiful repoussé silver Ormside Bowl (Yorkshire Museum, York), which has much of the liveliness of the Breedon sculpture, it is hard to decide whether it is actually Mercian or simply Anglo Saxon dating from c800. Exactly the same problem arises with lavishly painted and decorated books, such as the so-called Barberini Gospels (Vatican Library, Rome). In its initial letters it uses curious little fantastic animals reminiscent of the Breedon frieze but it is far from certain that this similarity indicates proximity of place of origin rather than simply contemporary manufacture. Clearly this problem arises because books and small precious objects were easily carried and because only a tiny, random selection of work has survived. However, as well as merely serving as an uncomfortable reminder of how little we really know, it may also indicate that although there were differences, for example between Northumbrian and Kentish art, Anglo-Saxon production as a whole often showed considerable uniformity of style and motif.

No early secular architecture survives above ground. All we know about Anglo-Saxon houses and halls comes from descriptions in early literature and from modern excavations. So although ground plans of timber buildings can be recovered we seldom have information about numbers of stories or designs of doors and windows. Happily the situation is not quite so obscure in the case of church building. With the introduction of Christianity stone building was reintroduced to England for the first time since the collapse of Romano-British civilization and fairly substantial fragments have come down to us. The 7th- and 8th-century churches fall into two geographical groups, northern and southern, and although, as in the case of manuscript painting, there were differences between them, they nonetheless had fairly similar plans and used the same range of ideas. Basically, an early Anglo-Saxon church consisted of a high rectangular room for the nave, with a chancel probably about half the size of the nave to the east. To north and south of this high central structure were small rooms called both collectively and in the singular *porticus*. We know that important people were buried in them, for instance St Augustine and King Ethelbert in the church of St Peter and St Paul in Canterbury, but perhaps they were more normally used as small chapels for private prayer. Access to these *porticus* was from the body of the church through small doorways. The main door to the church was usually at the west end and either had a covered porch or else was set in the base of a western tower. The buildings were small in scale, the nave seldom exceeded 60 ft by 40 ft (18 m by 12 m) and there would usually be three or four *porticus* along either side.

Of the southern churches only Bradwell-on-Sea in Essex has substantial surviving walls. Although, properly speaking, only the nave remains, scars of the lost *porticus* walls and the western porch can be seen and both their height and position can be reconstructed. In the eastern wall remnants of a triple

Right: A rare example of Mercian sculpture, the stone Madonna in the church at Breedon-on-the-Hill, Leicestershire; late 8th/early 9th century

arcade which formed a screen separating the nave from the chancel can also be seen. A few, small windows were set in the nave walls above the roofs of the surrounding *porticus*. We encounter the triple arcade used as a chancel screen at Reculver and apparently at Brixworth in Northamptonshire; both these churches had an apse at the east end. Unfortunately the eastern arrangement at Bradwell is not clear. The church at Brixworth is complete except for the loss of its *porticus* and the removal of the triple arcade. As at Bradwell-on-Sea, Roman building material was reused. The *porticus* at Brixworth were linked to each other by doorways, giving the impression of embryonic aisles on either side of the nave. At the west was a tower of two stories flanked by two high *porticus*. The purpose of this elaborate structure is unknown but a great deal of trouble was obviously taken over it.

Little survives of the churches built by St Wilfrid at Ripon, York, and Hexham, but descriptions indicate that one of the churches at Hexham had colonnaded aisles. Ripon, however, apparently had the normal arrangement with *porticus*, and both Ripon and Hexham had eastern crypts, the only parts of the original churches still in existence. At Jarrow and Monkwearmouth there are remains of Benedict Biscop's twin monasteries. Particularly impressive is the tower at Monkwearmouth. Like Brixworth it has two stories, the lower of which here forms an entrance porch with a barrel vault and turned baluster shafts supporting the arches. Practically nothing remains of the early monastic building at Monkwearmouth or Jarrow, or indeed of any of the other churches we have discussed so far. However, excavations indicate large stone halls, presumably the refectory, dormitory, and chapterhouse to the south. Here they were not grouped in a square about a cloister like later conventual buildings. Rather, at Jarrow, which is probably the later of the two, they formed a long line running parallel to the church.

The Danish incursions (c850–c950). The period c800 saw two important historical developments. One was the emergence of the powerful expansionist Frankish Empire under Charlemagne which led to an important revival in the arts, the Carolingian Renaissance or *renovatio* as it was called at the time. The second factor, one with more direct and immediate effect upon the Anglo-Saxons, was the beginning of Danish raids which threatened security of life and property throughout the coastal areas of western Europe. Monasteries and churches with their rich collections of gold and silver furnishings, their books and tapestries, were easy prey to Danish raiders, and had not Anglo-Saxon books and metalwork been exported to the Continent even less early English culture would have survived.

Fortunately, due to the missionary activity of such Anglo-Saxon saints as St Boniface and St Willibrord in Germany and the Netherlands, a certain number of works did travel abroad,

and some of them, the Book of Echternach for instance, still exist (the latter in the Bibliothèque Nationale, Paris). Of even greater general importance was Charlemagne's employment of Alcuin of York as principal scholar and cultural adviser to the Frankish court, for through him much of the literature and learning salvaged by the English from Italy passed back to the Continent before England herself suffered at the hands of the barbarian invaders.

Although English society was badly dislocated by the Danish attacks, artistic production did not altogether stop. But only the jewelers seem to have produced work throughout this troubled time. Again, we have no precisely dated examples, but the Trewhiddle Hoard from Cornwall seems to have been buried c875. The style of this treasure is best characterized as derivative of late Mercian art. The majority of the pieces, now in the British Museum, London, were made of nielloed silver, apparently a favorite technique of the period. Also of nielloed silver and in a similar style is the Fuller Brooch, in the British Museum, London. The figures on the brooch confirm the impression given by the interlaced animals that the style derived from earlier Anglo-Saxon art.

The late 870s were to prove decisive for the survival of Anglo-Saxon England. The Danes came within an ace of conquering the whole of the country and it was only a brilliant rearguard action by Alfred the Great, King of Wessex, that averted total domination. The turning point was Alfred's victory at Edington in 878. In culture too Alfred's reign proved to be something of a turning point. The King was a dedicated educationalist and personally translated important Christian texts, such as Pope Gregory's *Pastoral Care* and St Augustine's *Soliloquies*, from Latin into English to make them accessible to a wider audience. The resulting manuscripts were not lavishly decorated, but the few initials in them give evidence of a change of interest from the abstract interlace of earlier years to a primitive foliage which was to grow in size and quality in succeeding generations.

King Alfred died in 899 having reestablished Anglo-Saxon rule in at least a large area of England. With this greater security people once again began to produce luxury objects, though this did not properly develop until the second half of the 10th century. But by the second decade it was already apparent that in Wessex at least a change of style and artistic allegiance had occurred. The two principal items of evidence for this are a stole and maniple, embroidered at Winchester between 909 and 916 and later presented to the shrine of St Cuthbert, and some small illuminations added to a Psalter, probably during the reign of King Athelstan (924–39). Both these objects indicate artistic links with the Carolingian Empire. More particularly the foliage and the figure-style seem to derive from the illuminations in manuscripts of the Court School of Charlemagne, such as the Soissons Gospels (Bibliothèque Nationale, Paris). On the other hand the iconography of two of the scenes in the Psalter is ultimately Byzantine and we cannot rule out the possibility of stylistic influences from that source. As yet English work did not dis-

The north porticus of the church of St Lawrence, Bradford-on-Avon, Wiltshire; late 10th century (see page 413)

The Winchester Style

In the mid 870s the Danish invaders came very close to conquering England. However, Alfred the Great, King of Wessex, defeated them and he and his successors became sole kings of the Anglo-Saxon peoples. Winchester, the ancestral capital of his dynasty, became the virtual capital of England, and such evidence as we have suggests that the major artistic recovery of the 10th century was based there.

An embroidered stole and maniple, later presented at the shrine of St Cuthbert by King Athelstan, was originally made for Frithstan, Bishop of Winchester, by order of Queen Aelfleda between 909 and 916 (now in the Monk's Dormitory Museum,

Durham). In its figure-style it contains the germ of much to come, as a comparison with a drawing made about 40 years later will show (Bodleian Library, Oxford; MS. Auct. F.4.32). Both are essentially linear, but St Dunstan's drawing has developed the extent to which hem lines flutter and folds flick up around the feet. The end of the prophet Hosea's cloak merely hangs below the hand holding his book, while Christ, in the drawing, has a flying band of drapery curving into space behind him.

The classical apogee of this style is the book of benedictions made for Ethelwold, Bishop of Winchester (British Library, London). It almost certainly dates from the 970s and shows a fully painted and even more animated version of the earlier art of Winchester. The calligraphers' interest in swirling cloud and frilly edges is supplemented here by a grand use of gold and color on a scale unknown in English painting for nearly 200 years.

Although expensive pigment and gold were available, the English retained their affection for drawing, though outlines were often in several different colors. Even the

▲ King Cnut and Aelfgyfu present a gold cross to the New Minster at Winchester; c1031? A drawing in Stowe MS. 944, British Library, London

◄ The Annunciation, from the Ethelwold Benedictional; c973. British Library, London

Far left The Prophet Hosea, a detail from the embroidered stole made for Bishop Frithstan of Winchester; c909–16. Monks' Dormitory Museum, Durham

◀ The Crucifixion, the frontispiece of a Psalter, Harley MS. 2904; c980. British Library, London

▶ Christ in Majesty, an illumination from the Trinity Gospels. Trinity College Library, Cambridge

Below right Monks presenting a book to St Benedict; c1020. An illumination in Arundel MS. 155, British Library, London

▼ St Matthew, an illuminated page from the Grimbald Gospels; c1030. British Library, London

...rge-scale frontispiece of a splendid manu-...ript such as the Harley Psalter (British ...ibrary, London) might be drawn. Here the ...sual zigzag hems are combined with a new ...yle of broken outline, particularly apparent ...n the Virgin Mary's cloak. This method of ...rawing derives from the Utrecht Psalter, a ...ook made near Reims in France c830 (Uni-...ersity Library, Utrecht). The Virgin's pose, ...er large head and shoulders set on a taper-...g body, also comes from the Carolingian ...ork. The emotional effect of the rapid ...enwork is clearly apparent.

The Winchester style traveled through ...ost of England in the wake of the reformed ...onasticism of the later 10th century, so it is ...ot certain where the Harley Psalter, for ...xample, was made. By soon after 1000, ...hough, Canterbury had become an impor-...nt artistic center, producing such works as ...e Trinity Gospels (Trinity College Library, ...ambridge), whose lavish foliage is paral-...led in other media, notably ivory carving ...ke the beautiful staff top found in Warwick-...ire.

Although the style was widely dissemi-...ated it does not seem to have broken down ...to a series of local variants. One possible ...eason for this would be the unifying in-...uence of court patronage. King Cnut was a ...onsiderable benefactor and among his many ...recious gifts to churches was a gold cross ...onated to the New Minster at Winchester ...British Museum, London). The drawing ...ade at Winchester showing the presenta-...on is close in style to a contemporary ...anterbury illumination of monks presenting ... book to St Benedict. Both of these pictures ...re in books written by monks, the former by ...elsinus of Winchester, the latter by Edwi of ...anterbury, and one would have supposed ...ach community to have been artistically self-

sufficient (both books in the British Library, London). However, the Canterbury monk Edwi wrote part of a book known as the Grimbald Gospels (British Library) which was at Winchester within a few years. The pattern of patronage and artistic interchange is therefore quite complicated and though the details are not clear, it helps explain the homogeneity of the style, which although no longer based exclusively in Winchester, was formed there during the 10th century.

T.A. HESLOP

Further reading. Beckwith, J. *Ivory Carvings in Early Medieval England*, London (1972). Deshman, R. "Anglo-Saxon Art after Alfred" *Art Bulletin* vol. LVI, (1974) pp176–200. Temple, E. *Anglo-Saxon Manuscripts 900–1066*, London (1966). Wormald, F. *English Drawings of the Tenth and Eleventh Centuries*, London (1952). Wormald, F. "The Winchester School before Ethelwold" in Clemoes, P. and Hughes, K. (eds.) *England before the Conquest*, Cambridge (1971).

play the freedom in handling or the breadth of conception of its Continental prototypes: memories remain of the rather deliberately linear Anglo-Saxon art of the 8th century. Nevertheless there was a considerable relaxation of line, and this is as obvious in the acanthus foliage as it is in the drapery.

From now on acanthus foliage, a fleshy plant form ultimately of classical origin which passed from the early Christian era into Carolingian art and thence to England, was to be the dominant decorative motif, replacing almost totally interlace and vine-scroll. Equally, certain trends in drapery style, such as fluttering hems, which were to develop much further in the succeeding decades, were seen in embryo in the figure art of the early 10th century. Thus, despite their apparent simplicity, the stole and maniple and the Psalter contain in essence the germs of later Anglo-Saxon styles.

The Monastic Reform to the Norman Conquest (c960–1066). The greatest impetus to the revival of art in England in the second half of the 10th century was provided by the monastic reforms of St Dunstan, Archbishop of Canterbury from 960, St Ethelwold, Bishop of Winchester, and St Oswald, Bishop of Worcester and Archbishop of York. The ravages of the Norsemen made it necessary to restock libraries and replace service books and church furnishings that had been taken as plunder.

We know that St Dunstan was a considerable artist himself, and a drawing of him at the feet of Christ, now in Oxford (Bodleian Library), was apparently the work of the Saint. It probably dates from the 950s and is related in style to the Cuthbert Stole and the Athelstan Psalter, although its greater monumentality and its success in conveying a sense of the roundness of bodily forms seem to indicate that the influence from the Court School of Charlemagne had now been more thoroughly assimilated. However it is not this style, sometimes called the "Quiet style" that is normally associated with the period of the monastic reform.

A great change came over Anglo-Saxon drawing in particular in the last quarter of the 10th century and this can be largely explained as the result of influence from Carolingian drawing of the Reims School. We know that the finest representative of Reims drawing, the so-called Utrecht Psalter (University Library, Utrecht), written and illustrated in northeastern France c830, was at Canterbury by c1000. At that time it was copied, with remarkable accuracy, by Anglo-Saxon artists. However, its influence may be seen even earlier in a drawing of Christ on the Cross between Mary and John which occurs at the beginning of a Psalter now in the British Library, London. This drawing, in red, blue, and brown outline, was perhaps originally made c980 for a monastery in the East Anglian fens. The large hunched shoulders of the Virgin Mary and her tapering body balanced on diminutive feet were clearly derived from the Reims manuscript. However, the most important effect of the Utrecht Psalter in terms of the future development of Anglo-Saxon art lay in the change that it has brought about in the making of pen lines. Whereas in

The Ethelwold Benedictional, the Adoration of the Magi; c973. British Library, London

the drawing of Christ with St Dunstan the figures have a continuous outline of graceful curves, in the crucifixion drawing a broken series of agitated lines *suggests* rather than *defines* the limits of the figures. The lively penwork, which in the Utrecht Psalter so wonderfully conveys form and movement, is here used, by subtle change of emphasis, for largely expressive purposes. The fluttering hemlines, the poignant faces, and the tenderly and powerfully conceived poses were the legacy of the Reims style but they have been transformed by an artist who has realized their emotional potential.

It is far harder to assess the influence of this new expressive style on painting. The seminal work for understanding the development of Anglo-Saxon painting in its last hundred years is a manuscript, a Benedictional, made c973 for Ethelwold, Bishop of Winchester (now in the British Library, London). It is sumptuously decorated with full-page pictures surrounded with lavish acanthus borders. Gold is profusely used throughout, and the coloring is a wonderful combination of richness and delicate pastel shades. Some of the colors were applied opaquely and others in bold washes. Indeed the development of a "watercolor" school of painting in England, using transparent washes over a white ground to give luminosity and depth to the scene, started with the Anglo-Saxons. Many of the illuminations of the later Anglo-Saxon period were little more than "washed" drawings and both on them and on others where opaque paint was used, details such as drapery folds tended to be painted on afterwards in line. This use of white and black line for highlighting and shading a colored area obviously approximated to drawing and the net result has the same ethereal, emotional quality so apparent in the crucifixion drawing influenced by the Utrecht Psalter.

However, of itself this does not prove it was the Utrecht Psalter that affected late Anglo-Saxon painting. One reason for caution is that the iconography of several of the Benedictional's narrative scenes was copied directly from a manuscript of the Carolingian Metz School, which is now unfortunately lost so we can have no clear idea about its date or style. But its impact on the iconography was so strong that it would be foolhardy to ignore its possible stylistic effects. The other reason for caution is that the method of representing relief by means of light and dark lines had been used since at least the early 10th century, for example in the initials of a Psalter now in Oxford (Bodleian Library; MS. Junius 27), and the Benedictional simply represents a development from this.

Because several of the most important representatives of late Anglo-Saxon illuminated books have associations with Winchester, the style as a whole is often referred to as the Winchester style. Although this is misleading, since at least Canterbury among the large English monasteries of the period produced important decorated books, it is a convenient and by now time-honored way of referring to the art of the century before the Norman Conquest. The Winchester style may be defined above all by its use of agitated line for expressive effect; and if we so define it then it is easy to see that it did not stop with the Conquest but remained an important ingredient of English art until the middle of the 12th century.

Although elements of the Winchester style's character survived for 200 years their emphasis changed. By the mid 11th century two divergent streams appeared. One, represented by two Gospel books made for Judith of Flanders and now in New York (Pierpont Morgan Library), was a very mannered version of the agitated style, using attenuated figures and exaggerated gestures; the other was a hard, sometimes angular version which in its organization and interest in pattern-making was the English equivalent of the early Romanesque styles emerging on the continent. A good example of this is the crucifixion drawing in a Psalter in the British Library, London (MS. Arundel 60). As one might expect, the flickering, linear Winchester style was difficult to adapt to large-scale sculpture, and the result was that the "Quiet style", or at least a quiet version of the Winchester style, predominated. The loincloth of Christ on the large stone Romsey rood at Romsey Abbey in Hampshire shows none of the agitation of the Ethelwold Benedictional. Similarly, his upright figure lacks the sinuous outline of contemporary figure painting. In ivory carving the situation was rather different. The Winchester style was suitable for small-scale works, and ivories represent some of the most beautiful and certainly the best-preserved sculpture to survive, for instance the Virgin and St John now in the Musée Hôtel Sandelin, St-Omer.

No important late Anglo-Saxon architecture, such as a

The Winchester style: David playing his harp, a folio from a Winchester psalter of c 1060, MS. Tiberius CVI, British Library, London

cathedral or major abbey, has survived. For knowledge of large-scale building we are dependent upon contemporary descriptions, and in many cases the interpretation of these is so difficult as to provide little unequivocal information. However, several smaller churches or parts of them exist, giving some idea of the range of styles and motifs and techniques favored by the late Anglo-Saxon builder. At Earls Barton and Barnack there are western towers on which one can see eccentric and rather rustic articulation, known as strip-work, which is associated with late Anglo-Saxon architecture. This decoration no doubt originated in timber buildings, some of the projecting stones at Earls Barton being visual substitutes for the structural timbers of a wooden church. The small church of St Lawrence at Bradford-on-Avon in Wiltshire, however, which seems to date from the second half of the 10th century, is rather different. Rather than the basic rendered cement-and-rubble walling of Earls Barton it uses large, well-squared blocks of stone. Its whole effect is one of precision. It has low-relief blind arcading of a convincingly geometrical appearance rather than picturesque, erratic strip-work. This is important because it shows that English masons were quite capable of careful design and stone-cutting, and it raises the question whether the apparently rustic style of Earls Barton might not be deliberately contrived for aesthetic effect rather than simply showing a low level of competence.

From the patchy and often ambiguous archaeological and documentary evidence we can only speculate about the appearance of most of the buildings. This is particularly true at this period because many, if not the majority, were built of wood and practically all trace of them has vanished. The stone churches do show some variety. Although most kept to the simple rectangular box nave, Wing in Buckinghamshire and Great Paxton in Huntingdonshire had aisles. There also seems to have been a development in the building of complex western blocks, for which continental parallels can be found. On the other hand, as early as the eastern church at Jarrow of the late 7th century, there is evidence for a raised western gallery which may show that the genesis of the storied western element was in part English. One feature which did come to England from the Continent was the transept. To some extent this cross arm of the church can, in Anglo-Saxon England, be regarded as two large *porticus* flanking the junction of the nave and chancel. However, we can legitimately ask why the *porticus* had been enlarged and correspondingly why the arches leading into it had grown from small doorways to grand openings? The easy answer is influence from abroad, but until we know more about the function of these areas it would be dangerous to be too categorical about their introduction and development.

Despite these tendencies to open out the interior of the church, to enlarge openings and increase the sense of spatial play by means of moldings, late Anglo-Saxon architecture seems to have retained much of the *porticus* mentality, with its liking for small rooms leading off a central space. The Anglo-Saxons revered their ancient churches and would preserve and enlarge a venerable structure, perhaps by linking it with other small buildings, rather than knock it down and start again. The result was churches with piecemeal additions and *ad hoc* solutions which can rarely have presented a unified architectural composition. This must have given to many important ecclesiastical buildings, such as the Old Minster at Winchester and St Augustine's at Canterbury, an endearingly eccentric appearance.

The Norman Conquest transformed architecture in England out of all recognition. A great deal was demolished, and large, impressive, organized buildings, such as Durham Cathedral and the Tower of London, replaced the pleasantly amateurish structures of the Anglo-Saxons. The Normans also introduced architectural sculpture as practiced on the Continent. Anglo-Saxon sculpture, when it decorated buildings, was seldom integrated with the architecture. Norman sculpture on the other hand was strictly architectural from the start and largely confined to the decoration of capitals and archways. The same transformation did not occur in the other arts, however. Norman manuscript illumination and metalwork were essentially offshoots of the Winchester School style, so that in conquering England they did little more than bring the style back home. The Bayeux Tapestry at Bayeux Cathedral, almost certainly an Anglo-Saxon work, postdates the conquest, and yet is completely within the old tradition.

When reviewing any ancient art we must be constantly aware of appalling losses. This is especially true of Anglo-Saxon art. We have only one minute fragment of wall-painting where once there must have been literally acres. Similarly, for every piece of metalwork that remains thousands have been melted down to pay debts or taxes, or taken away as booty. The amazing richness of the few objects that do survive gives us a hint of what the Anglo-Saxons achieved. Certainly if one heeds the praise of their continental contemporaries it is apparent that the art of the Anglo-Saxons was held in very high regard indeed.

T.A. HESLOP

Bibliography. Alexander, J.J.G. *Insular Manuscripts from the Sixth to the Ninth Century*, London (1978). Beckwith, J. *Ivory Carvings in Early Medieval England*, London (1972). Bruce-Mitford, R.L.S. "The Reception by the Anglo-Saxons of Mediterranean Art following their Conversion from Ireland and Rome" in *La Conversione al Cristianesimo nell'Europa dell'Alto Medioevo*, Spoleto (1967). Clapham, A.W. *English Romanesque Architecture before the Conquest*, Oxford (1930). Kendrick, T.D. *Anglo-Saxon Art to AD 900*, London (1938). Kendrick, T.D. *Late Saxon and Viking Art*, London (1949). Nordenfalk, C. *Celtic and Anglo-Saxon Painting*, London (1977). Stone, L. *Sculpture in Britain in the Middle Ages*, Harmondsworth (1972). Taylor, H.M. and Joan *Anglo-Saxon Architecture* (3 vols.), Cambridge (vols. 1 and 2 1965; vol. 3 1978). Temple, E. *Anglo-Saxon Manuscripts 900–1066*, London (1976). Wilson, D.M. *Anglo-Saxon Ornamental Metalwork 700–1100 in the British Museum*, London (1964). Wormald, F. *The Miniatures in the Gospels of St Augustine*, Cambridge (1954). Wormald, F. *English Drawings of the Tenth and Eleventh Centuries*, London (1952).

23

VIKING ART

A slab with Ringerike-style beast and snake carved in low relief; c1016–35. Museum of London (see page 422)

FOR the inhabitants of Scandinavia the Viking age was a period of rapid expansion, a period which lasted from the 9th to the mid 11th century. For piracy, trade, and colonization the Vikings traveled from Russia to Byzantium, from Iceland to Gibraltar. At the beginning of the 9th century factors both inside and beyond Scandinavia made the expansion possible. Firstly, the population of Scandinavia rose and in the savage climate it only needed a few extra mouths to feed for small farms to become overcrowded. At the same time, the Viking ocean-going ship, the *knorr*, had reached a high stage of technical development which enabled men to sail to the Mediterranean and across the Atlantic. Secondly, the break-up of Charlemagne's empire and political disorders in the British Isles left a power vacuum which the Vikings were quick to exploit. Although they seldom missed the opportunity to raid a monastery or a town, the Vikings also had peaceful motives for travel. The Swedes conducted a profitable trade with eastern Europe and even with Asia Minor, moving up and down the Volga and Dnieper rivers. This accounts for the large amounts of Arabic silver found in eastern Swedish hoards. The Norwegians left their homes to settle around the north Atlantic, on the Scottish islands, Iceland, Greenland, and even, for a short while, in north America. They established themselves in Ireland, on the Isle of Man, and in northwest England: the fusions of cultures which occurred in these areas were to have important artistic results. On the other hand, the conquest of Normandy by the Norwegian or Danish Rollo, in 911, had practically no artistic effects on Viking styles. The Danes concentrated their activities on the northern part of the Holy Roman Empire and on eastern England. Here they were granted the Danelaw by King Alfred in 878 and under King Canute (reigned 1017–35) created the joint kingdom of England and Denmark.

Religion, rather than political conditions or commercial activity, had the greatest effect on Viking art. In the 9th century Scandinavia was pagan land, its inhabitants worshiping such gods as Odin, Thor, and Frey. They frequently, though not consistently, practised inhumation, burying their dead along with a wide variety of grave goods. A ship, either real or symbolic, was often associated with the grave, to carry a dead person on his spiritual journey. Unfortunately for archaeologists, the advent of Christianity brought an end to burial with possessions, but the Vikings continued to bury hoards of gold and silver.

Christianity made progress in Scandinavia for a variety of reasons, including the missionary efforts of such priests as Ansgar and Poppo, and the political ambitions of kings. Thus the attempts to convert Norway by King Olaf (the Saint) were closely linked to his desire to become sole ruler of the country. Denmark was converted under King Harold Bluetooth (c980); Norway with the help of Anglo-Saxon missionaries during the 11th and 12th centuries; and Sweden, finally, in the late 12th century.

Viking art can be divided into several distinct styles. They often overlap chronologically and so cannot be used for accurate dating, but they are useful when analyzing the content of a design. The styles take their names from the find-places of important objects. The approximate dates given to styles below are deduced from coins or from inscriptions that occasionally accompany finds.

Viking art is based on the abstract animal forms which flourished in northern Europe from the period of migration (cAD 400) onwards. The animal style consisted of contorted writhing snakes and beasts whose actual shape is often barely recognizable (see Steppe Art). Such designs were almost entirely devoid of plant ornament and were most frequently applied to objects in daily use, for example swords, bridles, and buckles. Some representational art is found on carved stones, but probably more once existed on tapestries or wooden carvings.

Most Viking buildings were made of wood and earth, and as such have mainly disappeared. However, excavations of the Danish military camps at Trelleborg and Fyrkat show that the Vikings could design settlements with mathematical precision. Houses themselves were long and low, with slightly convex walls made of posts and planks. They were buttressed by an additional row of inclined posts around the outside of the walls. Little is known about the architecture of the Vikings' shrines and temples.

The earliest Viking art emerged without a break from the traditions of the Migration period and is found, executed to an exceptionally high standard, on objects from the Oseberg ship burial (now in the University Museum of Northern Antiquities, Oslo). The grave at Oseberg in Norway (on the west side of Oslo fjord) was made some time between 800 and 850 for an important lady, perhaps a queen. She was buried with

Important places mentioned in the text

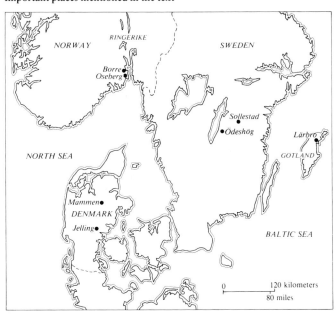

Right: A carved funerary stone from Gotland; 8th century.
State Historical Museum, Stockholm

The Oseberg Ship Burial

The Oseberg ship (University Museum of Northern Antiquities, Oslo) was discovered beneath an airtight burial mound of clay and peat beside the Oslo fjord. Although grave robbers had looted all the valuable jewels from the two female bodies buried with the boat, the soil condition had preserved a unique treasure of organic material. For the voyage of death the boat was loaded with a precious cargo of carts and sledges, kitchen equipment, weaving looms for the ladies, and a pile of cushions, quilts, and tapestries. The boat, built c AD 800, is the earliest sailing ship found in the north, but it is also fitted with 15 pairs of oars. Its sinuous shape and flexibility on the waves justified the names of Serpent and Dragon given to many Viking ships. On the prow and stern are panels carved with grotesque creatures like old men with long beards and fat thighs, gripping each other in every conceivable position.

The function of the animal-head posts is not fully understood. Their ferocious expression and, in one case, a bristly studding of silver nails, suggest they were to deter evil spirits. Their design ranges from the cool restraint of the so-called Academician's post to the stifling surfaces crammed with animals on another post. The fact that such varied styles were being produced, presumably at the same place and time, suggests there was a team of highly individual craftsmen being sponsored by a cultured, eclectic patron on the Oslo fjord.

Above The Oseberg ship, as reconstructed; oak with rails partly of beech; length 20m (22yds); c AD 800. University Museum of Northern Antiquities, Oslo

▲ The front end of the ornamental cart found in the Oseberg ship burial. The figure in the top left-hand corner is possibly Gunnar being tormented in a snake pit

▶ A carved panel from the stern of the Oseberg ship showing the men clasping each other's beards

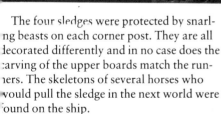

Above left The post carved by the so-called Academician, perhaps originally part of a chair

◄ A dragon head post found amongst the furniture in the Oseberg ship burial; *c* AD 850

▲ A detail from the tapestry found in the burial; carts and people in procession. Height about 20cm (8in)

▼ A detail from the side of the ornamental cart. A woman (right) restrains a man from attacking a man on horseback

The four sledges were protected by snarling beasts on each corner post. They are all decorated differently and in no case does the carving of the upper boards match the runners. The skeletons of several horses who would pull the sledge in the next world were found on the ship.

For summer transport the ladies were supplied with a highly ornamental cart, perhaps only used on ceremonial occasions before it was buried. At the front end, struggling for space among double-jointed beasts, is the scene of a man being cruelly bitten to death by snakes, with a toad leaping at his side. This probably represents Gunnar of the *Volsunga Saga* who was thrown to his death in a snake pit. Along the side of the cart is another figural scene, taut and vigorous, but enigmatic. The central character is trying

to attack a man on horseback, but his raised sword-arm is restrained by a very determined and aristocratic woman. She wears strings of necklaces and her hair, tied in a fashionable knot, wafts behind. On the cart frame there are some small human heads carved in the round, a rarity in Viking art. Here we can see a Viking perhaps as he saw himself. He has a trim beard and handlebar moustache. His eyes are staring wildly, and his mouth, snarling with teeth, opens in a yell. In a way this face typifies much of the Oseberg art: full of vitality but no gentleness.

The tapestry was found in fragments but enough survived to make an accurate reconstruction. It was woven with red, yellow, and blue wool, using about 20 different weaving techniques. The largest fragment depicts a stately procession of horses, riders, carts,

warriors, and women. Perhaps such a procession brought the grave goods down to the seashore at Oseberg in the early 9th century. Because the burial was so sumptuous, it has been suggested that the buried women were Asa, Queen of Vestfold, and her handmaid. Asa is known from legends as a formidable woman. Snatched by force from her father's home, she married the King of Vestfold and subsequently arranged his murder. The Oseberg art is a fitting memorial to a heroic age.

JANE GEDDES

Further reading. Anker, P. *The Art of Scandinavia* vol. 1, London (1970). Brøgger, A.W. and Shetelig, H. *The Viking Ships*, Oslo (1971). Wilson, D.M. and Klindt-Jensen, O. *Viking Art*, London (1966).

serving maid and a wealth of everyday artifacts including a cart, four sledges, a loom, buckets, and eiderdowns. She was placed inside a small cabin in the magnificent Oseberg ship with grave goods stacked around her on deck. The grave was robbed of its precious jewelry early in its history but soil conditions preserved the wooden objects until the burial mound was excavated in 1904.

The ship itself was an elegant fjord cruiser—too low in the beam for long-distance voyages. Its stem and stern posts, terminating in spirals, are lavishly carved with interlocking animals. They have small heads, double-contoured bodies, and pierced heart-shaped hips. Another part of the ship is carved with a variation of the "gripping beast". This motif was a new feature in the 9th century, its compact form contrasting with the running ribbon animals. It is recognized by its round head, bulging eyes, snub nose, exaggerated biceps and thighs, and omnipresent gripping paws. It usually resembles a feline creature but on this occasion looks like a group of old men gripping each other's long beards.

Several carvers worked on the collection of objects and some have been identified as artistic personalities, for example the so-called Academician and the Baroque Master who worked in contrasting ways. The Academician's animal head-post is a masterpiece of restraint, its head covered with a flat, well-spaced mesh of intertwined birds, its neck completely plain with a geometric ornament at the bottom. A comparable post made by the Baroque Master is totally covered with gripping beasts, carved with a good feeling for plasticity. The bodies are arranged around a series of oval shapes which give some rhythm to the overall design. The decoration of two bed posts and a sledge runner includes an important precedent for future Viking styles: they are carved with imposing beasts in a heraldic stance, which reappear as the main motif of the Mammen style.

Metalwork from the same stage of development as the Oseberg objects is represented by finds from Broa, Gotland (now in the State Historical Museum, Stockholm). They are mainly gilt-bronze bridle mounts, a bridle bit, and sword hilt etc. Most of the animal motifs found on them can be paralleled on the Oseberg objects.

Narrative art from this period survives on a few objects; on one of the Oseberg carts, for example, a man is seen struggling with a huge nest of snakes. Some tapestry fragments from the burial cabin show a procession of horses and figures and a gallows scene, possibly with reference to the god Odin. In Gotland there is a whole series of related stones carved in low relief, for instance those from Tjängvide (State Historical Museum, Stockholm) and Larbro (at Bunge, Gotland). They have a curved top, indented neck, and borders decorated with interlace. Scenes from legends are placed haphazardly over most of the surface. The motif most commonly represented is a splendid ship, looking rather like the Oseberg vessel, with a spiral prow and stern, a large square sail, and a company of warriors armed for battle.

The Borre style flourished from c840 to c980 and is named after the bridle mounts from Borre in Norway (University Museum of Northern Antiquities, Oslo). The style has three main elements, the most obvious being the ring-chain motif: a two-stranded plait whose intersections are bound by a ring. Secondly there is a type of gripping beast with a ribbon body whose claws clasp the frame in which it is placed, and finally a backward-looking quadruped with spirals on its hips and a pigtail.

The Borre style is found on jewelry throughout Scandinavia and even as far away as Russia. In Britain it can be seen on stone crosses, for example the stone of Gaut Bjornsson at Kirk Michael, Isle of Man. Gaut's ring chain, an insular variation of the Borre type, is also found on a wooden gaming board from Ballinderry, Ireland (National Museum, Dublin). The Borre style can be roughly dated from coins in the Hon hoard which includes Borre-type jewelry—treasure buried c860.

The Jellinge style (c870–c1000) is often found in conjunction with the Borre style. For example, a brooch from Odeshog, Ostergotland, has Borre interlace at its center and typical Jellinge animals around its sides (State Historical Museum, Stockholm). The style's name is derived from a

The stone of Gaut Bjornsson carved in the Borre style (c840–c980). Kirk Michael, Isle of Man

The Bamberg casket, decorated in the Mammen style (c960–c1020). Bayerisches Nationalmuseum, Munich

silver cup from Jelling, Jutland (National Museum, Copenhagen). Each animal has a ribbon-like body, outlined by a double contour. Its head with a long pigtail is in profile and the upper jaw extends into a lip-lappet: the creature is derived from the elongated gripping beast found at Borre.

A florid example of the style is seen on a horse collar from Sollestad, Denmark (National Museum, Copenhagen). In England, the Jellinge style is found in a strangely modified form on a series of Yorkshire crosses, for example those at Middleton and Collingham. On these the delicate ribbon interlace is rendered in a thick doughy form, probably by an Anglo-Saxon who did not fully understand the style. An interesting fusion of cultures is shown by the Gosforth cross (in situ), the result of close connections between the Vikings in Cumbria and their confederates in Ireland. Its decoration includes elements of the Borre and Jellinge styles plus figural scenes deriving from the high crosses of Ireland (see Irish Art). The scenes are selected from both the Bible and Scandinavian legends. On the Isle of Man, at Kirk Michael, there are perfect examples of Jellinge animals with twining pigtails, found on stone crosses. Here also, the Scandinavian tradition of picture stones is fully represented with stories about Gunnar, Sigurd, and Loki. Although details of costume, for example trailing skirts and knotted hair styles, show their Scandinavian derivation, the slabs are designed differently from those on Gotland because the narrative scenes are placed on either side of the cross shaft.

The Mammen style (c960–c1020) overlaps both in time and appearance with the Jellinge but shows a more emphatic form on the same theme. Animals have fuller bodies instead of ribbons, spirals on the hips, and often a total covering of billets: the new feature is plant-like tendrils, derived ultimately from Carolingian acanthus.

The style takes its name from an ax-head found at Mammen, Jutland, which has an inlaid wire design of a pelleted beast with spiral hips enmeshed in tendrils (National Museum, Copenhagen). A stone erected by Thorleif at Kirk Braddan, Isle of Man (in situ), is an early example of the style. He uses a combination of the Jellinge ribbon animal and the fuller, pelleted Mammen beast. Two famous caskets were made in the Mammen style, known as the Bamberg and Cammin caskets. The Bamberg Casket is in the Bayerisches Nationalmuseum, Munich; the Cammin Casket was destroyed in the Second World War but photographs of it survive. Both are squat chests, with lids that slope like roofs, made of thin panels of ivory and horn joined together by bronze bands. The panels are completely filled with pelleted beasts and tendrils while the metal bands are more simply decorated with raised animal heads.

The great stone raised by Harold Bluetooth in memory of his parents (in Jelling churchyard, Jutland) is historically the most important example of the Mammen style. It can be dated, from an inscription, to 983–5. On one face is a low-relief carving of the crucified Christ, surrounded by interlocking loops and circles: the first dated Christian monument in Scandinavia. On the other face stands a great "heraldic" beast entangled with a snake. The Jelling stone probably started a fashion for erecting carved stone memorials in Scandinavia which became more common in the 11th century.

The Ringerike style (c980–c1090) developed one element of the Mammen style still further: now thrusting tendrils threaten to dominate the animals they usually surround. The ragged tendrils derive ultimately from acanthus decoration in Ottonian and Anglo-Saxon manuscripts, especially those of the Winchester School (see Anglo-Saxon Art). The so-called

Great Beast of the Jelling stone, fighting with a snake, is often represented in the Ringerike style, the name of which comes from a group of carved stones in the Ringerike district of Norway. One vigorous example of its use is on the Vang stone, from Vang in the Valdres region of Norway (*in situ*), while a more refined version of the style, in metal, is shown on the Kallunge weather vane (State Historical Museum, Stockholm). On one side are the Great Beast and snake, on the other, two interlaced fighting snakes with tendrils sprouting from all parts of their bodies.

The Ringerike style flourished especially well in England during the reign of King Canute (1016–35), because there were so many Viking patrons in England and because the style was easily assimilated by artists versed in the contemporary Winchester style. In manuscripts the subtle change from Winchester acanthus to Ringerike can be seen by comparing the Harley Psalter (British Library, London; MS. Harley 2904) with a manuscript in the University Library, Cambridge (Ff I 23). In the former, acanthus ornament is lush but controlled; in the latter thinner and thrusting, forever exceeding its boundaries. A sketch in the back of the Caedmon manuscript (Bodleian Library, Oxford; MS. Jun. 11) shows a perfect combination of Winchester rosettes in a Ringerike style border. A grave slab from St Paul's churchyard, London, is one of the better renderings in stone, depicting the beast and snake in struggle, carved in low relief (Museum of London). The background was painted in blue and black while the beast was covered in white dots. The style is admirably represented in English metalwork by the weather vane found at Winchester (Winchester Cathedral Library) and by the silver disc brooch from Sutton, Isle of Ely (British Museum, London). The Ringerike style was very influential in Ireland and can be seen on such objects as the crozier of the Abbots of Clonmacnoise (c1120) and on the book shrines of the *Cathach* and the *Misach* (both c1090; all in the National Museum, Dublin). In England the style lost favor in the 1050s, shortly before the Norman Conquest, but it continued in Ireland until the 1120s.

The last artistic invention of the Viking world was the Urnes style. It can be seen evolving from the Ringerike on a series of rune stones in Sweden. The series begins at Boge, Gotland, with a thick-set beast extruding tendrils like those on the Kallunge vane. Gradually the beast becomes more attenuated and elegant, as seen at Strangnas, Sodermanland, and Ardre III, Gotland.

The style takes its name from wood carvings at Urnes church, Norway. Here two techniques were used: one, a high, round relief with some threads almost 5 in (12 cm) deep but as thin as a knife edge; the other was a quieter echo of the same patterns in a low, flat relief. The motifs are a slender quadruped, a lizard-like animal with only one front and back leg, and a thin thread sometimes ending in an animal head. The forms are very sinuous and graceful, curling around each other in wide loops, and each animal can be easily distinguished from its fighting foe because they are all of varying thicknesses. At Urnes these carvings found on the doorway, gable, and two planks and a corner post, have been incorporated into a later church of c1160.

Several high-quality examples of the style are to be found in England and Ireland where it continued to be popular long after Romanesque art had more or less become dominant in Scandinavia. The Pitney Brooch, found in Somerset though perhaps made in Scandinavia (British Museum, London) is decorated with the two-legged lizard struggling through threads. The crozier of Bishop Rannulf Flambard of Durham (Bishop 1099–1128) is decorated with Urnes animals (Monks' Dormitory Museum, Durham). Stone sculptures in the Urnes style are found on a capital of Norwich cathedral (c1140) and at Jevington in Sussex. In Ireland the style was slightly modified so that animals are arranged in more compact, symmetrical designs, as on the Cross of Cong (c1123; National Museum, Dublin) and on the Cashel Sarcophagus (*see* Irish Art).

The coming of Romanesque art to the North considerably curtailed indigenous artistic design. Christianity required Christian architecture and for this Scandinavians were dependent on foreign examples: the countries are covered with hundreds of small, stone churches—and a few large ones—inspired by examples in the Rhineland, England, and Lombardy. Nonetheless, native forms continued in use for wood carving in the 12th and 13th centuries, while the remarkable sculpture and architecture of the Norwegian stave churches show the persistence of fighting dragon motifs well into Christian times.

JANE GEDDES

Bibliography. Anker, P. *The Art of Scandinavia*, London (1969). Collingwood, W.G. *Northumbrian Crosses of the Pre-Norman Age*, London (1927). Graham-Campbell, J. *Viking Artefacts*, London (1980). Graham-Campbell, J. *The Viking World*, London (1980). Kendrick, T. *Late Saxon and Viking Art*, London (1949). Lindqvist, S. *Gotlands Bildsteine*, Stockholm (1941). Wilson, D.M. and Klindt-Jensen, O. *Viking Art*, London (1966).

24

ISLAMIC ART

Lovers Drinking Wine, from the Large Clive Album; signed by Afzal al-husaini of Isfahan
11×18cm (4×7in); dated 1646. Victoria and Albert Museum, London

THERE is under Islam no distinction between sacred and secular, thus giving Islamic art a unity which has been absent at least from post-medieval Christian art. This essay describes the establishment and development of this art within the area of the first conquests and its extension from the Atlantic coasts of Spain and north Africa to central Asia and what is now Afghanistan. From the 9th century AD onwards, Islam has also been established in the Indian peninsula and from the 15th century in Indonesia and Southeast Asia. The arts of these two areas are covered elsewhere in this encyclopedia because of their ties with the earlier art of the Subcontinent and will here receive only slight attention (see Indian Art and Southeast Asian Art).

The manner of designing and decorating buildings throughout the whole area of Islamic conquest was remarkably enduring. Architecture was the primary art of Islam, but through much of this area the carpet was also a major art and, so far as we know, shows a similar constancy in its principles of design.

It is sometimes alleged that there is no such thing as Islamic art, on two main grounds. First, that there is no connection between the art of the Islamic lands and the faith of Islam since it has no use for didactic or figural art. Secondly that the Arabs brought no art with them when they overwhelmed the ancient lands of Egypt, Syria, and the Fertile Crescent with the Iranian plateau, but employed the craftsmen of these conquered lands to continue to use the skills and styles of design they had inherited.

The truth behind the first allegation is that art was not for didactic enhancement of the faith nor for its expression except through the repetition of its profession or simply the names of God and the Prophet, but to decorate and to dignify public buildings. Mosques were for communal worship by the whole congregation of the Faithful and for their instruction; there was no altar and no liturgy, there were teachers but no priesthood. The *mihrab*, which marked with a niche the focal point in the *qibla* wall indicating the direction of the *Ka'ba* or holy place of Mecca, was not specifically sacred: it was originally the place in front of which stood the leader of the congregation, the *Imam*, in the Friday prayers of the community.

Beside it stood the *mimbar*, the pulpit from the steps of which pronouncements were made in the name of the ruler. The *mimbar* represents the throne from which the Prophet taught and it retains the canopy of dignity; but no successor has sat under it: the sermon is always given from the lower steps. Its political significance was as the place from which alone the *khutba* or naming of the ruler could be made. Although coronation was a rite used later under Persian traditional influence, it was never of decisive importance.

The truth behind the second allegation is that the Arabs at the time of the invasion had been in touch through trade and diplomacy with the Byzantine and Sassanian empires for many years previously and were thus able to take at once what they chose from the arts of both these great cultures. Consequently they could adopt the varied techniques in building and the applied arts and use them for their own purposes.

The 30 years following the death of the Prophet in AD 632 was the period of the conquest, during which four Orthodox Caliphs or Successors ruled from Medina in Arabia. Ali, the fourth Caliph, established his capital at Kufa in Mesopotamia, the newly founded city of Arab settlement, and claimed to combine religious with secular authority over all the conquests of the Muslim ("Faithful Acceptors of Islam", or "Submission to the Word of God"). Both Uthman and Ali were murdered and the first Umayyad Caliph Mu'awiyah emerged as ruler of the Arab empire, from 661, with his seat at Damascus and his authority supported by the army of Syria. Thereafter only the Alids believed in a theocratic government. The Arabs, with their tradition of tribal independence, proved difficult to control. Mu'awiyah's solution was to keep the warriors active with annual raids into Byzantine territory and into the still unconquered parts of Khurasan and central Asia beyond the Oxus. Merv, now in Soviet central Asia, became an advanced base for these raids. The warriors brought much needed treasure to the central administration.

The main source of regular income was from taxation of the conquered, assessed on their persons and property. The coinage of the defeated empires suffed at first to meet the needs of the conquerors, but by the 690s under the Caliph Abd al-

The main centers of Islamic art discussed in the text

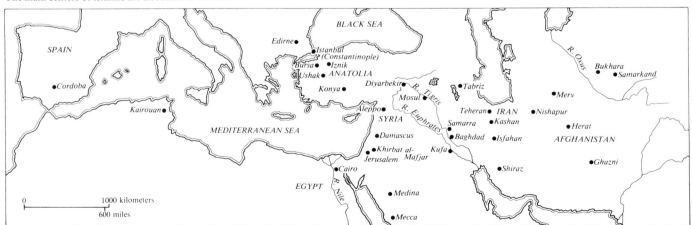

Malik (685–705) a decisive change was made: first by the addition of inscriptions in Arabic to the Byzantine types and then by the substitution for a short time of the figure of the Caliph for the Emperor (693–7) before the adoption of an aniconic style of coinage. In the Sassanian provinces the familiar heads of the last Persian rulers, especially Khusrau II (591–628), continued to appear on the new silver *dirhams* but with the addition of the name of the Arab governor in Pahlavi with *bismillah* ("in the name of Allah") in the margin. In both east and west the old mints were used, no doubt with the former die-cutters. In 695 a new reverse design showing the *mihrab* first appeared with the legend *Amir al-mu'minin* (Commander of the Faithful). Two rare coins with the standing figures of the Caliph are from the same year.

Two years later, in 697, Abd al-Malik reformed the currency by causing the design and execution of a specifically Islamic coinage, first in gold and, in 699, in silver which everywhere superseded the two different coinages of east and west. Henceforth, with rare exceptions, no figure appears on any Islamic coinage.

The end of the 7th century may thus be taken as the moment of the assertion of a distinctive personality in Islamic art: and it is significant that this takes the form of Arabic legends in Kufic script of the Profession of the Faith. The script thus attributed to the new city of Kufa had preeminent status as the medium for the copying of the Koran, the revealed Word of God through Muhammad his Prophet. Thus all religious writing and monumental inscriptions are in Arabic in every part of the Islamic lands. Since it was expected of the Muslim that he should learn the Koran by heart, easy legibility of these texts was not essential, but dignity and beauty were sought. So from the earliest times the Arabic script developed formal style, while the scribe or calligraphic designer ranked as the highest of artists.

Although there is no prohibition of figural art in the Koran there is a strong condemnation of idolatry, and the abstract unknowable nature of Allah could be revealed only in his Word with the consequent unacceptability of any icon. Figural art was thus excluded from religious buildings and books, but from the beginning it was allowed in secular and private works.

This stance is at once seen in the first major buildings of the Umayyad caliphs, the Dome of the Rock in Jerusalem and the Great Mosque in Damascus. Abd al-Malik built the Dome of the Rock in 691–2 as a shrine, not a mosque, consisting of a circle set in an octagon, with two rows of columns and piers supporting a high central dome, and a roofed ambulatory for circulation around the Rock, associated with both Abraham and Muhammad. It stands in the wide open space left empty after the destruction of the Jewish Temple built by Herod. This area is known as the Haram al-Sharif ("the noble Sanctuary") and is considered to be the site on which the Prophet Muhammad descended from his night ride through the heavens on the miraculous steed Buraq whose footprint is considered to be visible on the Rock under the Dome. But this belief does not go back to the earliest centuries of Islam and it is now accepted that the Dome of the Rock was built as a symbol of the status of Islam as superseding Christianity as well as Judaism. It bears inscriptions which specifically challenge the divine nature of Christ and the Trinity and is evidently meant as an answer to the domed structure built by Constantine over the Holy Sepulcher.

It was thus necessary for the unknown architect to plan a building in that same tradition and no doubt the lavish and beautiful mosaic decoration must have been carried out by local Syrian craftsmen of Christian origin. The exquisite beauty consists in its harmonious proportions and rich ornamentation, especially the mosaic cladding of the arcades and the drum above and in the decoration of the bronze-clad tie-beams on soffits supporting the dome. A first impression of the design in mosaic is of vases from which grow great scrolling plants, the kind of subject to be seen in the marble floor-mosaics of Christian churches of Syria and Jordan; but apart from the greater brilliance of glass tesserae in wall mosaic, this vegetation is enhanced by the addition of jewels and crowns. In suggesting that these are intended as royal symbols, Professor Grabar has put forward his view that the Dome of the Rock was intended as an assertion of the supremacy of the Muslim faith over all older realms, and to emphasize by the inscriptions the finality of the Islamic revelation. Although the structural and decorative elements had all been used previously in Christian buildings, the actual form of the building is new, to match the novelty of its purpose.

By this time the mosque had acquired a specific if not regulated form. Even in the lifetime of the Prophet the weekly communal prayers of the whole community had required a place of worship of adequate size, and capable of expansion, but affording protection from the weather—in the central area of Islam, from the heat of the sun. A roof supported on regular rows of columns arranged in a rectangle was the natural solution; and since there were on every hand ruined or deserted Christian churches there was at first no lack of marble columns within the bounds of the former Byzantine Empire ready for reuse. In this Mediterranean area a system of enlargement by the addition of extra units was evolved, as is most clearly to be seen in the Great Mosque of Cordoba. This was three times extended in different directions until it came to be supported by 581 columns. Founded in 785 by Abd al-Rahman I, it originally consisted of a square enclosure of 81 yds (74 m), each side with a covered area on the *qibla* side of 11 aisles supported by 11 columns each, giving an original total of 121 columns. After the final enlargement by al-Mansur in 987–8 the area of the mosque was increased to 197 yds (180 m) from north to south and 142 yds (130 m) from east to west, with a new facade towards the open court; while the covered prayer hall had 19 aisles. The middle aisle was always wider than the others, to mark its direction to the *mihrab*.

In 965 Hakam II added to the Great Mosque of Cordoba the most splendid *mihrab* anywhere in the Islamic world. It was a six-sided domed chamber, approached through a horse-

shoe arch, in front of which was a royal enclosure (*maqsura*) also domed and opening on the south side to the Caliphal palace of the Alcazar through a similar arch. Both arches were framed in rich mosaic wall decoration of arabesque patterns and Kufic inscriptions, as was the dome over the *mihrab* and its supporting ribs and their spandrels. The Byzantine Emperor Nikephoros II Phokas sent a master mosaicist from Constantinople who set up a workshop in Cordoba; but the designs are entirely Islamic and the names of the architect and principal craftsmen who worked on the *mihrab* chamber, recorded in the inscriptions over it, are Muslim. They had also worked on the royal palace of Madina al-Zahra for Abd al-Rahman III (936–61). This terraced structure with its rich stucco and marble decoration and sumptuous furnishing was sacked and largely destroyed by the puritanical Berber conquerors from north Africa, the Almoravids, in 1010, but is now under reconstruction.

These Cordoban monuments are of unique importance because they deliberately reflect the styles of the Umayyad Caliphate, while the great Aqsa mosque in Jerusalem, originally built *c*716, was twice reconstructed, first by the Abbasid al-Mahdi and then by the Fatimid al-Zahir in 1035. All that remains from the earlier mosque are the decorated tie-beams of painted wood and the carved wood consoles which supported the roof. Natural vegetal forms are converted into arabesque patterns at Madina al-Zahra. Al-Aqsa, built in the great space of the Haram al-Sharif, could be freely planned and again it shows the emphasis on the central aisle and the partial enclosure of the first four bays next to the *qibla* wall as a place set aside for the ruler. The "T" shape thus formed was repeated many times in the mosques of Syria and north Africa.

Exceptional is the other great work of al-Walid, the Great Mosque at Damascus (706–14). It was fitted into the *temenos* of the pagan temple of Augustus which had meanwhile housed the Christian cathedral of St John. This was demolished and within the walled area of 167 yds by 108 yds (153 m by 99 m) a covered prayer chamber was constructed with three wide aisles and a dome over the much wider central aisle, but open towards the courtyard. The roof was supported by alternate piers and columns; and this system was continued round the remaining three sides of the court, thus giving it unity. A great fire in 1893 destroyed the covered part. When reconstructed, the side towards the court was filled in, thus negating the unity of space. All the lower surfaces of walls and piers were covered with a revetment of thin figured marble cut so as to make a symmetrical pattern among every four slabs. This was a Byzantine manner of palace decoration, as was the glass-mosaic cladding of the upper surfaces including the spandrels above the columns and the reveals of the arcading. The specialist mosaic workers for this great decorative scheme may have been recruited from Constantinople itself, as they were for the mosque at Medina which was reconstructed in 707–9. The metropolitan style of the Damas-

The Great Mosque of Damascus, a mosaic in an arcade on the west wall; c715

cus mosaics, in contrast with the Syrian style seen in the Dome of the Rock, would support this attribution. The surviving portions show buildings in classical style, but with fantastic detail, standing in park-like landscapes beside wide streams. These were believed by some to represent the Barada, always a favorite resort for the inhabitants of Damascus. Whether these views in fact represent the capitals of the world or rather the heavenly mansions of paradise remains unclear. Certainly there is no sign of fortified or enclosed buildings, so that the scene is always one of peace; while the absence not only of human but even of animal figures would at once set these apart from any Christian building. Evidently the intention was to produce an effect of overwhelming splendor; the intense blue and green foliage against a gold ground conveys palatial rather than religious feeling, pleasure rather than power. It has only a formal and not a structural relation to the architecture. This is in general the norm to which Islamic art reverts (although there is on occasion strong emphasis on structural line, as in Seljuk architecture).

Construction of palaces outside the main centers of population had a political aim: to assume a position of power *vis-à-vis* the Arab tribes as well as the conquered peoples; to weld together subjects unaccustomed to loyalty into units larger than the tribe, while agriculture and trade were still in the hands of non-Muslims. In Syria there was no royal palace to take over: hence the need to invent a new type of building, neither castle nor villa, but a setting for personal display, as at Khirbat al-Mafjar near Jericho, or Mshatta, in the Jordanian desert. An essential feature of these palaces was the imposing gateway without military function, and a throne room for the ruler approached through an anteroom. There was also provision for pleasure in the bath-chamber which, as at Qusayr Amra, also in Jordan, might be painted with scenes of hunting, bathing, and music, and also of victory symbolized by figures of the kings overcome by the Islamic conquests, from Visigothic Spain to central Asia. Finally, on the roof there was

Left: The interior of the Dome of the Rock, Jerusalem; 691–2

The "Tree of Wisdom" mosaic in the unfinished palace of Khirbat al-Mafjar, near Jericho; c730

an astronomical map of the heavens. There are Greek labels for some parts and the whole concept is of Greco-Roman origin. This is a work of Walid I soon after 711; but Khirbat al-Mafjar, which was never finished, is a work under the Caliph Hisham (723–43) though perhaps for his nephew Walid II.

It is remarkable above all for the splendid floor mosaics, especially one depicting two deer feeding beneath a great fruiting tree while a lion has pounced upon another deer on the opposite side. According to Ettinghausen, this may symbolize the Tree of Wisdom under which the peace of Islam is contrasted with the rule of force outside. There are also stucco figures in the full round in this palace probably representing the Caliph attended by serving girls, evidence of Iranian in-

fluence which is most clearly seen at Qasr al-Hayr al-Gharbi, in the Syrian desert half-way between Damascus and Palmyra. Here, c730, a much larger palace complex was built for the Caliph Hisham in brick with stucco enrichment. On the great east gateway, now reconstituted in the garden of the National Museum in Damascus, the decoration includes arcades and floral patterns with some small trees in full relief; but it is noteworthy that Kufic inscriptions do not figure in the decoration of any of these palaces, unlike the religious buildings of the Umayyads.

Unique to Qasr al-Hayr al-Gharbi are the floors painted in a kind of fresco technique on hard gypsum. One is laid out like a Roman floor mosaic with vine border and semi-human marine figures round a bust of Gaea, the earth goddess, but orientalized and with the favorite Sassanian pearl border. The second, even more oriental in theme as well as style, shows a huntsman shooting from a bow and musicians standing under an arcade. This is laid out like a wall-painting and reflects late Sassanian decorative art, in which the Caliph Hisham is known to have been interested. This site thus represents a definite turning eastwards before the end of the Umayyad period.

So the arts of this period represent the attempt to enhance the prestige of the Caliphate by the choice of themes and techniques alternately from those current under the Sassanians with their orientalizing tendency and Byzantium. The beginning of a specifically Islamic art is to be seen mainly in the new coinage and the development of the Arabic script, both in the Koran manuscript and on monuments.

The Abbasid Period (AD 750–940). The rise to power of the Abbasid house and the shift of the capital of Islam from Damascus to Mesopotamia represent an ideological revolution marking the end of the Arab tribal empire and the rise of international Islam. The new capital city of Baghdad, founded in 762, was designed as a round shape with gates at the four quarters to symbolize the central point of an empire which revolved around the caliph in his palace at its heart. Although nothing now remains of this city it can be reconstructed from the full descriptions, especially that of the late-9th-century historian Ya'qubi. The founder, the Caliph Mansur (754–75) collected a great army of builders from many quarters and pushed ahead with great energy. Since the material was brick, local resources were available including part of the Sassanian palace at Ktesiphon lower down the Tigris. In addition to the city palace at the center of the Round City, Mansur built himself a residential palace complex by the Tigris called the Palace of Eternity (*Kasr al-Kuld*) and upstream a suburb for the army at Rusafa with its own great mosque and living quarters. Other quarters and palaces were built by Mansur's successors especially Mut'adid (892–902), the *Firdus* (Paradise) and the *Taj* (Crown). From a vivid and detailed description of the visit in 917 of the Byzantine ambassador and his reception at the Taj Palace given by al Katib, the ceremonial of the Abbasid court can be envisaged in all its splendor. The traditional oriental interest in automata is reflected in the display of silver trees with moving leaves and singing birds and also by the attendance of 100 lions, the royal beasts, with their keepers. But the new products of the Islamic world are represented by the hundreds of carpets which were spread the whole way from the gate to the Caliph's presence, in addition to a vast display of woven silks. Such a ceremonial background to the court of Baghdad had a prolonged effect in the Islamic world; it was imitated in Spain by the Caliphs of Cordoba, by the Fatimids in Cairo, and by the successor rulers in Iran. By 917 the Caliphate had ceased to hold the unrivaled position which it held in the time of Mansur and Harun al-Rashid (786–809), whose legendary state is recalled in the Arabian Nights in which the City of Brass reflects memories of

The minaret of the Great Mosque of al-Mutawakkil at Samarra; 848–52

the Round City.

Meanwhile the attempt was made by the Caliph Mu'tasim (833–42) to escape from popular pressure and to separate his troops from the populace by constructing a new palace-city some 70 miles (112 km) higher up the Tigris at Samarra. A vast congregational mosque was built to contain the Caliph's household, a great walled enclosure (*sahn*) with eight bays on the south side and four each on the other three. The most remarkable feature of this mosque is the minaret which is the oldest surviving example of this feature. All that was required was a place from which to make the call to prayer at the five stated hours; and for this the roof would normally have sufficed. Here at Samarra the minaret is a separate structure, a tapering spiral tower to be ascended by a ramp round the outside, and without decoration; but its height and monumental scale recall the ancient ziggurat and its purpose must have been to impress. The form was copied at Cairo in the mosque of ibn Tulun; but earlier is the tower minaret of the Great Mosque at Qairawan (724–7 or 836) and this square shape was the usual form in Syria until the 12th century.

On a hill overlooking the Tigris, the palaces of Samarra were laid out in as axial and symmetrical a shape as the site would allow. Construction started in 836 and continued until 892. The seat of the Caliph was placed in an *aiwan*, the recessed arch of Sassanian form, across the front of which a curtain was suspended and drawn aside at an audience to reveal the august figure on his couch wearing a tall, soft hat, the *tawila*. To maintain his state the Caliph was carried under a pavilion and a state parasol was held over him. The more real political power passed away from the Caliph, the more carefully were the state and protocol preserved. The buildings were of brick and the inside surfaces all had dados of stucco, either molded or carved, with stylized arabesque designs endlessly repeated. Stucco had been the favorite Sassanian decoration and it is likely that there was no break in the tradition of its use. It was now used in all good quality buildings, religious or secular, public or private, throughout Mesopotamia, Iran, and beyond. These building techniques by groups of specialist craftsmen who were mobile and could find their raw material near their building operations permitted rapid construction, but also meant that the architecture was regarded as ephemeral. While Syria is an area of good stone and marble quarries, in Mesopotamia and Iran there is little good building stone and the traditional building material is brick, generally sun-dried except for important buildings.

The 9th century also saw the beginning of an important ceramic industry, first to serve the capital but later exporting as far as Egypt and Khurasan. In an attempt to produce a ware comparable to Chinese porcelain, already reaching the Islamic world by this period, the pottery body was covered with an opaque tin glaze producing a mat white ground on which decoration could be painted in colored glazes, limited at first to cobalt blue and green. This might be in radial stripes or in floral units, sometimes combined with Arabic legends—either blessings on the owner or the signature of the potter. A more

A dish with a lustrous surface decoration produced by a second firing; height 10cm (4in); diameter 36cm (14in); 10th century. Freer Gallery of Art, Washington, D.C.

impressive invention was the use of silver and copper oxides compounded with sulphur to form a lustrous surface decoration applied in a second firing over the tin glaze. This luster technique was a secret held by the potters who conveyed it first to Egypt and then to Syria and Iran in the late 12th century. By the 10th century there was a tendency to cover the whole ground with patterns of dots or eyes against which stylized figures of men or birds might be drawn; and this type formed the basis of the industry when extended to Egypt under the Fatimids. The technique was also used in the 9th century for decoration of tiles, fragments of which were found in excavations at Samarra and in Tunisia.

Under ibn Tulun and his son Khumawaya, descendants of a Turkish slave, Egypt was semi-independent but under cultural domination of the Abbasid caliphate. Tulun and Khumawaya sought to rival Baghdad in public works and the production of luxury craftsmanship, especially in textiles and ceramics. Khumawaya was notorious for his luxurious living and ostentatious display of gold and silver plate. The permanent memorial in Cairo of Tulunid rule is the great mosque of 876–9, known as al-Maydan because it faced a large polo ground. It was connected by a wide processional way with the ruler's palace which was entered by triple gates. Nothing remains of this palace, but the mosque is mostly well-preserved though no longer in cult. Following the precedent of Samarra, the great courtyard (*sahn*) is surrounded by arcades on brick piers, two deep on three sides, four on the side of the *qibla*, and with the minaret outside the walls, but inside an outer crenellated wall which effectively screened the mosque from the noise of busy streets and bazaars. The six main gates are simple. The openings are framed with carved wood revetment and the decoration is concentrated within the court of the mosque. Here the piers each have four attached pilasters with capitals in stucco, while the profiles of the arches are outlined with a rich carved ornament in stucco which covers the whole surface, in the Samarra style. Even richer is the decoration of the soffits of the arches and the marble ajouré window slabs, all of different designs. Above each pier are decorative rosettes on either side of pointed arches pierced through the spandrels. Above the tops of the windows, and all round the mosque, is a decorative stucco frieze and above this a continuous Kufic inscription more than a mile (1.6 km) long in carved wood, while the roof over the arcades is also carved. The decoration was thus very rich but all was subordinated to the sober monumental effect of the general design of the building. The original minaret, derived from Samarra in its corkscrew form, is now represented by a renewal of 1296. At that time the Mamluk, Lajin, dedicated a beautiful carved wood *mimbar* and adorned the original *mihrab* with marble and mosaic enhancement. During the past century the mosque has been extensively restored.

Another fine example of the influence from Baghdad introduced into Cairo is found in a long wooden frieze from the great cemetery, now in the Museum of Islamic Art. This contains elements of Sassanian design, a winged diadem alternat-

Decorated arcades in the court of the al-Maydan, ibn Tulun's great mosque in Cairo; 876–9

ing with a tree of life and palmettes but here combined with Coptic style vegetation, the whole being framed with Koranic texts in an elongated Kufic of 9th-century style.

Another Abbasid governor who made himself independent was Ibrahim ibn Aghlab (800–11), governor of Ifriqiyah (Africa), the modern Tunisia, with his capital at Kairouan (Qayrawan). There his successor Ziyadat Allah (817–38) started in 836 to build a great congregational mosque on the site of two earlier mosques. The covered area of the sanctuary was later extended to 16 arcades parallel to the *qibla* wall over 17 aisles, with a dome raised over the central space by Abu Ibrahim Ahmad (856–63). The arcades all rest on columns, as at Cordoba, thus giving this sanctuary a primitive appearance. But the *mihrab* itself is almost as highly decorated as that of the following century at Cordoba. The niche is formed of 28 marble plaques arranged in four registers with the central panels each carved with a conchoid form, as was the surviving niche from the mosque of al-Mansur at Baghdad of which this is the sole relic. The three rows on each side are ajouré carvings of Sassanian style vegetal motifs framed at the sides by a running frieze of plant scrolls. Below the upper row of panels runs a Kufic inscription in relief. The niche is flanked by two Byzantine columns with capitals while the arch above is covered with luster tiles which, according to ibn Naji, quoting an 11th-century writer, were imported from Baghdad, as well as teak wood, originally no doubt from India, that was used to form the top of the *mihrab* niche.

Iran under the Samanids and the Buyids (874–1037). Politically this period marks the beginning of the decline of the Abbasid caliphate as a power center; in the history of art it is notable for the revival of specific Persian art forms based on the pre-Islamic traditions of the Sassanian era. But the 9th and 10th centuries still witnessed the dominance of Arabic as the language of administration and trade in Iran as well as of scholarship, and both Samanids and Buyids continued to seek recognition of their position from the Caliphs in Baghdad. Balkh and Herat became centers of Arab armed camps which were established outside these cities. By the late 8th century, after the Abbasid revolution which was based on this area of Khurasan, conversion to Islam became general and religious differences were not significantly divisive.

The first Iranian mosques were not much influenced by local tradition and differed mainly from those of the west only in there being here no Roman buildings to rob for their marble columns. Thus the early mosques at Damghan, Siraf, Nayin, and Bukhara had, like those in the west, three arcades parallel to the *qibla* wall and one on the other three sides of the court. At Damghan a square minaret was placed outside the court but at Siraf (815–25) it was integrated into the wall of the court, and was probably not much taller than it. This mosque was built of stone, no doubt because it was available on the Gulf; but in general mud-brick was used for the walls of the earliest mosques of Iran and wood for their columns, which accounts for their quick decay and the consequent lack of survivors. However the Sassanian tradition of the barrel vault was continued, as at Damghan.

By the 10th century fired brick was general, with better chance of survival. The mosque at Nayin on the western edge of the central desert of Iran is the earliest, with its rich internal

Acorn-filled carved stucco decoration on the mosque at Nayin, Iran

both been explored archaeologically, but there is much more to be learnt from both sites. Large quantities of pottery have been found at both; and since we do not know which types were made at either they may be considered together. Unfortunately at neither site is there satisfactory established stratification.

At both Chinese influence is apparent, but confined to the splashed wares of orange and green on a clear white ground. It used to be thought that these types derived directly from the well-known T'ang dynasty three-color ware; but it is now clear that it was rather from the ware of the Liao of North China (916–1125) that this influence on Islamic pottery can be derived, as successors to the T'ang art tradition. The Samanid examples showing this influence are mostly bowls but include vases, one of which found at Samarkand is of clear Chinese shape. Later the Samanid potters added to the splashing *graffiato* decoration under the glaze leaving petal-shaped areas unsplashed, a gay and effective type of decoration. Since they could not make a fine or white body they had to rely on an opaque white glaze to produce a clean field on which they developed two variant types of colored slip painting, apparently simultaneously. One style is probably a vernacular version of earlier perhaps pre-Islamic astronomical figural subjects. The second type is explicitly Islamic, relying only on Arabic legends as sole decor, in an elegant form of Eastern bent Kufic, sometimes combined with abstract knotted or plaited forms from the common Islamic repertory. These are among the most beautiful of Islamic ceramic wares. A less sophisticated but decorative type has a dark ground, generally aubergine or yellow, on which abstract patterns are laid out in two- or three-colored slips. Neither of these types is found in any other area or period of Islamic pottery. Luster-painted wares were also found, while local imitations were made which lack the sheen of true luster.

At this period under the Samanids the silver mines in their control situated at Panjhir in Seistan, at Badghir in Khurasan, and at Bamiyan were exploited, and the metal no doubt mostly minted as *dirhams*. But enough examples of silver plate survive as evidence for survival of a skilled industry founded under the Sassanids. Many examples of silver plate have been found in Russia, sometimes accompanied by coins of as late as the 11th century. A characteristic of these Sassanian-style vessels is the use of hammering and chasing, and niello was sometimes employed for detail color, as it was also in contemporary Byzantium. Oleg Grabar has suggested that this production continued as the princely art of the Samanids—in contrast with the popular art of the ceramics or bronze. Such a conclusion is supported by the shapes of the bronze vessels of the period, several of which, especially ewers and bottles, are closely dependent on Sassanian silver shapes. In bronze the usual technique is casting: the vessels are pierced or engraved with inscriptions or floral patterns, leaving much of the surface plain. They rely on shape for their aesthetic appeal and this combines strength with elegance.

carved stucco decor, including decorated Kufic inscriptions framing the sanctuary arch and interlacing on the heavy round columns against an acorn background pattern. In the soffits of the arches are linked polylobed medallions, not far removed from Mesopotamian design of the previous century; but these Persian mosques begin to give added height to the central arch of the sanctuary facade and so to prepare the way for the great *aiwan* (portal) mosques of the 11th and 12th centuries.

In the 10th century the two principal powers controlling Iran were the Samanids in the east and the Buyids in the center and west. The Samanids emerged earlier and were enriched by their control of the international trade route between central and eastern Asia and the West by way of the Russian rivers north of the Caspian Sea. From 892 they minted silver *dirhams*, and gold dinars from about the same date, coins that traveled far. Found in quantity in Poland and even round the Baltic and also in the Balkans, they witness to the extent of the Samanids' overseas trade connections. Their twin capitals of Nishapur in Khurasan and Samarkand in Transoxiana have

The Buyids originated from Dailam, south of the Caspian

Sea, but by 930 they had established their capital in Isfahan and dominated all of western Iran and by 946 had reached Baghdad and been honored by the Caliph as *Amir al-Umara*. They built themselves a palace in Baghdad and received a formal coronation from the Caliph, a revived Persian ceremony without Islamic significance. Although originally rough soldiers, they soon became patrons of learning and art and collectors of manuscripts, though none survive to illustrate this aspect of the arts of the period. That they also patronized goldsmiths is seen in a gold ewer (Freer Gallery of Art, Washington, D.C.) bearing the name of a Buyid prince who ruled in central Iran from 967 to 977. It is chased with deer in roundels formed of stylized floral scrolls which completely cover the ground, as with the stucco patterns of the 9th and 10th centuries. Like the Samanids, the Buyids were interested in foreign trade, an outlet for which was by way of the Persian Gulf through the ports of Basra on the Tigris and Siraf due south of Shiraz, a flourishing entrepôt for imports from India, China, Southeast Asia, and East Africa. Excavations have confirmed written evidence for the wealth of its merchants and for the large scale import of Chinese porcelain in this period.

There is ample evidence for the existence of a major textile industry; silk was long cultivated in the Caspian area of northern Iran, and Khuzistan was noted for its silk-weaving, centered on the city of Ahwaz. The Buyid courtiers all wore silk dresses, and silk cloth was evidently a major export commodity. A find of silks of the period was made in Ray some 50 years ago and these are now scattered among the museums of the world. But the earliest datable Iranian silk of the Islamic period was preserved for centuries in a French country church at St Josse (now in the Louvre, Paris). This is woven with the titles of a Samanid general who was killed in 961. It is decorated with pairs of confronted elephants and a border frieze of camels. Its history illustrates the wide repute of Iranian silk and the far-flung trade connections of the Samanids.

The Fatimids and the Islamic world (915–1171). Nothing shows more clearly the decline in authority of the Abbasid Caliphs than the rise to power of the Fatimids. For they went so far as to set themselves up as a rival Caliphate and by their propaganda did all in their power to discredit the Abbasids in Baghdad. Claiming descent from the daughter of the Prophet, Fatima, the founder of the line Ubayd Allah Sa'id, after the preparation of Isma'ili missionaries, left Syria in 903 and took the title of *Mahdi*, or Divinely Designated Leader, in 910 at Rakkada in Tunisia.

The first four Fatimid Caliphs remained in Africa but in 973 al-Mu'izz moved to Egypt in the hope of deposing the Abbasids in Baghdad. Thus Shi'i rule was brought to Egypt and even to the holy cities of Mecca and Medina; but Syria was only temporarily in their power and their emissaries were present in Iran, where the extreme Isma'ili established themselves in castle strongholds in the mountain valleys of Dailam. From Africa they had conquered Sicily between 916 and 965. Subsequently the island became virtually independent; while soon

after, before 1051, Africa also fell from their grasp. It is therefore as rulers of Egypt that the Fatimids made their major impact on the Islamic world and by their contacts with Europe through the Normans in Sicily.

As the successors of Ali, they united in their persons spiritual and temporal power, as the Abbasids never did. So, although the Fatimids imitated the palace plan and the ritual of the court at Baghdad, they sought to surpass it. In addition therefore to the rite of unveiling the Caliph which the Abbasids had inherited from the Sassanians, the Fatimids derived from Byzantium prostration when approaching the Caliph, kissing of his stirrup, his foot, and his knee, and withdrawal without turning the back towards him. They wore a turban instead of a high cap but wound in such a way as to reach a peak round a jeweled support to which the name of *taj* was attached, though it was not a crown in the usual sense.

The new capital, Cairo, was founded in 969 by general Jawahar, a Sicilian, and probably with help from Amalfi. In the 12th century Amalfi was eclipsed by Pisa: this trade was protected by the Caliphs who allowed the establishment of a factory of these merchants. Cairo was thus a cosmopolitan society, tolerant and well-equipped with hospitals and other public services. The great congregational mosque of al-Azhar was built in 970–2 laid out like ibn Tulun round a wide court, but the present structure dates only from the 12th century and has been extensively restored. It has also been greatly enlarged because of its function as an Islamic University. Originally founded for the training of Isma'ili missionaries, it has become the greatest center of orthodox teaching in the Islamic world. The mosque retains its original style of decoration, austere Kufic lettering round simple stylized motifs in stucco which fill the spandrels of the arches resting on many marble columns both in the courtyard and in the sanctuary area in which the *mihrab* niche is also set in a wall clad with stucco panels of strapwork design.

The mosque of al-Aqmar (1125) is a more revolutionary building, for it begins the new practice of aligning the facade of the mosque to the main street on which it was built. This often, as here, produced problems in that the street was not straight and it was difficult to arrange for the orientation of the *qibla* wall towards Mecca. The treatment of the facade is all the more to be praised for lively variety within general unity. The masonry is finely carved with a frontispiece round the entrance divided into three units each with its conchoid niche, a great one over the entrance and smaller ones flanking it, above which are secondary small niches. To the left of this facade is a more shallow blind niche again surmounted by a conchoid semicircle. The whole is united by bands of Kufic inscriptions running the whole width of the street frontage.

Of the Fatimid palace only some carved wooden friezes remain from the great hall, now in the Museum of Islamic Art in Cairo. They show lively scenes of hunting and music playing and were originally colored but give a fair idea of the splendors recorded in literature. The princely themes of these carvings and the naturalism of the style are characteristic of

The interior of the congregational mosque of al-Azhar, Cairo; 12th century

the period and are also reflected in the ceramics. The fortification of Cairo dates only from the time of al-Mustansir, who built the three great gates Bab al-Futuh and Bab al-Nasr (1087) and Bab Zuwayla (1091) to the design of an engineer from Urfa (ancient Edessa) and forming parts of the walls built to ward off an expected attack by Seljuk Turks. The gates are extremely impressive and flanked by great square or round bastions.

The most conspicuous art of the Fatimids must have been textiles. It was with silk brocades that the processional route of the Caliph was decorated while he rode his horse out of the palace over carpets laid on the marble floor to avoid the risk of slipping. The textile tradition in Egypt inherited by the Arab conquerors is known to us from the linen cloth with wool tapestry woven designs of the Coptic workshops which continued into the Islamic period. It was the Tulunids who introduced the craft of silk-weaving from Baghdad and under the Fatimids the application of tapestry woven silk decorative and inscriptional bands to linen of extreme fineness of weave was developed as a high art at the Caliphal factory at Timis and elsewhere in the Fayum. The factory and its products were known as *tiraz*, a term referring to the royal titles and name of the ruler which adorned the garments made for distribution at the court of the Caliph, who thus asserted his

claim to their allegiance. Examples have survived in the dry soil showing bands decorated with animal processions and elegant Kufic inscriptions.

The technique of luster pottery, invented at the Abbasid court, was probably introduced to Egypt by the Tulunids in the second half of the 9th century. But practically all that has survived is from the 11th or 12th centuries. Not a single piece is dated, nor do we have any precise information on the potters whose names occur on some. The product is considered by Grabar to have been made for a wide public, probably of the merchant class: he points out that the subjects, although princely in theme, are not specifically royal. There are no symbols of power—rulers, thrones, crowns, royal titles—but of what the average man might aspire to of the good life. We see musicians, hunters, drinking and dancing, and good wishes, animals or birds, which may all refer to favorable astrological prognosis. Similar subjects carved in ivory and in wood, the former undercut with great skill against a background of vine-scrolls, witness to the diffusion of realistic and luxurious taste among a wider public, after sales from the palace and its subsequent sack in 1067.

The most famous of these luxury products is in rock crystal, a material of high value and difficult to work. It was therefore necessarily a product of royal workshops. The Fatimid treasures once included 18,000 items in rock crystal, not necessarily all of local workmanship. For the craft is probably of Sassanian origin from which period many crystal seals are known, and it was practiced in Mesopotamia, where Basra is said to have been a leading center, before its introduction to Egypt. The greatest collection of the Fatimid rock crystal vessels is now in the Tesoro di San Marco in Venice, representing part of the loot from the sack of Constantinople by the Crusaders in 1204. Many other pieces have survived in the West in church treasuries, probably already in Europe in the Middle Ages. Those carved with the names of rulers confirm a Fatimid origin, datable examples falling between 975 and 1036. Two of these are ewers with relief-cut animals and birds and with Kufic inscriptions giving the titles of the Caliph al-Aziz (975–6) and of Husayn, the son of Jawahar, the founder of Cairo, in power between 1000 and 1008. Four similar ewers are in European collections, including the finest which is in the Victoria and Albert Museum, London.

Fatimid paintings must have been of importance for decorating buildings, as well as portable objects such as textiles and ivory, but almost nothing has survived. One ivory box made for the Caliph al-Muizz (972–5) is preserved in Madrid, (Archaeological Museum), but its decoration is limited to foliate scrolls in red and green. A number of ivory caskets of coffer or cylindrical shape have survived in cathedral treasuries, the painted decoration including birds and small figures as well as Kufic letters, princely themes of rulers, hunters, and arabesque patterns. But some are specifically Christian and the whole group is attributable to Sicilian workshops of the 12th and early 13th centuries.

More important evidence for Fatimid painting is in Palermo, the capital of the Norman King Roger II. When he built his richly adorned palace chapel in the early 1140s he had the wooden coffered ceiling painted by Muslim craftsmen from Egypt or Syria. The central nave of the chapel is covered with a nonstructural system of coves used to give variety of light and shade. The only earlier surviving painted wooden ceilings are in the mosques of Cordoba and Qairawan but in these only abstract patterns are used. Owing to the structure the field for the painter is varied in shape and size: in some are Kufic inscriptions, in others mock Kufic; the script is in good Fatimid style, with floral adornment that may be more eastern. In the pictorial repertory there is a good deal of repetition. The most frequent are addorsed birds and animals, stylized palm trees, and dragons, but not of a Chinese kind, and without wings. The most significant subjects are human; and here the old image of the enthroned ruler seen frontally is flanked by musicians and dancers in vigorous action. The plastic sense here seen is said by R. Ettinghausen to be a special feature of Fatimid painting but Monneret de Villard detects the influence of Byzantium. Purely Islamic is the tendency to set the figure against a background filled with arabesque, thus excluding any idea of defined space for the action.

Sicily was, with Spain, a principal route for the entry of Muslim art to Europe. Among the regalia of the Holy Roman Emperors, transferred to Germany in 1194 by the Hohenstaufen Henry VI on his marriage with Constance, daughter of Roger II, was the coronation robe made for Roger in Palermo in 1133–4, in accordance with the Kufic inscription embroidered in gold along its lower circular edge. The main element of the design embroidered in gold on a Byzantine red silk ground shows identical images in reverse of a lion bringing down a camel and with a stylized date-palm in the center. The outline is vigorous and the action almost natural but the detail is highly stylized and completely flat, the indication of mane and ribs being reduced to a pattern, while the lion mask is

A rock crystal ewer inscribed with the titles of Caliph al-Aziz (975–6). Tesoro di San Marco, Venice

almost floral. Space-filling floral arabesque elements are introduced on the bodies of both lion and camel, while stars of different magnitudes are indicated at several points, as in astronomical illustrations found in manuscripts of as-Sufi who wrote his book on the *Forms of the Fixed Stars* under the Buyids in 960, and of which a copy dated 1009 is in the Bodleian Library, Oxford, and also on the related celestial globes, the earliest surviving examples of which were made in Spain in the 11th century.

A fine globe dated 1274–5 and made by an astronomer of Mosul in Iraq, reached the British Museum in London in 1871. On it the lion's head is still recognizably of the same form as on the coronation robe. This is also adorned with a series of small square enameled gold plaques placed along the straight edges and with two much larger enameled clasps believed to be contemporary work and also made by Muslim craftsmen in Palermo when the city was full of Arabs, especially around the Court.

In textiles, Italian looms first imitated the brocades at Genoa and their designs appear in inlaid marble pavements, for instance in S. Miniato al Monte (1207) and the Baptistery at Florence (1209), in both of which Signs of the Zodiac and affronted lions are of Islamic derivation. By the following century the carpet, another product of the Islamic East, was finding its way to Italy and was destined to greater popularity and a much longer reign in Western taste, indeed down to our own times. Again in this medium it was evidently the animal designs that were first appreciated, for such carpets of Seljuk type are represented in early Sienese paintings where they can be identified as Anatolian—a type that continued through the 15th century. Incidentally these paintings provide vital evidence for the knowledge of early Turkish carpets, of which only small fragments survive.

Iran and the East under the Ghaznevids (977–1164), the Ghurids (1148–1215), and the Seljuks (1038–1194).

The Iranian revival was carried further under the Ghaznevids. Mahmud (971–1030), son of the dynasty's founder, was a fervent supporter of Iranian traditions of government and culture. He carried Islam further east but his conquests in India were essentially in quest of prestige, and loot—the finance required for his army and building operations. Ghazni, his capital, was strategically placed on the trade route to India and near the debouchment of the north–south passes through the Hindukush. It lies in a quite extensive oasis but not in a fertile plain like Merv and Balkh, and it had not hitherto been an important city. Its position enabled the Ghaznevids to acquire great wealth. Like other freshly settled rulers they liked great display and fine buildings. Enormous structures were rushed up by employing unfired brick covered with rich revetment of painted plaster and white marble sheaths. Fire, earthquake, and conquest soon destroyed most of their works, so nothing remains in Ghazni of the great mosque of Mahmud, known as the Bride of Heaven (built c1020).

The palace of Mas'ud I (1030–41), finished in 1038, was most luxurious, with a jeweled golden throne above which the crown was suspended by a golden chain, thus copying the state of the Sassanian Khusrau II. Three hundred and eighty gold dishes were set out in this hall which was spread with carpets. Round the palace, gardens were laid out with great expenditure of labor and there were countless musicians and dancers at his court. In all he imitated Samanids and beyond them the Abbasid court.

Literary culture too was predominantly Persian and Mahmud formed a splendid library and patronized the poets Firdawsi and Farrukhi. Even as late as Mas'ud III (1099–1115), the layout of the palace c1114 was thoroughly Persian and a long Persian verse inscription in the meter of the *Shahnama* was carved on marble slabs forming a dado round the courtyard. Ghazni had a short life as the capital of an empire; it was destroyed in 1149 by Ala al-Din the Ghurid. All that remained above ground until the Italian excavations in the 1960s were the two great minarets, probably also victory towers, although air photographs show that they were once attached to mosques.

That of Mas'ud III (*ob.* 1115) now consists only of a high prismatic octagonal base about 66 ft (20 m) tall but crowned until 1902 by a high cylindrical tower, in the decoration of which cast terracotta is used as well as carved brick for the monumental Kufic inscriptions and small *naskhi* inscriptions round the panels. Below are geometrical and floral patterns and the sections are separated by wooden platforms as a precaution against earthquakes. This patterning was new, but by the early 12th century there was already a century-old tradition of building monumental tomb towers, starting with the Gunbad i-Qabus of 1006–7 in Gurgan, a "great personal assertion" by its builder Shams al-Ma'ali Qabus. This tower is faceted, but the inscriptions are not yet a main decorative feature as they are at Ghazni. Virtually contemporary with the minaret of Mas'ud III are two minarets at Saveh dated 1110–11, Seljuk constructions of Muhammad ibn Malikshah, in which the monumental brick inscriptions are again a major element. The 11th-century minarets of Damghan are smooth cylindrical structures. By 1067–8 we can see at Kharraqan and Zavareh the first use of square Kufic brickwork inscriptions.

The splendid marble tomb of Mahmud at Rauza in the garden outside Ghazni, said to have been his favorite place of recreation, consists of a marble, prism-shaped sarcophagus raised on a high marble plinth, with applied pilasters at the corners and with a *mihrab*-shaped niche at either end. The main inscriptions on the two long faces of the prism are in Kufic against a floral scroll, but at one end of the prism is an inscription in *naskhi* giving the names and titles of Mahmud with the date of his death in 1030. *Naskhi* had been introduced into a subsidiary inscription in brick on the minaret of Mas'ud III and here this script, which was habitually used in the Ghaznevid chancery, was first used monumentally. It is therefore likely that the tomb of Mahmud is to be dated to the time of his grandson Ibrahim (1059–99) or even of Mas'ud III. A date in the 12th century rather than the 11th is also

The minaret of Mas'ud III at Ghazni, Afghanistan; c 1100

probable for the splendid carved wood doors of his tomb chamber.

The only considerable remains of the Ghaznevid period outside Ghazni itself are in the palace-castle of Lashkar-i Bazaar, on the Helmand river west of Qandahar. This complex of buildings, rediscoverd by Daniel Schlumberger of the French Archaeological Mission in Afghanistan in 1948, yielded precious evidence for the structure and decoration of a major secular building of the 11th or 12th century. The great audience hall is to be attributed to the time of Mas'ud III (1099–1115) or of Bahram Shah (1118–52) with its stucco dado below a great frieze of figures of the royal guard painted on plaster running right round the hall. The tradition of such a subject goes back to Sassanian times and is evidence for its survival here in the east long after its use in the Abbasid palaces at Samarra. The palace was sacked in 1150 by Ala al-Din Husayn Jahan-suz, the Ghurid conqueror, but was extensively restored by his successor Ghiyath al-Din (1156–65) as his winter palace. From this time there survives a great gateway with monumental brick inscription and the walls of a small, richly decorated palace chapel covered by stucco revetment in an eastern version of the classic Abbasid style.

The Ghurids, who destroyed the Ghaznevid empire in 1150, were a native Persian tribe who had only been converted to Islam little more than 50 years before that date. They rapidly extended their power over all the eastern Iranian world from their capital in their homeland on the upper Hari-rud. Here Ghiyath al-Din Muhammad (1162–1202) embellished his capital Firuzkuh, destroyed by the Mongols under Chingiz-khan in 1222. All that now remains of his great mosque is the minaret of Jam, dated 1194 but unknown to the world until 1957, now famous for its beauty and monumental dominance of the river valley in which it stands.

Like the two minarets at Ghazni, it is to be regarded as a victory memorial as well as minaret, for the name and titles of the ruler are picked out in blue tile, whereas the rest of the decoration including the Koranic text is in cut brick. Its richness and its great height of 213 ft (65 m) are impressive; but it is only a continuation of the Ghaznevid tradition which was extended further into India with the building of the Qutb Minar in Delhi, 26 ft (8 m) taller than the minaret at Jam. It is a stone structure which can therefore have a shaft of multiple reeded form, whereas the Jam minaret is of brick with an octagonal shaft laid out in panels connected by interlacing ribbons of inscriptions. At Delhi the inscriptions are in the new monumental *thuluth* while at Jam the traditional Kufic is used. The Ghurid general in Delhi, Qutb al-Din Aybaq, used the local skill of the stonemason and sculptor in treating the inscriptions as the major decoration, just as did his master at Jam.

The Ghurids were also patrons of the book; with the zeal of the recent convert Ghiyath al-Din commissioned a splendid Koran in four volumes copied in 1188 in *naskhi* with rich illumination. He also built an early *madrasa* at Shah i-Mashhad in northern Afghanistan in 1165–6 with rich adornments in brick and terracotta, including inscriptions.

The Seljuks were already powerful in central Asia and Transoxiana in the 10th century. About the year 1000 they were converted to Islam and became fervent protagonists of the conservative Sunni orthodoxy. In 1028–9 their leaders Chaghri and Tughril overran eastern Khurasan when Merv and Nishapur submitted to them. In 1040 Mas'ud I was defeated by the Seljuks and fled to India, thus opening the whole of central Iran to the Turks. Throughout their expansion the spearhead of their advance was formed by the Turkman tribes who remained nomads and aimed only at plunder rather than settlement, while the Seljuks accepted the heritage of Persian-Arab civilization, with its administrative bureaucracy, learning, and artistic tradition of craftsmanship. Their advance was very rapid; by 1055 Tughril, the first Great Seljuk Sultan (1038–63), entered Baghdad. His successor Alp Arslan appointed as his vizier the Persian Nizam al-Mulk (*ob.* 1092), the most enlightened and expert administrator of the period. In 1071 he won the decisive victory of Manzikert on the Upper Euphrates over the Byzantine Empire, which opened the way for the overrunning of most of Anatolia; while in 1079 Malik Shah took Damascus and soon afterwards Antioch. At his death in 1092 the Seljuk Empire had reached its height.

Inasmuch as the Seljuks relied upon local traditions of building and architectural decoration they cannot be considered creators of new styles. For this reason it seems best to treat of their period in Iran first before turning to their achievements in Anatolia, where their rule lasted longer. Although Nizam al-Mulk founded and built many *madrasas* for the teaching of orthodox Islamic law and theology, he was not an innovator. But the *nizamiya*, as the *madrasas* were now called, were foundations of the state and therefore uniform in organization though not necessarily in architecture. Unfortunately not one has survived. So too the monumental Seljuk mosque with courtyard marked by four *aiwan* portals in the center of each of its sides and a dome in front of the *mihrab* seems to be no more than the regularization of widespread previous practice for public buildings, from the palace to the caravansary. The Seljuk palaces of Iran have also vanished but a caravansary at Ribat i-Sharaf built by Sanjar in the 1120s on the Merv–Nishapur road survives to witness to a monumental axial court from this period.

Mausolea evidently had a major significance for the Seljuks; the finest is that of Sanjar (*ob.* 1157) at Merv built for the last of the Great Seljuks but lost to the Ghuzz Turks in 1152. It had originally a blue covered tiled dome remarkable also as the first of the double skinned domes in which the external profile could rise far above the interior, a major architectural development which was to be followed under the Mongol rule in Iran. So by the mid 12th century color was added to the repertory of decoration of the exterior of these structures.

It was, however, only after this date that we can see evi-dence for the revival of the major industries of ceramics and metalwork in cities that had not been Seljuk capitals like Isfahan and Merv, but in places like Ray and Kashan which were then not even under Seljuk control. This revival was due to these commercial centers and to their merchant class. Many of the luster-painted bowls and dishes of Kashan dating from *c* 1200 carry poetical inscriptions and these are also found on luster tiles even when intended for religious buildings. This strongly suggests their appeal to a literate public, familiar with the stories of the *Shah-nama*. Thus the princely themes also found on the ceramics would not imply that they were made for princely patrons but for people who knew and enjoyed references to princely incidents in literature—to a romantic public in fact.

The production of luster pottery in Iran can be dated between the last quarter of the 12th century until the Mongol invasions of 1220 onwards, after which there is a gap, at least in superior products, of a generation or so. The earliest dated vessel is of 1179–80 and the factory may have been working for a decade or so already, suggesting that the luster technique may have been brought to Iran by refugee potters fleeing after the fall of the Fatimids in Cairo in 1171. A superior type of luster, considered to be early in the series, is nearer to the Fatimid single figure, rather than overall patterns of many small figures. This early "monumental" type used to be attributed to Ray, but there are strong formal connections as well as signatures in common with Kashan. Kashan is now established as the chief, if not the only, kiln center for luster in Iran at this time. Its products were exported to Syria, Egypt, and as far afield as Ghazni. The kilns also produced major architectural elements including large *mihrab* units and other compositions for mosques and public buildings. The revival of luster at Kashan under the Ilkhans shows no falling away in quality as in the 1270s at the palace kiosk at Takht i-Sulayman of Abaqa Khan as well as in the series of luster tiles from Veramin (1260s) scattered among many western collections.

Another product of the Kashan kilns is the so-called *mina'i* or polychrome enameled ware which enjoyed a brief period of great favor in the decades before the Mongol conquest. The bowls and larger dishes were adorned with figural subjects, arabesque patterns, and *naskhi* or false Kufic inscriptions on a white or more rarely a turquoise ground, often enhanced with gold as well as the gay overglaze enamels. This luxury product was not revived after the Mongol conquest, but, instead, overglaze decoration in gold and red enamels was added to a special class of tiles and vessels now known as *lajvardina* (lapis lazuli type, though this mineral was not in fact employed). This type is also found at Takht i-Sulayman and dates therefore from the second half of the 13th century.

Many other types of pottery were made in Iran in this, the greatest period of her ceramic production. In these, unlike the types already discussed, it is Chinese influence that is forma-

Detail of the carving on the minaret at Jam, central Afghanistan; dated 1194

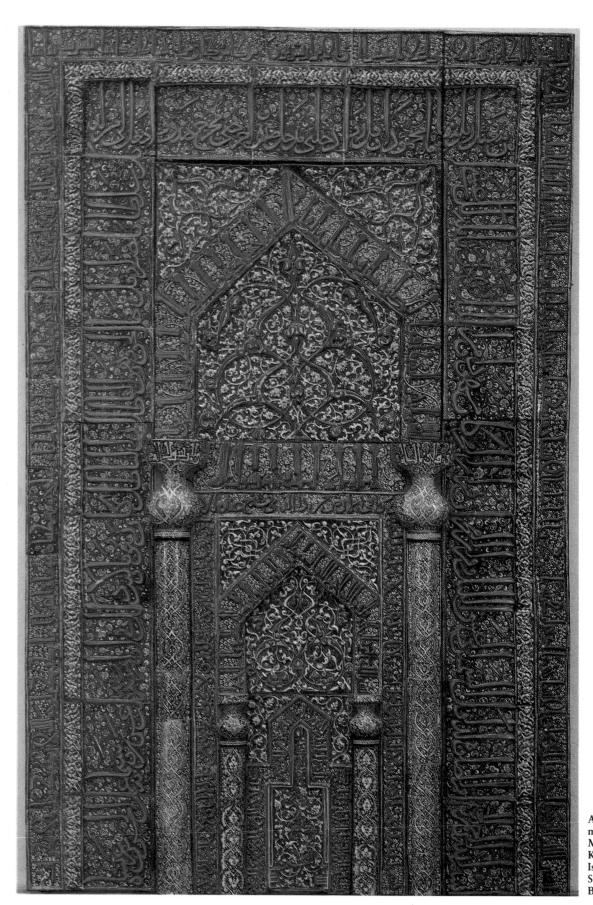

A luster-painted
mihrab unit from the
Masjid-i Maydan,
Kashan; dated 1226;
Islamisches Museum,
Staatliche Museen,
Berlin

tive—most obviously with the monochrome wares in which decoration depends on the carving or molding of the body under a white or blue glaze. The Persian potter could not match the hardness or transparency achieved by the Chinese Sung dynasty potter but the invention of frit, in which ground quartz was mixed with the levigated clay and glaze so that when fired the whole was fused into a compact whole, produced crisp and thin, near translucent, bodies. The use of molds enabled cheap and varied products with turquoise, cobalt blue, or colorless glaze to be made. Some of the shapes were of considerable size, *albarelli* or ewers, very handsome as adornments for houses. Another technique developed at this time, probably also at Kashan, was carving through a black slip and covering with a turquoise translucent glaze. Finally we find the use of underglaze painting in black or blue under a colorless glaze or a transparent turquoise glaze.

The production of the numerous fine brass and bronze vessels inlaid with copper and silver for which Khurasan was the major workshop is also to be placed after the mid 12th century. Far fewer surviving silver vessels were made before *c*1100 in the time of the Great Seljuks; but unlike the brass and bronze, many of which are dated, these silver and the few gold objects are not dated and the range of possible dating is therefore wide. After 1100 silver was scarce throughout the Middle East, leading to a decline in silversmiths' work and so to the development of the inlay technique to compensate for the use of base metal for the vessel itself. The earliest dated example of this new technique is from 1148, on a pen box of cast bronze; it is followed by a major creation, a bucket of beaten bronze dated 1163 and made in Herat, as was a ewer dated 1181, thus bearing out the statement of the 13th-century geographer Qazwini that metal vessels inlaid with silver were made in Herat and widely exported. Two other vessels of the same period made by craftsmen of Nishapur confirm the role of Khurasan in the industry. That casting was still employed, at least for unusual pieces, is proved by the extraordinary ewer in the form of a cow and calf attacked by a lioness and dated 1206. This and the bucket of 1163 (both now in the Hermitage Museum, St Petersburg) are inscribed in both Kufic and *naskhi*, then first used for monumental inscriptions; and human-headed script is found in both scripts.

The Seljuks of Rum (1077–1278) and the Atabeg dynasties. The Turkish absorption of Anatolia (modern Turkey) into its hegemony was gradual, and proceeded at two levels. At the top the Great Seljuk Alp Arslan (1063–72) destroyed the Armenian Kingdom at Ani in 1065 and defeated the Byzantine Emperor Romanus Diogenes at Manzikert in 1071, marking the permanent loss to Byzantium of eastern Anatolia. On the demographic level, the Turkman nomad tribes which provided the rank and file of the Seljuk army found the high tablelands of central Anatolia congenial to their way of life and started to settle. This explains the extent to which local building traditions were accepted by the Seljuks in Anatolia, in stone structure and sculpture, in which Armenian influence

is clearly seen in octagonal form and conical roofs and above all in the use of relief carving to decorate the outside of buildings. The Seljuks entered the area as Muslims but accompanied by many Persian administrators and craftsmen. Thus the Gok *madrasa* at Sivas (1271–2) is signed by a Muslim Armenian, Ustad Kaluyan, and a fine carved wood *mimbar* from Mosul was signed by Georgian craftsmen with Muslim names in 1153. But the most striking feature of the great Anatolian buildings of the Seljuk period, the monumental frontal (*pishtaq*) gateway, is a local invention. It derives from the *aiwan* of Persia but instead of being an arched recess with surface decoration, it has become a flat facade often flanked by towers and adorned with elaborate carvings in high relief in which the different levels are of great importance. At Erzerum, conquered in 1080, the *madrasa* of Khurdı Khatun of 1242, known as the Cifte Minare, has a very high stone facade in which the arabesque carving of the portal and niches on either side contrast with areas of fine plain masonry; while brick towers flank the portal relieved by calligraphy and patterned in blue-glazed tiles of Persian origin. Similar monumental gateways survive at the Sahib Ata mosque at Konya (1258) and the Cifte Minare *madrasa* at Sivas (1271–2) but with even more strongly accented stone decoration in which the recessed gate under stalactite roof (*muqarnas*) is prominent. Without the brick towers or the relief of colored tile are the severe facades of the mosques at Nigde (1222–3) and Divrigi (1228), the former with *pishtaq* decorated only in low relief arabesque, but the latter with high relief stylized wing or palmette motifs, treated as though they were applied in stucco. Finally, at Konya the Ince Minare *madrasa* of 1258 has a *pishtaq* in which the decor consists of inscriptional bands interlacing and outlining the whole facade. This entirely original treatment of the monumental entry is the greatest contribution of Seljuk architecture of Anatolia, and not found in the Armenian or Georgian architecture of the region.

The Seljuks were also great builders of walls, bridges, and caravansaries. These reveal a capacity for engineering and mastery of structural form. The most completely surviving fortifications are at Diyarbakr (formerly Amid) conquered in 1084–5. The base of the 3 miles (5 km) long city wall is Byzantine, but largely rebuilt in the 11th century and with 12th-century bastions adorned with inscriptions and relief animal sculptures and blazons in the Seljuk style added by the Artukid Atabeks, who ruled here from 1183. Similar austere decoration is found on other Seljuk buildings on which motifs like the dragon, tree of life, and lion-killing bull are represented. The Artukids were also great bridge-builders during the 12th century, one of which was decorated with carved signs of the Zodiac. The trade routes were served by these bridges and between them were built a string of caravansaries. The best known of these walled resting places (Turkish *han*) are the Karatay *han* of 1229–48 and the Sultan *han* at Aksaray, restored in 1278. These are both foundations of the ruling prince, unlike nearly all the remaining *hans* which were founded by emirs. They are major architectural works consist-

The west door of the mosque at Divrigi, Turkey; 1228

ing of an open courtyard surrounded by small chambers for animals below, with an upper floor for goods and a large pillared hall with three naves and vaulted roof. The treatment is monumental, with decoration similar to that on the *madrasa* of bold dog-tooth or meander or cable patterns. These works are all of the 13th century, more than 100 years after the original Seljuk conquest, thus giving time for the evolution of a new style, in which influence from Syria of the bichrome marble or stone in alternate courses had been absorbed while layout remained little changed from the plan seen in the mid-12th-century Ribat i-Sharaf.

Another major architectural form in Seljuk Anatolia is the free-standing mausoleum, a tower of circular, octagonal, or decagonal plan, usually with a conical stone roof, and often with external decorative arcading. These features derive from Armenian church architecture in which the conical roof is usual, as is polygonal form and external arcading, dating from the 10th and 11th centuries. The tomb tower was an architec-

tural form in Iran in the 11th century but only for the very great. In Anatolia the form became more common and the scale smaller; there is a fine group of tombs at Ahlat by Lake Van, dating from the last quarter of the 13th century onwards, and others at Erzerum. The form continued after Mongol rule in eastern Anatolia became direct, in 1278; the beautiful tomb of a Mongol princess at Gevash, south of Lake Van, is a fine example, with tomb chamber below the decagon with its paneled decoration and *thuluth* inscription under the conical roof.

While the Ayyubid and Mamluk influence in Anatolia gradually increased this was not at the expense of the decorative influence from Iran. A striking instance is the Great Mosque at Malatya, built of brick with extensive tile-mosaic, blue, turquoise, and manganese, from 1224 onwards. The stone doors are of 1247 and 1274. The dome over the sanctuary is raised on a high octagonal drum over squinches and the *aiwan* arch is framed in tiled *naskhi* inscriptions, while knotted Kufic inscriptions are found above the courtyard arcades. It thus descends directly from the Seljuk period mosques of Iran, although the architect was a local man. The use of tile mosaic is extended in the mosque at Beysehir built in the last years of the 13th century. The congregational area is roofed over on rows of wooden columns but the doorway and the tall *mihrab* are completely clad in tile mosaic in cobalt blue, turquoise, and manganese. This use of color was extended still further in the tomb chamber attached to the Sahib Ata mosque in Konya of 1282 where the walls, arches, and cenotaphs are all clad in tiles or tile-mosaic in the same coloring. This use of tilework leads on to the splendid decoration of the early Ottoman buildings in Bursa of the 15th century.

We are reminded of the importance of color in Islamic living, as evidenced in costume, above all in the carpet. The knotted woolen rug is of great antiquity in Inner Asia. Not only in the tented life of the nomad but in the settled communities of the Middle East the floor-covering is of far more importance than in the West because of the lack of furniture and the habit of sitting on the floor. The carpet is especially prominent in the mosque where the floor in the roofed areas of the Ottoman Empire from the Caucasus to Morocco are covered with carpets, usually several layers thick. The earliest surviving carpets are in fact from mosques in central Anatolia and date from the 13th century. One group was found early in this century in the Ala al-Din mosque in Konya, which was extended 1218–20, and might date from that time. Another group was discovered in 1929 in the Beysehir mosque, built *c* 1298, and therefore presumably not earlier than that date. In style and design there is not much difference between the two groups, and probably not more than a generation. K. Erdmann has pointed out that these carpets were made on wide looms and that they must therefore be the work of town-dwellers and not of nomads, but no factory has been identified. Ibn Said (*ob.* 1274) wrote of a carpet factory in Aksaray and of export thence to "all the countries of the world". This export trade is confirmed by discovery at Fustat of numerous fragments of carpets resembling those from the Anatolian mosques.

The most striking feature of this group is the border design of bold Kufic style letters in white on a red ground or in shades of blue or red on another shade of the same color. The designs in the main field are rather small-scale allover geometrical or highly stylized plant motifs, again largely in two tones of a single color but with accents in another color, thus forming a sophisticated system of design which implies a considerable previous development of the craft. The Seljuks probably introduced carpet-making into Anatolia, where there is no evidence of previous carpet-making. In the 14th century a new style of design appears, in which the dominant motif is a stylized animal, eagle, or dragon, within a frame, arranged as a repeat pattern in groups of six or more. This type is best known from its representation in Italian paintings of the 14th and 15th centuries. Such designs might have derived from Byzantine silk textiles in which roundels containing animals, eagles, or confronted birds are common; but they are also found in stone carvings of the Seljuk period as at Diyarbakr, while a double-headed eagle is painted in gold on a red ground on the inner surface of a carved wood Koran stand in Konya, dated

The dedicatory inscription and decoration on a wood Koran stand dated 1279/80. Konya Museums

1279/80, with a carved inscription of dedication to the mausoleum of the great mystic Jalal al-Din Rumi (ob. 1273). The dragon and phoenix are not likely to have appeared in Anatolia before the Mongol conquest of 1243.

This Koran stand is but one example of the accomplished school of wood carving under the Seljuks, which provided doors and pulpits (mimbar) for the mosques and other religious foundations of Anatolia. One center was at Karaman. A splendid door from Karaman, now preserved in Istanbul (Museum of Turkish and Islamic Art), is carved in high relief with figures of lions (mutilated by some fanatic) and even small stylized human figures, as well as arabesque patterns. This work, attributed to the mid 13th century, is one of a series of such doors from Ermenak, the Karamanid capital, as well as from Konya. Fine carved mimbar in the Ethnographical Museum, Ankara, include examples with decorative Kufic and arabesque panels from Malatya, Siirt and Damarsa, the last with inlaid panels, of the 14th century.

The office of Atabeg arose out of the need to provide the young princes of the Seljuk rulers with guardians who would perform the duties of the command to which the prince was nominally appointed. Some of these Atabegs succeeded in making their positions heritable; hence the foundation of dynasties like the Artukids (1102–1408) and the Zangids (1127–1222). The Turkman General Artuk had served Malik-shah in the later 11th century and his sons were granted the fiefs of Hisn Kayfa and Mardin in southeastern Anatolia near the border with Mesopotamia, nominally for their lifetime. Their descendants managed to preserve almost independent rule in this area until they were obliged to become clients of Saladin in 1283 but remained local rulers until 1408, though only in Mardin after 1232. It was in the opening decades of the 13th century that their capital Amid (Diyarbakr) and their more easterly outpost on the upper Tigris, Siirt, became centers for the casting of fine bronzes. The specialists in inlay who worked for them may have come from Iran, but their workshop was established before the Mongol invasions, and was capable of original design and technical innovation. The back of a bronze mirror (Collection of Prince Öttingen-Wallenstein) shows signs of the Zodiac arranged round a spread-eagle, like those on the walls of Amid, and seven busts of men, like figures in Armenian churches. Two great bronze kettledrums from Amid, now in Istanbul (Museum of Turkish and Islamic Art), with only inscriptions for decoration, in splendid human-headed Kufic, are now attributed to this school of casting; while a pair of bronze door-knockers with confronted dragons on either side of a feline mask, coming from Cizre on the Tigris but now divided between two Western museums (Staatliche Museen, Berlin, and C.L. David Collection, Copenhagen), show even greater mastery of plastic form. Recently a group of footed bowls and another of candlesticks have been convincingly attributed to the Siirt workshop. They are perhaps slightly later, since they are extensively inlaid in silver, with designs of rosettes and strapwork and with friezes of naskhi inscriptions. The area is rich in copper: the mines at

Maden lie to the northwest of Amid near Kharput. Mustawfi wrote (c1340) that in his day Siirt (Sa'ird) was still famous for its manufacture of copper pots and cups.

The Artukids showed an interest, at first sight strange, in Antiquity. A Roman theater facade of the 4th century was reerected to form one side of the courtyard of the Great Mosque of Amid in 1155. In the same decade the Artukid Najm al-Din minted copper coins with Christian subjects on the reverse and his own portrait on the obverse; his successors c1200 put signs of the Zodiac on their coins, while the Zangids imitated the coins of the Seleucids and of Constantine the Great. This area was not only an ancient cradle of past civilizations but still contained a large Christian population, both Armenian and Monophysite (Syriac). This is the context for the production of a unique work of art (now in the Tiroler Landesmuseum Ferdinandeum, Innsbruck), a bronze two-handled dish decorated in opaque cloisonné enamels with a central roundel of the legend of Alexander the Great ascending to heaven borne by four eagles, surrounded by six roundels (and another six corresponding on the outside), of which five show an eagle heraldically displayed, five more the combat of a winged griffin with bull, and the last two, musicians between alternating palm trees and dancing figures, types that go back to the Umayyad mosaics in the Dome of the Rock and the Abbasid palace wall-paintings in Samarra—altogether a set of archaic subjects as discrepant but as evocative as those on the coins. Round the rim is a Persian inscription in *naskhi* dedicated to the Artukid Rukn al-Dawla Da'ud (1114–44). It is unique in Islamic lands both in shape and in technique of decoration.

Alternating dancers and trees also form the decoration in fired gold wash on a glass flask dedicated to Imad al-Din, the first Zangid Atabeg of Mosul and from 1129 of Aleppo (1127–46). This now fragmentary object, in the British Museum, London, is almost unique evidence for this sophisticated technique, probably established in Aleppo which was to be one of the centers for the enameled glass of the next century.

The greatest patron of the arts among the Zangids was Badr al-Din Lu'lu (1218–58) who made himself independent of the Ayyubids from 1231 but whose rule did not extend far from his capital Mosul. There a workshop of inlaid brassware was established, whose pupils later moved on to Syria and Egypt to work for the Ayyubids and the Mamluks, providing many of the finest and most famous works in this medium. That the school was already established by 1223 is illustrated by a ewer (now in the Cleveland Museum of Art), with interlaced Kufic inscription on the shoulder and two signatures in *naskhi* of the engraver Ahmad al-Dhaqi of Mosul. The whole surface is densely covered with silver inlay in which pastoral and country scenes appear in lobed medallions against a background of arabesque convolutions. From 1232 comes a brass polygonal ewer in the British Museum, London, on which the signature Shu'ja ibn Man'a includes the fact that it was made at Mosul but without a princely dedication. Two contemporary texts refer to Mosul as a source of inlaid brass vessels, "which are exported to rulers". Ahmad al-Dhaqi worked afterwards for the Ayyubid al-Malik al-Adil and introduced the art of inlay to Syria whence it was carried to Egypt in 1260. The Jazira was overrun by the Mongols under Hulagu in 1258–60 and, athough Mosul was not sacked by them, the Zangids fell and local patronage failed.

Also connected with Badr al-Din is a copy of the great Arabic anthology the *Kitab al-Aghani* (*Book of Songs*) in 20 volumes, dated 1219, of which six whole-page frontispieces survive, painted with scenes of hunting, dancing, and bathing girls. The prince depicted wears the arm-band (*tiraz*) of Badr al-Din Lu'lu and the manuscript must have been made for him or at least for one of his emirs. These miniatures are sumptuous, with free use of gold, and represent the same school of design as the inlaid brasses. A similar layout is found in a Arabic version of the *Book of Antidotes* (*Kitab al-Diryaq*), that goes under the name of Galen. In a copy dated 1199 pastoral scenes resemble those on the inlaid brasses and it comes, no doubt, from the same area (Bibliothèque Nationale, Paris).

Scientific manuscripts of this kind had been provided with illustrations in Byzantine versions. A striking example of Islamization in such miniatures is a manuscript of the *De materia medica* of Dioscorides, finished in Baghdad in 1224. The manuscript remains in Istanbul, but 31 miniatures cut from it many years ago are in various Western museum collections (including those of the Freer Gallery of Art, Washington, D.C.; the Metropolitan Museum, New York; the Louvre, Paris; and the British Museum, London). In the last years of the Abbasid Caliphate before the Mongol sack of Baghdad in 1258, the city was a cosmopolitan center in which Persian, Turkish, and Christian traditions mingled with the Arab. The painting style may justifiably be called "international".

Architecture is purely conceptual or diagrammatic and space is divided into horizontal zones by conventional landscape symbols, strips of grass with flowers emerging in a frieze above. Figures of men and animals are more realistically depicted and show real observation. In several richly illustrated manuscripts of the *Maqamat* of Hariri, a series of anecdotes of amusing incidents befalling a plausible braggart *poseur* Abu Zayd, the miniatures add a fresh commentary on life in the street or tent in which there is much realism. Two of these manuscripts are dated 1210 and 1237, and the latter also shows in a miniature an inscription in honor of al-Musta'sim (1242–58), the last Caliph of Baghdad; but none gives that city as its place of production. However, the 1237 manuscript was copied by a scribe of Wasit in Mesopotamia who was also its illustrator, and they must all be from that area. In undated manuscripts of the animal fables of *Kalila wa Dimna*, a work of Sanskrit origin but descended through the Middle Persian version to Arabic, the animals show a vivid and lively realism which is combined with an overall symmetrical layout in which trees and other natural features have only a formal and symbolic value.

The great Muslim leader Saladin (correctly Salah al-Din) grew up in the service of the Zangids. His father and uncle had served Zangi from 1138 and been granted the fief of Hims by his son Nur al-Din, who built the Great Mosque there in 1146 with its 66 ft (20 m) tall square minaret of north Syrian form, similar to that at Aleppo of 1089, a Seljuk commission; and also the mosque by the bridge over the Orontes at Hama. Nur al-Din remained the suzerain of Saladin until his death in 1174; but Saladin, who was of Kurdish origin, showed himself a master of generalship and built up supreme power throughout the Middle East. In 1170 he secured Egypt from the Fatimids and in 1187 inflicted a decisive defeat on the Crusaders at Hattin, followed by the capture of Jerusalem. Nur al Din had made Aleppo his fortress capital and Saladin installed his brother al-Adil there and the immensely impressive facade and portal to the citadel are Ayyubid work.

The Mongol period: the Il-Khans and their successors in Persia, Mawarannahr, and eastern Anatolia (1256–1370).

The great destructive sweeps of the Mongol hordes through Iran between 1220 and 1230 and the defeat of the Seljuks in Anatolia in 1243 were followed by the permanent rule of the grandson of Chingiz, Hulagu (1256–65), as first Il-Khan of the west, who extended the conquest to Baghdad (1258), Aleppo and Damascus (1260) and under Abaqa (1265–81) his son, from 1278 to eastern Anatolia.

The Mongols continued to prefer a seminomadic existence, moving each year between summer pastures in the lower mountains and winter pastures in the plain. At the Takht-i Suleyman, a former site of a Sassanian fire-temple in the crater of an extinct volcano in southern Azarbayjan, Abaqa had a palace built c1270 called Saturiq to be the summer hunting lodge. The main rooms were paneled with ceramic tiled dado and stucco reliefs above in the vaults. It was built round a courtyard, in the center of which was a natural lake, and with a four-aiwan plan, usual for all public buildings at this time. The interiors were completely clothed in tiles and stucco and even the exteriors were tiled. In the principal room tiles of elaborate technique were used to make panels with star and cross tiles with designs of dragon and phoenix in relief under turquoise or cobalt glaze and with overglaze gold enhancement. Friezes of tiles in similar technique show high-relief designs of hunting and battle scenes, while the same molds were also used for luster-painted tiles.

Other types of pottery characteristic of the Il-Khanid period and also represented by finds of sherds at Takht-i Suleyman are imitations of Chinese celadon with molded relief designs under a green glaze and painted designs in black under a blue glaze or painted in cobalt or turquoise under a colorless glaze. This latter technique was used in the very early 13th century, before the Mongol invasion, but these so-called "Sultanabad" wares continued after the Mongol conquest and into the 14th century. The type in which the design is first outlined in greenish black on the white body and the background then filled in with dark blue or hatched backgrounds on a white slip ground

dates only from this time. Both shapes and exterior petal-design derive from the imported Chinese celadon. Other types of decoration show figures in typical Mongol dress, often against a background dominated by a design in which lotus flowers are prominent, a motif introduced from the Far East or central Asia by the invaders.

Similar lotus flowers are also prominent in the decoration of the inlaid metal vessels, but on these the figures are more slender and elegant, wearing close-fitting caps. Usually, however, the main theme in the decoration is now provided by honorific inscriptions in bold naskhi script. Favorite shapes are faceted candlesticks and water bowls with inturned mouths, a shape also deriving from Chinese celadon (there are dated examples of 1338, 1347, and 1351). Other shapes are rectangular caskets, pen-boxes, and elegant cups with a splayed foot; and the figural subjects on them are peaceful scenes of feasting, music, and hunting. The main center of production was in Fars.

The Il-Khans were great builders of mosques, madrasas, and tombs after their conversion to Islam in 1295. The most impressive surviving monuments are the congregational mosque at Veramin (1322–6); the shrine of Pir-i Bakran at Linjan outside Isfahan (1303–12); the great mihrab niche supplied to the Friday mosque at Isfahan in 1310; the complex of mosque, tomb, and khanqah (Sufi foundation) at Natanz (1306–8); and the great domed tomb of Uljaytu at Sultaniya (1303–13). In these buildings it is the lavish decoration that is the most striking feature. The interiors are richly clad in stucco with inscriptions in both naskhi and Kufic intertwined with foliage and geometric elements, often in high relief and originally painted. On the outside tile-mosaic patterns of geometric form occur, in which stylized Kufic can be distinguished, in two blues, turquoise and cobalt, most notably on the Uljaytu mausoleum, where the vaults under the dome are laid out in star-shaped elements. The stucco reliefs of the period represent the highest achievement in this ancient art; but the tile mosaics were employed with even greater finesse and variety later.

The later Il-Khanid period also saw the development of the arts of the book to its supremacy in Islamic art. When Dust Muhammad wrote a short account for the Safavid prince Bahram Mirza (1544), it was to the reign of the last Il-Khan Abu Sa'id (1316–35) that the emergence of the miniature as an art form was attributed. Then the master (ustad) Ahmad Musa is said to have "invented the kind of painting which is current at the present time". Continuity is thus recognized between the Il-Khanid masters and the school flourishing under Shah Tahmasp. Although we cannot point to any work by Ahmad Musa, we do have a great series of illustrations to the Book of Kings, the Shah-nama of Firdawsi, which belong to this period. Dust Muhammad charts a system of descent by training from master to pupil from Ahmad Musa to Shams al-Din, the protégé and afterwards master under the Jalayrid Sultan Uways (1356–74) and from him to Abd al-Hayy and Junayd who worked for his successor Sultan Ahmad Jalayr.

Calligraphy in Islamic Art

Arabic calligraphy differs from Western calligraphy in two separate and fundamental ways. It originated not as a utilitarian means of communication between man and man, but as a sacred means of communication from God to man. The Arabic script was scarcely evolved, and little used before the time of Muhammad; it was developed within a century into majestic form as a vehicle for the transmission of the Koran and thus became the heritage of all Islamic peoples. For both the calligrapher and the beholder this factor gives this art its character and importance, and explains its function not only in the book, but as a dominant element in architectural decoration, and in almost all the other art forms—metal, ceramic, glass, textile—of the Islamic world.

Secondly, Arabic script is differentiated from Latin by its composition. Both are alphabetic; but whereas Latin letters are always separate entities, in Arabic writing they are part of a unit. All letters, except those beginning a word, join on to the preceding letter, and also, with four exceptions, to the succeeding one. The script therefore moves horizontally from right to left with breaks only at the ends of words or where these final letters occur. The number of letter-forms is also fewer; certain forms are only differentiated by dots; and these together with diacritical signs, which indicate short vowels, in some scripts make an important background accompaniment to the linear pattern of the letters.

As in Latin lettering with its Roman, Gothic, Uncial, Italic, and other forms, there are many distinct styles of Arabic script. Here it is only possible to show the most important, and to suggest a few of the ways in which they have been used.

▲ Calligraphy in ceramic tiles used on the dome of the Madrasa Sultani at Isfahan, 1706–14. The top band on the drum bears a pattern of *thuluth* in several layers; below is Kufic with a background of square Kufic; below that, square Kufic in medallions

▶ *Maghribi* script, used in North Africa and Spain; 1599. Escorial Library, near Madrid, MS. 1340

▼ *Nasta'liq* script

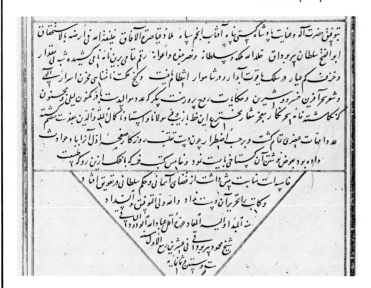

The earliest style is known as Kufic and has many forms. In the earliest type of Koran great horizontal elongations, spacing the words within the line, are characteristic. The writing is done with a broad-edged reed pen, but already this is manipulated with great sophistication; all the strokes are wide, making great rounded bowls which, with the diagonal terminations, counterbalance the long horizontals. The sacred import of the text is expressed in deliberate, abstract terms. Eastern Kufic stresses diagonal movement in its diamond shaped bowls and the vertical element; the tall letters *alif* and *lam* which frequently come together make strong parallels, and if reversed, a composite letter with a double curve, thus dominating the pattern. Yet another pattern was created by North African and Spanish calligraphers stressing terminal letters by extending them in great curves; the ink is characteristically thin and modulated, and diacritical marks are used to enhance the color contrast.

A more legible and informal script had developed contemporaneously with Kufic, and in the 10th century rules of proportion for each letter were formulated by the calligrapher Ibn Muqlah. Six classic, closely related styles were evolved, including *naskhi, thuluth,* and *muhaqqaq.* The discipline of these canons of proportion allows a new freedom to develop without loss of control. The baseline which gives Kufic its stability is no longer important—letters can overlap and the pen moves with a new fluency creating a different rhythm and making a more complex and dynamic pattern.

At different times and in different countries other styles developed, of which the most important is *nasta'liq,* invented in the late 14th century and used in Iran, Turkey, and India. It has a new lyrical quality; delicate line movements replace the sinuous strength of *thuluth.* Characteristically it is used to transcribe poetry rather than the Koran.

In architectural decoration, and in its application to various materials, the great achievements in cursive scripts are the creation of complex patterns within a given area: often also against a background arabesque. In Kufic new styles were invented for three-dimensional usage; chunky forms with a strong base line, completely geometric forms for built-in brick inscriptions, or forms where the verticals twist themselves into elaborate patterns. And almost all these varieties of calligraphy can be combined together. The variety of Islamic script is immense and its incidence and importance omnipresent in the Islamic world.

NICOLETE GRAY

Further reading. Khatibi, A. and Sijelmassi, M. (trans. Hughes, J.) *The Splendour of Islamic Calligraphy,* London (1976). Lings, M. *The Quranic Art of Calligraphy and Illumination,* London (1976). Safadi, Y.H. *Islamic Calligraphy,* London (1978). Schimmel, A. *Islamic Calligraphy,* London (1970).

An example of eastern Kufic from Iraq or Iran; late 11th century. Collection of H.H. Prince Sadruddin Agha Khan, Geneva

Below right An example of *muhaqqaq* script written by Muhammad ibn Aybak in Baghdad in 1307. Topkapi Saray Library, Istanbul

▶ A section of the monumental Kufic round the courtyard of the Great Mosque at Sousse, Tunisia; built in 851

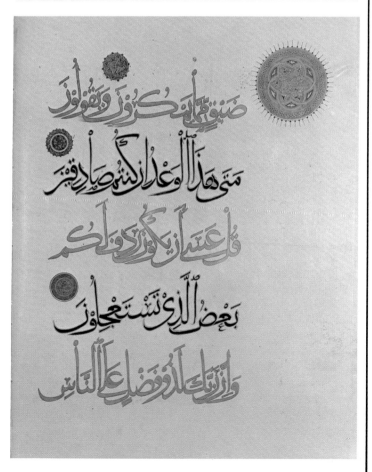

The bier of Alexander the Great from the "Demotte" Shah-nama; mid 14th century. Freer Gallery of Art, Washington, D.C.

We can attribute to the court of Uways a fragmentary copy of the Fable Book *Kalila wa Dimna* (University of Istanbul). In these splendid and richly colored pages the drawing of the animals is most sympathetic and the landscape, while still showing evident Chinese influence, begins a practice of extension into the margins of the manuscript, thus allowing trees and plants and birds to appear against the clear space of the blank paper, which is in line with Chinese precedent.

The Abu Sa'id *Shah-nama* (now dispersed but often called "Demotte" after its former owner), was lavishly illustrated with more than 100 miniatures, and the ample page permitted a large-scale treatment (nearly 12 in, 30 cm, in width by 6 in,

16 cm, to 7 in, 18 cm, in height). The action in the foreground dominates the scene with large figures, expressive and eloquent gestures and, on occasion, unrestrained grief. These figures are either silhouetted against a gold or a deep blue sky or framed by an architectural proscenium; but what was wholly new was the landscape setting for almost every scene. This new element owes its vocabulary to Chinese tradition, but instead of dwarfing the human as it does in that tradition, they are juxtaposed without resolution or scale or relation. So though both these elements are expressively drawn with all the freshness of a new vision, the whole bursts the bounds of the book.

In the *Shah-nama* of Uways a generation later (in part preserved in an album in the Topkapi Saray Museum, Istanbul), the two elements are reconciled and a single unified vision is achieved in which action is placed in a natural world to which it can be seen to belong, though in the interior scenes the old-fashioned flat architecture is not completely abandoned. This further step was taken under Sultan Ahmad (1382–1410), from whose reign two notable manuscripts survive, a *Diwan* of Khwaju of Kirman in the British Library, London, dated 1396 from Baghdad and with the precious indication of a signed miniature by Junayd; and a *Khusrau and Shirin* of Nizami in the Freer Gallery of Art, Washington, D.C., from Tabriz, probably between 1406 and 1410. In both of these the architecture, although still screen-like, is articulated so as to give some indication of depth. Thus the style was formed which was to be used through the 15th century at the courts of the Timurids and later the Turkmen rulers.

This same period saw the culmination of the abstract art of illumination with the provision of double-page frontispieces of arabesque patterns in blue and green framing the title of the work. In the case of a splendid 30-volume copy of the Koran of noble proportions, 21½ by 15 in (55 by 38 cm), prepared for the Il-Khan Uljaytu in 1314–15 in Hamadan, each great volume has a double-page frontispiece consisting of different geometric patterns in colors of extreme beauty and accomplishment (now in the National Library, Cairo). In binding, too, the period witnessed the perfection of leather tooling in gold on the outer covers and at its end the invention for Sultan Ahmad Jalayr at Baghdad of the use of filigree arabesque patterns on a colored ground panel on the inside of the covers.

The Mamluks (1250–1517). The Mamluks were recruited as slave troops under the Ayyubids, mainly from the region north of the Black Sea, then in the hands of the Golden Horde, the westernmost branch of the Mongols. The word "Mamluk" means "freed" and only the slaves who had been given their freedom after conversion to Islam and meritorious service were entitled to the name and were then eligible for civilian as well as military office of high rank. In 1259 the Mamluk Baybars succeeded to the Ayyubid Empire in the control of which he was aided by other Mamluk emirs. Their offices were not hereditary but had to be filled by new generations of Mamluks. Their sons, having been born free, were disqualified. It was remarkable that such a regime retained power for 250 years, though there was a change of line in 1382 when the rule passed to the Circassian or Burji Mamluk emirs with Barquq (1382–99) as the first of this new line.

The period until 1322 was dominated by the struggle to stem the advance of the Mongol armies into Syria. In 1322 a truce was arranged in Aleppo with provision for duty-free trade between Mamluk and Mongol lands, under which the Mongols imported only raw materials whereas the Mamluks were eager to acquire finished products. The Uljaytu Koran of 1313 may have reached Egypt as a direct fruit of these negotiations. Earlier Mongol influence may have been conveyed

through migrant craftsmen, such as those who worked on the *mihrab* in the *madrasa* of al-Nasir Muhammad (1295–1303), the stucco work at the mausoleum of Qarasunqur (1300–1), and the *mihrab* added to the mosque of ibn Tulun in 1297.

The craftsmen who worked for al-Nasir may have left Iran before the conversion of Ghazan in 1295, in search of commissions among the Mamluks. There is no doubt of their introduction of their fine skill in high relief stucco.

The first Bahri Mamluk Sultan Aybak (1250–7) was succeeded by Baybars (1260–77) and Qala'un (1279–90) whose descendants retained power for over 100 years. These rulers were not only successful generals but great builders in their two capitals Cairo and Damascus. Baybars reopened the Red Sea ports to international trade in Chinese silks and ceramics which from then on arrived in quantity. Hitherto there had been only sporadic instances of the impact of Chinese influence in the arts and in Mamluk decoration. The full impact came only from c1285, when Mongol figures first appear in the decoration of the enameled glass of Syria, while in the 14th century some mosque lamps like those made for hanging in the mosque of Sultan Hasan in Cairo (1356–63) are entirely covered with decoration of lotus flowers and peonies. On other lamps, on which the main decoration is of Koranic texts in *thuluth* script, the chinoiserie patterns are confined to the area below the shoulder. From c1290 Mongol figures begin to appear also on inlaid metalwork, including some pieces made especially for the Yemen which was under Mamluk control and vital to the Far Eastern trade. So both these luxury products were also exported to China, where examples were found still in use in the 19th and 20th centuries. Aleppo was no longer a glass center at this time after its sack in 1260 and Damascus remained the major factory until it was captured by Tamerlane in 1400, when he stripped the city of many of its skilled workers.

In the earlier Mamluk metalwork the place of chinoiserie had been filled by medallions showing scenes of hunting and polo-playing. But exceptionally on the most famous vessel of the period, the so-called "Baptistère de Saint Louis", an ancient possession of the French crown but probably in fact made for Salar, Mamluk Viceroy of Egypt (*ob.* 1310), battle scenes are prominent in the decoration, though there are also hunting scenes as well. The armor and some headdresses of the emirs are of Mongol type which the emirs are known to have adopted. It bears the signature, six times repeated, of Muhammad al-Zain, the leading craftsman of his day. Copper ceased to be used for inlay after 1293 while from 1290 gold was added to the decoration and continued until the decline of the inlaid metal craft c1375.

Wealth flowed into Egypt and Syria through international trade, thus making possible the great burst of building by the Mamluk emirs of tombs and palaces as well as religious foundations. They were not scrupulous over robbing previous structures of rare materials, such as cypress wood or marble. The Sultan Qala'un (1284–5) founded a hospital on the site of the Fatimid palace; the youthful Sultan Hasan who succeeded

One of the surviving lamps made for Sultan Hasan's mosque in Cairo; 1356–63. British Museum, London

in 1347 began in 1356 to build a great mosque attached to his own mausoleum. This was a large complex, for the cruciform mosque was to have a *madrasa* in each of the four corners for the four orthodox theological schools. On the street was a tall porch above which it was planned to build a pair of minarets in imitation of the Seljuk mosques of Anatolia. This grand entrance led through a domed vestibule into a courtyard centered on an ablution fountain and then, changing direction, into the mosque courtyard, and beyond the *qibla* wall, into the tomb chamber of the sultan. It continued the Ayyubid practice of alternating color in the stone structure, while colored marbles enriched the whole *qibla* wall and the deep *mihrab* niche was paneled with marble veneers arranged in arcades and geometric patterns. Sultan Hasan was assassinated in 1362 before he could finish this immense building and the entrance never received its marble paneling; while the great bronze doors were removed 100 years later by the Burji Sultan al-Mu'ayyad Shaykh to adorn his own mosque. This pattern of *madrasas* attached to the mausoleum of the founder was common in 14th century Mamluk Cairo, but in the 15th century the mausolea of the Burji Mamluk Sultans were built in the eastern cemetery of the city outside the walls, conspicuous for their high ribbed domes in their desert setting, and surrounded by smaller domes of lesser men. These great stone

domes mark a further achievement in Mamluk architectural engineering.

The wealth of the Mamluks is further demonstrated in the manuscript arts of illumination, miniatures, and book-binding. Inspired probably by the Uljaytu Koran, monumental copies of the Holy Book were produced in Cairo through the 14th century, their great opening pages more than 2 ft (61 cm) tall with their central pattern generally based on the star, as in architectural layout, and Kufic inscriptions in panels above and below, also monumental in style. As the century advanced the coloring became stronger with blue and gold predominating instead of the pale Il-Khanid colors. The Mamluk bindings are tooled with medallions and geometric designs simplified as compared with the illumination, but reaching in the 15th century elaborate tooling, in which gold enhances the whole design including an inscriptional border. These Mamluk Korans are some of the most sumptuous books ever produced; most are now preserved in the Egyptian National Library.

The art of miniature painting was more conservative, prolonging the tradition of illustration of scientific works and the *Maqamat* of Hariri which had matured under the Atabegs and Ayyubids. The making of ingenious waterclocks and other semi-scientific toys for mixing and dispensing wine had long fascinated rulers. Very popular was a work composed for the Artukid Nasir al-Din Mahmud (1200–22) by al-Jazari, the *Book of the Knowledge of Mechanical Devices*. The finest surviving copy, though now broken up and dispersed, is dated 1315 and was produced in Syria. A group of the miniatures is now in the Freer Gallery of Art, Washington, D.C. Similar are copies of the cosmology composed by al-Qazwini (1203–83) under the last Abbasid Caliph al-Mustasim with the title *The Wonders of Creation*. The finest surviving copy is divided between the New York Public Library and the Freer Gallery. Here the great decorative quality of the illustrations exceeds their scientific interest (c1400).

Further removed from the versions produced in pre-Mongol Mesopotamia, a beautiful copy of the *Maqamat* of Hariri, made in 1334 in Egypt and now preserved in Vienna (Nationalbibliothek), shows figures silhouetted against a gold background, while the landscape, tent, or interior are reduced to stylized patterns. A decorative frontispiece shows on a gold ground an enthroned ruler attended by cupbearer and musicians and even a contortionist, while overhead are a pair of confronted winged and crowned Victories.

Still popular under the Mamluks was the Arabic version of the animal fables, the *Kalila wa Dimna*, in the illustrations to which is a strong tendency towards pattern-making especially in the use of standard types for mountain, water, and plants, with a corresponding excellence in decorative composing.

Influence from Inner Asia must have reached Egypt without passing through Iran, for the design and knotting of the Mamluk carpets of Cairo are distinct from the Persian in every way. The central design is of a star set in an octagon with the corners filled to make a square. This design originated in the Cloud Collar, a cosmological symbol which surrounded the peak of the nomad tent but had started as a Buddhist four-pointed cape. It can always be identified by the multiples of four and must have reached Mamluk Egypt through the Qipjaq on the Volga. The Cairene carpets are luxury products, knotted in fine lustrous wool dyed cherry red, pale green, and a more sparing use of sky blue. They were much sought after and reached Europe by 1474 at the latest; but their manufacture continued after the Ottoman conquest of Egypt in 1517.

The Timurid and Turkmen rule of eastern Anatolia, Iran, and central Asia (1370–1506). The world-conqueror Timur Leng (Tamerlane) in spite of his Muslim commitment, inflicted as great damage on the lands which he subdued between 1370 and 1405 from Transoxiana to Turkey and Syria as had the Mongols 150 years earlier. At his death in 1405 he was leading a great army to the conquest of China where the first Emperor of the Ming dynasty Hung Wu was as ruthless a general as himself; both rulers, however, were builders and patrons of the traditional arts. At his capital Samarkand, Timur erected palaces, mosques, and tombs of splendor, even more strikingly seen in the tented camps in gardens in the suburbs. In these the mosaic tiling of the permanent brick buildings was replaced by embroidered tent hangings and woven carpets, great canopies with bird finials, and all the splendors of costume and display depicted in miniatures in which alone they survive. Of the larger buildings of Samarkand, especially the immense congregational mosque called the Bibi Khanum after his favorite wife, in spite of severe damage by earthquake, enough remains to represent the boldness and scale of conception and skills in execution by the craftsmen that Timur brought to his capital from the conquered provinces of Iran and Turkey.

The plan was laid out on a grid system mathematically drawn and under the influence of the Uljaytu mausoleum at Sultaniya. This monument, like the mosque, once had a great portal (*pishtaq*) with two flanking minarets. Domes raised on high drums in the center of the east and west sides of the court dominate it. Stone as well as brick was used in the structure, no doubt worked by Indian labor imported after his sack of Delhi, but as usual the brick surfaces are covered in inlaid tilework while only the inscriptional panels and the spandrels of the arches are decorated in tile mosaic, all in turquoise, manganese, and cobalt.

The most extensive remaining complex in Samarkand is at the Shah-i-Zindeh which grew up as an approach to the shrine of Qutham ibn' Abbas. The present sanctuary is of 14th-century date, domed and tiled; but it is the portals to other tombs which line the route to the shrine that illustrate the rich variety of technique available in Samarkand in the lifetime of Timur. The carved and glazed terracotta relief inscriptions stand out proud against a low relief arabesque of floral sprays in white and two blues (turquoise and cobalt). The doorways are surmounted by *muqarnas*, corbeled niches, and framed by pilasters while the reveals show panels of star-shaped compositions

The enthroned ruler on a frontispiece of a copy of the Maqamat of Hariri made in Egypt in 1334. Österreichische Nationalbibliothek, Vienna

in blue and gold. The dome drums and the outer walls are in cut tile mosaic patterns including monumental Kufic inscriptions, below turquoise-clad domes.

Similar rich tilework and glazed brick decorate the walls of the well-preserved Gur Emir with a tall drum below a high ribbed dome with patterned turquoise tiling, constructed by Timur in 1403–4 for his son, Muhammad Sultan (*ob.* 1403), but to become his own tomb in 1405. His son Ulugh Beg later provided a dark green jade catafalque in the upper chamber, the largest block of jade known. Ulugh Beg is also remembered in Samarkand, where he was governor, for his beautiful *madrasa* (1420) with tile-clad facade towards the city square, the Registan, framed by twin minarets and with deeply recessed portal over the entrance, and for his famous observatory.

The palace of Aq Saray was built by Timur (1380–96) at Kesh, the city of his birth renamed Shah-i-Sabz, 50 miles (80 km) south of Samarkand, but never finished. Here there is bold use of inlay on the massive towers of the portal, but with tile mosaic on the reveal of the great *aiwan* arch, which is 72 ft (22 m) wide and 41 ft (12.6 m) deep with hexagonal tiles in blue and gold framed by tile mosaic white inscriptions in *thuluth* on a deep blue ground enhanced with floral patterns in two blues and yellow.

At Turkestan city is a pilgrim shrine (*mazar*), a mosque, and

Tile inscription and arabesques in mausoleum 15 in the Shah-i-Zindeh, the shrine complex at Samarkand; c1380–9

mausoleum for Ahmad Yasavi (1396–7), cruciform in plan with a great central dome and a second high-ribbed dome over the tomb chamber by the architect Khawja Hasan of Shiraz. All the external walls are decorated with brick inlay and tiles with inscriptions in Persian and Arabic painted in Kufic under the glaze.

Shah Rukh succeeded in establishing himself as his father's successor in most of his wide empire. He moved the capital to Herat in Khurasan, where he had ruled as governor, until his death in 1447. He too was a builder and his wife Gawhar Shad built the first cruciform mosque at Mashhad, dated 1418–19 and with inscriptions designed by their son Baysunghur. The architect was Qiwam al-Din Zayn al-Din of Shiraz, one of the four leading lights at his court. The tile revetment is now much restored but the tile mosaic in the spandrels and the framed inscriptions are better preserved.

Herat has suffered greatly from repeated sacks and from earthquake, so that little survives from its 15th-century splendors. Of the large *musalla* of Gawhar Shad only one minaret survives with polygonal base and with three cornices above on the cylindrical shaft with mosaic tiles between them (1417–38). The *madrasa* by Qiwam al-Din of 1432 resembles that of Ulugh Beg in Samarkand but only one minaret survives with the west chamber now known as the mausoleum of Baysunghur. This has a high ribbed dome clad in tile inlay in two blues, black, white, and red and with painted tile Kufic inscription outlining its base line.

At Khargird, also in Khurasan, a *madrasa* was built by Ghiyath al-Din, a minister of Shah Rukh, in 1435–44 with a similar internal membrane structure beneath each of the four domed chambers. The period was rich in shrines, such as that of the Imam Riza at Mashhad and that of Khwaja Abd Allah Ansari at Gazur Gah near Herat, where the enclosure (*hazira*) surrounding the tomb of the saint was constructed in 1425 by Shah Rukh himself and became the burial place of many of his family. At Turbat i-Shaykh Jam, an older foundation, Shah Rukh added a new mosque and *madrasa* in 1440–3, built by the architect Hajji Mahmud of Shiraz. Finally at Taiyabad, near the present Afghan frontier with Iran, the mosque Masjid i-Mawlana of 1444–5 retains much of its original surface decoration in tile work and interior painted designs which were much developed at this time.

No major Timurid building survives in the west or south; but the Qaraqoyunlu Turkman Jahan Shah built a major mosque in his capital Tabriz in 1465, of which enough survives to give an idea of the plan and sumptuous decoration of this "Blue Mosque". The Aq-Qoyunlu Uzun Hasan moved his winter capital to Isfahan and restored the congregational mosque there. His son Ya'qub built a sumptuous palace in Tabriz, and its description by Venetian envoys survives to give an idea of this *Hasht Bihisht*. All the work for the Turkman court was carried out by Persian craftsmen and they drew on the Khurasani capital of Herat as well as on Shiraz for their artists.

Herat at the end of the Timurid period was described by the future Emperor Babur in 1506, before its capture by Shaybani Khan in 1507, as full of learned men: poets, musicians, artists, calligraphers, bringing every work to perfection. But of all the palaces and gardens he visited, nothing remains today.

After architecture the major arts of the Timurid period were those of the book: calligraphy, illumination, miniature painting, and binding. We have seen how these developed in the late Mongol period and came to full fruition in the twin capitals of the Jalayrids, Tabriz and Baghdad. Under Shah Rukh these cities lost their primacy. Baghdad indeed recovered briefly when it was for five years, 1460–5, the seat of government of Pir Budaq, a Turkman princely connoisseur.

The first Timurid center was Shiraz under the government of Umar Shaykh and his son Iskandar (1393–1414) to which some of the best Jalayrid painters must have moved. This school reached its height in two anthologies produced for Iskandar in 1410–11. Some of the compositions illustrating these had already been devised under the Mongols, but many were here first invented to become the source for many later Timurid versions at Herat and Shiraz itself. One special feature of these two manuscripts (now in the Gulbenkian Foundation, Lisbon, and the British Library, London), vividly illustrate a new encounter with Chinese art. Timur had established contact with the new Ming court in 1387 and maintained it until a break in 1395. These diplomatic contacts were renewed by Shah Rukh in 1407 and remained intense until 1435. Many designs survive, having been mounted later in albums at the Ottoman court in Istanbul, to witness to the use of Chinese motifs in Persian-Islamic versions. Their impact can be traced in manuscript illumination and on book-bindings. Shiraz had been a pioneer in the introduction of elegant floral decoration into illumination in the final decades of the 14th century; now there were added numerous Chinese motifs—dragon and phoenix, lions playing with ribbons, ducks and wild geese.

The connection between Shiraz and Herat was close and the first Timurid atelier at Shiraz certainly contributed both examples and artists to that established at Herat by Baysunghur in 1420. He was able to attract the leading calligraphers, binders, illuminators, and miniaturists from Tabriz; and until his death in 1433, they produced for him the most accomplished work of the time. Half a dozen of his fine books survive, to witness to the taste and skills of the time. Apart from the rich and well-matched palette, their most outstanding feature is the perfect harmony between figures and their setting, whether natural or architectural, and their perfect relation to the manuscript. The most important of these manuscripts is a *Shahnama*, 1430, now in the Gulistan Library, Teheran. This was written by Mawlana Ja'far of Tabriz, is beautifully illuminated and contains 21 miniatures, including a double-page frontispiece on which Baysunghur is represented on horseback attending a hunting party. These are not signed but we know that the two leading painters were the master Sayyid Ahmad and Amir Khalil, while the leading illuminator was Khwaja Ali. The compositions are probably traditional; three at least derive from a manuscript of 60 years earlier, Tabriz work under the Jalayr, but up-dated in accordance with the new, more decorative conventions of coral-edged rocks and more

disciplined trees. One half of the miniatures are extended into one of the side margins and the upper margin: a practice of Jalayrid origin.

Also copied by Ja'far in 1431 is a fable book the *Kalila wa Dimna* now in the Topkapi Saray Library, Istanbul, with 19 miniatures in a more refined and lyrical style. These miniatures are to be contrasted with those illustrating a 1430 version of the same work, copied by Shams al-Din. These 22 miniatures show the same academic perfection as the *Shahnama* of 1430, with the same free use of the margin.

Meanwhile Baysunghur's father Shah Rukh had his own library studio, in which he had the *World History* of Rashid al-Din reconstituted and brought up to date by his own historian Hafiz i Abru. He commissioned a *Khamsa* of Nizami for himself, dated 1431, now in the Hermitage Museum, Leningrad. The miniatures, particularly that of Iskandar watching the Sirens swimming, have an intimate charm but look more old-fashioned than Baysunghur's and may well be by artists recently recruited from Shiraz. Shah Rukh is known to have protected and encouraged central Asian Turki scholars and poets and a unique manuscript of the *Mi'rajnama*, the *Journey of the Prophet Muhammad to Heaven and Hell* is attributed to his library. This manuscript (Bibliothèque Nationale, Paris) written in Uighur-Turki script by a skilled secretary (*bakhshi*) and dated 1436 is illustrated by 57 miniatures lavishly enhanced with gold and brilliant colors in contrasting scenes of punishment and bliss.

Baysunghur's younger brother Muhammad Juki (*ob.* 1445) was a major patron. About 1440 a *Shah-nama* manuscript, now in the keeping of the Royal Asiatic Society of London, was prepared for him with 31 miniatures, which reach the highest pitch of romantic feeling in their ethereal landscapes and chivalrous battle scenes. After Shah Rukh's death in 1447, his family retained supreme power for only two more years under his son Ulugh Beg. He too may have patronized the miniature art, for 19 miniatures illustrating a *Nizami* dated 1446 by a certain Sultan Ali *al-Bavardi* (the Taster) survive with angels in the four corners of the frontispiece with a central dedication to him. He died in 1449.

The Empire then fell apart and all western and central Iran were overwhelmed by the Black Sheep Turkman Jahan Shah by 1453. He had been established in Tabriz since 1436, and his son Pir Budaq gathered artists round him in his two seats of government, first in Shiraz, 1453–60, and then in Baghdad, 1460–5. Pir Budaq was killed in 1466 and Jahan Shah in 1467, when the Turkman leadership passed to the White Sheep confederacy under Uzun Hasan. He too, like Jahan Shah, seems not to have had much time for the arts, but his son Ya'qub (1478–90) was a major patron and under him the style of miniature art became increasingly exuberant and colorful, trees and plants forming a tapestry-like ensemble for the richly dressed figures of his court.

This style, though originally based upon the Herat school, contrasted with the contemporary work in Herat where Sultan Husayn Bayqara, the last Timurid ruler of note, pre-

From an anthology produced for the Sultan Iskandar at Shiraz, The Battle between the Tribes of Layla and Majnun; 1411; British Library, London

five poems with wonderful illumination and miniatures survives in the Bodleian Library, Oxford (four parts) and the John Rylands Library, Manchester (one part), all dated 1485. Like so many of the fine books of this school this passed afterwards into the Mughal Imperial library.

The Ottoman period (1326–1922). From a modest nucleus in west central Anatolia the Osmanli or Ottoman Turks developed rapidly first a central state by absorbing the other successors to the Seljuks and then from the early 16th century, an empire which stretched from the Atlantic to the border of Iran and Arabia. Even before the final capture of Constantinople in 1453 they had absorbed the greater part of the Balkans, much indeed before 1402. The Osmanli or House of Osman were for some 300 years an exceptionally able and vigorous ruling line which persisted until the end of the Empire at the close of the 1914–18 war. Their subjects included peoples of many different races and traditions but the Turks remained a governing class. Thus Ottoman art is an imperial art in which craftsmen and artists might come from many different races but, in a strong centralized state, the direction of the court and the capital was decisive. There were regional differences in materials and village crafts like carpet weaving or embroidery, but the main line of development was set by the court and its styles were carried everywhere. Thus Ottoman-style mosques were built in Cairo and Damascus, and their decoration followed the designs laid down for the official Iznik kilns for tiles or pottery vessels. We will therefore be following the progress of the arts only in the central area.

At the same time there were other forces behind Ottoman culture which affected the visual arts, especially the power and prestige of the mystical orders, in particular of the Bekhtashi. Founded in the second half of the 13th century, this order spread rapidly among the nomads and peasants and became identified with the Janissary corps, the Imperial guard formed from Christian boys. The Bekhtashi founded *tekkes* or monastic houses and propagated a cult combining old Turkish shamanism with Shi'a and Sufi mysticism. Another powerful cultural influence was from the Mevlevi order of dervishes whose patron saint was Jalal al-Din Rumi (1207–73). With its headquarters in Konya it propagated a more extreme form of mysticism especially among the intellectual and governing classes. Further cohesion was brought to the urban societies by the *Zaviye* or clubs of artists calling themselves *ahi* or "brotherhoods of virtue", a kind of cooperative or guild with pooled income. They were formed of men of different trades and operated to preserve traditions of skill. Thus local methods of craftsmanship survived.

The Yesil Cami or Green Mosque at Iznik (built 1378–91) already shows the Ottoman liking for the spacious portico, for carved stone door and window frames. The prayer hall is still a domed square and wood is still used, not only for the splendid *mimbar* but also structurally, as at Beysehir, where tall wooden columns support the roof of the Esrefoglu mosque. Carved wood doors carry on the Seljuk and Karaman tra-

sided for 35 years, until 1506, over a court at which the arts of the book reached their peak. The calligrapher Sultan Ali Mashhadi and the painters Mirak and Bihzad shone in the circle dominated by the poet and mystic Jami (1414–92) who composed biographies of the Sufi saints and a collection of stories about them in the *Baharistan* or *Spring Land*, and the *Haft Aurang* of seven poems with allegorical meaning, as well as lyrical poems (*ghazals*). His dominance does not mean that the earlier poets Sa'di, Nizami, or Amir Khusrau were neglected and indeed the best attested work of Bihzad illustrate these poets. It follows that the central point of the work of his school was man; but men in quiet relation to one another rather than in action. Architecture too plays its part as a support for the brilliant blue-dominated harmony, conveying an ideal picture of life. In all this Sultan Husayn was rivaled as patron by his minister the poet Ali Shir Nawa'i, who wrote equally in Turki and Persian: a fine contemporary copy of his

dition through the 14th century, as at Kasabakoy, behind Sinope.

Bursa was captured by Orhan in 1326 and became the first Ottoman capital. Beside the great silk bazaar Yilderim (Thunderbolt) Bayazit (1382–1402) built the congregational mosque (1396–1400), raising 20 domes on 12 great cruciform piers. This enabled the walls to carry no weight and so to admit plenty of light. But this mosque must yield to the splendors of the much smaller Yesil Cami (Green Mosque) of Bursa (1419). Though damaged by earthquake in 1855, it retains the extensive tiling inside the Sultan's loge and the *mihrab* and inscription above the *qibla* arch. The tiles are in *cuerda seca* technique, as in Iran and central Asia, and are glazed in deep blue, green, white, and yellow. This work is in fact signed by the "Masters of Tabriz", while the inscription in the royal box is in Persian and signed by Mehmet the Eccentric. So this work in the Iranian tradition, not that of the Seljuks, represents a new departure in Anatolia. The painted decoration above the tiles, on the other hand, is by a local man Ali ibn Ilyas Ali-*naqqash*. Owing to the death of Mehmet I in 1421 the mosque was left without a portico. His tomb on the slope above the mosque was built 1421–5 and has lost by earthquake the green tiles that sheathed the dome and gave it its name; but it retains its great dome, the first Ottoman on this scale. Its chief glory is the tile-clad catafalque and the *mihrab* behind it, which are in the same style and technique as the tiles in the mosque.

Murat II (1421–51) built his own mosque and tomb at Bursa in a more austere style, but at Edirne in Thrace, the second Ottoman capital, he built a royal mosque, the Muradiye, in 1434, with panels of hexagonal painted tiles in blue and white after Chinese example with floral designs giving an Islamic arabesque flavor. Since the copying of Chinese blue and white vessels in ceramics is not found at Iznik before 1500 and there is no evidence for Chinese porcelain in the collections of the Sultans before 1495, the designs on these tiles of 1435–6 must have been brought from Tabriz by the potters. In this mosque there are also *cuerda seca* tiles round the *mihrab* like those at Bursa. The architect of the Uc Serefeli mosque at Edirne (1438–47) has achieved a dome 79 ft (24 m) in diameter supported by massive piers tied together by pairs of tie-beams. The courtyard is larger than the mosque and the entry is through a raised portico of verd antique columns: there are four minarets, the tallest being over 220 ft (67 m) with three galleries round the shaft.

The first building of Mehmet II, the Conqueror (1444–81), was the castle of Rumeli Hisar, built on the European shore of the Bosphorus (1452), with walls 220 yds (200 m) long, stretching from the hill behind down to the water's edge. After the capture of Constantinople in 1453 time was needed to clear up the city and induce Turks to reside there. The Fatih (Conqueror's) mosque was started only in 1463, although the cathedral of Hagia Sophia was immediately converted for use as a mosque. The first palace of Topkapisaray was completed in 1472, but the oldest surviving monument in the city is the

turbe of the Vizier Mehmet Pasa of 1473 with glazed brick exterior. Of the same year is the Cinili Kiosk in the palace garden, an elegant porticoed building raised on a podium and with blue and black tiling on the facade, including inscriptions in Persian. It derives its plan as well as its decoration from Timurid Iran or Samarkand and internally has a central chamber under an eight-ribbed dome and with four *aiwans* opening off it. Little of the Fatih Cami survived an earthquake in 1766 but the dome was 85 ft (26 m) in diameter and in the courtyard carved marble lunettes survive above the windows and tile inscriptions under the portico in *cuerda seca* tiles as in the Muradiye.

Mehmet's successor Bayazid II (1484–1512) built two great endowed complexes, one outside Istanbul of a hexagonal hospital, medical school, mosque, and lodging for dervishes—in all providing for 167 persons; the second foundation was of schools of music, theology and cosmography attached to a mosque at Amasya built 1481–6.

It was only later in the reign that his great mosque in Istanbul was built in 1501–6, when the population of the city was once again reaching the half-million mark. This building is remarkable for its geometrical plan and for the carved marble inscriptions by Hamdullah (*ob.* 1520), regarded as the founder of a distinctive and distinguished style of calligraphy, in which he was followed by Hamza as-Sarafi who developed large floral terminals to decorative angular Kufic script as well as a *thuluth* with floral arabesque enhancement. The greatest exponent of decorative script was Ahmet Karahisari (*ob.* 1556) who excelled also in floral decoration, but in natural growth rather than arabesque pattern; he is best known for his highly fluid but eccentric calligraphy. All these calligraphers worked both in manuscripts and in architectural lettering.

In 1509 a heavy earthquake did immense damage in Istanbul and Thrace, including Edirne. All resources were needed for repair; moreover Selim (1512–20) was occupied with his wide-ranging campaigns, as a result of which eastern Anatolia, Syria, and Egypt were added to the Empire. Many craftsmen from these conquered lands were brought to Istanbul, including 700 potters from Tabriz, moved to Iznik, and many marble craftsmen from Egypt. Selim's own mosque in the capital was completed only in 1522 and must be due to his successor Suleyman (1520–66). In it are the first *cuerda seca* tiles from the Iznik kilns on a lighter body than those at Bursa and in polychrome. Before that date, these kilns had produced in 1495 vessels with underglaze blue painted decoration. Chinese inspiration underlies the whole group but the Islamic element in the design predominates; on several mosque lamps made for the *turbe* of Bayazid II calligraphy is the main decoration in the style of Hamdullah but evidently executed by craftsmen ignorant of Arabic. Among the vessels of this early period the shapes are mostly derived from metal prototypes, but they also include some special shapes such as great footed bowls and ewers, as well as mosque lamps of glass shape. The Iznik kilns were the main official source for wall tiles as well

as vessels for the palace, but throughout the 16th and 17th centuries secondary kilns were working at Kutahya, probably under local Armenian control as is demonstrated by two vessels in the Godman Collection, Horsham, with inscriptions in Armenian and dates of 1510 and 1529. About 1520 turquoise was added to the Iznik palette and from c1525 sage-green and manganese purple appear at the same time that natural flowers begin to supersede arabesque patterns. Conspicuous are the tulips and carnations (*dianthus*) which had earlier been introduced into textile fabrics under Mehmet II, when they figure in bold designs on the velvet woven kaftans combined with stars and stylized clouds. The main center of the important weaving industry was at Bursa where satins as well as velvets were woven. Looms for the exclusive supply of sumptuous robes for the court were set up in Istanbul in the 16th century when the designs led the way for tile decoration in increasingly flowing and complex designs and rich coloring. The famous so-called "Rhodian" red (Armenian bole) first appears in the potters' palette in the great mosque of Suleyman (1550–7) and the beautiful tile-clad interior of the much smaller mosque of Rustam Pasa (1561).

By this date we enter the period of activity of the greatest Ottoman architect and engineer Sinan. Only one other Ottoman architect merits mention here, Mehmet Aga, appointed architect to Ahmet I in 1606, when he was already over 60. In contrast to Sinan he was essentially a decorator, indeed a specialist in inlay of ivory and tortoiseshell on wood, in which materials he constructed an inlaid ebony throne for this Sultan. He began to build the Sultan's mosque in 1609 and finished it in 1617, just before his master's death. The interior is vast and spacious but the low dome rests on huge reeded piers which have been compared to elephant's feet. Ahmet had a passion for tiles and the interior is clad with no less than 20,000, arranged in panels in which blue is the dominant color, hence the popular name, "The Blue Mosque". Not unnaturally quality varies, for this order must have overwhelmed the official kilns and led to outfarming. The Sultan Ahmet mosque is the last major work of the classic age; but Murad IV (1623–40) built two delightful kiosks to ornament the Topkapisaray, that of Revan in 1635 to celebrate the capture of Erivan and that of Baghdad in 1638 when that city was taken from the Safavids. They form viewing rooms overlooking the gardens, so characteristic of Turkish palaces, and are domed, tile-lined above marble dados and with marble balustrading outside the windows under the wide projecting roof eaves.

By the end of the 17th century there began the construction of wooden villas (*yalis*) along both shores of the Bosphorus in delightful shaded gardens, with jetties for access by water. The interiors were enlivened by decorative paintings of flowers in vases and fruit in baskets, which show Dutch influence. After 1700 Western influence, mainly French, increasingly affected

Left: The interior of the Yesil Cami (Green Mosque) at Bursa, Turkey; 1419

An Iznik pottery bowl decorated in blue on white slip; c1520. Victoria and Albert Museum, London

all Turkish art but especially architecture, and Baroque and later Rococo forms and decoration were favored. As applied to such buildings as public fountains for drinking water, with taps not sprays, charming effects were achieved; but when this style extended to the Sultans' palaces on the Bosphorus it became no more than a pastiche of the western. So with painting, the work of Levni (*ob.* 1732) illustrator and portraitist, a certain native vigor of folk origin still informs his costume studies; whereas the flower paintings in the *Sunbulnama* of 1736 (Topkapi Saray Library, Istanbul), charming as they are, are again pastiches from Western flower books, by Isma'il, Ali, and Husayn. Hitherto the Turkish school of miniature painting had represented a vigorous offshoot from the Persian school, to which it added fresh genres in extensive treatment of history, and the court ceremonies and processions of the later 16th century. In these and some geographical and astronomical works the Turkish interest in the world as observed lent a vitality to a new sort of historical and topographical art which preceded the Mughal School of India. But this school faded in the early 17th century.

Very different has been the continuing vitality of the best-known in the west of all Turkish arts, that of the carpet, widely exported since the 15th century. Modern studies of its development have relied, in default of dated examples, on the evidence of Western paintings for the establishment of a chronology. The popularity of the so-called Holbein carpet named from his portrait of the merchant Gisze (1532; Staatliche Museen, Berlin) in which one is depicted as a table cover, is also clearly shown in Italian and rather later Northern paintings from the mid 15th century onwards. The type shows linked octagons of cusped or angular outline in red and white on a dull blue ground covering the whole field, with a border of degenerate Kufic script. A second type associated with the name of Lorenzo Lotto (c1480–1556), who depicted one in an altarpiece (in the church of SS. Giovanni e Paolo, Venice), shows a striking allover design in yellow on a red ground in the form of a strongly angular type of floral arabesque, also forming crosses at the junction of these design units and again with mock Kufic borders. Venetian inventories of the early 16th century frequently include Turkish carpets, though sometimes mistakenly attributed to Rhodes or Damascus. Both "Holbein" and "Lotto" carpets are believed to come from the Ushak region of west-central Anatolia. By 1584 the overseas trade was sufficiently well organized to permit orders being specially placed for clients.

In the late 15th or early 16th century the Ushak area looms introduced a new type of design, apparently under Persian influence, centered on a star or medallion. The first Turkish capture of Tabriz in 1514 may have caused this move. Many prayer rugs were also made in this area and in the neighboring center of Gordes. The sheep of the high Anatolian pastures provided the fine wool for these knotted carpets, produced in many villages, each with its own tradition, modified by contact with the major centers. After the conquest of Cairo in 1517 some weavers used to mixing silk with the wool were brought to Bursa to start a court carpet factory for the Sultan's use. Not surprisingly the designs follow the same style of wind-swept floral pattern as the court textiles. The strong coloring and vigorous sweeping designs seen in Ottoman textiles and ceramics witness to the confident spirit of their classic age, the 16th and early 17th century, when their Empire was at its height and they had assumed the leadership of the Islamic world.

Iran: the Safavid period (1502–1730). It is a paradox that the rapid conquest of Iran by Shah Isma'il Safavi, 1502–14, should appear as a great national revival, for the army of the religious leader was drawn almost entirely from the Turkoman tribes of Anatolia and Azarbayjan and the ruling elite remained Turkish-speaking and with strong tribal affiliations at least until the accession of Shah Abbas I in 1587. In the cultural field the rise of the new dynasty did not make for an immediate break; both in letters and art there was a steady development in the centers previously dominated by the Aqqoyunlu in the west and south and by the last Timurids in the east. The wholesale adoption of the Shi'a faith tended towards isolation of the country from their neighbors, the Ottoman Turks to the west and the Uzbeks to the north, both strong supporters of orthodox Sunni belief.

The period falls into two distinct parts. Until the accession of Shah Abbas I (1587) development was traditionalist and isolationist. Architecture continued to be clad in tile-mosaic with inscriptions as the major decoration, as in several buildings of Isma'il and Tahmasp at the shrine of their ancestor Shaykh Safi at Ardebil and in the mid-century palace built for Shah Tahmasp in Qazwin, the Dawlat-khaneh (1548). He prepared a splendid tomb for his father Isma'il at Ardebil, with inlaid ivory and enameled silver inscriptions.

It was left to his brothers Bahram Mirza (1517–49) and Sam Mirza (1517–76, but in prison from 1561) and his nephew Ibrahim (1543–76) to develop a wider interest in the arts, including especially the use of painting, stucco, and

From the period of Ottoman architecture, the mihrab of the Ulu Camii at Adana, Turkey; 1560s

mirror-glass as internal decoration of palace buildings. The Mirror House of Bahram Mirza (before 1544) has vanished, but a beautiful pavilion of c1560 survives at Nay'in, east of Isfahan with painted cut plaster decoration in the vaults depicting hunting and feasting scenes, as well as the heavenly Peri. Colored glass was set in the dome—all resembling the painted lacquer bookcovers fashionable at this time. Such was the modest role of architecture in the first century of Safavid rule.

The most favored of the arts were those of the book. Shah Tahmasp, even before his accession in 1524, took personal interest in these arts and was himself both calligrapher and painter. A poem by Arifi, the *Guy y Chawgan* (Polo ball and stick) in his own hand is preserved in the Leningrad Public Library, dated 1524–5 and with some traditional miniatures. More ambitious are some fine illustrations added c1526 to a manuscript *History of the Faithful Imams* (in the same library) dedicated to the Shah. The massed figures of spectators in these pages are still in the tradition of the Tabriz school of Ya'qub Aqqoyunlu (*ob.* 1491), with brilliant coloring, flat architecture, and restrained gestures. But the new medallion carpets without false Kufic borders are depicted. The painter, whose signature Qasim ibn'Ali appears on one of them, is not otherwise known but must have been trained in Tabriz, rather than Herat.

This is the first of a large family of splendid miniatures produced in the royal workshop of Isma'il and Tahmasp, of which only the most important can be mentioned here. The earliest closely dated works are 11 miniatures added to a Nizami manuscript of 1481 in the years 1504–5 (Topkapi Saray Library, Istanbul, and the Keir Collection, The Manor House, Ham, London) and in a *Jamal u Jalal* (Uppsala University), copied in Herat in 1501 but the miniatures added in Tabriz, two dated to 1504. Both series are richly colored, with the luxuriant vegetation that had characterized the later Aqqoyunlu school.

Meanwhile the school of Herat, so famous in the time of Sultan Husayn (*ob.* 1506) did not at once fade, though it is not always easy to see whether work is from that center or represents the removal of artists trained there to the Safavid capital, Tabriz. For instance a *Bustan* of Sa'di dated 1515 (Keir Collection, The Manor House, Ham, London), the year after Isma'il recovered Herat from the Uzbeks, is illustrated in a strongly Herati style and may well have been produced in Herat. Three other manuscripts of the *Bustan* are illustrated in Herat in 1519–24, and an Arifi in 1523, together with a manuscript of Amir Khusrau copied in Herat in 1514.

These small manuscripts are completely eclipsed by the major achievements of the Tabriz royal workshop. Earliest of these is a *Khamsa* of Nazami in the Metropolitan Museum, New York, dated 1525 on one of its miniatures. The connection with the Herat school is still close, some groups of figures in the "Battle of Iskandar with Dara" deriving directly from a Bihzadian miniature in the British Library *Khamsa* of 1494; but the final miniature of "Iskandar capturing the Khaqan" is in the full new court style of Tabriz and probably by Sultan Muhammad, its director. Next comes the *de luxe* copy of the Turki poems of Ali Shir Nawai in the Bibliothèque Nationale, Paris, copied in Herat in 1526–7 but with six miniatures added in Tabriz by leading court artists, one of whom also used established Bihzadian figure groups.

While the large format allows a spaciousness which recalls wall-painting, the rich coloring and lavish use of gold and silver make these pages comparable with those in the greatest undertaking of the library under Tahmasp, a *Shah-nama* with 256 miniatures, whose production must have been proceeding at the same time. This can hardly have taken less than ten years to complete, while its only date is of 1527/8 from a miniature towards the end. It is reasonable to suggest a bracket of 1520–30 for its production, bringing its commencement into the reign of Isma'il (*ob.* 1524); in the earlier part of the epic poem some are still in the Aqqoyunlu style; others are in a more Bihzadian, Herati style; while a few have advanced towards the new synthesis achieved under the Safavids. The head of the royal library in Tabriz was Sultan Muhammad, who had received his training there, since he signs himself thus in the Hafiz of Sam Mirza.

Typical of Tabriz is his "Golden Age of Gayumars" depicted against a fantastically rich background of luxuriant vegetation and brilliant rocky peaks among which the wild animals move in harmony with the fur-clad men, thus corresponding to the near-contemporary reference by Dust Muhammad (1544) to the skill of Sultan Muhammad in drawing "people clothed in leopard skins, such that the hearts of the boldest of painters were dismayed". This whole enterprise implies the organization of a large workshop of highly qualified masters.

In general human figures now dominate the landscape, with their graceful forms and subtle relationships. On a more intimate scale this can be seen in five miniatures added *c*1530 to a *Khamsa* of Nizami, originally, copied in 1442 in Herat and already adorned with Bihzadian miniatures of *c*1493 (British Library, London; Add. MS. 25900). A *Diwan* of Hafiz, dedicated to Sam Mirza, must date from his youth, probably from *c*1533–5; it shows the ability of Sultan Muhammad to control large groups of figures with expressive gestures in rhythmic patterns in keeping with the poet's Sufi intention. Shaykh Zadeh who collaborated in this manuscript is evidently a Herat-trained painter; but he too can control more heavily peopled scenes than had been usual under Bihzad's supremacy.

The school of Tahmasp reached its height in the illustration of a large-page *Khamsa* of Nizami between 1539 and 1543 (British Library, London). By the latter date Mir Musavvir had succeeded to the direction of the court library *c*1540, on the death of Sultan Muhammad. A lyrical spirit fills these miniatures in a perfect balance between the natural world and the human actors, above all in the *Khusrau's First Sight of Shirin* by Sultan Muhammad, perhaps his last work, the *Majnun attended by the Wild Beasts in the Desert* by Aqa Miraq, and the anonymous *Flight of Muhammad through the Heavens*.

About 1545 Tahmasp began to turn away from the visual arts under a puritanical urge, and his artists had to seek other patrons. Poets, calligraphers, and painters moved to the Uzbek court in Bukhara or to India, to the Mughal court or to one of the courts of the Deccan, where they received a royal welcome. Among those who left Iran were Shaykh Zadeh, Mir Musavvir and his son Mir Sayyid Ali, and Abd al-Samad, the last two to be founders of the Mughal court school (*see* Indian Art).

In the third quarter of the 16th century court patronage fell to Sam Mirza, until his fall in 1561, and then to his young nephew Ibrahim Mirza, who was sent as a boy of 13 to govern Mashhad in Khurasan. During his nine years there, 1556 to 1565, he commissioned a splendid copy of the *Haft Aurang (Seven Thrones)*, a mystical poem by the Herat poet Jami, with 28 full-page miniatures, now in the Freer Gallery of Art, Washington, D.C., perhaps not quite finished at the time of his removal from office. Although we have the signatures of three scribes who worked on this book, the miniatures are unsigned; but we know from Qadi Ahmad that the leading painters who worked at the Mashhad court at this time were Shaykh Muhammad, Ali Asghar, and Abdallah. The first is likely to have been the principal miniaturist.

Ushak Medallion Carpets

The most popular and long-lived type of Turkish carpet, known in the West as the Ushak medallion carpet, was evolved in western Anatolia in the area round Ushak city, from which it reached the Mediterranean port of Izmir (Smyrna) in the early 16th century. A lost painting of Henry VIII and his family (1538), known from a copy in Sudeley Castle, Gloucestershire, shows a large carpet spread underfoot with star-medallion design. It resembles a carpet formerly in the Stroganov Collection. These carpets were extensively exported to the West and appear as furnishings, often as table-covers, in Western paintings of the 16th and 17th centuries.

The original design scheme, of a central medallion with four quarter medallions in the corners, derives from the layout of leather bookbindings as developed in Herat in the 1440s when it was the capital of the Timurid ruler Shah Rukh (*ob.* 1447), of which a fine example preserved in the Topkapi Saray Library in Istanbul is best known (Ahmet III 3059). From Herat the type was introduced to Tabriz, capital of the rulers in northwest Iran, as, for instance, in a manuscript of 1478 in the Chester Beatty Library, Dublin (T.401) and one of 1482 in Istanbul (Topkapi Saray Library; Hazine 762). From Tabriz this type of binding passed to Istanbul, especially after the sack of Tabriz by the Ottoman army in 1514. These bindings would have been sufficient inspiration for the carpet-designers;

but it is likely that carpet weavers were transferred at that time from Tabriz to Anatolia, where there were plentiful flocks of sheep producing fine wool. However, the design of the Ushak medallion carpets differs widely from that of medallion carpets of Safavid Iran, which are more complex and not so strong in composition or color.

The classic design of the Ushak medallion carpet is dominated by the circular or ovoid central medallion which is filled with a symmetrically developed stylized floral pattern. The ground color of the medallion is generally dark blue, as in an example from the Victoria and Albert Museum, London (T.71.1914). Originally the only other decoration of the field, which is either red as here, or white, was the quarter medallion in each corner repeating the design of the central medallion. But quite early the field outside the medallion was filled with star medallions split symmetrically in the four corners. This design quickly developed into the star-Ushak, in which the central element also became a star, now generally surrounded on all four sides by six half-stars, as in a carpet at Hardwick Hall, Derbyshire, and another in the Keir Collection (The Manor House, Ham, London). Alternatively, the star-medallion might be repeated in full down the length of the carpet, as on an example in the Islamic Museum in the Staatliche Museen, West Berlin; or the medallion might be

▲ The classic design; an example in the Victoria and Albert Museum, London; 530×250cm (208×98in)

▼ A central star and six half-stars; an example in the Keir Collection, the Manor House, Ham, London

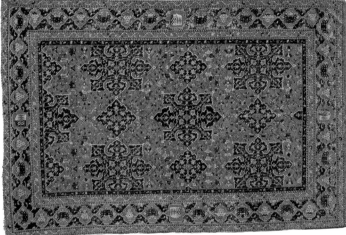

◄ A star-medallion carpet shown in a later copy of an early-16th-century painting of Henry VIII and his family possibly by Hans

Eworth; oil on panel; approx. 122×213cm (48×84in). Sudeley Castle, Gloucestershire

► Two stars with two half-stars on a 17th-century carpet in the Textile Museum,

Washington, D.C.; 528×308cm (208×121in)

► A late-16th-century Flemish (?) imitation of an Ushak medallion carpet bearing the arms of Montagu. Boughton House, Kettering

▼ Two stars, two half-stars, and quarter medallions in the corners; a 16th-century carpet at Hardwick Hall, Derbyshire

duplicated and the ground occupied by two half-stars fitted between them, as on an example in the Wolf Collection, Textile Museum, Washington, D.C.

The Turkish knot is used in all Ushak carpets, generally 12 or 13 to each square centimeter, on a white or natural warp with red shoots of wool. Some carpets are over 16 ft (5 m) in length and it is clear that the weaving must have been organized as an industry and not on a tribal basis. Prayer carpets were also made on these looms; naturally much smaller, but differing in design only in having the *qibla* direction indicated by a hanging lamp or the arched outline of the *mihrab* niche.

Medallion carpets were imitated in the West because of their wide popularity and a famous carpet in England in the collection of the Duke of Buccleugh dated 1585 (Boughton House, Kettering) is now recognized as such an imitation, probably made in Flanders. It bears the coat of arms of Montagu, while others bear arms of Polish families.

BASIL GRAY

Further reading. Erdmann, K. *Seven Hundred Years of Oriental Carpets*, London (1970). Mackie, L.W. *The Splendor of Turkish Weaving*, Washington (1974). Spuhler, F. *Islamic Carpets and Textiles in the Keir Collection*, London (1978). Von Bode, W. and Kühnel, E. (trans. Ellis, C.G.) *Antique Rugs of the Near East*, London (1970).

Not all the artists deserted the Shah's library in Qazwin. Near the end of his long reign, a fine manuscript of the epic *Garshaspnama* (British Library, London) was produced there in 1573, to which Muzaffar Ali, one of the masters who had worked on the 1539–48 *Nizami*, contributed two miniatures; one of the *Court Poets of Ghazni testing Firdawsi on his Arrival* in the garden where they were picnicking. This shows both psychological insight and a fine color-sense. It served four years later as inspiration for a younger artist, perhaps one

A beggar professing his love for the Prince, a miniature from the Attar, Conference of the Birds (Mantiq at-Tayr) of 1483. Metropolitan Museum, New York

of Muzaffar's own pupils in the *Shah-nama* of Shah Isma'il II (1577–8). Owing to his short reign of no more than 18 months, this manuscript, now dispersed, remained half-finished but it marked a courageous attempt to revive the patronage of the previous generation and introduced two artists trained by Muzaffar Ali, Siyawush the Georgian and Sadiqi Beg, who together dominated the last quarter of the century. They represent a fresh movement towards more dynamic composition and also towards more individual styles, no longer conforming to a house style.

The reign of Shah Abbas I the Great (1587–1629) marks a shift in the ethos, economy, and cultural life of Iran. From being isolated and inward-looking, the country was led to accept the position of a world power; the role of the Safavid house changed from one of religious leadership based on tribal support to a centralized monarchy with a regular army paid for by revenues from large crown demesnes and from the profits of monopolistic royal workshops working for the export market. So the industrial arts—silk weaving, carpets, ceramics, arms, and metalwork—came to the fore. The Shah needed to replace the religious charisma with the splendor of his new capital, Isfahan. The removal of the administration to that city took place only in 1598 and the intermediary period after 1587 was one of transition during which the *kitab-khaneh* continued in the tradition of splendid production, including a large and sumptuous *Shah-nama* from which only a portion (Chester Beatty Library, Dublin) is known to survive; and extensive illustrated manuscripts of the Fables, *Anwar i-Suhayli* (1593) and of the *Annals of the Prophets* (Bibliothèque Nationale, Paris) of the 1590s, an early work of Riza. Another aspect of the Shah's patronage is seen in his revivalism in the four miniatures which he added to the Attar, *Conference of the Birds (Mantiq at-Tayr)* of 1483 (Metropolitan Museum, New York), before presenting it to the shrine of Shaykh Safi at Ardebil; and in a Timurid style *Shahnama* of 1614 (New York Public Library, Spencer Collection), directly inspired by the Baysunghur manuscript of 1430.

During the first decade of the reign Sadiqi Beg was head of the library workshop and the manuscript of 1593 is dedicated to him by his pupils. But already the rising star of Riza was starting to eclipse his with further emphasis on the personality and prestige of the artist. From then on most drawings and many miniatures bear the signature of the painter quite prominently written. Riza's earlier work is signed with his personal name alone, without *nisbah*, but from about 1600 he used the style Riza i-'Abbasi, until his death c1635, leaving his son Shafi to carry on the same tradition and to use the same *nisbah* Abbasi. His best pupil, however, was Mu'in who must have been quite young when his master died, for he was still working as late as 1697. The fluent draughtsmanship and strong color-sense of these three masters dominated the whole of the 17th century. It was due to the strength of this tradition that western influence only became apparent in Iranian painting in the last 30 years of the century in the time of Shah Sulayman (1671–95). He patronized Muhammad Zaman and Ali Quli

The Lutfallah mosque in Isfahan; 1602–16

Jabbadar, who adopted a chiaroscuro style based on northern Caravaggiesque masters.

Architecture was the major art in Iran in the 17th century, and was concentrated in the capital Isfahan. With its new layout planned by Shah Abbas on a scale greater than had ever been conceived of in Iran, and improved by his successors right up to the end of the dynasty, it became the finest city in the world.

There were two separate focuses in the new city: first a more conservative one developed round the Maidan, the polo ground which was also a parade ground, market center, social promenade, and place of contact between the Shah and his people. This very long piazza surrounded by arcaded shops led up to the Royal Mosque (*Masjid i-Shah*) at one narrow end with the gateway to the great bazaar at the other. Opposite the Ali Qapu (a royal pavilion) was a second mosque, the Lutfallah, remarkable for its entrance to the square domed prayer chamber, bent to adjust the direction towards the *qibla* Mecca, but also thus psychologically separated from the outer world. Built between 1602 and 1616, it was intended as the private mosque of the Shah and his court. It is distinguished by its splendid tilework of polychrome painted tile (*haft aurang*) and for the design of the interior of the saucer dome, over 59 ft (18 m) in diameter, laid out in a pattern of arabesque medallions radiating from the center in widening linked circles over an octagonal drum in which are set 16 windows which flood it with light.

The Shah mosque is more conventional in its planning but it was conceived on a vast scale with an immensely tall entrance portal flanked by twin minarets. The courtyard is of the usual four *aiwan* shape but with the *qibla* side given enhanced importance by the use of a double dome, the outer skin being raised a further 46 ft (14 m) above the inner, to a total height of 170 ft (52 m). The whole structure is clad in the *haft aurang* tilework in which inscriptions were the major decorative element. The building was begun in 1612 and the structure, designed by the architect *ustad* (master) Ali Akbar, was completed in 1630, but the marble dado was not finished till 1638. These works on the Maidan were on an unprecedented scale but basically of traditional form and decor.

More revolutionary was the conception behind the second focal scheme of a boulevard linking the center of Isfahan in the royal palace with a new bridge over the Zayanda-rud, running north–south, lined with trees and bordered by a stream. It thus combined the old Persian preference for bringing the garden into close relation with the city with a new sense of space and scale. The principal palace, the Chihil Sutun, is mostly the work of Shah Abbas II (1647) though the first building is earlier. Its main feature, which gives it its name, is the elegant open veranda on the east side with a roof supported by 18 slender wooden columns and coffered with mirror inlay and with a fountain in the center. Even if you count the reflection of these columns in the pool in the garden before it there are not Forty Columns as the name literally implies. There is a throne room behind and side rooms, while shallower verandas open on the other three sides. Wall-paintings in these also belong to the work of 1647, and are in a style dependent on the tradition of book-painting.

The only other of the many royal and private palaces to survive, though now much restored, is the Hasht Bihisht erected by Shah Sulayman in 1669–70 near the Chahar Bagh. This is a complex structure consisting of four *talar* on the principal directions with octagonal corner towers between. The side vaults are open to the roof so that the rooms are all in the octagons and quite small. The main decorative features are in the spandrels of the *talar* arches, each laid out with a different design in bold figural tilework in which blue, yellow, and white are the main colors. These designs are almost certainly by Mu'in and other miniaturists. Chardin described the now vanished interior with its 10 ft (3 m) high marble dado, wall-paintings and crystal mirrors, and added that the whole was no more than a *château de carte*, a cardboard palace.

In the greatly expanded ceramic production of the 17th century, Chinese example was predominant, since these wares were intended to compete in the international market with the blue and white porcelain of China and Japan. Some were copied directly from Chinese porcelain of the Wan-li period (1573–1619), while a large group show "Chinese" figures set in a more or less Chinese landscape. Western travelers mention Mashhad, Kirman, and Yazd as centers of ceramic kilns at this time, but there is no sure evidence to identify their products. A specific type is associated with Daghestan, now in Soviet Azarbayjan, because many examples were found there in domestic use; but they may well have been made in Kashan and certainly go back to the 16th century. But the rare dated pieces of blue and white from the early 16th century are from another center (two dated 1523 and 1525) and less closely connected with Chinese prototypes. More in native taste are two other decorative techniques used in this ceramic revival in the second half of the 17th century and allegedly in Kirman—one polychrome painted under the glaze in blue, black, sage-green, and red; the other in the luster technique, either on a blue ground or on alternate segments of blue and white. These techniques continued into the 18th century, but in declining quality.

Far surpassing the pottery in value were the manufactures of silk brocades and carpets. In addition to the court workshops in Isfahan there were state factories established by Shah Abbas I in provincial centers where both silk and woolen carpets were made. The court would have required great supplies of brocades, velvets, and satins not only for the dress of the monarch, but for those distributed to courtiers and distinguished foreigners. The velvets were used as hangings in halls and tents and their patterns are often figural with mirror image repeats, some certainly earlier than Abbas I. These designs were made by miniaturists, as by Shafi Abbasi under Shah Abbas II. They even include scenes from well-known poetical stories familiar from miniatures. In the 17th century single figures of young men and girls show a good selection of modish costumes.

Although the knotted carpet is of great antiquity in the area, nothing survives earlier than the Safavid period and very little even from the 16th century. The carpets of the 14th and 15th centuries can be known only from their depiction in miniatures, where we can see that they passed through successive stages in design, from the broad two-colored chevron design through one of allover linked medallions in two colors, generally red and green with a pseudo-Kufic border pattern, to the types of unitary design based on central motifs, beginning in the late 15th century but only fully developed in the 16th. As with ceramics no identification of the places of origin for any of the well-known types is possible; and it is from European travelers that we hear of places other than Isfahan—Kashan, Yazd, and Kirman—as centers of carpet manufacture on a large scale. This factory work would be distinct from village or nomad weaving, always on a much smaller scale and with less well-controlled design. Brocading of carpets with gold and silver thread was practiced in the main centers, as well as weaving in silk for court use. Only a handful of carpets from the Safavid period are dated, the most famous being one of 1522 in the Museo Poldi Pezzoli, Milan, and one woven for the shrine of Shaykh Safi at Ardebil in 1540 and now in the Victoria and Albert Museum, London. The latter, which is very large, had been restored before its acquisition by patching from a second similar carpet, the remains of which are now in Los Angeles County Museum, Los Angeles (Paul Getty Gift).

It is sometimes suggested that the more elaborate carpet designs were the work of miniaturists. This would seem improbable, because of the different techniques requiring close involvement of the designer with the manufacture. The basic arabesque carpet designs were traditional, but in the 16th century the weavers added pictorial elements, especially the garden, trees, birds and animals, vases, lamps, and even human figures and angels. There are a small number of pictorial carpets framed and directed like a picture; but even these contain mostly symmetrically arranged figures. One fea-

A Persian velvet hanging with mirror-image figures and patterns; early 17th century. Royal Ontario Museum, Toronto

ture is common to binding and carpet design, the renewed presence of chinoiserie elements, especially the mythical animals *ch'i-lin*, dragon and phoenix. The organization of these patterns is conservative, with the border separate and generally filled with an abstract running design of lozenges and medallions; in the field are brilliant colors against a brown, white, deep blue, or red ground. Successful types were repeated for more than a century, but generally with increasing stiffness and loss of the fine color-sense. In the time of Chardin (1666) 32 royal workshops were under central control and their staff received salaries, partly in kind, under royal warrant for life; but they were allowed to accept private commissions when not engaged on official orders; this applied also to the painters and favored the growth of the separate drawing or painting. In metalwork only the armorers and swordsmiths had now preserved reputation for fine work.

In 1674 the trade passing through the port of Bandar Abbas (the former Gombroon), the main commercial center on the Persian Gulf, was still considerable, carried mainly in Dutch and English ships. According to Chardin the main export was of silks and carpets. But the Safavid state was by then already in disarray and declining. Sulayman was succeeded in 1694 by Husayn, a weak man unable to rally the state, assailed on every side. In 1722 the Afghan adventurer Mahmud boldly crossed the desert and attacked the capital with a small force. In October the city surrendered and was sacked by the invaders. A man of obscure origin, Nadir Shah, drove out the Afghans in 1728 and by 1730 had deposed the last of the Safavids and ascended the throne. In spite of brilliant military successes and his seizure of Delhi with the Mughal Emperor Muhammad Shah in 1739, Nadir Shah emerged as a cruel tyrant and his assassination in 1747 plunged the country again into chaos. These events and the immense damage caused to the industrial basis of Iran brought a complete break in her cultural history. The land fell into the power of several tribal chiefs.

Iran: the Qajar dynasty (1788–1907). Agha Muhammad Khan, a chief of the Qajar tribe with its center at Astarabad, settled in Teheran as capital in 1788. By the time of his assassination in 1796 he had established his rule all over Iran and the peace he imposed led quickly to a revival of manufacture and trade. His nephew and successor Fath Ali Shah (1797–1834) was more impressive in appearance and manner than in action or character; he is noted as "looking the majesty he felt" with his long, black beard, jeweled crown, and dress, surrounded by numerous sons and sycophantic courtiers. He liked to have luxurious adornments and the walls of his palaces and pavilions were covered with oil paintings on canvas and mirror glass, a taste imitated by his family and courtiers. Life-size figures of the Shah and (on a smaller scale in accordance with ancient Persian tradition) his sons and courtiers, of dancing girls and more rarely boys, are painted in this Western medium though in a "primitive", unsophisticated manner in a genuine local style of considerable charm. The names of the chief painters at the court are Mir Baba (*ob.* 1805) and Mihr Ali (1805–13), Abdullah Khan (1813–48) and Abul Hasan Ghaffari (*fl.* 1850–61), the last of whom alone actually studied painting in Europe. Some of their signed work survives and there is a collection in Teheran installed in the Negarestan Museum, which specializes in Qajar art.

By the mid 19th century under Nasir al-Din Shah (1848–96) oil painting had been largely superseded in esteem by painting in lacquer in a similar naive manner and with borrowings from Western art, on small portable objects such as bindings, mirror-cases, and pen-boxes, and also by enameling on gold and other metals. The painter Baba, who had also worked in lacquer, founded a family of artists, his two sons Najaf Ali (*ob.* 1865) and Muhammad Isma'il (*ob.* 1871) who both became in turn *naqash-bashi* or head painter; while his grandsons Kazim and Ahmad worked in enamels. This style of lacquer painting originated under the Zand dynasty (1750–87) in Shiraz, its leading executant being Muhammad Sadiq. Painted enameling on gold introduced as a court art from the beginning of the reign of Fath Ali Shah probably derived from Russia but in style was similar to that used in lacquer painting and by the same artists, still in manner and subject in the Persian tradition. The semi-translucent enamels are given brilliance by the gold ground. The leading masters of the craft were Ali and Baqir. In the mid 19th century the leaders were the two sons of Najaf Ali, Ahmad and Kazim, who survived until *c*1880. Painting in all media declined during the second half of the 19th century into skilful pastiche. Nasir al-Din and his successor, the last Qajar Shah, Muzaffar al-Din (1896–1907) were unable to resist the prestige of Western art.

BASIL GRAY

Bibliography. Atasoy, N. and Çagman, F. *Turkish Miniature Painting*, Istanbul (1974). Atil, E. *Ceramics from the World of Islam*, Washington, D.C. (1973). Erdmann, K. *Seven Hundred Years of Oriental Carpets*, London (1970). Ettinghausen, R. *Arab Painting*, Geneva (1962), London (1977). Fehervari, G. *Islamic Pottery, a Comprehensive Study based on the Barlow Collection*, London (1973). Grabar, O. *The Formation of Islamic Art*, Yale (1973). Gray, B. *Persian Painting*, Geneva (1961), London (1977). Lane, A. *Early Islamic Pottery*, London (1948). Lane, A. *Later Islamic Pottery*, London (1971). Rogers, M. *The Spread of Islam*, Oxford (1976). Sourdel, D. and Sourdel-Thomine, J. *La Civilisation de l'Islam Classique*, Paris (1968). Sourdel-Thomine, J. and Spuler, B. *Die Kunst des Islam*, Berlin (1973). Stchoukine, I. *La Peinture Iranienne sous les derniers Abbasides et les Il-Khans*, Bruges (1936). Stchoukine, I. *Les Peintures des Manuscrits de Shah Abbas Ier à la Fin des Safavis*, Paris (1964). Stchoukine, I. *Les Peintures des Manuscrits Safavis de 1502 à 1587*, Paris (1959). Stchoukine, I. *Les Peintures des Manuscrits Timurides*, Paris (1953). Stchoukine, I. *La Peinture Turque d'après les Manuscrits Illustrés*, (2 vols.) Paris (1966 and 1969). Von Bode, W. and Kühnel, E. (trans. Ellis, C.G.) *Antique Rugs from the Near East*, London (1970). Wilkinson, C.K. *Iranian Ceramics*, New York (1963). Wilkinson, C.K. *Nishapur Pottery of the early Islamic Period*, Greenwich, Conn. (1973).

25

PRE-COLUMBIAN ART

Colossal Head number one from the Olmec site San Lorenzo, Mexico; height 284cm (112in)
c1250–900 BC. University Museum of Jalapa, Mexico (see page 472)

ANCIENT Indian civilizations in the New World were distributed from North America down into northwest Argentina. Two areas achieved the highest levels of cultural development: Mesoamerica, or Middle America (including Guatemala and southern Mexico, with Belize, El Salvador, western Honduras, and western Costa Rica on the periphery), and the Central Andes (Peru and adjacent parts of Bolivia).

In both areas "civilization" was under way by *c*1250 BC, and continued in a succession of different cultures, represented by distinct art styles, until the arrival of the Spanish conquerors in the early 16th century. Throughout the Pre-Columbian world, art was closely related to both religion and nature; it was also connected with secular power: architecture and sculpture were displays of political, as well as religious, strength. Powerful rulers could command large labor forces to build grandiose ceremonial centers. For the most part, this labor worked with stone tools. They did not use the wheel, either for transport or for pottery-making. Considering these limitations, their accomplishments are astonishing.

Only the Maya, in southern Mesoamerica (AD 300–900), had a true form of writing. There are, therefore, virtually no written sources to aid the understanding of these ancient civilizations. Information may come from ethnographic data and early accounts by Indians or Europeans, but it is chiefly the material remains of these peoples—their buildings, sculpture, pottery, lapidary work, and, in a few cases, textiles—that provide material for study. The spread of pottery types and architectural and sculptural styles is informative in defining the influences of one people on another. Materials like obsidian, jade, flint, and shells, when they appear in places where they are not indigenous, indicate trade.

One of the best sources of information is the content of artistic works, for, although they lacked writing, the high cultures had well-developed symbolic languages. The important elements of their universe—their myths, deities, ceremonies, and historical heroes—are represented in art. Although little is yet known about how to interpret these elements, they hold a great deal of coded information.

Objective reality may be depicted in Pre-Columbian art (for example, the stone and stucco portraits of Maya kings, or the portrait vases and representations of animal and plant species of the Mochica in Peru), but mythical elements are often mixed in, elements that were probably equally "real" to these peoples. The attributes of what appear to be surreal monsters—deities or supernatural beings—can generally be traced to elements in nature, although they are combined in ways unnatural to the eye of an outsider. Human traits may be combined with those of large felines (especially jaguars), raptorial birds, snakes, crocodilians, toads and frogs, or sea creatures. The jaguar, the largest cat in the New World, was a powerful predator with whose hunting prowess man wanted to identify. Jaguars, whose preferred environment is tropical rain forest, are variously associated with night, the earth, caves, waterways, rain, and fertility. Jaguars are perhaps sometimes thought of as supernatural ancestors. Other creatures, often also hunters and carnivores, are associated with life in more than one realm and can change from one form into another or shed their dead skins. These are all creatures whose attributes were significant to Pre-Columbian peoples.

Death imagery is common, and is probably associated with fertility and regeneration. As plants are reborn from the earth,

The main sites of Mesoamerica

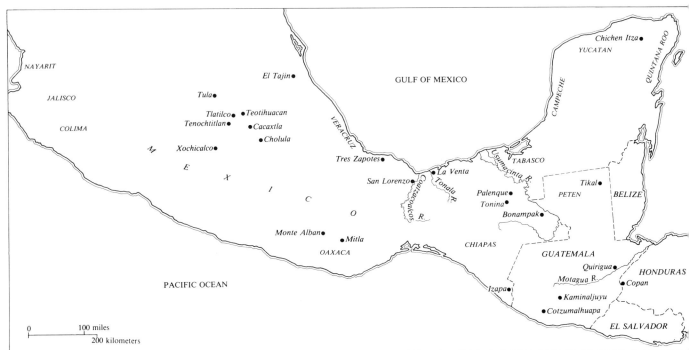

so the life of man was thought of as cyclical. High Pre-Columbian cultures all believed in an afterlife and produced burials equipped with rich grave goods. Some works must have been made specifically as burial objects—it is even possible that a majority of fine objects were made to accompany the dead to the other world.

Additional traits that are also elements in their art, shared throughout high Pre-Columbian civilizations, are the use of significant headdresses and garments, the wearing of ear and nose ornaments by high-status people, scarification, tattooing, or painting on the face or body, the carrying or wearing of warrior's paraphernalia as status symbols, the practice of ritual human sacrifice, the importance of prisoners or sacrificial victims, the use of fine pottery and cloth as ritual objects, utilization of metal for adornment or ritual objects rather than for utilitarian purposes, and cosmological emphasis on the four world directions. Although the same themes are repeated within the art of a particular style, there are never exact repetitions—even mold-made ceramics are variously finished. This lack of repetitiveness is another trait of high Pre-Columbian cultures.

Ceremonial architecture consists of stone or adobe-brick buildings placed on platforms or pyramids, which are situated around a plaza. Structures were frequently built over earlier structures. Sites are often located in relation to a hill.

We must postulate considerable movement of peoples throughout Pre-Columbian history. Within the two major areas, people surely knew about each other, at times traded with each other, proselytized each other, and sometimes conquered each other. The question arises of whether the peoples of one area, at any time, knew about the other area. Certain similar traits suggest that there must sometimes have been contact. For example, a scroll-and-stepped-triangle motif apparently came from the Andean area to Mesoamerica just before the time of Christ. It is widely distributed in both areas, and probably has varying significance in different times and places. In the past, it was proposed that there might have been ties between the two earliest civilizations, the Olmec, in Mexico, and Chavin, in Peru. Now, however, it is thought that there may have been a people, ancestral to the peoples of both Mesoamerica and the Central Andes, somewhere in the tropical forest of the northern lowlands of South America. This would explain many basic similarities, particularly the use of certain symbolic motifs, as well as individual differences—for example, the existence of early metallurgy in the Central Andes, but not in Mesoamerica.

The question of direct contact with peoples across the Pacific has also been raised. It is generally agreed now that the early New World populations came from the Far East in a series of small, migratory bands across a then-existing Bering Strait land-bridge. Although radiocarbon evidence for man to date goes back only about 10,000 years, it is possible that man was in the New World as early as 30,000 years ago. Originally nomadic hunters and gatherers who wandered on the American continents, the migrants became sedentary farmers who domesticated plants, made pottery, lived in villages, and began to build mounds and sacred structures—for a complex ritual life began early. There are many visual and trait similarities all around the Pacific Basin, and many items from the New World and the Orient stand comparison. How much of this came from the Oriental inheritance of New World peoples, and how much might have come from possible direct contact? The argument for contact is virtually impossible to prove or disprove, given the fact that no object has yet been found that was undoubtedly traded across the sea in either direction. Whether or not there was direct contact, the original works of peoples in the New World are more accomplished than anything that could have been brought by export from Asia. The development of New World civilization was not directly dependent on that of the Old World.

Mesoamerica. The cultural area called Mesoamerica was, in turn, the home of the Olmec, the Zapotec, the Maya, the peoples of Teotihuacan and El Tajin, the Toltec, the Mixtec, and the Aztec. To the north, nomadic peoples wandered; to the southeast, lay Central American countries with a less integrated cultural development.

Mesoamerica has considerable geographical variety. A spine of mountains runs down the center, northwest to southeast, with the land sloping off into humid forests as it approaches the coasts. The Yucatan Peninsula juts northwards from the mountain chain, an area largely of lowland forest which becomes drier toward its northern tip. Mesoamerica includes temperate and tropical climate, highlands and lowlands. It is extremely diverse in flora and fauna. The geography must have greatly influenced the development of civilization, which was largely based on the trade of ideas and goods from one environment to another.

Mesoamerica is defined by shared cultural traits. Its inhabitants were farmers whose staple crops were maize, beans, and squash. There were populations of relatively great size and density, with a hierarchical social structure. Its large source of manpower could be concentrated in the ceremonial centers, to work on the stone mounds and stepped pyramids with structures on top, plazas, courts for ritual ball games, and monumental sculptures. Impressive art styles were produced in many media: books and maps, astronomical calculations, complex calendars, and numerical notation systems. The peoples of the area flattened the skulls of the elite in infancy, valued carved jade objects, sprinkled burials with cinnabar, and shared various other customs.

The earliest known civilization in Mesoamerica was that of a people now called "Olmec". Their principal ceremonial centers were erected in their "heartland", the humid, lowland forest of the Gulf of Mexico, in the states of Veracruz and Tabasco, c1250–300 BC.

The two principal excavated sites are San Lorenzo and La Venta. San Lorenzo lies on a man-made pre-Olmec platform raised about 165 ft (50 m) above the surrounding savannas and the Coatzacoalcos River. La Venta, on the Tonala River,

Maya and Central Mexican Codices

The Maya made folding-screen books from a single sheet of pounded-bark paper, coated with lime sizing and painted on both sides with depictions of deities, hieroglyphic texts, and bar-and-dot numbers. These books were presumably copied and recopied, as European medieval manuscripts were. Although most of the books existing at the time of the Conquest (1520) were destroyed by the first Bishop of Yucatan, Diego de Landa, and other early missionaries as "works of the devil", four pre-Conquest codices still exist, all Postclassic (900–1520), but presumably copies of earlier texts. Three are known by the names of the cities where they can be found today. The Dresden Codex, probably made in the 13th century, is the finest. It is essentially a treatise on astronomy, astrology, and divination, with eclipse tables and

tables for the synodic revolutions of Venus, divinatory almanacs, and information on ceremonies. The Madrid (or Tro-Cortesianus) Codex, the longest of the Maya books—about 21 ft 6 in (6.6 m) in length—was found in two parts. A book of horoscopes for use in divination, it was probably made in the 15th century. The Paris (or Perez) Codex is a fragment, which deals with ceremonies on one side and with divination on the other. The fourth codex was discovered recently, and at the time of writing its authenticity is still under debate. It shows one synodic position of the Venus calendar.

Pre-Conquest manuscripts in other styles, painted on animal hide, have come from various parts of Mexico. Notable are five known as the Borgia Group (the major codex

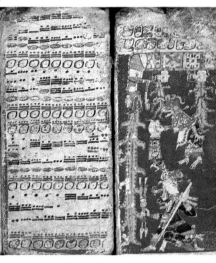

▼ A *tonalpohualli* (calendar) page, from the Aztec Codex Borbonicus. Bibliothèque du Palais Bourbon, Paris

▲ Two pages of the Dresden Codex; 13th century. Sächsische Landesbibliothek, Dresden

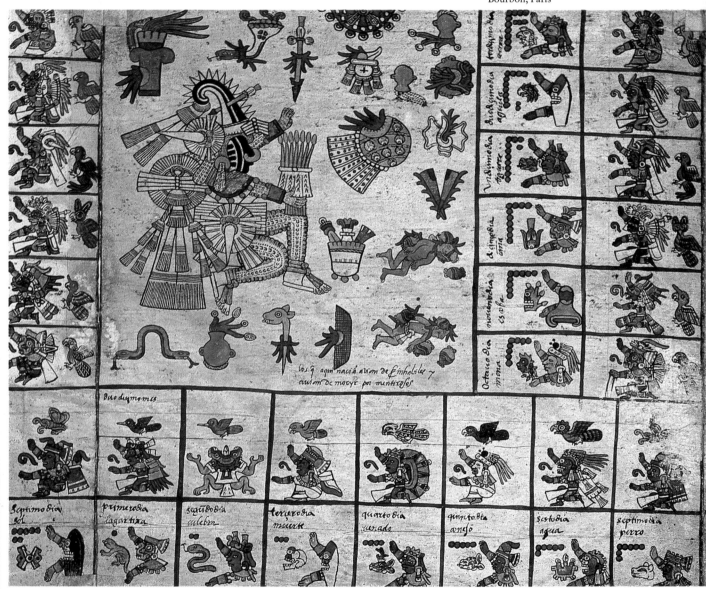

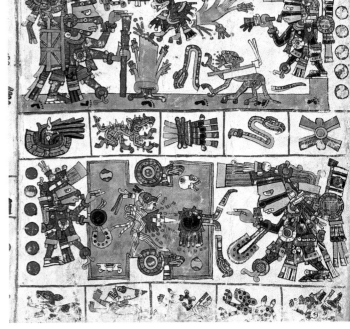

n this group once belonged to the Borgia family). Their place of origin is uncertain, but these screen-fold books share a similar art style and iconography.

One of the most important sections of these and other early manuscripts is the *tonalpohualli*, "the count of days", a calendar of 20 named days in fixed sequence, accompanied by a rotating series of the numbers one to 13, so that 260 days passed before the same name appeared with the same number. Deities, ceremonies, and auguries were associated with this calendar, which was the sacred, ritual calendar prevalent throughout Mesoamerica. This was combined with a 365-day, approximate-solar calendar of 18 20-day months, plus five "dead" days, to make up the Calendar Round.

Contrasting with the ritual manuscripts is a group of codices, made by a Mixtec-speaking people in Oaxaca, that record the history of the ruling dynasty of the town of Tilantongo, especially the history of the 11th-century ruler known as "Eight Deer". (Mixtec ruling families took calendrical names—Eight Deer is the name of a day in the *tonalpohualli*.) There are also other Mixtec genealogical-historical manuscripts painted in a pre-Conquest style.

Many post-Conquest manuscripts are painted in a manner showing Spanish influence, but give information about earlier matters. They may be histories, migration maps, or lists of tribute items paid to the Aztec. The most important of these is the Florentine Codex. It was a large compendium of pictures and text compiled from native informants by Fray Bernardino de

▲ A snared deer, a detail from the Madrid (or Tro-Cortesianus) Codex; 15th century. Archaeological Museum, Madrid

▲ A section of the Codex Borgia; the main figures are Aztec deities; 14th–16th centuries. Vatican Library, Rome

▼ A section of the story of Eight Deer as told in the Nuttall Codex; 1011–63. British Museum, London

Sahagun, a 16th-century Franciscan who was the first ethnographer in Mexico. In it, he gathered information on the beliefs and rituals of the Aztec, their craft techniques, and the flora and fauna of their world.

ELIZABETH P. BENSON

Further reading. Kelley, D.H. *Deciphering the Maya Script*, Austin and London (1976). Robertson, D. *Mexican Manuscript Painting of the Early Colonial Period*, New Haven (1959). Smith, M.E. *Picture Writing from Ancient Southern Mexico: Mixtec Place Signs and Maps*, Norman (1973). Thompson, J.E.S. *A Commentary on the Dresden Codex: a Maya Hieroglyphic Book*, Philadelphia (1972).

has a pyramid about 100 ft (30.5 m) high.

Both sites lack stone architecture but are rich in large stone sculpture, usually of basalt. The earliest Olmec stone monuments probably date from *c*1250 BC. A prominent form is the Colossal Head; 13 are now known, ranging from 5 ft (1.5 m) to nearly 10 ft (3 m) high, and weighing from about 7 tons (7.1 tonnes) to more than 28 tons (28.5 tonnes). They have portrait features, flattened in conformity with the shape of the stone, and wear tight-fitting helmets. Carved as bodiless heads, they probably depict chieftains. There are also "altars"—massive rectangular stones now thought to have been thrones. These commonly show a half-round human figure emerging from a cave. Other monumental sculpture represents figures in the round. The heads of many have been destroyed; some of the existing heads have feline traits, which may relate to ancestor myths or to the transformation of human beings into jaguars. Human-faced figures may hold an infant with a partially feline face. Bird, toad, monkey, and snake attributes also appear in Olmec art, and a notable aspect is the use of glyph-like symbolic designs, thought to be precursive to writing. Late in the Olmec sequence, when a low-relief style dominates sculpture, stelae (vertical shafts of stone) were carved with a number of figures.

The Olmec had a penchant for burying offerings to an earth-god. At La Venta, five large mosaic "pavements" of dressed and polished serpentine blocks were found buried as deeply as 16 ft (4.9 m) and elaborately covered with colored clays. Most of the stone monuments found at San Lorenzo had also been ritually buried in alignments after disfiguration. It is surmised that *c*900 BC there was a disruption in the Olmec world, and monuments at both San Lorenzo and La Venta were mutilated.

The Olmec were fine lapidaries who carved figurines and other objects from jade and serpentine. Figurines are usually nude but have no identifying sex characteristics. In the excavations at La Venta, a scene was found made up of carefully buried figurines and celts. No jade objects have been found at San Lorenzo, but a number have come from other sites and some from as far away as Costa Rica.

Pottery is not well preserved in the heartland, but fragments of handmade figurines have been found, both solid and hollow; among them are white-slipped, baby-faced figurines. There are a number of pottery wares, including a fine-paste "kaolin" ware, and also various vessel shapes, some of which have stamped or incised designs.

The Olmec probably traded widely for obsidian, serpentine, and jade, across the mountains to the West Coast and possibly down as far as eastern Costa Rica, where jade is known to have been worked in later times. Sculpture that is surely Olmec-influenced, and may be contemporary, appears in central Mexico, in southern Chiapas, and in El Salvador. Other faraway relief sculpture also relates to that of the Olmec, and two groups of the only known Olmec-style paintings have been found in central Mexico. Pottery similar to that of the heartland has been found in the Mexican state of Oaxaca, in the central Mexican highlands, and on the Pacific Coast. It is not always clear whether this art is contemporary or later, for not only has the Olmec style been found over a wide region but it influenced the art of succeeding peoples.

The exact nature of Olmec influence outside the heartland is unclear. Certainly, trade was involved. The prevalence of Olmec iconography also strongly suggests the spread of a belief system. Military conquest and colonization are also possibilities. Such influence, however, did not spread in a vacuum, for the sites with which the Olmec dealt had highly developed cultures of their own.

At the beginning of the Late Preclassic period (*c*300 BC) attenuated Olmec traits continued in the sculpture of faraway sites, but traits from across the mountains were found in the Olmec region where monuments depict the triumph of people of different features and Olmec figures in postures of submission. The Olmec style slipped into a developing post-Olmec art which traveled, apparently, along old Olmec trade routes. In Oaxaca a number of sculptures have been found from this period, notably the "danzantes"—linear relief depictions of presumably dead "floating" figures. In the highlands of Guatemala an important site was Kaminaljuyu, the remains of which have been virtually destroyed by the spread of present-day Guatemala City. Located at an important crossroads in the mountains, it has been a strategic place for millennia. Other post-Olmec material comes from southern Chiapas and coastal Guatemala.

The most important manifestation of this style today is at Izapa, in the southeastern corner of Mexico, where there are stone-faced, pyramidal mounds, and stelae accompanied by round "altars". The stela-and-altar complex, with low-relief carving, is a Maya trait, and, for this and other reasons of style and iconography, the Izapan style is considered transitional between Olmec and Maya.

This art contains many new elements: its low-relief sculpture shows active figures in asymmetrical compositions; there are new themes of war, sacrifice, and death, new deity faces, and the use of compositional zones and borders with scrolls and stepped and diagonal bands.

A post-Olmec-style monument from Tres Zapotes, Veracruz, is dated 31 BC. This monument and another from Chiapas, inscribed 36 BC—the two earliest dated monuments in Mesoamerica—make it certain that the Long Count system of dating, used prominently by the later Maya, began in this period.

Of the several civilizations flourishing in the great Classic period of Mesoamerica (AD 250–900), the Maya is the most impressive and best known. The Classic Maya inhabited the Mexican states of Yucatan, Campeche, Quintana Roo, Chiapas, and Tabasco, as well as Guatemala, Belize, and western Honduras. The core of this region is the tropical lowland forest of the Guatemalan state of the Peten. To the south, the land rises to the mountains.

The beginning of the Classic period is marked by the common appearance of the corbel vault, polychrome pottery, and Initial Series inscriptions on monuments. The Early Classic period, AD 250–550, produced sculpture carved in a crisp, tight, curvilinear style, and pottery, often in the form of large, four-footed, lidded vessels. About AD 550–600 there was a lessening of Maya activity, probably the result of the activities of other Mesoamerican civilizations active in the Middle Classic period (AD 400–700). In the Late Classic period (AD 600–900) there were more naturalistic styles, new pottery forms, and an increase in building and sculpture in the ceremonial centers. The site that has been most thoroughly investigated is Tikal, in the center of the Peten, a large and important site in the Late Preclassic and Classic periods.

Two general types of Maya buildings are recognized: "temples", usually one-to-three-room structures placed on a high pyramid, and "palaces", or "range-type structures", multi-room buildings on a lower platform. Many structures have a number of building layers; an old platform or pyramid may have been covered with rubble and a new structure built over it. Classic Maya buildings show considerable variation in the construction of the vaults, in the kinds of roof-combs that decorated building tops, in the size of rooms, and in wall ornamentation. Facades at Palenque, for example, are decorated with stucco figures on armatures, whereas Puuc buildings in the north have upper registers of mosaic-like stone with rain-god heads projecting at the corners. Structures might be embellished with carved stone or wooden lintels, and with interior wall panels of relief-carved stone. Walls were coated with lime plaster, and might be painted. The most complete existing paintings are at Bonampak, near the Usumacinta River.

Monumental sculpture was also painted. The most common sculptural form was the stela. Carving might be in very low relief, as at the Peten and Usumacinta sites, deeply carved, as at Copan and Quirigua, in the southeastern area, or in full-round, as at Tonina, in Chiapas. Stelae generally depict the rulers of the sites, with inscriptions giving their dates of birth and accession, their ancestry, including mythological as well as real ancestors, the rituals they performed, and astronomical-astrologically propitious dates. Stelae were usually accompanied by "altars" in a variety of shapes, from drum- or box-shaped to complex, mixed zoomorphic forms.

Maya inscriptions, sometimes carved with remarkable beauty, are read in two columns, from left to right, generally beginning with a Long Count date—a series of glyphs with bar-and-dot numerals giving the number of days, months, years, 20-year cycles, and 400-year cycles since the beginning of the current creation of the universe.

The Maya carved figurative pendants and ornaments from jade. The greatest Maya burial yet found lies under a temple at Palenque. Inside a large, carved stone sarcophagus a great ruler was buried, his face covered with a jade mask, his head enclosed in a jade headdress, and with jade jewelry covering his wrists, hands, and chest. Little is yet known about the sources of Maya jade, but one source has been found in the Motagua River Valley in Guatemala. Objects were also cut

Stela B at the Maya site of Copan; a Maya king surrounded by symbolic paraphernalia with a glyphic text to the left, carved in relief; 8th century AD

from shell and bone, and, in the Peten, flint was formed into "eccentric" shapes. Many small artifacts were placed in dedicatory caches under buildings, plazas, and sculptures, as well as in tombs.

Maya pottery wares are generally coarse, but cylindrical vases were used for finely painted scenes, some of which illustrate Maya deities and myths (sometimes identifiable from a 16th-century Maya manuscript, the *Popol Vuh*), while others seem to depict a ruler and retinue, possibly in an Underworld palace. Attractive figurines, although quite naturalistic, probably depict supernatural beings.

Little is known about Maya deities, but many supernatural creatures are depicted: a skeletal god, a long-nosed or long-lipped deity who is associated with water and rain, a moon-

A Maya jade plaque from Copan carved in relief: a ruler sits on a throne with a dwarf at his feet; Late Classic period (AD 600–900)

goddess, various old, Underworld gods, a deity who wears a shell and is thought to be an earth god, and a deity associated with kingship, whose effigy is often held by a ruler like a royal scepter.

By c AD 900, the central Maya area was largely abandoned, for reasons that are not yet fully understood. Peripheral Maya centers (Kaminaljuyu and Chichen Itza) continued to thrive under influence from central Mexico.

In the coastal lowlands of central Veracruz, just north of the Olmec region, a Classic-period culture developed. The architecture of El Tajin, which shows influences from central Mexico, Oaxaca, and the Maya area, is distinguished by the use of step-scroll elements and niches. The major pyramid has 365 niches, probably referring to the number of days in the solar year.

Rubber is indigenous in this region, and a ritual ballgame was played. Ballcourts are widely distributed in Mesoamerica, in the heart of ceremonial centers, but ballgame-related architecture and sculpture is particularly prevalent in central Veracruz. El Tajin has 11 ballcourts. Judging from the relief sculpture that adorns the major ballcourt, and ballcourts elsewhere, the game was a decapitation ritual in which blood was probably an offering to sky deities who kept the earth fertile.

Ballplayers shown on relief sculpture and pottery wear belts and protective equipment, probably made of wood or woven material so no examples of these have survived. But what may be stone replicas of these objects have been found widely and were possibly used for both ritual and burial, or burial only. "Yokes", U-shaped objects, weighing about 50 lb (22.5 kg),

represent a kind of belt worn by ballplayers. These are usually elaborately carved, often with the depiction of a frog-like earth monster. *Hachas* ("axes") have a blade-shaped top and an undercut at the bottom rear; they may represent a variety of subjects and carving styles. A similar form is the *palma*, which has a broader top. The Tajin carving style, which grew out of the post-Olmec style, consists of images embellished by intricate scroll designs. Numerous attractive figurines also come from Veracruz, of which the best known are mold-made human figures with smiling faces.

The highland region around the modern city of Oaxaca had a long Pre-Columbian history going back at least as far as the Early Preclassic period (1500–900 BC) when it traded with the Olmec. Writing and the Mesoamerican calendar presumably began in Oaxaca in the Middle Preclassic (900–300 BC), for the sculpture of that time is sometimes inscribed with hieroglyphs of names of people and places as well as dates in a bar-and-dot system (a dot is one; a bar is five) of vigesimal numeration, basic to later Maya arithmetic.

Monte Alban, a great site on the flattened top of a mountain, surrounded by higher mountains, flourished c AD 200–700 when the site was expanded by a Zapotec-speaking people. Both stelae and architectural members bear inscriptions from this period.

In addition to plastered stepped mounds in a vast plaza space, about 150 masonry slab tombs have been found under plaza and patio floors. Some are miniature replicas of temple structures and a few have mural paintings. In a patio over one tomb, an offering scene was found consisting of five richly dressed pottery figurines, a seated fire-god figure, an orchestra, and, in the center, a stone mask placed on a form that may represent the bundled body of the deceased. The most common burial-pottery form was an urn depicting a vegetation, weather, or astronomical deity with a mask face and elaborate headdress. Such urns represent the complex development of a simple form that began in the Preclassic (900 BC). Jade pendants, showing full figures or heads with dead faces, have been found in pottery vessels placed in burial caches.

The city of Teotihuacan in the highlands just north of Mexico City had been inhabited in the Preclassic period, dominated the early Middle Classic, and declined c AD 700. It was a true urban complex—probably the largest city in Mesoamerica—covering 7.5 sq miles (20 sq km) with compounds for palaces and apartments. Its population has been estimated in hundreds of thousands.

The ceremonial center was laid out with two large pyramids at one end and a long series of plazas, flanked by stone buildings in *talud-tablero* architecture (a system of alternating straight and sloping panels). Buildings were decorated with sculpture—roof decoration and tenoned heads—and with paintings, many of which still exist. The paintings represent highly stylized figures with flat forms and rigid poses. They wear, or are accompanied by, symbolic elements of near-glyphic character: bird headdresses, the eye-rings of the rain

An urn from Monte Alban depicting a deity with a serpent-mouth mask; AD 200–700. National Anthropology Museum, Mexico City

god, shields and arrows, incense bags, "speech scrolls", netting, drops of water, and cut conch-shells, among other motifs. Composite animals also appear. The most naturalistic mural depicts what is thought to be the paradise of the rain god.

Although freestanding sculpture was not a notable Teotihuacan art form, there are small sculptures, stone figurines in rigid poses, and masks of impersonal, open-mouthed faces.

The influence of Teotihuacan art was felt throughout Mesoamerica. Because Teotihuacan symbolic elements are found on Classic Maya monuments, at least one ruling Maya family may have come originally from Teotihuacan. *Talud-tablero* structures are found widely in the Maya area, and also

at Monte Alban and El Tajin, at Xochicalco in the Mexican state of Morelos, and at Cholula in Puebla. The latter three sites may have had quite close relationships with Teotihuacan. Teotihuacan and Cholula have the largest pyramids in Mesoamerica; Cholula also has mural paintings, although they are generally of a more naturalistic style than those of Teotihuacan. Teotihuacan influence is also seen in the recently discovered murals at Cacaxtla near Mexico City, and in sculpture on the Pacific slopes of Guatemala, around Cotzumalhuapa.

Another indication of Teotihuacan influence was the spread of a pottery form, a slab-footed cylindrical tripod pot with a lid. Locally made examples have been found in Kaminaljuyu and Tikal. Most of those from Teotihuacan, however, are of a Fine Orange ware which does not appear in the other sites at this time.

Teotihuacan was intimately connected with the life of other Classic-period peoples, and its fall probably had much to do with the fall of other Classic civilizations. Monte Alban collapsed at about the same time as Teotihuacan; the Classic Maya lasted only a little longer. Situated near the shifting northern border of Mesoamerica, the downfall and partial destruction of Teotihuacan (there is evidence of burning) were probably caused by the invasion of less civilized people from the north.

The site of Tula, believed to have been the ancient Toltec capital, Tollan, lies in the highlands north of Teotihuacan, again on the northern edge of civilized Mesoamerica. According to legend, Tollan was founded in the late 10th century. Its most important ruler was Quetzalcoatl ("feathered serpent"). The concept of a supernatural feathered serpent is quite ancient in Mesoamerica; in the Postclassic period (AD 900–1520) Quetzalcoatl was an important deity—a creator god associated with agriculture and with the planet Venus. There is some confusion with the name, since it was both the name of a deity and a title as well as the name of a proto-historical king. Tula is full of Quetzalcoatl symbolism. The most important pyramid has giant caryatid columns carved like blocky human figures with the butterfly symbol of the god on their chests. Inside the structure, whose roof these columns once supported, small, painted, stone Atlantean figures, found at the site, probably held up an altar. At the base of the temple are friezes depicting prowling jaguars, eagles eating hearts, and a full-face depiction of the head of Quetzalcoatl. The temple is guarded by Chac Mools (simplified, supine figures, with a vessel on the stomach) and in front of the structure stand the remains of a building supported by columns.

There is a very striking resemblance between this complex and the Temple of the Warriors at Chichen Itza, in the center of the northern Yucatan Peninsula, a site that also has Classic Maya remains. Not only are the above-mentioned Toltec elements present at Chichen Itza, but the shapes of the pyramidal structures are similar, the Atlantean altar actually exists at Chichen Itza, and both sites have similar small standard-

Stone caryatid columns at Tula which originally supported the roof of a temple pyramid; height 460cm (180in); 10th–13th centuries AD

bearer figures and other sculpture traits. Figures at Chichen Itza wear Toltec clothing, and there are a number of other central Mexican motifs.

Legend tells that King Quetzalcoatl, driven out of Tollan, went east, out into the Gulf of Mexico, and disappeared. A week later he reappeared as the planet Venus the morning star. This legend may be based on a Toltec migration that led to Chichen Itza. In later, Aztec times, "Toltec" stood for all that was civilized, aristocratic, intellectual, and artistic, and Aztec kings went to considerable trouble to claim Toltec ancestry.

The finest craftsmen of the Postclassic period were the so-called Mixtec people in Oaxaca who became dominant after the decline of the Classic-period Zapotec people. Of the Postclassic sites in the Valley of Oaxaca, Mitla is the best-known and perhaps the most handsome with its mosaic stonework in various textile-like fret designs. The Mixtec did not add new structures to Monte Alban, but they did use some of the Classic-period tombs where they made their own burials, accompanied by gold-work and pottery.

Gold-working became important *c* AD 1000, and the Mixtec were the most skillful craftsmen in this medium. They cast gold by the *cire perdue* process, making necklaces with shell-shaped beads and pendant bells, pectorals with the face of a death-god or a warrior in an eagle headdress, and ear,

nose, and lip ornaments. One Mixtec burial at Monte Alban, guarded by Zapotec urns, yielded more than 500 ornaments, many of them of gold. There were also intricately carved deer bones and objects of jade, for the Mixtec were also fine lapidaries. They made masks and disks of, or covered human skulls with, turquoise mosaic. They also carved earspools of obsidian—brittle volcanic glass. In the pottery of this period, polychrome pedestal bowls and pitchers, decorated with step-scroll designs and animal and bird heads, replace the urns of the earlier people.

Whereas the Toltec people more or less disappeared in the Late Postclassic (AD 1200–1520), the Mixtec civilization continued: many of the finest objects of the Aztec period were made by Mixtec craftsmen.

In 1518, when the Spanish conquistadors reached the Aztec capital, Tenochtitlan, in the Valley of Mexico, they found a handsome, imperial city, with palaces and canals laid out in a four-quartered grid pattern and a great ceremonial center with temple-pyramids. The ruins of this capital now lie under Mexico City.

The Valley of Mexico had long been occupied. In the Early Preclassic period (1500–900 BC), pottery-making villages had interacted with the Olmec civilization: Tlatilco, on the outskirts of the present city, controlled obsidian mines in Teotihuacan and made fine pottery in its own style. The

Valley was a crossroads for trade and movement north and south through the mountains, and east and west across them. Teotihuacan lies at the edge of the Valley; Tula is not far to the north.

Tenochtitlan was founded *c*1325 by a wandering band of people who settled on the edge of Lake Texcoco. They quickly gained dominance in the Valley, and in the succeeding two centuries conquered territory from the Gulf of Mexico to the Pacific.

The Aztec had a large pantheon of deities who are represented in their art. Huitzilopochtli, the patron god of the Aztec, was a sun god nourished by sacrificial human blood. Xipe Totec, a pre-Aztec god concept, was the flayed god, a god of regeneration and the springtime renewal of vegetation. Tezcatlipoca was another god who probably originated far back in Mesoamerican prehistory. For the Aztec, he was a creator god, associated with the night sky. Quetzalcoatl was also prominent. Coyolxauhqui was the moon-goddess, who was slain by the sun (Huitzilopochtli). The Aztec took on the gods of the peoples they conquered, adding to the number and complexity of deity representations. Some prominent Aztec deities were probably taken over from the Huastec, a Postclassic people in Veracruz who made handsome sculptures of their gods.

Aztec deity sculptures are often monumental, symmetrical,

A Mixtec gold-copper alloy pectoral, from tomb 7 at Monte Alban, representing the god of death

and blocky: more a collection of attributes that tell the story of the deity than realistic representations. Skulls, snakes, and human hands and hearts are among the accoutrements of these gods.

But Aztec sculptors also made elegant and naturalistic depictions of animals and vegetables. Some finely carved wooden objects also remain—drums, spearthrowers, and frames for obsidian mirrors—and there is lapidary work in turquoise, rock crystal, and obsidian. And, of course, there were the gold objects that caught the eyes of the Spanish conquerors, whose writings show how impressed they were by the art of these last Pre-Columbian people in Mesoamerica, although they were more interested in the value of the gold than in the craftsmanship with which it was worked. Some Aztec objects were sent back and shown in Europe, where Albrecht Dürer (1471–1528) saw them and wrote in his diary: "All the days of my life I have seen nothing that has gladdened my heart so much as these things, for I saw amongst them wonderful works of art."

The west coast of Mexico—particularly the states of Colima, Jalisco, and Nayarit—in general developed independently of the rest of Mesoamerica. It seems at times to have had contact with northern South America. Radiocarbon dates indicate that the village cultures of this region, which consists of both highlands and coastal plain, had their greatest development *c*200 BC–AD 330. Shaft tombs have yielded mortuary offerings of pottery in the form of effigy dogs and other animals (dogs were eaten in Mesoamerica), warriors, shamans with horns on their heads, women (sometimes pregnant), and elaborate scenes with many figures in houses and plazas. Figures and vessels were modeled by hand. Colima and Jalisco pottery is usually polished, and Nayarit pieces are painted.

Central Andes. This term refers to the Peruvian desert, on the west coast of South America, and to the adjacent, parallel chain of mountains and highland plateaus extending southeast into Bolivia. Northwest Argentina and northern Chile are peripheral to the Central Andean region, to the south; to the north lies Ecuador, which has produced a great deal of early pottery, and Colombia, where early pottery has also been found as well as an abundance of gold artifacts.

The coast of Peru is one of the driest deserts in the world. Offshore flows the Humboldt Current, cold waters from the Antarctic that normally provide one of the world's richest fishing grounds. The coastal desert is cut by rivers, perpendicular to the coast, which bring water from the high sierras. The control of this water has always been of great importance. In the river valleys, agriculture by irrigation has been practiced for several millennia, with maize as an important crop. In the mountains, there is farming in the valleys and on terraced hillsides. At higher altitudes, root crops are grown and llamas and alpacas graze. A great altiplano, at 13,000 ft (4,000 m) above sea level, stretches about 500 miles (800 km) from the southern highlands of Peru down into Bolivia. To the east, the mountains descend quickly to the tropical forest of

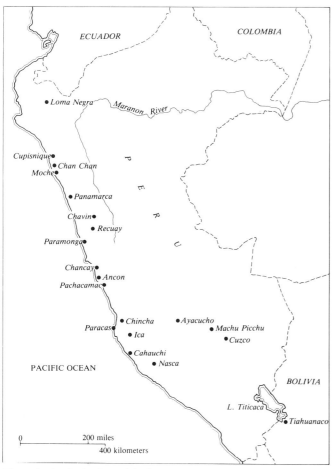

The main sites in the Central Andes

the Amazon Basin. Some of the earliest archaeological material in Peru has been found on the lower slopes of the eastern Andes.

For millennia there has been contact between the inhabitants of the coast, the sierra, and the edge of the forest. Influences and goods have flowed from one to the other. There are, however, basic differences in the art and the way of life of these peoples. Stone architecture and sculpture are mountain traits; sometimes natural hills are faced with stone to imitate structures. On the coast, buildings are made of sun-dried adobe bricks, and there is little sculpture. Pottery forms tend to differ between north and south, rather than between highland and coast. The stirrup-spout pot is an ancient northern form for special pottery, whereas bridge-spouted vessels are a southern form. Effigy vessels—representing anthropomorphic figures, animals, vegetables, and complex scenes—are widespread, particularly during the early periods, and globular vessels with modeled human heads are generally common.

The art of the coast often depicts fishermen and sea life, and many decorative objects of worked shell have been found. Yet sea shells may be shown on sculpture made in the sierra, and pottery made on the coast may represent mountain scenes.

Textiles were important symbolic goods throughout the Andes. Because of preservation conditions, most of those ex-

isting today come from the central and south coasts, although cloth of twined, cultivated cotton, dating as far back as 2000 BC, was found on the north coast. Painted cotton textiles appear in various times and places. Cotton was also used with llama or alpaca wool to make plain cloth, double cloth, tapestry, and other weaves. Many garments were made from the feathers of brilliant tropical birds tied into cloth. The most common garment was a *poncho* (a shirt or tunic), a rectangle of cloth woven on a back-strap loom in varying sizes and proportions with slits for the neck and arms.

One of the dominant themes of Andean art relates to the "trophy-head cult". Decapitated heads appear in Mesoamerican art, but they are shown with much greater frequency in the art of the Andes. Supernatural monsters are often seen holding a knife and a human head that must have been offered in sacrifice. Little is known about religion, but art themes suggest that there were sacrifices to mountains, to the sea, and to felines.

Various chronological terms have been used for the history of the Central Andes, but most common in present usage is the division of the archaeological periods into stages of "horizon" or widespread styles, and intermediate periods of regional styles, for there is a pattern to the ebb and flow and transfer of power through time. In some places, of course, periods are longer or shorter than in others.

The first civilization in Peru, for which radiocarbon dates go back to c1250 BC, was that called Chavin. It is named after a modern village, Chavin de Huantar, which lies next to what must have been the major temple of the ancient civilization. The small valley containing the ruins lies at the junction of two tributaries of the Maranon River, on the eastern slopes of the Andes, at about 10,500 ft (3,200 m) on the way down to the Amazon Basin. From the coastal point of view, its remote position suggests that the site was deliberately placed to provide an inaccessible *sanctum sanctorum*; but there are other sites nearby with Chavinoid and earlier remains, and the activity in this region may reflect closeness to an ancestral tropical-forest people in the Amazon Basin where all Pre-Columbian high civilization may have begun.

The intricate stone structure at Chavin, built in four major stages, faces a sunken courtyard and has interior rooms, galleries, ramps, stairs, and air vents. The outside of the building is of dressed stone, garnished with stone sculpture—tenoned heads of monstrous faces, lintels, panels, and columns flanking the main portal. Although the tenoned heads and a few other sculptures, for example, the Lanzon or Great Image, placed in a small cruciform room in the oldest part of the building, are carved in the round, most of the sculpture is in low-relief or incised techniques, and even sculpture in the round does not have deep carving. The Great Image represents a deity with a smiling mouth and snaky hair, thought to be the earliest important god represented at the site. Other particularly significant sculptures from Chavin are the Raimondi Stela, a plaque showing a figure holding an elaborate snake-headed staff in each hand, and the Tello Obelisk, a shaft of stone carved on four sides with crocodilian and other motifs. In general, figures in Chavin art have human bodies, with a round eye, which may derive from a snake, a bird, or a feline (although an eye with squarish corners and a pupil at top center is also common); feline fangs; snake appendages; bird feet and wings; the crest of a harpy eagle; extended mouths, which look like zippers on the body; masks on the rump or tail; and crocodilian attributes. The designs sometimes consist of modular repetitions of these motifs. Small stone vessels have the same iconography in the same incised technique.

Earlier Chavin pottery has low-relief carved decoration and fat stirrup spouts; later pottery may be painted and slimmer in form. The variation in the shape of stirrup spouts is a useful chronological marker in Chavin and later times. In addition to stirrup-spout pots—which may have effigy bodies—there are bowls and narrow-mouthed bottles.

A Chavin hammered gold plaque; 22×11cm (9×4in); c1250–300 BC. Dumbarton Oaks Research Library and Collection, Washington, D.C.

Gold was already worked in Chavin times by simple processes of hammering and cutting. Gold pendants and ear ornaments repeat the same motifs found on sculpture.

Little is known about the nature of the power of the Chavin cult, but it is clear that it affected wide areas. Architecture, sculpture, and pottery of Chavin style have been found across the mountains on the central and north coasts (north-coast Chavin-style pottery is often called "Cupisnique", after the narrow valley where some of it was found), and Chavin-style pottery has also been found on the south coast. Moreover, the only known Chavin textiles come from the south coast. It is not known whether these were made there or were imported from the north. Because they were highly portable, they may have been a means of transporting the style from Chavin de Huantar.

Late in the Chavin period, new influences entered the mountain site, probably from the north coast, and artistic work became simpler and more naturalistic; but Chavin concepts and motifs continued over a wide region and for a long time.

There were other Chavin-descended early art styles on the north coast (Salinar, Gallinazo, Vicus), but it is the Mochica, or Moche, style that came to dominate the north-coast valleys in the early centuries of the Christian era. Inhabitants here must have considered themselves descendants of the Chavin people. A few Mochica vessels have been found at Chavin, indicating some contact with the earlier site; a deity closely resembling Chavin deity depictions appears in Mochica art; and the stirrup-spout form was perpetuated in much of the fine pottery found in burials. The chronological sequence established by archaeologists for Mochica subperiods is based, to a large extent, on the variations in the shape of stirrup-spout pottery.

The Huaca ("sacred place") of the Sun, at the village of Moche, is the largest single adobe structure in the New World. Moche ceremonial buildings once had walls with painted scenes, but few remain except at the site of Panamarca in the Nepena Valley. No stone Mochica sculpture exists, but there is lapidary work as well as carved and inlaid wooden objects. Only a few textile fragments remain, for there are destructive salts in the north-coast sands. The figured textiles have tapestry designs showing mythical creatures.

The Mochica were fine metalworkers who made great technological advances in gilding copper, combining silver and gold, and inlaying to make ear and nose ornaments, headdress decorations, and masks. A handsome mask was found at Moche, but the most important finds come from a site in the far north, Loma Negra, where more than 500 pieces of hammered metal were discovered a few years ago.

The largest body of Mochica art, however, is the quantity of fine pottery vessels with figures and scenes depicting a broad variety of ritually important matter. In addition to the stirrup-spout pots, there are wide-flanged bowls (floreros), "dippers", cruet-shaped pots, broad-shouldered vases, and double-vessel whistling jars.

Mochica Effigy Vases

The stirrup spouted vases made by the Mochica between c100 BC and AD 700 vary greatly in shape and subject. Some pots show single figures, some represent complicated scenes. Some are simple globular vessels with painted scenes, but even these may have a modeled "deck" figure on the top. Many pots were mold-made. The basic decorative techniques are full-round modeling, low relief, and painting.

Many "realistic" subjects appear. There are portrait heads of individuals—a number of pots bear not only the recognizable features of the same man but even his scars. Some vessels show the diseased or the blind, who wear special garments and are depicted with what were probably burial offerings. Other pots may be in the form of identifiable

species of birds, felines, llamas, frogs, deer, or foxes; some show plants. Houses and boats may be depicted in modeled form, as may ritual scenes in the mountains or on the offshore guano islands. Full-figure warriors are common subjects; naked, roped prisoners also appear, and pots may imitate helmets and war-clubs. Music was an important theme: vessels show figures playing panpipes, flutes, and drums, and there are clay trumpets with effigy figures on the bell.

Many full-figure effigy vases show a man in specific kinds of dress with paraphernalia for the ritual chewing of coca leaves. The leaves were carried in a small bag with a long woven cord around the neck. They were chewed with a bit of lime which was carried in a gourd and removed with a stick.

Such remarkably realistic vases tell a great deal about both the environment and the ritual of the Mochica people. Yet many pots depict worlds that seem surreal. Some of the "portrait" heads represent an animal in a headdress or a deity with a fanged mouth, round animal eyes, and snakehead ear ornaments. A modeled warrior may have the head of an owl. Scenes of sexual activity show skeletal figures. A frog has vegetation on its

▲ A man with a diseased, scarred face sitting above a scene of offering preparation. Linden-Museum, Stuttgart

▼ A frog, with a landscape painted on its back, and a snake. University Museum, Philadelphia

◄ A stirrup-spout vase portrait of a man. Dayton Art Institute

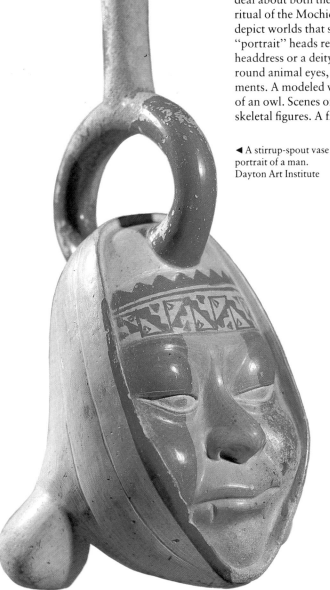

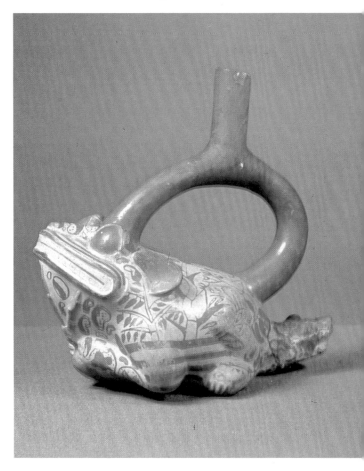

...ack; its tail may end in an animal head. An ...nthropomorphized peanut plays a flute, and ...otatoes bear the faces of diseased men. ...nthropomorphic seals and cormorants play ...rums.

Such representations may have seemed just ...s "real" as the naturalistic ones in terms of ...Iochica myth, religion, and cosmology. It is ...kely that these vessels were made only for ...lacing in graves; their subject matter would ...e in with beliefs about the other world and ...hat was important to take into it.

For Pre-Columbian peoples, pottery was a ...cred medium. The fine pottery, on which ...are and skill were lavished, was produced in ...rms significant in themselves—the stirrup-...pout pot was an ancient, ancestral form for ...e Mochica—and the pottery was used to ...epict subjects of great importance. Perhaps ...e should not look at conventional Mochica ...presentations as realistic, but should con-...der even these vessels as charged with ...upernatural, religious meaning.

ELIZABETH P. BENSON

...urther reading. Benson, E.P. *The Mochica: a Culture*
...*Peru*, New York and London (1972). Donnan, C.B.
...*oche Art of Peru: Pre-Columbian Symbolic Com-*
...*unication*, Los Angeles (1978). Kutscher, G. *Chimu:*
...*ne Altindianische Hochkultur*, Berlin (1950).
...wyer, A.R. *Ancient Peruvian Ceramics: the Nathan*
...*ummings Collection*, New York (1966).

A vase in the form of ...anthropomorphic seal ...aying a drum. Art ...stitute of Chicago

▶ A mountain scene: an offering is presented to a deity. Staatliche Museen, Berlin

op left A vase depicting ...naturalistic bird. Art ...useum, Princeton

Top right A man with a lime gourd and coca bag sitting among cacti; Metropolitan Museum, New York

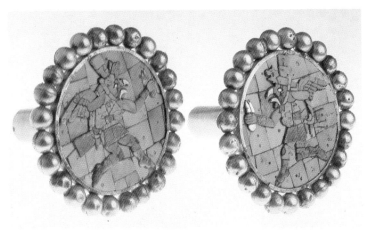

A pair of Mochica ear plugs; gold with stone and shell inlay; diameter of each 9cm (3½in); 3rd–4th century AD. Metropolitan Museum, New York

In the mountains, between the Mochica coastal valleys and the old Chavin heartland, a culture called Recuay or Huaylas made hand-formed, resist-decorated pottery showing some of the same motifs found in Mochica art—warriors, women, felines, birds, llamas, and various clothing details and ritual objects—but used in a different symbolic system. Moreover, Mochica faces may be portraits, but Recuay faces are always expressionless and stylized. A central figure is often flanked by two felines or a pair of figures. As in Mochica art, the pots are usually combinations of modeled forms and flat, painted surfaces, but the basic pottery forms are different. Wide-rimmed jars with strap handles are common; stirrup-spout vessels are rare.

Stone sculpture from this region consists of bulky, stylized human forms, sometimes holding trophy heads and with human hands on their headdresses. There are also tenoned heads that are cruder than, but probably derived from, Chavin prototypes. The Recuay style probably starts somewhat earlier than the Mochica, c200 BC, and also ends somewhat earlier, c AD 600.

The south coast of Peru was also an inheritor of the Chavin style. Pottery and textiles bear motifs resembling those of Chavin. But a distinct local art, known as the Paracas style, began by c600 BC. It is represented most strikingly by elaborately embroidered garments, particularly enormous mantles, about 10 ft (3 m) by more than 3 ft (1 m) which, it has been estimated, may have taken 30 years to make. The mantles have checkerboard patterns, with plain squares alternating with embroidered ones, which depict monstrous anthropomorphic figures with snake, fish, and bird attributes, brow and nose masks, trophy heads, knives, and other ritual paraphernalia. No two mantles have the same basic design unit, and, even within a mantle, although the figures are essentially the same, no two are identical. The mantles, presumably only made for burial, were found in mummy bundles which sometimes included dozens of embroidered textiles: shirts, turbans, kilts, and loincloths. Although cloth dominates the contents of the mummy bundles, white-slipped, double-spout-

and-bridge ceramics and simple gold ornaments were also found.

In another context in the same region, small, painted cotton cloths, with long fringes at the top, were discovered; these were used as masks for mummy bundles. They seem to derive from Chavin painted textiles, but are simpler in style. They were accompanied by pottery with incised designs and a resinous paint applied after firing.

The Nasca style followed the Paracas in the same region, in the river valleys inland from the Paracas Peninsula. Early Nasca pottery exhibits the incised technique of Paracas and some of the same iconography. In time, however, a distinctive polychrome style takes over, with agricultural and sea subjects and whiskered deities, or deities who wear whiskered mouth masks. Toward the end of the Nasca style, pottery designs become more florid with repetitions of motifs and appendages.

The brow and mouth masks seen on Paracas mantles and on Nasca pottery are actually found among Nasca metalwork. Most Nasca metalwork consists of simple, hammered-and-cut gold and is less sophisticated than that produced by their north-coast contemporaries, the Mochica.

There are textiles of cotton and wool: shirts, loincloths, and bags to hold coca leaves to be chewed in a ritual. The designs are spaced in a manner reminiscent of Paracas textiles, but are simplified and more abstract.

A Nasca figure with mask and trophy head; height 25cm (10in); 200 BC–AD 900. Staatliche Museen, Berlin

The Gate of the Sun at Tiahuanaco; height about 300cm (120in); AD 400–700

Architecture, mostly of adobe and cane construction, is less ambitious in the south at this period than elsewhere. The site of Cahuachi, in the Nasca Valley, however, is large, includes a plaza, and boasts a 65 ft (20 m) high pyramid, which is actually a natural hill capped with adobes.

The most famous remains are the ground markings in the Nasca Valley: straight lines, geometrical forms, and sometimes animals or birds, drawn on the surface of the desert by removing the surface to expose a lighter-colored soil beneath. Such markings may well have astronomical meaning; they may also be offerings to sky gods.

At nearly 13,000 ft (4,000 m) above sea level, the site of Tiahuanaco lies in the altiplano on the Bolivian side (the southern end) of Lake Titicaca: the highest navigable lake in the world. The lake is still plied by reed rafts that must be of ancient design. A desolate, treeless landscape, without human scale, the altiplano has been occupied for millennia, and Tiahuanaco, in the Early Intermediate period (400 BC– AD 550), was a great ceremonial center.

The site has impressive stone sculpture and architecture,

including a stone-faced natural hillside, a sunken court and tenoned heads reminiscent of those of Chavin, and monumental standing human figures with low-relief modeling and incised lines like tattooing and textile designs on faces and garments. These figures stand to attention, holding symbolic objects, their eyes surrounded by the drawing of a bird head and wing.

The greatest sculpture at the site is the Gate of the Sun, a single piece of finely dressed and carved andesite, about 10 ft (3 m) high, and nearly 13 ft (4 m) wide. Rows of small profile figures of anthropomorphic birds, holding a staff, run toward a large central frontal figure, which stands on a platform and holds in each hand a snake-headed staff. Bands of incised trophy and snake heads embellish his garments. The face, which protrudes in higher relief than the rest of the sculpture, is square and mask-like. Bird-headed tears run from the eyes. Medusa hair ends in snake-heads.

Characteristic pottery shapes are the *kero*, a flaring-topped tumbler form, and a shorter, flaring-topped vessel with a modeled feline head on a plaque at one end and a tail at the other, resembling a modern gravy boat.

The Gate of the Sun at Tiahuanaco encapsulates the style that spread from there: through the site of Wari, near Ayacucho, in the southern highlands of Peru, down to the coast, where it left its imprint on south-coast art, then up to the far north for a brief, but telling, impact. The relationship between Wari and Tiahuanaco is not yet fully understood, but the spread of traits from these sites seems to have followed both military and religious activity.

Wari is a vast site, consisting of groups of rectangular buildings of solid stone, surrounded by walls hundreds of yards long and from 20 to 40 ft (6 to 12m) high. Other large walled cities began to develop at this time. Elsewhere there are stone-slab structures that must have been ceremonial buildings, but such architecture and sculpture is not as impressive as at Tiahuanaco. Wari sculpture is similar to that at the altiplano site—its blocky, monolithic figures have the same mask-like square face, a headband headdress, and generally similar garments—but it is smaller, simpler, and less finely worked, as if the attention of its creators was on other things: possibly the political domination of other peoples. Wari probably administered a great empire, for a number of large centers with architecture, pottery, and textiles of the Wari-Tiahuanaco style are found scattered throughout Peru. The Wari-Tiahuanaco style, as it fanned out from the southern highlands, influenced, and was combined with, local contemporary styles, and left its impression on later art.

There are many surviving Middle Horizon textiles from the south coast, notably large tunics with figures deriving from the running bird-men on the Gate of the Sun—staff-holding figures with a snake headdress, prominent teeth, and a shirt and a kilt—and simplified elements of these designs; for example, an eye and a mouth combined with a step-scroll motif. There are also four-cornered pile-cloth hats with these designs.

On the north coast, in the Moche Valley, near the sea, the great city of Chan Chan arose in the Late Intermediate period (AD 900–1430). Built by the Chimu people, the capital of the kingdom of Chimor covers 9 sq miles (23.5 sq km), and has nine compounds with high walls, and large plazas and small rooms within the walls, some of which seem to be ritual rooms, some storerooms. Walls are sometimes partly open, with a latticework design of adobes; solid walls may have a coating of clay with designs that look like, and may have derived from, textile patterns. It is thought that these compounds were the palaces, storerooms, and mausoleums of nine divine rulers of the city. When a king died, he was richly buried, his compound was abandoned, and his successor began his own compound.

Stirrup-spout pottery continued in use, and many inherited Mochica motifs appear on the mold-made, mass-produced Chimu vessels, for example, effigy fruits and vegetables, and relief designs showing a deity fighting a fish monster. The themes are fewer, however, and more simply presented, and the pottery is not as beautiful or as varied as that of the

A detail of a Chimu poncho decorated with large birds carried on litters by small birds; height 69cm (27in). Textile Museum, Washington, D.C.

Mochica. The stirrup spout usually has a small monkey nestling in the angle between the stirrup and the spout.

Extant textiles include *ponchos* of gauze, or wool and cotton, sometimes elaborated with the addition of feathers and metal plaques.

Goldwork was splendid, but not much more technically advanced than that of the Mochica. There were sheet-gold crowns; enormous embossed ear disks on rods; gold or silver-gilt mummy masks, broad and flat, and often decorated with danglers or stone inlays or attachments; *keros* with hammered designs; and elaborate knives with a handle that might be a deity with intricate filigree headdress and turquoise or chrysocolla inlay. Elaborate figurative ornaments were made of cast copper.

The Chimu conquered the northern valleys as far south as Paramonga, farther than the extent of the Mochica realm. In *c*1470 the empire was conquered by the Inca, who brought Chimu metalworkers to Cuzco; so greatly did they admire their skills.

Other cultures flourished in the Late Intermediate period (AD 900–1430) on the central and south coasts. From the Chancay Valley, north of Lima, come tapestry and painted cloth showing figures with elaborate headdresses, and repeated bird and fish designs, as well as fine gauzes. The textiles are generally more sophisticated than the pottery. Effigy vessels representing nude figures, with a few crudely painted lines on slip on rough-textured, gritty clay, and dolls made of textile clothing on wooden frames were probably created solely for mortuary use. The site of Ancon, which has produced Early Horizon material (1400–400 BC), is the source of some of this Late Intermediate material.

The site of Pachacamac, south of Lima, was the sanctuary of a creator deity of the same name. Long an important site, Pachamacac has material from the Early Intermediate period, and a great deal of pottery from the Tiahuanaco-Huari expansion. The sanctuary and oracle there were so influential that, when it was conquered by the Inca in the Late Horizon (1430–1532) Inca structures were added, but the basic integrity of the site was left intact.

On the south coast, where Paracas and Nasca styles once flourished, the Inca and Chincha styles dominated the Late Intermediate period. Flaring-rimmed globular vessels, often with handles, had small, abstract polychrome designs repeated like those on textiles. The textiles themselves have designs reminiscent of patchwork quilts.

The Inca people rose out of obscurity in the southern highlands of Peru *c* AD 1200, and gradually increased their power until, by the time of the Spanish arrival in 1532, their empire extended, southwards down into Chile and Argentina, and, to the north, up through Ecuador to the Colombian border. The great expansion began *c*1470, under the Inca Pachacuti. ("Inca" was the term for the divine ruler; the word has since come to be used for the whole people.)

The capital city, Cuzco ("navel of the world"), is situated

The entrance of the so-called Royal Tomb at Machu Picchu

A Chimu knife of cast and hammered gold and turquoise inlay, with a deity figure; height 34cm (13in); c1200–1440. Art Institute of Chicago

about 11,000 ft (3,400 m) above sea level, in a small valley accessible both to the coast and to the Amazon Basin, as well as to intermontane valleys. The city was divided into four quarters, as was the empire itself, which was called Tawantin-suyu, "world of the four quarters".

The empire was carefully defined and controlled, and linked by roads, which carried official movements of peoples, llama trains bearing goods, and runners who relayed messages. One main road ran along the coast, the other through the mountains. Storage depots and way stations were placed along them. Inca skill in engineering roads and in constructing precisely fitting, mortarless stone walls for their ceremonial buildings is well known. Remains of Inca architecture, characterized by trapezoidal doorways, can still be found all over the former empire.

Stones were sacred to the Inca people, and stories of stones changing into men, or men turning to stone, abound in Inca legend. Inca sacred structures sometimes combine natural rock formations, particularly cave-like places, with carefully dressed and fitted man-made walls. A notable example is the so-called Royal Tomb at Machu Picchu. There is little naturalistic monumental Inca sculpture, but large rocks were carved with forms from nature, as well as with architectural and abstract shapes. Small stone ceremonial bowls were also carefully carved and decorated with animals, as were spoons and snuffing tubes for ceremonial use.

The Inca were fine craftsmen, achieving the greatest advances in metallurgy since those on the north coast in the Early Intermediate period. In addition to making human figures and llamas of hammered gold and silver, they cast knives, tools, and ornaments in bronze and inlaid them with copper and silver. The temples of the Sun and the Moon in Cuzco were lined with silver and gold, and the central patio contained a garden with a stone fountain sheathed in gold, as well as artificial golden plants.

The Inca were also excellent potters. Although effigy vessels were still produced in this period, the characteristic pottery shape is an *aryballo*—a jar with a pointed bottom, handles, and a long neck with flaring rim. Designs on these were more geometrical, less figurative, than those on most previous pottery. The same is true of textile designs, especially the finely woven tunics or *uncus*. Featherwork was still prominent, and there are also a number of wooden objects, including *keros* and elaborately carved tomb posts.

Even with the regimentation enforced by the Inca empire, there were still elements of local styles in the art of the Late Horizon, and it is often possible to identify the area where objects were manufactured.

The empire was beginning to disintegrate when the Spaniards arrived to destroy it. The ransom of the Inca Atahuallpa, a roomful of gold artifacts, marked the end of Pre-Columbian art.

ELIZABETH P. BENSON

Bibliography: MESOAMERICA: Coe, M.D. *Mexico*, New York and London (1977). Coe, M.D. *The Maya*, New York and London (1980). von Winning, H. *Pre-Columbian Art of Mexico and Central America*, New York (1968). Wauchope, R. (ed.) *Handbook of Middle American Indians* (16 vols.), Austin (1964–76). CENTRAL ANDES: Bushnell, G.H.S. *Peru*, London and New York (1957). Lapiner, A. *Pre-Columbian Art of South America*, New York (1976). Lumbreras, L.G. *The Peoples and Cultures of Ancient Peru*, Washington, D.C. (1974). Rowe, J.H. and Menzel, D. *Peruvian Archaeology: Selected Readings*, Palo Alto (1974).

26

NORTH AMERICAN INDIAN
AND INUIT ART

A Navajo Indian blanket (Southwest); c1920. Schindler Collection, New York (see page 497)

THE world into which the Native American migrated from Siberia across the Bering Straits into present-day Alaska some 40,000 years ago, according to generally accepted belief, was one that offered a wealth of resources to the potential artist. Not only was the New World richly endowed in fauna, but flora was equally plentiful and adaptable. It offered the people food, shelter, and clothing from a great variety of wood, stone, and animal substances which provided materials from which to create exciting new designs, as well as to develop gradually techniques needed for their manufacture, many of which are to be found nowhere in the Old World.

Indeed, this factor of variety requires emphasis, for it is a common error to consider the aboriginal inhabitants as "one" American Indian and to think that the product of this collective person is "Indian Art". While it is true that the product of the Native American is, indeed, Indian Art, it is the product of well over 300 distinct tribes, speaking almost as many languages. Many of these are as dissimilar as Chinese is from English, with social patterns equally diverse: they have no more in common than ancient bloodlines. So complex is this topic that any individual treatment will be somewhat imbalanced. An art style may be similar, but not identical, from one group to another, and in many styles of design the difference will be quite dramatic. As new materials were gradually introduced into the manufacturing process, and techniques developed for making best use of them, not only were exciting new patterns and forms created but also stylistic varieties which slowly evolved into styles we now regard as "traditional". In considering evolution, we should remember that with these forms went a cultural pattern which itself changed continually; what was customary for one group at one place in time frequently underwent a considerable change with another generation as new ideas and applications filtered in.

Absolute "firsts" in prehistoric art continually change with new discoveries, but for the New World it is possible to give a fairly accurate account of the development of cultural activities. It is usually believed that the earliest artistic developments arose in the forming of stone implements for hunting food and self-protection. As we examine these implements and projectile points it becomes immediately obvious that many are true *objets d'art* in themselves; the skillful handling of flint, chert, and slate required to create the Clovis, Sandia, and Folsom points by which the earliest cultures are known required the greatest sophistication in stoneworking. Dating from *c* 10,000–8,000 BC, their careful forming and fluted section make them aesthetically outstanding. The use of wood may or may not have preceded stone. Along with wood, bone was easier to work than stone, but and all three became major sculptural media; knife-handles, clubs, ornaments, and similar implements offered a surface for decoration which was executed by incision, in low relief, or in-the-round. Many of the earliest archaeological finds indicate a completely successful aesthetic level of maturity in these materials.

Of the more complex arts, basketry was probably the first to reach maturity. The use of the wide variety of grasses, luxuriant in the New World along with vines and long-leaved tree materials, allowed the manufacture of a great range of shapes and sizes. The combination of different types of fibers, along with the relatively quick mastery of plant dyes necessary to produce colors, introduced many design styles which created a colorful basketry art and allowed the maker to identify her work against another's. This factor of identifica-

Two Sandia points from Sandia cave near Albuquerque; heights 6cm (2½in and 7cm (2¾in); c10,000–8,000 BC. Maxwell Museum of Anthropology, Albuquerque

North American Indian cultural areas

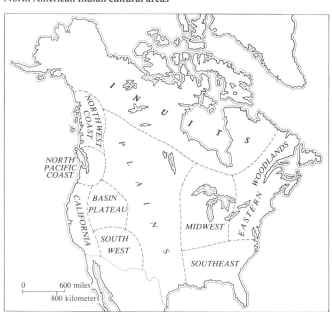

tion is important in the arts, for by it one could indicate tribal affiliation, social classification, and religious symbolism.

Basket-making was followed closely by textile-weaving. The differences are based largely on the use of a loom, the creation of a different type of finished product, and the introduction of more pliant fibers—notably more delicate plants, animal fur and wool, and human hair. Several distinct types of looms were known to prehistoric people, particularly the simple frame loom involving a back-and-forth warp and an interwoven weft. There was also the backstrap (or waist) loom, in which the tension was produced by the weaver adjusting her body as she proceeded; and the true loom, in which a shed was created by the introduction of a heddle and the weft introduced by a type of shuttle.

There were many subtle variations on the basic loom styles. These were distributed from the northern area of North America into most southerly South America, and all are still in use. Their complexity varies with the degree of skill of the weaver, and the extent to which they became important in a particular area. From them came the tremendous range of garments—containers, pouches, belting, head coverings, and similar woven materials—used by ancient and contemporary Indian people to provide themselves with the comforts needed to develop a comfortable life and a sophisticated civilization.

The next of the ancient arts in the sequence of development is usually thought to be the use of clay. While pottery is almost as old as any of man's activities, it probably developed out of a coincidental use with basketry. One theory is that baskets coated for waterproofing were placed over a fire to heat the contents; somehow, probably by accident, the basket was burned, and when the astonished woman pulled the hardened form from the ashes she had a new container—fired clay—made from what had been the earthen coat of the basket. A new art was thus born, since it was soon realized that the use of a basketry "jacket" was unnecessary, and ceramics became a major art with the experimental uses of clay combined with other earthen materials to give strength, shape, size, and color.

Although weaving, pottery, and basketry are known from early archaeological sites throughout the Americas, datable examples of weaving in North America seem to be later than those in South America. Part of the reason may be that more older pieces have survived from the desert regions of Peru. The few examples from the desert Southwest in North America all seem to date from later Horizons. But, on the other hand, pottery from North America is notable because some of the earliest-known examples are found in the southeastern area: Stallings Island, in Georgia, for example, was producing well-formed and fired pottery as early as 3500 BC, and some very recent radiocarbon dating in southern California argues for a pottery period of c4000 BC. (The earliest ceramic production in South America so far found seems to be at Valdivia, El Ecuador, c3500 BC.)

While wood was sculptured almost everywhere, and a few examples have survived in North America, the evidence is too scant to form anything other than conjectures about the scope, style, and, most important, the degree to which this was a major art. In areas where large forests were known, it is certain that the wood sculptor's art was of major importance—as it is today; it was peripheral in regions lacking substantial tree growth.

Wood seems to have been used for almost every conceivable purpose: shafts, handles, containers, masks, paneling, small charms, ornaments, and decorations of every type. Large planks were cut from trees to construct dwellings, many of which were large enough to house comfortably several dozen individuals. Most of the wooden art objects were carved, incised, or worked in an effort to make them visually more attractive; many were further decorated with colors.

Metal was not commonly used in Pre-Columbian North America to any considerable degree until the introduction of iron by the European. Some float or surface copper was used, and there is an indication that lead was employed; but gold, silver, and iron remained largely unknown and unused until later. Copper knife blades have been found, along with projectile points, and some small containers, spoons, and needles or awls; beyond these, copper was not widely used.

With the development of these skills to varying extents throughout the continent, the introduction of new techniques and materials by Europeans made a critical impact. The phenomenon of insinuation of new materials or techniques requires a hospitable recipient to become effective; unless a culture is sufficiently advanced to be able to make use of the novelty, that introduction can be of little importance. In most of these arts, the Indian was well-advanced—indeed, in some instances ahead of the introduction of a given skill—and was immediately able to adapt it for his own benefit. Weaving skills were such that the introduction of the horizontal loom had only modest impact, outmoding the vertical loom only for producing vast quantities of cloth. The potter's wheel was not used before the coming of the European, although a primitive form of platform base was known which was rotated by one hand or the feet. A type of "walk-around wheel" was used in a limited area (the potter walked around the vessel, forming it as she progressed). Only in modern times, however, has the wheel assumed any real importance in Indian America, largely in Latin lands.

Almost every variety of stone was used in sculpture or the production of implements; the three most commonly carved for artistic purposes were steatite, limestone, and catlinite. The first, also known as soapstone, was used to create a vast array of bowls, pipes, and ornaments, while large effigies, statues, zoomorphic forms and related figures were sculptured in sandstone and limestone. Catlinite, a special form of red-colored indurated clay, was used not only for pipe bowls and occasionally for stems but was also sculptured into figures and some bowls.

The prehistoric palette was derived largely from plants, berries, and natural materials, usually in black, red, brown, and yellow; mineral pigments supplied ocher, white, and green or blue-green. All of these were relatively muted hues; it was not

A platform effigy pipe, depicting a frog; Hopewell culture
(Eastern Woodlands); length 10cm (4in); 300 BC–AD 500;
Ohio State Museum, Columbus

A shell disk, with crested woodpeckers; Mississippian culture
(Southeast Woodlands); c AD 1000. Museum of the American Indian,
New York

until the European introduction of aniline dyes, c1880, that the brilliant colors so often mistaken for "Indian colors" became prevalent. However, when these did become available, the native artist embraced them wholeheartedly, though traditionalists often disapprove of their use. To Indian eyes a carving painted in brilliant colors is far more desirable than the somber or subdued tones obtainable earlier.

Many other decorative materials were commonly employed by Indian artists, especially porcupine quills, animal fur, claws, teeth, human hair, shell, and plant materials. Shell had a particular attraction for the individual, coming as it did from the water. Many of the charms, pendants, and carved adornments made from shell have a quasi-sacred importance, and some of the most creative and delightfully artistic designs are to be found carved or incised on large rounded shell discs.

All of these techniques and applications were the result of a long period of development, experimentation, and practice, and helped to create a cultural peak which remains today. One comment frequently heard maintains that the Indian artist never created "art for art's sake", arguing that everything had a mundane function. This is an oversimplification; while the limited storage facilities of the native home gives this observation a certain truth, there are many examples known whose functional value seems by any reasonable standard to be measurable only in visual terms. The most obvious are those open cut-out work vessels made by the prehistoric Florida people; it seems clear these could never have served as containers, but were made solely for their aesthetic appeal.

What is Indian art? Basically, a folk art made by Indian people; at its best it was made for indigenous needs to serve indigenous purposes. When exposed to outside demands, the art often loses much of its original integrity and assumes alien shapes, purposes, or sizes. Indeed, one of the major European influences upon Indian art has been that of size: vessels in-

tended for cooking family portions became held-in-the-hand bowls; and textiles were no longer used as body coverings but became important as wall hangings or floor coverings. Huge storage baskets and winnowing trays became small containers for the mantelpiece, or trays for flowerpots. The major need was no longer an object for daily use, but one made for admiration which could be easily transported. Shapes had also to be adjusted to those needs, or, unfortunately, forced into "cute" designs and patterns, such as the basketry hats, vases, and fancy bowls based on European prototypes made early this century.

Indian Art is not unique in and of itself; while it reflects certain individual qualities, predominantly in design, color, form, and style by which the initiated viewer can readily identify the cultural origin of the object, there are many close parallels with the native arts of the Old World. It is possible, in fact, to confuse certain clay vessels from Cyprus with those of the Southwest; a flaked point from Arkansas would be lost among a tray of prehistoric European points; and some Navajo weaving is very similar to the textiles from certain weaving areas of the Middle East. All of these were natural responses to local needs and environment.

Yet when it comes to judging "traditional North American Indian art", there is little confusion between the products of the Old World and the New. And it is this traditional, readily recognized form that becomes the standard by which we judge. The discrete qualities of Indian art may be regarded as a great use of mass; specific forms and types of objects which reflect the New World's environmental resources; linear motifs, either angular or curvilinear; predominant use of repeated patterns, often to the point of completely filling in a given area or surface; solid combinations of color, with a relatively limited palette; and designs applied to the surface, with a greater use of flat or low-relief designs than in the round. Much of the production of the artist had an eye to portability, due in no small part to the mobile nature of many Indian tribes; this was perhaps slightly less true of the sedentary Pueblo and Northwest Coast folk.

Certain arts were more advanced than others: basketry was one of the most remarkable achievements of the native artist, and, on balance, the claim can be made that no other region of the world equalled the skills of the California basket-weaver. In pottery, the range, variety, and aesthetic quality was of a high order; many of the relatively low-fired wares of the Southwestern potters equaled those of the Oriental ceramists in form, design, and imaginative variation. The weaving of many fibers, careful cording, and skillful design gave the Indian a textile art that can hold its own in any exhibition. Only in metal and stone was the North American native artist less impressive, probably because the need for transportable objects impeded the development of heavy sculpture. It may also be claimed that each major region of North America seems to have excelled in one particular art.

This thought introduces the question of specialization in native art. In one sense every man was an artist: each person made his own objects for a particular purpose. Those who were more gifted produced better-quality objects; through being sought after, they became artists in the sense of being creative individuals—although this concept seems not to have existed in most early civilizations. A few groups did have "professional artists" or persons who made their living by producing objects for sale or exchange. We know that they were highly regarded; some artistically or technically skilled individuals were even the targets of tribal raids—the conquerors kidnapped the artist for productive slavery at home.

On the Northwest Coast, wood carving was the preeminent art; in the Southwest, applied art, particularly weaving and pottery, were dominant. California basketry has already been mentioned as the supreme accomplishment of that region; the Plains people made maximum use of hides, with colorfully painted and decorated buffalo robes and costumes. The Plateau people used woven cornhusks in a unique manner, while Inuit ivory-carving is a technique still masterfully employed by the western Alaskan artists. The Indians of the Great Lakes were most active in wood, although not on the monumental scale of their distant brothers in Alaska; the peoples of the Eastern Woodlands culture, comprising the balance of the continent, expressed their creativity in unusual materials, particularly moose hair and birch bark, as well as in wood and quills. Finally, throughout the Southeast, clay modeling and pottery work, coupled with superb stone sculpture, provided a remarkably high level of aesthetic accomplishment.

A major influence upon native art resulted from the wide-ranging trade routes of prehistoric and recent times. It is often erroneously thought that early people lived in a vacuum, knowing only the general area in which they lived. We now know this was not true—peoples of the ocean shores were frequently visited by traders, coming for the colorful seashells,

bringing with them precious objects from inland. They returned not only with the shells, but also with stories of what they had seen, including new ideas, new cultural concepts, and often totally new materials which in time gave rise to a wholly new art form. It is this wide-ranging intertribal trade that frequently leads scholars astray in their attempt to establish design origins.

Although a certain homogeneity exists whereby the craft materials and regions can be distinguished and identified, variations in form, style, and design are present so that we need never be seriously concerned about an ability to identify, if only in general terms, the origin of the object. In the regional discussion that follows, it will be most helpful also to consider them in three major chronological sequences: the prehistoric art forms from the area; the traditional and transitional styles which developed over the centuries, which are today the primary bases for identification and thereby the indicator of a given regional or tribal style; and the contemporary patterns in those areas where there is a traceable continuum. The latter also allows a brief consideration of the changes which have evolved from various influences levied during the past century.

The Inuit. From the earliest Okvik form of c4000 BC the major art of these Alaskan people was sculpture. Other arts certainly existed, including the working of wood, hide, bone, and shell, as well as the more permanent clay, stone, and ivory; the latter, in particular, provide ample evidence of the widespread creation of beautifully worked figurines and ivory implements with deeply incised, carefully designed linear surface motifs. The figurines have a characteristic diamond-shaped head with straight line-and-circle incision; the harpoon and dart heads have similar linear designs.

Since the more perishable materials long ago disappeared in the hostile Arctic climate, the only surviving evidence is to be found in the ivory, stone, and occasional bone objects excavated in the ancient graves. However, enough parallels have been discovered between prehistoric and more recent forms to make it clear that there has been minimal change over the centuries. The traditional period of Inuit art is exemplified by the bizarre wooden masks, ivory toggles, buttons, charms, and other small ornaments produced between AD 1500 and 1900. It is interesting that of all Native American arts the abstract and surrealistic styles had their most imaginative development among the Inuit, and are particularly well-demonstrated in the fantastic carved and decorated dance masks used in ceremonies.

The artistic skills of the Inuit people tend to diminish in aesthetic quality as we move from west to east. The most sophisticated and technically superior work is found among the western Inuits, inhabiting Alaska; the central Inuits of Canada have a less exuberant art style, most of which is expressed today in stone. Here far less ivory is found, although both groups demonstrate the wonderful sense of humor so prevalent in Inuit art. The far-eastern Inuits, including the people living in Greenland, have a more static

A mask with black eye and feathers from West Alaska; 19th century. Robert H. Lowie Museum of Anthropology, Berkeley, Calif.

art form and show less of the humorous treatment.

The cumbersome fur costumes of the Inuit create a need for small buttons and fasteners; examples of these carved in ivory are works of art in themselves. Wooden utensils, also widely used, were not only well carved but frequently ornamented with similar ivory ornaments. But it is the small charms, fetishes, and effigies that are perhaps best known among the smaller objects, and many of these are true masterpieces.

Most contemporary Inuit art activities have developed directly as responses to White demands; the widely distributed and extremely popular steatite carvings made from a local soft stone in designs reflecting the daily lives of the people, or mythological creatures and events, grew out of the introduction of this art *c*1946 by non-Inuit individuals connected with the Canadian and United States arts and crafts organizations. Some years later a similar outside influence was responsible for the introduction of Japanese-style printmaking. Both activities are now pursued to provide income. Inuit artists have indeed brought their own talents to bear on these two art activities, but it is equally true that there is no traditional ancestry nor purpose in Inuit life for these objects. This is a sophisticated, albeit aesthetically excellent, tourist art.

Today several factors have made Inuit art a major activity in which professional artists take considerable pride. Among these are the change from an isolated village carver to an individual working with businesslike craft groups or cooperative organizations in which facilities and buildings are available. The artist comes to the studio to work, often on a regular daily basis, obtaining his livelihood from his art. Some cooperatives retail directly, others sell through curio stores or other outlets. They continue to produce the traditional ivory figures, ornaments, and decorations, wooden masks and implements, or steatite carvings and stone prints.

The Northwest Coast. Along the Alaskan coast and in British Columbia live some of the most remarkable wood sculptors in the world. Not only did they surpass all other native wood artists in the New World, but their monumental designs hold their own favorably with Old World artists as well. Their elaborately carved totem poles, stretching well over 60 ft (18 m) towards the sky, are eloquent testimony to their aesthetic talent, technical skill, and political grandiosity; all of these were combined in their art forms. Ranging from tall totem poles 60 to 70 ft (18 to 21 m) in height; stout houseposts 10 to 15 ft (3 to 4.5 m) tall for supporting the roofs of the frame dwellings; and the long staffs, paddles, and statues to small hand-sized charms and ornaments, we sense a powerful sense of complex, controlled design which is at once intricate yet beautifully organized and balanced.

The Tlingit and Haida people mastered the art of wood sculpture better than most, both in devising objects, designs, and motifs, as well as in large-scale execution. Equally exciting work was produced by the Tsimshian, Kitksan, and Niska, but in smaller numbers. The Kwakiutl favored more massive designs and concepts, in which the elements were frequently accentuated by color—usually red and blue-green, on a black-and-white background. While most Northwest Coast wooden art was also painted, the color schemes of the Tlingit and Haida were more subtle in contrast.

A further dynamic elaboration was the use of mechanical masks, also called "transformation masks", in which the dancer pulled strings attached to various sections of the carvings. This manipulation caused the masks to move, open out, or show sudden, startling action, thereby bringing the masks to life (simulating the swimming of a whale, for example) or revealing the inner "soul" of the animal depicted on the closed mask. These movable headdresses, when seen *en masse* accompanied by throbbing music, percussive drumbeats, and rhythmic foot or body movement, amid flickering fire and smoke of the ceremonial house, inevitably produced a hypnosis which tremendously augmented the dramatic effect.

Since much of this art was connected with wealth and prestige, both political and social, the artists themselves were of more than casual importance. They were a true professional group hired to create objects, highly paid for their skills, and valued for their ability. They enjoyed special privileges and their status often became equal to that of a village chief. Most of their designs were totemic, serving in much the same manner as the British heraldic system to provide a means whereby an outsider could readily identify the individual in relation to his clan, family lineage, social position, and mythical ancestors.

The function of this art was based on ritual. Unlike many cultures where fine art was dedicated to religious needs, among the Northwest Coast people these beautiful objects were made to demonstrate the importance of the person who bought them. They would be given away to friends, relatives, or rivals as direct indication of the political, social, or economic position of the owner at a special *potlatch* ceremony held for the specific purpose. Some art objects were even destroyed. This was intended to indicate the unimportance attached to wealth.

There was a canny psychology attached to this seemingly flagrant extravagance: it was incumbent upon the recipient to reciprocate in kind. He was required by social ethic to hold a similar party at a future date, invite his host, and then show his own wealth, generosity, and hospitality by making even more lavish gifts: an economic merry-go-round in which individuals often bankrupted themselves and their whole village simply to establish prestige. It became a seesaw with poverty as the inevitable consequence.

Materials used by the artists included walrus hide as a "canvas" for a painted robe or garments. Large flat-adzed planks were made into panels and subsequently painted or carved. Great woven textiles, used for ceremonial curtains, had powerful swooping patterns painted on them, as well as on the stone and wood used for smaller objects. Metal was very familiar: probably the earliest was surface copper, hammered into the desired shape and then decorated. The early "war knives" were of this type; later, with greater sophistication, the acquisition of sheet copper, and a knowledge of smelting, superb works of metal art were executed, often decorated with carved wooden or ivory handles.

The designs themselves were rigidly prescribed, yet in a manner that allowed a great degree of individual freedom. The so-called "X-ray style", in which the body, limbs, and vital organs of an animal were laid out in a symmetrical pattern, with all the features presented abstractly in a flattened-out arrangement, is best seen in the famous "Chilkat blankets" of the Tlingit people. Other designs were executed in strong, clean lines with as much or as little detail as the artist wished, although there were also specific clues for identifying the animal intended: a lolling tongue and sharp teeth for the bear, two flat incisors to portray a beaver, a long sharp beak to distinguish the raven.

Today, several younger carvers have taken up the art of the sculptor and distinguished themselves by their remarkable craftsmanship. Some of these work individually; others have organized themselves into cooperative groups, encouraging and supporting one another; some are local people of Indian blood. Some are descendants of Indians from distant tribal affiliation, often quite unrelated in culture but interested in art as a career. All these artists have developed their skills to a fine point, concerned with keeping a tradition alive. The unfortunate truth is that most of them tend to copy old objects, seen in museum exhibits, inevitably resulting in a strong art activity somewhat sterile in aesthetic concept.

A Chilkat weave shirt (Tlingit people, Northwest Coast). Portland Art Museum, Oregon

North Pacific Coast. Adjacent to, but slightly removed from the preceding tribal group is an area of Salish-speaking peoples commonly known as the Nootka, Makah, Fraser River, and Thompson River tribes. (They prefer the term "Westcoast" among themselves, but this name has yet to find general acceptance.) Their major artistic accomplishments are in basketry and wood sculpture of a special type. Some of the fine Nootka and Makah basketry is among the better products of the western region, while the strong imbricated-weave basketry of the Lillooet and related Fraser people is excellent. Most of their carved objects are solid and bulky, with only limited amounts of fine detail frequently painted to emphasize the contrast. While less classically worked than the carving of the Tlingit or Haida, Salish masks suggest the design styles of the Kwakiutl, and Nootka work has a characteristic form and quality of its own. The contemporary art of the region is limited; some wool-weaving continues and a few women are

Northwest Coast Sculpture

The coastal and adjacent interior area of Alaska, including parts of British Columbia, was inhabited by many tribal groups, of which the most important for aesthetic consideration were the Tlingit, Haida, Kitksan, Niska, Kwakiutl, and Tsimshian peoples. By *c* AD 1000 they had settled in the vast forests of the Northwest and quickly took advantage of these natural resources to become some of the most remarkable sculptors of Native America. The tall, straight cedar and spruce trees supplied the Indians with wood ideal for the construction of their large gabled dwellings, oceangoing canoes, totem poles, and houseposts needed to support the roofs of their homes.

Carving was effected by stone tools, including jade, until the introduction of iron and steel by Europeans—following which the art literally exploded into active production. The crisp, clean linear designs provided a sharp balanced form which distinguishes it from all other art styles. Smaller objects such as dance rattles, bowls, masks, helmets, and religious charms were stored in large carved treasure boxes; speaker's staffs, long clubs, and panels were carved for ceremonial purposes.

War canoes and whale-hunting vessels, many capable of holding 40 or 50 people, were carved from a single tree trunk and often went several hundred miles off the coast in search of their prey. They were decorated with mythological beings, such as the Land Otter Man, which were placed in the prow of the boat to assure its safe return. Tall totem poles, many reaching upwards of 60 to 70 ft (18 to 21 m), were decorated with the family crest and history; these were intended to announce the clan, background, wealth, and social position of the man who hired an outstanding artist to create the pole. Houseposts, usually between 10 and 15 ft (to 4.5 m) in height, were similarly decorated.

Best known to art collectors are the masks carved with designs of mythical creatures, supernatural beings, portraits of important individuals, or zoomorphic performers in the ceremonies held in large structures built for the purpose. Everything was done on a magnificent scale; dances were accompanied by chanting, incessant drumming, or singing, and with the hoots, growls, and shrieks of the animals being represented, this provided a tremendously dramatic performance. With the masks went elaborate costumes which completed the illusion of the supernatural performers. Movable masks, in which the performer activated the articulated carvings, added to the quasi-magical effect.

◄ A Tsimshian chief's headdress, inlaid with abalone shell, worn at *potlatch* ceremonies. Royal Ontario Museum, Toronto

▲ A Tlingit canoe prow ornament, the Land Otter Man; length 97cm (38in). University Museum, Philadelphia

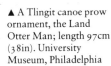

▼ A Haida Thunderbird or human transformation (movable) mask. Vancouver Centennial Museum

◄ A Haida shaman's rattle, inlaid with abalone shell. Private collection

Far Left A Tlingit ladle, length of handle 31cm (12in); late 19th century. Cleveland Museum of Art

◄ A carved and painted
cedar Tlingit housepost;
height 240cm (94in).
University Museum,
Philadelphia

▲ A Northwest Coast
totem pole

Almost everything the wealthy individual used was decorated with these elaborately carved designs. They were remarkably intricate—including motifs representing heraldic crests, legendary records, or supernatural guardians—and were often inlaid with precious *haliotis* (a form of abalone) shell. Spoons, ladles, food bowls, garment ornaments, and headdress plaques were all carefully worked to bring out the beauty of the design and to impress the viewer with the importance of the wearer. The Haida made great use of the deposit of argillite (an argillaceous shale found on their home island) to carve exquisite, small black miniature totem poles, pipes, and other sculptures intended for the tourist market. All reached the height of technical skill.

These sculptures were created for one purpose: to enhance and emphasize the prestige of the individual. They were bought, sold, traded, and given away in the complex ego-building surge of self-esteem and ladder-climbing which often resulted in bankruptcy, when the owner would give his entire possessions away at a *potlatch*. The recipient, usually a rival chief from a neighboring village, was then obligated to surpass this munificence; the inevitable result was an ever-escalating trade war with ruin at the end. The winner was he who, at least temporarily, had given away the most at a ceremonial occasion. It remains a remarkable example of art-induced social warfare.

FREDERICK J. DOCKSTADER

Further reading. Davis, R.T. *Native Arts of the Pacific Northwest Coast*, Stanford (1949). Gunther, E. *Art in the Life of the Northwest Coast Indians*, Portland (1966). Hawthorn, A. *Kwakiutl Art*, Seattle (1979). Holm, B. *Northwest Coast Indian Art*, Seattle (1965). Inverarity, R.B. *Art of the Northwest Coast Indians*, Berkeley (1941).

still able to produce the fine basketry of their ancestors, but wood carving has declined in quantity and is only occasionally produced in any quality.

California. Basketry weaving was the art *par excellence* not only of this Pacific Coast region but throughout the Native world. The lush grass that covered the countryside provided a resource that allowed the deft fingers of the Pomo Indians to produce some of the most remarkably detailed weaves known. Although we do not have good evidence of the extent of this art in prehistoric times, it could have been no less than is known traditionally; a long history of experience was responsible for the high state of the art. The list of tribes skilled in the art is a lengthy one, but the Pomo, Chumash, and Hupa come first to mind, followed closely by the Yurok, Karok, Diegueño, Kawia, and a host of others. The design styles change, but the technical skill is remarkable throughout.

Some of the tightly woven Pomo baskets are among the smallest known, as well as the most finely woven. With other sizes they introduced unusual materials—shell beads, bird feathers, quills, and similar natural substances—to serve as decorative elements, and mastered a wide range of shapes and forms. These varied in size from miniatures less than $\frac{1}{16}$ in (1.6 mm) in diameter to large storage vessels often 3 or 4 ft (0.9 to 1.2 m) in size. Some baskets had covers, while others were of the open-mouth type; all were fashioned perfectly in design and silhouette with colors in black, natural tan, and an occasional red or white.

Only a limited amount of stone or wood carving was produced by these people; the Chumash created large planked houses and canoes, but little else has survived in wood. Most of the evidence of their artistic talent lies in the carved shell ornaments and small steatite charms, fetishes, and smoking pipes recovered from burials. With the Gold Rush of 1849, the resulting massacre of the native population, combined with the diseases introduced by the White immigrants, decimated the Indians to such an extent that few people with measurable native blood survived. A few individuals in scattered areas still make baskets of high quality. The surprising fact that the art still survives in the face of this adversity is a tribute to Indian tenacity, pride, and the recent increase of interest in Indian arts.

The Basin-Plateau area. Isolated in times past, this area is still set apart in Indian life today. Made up of Nez Percé, Shoshoni, Washo, Ute, Paiute, and related tribes, these resilient people continue to live as hunters and farmers; their land is mountain and upland country, scenically beautiful but with relatively limited resources. The inhabitants were greatly influenced by the Plains Indians to the east and the Northwestern tribes of Washington and Oregon; their arts reflect this interchange. The most original technique to be found here—if, indeed, it is original on the Plateau—is the woven cornhusk wallet, nominally credited to the Nez Percé. The technique is shared with several neighboring tribes, notably the Yakima

Nez Percé beadwork: a detail of a cradle board. State Capitol Museum, Olympia, Washington State

and Umatilla, who produce an almost identical "sally bag", as these are also commonly known.

Plateau beadwork has a colorful resemblance to that of the Crow and Shoshoni people, and uses many similar motifs and colors. Since they are among the more active horsemen of the western United States, it is not surprising that they have developed a wide array of spectacular ornaments, decorations, and equipment for their mounts. These similarities may have resulted from their far-ranging travel and trade.

The Southwest. This major art region of native North America had its beginnings some 4,000 years ago in Utah, Nevada, Arizona, and New Mexico. The so-called "cliff dwellers", who lived in well-constructed structures built into the caves and clefts in the huge rock canyons and valleys of the Southwest, subsequently moved out on to the more exposed areas, constructing sturdy stone-mud-and-adobe structures which the early Spanish explorers called *pueblos*. The oldest village still inhabited is Oraibi in northeastern Arizona, constructed *c*1125; the most recent is Bakabi, dating from *c*1907. Many of these were dramatically affected by the Pueblo Revolt of 1680 during which the people abandoned (at least temporarily) their ancient homes and fled to other villages to take refuge from the Spaniards. This interval greatly affected tribal art styles and designs, as well as the forms of objects, and is still seen today in much of the more recent pottery and weaving designs as well as in social patterns.

The vigor of Southwestern Indian art is difficult to evaluate, but one of the major arts was pottery. The gradual development of pottery has been a continuing improvement in technical skills, accompanied by an ever-increasing attention to form and design. The forms and styles vary, as do the motifs, but they all remind us of the variety between the several Pueblos, as well as the interaction which has apparently always existed. Strong black-on-white designs, boldly executed

A Mimbres painted ceramic bowl from southwest New Mexico decorated with human figures; diameter 30cm (12in); c AD 950.
Maxwell Museum of Anthropology, Albuquerque

or delicately expressed, have all been part of this exciting art form.

Comparison between Pueblos is invidious; each had its own particular approach to ceramic form and decoration, and each had a particular success. The most realistic was probably that of the Mimbres people of southwestern New Mexico, c AD 900–1100; their often humorous representation of the life and times of the people remains one of the great visual documents of American antiquity.

Weaving was practiced throughout the Southwest at an early date and Spanish chroniclers record taxes paid in large quantities of blankets, attesting to the industry of the Pueblo weavers. Later, with the migration of the Navajo into the Southwest, they quickly learned to weave and surpassed their teachers—today the finest textiles produced in North America are the achievements of these weavers. Much of this improvement was due to the introduction of sheep; but nevertheless the ability of the nomadic Athapascans to adopt the sedentary Pueblo skills and develop them to the present remarkable level is a testimonial to native American adaptability.

Insufficient evidence has survived to allow us to evaluate completely the basketry skills of the prehistoric Southwesterners. We know that basket-making was a widespread and successful craft, probably familiar to all Pueblo groups. Later, basket-weaving became dominant in every village and even the Navajo people took to the art, but it attained its greatest strength, surprisingly enough, among the Apache people. The Apache neither wove nor expressed themselves in pottery, beyond rudimentary culinary vessels; but because of their nomadic life, basketry filled a need no other art supplied.

Painting was used to cover the walls of underground Pueblo religious chambers called kivas; many examples have been recovered and preserved by excavations, and are witness to the strong colors and designs used to decorate such rooms. To

a certain degree hides were also painted and no doubt textiles were ornamented by painted designs. This tradition of painting textiles and hides has continued. Most of the motifs were geometric, although some quasi-realistic or anthropomorphic figures were common.

Metal was uncommon in the Southwest in ancient times, and only became important when Europeans introduced iron, copper, and silver. The great silversmithing art for which the Navajo and Zuni became so famous did not exist before c1853, when the Navajo learned to work metal from Mexican ironsmiths and saddlemakers. In the next half century this was to become the major income-producing art in the Indian Southwest.

Sculpture was never a preeminent art in this region, probably because suitable stone and wood resources were absent. The type of sandstone common in the area does not lend itself readily to carving, and the species of trees are not suitable for the finely worked carving found, for example, on the Northwest Coast. Such carving as existed was on a limited scale, and related primarily to religious effigies; almost no wooden sculpture has survived in prehistoric burials. Painted flat slabs, small effigies, and low-relief wooden art is characteristic of the early period. True work in-the-round did not become substantial until the middle of this century, seen for the most part in the small painted wood Kachina dolls of the Pueblos.

In the Southwest today the major art activities are in the fields of weaving, silversmithing, painting and pottery; a minor expression continues in sandpainting. The basket-weaving arts have almost died out, with only the Hopi carrying on in any strength. Navajo weaving, however, while perhaps not so numerically significant as it was, is probably of better quality than ever; the remarkably finely woven Two Gray Hills textiles are among the most eagerly sought-after weaving available, and command fantastically high prices. In smithing, the most remarkable new development has been the recent introduction of gold as a medium for cast jewelry; in times past this metal was rarely used. Silverwork continues in the more traditional forms, particularly in cast and overlay work. It is perhaps in Pueblo pottery that major strides have been made from competence to work of overwhelming design and technical skill. The work of a few individuals has become the test by which almost all other fine pottery is now judged and priced. Painting has departed from the older so-called "Studio school" of watercolors, branching out in many directions: collages, abstracts, oils, impressionistic works—all are found in Indian galleries today, with a receptive audience of collectors. Sculpture is represented not only by sophisticated and naturalistic Kachina dolls, eagerly sought by collectors, but by many fine sculptors in stone, bronze, and wood. The arts are alive and well in the native American Southwest; quality is high and, of equal importance, quantity abundant.

The Plains. Indian art of the Plains was traditionally adapted to the mobility of the early horsemen, though we have almost no evidence about the aesthetic achievements of the prehis-

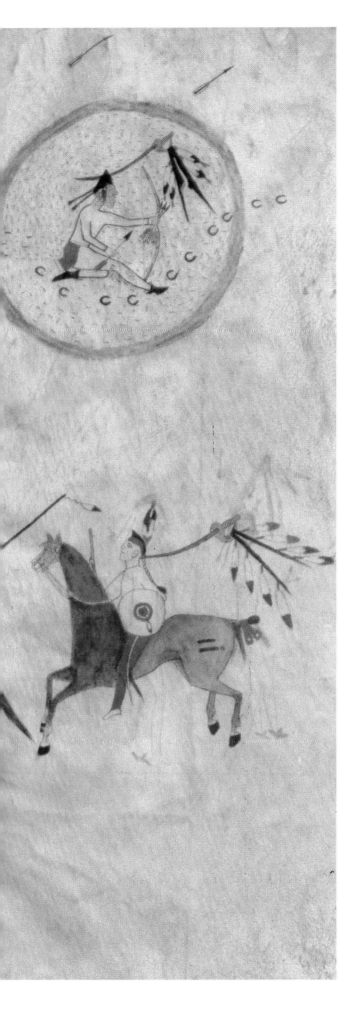

toric people of the area. With the coming of the White man and the acquisition of the horse, the whole tribal structure changed radically. The bison-culture peoples who moved into the Plains area—including the Sioux, Crow, Cheyenne, Arapaho, Mandan, and Assiniboin—created a demand for costuming, horse gear, and decorative materials which the artists of the various tribes soon satisfied. Painting on deer or elk hides was common (later, cow and horse hides were occasionally used) in a variety of geometrical and semi-realistic designs, for garments, bed covering, and robes. Rawhide and buckskin containers were decorated in strong colors, usually in straight-line geometric patterns. In addition to painting, surface decoration was applied with dyed porcupine quills; but following the arrival of traders, glass beads quickly replaced them almost entirely. Woven cloth, particularly the popular heavy wool Stroud cloth (also called trade cloth) was made into clothing, blankets, shawls, and other garments.

More recently, tourist demands have had a particular impact upon the Plains people. No longer do they make use of the painted rawhide "luggage" which the women once made for the annual trips following the buffalo. These containers have become redundant, as have bow-and-arrow quivers, feather bonnet cases, and the large hide robes. With the resurgence of social and ceremonial affairs costumes are still important, and a certain amount of decorative objects for Indian use still find ready customers. But the type of object now offered by most artists is directed towards the White market, and reflects a less traditional function. Small beaded bags, pouches, and purses are common, as are elaborate "ceremonial paintings" on hide. They are well done, but lack the integrity of the earlier art. Some wheel-turned pottery is now being made; but most of the traditional Plains artwork was less adaptable to tourist demands, and the craftwork of these people has not been as successful in making the transition.

Perhaps the most effective response to outside influences in art has been in painting, into which most artistic effort is directed by the Plains Indians today. Many fine artists have developed, both male and female, producing fine watercolors, temperas, and oils of excellent quality. Most of their subjects involve the open prairie homeland and, with Indian genre scenes, find a ready audience. Some people have turned to more contemporary abstract, impressionist, or similar schools, and a few have even undertaken collage. Sculpture is not yet of major importance in this market, though this is certain to change with the years.

The Midwest and Central Woodlands. In this area artistic expression is almost unknown from prehistoric periods, largely because of the conditions of the environment. We also know little about the possible relationships of these people to the contemporary tribes inhabiting the Great Lakes region.

Detail of a Sioux painting on hide from the Plains showing a battle between the Sioux and the Blackfoot. Field Museum of Natural History, Chicago

Today they are known as Chippewa, Sauk, Fox, Menomini, Kickapoo, Potawatomi, and Winnebago; but certainly some of these came from other areas to settle. Such visual evidence of their skills as has survived is largely in stone, with many fine objects reflecting the aesthetic ability of the people. Bird-stones, bannerstones, fine flaked projectile points, effigy pipes, and similar small objects are beautifully designed and finished. Although we know that textiles existed, as well as wood carving, few examples have survived in a condition that demonstrates their original form. Some shell has been recovered—notably large circular gorgets with incised designs upon the surface—and copper implements have also been found in great quantity.

Later, during the transitional period, most of the Central Woodlands art styles were executed on animal hides, with quilling, moose hair, or bark as important decorative materials. The designs were primarily geometric or floral, the latter form more dominant after the entry of French nuns who taught motifs taken directly from colonial costumes of the day to girls in convents. With the introduction of glass beads, the Midwestern tribes followed the pattern of the Plains people and abandoned the use of the time-consuming porcupine quilling for the new, brighter material to ornament their costumes and accessories. The quantities of beads available were so great that they probably helped to stimulate the contemporaneous interest in beadwork in Europe.

Weaving is known to have been common during this same period, with native fibers supplanted by materials from Europe. Shredded bark from various plants and trees—cotton, apocynum (Indian hemp), milkweed, buffalo hair—along with the introduction of imported cottons, wool, silk, and related weaving threads were all important resources. Bark mats, wall weavings, and belting were common; garments which were originally of hide were gradually supplanted by cotton, gingham, wool, or even velvet, and design motifs were commonly geometric or floral, with an only occasional naturalistic representation.

Metal was not used to a great extent, as was true with the Plains and Plateau Indians. Only surface copper, found commonly throughout the region, was in fairly regular use. While iron ore abounded, the art of smelting did not come into Indian use until the advent of the European; then tools and implements were made in great number, and silver was introduced via trade objects, most of which were made in Montreal, Quebec, and London. Later, Indian smiths learned the art and produced ornaments for their people. Some lead or pewter was used as inlays on stone and wooden objects, but gold was almost totally unknown.

Such wood as has survived exhibits a talent for sculpture, even though the species available in the forests did not lend themselves well to large-scale figure work, and the art seems to have been of marginal importance. Clay was known, and a wide variety of vessels was produced; the abundance of wood and bark containers probably retarded the development of pottery as an important art. This may also reflect the fairly early introduction of metal pots and pans by colonists.

More recently, the use of fragments of silk and silk ribbon obtained from White settlers or traders has developed into a major art style. Throughout the Midwest we can find superb examples of garments beautifully trimmed in complicated appliqué patterns which employ this material. Shawls, blouses, skirts, leggings, and even moccasins were decorated with gaily colored bits of silk. Today this is replaced by rayon, but it is still important for costume ornamentation. The intricately cut, fitted, and sewn "patchwork" was executed in geometric or floral patterns for both personal use and as giveaway pieces. There has been no noticeable resurgence of wood or stone sculpture, and clay has almost died out in the region. Basketry, bark work, and some weaving are most frequently seen, and beadwork is continued by many of the younger women. The latter do most of this work on a loom, rather than by the surface-application technique of the Plains people.

The Eastern Woodlands. Closely related in cultural patterns to the Indians of the Midwest, although less so in language, this area divides roughly into three: firstly the Northeast, populated by Iroquoian tribes, the Abnaki Confederacy, the Lenni-Lenape (or Delaware), and many small Algonquian-speaking tribes in Massachusetts and Connecticut; secondly the Central, inhabited by the Shawnee, Erie, Wyandot, and the Powhatan Confederacy; and thirdly the Southeast, early home to the Five Civilized Tribes (later removed to Oklahoma), and the Catawba, Caddo, Alibamu-Koasati, and Natchez. There were also many tribes that have now disappeared entirely.

Each area varied more in prehistoric times than in the later traditional period, and each was tremendously affected by the coming of the White man. The forced removal of these tribes from their ancestral homeland almost destroyed their culture and the arts which beautified that lifestyle. As with the Midwest, the climate has adversely affected the survival of more perishable materials, so much of our knowledge is often mere surmise. Wood was commonly used, primarily for small figure sculpture, ceremonial masks, some construction, and ladles, many of which were decorated with lovely zoomorphic forms. A common pottery form was the bulbous-bodied vessel with constricted neck and pointed base. It was quickly replaced by European metal pots, kettles, and spoons, as were the bark containers and grass or plaited oak-splint baskets.

Shell and bone carving were widespread arts, and small charms, figures, and amulets were common. Bone combs were unique to the Iroquois, who carved them in a great variety of forms attesting to their importance. Deerhide provided most of the clothing, and was ornamented by porcupine quill, moose hair, and paint. Some copper was worked, although far less than was common with the Midwesterners; silver was not used until its later introduction by traders (aside from the very rare use by a few Southeastern artists). The only sculptures of consequence in monumental scope were the so-called "idols", or ancestral figures of seated or kneeling people. Many of the

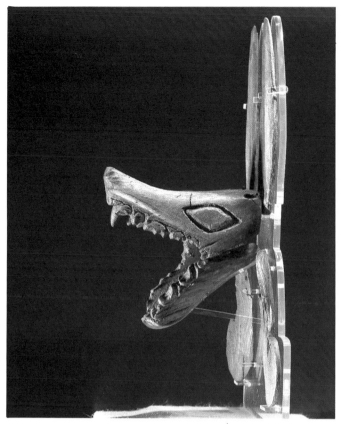

A wooden wolf mask from Key Marco, Florida; height 30cm (12in).
University Museum, Philadelphia

A Mohawk (Iroquois) pouch from the Eastern Woodlands; glass beads on
velveteen; c1850. Collection of R.A. Testudine, Saverna Park, Maryland

An example of modern Indian painting, an untitled work by Carl Tubby; oil on canvas; Institute of American Indian Arts Museum, Santa Fe

effigy pipes were important examples of true Pre-Columbian masterworks, and at Moundville, one of the greatest sculptural achievements of the ancient artist was the famous Moundville Bowl (Museum of the American Indian, New York). One other remarkable art area was Key Marco, in Florida, where many wooden objects have been recovered from underwater sites. This was one of the richest regions of art in native North America: materials excavated from such ceremonial centers as Etowah, Spiro, Cahokia, and Key Marco offer ample evidence of the aesthetic and technical skills of the ancient Southeastern people.

One of the remarkable aesthetic activities was in clay: pottery containers were created in such an astonishing range of sizes, forms, and designs that these objects seem to have no common traceable element. Large cooking utensils, storage urns, burial vessels, and ritual wares were obviously no problem to the makers. While most of these were in gray, black, or red, polychrome vessels in red, black, and white on gray, black, or buff are known, and for a brief period a negative-design ware (usually called "resist ware") was made.

In recent years, this clay work has continued in production; the Catawba and Cherokee are particularly active in making a burnished black ware. Wood sculpture is also continued by several competent people, notably the Cherokee working at Qualla, North Carolina. Basketry is still made from river cane, honeysuckle, oak, and similar materials by the Cherokee, Chitimacha, Creek, Catawba, and Koasati weavers.

Beadwork follows an early tradition of shell and stone bead ornament; with the introduction of trade beads, this became a more active art activity. Pouches, costume accessories, belts, and other decorative objects were executed in designs, many of which are traceable to earlier floral and scroll designs on prehistoric clay vessels.

Painting has continued to a certain extent. Many of the better-known contemporary artists showing in galleries today are related to Southeastern tribes, and while their work does not always reflect this affinity they do have a strong feeling of kinship with their heritage. Earlier, tattooing and body painting are known to have been commonly practiced in this region. None of this has continued to the present, although the watercolor and oil paintings clearly reflect this feeling. Working in acrylic, tempera, and oil, some of these people paint in the so-called "traditional" mode; others have developed a more contemporary aesthetic expression.

Conclusion. The earliest inhabitants of North America seem to have responded artistically to their environment soon after acquiring the means for survival. Since then, artistic effort, even under the most adverse conditions has always been a feature of Indian life, and, unlike native art in Africa and Oceania, a separate form of expression. Such was the Indians' esteem for their arts that they continually developed their forms and techniques, clinging to them tenaciously when Western settlers sought to eradicate Indian culture. The Native American has retained a surprising and impressive amount of his aboriginal identity. The influence of settlers has in time come to stimulate Indian art, but no less than the art of one tribe formerly levied the art of another: Western influence has caused greater damage to Indian self-esteem than intertribal conflicts. Only in our own century has the interest of collectors, museums, ethnologists, and anthropologists provoked new arts in many regions, and created a new sense of personal worth, individual dignity, and tribal affiliation for many younger Indian people.

FREDERICK J. DOCKSTADER

Bibliography. Adair, J. *The Navajo and Pueblo Silversmiths*, Norman (1944). Amsden, C.A. *Navaho Weaving: its Technic and History*, Santa Ana (1934). Bedinger, M. *Indian Silver: Navajo and Pueblo Indians*, Albuquerque (1973). Dockstader, F.J. *Indian Art in America*, Greenwich, N.Y. (1962). Dockstader, F.J. *Indian Art of the Americas*, New York (1973). Dockstader, F.J. *Weaving Arts of the North American Indians*, New York (1978). Dunn, D. *American Indian Painting of the Southwest and Plains*, Albuquerque (1968). Feder, N. *American Indian Art*, New York (1972). Hawthorn, A. *Art of the Kwakiutl Indians*, Washington, D.C. (1967). Mason, O.T. *Aboriginal American Basketry*, Washington, D.C. (1902). Snodgrass, J.O. *American Indian Painters*, New York (1968). Tanner, C.L. *Southwest Indian Craft Arts*, Tucson (1968).

27

AFRICAN ART

A *pwo* dance mask representing Tshokwe ideal female beauty; wood and fiber;
height 21cm (8in). Private collection (see page 517).

THE aim of this essay is to place African art in its social context rather than to discuss aesthetic appeal, stylistic zones, and the formal qualities of art objects. European art frequently uses symbols that are immediately meaningful to educated people—symbols of Christ, the saints, historical episodes. A knowledge of the meaning behind these symbols plays an important part in understanding and appreciating painting and sculpture. The same is true for African art: it is essential to discover whether a mask or a sculptured figure is made to entertain, frighten, promote fertility, or merely to be art for art's sake. We need to know whether a mask portrays a chief, a god, a slave, a were-animal, or a witch; whether a mask is worn on the head or over the face, carried, or secretly conserved in a cult-house.

Although African art is presented here as an integral element of economic, social, and political institutions, in the final analysis the prime element is aesthetic. This aesthetic imperative should be clear enough in most of the works mentioned without the need to refer to European-biased impressions about their "mystery", "magic", "awe", and "serenity". It is important to recognize the relationship between a mask and the identity of its wearer or the society that owns it, between a mask and economic or witching activities, between figurines and religious beliefs and rites. Despite the splendors of "classi-

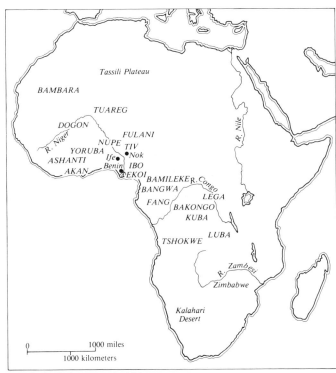

Principal ethnic groups in Africa

A rock painting at Jabbaren in the Tassili plateau

cal" African art—the sculptures of Nok, Ife, Benin—the main concern here is with the arts that continue to flourish in the chiefdoms, villages, and nomadic tents.

Rock paintings. African rock paintings and engravings were, curiously, discovered earlier than European ones: those in southern Africa as early as the mid 18th century, those in the North in 1847 when they were found by a group of French soldiers who reported engravings of elephants, lions, antelope, bovids, ostriches, gazelles, and human beings armed with bows and arrows. The best-known center of desert paintings in the north is the Tassili plateau, explored and described by Henri Lhote in the 1950s. This is a mountainous area—2000 sq miles (5180 sq km) of rock and shifting sand—now inhabited by only a few Tuareg shepherds. Thousands of years ago, when the paintings were made, the land was fruitful, covered with forests and crossed by rivers alive with fish. Some of the Saharan paintings depict Negroes and a hunting way of life (dating from the prehistoric Roundhead period), while others (from the Cattle period, 4000 BC–AD 800) show pastoralists, figures with copper-colored skin and straight hair who resemble the Fulani cattle-herders of the west African savanna. Art historians have tentatively suggested, and ethnographical research partly confirmed, that these paintings were the work of proto-Fulani groups: they contain elements that correspond to features of Fulani myths taught during boys' initiation rites, such as the hermaphroditic cow from whose chest emerge the heads of domestic animals, and the graphic portrayal of what resembles a Fulani initiation field (a circle with the sun in the center and heads of other cows, representing different phases of the moon, spaced around it).

Classical African sculpture. Thanks mainly to archaeologists, African bronzes and terracottas no longer belong to an "unknown" past. Detailed comparative studies aided by radiocarbon dating have located them in historical contexts and continuing traditions. One of the best-known examples of an early sculptural tradition is that of "Nok", a label covering many terracotta sculptures of human and animal figures found widely distributed across northern Nigeria. They first came to light in tin mines near the village of Nok in Zaria province and have since been dated to the 4th or 5th century BC. Some art historians have detected similarities between the stylized human figures and the naturalistic animals of Nok and the undated stone sculptures of Esie, the nomoli figures of Sierra Leone, and the Afro-Portuguese ivories carved at Sherbro. But a more convincing suggestion is that the Nok style— the main features of which are a spherical or conical head, and eyes represented as segments of a sphere with the upper lid horizontal and the lower lid forming a segment of the circle— has many features in common with that of Ife, the religious and one-time capital of the Yoruba people.

One thing is certain: the traditions of African art have not been without development. Frank Willett has shown the different natures of their evolutions. Radiocarbon dating and

oral traditions suggest, for example, that the naturalistic style of sculpture at Ife lasted for about as long as bronzecasting in Benin. However, the rich Ife style shows an unvarying canon from the 10th to the 14th centuries, while in Benin, from the 15th to the 19th centuries, the progression from a moderate naturalism to a considerable degree of naturalization is very marked.

Less is known about the arts and civilizations of Sao (Lake Chad) and Zimbabwe, but enough to show that they are indigenous African cultures: there is no longer need to invoke Egyptian, Phoenician, or Portuguese influences. Archaeologists have shown, for example, that the walls and towers of Zimbabwe were raised by African builders and from African sources of inspiration. Nor is there any doubt about the Afri-

A terracotta Nok head from Northern Nigeria; 4th or 5th century BC. National Museum, Lagos

The Tyi Wara Mask

The *tyi wara* mask is worn by members of a Bambara cult association concerned with fertility and farming. Societies of young men perform such communal agricultural tasks as tilling, sowing, and harvesting. The masks they wear are closely associated with them: their facial scarification recalls the patterns painted on the mask, which in turn recall Bambara agricultural myth. These marks consist of eight small scars: two vertical ones at the roots of the nose and three under each eye. The mask is said to represent a fabulous being, Tyi Wara, half man, half animal, who in the legendary past taught men the art of farming. He cultivated the soil with his claws, and through his efforts wild grasses became edible grains.

▼ A male wooden *tyi wara* mask; height about 110cm (43in). Dallas Museum of Fine Arts

Below right A female wooden *tyi wara* mask; height about 110cm (43in). Dallas Museum of Fine Arts

▲ A male horizontal mask with metal, fiber, and beads; length 53cm (21in). Dallas Museum of Fine Arts

▶ A vertical *tyi wara* mask with elongated, stylized horns. Dallas Museum of Fine Arts

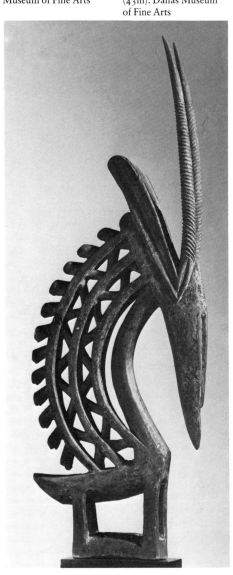

The *tyi wara* mask appears in masquerades. Representing the timeless snake-farmer of legend, the mask participates in a day of ritual farming, singing, dancing, and sacrifice. During the ceremony a figure appears wearing the male "antelope" headdress, followed by a female figure. Dancers imitate the actions of the animal, its wild cries, and its leaping movements.

The Chief of the cult association is the Bambara blacksmith who also carves the masks. *Tyi wara* masks are remarkably homogeneous: their style is immediately recognizable. Nevertheless, none is identical. Both male and female masks, the former representing the sun and the latter the earth, are made in the image of the antelope, which is seen as a worldly intermediary between sky and earth. The antelope is provided with a mane, the construction of which lends itself to an extremely stylized design executed in openwork. The male mask sometimes has a penis, while the female, which portrays a roan antelope, is accompanied by a child.

Tyi wara masks are both vertical and horizontal in form. In the vertical ones the sculptor reduces the animal's body and legs to minimal proportions, and develops the neck, muzzle, horns, and mane in a pattern of flowing lines within an elongated vertical curve. A mask representing the hippotragus (a roan antelope) has a series of triangular shapes to represent the fur mane on its neck and back. Horizontal masks are more naturalistic, and on these the head and neck of the hornbill are sometimes represented.

The headdresses are decorated with pieces of red cloth. They are worn with a costume composed of black-dyed fibers which are also used for making the circular veil that hangs from the basket cap below the masks.

One interesting substyle of the *tyi wara* is found in the Bougouni area. It has a stylized male-female torso and the antelope is carved together with an aardvark.

The symbolism of these agricultural masks—the horns, the eight scars, the antelope itself—is to encourage fertility on the farms. The endlessly elaborated horns, with their curving motions, create a source of artistic inspiration associated with human fertility.

ROBERT BRAIN

◀ A *tyi wara* mask of the Bougouni area. Institute of Ethnography, St Petersburg

▼ Male (*left*) and female (*right*) horizontal *tyi wara* masks; height 30cm (12in). Anspach Collection, New York

Further reading. Brain, R. *Art and Society in Africa*, London (1980). Goldwater, R.J. *Bambara Sculpture from the Western Sudan*, New York (1960).

canness of the Cross River *akwanshi* of southeastern Nigeria and neighboring Cameroon—stone figures that resemble no other works of art in any medium in the whole of Africa. They are phallic in shape, with a general stylistic progression from phallus to human form. Some are little more than dressed and decorated boulders but they are distinguished by profuse surface decoration centered on the face, breasts, and navel.

Other less well-known examples of "classical" African art are the bronzes of Nupe and Ibo, in Nigeria. The bronzes of Igbo (or Ibo) Ukwu were discovered in 1938 when a cistern was dug in the village. The site proved to be a repository for elaborately decorated objects—vessels, mace-heads, a belt, and other items of ceremonial wear. A grave excavated nearby contained a crown, a pectoral, a fan, a fly-whisk, and beaded metal armlets, together with more than 10,000 beads. Radiocarbon tests agree in dating these objects to the end of the 1st millennium, which makes this the earliest bronze-using culture of Nigeria. The bronzes are extremely detailed castings with elaborate surface decorations, but they differ from other African traditions of casting, such as those of Benin and Ife. Moreover, the high standard of wealth they reveal has no parallel in "democratic" Ibo-land where there are no centralized chiefdoms or wealthy aristocracies as among the Yoruba and Benin.

African hunters. One of the most striking aspects of African art is that it is always very much an intimate part of social life, manifest in every aspect of Africans' work, play, and beliefs. The style and symbolism of paintings, figures, and masks, therefore, depend on their political, economic, social, and religious contexts, an examination of which often provides valuable insights into the meanings of African art. The Bushmen of the Kalahari desert, for example, hunt in an inhospital environment, leading a life dominated by their absolute dependence on immediately available resources for survival. There is an intense relationship between the hunters and the hunted, between life and rain. The Bushmen's anxieties are expressed in their myths, their ceremonies, and their rites, and they are represented too in their paintings and engravings. Bushman rock paintings not only depict the animals they hunt, rain rituals, and the hunters themselves, but the animal species that have greatest mythical meaning. Another group, the Kalabari Ijo, are fishermen who also depend on chance—the luck of the tides, the shifting shoals of fish. Their art also directly reflects their way of life, their anxieties, and their myths. Living in isolated, self-contained communities in the mangrove swamps of southeastern Nigeria, they believe in water spirits, "Lords of the creeks" who live in a fabulous underwater world, who are, like the sculptures that represent them, anthropomorphic or zoomorphic, or a mixture of the two. The essence of the spirits is contained in the masks and sculpted headdresses worn by the fishermen at masquerades. The types of animals depicted in the masks are selected not for their economic importance but for their symbolic meanings and roles in Ijo myth and ritual.

The art of the nomads. The numerous nomadic peoples of Africa are prevented by the very nature of their way of life from owning bulky or heavy works of art. In many cases they prefer literature, the most portable form of art—bucolic poems, epics, tales, and satirical pieces which vividly express a nomadic aesthetic. The Fulani of west Africa are a case in point. They have a positive disdain of the working of wood, iron, and leather; any cultural objects made from these materials which they possess are made by Negro groups on whose lands they graze their cattle. Even Fulani who have settled in villages prefer to give artistic expression to architecture, elaborate clothes, and ornaments. Authentic Fulani art is therefore rare, and restricted to details of dress, amulets, headdresses, girls' anklets, ceremonial tools, and containers—and the body itself. Indeed, the Fulani have developed a veritable aesthetic of personal appearance. From childhood they learn to decorate and paint themselves, fashion their hair into wonderful shapes and patterns, cultivate splendid styles of walking; mothers even massage the skulls of their babies to achieve ideal shapes. During annual ceremonies, which are both sadistic tests of manhood and male beauty contests, youths use all the arts of personal decoration—the body is oiled, painted, and ornamented. The men line up before the judges, "like sumptuous images of gods", their faces painted in red and indigo patterns, their hair decorated with cowries and surmounted by tall headdresses. On both sides of their faces hang fringes of ram's beards, chains, beads, and rings. Old women loudly berate those youths who do not come up to the highest standards of Fulani beauty.

Wooden sculpture. The greatest contribution Africa has made to world culture is its fine tradition of sculpture, although it was hardly known outside the "dark" continent until towards the end of the last century. Then, works that had previously been considered only as colonial trophies and weird museum objects attracted the attention of European artists keen for new experiences. Vlaminck, Derain, Picasso, and Matisse were in turn overwhelmed by the expressive and abstract qualities of the figures and masks that turned up in Paris from the distant Congo and the French Sudan. Juan Gris even made a cardboard copy of a funerary figure from Gabon. The interest of these painters led to a generally heightened sensitivity to the qualities of African sculpture, although for many years it was a sensitivity that could only react to the pure form and mystery of the sculpture from ignorance of its function or symbolism.

Today we are better informed, although whole corpora of African art remain mysterious entities since they were collected long ago, as curiosities, from people who had lost awareness of their uses or symbolic meanings.

Among the Dogon of Mali there are a number of famous old sculptures, known as *tellem*, about which neither the Dogon nor archaeology can tell us anything (although innumerable art historians continue to make more or less inspired guesses). *Tellem* figures usually have uplifted arms and are

Two tellem figures from the Dogon of Mali. Background figure, Dallas Museum of Fine Arts; foreground figure, Musée de l'Homme, Paris

mostly female or sometimes hermaphrodite. Others include animals or anthropomorphic figures carved along the lines of the original curved pieces of wood. With sculptures of this kind we are restricted to formal comparisons of style and subjective aesthetic appreciation. To this class belong the Fang masks and Kota figures, once the new-found "idols" of Derain and Epstein. The plaque behind the head of the Kota figure has been described, confidently, as "rays of the sun", "horns of a goat", "a crescent moon", and a "Christian cross".

Bambara farmers and their art. The majority of Africans are not kings, priests, witchdoctors, and sorcerers, but farmers who spend the greater parts of their lives producing grain or cultivating root crops. Their aesthetic life is closely linked to this fact of their existence. Some of the greatest sculptural traditions of Africa are represented by masks and figures pro-

duced to assure the fertility of the fields and the survival of their cultivators. The Bambara, a Mandinka group of more than one million people living in Mali, have become well-known for their metalwork, basketry, leatherwork, weaving, dyeing, and, particularly, their woodcarving. Bambara masks are associated with four major cult associations: the *n'domo*, *komo*, *kove*, and *tyi wara*. These societies bring out their masks during both dry and wet seasons; they "help" with the sowing, weeding, and harvesting of the Bambara's staple crop, millet, and celebrate the coming and going of rain.

The *n'domo* mask, with its vertical horns, symbolizes growing millet—the corn will stand up strong and erect like the horns of the mask. The horns are eight in number and rise up straight in a row, like stretched fingers above the top of the head and on the same plane as the ears. According to Germain Dieterlen the horns represent, in a schematic way, the various episodes of the Bambara creation myth, the eight horns in the ideal mask representing the eight primordial seeds created by God for the building of the universe. Dominique Zahan writes that the basic meaning of the horn symbolism derives from the assimilation of these organs to the growth of grain and the human liver—Bambara farmers say that animal horns are to animals what the liver is to humans and what vegetable shoots are to the earth.

The symbolism and rites of other Bambara societies and masks are also closely related to the prosaic activity of farming. The *komo* mask represents the hyena, the great laborer of the soil and guardian of life. The *tyi wara* represents a fabulous being, half man, half animal, who in the past taught men how to farm. During the sowing and growing seasons the *tyi wara* antelope mask represents the spirits of the forest and water, and assures fertility to the fields and to man.

The art of the African kingdoms. Art is universally a means of glorifying persons of rank. The presence of objects elaborately carved in such precious materials as gold, silver, or ivory usually indicates the presence of a ruling class, surplus wealth, and the wherewithal to employ specialized craftsmen. In Africa, most *cire perdue* castings, for example, require a highly specialized production technique and although it is not an art entirely restricted to kingdoms, it receives its greatest elaboration where the chief or a wealthy caste can afford to maintain a group of specialized artists. In Benin the privilege of working bronze was reserved for a special corporation who lived in a special quarter of the town and who came under the control of the Oba—the ruler. Among the Bamileke, artists were thought of and treated as servants, even slaves, of their chiefs in whose palaces they lived and through whom they sold their work. In these situations African art is not the result of "instinct"—capturing the soul of an animal or object through a "primitive ecstatic imagination"—but the product of training, apprenticeship, and a close knowledge of tradition.

The artist in an African chiefdom worked portraits, insignia, and emblems to portray the king and his royal relatives as

Benin Bronzes

Although the Portuguese visited Benin City in the 15th century, Benin art was only revealed for most Europeans in 1897 when the treasures of the Oba, the Benin king, were looted by the British during a punitive military expedition. Since then, Benin heads and plaques have become dispersed in Great Britain, the United States, and Europe. After the Second World War, heightened interest in West Africa and its ethnography and history caused Benin art to leave the ranks of curious "primitive" art and stand in auction rooms alongside works by such artists as Matisse and van Dyck. Even Nigeria must now pay huge sums of money to purchase objects originally made in Benin City to build up her national collections.

The bronze memorial heads of the Obas of Benin can only be dated approximately. When a king died, his successor had a head cast in bronze. One hundred and sixty survive, the earliest probably dating from the 12th century. The earlier ones, which recall the splendid sculptures of Ife, are the more naturalistic, the later, from as late as the 19th century, more stylized.

Philip Dark has established five main types. The earliest includes heads with a collar under the chin. Heads of the second type have rolled collars, the bases of which are flayed in the third type. Types four and five are heads with a high collar, flayed base, and often a winged cap. Each set of masks is

◄ A Benin plaque showing an Oba, or king. British Museum, London

associated with a series of reigns; those of the 18th and 19th centuries show increased decoration and symbolic elements along with a growing coarseness in the bronzeworking. Examples of the fifth type, made during the 19th century, are rigidly stylized. In the 20th century, contact with the West has led to the reproduction of old forms, which are, however, little more than "tourist art".

The bronzeworkers of Benin were formerly organized into a guild under royal patronage and control. Iron and bronze were usually combined for making the heads, though sometimes bronze was cast on iron. The process of casting used was the *cire perdue* method: the artist modeled the head in beeswax which was then invested with clay. After being dried by the sun, the molds were placed in a fire. The wax melted, the clay mold was fired further, and then molten bronze poured in. Once cooled, the clay was knocked off and the head was polished smooth.

ROBERT BRAIN

Further reading. Dark. P.J.C. *Benin Art and Technology*, Oxford (1973). Fagg, W. *Nigerian Images*, London (1963).

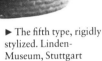

▲ A head of the first type, originally inlaid with iron; 14th century. National Museum, Lagos

▼ The second type. Royal Scottish Museum, Edinburgh

► The fifth type, rigidly stylized. Linden-Museum, Stuttgart

▼ A head of the third type, showing increasing distortion. City Museum, Bristol

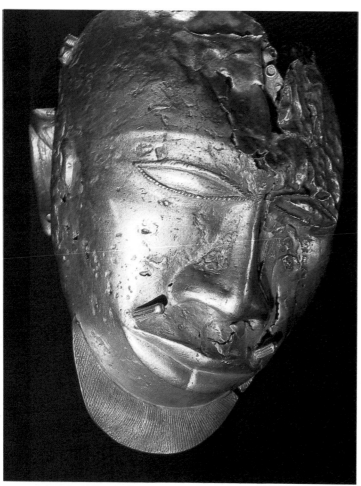

The gold mask from the treasury of the Ashanti King Kofi Kakari.
Wallace Collection, London

special, awe-inspiring figures, and to make them outlast the short periods of their lifetimes by commemorating them in art. So kings are shown as powerful and beautiful, without blemish and usually without expression, bedecked with royal symbols. The chiefs themselves wear splendid cloths and ornaments, sit on high, ornate stools, and sleep on elaborately carved beds. Artistic production under royal control is also used to emphasize the need for the royal caste to control its subjects, and princes often use art objects to terrify citizens.

In Africa, as well as in Europe, the concentration of wealth and power in the hands of a chief or an oligarchy often results in a local renaissance of the arts. Ashanti and Dahomey are good modern examples, where brilliant courts, receptive to multiple influences, produced distinctive and sumptuous art styles. In Dahomey the king concentrated on the working of silver, brass, and the production of appliqué work in his court. Wall sculptures decorated the palace, depicting historical and allegorical scenes and battles. Among the Ashanti, trade in gold and slaves brought great wealth to the kings who made the working of gold a court monopoly. Their goldsmiths formed a respected and privileged caste and produced ceremonial objects and portraits, the most famous of which is the

gold mask from the treasury of King Kofi Kakari (Wallace Collection, London). Small weights cast in brass were also produced in order to weigh gold dust.

Kuba-Bushong art. One of the richest artistic zones in Africa covers the basins of the Kwango, Kasai, Katanga, and northwestern Angola. This is an intermediary zone between forest and savanna occupied by farmers whose ancestors were the subjects of powerful kingdoms—the Luba, Tshokwe, Lunda, and Kuba. In each the artists were closely tied to the court and the royal cults. Among the Luba, for example, statues of kings and queens, caryatid stools, headrests, scepters, maces, and arms were produced to reflect the might and glory of the rulers. Among the Kuba the dominant Bushong group inspired an aristocratic culture that imbued social life with a passion for beauty and decoration. Kuba art and decoration flourished in all aspects of daily life—in building, metalworking, basketry, and weaving. Artistic endeavor became a way of life for many: even rulers were often artists and sculptors.

Art was used to glorify Bushong kings, statues of whom are masterpieces of Kuba sculpture and have been made since the 17th century. All show the king seated, his legs crossed, wearing emblems of sacred kingship. They are small, barely more than 20 in (50 cm) high. Their faces are expressionless, their eyelids half closed; the artists have achieved remarkable appearances of timeless repose and deep gravity. Like all good kings they are fat and adorned with bracelets, anklets, belts, and necklaces. While the statues have a similar general form, they are not identical and individual details have been given to their faces. Yet they are hardly lifelike portraits: rather, conventionalized representations of kings with distinguishing characteristics. The main aim of the sculptor was to suggest the essence of kingship, an essence that is transferred from one king to the next.

Secret societies and their masks. Chiefs and wealthy individuals are not the only patrons of art. In Africa important objects may be commissioned by lineage groups and, in societies without chiefs, works of art are most frequently held in common by members of associations of important men which perform governing as well as religious functions. The qualifications for membership of such cult associations, age grades, or secret societies differ from society to society. Sometimes all adult males are included; sometimes membership is restricted to individuals with special abilities or to those who possess particular statues or other sacred paraphernalia.

Perhaps the most famous "secret society" is that of the *poro*, the membership of which is most densely concentrated among the Mande- and Kpe-speaking peoples of Liberia and southern Sierra Leone although it also spreads, usually under different names, into Guinea and the Ivory Coast. Closely connected with the men's *poro* are the *sande* or *bundu*, women's associations which take the form of lodges among the women of specific chiefdoms. Both male and female societies maintain cycles of ceremonies connected with the

recruitment and initiation of members. The main actors in the ceremonies are the uninitiated youths, all the adult men of the *poro*, the adult women of the *sande*, and the sacred elders representing the ancestors. They are joined by the masked impersonators of the nature spirits who are allied with the founders of the country.

Throughout the area of the *poro* and *sande* we find generally two types of mask: the sleek, naturalistic masks associated with the name Dan, and the violently contrasting, roughly finished "Great Masks". There are also subsidiary masks used to enforce law and order and to educate the youths during the *poro* initiation rites. Dan masks are well-balanced and harmonious. Their beauty derives from their naturalistic but highly simplified form. There are also miniature copies of the large masks, 3 to 4 in (7.5 to 10 cm) long, which are worn by those initiated into the secret societies.

The Great Mask of the *poro* is a fierce, abstract representation of the demon of the forest. Its stylized face is supposed to represent a long-dead, almost mythical ancestor of great wisdom—the culture hero who introduced the *poro* to the land of men. The Mask is the symbol and oracle of the priest, who, as judge and clan leader, is allowed to keep the mask on behalf of the *poro*. Using it he can obtain the sanction of the ancestors to punish criminal and civil offenders. When important disputes are to be settled, the priest carries the Mask to the meeting of the elders and places it on the ground under a white cloth. Any human judgment reached is considered tentative until the Mask has indicated its approval.

The use of the Great Mask in such a manner usefully provides divine ratification: judgment is considered to come from the spirit world, via the Mask, not from human beings. The Mask takes responsibility, for example, for the death from poisoning of someone who has undergone the sasswood ordeal. At important council meetings the Mask attends to ensure the presence and approval of ancestors. During violent quarrels the priest puts on the Mask and stops the litigants with his word. Lesser Masks are also used to act as messengers or policemen.

The Great Mask itself is characterized by protuberant eyes, faced with perforated china or metal disks, red felt lips, and a long beard hung with palm nuts or beads. Its typical thick patina comes from black, dried blood from sacrifices and the reddish remains of chewed kola nuts spat into the mouth of the Mask by the priest.

During the actual *poro* initiation rites the Great Mask appears mysteriously four times, merely to utter a secret phrase at which all fall prostrate to the ground. Minor masks, known as *ge*, are used to discipline and educate the initiates. The masks act as officials controlling the women and children outside the village, or work as scavengers rounding up food by begging, borrowing, and stealing from citizens.

In appearance *ge* masks are hideous, combining animal and

A Kuba wooden portrait statue of Bom Bosh, 96th Nyimi of Kuba; c1650. The Brooklyn Museum, New York

human features. They are said to be artistic attempts to represent the belief that spirit power has both animal and spiritual attributes—the combination of traits, plus distortion, suggesting that there are certain unexplained phenomena more potent than the forces possessed by animals and humans separately.

During the long initiation rites the women are led to believe that their children are swallowed by the masks, and scarification is said to be caused by the masks when they ingest the boys and later give birth to them. After their rebirth from the stomachs of the masks, the initiates sit on mats with blankets over their faces and in two days the masks teach them everything all over again— how to walk, eat, and defecate. Near the end of the session the Great Mask, with its deep growling voice, takes the boys to the waterside where they are washed and given new names.

Girls are also initiated into the *bundu* or *sande* societies. At their coming-out ceremony they are anointed with oil, their hair is beautifully coiffed, and they wear rich clothes and jewelry. They parade to the accompaniment of songs, dances, and acrobatic performances, all performed by the masks. The *sande* mask is shining black and the women bearers are hidden behind a cloth costume and raffia veils. The form and symbolism of the mask vary little. The most conspicuous features are the spiral neck, the complicated decoration of the hairstyle, and the small triangular face.

Art and kinship. The most important feature of many African societies, and the source of political action within them, is kinship, in the form of corporate lineage organizations. Art fequently serves as an adjunct and symbol of the powers of lineage and clan. Among the Bakwele, lineage elders meet together in times of crisis and attempt to circumvent the trouble through the use of masks. Among the Fang and the Tiv, where political power is transmitted through lineages, masks and statues are symbols of the rights of lineage heads to succeed and are used in the administration of social affairs. Similarly, among the Lega of eastern Zaire where chiefship does not exist and the lineage system functions without political leaders there are men of prestige who gain influence through their age, their personal magic, and their possession of art objects. The Lega have included carvers able to produce original and skillfully-made work in a variety of materials; their masks and figurines are used by the *bwame* association in its dramatic and ritual performances. The objects used in initiation ceremonies present a complex of symbols that help translate the essence of Lega society and thinking from *bwame* elders to initiates. They are corporately owned by lineages and as they pass from hand to hand they act as symbols of the continuity of Lega lineages and as the link between the dead and living members of the patrilineal family.

In Ghana matrilineal lineages play an important part in

maintaining the well-being of the Akan community, even when this community, as in the case of the Ashanti, is a centralized kingdom. Everybody traces his descent through his mother and belongs to his mother's lineage which consists of all the descendants of a common ancestress. The shrine of the lineage is in the form of a stool to which the head of the lineage offers food for the ancestors. In the main rite in the installation of an Ashanti chief, the new chief is lowered and raised three times over the sacred stool of the founder of his lineage. So the Ashanti stool is a symbol of the ancestors and of the lineage. It consists of a rectangular pedestal with a curved seat supported by carved stanchions. In the Kumasi stoolhouse there are ten black stools preserved in memory of ten Ashanti kings. The Golden Stool, traditionally believed to have been brought from the sky by the first king's priest and councillor, is a mass of solid gold with bells of copper, brass, and gold attached to it.

Religious art. Although our increased knowledge of African societies means that social and aesthetic functions are now assigned to many works of art previously considered as items for religious use only, much African art essentially has a religious and symbolic role. Members of the Yoruba, for example, are the most prolific African carvers and the largest concentration of their art is devoted to the cults of the various *orishas* or gods. Elsewhere, masquerades and other ritual performances use masks and carved figures to enact basic myths.

Dogon art is explicitly religious in character: it depicts the ancestors, the first mythical beings, the atavistic blacksmith, the horseman with the ark carrying skills and crafts, and mythical animals. Their cosmological system and its relation to the content of their art has been explored in marvelous detail by a team of French anthropologists and art historians. So in order to comprehend the meaning of the Dogon Grand Mask we have to understand the meaning of the Dogon creation myth and the periodical *sigi* festival which regulate Dogon religious life. The Grand Mask is the double of the

An Ashanti stool. British Museum, London

Left: A wooden Dan mask of the poro society; height 21cm (8in). Private collection

mythical ancestor; in making the new mask the carver deceives the soul of the ancestor and persuades it to enter into its new abode. When the Grand Mask is exposed to public view only the base pole is visible, since the head is buried in a pile of stones. Other Dogon masks are less sacred although their performances may reflect special signs and symbols and parts of the creation myth.

Much of the cosmological thought of many African societies centers on twinness and androgyny. Among the Bangwa, a Bamileke people of Cameroon, twins and their parents are revered, twin births being considered perfect births representing a primordial and androgynous world when dual births were the rule. A woman who produces twins is feted by the whole village and elaborate sculptures are carved in the twins' honor. Both parents are given special attention and they are initiated into a religious association which plays an important role at fertility ceremonies and funerals. Bangwa sculpture has drawn inspiration from these twin parents and there are a number of statues of women and men carrying twins or wearing the symbols of twinship. Perhaps the best known of all Bangwa sculptures is a danc-

ing figure, wearing a cowrie necklace and carrying a rattle and bamboo trumpet of the kind worn by mother-of-twin priestesses when calling the gods.

Among the Yoruba, twins are also given special attention and there is a tradition of making images of them if one or both of them should die. These *ibeji* figurines are nourished and cared for like real children, since each is believed to contain the soul of a dead twin. Everything done for a live child is done for the *ibeji*: it receives gifts and new clothes. Regular sacrifices are also made to it in an attempt to prevent the soul of the deceased from harming his living twin or mother. The carrying of the *ibeji* also prevents the mother from becoming infertile.

Ibeji figurines are homogeneous in form—small, standing statuettes, nude in most cases although some are carved with an apron-like garment. Usually the proportional size of the head to the body is larger than that of the model; the genitals are carved, and the finished object colored—the head often stained a different color from the body. The face is oval with prominent eyeballs, the forehead convex, the nose broad, the ears stylized. The lips are generally prominent, carved to form

Five ibeji figurines from the Yoruba of Nigeria. Philip Goldman Collection, London

a kind of shelf because mothers feed them like their other babies. The arms are heavy and long, the hands stylized and joined to the thighs. *Ibeji* have a variety of scarification marks and hairstyles.

The "art" of witchcraft. Throughout Africa, witchcraft has some remarkably common features, the term itself usually referring to malign activities attributed to human beings who activate supernatural powers in order to harm others. Most witches work by night; they have the ability to fly and cover long distances in a flash. During peregrinations the body of the witch remains behind, the other self traveling invisibly or in animal form. They are fond of human flesh, making their victims ill and consuming their bodies after burial.

So illness and death can be imputed to supernatural causes, and art objects, in association with magical techniques and ritual, are used to combat them. These objects are usually known as fetishes, a word that should really be reserved for a kind of "machine"—the word "fetish" comes from the Portuguese *fetico* which means an object made by the hand of man fabricated by diviners or sorcerers and composed of various materials and medicines in order to draw upon the immanent life-forces of these substances. In fact the additive material may be more important than the basic sculpture and consists of miscellaneous objects—crabs, animal bones and horns, teeth, feathers, parts of birds, buttons, cloth, and pieces of iron. Even if at first sight this conglomerate of objects seems haphazard and mundane, the accoutrements of a fetish all have symbolic value and meaning for their owners and the persons affected by them.

The best-known fetishes were originally found in the Zaire region: some very early pieces are extant. In 1514 the Christian king of the Congo, Alfonso, is reported to have lamented the idolatry then prevailing among his subjects, declaring, "Our Lord gave, in the stone and wood you worship, for to build houses and kindle fire". Hundreds of types of fetishes have since been collected among the Bakongo and neighboring peoples; they are known as *nkisi* and all have the same general property of magical figures: they are able to inflict serious illnesses upon persons believed to be the cause of supernatural harm to others. In spite of its fame, this art form has not been studied in great detail.

Throughout Africa, art objects are used in the divination of the supernatural causes of illness. Among the Bamileke, the traditional anti-witchcraft society, the *kungang*, is called together during times of crisis and epidemic to purify the country and decimate witches through the agency of their powerful fetishes. *Kungang* figures are carved with great skill; they usually have exaggeratedly swollen stomachs to indicate the dreadful dropsy which is one of the supernatural sanctions of the fetish. They also symbolize a more sympathetic magic: the bent arms represent the attitude of a begging orphan or a friendless person; the crouching position is the stance of a lowly slave. The *kungang* figures are believed to be imbued with powers accumulated over generations: these powers are concentrated in a thick patina formed from the blood of chickens sacrificed during anti-witchcraft oathing rites. Most of them have a small panel in their stomach or back which can be opened for the insertion of medicines.

"The eternal feminine". While there are few, if any, women carvers, women play major roles in the production of African art as dyers, potters, and weavers. Women also provide many of the themes of art, as mothers, queens, fertility figures, or merely as "women". Mother-and-child figures have been found in various parts of western and central Africa; the Bangwa and Congo figures celebrate womanhood and the joy of being a mother and exult the general notions of maternity and fecundity. Figures and masks elsewhere portray women as ideals of female beauty. Among the Dogon, certain female masks were made for no other reason than that the models for them had vividly impressed the artist by their beauty. Among the Tshokwe of Angola the dance mask *pwo* is the image of a

Overleaf: masked Dogon dancers performing a funeral rite in Mali

A miniature fetish from the Basongye of Zaire; height 10cm (4in). Private collection

female ancestor; it is supposed to encourage fertility by depicting the features of ideal Tshokwe beauty. Among the Ibo, masks are often carved to portray beautiful spirit maidens in a refined and delicate style. These masks are small, with sharply defined features. They are often painted white with the hair and tribal markings on the face picked out in black or another color in a decorative way. These "maiden spirit" masks are said to represent beautiful local girls and in most of them, if not all, we have an idealized type of Ibo beauty.

Art for art's sake. African art is multi-functional: it serves as a handmaiden of government, religion, and even economics. It also serves to entertain. West African masquerades, in particular, belie the generalization that in traditional African cultures there is no such thing as art for art's sake. Even when performances are associated with ritual and belief, aesthetics and theatricality are never ignored. In many West African societies, masquerades appear during the second burial ceremonies performed for all dead adults. In most cases the aim of the performance is not only to imbue religious awe or to seek ancestral protection, although these play a part, but to entertain the mourners and bring glory to the memory of the dead man and his successor. In all these dances it is the mask that matters and for this reason the personality of the dancers is entirely subordinate to that of the mask. For the member of the masquerades the masks should be as spectacular as possible, and nothing—not even a monkey's skull or a European doll—is unacceptable on a mask which usually becomes much more elaborate once it has left the hands of its sculptor. Dyed plumes are added to the top and striated horns to each corner. Cockades are made from the fine hair of a ram's beard, and raffia is plaited and added to the chin in the form of a bear or attached to the front and back of the head of the masks. Skin-covering may be used, as among the Bangwa and Ekoi, to achieve textural rather than symbolic effects. Other Bangwa masks are beaded, while most of them are colored brightly with vegetable dyes or modern polychrome paints.

A consideration of the decoration of the Ibo *mbari* houses will demonstrate that an art form cannot simply be categorized as "primarily religious" or even "primarily aesthetic". Here, elaborate stucco embellishments are created in honor of the goddess Ala at the beginning of the yam farming cycle. During a period of seclusion, specially selected persons create a profusion of sculptures and reliefs which are then displayed to the general public. During this period they sing songs in honor of the earth goddess and subsidiary gods. The *mbari* objects are diverse and may represent gods, human beings, hunting scenes, women and men copulating, and women giving birth. The main figure is Ala who is sculpted and painted last, sometimes with her two children. Associated with her are phallic figures, constructed for the invocation of human and farm fertility. *Mbari* is not only religious art but also a source of pleasure. Many of the figures are comic; some are obscene. Unnatural practices are illustrated with glee; women brazenly display their private parts; and scenes of copulation include sodomy between man and beast. Gross indecencies are explained on the ground that a *mbari* should reveal every phase of human existence because it is a concentration of the whole of human life, including its taboos. Ibo art, like all African art, is marvelously eclectic. In the *mbari*, Christ on his cross stands alongside Ala the earth goddess. Nor are sexuality, entertainment, and religion seen to be incompatible. Tradition is renewed by the artist's individual inspiration and the use of external influences. Profound moral purpose and pure entertainment combine to make *mbari* a dynamic and immediate art form.

ROBERT BRAIN

Bibliography. Brain, R. and Pollock, A. *Bangwa Funerary Sculpture*, London (1971). Fagg, W. *Tribes and Forms in African Art*, London (1965). Griaule, M. *Les Masques Dogon*, Paris (1933 repr. 1963). Laude, J. *Les Arts de l'Afrique Noire*, Paris (1933). Leiris, M. and Delange, J. *Afrique Noire—La Creation Plastique*, Paris (1967). Leuzinger, E. *Africa—the Art of the Negro Peoples*, London and New York (1960). Paulme, D. *African Sculpture*, London (1962). Willett, F. *African Art, an Introduction*, London (1971).

28

OCEANIC ART

A ceremonial dance mask used by members of the Elema tribe of New Guinea,
Melanesia; bark cloth on cane frame; height excluding skirt 95cm (37in)
Pitt Rivers Museum, Oxford (see page 531)

THE islands of Oceania extend from New Guinea across the South Pacific Ocean to Easter Island, north to Hawaii and south to New Zealand. Most lie within the Tropics and have flora and fauna predominantly of southeast Asian origin. Conventionally Oceania is divided into three areas. The most diverse is Melanesia, which includes New Guinea and a string of islands eastwards to Fiji. Northwards is Micronesia, four festoons of small islands spread across the Pacific east of the Philippines and southeast of Japan. Most but not all are atolls. Further to the east in the open central Pacific is the enormous triangle of Polynesia, comprising both high volcanic islands and atolls, found sometimes in groups, sometimes in isolation. Polynesia and Micronesia are much more limited in their floral and faunal resources than Melanesia. To the southwest of Oceania proper lies the continent of Australia. Its extremely diverse topography and climate vary from the northern tropics to the arid central deserts and the more temperate regions of the south.

In terms of human settlement, Australia and New Guinea are by far the oldest. Hunting-and-gathering groups from southeast Asia began to occupy Australia at least 40,000 years ago, at a time when New Guinea, Australia, and Tasmania constituted one large land mass. Many thousands of years later, when island topographies conformed much more to those of today, settlements based on agriculture began in New Guinea and, subsequently, along with fishing, in the more easterly islands of Melanesia, and eventually in Micronesia and Polynesia. Archaeological research still has to clarify the detailed chronology and nature of this settlement, but it is now known that by the end of the 2nd millennium BC seafaring populations occupied much of island Melanesia and some of the Micronesian islands as well as Tonga and Samoa in western Polynesia. Most of the remaining inhabitable islands of the South Pacific were occupied by c AD 1000.

Culturally, Australia and Tasmania remained isolated and their inhabitants never adopted agriculture. Melanesia became extremely diverse, with hundreds of cultural and linguistic groups, although many, especially in the east, possessed certain common traits. Polynesia was much more unified in language and culture, developing from one "proto"-Polynesian group in eastern Melanesia. Micronesians and Polynesians were skilled agriculturalists, fishermen, and seamen, well-adapted to the environmental conditions of isolated tropical islands. Oceanic communities developed extensive exchange systems, sometimes over considerable distances; so trade was often reflected in their art. In Micronesia and Polynesia craft, ritual, and other specializations became institutionalized within a hierarchical social order.

Social organization was extremely varied throughout Oceania. In Melanesia, where societies were generally non-hierarchical and competitive, leaders and their rivals vied for control of politically independent communities. In Micronesian and Polynesian societies, normally organized into stratified groups, power was held by chiefs whose authority was sanctioned by their inherited lineage status.

Oceania was therefore a region of considerable antiquity and cultural diversity, supporting populations which, before European contact, were highly attuned to their environments and capable of exploiting them with marked sophistication.

Materials used in the manufacture of art objects included some taken unmodified from the environment such as leaves, flowers, seeds, stones, earth, shells, and feathers. More commonly, materials capable of extensive modification were employed: wood, tree bark, stone, bone, fibers, and dyes. Tools were generally of stone, bone, or shell. The loom was used in Micronesia and parts of Melanesia west of Santa Cruz. Pottery was manufactured in much of the area. It is known from archaeological evidence as far east as Samoa and Tonga in (locally) early prehistoric times, and a few shards have been recorded as far east as the Marquesas Islands. However, pottery was not reported in Polynesia at the time of European contact in the 18th century—except in Tonga.

Oceanic peoples often regarded objects as expressions of personal power or prestige, as temporary repositories of spirits, or as forms of social control. Oceangoing canoes and community houses were built and decorated by groups under specialist direction. These objects had high status and were symbolic expressions of social cohesion. Portable artifacts, clothing, body decoration, or mutilation often stated symbolically one person's status within a web of ranked or competing individuals.

Western observers have often concentrated attention on the form rather than on the content of Oceanic art, because much of the cultural history of the area is inadequately recorded and form can be more easily appreciated in terms of Western cultural norms. But to regard the traditional arts of Oceanic societies as "primitive" shows a profound misunderstanding of the many complex relationships that exist, or once existed, between the arts and other aspects of social behavior. Oceanic art should not be regarded as "above" society. Integral to behavior and thought, and linked with technology and economics as well as with politics and religion, it cannot be properly understood without reference to its cultural setting.

A growing number of art historians and anthropologists are studying Oceanic arts from the standpoint of the societies concerned. However, because of gaps in the distribution of

The subdivisions and main islands of Oceania

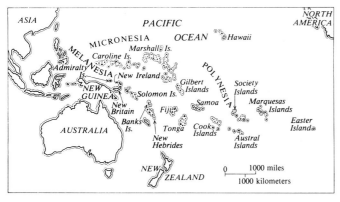

Decorated Mt Hageners of New Guinea during a moka exchange festival

fieldwork, many of the arts are imperfectly known. It is difficult to define them precisely and to illustrate their relationship to each other. The state of research is very uneven and does not allow for simple generalizations about character and meaning. This situation is exacerbated because adequate terminologies for accurate description and analysis have not yet been properly formulated. Such words as "art", "craft", "style", and "form" are imprecisely used because they carry overtones of meaning related to their use in Western art history. It is not Oceanic art that is primitive, but the appreciation of it by the non-Oceanic world. The following survey is therefore only a summary of present knowledge, not of the "total" ethnographic position that once existed.

Melanesia. Essentially, art in Melanesia was, and in some areas still is, an important form of communication. It made statements about the relationships people formed with other people, with their physical environment, and with their gods. The ceremonies and rituals that reordered and reaffirmed these relationships may themselves have been dramatic productions, to be viewed as expressive phenomena over and above their component songs, dances, music, body decoration, sculpture, or painting.

In New Guinea, now recognized as one of the major art areas of the world, the visual arts adopted such diverse regional forms that scholars usually distinguished a number of stylistic regions (see Gathercole, Kaeppler, and Newton, 1979, pp56–64). These have proved useful in organizing public and private ethnographic collections, but within each

region there existed a wealth of creative activity, much of which lay outside the range of attractive and collectable objects and was often discounted.

The arts of New Guinea clearly reflected the spirit of exchange and competition that permeated Melanesian societies. The belief that both human contact and spiritual sanction were essential to successful exchanges accounted for the efficient and magically protected canoes of the coasts, islands, and riverways. Among the most famous seagoing vessels which still illustrate this role are the handsome Massim District outrigger canoes. Their crews navigate the ring of islands involved in the *kula*, a highly organized system of ceremonial exchange. The *kula* valuables traded on such expeditions never stop circulating, for the prestige they symbolize is owned by no man for life. Rather, his temporary ownership is an emblem of the standing of his credit with other partners in the ring.

This typically Melanesian theme of ephemeral display also characterizes the Mt Hagen *moka* exchange festivals, for on these occasions a man's prestige is judged by what he is *seen* to possess and to give away. Mt Hageners compete with other Highland groups for recognition in dancing, elaborate self-decoration, and oratory. But the Hageners are their own most exacting critics, seeking a balance between the bright and dark elements of their body art, fluidity in dance, and logic and bravado in oratory.

The display theme was equally well developed in other settings where supernatural contact was sought and dramatized. During his initiation into adult society, a Namau boy from the

Papuan Gulf was "danced" through the men's ceremonial house in the jaws of the *kaiaimunu* spirit. The spirit itself was a huge wickerwork quadruped whose voice was the sound of bullroarers. Musical instruments such as drums, slit gongs, flutes, and bullroarers commonly play, or played, such sacred roles in New Guinea.

Wherever secret societies existed in New Guinea, ceremonial cult-houses functioned as composite symbols of male solidarity and authority. The Abelam of the Maprik region still build these sacred structures—some of them 80 ft (24 m) in height—which are brightly polychromed and adorned with woven gable masks. Inside, wickerwork masks are constructed for the long yams (some 12 to 15 ft (3.5 to 4.5 m) in length) which feature in cult festivities. The house interiors are female, and initiated men who enter there are born in reverse into a sacred realm where even the paint applied to ancestral carvings is powerful magic.

In stark stylistic contrast are the small *korwar* ancestor figure carvings of the northwest coast, where form is emphasized over color. Some of the *korwar* figures hold openwork screens; others, the skull of the deceased. Stylistic links between parts of New Guinea and Indonesia have been suggested. But "style" in New Guinea is not yet fully defined. This is not to imply that anonymity or slavish copying is the rule. Contemporary Asmat carvers (*wow-ipits*), now known from several documentary films, interpret the visual symbols of their culture quite freely and some even develop "signature" motifs. A carver's reputation is established on the basis of his creative insight and technical skill. But it is the effectiveness of the object, more than its authorship, that is important to the Asmat people. Ambitiously carved ancestor poles standing near the central hearths of the large ceremonial men's houses must be perceived in the context of the performance of sacred songs and ritual drumming which occurs when the houses are rebuilt. These activities once promoted successful headhunts.

Armed conflict remains a common form of settling disputes in those parts of New Guinea where Western influence is still minimal or disregarded. Weapons and shields such as those of the Chambri Lakes District (Middle Sepik Region) may be inoculated against the effect of enemy sorcery by means of carved relief or paint. The forms and surfaces of even the most utilitarian objects are frequently quite elaborate: for example, Lake Sentani bowls, Huon Gulf suspension hooks, Massim District lime spatulae, and Geelvink Bay headrests. Some of these forms may seem to be only decorative, but even abstract designs are likely to be conventionally expressed codes reflecting patterns of daily interaction.

Throughout the islands of the Bismarck Archipelago, supernatural forces which inhabited the sea and bush were the focus of highly developed ritual and artistic activities.

In southern New Ireland chalk figures of mythical ancestors portrayed the "quiet side" of sacred art; in the north, dramatic displays of religious beliefs, as well as of community wealth, were expressed in the *malanggan* ceremonies. Here each clan owned the design blueprint for an intricate *malanggan* assemblage. These spirit-charged polychrome carvings of symbolic shapes formed a gallery of mythological events and figures. When a *malanggan* piece was destroyed at the completion of a ritual cycle, its design was retained in the memory of the clan headman. It could be purchased from him by a neighboring clan, or stored as instructions for future craftsmen. The carving process itself was intertwined with magical rites, each step occurring at a precise point in the seasonal calendar. Some *malanggan* masks, however, such as *tatanua* (images of particular ancestors), were never destroyed. These masks were intrinsically powerful and capable of transforming human wearers into the spirits they represented.

A bonito- or shark-shaped fish sculpture from the Solomon Islands, Melanesia; length 91cm (36in). British Museum, London

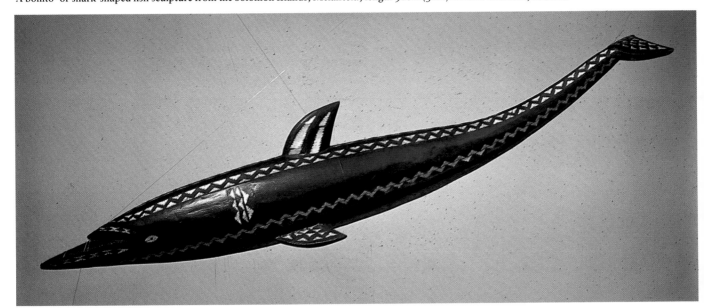

Cult activity was also the stimulus for flamboyant masquerade complexes in neighboring New Britain. Among the Baining of the Gazelle Peninsula, painted barkcloth masks of secret society members functioned as powerful agents of social control. Being spirits, they often acted outside the laws of society—for example by stealing and killing in the process of enforcing order.

In contrast to New Ireland and New Britain, masquerades were unknown in the nearby Admiralty Islands. However, *malai* ancestral spirits, which manifested themselves as crocodiles and snakes, were well-represented in carvings. These included elegant bowls, ladders, bedlegs, and doorposts. Obsidian blade daggers and spears with points of obsidian or stingray spine were also elegantly decorated.

In the Solomon Islands, socially oriented activities were considered highly appropriate art contexts. The construction of large-scale objects such as canoes, ceremonial food bowls, and houseposts was explicitly linked to rites commemorating tutelary deities and ancestors.

In the eastern Solomons, the focal point for such activities was the canoe house where large seagoing vessels and sacred bonito fishing canoes were housed. These were lavishly ornamented, in the latter case to attract bonito schools which only appear seasonally. The bait that lures the bonito is shared by swarms of fishing birds, and the bonito themselves are bait for the sharks that hover on the fringes of the schools. This spectacle of birds and fish was regarded as a supernatural phenomenon, and its occurrence indicated man's standing with the gods. The motifs occurred elsewhere in the Solomons, for example as freestanding shark and bird sculpture in the western islands, and possibly in the patterns of circle dances and songs.

Not surprisingly, the spirits were also responsible for commissioning or inspiring the thoughts of the Solomon Islands' artists, known as "talented men". An artist's visions seldom overruled his preference for producing one item as opposed to another, a preference that often reflected local specialities. In Santa Ana, "talented men" were known for their houseposts, while ritual bowls, the "preference" of Santa Cruz artists, were never carved in Santa Ana. These bowls have become a symbol of eastern Solomons style just as shell-inlaid canoe prows have for the central islands and freestanding *watawut* sculptures for the west. As the regions differ linguistically and culturally, artistic preferences communicate these differences to Solomon Islanders themselves.

Throughout the Solomons "talented men" were also responsible for the delicate geometric patterns cut into the faces of children during initiation ceremonies. Such marks added to the body a dimension of spiritually sanctioned rank in a way that tattooing, executed by "talented women", did not. Removable ornaments were also part of the vocabulary of body art but were worn primarily on ceremonial occasions. Men of high status displayed delicate shell combs, nose-pendants, and earplugs. Women also wore their wealth, but more literally in the form of strands of shell currency.

Traditional values of Solomon Islands life have undergone considerable change in response to European contact. With the eclipse of primary deities, and increasing adoption of Western ways of living, the foundations of traditional art have been seriously shaken. One significant recent response has been the rise of the Moro cult at Makaruka in western Guadalcanal. This movement advocated a return to what are perceived to be traditional values, expressed partly in carving. Their headquarters possesses a museum of objects regarded as traditional, which serve as models for artistic and ritual designs for the future.

The major art forms of the New Hebrides were concerned with initiation rites, social grade or rank-taking ceremonies, and funerary rituals. Materials used were wood, tree-fern, stone, or an over-modeling paste made of shredded creeper, tree-fern pith, coconut milk, and bread-fruit juice. The best-known pieces come from the islands of Malekula and Ambrym, where there were male graded-society systems known as Maki or variants. In most islands social rank, power, prestige, and material and spiritual wealth were obtained by the acquisition, raising, loaning, and sacrificing of pigs. Their upper canines were removed and their lower canines grew into tusks. The greater the curvature of the tusks the more valuable the pig became, especially for sacrifice in the graded-society rituals. Pigs were used not only as sacrifices but also as payment for ritual and artistic works.

In north-central New Hebrides, most art objects were made and used through the payment, loan, and sacrifice of tusked pigs. In central Malekula, objects erected during initiation rites for young males were paid for in this way. In southern Malekula, masks made of tree-fern, overmodeled with vegetable fiber paste and painted, were worn in sacred pig killing rites. After initiation and entry into the sacred men's house, men were allowed to acquire and subsequently to sacrifice tusked pigs which enabled them to climb the social ladder. During these graded-society sacrifices, images of tree-fern or stone were erected to represent ancestral figures and to symbolize the grade the individual was assuming.

The grade an individual possessed at his time of death determined the type of funerary rituals held for him. The dead person's skull was removed and overmodeled with vegetable fiber paste to reform his features. If a man reached high rank a *rambaramb* was made for him after death. It consisted of his over-modeled skull (often elongated), and a life-size body of bamboo or tree fern overmodeled and painted with the insignia of the person's rank. Small overmodeled puppet figures with arms known as *temes nevimbur* were used in initiation ceremonies in central Malekula, and were formerly used further south in pantomime performances which reenacted ancient myths. *Nampuki* masks, overmodeled on a spider's web base, were worn in central Malekula at certain stages of the ceremonies after the death of a high-ranking male.

Most villages possessed orchestras of slit drums which were played during such ceremonies. The more important drums, some 10 ft (3 m) high, were hollowed out tree trunks, often incorporating representations of a human face at the top.

Today, only three major areas of the New Hebrides produce and use art pieces in the traditional manner: Mota Lava (Banks Island) in the Banks group, north-central and south-central Malekula, and north-central Ambrym.

New Caledonia shared with its western Polynesian neighbors a more hierarchical concept of authority than existed in the nearby New Hebrides. Regalia such as circular shaped nephrite "axes" were employed by chiefs as emblems of authority. Dwellings were sometimes surmounted with carved ornaments, and door-jambs incorporated superb human images. Composite costumes of wooden masks and feather capes were worn for certain rituals.

Polynesia. The arts of Polynesian societies possessed similarities derived from a prototype ancestral culture in eastern Melanesia. Some of these similarities persisted in spite of the isolation of islands and local innovations in style. Polynesian societies were stratified into status groups: chiefs (and their high-ranking kin), commoners, and sometimes slaves. Within this ranked structure specialists functioned, including priests and artist-craftsmen, who took charge when certain rituals were to be enacted, important objects made, or dances performed. Traveling experts were also employed in the elaborate tattooing which flourished in Polynesia. The whole social system was sanctified by belief in a hierarchy of gods, many of whom had interests in particular aspects of human behavior. Ancestors also had a revered place in the social order. Polynesian life was much concerned with fishing, gathering, and agriculture in small island environments, and existed within an embracing mythological world where gods, ancestors, and humans were closely interrelated in sacred and secular contexts.

Visual art was integral to this interlocking situation. The human figure, representing gods or ancestors, was often represented in carving, generally in wood, with particular attention given to the head. Styles were sculptural and restrained, and areas of relief decoration carefully controlled. Simple, undecorated artifacts were often functionally beautiful. Decorative carving was widely used on a range of objects: community buildings, canoes, bailers, paddles, weapons, tools, bowls, personal ornaments, musical instruments, and the handles of fans and fly whisks. Shell, ivory, and more rarely bone, stone, teeth, hair, and feathers were important components of ornaments. Human figures were carved in stone, particularly in the east where rock-carving, both incised and in relief, was also a significant activity. Painting and color ranges were limited in extent. The manufacture and decoration of bark cloth (*tapa*) was of a high order, methods of fabrication and decorative patterns varying between island groups. Fine *tapa* clothing, body ornamentation (particularly tattoo), and the carving of regalia all signified status, and were often ex-

A nampuki mask from Malekula, New Hebrides, Melanesia;
height 140cm (55in). British Museum, London

plicit artistic statements of the position of an individual in the social order. Polynesians exhibited high standards of workmanship in finger weaving and plaiting split leaves (particularly of pandanus) to produce mats, baskets, belts, and sails, in making cordage from coconut or hibiscus fiber, and in working stone. Categorizations that divide "art" from "craft", and both from technology, are therefore inappropriate.

Ethnographic evidence, particularly from the late 18th and early 19th centuries, gives some indication of the high development of certain visual arts in various islands. In Tonga, perhaps the oldest and most formalized Polynesian society, female figures were delicately carved in wood or ivory; the ivory figures were used as neck pendants and ceremonial suspension hooks. Neck rests and oil dishes were beautifully simple in line and finish, while war clubs were elaborately incised and sometimes inlaid with ivory. Some of these forms, as well as the making of large sheets of decorated *tapa*, also occurred in Fiji. Trade between Fiji, Tonga, and Samoa for raw materials and finished objects significantly influenced the local styles of the three areas, although resin-glazed pottery was a notable and specifically Fijian product.

Figure sculpture was also of considerable importance in eastern Polynesia. Simple but powerful wooden figures were made in the Society Islands, the Cooks and Australs, both as freestanding sculpture and as whisk handles. Some were formal and stylized, like the squat male fishermen's gods from Rarotonga. Others were more abstract, like the staff gods from the same island. The flexed human figure was elaborately employed on adze and fan handles, canoe prows, and stern boards; a dramatic representation of this motif in stone is the figure from Raivavae (Pitt Rivers Museum, Oxford). More ornate representations of the human figure were made in the Austral Islands not only in figure sculpture but also incorporated in the design of drums. Bowls, ladles, and paddles had equally elaborate decoration. Magnificent examples of composite art were the Tahitian mourning dresses, made of *tapa*, bird feathers, pearl and turtle shell, and wood. These were worn by the chief mourners at ceremonies following the death of a person of high rank.

Sculpture in wood, bone, and stone was also well-represented in Marquesan art. On such wooden objects as freestanding figures, clubs, canoe ornaments, and stilt footrests, the quality of workmanship was particularly high, as it was in small-scale ivory carving on fan handles, earrings, and other personal ornaments. Status objects of shell, feathers, and coconut fiber were made with great finesse; they reflected the power of the chiefs in a society where warfare was rampant between valley-based groups and cannibalism widely practiced.

Hawaiian art can be characterized as dramatic and powerful, involving great technical virtuosity. Cloaks, capes, helmets, and images of gods incorporated thousands of brilliant red and yellow feathers with fiber and wicker bases to form the most dramatic of Polynesian clothing. Huge wooden images set in outdoor temples looked after the well-being of

A stone figure of a deity from Raivavae, Austral Islands, Polynesia; height 97cm (38in). Pitt Rivers Museum, Oxford

the people, while small images on pointed props were called upon for help by fishermen, canoe-builders, and sorcerers. The figures are squat and muscular, with body parts juxtaposed in angular planes. Such figures were also carved in servile positions on food bowls to insult conquered chiefs, and some of the most superb examples were incorporated into drum bases. Hawaiian *tapa* was unequaled both in its fine

A chief's cloak from Hawaii, Polynesia; feathers on a net base; 122×269cm (48×106in); c1840. Pitt Rivers Museum, Oxford

quality and in its decoration, which included grooving, watermarking, lining, and stamping, creating both direct designs and designs out of negative space.

The arts of Easter Islanders and of the Maoris of New Zealand were much influenced by the nature of their local environments, resulting in numerous unique forms. Easter Islanders developed unusual stone ancestor figures, wooden cult-carvings, and unique god figures modeled in painted *tapa*

A nephrite hei tiki (breast pendant in human form) from New Zealand; height 10cm (4in). Pitt Rivers Museum, Oxford

which were clearly much influenced in form by limitations in the available raw materials. These objects reflected in a massively purposeful way the power of Polynesian art in stating the interdependence of man, ancestors, and gods in isolated environments.

There are similar powerful themes of cosmological interdependence to be found in Maori carving, the best documented art form within Polynesia. Wood carving was probably the most important of the visual arts, exemplified by the shape and decoration of houses, canoes and canoe equipment, palisades, musical instruments, ritual objects, weapons, and tools.

Gods were rarely, ancestors commonly, portrayed. Forms and decoration were curvilinear with recognizable regional styles, in contrast to the predominance of rectilinear styles in tropical Polynesia. Tattooing, stone-carving, particularly of nephrite ornaments, and rock-painting and engraving also employed curvilinear motifs, and were thus symbolically and aesthetically linked to wood carving. The large carved meeting houses, often regarded as traditional but predominantly products of the latter half of the 19th century, contained carvings of important ancestors and other features, symbolizing the political and ideological unity of the tribe in the face of control by the British colonial government. This particular manifestation of carving reflected race relationships of the time. Like more traditional forms of art, it also demonstrated the long-standing and pervasive role of the arts in Maori society. The technical virtuosity involved was also evident in the manufacture of finger-woven flaxen garments, cordage and nets, leaf baskets, bone fish-hooks, and stone tools.

Micronesia. The visual arts of Micronesia were for the most part neither as elaborate nor as dramatic as those of other parts of Oceania. The relative poverty of many Micronesian environments entailed the maximum use of resources, particularly wood, stone, fibers, leaves, coral, and shell. This may help to account for the production of objects of elegant but simple form, and great constraint in style. This situation has sometimes been overlooked by outside observers, who have disregarded the fact that many utilitarian objects, such as adze handles, coconut graters, bowls, and fishing tackle boxes, were often made with aesthetic sensibility and self-discipline. Body decoration included ornaments for artificially distended earlobes, and elaborate tattooing was ritually performed with aesthetic intent.

The hierarchical societies of Micronesia lacked the elaborate public rituals associated with rank, typical of Polynesia, and religion was only moderately formalized. Stone and wood sculptures were generally absent, except for isolated examples such as wooden gable figures which surmounted men's meeting houses and the carved and painted story boards in Palau. Architectural wood-working and the lashing of timbers with sennit fiber were of high standard. In the western Carolines, lashing of house beams was a task for the master carpenter. Canoe houses and canoes were constructed with the same

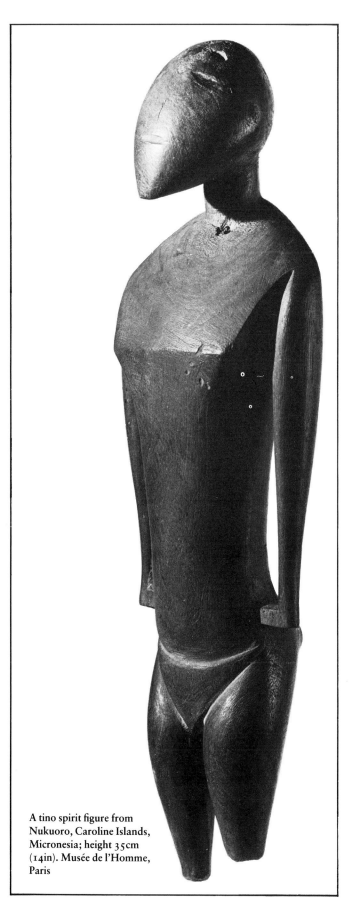

A tino spirit figure from
Nukuoro, Caroline Islands,
Micronesia; height 35cm
(14in). Musée de l'Homme,
Paris

precision. Indeed, the oceangoing canoe with its assymetrical hull and fine finish is one of the highest expressions of Micronesian art. From the few surviving pieces, such as those from Truk, Palau, and the Mortlock Islands, it is clear that house carvings, canoe ornaments, and human figures were made with great sensitivity. The most famous objects are probably the *tino* spirit figures from Nukuoro, a Polynesian outlier in the eastern Carolines, which appeal primarily because of their powerfully abstract quality. These figures are often regarded as Polynesian in style, but they may be expressions of a lengthy, common artistic tradition.

Some societies were extremely warlike. In the Gilbert Islands, wooden spears and daggers were edged with sharks' teeth, carefully seated in notches and bound with sennit. The placing of the teeth and the spacing of the fibers were both functional and decorative. Warriors of high status wore heavy armor of intricately woven coconut fiber.

Weaving and plaiting were generally highly developed, and clothing, bags, baskets, and mats of many kinds were woven throughout the area. Some were of outstanding quality, such as the plaited skirt mats and the loom-woven banana fiber belts of the Marshall Islands. The range of personal ornaments was varied, including wooden combs, shell necklaces, ear ornaments, fiber headbands, and flower necklaces. Tattooing was normal for both men and women, with geometric designs. Some influence, seen in the use of the loom, is thought to have come from Indonesia, but it has often been claimed that Melanesian influences were strong in the south and western Polynesian influences evident in the southeast. Limited knowledge of metal tools may also have come from Indonesia before the Spaniards arrived in Guam in 1520, but the settlement of Micronesia probably goes back at least to the 2nd millennium BC and the subsequent pattern of outside influences was undoubtedly complex. Some structures, such as the artificial islands with upright stones off the coast of Ponape, have not yet been satisfactorily explained.

Australia. The arts of the Australian Aborigines differed greatly from those of the islands of Oceania; they were expressions of societies that never practiced agriculture and possessed no permanent settlements. Aboriginal tribes were seminomadic hunters and gatherers, their technology simple but well attuned to their needs. More important to them were their economies and their religion which gave them understanding and control over their environment. Much time was devoted to rituals which included music, song, dance, and the telling of myths, all of which helped to make them secure within their environment and its history. "The Dreaming" was a state of mind which united members of society with their surroundings and activated links with mythical beings.

Art was religious, and as necessary as hunting to the well-being of the group and the individual. Totemic ancestors—animals, plants, or features of the landscape—were often symbolically represented in carvings on objects, in rock-engravings and paintings, and in ground paintings. These art forms were selectively distributed according to local traditions. The *churinga* of central Australia were stone or wooden oval plaques incised with geometric designs, usually of concentric circles or arcs, which symbolized the totemic affiliations of the owner. Ground paintings and body painting found in the same area were important in the cycle of rituals carried out by initiated males and from which uninitiated young men and all women were excluded. Painting was done in curvilinear designs on hard level surfaces with ochers, charcoal, and white bird down. Body decorations were similar: the down was fixed by the blood of the initiate.

Painting and engraving on flat stone surfaces was executed at thousands of localities throughout much of the continent. In the 1970s archaeologists discovered many new sites and it is now recognized that Australia has one of the largest and richest continuing traditions of rock art in the world. At Koonalda cave in South Australia, many wall markings of meandering and linear V-sectioned grooves have been found deep underground. They are probably more than 20,000 years old. Of later date, buried between 5000 and 7000 years ago, are sandstone fragments incised with linear and "bird track" designs found at Ingaladdi in the Northern Territory. Fragments of ocher at other widely distributed sites, dated up to 30,000 years ago, suggest that body decoration and/or rupestrian art may be as old as man himself in Australia. It is not surprising, therefore, that rock art has such a wide distribution. Painted galleries occur from the Kimberleys, in Western Australia, across Arnhem Land to the Cape York Peninsula. Other paintings are found in the central deserts and less commonly in the south. Engravings are certainly known in the north, but they predominate to the south, from Port Hedland in Western Australia to the Warburton Range and across into western New South Wales. Other sites occur in northern Queensland and between the Hunter and Hawksbury Rivers north of Sydney. There are also many more isolated locations.

The commonest engraved motifs are animal tracks and circles. In some areas animal forms are dominant. Some are of enormous size, as are human figures which represent mythical beings from "the Dreaming". Human beings are often an impressive feature of the painted galleries. In the Kimberley district are the Wandjina paintings, illustrating myths that belong to "the Dreaming" when ancestral beings created the landscape. These beings are said to have made the paintings as well as the outline human figures and heads of great dramatic power. In Arnhem Land are remarkable "X-ray" paintings of animals and sometimes human beings, incorporating anatomical details, and the so-called *mimi* figures, which represent potentially hostile spirits dancing, hunting, or fighting. The paintings of the Cape York Peninsula are predominantly of human beings, although animals, weapons, and plants have also been recorded. Many galleries are now known in this area, some containing hundreds of figures.

Two other art forms should be mentioned. The first is bark painting, once widespread but now practiced in traditional form only in Arnhem Land. The second is sculpture, perhaps

An Australian aboriginal rock painting

also once widely distributed but best exemplified today in northeast Arnhem Land, on Bathurst and Melville Islands, north of Darwin, and in the Aurukum area of Cape York. Almost all aboriginal sculpture had a sacred purpose. The mortuary posts of Bathurst and Melville islands are still ritually placed over or near a grave and allowed to decay. All Aboriginal art was, and in some areas still is, an expression of the relationship of an individual within a group to the past history of the group. That expression was transient, but the arts themselves were continuing integral elements of Aboriginal life.

Music, Dance and Oral Literature. Many commentaries on Oceanic arts have concentrated on sculpture and ornamented artifacts with little regard for other arts with which these objects were often associated in function and meaning. The performing arts—music and dance—have not been studied to the same extent as carving because they were thought to be of lesser significance in artistic terms and were more difficult to record and interpret. Although some Torres Straits' music was recorded as long ago as 1898, and that of parts of New Guinea in 1904–6, the amount of competent ethnomusicological analysis available is still limited, and much information has been lost. The study of dance ethnology is even less developed. It is fair to add, though, that more rapid progress is now being made by specialists in both fields.

Music and dance in Melanesia were used primarily in elaborate displays at times of ritual or life crisis, whereas in Polynesia and Micronesia they were typically accompaniments of poetry. This difference reflects the broad distinction between "big-men" societies and chiefdoms. In Melanesia two types of dance have been characterized: of impersonation and participation. In the former the dancer can be regarded as an actor representing mythical or ancestral beings. He was often masked, and the masks themselves are works of art. In participation dances, members of the audience could join to form a mass expression of rhythm. Where they occurred, words were relatively insignificant. Both types of dance were used when leaders organized dramatic public occasions to portray their wealth and power.

In Polynesia, on the other hand, poetry was usually central to dance, the latter illustrating the poetry of the chant. The dancer was a storyteller. Performances of song and poetry accompanied by dance often expressed the unity of society at such times as first-fruit festivals and other large public ceremonies. Detailed knowledge of Polynesian music and dance is available, particularly for Tonga, where poetry accompanied by dance referred to mythology, important places, and historical events. In Micronesia, music and dance had somewhat similar roles although in some islands dance had other functions. In the Gilbert Islands and Ifalik in the western Carolines dance ornamented poetry rather than illustrated it. In the Yap

empire this applied in a very specific sense, for there dances acknowledged the domination of Yap over neighboring islands.

Oceanic musical instruments included drums, musical bows, zithers, slit-drums, shell trumpets, flutes, and panpipes. These had a variable distribution and some island groups had few instruments. The Maoris used the body in lieu of the drum, an important instrument in tropical eastern Polynesia. The human voice, though, was more important than instruments, although the latter sometimes had considerable ritual significance and were decorated accordingly.

Music and dance were essential components of the rituals of the Aborigines of Australia, concerned with dramatic expressions of mythological origins and relationships with totemic phenomena. These arts were often visual demonstrations of oral literature. They had esoteric links with the decorative arts, but the nature of these relationships has rarely been studied in detail.

The oral literatures of Oceanic peoples are also inadequately known: a systematic comparative study could do much to clarify the function and meaning of other arts, particularly in areas such as central Polynesia where missionary influence led to the wholesale destruction of many objects. Common themes were origin myths reflecting cosmological beliefs, genealogical recitations embodying statements of political status, and legends and stories expressing aspects of daily life heightened by poetic imagery.

Changes in the visual arts after Western contact. The history of Oceania since Western contact has been extremely complex, and the response of individual cultures to differing forms and intensities of external influence far from uniform. This influence has been economic, political, and ideological. Some traditional arts still exist in a few areas of Oceania, especially in New Guinea. In most of Micronesia and Polynesia, however, where communities have often been under direct European, American, or Japanese control for longer periods, indigenous visual arts no longer exist as elements of independent cultures. Some scholars have assumed that all traditional arts were necessarily doomed once outside influences began to affect local ways of life and belief. This is not the case, and changes have operated quite subtly. A few arts can remain relatively unaffected. More commonly they show elements of acculturation, or develop forms of non-traditional folk art, or produce quantities of so-called "airport" art for an external, predominantly tourist, market. Two or more of these types of art often occur concurrently, the balance between them varying over time. Here we can only mention certain trends to indicate the complexities of the situation.

In Melanesia, certain functional arts have persisted in relation to specific needs. Sometimes these needs are new, born of new forms of cultural contact. Thus carving, painting, and body decoration are still extremely important in parts of New Guinea and in some islands of the New Hebrides. In these areas, the purchase of declining numbers of traditional objects

Female and male wooden figures representing spirits or minor deities from the Society Islands, Polynesia; height 30 and 33cm (12×13in). Pitt Rivers Museum, Oxford

by dealers, collectors, and tourists is often accompanied by the manufacture of an increasing number of objects made expressly for sale, some being specifically "airport" art. The character, quality, size, and range of types now made reflect international rather than local needs, but this does not imply it is necessarily bad. These changes, however, often profoundly affect the attitude of local societies towards their art.

Polynesia and Micronesia have been influenced by similar factors for many years. In islands where the visual arts were not suppressed by missionary or administrative insistence in the 19th century, or where they became irrelevant to the people as social norms changed, carving, personal ornamentation, and *tapa* manufacture were modified in several ways. In central Polynesia, though, many visual arts disappeared during the first half of the 19th century. The position in Hawaii was similar, although initially a wider range of figure carvings were made and *tapa*-making persisted well into the 19th century. An example of Hawaiian folk art was the manufacture of bed quilts, which took over one of the functions of *tapa* and used designs in conceptually similar ways. In smaller isolated islands like Mangareva, Easter, and the Chathams, the decline of traditional arts was much more rapid. In western Polynesia and New Zealand, however, certain arts have remained important in everyday life and often reflect Polynesian reactions to European control. *Tapa* and mats still have an important function in western Polynesia, particularly on state occasions or in certain *rites de passage* such as weddings and funerals. *Tapa* pieces are also popular trade items, and many are made up into hand bags and similar items. *Tapa* and other designs based on wood carving and petroglyphs now appear on imported woven fabrics and table mats.

Maori carving became sufficiently important in the 19th century in the decoration of meeting houses and other structures that, to some extent, we can speak of an artistic renaissance prompted by local reactions to the technical, economic, and political innovations introduced by the British settlers. New musical forms such as action songs and *poi* dances developed, leading ultimately to the emergence of the "concert party" in the early 20th century. Two artistic tendencies have become apparent. On the one hand, carvers and some other craftsmen have continued to work in traditional styles (for example at Rotorua). On the other, a number of Maori artists, sometimes using Western art forms, have sought direct inspiration from the New Zealand environment or Maori myth-

ology, as have some non-Maori artists. Schematic versions of traditional Maori designs are often used to symbolize a collective identity for all New Zealanders, not always successfully. Among contemporary Maoris, as in Tonga, Samoa, Fiji, and to a more limited degree in Hawaii, song and dance have survived more readily. Form and content have often changed, partly because of the influence of church music, but also because music often develops folk idioms in response to popular Western music. Tourist "airport" art carvings and other objects are now widely made. Some of these are related to local traditions, although many use spurious or conjectural "history". The scholar of traditional art might spurn "airport" art as debased, but to the art historian and anthropologist it has become an important aspect of social history.

Today, there is a growing interest in the art history of the whole of the South Pacific, closely linked to the development of more systematic research in anthropology, documentary history, and archaeology. The arts are becoming recognized as highly significant expressions of identity among the new nation states in Oceania. Pan-Pacific festivals of the arts are held every few years, and these will surely grow in scope and significance. The work of indigenous novelists, poets, and painters, though small in quantity at present, may soon be as representative of Oceanic art as are the productions of carvers and similar artists. They are all seeking to reestablish or redefine certain traditional values which have cultural and aesthetic meaning for the varied inhabitants of the Oceanic islands.

PETER GATHERCOLE

Bibliography. Barrow, T.T. *Art and Life in Polynesia*, Wellington (1971). Bellwood, P. *Man's Conquest of the Pacific*, Auckland, Sydney, London (1978). Berndt, R.M. (ed.) *Australian Aboriginal Art*, London and New York (1964). Bodrogi, T. *Art in North-East New Guinea*, Budapest (1961). Bühler, A., Barrow, T., and Mountford, C.P. *Oceania and Australia: the Art of the South Seas*, London (1962). Burrows, E.G. *A Flower in my Ear*, Seattle (1963). Christensen, D. and Kaeppler, A. "Oceanian Peoples, Arts of, III. The Performing Arts: Music and Dance", *Encyclopaedia Britannica*, Chicago (1974) Vol. 13 pp456–61. Dodd, E.H. *Polynesian Art*, London (1969). Gathercole, P., Kaeppler, A.L., and Newton, D. *The Art of the Pacific Islands*, Washington (1979). Gerbrands, A.A. *Wow-ipits*, The Hague (1967). Mead, S.M. (ed.) *Exploring the Visual Art of Oceania*, Honolulu (1979). Strathern, A. and M. *Self-Decoration in Mt Hagen*, London (1971).

29

CAROLINGIAN ART

The presentation of the Vivian Bible to Charles the Bald, folio 423 recto of the Vivian Bible
c851. Bibliothèque Nationale, Paris (see page 542)

WHEN Charlemagne was crowned Holy Roman Emperor by Pope Leo III on Christmas Day of the year 800 in St Peter's, Rome, he gave his name to a period and laid the foundation of a dynasty that was to rule Western Europe for 100 years. Charles had been crowned King of the Franks jointly with his younger brother Carloman in 768. In 771 Carloman died and left only one possible infant successor. The Franks therefore wisely accepted Charlemagne as their sole ruler—a position of power that enabled him to build partly by conquest, partly by diplomacy, partly by creating a new form of centralized bureaucratic and fiscal control, a new Western Empire, the largest since Antiquity. At his death in 814, Charlemagne's Empire extended to southern Italy, the River Ebro in Spain, and eastwards as far as the River Elbe in the north and the Hungarian plain in the south.

Political and military activity dominated the early decades of Charlemagne's long reign, but by the 780s the first evidence of his cultural revolution can be discerned; it was to increase in scope and magnitude in the last 20 years of his life. It may well be that the enormous treasure of the Avars (it is said to have taken 15 carts, each drawn by four oxen, to carry only the gold and silver and precious garments), captured in 795, played an important part in providing the necessary surplus wealth to pay for the lavish patronage at the court. Clearly the basic intention of this patronage was to create a new image for a "barbarian" ruler—an image to rival the great past, the Roman Empire. Court poets were to call Aachen, Charlemagne's favorite palace and the major center of the Empire, the "New Rome", a name applied hitherto only to Constantinople.

The most obvious symbol of this New Rome was the palace itself. A court scholar described Charles supervising its layout from a high vantage point, pointing to where the "forum", the "senate", the "theater", the "baths", the "Lateran", and even the "aqueduct" were to be built. The palace chapel itself, planned on a central octagon and under construction by 786, was not only based in its design on S. Vitale, built by the Byzantine Emperor Justinian in the 6th century in Ravenna, but Charlemagne actually ordered columns and carved capitals to be imported for it from there. Bronze doors with lion-head handles and finely chiseled Classical moldings, bronze railings with Classical pilasters, Corinthian capitals, and entablatures decorated with acanthus-scrolls, again emphasize the debt to Antiquity. Molds for the doors, excavated at Aachen in 1911, prove that this technically highly competent casting was undertaken on the spot. In 801 Charles brought the life-size equestrian bronze-gilt statue of what was believed to be the first "Germanic" Emperor Theodoric (it was probably the late-5th-century Emperor Zeno) from Ravenna, and set it up between the palace chapel and the palace. The statue itself perished later, but a miniature equestrian bronze now in the Louvre, Paris, probably a representation of Charlemagne himself, was no doubt inspired by it. That statue and the large bronze pinecone, intended to be set up as a fountain in the *atrium* in front of the chapel, in direct imitation of a similar fountain in front of St Peter's Rome, prove how self-conscious this revival, or *Renovatio* as it was called at the time, of Classical Antiquity was at the court.

As well as architectural details, some figurative and decorative sculpture survives from the period. Outstanding among it is work in stucco, like the life-size figure of Charlemagne in the church of St John, Müstair, and the decoration of the church of S. Maria in Valle at Cividale, the capital of the first Duchy of Lombardy in Italy. The Müstair figure is identified as Charlemagne by a late medieval inscription; although its date is controversial, it is likely to have been made during the period from 806 to 881 when the monastery was an Imperial possession. The stucco decoration at Cividale is of an elaborate kind. It includes a superb arch made of pierced vine-scrolls and six life-size female figures, and is combined with wall-painting. The work probably dates from just before Charlemagne's conquest of Lombardy in 774, and may well have been derived from eastern Mediterranean sources; it is possibly even the work of imported Syrian craftsmen, whose work at Khirbat-al-Mafjar, a private mansion in the Jordan Valley built between 724 and 743, shows a similar decorative vocabulary, though no large-scale figure-work. The technically far less skilled work of the figures at Cividale, when compared to the decoration, might seem to strengthen the argument that craftsmen, not practiced in this part of the work, were imported. Such fine remains in a somewhat fugitive medium suggest that this kind of sculpture was probably far more common in the Carolingian era than the few survivals indicate.

Sculpture in stone, apart from architectural details, seems to have been restricted to church furnishings, like choir enclosures, as seen in St Peter, Metz, S. Benedetto, Malles, and Schänis, Switzerland. In quality, the surviving carved slabs of such enclosures are far less sophisticated than the Cividale

The main artistic centers of the Carolingian Empire

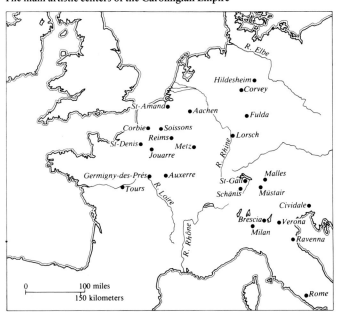

The bronze doors of Charlemagne's palace chapel at Aachen; c800

stuccos and are more likely to belong to a long established pre-Carolingian tradition. Both the occasional insular influence and the uncertainty scholars have to admit about whether panels such as those of St Peter's, Metz, should be dated to the early 7th or the late 8th century, emphasize this continuity. The recently discovered fragments of a screen from a church founded in 783 at Cheminot, attributed to the same workshop as those at Metz, lend strong support to a Carolingian date for much of this work.

In ivory-carving, a kind of miniature sculpture, such a sense of continuity with earlier traditions cannot be found. Here, models of the Antique, ranging in date from the late 4th to the 6th century, were closely imitated. The ivory bookcovers for Court School manuscripts, like the great covers of the Lorsch Gospels (now divided between the Vatican Library, Rome, and the Victoria and Albert Museum, London) based on the 6th-century style patronized by Justinian's Archbishop Maximian at Ravenna and on the five-part consular diptychs fashionable in the 5th and 6th centuries, show this intention clearly. Occasionally, as in the bookcover of the Bodleian Library manuscript Douce 176 in Oxford, the exact 5th-century models, showing identical iconography and closely related styles, actually survive.

In manuscript illumination, two very distinct styles were developed at the court. The first, not only again based on late antique models, but actually enshrining the loosely handled painting style of the late Antique, is best represented by the superb Coronation Gospels, painted on Imperial purple stained vellum now preserved in Vienna (Weltliche und Geistliche Schatzkammer). Here we cannot speak of a revival of a Classical model, but must assume that the painter was actually trained in the antique tradition itself; perhaps the name of the priest, "Demetrius", mysteriously written in gold into the margin at the beginning of the Gospel of St Luke, gives us a clue, pointing to Byzantium itself where such a living tradition is more likely to have survived into the late 8th century. The book itself is said by tradition to have been found on Charlemagne's knees when his tomb was opened at Aachen by the Emperor Otto III in the year 1000; it was used thereafter at German Imperial coronations.

Perhaps more creative than the astonishing and almost academic conservatism of the Coronation Gospels is a group of major gospel books made for the Imperial chapel at Aachen, now known as the Court School though called the Ada School in earlier literature. The earliest manuscript in this group, the Godescalc Pericopes in Paris (Bibliothèque Nationale), dated 781–3 and made as a gift for Pope Hadrian I, gives us a clear indication of the kind of sources available at the court at the beginning of the School's existence. The figurative elements tend to be derived from provincial Byzantine sources, probably transmitted mainly through northern Italy, while the decorative vocabulary, especially in the elaborate opening folios of text, is enriched by British (Insular) influence. This may in part be a traditional and long-established element in the Frankish Kingdom, and in part the result of a renewed contact with English artistic traditions through such eminent scholars as Alcuin, who was summoned from York to the court by Charlemagne in 781. A similar fusion of Insular and Byzantine styles can be found in the ivory bookcovers from Genoels-Elderen (Musées Royaux d'Art et d'Histoire, Brussels) probably contemporary with the Godescalc Codex. The mature Court School style, developed first in the Abbeville Gospels (Bibliothèque Municipale, Abbeville) and then in the Trier Gospels (Stadtbibliothek, Trier) and the Lorsch Gospels (Vatican Library, Rome) is more linear than painterly, and in its technique finally establishes the medieval method of laying in a middle tone and working both light and dark variation on it, ending in white or gold highlights, each applied when the previous stage of the work has dried. The artistic antecedents of this style are found in the 6th-century "Byzantine antique" of Justinian's art of Ravenna, also found in the magnificent Lorsch ivory bookcovers on the one hand (Victoria and Albert Museum, London), and in north Italian painting, exemplified both by wall-painting as at Cividale and by the unique survival of a high-quality north Italian manuscript, the Egino Codex (Staatsbibliothek, Berlin) produced at Verona between 796 and 799, on the other. Although little Carolingian wall-painting survives north of the Alps, there can be little doubt that it

The opening folios of the Godescalc Pericopes; 781–3. Bibliothèque Nationale, Paris

was not only inspired but may even have been executed by Italians.

In Italy, a much fuller picture can be gained of the importance of wall-painting as a form of architectural decoration in the Carolingian period. Here, both the earlier traditions and their continuation into the 9th century are fully documented by the survival of examples spanning the centuries from the beginnings of Christian wall-paintings in the Catacombs of Rome to the Carolingian era. In the church of S. Clemente in Rome, a series of frescoes which includes the Ascension, the Harrowing of Hell, and a Madonna, are found in the early basilica below the later church, and can be dated by the votive portrait of Pope Leo IV (847–55) included in the scheme. Here, the earlier painterly illusionism of the Classical tradition is transformed into a harder and more linear idiom which already foreshadows the later Romanesque style of the 12th century. So what appears at first sight to be painting of rather limited and indeed almost crude quality may be, in a very real sense, progressive.

The decoration recently uncovered and studied at S. Salvatore in Brescia includes both wall-painting and fine stucco work. It is found in the monastic church founded in the 8th century and rebuilt in the time of Louis the Pious. Stylistically, the painting here is in much closer touch with older Italian painterly traditions, which serve far better as models for the kind of wall-painting known in the Alpine area and north of the Alps. At Malles, in the Italian Tyrol, and at Müstair in Switzerland, painting strongly influenced by such Italian sources survives; and at Müstair the style is so close to the Brescian model that the work may well be by painters trained there. In the church of St John, Müstair, the largest cycle to survive outside Italy is very important both for its iconography, as well as for its style. No less than 62 scenes from the New Testament decorate its walls, unusual in the period when Old Testament scenes are found far more commonly in Carolingian manuscripts. Müstair serves as a useful reminder that only a small proportion of the work executed has survived. Documentary evidence also shows clearly how common painted decoration was in the 9th century, and how important Italian artists were to the North. It is known, for example, that the original decoration of the palace chapel at Aachen itself was undertaken by Italians called specially for the task. The rare survival of mosaic decoration north of the Alps at Germigny-des-Prés, finished c806, was no doubt also inspired by Italian work and almost certainly executed by such traveling craftsmen.

More difficult to establish than the *Renovatio* at the court is the continuation of older traditions, both Merovingian and insular, in the rest of Charlemagne's Empire, away from the scholarly atmosphere at the court. Some evidence, however, suggests that it must have existed. One example may well be the richly decorated purse reliquary from Enger (Staatliche Museen, West Berlin) traditionally said to have been given to Count Widukind of Saxony by Charlemagne on the occasion of his baptism in 785, but more likely to have been given by the Count to Enger at its foundation in or soon after 807. The later date is suggested by the reverse of the reliquary, where the iconography appears to be influenced by the Lorsch ivory covers produced at the court in the early 9th century. Another example of the continuing importance of insular influence is the back bookcover of the Lindau Gospels (Pierpont Morgan Library, New York) which, because it contains elements of the Scandinavian "gripping beasts" style (*see* Viking Art), is likely to date from no earlier than the early 9th century.

In architecture, too, where continuing traditions of craftsmanship and knowledge of construction techniques are even more likely to be of great importance, no matter what the immediate sources or the intentions of patrons, there is some evidence that the 8th-century Frankish background, badly documented though it is, was a significant factor alongside new ambitions. The structure, for example, as distinct from the design of the Aachen palace chapel, does not relate at all to its Ravenna model, and the exterior decorative treatment of the early-9th-century Lorsch Abbey gateway has alongside its purely Classical half-columns, pilasters, Corinthian capitals,

The reverse of the Enger purse reliquary; repoussé silver-gilt on wood; probably c807; Staatliche Museen, Berlin

and elaborate cornice, a traditional triangular arcade on the upper level and a decorative mosaic treatment of wall surface—clearly a Merovingian technique found in the crypt of Jouarre Abbey, near Paris, and dating from the 7th century.

Although it is more difficult to sketch a consistent development for Carolingian architecture than for the figurative arts, the lasting contributions made in the 9th century to medieval architecture are obvious and outstanding. The elaborate plan drawn for Abbot Gozbert of St-Gall, who began rebuilding his abbey in 830, was probably drawn by Heito, Bishop of Basel and Abbot of Reichenau from 803 to 823. It shows a large abbey church with both eastern and western choirs, cloisters, and a vast variety of abbey buildings, from the abbot's lodgings, infirmary, and guest houses, to kitchens, barns, and even chicken coops. It lays down a kind of "ideal monastery" that was to remain a model throughout the Middle Ages. Although monastic life had been vigorous and constantly expanding in Europe since the 6th century, the kind of sophisticated physical organization we see reflected in this plan is a new contribution much influenced by the monastic reforms introduced by Louis the Pious' tutor Benedict of Aniane.

Also of great importance was the development of the crypt as an important part of major churches. Although the surviving examples seem to have some basic characteristics in common, their precise forms are by no means closely related. This is typical of a period in which uniform customs and functions were being established, but architectural solutions accepted by tradition were not yet available. The reason for the appearance of crypts was the growing popularity of the worship of saints and their mortal remains. Almost like a second church, a smaller, more intimate space was created at the east end of the church, often on the same level as the nave, covered by groined and barrel vaulting of very limited span to carry a raised eastern sanctuary reached by steps up from the nave. At the church of St-Germain, Auxerre, a large crypt was built between 841 and 865 which has quite a large central chamber surrounded by a three-sided ambulatory walk and another chamber to the east. This probably led originally to a circular oratory beyond. At St-Médard, Soissons, erected between 826 and 841, a series of seven small barrel-vaulted chambers cross the whole width of the church, linked by a narrow groin-vaulted walk running north to south, with yet another three tunnel-like extensions running towards the west. We are reminded, in such an array of small funerary chambers, of the catacombs of Rome. Such crypts, in all their variety of forms, had one added advantage in common: in the raised sanctuary of the upper church, the high altar stood immediately above the most holy relics of the saints below, while at the same time a more intimate contact with such relics was possible in the crypt itself.

As well as developing new architectural forms at the east end of churches, Carolingian architects also paid new attention to the west end of their major buildings. Here great massive structures were built, always at least two stories high, usually square or rectangular in plan and normally sur-

Carolingian Bookcovers

The Carolingian period began with the reig[n] of Charlemagne, King of the Franks from AD 768, crowned Emperor by Pope Leo III [on] Christmas Day of the year 800, and came t[o] an end soon after the last great Carolingian patron of the arts, Charles the Bald, died in 877.

Throughout it, precious bookcovers for great Bibles and service books were produc[ed] for the important abbeys of the Empire and for royal patrons; they are among the most splendid works of art to survive from the period.

The earliest in style—although not neces[s]arily in date—is now mounted as the back cover of the Lindau Gospels in New York (Pierpont Morgan Library). It combines animal ornament, between the arms of the cross, of a kind first developed in the Britis[h] Isles, but is used here by a south German workshop, along with colored cloisonné enamel—powdered glass fused in small gol[d] cells—found in the top, left-hand border.

▲ The back cover of the Lindau Gospels; silver gilt, niello with inset enamel and garnets; 34×25cm (13×10in); early 9th century. Pierpont Morgan Library, New York

▼ A bookcover made at Metz; ivory relief panel in a gold frame set with cloisonné enamels and precious stones; c840. Bibliothèque Nationale, Paris (MS. Lat 9383)

◄ Christ treading the beasts, and scenes from His life on an ivory bookcover; 21×13cm (8×5in); early 9th century. Bodleian Library, Oxford

▼ Bookcover made in Metz, c840–5; from top to bottom, the Annunciation, the Adoration of the Mag[i], the Massacre of the Innocents; Bibliothèq[ue] Nationale, Paris

◄ The front cover of the
Lindau Gospels; gold,
gems, and pearls;
34×26cm (13×10in);
870. Pierpont Morgan
Library, New York

▶ The front cover of the
Codex Aureus of St
Emmeran; 42×33cm
(17×13in); 870.
Bayerische
Staatsbibliothek,
Munich

In contrast to the somewhat "barbaric" splendor of the Lindau cover, the two covers made entirely of ivory (although they may originally have had settings in precious metals) in the Bodleian Library, Oxford, and in the Victoria and Albert Museum, London, present us with examples of the revival of Mediterranean humanist Classical art sponsored in the Court School of Charlemagne. The larger of the two, with the Virgin and Child in the center, originally the front cover of the Lorsch Gospels written in Charlemagne's scriptorium early in the 9th century, wholly takes the form of what is called a "six-part" diptych, originally developed in the late antique period of the 6th century. The smaller one, in Oxford, adopts the same format and combines it in a simplified way within a single panel. But in both, the ancient ancestry of form and figure-style is obvious.

During the reign of Louis the Pious (814–40) the most important bookcovers were made at Metz, where Louis' half brother Drogo was Archbishop. One showing a Crucifixion in ivory, surrounded by a very richly decorated gold frame, mounted with cloisonné enamels, can be dated by the Gospel manuscript it covers to c840; the other, perhaps not much later, shows pierced ivory carving of superb quality, probably originally set off against a gold background (both in the Bibliothèque Nationale, Paris). In this, the carver has succeeded to a remarkable extent in translating a free and painterly late antique pictorial style into three-

dimensional relief carving.

The remaining three covers were all made for perhaps the greatest patron of the 9th century: Charles the Bald, King of the western Franks (843–77) and Emperor (875–7).

The earliest, the relatively modest cover of Charles' Psalter, was written in the 850s, but the ivory mounted in the center illustrating Psalm 56 may have been carved as many as 20 years earlier (Bibliothèque Nationale, Paris). The front cover of the Lindau Gospels (Pierpont Morgan Library, New York) is a much richer example, with the figures of the crucifixion in embossed gold in the center. Surrounding it is a gold-and-jeweled border of great splendor. It was made c870, perhaps in Charles' favorite abbey, St-Denis, near Paris, of which he was lay abbot.

By far the most magnificent Carolingian cover to survive is the front cover of the

Codex Aureus of St Emmeran, Regensburg, now in Munich (Bayerische Staatsbibliothek). In the center is Christ in Majesty, surrounded by a gem-encrusted frame carried on small golden chalices in full three-dimension which can only be seen when looking sideways at the cover. In the four fields the four seated Evangelists are depicted, as well as scenes from the Gospels. An outer border set with huge gems on massive mountings carried on filigree arcades completes an almost too ostentatious display of glittering wealth.

PETER LASKO

Further reading. Beckwith, J. *Early Medieval Art*, London (1964). Lasko, P. *Ars Sacra: 800–1200*, Harmondsworth (1972). Steenbock, F. *Der Kirchliche Prachteinband im Frühen Mittelalter*, Berlin (1965). Swarzenski, H. *Monuments of Romanesque Art: the Art of Church Treasures in North Western Europe*, Chicago (1967).

The gateway of Lorsch Abbey; early 9th century

mounted by one central or two lateral towers. These structures have been given the name *Westwerk*. One of the finest to survive is at the abbey church of Corvey in Westphalia, built 873–85. At the entrance level there is an open hall, where 16 supports carry a groined vault surrounded by a narrow aisle on all four sides. Above this, no doubt on the level of the tribune galleries of the original church, is a spacious chamber reaching through two stories in height; its windows with double openings look into it from the surrounding walks on the upper level. The function for which these enormous western structures were built has never been established beyond doubt, although it is clear that baptisms took place in some, while others were used as a kind of Royal or Imperial tribune

gallery, looking from an upper level into the nave of the church and towards the high altar. Altars in the *Westwerk* were often dedicated to the warrior saint St Michael: so were these structures simply, or even mainly, the defence against the powers of darkness coming from the west? Much clearer than their original purpose is the fact that in its monumental emphasis on the west end of the "Great Church", the *Westwerk* is the ancestor of the two-tower facade which was to become the conceptual hallmark of many churches.

After the death of Charlemagne in 814, the idea of the Renaissance of Antiquity certainly persisted and was even heightened during the reign of his son, Louis the Pious (*ob.* 840). Whereas the Court School in its ostentation reflects the

Corvey Abbey (built 873–85): left, a ground plan of the church; right, the Westwerk

Folio 15 (Psalm 26) of the Utrecht Psalter; University Library, Utrecht

aste of Charlemagne, the more scholarly academic style seen in the Coronation Gospels may have been patronized by Louis, crowned King in 781 and co-Emperor in 813. Certainly, while the Court School ceases with Charlemagne's death, the influence of the Coronation Gospels and similar precise classical revivals gains ground after 814. Outstanding works of art like the Utrecht Psalter (University Library, Utrecht) and more particularly the Ebbo Gospels (Bibliothèque Municipale, Epernay) written for Archbishop Ebbo of Reims (elected 810, deposed 845) descend directly from the Vienna Gospels. But whereas the latter retains the calm, restrained grandeur of the late Classical style, the Ebbo Gospels are painted with a violent fervor of expressionistic intensity. The painterly impressionistic touches of strong, clear color are identical in both, but in the Ebbo Codex this technique is combined with a more linear use of paint and far more contrast in light and dark, heightened in the final touches with black lines and gold highlights. It is in this linear treatment that the style developed in the Utrecht Psalter is seen most clearly, where illustrations are drawn throughout in brown ink. Each Psalm is illustrated by unframed compositions, each occupying about one third of a page. Closely bunched groups of figures enact a kind of literal translation of the narrative content of the text in pictorial form. Landscape and architectural details are drawn with the same rapid line and delicate illusionism, and all parts

of the drawings are swept along in ecstatic movement. Because of the book's connection with the Archbishop of Reims, it is known as the Reims style; it was to be one of the most influential contributions to medieval art.

In a way, the continuing interest in the art of the late Antique during the reign of Louis the Pious is shown even more clearly in an ivory panel now in the Merseyside County Museums, Liverpool. It shows the Crucifixion with the Virgin, St John, and Stephaton and Longinus above, and the three Maries at the Tomb below. The latter scene is an exact imitation of an early-5th-century ivory now in the Bayerisches Nationalmuseum, Munich.

After the death of Louis the Pious in 840, the Empire was divided into three parts by the Treaty of Verdun in 843. The central area of Europe, from Lower Lorraine in the north to Italy in the south, and the Imperial title, were given to Louis' eldest son Lothar I; the eastern regions went to Louis the German, and the western area, mainly ancient Gaul, was received by Charles the Bald, Louis' youngest son by his second wife, Judith. This division lasted until the Treaty of Meersen in 870, when on the death of Lothar II (second son of Lothar I), Louis the German and Charles the Bald divided the central Kingdom between them, leaving only Italy to the descendants of Lothar I; the boundary was drawn more or less along the line between modern Germany and France. As a direct result

An ivory panel; above, the Crucifixion; below, the three Maries
at the Tomb; 16×11cm (6×4in); 9th century.
Merseyside County Museums, Liverpool

of such divisions, the centralized patronage of Charlemagne
and Louis ceased. Under new rulers and powerful churchmen,
new centers of activity developed: Tours, Corbie, St-Amand,
and St-Denis in the west; Corvey, St-Gall, and Fulda in the
east, and Metz and Milan in the central kingdom.

The last phase of ivory-carving at Metz, long known as the
Younger Metz School, begins with a Crucifixion plaque
mounted on the cover of a manuscript dated to c840, now in
the Bibliothèque Nationale, Paris, (MS. Lat. 9383) where it is
surrounded by a magnificent border of goldsmith's work including gems and gold cloisonné enamels closely related to
those found on the Golden Altar of S. Ambrogio in Milan of
c850. A large number of related Crucifixion panels survive, as
well as plaques with scenes from the New Testament made as
back covers for the same books. They must date from the
period of high activity at Metz which ceased when Metz declined as an artistic center after the Treaty of Meersen in
870—a decline also reflected in the fact that the production of
illuminated manuscripts virtually ceases in Metz at that time.

The great abbey of Tours first established a tradition of

scholarship under Alcuin in the late 8th century. It then de
veloped important artistic production under the patronage o
its Abbots Adelhard (834–43) and Count Vivian (843–51), a
production which flourished until the destruction of the
Abbey by invading Norsemen in 853. The Old Testamen
illustrations created there, probably based on 6th-century
Mediterranean models, were to lay a foundation in both
iconography and style which was to be vividly exploited a
Hildesheim as late as the 11th century.

In the large Tours Bibles, the whole-page illuminations are
either single subjects, like the Christ in Majesty at the begin
ning of the Gospels and the dedication pictures, or they are
organized in three or four strips across a page in continuou
narrative form—almost like a strip cartoon. The obviou
source for this is the tradition of the antique scroll, seen i
sculptural form winding up Trajan's column in Rome (se
Roman Art). The same tradition is also seen in the horizonta
strips of color in the background of the Old Testament scenes
a somewhat misunderstood adaptation of the graduated colo
background of late antique painting intended to simulate th
aerial perspective of the original. One of the great Tour
Bibles, the Vivian Bible (Bibliothèque Nationale, Paris: MS
lat. 1), ordered by Count Vivian in 845 and dedicated t
Charles the Bald, links the Tours style with the last grea
Carolingian school to have been created, that of Charles th
Bald.

It was especially at Metz and Milan that the characteristic
of the earlier Renovatio were further developed. Drogo, Arch
bishop of Metz, half-brother of Louis and Chaplain to th
Emperor Lothar I, based his patronage on the traditions of th
court, while at Milan, works like the great Golden Alta
frontal of S. Ambrogio (c850) enjoyed the advantages o
having fine Early Christian models close at hand. The develop
ment of Metz as an artistic center is a long and complicate
story. After Drogo was appointed to the see in 823, clos
relations with the court of Louis the Pious were establishe
and maintained throughout its subsequent history. After th
accession of Lothar I and Drogo's elevation to Archbishop i
844, relations with the court were probably even closer. Fror
the beginning, the painterly late antique "Court" style c
Louis was of greatest importance. Also, Classical influenc
was not only stylistic—the earliest known manuscript, prot
ably written for Metz in the early 820s, was an astronomica
compilation, now in Madrid (National Library; Cod. 3307
The vast majority of Classical texts, literary and scientifi
survived into later periods only through the enlightened activ
ty of Carolingian scholars and scribes. Drogo's own sac
ramentary (Bibliothèque Nationale, Paris; Nat. Lat. 9428) n
only continued this painterly late antique style, but also estab
lished a decorative vocabulary based mainly on Antiquity
favorite acanthus ornament, and developed the art of the in
tial filled with figure scenes to illustrate the text ("historiated
initials), which was to become one of the great artistic con
tributions of medieval illumination. The ivory bookcovers c
this same manuscript, of better quality than reproductions c

t suggest, survive only in fragmentary form. They show scenes from the liturgy, which, although it is an unusual series of subjects—indeed, unique among bookcovers—are highly suitable decorations for a personal sacramentary. Stylistically, these covers can be related to another now in Frankfurt (Stadtbibliothek; MS. Barth. 180) where a large central panel showing Christ's Temptation indicates that the Metz school had an astonishing mastery of the classical style in the 840s. A number of other carvings with the same strong element of classicism must be the work of the same school, such as the covers of a gospel book now in Munich (Bayerische Staatsbibliothek; Clm. 4451) with the Baptism of Christ on the front, and the Annunciation and the Nativity on the back, attributed by some scholars to the 10th century.

One of the centers in which the Court school of Charles the Bald was probably active was the royal abbey of St-Denis, of which Charles became lay abbot in 867. A great wealth of manuscript illumination and goldsmith's work was commissioned, especially in the last decade of his long reign ending in 877; perhaps the decline of Metz after the death of Lothar II in 869 enabled Charles to add a rich stream of artistic talent to the established traditions active in his kingdom. In many ways, technically and stylistically, a manuscript like the Codex Aureus (Bayerische Staatsbibliothek, Munich; Clm. 14000), written by Beringar and Luithard in 870, and its magnificent golden bookcover, sum up all the achievements of Carolingian art. Whereas earlier in the century, schools like Metz or Aachen could for the most part only exploit the heritage of Antiquity, the artists employed by Charles were able to enrich that heritage by transforming it into a wholly Carolingian idiom, at the same time as summing up all that had been achieved before. Charles the Bald might even have been aware of this, when, in a charter granted in 877 to his favorite foundation at Compiègne, he states specifically that he wished to follow the example of Charlemagne in presenting a large number of relics to his new church as his illustrious grandfather had done at Aachen. Certainly, the enormously rich style of decoration evolved in the Codex Aureus and its related manuscripts rivals and and even surpasses the work at Charlemagne's Court School in richness and ostentation. In goldsmith's work like the Codex Aureus cover, the late Lindau bookcover (Pierpont Morgan Library, New York;

An illuminated initial from Drogo's sacramentary; c826–55. Bibliothèque Nationale, Paris

Christ in Majesty, from the Codex Aureus; 870. Bayerische Staatsbibliothek, Munich

MS. 1), or the golden altar frontal for his Royal Abbey of St-Denis (now only known from a painting by the Master of the Mass of St Giles, of *c*1500; National Gallery, London) the same splendor is found and the same technical and stylistic summing up of all previous achievement. The iconography of the Codex Aureus cover, as well as its Christ in Majesty page, is based closely on the Tours tradition found in the Vivian Bible. The painterly and vivid expression of Charles' personal Psalter of *c*860 (Bibliothèque Nationale, Paris; MS. Lat. 1152) owes much to the Metz school, and the goldsmithing techniques employed at the court draw fully on all previous work—especially the more sophisticated traditions of northern Italy seen so clearly in the Milan Golden Altar. Only in ivory-carving does the same wealth of material not seem to be available. Recent research has shown, however, that the great "Throne of St Peter" in the Vatican was made for Charles the Bald; but here, as elsewhere in this period, ivory panels seem to have been turned and carved a second time, and more often than is usual. Also ivories very closely connected with the style of the Utrecht Psalter, and perhaps carved nearer 830 than 870, were used, perhaps reused, by Charles' craftsmen. Perhaps the trade in the raw material of ivory tusks was declining in the second half of the 9th century. Also, the great variety of styles patronized by Charles is obvious; alongside those already mentioned there is still the Franco-Saxon style of the so-called "Second Bible" of Charles the Bald (Bibliothèque Nationale, Paris), a decorative art of great elegance and precision derived from earlier Insular sources. It would be wrong to call this great variety of work the "School of Charles the Bald"; it is the work of an era rather than of a school, but more truly creative and more truly Carolingian than any that had gone before. None of the successors of Charles the Bald in the last quarter of the 9th century was able to create sufficient stability to encourage the arts at their courts.

The Carolingian achievement as a whole was of the greatest importance to the civilization of northern Europe. The long-established predominance of the Mediterranean tradition was finally broken, not by any fundamentally opposed aesthetic but more by the absorption of its humanist tradition. Throughout the Middle Ages, from the 9th century onwards, whatever influence the Classical tradition was to have on the art of the west, be it in its antique, its Early Christian, or in its Byzantine guise, it has always to be qualified by what might be called an indigenous northern classicism created by Carolingian artists.

PETER LASKO

Bibliography. Beckwith, J. *Early Medieval Art*, London (1964). Conant, K.J. *Carolingian and Romanesque Architecture: 800–1200*, Harmondsworth (1978). Dodwell, C.R. *Painting in Europe: 800–1200*, Harmondsworth (1971). Henderson, G. *Early Medieval*, Harmondsworth (1972). Hinks, R. *Carolingian Art*, Ann Arbor (1962). Hubert, J., Porcher, J., and Volbach, W.F. *Carolingian Art*, London (1970). Lasko, P. *Ars Sacra: 800–1200*, Harmondsworth (1973).

30

OTTONIAN ART

The Imperial crown of Otto I; height of front panel 15cm (6in); c962
Weltliche und Geistliche Schatzkammer, Vienna (see page 554)

B Y THE beginning of the 10th century, the Carolingian Empire had disintegrated as a result of internal dissension and the attacks of external enemies—Norsemen in the west, and Slavs and Magyars in the east. With the election of Henry the Fowler, Duke of Saxony, as King of the eastern Franks in 918, a process of consolidation began. It culminated in the establishment of the Ottonian Empire under Henry's son Otto the Great, who was crowned Holy Roman Emperor in Rome in 962 and who gave his name to both the dynasty and the period. The Saxon Emperors reorganized the means of government, developing close cooperation between Church and State in which the Emperor acted both as divinely appointed ruler and as God's vicar on earth—*Rex et Sacerdos* (King and Priest)—while the great princes of the Church and their clergy acted as a civil service working in close harmony with, and indeed forming, the royal chancellery. Under the Ottonian dynasty the eastern Franks became the undisputed leaders of western Christendom. The princes of the Church, nominees of the Emperor, were not only spiritual prelates, but also feudal lords, and archbishops and bishops themselves took up arms for the Emperor. Bruno of Cologne, Otto I's brother, for example, held the Duchy of Lotharingia as well as the vital archbishopric of Cologne.

Another important development was the great movement of monastic reform. In 910, William, Duke of Aquitaine, founded a new kind of independent monastery at Cluny, and similar reforms were undertaken in Lotharingia by St Gerard of Brogue (*ob.* 959) and at Gorze by St John of Vendières (*ob. c*975). The powerful, well-organized monastic houses, with an ever increasing income resulting from more efficient use of land, reached the peak of their power and influence somewhat later, but during the 11th century the established cooperation of Church and State began to break down. The "Investiture Conflict", when the Church, conscious of its growing economic strength, was no longer prepared to accept the appointment of bishops by the secular arm, was both symptom and cause of a new situation.

During the 10th century, however, the reform movement was still firmly under the control of the prelates who were often linked by blood and always by common interest to the Imperial power. It was these prelates who created great centers of artistic patronage, competing with the Imperial court itself in generosity and splendor. Such centers, comparable to the courts of Carolingian kings, were created by Egbert at Trier, by Meinwerk at Paderborn, by Bruno at Cologne, and by Bernward at Hildesheim, as well as by the great ladies of the Ottonian aristocracy, like Mathilde, granddaughter of Otto the Great at Essen, and her sister Adelheid, who was simultaneously Abbess of no less than four convents—Quedlinburg, Gernrode, Vreden, and Gandersheim. If Carolingian patronage was mainly royal and Imperial, Ottonian art, although more broadly based, was still almost exclusively aristocratic.

Ottonian art was the result of three major influences: a revival of the northern Carolingian heritage, a renewed interest in northern Italian art, and a more direct contact with Byzantine art so brilliantly revived under the Macedonian emperors after the final abandonment of Iconoclasm in 842. The interest in their own Imperial past seems natural enough, and the influence of Italy was the direct result of political involvement with the papacy. This began with a first campaign in 951, when the Pope asked for Otto's help against the Lombards; it resulted in Otto being crowned King of Lombardy at Pavia in the same year. A passionate interest in Italy and things Italian continued under Otto's successors, who have often been accused of neglecting their northern homelands, both politically and artistically. Not until the reign of Henry II (1002–24) did a German emperor again reside north of the Alps for any length of time. The intimate and personal contact with the Byzantine court led to the marriage of Otto's son to a Greek princess, Theophanu, one year before Otto the Great's death in 973. On Otto II's death in 983, this powerful lady became regent for her son Otto III, born in 980, and she continued to rule the Empire until her death in 991.

In architecture, however, Carolingian traditions predominated and were developed. The emphasis on western blocks with towers and on crypts continued, but a number of innovations were developed during the 10th century which all led towards a more precise articulation of architectural forms both internally and externally. Unfortunately, little survives from the earlier phases of this development, begun, no doubt, with the reconstructions and new foundations initiated by Henry the Fowler and Otto I—for example Henry's favorite foundation at Quedlinburg (*post* 922) and Otto's at Magdeburg, begun in 955.

These innovations include the elaboration and more extensive use of galleries, often, in the 9th century, restricted to use in the western blocks (*Westwerk*), the development of an alternating system of supports—columns and heavy piers—which divide a wall into a repeating pattern of bays, and clearly defined crossings of transept and nave, again seen as four bays meeting and reflecting each other. Externally, wall arcades, blind arches around windows, and both horizontal

The main artistic centers of the Ottonian Empire

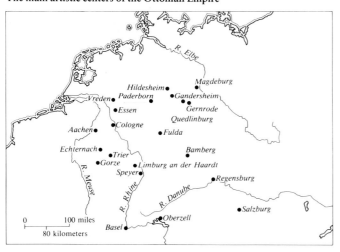

The nave and east apse of St Michael's, Hildesheim; c1001–33

stringcourses and vertical pilaster shafts were used to divide wall surfaces into well-defined areas to emphasize and explain structure. All this imposed on buildings a far more clearly expressed and self-conscious "design" of both space and wall. Proportions are often simple geometric relationships, harmonious and easily understood.

One of the rare surviving buildings of earlier Ottonian architecture is St Cyriakus at Gernrode, founded by Margrave Gero in 961. The western part is heavily emphasized by two strong staircase towers flanking a large western block with an internal western gallery, very much in the Carolingian tradition. But externally, blind arcades, stringcourses, and pilasters divide up the wall surfaces into units, relating to windows, internal floor levels, and bay divisions. Internally, the crossing of a transept, which hardly projects beyond the aisle walls, is clearly defined by high arches carried on at-

tached pilasters across the nave and the chancel. The nave is articulated by alternating columns and piers, and each bay of two arches in the nave is surmounted by a gallery opening, divided by four arches, carried on small columns, again separated from the next bay by a heavy pier. In all this a clear sense of harmony is expressed, achieved by balance and the regular repetition of geometric units. It is these qualities of order and harmony that were further developed during the 11th century, both within the Ottonian Empire and elsewhere, and were fundamental to the creation of the great Romanesque church.

Indeed, architectural historians usually discuss the beginnings of Romanesque architecture in terms of the abbeys of St Michael at Hildesheim and Limburg an der Haardt, one founded by St Bernward of Hildesheim in 1001, the other by the Emperor Conrad II in 1025. They find it difficult to make any valid stylistic distinctions between these and a more fully developed Romanesque building, like the second cathedral of Speyer, built between 1092 and 1106 by Henry IV, after its main outlines had been determined by Conrad II's Speyer, begun in 1030 and consecrated in 1061. Only in two respects was the great church of the late 11th and 12th centuries to go beyond the achievements of the 10th- and early-11th-century builders. One was the ability to construct the high stone vaults of choir and nave, first by barrel or groin and then by ribbed vaults; the other was the growing importance of sculptural decoration, which began almost to dominate purely architectural principles towards the beginning of the 12th century.

In the Ottonian period, the decorative and sculptural treatment of architecture remained concentrated on church furnishings—doors, altars, tombs, Easter candlesticks, and sepulchers—rather than indulging in the interpenetration of architecture and sculpture so typical from the Romanesque onwards. It is true that more ephemeral decoration, such as painting and stucco, may have played a larger part in architecture than their rare survival allows us to assume, but where architectural sculpture does survive in some quantity, as for example on carved capitals, it is clear that architectural traditions rather than pictorial principles predominated. The ubiquitous Corinthian-derived capital and simpler forms like chamfered or cushion capitals—the latter perhaps originally decorated by painting—seem to be the only parts of the buildings that gave opportunities to the masons to exercise their carving skills. It was not until the second half of the 11th century, first on capitals and then in decorative moldings, figural decoration on portals, tympana, wall-surfaces, and especially on the west fronts of most churches, that the sculptural ability of craftsmen, for so long restricted to the relatively small scale of furnishings, were given new and vast fields to conquer.

The Ottonian desire to increase the articulation of architecture, to produce a structured sense of order and harmony, may also have been achieved by large, decorative schemes of wall-painting—but, alas, very few fragments have survived. The only major scheme still to be found north of the Alps can be seen in the church of St George of the monastery of Oberzell on the island of Reichenau. Although much damaged and much restored, it is still clear that the large, plain surfaces of the nave walls above the arcades and below the clerestory windows were divided by broad bands decorated with illusionistic multi-colored meander strips separating the arcade, with roundels in the spandrels, from the large scenes showing the miracles of Christ above them. Both in style and technique these paintings owe much to north Italy, as most major architectural decoration had done already in the 9th century. But they can also be compared to manuscript illumination of c1000, especially to the work of schools patronized at the Imperial court which themselves owed much to the same sources. Large, imposing figures dominate the scenes, placed against architectural backcloths with buildings in rudimentary perspective as in late antique paintings. The horizontal strips of blue, green, and brown, of the background, are also derived

St Matthew, from the Gero Codex; c960. Landesbibliothek, Darmstadt

from the same illusionistic late antique tradition.

Ottonian illumination is far better documented by a surprising quantity of surviving manuscripts. It begins with what seems almost a self-conscious revival of early Carolingian forms, in the Gero Codex (Landesbibliothek, Darmstadt), a Gospel lectionary closely copied from the Lorsch Gospels of the Court School of Charlemagne (which survives in two halves, one in the Vatican Library, Rome, the other in the Biblioteca Documentata Batthayneum, Alba Julia, Rumania), and produced c960 for a "Custos Gero", perhaps the later Archbishop of Cologne (969–76). The Codex Wittikindeus painted in the late 10th century at Fulda (Staatsbibliothek, Berlin) is another manuscript that clearly illustrates the strength of the early Carolingian tradition in the second half of the 10th century. The latter is almost indistinguishable in style from the Court School of Charlemagne, while in the Gero Codex there is a degree of simplification, a somewhat broader use of forms, an emphasis of essentials and the elimination of the at times rather fussy detail of Carolingian painting, as well as the use of a lighter, more chalky palette, which more clearly differentiates it from its Carolingian model.

The finest achievements of Ottonian illumination are connected with the patronage of Egbert, Archbishop of Trier (977–93), and the Imperial court. The origin of this interrelated series of manuscripts has long been connected with the Imperial monastery of Reichenau, believed to have been the seat of the chancellery of the Emperors, but it has been argued more recently that most of the manuscripts were produced at Trier. What is quite clear is that the scriptorium worked both for Egbert and for the Emperors Otto II (973–83), Otto III (996–1002), and even on until the reign of Henry II (1002–24), and that it should be seen first and foremost as an Imperial scriptorium.

One of the manuscripts of this closely interrelated group of masterpieces of illumination—a gospel lectionary which sets out the readings from the gospels throughout the liturgical year, known as the Egbert Codex (Stadtbibliothek, Trier; Cod. 24)—was certainly made for the personal use of Egbert. Born c950 in Flanders, Egbert was made Archbishop of Trier in 977 by Otto II after only one year as head of the German Imperial Chancellery. He had probably entered the Imperial household under Otto I and went to Italy with Otto II and Theophanu in 980. He attended the Diet at Verona in 983, and, after the death of Otto II in the same year, supported the claim of Henry the Wrangler to the regency during the infancy of Otto III, who was only three years old when his father died. Egbert returned to Germany, and in 985 made his peace with Theophanu who had succeeded in her ambition to assume the regency. But Egbert played no major part in politics thereafter.

Under Egbert's rule, Trier became a flourishing center for scholarship and the arts. The Egbert codex was produced certainly after 977—Egbert appears as an Archbishop on its dedication page—probably after 983, and before his death in 993. Both in style and iconography this codex is closely related to a number of manuscripts known as the "Liuthar group", named after the monk Liuthar. He is portrayed as the scribe in the gospels of Otto III, written between 997 and 1002, now in Munich (Bayerische Staatsbibliothek; Cod. 4453). The other major manuscripts of the group are the early-11th-century lectionary of Henry II (Bayerische Staatsbibliothek, Munich; Cod. 4452) and the Aachen Treasury Gospels, often attributed to the reign of Otto III (c1000), but more probably made for Otto II shortly before his death in 983.

This Imperial scriptorium drew on a combination of late antique and Byzantine influences. From the late antique tradition of northern Italy came the rich, atmospheric settings, the pale, delicate color, the loosely painted figure-style, and the architectural details—all characteristics also found in the so-called "Gregory Master", named after the *Registrum Gregorii* (Musée Condé, Chantilly) who worked for Egbert in Trier in the 980s. Byzantine illumination contributed new, post-Iconoclastic iconographic themes, and provided models for solid gold-leaf backgrounds, increasingly popular in Ottonian painting. An even stronger reliance on Byzantine tra-

The marriage at Cana-in-Galilee, from the Hitda Gospels; 29×22cm (11×9in); c1000–25; Landesbibliothek, Darmstadt

ditions, especially in the use of full and vivid brushwork, was found in the Cologne region, where the Gospels produced for the Abbess Hitda of Meschede (Landesbibliothek, Darmstadt; Cod. 1640) and the Sacramentary of St Gereon (Bibliothèque Nationale, Paris; Cod. Lat. 817) were produced in the early 11th century.

At the same time—indeed, already in Henry II's lectionary, but in an even more pronounced manner—in the somewhat later Bamberg Apocalypse (Staatliche Bibliothek, Bamberg; A1142) a hardening of forms occurs: a new insistence on flat color with a strict formal balance, not unrelated to the search for pattern and harmony as in architectural design, which enabled powerful and expressive images to be created. A similar emphasis on pattern, although very different in character, being based more on an almost metallic brilliance and jewel-like details, was developed in another scriptorium which also enjoyed the Imperial patronage of Henry II, at Regensburg, where outstanding manuscripts like the Sacramentary of Henry II (Bayerische Staatsbibliothek, Munich; Cod. 4456)

The Egbert Codex

The Egbert Codex, in the Stadtbibliothek, Trier, is a Gospel Lectionary—a service book with extracts from the New Testament arranged according to the liturgical year—and was written and lavishly illustrated *c*980 for Egbert, Archbishop of Trier from 977 until his death in 993.

In the opening folio are the dedication pages. On the right, the Archbishop is enthroned and the manuscript is handed to him by two smaller figures of monks named in the inscription as Keraldus and Heribertus "Augienses"—probably the scribe and the illuminator. There is a dedicatory verse on the facing page.

O Egbert, on taking this book full of divine teaching, fare thee well. And do thou, O fortunate "Augia", rejoice for evermore in the honor which the prelate pays thee.

Much controversy surrounds this book. Although the "Augia" of the inscriptions is usually accepted as referring to the monastery on the island of Reichenau in Lake Constance, it is by no means certain that the manuscript was produced there. It has been argued very cogently that it was created under Egbert's patronage in his city of Trier.

What is certain, however, is that it is not only among the finest illuminated manu-

◄ Otto II receiving homage from the four provinces of the Empire, the leaf after which the Gregory Master of the Egbert Codex is named; *c*983. Musée Condé, Chantilly

▲ The dedicatory verse of the Egbert Codex, folio 2r.; *c*980. Stadtbibliothek, Trier

scripts to survive from the early Middle ages, but also that the Egbert Codex itself and the late antique model on which it is based were immensely influential on a whole series of splendid manuscripts produced for the court in the time of the emperors Otto III (996–1002), Henry II (1002–24), and perhaps even Otto II (973–983).

The earliest related book is the Aachen Treasury Gospels (Domschatzkammer, Aachen), which may well have been produced as early as *c*980 for Otto II, or possibly for Otto III towards the end of the 10th century. If the Crucifixions in the two codices are compared—the unusual way the two thieves are crucified and the two soldiers throwing dice for Christ's cloak in the Egbert Codex reflecting the four small figures in the Aachen Gospels—they show that a similar model lies behind them. The same can be said for the Crucifixion scenes in the Otto III Gospels of *c*1000 and the Henry II Lectionary which can be dated to between 1002 and 1014 (both in the Staatsbibliothek, Munich), where in each case similarities exist. Take, for example, the figure of Stephaton with a spear, on the right of the cross: it looks very like the same figure in the Aachen Gospels; while the two figures of soldiers dicing seem to reflect a knowledge of the Egbert Codex rather than the Aachen book, and the thin border frame in the Otto III Gospels copies the Egbert borders precisely. No doubt the illuminators of the two later books knew both the earliest or the original prototype used for the Egbert Codex.

◄ The Crucifixion in the Aachen Treasury Gospels; c980 or c1000. Domschatzkammer, Aachen

Below left The Crucifixion in the Henry II Lectionary; 1002–14. Staatsbibliothek, Munich

► The Annunciation, an illumination in the Egbert Codex by the Gregory Master

▼ The Crucifixion in the Egbert Codex; c980. Stadtbibliothek, Trier

It is the Egbert Codex that reflects the early model most exactly. The use of the thin, red borders with lozenge-shaped gold ornament, and the whole concept of the painterly aerial perspective to be seen in the Egbert Codex, closely resembles one of those very rare survivals of illuminated late antique books, the Vatican Virgil, which dates from c AD 400. The earlier illuminations in the Egbert Codex, like the Annunciation on fol. 9v., have been attributed to an artist who has been called the "Gregory Master" after a superb leaf, once in a manuscript with the letters of St Gregory, dated 983, and now in the Musée Condé, Chantilly. It shows Otto II enthroned, in the same border and against the same softly painted infinity, and with a softly modeled figure so clearly in the late antique humanist tradition.

PETER LASKO

The Annunciation to the Shepherds, from the Bamberg Apocalypse;
c1020. Staatliche Bibliothek, Bamberg

and the lectionary of Abbess Uta of Niedermünster (Bayerische Staatsbibliothek, Munich; Cod. 13601) were written.

Towards the end of the Ottonian period, around the middle of the 11th century, both at Salzburg and at Echternach, hardened forms again dominate, but here solid figures almost sculptural in three-dimensional solidity contribute yet another important characteristic as source material for the beginnings of Romanesque style of the 12th century. Outstanding among these manuscripts is the so-called "Golden Gospels" of Henry III (The Escorial, near Madrid; Cod. Vetrinas 17) given to Speyer Cathedral, the burial church of his dynasty, painted at Echternach 1045–6, where there is also a strong dependence on the Carolingian traditions of the Tours school. At Salzburg, this "solid figure" style is much more profoundly influenced by middle Byzantine illumination, as can be seen in the lectionary from the library of the Archbishops of Salzburg (Bayerische Staatsbibliothek, Munich; Cod. 15713).

It is not surprising that during the Ottonian period, when art was so heavily dependent on both Imperial and aristocratic patronage, there should also have been major contributions in the luxury arts of goldsmiths' work and ivory carving.

It has been difficult to attribute surviving work to the reign of the founder of the dynasty, Henry I, but a splendid ivory casket survives in the monastery of St Servatius at Quedlinburg that may well have been donated by him. Not only was this monastery his favorite foundation, begun in 922, and where both the king and his wife were buried, but three ivory shrines were recorded in its treasury as early as the beginning of the 11th century, and it seems more than likely that the handsome casket was one of them. An inscription on its base records that a restoration of it was undertaken under Abbess Agnes (1184–1203) and it is clear that some parts of the rich silver-gilt foliate filigree were added to it then. But the remainder of the metalwork—especially the oblong cloisonné enamels—would fit better into the early 10th century. Similar enamels were employed in the middle of the 9th century on the Golden Altar of S. Ambrogio in Milan.

The figure carving of the single apostles under arcades also shows both strong links with Carolingian traditions—especially those of St-Gall c900—as well as the kind of thickening of form and more solid and somewhat more static treatment of figures characteristic of the transition from Carolingian to Ottonian styles at the beginning of the 10th century. More convincing still is the decoration of engraved snakes in the spandrels of the ivories in the Quedlinburg casket, now hidden under the metal mounts but revealed during a restoration, which can be compared to exactly similar decoration between arches in the Folchard Psalter, illuminated at St-Gall between 855 and 895.

During the reign of Otto I, material becomes more plentiful. In ivory-carving there is the more securely dated *antependium* (altar-frontal), commissioned by the Emperor for his new cathedral of Magdeburg begun in 955. Some 16 panels survive scattered in various museum collections and libraries reused as bookcovers. Among the surviving panels, (approximately 5 × 4½ in, 13 × 12 cm) most of which are decorated with scenes from Christ's ministry in the New Testament, there is a dedication scene (now in the Metropolitan Museum, New York), in which Otto is shown, attended by St Peter and probably St Mauritius, the patron saint of Magdeburg, presenting the model of the new church to Christ enthroned. The figures are stiff and massive against a pierced background of heavy pattern, probably originally set against gilt-bronze. The borders are broad, undecorated, and flat, and were probably intended to be covered by decorated metal framework. Although it is known that for the building itself at Magdeburg Italian materials like columns and marbles were imported, the style of these ivories is not difficult to see as one derived from northern Carolingian traditions. When attempting to locate the style to a particular region, however, a perennial problem of Ottonian art arises—especially when dealing with court commissions. Either craftsmen practiced their art while on the

Right: St Erhard celebrating The Mass, from the codex written for
Abbess Uta of Niedermünster; 1002–25.
Bayerische Staatsbibliothek, Munich

Otto I presents a model of Magdeburg Cathedral to Christ; ivory; height 14cm (5½in); c962–73. Metropolitan Museum, New York

move with the peripatetic Imperial court, or the Emperors gave their orders to the various abbeys patronized by them. In the end, it must be more important to discover in what kind of milieu artists formed their style, and what sources were available to them, rather than attempt to define the precise location of any given workshop.

In the case of one of the most important objects associated with Otto I, the great Imperial crown now in Vienna (Weltliche und Geistliche Schatzkammer), such an approach must lead to the conclusion that it is unlikely this masterpiece of the goldsmith's craft could have been made north of the Alps. The techniques of stone settings, and the large figurative cloisonné enamels found on four of the large eight panels hinged together to form the crown, have no antecedents in northern Europe. Only in Italy and in the Byzantine tradition could any craftsman have acquired these skills. It was also customary in the early Middle Ages for the Pope to provide the crown for Imperial coronations; no one would have been more deserving of special papal generosity than Otto who had come to the aid of the Holy Father in his struggle against the Lombard kings.

Was the crown, then, made for Otto I's Imperial coronation in Rome in 962? The internal evidence of the crown itself lends strong support to this attribution. The arch that now spans the crown from front to back bears an inscription giving the name of the Emperor Conrad, who was crowned in 1027. The arch is clearly an addition to the original, quite different

in style: the crown must therefore have been made for an earlier occasion. Yet another piece, now part of the crown, a small cross mounted rather awkwardly on the front, is by yet a different workshop, which can be paralleled in the court commissions of c980 and is most likely therefore to have been added for Otto II after his succession in 973—especially as Otto III was only three years old when his father died and only 16 when he assumed the Imperial title in 996: the crown is unusually large even for a fully grown man. There seems little doubt, then, that the crown was in its original form intended for Otto I in 962.

Although no exact parallel to the general form of the crown survives, it is true to say that large, figurative enamels with semicircular tops are found only on Byzantine crowns—like the 11th-century Byzantine crown of Constantine Monomachus, in the National Museum, Budapest.

An increasing interest in Byzantine fashions was clearly evident at the Ottonian court, especially after the marriage of Otto's son to the Byzantine princess Theophanu in 972. A large number of pieces of jewelry, including half-moon shaped earrings of pure Byzantine form and a lorum, a kind of breast ornament fashionable in Byzantine court dress, were found in Mainz in 1880 and named the "Gisela" treasure after the wife of the Emperor Conrad II, who died in 1043. The treasure may well have been lost or hidden in the 11th century, but the workmanship and the strong Byzantine connections make it far more likely that it had once belonged to a lady of the earlier Ottonian court, probably Theophanu herself. She and her husband, Otto II, are certainly shown in pure Byzantine court dress on an ivory panel (Musée Cluny, Paris), a close western copy of a Byzantine type of ivory. The Imperial pair are represented being crowned by Christ, exactly as on a panel on which Christ crowns the eastern Emperor Romanos and his consort Eudoxia (Cabinet des Médailles, Paris) probably carved in Constantinople between 959 and 963. Even the inscription on the Ottonian panel is for the most part in Greek.

Style, as well as fashion and iconography, fell under the spell of Byzantine art during the reign of Otto II. A superb, small panel (Castello Sforzesco, Milan) shows Christ in Majesty attended by St Mauritius and the Virgin with the Emperor to the left and Theophanu with her infant son on the right and the inscription below: "OTTO IMPERATOR". It was perhaps a gift from the Abbey of St Mauritius in Milan. Here the broad, massive forms, the flat relief, and the strict placing of the figure within a tightly drawn frame are all reminiscent of the style already seen on the Magdeburg antependium. But while the northern panels show a dry, linear treatment of drapery, the later panel has a smoother overlapping of folds, better understood modeling, and a far more subtle and sophisticated handling of relief—all derived from Byzantine models. The large, ivory situla (holy water bucket), now in the treasury of Milan Cathedral, with an inscription stating it was made for Archbishop Gotfredus of Milan (975–80) to be given to the Emperor during his visit to Milan, is from the same workshop.

Otto II and Theophanu being crowned by Christ; an ivory panel; 982/3. Musée Cluny, Paris

A reliquary statue of the Virgin and Child; gold sheet on wood; height 74cm (29in); late 10th century. Domschatzkammer, Essen

Once art at the court had been saturated by north Italian and Byzantine taste—neither Otto II nor Otto III spent much time north of the Alps—the influence of such work increased in aristocratic circles in Germany. Two workshops were created: one at Trier by Egbert, and another by Mathilde, granddaughter of Otto I at Essen, where she was Abbess from 973 until her death in 1011. A series of three gold altar crosses, decorated with precious stones and large cloisonné enamels, all given by her to the Abbey, are still to be seen in the Domschatzkammer, but the major masterpiece was the great three-quarter-life-size reliquary of the Virgin and Child, now in Essen Cathedral. Gold sheet nailed to the wooden core of the

seated figure, enameled eyes, and a jewel-studded halo decorated with filigree for the Christ child, enrich this astonishing cult-figure. She is sensitively modeled with fluid, broad flat forms, overlapping and sweeping across her figure, not unrelated to the Milanese ivories already mentioned. But there is something immature about her: the detail is not in complete harmony with the whole sculpture, perhaps because the more usual miniature scale of goldsmiths' work has here been enlarged to an almost life-size piece of freestanding sculpture.

At Trier, three fine pieces of goldsmiths' work survive of those commissioned by Archbishop Egbert; all are technically related to those produced at Essen, especially in the use of

Bernward's Column

Bronzecasting on a grand scale was the major achievement of Bishop Bernward of Hildesheim's art patronage. He was elected to his see in 993 after he had spent six years at the German Imperial court where he was tutor to the Empress Theophanu's son, later Emperor Otto III. Most of these years were spent in Italy, and the obvious inspiration for Bernward's column was the antique triumphal column set up by Trajan in Rome in AD 113—the most famous, and one that was certainly well-known to Bernward.

As Trajan's column tells the story of the Dacian wars, winding upwards, ending in the climax of the death of Decebalus under the walls of his capital, so Bernward's unwinds the story of the ministry of Christ from the Baptism in the River Jordan at the bottom, to the Entry into Jerusalem at the top. The story received its climax originally in the large crucifix mounted on the column, which was destroyed in 1544.

The column, cast by the *cire perdue* method in a single hollow piece, is nearly 13 ft (4 m) high, and stands alongside a great pair of bronze doors, 16 ft (5 m) high, decorated with 16 scenes from the Old and New Testaments. It is among the greatest technical achievements of the early Middle Ages. An inscription on the doors tells us that Bishop Bernward had them cast for his own foundation, the church of St Michael at Hildesheim, in 1015, and that Bishop Godehard of Hildesheim had them installed in the cathedral after Bernward's death in 1022.

The column, no doubt also made for St Michael's and in the same workshop, must be of much the same date. Most scholars have seen it as a more mature work, technically more difficult to cast, and have dated it later than the doors; some have even suggested that it was made after Bernward's death, towards the middle of the 11th century. Against this, the column is certainly an altogether less-well-finished work, both in the original modeling and in the chasing done after casting, and is more closely related in its iconography and its style to the earlier traditions of the Carolingian "Metz" School. The scene of the "Healing of the Blind Man", compared with the same scene on a Metz School ivory of *c*870 (Universitätsbibliothek, Würzburg; M.P. theol. fol. 65), shows a similar parallelism of the drapery and close grouping of the figures, and the same undulating ground on which they stand. On the doors, however, the handling of relief is much more complicated. The sculptors here are more adventurous: they release the upper parts of the figures from the background, and the heads and shoulders are often modeled fully in the round. Yet the hand that worked most of the relief on the column undoubtedly also worked on the doors.

It is not surprising that scholars have wanted to see a more mature and therefore later work in the column. The firm handling of relief, the harsh, uncompromising surface, and the sense of mass and weight achieved in its figure compositions, are qualities that laid the foundation for much that was to be fully exploited only in the Romanesque period—and perhaps especially in architectural stonecarving rather than in the usually more

Above The meeting of Adam and Eve, a panel of Bishop Bernward's bronze doors. Hildesheim Cathedral

▲ Christ healing the Blind Man, a scene on Bernward's column. Hildesheim Cathedral

▲ Christ healing the Blind Man, a scene from a Metz School ivory; *c*870. Universitäts-bibliothek, Würzburg

► St John, a detail from Bernward's column

efined arts of the metalworkers and ivory-
carvers. And yet the sources for the relief
tyle column are more obviously derivative,
ontinuing the well-established techniques of
he Carolingian tradition; in contrast the
loors are far more sophisticated and certain-
y more original. It would therefore seem
robable that the Bernward column is the
arlier work cast in the early years of the
11th century, and that the workshop,
erhaps with the addition of a more talented,
reative master, developed the more original
nd sophisticated style of the doors after the
column had been made.

PETER LASKO

▶ Bernward's column;
the capital was cast in
1871, but probably in
imitation of the original;
height almost 400cm
(157in). Hildesheim
Cathedral

▼ The bronze doors cast
for the church of St
Michael, Hildesheim;
height 500cm (197in).
Hildesheim Cathedral

cloisonné enamel of astonishing quality and precision. While the earliest of the altar crosses at Essen was made for Mathilde and her brother Otto, Duke of Bavaria, after 973 and before Otto's death in 982, the workshop at Trier was probably not very active until after Egbert settled there in 985. But one piece, and certainly the earliest, the staff reliquary of St Peter (now in Limburger Domschatz), is dated by inscription to 980. The full length of the staff is covered with gold foil decorated with relief busts (now badly damaged) of ten popes and ten archbishops of Trier, while the spherical knop is enriched with small enamels showing Evangelist symbols, four busts of Saints—St Peter among them—and the 12 Apostles. A second work, and the major surviving commission, is the Reliquary of the Sandal of St Andrew (Domschatzkammer, Trier). The large rectangular box, which served also as a portable altar, over 17 in (44 cm) long, has a fully three-dimensional foot covered in gold on top, decorated with a strap sandal set with gems, in imitation of the precious relic inside the box. Four very large cloisonné enamels with the symbols of the Evangelists are mounted in the sides and at both ends, while elaborate decoration of pierced gold repeat patterns, set off against red glass enriched with strings of small pearls, show in both technique and style very close relationships with Byzantine goldsmiths' work.

The third piece is smaller but of even more astonishing precision, and an unprecedented technical mastery of enameling which covers all its surfaces: the reliquary of the Holy Nail of the Crucifixion (Domschatzkammer, Trier).

The same workshop, or at least one of the masters trained there, must also have been responsible for a gold bookcover commissioned by the Regent, the Empress Theophanu, between 983 and 991. She is represented on it, along with her son Otto III, as well as a number of saints all closely connected with the Abbey of Echternach, near Trier. The central ivory panel with a crucifixion was inserted into the cover when it was reused for a new manuscript during the reign of Henry III in the middle of the 11th century. Such close collaboration between Egbert and Theophanu would only have been possible after their reconciliation in 985.

Another, and possibly somewhat earlier Imperial commission, the so-called Lothar Cross at Aachen (Domschatzkammer), cannot be attributed to either of these two outstanding workshops with any certainty, but the shape of the cross, set with filigree and gems and small strips of blue and white step-pattern enamels, relates it to the Essen series, and it may well have inspired them. On the reverse of the Lothar Cross, a superb engraving of the suffering Christ on the cross again reveals the strong dependence on Byzantine models in court circles.

The life-size wooden crucifix figure (Domschatzkammer, Cologne) believed to have been ordered by Archbishop Gero of Cologne (*ob.* 976) has often been compared to this engrav-

The Gero Crucifix; oak; height of Christ 186cm (73in).
Domschatzkammer, Cologne

ing, but the Gero Crucifix is a far more powerful image and perhaps the most seminal sculptural creation of the Ottonian period. Christ is suspended from the cross, arms strained, and the severely modeled head falls on to his right shoulder. The sagging body twists first one way, then the other, and the sharply drawn loincloth jaggedly contrasts with the softly modeled, almost swollen flesh. The thin, twisted legs below are no longer capable of bearing any of the massive weight of the straining body. The harshness of its conception was to be of considerable importance for the next two centuries, and it foreshadows many of the most powerful Romanesque sculptural achievements.

A growing awareness of sculpture, both on the miniature scale of ivory-carving and of larger work for church furnishings, including work in both bronze and stone, became increasingly important during the 11th century.

With the premature death of Otto III in 1002 the direct line of Ottonian emperors of the Saxon dynasty came to an end, and Henry II (1002–24), Duke of Bavaria, grandson of Otto I's brother Henry, was elected by the German nobles. In character, Henry was a very different man from his predecessors. At home in his native Saxony rather than in Italy, he enjoyed the chase, was a shrewd and practical politician with a passion for law and order, and a zealous reformer of the church. He had a reputation for piety which led eventually to his canonization in 1146. His gifts to the church were lavish, and the workshops assembled at the end of the 10th century, stimulated by contacts with Italy and the Byzantine tradition, were now fully employed north of the Alps for the first time. Among his gifts survive the Golden Altars for Aachen and for Basel (now Musée Cluny, Paris), the great pulpit for Aachen, the Reliquary of the Holy Cross for Bamberg (Reiche Kapelle, Munich), his favorite foundation, where there are four splendid vestments, including two great copes, with figure scenes embroidered in gold thread and appliqué work in deep purple silk. In goldsmiths' work, like the Golden Altar of Basel and the Aachen pulpit, sheer scale is unprecedented. The five great figures at Basel, under an arcade and the full height of the altar, are in high-relief sculpture with a sculptural presence not generally found in major stone sculpture until the end of the 11th century; the great pulpit seems to enlarge a bookcover to an almost heroic scale more than a yard in height. While gems are set on bookcovers, the pulpit has large crystal and semi-precious agate bowls mounted on it.

The outstanding contribution, however, to this new awareness of monumental scale and sculptural potential in church furnishings was made by the workshop created by St Bernward, Bishop of Hildesheim (993–1022). Early in his episcopacy, the workshop produced some very fine small-scale silver castings, including a pair of silver candlesticks, a crozier head made for Abbot Erkanbaldus of Fulda who was appointed in 996, and a small crucifix and Reliquary of very high quality made to contain relics of St Dionysius, acquired by Bernward in Paris in 1006 (all preserved in Hildesheimer Domschatz). After these early experiments in *cire perdue* casting, Bernward commissioned two major works: a hollow, cast bronze column nearly 13 ft (4 m) high which once supported a crucifix, and a pair of bronze doors nearly 16 ft (5 m) high for his foundation of the Abbey of St Michael, dated 1015. With these, sculptors took the first steps towards a new monumental art, without which the achievements in architectural sculpture of the late 11th and early 12th centuries would hardly have been possible.

PETER LASKO

Bibliography. Beckwith, J. *Early Medieval Art*, London (1964). Conant, K.J. *Carolingian and Romanesque Architecture: 800–1200*, Harmondsworth (1978). Dodwell, C.R. *Painting in Europe: 800–1200*, Harmondsworth (1971). Dodwell, C.R. and Turner, D.H. *Reichenau Reconsidered*, London (1965). Jantzen, H. *Ottonische Kunst*, Munich (1946). Kitzinger, E. *Early Medieval Art in the British Museum*, London (1969). Lasko, P. *Ars Sacra: 800–1200*, Harmondsworth (1973).

31

ROMANESQUE ART

The Ascension: detail of stained glass in Le Mans Cathedral; c1145 (see page 573)

R OMANESQUE art emerged during the 11th century and flourished in the 12th, giving way to Proto-Gothic or Gothic. No single country or region "invented" Romanesque art; the process of its creation was a slow one and took place almost simultaneously in Italy, France, Germany, and Spain. Greater political stability, economic growth, and the reform of religious institutions created conditions more favorable for the renewal of artistic activity than in the preceding period, when civilized life in Europe was threatened with extinction. The revival first took root in Germany (*see* Ottonian Art), which extended its rule over large parts of Italy. The decline of the Roman Church was halted by the revival of monastic life and discipline, led by the Abbey of Cluny in Burgundy which stood at the head of a network of dependent monasteries throughout Western Europe, and also by the reforming activity of the Papacy. At first, the interests of the Holy German Empire and the Papacy were complementary and their relations harmonious. But before long, the emperors and secular rulers in other countries could not accept the divided loyalties of their clergy, controlled from Rome, and bitter conflicts erupted which were to weaken Germany.

The triumphant Papacy extended its influence to the newly converted Scandinavian countries, and to Poland and Hungary. Wherever Rome established its influence, wherever monastic orders were founded, Romanesque art made its

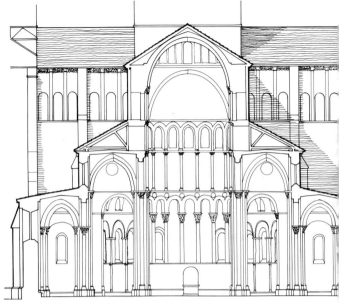

A transverse section of Cluny Abbey, looking towards the apse and ambulatory, as it was in the mid 12th century

appearance. Western Christianity, led by energetic popes, thriving monasteries, and pious rulers, entered a period of expansion. The Crusades and the reconquest of the Holy Land, Sicily, and the partial reconquest of Spain from the Moors started in the 11th century and opened new territories

Map of places mentioned in the text

in which Romanesque art could flourish. The emergence of Germany as a political power of the first order was soon followed by the revival of strong centralized power in France, although, for most of the 12th century, France was still divided into semi-independent units. The Norman rule in England, after the victory at Hastings in 1066, brought the British Isles into close contact with the rest of Europe and introduced Romanesque art there, chiefly, though not exclusively, from Normandy.

It is often said that Romanesque art was predominantly monastic, but this is only partly true. The revival of civilized life in Western Europe was chiefly due to the monastic communities emerging from a period of corruption and decline. In the early stages of this process, Cluny and its dependencies played a decisive role. The Benedictines were the most numerous and their influence was powerful. Many new orders came into being at this time—Carthusians, Premonstratensians, Cistercians, for example. The latter were to assume a leading role during the abbacy of St Bernard (ob. 1153), and had a profound influence on the art of the 12th century and on the emergence of Gothic architecture. Monastic orders were not only the centers of a religious revival but also of a revival of learning, letters, and the arts. By the 12th century, however, their leadership in the sphere of intellectual life had passed to schools and universities, and the blossoming of intellectual life that ensued has been rightly called the Twelfth Century Renaissance.

Romanesque art was an integral part of this revival, but our knowledge of the art of this period is very imperfect; it relies on the accidental survival of buildings and works of art, which are only a small part of what once existed. This is particularly true of England, where the deliberate destruction of the majority of the monastic churches and vast quantities of figural religious art during the Reformation was followed by the further ravages of the Puritans.

The term "Romanesque" art (in French l'art roman, in Italian arte romanico, in German romanische Kunst) is a comparatively modern creation, intended to indicate a style derived from Roman art but distinct from it. The English term "Norman", often used as synonymous with Romanesque, should be avoided, for not all Romanesque art in England was of Norman inspiration or due to Norman patronage. Roman sources for Romanesque art are undeniable, but there were also others: Early Christian, Byzantine, Carolingian, Ottonian, even Islamic. Moreover, each country or region blended Romanesque art with the local art of preceding ages, whether Christian or pagan, as, for instance, in Norway, where the Romanesque style absorbed many elements from Viking art. Because of this variety of sources, Romanesque art differs greatly from country to country and even from region to region. Nevertheless, there are certain underlying common tendencies in all Romanesque art which fully justify the use of the term "Romanesque style".

Architecture. The first result of the more settled conditions in Western Europe in the 11th century was a great improvement in building techniques and the planning of churches, which had to take account of the more elaborate liturgy that was being evolved, especially in the Cluniac order. During the 10th century, the stone used for building was predominantly unhewn rubble. In the 11th century, carefully wrought ashlar became almost the rule. In some regions, brick was preferred, as, for instance, in Sahagun in Spain, from which center the fashion for brick buildings spread widely, eventually reaching as far south as Toledo. This technique was popularized by the Arab builders settled among the Christians of northern Spain.

One of the preoccupations of masons during the Romanesque period was to reduce the risk of fire. Medieval chronicles are full of accounts of fires that destroyed or damaged churches. These churches were lit by candles, there was a considerable amount of wooden furniture and equipment, textiles were used for curtains and hangings, and ceilings were usually of timber, so the risk of fire was always great. The need to replace the ceiling by stone vaulting was therefore given priority. Experiments were carried out in many regions and were particularly energetic and fruitful in the Mediterranean countries, where Roman buildings provided inspiration and models. The vaulting of narrow spaces presented no great difficulty, so apses and aisles were the first to be vaulted. But gradually the vaulting of the nave was mastered as well. The dome also came into use.

The earliest experiments in vaulting were in a group of churches to which the name "First Romanesque" is given. The earliest of these churches were built in Lombardy at the end of the 9th century, but the greatest number of the buildings in this group date from the first half of the 11th century. The style of these distinct buildings spread from Lombardy along the Mediterranean coast west to Catalonia, through northern Italy to Dalmatia, north to Switzerland, and along the rivers Rhône and Rhine as far as the Low Countries. Apart from the characteristic external decoration, consisting of pilasters and corbel-tables in the form of small arcades under the eaves (called "Lombard arches"), these churches are most notable for their vaults which are either of the simple barrel (or tunnel) type, or groin vaults, a form well-known to the Romans and the result of intersecting two barrel vaults at right angles. The barrel vault was given a pointed section in some regions (for example, Burgundy and Provence), so the pressure of its weight does not cause supporting walls to be pushed outwards. The groin vault had the advantage of directing the stress to the four corners which could be suitably supported by heavy piers. A great step forward was the invention of the rib vault, an improved version of the groin vault with two arches placed at the intersection. By this method, the masonry between these arches, which no longer had any structural function, was reduced in weight, so that much wider spans could be covered by vaults. Rib vaulting was to revolutionize medieval architecture and led to the evolution of the Gothic style.

In their plans, large Romanesque churches followed the traditional basilican forms of naves with aisles, transepts, and apsidal choirs. But they differ from Early Christian basilicas in many respects—especially in the treatment of the two extremities, the choirs and the facades. The elaborate liturgy, which had developed over the ages, though notably during the monastic revival of the 11th century, required large choirs and numerous chapels. Side by side with this development went the increased cult of relics, displayed in shrines of precious materials placed in the choir and not, as in the past, in a dark, underground crypt. The architects' reaction to the spatial problems caused by these changes in religious practices was to design two basic types of choir. Both were spacious enough to allow large numbers of monks or secular clergy to participate in services and ceremonies, and vast crowds of the faithful to have access to the shrines and to take part in processions and other rituals. One of these types had staggered apses in the choir and the transepts, the other an ambulatory: an aisle encircling the apse from which chapels usually radiate. Extensive crypts were often built under such choirs for burials and as additional space for services.

Romanesque facades differed from those of the Early Christian churches just as much as did the choirs, and here the influence of Carolingian and Ottonian buildings was decisive. The western block, usually with twin towers, was adopted in many important churches, especially in Germany, France, and England, and the tradition continued during the Gothic period. In Italy, however, towers were frequently separate, isolated structures and the facades were usually "sectional": they consist of a wall that repeats the form of the interior. In other cases, as in S. Michele, Pavia, the facades extend upwards above the roof, as if pretending that the building behind is more extensive than it is in reality. Such screen-facades became particularly popular in Western France and England, and in the latter the tradition continued well into the Gothic period, producing such gigantic screen-facades as the one at Wells.

Whichever type of facade was used by Romanesque builders, it was always divided into smaller units by stringcourses, buttresses, and other means. Certain features are emphasized by moldings and sculpture; portals in particular were given a rich decoration. This division into units applies to interiors as well. Everything consists of units. The nave and aisles, the transepts and the choir are all made up of well-defined bays, each separated from its neighbor by piers or columns, by wall shafts, and by pilasters. This division is carried upwards into the vaulting by means of transverse arches, which, while strengthening the vault, also provide the customary division. Even in cases where barrel vaulting has no transverse arches, the division into bays is achieved by painted decoration. Within each bay, the elevation is also subdivided into a main arcade, a tribune, and a clerestory. Thus the whole building consists of the sum of its rhythmical parts, the proportions of which are determined by simple, mathematical relationships. Romanesque builders acquired their knowledge and art by experience and the study of older structures, especially

The pilgrimage church of Ste-Foy at Conques; 2nd half of 11th century

Roman, and they passed their craft from generation to generation, each trying to improve on previous achievements. In spite of common features, Romanesque buildings vary a great deal from country to country and from region to region, although certain types of churches, which are closely related, are found far apart. The so-called pilgrimage churches belong to this last group, the best-known being Ste-Foy at Conques, St-Sernin at Toulouse, and the cathedral of Santiago at Compostela.

Pilgrimages, which started during the Early Christian period out of the desire of the pious to visit and pray at the places associated with the life of Christ, the apostles, and other saints, developed during the Romanesque period into a well organized mass movement of thousands of pilgrims crossing Europe and the Near East in all directions and stopping at numerous famous shrines to pray. The most celebrated pilgrimage places were, of course, those in the Holy Land and Rome, but during the 11th century, the shrine of St James the Great in Santiago de Compostela in western Spain acquired almost equal fame. St James was the patron saint of the *Reconquista*, the holy war to free Spain from Arab rule, and pilgrimages to his reputed tomb were, in part at least, inspired by a pious zeal to be associated with this struggle. Along the routes to Santiago, the troubadours encouraged this spirit by their epic poems, of which the *Song of Roland* was based on the war of Charlemagne against the Moors. Special hospices were built along the pilgrims' routes, roads were improved, bridges repaired and built, and, above all, churches capable of holding large numbers of pilgrims sprang up along the principal roads used by them.

The pilgrimage churches are all of the ambulatory type and their transepts provided with aisles so the crowds had more room to circulate. All of them employ sculpture lavishly. One of the landmarks in Romanesque architecture was the rebuild ing of the Abbey of Cluny, which started in 1088. Until the rebuilding of St Peter's in Rome in the 16th century, it was the largest Christian building. In order to provide sufficient room for the resident and visiting monks, and for the vast congregations attracted to Cluny by its fame, the church was built with two transepts, each with apsidal chapels and each with a tower over its crossing. In addition, there was a further tower over each arm of the western transept. In front of the facade was a narthex flanked by twin towers. This massive building must have been an unforgettable sight, but all that remains of it today is the arm of the southwest transept; the rest was pulled down after the French Revolution.

Some of the self-evident features of Cluny—the pointed barrel vaulting, the fluted pilasters, and the pointed arches of the arcades—were imitated elsewhere. The double transept plan found only one follower, the Cluniac Priory at Lewes in England. However, on the whole, Cluny was too vast to have inspired close imitations. The majority of Cluniac churches followed, in the design of their churches, the example of churches in their own regions rather than that of the awe-

The elevation of the nave of Durham Cathedral; 1093–c1130

inspiring mother church in Burgundy.

Regional schools of Romanesque architecture are most distinct in the countries that lacked strong, central political power, like France and Italy. In England, the strong monarchy, imposed by military conquest, used the monasteries, which were filled with Norman monks, as one of the means of keeping the country under control. The Norman monks imported to England Romanesque architecture of the most advanced kind, for 11th-century Normandy witnessed a development in the field of architecture that ranked among the most progressive in Europe. The abbey churches at Bernay and Jumièges are the earliest surviving examples of those large and massive buildings. The two abbeys at Caen—one for the monks, St-Étienne, the other for the nuns, La Trinité—were founded by William the Conqueror and his wife. They, and a string of other major churches, set the pattern for the future development of Anglo-Norman architecture in England. With the great financial resources available to them in their new country, the Normans built on a far larger scale than in their own Duchy; Norwich Cathedral, for example, has no less than 14 bays. As in Normandy, Anglo-Norman churches were of the three-apse or ambulatory type and, in elevation, they usually have three stories: the main arcade, the tribunes, and the clerestory with a wall-passage for circulation at window level, a useful device for diminishing the weight of the wall and for the maintenance of the building. Jumièges, St-Étienne and La Trinité, Caen, and many other Norman churches, are notable for their two-towered facades, a scheme frequently followed in England, although in the later Romanesque churches screen-facades became popular.

The most famous of all Anglo-Norman buildings is Durham Cathedral (1093–c1130), which, in many of its features, followed the earlier Norman models (like Jumièges, for example, it has an alternating system of supports with cylindrical and compound piers) but introduced ribbed vaulting which had never before been used on such a scale. This type of vaulting was further experimented with in Normandy, and from there passed on to the Île-de-France (the royal domain round Paris) where it laid the foundations for Gothic architecture.

With the exception of a group of buildings in the West of England (Gloucester, Tewkesbury, Pershore) characterized by tall, heavy columns and four-story elevations, which can be considered as a local school, English Romanesque churches do not form regional types as in France or Italy. The most distinctive regional school of the French Romanesque, apart from Normandy, is the group of domed churches in Aquitaine—probably the result of influences from Cyprus.

Italian churches varied greatly in type. The Lombard school evolved from the "First Romanesque" and frequently employed exterior galleries and distinctive decorative sculpture. It had a wide influence in the whole of Europe from western France to Hungary and Poland. The metropolitan church of Scandinavia, Lund Cathedral, is a pure Lombard building.

The Tuscan Romanesque, with Pisa Cathedral, the Leaning Tower, and the Baptistery as the most famous examples, relies

Pisa Cathedral, begun in 1063, enlarged 1150–60, and the Leaning Tower, begun in 1174, completed in 1372

German Romanesque: the west end of the Abbey church of Maria Laach; 1093–1230

largely for effect on the multi-colored marbles and external galleries. Much of the detail is classical, deriving from Roman models. Venice and the Adriatic coastline were much affected by Byzantine influences. In the Norman kingdom of Sicily and southern Italy, a blending of many cultures took place, with considerable elements from Arab art, especially in the lavish decoration of buildings. In Spain, too, Arab influences affected Romanesque buildings.

Perhaps the most distinctive was Romanesque architecture in Germany, which emerged gradually out of the Ottonian style. Although Lombard exterior galleries were frequently employed, the character of German Romanesque churches is quite un-Italian. In their plans, the use of apsidal terminations at both the east and west ends of the buildings was frequent— as was also the employment of numerous towers, not only at the west end but over the transepts or flanking the choir. Especially impressive are the Imperial cathedrals of Speyer (with groin vaults over the nave, built before 1100), Mainz, and Worms.

From Early Christian times onwards, certain structures were built on round or polygonal plans—for instance, mausolea and baptisteries. One of the most venerated buildings of Christianity was the Holy Sepulcher in Jerusalem which became a model for endless imitation over the centuries. During the Romanesque period, many imitations (few actually resembling the Holy Sepulcher) were made and many of these were connected with the buildings of the military orders, set up in the Crusading Kingdom for the defence of the holy places and the protection of the pilgrims. These orders, the Templars and the Hospitalers, had many wealthy branches in the West and their churches are invariably centrally planned.

An important place in the architectural history of the Romanesque period is held by Cistercian buildings. Founded as a reaction against the worldly mode of life of the Cluniacs and the Benedictines, the Cistercians aimed at an austere life in isolation, away from towns and even villages. Their monasteries were to be self-sufficient in everything the soul and body needed. Their churches were simple in plan, rectangular, without towers, and without sculpture or painting. Their beauty lies in their simplicity and fine craftsmanship. The order was born in Burgundy, and, in spite of great animosity between the Cistercians and the Cluniacs, Cistercian builders adopted the pointed arch from Cluny. The newly emerging Gothic architecture was much to their liking because of its simple, logical structural qualities. The prodigious success and expansion of the Cistercians throughout Europe helped the expansion of the early Gothic style which they adopted. Unfortunately, many early Cistercian monasteries in Burgundy have perished, but Fontenay Abbey survives as an example of the Cistercian type of church, monastic buildings, workshops, and agricultural structures. In the early stages of their history, before they too became as worldly as the orders they aimed to replace, wherever the Cistercians built a monastery it was based on the standard type: Fontenay is an example.

Of secular Romanesque buildings, many town houses and public structures survive—usually in a much altered condition. Some monastic buildings, such as chapter houses, dormitories, and even kitchens, still exist. The most spectacular Romanesque kitchen in existence is at Fontevrault Abbey, built with great attention to the decorative use of stonework. In these monasteries, the most beautiful structure after the church was invariably the cloister, the place where the monks read, kept their books, and performed many of their allotted tasks. The cloisters of Silos Abbey in Spain and of Moissac Abbey in Languedoc in southern France are among the most spectacular buildings of this type (both c1100).

The castles of the period are more works of utility than beauty, but often, in their massive solidity and picturesque situation, they are a memorable sight. Some of the most inventive castles were built by the Normans, both in the Duchy and in England; they are credited with the invention of the keep, the towerlike structure within the defensive walls and moats. The greatest advances in castle-design were made by the Crusaders, who, under Byzantine influence, introduced curtain-walls incorporating defensive towers at frequent intervals.

The first Gothic building, the choir of St-Denis Abbey, (built 1140–4), started a new development in European architecture, at first confined to the Île-de-France and the adjoining regions. In many parts of France and the rest of Europe, the Romanesque style in building continued to be used until the

Norman castle-building: the keep of Hedingham Castle, Essex, England; 1130–52

end of the 12th century and even later. In contrast to the severity of the early development, this late phase was characterized by a complexity of forms and a richness of sculptural decoration. This Romanesque "Baroque" lost the vigor and inventiveness of the earlier works. It was the swan song of a style which, at its height, produced buildings that still rank among the great achievements of human culture.

Painting and glass. The interiors of Romanesque churches were, almost without exception, covered with plaster and then painted. Many of these churches were cleaned and their paint removed in the 19th century, as it was then believed that the beautifully cut ashlar was originally uncovered. In fact, it can be shown that, in some cases, walls were plastered and painted in imitation of ashlar blocks, as if the idea of an unpainted surface was repugnant to medieval men. Romanesque interiors, with their vast expanses of walls and comparatively small windows, provided far greater opportunities for painters than, say, Gothic interiors, in which walls were reduced to an absolute minimum and large windows took their place. This explains the blossoming of stained-glass painting in the Gothic period and its rather modest role in the 11th and 12th centuries.

By far the most durable technique of covering walls with decoration was that of mosaic. After the distintegration of the Carolingian Empire in the 9th century, this technique, requir-

The apse mosaics in S. Maria in Trastevere, Rome; 1140

ing costly materials and great skill, practically went out of use in Western Europe. It was revived at the celebrated monastery of Monte Cassino, the cradle of western monasticism, when it was being rebuilt by Abbot Desiderius (*ob.* 1087). He obtained the services of Greek craftsmen from Constantinople, and used them to decorate his church and to train local people, so that the craft would not be lost again. None of the mosaics by these Greek artists survive, but the example of Desiderius was followed in Rome, where two cycles were carried out: one in S. Clemente (1128) and the other in S. Maria in Trastevere (1140). Outside Rome, two centers are oustanding for their mosaic works—Sicily and Venice—and both imitate Byzantine models. The Norman Kings of Sicily, jealous of the splendors of Constantinople, sponsored a colossal scheme of decorating the churches under their patronage, and their palaces, with Byzantine-inspired mosaics: for example, Cefalù, Palermo, Monreale. Venice, whose power was based on trade with the East, was able to commission Greek artists to work in its territories, but simultaneously many local craftsmen acquired a mastery of Greek techniques and styles, and sometimes blended them with Romanesque forms.

Among the mosaics of St Mark's in Venice and those on the neighboring islands of Torcello and Murano, cycles survive dating from the 11th to the 14th centuries.

A related technique was that of making mosaic pavements, of which the most extensive examples also survive in Italy, at Otranto for example. Wall-painting as practiced during the Romanesque period included frescoes; this was frequently combined with other techniques such as *a secco* and tempera. Even in the best conditions, wall-paintings deteriorate with time, so they were usually replaced at one time or another, frequently by painting a new scheme on top of the old. Thus, the wall-paintings that now survive were often uncovered by painstakingly removing the later layers of paint. In all cases, what survives gives only a very imperfect idea of what must have been one of the most important branches of artistic production in the period.

As far as can be judged from the existing material, there was, unlike in Byzantium, no universally followed method of allocating subjects to any given place in the building. Generally speaking, the central apse was considered the most important part of the building, reserved for Christ, with subsidiary

Christ and the Adulteress: a wall-painting in S. Angelo in Formis, near Capua; late 11th century

apses frequently decorated with the figures of the Virgin Mary and the patron saint of the church, whoever he or she might be. The long stretches of the nave walls above the arcade were usually divided into bay units, each devoted to a scene from the Scriptures, Old and New Testament episodes on opposite walls. The west wall was frequently allocated to the Last Judgment.

One of the best-preserved cycles of wall-paintings is at the Abbey of S. Angelo in Formis near Capua, a dependency of Monte Cassino. These wall-paintings probably reflect, in a distant way, the now lost mosaics of the motherhouse, for they are strongly Byzantine in style and iconography. However, there seems little doubt that if the painters of S. Angelo in Formis were influenced by Byzantine art, they were also deeply indebted to late Roman illusionism with which they were familiar through the study of Early Christian wall-paintings in the old churches of Rome. But their figures are indisputably Romanesque in the linear, stylized treatment of the faces (especially the schematic hair) and the draperies. The paintings include the figure of Abbot Desiderius of Monte Cassino, shown with a square nimbus (signifying a person of

importance, still alive), a detail which makes it possible to date at least the earliest of these wall-paintings to before 1087, the date of Desiderius' death.

The Byzantine elements in these south Italian paintings are easily explained by the proximity of Monte Cassino. But in other parts of Europe, in Austria (Salzburg), France (Berzé-la-Ville), England (Canterbury, Winchester), and elsewhere, Romanesque painters were clearly aware of the Byzantine style and made use of it, modifying it in various ways. Their Byzantine models were presumably portable objects, such as illuminated books; in other cases they probably knew Byzantine art second-hand, from visiting Italy, especially Sicily. In some cases, they could have traveled through Constantinople on the way to the Holy Land and have seen Greek paintings. It is easy to see the difference between Romanesque painting affected by Byzantine art (as at Berzé-la-Ville), and that which was not (as at Tahull). In the former, there is a striving for naturalism in the way the folds of the draperies are used to emphasize the structure of the human body, and the highlights attempt to convey its three-dimensional quality and roundness of forms. Modeling is achieved not only by the use of high-

lights but also by many dynamic lines which help to define the shapes and postures of the figures, while other such lines are used merely as patterns in order to enrich the surface of the picture. This last feature is not Byzantine but Romanesque. Berzé-la-Ville is a small church near Cluny, belonging to it, and the place of rest for Abbot Hugh (*ob.* 1109), who built the great church at Cluny. As S. Angelo in Formis is thought to reflect the style of the lost mosaics of Monte Cassino, so the wall-paintings of Berzé are believed to reflect the style and quality of the frescoes that we know decorated the great church at Cluny.

In contrast to Berzé, the wall-paintings in the Catalan church of S. Clemente at Tahull (removed to the Museum of Catalan Art at Barcelona) are thoroughly Romanesque in style, without any attempt at Byzantine naturalism. They are linear, stylized in the extreme, and two-dimensional. The features are simplified and geometrical, the colors vivid and arbitrary. The whole is a powerful image, only distantly related to natural forms and proportions.

Not all Romanesque paintings were as uncompromising, but many share with Tahull the predilection for the simplification, almost geometrization, of human forms. This tendency towards abstraction, for changing natural forms almost into geometric patterns, was one of the features of Romanesque art as a whole.

In western France, a number of wall-paintings of the Romanesque period survive and illustrate well the great variety of styles that existed even in one geographical area. The most extensive of these are the wall-paintings at St-Savin-sur-Gartempe, where in one church it is possible to distinguish different styles because of the employment of a number of painters trained in somewhat different traditions.

Much better known than Romanesque wall-painting is the book-illumination of that period. Although here also the loss through destroyed libraries is heavy, a sufficient number of books exist to give us a much fuller picture of the development in this important field. Not all medieval books were illuminated: in fact only a small proportion of them were. In that age of intellectual curiosity, a great many texts were copied for their content only. Illuminations are found chiefly in books for liturgical use at special ceremonies and also in books intended as gifts to some highborn person. Some books depended on pictures as much as on the text, for instance the Bestiaries and Herbals. Not all books were illustrated in the same way in all countries. It became a custom in England to precede the text of the Psalter with full-page illustrations of episodes from the Gospels, although the pictures had nothing to do with the text.

In the past, it was assumed that all Romanesque illuminations were the work of monks, but today it is generally accepted that, in many cases, the illuminators were lay artists. It is of course true that most monasteries had their scriptoria,

Christ in Majesty, from the Bury Bible; 2nd quarter of 12th century. Corpus Christi College Library, Cambridge

where monks copied books and decorated them. But there are also numerous examples of books commissioned by monasteries from lay artists. One such book is the Bury Bible (Corpus Christi College Library, Cambridge) which, we know from a document, was executed by a secular master, Magister Hugo, for the Abbey of Bury St Edmunds. Two other celebrated books, the Eadwine Psalter (Trinity College Library, Cambridge) and the Dover Bible (Corpus Christi College Library, Cambridge) were written by a monk of Christ Church Cathedral in Canterbury, but illuminated by lay painters who are portrayed in the Dover Bible painting in an initial.

The Eadwine Psalter is a good example of the method of "copying". This book was one of three copies, made at different times, *c*1000, *c*1150, and *c*1200, from a Carolingian original, the Utrecht Psalter (University Library, Utrecht), which was at Canterbury from about the year 1000 until the Reformation. None is an exact copy, but the closest to the original is the earliest of the three. The Eadwine Psalter is

Wall-paintings from S. Clemente at Tahull; early 12th century. Museum of Catalan Art, Barcelona

thoroughly Romanesque in style, and follows the original only in iconography and layout. Thus copying was not slavish, but, on the contrary, the artist felt free to modify the model to the taste of the period.

As can be expected, Romanesque illumination evolved gradually from pre-Romanesque styles. In Germany, for example, the transition from the Ottonian style was a slow process. It is difficult to say precisely when the Ottonian style, based so strongly on Byzantine and Classical models, was abandoned in favor of the more decorative and linear Romanesque. Among the various regional styles or schools of illumination, those of Regensburg, Salzburg, and Cologne are the most distinctive. The Mosan region (the valley of the River Meuse in Belgium) was one of the most inventive artistic centers during the Romanesque period; some highly original books were produced there, in which Byzantine elements played an important part. The Italian illumination of the period is best known by the so-called gigantic Bibles, produced in Rome and Umbria, and the Exulted Rolls, a peculiarity of southern Italy. These were long parchment scrolls, with the text for the blessing of the paschal candle and its appropriate pictures; they were read from the pulpit, and unrolled for the congregation to see the pictures at the ceremony of the blessing of candles on the Saturday before Easter.

In France, there were several regional centers of book-illumination, Limoges, Normandy, and Burgundy among others. Unfortunately, little is known about the books produced at Cluny, for few manuscripts from there have survived. Those that do, however, show fairly close links with German illumination, both Ottonian and Romanesque. Burgundian manuscripts produced in Cistercian monasteries are better known. They include some striking books from the early 12th century, full of humor in depicting the occupations of the monks. In this respect, they are exceptional. Towards the

middle of the 12th century, the character of Cistercian illumination changed considerably under the influence of Byzantine models and in response to the austere directives of St Bernard.

The country that produced an astonishing number of masterpieces in the field of book-illumination was England, where the tradition of book-painting of the highest quality went back to the early Middle Ages. The Norman Conquest, and the resulting reorganization of the English Church and the great influx of Norman monks, introduced into England Norman forms of illumination. These consisted chiefly of "inhabited" initials, that is, initials made up of scrolls of conventional foliage in which human figures, animals, and monsters were entangled. Of the many centers producing books with such initials, the most prolific was at Canterbury. But the tradition of lavishly illuminated books with full-page pictures was revived *c*1120 with the St Albans Psalter (now in St Godehard, Hildesheim) made for a recluse, Christina, and followed by a number of other, equally rich books: the *Life of St Edmund* (Pierpont Morgan Library, New York), executed by one of the painters of the St Albans Psalter, for Bury St Edmunds, the Bury Bible by Magister Hugo, already mentioned, the Lambeth Bible, made at Canterbury, and many others.

The Bury Bible (*c*1140) is a manuscript of great importance. It contains a strong Byzantine element, which was increasingly to influence English painting in the 12th century. The vivid colors and considerable amount of gold give the book a lavish appearance. The figures are solid, and covered by clinging draperies, enriched with double-line patterns, which help to indicate the form of the bodies. This so-called damp-fold drapery is of Byzantine derivation, a device used by other painters in many other centers, notably at Canterbury (the Lambeth Bible, Lambeth Palace Library, London) and Winchester (the Winchester Psalter, British Library, London) where it was used with a passion for rich, dynamic patterns. Here the Byzantine forms were made truly Romanesque. But by *c*1170–80, this agitated style gave way to a softer, more naturalistic method of depicting the human figure. This new trend was not restricted to England alone, but was almost universal and was also present in media other than painting. This "classicizing" trend was due, once again, to a wave of Byzantine influences, partly from Sicily but also presumably by direct contacts with Greek art. A manuscript in which this Byzantine element is seen very strongly is the Winchester Bible (in Winchester Cathedral Library), a colossal book now bound in four volumes, which dates to *c*1180. A leaf by one of the painters of this famous work is in the Pierpont Morgan Library, New York (MS. 619), and it is thought that the wall-paintings in the Aragonese royal chapel at Sigena (damaged during the Spanish Civil War and now in the Museum of Catalan Art, Barcelona), are by the hand of this Winchester master, who was probably trained in Sicily.

This development away from the Romanesque style, imbued so strongly with classical elements absorbed from By-

An example of French Romanesque book-illumination: a monk cutting corn. Bibliothèque Municipale, Dijon

zantine art, is usually termed the Transitional or Proto-Gothic style.

Romanesque stained glass is stylistically closely related to wall-painting and book illumination. Its aesthetic effect is, of course, very different by the nature of the technique for the translucent colors of glass are more lively, especially if seen against strong outside light. The technique of glass-painting is described in the celebrated artists' manual *De Diversis Artibus*, written *c*1100 by a monk who wished to remain anonymous, and who signed his work with a pseudonym, Theophilus. The design of the glass panel was made on a flat surface and pieces of glass of appropriate colors were then cut to shape. On these were painted, with enamel colors, the details of the draperies, the faces, the hands, or whatever was required; these painted pieces were fired so the colors would fuse with the glass. The pieces were then put on the flat surface and joined with strips of lead; these formed an important part of the design, providing black outlines and accents. In spite of the use of highlights for modeling the figures in early Romanesque glass, they appear very flat and highly stylized (for example, the head of Christ from Wissembourg in Alsace, now in Strasbourg; late 11th century). The figures were large and hieratic, and there was a predilection for much ornamental detail (for example, the Prophets in Augsburg Cathedral; *c*1135).

France was renowned for its glass during the Romanesque period, and, not surprisingly, most of the surviving glass is found there. Not all this glass was made by Frenchmen: the glass preserved at Châlons-sur-Marne Cathedral was executed *c*1150 by Mosan artists. The person who stimulated the development of stained glass in France was Abbot Suger of St-Denis, but unfortunately much of this glass was destroyed or dispersed during the French Revolution. His famous Tree of Jesse window started the fashion for this iconography in which Christ's descent from the line of Jewish kings was represented. This composition in glass was, for instance, repeated in Chartres Cathedral, in York Minster, and many other places. Closely connected with the styles of the local schools of book illuminations is the glass in Le Mans, Angers, and Poitiers. But gradually the monumental and hieratic style of the early Romanesque glass was replaced by a more agitated, narrative type of painting, in which the scenes were small, and contained in roundels with decorative borders. As in other media, the Transitional style of Byzantine inspiration also dominated the late-12th-century production of glass everywhere, paving the way for the stylistic changes that took place in the 13th century with the triumph of Gothic.

Sculpture. The revival of sculpture after the period of neglect during the 10th century was due, in the first place, to Ottonian art. But Ottonian sculptors were chiefly concerned with sculpture in the round, such as cult-images and church furnishings

Paintings on a leaf by one of the Winchester Bible artists; late 12th century. Pierpont Morgan Library, New York (*see* Ottonian Art). The architectural sculpture of the Ottonian period was negligible. One of the great merits of the Romanesque period was the revival of sculpture in stone which formed part of a building; in this field, the achievements were truly astonishing.

The beginnings of this development were modest, tentative, and experimental. There were enough craftsmen in different countries during the 11th century, who were presumably masters in several media and who were capable of carving, when required, such objects as altar frontals (though these were usually made of precious metals), bishops' thrones, screens, and tombs. The first tomb with an effigy, since Classical times, was that of Abbot Isarn (*ob.* 1048) of St-Victor at Marseilles, and it is not surprising that it was based on a Roman model. The next surviving one is that of Rudolf of Swabia who died in battle in 1080 and was buried in Merseburg Cathedral. This time the tomb was cast in bronze, a technique German craftsmen were more familiar with than carving in stone.

It was one thing to carve an isolated object which was then set up inside a church, and quite another to work side by side with a team of masons decorating selected features of a building. It was from the close collaboration between a sculptor and an architect that truly Romanesque sculpture was born, and achievements in monumental sculpture became possible. At its best, Romanesque sculpture is an organic part of the building of which it forms a part. The collaboration between the carver and the builder led to a mutual understanding of problems and difficulties, and resulted in happy solutions.

At first, sculpture was presumably commissioned from sculptors working near quarries, so there was hardly any need for the sculptor even to see the building for which his work was intended. The celebrated marble lintel over the west doorway of the Abbey of St-Genis-des-Fontaines (dated 1019–20) in the Roussillon region on the French side of the Pyrenees could well be a work of this type, for it is inserted into the facade without in any way being integrated into its design. The carving is flat, in two planes, with arbitrary forms, executed in the so-called chip-carved technique. The subject is Christ in Majesty enthroned between two angels and six apostles. Chip-carving was practiced in many periods, but in this case it was probably inspired by works in Islamic Spain. However, Arab art was predominantly nonfigurative; the St-Genis-des-Fontaines' carver could well have had in front of him an Ottonian ivory as a model for the composition and, above all, for the facial types. In the same region, there are related but later works, a lintel at St-André-de-Sorrède, a cross, set above the doorway, at Arles-sur-Tech, and, on the Catalan side of the Pyrenees, a series of capitals at S. Pedro de Roda. This regional development was the first sign of the intensive sculptural activity that was to blossom in the last two decades of the 11th century. Its chief center was Toulouse.

The collegiate church of St-Sernin at Toulouse has already been mentioned as one of the "pilgrimage churches". Its earliest sculptures consisted of interior capitals and a portal known as the Porte des Comtes, with "historiated", that is to

Christ in Majesty: a relief by Gilduinus in the choir of St-Sernin, Toulouse; c1090

say, narrative capitals and sculptured figures in niches, flanking the portal. Around 1090, a remarkable sculptor called Gilduinus took over, first producing a marble altar, and then carving a number of capitals in the interior and seven large reliefs which were probably part of the screen. One of these is Christ in Majesty, still a timid work. The sculptor must have used a work in metal or ivory as a model, and enlarged it in marble. The relief is flat and the draperies indicated by double lines. Yet the composition is powerful in its simplicity. In other reliefs, Gilduinus tried to introduce a different, more naturalistic type of drapery, clearly imitating Roman sculpture, of which the district still has numerous examples. The work of Gilduinus and his workshop at Toulouse must have been much admired, for the rich and powerful Cluniac Abbey at Moissac obtained the services of sculptors trained by Gilduinus. To them we owe the beautiful cloister with its wealth of capitals and marble plaques on cloister piers. An inscription tells us it was finished in 1100. The rapid evolution of the style initiated by Gilduinus at St-Sernin can be seen in a doorway there, known as the Porte Miégeville (of before 1118), which repeats the arrangement of the earlier Porte des Comtes, with the addition of a tympanum and lintel representing the Ascension of Christ. The portal is recessed by two orders: arches and columns; as time went on, the number of orders in a portal increased, providing a rich frame for the entrance, and leading the eye by gradual stages into the interior. The style of the Porte Miégeville is more lively, the relief more pronounced, and the details more decorative than the earlier works of Gilduinus. It is at this stage that the sculptors from Toulouse must have moved to the principal pilgrimage church, Santiago de Compostela, where they worked on the transept portals of the cathedral. A similar style is also found in two portals of S. Isidoro at Leon, at Jaca, and at other places on or near the route to Santiago. If we were to use the term "pilgrimage sculpture", it would be for this series of works.

The extraordinary blossoming of sculpture in Toulouse and elsewhere was largely due to the collaboration of the craftsmen, who, in the 11th century, worked in many media, chiefly making church furnishings, with the masons on a building site. As sculpture was increasingly in demand for decorating buildings, the craftsmen began to specialize more and more in stone sculpture—but they did not always become members of the masons' teams. This can be demonstrated in many regions where similar types of buildings do not necessarily contain similar types of sculpture; on the contrary, very different buildings incorporate sculpture by the same sculptors.

Languedoc, with Toulouse as its main center, was one of the many regions of Europe where, at the close of the 11th century, a veritable school of sculpture arose. Burgundy was another important region where, out of modest beginnings in the 11th century, a flourishing school of sculpture developed. This can be seen, for instance, in the series of capitals in the crypt of St-Bénigne Abbey at Dijon (before 1018). The center where most important innovations were made, was, not surprisingly, Cluny Abbey. Here, at the close of the 11th century, the new church was adorned with a series of capitals in the ambulatory, now in the Musée du Farinier, Cluny, which are as refined in their execution as in their iconography. The crisp, delicate forms of the acanthus leaves and the figures show a complete mastery of the stone-carving technique. The subjects represented on these capitals include the Seasons, the Virtues, and the Tones of the Gregorian chant, personified by musicians playing various instruments. The main portal of the abbey is known from drawings made before its destruction and from a few fragments. It had a majestic tympanum, with Christ surrounded by the symbols of the Evangelists and seated in a mandorla supported by two angels. As on the portals of St-Sernin at Toulouse, there were flanking figures in the spandrels of the square frame (of Arab derivation) and, in addition, there were carved archivolts around the tympanum.

The sculptural workshop of Cluny must have attracted the best talent of the region. Once the work in the abbey was completed, the sculptors dispersed over the whole of Burgundy to produce some of the greatest masterpieces of Romanesque sculpture. The two most talented masters were Gislebertus, whose name is recorded in an inscription at Autun, and the unknown author of the tympanum at Vézelay. The fame of Gislebertus rests on a series of interior, historiated capitals, and the two large tympana at Autun. The style of the master of the Vézelay tympanum is more dynamic than that of his rival's at Autun, and more akin to the wall-paintings at Berzé-la-Ville. The innovation in their portals (c1130) was the use of the *trumeau*, a supporting pillar in the center of the doorway, technically essential because of the great size of the tympana employed by them. Such large tympana had to be carved on several slabs joined together; although they rested on strong lintels, the weight of the whole work required additional support. This provided sculptors with the welcome opportunity of extending the sculptural program by carving additional reliefs on *trumeaux*—the statue of St Lazarus, the patron saint of the church, at Autun (destroyed in the 18th century and replaced in the next) and that of John the Baptist at Vézelay. Moreover, at Vézelay there are additional pairs of figures of apostles flanking the doorway on either side. At both Autun and Vézelay, the west facade also included two lateral portals of a smaller size.

Contemporary with, or even a little earlier than, these two major works was the portal of Moissac (c1125) with its gigantic tympanum representing the Apocalyptic vision of the Second Coming: Christ, the austere Judge, in the center flanked by two angels, the symbols of the Evangelists, and the 24 Elders of the Apocalypse. Below, on the *trumeau*, there are fierce beasts and, fitting skillfully into the sides of the *trumeau*, are the elongated figures of Jeremiah and St Paul. On the jambs on either side are the figures of St Peter and Isaiah. The portal is within a shallow porch, and here the sculptor took advantage of the opportunity to cover the side walls with narrative reliefs. Portal sculpture, so modestly initiated 100 years earlier at St-Genis-des-Fontaines, had developed into a complex and extensive program of decoration. The Moissac tympanum is a work of great power and beauty that ranks among the masterpieces of human artistic achievement. It expresses forcefully medieval man's piety, and his fear of the severe judgment that awaits the sinner. Although the tympanum or the *trumeau* are unified works in themselves, the individual parts of the portal and porch are not fully integrated into an harmonious whole. As with the bay system of a Romanesque interior, these are still individual units. True unity in portal decoration was not achieved until the portals of St-Denis Abbey were created a short time later.

In the meantime, Romanesque sculpture had made parallel advances in many parts of Europe. In Spain, a similar development to that in Languedoc was taking place. The cloister of Silos Abbey is contemporary with the cloister of Moissac. Its capitals have the delicacy and refinement akin to that found in

The Burgundian School of Sculpture

The beginnings of the Burgundian School of sculpture are linked with the rebuilding of Cluny Abbey, the motherhouse of a vast and influential monastic order. Work on the huge building, to be the largest in Christendom, was started in 1088, and the consecration of the finished church took place in 1130. Only a small portion of this structure survives, but eight capitals from the ambulatory are preserved (in the Musée du Farinier, Cluny) and excavations have brought to light numerous carved fragments from various parts of the building. These include the majestic west portal, recorded by drawings and engravings before its destruction.

Cluny sculpture is of great refinement; the acanthus of the Corinthianesque capitals imitates the best Classical models, the figures are modeled with delicacy, the draperies are rendered by rhythmical incised lines, while the contours are agitated, expressing a dynamic mood. The subject matter of the capitals is allegorical, and includes the Tones of the Gregorian chant, the Seasons, and the Virtues.

On the great portal was the Apocalyptic Vision of Christ between the symbols of the Evangelists, the Elders of the Apocalypse, and the angels. There were originally many hundreds of carved capitals in the church, and altar frontals, tombs, screens, and many other furnishings and embellishments in marble, stone, and wood, which must have occupied a large team of sculptors until, c1120, many of them moved to other building sites throughout Burgundy and beyond.

The great sculptor who carved the ambulatory capitals at Cluny found employment in the pilgrimage church of St Mary Magdalen at Vézelay, where he produced

◄ A Corinthianesque capital, of the Four Rivers of Paradise, from Cluny Abbey; late 11th–early 12th century. Musée du Farinier, Cluny

▼ The figure of Eve from the lintel of the transept portal of Autun Cathedral; height 70cm (28in); 12th century. Musée Rolin, Autun

▲ The tympanum of the Last Judgment at Autun Cathedral by Gislebertus; c1120–30

two side-tympana, though the greatest glory of this church is the central portal with the Mission of the Apostles on its tympanum, the expressive work of a sculptor who was no doubt trained at Cluny. Some of the nave capitals at Vézelay by this sculptor faithfully repeat the designs first used at Cluny.

The portal of Vézelay holds an important place in the development of sculpture, for here figure-sculpture was applied not only to the tympanum but also to its supporting pillar or *trumeau*, and to the door-jambs, thus taking a step towards the "royal portals" of the Gothic period, in which rows of column-figures flank the portal.

Another great sculptor, also trained at Cluny, was Gislebertus, whose chief works survive in the cathedral of St Lazarus at Autun, another popular pilgrimage church in Burgundy. From c1120, for ten years or more, he carved, practically single-handed, the narrative capitals inside the church and the two portals (both with *trumeaux*), one in the north transept, and now largely destroyed, and the gigantic west portal with the Last Judgment on its tympanum. This is a work of great expressive power and feeling, executed in bold, arbitrary forms, visionary rather than naturalistic. The Eve from the transept portal is, in contrast, a work of great tenderness and almost sensuality.

Numerous other buildings throughout Burgundy were decorated with sculpture showing the influence of the style initiated at Cluny and thus deserving to be called a School. There are considerable differences

etween individual works, and yet they share
nough common characteristics of style and
ubject matter to be instantly recognized as
aving been created in Burgundy.

Towards the middle of the 12th century, a
ew, even more agitated style had begun to
ominate Burgundian sculpture (seen, for
xample, at Charlieu and St-Julien de Jonzy).
Works in this style rely on contrasts of light
nd shade and on expressions and poses
erging on caricature.

Burgundy had a widespread influence on
Lomanesque sculpture not only in other
egions of France but also beyond its borders,
or instance in Spain and England. More
mportant, however, was the impact of the
urgundian style and portal decoration on
te early Gothic sculpture of the Île-de-
rance.

GEORGE ZARNECKI

The central portal
mpanum of the
Mission of the Apostles
St Mary Magdalen,
ézelay; c1130

▶ An example of the
later, more agitated
style: a tympanum at
Charlieu Abbey; mid
12th century

Christ on the journey to Emmaus; a relief in Silos Abbey, Spain; late 11th century

Islamic ivory works from Cordoba; it is possible that Arab craftsmen were employed there. As at Moissac, the piers of the cloister are decorated with carved plaques: not with the single figures that are found at Moissac, but with narrative scenes, like the Journey to Emmaus, in which Christ is represented as a pilgrim to Santiago with the shell, the emblem of St James, on his crib. Some scholars believe that in the early stages of its development Romanesque sculpture in Spain anticipated by a decade or two many of the features of French sculpture. Whatever the truth of such claims, it is a fact that Spanish sculptors were highly original throughout this period, and that Spain possesses some of the most spectacular of Romanesque sculptures.

Italy, as can be expected from a country so rich in Classical remains, developed a number of regional schools in which the influence of Roman sculpture was very marked. The marble throne in S. Nicola at Bari, an important pilgrimage center for the cult of St Nicholas, is a late-11th-century work of extraordinary naturalism, based on some Roman models. This throne is one of a series surviving in Apulia and Campania. There, as in Languedoc at precisely the same time, marble carvers were put on building sites to decorate portals and other architectural details of buildings. These thrones are invariably supported by lions, elephants, or human Atlas figures, and it is not surprising to find similar supports employed under the columns in portals. One such portal, perhaps the earliest (before 1105), is found in S. Nicola, where lions support the freestanding portal columns, an Italian revival of this Classical motif. Such portals, with columns standing some distance in front of them, eventually developed into large porches as in Modena Cathedral, Ferrara Cathedral, and in many others. Their echo is found in the transept porches of Chartres in the 13th century.

Two Italian Romanesque sculptors stand out by the individuality of their styles: Wiligelmo and Niccolò. The first was responsible for the decoration of Modena Cathedral (c1099–1120) and stands at the beginning of the school of sculpture in Emilia; the second was active c1120–50 at several places, but his most mature works are in Ferrara and Verona. Wiligelmo was a powerful, expressive sculptor, deeply indebted to Antiquity. Niccolò was more lyrical in mood and softer in modeling his figures. His late portals include a feature that was only hinted at by Wiligelmo: figures carved on door-jambs. This method was only one step from the Proto-Gothic portals of St-Denis.

The most influential of all regional schools of sculpture in Italy was that of Lombardy, characterized by the exuberant decoration of portals, windows, capitals, and, at times, whole facades (as at S. Michele, Pavia) with interlaces, foliage, animals, and monsters intermingling with occasional religious motifs. It was obviously because of the almost light-hearted, playful character of this decoration that it found numerous followers in other parts of Italy, and, above all, in Germany, the Scandinavian countries, Hungary, and Poland. A group of late-12th-century churches in Russia also shows a distant influence from this sculpture. Romanesque churches in Tuscany relied for their decoration as much on marble inlays as on sculpture. Pisa was an important center where, in the third quarter of the century, the master Guglielmo was active. His style is related to that of the school of Provence where the facades of St-Gilles Abbey and St-Trophime, Arles, are the most outstanding monuments (third quarter of the 12th century), and were inspired by Roman architecture and sculpture. In those facades, portals are flanked by statues in niches, Roman fashion, and the lintels extend beyond the portal to form a frieze, again an imitation of Roman friezes on triumphal arches. These Provençal works not only show a strong stylistic link with Italy, but also with Burgundy and other French schools. Artists traveled a great deal and accepted

The facade of Notre-Dame-La-Grande at Poitiers; mid 12th century

commissions in places far apart, transmitting the style of one region, and even from one country, to another. A sculptor known in literature as the Master of Cabestany, whose works are found in Catalonia, Roussillon, and in Tuscany, is a good example.

One of the most prolific regional schools was that of western France, embracing Poitou, Saintonge, and Angoumois, and extending even beyond those provinces. The original inspiration for the style and type of decoration probably came from Lombardy and Languedoc, but in their exuberance the churches of this school surpassed even Lombardy. The sculptors have used every known method of decoration, lavishing it on capitals, portals (which avoid tympana), niches (frequently with tympana), friezes, and corbel-tables, and at times even covering whole wall surfaces with sculpture. In the earlier

stages of its development, the school was characterized by the very rich archivolts of the portals, niches, and windows, carved radially with small, repetitive motifs, as, for example, in Notre-Dame-la-Grande at Poitiers. This method was comparatively easy and effective and it was adopted in Spain and England with great enthusiasm. In England, especially, radiating voussoirs became a favorite form for the decoration of arches, and remained so throughout the 12th century, long after the fashion for them in their country of origin had died out.

The new method of decorating arches in western France was invented in the third decade of the 12th century. Ultimately, it was of far greater importance, for it was adopted in Gothic portal sculpture. This new method was evolved out of the dissatisfaction with radiating voussoirs, which allowed only small-scale sculpture. The sculptors, therefore, began to carve figures along the curve of the arch, thus increasing their length. The method had one disadvantage. Arches are formed of small segmental voussoirs; to carve a large figure on them necessitated using four, five, or more voussoirs for the purpose. To achieve a perfect fit for the various pieces, great sculptural technical virtuosity was needed and achieved. The figures on the arches carved in this technique are usually of the Virtues and Vices, the Wise and Foolish Virgins, and of angels; in the apex, there is often, carved vertically, the Agnus Dei and a bust of Christ. This change from the purely decorative sculpture of the previous method to more meaningful, symbolic or narrative themes was perhaps the result of the increasing influence of the Cistercians and especially of St Bernard. At precisely the time when the change in the character of west French sculpture was taking place, St Bernard wrote his famous indictment of frivolous subjects in art. It is true that the great Cistercian chiefly objected to the use of luxurious art objects in monastic houses, but he also criticized grotesque subjects in sculpture because, as he put it, "we are more tempted to read in the marble than in our books".

Romanesque sculpture in England was, generally speaking, of the kind that was so offensive to St Bernard. Even before the political union with Aquitaine under Henry II, when the influence of western French sculpture became prevalent, the sculpture used in Anglo-Norman churches was predominantly decorative, using all kinds of grotesque motifs similar to those found in the contemporary "inhabited" initials in illuminated books. The capitals in the crypt of Canterbury Cathedral, built c1100, are an admirable example of this, and it is, in fact, possible to find numerous close parallels in subject matter and in style to these capitals in initials painted at Canterbury at that time. The similarity of the two is in many cases so striking that it is quite possible the painters and the sculptors were the same people. The likelihood of this is further suggested by a documented case of the artist Magister Hugo who obviously practiced several techniques—book-illumination, casting in bronze, and the carving of large figures.

The sources of the English sculpture of the period were varied. Of foreign influences, those from Lombardy and the west of France were the most widespread. But English sculptors were, nevertheless, faithful to local traditions and of these, the Winchester School style and the Viking animal styles were the most persistent (see Anglo-Saxon Art and Viking Art). On the whole, English Romanesque sculpture is not monumental, but employs small-scale delicate ornamentation of every kind. In no other part of Europe did geometric patterns enjoy greater popularity than in this sculpture. Religious themes were rare except on screens (of which there are several fragmentary remains, for example at Chichester and Durham Cathedrals), and their presence on doorways usually signifies foreign inspiration (for example, Ely from Lombardy and Burgundy, Malmesbury from Languedoc and western France). One of the few schools of sculpture with a clear geographical boundary and an individual style was what is called the Herefordshire School. It flourished c1130–60 in the west of England: its principal monuments are at Shobdon and Kilpeck. The latter contains one of the best preserved village churches in the country from the Romanesque period, and is lavishly decorated both inside and out. It can be shown that the origin of this school was due to the pilgrimage of a local patron to Santiago, accompanied by the principal sculptor of the School. This sculptor must have made numerous sketches of decorative schemes on churches he visited, and he and his assistants used these as models for work on many buildings over a number of years.

In Germany and the territories under German influence, Romanesque sculpture falls more clearly than elsewhere into two categories. Architectural sculpture was strongly influenced by Italy, a fact easily explained by the German political involvement in Italy; but in the sculpture of cult-images and church furnishings, such as fonts, screens, and lecterns, German sculptors followed local traditions, mainly from Ottonian art. This type of sculpture was stylistically close to contemporary metalwork and ivory-carving; it is possible that, as in England, many craftsmen worked in all these media throughout the Romanesque period.

Of the newly converted Christian countries, the most original contribution to Romanesque sculpture was made by Norway. There, timber remained the favorite building material for a long time. The Norwegian stave churches, as a rule, were provided with carved portals of great richness, in which Romanesque motifs were modified by the survival of Viking animal forms—mainly large dragons, whose bodies are carved the whole height of the portal, one on each side and interlaced with stems of complicated foliage design. These carvings are fairly flat, but crisp and dynamic. Religious motifs are practically unknown. The spirit of this art is still entirely Viking.

It is no exaggeration to say that the course of European sculpture north of the Alps was influenced by one single building and one person. The building was St-Denis Abbey, and the person was its Abbot, Suger.

The rebuilding of the abbey involved the addition of the western block, carried out 1137–40, and the new choir, 1140–4. The western block consists of a narthex between two towers and the three portals. In his fairly detailed account of the work carried out on his initiative and under his guidance, Suger tells us very little about the portals—but this is consistent with other medieval writings, which, while describing works in precious materials, are usually silent about stone sculpture. Suger was a cultivated and much traveled man; this must have made him conscious that, by contemporary standards, the Abbey under his charge was old-fashioned. He resolved, therefore, not only to improve it, but to make his Abbey more impressive and more lavish than any he had seen. For this purpose he assembled the best craftsmen from many regions, and it seems that, among his sculptors were men from Languedoc and western France, and possibly even an Italian. Of the three portals of the west front, one had a mosaic tympanum which certainly suggests some Italian participation in the work. The portals as they exist today are but a sad remnant of the original work, but drawings exist of the statues that were destroyed during the French Revolution.

The central doorway has the scene of the Last Judgment on the tympanum (with Suger prostrate at Christ's feet) and there was an inscription (quoted in Suger's account of the work) on the lintel. The lintel and the *trumeau* no longer exist. Surrounding the tympanum are four archivolts with the Elders of the Apocalypse and other figures carved along the curve of the archivolts. Suger must have seen this new method of carving arches in Aquitaine when he went there to arrange the marriage of King Louis VII with Eleanor, the heiress to the Dukedom. The door-jambs either side of the entrance are carved with the Wise and Foolish Virgins, a subject favored in western France, but the actual arrangement of the figures under the arches is taken from Wiligelmo's portal at Modena. What was, however, entirely novel (but is now destroyed) was the use of so-called column-figures, four on either side. They were less than life-size and were statues in the round projecting from the colonette of the portal and carved from the same block of stone. This was a logical development of what had been done at Moissac or Vézelay, where large figures flank the portals without being incorporated into them. The sculptor Niccolò made such figures a part of portal composition, but placed them on rectangular jambs. The sculptor of St-Denis, by placing the figures on columns, brought them into much closer unity with the portal, at the same time allowing the figures more life and freedom. Future development demonstrates to what extent this was a revolutionary invention.

The lateral portals repeated the design of the central one, though on a somewhat more modest scale, but the three portals were separate units, isolated from each other by buttresses. The next step (1145–55) was taken in Chartres Cathedral, where the three western portals are brought together into a whole, the 24 column-figures and the frieze-capitals providing a link between the three. The iconographic program at Chartres is much fuller and more logical than at St-Denis. The tympana illustrate the Infancy of Christ, the Ascension, and the Second Coming. The archivolts are devoted to the Labors of the Months and the Liberal Arts, thus indicating that a good life on earth should follow the orderly pattern of manual work month by month, and of worthy intellectual pursuits. Episodes from the life of Christ are carved on the capitals, while the column-figures represent the Old Testament figures of kings, queens, and the forerunners of Christ. Many sculptors contributed to this gigantic work. One could well have been the St-Denis Master; another is known as the Étampes Master because he was also responsible for the portal of Notre-Dame at Étampes, not far from Chartres. But the truly great artist was the author of the central portal with its elongated column-figures, which have the simple beauty similar to some of the Greek figures of the Archaic period (*see* Archaic Greek Art). These figures, attached to the columns, took the form of columns. They are hieratic and immobile, as

if suspended between heaven and earth. They were imitated widely in France, and occasionally in Spain and England, but nobody could equal the artistic quality and spirituality of these statues.

The achievements of the Chartres workshop, unique though they are, were made possible by the experiments carried out previously elsewhere, and in Languedoc and Burgundy in particular. The Île-de-France, with Paris as its capital, had played little or no part in these experiments. From now on, after St-Denis and Chartres, the leadership was to pass to that part of the country, reflecting the new prestige of the French monarchy. St-Denis was an Abbey, Chartres was not. St-Denis and Chartres are still largely Romanesque, but contain the seeds of new developments which were to lead to Gothic art. In St-Denis the long line of monastic patronage that had so dominated the Romanesque period was to end. The future belonged to the city cathedrals and to secular patronage. The main steps in the evolution of the sculpture of the Proto-Gothic period must be studied in cathedrals such as Senlis or Laon. During this period of transition, the main inspiration came from the prosperous, industrial Mosan region. Senlis (*c*1170) follows St-Denis and Chartres in some respects, but its column-figures, invested with a new naturalism, are quite foreign to Romanesque art. Its iconography, the Triumph of the Virgin, also marks the new period, less haunted by fear of the Last Judgment and the punishments that would follow. It was a period of greater gentleness and hope.

Luxury arts. It is clear from contemporary texts that works in gold, silver, and bronze, ivory-carvings, embroideries, and the other so-called "minor arts" were highly valued, not only because the materials from which they were made were expensive, but chiefly because of their beauty. Reference has already been made to the manual *De Diversis Artibus*, written by the monk Theophilus *c*1100, in which many techniques are described in detail. From this we know that many craftsmen were masters of several techniques and they could switch from one to another as a commission required. This explains the close stylistic links that exist between works in different media. What in the past was believed to be the result of the influences of one medium on another was probably due to the common authorship of such works. Magister Hugo is a good example of an artist who was able to use several techniques. The praises lavished on him by his contemporaries testify to the high esteem in which he was held. To use the somewhat derogatory term "minor arts" for the works of such men seems inappropriate and so the term "luxury arts" has been introduced in recent years. It gives a far better idea of the status this type of art had attained in the Middle Ages.

Many of the objects that fall within this category had additional prestige because of their function as reliquaries, altar frontals, or covers of liturgical books. In other words, they were intimately related to the liturgy and they acquired special sanctity because of this association. Unfortunately, the precious materials from which many of these objects were made rendered them vulnerable to plunder and theft. It was also quite a common occurrence to pawn or sell them in times of need. But in spite of the destruction of so many of these objects over the ages, there are still enough left to give an idea of what these luxury arts were like during the Romanesque period.

The altar was the most important place in a church, and was often embellished with either a sculptured or painted altar frontal. In the richer churches, such altar frontals were made of ivory, gold, or silver and were usually decorated with reliefs hammered out from behind (the repoussé technique), enamels, and precious stones. Some spectacular examples survive in Spain, Germany, and the Scandinavian countries. When on a journey, an abbot or a bishop would use a richly decorated portable altar containing relics. Two such altars are the work of a celebrated artist, Roger of Helmarshausen, who is probably identical with Theophilus, the author of the manual. The

The ivory cross given by Ferdinand I and Sancha to S. Isidoro, León; height 52cm (20in); c1063. Archaeological Museum, Madrid

linear and dynamic style of Roger's work is thought to show an Italo-Byzantine influence.

Of the objects on an altar, the most important was the crucifix which was usually made of wood, metal, or ivory. The crucifix given by Ferdinand I of Spain and his wife Sancha to S. Isidoro at León in 1063 (Archaeological Museum, Madrid) is a splendid example of such a cross, 20 in (52 cm) high and carved on two sides. Another famous cross of the late Romanesque period is now in the Metropolitan Museum, New York, and is attributed to the Abbey of Bury St Edmunds. Of 12th-century crosses, an important example, over 19 ft (6 m) high, existed at St-Denis Abbey where it stood by the entrance to the crypt. Made at the order of Suger and consecrated by Pope Eugenius in 1147, it consisted of a gilt-bronze base adorned with figures of the Evangelists and enamel plaques. The cross no longer exists, but its appearance is known from descriptions. A small version of it was in the Abbey of St Bertin and the foot of this cross is preserved in the Musée Hôtel Sandelin, St Omer.

Besides the cross, there were numerous candles on and in front of the altar: the number depended on the solemnity of the occasion. They were placed in gilt or silver candlesticks of which the Gloucester Candlestick (early 12th century) in the Victoria and Albert Museum, London, is an elaborate English example. Further light was provided by the candles in *coronae* hanging from the vaulting.

> The church is adorned with gemmed crowns of light, nay, with lusters like cartwheels, girt all round with lamps, but no less brilliant with the precious stones that stud them. Moreover, we see candelabra standing like trees of massive bronze, fashioned with marvelous subtlety of art, and glistening no less brightly with gems than with the lights they carry.

These are the words of St Bernard—words of disapproval, but carrying more than a hint of his admiration for the "marvelous subtlety of art" of these objects, an opinion borne out by the surviving objects. "The trees of bronze" to which St Bernard refers were the seven-branched candlesticks used in large churches for special occasions. At Durham, the branches are said to have stretched from one wall of the choir to the other. A particularly beautiful candlestick of this kind is in Milan Cathedral, dating from the late 12th century.

The vessels used to celebrate Mass, especially chalices, were particularly lavish and of high artistic quality. In a class apart were reliquaries, some taking the form of the part of the body contained in it—an arm, head, or foot—others resembling large sarcophagi made of gold, silver, precious stones, ivory plaques, and enamels. Conques Abbey preserves in its treasury a number of reliquaries, the most precious of which is that of the local saint to which the Abbey was dedicated, St Faith (Ste-Foy). Her relics are enclosed in a golden image of the seated saint, her face made of a reused Roman mask. Occasionally, reliquaries were given the form of a domed building, a kind of a golden *martyrium*, with ivory figures placed in niches.

Norman knights charge the English lines, a scene from the Bayeux Tapestry; height 52cm (20in); c1080. Musée de la Reine Mathilde, Bayeux

Connected with the altar were liturgical books, some of which were actually kept on the altar or near it, others in the sacristy, and, on occasions, if their bindings contained relics, with the reliquaries. The bindings of many books incorporated ivory plaques, enamels, or engraved designs, and were works of art of the highest order.

Apart from the altar, there were, in a Romanesque church, numerous other objects of beauty: lecterns, statues, fonts, screens, and precious hangings. The Bayeux Tapestry (which is in fact an embroidery) with its incomparable history of the Conquest of England, used to be draped at one time round the nave of Bayeux Cathedral on the Feast of the Relics, July 1st. Many churches must have had decorative textiles for such occasions. Other textiles, often imported Byzantine or Islamic silks, were used for vestments.

Fonts were, as a rule, made of stone or marble, and their decoration was frequently elaborate. Some of the richest stone fonts are found in England and the Scandinavian countries, while in Sweden, exceptionally, there are even wooden fonts. Probably the most celebrated font of the period is of bronze. It was originally in Notre-Dame-aux-Fonts at Liège (now in St-Barthélémy's), commissioned by Abbot Hellinus (1107–18) and is the work of Renier de Huy. Although almost contemporary with the portable altars of Roger of Helmarshausen, it represents a very different style. Roger's work is linear and dynamic, and the figures are covered by the arbitrary lines of the draperies. In contrast, Renier's figures are modeled in high relief; their draperies are soft, the expressions gentle, and the movements and gestures natural. The difference between these two styles is fundamental to the understanding of the stylistic

development of 12th-century art. Roger's style is thoroughly Romanesque, though its sources may be, at least in part, Byzantine. Renier's style, on the other hand, is basically Classical, even if it was formed without a deep, personal knowledge of Classical art by the artist. Classical forms could have been transmitted by a series of Carolingian and Ottonian intermediaries, and these were already present in the Mosan region in the 11th century in manuscript painting and ivory carvings.

The bronze font by Renier de Huy; c1107–18. St-Barthélémy. Liège

Thus, Renier's style was not as unexpected as it may appear at first sight. For a time, this classicism was a purely Mosan development, but in time it became of European significance when Mosan artists and their works started to influence the artistic production of neighboring countries, especially France. The great cross at St-Denis was made by Lotharingian (or Mosan) goldsmiths. The stained-glass windows at Châlons-sur-Marne were also the work of artists from the Meuse valley. By c1170 the influence of this art was already present in the portal sculpture of Senlis. In the last quarter of the 12th century Mosan classicism can be found affecting sculpture, painting, metalwork, and ivory-carving, not only in large areas of northern France, but also in Germany and England. The Proto-Gothic Style was, in large measure, of Mosan inspiration.

The late state of this development, which is towards an even greater naturalism, was due to yet another and probably the greatest of Mosan artists, Nicholas of Verdun. His reputation must have been sufficiently established in the late 1170s for him to be called to Klosterneuburg, near Vienna, to execute a pulpit (converted into an altar retable in the 14th century) for the Augustinian monastery, a task he finished in 1181. The pulpit consisted of numerous enamel plaques of related Old and New Testament scenes (in what is termed the typological program) which, in their style, depart from the gentleness of the earlier Mosan works and depict a mood of great intensity and drama. This is further augmented in his other works, the shrines in the cathedrals of Cologne and Tournai. The art of Nicholas of Verdun is no longer Romanesque, and it foreshadows the style that was to be widespread in the first decades of the 13th century.

The contribution of different countries in the production of luxury arts is difficult to assess: in many instances, the attribution of a given work, so easily portable, is uncertain. We know that Spain produced some early champlevé enamels, and that Limoges was a center for similar enamels in the later 12th and 13th centuries. But it is difficult to be absolutely sure, when dealing with mid-12th-century works, whether they are Spanish or French. The same applies to Mosan and English enamels, which are close in style. However, generally speaking, in the field of metalwork, German lands and those under the rule of the emperors (for example, the Meuse Valley) were especially famous, but this does not mean that England, France, Spain, and Italy were not capable of producing masterpieces in this medium. Important ivories originated in the 11th century in Spain and southern Italy, but in the 12th, Germany and England were the most inventive in this field. Bronze doors were, in the earlier Middle Ages, exclusively of German workmanship, but during the Romanesque period Italy produced the greatest number of them. Lead fonts were an English speciality.

The luxury arts, far from being a reflection of monumental works such as wall-paintings and stone sculpture, were, in many instances, in the forefront of the artistic development of the period. In the eyes of contemporaries they were the most praiseworthy. It is therefore essential in the assessment of Romanesque art to give them their due.

GEORGE ZARNECKI

Bibliography. Clapham, A.W. *Romanesque Architecture in Western Europe*, Oxford (1936). Conant, K.J. *Carolingian and Romanesque Architecture: 800–1200*, Harmondsworth (1978). Dodwell, C.R. *Painting in Europe: 800–1200*, Harmondsworth (1971). Lasko, P. *Ars Sacra: 800–1200*, Harmondsworth (1973). Rickert, M. *Painting in Britain: the Middle Ages*, Harmondsworth (1965). Stone, L. *Sculpture in Britain: the Middle Ages*, Harmondsworth (1972). Zarnecki, G. *Romanesque Art*, London and New York (1971).

32

GOTHIC ART

Panels in the Resurrection window of St Lawrence's Chapel, Strasbourg Cathedral; c1345 (see page 603)

THE term Gothic is liable to be misunderstood and misused, so it is best to begin by explaining its descriptive limitations. It was coined at the very end of the artistic period to which it is normally applied. Its inventors were the Italian art historians and critics of the 16th century who were seeking a word to describe art that was either pre-Renaissance or non-Italian or both. The Goths in question were the Ostrogoths and Vizigoths of the 4th and 5th centuries AD who, by their persistent attacks on and occupations of the Italian and Iberian peninsulas, contributed largely to the collapse of the western Roman Empire and, so it was held, to the destruction of the artistic culture of Classical Antiquity. What they put in its place was, to later Italians, a virtually undifferentiated mass of art and architecture strung across the centuries up to *c*1300—art that was at best grandiose, but in general barbaric and retrogressive. Thus "Gothic" was a derogatory adjective and, a little like the connotations often attached to "medieval" now, implied something strikingly old-fashioned from a background that was certainly unenlightened and probably repressive. Needless to say, the reappraisal of Gothic art in the 19th century has dispelled most of these unpleasant overtones, and the adjective, scaled down in its application, has become a useful descriptive word.

The main subsequent development of terminology came with the distinction made in the 19th century between the high- and late-medieval Gothic styles of art and architecture and the earlier Romanesque style. The dividing line between the two, largely under the influence of architectural historians, was drawn through the period when pointed-arch architecture was superseding the use of round arches, *c*1150. At the other end of the time-scale, the Gothic period was held to have come to an end with the introduction of the Classical orders into architecture, *c*1400 in Italy and *c*1500 north of the Alps. In practice, this isolation of the period *c*1150–*c*1400 or *c*1500 is

Gothic Europe

also useful for the figurative arts. During the period *c*1150–1250, European painting and sculpture underwent one of its most fundamental periods of transition in which a style still heavily influenced by the pattern and symbolism of Byzantine art was replaced by an interest in realism, naturalism, and humanitarian feeling. On the other hand, from *c*1400 onwards, European art became increasingly involved in the academic, antiquarian, and often frankly revivalist aspects of the Italian Renaissance. Thus Gothic art is what lies in between these dates. It is neither Romanesque nor Byzantine nor Renaissance—but it is much easier to say what it is *not* than to give an account not merely of what happened during this period, but why it happened.

Much did happen during this period, and in fact, of course, Gothic style (like Renaissance style) is many styles. Within the term have to be accommodated, by way of example, Canterbury Cathedral and Prague Cathedral, the sculpture of the Naumburg Master (*fl.* 1230–70) and at least the early sculpture of Lorenzo Ghiberti (1378–1455), the painting of Matthew Paris (*ob.* 1259) and the painting of Jan van Eyck (*fl.* 1422–41). This observation brings out immediately the very limited use of "Gothic" when applied without qualification; in practice, historians have evolved a great many qualifying phrases. For instance, *formulae* such as the "International Gothic style" have been devised in order to evoke a whole episode within the Gothic period (in this case, *c*1400), and English architectural historians have long been familiar with the famous sequence of Early English, Decorated, and Perpendicular styles into which English Gothic architecture is, by now, traditionally divided (another distinction made in the 19th century). By contrast, attempts to invest Gothic as a whole with specific qualities are doomed to failure. It is nevertheless common for Gothic art *tout court* to be dubbed by such adjectives as "spiritual", "naive", "linear", and "hieratic". The reasons for this insensitivity are worth examining, since they bring out some of the historical problems which have collected round the period.

One of the chief enemies of any art is ignorance—and ignorance of the Middle Ages is widespread. To many people, the history of Europe before 1500 is as remote and inscrutable as Chinese Mongolia. It is true that, to anybody living in the post-industrial age, there is much in Early European history that is unfamiliar and foreign. But there are many situations which are instantly recognizable—and, in terms of art, its patrons and producers, many of the practical conditions in which "Gothic" aesthetic taste developed and artistic skill flourished, long survived the demise of "Gothic art". In terms of training to be an artist or architect, attaining success and gaining a reputation, the change between the 14th century and, for instance, the 18th century is not so complete as might be imagined.

One of the most striking developments of the Gothic period is the thorough secularization of its artists. Romanesque art was almost certainly ecclesiastically based. But already by the 12th century there is evidence that architects were increasingly

The Trinity Chapel of Canterbury Cathedral; 1174–85

secular persons—and further indications suggest that some even of the more famous monastic craftsmen, such as Roger of Helmarshausen (fl. early 12th century), may have been secular professionals who entered monastic life at a late age. This does not mean that "ecclesiastical" artists vanish from the scene c1200. Matthew Paris was a Benedictine monk, Lorenzo Monaco (c1370–1425) a Camaldolese monk, Fra Angelico (c1395/1400–55) a Dominican friar, Fra Filippo Lippi (c1406–69) a Carmelite friar. But by the late 13th century, these conventuals had at the top professional level been decisively challenged by people such as Master Honoré in Paris (fl. late 13th/early 14th centuries), Erwin von Steinbach (fl. 1277–1318) at Strasbourg, or Giotto (1266–1337) in Florence. So the conception of Gothic art as the product of devout clergymen working to the greater glory of God is extremely misleading.

Indeed, alongside the work of the great master, there flourished by the end of the 14th century a degree of commercialization and mass production—perhaps surprising for a preindustrial age. For instance, the growth of the universities and the increasing numbers of people entering some form of academic discipline meant that large numbers of standard texts—especially Bibles, the writings of the Church Fathers, and law books, all with their appropriate commentaries—had to be produced and marketed. The concept of "mass production" in the Middle Ages is easily grasped by examining the detailed carving of a building such as the nave of Canterbury Cathedral (late 14th century). The degree of imagination required of the stone-carvers is nil: the architect made his effect partly through a restricted number of seemingly endlessly repeated moldings and motifs. Buildings of this sort could only be completed successfully if the architect had at his disposal a team of carvers who could work with meticulous precision on a production line.

So in the 13th and 14th centuries, the production of art became increasingly secularized. In general, this reflected the prosperity of towns and cities and the benefits of civic life which followed. More and more, these must have outweighed the security offered to those who belonged to a religious order. Members of collegiate and monastic communities have always been offered protection against the ruder buffets and pressures of the outside world, and there was a long period when these institutions offered a natural haven for virtually all cultural pursuits. As a haven for artists, however, they had various severe disadvantages. For one thing, a member of an enclosed community would have had considerable restrictions placed on his ability to travel. But the attitudes to his work to which he was at least supposed to pay lip-service must also have seemed increasingly unrealistic. These are clearly stated both in the *Rule of St Benedict*, and in the fundamentally important 12th-century treatise *De Diversis Artibus*, written by a monastic writer calling himself Theophilus, now thought on good grounds to be the German metal sculptor Roger of Helmarshausen. On all artistic counts, Theophilus belongs firmly to the Romanesque period (*see* Romanesque Art); but his principles of work hold good effectively for all members of all religious communities at all times. A conventual artist must be humble, not proud of his achievement, and not interested in financial reward. For him, the sins of Pride and Avarice always lie in wait. But humility is not the first quality we normally associate with the great masters, and what we know about the careers of Giotto or Henry Yevele suggests that making money and gaining recognition were high on their list of priorities. The secularization of artists is not surprising; by the late 13th century, communities of artists and craftsmen were established in the major European cities. In Paris in 1292, according to the taxation rolls, there were 33 painters, 24 image-makers, 13 illuminators, and 104 people listed as masons. The earliest ordinances for London's painters date from 1283.

This immediately introduces the subject of guilds. They have in general acquired a bad reputation for being obscurantist and restrictive in their operations. Indeed, it is sometimes suggested that the alleged freedom of the Renaissance artist was in some sense due to the break-up of a "guild system". All this is very misleading. In the first place, guild regulations never seem to have restricted the achievements, movements, or operations of a really good artist. In order to work on Siena Cathedral, Giovanni Pisano (*c*1245/50–1314) moved to Siena and was granted Sienese citizenship. Later, he moved back to Pisa to work on the cathedral there. The Savoyard James of St George (active in England 1278–1307) moved to England during the same period to mastermind the construction of castles in Wales for Edward I. Giotto in the 1320s and the 1330s moved from Florence to Naples and back again. Simone Martini (1280/5–1344) in the 1330s moved to Avignon (where he died). The Roman marble-workers under Petrus and Odoricus came to Westminster in the 1260s and 1270s to fit out the presbytery of Henry III's new abbey church. The practical effects of guild activities in the Middle Ages are too little known; but surviving regulations suggest that their primary aim was not to restrict first-rate artists, but to protect good second-rate ones. Guild ordinances veered between general regulations about meetings and conduct, and precise instructions about particular types of work. General

The west front of Siena Cathedral, by Giovanni Pisano and Giovanni di Cecco; late 13th century

regulations aimed mostly at welding a guild's members into a unit and giving them an *esprit de corps*. Annual general meetings were ordered and processions were arranged, especially on the patronal saint's day, when all members might be expected to attend. Indeed, most guilds might be expected to have their own altar in a local church as a focus for corporate worship. Similar attendance was sometimes urged at a member's funeral, and more fortunate members might be enjoined to visit sick and needy brethren. The most public ceremonies would have demonstrated to the world at large the existence, composition, and status of the guild, and to some extent must have fostered a sense of solidarity and purpose among the artists taking part. But if the members were then offered a sense of protection as being a part of a greater (and beneficent) whole, it was still necessary to protect the good name of the profession by guarding its members against cheats and swindlers within its ranks. So, the detailed regulations are mainly about specific jobs (for instance, the manufacture and decorations of shields, saddles, or religious images) especially, for example, shoddy refurbished goods which might be placed on the market as brand-new.

It is difficult to make generalizations about the members' workshops. It is, however, quite clear that members often formed family units. Many great artists produced sons who worked under them; occasionally, as in the case of the Pisano or Bellini families, the genius of the father was passed on to the son. Where no son existed, the most promising apprentice might marry the master's daughter—Richard of Verdun (*fl.* 1288–1318) was the son-in-law of Master Honoré—and in practice there must have been a large number of these small working groups created partly by procreation and partly by intermarriage. Simone Martini was the most distinguished member of a group consisting of himself, his brother, his father-in-law, and his brother-in-law (Lippo Memmi; *fl.* 1317–47).

It was normal to train for several years as a pupil in an established workshop. From the 15th century, contracts survive to demonstrate a legal relationship between master and pupil, although the actual length of the apprenticeship seems to have varied. Albrecht Dürer (1471–1528) trained for three years under Michael Wolgemut (1434–1519); Rogier van der Weyden (1399/1400–64) was for five years under Robert Campin (1378/9–1444). The purpose of this training was first and foremost to protect standards. It was assumed that five years spent watching Robert Campin at work would at least turn an apprentice into a reliable painter (though not necessarily an inspiring or memorable one). However, it also produced a respect for tradition which forms a prominent trait in medieval art. It comes out clearly in one of the surviving medieval painters' manuals, the *Libro dell'Arte* of Cennino Cennini (*fl. c*1370–*c*1440), written probably in the late 14th century. Cennini stressed two distinct elements in the development of a young painter's potential: learning from a good master, and copying nature. With regard to nature, it is difficult to know whether, say, a 13th-century artist would have expressed himself in quite this way (although there is plenty of 13th-century sculpture with a very direct underlying basis in nature); but Cennini's sense of the importance of having a good master extends to implying that that master, too, should have had a good master. He himself, he wrote, had learnt his precepts from Agnolo Gaddi (*c*1350–96), who was the son and pupil of Taddeo Gaddi (1300–66) who, in turn, was the pupil of Giotto. There is no reason to suppose that a 13th-century artist would not have thought in similar terms—although Cennini's inclusion of his "pedigree" was certainly influenced by the high reputation Giotto had already achieved by the end of the 14th century. However, in a perfectly practical way, possession of a good training has always been taken as *prima facie* evidence of reliability, with simple consequences in the case of architecture. Any patron who knew the buildings of Heinrich Parler (mid 14th century) would have felt immediate confidence in employing his son, Peter Parler (1330–1399).

It is sometimes suggested that this respect for tradition had a stultifying effect on art, and that an innate conservatism has left its mark on the Middle ages. This is partly true: from a 20th-century viewpoint, changes seem to occur slowly, although it seems unlikely that this particular characteristic would have struck many people with any particular force at any period before the mid 19th century. Up to that point, changes in art normally occurred gradually and originality was almost invariably tempered with a strong respect for tradition. Nor, clearly, did the balance thus struck inhibit at any point the production of works of art of breathtaking beauty. But, for the Gothic period, it is much harder than at any period since to discover what artists and architects themselves felt about this balance.

There is also a further class of persons to be taken into account here—the patrons. The large majority of surviving medieval art is ecclesiastical in its application; during the Romanesque period (11th and 12th centuries) it would probably be true to say that the church, in its many forms, exercised a near monopoly in the patronage of art. However, from the 13th century onwards, two particular types of secular patron appear on the scene—the king and the city council.

Kings had at all times, according to their means, exercised their patronage in the field of architecture, since their status was in part judged by outsiders according to the state they kept. Charlemagne's Chapel Royal at Aachen (built *c*785–800), and William Rufus' Great Palace Hall at Westminster (1090s), are magnificent surviving examples (the latter is now much altered). However, during the 13th century there is increasing evidence of a more detailed interest in the decorative arts from members of royal families. Louix IX of France (St Louis; reigned 1226–70) and Henry III of England (reigned 1216–72) are particularly important. Much is known about the interest Henry III took in the decoration of the Palace and Abbey of Westminster, and of his palace at Clarendon, Wiltshire. St Louis had a major artistic project in the new palace chapel in Paris (the Sainte Chapelle); we also know he started to build up a library of manuscripts. It was a collection his successors continued, and which, by the end of the 14th century, was one of the most impressive in Europe, containing about 1,000 items. Other secular libraries were built up concurrently, notably the library of the Visconti lords of Milan. By the late 14th century this was similar in size. This type of activity does not amount to anything as abstract as collecting "art". Libraries were respectable, and these libraries have the character of 18th-century gentlemen's libraries with their large preponderance of standard works of reference and literature. Otherwise, kings collected not "art" but curiosities, such as wild animals (Henry III of England had an elephant in the Tower of London). Later in the 15th century, the great men of Italy came to collect antique sculpture, gem stones, medals, and cameos. The concept of collecting "art" was a late arrival on the scene. Nevertheless, the spectacle of important men from distinguished families taking a close interest in art can have had nothing but beneficial effect on artists. Not only did it confer a kind of nobility on their profession, but it also opened up vistas of social advancement such as had not apparently existed before. During the 14th century, small groups of artists are found in Italy and France, on court establishments and associating closely with the relevant prince or monarch. The French court office of *Valet de Chambre* is the

Sculpture and Glass at Chartres

For many people, the cathedral of Chartres will sum up everything they feel a Gothic cathedral ought to be. It must always have been one of the most completely decorated of medieval ecclesiastical buildings, and by great good fortune the main constituents of this decoration—the glass and the portal sculpture—have survived virtually intact. At Chartres, more than anywhere else, it is still possible to sense the impact of a large medieval church in all its pristine glory, and to see an important part of the development of early Gothic glass-painting and sculpture.

The main areas of sculpture surround the portals of the west end and the transepts (the 13th-century choir screen was demolished in the 18th century and survives only in fragments). The west portals were carved c1150. In their general layout and style, they strongly resemble the west front of St-Denis, Paris. The style is not indeed uniform, but at its best it exemplifies mid-12th-century sculpture at its peak. Chartres was imitated several times (for instance at Angers and Bourges), but never surpassed.

The themes with which the sculptors involved themselves embrace the whole history of the world—past, present, and to come. The tall figures flanking the portals are almost certainly from the Old Testament—probably, in part, Kings and Queens of Judah. The capitals display the life of Christ in a continuous horizontal band. Above are visible carvings of the Ascension, the Virgin and Child, and, in the center, Christ at the Second Coming surrounded by the Apocalyptic Beasts. This sculpture forms part of a porch or narthex which was added to the 11th-century church. The original glass of this building survives in the three west lancet windows. Together with the famous Notre Dame de la Belle Verrière, preserved in the south choir aisle, they constitute precious survivals from the 12th century—nearly contemporary with the famous glass of Abbot Suger of St-Denis.

The 12th-century sculpture and glass at Chartres are famous in their own right. But in 1194 a disastrous fire destroyed the main part of the old church (except for its crypt), and the glass and sculpture to the east of the porch belong for the most part to the rebuilding. Miscellaneous dating evidence suggests a

▲ Chartres Cathedral, seen from the southeast; built 1194–1260; north steeple added 1507–13

◀ Christ at the Second Coming, the tympanum of the central portal of the west facade of Chartres Cathedral; c1150

period c1210–30. The sculpture is concentrated in two enormous transept porches. Although these may look as if they were planned from the start, appearances are deceptive. Archaeological evidence suggests that, like many medieval projects, they were altered in form, and enlarged during the making.

The final "program" of sculpture is one of the most extensive to survive. It embraces the Life of the Virgin, the Final Coming, Apostles, Prophets, Confessors, and Martyrs, many other Saints and various subsidiary themes such as Virtues and Vices and the Labors of the Months. The work in general is remarkably high in quality, and the style probably derives from that of the workshop of the cathedral at Laon (1190s). Interestingly, the two porches are quite different in character and must have been designed by different people.

The magnificent program of 13th-century glass at Chartres in many ways echoes the style of the portals—at least in the figures and drapery. The iconography is, however, less clearly organized. The two huge transept rose windows glorify the Virgin and comment on the Second Coming. In the clerestory of the

► Column figures on the north porch of Chartres Cathedral; from left to right, Melchizedek, Abraham and Isaac, Moses, Samuel, and David; c1200–10

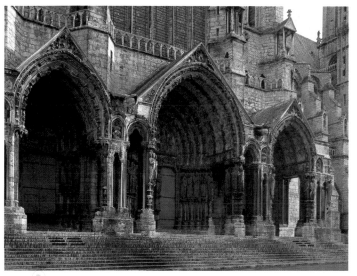

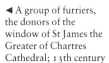

◀ A group of furriers, the donors of the window of St James the Greater of Chartres Cathedral; 13th century

Above left The porches of the north transept; *c*1210–30

▲ The porches of the south transept; *c*1210–30

▼ The rose window and lancets of the south transept; 1224

main apse, we see the Virgin and Child surrounded by the major Old Testament Prophets. But throughout the remainder of the cathedral, the visitor is overwhelmed by a fantastic and somewhat miscellaneous wealth of imagery. The donors of individual windows often had themselves portrayed, or indicated their contributions by heraldry. Many of these donors were royal or noble. But a large number of windows offer tiny vignettes of bakers, carpenters, wine merchants, furriers, and many other secular professions. Cumulatively, the effect is almost complete and very impressive—and crucial to the history of early Gothic glass painting.

ANDREW MARTINDALE

Further reading. Delaporte, Abbé Y. and Houvet, E. *Les Vitraux de la Cathédrale de Chartres*, Chartres (1926). Henderson, G. *Chartres*, Harmondsworth (1968). Katzenellenbogen, A. *The Sculptural Programs of Chartres Cathedral*, Baltimore (1959). Kidson, P. and Pariser, U. *Sculpture at Chartres*, London (1958). Mâle, E. *L'Art Religieux du XII*e *Siècle en France*, Paris (1928). Mâle, E. *L'Art Religieux du XIII*e *Siècle en France*, Paris (1925). Merlet, R. *La Cathédrale de Chartres*, Paris (1926). Sauerländer, W. *Gothic Sculpture in France 1140–1270*, London (1970).

best known of these established posts—later, Pol de Limburg (*c*1410–15) and Jan van Eyck (*c*1425–41) were *valets de chambre* of the Dukes of Berry and Burgundy respectively. They were preceded by many others, including Giotto who, as *familiaris* (a member of the household establishment), held a similar position at the court of Naples (*c*1330–3).

This extension of secular interest in the activities of artists had beneficial effects in other directions. The most obvious was the way in which town councils sought to emulate the activities of royal courts. Town councils, too, needed palaces and splendid chapels. We have only to see the Guildhall in London, and the close association between the Mayor and Aldermen and St Paul's Cathedral, to realize that the state a city "officially" kept was also of the greatest consequence. Most medieval cities would have had city halls and offices, although in many cases these have necessarily since been rebuilt. London's Guildhall may go back to the 13th century (the Hall is now mainly early 15th); the Guildhall of Norwich is fundamentally early 14th century. But the earliest and most splendid city palaces were in Italy. The establishment of the Italian communes from the 12th century onwards led, in the 13th and 14th centuries, to the building of a number of enormous civic buildings, often modeled on the Imperial palaces of Germany. The original decoration of these municipal palaces has survived far less frequently than the buildings, and their most popular theme seems to have been the cycle of images of the great men of Antiquity and Biblical history by which, presumably, a regime might seek to link its aspirations to a respectable past. However, that more ambitious undertakings were possible is shown by the sequence of decorations in the Palazzo Publico at Siena, where the surviving paintings cover a wide range of religious imagery, allegory, and fairly recent history.

The determination of the Italian communes to have impressive civic buildings also extended to removing the supervision of the fabric of the local large church (usually a cathedral) from the ecclesiastical authorities and vesting it either in a council committee or in an existing guild. In this way, the rebuilding of the cathedrals of Florence and Siena, for example, became civic enterprises, paid for largely out of local taxation.

It might be expected that there would have been a civic development parallel to that of the *valet de chambre*—that is, a development by which artists might have been officially designated as serving the town council. For architects, this indeed took place. But there was always the need for a city engineer, since, apart from any work of aesthetic merit, roads, walls, bridges, and drains required permanent maintenance. Imitation of the royal courts to the extent of having an official "town painter", however, occurred so seldom as to be negligible; presumably it was a form of luxury expenditure unacceptable to the majority of councillors.

Nevertheless, the lot of the artist and architect continued to improve throughout the Gothic period as a result of the increasing interest in the arts taken by those at the highest level of aristocratic and civic society. By the 14th century, architecture, sculpture, and painting were all activities in which educated men could take an interest without necessarily appearing ridiculous to their peers, and artists, in a sort of reciprocal development, attracted something of the gentility associated with this interest. The first knighthoods conferred on artists appear at the end of this period in the late 15th century. (Andrea Mantegna (1431–1506), Gentile Bellini (1429–1507) and Carlo Crivelli (1430/5–*c*1495) were all created Knights.)

The situation thus far described is, in the main, unmysterious and requires no great effort of the imagination to resurrect it. Why, then, does Gothic art create for itself such problems of interpretation? The answer lies partly in the fact that Gothic art was inarticulate in a quite easily perceptible way. In spite of this apparent interest in art by educated men, and in spite of the apparent increase in the social acceptability of artists, the practice of writing about art never developed in the Middle Ages. The reason for this must lie partly in the bias given to all formal education by its classical antecedents: "art", in the modern sense, was a craft, a "mechanical" operation, and, as such, incapable and unworthy of intellectual analysis. It is, in fact, confusing that the medieval use of the Latin word *Ars* denoted a craft, as apposed to *Scientia*, for which intellectual accomplishment was necessary. Artists were not thought worthy of biographies, and their activities were not considered worthy of written comment. Consequently, very little is known about the lives of medieval artists, and even less is known for certain about the way in which people talked about art in the Middle Ages. We know almost nothing of the way in which patrons and artists distinguished between good art and bad, talked about the interplay of tradition and originality, or noticed the development of a new style.

The absence of literary exposition on these points, however, cannot mean that artists and patrons alike were reduced to incoherence when confronted by them. The Abbot Suger (*c*1081–1151) did not pick the names of his artists and architects out of a miter when he was planning his operation at St-Denis, and his writings show, almost in parenthesis, that he was conscious there was such a thing as a "modern" architectural style. The monk Gervase of Canterbury (*c*1200) left a long and famous account of the building works at Canterbury following the fire of 1174 in which he showed quite clearly that the architectural style of the new building was novel, memorable, and to be distinguished in detail from the building of the early 12th century. Cennino Cennini saw (rather less clearly) that artistic creativity in painting depended on the balance struck between the demands of tradition, the claims of the visible world, and the operation of the artist's imagination. His writing has great interest because of the difficulty he reveals in framing these somewhat abstract concepts. In fact, the language he used was heavily indebted to Horace's *Ars Poetica* and to a somewhat cloudy Platonism. An academically trained mind might have made easier going of this, but we must infer that for most of this period no educated person attempted a reasoned written study of the subject. The idea that the activities of an artist could be reduced to the form of a literary treatise had to wait for Alberti's *Della Pittura* (*c*1435; first written in Latin).

This unwillingness of the educated classes to concern themselves with art in literary terms places a permanent limit on our knowledge of these aspects of the development of art and architecture. This reticence may be inferred from the positive way in which artists' names were excluded from accounts of their achievements. A 13th-century chronicler of St Alban's Abbey, England, wrote that "he by whose authority a thing is done, does it", and there is an almost universal tendency on the part of medieval writers to remember things by the name of the person who paid for them or otherwise instigated their creation. Thus, churches have come down to us as "by" the bishop, abbot, or prior who was in charge at the time, and, as often as not, manuscripts are known by the name of the bibliophile for whom they were produced.

The apparent thoughtlessness by which an artist's name was almost never attached to his achievement brings us to one of the features of medieval and Gothic art which is perhaps most difficult to comprehend: the apparent anonymity of its practitioners. We cannot believe that the artist of the Oscott Psalter (British Library, London) or the architect of St Augustine's, Bristol, were nonentities, even though we do not know their names. It is also impossible to believe that works of this caliber and individuality did not go with a considerable reputation which circulated within a perhaps restricted circle of connoisseurs. So we must examine the sort of reputation sought by these artists, as implied by the surviving evidence.

The first conclusion that becomes apparent is that few artists saw their work as monuments to keep their names alive and in the minds of posterity. Today, when virtually all paintings are signed, many buildings have a foundation stone naming the architect, and most people think it desirable to be commemorated by a personalized tombstone inscribed with their name, this attitude may seem puzzling. In the Middle Ages, however, the problem seems to have been approached from a somewhat more realistic angle: what people and deeds were worth a monument? In general terms the answer was "very few", but especially the deeds of those who were mighty and powerful and of those who were charitable. In practice, the biggest charitable foundations tended to be endowed by those who were also powerful. The idea that art might become a personal monument to its creator seems seldom to have entered the consciousness of artists.

The most prolific source of inscriptions naming the artist on a work of art is, for all of the Middle Ages, Italy. This may say something about the Italians, but it more likely that it represents a dim survival of the Classical concept of Fame as being something desirable. In the north, few works of art are signed before the 15th century; we can only assume that the inclusion of an artist's name on a tomb or in a manuscript was an act of presumption—a sort of lapse of good manners—undesirable to both patron and artist. This did not mean that an artist, in

common with all humans, was unconcerned about himself after his death. But, as with others, he would consider the most useful and efficacious form of commemoration to be a posthumous liturgical one provided by his guild or a religious institution. Seemingly *in perpetuo*, they would remember him annually by name, and suitable prayers would be offered for his progress in the afterlife.

The anonymity of Gothic art does not imply, therefore, that artists and architects were an oppressed class, nor that they were excessively devout and humble. It does not tell us that the development of the current stylistic ideas was carried out in subdued religious undertones. Indeed, judging from the occasional glimpses behind the scenes, it is more realistic to imagine the period as full of drama and excitement, peopled by colorful personalities with the most exacting standards of work. Moreover, increasingly during this period we must imagine a widening class of patrons, both secular and ecclesiastical, who possessed equally high standards of connoisseurship and the ability to choose particular artists for particular commissions. Ultimately, the records compiled by the literate begin to reveal this situation in greater detail before the Gothic period closes.

European art (except Italy) *c*1150–1300. At the opening of the period under consideration, we immediately confront all the problems mentioned. The period 1150–1250 has a certain convenience for the historian. In architecture, it is possible to chronicle the exploitation of the potential of pointed arch, ribbed vault, and flying buttress; and in the figurative arts, the historian can note the dramatic moves towards a realistic and humane figure-style. However, it takes imagination and a certain amount of courage to infer from monuments what each master thought he was doing, and it is often equally difficult to assess the qualities for which a particular masterpiece was in its time admired.

The man who traditionally dominates the beginnings of Gothic art is not an artist but a patron near Paris, the Abbot Suger of St-Denis. Much is known about him: he left two lengthy autobiographical writings, a considerable proportion of which concern his rebuilding and refurbishing of his abbey church. These writings exhibit many of the less admirable qualities of the successful business executive (Suger was highly successful): an inordinate admiration for the evidence of well-managed finances, a love of sumptuous effects, a sense of taste that sometimes seems to go awry, and a superficial interest in the past that may be specious. But Suger had an unerring eye for technical quality, and although (characteristically for this period) he never mentioned an artist's name it was certainly no accident that he acquired at least two architects of first-rate ability. Their place in the history of European architecture and sculpture will become clear.

One of Suger's main achievements was to replace the Carolingian apse of St-Denis by a new choir, an ambulatory, and radiating chapels. Unfortunately, the choir itself was later drastically remodeled in the 13th century, but the ambulatory

and chapels, begun in 1140, are much as Suger left them. Up to this date, the east end of the church had usually been planned as a series of separate units; chapels clearly divided from each other and opening individually off the ambulatory. Suger's architect, by breaking down all internal divisions, opened up a large, exciting hall-like space within the church and streamlined the external appearance into a series of smooth, regular undulations. The effect he achieved was made possible by his superb technical expertise in the calculation and construction of pointed vaults: this in itself must have set new standards for technical excellence. But his rethinking of the interior space had a number of notable imitations, for instance at Notre Dame, Paris, (1163) where the idea of streamlining the external perimeter of the building was carried still farther. Nothing else in France or Europe survives from this date to approach Suger's architect's mastery of his materials; it is a matter for regret that we have lost the internal elevation of his choir at St-Denis.

The interior elevation of a great church was treated in various ways during this period though almost all the solutions adopted had been invented in their broad outlines during the Romanesque period (see Romanesque Art). Basically, it was agreed that churches should have aisles and therefore arcades separating the aisles from the main body of the church. But on almost every other conceivable point there was disagreement. What should happen above the arcade? Was it desirable to have transepts? If so, how far should they project and what form should they take? How many towers should there be and where should they be placed? The answers depended in part on the area of France concerned. Most of the solutions had their own merits. The large and indubitably Gothic cathedral of Poitiers (begun in 1162) has the form of a "hall-church": the aisles are similar in height to the nave and choir, and there is no clerestory or other feature rising up above. This is in keeping with local 12th-century traditions governing the appearance of a great church, and the result is, in its way, spacious and impressive. Sens Cathedral (begun c1140) originally, like Poitiers, had no transept (one was added later), but, unlike Poitiers, it possesses a large and spacious arcade with a tribune and clerestory rising up to the high vault. It reminds us that, as in many Romanesque buildings, height and size played a part in the aesthetic preoccupations of the age.

This is especially brought home in a group of churches in the northeast of France and the western Empire, of which the most striking survivor is Laon Cathedral (begun c1165). Inside, the elevation of Laon has four stages: above a comparatively low arcade rise a tribune gallery, triforium gallery, and clerestory. The whole is capped by a vault. The insistent "layering" of Laon is impressive and the Romanesque prototypes probably derive from antique examples such as the exterior of the Colosseum in Rome. Laon itself, however, would

The west front of Notre Dame, Paris; c1200–45

The four-stage nave and choir elevations of Laon Cathedral; 1165–1200

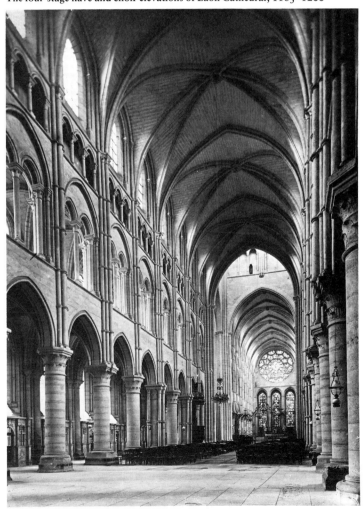

Left: The choir of St-Denis, Paris, built for Abbot Suger; 1140–4; clerestory and transepts rebuilt 1230s

have been impossible without an elaborate, if concealed, support and buttressing system which captures and distributes the weight of the high vault. The rudiments of this system had already appeared in Romanesque architecture along with other "Gothic" features such as vault ribbing. Up to the second half of the 12th century it seems to have been accepted that this buttressing system should be concealed beneath the aisle roofs—a preference that had important effects on the dispositions of the interior elevation. However, during the second half of the 12th century—it is not clear where it first occurred—architects made it possible to disassociate the height of this buttressing from the height of the aisle roof by exposing externally the arched support system (henceforth known as flying buttresses). This in turn led to some radical rethinking of the interior design.

The most influential church in this respect was the cathedral of Chartres, a major rebuilding of which began in 1194. Here the supporting buttressing rises clearly up above the aisle roof on the outside; the tribune gallery has been abandoned on the inside and the clerestory greatly enlarged (downwards) so that it nearly approaches the main arcade in height (the two are separated by a small triforium gallery). This solution must have won almost instant approval, since it was adopted, with modifications, in a number of major churches including Reims Cathedral (begun in 1210) and Amiens Cathedral (begun c1220). In fact, by concentrating their attention on the means by which the structural exigencies of a building could be tightly controlled and concentrated in a few places, this development set architects thinking along new lines. Initially, the most striking achievements were greater height and size. But with the collapse of the vault of Beauvais Cathedral in 1284, it was realized that the limits in this direction had been reached; architects turned instead to other aspects of the building.

It is worth noting, if only to demonstrate the selectiveness of architects, that the exterior appearance of Chartres had no imitators; in fact, it belonged to a fashion that was already passing away. Like Laon Cathedral, it was intended to have four transept towers as well as its two western ones (which derive from the church of the mid 12th century). The tradition of clusters of towers round the transepts of a great church is Romanesque in origin and has an extensive history in northern France and the Empire. The results, where completed (or nearly so, as at Laon), offer an exciting configuration of shapes, and its general abandonment in favor of a simple pair of towers at the west end of a church is hard to understand. The change of fashion was probably confirmed at the Cathedral of Notre Dame, Paris; in the 13th century, twin western towers became the norm.

The Gothic style of architecture thus far described was not a unified development. The Gothic qualities these buildings have in common are probably most apparent when reduced to points of decorative detail—rib and arch moldings, for example, or the development of a simplified type of Corinthian capital known as the crocket capital. But in whatever sense we choose to understand the development of Gothic architecture,

it is apparent that France was considerably in advance of other European countries. The earliest important Gothic buildings in England appear in c1170–80, but elsewhere the main developments belong to the 13th century.

It has sometimes been suggested that the Cistercian monastic order was important in the spread of French Gothic ideas. Founded in 1098, the other grew rapidly during the first half of the 12th century and established itself throughout Europe. Originally, its habits were intended to be dominated by an extreme sort of uniformity with annual visitations for every house and annual general meetings at the mother-house in France. This uniformity extended to architecture and Cistercian monastic ground plans, for example, bear a general resemblance to each other. However, the chief architectural principle of the Cistercians was simplicity—not in itself very positive—so although many early Cistercian churches bear a general resemblance to a French Burgundian Cistercian church such as Fontenay (begun in 1139), the architectural stimulus promoted by such a resemblance is not a particularly invigorating one. In practice, especially after the death of St Bernard (1153), simplicity was gradually abandoned by the Cistercians and their architecture achieved its own interest within the appropriate regional context.

The most important early Gothic building in England is the eastern arm of Canterbury Cathedral (1174–84). Although designed by a Frenchman, William of Sens, the structure still incorporates features from the Anglo-Norman Romanesque tradition in, for example, the tribune gallery and clerestory passage. But the capitals and coupled columns are derived from France, and the decorative colonnettes, an outstanding feature, are familiar from Laon Cathedral. Although the strength of these older traditions is still apparent (though chiefly in heavy proportions) in a building such as Wells Cathedral (begun c1180), the rebuilding of Lincoln Cathedral (1192) showed most clearly the characteristics of this first phase of English Gothic architecture—notably in the elaborate arch moldings, densely grouped colonnettes, and multiplication of vault ribs—producing a rich effect without any continental rival.

Gothic architectural developments elsewhere in Europe occur slightly later. In Germany, early-13th-century churches still often appear Romanesque in style, and even the interesting four-storied interior of the cathedral of Limburg is so heavy and graceless in its proportions and detail that it is surprising to learn it was begun c1220, making it a contemporary of Amiens. The earliest churches that by French standards might be called Gothic are the Liebfrauenkirche at Trier (begun c1235, finished in 1253) and the church of St Elizabeth at Marburg (begun in 1235). Both are reasonably up-to-date in architectural detail and St Elizabeth's has the additional interest of being a hall-church. This form, not much used in France after the 12th century, had a continuing popularity in Germany and ultimately became the occasion for daring experiments in vault design.

In Spain, the main early Gothic churches of Burgos (begun

The nave of Bourges Cathedral; c1195–1245

The west front of St-Denis, Paris, built c1137 for Abbot Suger

in 1222) and Toledo (begun in 1226) show, as Canterbury had earlier, unmistakable French connections—but with one particular French cathedral: Bourges. Although contemporary with Chartres, Bourges Cathedral (begun c1195) has a quite different interior design. The architect here used his engineering expertise to build a church of enormous height spread across five aisles, and the main arcade is of gigantic size. Here again, he was drawing on a Romanesque tradition but building to greatly enlarged proportions. He had French imitators at Le Mans (begun in 1216) and at Coutances (begun c1250); but the giant "arcade" type of church achieved its greatest popularity in Spain and, in various manifestations, became the commonest form of large Gothic church there: Toledo Cathedral is a good example.

The choir of Abbot Suger's abbey church of St-Denis was begun in 1140. Shortly before then, in the years following 1137, a different architect had rebuilt the west end of this church. He was undistinguished as an engineer, but as an architectural decorator he was a designer of crucial importance for the developments in France over the following 100 years. His achievement was to bring together on one facade various architectural elements that had already appeared in different parts of France, and to weld them together into a single whole. Thus he grouped beneath his two towers a circular window, some rows of arcading, and three large portals, each containing voussoir carvings, column figures on the jambs, and a decorated tympanum. Unfortunately, much of this carving has subsequently been destroyed, or restored almost out of existence, so Suger's facade is now a mere shadow of its former self. But in any case it is the design that seems to have been important. The sculptural style, as far as it is visible, was shortly superseded by a style far more distinguished whose chief focus seems to be found in the west front of Chartres Cathedral (c1150). Although various different hands can be detected here—this is true of all large assemblages of medieval sculpture—the "main" style is characterized by extreme gravity and restraint underlined by the method of drawing out the drapery folds into innumerable, thin parallel folds with pleated edges. It was a style that commanded great respect in the mid 12th century, if we can judge from its imitators at Bourges and Le Mans.

Two features are worth emphasizing about these churches. Firstly, they continue a Romanesque tradition whereby available virtuosi sculptors were employed by architects to make sizable, significant, and individual contributions to the architecture—a tradition that did not survive long into the Gothic period. Secondly, it is the beginning of a general development towards greater humanity in figure sculpture. Not all the Chartres west-end sculpture could be called life-like, but the figure of Christ in the center is strikingly more humane than previous representations of Christ, as at Vézelay or Moissac. This development towards greater humanity is one of the keys to sculpture of the following century. It is not a smooth, even development, but a succession of stylistic fashions with different antecedents and starting points. The result was a series of

Antique Figure Sculpture at Reims

The main portal sculpture of Reims Cathedral is commonly dated on archaeological grounds to between *c*1220 and *c*1240. Amongst the earliest work is a group of figures which looks unmistakably Classical. It includes the famous pair of statues portraying the Visitation on the west front, but much of the sculpture on the north transept portals shows similar characteristics. Together, these sculptures raise the question of the part played by Classical sculpture in the evolution of early Gothic art. The answers are intriguing, but by no means straightforward.

The distinctive drapery style of the Reims figures is not a creation of the Reims masons' workshop. The Reims sculpture, indeed, marks the final phases of a development, rather than a beginning. The characteristics of this style are to be found *c*1180 in the Mosan workshop of Nicholas of Verdun,

where a soft undulation of troughs and ridges—the so-called *Muldenstil* of German art historians—was devised as a replacement for the crisp, linear patterns of the previous decades. The initial inspiration for this particular stylistic trick was almost certainly Classical, but its application proceeded for the most part without obvious reference to original Classical art—especially at Laon and Chartres cathedrals (*c*1190–1210). It was also a style adaptable to painting, and in England, at least, had a history lasting to the middle of the 13th century. It makes an

▼ Figures of saints, influenced by Classical sculpture, on the north transept front of Reims Cathedral; St Bartholomew (*left*) and St Peter (*right*); *c*1220

▼ Mary and Martha, the Visitation scene by the Virgin's portal in the west front of Reims Cathedral; *c*1220

illustrious appearance in the sketchbook of the mason Villard de Honnecourt (*c*1220), the only survival of this kind from the period. Villard knew the workshops of both Chartres and Reims.

Part of the interest of the Reims figures lies precisely in their heightened classicism. But the character of the sculpture does not depend solely on this. From the start, the figures, though heavily dependent on the Chartres style, are altogether stockier. It is as if the principal sculptor had aimed at increasing their impact by diminishing their grace. At the same time, the impression of liveliness is enhanced by the use of head-types derived from Classical sculpture. The effects certainly made an impression on men like Villard de Honnecourt, and notable reflections of this style are also found in the Empire at Strasbourg and Bamberg (1230s); and in England at Wells Cathedral (*c*1230). Yet the classicism of the style as a whole is, at best, fitful. Classical sculpture usually acted as a reser-

voir of ideas for artists interested in lifelike results, and the example of Nicola Pisano can be used to demonstrate a 13th-century artist using the Antique with dramatically different results. Eventually, the somewhat baroque appearance of the *Muldenstil* must have grated on someone's susceptibilities and it was replaced (at Paris *c*1210–20 and Amiens *c*1220–30) by a style notably simpler—at Amiens almost to a point of dullness. The antique figures at Reims are thus in no sense a part of a general renaissance of the Antique, but a chapter in the complicated history of the development of a more lifelike form of art.

ANDREW MARTINDALE

Further reading. Hahnloser, H.R. *Villard de Honnecourt*, Vienna (1935). *Rhein und Maas* (2 vols.), Cologne (1973). Sauerländer, W. *Gothic Sculpture in France 1140–1270*, London (1970). Swarzenski, H. *Nicola Pisano*, Frankfurt am Main (1926).

The west front of Reims Cathedral; 13th century; upper gallery and towers 15th century

▼ The Adoration of the Magi, a relief panel on the Pisa Baptistry pulpit by Nicola Pisano; *c*1258–60

Below right The Death of the Virgin, the tympanum of the south transept portal of Strasbourg Cathedral; *c*1230–9

► An early example of Classical influence in the Gothic period, the Nativity from an altarpiece by Nicholas of Verdun; 1181. Museum des Chorherrenstiftes, Klosterneuburg

changes which by any pre-19th-century standards would be regarded as rapid.

The rather tight linearity of the Chartres convention had its limitations. It could be worked into a portal of elaborate richness at Avalon (c1150–60) in which all suggestions of decorative restraint have gone; or it could be applied to figures like those of Senlis (c1175) whose strange, abrupt, and contorted postures seem clearly designed to suggest drama and unease. It was about this time that a new drapery style developed which was quite unlike Chartres' and, in its own way, much more realistic. This style is usually called, from its characteristic fold pattern, the "troughed" style, or (in German) *muldenstil*, and its origins appear to be in the region of the River Meuse.

One of its earliest and most complete statements is in an *ambo*, later transformed into an altarpiece (Museum des Chorherrenstiftes, Klosterneuburg). This is dated 1181 and is the work of a metalworker called Nicholas of Verdun whose subsequent career can be traced into the early years of the 13th century. The *muldenstil* owes much to antique sculpture—ultimately to sculpture of the 5th century BC, although we are not sure whether this was known through originals or Roman copies. The achievement of this style is to give credible substance to the drapery (contrast the style of Chartres), to allow both a display of fold patterns and the form of the body to emerge from beneath the folds. Nicholas' debt to the antique is not especially surprising since there is spasmodic evidence from earlier in the 12th century that Classical art and architecture had a continuing fascination. Nicholas' particular achievement, however, was to extract, use, and (apparently) to popularize an antique drapery style without the least trace of arid antiquarianism. It is a tribute to the creative possibilities of this style that it could be used in very different circumstances—on the transept portals of Chartres (c1200–10), for instance. In fact, it was not until its final phases (c1220) that any sculptor thought of pressing the style's antiquarian aspects to the limit to produce statues that look unmistakably antique. These well-known figures are to be found on the west front and transepts at Reims (c1220), and include the famous Visitation group.

The two stylistic trends so far described flourished in the provincial areas of France and the low countries. At this point, c1200, Paris again became a focus of development. This is difficult to demonstrate: comparatively little good sculpture in Paris survived 18th-century destruction and 19th-century restorations. Thus, although the next important monument is the northwest portal of Notre Dame (c1205), the best surviving example of this new style is now the west front of Amiens Cathedral (c1225). The taste exhibited by these figures is extremely sedate and restrained. Nicholas of Verdun's drapery troughs have vanished, almost as if they had never existed; instead the clothes have voluminous folds. The origins of this style could lie in 10th-century Byzantine ivories.

Ultimately, also probably in Paris and presumably out of this new sculptural style, there developed a style best known in the work of the so-called Joseph Master at Reims Cathedral

(c1240). The V-shaped folds of the Amiens style became more pronounced and enveloping, the figures more graceful and animated, and a characteristic daintiness developed. This is really the general style of French sculpture as it remained for at least 100 years—and is therefore a significant point of arrival. As a drapery and figure convention, it received somewhat exaggerated expression in the Apostle figures of Louis IX's palace chapel, the Sainte Chapelle, built in the 1240s.

By the time of Reims Cathedral, the St-Denis architect's conceptions concerning the west front of a large church, while still recognizable, had been considerably modified. The main change architects had to cope with was the increased height of the buildings behind the facades; a long succession of cathedrals, including Laon, Chartres, Amiens, and Reims testify to the various solutions tried. The chief problem was to establish a visual connection between the central rose window, of necessity just beneath the vault, and the portals at ground level beneath. The Reims solution is notable because the architect boldly increased the size of the central portal gable so that it penetrates right up to the center of the rose window—and is indeed freestanding in front of it. This contains the element of an important idea in later Gothic architecture when architects increasingly experimented with superimposed layers of decorative work and tracery. At Strasbourg, the great central portal gable became a part of this decorative fretwork.

One further sculptural innovation from the early 13th century should be mentioned: the decoration of capitals and roof bosses with realistic carved botanical foliage. These are especially prominent at Reims, but occur early at Chartres and are to be found on a large number of French 13th-century churches.

In view of the enormous success of the St-Denis type of portal, and the extensive evidence of a lively and vigorous sculptural tradition in France, it is surprising that foreigners reacted either slowly or not at all. The most complete imitation of a French portal occurs in Spain at Burgos Cathedral c1235, where the Portada del Sarmental has close affinities to the west portals of Amiens. In England, there is little to suggest French Gothic influence until the 13th century; the first surviving complex of Gothic sculpture is on the screen-like west facade of Wells Cathedral (begun c1225), an architectural concept with clear Romanesque antecedents in the west of France. Although the sculptural style is reasonably close to contemporary developments in France, the architectural framework would hardly have been acceptable to a metropolitan French mason. Something similar is true of the south portal of Strasbourg Cathedral (c1230). Here the sculpture, of the highest quality, is close in style to the graceful porch sculpture of Chartres. But architecturally, the doorway itself is a strange mixture of elements with a strong Romanesque feeling. Equally strangely ambivalent is the sculpture of Bamberg Cathedral (c1235). The high quality, striking figures are carved in the almost outmoded *muldenstil*. But it is not at all clear what they were intended to decorate: several are inside the Cathedral in unrelated positions round the choir. Of all the German early Gothic sculpture, the easternmost examples are among the most exciting. The Wise and Foolish Virgins of Magdeburg Cathedral (c1245) demonstrate an extremely exaggerated emotion, as yet unequalled. But the far more restrained drama of Naumburg Cathedral (c1245–50) with its large, illusionistically conceived statues of secular benefactors round its west choir, is probably more arresting and memorable.

Twelfth-century European painting was, for the most part, still dominated by varying degrees of Byzantinism. There is no real equivalent to the Chartres style, nor any center or school that produced work of the significance of the architectural and sculptural complex of St-Denis. But the Klosterneuburg Altar was composed chiefly of enameled plaques and, to that extent, was pictorial rather than sculptural; so it is not surprising to find the *muldenstil* being adopted by painters as well as by sculptors. That it in any case achieved a two-dimensional existence in masons' notebooks is clear from a remarkable survival: the sketchbook of Villard de Honnecourt, a north-French mason who visited Reims Cathedral c1220—about the period when the so-called "classical" masters were at work. But even before this at the beginning of the century, a sumptuous Psalter was made for Queen Ingeborg of France (the Ingeborg Psalter; Musée Condé, Chantilly) in which pictorial illustrations were executed in the same general style. The attraction of this style was probably the bulk, roundness, and definition it gave the figures, as well as its decorative characteristics. At all events, parallel development can be found elsewhere c1200 in which a softer and heavier drapery style is achieved by similar means, although without the ubiquitous troughed effects of the *muldenstil*. This is particularly clear in a magnificent series of Psalters painted in England, and, indeed, changes in pictorial approach are virtually "chronicled" in a large work such as the Winchester Bible (Winchester Cathedral) in which the painting was done over a lengthy period. Here, the very latest contributions, made towards the end of the 12th century, are far removed from the Romanesque style of the first illustrations.

In England and France, however, the pictorial style that prevailed for much of the first half of the 13th century was a version of the *muldenstil*: the drapery, although no longer dominated by troughs and ridges, is still strongly curvilinear in its patterns; the figures, as a complement, are arranged in graceful, curving attitudes. This general style is strongly in evidence in a number of sumptuous French books, including a series of *Bibles Moralisées*—books of selected passages from the Old and New Testaments, each selection carrying with it an allegorical gloss—some of which were probably produced for the French court. It is also the style in which a large amount of France's early-13th-century stained glass was painted. It survived until the 1240s, and is found in the window painting of the Sainte Chapelle and also in part of an Evangelary ordered at the same period by Louis IX for his new foundation of the Sainte Chapelle. In England, it survived longer. It is the stylistic language of Matthew Paris, and a

The outpouring of the Holy Spirit at Pentecost, from the Ingeborg Psalter; early 13th century. Musée Condé, Chantilly

series of illustrated Apocalypse manuscripts and further sumptuous Psalters were similarly decorated. Some of this English illustration takes the form of tinted outline drawing (especially that of Matthew Paris), a curious and effective revival of an English tradition dating back to the 11th century.

Germany stood somewhat apart from this general development. In fact, the Byzantine tendencies of the 12th century seem to have been reinforced in a book such as the Weingarten Missal (c1216; Pierpont Morgan Library, New York; MS. 710) and the ceiling of St Michael's church, Hildesheim (c1230–40). Far from developing anything as graceful as the *muldenstil*, artists within the Empire produced a highly mannered version of stylistic elements, visible, for instance, in the 12th-century mosaics of Sicily or the 13th-century mosaics of St Mark's, Venice. Figures and drapery tend to assume angular spiky shapes. One of the more striking manifestations of this style is the painted altarpiece of the Trinity from Soest (Westphalia), probably c1230–40 (Staatliche Museen, Berlin). It flourished for about 80 years in the Rhineland, Westphalia, and Saxony, but eventually came to be superseded by something altogether more elegant and ultimately dependent on Paris.

It is at about this point in the history of Gothic art that the almost total absence of a contemporary tradition of literary commentary on the aims and achievements of artists is strongly felt. All artistic production involves choice—by artists as well as patrons. Human choice may not always be the product of reason, but is often the product of argument. Some of the arguments of the Gothic period, such as the aesthetic defensibility of flying buttresses, must have occupied professional architects at a general level over a considerable period. Others, such as the employment of especially idiosyncratic masters like the sculptor of Senlis, must have occupied the Cathedral authorities there for a comparatively short time. William of Sens at Canterbury is known to have been selected from a large group of contending masons. But although we can infer from the results the kind of aesthetic preferences current during this period, we can hardly begin to reconstruct the character of the argument by which these preferences were defended or supported. It is clear from the results, for instance, that during the first half of the 13th century, realism in sculpture was much appreciated. Sculptors seem to have been consciously attempting to impress the physical presence of their work on the spectator by its realistic and humane qualities. This is manifested as much in the extreme realism of some of the carved foliage as in the sometimes startling essays in emotional expressions. The statues of Wise and Foolish Virgins on the portal of Magdeburg Cathedral show contrasting degrees of smug self-satisfaction and despairing grief and frustration of a sort probably never explored since Classical Antiquity. The changing drapery conventions and the spasmodic classicism may be seen as successive attempts to reach a realistic solution, without sacrificing the aesthetic demands of decorative pattern. However, it is equally apparent that the figurative arts were not in step. In the second half of the century, the painters ultimately adopted a drapery style that had much in common with that of the Joseph Master (fl. c1230–45). But as far as the ideal of realism went, earlier-13th-century painters ignored the element of the third dimension almost entirely—although this was one of the things sculptors were successfully exploiting. The jambs of the portals of Reims, for instance, became progressively more of a stage on which action took place. The west choir of Naumburg Cathedral possesses a complicated series of cross-relationships between the carved figures which are set at intervals round the choir. But the idea of making figures act and move in a spatially described setting was almost totally ignored by northern 13th-century painters. (It was eventually developed in the quite different context of Italian wall-painting.) The northern painters were self-evidently not insensitive, and they were probably aware of the course taken by the sculptors. Yet virtually no steps were taken in the exploration of linear perspective, and the pictorial style as a whole seems to have been directed against the sort of experiments in facial description and characterization common in sculpture. These differences point to a positive sense of fitness and taste, and a strong sense of tradition, to balance against the desire for innovation. But the language in which these preferences and reservations were couched is now largely a matter for speculation.

Two wise virgins on the portal of Magdeburg Cathedral; c1237

The high Gothic period (outside Italy) 1250–1300. Up to c1230, the major architects of France had been preoccupied with structure and engineering, following the liberating acceptance of the flying buttress. Around 1230, however, they must have realized that building enlarged versions of Chartres Cathedral could no longer constitute progress: in practice, the highest vault ever built, at Beauvais Cathedral—158 ft (48 m)—later collapsed in 1284. Thus in the years after 1240 there was a radical reorientation of architectural thinking, and the first major building in which this is apparent is, again, the abbey church of St-Denis.

At some date after 1231, the Abbot and monks decided to pull down the Carolingian church and rebuild the nave and transepts to form a more splendid link between Abbot Suger's choir and the west front. The designer was Pierre de Montreuil (fl. 1231–67). In its interior elevations, the church retains the clerestory-triforium-arcade arrangement of Chartres but with an entirely new stress on glazing and tracery, though window tracery first appeared on a large scale at Reims Cathedral. The architect of St-Denis realized that with the main structural stresses and strains now concentrated in the major piers and buttresses, much of the wall space in between was superfluous for keeping the building up. Consequently, he dissolved it into window space, heightening the effect by bringing the glazed area down into the triforium gallery. Thus the entire upper half of the main elevation of the interior of St-Denis is a succession of huge windows, filled with patterns of window tracery. At the same time, huge rose windows were inserted into the transept ends: it is this particular "radiating" feature that has given the name *Rayonnant* to the architectural style as a whole. The lightness and grace of this type of architecture remained a feature of most subsequent Gothic architectural development in France; the manipulations of two features of St-Denis, the tracery pattern and the tracery screen, became the preoccupations that most occupied subsequent masons. Of the numerous cathedrals and churches that might be selected to show the course of this development, one of the smaller and most complete examples is the church of St-Urbain at Troyes, begun in 1262. One of the largest and most magnificent *pièces de résistance* of the style is to be found in the transept facades of Notre Dame, Paris (designed by Jean de Chelles); the north belongs to the 1250s, the south was begun in 1258, and both were added to the 12th-century building to bring it more into line with current architectural practice.

Outside France, the impact of this new style was very soon apparent. Two large German buildings, Cologne Cathedral, begun in 1248, and Strasbourg Cathedral, begun *c*1245, repeated the essential features of St-Denis—though on a colossal scale. At Strasbourg, the west facade, planned in 1277 by a German architect called Erwin, shows an extraordinary virtuoso use of tracery in windows and on screens of masonry. The facade was later much modified, but even at this date was intended to have its towers surmounted by slender, open, lantern-like octagonal structures capped by spires. Spain also possesses a Rayonnant cathedral at Leon, begun in 1255, and in England, the transept facades of Westminster Abbey (after 1245) and the east facade of the medieval cathedral of St Paul in London (begun in 1258), dominated by their great rose windows, would both have seemed familiar to a Parisian architect.

Yet alongside these achievements, deeply rooted local preferences persisted. In Spain, for instance, the great architects active *c*1300 reverted to the type of interior elevation dominated by a giant arcade: for example, Gerona Cathedral, begun *c*1291, Barcelona, begun in 1298, and Palma de Mallorca, begun *c*1300. In the Empire, the chief type of church built from *c*1300 onwards was the hall-church as already seen in St Elizabeth, Marburg (the most notable hall-churches belong to the 15th century); while in England, Westminster Abbey has always seemed to stand apart from the main line of developments—although it had great importance in some respects, such as the popularization of window tracery.

Westminster Abbey (rebuilt from 1245 onwards) was designed by an architect called Henry of Reyns—it is still not clear whether he was from Raynes (Essex), Reims, or somewhere else. His building was nevertheless deeply influenced in its interior effect by Louis IX's Sainte Chapelle, built in the 1240s. This palace chapel, designed to house, among others, a relic of the True Cross, was of unparalleled richness inside; in its wealth of carving, painting, and deeply colored glass, it was unlike most other contemporary French building. The Sainte

Chapelle must be one of the last major ecclesiastical buildings in France in which expert performances in the various applied arts were allowed to make a decisive contribution to the architectural effect. This change of attitude, already mentioned, must represent some sort of professional change within the masons' ranks. Those who designed buildings from the 1240s onwards became increasingly preoccupied with the intellectual exercises of tracery patterns (and later, vault designs). From *c*1280 onwards, major works of sculpture seldom appear on architecture.

Westminster Abbey followed the Sainte Chapelle to the extent that most of its interior surfaces were either carved or painted. This love of rich surfaces was imitated, for instance, in the Angel choir of Lincoln Cathedral, begun in 1256; but in two respects Westminster was seriously out-of-line with English practice (and, perhaps, in line with that of France): it is sparing in the use of colonnettes and vaulting ribs. The fashion for both features continued in England up to the end of the century, and when combined with the new possibilities of window tracery produced some overwhelmingly rich interiors, such as Exeter Cathedral, begun before 1280.

From some points of view, English architects lagged behind the Continent in their practice. It is true that England preserves one of the last great assemblages of realistic botanical foliage sculpture at Southwell Minster, Nottinghamshire, executed at a time in the 1290s when it was falling out of fashion elsewhere in Europe. It is also remarkable that tribune galleries should have survived as an element in the elevations of large churches into the second half of the 13th century. However, the intense amount of English experiment in tracery design and vault patterning were very important, and, in both, English architects made significant contributions to the development of European Gothic architecture.

This became apparent at the end of the 13th century in the nave of York Minster (begun in 1291) which, with the palace chapel of St Stephen, Westminster (begun in 1291, now mostly destroyed) is perhaps the most important building towards the turn of the century. The architect of York abandoned almost all the decorative features of, for example, Lincoln, and also abolished the tribune gallery. The elevation came much closer to a Rayonnant conception and is by earlier standards rather austere. However, the interior is roofed by an elaborate vault of intersecting tracery containing one of the first instances of lierne ribs. At St Stephen's, the architect combined a lierne vault with the elaborate extensions of window tracery over wall surfaces in the form of tracery panels. Perhaps the best impression of this general effect can now be gained from the choir of Gloucester Cathedral (refurbished soon after 1330). Gloucester choir is, of course, traditionally known as one of the earliest examples of Perpendicular style—from this it can be seen how Perpendicular is really the English equivalent of Rayonnant.

In the years following 1250, European sculpture ceased to undergo the dramatic and rapid transformation that had been a characteristic of its history over the previous 100 years. The

style visible in the later sculpture of Reims is not particularly different from that of sculpture carved 100 years later. The most interesting developments of that period relate not so much to the detailed appearance of sculpture as to the way in which it was used. There are indeed some notable exceptions to these observations. The "leaves of Southwell" were perhaps the last time in European art that capitals were given such minute individual attention. English figure sculpture in general lagged a little behind French developments. The mid-13th-century figure sculpture of Westminster Abbey contains none of the heavy drapery folds of the Joseph Master; only with the Angel choir at Lincoln, after 1256, did these enter the English repertoire.

One curious feature of this period is the virtual absence of commanding portal sculpture. The extremely vivid and dramatic figures on the west front of Strasbourg Cathedral (probably c1280–1300) only make the general absence more striking. It is true that major facades of this kind were appar-

ently less frequently built; but it seems that major sculptors were less willing to be involved in this type of work, seeking to make their mark in other fields.

In fact, first-class sculptors seem to have moved away from architecture (perhaps with the encouragement of architects) and to have worked instead on smaller commissions for which they took full responsibility and control. By far the largest surviving number of examples are sepulchral monuments. Before 1250, the tomb as a work of art has a modest history in northern Europe. But part of the history of the secularization of art lies in the increasing demand by secular patrons for personal memorials. Louis IX was an important figure in this respect since he reorganized the remains of his Capetian ancestors and his own family into two mausolea, at Royaumont and St-Denis, and provided a series of monuments for many of the remains. Unfortunately, French tombs as a whole suffered irreparable damage during the French Revolution; the best surviving medieval mausoleum is Westminster Abbey,

Left: Spanish Gothic: the choir and the ambulatory of Gerona Cathedral; begun c1291

English Gothic: the choir and part of the north transept of Gloucester Cathedral; mid 14th century

followed closely by the 14th-century burial place of the Despenser family, Tewkesbury Abbey, Gloucestershire. In Westminster Abbey, the most important monument for its style is that of Edmund Crouchback (*ob.* 1296) which with its great canopy, multiple gables and pinnacles, numerous figures, and lavish coloring set a standard of decorative ostentation which influenced English sculptors for the next half century. However, this particular decorative ideal had probably in its turn been influenced by the work of some itinerant Roman marble-workers, brought to the Abbey during the 1260s and 1270s to execute the presbytery pavement, the tomb of Henry III, the shrine of Edward the Confessor, and a number of lesser items. These survive, an oddly foreign contribution to the ensemble. Henry III's tomb (which is a Roman altar made to contain relics and may have been originally intended for the body of St Edward) was eventually completed by Edward I with the addition of a bronze effigy of Henry by William Torel (active 1290s).

But even as this fashion for magnificence was being established in England, something more restrained and sober was being evolved in France where royal tombs were normally composed of alabaster effigies on black marble sarcophagi. Color was in general limited to costume detail, accoutrements, and heraldry. The best examples of this ideal also survive in England, one of them, in Westminster Abbey, to Queen Philippa of Hainault, actually designed and made *c*1365–7 by the French court sculptor Jean Hennequin de Liège (*fl.* 1361–82). In the same tradition is the monument to Edward II (in Gloucester Cathedral; *c*1330–5); but this has in addition a fantastic canopy which, apart from a few English derivations and some unexplained parallels at Avignon, stands outside the canon of general European taste. These tombs were intensely personal memorials, and predictably heraldry—as an organized system virtually a creation of the 13th century—played an important part. Louis IX's monuments included sarcophagi some of which were decorated with small figures, traditionally called "weeper-figures" and intended to remind the spectator of the relatives of the dead person. But the most striking piece of personalization, which became common from now on, lay in the treatment of the effigy itself. Here half a century of experiment in facial characterization now bore fruit in the endowment of effigies with "portrait" faces. In many cases, of course, there is no evidence that a face is a real portrait, but often a face displays distinct characterization aimed at making it look different from other faces, and so unique. Ultimately (towards the end of the 14th century) evidence indicates that artists could and did take death masks.

Around 1250, Parisian court painting acquired many of the characteristics of the sculptural style of the Joseph Master and the sculpture of the Sainte Chapelle. Almost all trace of the *muldenstil* finally disappeared and was replaced by a type of "broad-fold" drapery, soft and voluminous, which hangs rather than clings, and which tends to fall in the V-shaped folds already familiar in sculpture. At the same time, figures tend to become daintier, and faces in particular lose the roundness and substance of previous work and become somewhat pallid essays in minute virtuoso penmanship. All these features are visible in a Psalter done for Louis IX himself (Bibliothèque Nationale, Paris; MS. Lat. 10525) and in a number of other books executed in Paris around this time.

The position of Louis in this development is central because we know he began to build up a library of books specially executed for himself. Another early example of this style is in an Evangelary executed for the Sainte Chapelle (Bibliothèque Nationale, Paris; MSS. Lat. 8892 and 17326); a further example is in a Psalter done for his sister Isabella of France (Fitzwilliam Museum, Cambridge; MS. 300). Moreover, the center for the further development of this style remained Paris, and one of its subsequent exponents known by name is Master Honoré, an artist who worked for Louis IX's grandson, Philip the Fair (1285–1314). Honoré's documented career belongs to the late 13th century; and while his painting has much in common with the so-called St Louis style, he managed by modeling his drapery into white highlights to give it a bulk and solidity previously lacking. The discovery of light as a pictorial factor should, from every point of view, have a European significance and it is a teasing problem that its discovery is evident at about the same time in Italy in the painting of Pietro Cavallini (*c*1250–1330). This could be early evi-

A folio from the **Psalter of Louis IX**; 1253–70. Bibliothèque Nationale, Paris

dence of stylistic influence of Italy on northern Gothic art, but the firm testimony of dated work is unfortunately lacking.

Nevertheless, the influence of Italian art became a pervasive factor in 14th-century Paris. The reasons for this were in part ones of circumstance. It is not known when Honoré died, although his workshop tradition was presumably continued by his son-in-law, Richard of Verdun (*fl.* 1288–1318). At this time, three Roman painters were living in Paris where they had moved when the Papal court left Rome for the south of France (1305). They were employed in Paris for two decades and it is hard to believe that their work (now entirely destroyed) did not make some sort of impact. No work by Richard of Verdun is known; but his successor as court painter, Jean Pucelle, was very much a student of Italian art. Pucelle is now known to have died in 1334 and his working life seems to have been comparatively short. During the 1320s, however, he probably supervised the production of a small number of important manuscripts, especially for members of the royal family: his workshop was apparently active up to the middle of the century. Pucelle introduced Italianate perspective into Parisian painting (he could have been to Italy and known Duccio's *Maestà*). He also popularized a fashion for monochrome painting (usually called grisaille) which followed the developments under Honoré: it necessarily entailed the description of forms chiefly in terms of shadows and highlights. There are distinguished earlier examples of grisaille painting in Giotto's Capella dell'Arena at Padua (*c*1305–10). These importations were of great consequence because they launched northern painting, in the wake of the Italians, in the pursuit of realistic pictorial space. The advance was gradual, and, once again, the pressure of tradition and, presumably, ideas of pictorial decorum were always important, but the change of direction is clearly perceptible.

The distinguishing features of the St Louis style appeared in English court art during the third quarter of the 13th century. A book such as the so-called Douce Apocalypse (before 1272; Bodleian Library, Oxford) has the soft hanging drapery with the V-shaped folds, and also the minute, carefully drawn faces. This book seems to have been intended for Edward I, before his accession. Another important book in a similar style is a Psalter (British Library, London; MS. 24686) begun for Edward I's son Alfonso (*ob.* 1284). In England, a unique group of large-scale paintings in the same style and from a similar date survives in Westminster Abbey, including notably the so-called Westminster Retable. This is a large panel-painting, meticulously and finely painted, with the heavy modeling associated with Master Honoré's work.

In following this English style into the 14th century, the formal characteristics of the decorated manuscripts become more important than the exact way in which the figures are painted. The so-called East Anglian School of manuscript painters is distinguished by the elaborate quality of its border

Right: St Peter, a panel of the Westminster Retable; late 13th century. Westminster Abbey, London

English Manuscript Painting c1280-1350

By any standards, the late 13th century and the first half of the 14th must count as one of the golden periods of English painting and figurative design. Works of the highest quality survive in all manner of different media, including manuscripts, panel-painting, stained glass, and needlework. The various media are interrelated, and together offer a beautifully complete pattern of artistic production.

The period is best seen as one in which a number of individual artists with their workshops responded in various highly personal ways to the style associated with the royal court and abbey at Westminster. Important in the exposition of that style is the Psalter begun for Edward I's son, Alphonso, shortly before his death in 1284 (the Alphonso Psalter; British Library, London). This has much in common with contemporary French art, particularly in the delicacy of the figure drawing and painting. But the vitality and variety of the border decoration go far beyond anything in contemporary Parisian work, and it was in the development of this

particular potential that many of the subsequent manuscripts excelled.

One group of these manuscripts, a reasonably coherent one, is associated with the Abbey of Peterborough and a number of neighboring institutions. Probably the oldest, and certainly the most sumptuous, member of the group was actually made for the Abbot of Peterborough, Godfrey de Croyland (the Peterborough Psalter; Bibliothèque Royale Albert I, Brussels). The painting shows a vivid awareness of the visible world, and a remarkable observation of human beings, animals, birds, and plants. Even more elaborate are two books from a different group associated with the diocese of Norwich: the Ormesby Psalter (Bodleian Library, Oxford) and the Gorleston Psalter (British Library, London).

The richness of the inspiration underlying English painting becomes clear when these books are contrasted with a further contemporary group of manuscripts of which the most exquisite example is the Queen Mary Psalter (British Library, London). In these,

the emphasis is on delicacy and restraint. Border decoration is far less exuberant than in the works already noted, and the colors are less brilliant and strident. In general, their aesthetic impression is more in keeping with the contemporary Parisian style of Master Honoré and Jean Pucelle.

These works form only a small part of a total output. Many of the others are well-known. A late example from this period is the Luttrell Psalter (British Library, London), not perhaps of the highest quality but famous for its border paintings showing scenes from everyday life. The patrons for whom these manuscripts were produced varied considerably. Some were ecclesiastics like Godfrey de Croyland. Others seem to have been laymen and women—often of considerable means, since the most elaborate of these books have characteristically been the possessions of rich people. The geographical distribution of these patrons is of some interest: many of the

◄ An illuminated initial from the Gorleston Psalter; c1300–25. British Library, London

► An illuminated initial from the Alphonso Psalter, painted shortly before 1284. British Library, London

▼ A detail from a processional scene in a border of the Luttrell Psalter; c1340. British Library, London

◄ A folio showing the more restrained style of the Queen Mary Psalter; c1300–10. British Library, London

Above left Italian influence, the Sienese-style leaf added to the Gorleston Psalter; c1300–25. British Library, London

▲ An early folio from the St-Omer Psalter; c1330. British Library, London

books have connections with the eastern counties of England, which leads to the proposition that here we are dealing in some sense with an East Anglian school of painting.

The tendency in the past has been to emphasize the role of East Anglian religious houses in its development. But virtually no documentary evidence about the artists survives, and current scholarly opinion tends to play down both the importance of monasteries in general, and East Anglian monasteries in particular, as decisive factors. These books were probably the product of groups of secular painters, often trained in London, who worked either there or in important provincial centers such as Norwich. The actual impetus towards change and development probably gathered force in the capital too.

Some indication of the nature of subse-quent developments is already clear in the later manuscripts, c1320. They amount in various forms to Italian influence. An added leaf in the Gorleston Psalter shows a very Italianate Crucifixion reminiscent of Sienese art; the earliest work in the St-Omer Psalter (British Library, London) shows, within the traditional ornate border setting, figures whose foreshortened limbs and modeled faces with beady, black eyes represent a general reappraisal of the importance of structure in pictorial composition. The precedents for this also lie in Italy. Thus these manuscripts offer hints of the direction taken by painting in the second half of the century.

ANDREW MARTINDALE

Further reading. *Medieval Art in East Anglia 1300–1520*, Norwich (1973). Rickett, M. *Painting in Britain: the Middle Ages*, Harmondsworth (1965). Sandler, L.P. *The Peterborough Psalter in Brussels and other Fenland Manuscripts*, London (1974).

decorations and the inventiveness of its grotesques. Many of the manuscripts (chiefly Psalters) have definite connections with East Anglia, interpreted to include Peterborough as well as Ramsey and Norwich. Others, such as the so-called Queen Mary Psalter (British Library, London), may have been court works done in London; indeed, aesthetically this manuscript has much in common with Pucelle's work (it is probably earlier). English painting of the first part of the 14th century frequently exhibits minor Italianisms, mainly of figure-style; one leaf added to the Gorleston Psalter (probably c1330; British Library, London) is painted with a Crucifixion strikingly reminiscent of Sienese art. Yet, on the whole, Pucelle's penetrating grasp of the rudiments of Italian spatial construction is not found in England until much later in the 14th century.

The attractions first of the St Louis style and then of Italian art are also in evidence in the Empire during this period; some of the paintings added to the Klosterneuburg Altar (1324–9), for instance, contain some very obvious examples of Italian iconography. The tiny faces and dainty gestures remain a legacy from the 13th century. In Spain, on the other hand, the impact of the Italian Trecento (14th century) style seems to have been more profound and far-reaching. In particular, the works of Ferrer Bassa (c1290–1348) are thoroughly Italian-ate—they might almost be mistaken for the work of a provincial Italian (but Ferrer Bassa came from Barcelona); and this striking Italian bias remained a characteristic of Spanish painting for the remainder of the century.

Italian Gothic Art to c1350. We have postponed a consideration of Italian Gothic art for two reasons. First, in European terms it developed at a comparatively late stage; second, its characteristics set it apart from the developments so far considered. There were, in fact, some tangible physical differences about Italian art. Sculpture was mainly in marble, buildings were predominantly of brick, and the most important pictorial work was on a large scale—panel or mural. However, Italy's geographical position must also be taken into account. Italy is a Mediterranean country, and in the figurative arts, at least, the influence of Byzantium remained strong until the middle of the 13th century.

The gigantic differences between Italy and the North emerge immediately one looks at the history of Italian Gothic architecture. Elsewhere in Europe, there is evidence that in most countries there were architects interested in and ready to experiment with the Rayonnant style. This feature is almost entirely missing in Italy. In the North, the Cistercians, in the 12th century, played a modest role in the dissemination of basic Gothic moldings, pointed arches, and ribbed vaults. In Italy, a small number of Cistercian churches, although later than their northern counterparts, stand out as exceptional in a country in which the characteristics of Romanesque architecture survive up to the end of the 13th century. A church such as Fossanova (Cistercian, consecrated in 1208) will seem revolutionary in a century that in 1290 was still producing the enormous Romanesque nave of Orvieto Cathedral.

In fact, Italian architectural ideals were totally different from those of northern masons, and in many ways much simpler. Window tracery, the glazed triforium, vaulting patterns, and multi-storey elevations played virtually no part in Italian building. Architects made almost no use of flying buttresses, but this did not stop them building large buildings—the nave of Florence Cathedral, built in the late 14th century, is as tall as most French naves. Italian expertise for the most part was put into providing wide churches with enormously high arcades. The most striking—the cathedrals of Florence and Orvieto, S. Croce (in Florence), and S. Petronio in Bologna among them— offer the visitor height and spaciousness, but not much else.

Against this general background, a few of the essays in external adornment stand out. The campanile of Florence Cathedral was originally intended, in the 1330s, to have an octagonal openwork tower on its top, capped with a spire, in a manner similar to the spires of Cologne and Freiburg. Siena Cathedral has a facade whose lower half, begun in the 1280s, has three deep gabled porches similar to French portals of half a century earlier. Orvieto Cathedral has a facade begun in 1310 which comes closest to a piece of Rayonnant architecture with large porches and gables thrusting through into the upper stories. The impression this creates, however, is of a series of individual essays rather than a development backed up by any coherent community of thought.

By contrast, the history of sculpture offers a quite coherent story of development—even if it is conducted on a regional basis. Once again, Italian Gothic developments are somewhat later than those in the North: the earliest indubitably Gothic sculpture appeared around the middle of the 13th century in the work of Nicola Pisano (fl. 1258–78). The circumstances in which Nicola was trained to carve are entirely mysterious. Nothing survives in Tuscany from before this date which remotely touches his imaginative powers and expertise. The pulpit in the Baptistery of Pisa Cathedral (signed by him in 1259) combines the heavy V-shaped folds of mid-13th-century drapery with some remarkable imitations of Classical heads and other antique features. Nicola's narrative reliefs, moreover, bear little resemblance to northern reliefs, but seem to be constructed after the principles of Classical sarcophagi. It is interesting and reminiscent of Nicholas of Verdun, that Nicola should have gone to Classical art when evolving a realistic sculptural style; and, as with Nicholas of Verdun, his later sculpture is less Classical than his earlier work and in many details more like northern Gothic.

A combination of documents and signatures give us some idea of the composition of Nicola's workshop (contrast those of the northern masons). From his next monument, the pulpit of Siena Cathedral, a contract survives in which the sculptors are named as Nicola, his son Giovanni, Arnolfo di Cambio, and Lapo and Donato (otherwise unknown). Both Giovanni and Arnolfo were still alive and working 30 years later (c1300), each with an individual style which may nevertheless be seen to emerge from Nicola's training. This type of information can presumably be applied in northern circumstances

The nave, the aisles, and apse of Florence Cathedral; late 14th century

and to northern monuments.

Within Nicola's family circle, the speciality seems to have been pulpits. He and his son Giovanni (with assistants) between them produced four; the last (in Pisa Cathedral, of 1302–10) by Giovanni is artistically the least interesting. In sheer size, however, it must be one of the largest pulpits ever built, and it has many curious details and a very elaborate iconography. Giovanni's greatest work, however, is the truly monumental facade of Siena Cathedral, built in the 1280s and 1290s. Unfortunately, the upper half was not completed at this time and only the portals with figure sculpture can be considered as Giovanni's. But the application of the enormous figures *above* the portal gables is highly original, and the extraordinarily dramatic twist given to the whole ensemble shows Giovanni Pisano to be an impresario and stage manager of a high order.

Giovanni Pisano specialized in pathos, emotion, and deeply cut dramatic drapery. By comparison, the work of his contemporaries and successors seems rather tame. Arnolfo di Cambio went to Rome in the 1270s where he, too, established a flourishing workshop. His style, more solid and pedestrian than Giovanni's, is nevertheless at its best of an extremely high technical order. In Rome, he became a designer of church furniture and tombs, adapting to his own uses much of the brilliant decorative ideas of the local cosmati mosaic workers (already familiar in this context from their almost concurrent work in Westminster Abbey). Some of his work is startlingly magnificent and highly imaginative, for instance the tomb of the Cardinal De Braye (*ob.* 1281) in S. Domenico, Orvieto. Late in life (1296) Arnolfo was recalled to Florence, his original home, to design the new cathedral. He built part of a new west facade, though little of this now survives; but the event is of some interest because elsewhere in Europe the employment of first-rate sculptors as architects seems by this date to have been uncommon.

The sculpture on the west facade of Orvieto (*c*1310–30) is normally attributed to the master mason Lorenzo Maitani (*fl.* 1302–30). Some of it is reminiscent of the style of Giovanni Pisano, but it demonstrates a regard for low relief and fine finish which suggests the sculptor in charge had a different training. However, the immediate origins of both the style of the sculpture and the way it is applied to the facade in large reliefs flanking the portals are very far from clear. The Orvieto sculpture is not alone in this. Another high-quality work, the pair of bronze doors by Andrea Pisano (*fl.* 1330–49) on the Florentine Baptistery (1330–6), also has an enigmatic quality.

Statues carved by Giovanni Pisano for the facade of Siena Cathedral;
in the foreground, Mary the sister of Moses; marble; height 194cm (76in);
late 13th century. Museo dell'Opera del Duomo, Siena

Andrea Pisano was a designer of the first order who, perhaps
more than any other artist, exploited the economy and directness of Giotto's early style. His name indicates he came from
Pisa, and documents make it clear he was a goldsmith; but
although his style contains reminiscences of the Orvieto reliefs, the material as a whole produces no conclusive evidence
about his original training. Taking his work and the Orvieto
sculpture together, we are merely left with the impression that
there is a missing chapter in the development of Italian Gothic
sculpture which ought to complement the pervasive influence
of Nicola Pisano and his workshop.

This influence, indeed, extended throughout the first half of
the 14th century, visible alike in the work of Giovanni Balduc-
cio in Milan (fl. 1315–49) and Tino di Camaino in Naples
(c1295–1337) and of their respective followers. The general
development is similar to that of northern sculpture. There are
very few stylistic surprises, and the main interest lies not in the
way sculpture is carved but how it is applied. Prevailing taste

and fashion led to the production of two memorable family
mausolea: of the Angevins in Naples and of the Scaliger family
in Verona.

The changes in Italian painting c1240–1340 were in their
way as complete and dramatic as the development between
the sculpture of the west front of Chartres Cathedral and the
work of the Master of Naumberg a century later. At the same
time, however, the propensity of Italian artists to sign their
names, coupled with considerable survival of documentary
evidence, means that the study also becomes transformed. Far
more than in the North, the historian is dealing with names
and artistic personalities. The general outlines of the study,
however, remain clear. The change is from the stylization and
decorative patterns of an art still dominated by Byzantine
traditions to something in which lifelike qualities were accepted as desirable. Given the preceding developments in the
North and the example set by the Tuscan sculptors, the fact
that this happened at all is not surprising. The models available to the painter, however, produced a development
towards realism that achieved a scale quite different from
anything that had happened in the North. It is still not clear
how far the impulse towards the particular sort of change
came from Constantinople itself, and how far it was stimulated by the study of late antique frescoes in the basilicas of
Rome. The result, however, was a new appreciation of the
role of light and linear perspective in the manipulation of
space, and a new vocabulary of gesture and expression in the
human figure. Large losses of wall-painting in Rome have
permanently deprived the historian of much of the evidence
for the precise course of these changes. But they may still be
perceived in the Basilica of St Francis, Assisi. The most important personalities known to us who worked on a large scale
were Pietro Cavallini (c1250–1330), the so-called Isaac
Master (fl. late 13th century), and, of course, Giotto (1266–
1337).

The upper church of St Francis, in Assisi, decorated probably c1280–1300, demonstrates many of the novel features of
this extraordinarily rapid development. The work of the Isaac
Master shows an astonishing grasp of form and great sensitivity to the nuances of human reaction. His dramas are related with fine economy and directness. The chief master of
the St Francis cycle was a very different character. The first
striking feature is the remarkable illusionistic architecture
with which he surrounded his scenes. But the scenes themselves, although they never attain the dramatic intensity of the
Isaac Master's, display an exciting command of different types
of setting and different interpretations of narrative. Clearly,
he was a man with a lively imagination. At the same time, the
whole ensemble demonstrates the problems of realistic representation and the choices painters faced. The interpretation
of the "real world" merely adds another dimension to the
artist's ever-present problems of choosing what to represent—
and how to represent it.

Right: The Capella dell'Arena, Padua, frescoed by Giotto c1303–6

At the start of his carer, Giotto's solution to the problem of choice was simplification. His *tour de force* in this respect was the Capella dell'Arena, Padua—and this achievement has an air of austerity and singlemindedness which has always been treated with respect by artists and with reverence by non-artists. It was not, apparently, the most likable solution at the time, and in many ways the imaginative extravagance of the St Francis Master has greater relevance to future developments. Even Giotto, in the late Peruzzi Chapel frescoes (S. Croce, Florence), was developing a more discursive and experimental sort of narrative; this became far more apparent in the works of his most important followers, such as Taddeo Gaddi (1300–66). However, it is also a development particularly associated with the painters of Siena.

The history of Sienese Gothic art traditionally starts with Duccio (*c*1255–1319), an artist belonging to a rather older generation than Giotto. In many ways his ultimate achievements are even more remarkable than those of Giotto and it is a pity that so little is known about his painting until the very end of his life when he was working on the *Maestà* (Siena Cathedral, 1308–11). Duccio combined in this enormous altar a purely material magnificence with a sparkling display of storytelling which has never been surpassed. It is true that his work never has the gravity of Giotto's, but it makes up for this in the enormous variety and liveliness of the spectator's experience.

The priority given to pictorial variety and description in Duccio's painting became an important feature of scene painting, although a great artist like Simone Martini (1280/5–1344) seems to have been able to shift at will from this to a

The Temptation of Christ, a panel from Duccio's Maestà; 1308–11. Museo dell'Opera del Duomo, Siena

Giottesque selectivity and intensity (as in the *Holy Family*; Walker Art Gallery, Liverpool), and again to scenes of high pathos and drama (as in the polyptych of the Passion; panels divided between the Royal Museum of Fine Arts, Antwerp, Staatliche Museen, Berlin, and the Louvre, Paris). But the concept of a Sienese style is probably best exemplified in the work of the brothers Ambrogio and Pietro Lorenzetti (Ambrogio *ob*. ?1348; Pietro *c*1280–?1348) in both the lower church of St Francis, Assisi, and the Sala della Pace in the Palazzo Pubblico, Siena, where new realistic devices were devoted to characterizing the towns of Good and Bad Government (1338–40).

European art *c*1350–1420. European art of the second half of the 14th century has received extremely varied treatment at the hands of historians. It is the half century of moral, political, and economic crisis following the Black Death in the middle years of the century. Various attempts have been made to demonstrate the presence of moral and political uncertainty and, indeed, also class distinctions and struggles in the forms of art produced. Even attempts to show that the plague seriously interrupted the production of art are unconvincing. Florence Cathedral is primarily the creation of Francesco Talenti (?*c*1300–69) in the second half of the 14th century—years that also saw the immensely individual creations of Tommaso da Modena (1325–76), Guariento (*fl.* 1338–68), and Altichiero (*fl.* 1369–90). In the Prague of the Emperor Charles IV (1355–78), there sprang up a new cultural center with its own vital, novel, and interesting style. Attempts to discern peculiar spiritual or political values in the art of this period merely draw attention to the general problem of the medieval period—that of interpreting an art for which there is almost no contemporary literary comment.

The general character of this half-century is one of synthesis leading to what is commonly called the International Gothic style. This was mainly a court, aristocratic style promoted in Paris, Prague, London, and Milan. Its artists exploited the grace and elegance of France combined with the realistic tricks learnt from the Italians. In much of this, there seems to have been a real interchange of ideas; the resulting *rapprochement* of style offers a European phenomenon of interest and rarity. The like was not to be seen again until the 17th century, when Europe once more achieved an international style following the inspiration of the Italian Renaissance and the art of Antiquity.

European art in the 15th century. The phenomenon of the International Gothic style had a comparatively short existence, and by *c*1420 new approaches to painting and sculpture were emerging. Florence parted company irrevocably with the North, and although in the work of north Italian artists of the generation of Antonio Pisanello (*c*1395–1455) and Jacopo

Right: Thief on the Cross by Robert Campin (the Master of Flémalle); *c*1425–30. Städelsches Kunstinstitut, Frankfurt am Main.

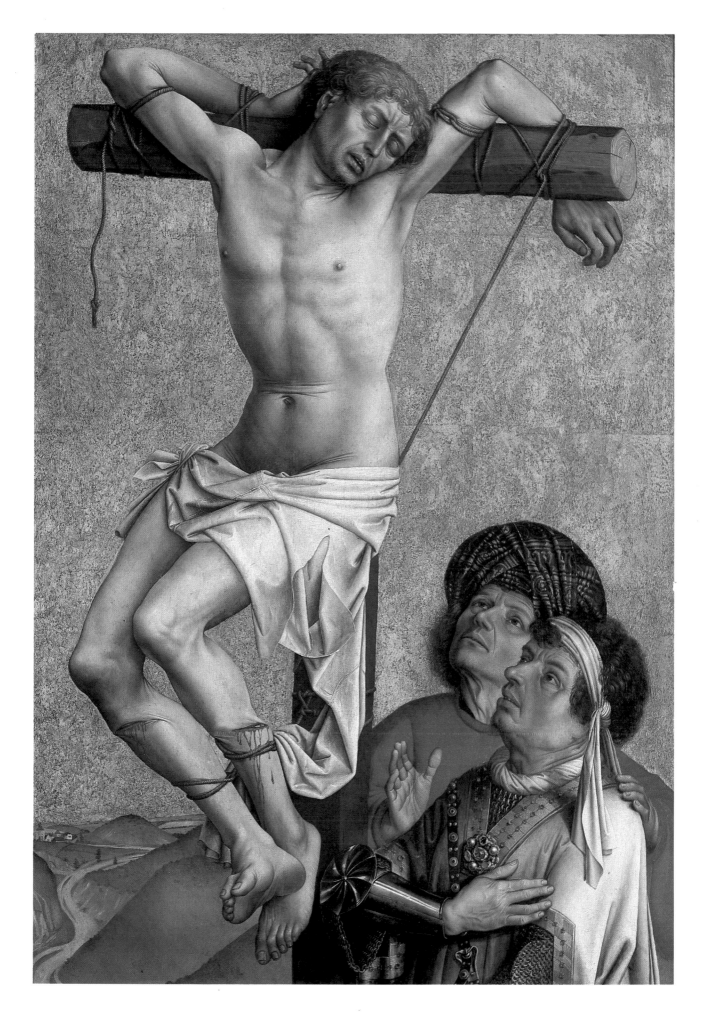

Bellini (c1400–70/1) many of the characteristics of the International style continue, their work came to be much influenced by the specifically Florentine preoccupation with pictorial structure, foreshortening, and one-point perspective.

In the North, the most striking changes in the first half of the 15th century took place in the Low Countries. The whole linguistic area of Low Germany during this period is interesting. From the late 14th century, it was able to "export" major artists or potential artists who trained and became famous elsewhere. Thus the court of Philip the Bold of Burgundy was served by some distinguished Low Germans—Jean Malouel (fl. c1390–1415), the Limburg brothers, Claus Sluter, Melchior Broederlam (fl. c1381–1409) among them. With the exception of Broederlam, it seems clear that those who were left at home, such as Conrad von Soest (fl. c1390–c1425) were of the second rank. But in the 1420s Philip the Good of Burgundy abandoned Dijon irrevocably as a political center and moved to Brussels. This led to that area becoming one of the most important centers of patronage in Europe.

A number of specific features contribute to give Flemish painting of this period its peculiar character. New facial types and characterizations appear in the work of Robert Campin (the Master of Flémalle; 1378/9–?1444) and his workshop which exercised great influence throughout the century. A new distinctive "crumpled" drapery was devised c1420. Many painters developed a particular sensitivity for landscape settings, taking further ideas that had already received attention in Parisian art of the International style. Precise foreshortening and one-point perspective do not on the whole seem to have attracted much attention, or to have been seen as possessing any special merit. But one area in which Flemish artists excelled was in their observation of the effects of light. This was not simply a matter of correctly painting the fall of shadows—their observation in this respect was often faulty. It concerned much more the effects of light on landscape and distance, on interior settings, and on different substances and materials, such as metal, brocade, or wood. The unsurpassed genius in this art was Jan van Eyck (fl. c1390–1444).

Nevertheless, the most influential northern artist of the first half of the 15th century was probably Rogier van der Weyden (c1399/1400–64) who had a long life and an extensive workshop and output. It was Rogier who painted the portraits of Philip the Good, his family, and his courtiers, and his workshop is an early example of one that provided precise, high-quality replicas of its own works. Rogier's work, though doubtless very expensive, was much in demand; and Rogierian conventions of presentation and style left their mark for the rest of the century. They are clearly visible in the work of Dieric Bouts (c1415–75) and Albert van Ouwater (fl. 1430–60), and, to a lesser extent, in the more eccentric work of Hugo van der Goes (c1436–82). At the same time, the continuing impact of van Eyck's painting cannot be entirely discounted, especially in the subsequent painters of van Eyck's home town, Bruges. Petrus Christus (fl. 1444–72/3), Hans Memling (c1440–94), and Gerard David (c1460–1523) offer

Madonna in Church by Jan van Eyck; 31×14cm (12×5½in); originally the left wing of a diptych; c1425–30. Staatliche Museen, Berlin

an interesting line of stylistic descent. Only with painters like Geertgen tot Sint Jans (c1455/65–c1485/95), Hieronymus Bosch (c1450–1516), and Joachim Patenier (fl. 1515–25) do we reach a style of painting that seems substantially "foreign" and different.

The impact of the new control over lighting effects achieved in Flemish painting was extremely important. It had almost incalculable consequences on religious subject-matter, because all the symbolic detail—and the paintings of the Campin workshop and Jan van Eyck contain a great deal—came to be incredibly sharply focused, and the scenes themselves were bathed in an intense other-worldly light previously unimagined. At the same time, portraiture assumed a new dimension. From being routine exercise in familial piety by which the general appearance of a family's members might be handed down, it became a far more aggressive projection of the sitter's presence behind the picture frame.

The lighting effects seem to have first caught the attention of non-Flemish artists. One of the earliest instances is the Tiefenbronn Altar of Lukas Moser (1431; in Tiefenbronn parish church) which strongly suggests that Moser knew the work of Campin's studio. Another brilliant, if eccentric, interpreter of the Eyckian style was Konrad Witz (c1400–45) seen, for example, in his Altar of St Peter, Geneva, of 1444. In the south, an uncertain chain of Eyckian characteristics leads *via* the Master of the Aix Annunciation (from Église des Prêcheurs, Aix-en-Provence; wings in Brussels, Amsterdam, and Rotterdam; 1445) and Colantonio (fl. 1440–70) to Antonello de Messina (c1430–79). The brilliant interplay of light and shadow and contrasted texture is also a feature of the work of Master Franke (active c1405–post 1424) and Stefan Lochner (c1400–51).

In practice, however, art is not simply a matter of technical brilliance; in the long run, it was probably the compositional style and emotional range of Rogier's painting that had more general influence. A long list of names spread around Europe testify to this fact—a list including artists like Hans Pleydenwurff (c1420–72) and Martin Schongauer (c1430–91) in the Empire, and Nuno Goncalves (fl. 1450–71) in Portugal. The painters of the chapel of Eton College, Windsor, (c1480) spread this style to England. It is hard to generalize about the contribution made by these artists to the development of this style, although it seems clear that to the German-speaking community, "progress" meant exaggeration (often to the point of grotesqueness) of the finely balanced emotional tone of Rogier's art.

The history of 15th-century sculpture is usually taken to start with the work of Claus Sluter. Although he died in 1406, his style was carried forward into the 15th century by his nephew Claus de Werve (ob. 1439), and (less certainly) by Juan de la Huerta (ob. 1462). The relevant sculpture is all in Dijon (Musée des Beaux-Arts and the Chartreuse de Champmol). It is by no means clear that it forms an adequate introduction to the line of distinguished German sculptors which begins with Hans Multscher (c1400–67) and Nikolaus Gerhaert van Leyden (c1430–73) in the middle of the century (from the areas of Ulm and Leyden respectively). We are almost totally ignorant about the sculpture of Brussels in the time of Philip the Good (Duke of Burgundy 1419–67). But the appearance in the sculpture of Multscher and Gerhaert of the "crumpled" drapery of the Flemish painters suggests that the role of Flanders was important for sculpture, too.

In many ways, however, Sluter set the tone for what was to follow; his preference for fantastic drapery, strong characteri-

zation, and minutely worked surfaces finds many echoes subsequently in the century, if few direct imitators. The most striking creations of the second half of the 15th century and the early 16th are a series of carved altarpieces, some with painted wings. These show not merely extraordinary authority in the handling of materials—usually wood—but often a bewildering combination of elaborately carved figures with complicated tracery work in the carvings: see, for example, the St Wolfgang Altar of Michael Pacher (1471–81; St Wolfgang, Austria). A similar aesthetic approach is visible in the tombs of the period, notably in Gerhaert's monument to Frederick III in St Stephen's Cathedral, Vienna, begun in 1469; and it may also be seen in the notable Sacrament tabernacle of Adam Krafft in the church of St Lawrence, Nuremberg (1493–6). These works, and those of Tilman Riemenschneider (c1460–1531) and Veit Stoss (c1447–1533), demonstrate the summits of imaginative invention reached in this style. Moreover, this fashion in monumental compositions was exported to Spain where German or Flemish sculptors are often in evidence (for instance in the high altar of Toledo Cathedral, begun in 1498).

Moses, on the Well of Moses by Claus Sluter; 1395–1403. Chartreuse de Champmol, Dijon

The 15th century was, above all, a century of tracery and vaulting. Many of these experiments had already been suggested in the work of English masons c1300; it is a matter of dispute how far the Parler family, for instance, was aware of their work. It is clear, however, that from the late 14th century onwards we find in Germany a considerable development of high vaults, with intersecting tracery, followed later in the 15th century by pendant vaults, and vaults whose ribs describe fantastic curvilinear patterns (for highly developed examples see the Annenkirche at Annaberg, begun in 1499, and St Barbara's, Kuttenberg, begun in 1512, both in the eastern part of the Empire). These experiments were frequently carried out in hall-churches in which the equality of height between nave and aisles offered a considerable area of more or less continuous surface on which the designs could be displayed. Notable intermediate examples exist at Landshut, Spitalkirche, St Martin; Nuremberg, St Lorenz, St Sebaldus; and Munich, Frauenkirche.

Extraordinary displays of tracery continue to be found throughout the late 14th and 15th centuries. Gigantic towers with spires were planned (many were only finished in the 19th century) following the earlier precedents of Cologne and Strasbourg cathedrals. In fact, the present spire of Strasbourg represents a redesigning of the late 14th century by Ulrich von Ensingen (c1350–1419), who also designed the tower and spire of Ulm. Other examples exist at St Stephen's, Vienna, and Prague Cathedral. At the same time, especially in France, architects were developing the tracery screen. This is evident in some notable facade elevations as at Rouen Cathedral (early 15th century) and St Maclou, Rouen (c1500–14), and, on a much smaller scale, on some secular architecture. The best surviving example is the chimneypiece in the Duc de Berry's great hall at Poitiers (1384–6), but more important for future fashions was the main staircase of the Louvre Palace (1363–6; now destroyed), a circular structure apparently encased in tracery and niches in which stood statues of the royal family. The curvilinear, flame-like patterns developed by French architects during the 15th century have imparted to their style the name "flamboyant". Milan Cathedral in Italy (begun in 1387) was designed (at least, its exterior was) by somebody entirely in sympathy with this general taste.

With much of this development English art seems out-of-step, chiefly because many of the crucial developments in curvilinear tracery had happened much earlier, to be superseded by the more rectilinear approach of the so-called Perpendicular style. English tracery from c1350 right through to the 16th century holds few surprises. The main English invention in vaulting, the so-called fan vault, as seen in the cloisters of Gloucester Cathedral, constructed by 1377, although a precocious development when it first appeared, by the time of its 16th-century versions presents a distinct atmosphere of *déjà vu*.

Left: The St Wolfgang Altar by Michael Pacher; 1471–81.
Church of St Wolfgang am Ambersee, Austria

Nevertheless, if we review north-European achievements of the late 15th and early 16th centuries—at least in sculpture and architecture—it will be apparent that there is a remarkable community of taste. This becomes clear when we compare the chapel of Henry VII at Westminster, the chapel at Brou (Franche-Comté; 1513–32), Pacher's St Wolfgang Altar (1471–81), or the pulpit in St Stephen's, Vienna, by Anton Pilgram (1512–14). Commitment to vivid, lifelike sculpture goes hand-in-hand with a desire to display intricate, decorative richness in the setting of the sculpture. The result combines in extreme form the virtuoso treatment of the sculptural surface found earlier in the work of Sluter with all the tricks and contrivances designed during the course of the 15th century by architects. This type of visual excess was not by any means universally perpetrated. The funerary chapel of Richard Beauchamp, Earl of Warwick, at Warwick (c1450), presents a reasonably restrained balance between accessory sculpture, stained glass, and sepulchral monument, and in France in particular there are monuments, like the castle chapel at Châteaudun (c1425), where the primacy of the sculpture over decoration is established. But, on the whole, visual richness was demanded and enjoyed.

The study of the late 15th century tends to be permeated by a sense of impending doom—to the extent that we have foreknowledge of the change of taste that occurred c1500–50. So it is important to emphasize that 15th-century northern art exhibits enormous vitality. It is true that it is still an "inarticulate" vitality: only fleetingly can we find direct evidence of the way in which contemporaries evaluated their art. The architectural drawings from the lodge of St Stephen's, Vienna, and the treatise of Matthäus Roriczer (*ob. c1492/5*), *On the Ordination of Pinnacles*, for instance, give some idea of the preoccupations of professional architects. Artists' responses to Italian art can offer similar information. Where artists borrowed from Italian art, it was (as indeed it always had been) from a position of strength: Italian elements were used as a means of securing a wholly individual end. This is particularly apparent in painting. Ever since the generation of Jean Pucelle, Italian art had exercised an influence on northern painters without, however, in any sense taking over. This type of creative response continued throughout the 15th century, and is visible in different ways in the paintings of Jean Fouquet (c1420–80), the René Master, and Michael Pacher. Some similar process was at work in the creation of the Shrine of St Sebaldus by Peter Vischer the Elder (1508–19; St Sebaldus, Nuremberg). The extra Italian dimension offered by these works to some extent facilitates conclusions about good and bad practice, orders of priority and, in general, the preoccupations of those creating the art.

It is therefore misleading to think of non-Italian art as being in some sort of decline c1500. However, a change of taste was occurring, and symptomatic of this was the tendency of non-Italian monarchs to invite Italian artists to their courts. This had hardly occurred during the earlier Gothic period. But in the late 15th century, Andrea Sansovino (c1467–1529) went to serve King John II of Portugal, and at the beginning of the next century Pietro Torrigiano (1472–1528) worked for England's Henry VIII. However, it was the French court under Louis XII and then Francis I that was probably most influential in this respect. Louis' own tomb was designed by the Giusti brothers (1515–31) and a long line of distinguished Italians, including Leonardo da Vinci (1452–1519), Rosso Fiomento, Primaticcio (1504–70), and Benvenuto Cellini (1500–71), worked for Francis. It was especially at the French court that the idea of the inherent desirability of Italian art was propagated. The general reason stemmed from the belief that Italian art represented the revival of the art of Antiquity. This had little or nothing to do with any general search for purity, restraint or balance. What came north was basically the art of Rome, Raphael (1483–1520) and Giulio Romano (c1499–1546); in their density of visual interest, the Borgia apartments (Vatican) or the Palazzo del Tè (Mantua) yield very little to the German altarpieces of c1500 or Henry VII's chapel (Westminster Abbey). But the architectural and figurative conventions used by the Italians carried with them all the sanctions of the Antique which by now had the support of about a century and a half of humanist propaganda. By the early 16th century, the Italians were thoroughly articulate on the subject of art; for the first time in the post-Classical period, principles in art emerge and aesthetic distinctions of right and wrong are enunciated in literary form. It seems to have been felt that the Italians, by their near monopoly of ancient art, also possessed the key to what was right and desirable. The antagonisms this situation might have produced were probably felt mainly among critics and patrons. Artists from the different traditions were certainly capable of respecting each other's talents—remember the mutual admiration of Albrecht Dürer (1471–1528) and Raphael, and Dürer and Giovanni Bellini. It is also clearly not the case that Italian art was desirable only for its classicism. Whoever was able to afford to employ Cellini, for example, was a very lucky person. But it did mean that the formal conventions of antique art and architecture quickly came to supplant those native to the North; and, with the change, came a critical language in which the transformation might be explained and justified.

So we come back to the only real failure of Gothic art: it never achieved an intellectual dimension. Of course, the workings of the Vienna masons reveal some highly involved and abstruse thought, and the painting of Jan van Eyck, with all its exotic and antiquarian interests, is plainly aimed at an intelligent, sensitive public. But Gothic artists generated no discernible body of theory suitable for propagation by educated laymen; they possessed no sanctions derived from some remote and venerable past. Nor, in spite of their respect for tradition, did they develop a sense of their own history. These things are not essential for the production of good art and architecture, but from c1500 onwards their existence was to be more and more taken for granted. Their apparent absence in the Gothic period may have contributed to the later impression that Gothic art was uncouth. Whatever the truth, art derived from Classical Antiquity possessed all those things, and from c1500 the lands of the Gothic North passed rapidly into the era of the Renaissance.

ANDREW MARTINDALE

Bibliography. *Ars Hispaniae* Vols. VII-IX, Madrid (1952–6). Aubert, M. *La Sculpture Française au Moyen Age*, Paris (1946). Boase, T.S.R. *English Art 1100–1216*, Oxford (1953). Brieger, P. *English Art 1216–1307*, Oxford (1957). Frankl, P. *Gothic Architecture*, London (1962). Mâle, E. *The Gothic Image*, London (1961). Meiss, M. *French Painting in the Time of Jean de Berry*, Vol. I *The Late Fourteenth Century*, Vol. II *The Boucicaut Master*, Vol. III *The Limbourgs and their Contemporaries*, London (1967, 1968, 1974). Panofsky, E. *Die Deutsche Plastik des 11. bis 13. Jahrhunderts*, Florence and Leipzig (1924). Panofsky, E. *Early Netherlandish Painting*, Cambridge, Mass. (1964). Pinder, W. *Die Deutsche Plastik des 14. Jahrhunderts*, Florence and Leipzig (1925). Pope-Hennessy, J. *Italian Gothic Sculpture*, London (1955). Porcher, J. *French Miniatures from Illuminated Manuscripts*, London (1960). Rickert, M. *Painting in Britain: the Middle Ages*, Harmondsworth (1965). Ring, G. *A Century of French Painting*, London (1949). Sauerländer, W. *Gothic Sculpture in France 1140–1270*, London (1972). Stange, A. *Deutsche Malerei der Gotik* (11 vols.), Munich (1934–59). Stone, L. *Sculpture in Britain: the Middle Ages*, Harmondsworth (1972). Wagner-Rieger, R. *Die Italienische Baukunst zu Beginn der Gotik*, Graz and Köln, (1956). Webb, G. *Architecture in Britain: the Middle Ages*, Harmondsworth (1965). White, J. *Art and Architecture in Italy: 1250–1400*, Harmondsworth (1966).

33

THE SURVIVAL OF ANTIQUITY

The Death of Laocoön and his Sons by Hagesandros, Polydoros, and Athanodoros, of c100 BC,
rediscovered in January 1506; marble; height 240cm (94in). Vatican Museums, Rome (see page 638)

THE rebirth of interest in the culture and ideals of Greco-Roman Antiquity which we call the "Renaissance" is too wide a phenomenon to be defined solely in terms of the history of art: it embraces the study of law, language and literature, stagecraft and philosophy, as well as various antiquarian interests—epigraphy, numismatics, topography, and the collecting of antiquities. In Italy, where antique traditions were strongest, the revival began about the time

of Giotto (1266–1337) and ended about the time of the death of Raphael (1520). In Northern Europe, on the other hand, the art of Albrecht Dürer (1471–1528) provides the first prolonged attempt to assimilate Classical models into a Northern style. While a Renaissance style flourished in Italy during the 15th century, the North accepted the influence of the Antique only in the 16th century (see The Northern Renaissance).

However, the term "Renaissance" is often used loosely to

The Massacre of the Innocents by Giotto, a fresco panel in the Capella dell'Arena, Padua; 198×180cm (78×71in); c1303–6

Right: The Marriage of the Virgin by Raphael; oil on panel; 170×120cm (67×47in); 1504. Pinacoteca di Brera, Milan

RAFFAELLO SANZIO
URBINO 1483 – ROMA 1520
Lo Sposalizio della Vergine

The Madonna of Chancellor Rolin by Jan van Eyck; oil on panel; 66×62cm (26×24in); c1435. Louvre, Paris

mean "a new departure", "something different". Doubtless, the art of the early Flemish masters like Jan van Eyck (c1390–1441) and Rogier van der Weyden (1399/1400–64) is radically different from earlier traditions in its mastery of the techniques of perspective and oil painting, and in a new concern for the depiction of the world, especially of the human figure, which such techniques permit. These qualities have elements in common with Italian preoccupations. Indeed, the Southerners were fascinated by the Northerners' ability to capture light and to depict nature and human physiognomy in detail. Nevertheless, the difference in intention between a painting by Jan van Eyck and one of similar date by Masaccio

(1401–?28) is immense; given a comparable skill in perspective, lighting, the articulation of the human body, and the suggestion of thoughts and emotions, the former draws on the heritage of Gothic, the latter on Classical Antiquity.

The concept of "Renaissance" is, indeed, a difficult one, because it is emotive. It assumes resurrection following death, and this in its turn implies a value judgment: after the "Middle Ages" (a term devoid of color), art, or literature, or scholarship, was "reborn" miraculously, after the yawning gulf between Antiquity and Renaissance which was the "middle" Age. The Renaissance becomes good and progressive, the Middle Ages are consequently labeled *retardataire*. Also implied is a notion of total change, from old to new: such overt simplification is perhaps inevitable if the Renaissance is seen as a period rather than as a variety of style.

The feature of the Italian Renaissance that distinguishes it from preceding renaissances is the extent and depth of its devotion to Classical Antiquity in many fields. By comparison, the Carolingian and Ottonian renaissances were incomplete; they did not embrace such a range of antique subject-matter, nor did they create a distinct and thorough-going classical style. Rather they imitated a variety of styles, usually from late Antiquity and confined to easily transportable objects. Sculpture in the round was rare, as was the use of Antiquity in architecture. Although study and comparison clearly reveal the antique sources of much Carolingian and Ottonian work, most pieces do not proclaim their "Antiquity" at first glance.

But they embodied ideas of the importance of ancient Rome, city and civilization—ideas which continued essentially unchanged into the Italian Renaissance. A study of Carolingian ideas on the importance of Rome quickly shows that the Renaissance as revival must comprehend the concept of survival as well: Charlemagne saw himself as a Roman Emperor, and perhaps appreciated antique art not just for aesthetic reasons, but for its political implications. When, therefore, he sought permission from the Pope to transport marble and columns from Ravenna to beautify his palace chapel at Aachen, he was stating in artistic terms the legitimacy of his rule. To emphasize still further his Imperial *numen* (spiritual power), he brought an equestrian statue (supposedly of Theodoric) from Ravenna and set it up outside his palace which he called the Lateran.

Although ruling from Rome itself was not a practical possibility, every Emperor longed to be crowned on the Capitol. Otto III even dreamed of building himself a palace on the Palatine Hill, and Ludwig of Bavaria, who entered Rome in triumph in 1328, may indeed have been crowned on the Capitol to shouts of "Long Live Caesar", rather than in St Peter's. Ludwig emphasized his connection with the city by having its image on his seal, with the legend ROMA CAPUT MUNDI REGIT ORBIS FRENA ROTUNDI ("Rome, the head of the world, controls the reins of the round sphere").

If the Emperors did not make Rome their permanent seat, the popes did—at least until they fled to Avignon in 1308. They converted pagan buildings, and raised new structures at the inevitable expense of the ancient monuments which provided a handy source of ready-cut stone. They were just as interested as their secular rivals in the implications of *Roma caput mundi*, and at least two popes had themselves buried in second-hand Imperial Roman sarcophagi. If Christians of the Counter-Reformation found pagan objects distasteful, most educated men of the Middle Ages and Renaissance were fascinated by their beauty or associations. Both secular and religious rulers could find a complete vocabulary of triumph and glory in antique art, which therefore shapes the nature of both religious and secular art. This is particularly true of Florence, where the Renaissance was, in effect, born.

The Holy Trinity and the Virgin by Masaccio; fresco; 667×317cm (263×125in); c1426–8. S. Maria Novella, Florence

If the city of Rome provided such a wealth of monuments and associations, why should this be so? The answer lies in the backwardness and instability of Rome throughout the 14th century and in the first decades of the 15th. The popes, by going to Avignon, deprived the city of stable government; its economy did not flourish and it had a miniscule population. One historian (Rodolfo Lanciani) has assessed this as about 20,000 at the beginning of the 15th century, and written that "three quarters of the space within the walls was put under cultivation. The inhabitants, stricken with fear and poverty, lived like their prehistoric ancestors in mud huts." The popes finally returned in 1420, and slowly put in hand the renovation of the city; the jubilee year of 1450 was a spur to the refurbishing and building of a modern city. The officials of the

The Flagellation of Christ

Dismissed for centuries as little more than an ingenious exercise in perspective drawing, *The Flagellation of Christ* (Galleria Nazionale della Marche, Urbino) is today widely regarded as one of the greatest masterpieces of 15th-century Italian painting. It is admired chiefly for the perfect delicacy of its painting. The dramatic use of mathematical perspective at once creates and helps to resolve a compositional problem of daunting complexity, and the fascination of the work is intensified by the enigma of its symbolic meaning.

The nominal theme is the Flagellation of Christ—ordered by Pontius Pilate before the Crucifixion. Piero shows the paved courtyard of Pilate's palace in Jerusalem. On the left is a judgment hall enclosed by a colonnade of Corinthian columns. There the enthroned Pilate and a turbaned, unidentified figure

watch two soldiers scourge Christ, who is bound to a column.

But in the right foreground are the looming figures of three bystanders, and it is almost certainly the spatial relationship existing between this group and the flagellation scene that is central to the work's intended symbolism; for as a painting of this time, the *Flagellation* would have a subject and a purpose to which every device and detail has a calculated relevance.

Perspective is used by Piero in a strikingly original way. A more conventional perspective drawing would have placed the "vanishing point" at the theological center of the picture: Christ's head. But in the *Flagellation*, Piero places the vanishing point unexpectedly low down to the right of the flagellator in green. This minimizes the apparent distance between the foreground and background

figures while emphasizing their difference in scale, and its effect is to stress the relationship between the two groups.

Piero was originally a mathematician, and in preparation for the *Flagellation* he designed an architectural setting—so exactly that it is possible to reconstruct the ground plan and precisely locate the figures.

The identity of the bystanders, upon which the symbolism and narrative meaning of the work turn, continues to tantalize art historians. They are not the conventional spectators; nor are they readily identifiable New Testament figures—although the central figure has been variously associated with the risen Christ, the Apostle Peter, and the repentant Judas.

The figure on the right is often thought to be a portrait of Ludovico III Gonzaga, Marquis of Mantua, 1412–78, possibly the artist's patron. The figure on the left may be a theological interpreter or, more particularly, Ludovico's astrologer Ottaviano Ubaldini. But it is on the blond youth that the riddle centers. Who is he or what does he signify? Is he an object of filial loss—known to have been suffered by both Ottaviano and Ludovico? Or is he an allegorical figure or a symbol of more universal significance? Perhaps there is a clue in the fact that both the supernaturally immense laurel that frames his head and the statue above Christ are symbols of glory.

Earlier works depicting the Flagellation provided Piero with much of the raw material for his composition. One of the most important examples is the *Flagellation*

◄ *The Flagellation of Christ* by the School of Pietro Lorenzetti; fresco; c1325. Lower church of S. Francesco, Assisi

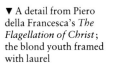

▼ A detail from Piero della Francesca's *The Flagellation of Christ*; the blond youth framed with laurel

▲ Byzantine Emperor John Paleologus and his entourage in Florence, a bronze relief by Filarete; c1439–45. St Peter's, Rome

▲ A medallion portrait of Ludovico III Gonzaga, Marquis of Mantua; a cast of an original by Pietro da Fano; c1452–7

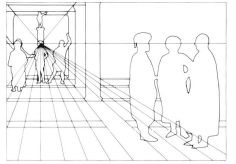 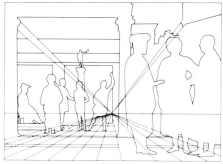

▲ *The Flagellation of Christ* by Piero della Francesca; oil on panel; 58×82cm (23×32in); *c*1460. Galleria Nazionale della Marche, Urbino

▶ The use of perspective: tradition would have required Christ to be at the vanishing point (*left*); Piero's use of perspective results in the points lying in an unexpected position (*right*)

(*c*1325) by the School of Pietro Lorenzetti. His asymmetrically organized fresco on the vault of the transept of the Lower Church of St Francis in Assisi would have been familiar to Piero.

The costumes of all except the second and third bystanders reflect contemporary Byzantine fashions. They closely resemble costumes worn by the Eastern Emperor John Paleologus and his entourage at a unification congress in Florence (1438–9), as recorded on Filarete's bronze doors at St Peter's, Rome. Piero, who studied and worked in Florence as a young man, may himself have been an eyewitness. Another source may have been the council of Mantua in 1459 called by Pope Pius II in response to the Turks' conquest of Constantinople in 1453.

▶ The reconstructed ground plan of *The Flagellation of Christ* showing the locations of the figures (after R. Wittkower and B.A.R. Carter in *Journal of the Warburg and Courtauld Institutes*, vol. 16 pp294f, 1953)

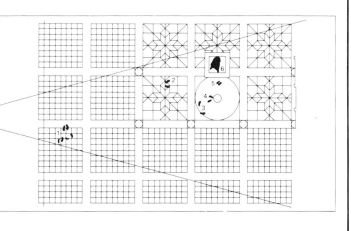

Papal Curia were often learned men, and their number included some of the most eminent humanists of the day, such as Poggio Bracciolini (1380–1459), the great hunter of ancient manuscripts, and Leon Battista Alberti (1404–72), artistic theorist and architect. Such a group was inevitably a civilizing force; we know, for example, that Pope Nicholas V sought Alberti's advice over the replanning of the city.

But the main reason for the preeminence of Florence proves that Renaissance art cannot be treated in a vacuum. Her primacy stems from the activities of intellectuals like Petrarch, Boccaccio, and Coluccio Salutati, whose study of the Antique and its relevance to contemporary life in fields as diverse as philology, epigraphy, law, and mythology in the 14th century prepared the way for further emulation of antique art. There is no satisfactory explanation of why a classical style was not conclusively adopted in the age of Petrarch; or of why, after the work of Nicola Pisano (fl. 1258–78) and Giotto, the preferred style of the 14th century should be a version of Gothic, which survived into the 15th century (and then formed an important element in the style of Lorenzo Ghiberti (1378–1455), as International Gothic). One suggestion has been that a return to traditional modes of art was a consequence of the Black Death.

Changes in the study of available antiquities are directly linked to the development of the Renaissance style. The pace of excavation, deliberate or fortuitous, is in its turn linked to the rate of building activities on Roman sites. The rebuilding of a splendid city like Rome had unfortunate consequences for those interested in ancient art: building required lime, which was easily obtained from hewn marble, so that the ancient city shrank while the new city expanded. With the destruction went many examples of Roman and Early Christian wall-painting and mosaic, whereas items that could be reused—like columns and capitals, decorative friezes and sarcophagi—were preserved, usually incorporated in Christian buildings. Sculpture in the round, so easily transported to the lime kilns, and in any case more breakable than relief work, was scarce in Rome until c1450, when the popes began their large building programs. From then on, with certain curbs on the destruction of antiquities and with the spread of collecting mania, the freestanding statue again assumed its natural importance.

Because of the paucity of painted remains, the Renaissance grew up on a diet of sculpture, mainly in relief; sarcophagi and other reliefs were the most important element in the development of Nicola Pisano's style, and the same is probably true for Giotto and Masaccio: not enough likely painted sources remain to show otherwise. Thus painting, as well as sculpture, was almost predisposed to a sculptural style because the exemplars were predominantly in that medium. The development of a painterly vocabulary for representing in two dimensions the effect of a three-dimensional object subjected to light is thereby linked to sculptural models. And because it is more difficult to reproduce in one medium effects which hitherto had been totally strange (and which involved the device of perspective), we might expect sculpture to be at first

rather more advanced than painting in the sense that it adopts the Renaissance style more speedily and comprehensively.

The development of a classical style in architecture proceeded at an intermediate rate. The transalpine extravagancies of Gothic never took a firm hold in Italy, and certainly not in Florence where the conspicuous churches were in a Romanesque style which Alberti was to find particularly congenial as the basis for his own formal experiments. There was, then, no basic incompatibility between Romanesque and ancient Roman architecture which the 15th century wished to imitate: the one stems from the other. And yet there were substantial problems in adapting Roman architecture to modern use. The unsettled political situation for much of the 15th century meant that palaces were built in towns and, for all their Renaissance detailing on the inside, tended to resemble the medieval fortresses from which they derived: the airy external loggias and broad walks of ancient Rome would have been too dangerous. The palace at Urbino exemplifies these features: it sits on an impregnable rock, its only external decoration a rather bleak triumphal arch motif. Yet inside is a courtyard, by Luciano Laurana (1420/5?–79), of measured beauty and delicacy—partly derived, of course, from the medieval cloister. A design by a Florentine architect, Antonio Filarete (c1400–69), of c1460/64 and therefore contemporary with the courtyard at Urbino, shows how his ideal palace looked: the sheer walls and small windows are replaced by elegant arched windows, echoing the continuous colonnaded loggia which surrounds the ground story.

To turn a building "inside out" in this manner would be possible only with the coming of political stability; it is therefore not until the first decades of the 16th century that the Renaissance villa comes into its own. This was often based on the ancient Roman villa in plan and motifs, for there were plenty of ruined examples available for imitation. The harbingers of the new type were Poggio a Caiano (built 1480 onwards), Poggio Reale, near Naples (c1490 onwards), and the Vatican Belvedere (1484 onwards; much altered). All these use a central portico—the type from which Andrea Palladio (1508–80) was to develop his series of villas in the Veneto, the vogue for which soon spread all over Europe. It has been suggested that such a villa type with portico and loggia is a Venetian tradition persisting from Antiquity; if we add to this Palladio's extensive researches into ancient Roman architecture, the antique nature of his inspiration is doubly plain.

If the antique models for secular architecture were easy to find, such was not the case with churches. The origin of the aisled nave was clearly the Roman basilica, but the height of the nave presented problems if the facade was to look antique. Alberti solved the problem in two different ways: for the church of S. Francesco at Rimini, which he rebuilt c1450, he demonstrated how the Roman triumphal arch, with its three entrances, one large and two small, was suited to the scheme of nave and aisles; at S. Sebastiano, Mantua, he used the antique temple front as the portico to the church. It is variations on these solutions which provide the vocabulary for

THE SURVIVAL OF ANTIQUITY 629

The main courtyard of the Palazzo Ducale, Urbino, designed by Luciano Laurana; c 1464–6

church architecture until the end of the Neoclassical period. (Indeed, the temple front is also an important element in the villa architecture of Palladio.)

A constantly recurring ideal for Renaissance architects was the church in variations of a centralized plan: the structure might be circular, hexagonal, octagonal, or a Greek cross (cruciform with equal arms). Philosophers from Plato onwards saw the circle as the perfect shape, a reflection on earth of heavenly perfection. In the 15th century the Neoplatonic and Christianized version of this idea, enunciated by such writers as Marsilio Ficino (1433–99), declared that God is the center of the universe, the hub of the world, and yet encompasses that world. The human shape itself can be contained within the circle, as demonstrated in the figure of the "Vitruvian man", whose outstretched limbs touch the circumference of a circle of which his navel is the center.

For the Renaissance architect, geometry was important for plan and elevation for two reasons. It provided him with a repertory of shapes which symbolized the Godhead. Aided by mathematics, it provided him with shapes which were numerically rational and therefore beautiful. Today, we know that the human eye cannot perceive intricate relationships between shapes and volumes, and we doubt whether beauty is the direct result of mathematics. For the Renaissance, the mathematical was beautiful.

The case of the central-plan church underlines another way in which information about the ancient world reached the Renaissance. For architectural detailing, the investigation of actual remains would provide plenty of motifs; but the question of the derivation of the plan is complicated. Few round temples survive from Antiquity, and there is no reason to believe that the position was substantially different in the 15th

The facade of S. Sebastiano, Mantua, by Alberti; begun in 1460.
It only partly reflects Alberti's original plans

"Vitruvian Man", a study of human proportions after Vitruvius
(1st century BC) by Leonardo da Vinci; drawing; 34×25cm (13×10in);
c1492. Gallerie dell'Accademia, Venice

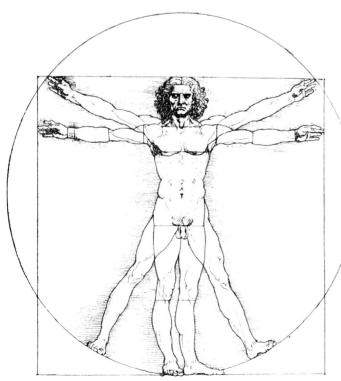

century. Most old central-plan buildings were Early Christian churches; some of them, it is true, derived from Roman circular mausolea, of which there were many examples in and around Rome. The 15th century was unclear about the true nature of the Early Christian churches, believing them to have been Roman foundations which had undergone a change of usage. The error is pardonable even in such a scholar as Alberti, who restored some of the early churches of Rome; but it does demonstrate the difficulties Renaissance men had in dating sources—sufficient historical equipment was as yet nonexistent. The main source for the Renaissance central-plan building was theoretical, and found in the only architectural handbook to have survived from Antiquity: the *De Archi-tectura* of Vitruvius, of the 1st century BC. This had been known in the 9th century by Einhard, Charlemagne's biographer, who had used Vitruvian principles in an attempt to erect truly antique architecture for his lord. Manuscripts of the work were rediscovered at the beginning of the 15th century, and architects studied it with enthusiasm: it provided a complete course of instruction—from the theory of siting a town or a building to the different types of construction—as well as information on how and when to use the orders depending on the purpose and type of work undertaken.

One drawback impeded a straightforward transposition of Vitruvius' theories into buildings: the illustrations which were evidently intended to accompany the text were lost and had to be supplied by editors. Unfortunately, the Latin of Vitruvius is far from clear and many of his prescriptions allow a wide latitude of interpretation. From the first printed edition of 1486, each architect-editor provided new suggestions so that a Vitruvian canon of what was or was not "correct" architectural practice developed without much reference to the text. Thus, the very drawback of having no ancient illustrations provided the Renaissance with an authentic antique textual tradition which they themselves could add to and develop; it endowed Renaissance architecture with both the sanction of Antiquity and a creative flexibility. Vitruvius, as it were, provided the ingredients and the Renaissance made up the prescription to suit themselves: but they could still claim that their architecture was formed in the antique mold.

The flexibility of the early years of the Vitruvian tradition did not outlive the High Renaissance. The whole point of Mannerist architecture is that it deliberately breaks the rules in the search for emotional effect or even shock: Michelangelo's vestibule to the Biblioteca Laurenziana (1524 onwards) exemplified this trend. But contemporary with Mannerism is an inclination to codify Vitruvian "rules" into a pedagogic system; such anti-mannerist retrenchment is a feature of the thought if not the practice of Pirro Ligorio (c1500–83), the designer of the Villa d'Este at Tivoli (c1565–72). We should call his architecture "mannerist", but he speaks of "stupidities" in the work of his contemporaries and continually looks back to the achievements of the High Renaissance. Attitudes such as this help to maintain the potency of the Renaissance tradition.

A central-plan church: the tempietto at S. Pietro in Montorio, Rome, by Bramante; dated 1502

If we except the occasional fresco, painters had to study the literary accounts when they wished to discover what antique painting had been like. Vitruvius provides the source for the architects; for the painters, it was the *Natural History* of Pliny the Elder (completed in AD 77), an encyclopedia containing descriptions not only of artistic techniques but also of famous paintings. With Pliny's help, artists could imitate not only the forms of antique art, gleaned from their study of sculpture, but also capture the spirit of Antiquity from accounts of works such as the *Calumny* of Apelles. This is best known in the painting by Alessandro Botticelli (1444–1510) in the Uffizi, Florence, (*c*1495?), but was suggested as a suitable subject by Alberti in his *De Pictura* of 1434, and very popular thereafter. Epic and lyric poetry, as well as episodes from ancient history, provided another source.

Fresco painting was one of the techniques described by Pliny: throughout the Renaissance, from Giotto onwards, the majority of great commissions were for work in fresco. Vasari maintained that the technique of *buon fresco* was the greatest test of an artist's skill, for it required a certain breadth of treatment, allied to a grandeur of conception, which was neither necessary nor possible when making smaller, more private, works in which the artist might choose to display his skill in details. Frescoes were usually made on large surfaces, for places essentially public: they might exalt or teach the faithful, as in Giotto's series in the Capella dell'Arena in

Padua (by *c*1306), or extol the power of the state through personifications and allegories, as in the notable episodes from Florentine history that Leonardo and Michelangelo were commissioned to represent in the hall of the Great Council in the Palazzo Vecchio in Florence (1503/5 and 1504 respectively).

Such desire for simplicity and antique grandeur is bound up with the Renaissance's own conception of Man and his potentialities. That such a desire was attainable is a result of the Renaissance ability to reconstruct the past, to write and think historically. When Hamlet exclaims in act two, scene two, of Shakespeare's *Hamlet*

> What a piece of work is man! How noble in reason! How infinite in faculties! In form, moving, how express and admirable! In action how like an angel! In apprehension how like a god! The beauty of the world! The paragon of animals!

he does so in frustration rather than in admiration, but the substance of his eulogy is the position of Man in the world—a commonplace to be found in the works of men as different as Pascal (1623–62), or Alexander Pope (1688–1744)

> Created half to rise, and half to fall;
> Great Lord of all things, yet a prey to all;
> Sole judge of truth, in endless error hurled:
> The glory, jest and riddle of the world!
> (*An Essay on Man* II, 13; 1733–4)

Man is seen as occupying a middle place in the scheme of things: a rational being, he can strive to be like God, but the nature of Man, "in endless error hurled", often steers him towards baser things. An essential element in this scheme is the notion of free will, not in the theological sense of Man's ability to choose between good and evil, but rather the potential that willpower gave him to change himself and the world around him for the better.

Given the potentiality of Man to incline either to base pleasure or toward higher things, it was naturally the latter which presented the Renaissance with their ideal man, the hero, formed from the antique mold. A hero was not simply bold, strong, and ingenious in battle, but led a life which reflected the nobility of his soul, his high morality, and his wisdom: he was magnanimous in his relations with others, and conducted himself with dignity. All his actions were founded in reason, on the domination of the emotions by the will. During the 15th century the cult of the hero, of the comparison of ancient prototype with modern men, would become a feature of art as it was of literature; the very idea of comparison could be seen in Plutarch's *Lives* (a clear source for stories of nobility), where eminent Greeks are paired with Roman counterparts, and then compared.

Epithets of the hero are applied to art and architecture—particularly to the latter, the public art *par excellence*. "Let us", writes Alberti in his *De Re Aedificatoria* (finished 1452), "erect grand buildings, so that we might appear magnanimous and powerful to posterity." And Lorenzo de' Medici (1449–92) writes of the "pomp and other honors, and public magnificence such as piazzas, temples, and other public buildings

The Calumny of Apelles by Botticelli; tempera on panel; 62×91cm (24×36in); c1495? Uffizi, Florence

which denote the ambitious men, and those who with great care seek honor." Naturally, a man desiring to be known for antique rather than specifically Christian virtues will prefer his art and architecture in a classical style.

The architectural style of an Alberti, a Bramante, or a Raphael has characteristics that link it to the heroic ideal it is intended to reflect. Magnificence is a public activity, and virtue is thereby proclaimed abroad. The forms of a work must be grand and dignified: magnificent in materials, choice and learned in decoration, yet not over-decorated in a way that would lead to vulgarity. Just as a man obeys the rules of conduct laid down by reason, so the architect must work according to the rules of Vitruvius: supplementing them by observation and imitation of the grandiose ruins of Antiquity.

The process of renascence, of "rebirth", requires a multitude of skills. These include a determination of the evidence on which to base a reconstruction, an understanding of why the facts, beliefs, or objects culled are of importance, and also an ability to set them in order. Above all, the practice of history requires historical perspective: a desire to understand how and why events or styles or beliefs are linked together. In the middle of the 14th century, Petrarch was deeply aware of the gulf separating his generation from the antique writers he admired. Indeed, he wrote letters to classical authors, letters which were more than literary exercises because the conceit was the assumption that he himself was their contemporary. The letter to Livy, whose work was crucial for an understanding of Roman history, was

> Written in the land of the living, in that part of Italy and in that city in which I am now living and where thou wert once born and buried, in the vestibule of the Temple of Justina Virgo, and in view of thy very tombstone ... (*Familiar Letters*, XXIV.8, trans. Cosenza, M.E. in *Petrarch's Letters to Classical Authors*, Chicago, 1910.)

Such an evocative attitude towards ruins of Antiquity was unusual in the 14th century; much more common and long-lasting was superstitious awe which tended to see the remains as the creation of giants or devils, and to attribute magical powers to the great figures of Antiquity. Throughout the Middle Ages and into the 16th century, Virgil, for example, was popularly believed to have been a sorcerer; Alexander the Great, about whose historical conquests sufficient written testimony remained, was transmuted into a chivalrous knight and his adventures recited to medieval audiences alongside those of Charlemagne, Roland, and Tristan and Iseult. These stories take place in a historical vacuum; even *La Chanson de Roland*, concerned as it is with the fight against the Moors, dresses Charlemagne and his knights in 12th-century costume and makes them behave strictly in accordance with the dictates of chivalry. Similarly, the ruins of Rome were generally considered throughout the Middle Ages as places with magical rather than historical associations. Indeed, a type of guidebook so popular that it lasted into the 18th century was called *The Marvels of the City of Rome*; in some printed editions, it includes, for no particular reason, a list and description of the Seven Wonders of the World.

Petrarch tends to be called—in an anachronistic and question-begging epithet—the "first modern man"; there is a grain of truth in the notion, apparent when his lively attitude to ancient Rome is compared with that of his great predecessor, Dante Alighieri (1265–1321). Dante's *Divine Comedy*, for all its connections with antique literary forms, shows little interest in the monuments of Roman civilization, for Dante's preoccupations were Christian; Petrarch, on the other hand, recognizes them, together with surviving manuscripts, as the essential elements in the revival and imitation of Roman forms and ideas.

Petrarch cultivated what we might call an historical mentality; he knew that not all things were possible in any one time, that style and practice developed and changed, and that society and institutions changed as well. When, therefore, in 1355 the Holy Roman Emperor Charles IV asked him whether he thought a document exempting Austria from Imperial rule was genuine, Petrarch examined the manuscript and pronounced it a forgery. He understood Roman forms of address, and complained that the supposed author of the document, Julius Caesar, did not use the royal "we", or call himself "king", or even "Augustus": such terms were anachronistic. Furthermore, every Roman letter bore the exact day on which it was written, and the consuls in office at that time: this one did not. His knowledge of the Latin language told him that "Austria" derives from the word for south: since the land concerned is north of Rome, the letter must be a nonsense. Petrarch therefore demolished the letter by both internal and external proofs, by applying to it the entire range of his antiquarian knowledge. The clinching proof is, for him, what he calls the "barbarous and modern" style in which it is written.

Petrarch's main concerns were literary ones. Monuments interested him because they called to mind the age of his Roman heroes. He was not an artist, and he does not seem to have collected anything except books, of which he formed a fabulous library. Inscriptions on monuments interested him greatly, but he was even more concerned with what coins and medals could tell him of antique practices. He was probably involved in the scheme for decorating a room in the University of Padua with images of famous antique figures. This, the *Sala Virorum Illustrium* ("Room of Illustrious Men"), follows the scheme of his *De Viris Illustribus* ("Of Illustrious Men", composed c1338), a book planned along the lines of his beloved Livy. Although the famous men in the room are in 14th-century costume, their iconography, and the appearance of the Roman monuments in some scenes, stem from the study of numismatics and actual monuments. Examples of such collaboration between a scholar and an artist (anonymous in this particular case) could be multiplied through the Renaissance period. It is for this reason that the activities of Petrarch and his fellow scholars are crucial in the development of a Renaissance attitude toward art.

Petrarch's interest in the dignity of Latin style could have but an indirect effect upon the development of art; his concern with antique topography—with the layout of the City of Rome, and determining what monuments were to be seen there in any span of years—was much more important. He tried, in Book Eight of his epic poem *Africa*, to describe a tour of Rome made by the envoys from Carthage to the Senate including only those monuments standing under the Scipios. He was only partially successful, but he made the attempt. We can parallel his topographical interests with the better-informed and more comprehensive surveys of the 15th and 16th centuries.

While bearing in mind the constant leitmotiv of the medieval and essentially non-historical *Mirabilia* tradition, it is easy to show the advances in historical scholarship made during the 15th century—often by scholars attached to the papal Curia. Flavio Biondo was one such scholar who was working in Rome by 1433 (Alberti was another). About 1446 Biondo wrote his *Roma Instaurata* in which research not only amongst the monuments themselves but also in literary sources enabled him to rebuild the ancient city in words. He was also the first to write the history of Italy, in his *Italia illustrata* (completed in 1453). Biondo's successors include men like Andrea Fulvio, who was to write one of the most popular books of historical biography illustrated from coins, both real and imaginary, the *Illustrium Imagines* of 1517; and also Raphael, who was commissioned in 1519 to prepare an ideal view of ancient Rome. We know no more about this scheme than about Alberti's scheme for a plan of the city (which could have been of ancient or modern Rome).

Such projects are indications of an historical state of mind, as well as of the frequent difficulty of disengaging scholarly from artistic activities. For it is thanks to the expanding knowledge of Antiquity during the 15th and 16th centuries that artists were commissioned to represent ancient Rome in their work, as a suitably grandiose setting for the action of the painting or bas-relief. Perhaps the best known reconstructions in miniature of cities in the antique manner are those seen in stage sets, particularly the permanent one designed by Andrea Palladio (1508–80) for his Teatro Olimpico at Vicenza (opened in 1585); of the *scena tragica* suggested by Serlio in his influential *L'Architettura*, issued in six parts between 1531 and 1551. We can usefully compare the latter with Serlio's prescription for a set for comedies: whereas that for the highest dramatic genre is an august Roman street with palaces and monuments, the lighter manner is provided with buildings in the Gothic style.

A guide to the nature and range of any culture's interest can be found in what it considers worth collecting. The Middle Ages indulged in the habit, although motives then were noticeably different from those of later centuries—at least as far as can be judged from the meager references. The majority of such collections were put together more for religious than aesthetic reasons: relics were regarded as possessing powers, rather than as representative objects from a past culture.

Renaissance Portraiture

Portraiture developed during the Renaissance from the Gothic depiction of people as generalized types to the representation of individuals whose characters and personalities were expressed in their faces. Increasingly, Italian artists attempted to portray their subjects accurately and even revived the ancient Roman practice of obtaining a likeness from a life or death mask cast in plaster. This method was especially popular with sculptors. But unflinching realism was avoided: Italian portraiture was also influenced by profiles on Roman coins and by Roman sculpted portrait busts. It was widely believed that character was revealed in the profile and that the possession of proper moral qualities was expressed in the structure of a classical Roman face. A classical profile in a woman attested her purity.

In Italy the leading political, mercantile, and intellectual figures regularly had portraits painted, whereas elsewhere in Europe most subjects came from royal families. German artists preferred to represent the faces of their rulers truthfully rather than idealize them, and in England the royal portrait principally celebrated the pomp and prestige of the monarch. The French tradition was more naturalistic but still elaborated the trappings of monarchy.

▲ The Roman model: a portrait bust of Agrippa; marble; early 1st century BC. Louvre, Paris

▶ A self-portrait in relief by Alberti; bronze; 16×12cm (6×5in); c1438. Cabinet des Médailles, Paris

In Italy, Roman coins and portrait busts established a type of appearance—the lofty forehead, the high cheekbones, the straight long nose, the firm mouth—to which everyone wanted their pictorial representation adjusted. Leon Battista Alberti's self portrait, c1445, derives from the profile image on a Classical gem or coin. Alberti's conception of himself was as a noble Roman in antique dress with hair cropped short, and whose upright sharp profile presents him as a stern and serious individual.

Two drawings by Pisanello of Filippo Maria Visconti, Duke of Milan, show how Pisanello changed the features and apparel of his subject—whom he drew from life—into those of a distinguished-looking ruler. Most sitters were transformed in this way; Pisanello's drawings are a rare surviving example of how it occurred. A death mask of Lorenzo the Magnificent of the Medici family was cast from his face immediately after his death, in 1492, to record his features for painters and sculptors. In a subsequent portrait bust, his nose, mouth, and eyebrows became more handsome and his cheekbones more prominent.

Settignano's bust of Marietta Strozzi and a portrait of a young girl by Pollaiudo depict charm and innocence. In contrast to the elaborate hairstyles and costumes the facial features are simple and delicate while the skin is very subtly portrayed. In Raphael's portrait of Pope Leo X, the Pope is seen with his two nephews. Endowed with qualities of Classical portrait busts, the three men acquire the dignity and gravity of Roman rulers while yet displaying their own powerful personalities. In the English tradition, Henry VIII is rendered by Holbein as a glorious ruler: his power is conveyed by his bulk and his magnificent costume, which dramatically emphasize the authority of his glance.

Further reading. Pope-Hennessy, J. *The Portrait in the Renaissance*, London (1966).

Lorenzo the Magnificent: *left* a death mask; 1492; Palazzo Medici, Florence. *Right* a bust; c1495–1500; Uffizi, Florence

◄ Two drawings of
Filippo Maria Visconti
by Pisanello; c1440.
Louvre, Paris

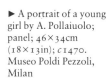

► A portrait of a young
girl by A. Pollaiuolo;
panel; 46×34cm
(18×13in); c1470.
Museo Poldi Pezzoli,
Milan

◄ Marietta Strozzi, a
bust by Settignano;
marble; height 52cm
(20in); c1455–60.
Staatliche Museen,
Berlin

Leo X with Cardinals
iulio de' Medici and
uigi de' Rossi by
aphael; panel;
;3×119cm (60×47in);
518. Uffizi, Florence

▼ Holbein's wedding
portrait of Henry VIII, a
copy probably by
Holbein; oil and tem-
pera; 86×75cm
(34×30in); 1539/40.
Galleria Nazionale
d'Arte Antica, Rome

When Classical antiquities were collected—and they certainly were treasured—it was generally for beautification probably associated with magical power, as, for example, in the cameo of Augustus set into the Cross of Lothair (Domschatzkammer, Aachen). The main example of what we would recognize as a collection put together presumably for aesthetic reasons was that of the Bishop of Winchester, Henry of Blois (Bishop, 1127–71), who imported antique statues from Rome; no trace of his collection remains, so we cannot assess its nature or its size.

We are similarly restricted in our knowledge of collections before the later Quattrocento, although written accounts make it clear that the collecting of classical antiquities was popular with humanists and useful to artists long before 1400. We have an account of the visit of a follower of Petrarch, Giovanni Dondi, to Rome c1375; he took measurements and copied inscriptions, and also wrote of contemporary interest in antique sculpture

> ... those which have survived somewhere are eagerly looked for and inspected by sensitive persons and command high prices. And if you compare them with what is produced nowadays, it will be evident that their authors were superior in natural genius ... when carefully observing ancient buildings, statues, reliefs and the like, the artists of our own times are amazed ... (As translated in Panofsky, E. *Renaissance and Renascences in Western Art*, Uppsala, 1960, pp208–9.)

This passage is important for the several hints it gives: evidently people were collecting antiquities, for high prices were offered for them; artists were looking to antique works because they realized their superiority; the study of such productions would help them to improve their own style. This is the spirit in which we may imagine Nicola Pisano, Giotto, or Ghiberti visiting Rome, and we might wonder whether the progressive artists described by Dondi were not, like himself, Florentines, for whom Rome meant an essential part of the developing civic humanism of their native city.

One early Quattrocento artist known to have collected antiquities was Lorenzo Ghiberti, the winner of the competition in 1401 for the Baptistery Doors in Florence. His relief won, partly because of the beauty of his main reference to the Antique in the torso of Isaac; he made use of his collection in his later work, particularly in the Gates of Paradise. Although his collection must have been in part a "paper museum"—of drawings from sarcophagi and statues, notes on architecture and perhaps sketches of the work of modern rivals—we know he possessed a big marble vase (supposedly from Greece), a leg in bronze, and many fragments of statues. His most important possession was one of the versions of the *Bed of Policleitos*—a work responsible for several popular motifs in Renaissance and post-Renaissance art. We may assume that Donatello (c1386–1466), whose art is similarly couched in the Antique, also collected; and Vasari reports that it was he who inspired an enthusiasm for collecting in Cosimo de' Medici the Elder

The stage set designed for the Teatro Olimpico, Vicenza, by Palladio; opened in 1585

The Sacrifice of Isaac, one of two reliefs produced by Ghiberti for the competition held in Florence in 1401 for the Baptistery Doors commission; 457×406cm (180×160in). Museo Nazionale, Florence

(1389–1464)—the possible origin, that is, of a collection amongst which Michelangelo received his early education.

Florence was not the only center of collecting, though the craze probably spread from there to Rome—perhaps helped by the curial officials, many of whom were Florentines. One was Poggio Bracciolini, who had been trained by the Chancellor of the Florentine Republic, Coluccio Salutati, at the beginning of the century. He used his spare time hunting for manuscripts of the Classics; he also sought antique statues with persistence (several of his letters on the subject survive), and was able to furnish his garden with antiquities.

But the first important collection in Rome, antedating those of the great Roman families by half a century, is that presented by Pope Sixtus IV to the town councillors of Rome, the Conservatori, in 1471, to place in their recently completed palace on the Capitol where it remains to this day. This collection, which includes the famous she-wolf (with 16th-century figures of Romulus and Remus suckling), and the Spinario (used by Brunelleschi in his relief for the 1401 competition for the Baptistery Doors), is really the first modern museum. But the importance of the exhibits was emotional rather than aesthetic, "tangible witnesses of Roman magnificence in the very seat of the city's government, so that visitors could be impressed by such relics of what Rome had been, almost, one might say, by a museum of former Roman splendour" (Weiss,

R., The Renaissance Discovery of Classical Antiquity, Oxford, 1969, p191). It was followed, c1506, by the building of a "museum" specially for the purpose of housing antiquities—the state court of the Vatican Belvedere, which housed the Laocoön after its discovery in January of that year, and where other now famous works, the Cleopatra, the Apollo, and later the Torso, were exhibited to an eager world.

We should view the statue court, like the Capitoline Museum, not as a collection of aesthetic objects, but as works evocative of ancient Rome. They were not an isolated phenomenon in the Vatican, but part of the creation of a modern version of a classical villa as described by Pliny—part of the area of which was organized to act as a theater for the production of antique plays. Their main effect on artists, however, (after the virtual destruction of the idea of the villa by rebuilding in the 1570s) was as individual exemplars of excellence in modeling, form, and expression. More than the works of any other collection, those of the statue court provided a standard of excellence which was as revered in the days of J.J. Winckelmann (1717–68) as it had been in those of Michelangelo and Dürer. A walk through any gallery will show the effects—often quite obvious, and intended to be so—of studying the Apollo Belvedere, or the Laocoön, available in plaster casts in art schools throughout Europe. We know, for example, that Titian had a plaster cast of the Laocoön in the 1520s, and although he is not an artist who at first sight appears as a great imitator of antique sculpture—as is plainly the case with, for example, Michelangelo—a study of his work demonstrates that it is permeated by the Antique. In other words, some artists assimilate the Antique into their style to such an extent that the original sources are hard to ascertain.

With the quickened pace of urban change in the Rome of the High Renaissance, the collections of antiquities increased enormously. Such collections were not private in the modern sense of the word, for collecting proclaimed the taste of the collector and artists must have found it relatively easy to gain access even to the noblest homes—some of which, indeed, had their own "house" artists, librarians, and scholars.

The invention of printing, and its diffusion throughout Europe in the 1460s, was a decisive influence in the dissemination of the Renaissance, but did not immediately transform its basic nature. For the first books printed were religious or popular, and inevitably expensive. The diffusion of the Classics (without which the spread of the Renaissance would have been slower) belongs to the end of the century; early items, like Cennini's edition of Virgil (Florence, 1471–2) were luxuries with restricted circulation.

There are two distinct stages, therefore, in the physical appearance and hence in the diffusion of the printed book. At first, printing was envisaged as a less costly version of the manuscript which, with the aid of decoration, and capital letters separately inked in bright colors, it sought to imitate. The use of parchment made the imitation more convincing. But by the end of the 15th century the price of paper had

The Spinario or Young Man taking out a Thorn, a Roman bronze copy of a 3rd-century BC original; height 73cm (29in). Palazzo dei Conservatori, Rome

ly copied manuscripts, teeming with stupid mistakes eternally recopied and enshrined in tradition: given a sensible editor consulting a cross-section of early and reliable manuscripts, a good version could be established and, after proof-reading (which Eramus did on the spot), transformed into an inexhaustible supply of printed sheets, all of which were identical. This factor was the main advantage (apart from price) of printing over the manuscript.

The same period saw the rise of repeatable reproductions in both woodcut and engraving, and the same reasons ensured their popularity. Woodcut is the earlier technique: the first dated print is a German *St Christopher* of 1423 (John Rylands Library, Manchester). Initially it is the more useful: it is a relief technique requiring relatively little pressure to print, and it can be set up alongside text to print illustrated books. Most woodcuts are very crude because of the difficulties of producing fine, expressive lines standing in relief from a block of wood; the technique, except in the work of Dürer and a few others, tends to remain in the domain of the popular print, crudely done and cheaply sold.

St Christopher, the earliest known dated woodcut; 1423. John Rylands Library, Manchester

dropped, and printers like Aldus Manutius in Venice were producing works with typefaces imitating the ancient Roman and Carolingian scripts—faces cheaper to cut because less fussy than the Gothic faces which nevertheless remained popular in the North. Aldus also perfected an italic face which, aesthetic attraction apart, meant more words per line than a standard face and thus lower costs.

We tend to underestimate the speed with which images and ideas could spread in earlier centuries. Printed sheets, usually packed in barrels, were sent to fairs and publishers all over Europe, perhaps to be bound on arrival. The absence of effective international copyright laws aided copying and imitation, and ensured the spread of Renaissance forms from Italy to the North.

One of the first men to grasp the power of the new invention was Erasmus (c1466–1536). His main works, written after 1511, are religious polemics, contributions to the debate on the Catholic Church; they prepared the way for the Reformation itself, and without the printed word, would have reached a far smaller audience. Gone was the age of imperfect-

Engraving produced much finer lines, and gave the artist the chance of capturing expression and detail—totally lost in most woodcuts. This enhanced "aesthetic" quality and, because prints were produced separate from books, engravings tended to become autonomous works of art.

Artists were quick to see the usefulness of prints. From the later 15th century onwards they formed an important method by which styles could be diffused and assimilated. The copying of sketchbooks—a practice which continued—provided the same problems as that involved in dealing with other manuscripts. The reproductive print is not as foolproof as the photograph: a work of art is transformed in being copied by another artist, and copies of prints could be made and sold by artists who had never seen the original model. Nevertheless, prints meant that artists and connoisseurs could build up portfolios of reference material. Such material might range from versions of drawings by Raphael (sometimes for unexecuted projects), reproductions of completed fresco or architectural designs, pictures of objects in private collections or otherwise of difficult access (like the top of Trajan's Column), to designs for decorative art.

It is via the graphic arts, therefore, including printing, that the North learnt about the Italian Renaissance. Dürer, for example, paid large sums for Italian prints—and the Italians of the Mannerist period were even keen to copy his own very northern designs. He complained to Willibald Pirckheimer in 1506, from Venice, that many Italians "are my enemies and they copy my work in the churches and wherever they find it; and then they revile it and say it is not in the antique manner and therefore not good". His widow was to have many problems trying to copyright his prints, so widely were they imitated. Little information survives about collections of prints from the late 15th and early 16th centuries, but we may assume that most artists collected prints as avidly as we know Rembrandt to have done.

Why, then, is the Italian antique manner so often misinterpreted, even mangled, in the North? The answer lies in the nature of the Renaissance style which is a spirit, a way of doing things, rather than just a collection of motifs. Reproductive illustrations, whether of figures or details or whole buildings, can convey only motifs, not essential principles: these can be thoroughly grasped only by studying antique art and Italian productions *in situ*. The North, with fundamentally different traditions from the South, attempted to graft Renaissance motifs on to a preexistent style; the result was often a confusing mixture of old and new, of Gothic and Renaissance, without those qualities of unity and simplicity so sought after by the Italians. Only when northern artists began to visit Italy in large numbers, from about the middle of the 16th century, did this state of affairs change.

MICHAEL GREENHALGH

Bibliography. Avery, C. *Italian Renaissance Sculpture*, London (1970). Baron, H. *The Crisis of the Early Italian Renaissance*, Princeton (1966). Blunt, A., *Artistic Theory in Italy, 1450–1600*, Oxford (1940). Burckhardt, J. *The Civilisation of the Renaissance in Italy* (illustrated English edn), London (1945). Burke, P. *Culture and Society in Renaissance Italy, 1420–1540*, London (1972). Burke, P. *The Renaissance Sense of the Past*, London (1969). Ferguson, W.K. *The Renaissance in Historial Thought*, Boston (1948). Freedberg, S.J. *Painting in Italy: 1500–1600*, Harmondsworth (1979). Gombrich, E. H. *Norm and Form: Studies in the Art of the Renaissance*, London (1966). Hay, D. *The Italian Renaissance in its Historical Background*, Cambridge (1961). Heydenreich, H. and Lotz, W. *Architecture in Italy: 1400–1600*, Harmondsworth (1974). Panofsky, E. *Renaissance and Renascences in Western Art*, Uppsala (1960). Pope-Hennessy, J. *Italian High Renaissance and Baroque Sculpture*, London (1971). Pope-Hennessy, J. *Italian Renaissance Sculpture*, London (1971). Weiss, R. *The Renaissance Discovery of Classical Antiquity*, Oxford (1969). Wittkower, R. *Architectural Principles in the Age of Humanism*, London (1962). Wölfflin, H. (trans. Murray, L. and P.) *Classic Art*, London (1952).

34

RENAISSANCE STYLE

Lady with an Ermine by Leonardo da Vinci; panel; 54×39cm (21×15in); c1483–4
Czartoryski Gallery, Krakow (see page 651)

IN recent times we have come to question the usefulness of the term "Renaissance" as applied to the visual arts of early modern Europe. The literal application of a word that originated to express the revival of, and building upon, the art of Antiquity after centuries of neglect has been challenged as we have recognized more clearly the lines of continuity between the arts of ancient civilizations and those of the medieval period. But this challenge cannot ignore a wealth of contemporary written evidence about works of art which evinces to an extraordinary degree the concern of this period to be articulate about its own achievements. It is the kind of commentary that is unprecedented in previous centuries. Renaissance writers believed they could identify a degree of progress in the arts that distinguished their own time from what had come before. This sense of mission, of there being certain goals to strive for, leads us back to the works of art themselves in search of some justification of the self-confidence displayed by their earliest critics and admirers.

We find that the visual arts became the vehicle of a new expression of certain ideals about man and society, and offer a new vision of the established beliefs of the Christian faith through the common vocabulary of human experience that their beholders share. Renaissance art demonstrates how the search for the idealization of form itself can be a spiritual exercise, summoning up for the onlooker a sense of the perfection of God *via* the perfection of the idealized human figure or the proportions of a building. The preliminary and most important stage of this exercise was the reexamination of nature by artists on whom new demands were being made in terms of skill and aesthetic judgment. The literature on art between about 1300 and the early 16th century also tells us that attitudes toward artists as social and creative beings changed significantly as a response to their success, so that by the end of the period the personal style of an individual artist was as much the key to a widespread admiration of his work as his technical competence or ability to work to order. We may no longer believe in the anonymity of the medieval artist, but the fragmentary evidence we have of him tells a very incomplete story beside the fame of the artist and his place in the literary traditions of art criticism that characterize the Renaissance period.

The concept of Renaissance became confused and has often been discredited because it has been much abused in the widest European context. Outside Italy, it has been applied not only to that period when, selectively, the surface qualities of Italian achievement, particularly ornament, were grafted on to native artistic styles, but also to earlier periods when Italy and other parts of Europe were achieving different things. The parallels across Europe in the 15th century, for example, are not always to be found in anything we might readily identify as a common "style" but rather in a common attitude towards expanding the possibilities of artistic expression. In both Italy and Flanders in the first half of the 15th century, artists were looking with scrupulous care at the world around them and forging new techniques to embody their findings. The Italian Antonio Pisanello's development of the medal form as a vehicle for portraiture and allegory is contemporary with the northerner van Eyck's use of what was probably the most refined technique of painting in oil known in Europe at that date, in order to render as faithfully as possible his extraordinary observations of the world around him.

During the longer period from the early 14th to the early 16th centuries, there are two truly international styles—one which we call "International Gothic", and another which marks the dawn of a culture more generally indebted to Italy which spread to other parts of Europe after 1500. The former was a last and splendid flowering of a common style based on the idea of Europe as a single Christian Empire, with such common aims as had expressed themselves in the repeated call for a crusade to deliver from infidel occupation those eastern Mediterranean lands in which Christianity was born. The second marks the emergence of Europe as a pattern of aggressive nation-states with imaginative horizons beyond the confines of Europe toward trade and empire overseas. Both these styles thrived on a common court culture and became disseminated by the procedures and protocol of court society in the exchange of works of art—and indeed artists—as diplomatic presents from one ruler to another. In the early 16th century, it was a pattern about to be fragmented and then given new alignment by the coming of the Reformation.

If it has generally been asserted that Italy was the chief stage on which the Renaissance was played out, it is because it is from Italy that we possess the greatest concentration of works of art and writing about them; together, these form a cumulative achievement of a consistent kind. The lack of written commentary from northern Europe in the 15th century and the destruction of a much greater part, through centuries of religious conflict, of the North's native artistic heritage, make the lines of development less clear. The powerful city-states of late medieval Italy patronized artists in the production of objects that are an important vehicle of propaganda, in the widest sense, on behalf of rulers, governments, and local corporate bodies. The Church in each community also sought the artistic embellishment of its buildings as a means of increasing prestige *vis-à-vis* its neighbors. There subsequently developed a healthy competitive artistic spirit between city-states, and between corporate and individual patrons within them. This encouraged the interchange of necessary expertise when required.

The first set of bronze doors commissioned *c*1329 for the Baptistery of Florence from Andrea Pisano (*c*1290–1348/9) can be seen as a deliberate attempt to rival the splendor of the bronze doors at Pisa, and it is indicative of the search for skilled hands that Florentines originally looked to Pisa or Venice for an artist to execute them. Moreover there was, as a kind of impetus to this sense of competitiveness, a common cultural identity between Italian city-states in their links with a common Italian past. Though politically fragmented at this time, Italians possessed the common heritage of the most numerous and splendid remains of the civilization of the

Roman Empire. It can be shown by reference to contemporary writing, and to the iconography of artistic commissions, that leading Italian cities wished to see themselves individually as the true heirs to the role of ancient Rome as the political and cultural arbiter of the civilized world. Thus the role of Classical Antiquity as inspiration and mentor to that of Renaissance Italy was a fundamental and long-formative process.

The medieval historian would rightly point out here that the concern with Antiquity had never been totally eclipsed in Italy or anywhere else in Europe. Yet it was the Renaissance that examined anew the form and subject matter of surviving antique art as an entity, and realized the importance of the essential indivisibility of spirit and function. The attraction of the gods and heroes of the Classical world for Christian society had long been rooted in the belief that there were worthwhile parallels in the Antique for the virtues of the Christian world. In medieval art, we invariably find that Classical subjects are dressed in contemporary costume to equate them in a direct sense with the world and teachings of the present. In the Renaissance, by a reexamination of the visual representation of the same figures, aided by archaeological discovery which clarified the varied vocabulary of antique art, and further by the correction of corrupt texts, the Classical figure was represented more accurately and with a sense of history. This meant in turn that the early Christian saints could be viewed historically as late antique figures. Donatello's *St George* for the armorers' guild (on the exterior of Orsanmichele, Florence) is shown in a freely imagined version of antique armor that renders him at once the Christian knight and an historical personage. By the later 15th century, Andrea Mantegna (1431–1506) had sufficient confidence in his ability to handle antique source material to recreate the antique world in his *Triumph of Caesar* series of paintings for the Mantuan court (now in Hampton Court Palace, London). As Antiquity became a touchstone by which contemporary arts were judged, as a standard to be matched and hopefully surpassed, so contemporary writers encouraged the belief that the age had particular and identifiable links with Antiquity across the gulf of medieval society. It was the 16th-century artist and historiographer Giorgio Vasari (1511–73), whose *Vite* (*Lives of the Artists*, 1550; second edition 1568) formulated a persuasive image of the Italian Renaissance as a restoration of the values and improvement of the achievements of antique art. But Vasari was only codifying and systematizing with a wealth of biographical material ideas that had long been current in Italy; he also gave them a particularly Tuscan, and therefore patriotic, dimension. The tradition begins, arguably, with Petrarch, though his concern for a revival of antique ideals is rooted mainly in hopes for political regeneration and a purification of language based on close attention to the modes of the ancient world. By the mid 15th century, the sculptor Lorenzo Ghiberti (1378–1455), in his *Commen-*

St George by Donatello, carved for Orsanmichele, Florence; marble; height 208cm (82in); c1417. Museo Nazionale, Florence

taries, asserts that art had lain dormant for 1,000 years before the arrival of Giotto. His contemporary Matteo Palmieri wrote

> Where was the painter's art till Giotto tardily restored it! A caricature of the art of human delineation! Sculpture and architecture, for long years sunk to the merest travesty of art, are only today in process of rescue from obscurity; only now are they being brought to a new pitch of perfection by men of genius and erudition.

This "new pitch" implies the setting of higher standards of achievement, engendered by the essentially competitive spirit already mentioned. This needs further definition, and the city of Florence provides the greatest evidence of its artistic results. Here there were open competitions for major public projects, one of the most famous being that for the second set of bronze doors for the Baptistery, announced in 1401, from which of the seven original trial reliefs only those of Ghiberti and Brunelleschi survive. A different kind of competition is evident from the degree of one-upmanship between the major guilds of Florence in the commissioning of statues for their respective niches on the outside of the guild-hall of Orsanmichele, one of which was the *St George* of Donatello. In 1423, a political body, the Parte Guelfa, commissioned from Donatello a statue of *St Louis of Toulouse* for their niche, specifying it was to be in bronze, and fire-gilded, in order to surpass in splendor the statues of other guilds to be seen on the building.

At yet another and more fundamental level, we can perceive a conscious rethinking and reworking of previous achievement by Florentine artists that seeks to build on the experience of others and depends for artistic merit partly on the recognition by its audience that this is in fact what is happening. Thus the role of informed beholder is crucial. Donatello's bronze *David* (Museo Nazionale, Florence) has eluded precise definition as to meaning and narrative content because the ambiguous, introspective mood of the sculpture makes it somewhat inscrutable. Its novelty as probably the first freestanding nude sculpture of its time asks the viewer to walk around it and admire the technical accomplishment. The exact date and circumstances of the commission of this work are not known, but it is first recorded in the Medici Palace in 1469, by which time Andrea del Verrocchio (1435–88) had cast his bronze *David* (Museo Nazionale, Florence) for the same family. Verrocchio rethinks the idea, primarily it seems in response to different circumstances of display since his work is not to be seen in the round, but also to turn the introspection into imminent action. To this end, he makes the sinuous Donatello outline into something more angular and assertive. Contemporary Florentines doubtless discussed the differences, and Verrocchio would have relied on the sense of dialogue with a previous idea for artistic impact.

The artist's concern to use the skills of the spectator based on his previous visual experience is one key to artistic criti-

David, by Donatello; bronze; height 158cm (62in); c1430. Museo Nazionale, Florence

cism. By the time Vasari was writing in the mid 16th century, there appears to have been much credit to be gained by the concealment of effort in the creation of the work of art: by a display of effortlessness of both design and technique. Vasari seeks to persuade us there had long been a desire on the part of the artist to court the spectator's admiration by offering him the most complex solution available, or even a variety of answers to the problem. In his Life of Masaccio, Vasari describes the painter's skill at foreshortening and mentions a now-lost work by him (possibly recorded for us in a copy in the Philadelphia Museum of Art) which he commends for its ingenuity for "besides the Christ delivering the man possessed, there are some very fine buildings so drawn in perspective that the interior and exterior are represented at the same time, as he took for the point of view not the front, but the side, for its greater difficulty." Vasari is using the terminology of his own period, but he reminds us of the fact that Masaccio is able to exploit the potential of perspectivized space because he himself has helped, through previous pictures, to ensure this is something the spectator would now take for granted in representation.

The perspectivized picture was one result of the recognition by Renaissance artists that the spectator needed a frame of reference with which to understand and interpret works of art, and that the world of visual experience needed to be ordered along recognizable and decipherable lines. It was a means by which the artist demanded of the viewer that he refer back to the real world, to check the fiction before him against his own experience. Primarily, that experience was focused on man himself and his central place in the order of things. In his book *On Painting* (Latin version 1435; translated into Italian 1436) the humanist Leon Battista Alberti (1404–72) outlines a way of constructing perspectivized space in painting by mathematical means. To arrive at this, he recommends the artist to use the figures in the painting as the means of establishing the unit of measurement; hence one third of the height of a figure in the foreground of the picture becomes the means of calculating distances and the relative position of one thing to another. Man is therefore seen as the determinant factor in this imagined world, echoing his supposed place in the real world of which the painting is conceived as the mirror image.

This was equally true with reference to man's physical proportions and particularly relevant for the devising of architecture. The Renaissance took its cue from the Classical writer Vitruvius, who, in his *De Architectura* (1st century AD) had argued that the proportions of the human form should serve as the paradigm for the proportions of man's creations. Perfection would result from the respect paid to this and the resulting symmetry: "since nature has designed the human body so that its members are duly proportioned to the frame as a whole, it appears that the ancients had good reason for

David, by Andrea del Verrocchio; bronze; height 126cm (50in); c1465. Museo Nazionale, Florence

S. Maria della Conciliazione, Todi, by Cola da Caprarola; begun in 1508

their rule, that in perfect buildings the different members must be in exact symmetrical relations to the whole general scheme." In a building such as the Pazzi Chapel, Florence, of Brunelleschi, the clarity of design is immediately comprehensible by a display of architectural logistics in the repetition of a module, or standard unit of measurement. This determines the height and width of the entire space and the relationship and spacing of the architectural members, emphasized here by the choice of materials so that the gray *pietra serena* marble of pilasters, base, and cornice stand out against the whiteness of the wall. We know that the building was barely begun at the time of the architect's death in 1446 and that its basic plan was probably largely determined by the preexisting layout of the friary of which it was to become part. These factors underline firstly the essential logic of structure, since it was possible to bring the building to completion out of the designer's hands, and secondly the ability of the individual architect to overcome constraints and still create something new and in a personal idiom. This, too, is what Vasari would have called part of the "difficulty" that roused the artist's sense of challenge.

The Renaissance expression of order in architecture, the

invitation to a spiritual response *via* an intellectual one, was perhaps best expressed in the concept of the centrally planned church. The visual inspiration for this came largely from the antique, from the round temples dedicated to pagan deities, but the form was sanctioned by some of the earliest Christian buildings also, particularly those commemorating death by martyrdom. Subsequently, it was the form consciously chosen by Donato Bramante (*c*1444–1514) *c*1500 for his Tempietto at the church of S. Pietro in Montorio, Rome, which traditionally marked the site of the martyrdom of St Peter. We know from 16th-century sources that Bramante intended to complete his scheme by an enclosing circular courtyard. A few years after this, the little-known architect Cola da Caprarola designed the church of S. Maria della Conciliazione at Todi, begun in 1508. The very isolation of this building underlines the impact of the centrally planned form. We are somehow acutely aware this is a building that will not suffer additions or subtractions to the fabric without being destroyed, in an aesthetic sense, in the process. The design of the medieval cathedral allows the eye to wander over its constructional and decorative features, but here the formal quality of design not only directs the eye in a very specific way but immediately gives us a sense of how the building fits together as interlocking regular shapes of circle and square.

Man could not only translate his physical shape and proportions into an understanding of what visually confronted him; often his own physical presence was positively necessary to complete the artistic idea. The viewer's involvement with a picture could be of a directly prompting kind; Alberti recommends there should be a figure in the painting gesturing to the spectator to encourage his participation in what was before him. This is best exemplified in large altarpieces of the Madonna and Child with Saints by the practice of having one of the forward saints beckoning to us, imploring us to share the visionary experience. The artist could also be sensitive to, and exploit, the viewer's surroundings, so that the visual experience in paint is part of the wider experience of setting. This could take the form of allowing the natural light in the room or chapel from window or door to determine the fall of light on the painted architectural surrounds to pictures; this occurs in the early 14th century in Giotto's famous fresco cycle in the Capella dell'Arena at Padua. More than a century later, in the 1420s, Masaccio (1401–?28) and Masolino (1383–1440/7) used the light from the window above the altar to determine the directional fall of light in their frescoes of the life of St Peter in the Brancacci Chapel at S. Maria del Carmine, Florence. Here, therefore, additional credence is offered to our experience of the painted world as actually happening behind the plane of the wall.

Planning works of art for the beholder also reveals itself in the artist's sensitivity to viewpoint. In different ways, Donatello's entire work in sculpture considers and continually re-

A view of the interior of the Pazzi Chapel, S. Croce, Florence, by Brunelleschi; begun c1430

St John the Evangelist by Donatello; marble; height 209cm (82in); 1408. Museo dell'Opera del Duomo, Florence

thinks this problem. It is indeed present from his earliest work. The *St John the Evangelist* of 1408 (Museo dell'Opera del Duomo, Florence) is characterized by certain figure distortions—such as the length of the torso and beard—to take account of its intended high position on the facade of Florence Cathedral; there the distortions would be corrected, and so justified, in the eye of the viewer. His later *St George* for Orsanmichele (Museo Nazionale, Florence) points out to us and then emphasizes the preparedness and alertness of the figure by turning him slightly forward of the shallow niche toward the spectator advancing along the street beneath him.

For a decade or so, from 1443 to 1453, Donatello worked in the north Italian city of Padua. It is interesting that Vasari claims Donatello decided to return to Florence because he missed the critical artistic sensitivity of his native city which induced him to further study and achievement. Contemporary

with Donatello's completion of bronze reliefs and standing figures for the high altar of the Basilica of Sant'Antonio at Padua, the painter Andrea Mantegna, in many ways Donatello's truest artistic heir, began his frescoes for the church of the Eremitani in the same city, with scenes from the lives of saints Christopher and James (destroyed in the Second World War). In the *St James led to Martyrdom*, Mantegna not only quotes from and rethinks Donatello's *St George* but also exploits the viewpoint for the work which was on the side wall of a chapel above eye-level; hence the subject is shown in sharp receding perspective. At the same time, he stresses the contact with the chapel space in which we are standing by the ambivalent presence of the forward soldier's foot which projects over the painted architectural framing.

A sense of illusion is also used by Mantegna for a secular setting, the so-called Camera degli Sposi in the Ducal Palace at Mantua. Here, painted fictive curtains cover two walls of the room; on the others the curtains are pulled back to reveal the Duke and his court, so holding up a mirror to those who would frequent the room. The result is something part imagined—and possibly part record of actual events, though this has never been agreed. The way Mantegna turns the awkward presence of a fireplace breaking into the design to advantage by painting steps either side, so that we read the top of the fireplace as part of a platform, shows a further dimension of the consciousness of the need to maximize the potential of the room setting. In the early 16th century, Raphael used similar limitations of wall space and shapes to advantage in the Stanze of the Vatican. The art of fresco, by which so much of the painted achievement of the Renaissance in Italy is carried, demanded a constant awareness of the need to overcome limitations by ingenuity and turn them into the impetus of design.

The Camera degli Sposi is unique in the history of wall-painting in terms of its content; in terms of its more general function, it served the purpose still largely filled at this time by tapestries or other wall-hangings. The fresco cycles in the great churches and public buildings of 14th- and 15th-century Italy had a more didactic message. The upsurge of building activity in the cities of northern and central Italy—particularly in the cities of Florence, Siena, Padua, and Assisi—provided large churches for the preaching orders; these required some visual commentary within the building on their teachings. This commentary depended for its source material on the Bible and other sacred texts on the one hand, and on the popular, semi-apocryphal tales of the saints of the Christian calendar, such as those found in the 13th-century collection, the *Golden Legend*, on the other. For the large, new public buildings, such as the Town Hall of Siena, wall-paintings were called for to demonstrate the dispensing of justice and the benefits of wise and beneficial government as a means of guiding the actions of the city authorities foregathered there. Wall-

St James led to Martyrdom, by Mantegna; fresco; width 330cm (130in); c1445–6. Formerly in the church of the Eremitani, Padua; destroyed on 11 March 1944

Ludovico II Gonzaga and his court on a wall of the Camera degli Sposi, Ducal Palace, Mantua, by Mantegna; fresco; width of base 600cm (236in); completed in 1474

The Tribute Money by Masaccio; fresco; 255×598cm (100×235in); c1425. Brancacci Chapel, S. Maria del Carmine, Florence

paintings of a similar kind were commissioned in Flanders at this time; Rogier van der Weyden (c1399–1464) painted now-lost scenes on the theme of justice in the Town Hall at Brussels, and two painted panels by Dieric Bouts (c1415–75), commissioned as part of a set of four by the city fathers of the same city, survive in the Musées Royaux des Beaux-Arts de Belgique, Brussels. The message and necessary ingredients of such paintings were codified out of an already developing practice by Alberti in *Della Pittura* (*On Painting*; 1436) where he suggests guidelines for narrative art.

In Alberti's words, the greatest work of the painter is the *istoria* or history picture, the depiction of narrative subject matter which will serve as moralistic guide to the observer. He outlines, in written form, much that was already becoming current practice in the Florence of his day and indeed had been anticipated in the work of Giotto and his school a century before. The *istoria* should be clear and instructional as an exemplar of human behavior; to this end it must be easy to read as narrative, and the sense of action must not be confused. Alberti recommends that pictures should be quite large, and that the relative sizes of figures and surroundings should approximate reality. The spectator's empathy with the scene represented will be best engaged by an economical number of figures, each of which should tell, by stance and gesture, of his emotions and reactions to the event taking place. Since the narrative should be uplifting, the figures themselves should be idealized; to this end, the artist should pay close attention to nature, and correct where she has faltered in creating that which is most perfect. A significant recent work that Alberti would have known, completed perhaps less than a decade before the completion of *Della Pittura*, was Masaccio's *The Tribute Money* in the Brancacci Chapel, S. Maria del Carmine, Florence. Here the language of gesture and reaction, the broadly sculptural rendering of the figures to give them weight and dignity in the consistent light and shade the artist uses, and the perspectivized outdoor landscape, all help to unify the three episodes of the story into a total design.

The implications of Alberti's demands on the artist's imagination and resourcefulness in the creation of the *istoria* are far-reaching for the status of the painter and his art in relation to craft skills and their social standing. The kinds of decision the artist here needs to make about his work and his source materials are achieved by inviting criticism, which, in turn, implies development of style rather than a repeated display of technical expertise. Moreover, Alberti seeks for the artist a kind of criticism that can only be found in intellectual circles —for he encourages the artist to frequent the society of poets and philosophers. His vision, therefore, of the artist's life-style suggests the patronage of the humanist prince and the world of the princely court rather than that of the city. "For their own enjoyment," Alberti says, "artists should associate with poets and orators who have many embellishments in common with painters and who have a broad knowledge of many things." It is clear from Alberti's constant reference to antique example that these "many things" will include a knowledge of

the Classics, and he draws extensively on Classical writings about celebrated pictures long since lost. If we examine a major example of an Albertian religious image, Mantegna's print of the *Entombment*, all the ingredients are there: the economical number of figures, the rendering of human emotion through a variety of gesture, the convincing landscape setting which reinforces and explains the story. But what is also clear is that Mantegna has looked closely at antique sculpture for his hard-edged style of linear description (the same is true, too, for his painting where sometimes he seeks to simulate the actual appearance of relief sculpture) and that antique texts have provided as much inspiration for his use of gestural language as the Biblical story.

The ability to select from available visual material became the means by which some Italian critics judged the work of Flemish artists and found them wanting. They marveled at the superlative control of the oil technique, and the ability to paint the infinitesimal with exactitude; but the giving of equal care and attention to all parts of the picture went against the advice of directing the attentions of the spectator that formed an essential part of the making of the history picture. Now we see this in a very different light, for the unity of a Flemish picture such as Jan van Eyck's *Arnolfini Wedding* of 1434 (National Gallery, London) rests with his care not simply to render minute detail for its own sake, but in order to give every object in the picture a spiritual significance which reflected the sacred rite taking place. Rather than exclude or generalize, van Eyck uses the whole range of his observed world as a celebration of divine presence and creativity. This selection process was less important for more straightforward portraiture, a lower genre in the hierarchy than narrative subjects; it is no accident that Flemish portraits were especially influential on Italian art, particularly in the closing decades of the 15th century.

The surviving evidence, from the 15th century especially, not only provides us with a wealth of painted portraits in numbers hitherto unknown, but also with an interest in the personalized physiognomy of the famous that is less stressed in medieval representation. The personalized portrayal is achieved at the expense of rank and station, so that the face and expression of the sitter now compete for prominence with the accoutrements of dress and perhaps regalia or some other symbol of office that denote a role in the world. One of the chief sources of medieval portrait representation is that of tomb effigies which we can categorize quite easily into types of king, bishop, knight, and so on, by dress. Renaissance painted portraits strike out in new directions of individual commemoration and suggest the dimensions of personal interest and environment. Several of Botticelli's portraits of the Medici, and other leading Florentine families, tell us little about the rank of the sitter, but suggest a contemporary room setting and a certain transience of facial expression and pose. During the years he worked at the court of Milan, Leonardo da Vinci (1452–1519) painted the portrait now in Krakow (Czartoryski Gallery), known as the *Lady with an Ermine*. This is usually

Renaissance Armor

The importance of hunting and warfare in pre-modern society meant that weaponry and protective clothing commanded a high degree of technical expertise not always found contemporaneously in other areas of applied knowledge. In the Renaissance, leading artists such as Leonardo da Vinci and Michelangelo turned their attentions to the problems of siege machinery and architectural fortification as the need arose and their patrons required. The Renaissance suit of armor was, in practical terms, a highly efficient piece of machinery. Its fully developed form, designed to give the wearer the maximum freedom of action, closely followed the shape of the human figure. This expression of the actions and flexibility of the man beneath generally contrasts with the armor of Eastern civilizations. The effect of strangely anthropomorphic form is captured by Paolo Uccello (1397–1475) in his painted vision of the *Battle of San Romano* (National Gallery, London).

Arms factories were found everywhere in Europe, but during the 15th century certain cities enjoyed a particular reputation as manufacturers of plate armor. Milan was the leading Italian center and here the Missaglia family were the most sought-after armorers, rivaling leading painters in fame and enjoying the confidence of princes. The kind of armor produced in Italy, as shown by Mantegna's painting of *St George* from the 1470s (Gallerie dell'Academia, Venice) with its smooth surfaces and rounded edges, contrasts with that produced by leading German manufacturers, notably at Nuremberg, which was more angular and decorated by fluting.

Armor was, like the other arts, open to the direct influence of political circumstances. Following the French invasion of Italy in 1494, the differing traditions north and south of the Alps came together to form the style known as "Maximilian" after the Emperor of the time. Here German fluting was applied to Italian form, though continuing to follow the basic contours of the design.

Sixteenth-century developments remind us that this was a time of fundamental transition in warfare since it was the last period in Western Europe when suit armor had any direct usefulness. As firearms developed and

◄ A detail from Paolo Uccello's *Battle of San Romano*; panel; height about 145cm (57in). National Gallery, London

▲ *St George* by Mantegna; tempera on canvas; 66×32cm (26×13in); 1470s. Gallerie dell'Academia, Venice

▼ Half-armor dated 1555 with etched decoration, by Michel Witz of Innsbruck. Wallace Collection, London

◀ A Gothic suit of armor of *c*1475–85 from south Germany. Wallace Collection, London

▶ The Judgment of Paris by Lucas Cranach the Elder; panel; 51×38cm (20×15in); 1527. State Art Museum, Copenhagen. Paris, on the left, wears German fluted armor adapted to Italian form

Below right An example of puffed and slashed armor of the early 16th century, a German suit of *c*1520. Wallace Collection, London

▼ A fanciful helmet from Augsburg, *c*1530. The visor takes the form of an eagle's head with etched plumage. Wallace Collection, London

the pattern of military engagement changed, so suit armor became increasingly redundant. Hence many features that developed for purely practical needs in the previous century became part of the trappings of court life and ceremonial, denoting rank and heraldic achievement. Suit armor underwent final changes for the needs of the tournament, but in the 16th century it tended to take on shape and contour more akin to other forms of dress, sometimes expressing soft materials and their effects, such as puffed and slashed garments. Thus the unity of function and materials of the 15th century was lost. Individual pieces of armor, particularly helmets, became less practical in their ceremonial guise and took on more fanciful and bizarre forms.

These developments encouraged more ornamentation. This could take the form of inlay or etching. It is no accident that the latter armorial skill developed in those same German cities where the potential of etching as a print medium was under experimentation at this time. Decoration could take the form of figural representation, perhaps of central Christian themes, or of saints, believed to be protective in times of danger or combat. Decorative motives increasingly took forms familiar to other kinds of Renaissance applied ornament, notably running vine and acanthus. This common vocabulary marks a further stage of the absorption of armor into the mainstream of applied design.

MAURICE HOWARD

Further reading. Blackmore, H.L. *Arms and Armour*, London (1965). Ffoulkes, C.J. *Armour and Weapons*, Oxford (1909). Ffoulkes, C.J. *Arms and Armament*, London (1945). Laking, C.F. *A Record of European Arms and Armour*, London (1920). Mann, J.G. "Notes on the Armour of the Maximilian Period and the Italian Wars", *Archaeologia*, London (1929). Mann, J.G. "The Etched Decoration of Armour", *Proceedings of the British Academy*, London (1940).

thought to be a portrait of Cecilia Gallerani, the mistress of Duke Sforza. The liveliness and challenge of the portrait rests in the turning pose, in the parallel placing of the ermine which appears to be part symbolic, part wordplay on the sitter's name, and the sense we get of her reaction to things outside the picture space. The quality of immediacy is underlined for us when we learn that in 1498, some years after the picture was painted, the sitter warns Isabella d'Este that when she sees the portrait she should bear in mind it shows her younger and not as she now appears. So this is not a timeless image in the medieval sense, summarizing the sitter's rank. Its creation was conditioned far more by the painter's reaction to the sitter and his concern to galvanize the spectator's reaction to the sense of movement—of her being, as was said of many Renaissance portraits in their own time, "about to speak".

That portraits were believed efficacious in prompting worthy attitudes in the viewer is shown by the original fittings for Duke Federico da Montefeltro's study in his palace at Urbino where, above the inlaid paneling and cupboards holding his books, there were portraits of famous scholars of the past as an inducement to study. The virtuous prince was no longer simply warrior and law-giver, but scholar and thinker in his painted representations. The search for new guises led to a consequent revival of quite specific antique forms—notably the sculpted portrait bust, a portable object for portraying the powerful, or the simply worthy and respected like the Florentine doctor Giovanni Chellini in the bust by Antonio Rossellino in the Victoria and Albert Museum, London, dated 1456.

Many Renaissance portraits remain anonymous to us where both the history of the picture gives no clues and the properties of insignia or coats-of-arms are also missing. The portrait played an important role in establishing the personal style, and thus fame, of the Renaissance artist because it was generally more portable than a large-scale historical or religious subject. Leonardo's portrait of *Mona Lisa* (Louvre, Paris) was painted in Florence in the first years of the 16th century. It became very famous in its day; its format was copied and rethought by artists at work in Florence during the few years it was there, for Leonardo took it with him to France in 1517 and it later passed into the French royal collection. The picture is rapturously and intimately described by Vasari half a

century later, even though it seems he never saw the original. Since we know very little about the sitter herself, it would be true to say that Mona Lisa was made more famous by Leonardo's portrait of her than she ever was in real life. It is a prime example of art taking the lead from history, making its own heroes out of painter and painted. This could operate at the highest political level and not simply among the kind of urban merchant class to which Mona Lisa belonged. In the annals of Renaissance history, we could well say that Leonardo Loredan, Doge of Venice from 1500 to 1516, is remembered not for his political or personal actions but as a haunting portrait by Giovanni Bellini in the National Gallery, London.

The fame of an artist's personal style could be established as much by the skill with which he handled his medium as by nature or novelty of the represented image. Certain technical skills, particularly that of fresco painting, were the means by which an artist showed whether he was worthy of inclusion in the most important traditions of art. As new kinds of representation developed, so new skills arose to express them. Portraiture itself provides one highly significant example of this in its promotion of the medal as a means of commemorating the famous. As a multiple and portable object, the medal became in the Renaissance a means of disseminating not only the likeness of the famous but also the virtuosity of the medalist's skill. Pisanello led the way in this development, and his employment at various Italian courts in the first half of the 15th century meant he recorded many leading figures in his medalic portraits. One of the most interesting is that of the Eastern Emperor, John Palaeologus, made when he visited Italy in 1438. This work particularly illuminates the way in which medals could become historical and physiognomic source material: the Emperor's profile and tall headgear became the prototype for many representations of Eastern figures in Italian narrative painting.

The development of new media encouraged new habits of collecting works of art, as skill came to be admired and so enjoyed for its own sake. The print media of woodcut and engraving embraced new forms of subject matter, and took on a new degree of linear sophistication in the second half of the 15th century. The emergence of the single print, liberated from accompanying text, begs interesting questions about the potential market for sale and its subsequent function in private hands. The print could demonstrate the artist's capabilities at full stretch to a wide audience. At the same time, since it is not an object intended for public display in the manner of a painted altarpiece, it must have been passed from hand to hand, and discussed by small groups of expert admirers. It certainly played an important part in encouraging special expertise on the part of the consumer in one particular area of the visual arts. We know that prints traveled relatively long distances very quickly. Drawings by Albrecht Dürer (1471–1528) confirm he was familiar with the prints of the Italians

Pisanello's medal to commemorate the visit of the Eastern Emperor John Palaeologus to Italy in 1438; bronze; diameter 10cm (4in). Museo Nazionale, Florence

St Jerome in his Study, an engraving by Albrecht Dürer; 25×19cm (10×7in); 1514

Mantegna and Pollaiuolo before his first visit to Italy in the mid 1490s. Later, when Dürer himself had become established as the most celebrated print-maker in the Europe of his day, he had a swift and direct impact on leading Italian artists. Vasari grudgingly admits that Dürer's work is commended in Italy for its "diligence" in engraving, and acknowledges his influence even though it undermines his concept of the art of central Italy as self-perpetuating and self-inspiring. Looking at one of Dürer's finest, fully mature works, the engraving of *St Jerome in his Study* of 1514, we can see the qualities that enthralled contemporaries. With every turn of the engraver's tool, Dürer has rendered by line and density of shadow an enormous range of texture and surface, of light and shade.

Even in the highest realms of narrative picture-making, where subject matter is often especially traditional and therefore delimiting, there comes a point at which the skills of art begin to upstage the image represented. Vasari tells us that when Leonardo was in Florence in the first years of the 16th century, he executed a cartoon, or life-size preparatory drawing, of the Virgin and St Anne with the Christ Child "which not only filled every artist with wonder, but, when it was finished and set up men and women, young and old, flocked to see it for two days, as if it had been a festival, and they marveled exceedingly." We know that the cartoon to which Vasari refers cannot be the one now in the National Gallery, London, because his further description of the activity contained in the cartoon seen publicly in Florence contains essential differences. Yet the probably earlier work (in London) must have provoked similar reactions when it was first seen, almost certainly in the city of Milan where Leonardo created it.

The quality at which we marvel is not based at all on any obvious truth to nature for which the earlier 15th century might have striven. It is rather Leonardo's own summation of narrative and figurative expression *via* a knowledge of the natural world—a knowledge he now takes for granted is within our understanding. On this he builds to explore new things. It is significant that Leonardo was largely responsible for a revolution in the potential of drawing as a means of thinking out compositional problems. The London cartoon is but one complex and obviously highly-worked idea in a long series of attempts to resolve the difficulties and challenge of combining several figures into a satisfactory compositional and spiritual relationship. As we see here, the drawing already tells us of a great sophistication and range of tone through effects of light and shade that would, if transferred to the medium of paint, be rendered as a convincing three-dimensionality not conceived of by his 15th-century predecessors. Leonardo has barely begun to draw the landscape surrounding the figures, but we can be sure, from the relative size of figures to picture field, even if we did not possess other, painted works by him, that it would not have been a carefully perspectivized setting. Figures are placed in landscape not to suggest actual physical surroundings as such, but to emphasize their timelessness.

Cartoon for a Madonna and Child with St Anne by Leonardo da Vinci; charcoal heightened with white on brown paper; size of cartoon 140×100cm (55×39in); c1495. National Gallery, London

The dimension of time has been similarly excluded from Michelangelo's contemporary sculpture group, the *Pietà* in St Peter's, Rome, where the Virgin is as youthful and ageless as the dead son she silently mourns. In 1504, Leonardo and Michelangelo were engaged in the preparation of cartoons for two scenes of famous Florentine victories in battle, to be frescoed on the walls of the Great Council Chamber in the Palazzo Vecchio, Florence. It was surely the greatest ever competition between two leading Renaissance artists, all the more competitive because there would be no declared winner, only everlasting debate about their respective merits. Their thinking out of the narrative possibilities, as well as their personal styles, had a great impact on the young Raphael—already with several large altarpieces to his credit in his native Umbria—on his arrival in Florence at this time. Under the impetus of these and other Florentine achievements, Raphael's style of painting changed quite dramatically and he prepared himself for the ambitious projects he found himself facing in Rome from 1509. In the sense that he feels free to choose a better or more intellectually rigorous style, to learn from others as the route to more perfect solutions, Raphael demonstrates in an emphatic way the artist's liberation from adherence to one singular, unchanging skill.

The Pietà by Michelangelo in St Peter's, Rome; marble; height 173cm (68in); 1498–9

Raphael's absorption of the lessons to be learned from Florentine contemporaries was intensive and quickly put to use when the opportunity presented itself. In Venice at the same period, we find the aged Giovanni Bellini (c1430–1516) both instructing and learning from younger Venetian artists and striving to keep abreast of the times and the changing fashion in pictures. Fashion here is not at all a trivializing term to use, for it is in the Venetian school in particular that we find direct evidence, in the early years of the 16th century, of patrons and collectors seeking out certain new types of subject-

picture from those artists capable of realizing them in paint. Prominent among these types were small pictures of landscape and poetical subjects, and they evoke the kind of picture always associated with the names of Giorgione and the young Titian. Once these artists had established their reputations in these fields, we find that the rarity value of their individual attainments begins to supersede the subject they are painting; collectors become anxious to acquire whatever works by their hand are available. We should beware of too simplistic a notion of the independent artist here. Venetian painters continued to seek prestigious commissions for churches and public buildings, and remained aware of their public role, but they also became famous for pictures that in type and sometimes in size were a far cry from Alberti's notion of the artist's true and worthy pictorial goals.

Part of the growing personal reputation of the artist, as the 16th century progressed, was based on the growing international reputation of Italian art. Leonardo passed the last years of his life in France under the protection of King Francis I, and he was to be followed there in later years by other leading Florentine and Roman artists. From the period following the French invasion of Italy in 1494, Italy came to have a significant influence on the arts of France and other areas of northern Europe. Sometimes Italian craftsmen worked in these places, but the influence shows itself in a more widespread fashion in the adoption by native-born craftsmen of Renaissance ornament—particularly in architectural decoration and interior design. Later in the century, this was to be codified through pattern books of ornament. Perhaps the greatest impetus in this direction came from the decorative concerns of Raphael and his workshop in their great religious and secular Roman commissions in the second decade of the 16th century and beyond. Their style was based on a wide vocabulary of decorative forms after the antique, especially from newly-discovered excavated material in Rome from such late antique buildings as the Golden House of Nero (see Roman Art).

The use of Renaissance motives in England in the early 16th century, carried out either by native craftsmen or by craftsmen far from direct contact with Italian sources, look to us certainly bold, perhaps even imaginative, but also unsophisticated beside Italian examples. The chantry chapel made for the de la Warr family at Boxgrove in Sussex is a particularly exuberant example of its kind, where Renaissance ornament in the form of cherubs and decorative motives are applied as a busy surface to what is essentially a Gothic canopied shape. Its impact is one of vitality, of a certain brinkmanship on the vulgar, emphasized originally by vibrant color. The chantry functioned for a very short time, as it was suppressed along with hundreds of other large and small religious foundations in the England of the 1530s. Continuity was broken therefore at the point where such structures were being built to look modern by the application of Italian ornament.

England was to make other false starts before establishing her own "classical" style from a mixture of native and continental forms. Not only do we miss here the refinement of ornament and design through materials as we find, for example, on an important 15th-century Florentine tomb, but also a confusion of traditions through the lack of an intellectual exercise—a process that would not have occurred to the craftsman at Boxgrove. Bernardo Rossellino (1409–64) conceived and carried out the tomb of the Florentine chancellor and humanist Leonardo Bruni in the church of S. Croce in the late 1440s. Bruni's book *De Studiis et Litteris* had defended the study of Classical authors, sought to demonstrate the core of truth in their writings as supportive to the Christian faith, and advocated education and knowledge as the keys to human creativity. His monument thus seeks to show us his elevation to heaven through a use of antique architectural forms and ornament more archaeologically purist, and governed by the eloquence of restraint. Both the inscription and the manner of his dress tell us it is his intellectual standing, rather than his social rank, that is the basis of his fame. The balance of forces here between figures and architectural setting, between the appropriateness of one form to another, between the portrait image turned toward the spectator and the sacred image above, all prompt our recognition of the Renaissance concern for order, for the conjunction of real and mystical and their expression through each other, that inspired the greatest achievements of the visual arts of the age.

MAURICE HOWARD

Bibliography. Baxandall, M. *Painting and Experience in Fifteenth Century Italy*, Oxford (1972). Benesch, O. *The Art of the Renaissance in Northern Europe*, London (1965). Blunt, A. *Artistic Theory in Italy 1450–1600*, Oxford (1940). Burckhardt, J. *The Civilization of the Renaissance in Italy* (illustrated English edn), London (1945). Gombrich, E.H. *Norm and Form: Studies in the Art of the Renaissance*, London (1966). Gombrich, E. H. *Symbolic Images*, London (1972). Panofsky, E. *Renaissance and Renascences in Western Art*, New York (1965). Seymour, C. *Sculpture in Italy: 1400–1500*, Harmondsworth (1966).

35

THE NORTHERN RENAISSANCE

Presumed self-portrait by Nikolaus Gerhaert van Leyden; sandstone; c1464
Musée de l'Oeuvre Notre-Dame, Strasbourg

THE Northern Renaissance is the overall heading usually given to non-Italian Western European art of the period c1420–c1600. It therefore parallels the Italian Renaissance and, like it, overlaps the so-called International Gothic at the beginning of its development and the Baroque at its end. As in Italy, the later stages of this period tend to be absorbed by the so-called Mannerist style (see Mannerism). The concept of "Renaissance" is based upon the idea of a rebirth of interest in the forms and content of Classical art, and was originally formulated with specific reference to Italian culture of the 15th and 16th centuries. However, Northern art of this period developed in a very different way. During the 15th century, the Northerners remained totally uninterested in the rediscoveries of the Italians. In the early years of the 16th century, their outlook altered dramatically: the Italian manner, previously shunned, was enthusiastically accepted almost overnight. So whereas Italian art of c1420–c1600 reveals a comparatively unbroken continuity of stylistic development, that of the North may be divided into two distinct phases. Many historians prefer to term 15th-century Northern art "Late Gothic", in distinction from a 16th century "Northern Renaissance".

We look in vain for an awareness of the idea of cultural rebirth in Northern writings of the 15th century. By the end of his life, Albrecht Dürer (1471–1528) had formulated such a notion, borrowed from Italian theory, but even he had only a very dim idea of the history of art as such. Carel van Mander (writing in c1604) and Joachim von Sandrart (writing in 1675–9) were the first Northern art historians. Both were heavily influenced by Vasari's Vite (Lives of the Artists) (1st edn 1550; 2nd edn 1568) which perpetuated the fame of Italian Renaissance art, to the detriment of that of the North which was generally stigmatized as retrogressive. This outlook was connected with that which regarded all medieval art with disfavor; both had an extremely long currency. Jakob Burckhardt in Die Kultur der Renaissance in Italien (The Civilization of the Renaissance in Italy, 1860) viewed the Renaissance as an almost exclusively Italian phenomenon, and even as great an apologist as Johan Huizinga (in The Waning of the Middle Ages, 1924) thought that 15th-century Northern art was the autumn fruitfulness of a dying mode of artistic expression. The fundamental problem was that the roots of art historical terminology were Italian based, and consequently lacked an appropriate vocabulary to express a positive opinion of 15th-century Northern art.

Yet much Northern art of this century can be considered "progressive". Contemporary Italian commentators were united in the high esteem they felt for Northern painting; they do not appear to have considered it in any way inferior to that of their own country. Quattrocento patrons paid large sums for Flemish paintings, and Italian artists frequently drew upon Northern models. Such quintessentially "Renaissance" departures in 15th-century art as portraiture and the accurate depiction of landscape depend primarily upon the Northern tradition. As the inventors and propagators of the new technique of oil painting, the early Netherlandish masters were once again in advance of their Italian contemporaries. Although Northern and Italian artists chose widely different modes of expression during the 15th century, their achievements remained complementary: both ultimately fed the development of Western European art.

In his masterful exposition of the Renaissance and Renascences in Western Art (published in 1960) Erwin Panofsky suggested a distinction between a "Naissance" without or even against Antiquity in 15th-century Northern art, as opposed to a Renaissance of Antiquity in that of Italy. This subtle but crucial differentiation allows us to separate the "birth" of naturalistic values in Northern art from the "rebirth" of a classicizing style incorporating naturalistic values in Italian art. During the 16th century, a rapprochement between North and South took place, setting the scene for the truly European style that followed: the Baroque.

The International Gothic. The International Gothic may be characterized as a tendency towards extreme elegance of form, combined with an often acute attention to naturalistic detail, which flourished in Western European art of the later 14th and early 15th centuries. This movement—too disparate to be readily termed a style—was "international" in manifesting itself in widely separate localities, notably Paris, Prague, London, and Milan. It was "Gothic" in springing directly from the 14th-century tradition. Although the International Gothic was not a new departure in the same sense as the realistic styles that arose in Florence and Flanders during the second and third decades of the 15th century, it fostered an interest in naturalism which did much to prepare the ground for the twin Renaissances of Italy and the North.

The International Gothic was essentially a court art; its decline coincided with a series of political crises which shook the major European courts in succession during the early 15th century. With a few notable exceptions, the major surviving monuments to this manner are all illuminated manuscripts. Many important works in other media have been destroyed, but the illuminated manuscript remains a particularly suitable medium for that combination of fine detail, delicate decoration, and glowing color which remains the supreme achievement of the International Gothic.

A vitally important unifying factor in European art of the later 14th century was the heritage of early Trecento Italian painting, which had been assimilated throughout most of the North in one way or another. However, the Parisian portrait of John the Good (c1356–9; Louvre) and the panels by Master Theodoric in Karlstein Castle, near Prague (c1357–67) reveal a weighty modeling of form which goes beyond Italian models. The dedication miniature of the Bible of King Charles V (1371; Rijksmuseum Meermanno-Westreenianum, The Hague) by Jean Bondol (fl. 1368–81) united this plasticity

The Flight into Egypt from the Hours of the Maréchal de Boucicaut by the Boucicaut Master; c1405–8. Musée Jacquemart-André, Paris

with a clearly defined spatial setting. This remarkable naturalism was not immediately followed. Illuminations produced for the Psalter of the Duke of Berry (*c*1380–5; Bibliothèque Nationale, Paris) by André Beauvenu (*c*1330–1400) and Master Bertram of Hamburg's Grabow Altarpiece (*c*1383; Hamburger Kunsthalle, Hamburg) incorporate voluminous figures within a two-dimensional setting which uncomfortably belies their weight. The illuminator of the Brussels Hours (*c*1385–1402; Bibliothèque Royale Albert I, Brussels), who is sometimes identified with Jacquemart de Hesdin, turned repeatedly to the problem of rendering three-dimensional space. His work was, however, overshadowed by Melchior Broederlam's Dijon Altarpiece shutters (*c*1394–9; Musée des Beaux-Arts, Dijon). These large panels exhibit a monumentality of form and a sureness of compositional and spatial handling which transcends their models.

The Boucicaut Master (*fl. c*1400–20) was heir to the achievements of the late 14th century, and, in his perspectival skill and precise observation of the effects of light and color, he was the prophet of early Netherlandish painting. Without his Hours of Marshal Boucicaut (*c*1409; Musée Jacquemart-André, Paris) the work of Robert Campin and of Jan van Eyck would be unthinkable. His sometime colleague, the Bedford Master (*fl.* 1405–35), was less innovatory, working in a related style which endured until the 1430s. The anonymous Master of the Rohan Hours (*c*1410–25) was a totally different personality, who perfected an expressionistic style which almost burst asunder the essential restraint of the International Gothic and the confines of the illuminated page to which it was so intimately linked. When all is said and done, elegance both of form and color were a keynote of the International Gothic. In Northern Europe, its supreme achievement was probably the last manuscript of the Limburg Brothers, the *Très Riches Heures* of the Duke of Berry (*c*1416; Musée Condé, Chantilly). Although the illuminations in this book include accurate landscapes and impressive night scenes, it is primarily memorable for its exquisite color harmonies and unfailing gracefulness of design.

The formulation of a new style. With the revival of the Hundred Years War (1337–1453) and the rise of an independent Burgundian state in the second decade of the 15th century, the epicenter of Northern art moved from Paris to Flanders. Throughout the century, the Netherlands remained a hive of artistic activity without European parallel. Tapestries, sculpture, paintings, and illuminated manuscripts were exported from there to every part of the West. Itinerant Flemish masters found employment in foreign cities, and artists from as far away as Spain and Italy visited the Low Countries to learn their trade. Netherlandish art found some degree of acceptance in every country in Western Europe and came to constitute the single most cohesive force in the style of the earlier Northern Renaissance.

In 1380, Philip the Bold, Duke of Burgundy and future ruler of the Netherlands, founded a Carthusian monastery at

Champmol, near his capital of Dijon. This charterhouse became a center of ducal patronage, providing employment for a galaxy of major artists. The greatest of these was the Dutch sculptor Claus Sluter (c1350–1406). Although he died as early as 1406 Sluter's surviving work marks a dramatic break with the still-flourishing International Gothic. Gone is the elegant flowing line; in its place is a bulky sense of mass. Sluter's weighty figures anticipate the gravity of Donatello by more than a decade. At the beginning of the 15th century their grim realism, which remains startling even today, must have seemed a revelation.

A painter who may have worked at Dijon and who was certainly impressed by Sluter's work was Robert Campin (the Master of Flémalle), who was active in Tournai c1406–44. Although many of his works retain the traditional "space-defying" gold ground, his figures are always massive, swathed in voluminous robes like those of Sluter's statues. Some of his paintings, such as the Dijon *Nativity* (c1420; Musée des Beaux-Arts), incorporate landscape backgrounds which reveal Campin's indebtedness to International Gothic manuscript calendar pages. In his Mérode Altarpiece (c1426; Cloisters, New York) he experimented with a naturalistic setting of a different sort, the so-called "bourgeois interior", which remained popular with Netherlandish painters throughout our period and beyond.

For over 500 years, one artist has been revered above all others as the "father" of early Netherlandish painting: Jan van Eyck (c1390–1441). Although modern opinion may differ as to his precise position within the historical development of the Early Netherlandish School, no painter of his generation left so distinct and lasting an impression upon his contemporaries as van Eyck and the permanent standard of excellence his art established remains incontestable.

For most of his documented life van Eyck was a court painter in the service of Philip the Good, third Valois Duke of Burgundy. A favorite and *confidant* of his employer, van Eyck was an early example of the urbane "courtier-artist", deeply admired for his skill and occasionally entrusted with affairs of state. That he was allowed considerable freedom is evident from the fact that none of his surviving works are ducal commissions. Whilst we know a great deal about Jan, we know next to nothing about his elder brother Hubert. The latter was already dead by 1426, predeceasing Jan by at least 15 years. He was also a considerable artist and it seems likely that the great Ghent Altarpiece (completed c1432; St-Bavon, Ghent) was their joint achievement. This enormous polyptych of at least 20 painted panels is the most important work in the history of 15th-century Northern art. It abounds in innovations, including accurate portraiture and representation of the nude, spatial illusionism, and careful attention to the effects of light and shadow. By precise observation of the effects of the fall of light upon different surfaces the van Eycks attained an analytical representation of nature which has, in its own way, never been surpassed. The old belief that they did so by the "invention" of oil paint is an oversimplification which can no longer be supported, but it is clear that they grasped the luminary, tonal, and textural possibilities of the oil medium in a new and innovatory way.

Although Jan van Eyck made exceedingly important excursions in the field of portraiture, his large-scale work remained tied to the fundamentally religious context of most 15th-century patronage. The remarkable realism with which he and his contemporaries depicted their subjects endowed the often hackneyed old motifs of Christian art with a pervasive new force. As reality became saturated with symbolism, so new devices were introduced to express ever more complex and exact levels of meaning. Thus the fall of light through a crystal vase of sparkling water could evoke the mystery of the Virgin Birth; or the accurate distinction between a Romanesque colonnade and a flamboyant Gothic portal express the supersession of the Old Testament by the New. The iconographic richness which this intimate relationship between form and content engendered remains one of the supreme achievements of 15th-century Northern art.

Apart from Jan, the artist most often praised in 15th-century sources is Rogier van der Weyden (c1399–1464). After studying under Robert Campin he settled in Brussels, where he was made Town Painter in 1435. His artistic aims are readily apparent in his best-known work, the *Descent from the Cross* (c1438) in the Prado, Madrid. Whereas Jan van Eyck made manifest the objective and immutable qualities of the new realism, Rogier van der Weyden explored its emotive and dynamic possibilities. In this aim he was aided by a brilliant sense of abstract design. The contorted poses of the mourners in his *Descent*, compressed within a claustrophobically enclosed space around the still twin forms of the dead Christ and the unconscious Virgin, convey unbearable anguish. Rogier's figure-types are generally melancholic and brooding, with long necks, aquiline noses, and sorrowful eyes. That this is true even of his portraits indicates just how essential to his art was the austere sense of tragedy which so impressed his contemporaries. More than any other artist of his generation, Rogier plumbed the psychological and emotional depths of the human spirit.

This illustrious trio—Robert Campin, Jan van Eyck, and Rogier van der Weyden—demonstrated the methods and outlined the aims of early Netherlandish painting. In doing so, they also established the general orientation of Northern art until the beginning of the 16th century.

The consolidation and propagation of the new style. In the second half of the 15th century the new manner of Jan van

St Joseph in his shop, the right-hand panel of the Mérode Altarpiece, a triptych by Robert Campin (the Master of Flémalle); oil on panel; 64×27cm (25×11in); c1426. Cloisters, New York

Overleaf: The interior panels of the Ghent Altarpiece by Jan and Hubert van Eyck (outer panels, left; central panel, right); height of central panel 350cm (138in); completed c1432. St-Bavon, Ghent

Arnolfini Wedding by Jan van Eyck

Arnolfini Wedding (National Gallery, London) is one of the best known of all early Netherlandish paintings. It was painted in the recently perfected oil technique, which enabled Flemish painters to depict the fall of light, and the varying textures of surfaces illuminated by it, with a degree of fidelity unattainable in tempera. The old belief that Jan van Eyck was the "inventor" of oil paint is misguided, but the inherent qualities of this new medium could only be fully exploited by a master of his stature. Working with meticulously applied translucent oil glazes, he has brilliantly characterized a wide range of substances. The highly polished metal of the brass chandelier, the heavy velvet of the man's patrician robe, and the wiry fur of the little dog, are all rendered with remarkable truth to nature. Every inch of the room, and of the people and objects in it, has been subjected to the same penetrating scrutiny. Although van Eyck was ignorant of "one-point" perspective, his exact observation of every detail, each of which is held in play by the even lighting, has created an astonishing approximation to actual optic experience.

The subject of the painting is clear enough: a fashionably dressed couple stand in a comfortably furnished bedroom. However, the realism of the Early Netherlandish School was directly linked to the requirements of a religious and symbolic art. As a full-length double portrait the *Arnolfini Wedding* is unique in 15th-century painting, so it is legitimate to suppose that the picture had some special significance. It is apparent from the ceremonial pose of the man and woman that a formal event is in progress; their discarded shoes suggest a religious occasion. That the holy scene in progress relates to matrimony is clear not only from the relationship between the two figures, but also from the symbolic meaning of the objects in the room. The bed is a marriage symbol, the oranges betoken fruitfulness, and the carving on the finial of the chairback next to the bed represents St Margaret—the patron saint of women in childbirth. The dog often personified faithfulness, and the rosary, hanging by the mirror, was a common artistic metaphor for Faith in general. During the Middle Ages a single candle was often required for the ceremony of oath-taking, referring in particular to marriage.

If the painting depicts a wedding in progress, we might ask where the priest is, and why the event is taking place in a house rather than a church. Unlike the other six sacraments, marriage was the only one not dispensed by the clergy but directly by the

▲ *Lady at her Toilet* by Jan van Eyck, a detail from *The Visit of Archduke Albert and Archduchess Isabella to the Collection of Willem van der Geest* by Willem van Haecht; 1628. Rubenshuis, Antwerp

recipients themselves. Until the reforms of the Council of Trent, instituted in 1563, it was legal for a man and a woman to marry without a priest and wherever they thought fit. In the mirror on the far wall of the chamber in which the *Arnolfini Wedding* is set are reflected two men, who face the standing couple. They are probably lay witnesses to the ceremony. If we assume that van Eyck himself was one of these men, his signature would take on a new significance: "Johannes de Eyck fuit hic" means literally "Jan van Eyck was here". Although van Eyck frequently signed his work, the elaborate Gothic calligraphy of this signature is reminiscent of the formal script reserved for legal documents. This would not be surprising if the *Arnolfini Wedding* was what it indeed appears to have been: a pictorial wedding certificate.

Although the bourgeois interior of the *Arnolfini Wedding* had an ancestry which may be traced back to the work of the Boucicaut Master and beyond, the iconography of the painting was an original invention. Interiors of this type recur throughout the

▼ *Wedding* by the Master of the Aachener Schranktüren; oil on panel; c1475. Aloisius-kolleg Collection, Bad Godesberg

▲ The compositional symmetry of the *Arnolfini Wedding* underscores its balance of tone and color, instilling the scene with a remarkable sense of calm and permanence which emphasizes the sacramental nature of marriage

▶ *Arnolfini Wedding* by Jan van Eyck; oil on panel; 82×60cm (32×24in) 1434. National Gallery, London

subsequent history of early Netherlandish painting, but only one later variant on van Eyck's theme is known: an indifferent German picture of the later 15th century by the so-called Master of the Aachener Schranktüren (*Wedding*; Aloisius-kolleg Collection, Bad Godesberg). The reason why such an undoubted masterpiece as the *Arnolfini Wedding* proved to have so little influence is because the unprecedented iconography of the picture must have been partly determined by the very imaginative decision of the couple portrayed. Another Eyckian composition of similar type depicting a lady bathing with the help of a female attendant is known from the background of a 17th-century painting, Willem van Haecht's *Visit of Archduke Albert...* (Rubenshuis, Antwerp). The original painting may have been a pendant to the *Arnolfini Wedding*, portraying the bride's ceremonial pre-nuptial bath. If this is so, then the symbolism of this pair of pictures would have been doubly recondite and proportionately less liable to imitation.

MARK EVANS

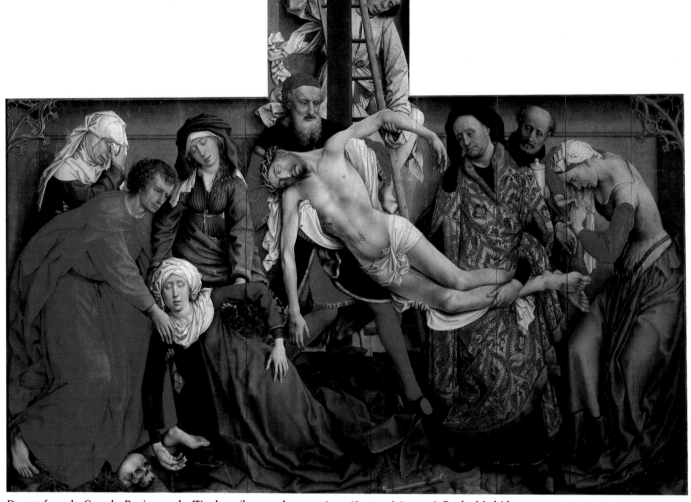

Descent from the Cross by Rogier van der Weyden; oil on panel; 220×260cm (87×102in); c1438. Prado, Madrid

Eyck and his contemporaries spread far and wide. The extensive trading links of the mercantile cities of Flanders facilitated this process, as did the international connections of the Northern aristocracy. Until 1477 the Dukes of Burgundy, who were also rulers of Flanders, possessed the most splendid court in Europe. In the eyes of the patronal classes, their political prestige may well have enhanced the evident excellence of the new style that had arisen in their domain. Whilst the influence of early Netherlandish painting never became in any sense "absolute", artists throughout Northern Europe gradually turned away from the forms of International Gothic in favor of the new realism. By the middle of the century what had in origin been a local development had become a general Northern European movement in the visual arts.

In the Netherlands, although Petrus Christus (fl. 1444–72/3) perpetuated the style of Jan van Eyck until the third quarter of the 15th century, the manner of Rogier van der Weyden proved to be more immediately influential upon younger artists. Dieric Bouts (c1415–75) reinterpreted Rogier's formal

vocabulary to create a remarkable art, at once apparently undemonstrative and yet painfully intense. Whilst both Christus and Bouts remained closely linked to the founding generation of early Netherlandish painting, they readily accepted Italianate "one-point" perspective, which found its way to Flanders c1450–60. With the exception of Justus of Ghent (fl. 1473–5), who actually emigrated to Italy, Flemish painters remained uninterested in the other stylistic qualities of Italian Renaissance art. Generally, the Netherlanders preferred to follow an independent line of inquiry; a characteristic example is Geertgen tot Sint Jans (c1455/65–85/95), who made important innovations in the depiction of nocturnal scenes. Hans Memling (c1440–94) possessed a less inquisitive mind, although he was an equally superb technician. His gentle religious compositions reveal a more contemplative

Right: St John and the Mourning Women, the right-hand panel of a diptych by Memling; oil on panel; 50×35cm (20×14in); Royal Chapel, Granada

Death of the Virgin by Hugo van der Goes; oil on panel; 125×120cm (49×47in); c1470–5. State Museum, Bruges

outlook. The most outstanding artistic personality in the third quarter of the century was undoubtedly Hugo van der Goes (c1436–82). A restless and passionate genius, his altarpieces seem to combine the monumental grandeur of Jan van Eyck with the emotive force of Rogier van der Weyden. In their variety of approaches, the work of these masters illustrates the many-sidedness of the early Netherlandish style.

The German-speaking lands covered a far wider area than the Netherlands and, as might be expected, they encompassed a much larger number of regional schools. Nevertheless, the art of these territories often reveals many points in common and may be examined under a single heading in the present context. Until the fourth decade of the 15th century, local variants of the International Gothic were firmly established in the major German art centers. The St Veronica Master in Cologne, Conrad von Soest in Westphalia (fl. c1390–c1425) and Meister Francke in Hamburg are all representative of this tendency.

By 1432, however, Lukas Moser's Tiefenbronn Altarpiece (Tiefenbronn parish church) indicates that the influence of the first generation of early Netherlandish painting had spread as far as Baden. Paintings by the Swiss master Konrad Witz (c1400–c45) which can only be slightly later in date reveal a similar orientation, although their dramatic lighting is an independent development. Similarly, although it is clear that Hans Multscher of Ulm (c1400–67) had some knowledge of Flemish art, the often brutal expressiveness of his paintings and sculpture is entirely personal. In Cologne Stephan Lochner (fl. 1439–51) absorbed many of the lessons of Jan van

Eyck without losing contact with an outlook essentially based in International Gothic.

During the second half of the 15th century the influence of Rogier van der Weyden was powerfully felt, as may be seen in the pictures of Hans Pleydenwurff (c1420–72) in Nuremberg (Germanisches Nationalmuseum), the Saint Bartholomew Master in Cologne and Martin Schongauer (c1430–91) in Colmar. The last of these was not only a painter, but also the first important print-maker whose name has survived. During this period, the revolutionary new technology of printing was already a potent force, although its precise artistic significance is often difficult to assess. Cheap, mass-produced woodcuts and engravings were capable of spreading new ideas with a speed that had hitherto been unimaginable. Ultimately, the graphic media became an essential factor in the later development of Northern Renaissance art.

During the years 1462 to 1473 Netherlandish influence was spread through German sculpture by the great Dutch sculptor Nikolaus Gerhaert (c1430–73), who worked at Trier, Strasbourg, Nördlingen, Constance, and Vienna. His full-blooded realism impressed a generation of sculptors, including such major artists as Jörg Syrlin (c1425–91) and Veit Stoss (c1447?–1533). Before the turn of the century, the painter Konrad Laib (fl. c1431–48) had established the Flemish style at Salzburg. Further South, the art of the Tyrol proved less susceptible to early Netherlandish painting, although this region produced one artist of major European significance: the painter and sculptor Michael Pacher (c1435–98). A visitor to northern Italy, he reinterpreted the perspectival effects of Andrea Mantegna (1431–1506) to produce a highly individualistic style.

The different ways in which German artists responded to the art of the Netherlands were extremely varied and seldom slavish. Generally, the Germans shared a common tendency to emphasize expressionistic rather than naturalistic values.

The history of 15th-century French art is closely connected with the fortunes of the Hundred Years War. Until the expulsion of the English from France in 1453, Paris was a beleaguered city and the king too concerned with military matters to have the leisure for artistic pursuits. The emergence of the provincial courts of the French princes as the most important centers of patronage mirrors the political fragmentation of the country. As the later Valois dukes of Burgundy spent most of their time in the Netherlands, Dijon declined as an art center, although the school of sculptors Sluter had established continued into the 1480s. Like the artists of Germany, those of France accepted the Flemish manner, although they favored the style of Jan van Eyck rather than that of Rogier van der Weyden. In the south, the territories of the cosmopolitan René, Duke of Anjou, attracted a number of major artists. The early Netherlandish style was introduced into the south as early as 1442 by the enigmatic Master of Aix and continued by Nicolas Froment until c1486. As a court artist to the Duke, the so-called René Master seems to have accompanied his patron to Italy. His exquisite Le Livre du Coeur d'Amour

The Virgin and Child receiving Homage, a miniature from the Hours of
Étienne Chevalier by Jean Fouquet; 15×12cm (6×5in); c1450.
Musée Condé, Chantilly

Épris (Nationalbibliothek, Vienna) reveals an emphasis upon
narrative which recalls Giotto and a skill in the handling of
light which is entirely Northern in derivation. Jean Fouquet of
Tours (*c*1420–*c*80) was the most important figure in the resurgence of French royal patronage which took place in the
second half of the century. Although his style was molded out
of the twin elements of late Parisian International Gothic and
early Netherlandish painting, he was also the first French
painter to employ Italian Renaissance motifs. His fascinating
hybrid style was already formed by 1450, presaging much
later developments in Northern art. Jean Bourdichon (*c*1457–
1521) continued Fouquet's Italianate manner well into the
16th century, by which time it had been absorbed by the
general rise of interest in Italian art.

Spain at the beginning of the 15th century was still very
much under the influence of Trecento Sienese art and the
International Gothic was a recent arrival. Luis Dalmau (*fl.*
1428–61), who had been trained in the Netherlands, introduced an extremely Eyckian style to Barcelona in 1443. In the
following two decades, a sub-Netherlandish style was established throughout the Peninsula with stunning rapidity. Its
two greatest exponents were the Spaniard Bartolomé Bermejo
(*fl.* 1474–95) and the Portuguese Nuno Gonçalves (*fl.* 1450–
71). Although working within what was basically an early

Netherlandish formal vocabulary, they creatively modified the
Flemish style to express a peculiarly Iberian intensity, allevi-
ated by rich decorative effects. The Castilian Pedro Berruguete
(1450–1504), who had worked at Urbino, marked the beginning of the introduction of Italian Renaissance ideas into
Spanish art. Even so, the majority of Spanish artists retained
their allegiance to early Netherlandish painting until long
after the beginning of the following century.

The reorientation in the visual arts *c*1500. At the end of the
15th century the artistic prospect of Europe was one of intense
variety. It is nevertheless possible to discern two underlying
trends; on the one hand, a tendency towards increasing formal
and iconographic complexity and, on the other, a search for a
more monumental simplicity of form. A comparison between
the art of Hieronymus Bosch (*c*1450–1516) and that of
Gerard David (*c*1460–1523) provides a vivid example of this
dichotomy. Some artists, including the German sculptor
Tilman Riemenschneider (*c*1460–1531), worked in a style
that combines aspects of both outlooks. In the course of the
following three decades a sudden and dramatic upsurge of
interest in Italian art swept away many of the artistic forms
that had dominated Northern art for most of the 15th century. The reasons behind this phenomenon have yet to be
satisfactorily explained. Whilst it is true that the intervention
of France and the Empire in Italian political affairs brought
the aristocracy of both states into increased contact with the
culture of the Italian Renaissance, the precise significance of
this development for Northern artists is far from clear. As we
have already seen, a number of Northern painters visited Italy
during the 15th century and were content to appropriate certain elements of Italian art while retaining an overall affiliation to their native style. Their successors had a much more
thoroughgoing interest in the classicizing art of the South,
which parallels the growth of humanist studies in Northern
literary circles during the same period. Whilst earlier borrowings had been occasional and haphazard, those of the 16th
century were part of a general infiltration of Italian ideas into
Northern culture.

The first Northerner to penetrate the theoretical basis of
Italian Renaissance art was Albrecht Dürer (1471–1528).
During visits to Venice in 1494–5 and again in 1505–7, he
read Vitruvius, Euclid, and probably Alberti. He was also in
direct contact with Italian artists, from whom he learned
about perspectival and proportional theory. His lifelong
friend, the humanist scholar Willibald Pirckheimer, assisted
his literary and philosophical endeavors, culminating in the
artist's publication of three treatises on art and architecture.
Dürer's decision to write these books was indicative both of
his dissatisfaction with the empirical nature of Northern style
and of his desire to establish a system of principles that would
foster the development of a "True Art" which concentrated
upon permanent values. As the innovatory iconography of his
engraving *Melencolia I* (1514) indicates, Dürer did not merely
copy the ideas of other men, be they Italian theorists whose

Melencolia I, engraving by Albrecht Dürer; 24×17cm (9×7in); 1514

from prosaic, Altdorfer's landscapes are lush and mysterious and sometimes possessed of a startling breadth of vision, such as may be seen in his *Battle of Alexander* (1529; Alte Pinakothek, Munich). The early works of Altdorfer's contemporary, Lucas Cranach, reveal an analogous interest in landscape and a similar vibrance of color. However, as he grew older, the latter's palette simplified and he concentrated increasingly upon portraiture and the nude. His mythological compositions are peopled with pale, languid goddesses and nymphs which established an extremely popular and purely Northern aesthetic for the portrayal of the nude. The eroticism of Cranach's work finds an echo in depictions of the human body by Hans Baldung Grien (1484/5–1545), although the moralizing subject matter of Baldung's work derives from the late medieval religious tradition, rather than that of Classical Antiquity. Like Dürer, Hans Burgkmair (1473–1531) discovered Italian art "first hand" on a visit to Venice. An accomplished painter, he was more significant as a graphic artist, particularly as a pioneer of the multicolored "Chiaroscuro" woodcut. Another visitor to Italy, Peter Vischer the Younger (1487–1528), introduced Italian Renaissance elements into German sculpture. In his family workshop, these were combined with traditional motifs to create a splendid hybrid style, of which the greatest example is the bronze St Sebaldus Shrine (1507–19) in Nuremberg (church of St Sebald). A more thoroughgoing classicism is apparent in the small-scale carvings of Conrad Meit (c1480–c1550) or the bronze Apollo Fountain (1532; Germanisches Nationalmuseum, Nuremberg) of Peter Flötner (1490/5–1546).

In the Netherlands in the closing years of the 15th century, Gerard David had formulated a monumental style by reviving the manner of Jan van Eyck. The younger artists Quentin Massys (1465/6–1530) and Jan Gossaert (c1478–1532) followed him in imitating the founding generation of early Netherlandish painting. However, in the first decade of the 16th century, the styles of both men were radically altered by the influence of Italian art. Athough Albrecht Dürer's prints would have been circulating in the Netherlands by this date and the hospitality with which he was received on his visit to the Low Countries in 1520–1 indicates the esteem with which he was regarded by the Flemings, the growth of an Italianate style seems to have been an independent development in these territories. In 1506 Michelangelo's marble *Madonna and Child* arrived at Bruges (in the church of Notre-Dame). Two years later, the Venetian artist Jacopo de' Barbari reached the Netherlands, after a long journey through Germany which had already brought him into contact with Dürer and Cranach. Although Massys is not known to have visited Italy, his Poznan *Madonna and Child with the Lamb* (c1513; National Museum) reveals an early familiarity with the work of Leonardo da Vinci which may have been gained from a study of prints or drawings after the great Florentine's work. In 1508–9 Gossaert was actually in Rome, as a member of a diplomatic mission. While there, he enthusiastically copied antique remains and after his return home adhered to a dis-

books he had read or the Northern Humanists within whose circle he was accepted. Like Leonardo da Vinci, he was an artist with an immensely fertile imagination and an intellectual with a profound artistic philosophy of his own. Nor was his genius confined primarily to theory. Over 400 woodcuts and engravings demonstrate his skill in the graphic arts, which he elevated to the status of artistic media of the first importance. Through these prints his ideas were broadcast throughout Europe with profound consequences. More than any other individual, he can be said to have molded the form of Northern European art for the first third of the 16th century.

After Dürer, the most outstanding painter in a generation of German artists of remarkable merit was Matthias Grünewald (1470/80–c1530). As his masterwork, the Isenheim Altarpiece (1515; Musée d'Unterlinden, Colmar) shows, he stood out against the Italianate style which was spreading through the North. Even so, the monumentality of his mighty figures compares favorably with Dürer's own work and far surpasses that of lesser artists. This sense of scale was combined with a pent-up dynamism and a brilliant sense of color to produce a style of awesome grandeur. Albrecht Altdorfer (c1480–1538) was his equal as a colorist, although primarily concerned with landscape, which he established as an independent genre. Far

The Crucifixion panel of the Isenheim Altarpiece by Matthias Grünewald; 270ft×300cm (106×118in); 1515. Musée d'Unterlinden, Colmar

tinctively classicizing style. Massys' attachment to Italian art was only partial and Gossaert's somewhat indiscriminate. The only Netherlandish artist able to approach the immense riches of the Italian Renaissance with comparative equanimity was Lucas van Leyden (1494–1533). A brilliant engraver and only slightly less skillful as a painter, Lucas was able to assimilate both Dürer's prints and Marcantonio Raimondi's engravings after Italian High Renaissance art without losing a highly individual artistic identity of his own. By comparison, the excessively Italianate compositions of such major figures as Bernaert van Orley (1491/2–1542), Joos van Cleve (c1490–1540/1), and Jan van Scorel (1495–1562) seem labored and derivative.

Under the patronage of Francis I, a host of Italian artists were invited to France. Their names read like a roll call of the alumni of early-16th-century Italian art: Leonardo da Vinci, Andrea del Sarto, Rosso Fiorentino, Primaticcio, Cellini, Vignola, and Serlio. Under their aegis early Italian Mannerism was introduced directly to France, where it gave rise to the so-called School of Fontainebleau. The aims of this school may be summarized as decorative abundance, incorporating extreme elegance of form. Its greatest surviving monument is the Galerie François Ier (c1533–40), a decorative scheme at Fontainebleau created by Rosso and Primaticcio in collaboration. Important French adherents of this new court style include the architect Philibert Delorme (c1510–70), the sculptors Jean Goujon (c1510–c68) and Germain Pilon (c1525/30–90), and the portraitist François Clouet (c1510–72).

Conclusion: Northern European art in the mid 16th century. By the middle of the 16th century most Northern artists had been directed into the fold of a "Mannerist" style, heavily dependent upon Italian sources. The nature and origins of this manner are complex as, indeed, are those of Italian Mannerism (*see* Mannerism). In the North, however, there was no "moment" of poise and equilibrium between the distinct but equally experimental styles of the 15th and 16th centuries, such as occurred during the period of the High Renaissance in Italy. With the exception of one or two figures, notably Dürer and Lucas van Leyden, the Northern art world was precipitated directly—from a native tradition derived ultimately from early Netherlandish art—into the mainstream of a flamboyant Mannerist style. It has been argued that this phenomenon reveals a recrudescence of late Gothic characteristics under the guise of an outwardly new Italianate style. However, it is interesting to note that some more traditional artists such as David and Grünewald, who eschewed Italian motifs, created a more monumental art than others, such as Cranach and Gossaert, who accepted the new forms. Only the School of Fontainebleau was actually created by transplanted Italian artists. The Mannerist style of Germany and the Netherlands was, by comparison, a native formulation, partially inspired by Italian models. We would not mistake even the work of Marten van Heemskerck (1498–1574) or Frans Floris (c1518–70) for Italian paintings. When, near the end of the century, Bartholomaeus Spranger (1546–1611) approached very close to contemporary Italian Mannerism, the era of the Baroque was about to begin.

Owing to its fundamentally representational nature, Northern portraiture was less affected by Italian ideas than other artistic genres. Even as committed a Mannerist as Frans Floris could produce so strikingly realistic a painting as his *Portrait of an Old Woman* (1558; Musée des Beaux-Arts, Caen). The greatest portraitist of the century was Hans Holbein the Younger (1497/8–1543). Although the presence of Italianate motifs in certain of his religious paintings recalls Holbein's visit to Italy, his portraits grow directly out of the 15th-century tradition, which he refined to an unsurpassed accuracy of characterization. In the Netherlands, Pieter Aertsen (1508–75) and Joachim Beuckelaer (c1533–74) continued the 15th-century taste for concealed religious or moralizing iconography with pictures that appear on first examination to be still lifes or domestic scenes. These paintings, within which the main theme is so artfully hidden as to be almost unrecognizable, illustrate a delight in caprice which is Mannerist in derivation. However, the ancestry of such scenes stretches back to the bourgeois interiors of early Netherlandish painting and they themselves served as an influential source for the more truly secular style of the following century.

The art of Pieter Bruegel the Elder (c1525–69) is a fitting point at which to conclude this survey, as it is in many respects a final statement of the old tradition and, in others, the beginning of the new realism which ultimately flourished in 17th-century Dutch painting. Early experience as a Bosch copyist left Bruegel with a sense of fantasy which never left him. However, his gentle irony channeled the catastrophic pessimism of the older painter into a more humane direction, as may readily be illustrated by a comparison of the Hell shutter of Bosch's *Garden of Earthly Delights* (c1505–10; Prado, Madrid) with Bruegel's *Dulle Griet* (1562; Museum Mayer van der Bergh, Antwerp). Although Bruegel traveled in Italy, Alpine scenery moved him much more profoundly than antique remains. Classicizing elements are rare in his work, whereas he repeatedly drew upon his memories of the Southern mountains in a series of breathtaking landscape views. These paintings were unprecedented in their clarity of observation, which extended to the painstakingly accurate depiction of the effects of weather. Equally memorable is the unfailing realism of his rustic compositions, such as the *Peasant Wedding* (1566–7; Kunsthistorisches Museum, Vienna). It is only necessary to examine the artist's last picture, the *Magpie on the Gallows* (1568; Hessisches Landesmuseum, Darmstadt) to appreciate how Bruegel's analytical vision embraced the whole range of human experience, from the miniscule to the enormous. Over a century earlier, Jan van Eyck's *Madonna with Chancellor Rolin* (c1433; Louvre, Paris) reveals a similar simultaneous concentration upon the microcosm and the macrocosm. This outlook, more than anything else, is the unifying thread in the history of Northern Renaissance art.

MARK EVANS

Bibliography. Baxandall, M. *The Limewood Sculptors of Renaissance Germany*, London and New Haven (1980). Benesch, O. *The Art of the Renaissance in Northern Europe: its Relationship to the Contemporary Spiritual and Intellectual Movements*, London (1965). Cuttler, C.D. *Northern Painting from Pucelle to Bruegel*, New York (1968). Müller, T. *Sculpture in the Netherlands, Germany, France, and Spain: 1400–1500*, Harmondsworth (1966). Panofsky, E. *Early Netherlandish painting: its Origin and Character* (2 vols.), Cambridge, Mass. (1953). Panofsky, E. *The Life and Art of Albrecht Dürer*, Princeton (1955). Von der Osten, G. and Vey, H. *Painting and Sculpture in Germany and the Netherlands: 1500–1600*, Harmondsworth (1969).

36

MANNERISM

The Saltcellar made by Benvenuto Cellini for Francis I of France; gold and enamel on an ebony base
height 26cm (10in); 1540–3. Kunsthistoriches Museum, Vienna (see page 678)

THE term "Mannerism" is normally understood to refer to the artistic style prevailing in Italy and northern Europe for the greater part of the 16th century. Its beginnings coincide approximately with the death of Raphael in 1520, and the disintegration of the High Renaissance; it was in turn superseded by the early Baroque from c1590 onwards. The term is derived from the Italian word *maniera*, originally meaning quite simply "style"; it first became current in art-historical usage in the early years of this century.

The main characteristics of the Mannerist style remain hard to define, since, even after more than half a century of critical discussion, the term remains highly controversial and no general agreement has been reached as to which artists and which works of art of the late Renaissance period may legitimately be categorized as Mannerist. In its broadest application, the term is used to embrace all the arts, and would include figures as diverse as Michelangelo (1475–1564), Bruegel (c1525–69), and Shakespeare (1564–1616). In its narrower sense, it is restricted to a particular trend in the figurative arts of central Italy around the middle of the 16th century, in which case its most typical exponents would be painters and sculptors such as Bronzino (1503–72), Salviati (1510–63), Vasari (1511–73), and Benvenuto Cellini (1500–71). Between these two extremes, an enormous variety of interpretations has been put forward, and, in face of the resulting confusion, some contemporary art historians have abandoned the concept of Mannerism altogether, choosing to see the whole period as an uninterrupted continuation of the High Renaissance. This, however, has not solved the problem either. The styles practiced by the leading artists around the middle of the 16th century are conspicuously different from those of Leonardo (1452–1519), Raphael (1483–1520), and the young Michelangelo; furthermore, several impressive cases have been made to demonstrate the essential unity of the Mannerist style, for all its many apparent contradictions.

Particularly homogeneous is the group active at the Florentine court in the mid-century, consisting of Bronzino, Salviati and the others; the term Mannerist is all the more appropriate to them, since the quality of *maniera* ("style", also used in the sense of "stylishness") was one they deliberately cultivated. Although it remains a matter of controversy how far these consciously stylish artists are to be seen as central or peripheral to the Mannerist style as a whole—and also how far their art reflects the broader political, religious, and artistic problems of the age—the majority of contemporary art historians would probably agree about the legitimacy of applying the term Mannerist to them. A characteristic work of Bronzino may therefore be chosen to illustrate some of the more striking features of the Mannerist style in painting.

Bronzino's *The Martyrdom of St Lawrence* (in the church of S. Lorenzo, Florence), painted in the late 1560s, is clearly indebted to the achievements of High Renaissance Rome, in particular to Raphael's multi-figured narrative compositions in the Vatican Stanze, and to the displays of heroic nudity in Michelangelo's Sistine Chapel Ceiling. Indeed, several of the figures appear as specific quotations from these authoritative prototypes—notably the reclining figure of St Lawrence himself, who is closely adapted from Michelangelo's *Adam*. The artist also shares the preoccupation of his High Renaissance predecessors with Classical Antiquity, and there is an almost archaeological attention to the details of Roman costume and architecture. Yet despite these learned references, the painting has an unnatural, over-contrived character, completely foreign to the High Renaissance. The pose of St Lawrence, so expressive when used by Michelangelo, has become merely ornamental and graceful, quite out of keeping with both the brutality of the subject, and its religious significance. Equally incongruous are the theatrical attitudes of the executioners and bystanders, whose improbable contortions and exaggerated muscularity are emphasized by their gratuitous nudity. The composition is excessively crowded, and since the classicizing architecture is not used to evoke any coherent sense of pictorial space, the effect resembles that of relief sculpture, with the limbs of the figures forming a complicated pattern of shapes on the picture surface. This effect is quite different from that of a classic work of the High Renaissance, such as Raphael's *School of Athens* (Stanza della Segnatura, Vatican, Rome), with its easy spaciousness and compositional lucidity. In Raphael, the formal grandeur and high idealization retain sufficient contact with nature still to appear completely plausible; in Bronzino, the contact with nature has been severed, gestures and expressions have become unashamedly artificial, and verisimilitude is sacrificed to self-conscious effects of elegance, virtuosity, and learned allusion.

There are striking analogues to the style of Bronzino's *St Lawrence* in the work of most central Italian and Emilian artists active in the middle decades of the century. Painters such as Giulio Romano (c1499–1546), Perino del Vaga (1501–47), Parmigianino (1503–40), Salviati, Vasari, Jacopino del Conte (1510–98), Daniele da Volterra (1509–66), and Pellegrino Tibaldi (1527–96) show a comparable dependence on the art of the High Renaissance, while at the same time subtly distorting it to create a more complex and artificial kind of beauty. In Parmigianino's *Madonna of the Rose* (Gemäldegalerie Alte Meister, Dresden), limbs and draperies have become aestheticized to form an abstract curvilinear pattern of the utmost grace; the figures are imbued with an unnatural elegance and sensuality that contrast disturbingly with the sacred subject. Much the same approach can be found in contemporary sculpture in the works of Cellini, Niccolò Tribolo (1500–50), Pierino da Vinci (c1530–53), Bartolommeo Ammanati (1511–92), and Vincenzo Danti (1530–76), as well as much work by Giambologna (c1524–1608). Like Bronzino, Danti represents *The Beheading of St John the Baptist* (the Baptistery, Florence) in a spirit of dispassionate ritual, with an elegantly Parmigianinesque Salome raising her hand in an attitude of fastidious distaste.

The Martyrdom of St Lawrence, by Bronzino; fresco; 1565–9. S. Lorenzo, Florence

The Madonna of the Rose by Parmigianino; panel; 108×87cm
(43×34in); c1528–30. Gemäldegalerie Alte Meister, Dresden

The Beheading of St John the Baptist by Vincenzo Danti; bronze;
heights of statues 243cm, 170cm, 270cm (96in, 67in, 106in); 1571.
The Baptistery, Florence

In a similar spirit, Benvenuto Cellini's exquisite Saltcellar (1540–3; Kunsthistorisches Museum, Vienna) made for Francis I of France, adapts the powerful and tragic figure of Michelangelo's *Dawn* (S. Lorenzo, Florence) for use as an ornamental figurine reclining on a miniature triumphal arch.

These and comparable works would have been seen by Vasari as perfect embodiments of *maniera*, for him one of the principal artistic virtues attained by the 16th century. As defined in the preface to the third part of the *Vite* (*Lives of the Artists*), *maniera* was the means by which pure beauty could be achieved. Instead of pedantically imitating raw and imperfect nature as the artists of the 15th century had done, those of his own age, guided by an innate sense of style, imitated only the most beautiful models, and selected, where necessary, only the most beautiful aspects even of these. In this way, the art of Bronzino and his contemporaries, taking the refining process of the early 16th century a stage further, would have represented a logical extension of the style of the High Renaissance. For Vasari, Leonardo, Michelangelo, and Raphael were also, in fact, artists supremely endowed with *maniera*. A similar attitude is adopted by Danti in his incomplete treatise *Delle Perfette Proporzioni* ("On Perfect Proportions"; 1567), which throughout invokes the example of Michelangelo as the ultimate authority on all artistic matters.

The first historiographical distinction between the generation of the High Renaissance and that of Bronzino and Vasari was made by the classicizing theorist Bellori in his *Vite de' Pittori* ("Lives of the Painters"; 1672). Interpreting the early

baroque classicism of Annibale Carracci (1560–1609) as a revival of the true spirit of Raphael, in reaction against the debased Raphaelitism and Michelangelism of the intervening period, Bellori gave Vasari's term *maniera* a pejorative twist, calling it "a capricious conceit founded on routine rather than on the imitation of reality". For Bellori, Bronzino and his generation were not so much stylish as stylized; having lost all vital contact with nature, their adoption of the grand manner was merely mannered. This disparaging attitude towards the art of the middle and late 16th century was to persist for most of the 18th and 19th centuries, with the term *maniera* and its cognates used to refer to what was regarded as its disagreeable and degenerate affectation. It was not until the second decade of the 20th century that the rehabilitation of Mannerist art began. This was partly as a result of a more systematic periodization of the history of Renaissance art, following the studies of H. Wölfflin and others, and partly following a shift in taste towards nonclassical and postclassical artistic styles. The two most influential contributions to the new positive evaluation of Mannerism as an artistic concept were short essays by Max Dvorak (1920) and by Walter Friedländer (1925), both of which had originated as lectures; at about the same time, Hermann Voss provided the first full-length study of the painting of the period as a whole (1920).

Under the influence of the contemporary aesthetic of German Expressionism, Dvorak interpreted Mannerism as a quest for the spiritual in art, in reaction to what he saw as the rationalism and materialism of the Renaissance. Concentrating his attention on the intensely religious works of El Greco (1541–1614), Tintoretto (1518–94) and the late Michelangelo, he drew attention to the distortions of the naturalistic representation of figures and space in the interest of a greater emotional and spiritual expressiveness. Friedländer, too, was concerned with a supposedly anticlassical reaction against the High Renaissance, and with the later works of Michelangelo, rather than his more harmonious early works. Unlike Dvorak, however, he concentrated on the beginnings of the period in Florence, and the emotionally highly charged paintings of the young Pontormo (1494–1557) and Rosso Fiorentino (1494–1540), with their intensely subjective reshapings of external reality. Friedländer's method was based on a searching visual analysis in the tradition of Wölfflin; he avoided Dvorak's attempt to explain the Mannerist style in terms of *Geistesgeschichte*, with its references to the religious and social upheavals of the age. Although the artistic currents discussed by Dvorak and Friedländer are now no longer normally seen as typical of Mannerism as a whole, their essays have provided important stimuli for further research.

Dvorak's approach was developed most notably by Nikolaus Pevsner, who, in an essay of 1925, closely identified Mannerism with the spirit of the Counter-Reformation. A sociological method was also the one adopted in the fulllength study of the style by Arnold Hauser (1965). Hauser's premise is that the 16th century was an age of crisis in a whole range of human experience—religion, politics, social institutions, science—and he sees Mannerism as the artistic reflection of this crisis not just in the visual arts, but in literature as well. So broad a conception of the style involves the inclusion of artists far removed from the Vasarian *maniera*, such as Pieter Bruegel the Elder, who, despite his apparent naturalism, is for Hauser a Mannerist by virtue of his expressive stylization and the essential subjectivity of his vision. The fullest developments of Friedländer's more visual, less intellectually abstract approach to Mannerism is to be found in the writings of S. J. Freedberg, who has subjected the various phases of Mannerist painting to a minutely detailed formal analysis.

Probably the most authoritative discussions of the concept of Mannerism to be published in recent years are two short books based on papers given at the International Congress in the History of Art in New York in 1961, by Craig Hugh Smyth (1962) and by John Shearman (1967). Both authors concentrate their attention on the artists of the *maniera*, and the formal origins of the style in High Renaissance Rome; both are intent on stressing the positive aspects of a trend that even the early-20th-century rehabilitators of Mannerism had regarded as hollow and imitative. Smyth sees Vasari and his generation as genuinely creative, extending the possibilities of the High Renaissance style by developing new formal conventions and methods of picture construction based on Antique reliefs. Shearman similarly sets out to evaluate the artists of the *maniera* on the basis of their own professed ideals; he characterizes Mannerism as a pursuit of sophisticated beauty, which deliberately introduces complexities in order effort-

lessly to overcome them. He emphatically denies the style any sense of crises or spiritual disquiet, insisting that its cultivation of elegance, nonchalance, and artificiality at the expense of energy, emotional expressiveness, and naturalistic plausibility was the outcome of conscious aesthetic choice.

Shearman's book has achieved wide currency, but his polemically presented interpretation has by no means won unanimous critical acceptance. For many scholars, his almost exclusive identification of Mannerism with the mid-century *maniera* and its influence is too restrictive, and they are unwilling to accept that the early works of Pontormo and Rosso, for instance, or Tintoretto, or El Greco, are peripheral to Mannerism as a whole. An even more serious objection to Shearman's thesis is that his reading of Vasari is too literal: by accepting the professed aims of the *maniera* artists at face value, he refuses to perceive their inner uncertainties. For all Vasari's assertions that the art of his own age was proceeding from strength to strength, there is an uneasy sense in his writings that perhaps his own generation did not, after all, compare favorably with the preceding one; after the great climax at the beginning of the century, a decline in art was to be feared. Vasari's observation that the painters of his own age surpassed even those of the High Renaissance, insofar that their technical dexterity enabled them to work at far greater speed, carries little inner conviction, especially when it is set against the apologetic references in his own *Life* to the defects of his notoriously hastily executed decorations in the Palazzo della Cancelleria in Rome. The exaggeratedly convoluted figures in these frescoes, as in Bronzino's *Martyrdom of St Lawrence*, may indeed be related to the artist's pursuit of a particular aesthetic ideal; but, at the same time, the very gratuitousness of the formal complexity, and the hollowness of the rhetoric, betray an underlying restlessness and uncertainty of direction. As Henri Zerner (1972) has pointed out, Shearman's deliberate underplaying of the more disquieting aspects of the style can involve a serious misunderstanding of many Mannerist works of art.

The tensions and uncertainties that, since Dvorak and Friedländer, have frequently been seen as the most striking characteristics of Mannerism, have been subjected to varying interpretations. One explanation is that the crisis was a purely professional one, and that the artists of the postclassical generation felt dwarfed by the colossal achievements of Leonardo, Raphael, and especially Michelangelo. This is the standpoint taken by Kenneth Clark in his lecture *Mannerism: A Failure of Nerve* (1967). Like Friedländer, Clark concentrates on the early works of Pontormo, Rosso, Giulio Romano, and Beccafumi—works excluded, on the whole, from Shearman's definition—and finds their tendencies towards melancholy, eccentricity, and violence symptomatic of a crumbling of the self-confidence of earlier Renaissance art.

Another explanation of the disturbed character of Mannerism relates it to the religious interest of the period, to the atmosphere of crisis generated by the Reformation, and to the movement of Catholic reaction culminating in the Counter-

Reformation. The most eloquent spokesman for this point of view is Nikolaus Pevsner, whose 1925 essay interprets the complexity and confusion of so much of Mannerist art as a reflection of the defeat of the anthropocentric ideal of Renaissance humanism by the reactionary forces of militant religion. For Pevsner, the subordination of the individual figure to anonymous crowds in the works of Bronzino, Salviati and Vasari, and also in Tintoretto, is paralleled by a similar suppression of the significance of the individual in the new religious orders, and in the many religious processions and solemnities of the period. Even the veiled eroticism of painters like Bronzino and Parmigianino may be seen in terms of a heightened religious sense, since nudity is portrayed with a more troubled conscience than before.

A cogent objection to Pevsner's approach, first put forward by W. Weisbach in "Gegenreformation—Manierismus—Barock" (*Repertorium für Kunstwissenschaft* vol. XLIV; 1928), is that, except in this inverted and indirect sense, rather few purely Mannerist artists—least of all those of the mid-century *maniera*—show any deep preoccupation with religion. The principal representatives of official Counter-Reformation views on art were, indeed, quite severe in their criticism of contemporary practice as disobedient to the directives issued at the Council of Trent in 1563. Gilio da Fabriano's *Dialoghi ... degli Errori de' Pittori* ("Dialogues ... on the Errors of Painters"; 1564), for instance, deplored the tendency of painters to treat the sufferings of Christ and his martyrs as mere exercises in virtuosity, instead of representing them in all their painful truth; by choosing the theme of St Lawrence on the gridiron as one of his examples, he implicitly condemned Bronzino's *Martyrdom of St Lawrence* even before it was painted. In a similar spirit, Raffaele Borghini's *Riposo* (1584), expressed the wish that Salviati in his *Deposition* (Museo dell'Opera di Santa Groce, Florence) had shown the body of Christ marked with the wounds of the Passion. The Tridentine ideals of simplicity, clarity, and doctrinal accuracy were completely opposed to the ingenious complexity and artificial beauty cultivated by the *maniera*, and Mannerist displays of nudity came under sharp attack for offending against decency and religious decorum.

In recent years, another style, first clearly identified by Federico Zeri (1957) and conveniently labelled "Counter-maniera" by Freedberg, has come to be seen as more representative of Tridentine attitudes. Typical of this are the severely chastened styles of such painters as Girolamo Siciolante (1521–c1580) and Marcello Venusti (1515–79), and, in a later phase, Santi di Tito (1536–1603), Girolamo Muziano (1528–92), Giuseppe Valeriano (1530–1606), and Scipione Pulzone (fl. 1550–80), all of which deliberately avoid the excesses of *maniera* in the interest of a clearer demonstration of piety. Even artists of the "high" *maniera* were influenced by this current: Bronzino, Jacopino del Conte, and Daniele da Volterra all modified their styles in their later careers, and the sculptor Ammanati went so far as to renounce his art altogether, in penitence, he said, for the many nudes he had

once made. Yet, as Freedberg makes clear, the Counter-*maniera* represents not so much an absolute contrast to the *maniera*—in the way the Baroque was to be—as a parallel tendency within the Mannerist style as a whole. The two currents remain closely related in their basic vocabulary of form, and the same artist might even alternate between them according to whether his commission was sacred or profane. Furthermore, many of the formal characteristics of the *maniera* were adopted by much greater artists, such as the aged Michelangelo, Tintoretto, and El Greco, who although frequently transgressing the letter of the Tridentine decrees, were unquestionably influenced by the intensely religious mood of the period.

Provided, then, that we do not follow Shearman in identifying Mannerism with the style and attitudes of the *maniera*, many of Pevsner's observations on the relationship between Mannerism in the broader sense and the Counter-Reformation movement hold good. In his introduction to the English edition of his paper (1968), Pevsner acknowledges the brilliance of Shearman's interpretation, but continues to insist on the deeply spiritual character of certain aspects of Mannerism ignored by Shearman.

Another explanation of Mannerism in terms of *Geistesgeschichte* relates it to the political and economic conditions of 16th-century Italy. These, too, were in a state of crisis, and F. Antal (1948) has drawn attention to the parallel between the decline of the wealthy bourgeoisie, with its rational and humanistic attitudes, and the development of an anti-natural, agitated and, at the same time, highly aristocratic style of art. The same theme is also sketched by A. Hauser as part of his sociologically oriented survey of the historical background of Mannerism. This approach has found little critical favor as an explanation of the origins of the style—the decisive steps that transformed the High Renaissance into Mannerism seem to have had little to do with political or economic factors—but it does usefully illuminate the social setting in which Mannerism was to flourish.

The restoration of the Medici in Florence in 1531, and the establishment of a grand-ducal court by Cosimo I, provided the ideal surroundings for the development of an art that was precious in form and abstruse in content. Cosimo was a munificent patron: it was he who commissioned not only Bronzino's *Martyrdom of St Lawrence*, with its learned visual references to previous works of art, but also the intellectually complicated *Allegory of Venus, Cupid, Folly, and Time* (c1542–5; National Gallery, London). He was also well aware of the value of art as political propaganda, and the primary purpose of much of the extensive decorations by Salviati and Vasari in the newly refurbished Palazzo Vecchio was to legitimize and glorify his authoritarian regime. It was principally through the international connections of the Medici court that Mannerism spread to northern Europe, to the courts of Francis I, at Fontainebleau, Rudolf II in Prague, and Albrecht V in Munich. There, even more than in Italy, the style was endowed with a strongly aristocratic and intellectual flavor, in conformity with the refined tastes of these princely connoisseurs.

However much historians are in disagreement about the character and origins of Mannerism, most would probably not now dispute it was essentially an Italian phenomenon, and, as applied to non-Italian art, it is used most appropriately to refer to a style created under the direct influence of Italy. The growing interest shown by northern European patrons in the achievements of the Italian Renaissance from about the beginning of the 16th century onwards resulted in a considerable export of Italian works of art, which, if only for chronological reasons, tended increasingly to be Mannerist in style. Several important Mannerist artists, notably Rosso, Primaticcio, and Cellini, were attracted to the French court at Fontainebleau; there they created a whole school of French painters practicing a highly refined, somewhat precious version of Mannerism. Since it was also increasingly becoming fashionable for northern artists to complete their training in Italy, large numbers of Netherlandish painters acquired a Mannerist sophistication and polish in Rome before taking the style back home with them.

Mannerism was all the more readily appreciated in the north for having certain characteristics in common with the still largely prevalent late Gothic. Its formal complexity, for instance, or its tendency towards elongation, could be much more easily assimilated into local traditions than the clear and harmonious classicism of the High Renaissance. The hybrid character of so much of Netherlandish art in the first half of the 16th century has, however, caused considerable terminological confusion in the past. Certain painters and schools active well before 1510 have been dubbed "Mannerist" more on account of supposed analogies with Italian Mannerism than because they were directly influenced by it. The works of Jacob Cornelisz. van Oorsanen (c1470–1533) and Cornelis Engelbrechtsz. (1468?–1533) in the northern Netherlands, for example, and of Jan de Beer (fl. 1490–1520) and a whole school of "Antwerp Mannerists" in the south, show crowded compositions, elongation of forms, and a certain elegant affectation of costume and gesture. But these tendencies, developed directly from local late Gothic tradition, and overlaid only superficially with Italianate motifs, appear long before the emergence of Mannerism in Italy. The term Mannerism implies not simply that a style is mannered in a nonclassical way, but that it is postclassical—and that its distortions of classicism are effected knowingly and wilfully. So it is probably equally inappropriate to apply it to the courtly style of Lucas Cranach (1472–1553), despite certain undeniable parallels with international courtly Mannerism, or to most art executed in England in the 16th century.

The definition of the term Mannerism as applied to architecture is even more problematic than with the figurative arts of painting and sculpture. Because architecture is a nonrepresentational art, there can be no question of idealizing and refining nature; because it has a more strictly functional purpose, there is less scope for indulgence in aesthetic caprice. Yet the architecture of the Mannerist period does show analogies with the figurative arts, particularly because so much of it was designed by artists who were painters or sculptors by training, such as Giulio Romano, Vasari, Ammanati, and Vignola.

Giulio's own house in Mantua, probably built in the mid 1540s, may conveniently be taken as an example of Mannerist architecture. Like Bronzino in his *Martyrdom of St Lawrence*, the artist takes as his starting point a classic work of the High Renaissance, in this case Bramante's Palazzo Caprini (House of Raphael) in Rome, destroyed in the 17th century. As in the prototype, a series of regularly spaced pedimented windows on the *piano nobile* is set on a rusticated base below an imposing entablature. But instead of the order and clarity of Bramante's composition, deliberate complications are introduced which are often in defiance of the rules of Classical architecture. What appears at first to be a pediment over the main entrance portal, becomes on closer inspection merely a kink in the horizontal stringcourse dividing the two stories. Any attempt to read the smooth bands running between the keystones on the ground floor as a continuation of the door lintel is frustrated by the flatness of the wall, which prevents the keystones from being unambiguously read as projecting in front of the bands. The pediments on the main floor windows have no proper bases, and continuous strips of ornament also replace the flanking members. The surmounting entablature is similarly unsupported by architectural members, and rests directly on the keystones of the arches. And the window frames, instead of projecting from the wall plane, are recessed into it.

All these liberties are taken with full consciousness of their implications, as any spectator versed in the classical language of architecture would have instantly recognized; they may be seen as exemplifying the kind of sophisticated artistic licence explicitly advocated by Vasari in his preface to Part III of the *Vite*. At the same time, the interpretative problem of Mannerist art in general remains. Is this to be seen merely as witty perversity, in pursuit of the aesthetic ideal of *maniera*? Or does it indicate some inner anxiety or disturbance within the artist? Critics inclining to the latter view would point to the uncomfortable way in which the window frames are squeezed into their niches, to the oppressive effect of the sagging entrance arch, or to the helplessly incarcerated appearance of the basement windows.

The same problem of interpretation applies to probably the most famous of all Mannerist buildings, Giulio's Palazzo del Tè, just outside Mantua. The way in which every third triglyph on the frieze of the inner courtyard appears to be slipping out of place has been compared in its effect to the illusion of dramatically collapsing architecture painted by Giulio in the Palazzo's Sala degli Giganti; to some critics, both communicate feelings of insecurity and alarm. But it is difficult to interpret the architectural and pictorial decoration of the palace as a whole in this way. Many critics would probably now agree with Shearman in seeing the ensemble as an exemplification of the Mannerist ideal of variety, providing the visitor with a dazzling display of contrasting sensations as

The Casino of Pius IV by Pirro Ligorio; 1558–62. Vatican gardens, Rome

he moves from facade to facade and from room to room. Giulio would certainly have been appreciated for his wit and ingenuity by his princely employer, and the informal function of the palace as a suburban villa would have allowed him greater inventive freedom than might have been possible, or appropriate, in a town palace or church.

Significantly, some of the most impressive creations of Mannerist architecture are of this type. In the Villa Giulia in Rome, for example, built by Vignola and Ammanati for Pope Julius III in the early 1550s, the visitor proceeds from the block-like severity of the outer facade, through a gracefully curving courtyard punctuated by a series of open loggias, towards a sunken garden and *nymphaeum* at the far end, where the architectural forms have fancifully begun to assume those

of nature. Another mid-century papal retreat, Pirro Ligorio's Casino of Pius IV in the Vatican gardens, shows a comparable concern with variety and inventiveness, and, in this case, a taste for superabundant small-scale ornament *all' antica*, which here replaces the architectural orders as wall decoration. With its gardens, fountains, loggias, screening walls, and changes of level, the Casino was probably intended, like the Palazzo del Tè and the Villa Giulia, to follow the example of Bramante's Belvedere in reviving the ancient Roman villa, as described by Pliny the Younger. This combination of enthusiastic antiquarianism in concept and motif, with an attitude of wilful licence towards the Vitruvian rules, may be seen as typically Mannerist.

The more serious aspect of Mannerist architecture may be

found in certain public and urban buildings, where preoccupations with style would certainly have been mixed with a concern for their symbolic effect. Vasari's Uffizi, for example, begun in 1560, violates the classical canon in the elegant slimness of its proportions, and the reduction to shallow layers of relief of the members flanking the windows, while the total effect of chill severity and uniformity perfectly matches the character of the authoritarian regime for whose administrative offices it was built. But the design here also seems to express the same inner tensions to be found in Vasari's paintings and writings. Although he shows himself to be a master of *maniera* in his brilliant and ingenious solution to the problems posed by the excessively long and narrow site, the cramped and fragile quality of the architectural membering scarcely reflects complete inner confidence and serenity. The same may be said of Vignola's unexecuted design for the façade of the Gesù in Rome (c1570), which exhibits a comparable formality, complexity, and fragility, and which Pevsner has characteristically interpreted as reflecting the "period of tormenting doubt" of the Counter-Reformation.

The case of architecture suggests that there is at least a grain of truth in most of the various current interpretations of Mannerism. Clearly, the ideal of *maniera*, with its concomitant virtues of ingenious complexity and effortless virtuosity, was fundamental to the great majority of central Italian artists coming to maturity between c1520 and 1590— even if this ideal concealed more inner uncertainties than some modern historians care to recognize. Various other artists of the period, though motivated by different, often more spiritual, ideals, nevertheless had many formal characteristics in common with the artists of the *maniera*, so they too can meaningfully be termed Mannerist. Understood in this dual sense— as both the period as a whole, and as a pronounced trend within the period—the term Mannerism would not necessarily be more ambiguous than many other stylistic labels applied to Western art. "Baroque" for instance, while referring especially to the style of Bernini or Rubens, may also be applied, with appropriate qualification, to Caravaggio, Poussin, Velazquez, Rembrandt, or Ruisdael (*see* Baroque Art).

But, in contrast to the Baroque, there remains one enormous stumbling block to any neat definition of the Mannerist style: the art of Michelangelo. By far the greatest and most influential central Italian artist of the period, he presented such a wealth of expressive possibility to his contemporaries that only certain aspects of his work could be successfully developed by them, and can so be categorized in the same terms as theirs. Michelangelo was one of the co-creators of the High Renaissance, but even before he had begun work on the Sistine Chapel Ceiling, he had carved the *St Matthew* (1506; Galleria dell' Accademia, Florence), which is proto-Baroque in its emotional and dynamic power. By contrast, the figurative language of his frail and poignant late *Pietàs* was to become so intensely personal as to transcend all stylistic categories. Despite the fact that Vasari developed the very notion of *maniera* from his observation of Michelangelo's

practice, seeing in it the ultimate triumph of nature, most of his work is divided from that of the leading exponents of the *maniera* by a broad gulf—and this has to do not merely with artistic quality, but with a fundamentally different artistic purpose. Yet, inevitably, the art of Michelangelo touches on that of his younger contemporaries at several points, and no attempt to define Mannerism can afford to ignore it.

There is no question about Michelangelo's overwhelming influence on the artists of the Mannerist generation. Works such as the Cartoon for the Battle of Cascina (now lost), or the Sistine Chapel Ceiling, with their displays of nude figures in a seemingly infinite variety of complex poses, provided the painters and sculptors of the *maniera* with an inexhaustible fund of inspiration. But until c1520, Michelangelo himself cannot properly be called a Mannerist artist. Despite the tensions underlying its surface harmony, the work of his early maturity clearly belongs to the High Renaissance with its dominant ideals of classical beauty and the perfect integration of form and content. This is true even of works like the Doni Tondo (c1504; Uffizi, Florence), which at first sight seems to anticipate the *maniera* directly in the highly artificial poses and the disjointed pictorial space, but which was certainly intended to have a serious expressive purpose going far beyond mere elegance and virtuosity.

The question of how far the art of Michelangelo may be called Mannerist becomes more complicated from the period of his middle age onwards, when he increasingly abandoned the ideals of the High Renaissance for the sake of greater expressive effect. The sculptures of the Medici Chapel, Florence, for example, with their tragic listlessness and tortured intensity, have much in common, both in terms of style and expressive purpose, with the early works of Pontormo and Rosso, painters who, in their deviation from the High Renaissance style of their master Andrea del Sarto, have often been seen as pioneers of Mannerism. Although the Medici chapel sculptures, no less than Michelangelo's earlier works, were extensively adapted and elaborated by the artists of the *maniera*, these adaptations seldom retained the disturbing qualities of the originals; it is still a matter of debate as to how far such qualities are compatible with Mannerism.

Another important work of which the Mannerist status is in doubt is the *Last Judgment* (1534-41), painted by Michelangelo on the west wall of the Sistine Chapel. A new appreciation of the artist's late style was one of the achievements of the early-20th-century rehabilitation of Mannerism, and both Dvorak and Friedländer saw the *Last Judgment* as a masterpiece central to their anticlassical conception of the style, standing in vivid contrast to the heroic idealism of the Ceiling. Although Michelangelo's close associate Condivi praised it in terms of *maniera*, saying that it "expressed all that art is able of the human body, omitting no act or gesture", polished elegance and ingeniousness seem completely remote from the artist's intentions. Most modern critics would unite in concentrating on the spiritual urgency and elemental power of the work. But whereas Shearman, in accordance with his own precise definition of the term, would therefore place it beyond the pale of Mannerism, it is nonetheless true that the work possesses striking analogies of a formal kind with the mid-century *maniera*. With its welter of contorted nudes, and its abandonment of the normative proportions and lucid space of the earlier Renaissance, it is comparable in purely stylistic terms to Bronzino's *Martyrdom of St Lawrence*—even if spiritually the two works remain worlds apart. From this point of view, the older critical traditions of Dvořák and Friedländer to a large extent retain their validity, and there is a strong case for continuing to class the *Last Judgment*, together with the Medici chapel sculptures and most of Michelangelo's works of his middle and old age, as Mannerist in the broader sense of the term.

But even in those works by Michelangelo that most critics would agree in calling Mannerist, there remains a difficult problem of interpretation. The *Victory* (Palazzo Vecchio, Florence), for example, originally included by Michelangelo for the Julius Tomb, but left behind in Florence on his final departure for Rome in 1534, approximates stylistically very

closely indeed to the *maniera*. With its composition in the form of a continuous upward spiral, the group is a characteristic example of the *figura serpentinata*, a type much favored by Florentine Mannerist sculptors in their pursuit of artificial elegance. Pierino da Vinci, Ammanati, Danti, and Giambologna all produced important variants of Michelangelo's theme, with a victor bestriding a prostrate foe with an air of effortless nonchalance. But whereas for Shearman, the smoothly serpentine twist of Michelangelo's main figure—so different from the passionate and abrupt *contrapposto* of his *St Matthew*—indicates that the artist's main preoccupation here, as with his followers, is aesthetic rather than emotional, not all critics would agree. Herbert von Einem (in *Michelangelo*, Stuttgart, 1959) reads into the languorous pose and enigmatically clouded features a paradoxical suggestion of exhaustion and defeat; consequently, he sees the figure as Mannerist in a quite different sense of the word.

Similarly conflicting interpretations are applied to Michelangelo's architecture of this period. Probably the most important of these, the vestibule of the Biblioteca Laurenziana,

Below left: The vestibule of the Biblioteca Laurenziana, Florence, by Michelangelo; begun in 1524, staircase designed and built after 1555

Below right: The Damned by Michelangelo, a detail from his Last Judgment in the Sistine Chapel, Vatican, Rome; 1536–41

Fire in the Borgo by Raphael; fresco; width of 670cm (264in); c1515. Stanza dell'Incendio, Vatican, Rome

Florence is characteristically unorthodox in its use of the classical vocabulary, and ever since an essay by R. Wittkower of 1934 ("Michelangelo's Biblioteca Laurenziana", *Art Bulletin* vol. XVI), it has been generally regarded as a key work of Mannerist architecture. Almost every architectural element—the paired columns, the blind tabernacles, the enormous consoles, the framing of the door, the staircase balusters—is treated in a completely uncanonical way, and the result is no less original than the contemporary activity of Giulio Romano in Mantua. Again in accordance with his interpretation of Mannerism, Shearman relates all this to Vasari's advocacy of variety and novelty, and to his admiration of the sovereign virtuosity that enabled Michelangelo to transcend all the rules of art. But especially in this case, it seems a misleading oversimplification to interpret the intentions of Michelangelo exclusively according to Vasari's ideal of *maniera*; most critics would probably still agree with Wittkower in seeing the reversed relationship between walls and orders as not merely ingenious, but as deeply expressive of uncertainty and conflict. In the Medici Chapel, too, the unorthodox treatment of the blind tabernacles, with their schematic pilasters and broken pediments, creates a sensation of tight compression and chill severity that is decidedly uncomfortable. Both these interiors seem, in fact, to deny "all human freedom and human power" (Pevsner), and are peculiarly oppressive in their overall effect.

Unless the term Mannerism is to become so restricted as to exclude the entire oeuvre of Michelangelo, it seems that any definition of it must, after all, take into account those qualities of tension and disturbance that pervaded his art throughout his middle and later career. In some cases, they may be plausibly related to the general spiritual climate of the period; the apocalyptic character of the *Last Judgment* certainly reflects the gloomy and uncertain mood prevailing in Rome immediately after the Sack of 1527. In other cases, Michelangelo's inner anguish was related to a more obviously personal crisis. But whatever its cause, the spiritual malaise apparent in his art struck a deeply sympathetic chord in the souls of many of his contemporaries, and artists as diverse as Pontormo, Tintoretto, and El Greco may similarly be seen as adapting the formal language of Mannerism to an expressive purpose far removed from the aesthetic ideal of *maniera*.

One of the many complicating factors in assessing Michelangelo's relation to Mannerism is the fact that his long career overlapped that of virtually every Mannerist artist of significance. As a result, as well as being a revered predecessor of the Mannerist generation, he himself seems on various occasions to have been influenced by the innovations of his younger contemporaries. The relation to Mannerism of its other great High Renaissance predecessor, Raphael, is less complicated, since the style was still in the process of formation at the time of his early death in 1520. During the course of his short career, Raphael sowed as many seeds for subsequent artistic development as did Michelangelo, progressing from the harmonious classicism of the Vatican Stanza della Segnatura to the dramatic proto-Baroque of the Stanza dell' Incendio within the span of little more than a year. But during the last few years of his life, his personal style evolved in a much more consistently Mannerist direction than Michelangelo's ever did, and after his death, the most talented members of his school, notably Giulio Romano and Perino del Vaga, were able to carry on directly where the master had ended. Many of the characteristics of mature Mannerism are already to be found in the third of the Vatican Stanze, especially in its principal scene, the *Fire in the Borgo* (c1515). The attitudes adopted by the figures dominating the foreground of this work, at once agitated and self-consciously elegant, seem curiously irrelevant to its real subject, which is the miracle being performed in the background. A similar combination of violence and grace, usually applied to a highly complex figure composition, is to be found in many of Raphael's other late works, such as in the lower half of the *Transfiguration* (1517–20; Vatican Museums, Rome). Raphael's activity as an architect in his later career was no less important in pioneering a Mannerist style. The ornamental richness and rhythmic complexity of his Palazzo Branconio dell' Acquila (1519–20; demolished) mark a decisive step away from the classic simplicity of Bramante's Palazzo Caprini, and the work provides the starting point for quintessentially Mannerist buildings of the mid century such as the Palazzo Spada and Pirro Ligorio's Casino of Pius IV (both in Rome).

It was during the 1520s that Mannerism became definitively established as the prevailing artistic style in Rome. The proto-Mannerist tendencies of the late Raphael underwent significant development in the earliest independent works of both Giulio and Perino; despite their differences of artistic personality, with Giulio tending towards the violent and romantic and Perino towards the refined and ornamental, each of them played a decisive role in this historical process. As the artistic capital of Italy, Rome inevitably attracted large numbers of young, ambitious artists, and it was largely through contact with the early Mannerism of the Raphael school that their styles acquired the polished sophistication and formal complexity that were to become hallmarks of the mid-century *maniera*. Parmigianino, for example, arriving in Rome in 1524, was encouraged to develop still further his innate feeling for ornamental and attenuated grace. Similarly, Rosso, who had tended towards the barbaric and brutally expressive, acquired on his arrival in the same year a completely new suavity and elegance. Any further tendency for Mannerism to remain a purely Roman phenomenon was dispelled in 1527, when the city was sacked and its artists caused to disperse all over Italy and even beyond. Giulio had already taken up a court appointment in Mantua in 1524, but the departures of Perino for Genoa, Polidoro da Caravaggio for Naples, Parmigianino for Parma, Sanmicheli for Verona, and Rosso for Fontainebleau immediately following the Sack, gave the style a new breadth of currency.

The Deposition from the Cross by Pontormo; panel; 313×192cm (123×76in); 1525–8. S. Felicita, Florence

Perino had already taken his highly refined version of Mannerism to Florence on a visit in 1522–3, where it was to make a considerable impact on Jacopo Pontormo (1494–1557) and other members of the postclassical generation. As early as 1518, in such works as the altarpiece for S. Michele Visdomini, Florence, Pontormo had developed the tendency of his master Andrea del Sarto towards instability, both in compositional structure and emotional expression, to a point no longer consistent with High Renaissance classicism. The question of how far Pontormo's early works until c1526 may be described as Mannerist is intimately linked with the whole controversy surrounding the term. Whereas for Friedländer, the tortured inwardness of the Certosa Frescoes of 1522–4 epitomized his anticlassical conception of Mannerism, for Shearman, the conspicuous lack of *maniera* in these works, explicitly deplored by Vasari, renders the term for them quite inappropriate. Similarly controversial are the early works of Pontormo's fellow pupil of Andrea, Rosso Fiorentino, whose *Deposition* (1521; Pinacoteca Comunale, Volterra) violates all classical norms in a way that is still harsh and eccentric, rather than ingenious and sophisticated. Yet during this phase, both painters exhibit many formal characteristics in

Frescoes by Perino del Vaga and others in the Sala Paolina, Castel Sant'Angelo, Rome; 1545–7

common with contemporary developments in Rome, such as elongated proportions, contorted poses, spatial ambiguity, and, above all, the imposition of an abstract sense of pattern on the human anatomy.

Since these characteristics were to remain fundamental to the Florentine *maniera* of the mid century, it is probably useful to continue to see the early works of Pontormo and Rosso, for all their subjective emotionalism, as direct predecessors of the mature style. These common elements inclined both artists to respond to Roman Mannerism once they had come into contact with it. Despite the persistent melancholy of his temperament, Pontormo's style acquired a new fluency and elegance after *c* 1526; in such works as the *Deposition* and *Annunciation* in S. Felicita, Florence, the tense angularity of his earlier manner is replaced by a more purely ornamental treatment of form, analogous to that of Perino, and to be of prime importance to his younger Florentine contemporaries. Rosso's move in this direction took place even earlier, and although on occasions he was to revert to the expressive urgency of the Volterra *Deposition*, it was the graceful and urbane style first acquired in Rome that he took with him to Fontainebleau. In this way, he inspired a whole generation of

French painters and sculptors with the ideal of *maniera*.

By the early 1530s, the previously different tendencies of early Mannerist painting in Rome and Florence had combined to form the basis for what may conveniently be termed "high" *maniera*, or mature Mannerism. Two of the leading exponents of this phase, Salviati and Vasari, were equally active in both cities; its most characteristic form of artistic expression was that of the large-scale decorative enterprise, often used for dynastic propaganda. Important examples of the type include the decoration of the Oratory of S. Giovanni Decollato, Rome (by Salviati and Jacopino del Conte, 1538), the Sala dell' Udienza in the Palazzo Vecchio, Florence (by Salviati, 1543–5), the Sala Paolina in the Castel Sant' Angelo, Rome (by Perino del Vaga, 1545–7), the Sala dei Cento Giorni in the Cancelleria, Rome (by Vasari, 1546), the Sala dei Fasti Farnesi in the Palazzo Farnese, Rome (by Salviati, 1549–63), the Sala del Cinquecento in the Palazzo Vecchio (by Vasari, 1555–71), and the Sala Regia in the Vatican (by Perino del Vaga, Daniele da Volterra, Salviati, the Zuccari, and Vasari, 1540–73). All these decorations were intended to emulate the achievements of Raphael and Michelangelo in the Vatican Stanze and Sistine Chapel; at the same time, they provided full scope for a

Assumption of the Virgin

This painting is the first great, public master-piece of the Venetian Renaissance. Commissioned for the high altar of the Frari, the Franciscan church in Venice, *c*1516, it showed that Venetian artists could match in scale and grandeur the monumental painting Raphael and Michelangelo were working on at the same time in Rome. Nonetheless it is completely Venetian: warm, sensuous, rich in its color and paint surface—a true celebration of its subject, which, through the resurrection of the corporeal body of the Virgin Mary into heaven, is the triumph of the flesh.

From contemporary sources, we know that while the picture was being painted, and even after it was put in place (on the Feast of S. Bernardino, 20 May 1518), the Friars were puzzled by and doubtful about it. The figures are far larger than lifesize—much bigger than in any earlier altarpiece—and the technique is very open and loose, quite different from the kind of precisely finished 15th-century altarpiece to which people were accustomed. But Titian knew what he was doing.

The painting had to be large, and broadly painted, because it was to be the focal point of a very large church, Gothic in style, down the whole length of which it could be seen. As the viewer walks down the church, he first sees the painting framed in the entrance arch of the choir, which echoes in shape the arched frame in which the picture itself is placed. This frame, with its great freestanding columns, is like a triumphal arch, and the main events in the painting are made to "tell" in relation to it. The Virgin herself is placed within a circle made by the arch of the frame, and the garland of sporting angels—her head is exactly in the center—and the silhouettes of the heads of the Apostles—the main horizontal division of the painting—are reinforced by being seen at the same height as the top of the high base on which the columns of the frame are placed. By these means, Titian organized the complex events of the painting into an orderly and harmonious design.

The giant Apostles all look upwards at the Virgin and we ourselves seem to be looking up between them, *di sotto in su* as the Italians say, at her spiraling figure. Above, God the Father, in a swirl of angels and mist, swoops down to receive her, swinging through the air like an eagle from the mountain tops—a reminder that Titian was born and brought up among mountains and must have been accustomed to looking upwards at their vertiginous mist-swathed heights in the same way as the Apostles look up at the Virgin.

Their vision is one of light and color. The Virgin is set against a glory of golden light—a luminous equivalent for the gilded half domes of Byzantine churches. Her cloak is carmine red and her robe blue, and these primary colors strike a harmonious chord which matches that of the forms. The upper zone of the picture is very broadly painted in large strokes, visible a long way off to match their distance from the eye; a detail of God the Father's head shows how the forms are evoked as if out of light by the minimum of strokes. The strokes match the perceptual evidence of tone and color presented to the eye in nature, and the impression of liveliness the head gives comes from the fact that we ourselves assemble them into form, as we do when we see things in life.

In this painting, Titian opposes to the linear, more intellectual art of the Roman High Renaissance a coloristic, pictorial style characteristically Venetian. It is direct, sensuous, and gloriously alive. It is also, like Roman art, idealized and on a monumental scale.

Above The nave and choir of S. Maria Gloriosa dei Frari, Venice, showing Titian's *Assumption* set behind the archway into the choir

▼ God receives the Virgin: a detail from Titian's *Assumption of the Virgin*

It may be compared, both for similarities and differences, with Raphael's *Transfiguration* (Vatican Museums, Rome) painted at almost the same time. Raphael's painting already shows some Venetian influence, but the sculptured forms, the clear separation of the two zones, and the balance between the contrasting elements of form, color, and chiaroscuro, show a harmony parallel to, but quite different from, that of Titian.

JOHN STEER

◄ Assumption of the Virgin by Titian; oil on panel; 690×360cm (272×142in); 1516–18. S. Maria dei Frari, Venice

Above An example of a Venetian altarpiece, earlier than Titian's *Assumption: The Resurrection of Christ* by Giovanni Bellini; oil on panel; 148×128cm (58×50in); c1475–9. Staatliche Museen, Berlin

▲ The *Transfiguration of Christ* by Raphael; oil on panel; 405×278cm (159×109in); 1518–20. Vatican Museums, Rome

Lucrezia Panciatichi by Bronzino; oil on canvas; 104×85cm (41×33in); c1540. Uffizi, Florence

typically Mannerist delight in ingenuity and complexity, both in form and content.

The career of the third great exponent of the "high" *maniera*, Bronzino, was, by contrast, more or less restricted to Florence, and he did not practice mural decoration on the same scale as his friends Salviati and Vasari. On the other hand, his extremely refined technique was well suited to the art of portraiture, and, with Parmigianino, Bronzino was probably the greatest Mannerist portrait-painter. It is paradoxical that a style so little concerned with the imitation of external reality should have produced so many portraits of so high a quality. But Bronzino mastered the art of combining his own artificially beautiful ideal of humanity with a sharp observation of individual detail; his courtly sitters are thus represented with an air of stiff formality and cool perfection, entirely appropriate to their social pretensions and yet with complete outward accuracy. The sitters of both Bronzino and Parmigianino tend to exude the quality of *maniera*, a term which in 16th-century usage was also frequently applied in a social sense to refer to good breeding, distinguished deportment, and general *savoir-faire*.

One of the most characteristic developments in Florentine sculpture of the mid century was the growing concern with the multiple viewpoint. Although Michelangelo's preference, almost reverence, for a single viewing point for sculpture was well-known, the spiraling composition of his *Victory* (Palazzo Vecchio, Florence) clearly suggested the possibility of dissolving pure frontality, thus presenting to the spectator an infinity of interesting views as he surveyed a freestanding sculpture from all sides. Michelangelo himself did, in fact, plan just such a work during the 1520s, a *Hercules and Cacus* group which was to be placed in the main Piazza alongside his earlier *David*; and although the project was abandoned in 1529, his clay model survived (now in the Casa Buonarroti, Florence), and was to exert a considerable influence on subsequent Mannerist sculpture.

The greatest sculptor active in Florence in the second half of the 16th century, Giambologna (c1524–1608), was obviously deeply impressed by both of these prototypes by Michelangelo. A group such as the *Rape of a Sabine* (Loggia dei Lanzi, Florence) is a mature example of the principle of the *figura serpentinata*, here applied to three figures larger than life, arranged in a continuously twisting spiral round a central core, and presenting a constantly shifting variety of silhouette. The sculptor's typically Mannerist concern with formal complexity and virtuosity, at the expense of the subject matter, emerges from a letter of 1579 in which he explicitly states that the subject was "chosen to give scope to the knowledge and study of art". It is known that the work was given its title only after it had been set up in the Piazza. The titles given to the various adaptations of Michelangelo's *Victory* by Pierino da Vinci, Ammanati, Danti, and again, Giambologna, seem similarly arbitrary. Despite the fact that, in contrast to these other sculptors, and also to Cellini, the art of Giambologna is frequently charged with dynamic energy out of character with the languid effortlessness of true *maniera*, it seems reasonable to categorize him as Mannerist in a generic sense.

The same may be said of Tintoretto (1518–94), who is excluded from Shearman's definition on account of his spiritual intensity and physical energy, but who frequently employed compositional devices and elongated proportions akin to those of central Italian Mannerism. In the *Finding the Body of St Mark* (Pinacoteca di Brera, Milan) the figures can no longer be called graceful, but there is an irrational handling of light and space, combined with a Michelangelesque plasticity of form, that indicates knowledge of Roman and Florentine developments during the 1520s. Within the context of Venice, however, Tintoretto is exceptional, and the dominating personality of Titian (c1485–1576) gave the mainstream of Venetian painting an abiding concern with the sensuous experience of reality alien to the abstracting and refining tendencies of Mannerism. Although Paolo Veronese (1528–88), and even Titian himself were sometimes influenced by leading north Italian exponents of the *maniera*, such as Giulio Romano and Parmigianino, such influences were to remain

Rape of the Sabines, by Giambologna; marble; height 410cm (161in); 1579–82. Loggia dei Lanzi, Florence

comparatively superficial. The essential naturalness and vitality of their art provided an uninterrupted continuity between the High Renaissance and Baroque. In Venetian architecture and sculpture, too, Titian's friend, Jacopo Sansovino, perpetuated the classical style of the High Renaissance, albeit in an enriched form, well into the second half of the century. The greatest architect active in the Veneto in the later Cinquecento, Andrea Palladio (1508–80), was equally restrained in his introduction of Mannerist forms.

Central Italian architecture from the mid century onwards, although dependent on the preceding phase in the same way that Bronzino was dependent on Pontormo, was less radically experimental than before. The daringly unorthodox works of the 1520s and 1530s by Giulio Romano and Michelangelo, and also by Peruzzi (1481–1536) and Sanmicheli (1484–1559), were followed after c1550 by a trend towards greater sobriety and reticence. Probably the most important representative of this tendency was Vignola, whose architectural treatise *Cinque Ordini di Architettura* (1562) reveals an academic desire to lay down uninfringeable rules based on a study of antique and High Renaissance practice. The stiff formality of Vignola's architecture, where a rigid conformity to a system of rules seems to conceal an inner uncertainty of direction, has much in common with central Italian painting of the high and later *maniera*, which also became increasingly academic and eclectic after the middle of the century.

This was unquestionably a period of general decline; the efforts of reformers such as Taddeo Zuccaro (1529–66) in Rome and Santi di Tito (1536–1603) in Florence to infuse new life into the art of painting may actually have had the opposite effect, since their advocacy of greater naturalness and simplicity was inimical to the original creative vitality of the Mannerist style. By the end of the century, this had become so dilute as to be completely effete, and, with the possible exception of the Cavalier d'Arpino (1568–1640), its Roman exponents could offer little resistance to the early Baroque innovations of Annibale Carracci and Caravaggio after the early 1590s. Yet, as late as 1570, it was still possible to create so perfect a masterpiece of Mannerist decoration as the Studiolo of Francesco I in the Palazzo Vecchio in Florence, a small chamber resembling the inside of a treasure-casket and studded with paintings and statuettes of a gem-like preciosity, all executed under the general supervision of Giorgio Vasari. In villa and garden architecture too, Mannerism continued as a highly inventive style throughout the second half of the century. Important examples include Pirro Ligorio's Villa d'Este at Tivoli (1565–72), Buontalenti's now destroyed Villa Medici at Pratolino, near Florence (1569–75), and the extraordinary Villa Orsini at Bomarzo, near Viterbo (c1550–80).

In tracing the development of the style outside Italy, it is often difficult, and even pointless, to attempt to distinguish between specifically Mannerist influences and the spread of the Italian Renaissance generally. The sudden grafting of Italianate forms from all phases of the Renaissance on to the vigorous local traditions of northern Europe frequently re-

The Studiolo of Francesco I, designed by Giorgio Vasari 1570–2. Palazzo Vecchio, Florence

A relief Nymph of the Seine by Jean Goujon; 1550. Louvre, Paris

sulted in a style too hybrid to be defined unambiguously as Mannerist. Yet despite the lack of any French equivalent of the High Renaissance, the style that grew up in Fontainebleau from the early 1530s may be seen as purely, almost quintessentially, Mannerist; being the creations of the transplanted Italians Rosso and Primaticcio. The Galerie François I, with its complicated fusion of allegorical paintings, stucco figures, and intricate ornament, is a perfect embodiment of *maniera*, a quality well-calculated to appeal to the refined tastes of the

French court. A whole generation of French artists was trained in this style, and although painters such as Jean Cousin the Elder and Antoine Caron were only modestly gifted, the sculptors Jean Goujon (*c*1510–*c*68) and Germain Pilon (*c*1525/30–90) developed its possibilities to a high level of accomplishment and expressiveness. Mid-16th-century French architecture, on the other hand, although equally inspired by the example of Italy, was more classically oriented; its greatest exponent, Philibert Delorme (*c*1510–70), explicitly disapproved of the fantasy and complexity of Mannerism.

While Mannerism in France flourished as a direct result of royal patronage, first under Francis I and then under his son Henry II, the style was introduced into the Netherlands, mainly at second hand, by native artists who had come into contact with it while visiting Italy. The term should not be applied to the first generation of Romanist painters, such as Jan Gossaert (*c*1478–1532), Bernaert van Orley (1491/2–1542), and Jan van Scorel (1495–1562), since their knowledge of Italian art was based on developments before 1520; but the contorted post-Raphaelite styles of Marten van Heemskerck (1498–1547), Frans Floris (*c*1518–70), Marten de Vos (1532–1603), and a whole generation of Netherlandish Italianizers, certainly do qualify as Mannerist—despite a certain tendency towards a coarseness and gaucheness alien to the *maniera*. Native artists with a pronounced bent towards elegance and sophistication tended to seek employment outside the Netherlands, and it was in the congenial environment of the courts of Albrecht V in Munich and Rudolf II in Prague that the sculptors Hubert Gerhard (*c*1545–1620) and Adriaen de Vries (*c*1560–1626), former pupils of Giambologna, and the painter Bartholomaeus Spranger (1546–1611), passed most of their careers. Probably the most significant Netherlandish contribution to Mannerist architecture were the pattern books (1565 and 1568) of Hans Vredeman de Vries (1527–?1604) whose fantastic designs, based on a variety of sources, including Peruzzi's Palazzo Massimi in Rome and the decorations at Fontainebleau, gave Mannerist motifs a wide circulation in the Netherlands and England.

In Spain, too, Mannerist forms in painting and sculpture were first introduced in the hybrid styles of artists such as Alonso Berruguete (*c*1489–1561), Juan de Juni (*c*1533–77), and Juan de Juanes (1500–79). Although some of these had visited Italy, they all remained closely tied to local traditions, and it was not until the 1570s, when Federico Zuccaro (1540/3–1609) and Pellegrino Tibaldi (1527–66) arrived to decorate Philip II's palace of the Escorial, that an authentically Italian version of Mannerism was imported. At about the same time, however, a much greater artistic personality, El Greco, made his appearance in Spain, practicing his own, highly individual version of the style. Despite its almost complete lack of the urbanity and polish of *maniera*, a deficiency that cost him all hope of success at court, the art of El Greco is recognizably related to central Italian Mannerism of the mid century—even if only in a formal sense. His *Martyrdom of St Maurice* (The Escorial, near Madrid) resembles Bronzino's *Martyrdom of St*

Lawrence in its stylized abstraction from reality, and its arrangement of limbs and draperies into a relief-like pattern, and there are many Italian Mannerist analogies for El Greco's tendencies towards elongation of form and spatial ambiguity. Thus, although the profoundly spiritual character of his art, as well as his increasing idiosyncrasy and his chronological position, make it impossible to accept Dvorak's estimate of it as typical of, or central to, the style as a whole, there still seems every reason to regard El Greco as one of the greatest exponents of Mannerism.

In England, Italian Mannerism was received at third hand only, introduced through Netherlandish or German intermediaries. Mannerist elements in the art of such painters as Guillaume Scrots (*fl. c*1546) and Hans Eworth (*fl.* 1540–74) are clumsy and provincial by Italian standards; even the refined and dainty art of the greatest native painter of the 16th

The Martyrdom of St Maurice, by El Greco; canvas; 448×300cm (176×118in); 1582. The Escorial, near Madrid

century, Nicholas Hilliard (*c*1547–1619), has too slight a basis in the Italian Renaissance properly to be called Mannerist. The same is true of the robustly creative tradition of Elizabethan architecture, where Mannerist motifs form part of a rich, chaotic mixture, derived from a variety of sources, and applied with no real understanding of the language of classical forms.

The central Italian preoccupation with *maniera*, with good style and the means of attaining it, produced an enormous crop of theoretical writings on art from the middle of the 16th century. By far the most important of these was Vasari's monumental *Vite*, first published in 1550, which although cast in a biographical form, contained numerous observations on the nature of artistic excellence. These ideas formed the basis for the more abstract and philosophical treatises of Lomazzo (1584), Armenini (1586), and Federigo Zuccaro (1607). The biographical tradition was continued in such works as Borghini's *Riposo* (1584), and in several autobiographies by Mannerist artists, the most famous of which is by Benvenuto Cellini (*c*1560). In northern Europe, the historical and theoretical approaches were combined in the copious writings of Carel van Mander, a painter and close friend of the arch-Mannerist engraver Hendrick Goltzius (1558–1617). Even in England, a short treatise on the art of miniature painting was produced by Nicholas Hilliard (*c*1600). A large number of architectural treatises were also published during the period, including those of Serlio (1537), Vignola (1562), Palladio (1570), and Scamozzi (1615) in Italy, and Ducerceau (1559), Bullant (1564), and Delorme (1568) in France. The proliferation of all these theoretical works reflects not only the Mannerists' concern with the processes of artistic creation—a concern reflected in the self-conscious character of the Mannerist style—but also the aspiration of their authors to raise the social and intellectual status of the artist. A post-medieval distinction between the creative genius of the artist and the purely manual skills of the craftsman had already appeared in the writings of Alberti, but it was not until the 16th century that the idea began to gain more general recognition. This was largely because of a widespread admiration for the achievements of the giants of the High Renaissance. Vasari reports approvingly that Raphael lived more like a prince than a painter, a rise in status later symbolized by the seigneurial residences of Mannerist artists such as Giulio Romano (in Mantua) and of Federigo Zuccaro (in Rome); the epithet

"divine", universally bestowed on Michelangelo, accorded with his own conception of art as the highest expression of the human spirit. Directly related to this sense of the enhanced social and intellectual dignity of the artist was Vasari's desire to found an academy of art, a project realized in the Accademia del Disegno in Florence (1563), and later imitated in Federigo Zuccaro's Accademia di San Luca in Rome (1593), and Van Mander's academy in Haarlem (1583). But embodied in the very notion of the academy was a paradox, of which Vasari himself seems to have been uneasily aware. On the one hand, it sought to gain prestige from the quasi-divine nature of artistic creation, reserving the very highest admiration for artists like Michelangelo, who retained a sovereign independence of tradition; on the other, it tended to reduce art to a teachable system of rules, encouraging study and imitation of the great masters of the past. This dualism, reflecting an underlying uncertainty of direction that could lead alternately to academic eclecticism and to purely subjective caprice, may be seen as entirely characteristic of Mannerist art and thought.

PETER HUMFREY

Bibliography. Antal, F. "The Social Background of Italian Mannerism", *Art Bulletin* vol. XXX (1938). Blunt, A. *Artistic Theory in Italy 1450–1600*, Oxford (1940). Dvorak, M. "Über Greco und den Manierismus" in Dvorak, M. (ed.) *Kunstgeschichte als Geistesgeschichte*, Munich (1924); English translation in the *Magazine of Art* (1953). Freedberg, S.J. *Painting in Italy: 1500–1600*, Harmondsworth (1979). Friedländer, W. "Die Entstehung des antiklassischen Stiles ... um 1520" *Repertorium für Kunstwissenschaft* vol. XLVI, (1925); English translation in Friedländer, W. *Mannerism and Anti-Mannerism in Italian Painting*, New York (1957). Hauser, A. *Mannerism*, (2 vols.) London (1965). Heydenreich, L.H. and Lotz, W. *Architecture in Italy: 1400–1600*, Harmondsworth (1974). Pevsner, N. "The Architecture of Mannerism" in Grigson, G. (ed.) *The Mint*, London (1946). Pevsner, N. "Gegenreformation und Manierismus" *Repertorium für Kunstwissenschaft* vol. XLVI, (1925); English translation in Pevsner, N. *Studies in Art, Architecture, and Design* vol. 1, London (1968). Pope-Hennessy, J. *Italian High Renaissance and Baroque Sculpture*, London (1963). Shearman, J. *Mannerism*, Harmondsworth (1967). Smyth, C.H. *Mannerism and Maniera*, Locust Valley, N.Y. (1962). Voss, F. *Die Malerei der Spätrenaissance in Rom und Florenz*, Berlin (1922). Zeri, F. *Pittura e Controriforma*, Turin (1957). Zerner, H. "Observations on the Use of the Concept of Mannerism" in Robinson, F.W. and Nichols, S.G. (eds.) *The Meaning of Mannerism*, Hanover, N.H. (1972).

37

THE BAROQUE

The Supper at Emmaus by Caravaggio; oil on canvas; 141×196cm (56×77in); c1596/8–c1602. National Gallery, London (see page 697)

THE word "baroque" was intended as a term of abuse; originally, it meant oddly shaped, and it grew to mean anything illogical, absurd, or bizarre. Eighteenth-century classicists used it to describe the 17th-century painter's neglect or defiance of classical rules, and perhaps more particularly the sculptor and architect's preference for eccentric and extravagant shapes. It was not until the 19th century that German scholars began to use the word neutrally to describe the art of the 17th century.

Historically, the art of this period must be seen in the context of the renewed power of the Roman Catholic Church and the increased centralization of political power. From the 1570s, the threat of Protestantism waned. The austerity of the Counter-Reformation consequently relaxed, and the more confident popes and cardinals of the 17th century became enthusiastic patrons of an art that should express their religious fervor and their enjoyment of life; the religious orders, particularly the Oratorians and the Jesuits, increased their power. The reassertion of the dogmas of the Roman Catholic Church became an important part of the painter's role; the glory of martyrdom, saintly visions and ecstasies, inflamed with highly charged emotion and presented with all the resources of a rhetorical language of gesture and expression, became common subjects for painter and sculptor. In the secular sphere, power was concentrated in the hands of the monarch, and buttressed by the doctrine of the divine right of kings; Philip IV of Spain, Louis XIV of France, and Charles I of England were quick to see the possibilities of the Baroque as an art of propaganda.

The confidence of the period is perhaps most apparent in the magnificence and sensuous visual beauty of many Baroque works; when we turn from the art of the Renaissance to the art of the Baroque we notice first the more radiant glow of color, the freer and more expressive brushwork, the richer contrasts of texture and of light and dark. Baroque architecture shares many of these qualities; a Baroque church interior, with its numerous decorative sculptures and paintings, its lavish use of gilt, stucco, and richly colored marbles, and its impression of movement and space, was designed to transport our thoughts to the glory of heaven.

One aspect of the Baroque, then, is that it is an art of persuasion; the artist was concerned above all to appeal to the emotions of the spectator. To make the scenes depicted vivid and enthralling, he attempted to capture the highest moment of dramatic action and to emphasize it by startling contrasts of light and shade. The spectator is often compelled to participate actively in a Baroque work either by a kind of composition in which the figures are pressed so close to the frontal plane that they seem to extend their movements into the world outside the painting, or, alternatively, he may be overwhelmed by a surge of figures moving in an upward spiraling movement into a seemingly endless space. The use of various illusionistic devices, often adapted from the theater, became more common in this period.

The effect of a Baroque work is immediate and overwhelming; there is a new sense of artistic unity in this period, of all the parts being subordinated to a dynamic rhythm that leads up to a climax. This principle contrasts sharply with the decentralized compositions of the Mannerists, whose works abounded in sophisticated rhythms and intricate details that the eye must carefully seek out and marvel over. In many ways, the Baroque was a return to the grandeur and monumentality of the High Renaissance; yet Baroque artists did not return to the Renaissance ideals of symmetry and clarity. They concentrated rather on daring effects of asymmetry and on diagonal movements into depth. There is a similar sense of unity and movement in Baroque architecture; forms and spaces are more dynamically organized than they had been in the Renaissance and tend to flow and merge into one another; facades are handled sculpturally and have a new plastic richness and depth. The unity of the effect is often emphasized by the merging of the three arts of painting, sculpture, and architecture into the production of a grandiose total effect; often, whole rooms and chapels are drawn into one work of art.

The Baroque was only one aspect of 17th-century art; the century saw an increasing variety of stylistic categories, and throughout the period a classical movement resisted the Baroque appeal to the senses and emotions. These artists, led by Nicolas Poussin (1594–1665), attempted to continue the tradition of Raphael (1483–1520) and concentrated on clarity, symmetry, and balance. There was also a widening of traditional subject matter; c1600, still life, genre, and landscape emerged as independent art forms. Painters of these subjects were for the most part neither classical nor Baroque, but realists; realism dominated Dutch art of the 17th century. All three styles shared a return to nature after the anti-naturalistic style of the Mannerists; this is apparent not only in Caravaggio's proletarian models, but in the Carracci's stress on drawing from life, in Rubens' and Bernini's treatment of flesh, and in Claude's and Ruysdael's observation of light and of the surface and texture of nature.

Italy. The artistic center for the greater part of the 17th century was Rome. The new mood of religious fervor was first manifest in the rapid and enthusiastic building of churches in the period from 1570 to 1620. The earliest of these, Il Gesù, planned by Giacomo Vignola (1507–73) in 1568, with a facade of 1575 by Giacomo della Porta (c1533–1602), became in both plan and elevation the standard type for the large congregational church; instead of the central plan common in the Renaissance, it has a single, broad longitudinal nave with side-chapels; the transept is short and the crossing surmounted by a splendid dome. The most important architect of the early Baroque was Carlo Maderno (1556–1629), whose facade of S. Susanna, Rome, of 1597–1603, transformed the broad amplitude and quietly accented center of the two-story facade of the Gesù into a tighter, more dynamically organized composition in which columns and bays progress more insistently to the center. S. Susanna initiated the Roman Baroque facade; later architects increased the crowding of the columns and the extravagance of the detailing.

To painters of this period, the most pressing concern was to renew a contact with nature after the excesses of Mannerism; they were concerned to return to a clear and lucid depiction of space, and to rid their paintings of both formal and psychological ambiguities. The most significant artists working in Rome in the 1590s were Michelangelo Merisi, called Caravaggio (1573–1609/10), and Annibale Carracci (1560–1609). Caravaggio came to Rome from Milan c1590–2; later he worked in Naples, Sicily, and Malta. He was a revolutionary artist whose originality lay in his insistence on realism, manifest first in a series of genre paintings of exotically dressed, somewhat decadent young men, and later in religious paintings of deep moral gravity in which he ignored earlier artistic conventions. His protagonists are unidealized, the disciples shown as rough peasants with wrinkled brows, torn clothes, and dirty feet. He aimed, too, at psychological realism, attempting, without recourse to established rhetoric, to comunicate the inward sense of the scenes described in the Bible. His compositions stress the physical, almost tangible presence of his figures; often they are arranged in a shallow space close to the picture plane, and dramatically foreshortened gestures break through the plane. Yet Caravaggio's realism is made dramatic and spiritually meaningful by non-realistic means: his pictures are illuminated by powerful and irrational contrasts of light and shade that are deeply poetic; his backgrounds are bare and dark, and empty spaces create an atmosphere of foreboding in his often violent scenes.

Annibale Carracci, the most important of a family of Bolognese artists, came to Rome c1595; his Roman easel paintings, and the frescoes in the Palazzo Farnese (1597–1604), established the fundamental principles of both the Baroque and classical styles. Annibale's style was an attempt to revitalize the tradition of the High Renaissance, based upon an intensive study of nature. The arrangement of the Farnese ceiling is a series of pictures showing the loves of the gods. These are presented as if easel paintings within an illusionistic architectural framework, supported by an abundance of motifs: imitation bronze medallions, imitation stone herms, "real" nudes, and putti. The clarity and logic of the ceiling, and its references to Raphael and the Antique, influenced the classicists; yet its illusionism, its decorative, sensuous, and lighthearted use of accessories, and its physical power, exuberance, and rich compositions of the individual paintings, anticipate the Baroque.

From 1610 to 1620, Caravaggio's followers and Annibale's pupils vied for supremacy. Caravaggio's influence was more diffuse, and rapidly spread through Europe; his early genre scenes were frequently imitated, and artists responded in a variety of ways to his chiaroscuro. Annibale's pupils, Guido Reni (1575–1642), Francesco Albani (1578–1660), and Domenichino (1581–1641), who had followed him from Bologna, received most of the commissions for frescoes in Rome. They developed Annibale's classical tendencies, and this decade was one of disciplined calm. Domenichino was the

St Cecilia distributes clothes to the Poor by Domenichino; fresco; c1611–14. S. Luigi dei Francesi, Rome

most rigorously classical; his colors are pale and clear, the space clearly defined with the figures parallel to the plane. Reni's response to Antiquity was more lyrical; his ceiling fresco *Dawn* (1613–14; Palazzo Rospigliosi, Rome) rejected both the illusionism and the exuberance of the Farnese; the movement is the gentle flow of a Classical relief; the figures have a more sweetly idealized beauty than their Raphaelesque prototypes. In his religious paintings, the heightened pathos of expression typifies this aspect of 17th-century sensibility.

A more exuberant style was introduced by Guercino (1591–1666), who arrived from Bologna in 1621. His use of light and shade is dramatic, his handling of paint rich and luscious. His ceiling fresco of 1621–3 in the Casino Ludovisi, Rome, shows Day's chariot now sweeping across the sky with true Baroque vigor; illusionistic architecture is boldly used to create a more unified space.

A lighter and more airy spatial illusionism, based on Correggio, was developed by Giovanni Lanfranco (1582–1647); he covered the vast area of the dome of S. Andrea della Valle in 1625–7 with a single composition showing the Assumption of the Virgin. A surge of figures sweep our eyes upwards into a painted heaven, and more than any other work of the 1620s this prepares us for the unity and complexity of the High Baroque.

The most important artists of the High Baroque who reached maturity in the 1630s were Gian Lorenzo Bernini (1598–1680), Francesco Borromini (1599–1667), and Pietro da Cortona (1596–1669).

Bernini, a Neapolitan, dominated the Roman artistic scene

Dawn, a ceiling fresco by Guido Reni; 1613–14. Palazzo Rospigliosi, Rome

David by Bernini; marble; height 170cm (67in); 1623. Museo e Galleria Borghese, Rome

for more than 50 years. Architect, sculptor, and painter, he had an astonishing virtuosity. He enjoyed the continuing esteem of eight popes, his works in and around St Peter's express, in a highly charged symbolic language, the renewed power and glory of the Catholic Church, and their decorative splendor is overwhelming.

In a series of figure groups executed for Scipione Borghese in the 1620s, Bernini broke away from the Renaissance sculptor's concept of an image enclosed within the limits of the block and from the spiraling complexity and multiple viewpoints of Mannerist sculpture. He attempted to involve the spectator emotionally by portraying, from a single viewpoint which concentrates the impression of energy, the highest moment of dramatic action. His works were based on an intense study of nature, of expression, and of surface detail; his capturing of the texture of flesh and hair in marble is unsurpassed. His figures seem to extend into the real space of the spectator; the *David* of 1623 (Museo e Galleria Borghese, Rome), his features tensely concentrated, is on the point of moving towards an unseen Goliath. The portrait busts were conceived on the same principles: the sitters, turning their heads sharply in response to the spectator, their eyes penetrating and lively, their lips parted, seem caught on the verge of speech.

Bernini's desire to involve the spectator's emotions lead him to explore the resources of illusionism, and to use the arts of painting, sculpture, and architecture together in the creation of an overwhelming effect that tends to break down the barriers between the three arts. The vividness is enhanced by concealed lighting and rich contrasts of color. The central group of the *Ecstasy of St Theresa* of 1645–8 (S. Maria della Vittoria, Rome), executed in highly polished white marble, is framed between dark columns as though it were a painting;

Right: The Ecstasy of St Theresa by Bernini; marble; 1645–8. S. Maria della Vittoria; Rome

S. Carlino, Rome, by Borromini; 1638–41

the swooning expression and feverish vitality of the draperies express the intensity of her vision. The group seems miraculously suspended before us, and this illusionistic effect is heightened by the presence of sculptured groups of the Cornaro family set into the chapel walls in what look like opera boxes. We, the spectators, tend to identify with them, and so grant reality to the vision. On the vault, stucco clouds that seem to blow across the architecture support painted angels. The light illuminating the central group with such supernatural radiance is natural light that falls from a concealed source through yellow glass. All the arts, and nature itself, thus combine in Bernini's work.

A more extreme fusion of sculpture and nature occurred in Bernini's fountains, in which powerful flowing water replaced the thin jets of 16th-century fountains. The Fountain of Four Rivers (1648–51; Piazza Navona, Rome) is an apparently natural rocky structure, covered with exotic sculptured vegetation and pierced by rushing waters, which supports four personified rivers who sit at the foot of an obelisk.

Bernini's most spectacular architectural achievement was the piazza of St Peter's. He enclosed the oval piazza by a free standing colonnade, which creates rich contrasts of light and shade and spatial effects; its shape seems to draw us physically towards the church with an impression of unity and movement typical of the Baroque. Bernini said that the oval colonnade symbolized the all-embracing arms of the Church.

In his designs for churches, Bernini returned to the most familiar of Renaissance ground plans: the Greek cross, circle, and oval. What was new was the importance of sculpture. We do not contemplate the harmony of the forms as in a Renaissance church; rather, Bernini charged the forms with energy, and the whole church became a setting for mystical experience revealed by the sculpture. In S. Andrea al Quirinale, Rome, (1658–70) a series of giant pilasters and massive entablature sweeps our eye around the oval plan to a climactic focal point above the altar where a sculptured St Andrew soars to heaven.

Borromini came to Rome from northern Italy, where he had been trained as a stonemason, in 1614; until 1633 he worked first as Maderno's assistant and later as Bernini's. He was a less traditional architect than Bernini; the drama in his works is inherent in the way that form and space are handled. He was fascinated by ingenious spatial compositions and by the idea of setting forms in movement; his walls sway and curve as if softly modeled. The basis of his approach was geometry; his plans did not aim, as did the mathematical plans of Renaissance architects, at spatial lucidity, but rather at a wealth of spatial relationships; forms flow into one another rather than being sharply divided. He used the most extravagant shapes in the towers, where strange spirals surge impetuously into space.

All these characteristics may be seen in the small church of S. Carlino, Rome (1638–41). Its plan is basically an oval. (Variations on the theme of the oval are one of the most interesting aspects of the Roman Baroque.) The quadrants of the oval are curved inward; the result is that the heavy cornice seems to flow rhythmically round the church in a sequence of concave and convex curves. The dome is decorated with sharply cut coffers of geometric shape, surprisingly light and graceful in feeling. The later facade (1665–82) shows a similar attempt to create dynamic effects of movement; the concave-convex-concave lower story is contrasted with the convex-concave-convex curves of the upper.

Pietro da Cortona was, like Bernini, both architect and painter, and, after Bernini, the most influential artist of his day. He came to Rome from southern Tuscany in 1612–13; he worked in Florence from 1640 to 1647. As an architect, he was less capricious than Borromini; his forms are graver, more Roman, and have a greater plastic richness. However, he shared Borromini's interest in setting forms in movement, and the theme of contrasting curves was taken up in his work. This is apparent in the facade of S. Maria della Pace, Rome (1656–7) where a semicircular portico invites us into the interior; its outward thrust is contrasted with the concave wings behind the first story. This portico was frequently repeated in European churches during the 17th century.

As a painter, Cortona excelled in organizing vast numbers of figures in works of the largest scale; his paintings have the ebullient vitality and robust physical power we associate with

The Marriage of Isaac and Rebecca (The Mill) by Claude; canvas; 149×196cm (59×77in); c1648. National Gallery, London

the Baroque. His forms are sculptural, his compositions complex, and his color glowing. The latter shows a deep indebtedness to Venetian art: in 1598 a group of paintings by Titian had been brought to Rome from Ferrara where they were copied by Rubens, Poussin, and Cortona. A neo-Venetian movement was an important aspect of the Baroque in the 1630s; of all High Renaissance painters, Titian most nearly anticipated the Baroque.

In 1633, Cortona began the ceiling decoration for the Great Saloon of the Palazzo Barberini, a work that epitomizes the Roman High Baroque and marks a turning point in its development. The painted architectural framework with imitation stucco figures at the corners was adapted from the Farnese, but the illusionism is taken much further: the figures appear above and below the architecture, and seem to sweep upwards towards an open space. A surge of flowing movement unites the whole composition; even the accessory figures are included in the turbulent action which leads up to the personification of Divine Providence. The effect is overwhelming, and, despite the intricacy of the subsidiary themes, unified. This unity is very different from the compartmentalized composition of Annibale Carracci's Farnese ceiling.

Throughout the 17th century, a classical movement op-

posed the Baroque; in the period of the High Baroque, this classicism became more painterly than it had been in the 1620s. The leaders were now Andrea Sacchi (1599–1661), the Frenchman Nicolas Poussin (1594–1665), the sculptor Alessandro Algardi (1598–1654) and the Flemish sculptor Francesco Duqesnoy (1594–1643). Cortona believed that a painting should be like an epic poem, with a central theme supported by many episodes. Sacchi believed that it should resemble a tragedy, with few figures and a highly concentrated simplicity of action. These contrasting doctrines were forcefully illustrated in the frescoes by both artists in the Palazzo Barberini; Sacchi's *Allegory of Divine Wisdom* (1629–c1633) is in every way opposed to Cortona's fresco; it shows comparatively few, rather static figures, and there is no illusionism, no foreshortenings, no swirl of movement. His style is seen at its best in his calm and meditative easel paintings.

The greatest classical artist of this century was Poussin. Although his influence was greatest in his native France, Poussin's development may better be studied in the context of interests he shared with his Roman contemporaries—he worked almost all his life in Rome. As a young artist, Poussin responded most powerfully to Titian: to his color, his free brushwork, and his poetic interpretation of mythological

Cortona's Barberini Ceiling

The spectator who enters the *gran salone* of the Barberini palace is immediately drawn into an imagined world of spectacular and overwhelming power. On the high ceiling, a painted architectural framework seems to open the huge vault to the sky; a swirling mass of twisting and weighty figures surge through the air, moving freely both in front and behind the framework. The vibrant atmosphere and skillful patterning of light and shade create the illusion of an infinite extension into space, fusing the world of the spectator with a world inhabited by the heroic figures of Classical mythology. The forms are grandiose; some are borne aloft on thick masses of cloud that in places cover the cornice. At one end, the wind-borne figure of Pallas forces downwards a tumbling mass of giants, involving the onlooker in the violent drama that takes place immediately above him. The decorative figures are themselves so vital that they seem to take part in the action.

This creation of a unified and spectacular vision inaugurated a new era in High Baroque ceiling decoration. Illusionism, and the breaking down of the barrier between the work of art and the spectator, are important Baroque principles. Yet within this unity are rich and diverse effects. The framework itself, painted in simulated stucco, in places weathered and cracked, is created from an immense variety of decorative details—shells, masks, dolphins, terms, feigned medallions in bronze. The structures at the corners are especially intricate, and it is these twisting figures that allow our eyes to move easily from one scene to another.

The framework also serves to divide the ceiling into five distinct areas, and each of the scenes painted along the coves demands to be looked at as an independent painting. Here the rich glow of Cortona's color, and his ability to breathe warmth and vitality into Classical myth and fable, may be most easily appreciated. The drunken Silenus sprawls in an exuberant composition illuminated by wonderful effects of flickering light, and, in the *Forge of Vulcan*, flashes of red and gold fall on antique armor.

The *gran salone* of the Palazzo Barberini was used for public receptions and entertainments, and the ceiling was intended to glorify the reigning Pope (Urban VIII) and the Barberini family. Again, Cortona's imagery broke new ground. Never before in Italy had courtly adulation been carried so far, nor the possibilities of the Baroque as an art of propaganda on behalf of the divine right of rulers been so systematically exploited. Domenichino, then in Naples, wrote that, from all accounts, it sounded more fitting for a secular prince than for a pope. Yet, although the central theme is clear, it is supported by erudite allusions.

The complex program was devised by Francesco Bracciolini, a favorite of Urban VIII. Bracciolini, already the author of a series of boring sycophantic poems in praise of members of the Barberini family, was well-versed in the art of flattery and had strong personal reasons for excelling himself on this occasion. Unfortunately the relevant poem has been lost, but an interpretation of the iconography was made by Girolamo Teti in 1642 in his *Aedes Barberini*.

The subject is an allegory of Divine Providence; Urban VIII, as her chosen agent, is shown as worthy of Immortality. In the

◄ Pietro da Cortona's fresco on the ceiling of the *gran salone* of the Palazzo Barberini, Rome; 1633–9

▲ The vault of the gallery in the Palazzo Farnese, Rome, by Annibale Carracci; fresco; between 1557 and 1600

Above right The *Triumph of Venice* by Paolo Veronese, a ceiling painting in the Sala del Maggior Consiglio, Palazzo Ducale, Venice; oil on canvas; 904×580cm (356×228in); 1583

central area, Divine Providence, borne aloft on clouds, commands Immortality to add the stellar crown to the three glittering bees who represent the Barberini coat of arms. The bees are surrounded by the laurel of immortality, carried by the theological virtues; held out above them are the papal tiara and the poet's crown (Urban VIII had a considerable reputation as a poet). The mythological scenes along the coving allude to the Pope's wisdom and virtues. Each is a detailed and carefully worked out allegory. At first sight their meaning seems fairly straightforward: the abandoned lust of Silenus and the satyrs are vanquished by the Pope's piety; his justice is represented by Hercules fighting the Vices; his dramatic war against heresy by Pallas destroying the giants. Other scenes refer to his encouragement of learning and to the blessings of peace and plenty. They could be interpreted by the more recondite at varying levels of precision and profundity; they seem

to have enjoyed reading into the frescoes precise references to individual members of the Barberini family.

In orchestrating so elaborate a display of literary and pictorial ideas, Pietro da Cortona turned back for guidance to the vault of the Farnese Gallery decorated by Annibale Carracci 30 years earlier. Most obviously dependent on Annibale are the simulated stucco framework, and the exuberant and sensuous response to Classical mythology; certain of the figures are direct derivations. Yet Pietro's ceiling is fully Baroque in the unity of his vision; the same sky unites the areas divided by the cornice in a way that is very different from the playful overlapping of layers of illusion in Annibale's work. It is also bound together by a sense of light and atmosphere that derives from Venetian models, particularly from Veronese. Cortona had visited Venice in 1637, and the dramatically foreshortened figures which fill the whole height

of his vault show a debt to a north Italian tradition of ceiling decoration. Cortona was perhaps particularly influenced by Veronese's *Triumph of Venice* in the Palazzo Ducale.

Cortona's works are the most spectacular performances of the Roman High Baroque, but his exuberance and daring illusionism were criticized by more classical artists. Slightly earlier (1629–31), Andrea Sacchi had frescoed another ceiling in the Barberini palace, illustrating the theme Divine Wisdom. In subject matter the two works are complementary. Sacchi's Divine Wisdom joins Cortona's Divine Providence and Immortality in praise of the Barberini family name. Yet Sacchi's illusionism is restrained, his composition clear and carefully balanced, and his figures relatively few. He aims for the classic qualities of restraint and simplicity, and his severity was to be answered by the tumultuous passion of Cortona. Both classical and Baroque styles were to be further developed throughout the century, at times opposing, at times complementing, one another.

HELEN LANGDON

scenes. The most attractive of Poussin's early paintings are Ovidian scenes, radiant in color, lyrical and delicately sensual, sometimes tinged with melancholy. Later, influenced by the antique statues and bas-reliefs he had studied in Rome and by the moral attitudes he had imbibed from a reading of Roman historians, Poussin moved towards a more solemn and austere style. He came to believe that art should appeal to the mind and not to the senses; he studied expression and gesture, and arranged the figures in his paintings parallel to the plane in clear, mathematically precise relationships so the spectator might study the significance of each participant. In one sense we "read" Poussin's late paintings as though we are reading a book; often the beauty is the abstract beauty of geometrically organized space. Yet although Poussin sacrificed spontaneity and warmth, his discipline was imposed on a naturally passionate temperament; it is perhaps this tension that prevented his works from appearing cold or insipid.

Poussin and another French artist, Claude Lorrain (1600–82), perfected a kind of classical landscape painting, known as ideal landscape, that had been introduced by Annibale Carracci. Claude came from Nancy, and spent most of his working life in Rome. Claude's landscapes were based on an intense study of nature, of the Roman Campagna, and of the coastline around Naples. Yet his intention was not naturalistic; Claude transformed the Campagna into an ideal world of the imagination, a setting for the pastoral life described in Virgil's poems; he evoked the mood of the Golden Age, a haunting vision of a lost era of peace and delight. It is the all-enveloping light that both unifies the space and creates the lyrical mood. In the harbor scenes, the path of the sun's rays creates effects of theatrical glamor; more often, a softer light shimmers over distances that melt into infinite space, or pinpoints tenderly depicted naturalistic detail in intimately enclosed foregrounds. His compositions are formal, and aim at harmony and balance; Classical buildings play an important part and there is usually some Biblical or mythological subject.

Algardi was the most successful Italian sculptor after Bernini. His most satisfying works are his portrait busts; less vivacious than Bernini's, they have a detailed surface naturalism and attractive solidity. Duquesnoy, who arrived in Rome in 1618, executed his *S. Susanna* in 1629–33 (S. Maria di Loreto, Rome), a religious statue consciously based on the Antique. He specialized in small reliefs and statuettes of cupids and putti.

The late Baroque style was predominantly one of fresco-painting; in the middle years of the century there had been a pause in the decoration of churches, but from 1670 onwards many domes and ceilings were frescoed. The main characteristics of the late Baroque style were that the whole ceiling was treated as a single unit; there were no longer many painted architectural frameworks; the individual forms were no longer massive and robust but rather graceful and elegant—they blended into one another and were illuminated by a more diffuse and flickering light. The beginning of this development

can be seen in the ceiling fresco of the church of the Gesù, showing the *Triumph of the Name of Jesus*, painted by Giovanni Battista Gaulli (1639–1709) between 1674 and 1679. The ceiling is executed in a bewildering mixture of painting, real stucco, and painted stucco, of real and simulated architecture; the whole roof appears open to the sky, and clouds seem to spill into the nave. The worshiper seems granted a vision of the glory of heaven.

The latest development in Baroque illusionism was the fresco of the *Apotheosis of St Ignatius* on the nave ceiling of S. Ignazio, Rome (1691–4). The painter was Fra Andrea Pozzo (1642–1709) who specialized in the virtuoso handling of perspective. Here, feigned architecture, painted in perspective, seems to continue the real architecture of the church and so create the effect of an imaginary upper story. Yet the illusion only works from one point in the nave; if we move from here, the structure seems to topple around us.

From the mid 1670s, painting was dominated by Carlo Maratti (1625–1713) who resisted the extravagances of Gaulli and Pozzo; he concentrated on the plastic mass and volume of the individual figure and became famous for a series of Raphaelesque madonnas.

The most interesting developments in late Baroque architecture took place in Turin. Guarino Guarini (1624–83) from Modena settled in Turin in 1666 and there produced a number of buildings of fantastic geometric complexity. He was influenced by Borromini, but made a more deliberate attempt to startle and confuse. The most exciting features of his churches are their domes; these have none of the robust vigor of the Roman dome, but are instead light and diaphanous. The dome of S. Lorenzo (1666–90) is vaulted by crossing ribs arranged like an eight-pointed star; in the dome of the Chapel of the Holy Shroud (1667–90), the ribs create a still more complex lattice-like effect. Guarini's style influenced the development of the Rococo in southern Germany.

Spain. Seventeenth-century Spanish art was strongly influenced by the Italian Baroque, but nonetheless retained a markedly individual character. Many of the greatest of the Counter-Reformation mystics—St Theresa, St Ignatius Loyola, St Francis Xavier, St John of the Cross—had been Spanish: saintly visions and ecstasies are treated by 17th-century Spanish artists with an extraordinary emotional directness, almost as though part of every day life. The artists aimed to make supernatural events real and comprehensible; their works were intended to appeal to the fervid and superstitious piety of the masses. There are few female nudes, few mythological paintings; references to the Antique seem to mock the great Classical tradition.

This intense piety inspired the peculiarly Spanish tradition of highly detailed and realistic colored wooden sculptures of Christ and Mary and various saints. Made to be carried

Triumph at the Name of Jesus by Gaulli, a fresco on the ceiling of the Gesù, Rome; 1674–9

through the streets at religious processions they have, at their best, the moving simplicity of appeal that may be associated with popular art. Gregorio Fernandez (c1576–1636) was the greatest sculptor of the Castilian school; his works are harshly realistic and express powerful emotions with deep sincerity; the carving has an almost Gothic sharpness and rhythm.

This tendency towards realism was strengthened by the influx of Caravaggism in the early years of the century. In the best works of Francisco Ribalta (1565–1628), the first painter of the new style, mystic experience is treated with a warm and human naturalism that contrasts sharply with the flickering insubstantiality of El Greco's visionary style. A remarkably solid and athletic angel appears before the quietly startled eyes of his St Francis in Ecstasy (Prado, Madrid); the details of his dress and his sparsely furnished cell are described with a precise and careful naturalism.

The most important source of Caravaggism in Spain was, however, the works of Jusepe de Ribera (1591–1652). Ribera left Spain as a young man. He arrived in Rome c1615, where he was profoundly influenced by Caravaggio. He had settled in Naples by 1616, and the Spanish viceroy sent many of his works to Spain. His realism was coarser and more aggressively earthy and vital than Caravaggio's; his brushstrokes create a richer and solider surface texture. He was particularly attracted to themes of torture and violence; the darkness and gloom that hang over his paintings is characteristic of Neapolitan Caravaggism.

Francisco de Zurbaran (1598–1664) moved away from a Riberesque realism towards a more deliberately archaic style suffused by an ascetic and unworldly religious feeling. The darkness of Zurbaran's paintings, which suggests the mystical union of the soul with God, is often reminiscent of the passionate poetry of St John of the Cross. Zurbaran simplified his forms and compositions: his forms have a sculptural, almost crystalline sharpness and precision, and the poetic Caravaggesque lighting, the abstract settings, and the lack of movement and depth create a haunting quality of stillness and remoteness. His figures appear suspended before us as though images from another world.

The earliest works of Diego Velazquez (1599–1660) were Caravaggesque genre scenes. Yet they have a profundity and solemnity that transforms their subject matter and already reveals Velazquez' personal genius. In The Water-Seller (Wellington Museum, London) of 1619, a young boy accepts a glass of water from an old man; the intensity with which each component of the composition is conceived, the delicate relationship between man and boy, and the stillness and beauty of the lighting suggest that we are witnesses to an almost religious rite.

In 1625 Velazquez became court painter and transferred his intense observation to the life of the Spanish court. Most of his subsequent paintings are portraits of the royal family and

of the court dwarfs and buffoons. He visited Italy twice, in 1629–31 and again in 1649–51: as a result of his knowledge of Italian painting, particularly Venetian, he developed a freer and more expressive brushwork and a greater interest in light and atmosphere. The stately formality of his royal portraits owed much to the example of Titian.

Yet as a court portraitist Velazquez had little in common with his contemporaries; his portraits have none of the flamboyant self-confidence of Rubens, nor the courtly grace and elegance of Van Dyck. Velazquez approached his sitters with greater detachment, albeit a sensitive and thoughtful one. He created remote images of absolute power, and recorded the stiffly formal atmosphere of the Spanish court. Yet somehow his sitters retain their humanity and look anxiously, even tentatively at the world around them. There is the suggestion of an elusive personality within the regal trappings.

In the 1630s, particularly in a group of equestrian Titianesque portraits, Velazquez' paintings had a robust vitality that brings them close to the Baroque. The later works were more muted and delicate. The Royal Family, popularly known as the "Maids of Honor" of c1656 (Prado, Madrid) illustrates his ability to combine stiff formality with intimacy. He shows himself painting a large canvas; the Infanta Margarita turns to look at the King and Queen who are reflected in the mirror; they would be standing outside the painting, in the real space of the spectator.

In these late years, Velazquez executed a series of portraits of the royal children who, like the Infanta Margarita, combine regality with a truly childlike quality; there is often an effect of pathos created by the stiff clothes, proud manners, and the suppressed playfulness of expression. In this period, his color harmonies of reds, blues, and silvery grays acquired a new richness. His remarkable brushwork attained its greatest freedom: dry and flickering, it makes a surface pattern independent of form, and creates both color and atmosphere.

In the second half of the century, Spanish painters moved towards a more emotional Baroque style. The religious painting of Bartolome Murillo (1617–82) have none of Zurbaran's austerity; instead he turned for inspiration to Titian and Rubens, although his works are sweeter and more delicate than theirs, his muted colors and soft brushwork more overtly charming. The movement towards the Baroque was continued by Juan de Valdes Leal (1622–90) and Claudio Coello (1642–93); in their works the dramatic movement of many figures, and the illusionistic treatment of space, indicate the direct influence of the Italian Baroque.

In architecture, the influence from the Baroque came late but in an extreme form. The most Baroque work in Spain is the Transparente in Toledo Cathedral by Narciso Tome (fl. 1715–42), completed in 1732, which carried the illusionism of Bernini's St Theresa still further. A richly sculptured altar is the setting for a glass case containing the Blessed Sacrament; it is lit from windows above and behind which have been let into the Gothic vault of the ambulatory and which are invisible to the spectator. The windows are surrounded by sculptured figures so that the whole space is drawn into the total effect.

For the most part, however, the Spanish Baroque is a style of surface decoration; Jose Benito de Churriguera (1665–1725) gave his name to an exuberant, often frenzied, use of twisting columns, scrolls, and thick and curving moldings that encrust the surfaces beneath.

France. Two factors determined the development of the arts in 17th-century France: the nature of the centralized autocracy of Louis XIV, which had been prepared for by the ministries of Mazarin and Richelieu (c1630–60), and a deeply rooted classical tradition. In the period from 1630 to 1660, French classicism achieved its most perfect expression in all the arts. In painting and architecture, the same pattern tended to be repeated; an influx of new ideas from Italy and Flanders invigorated the native school, but the most Baroque elements were invariably toned down and transmuted into a classical idiom. Baroque excesses, such as overwhelming illusionism, the fusion of the arts, and the emphasis on surprise and extravagant shapes, were rejected. After 1661, when Louis XIV began to rule as absolute monarch, France entered a spectacularly successful period in her history. The state now controlled every aspect of life, including the arts; these were efficiently directed, through the establishment or reorganization of academies, to one end: that of glorifying the King, the visible symbol of the power of the State. This state domination naturally did not encourage individuality; the achievement of this period lay rather in the creation, by a vast team of artists and craftsmen, of the spectacular decorative style at Versailles, whose influence was to spread through Europe.

The architects responsible for the creation of French classical architecture were Jacques Lemercier, (c1584–1654), François Mansart (1598–1666), and Louis Levau (1612–70). Lemercier, who had studied in Rome, designed the church of the Sorbonne, begun in 1635; this introduced to Paris a Roman facade ultimately derived from the Gesù; it was the first of a group of domed churches influenced by the Roman Baroque.

The purest expression of the French classical spirit in architecture, however, occurred in the works of Mansart, who had little interest in the Italian Baroque. The château of Maisons-Laffitte (1642–6) is conceived as a single plastic mass in three dimensions. Its effect depends on the intellectually satisfying relationship of the clear-cut rectangular blocks from which it is composed, and the detail is sharp, restrained, yet elegant. The quality of lucidity and the harmony of the parts is characteristic of Mansart's classical style. Like Poussin's paintings, it appeals to the mind as much as to the eye; Mansart had none of Borromini's interest in movement or surprise.

The break with the tired Mannerist tradition of the early years of the 17th century was brought about by French artists who traveled to Italy and responded to both Caravaggio and the Carracci. The most influential and interesting of the French Caravaggisti was Valentin de Boulogne (1594–1632) who settled in Rome c1612. He painted typical Caravagg-

The château of Maisons-Lafitte by François Mansart; 1642–6

esque themes—elegant musicians and soldiers idling in taverns—yet, unusually, he does not coarsen his subjects. He seems to have responded in an intensely personal manner to the sense of sadness and solitude in Caravaggio's works, and his own paintings are graceful, melancholic, and full of an awareness of the fragility of human contact.

In 1627 Simon Vouet, who in Rome had moved away from a Caravaggesque style towards Reni and Lanfranco, returned to France after 15 years in Italy. In France his style became more classical and he became the head of a large workshop and the founder of the great traditions of French decorative art; Charles Lebrun (1619–90) was his pupil. Vouet's decorative style draws on both the Roman Baroque and on Venetian traditions—particularly the works of Veronese. Yet these sources are toned down to satisfy the demands of French classicism.

Philippe de Champaigne (1602–74), a Flemish artist, arrived in France in 1621 with a painterly style indebted to Rubens and van Dyck. Later, under the influence of the Jansenists and of Poussin, he moved towards a style of almost startling simplicity and severity; his works are restrained and delicate in feeling, his color limited, his backgrounds bare.

Further interesting developments took place outside Paris over this period. Georges de La Tour (1593–1652), who worked in Lorraine, created one of the most personal forms of Caravaggism, possibly influenced by the Dutch Caravaggisti; like them he specialized in night scenes lit by candles. In his later works, as in the *St Sebastian tended by St Irene* of c1650 (Louvre, Paris), the surfaces are clear and smooth and all descriptive detail eliminated; the figures are clearly arranged and the poetic play of light creates a deeply moving atmosphere of stillness and contemplation. In a classical spirit, La Tour has distilled the poetry of Caravaggio's light while rejecting his violence and naturalism.

A similarly classicizing spirit was fundamental to the remarkable peasant paintings of Louis Lenain (c1593–1648). Comparable subjects were painted by Dutch artists working in Rome in the early 17th century, but Lenain did not share their tendency to satire and humor; his peasants are depicted with an exceptional dignity and even solemnity. His compositions are lucid; the figures are usually still and rarely seem to communicate with one another; they have an air of hushed watchfulness and expectancy that creates a strangely enigmatic atmosphere.

In the 1660s and 1670s, a team of architects, sculptors, painters, and craftsmen, controlled by Charles Lebrun (1619–90) who, as Director of the Royal Academy and of the Gobelins tapestry manufactory, virtually dictated the course of the arts, created for Louis XIV the splendors of the palace at Versailles. By this date, the artistic center of Europe had been transferred from Rome to Paris; this was symbolized by the rejection of Bernini's plans for the Louvre which he had made a journey to Paris to prepare in 1665. The new self-confidence of the French in art may be seen in their preference for the strictly classical facade for the Louvre, designed by Levau and Claude Perrault (1667–70).

In 1669 Levau designed the new château at Versailles to replace Louis XIII's small shooting box. Levau's design was, again, for a classical building which depended for its effect on the grandeur of clear-cut masses. The sheer scale of later developments at Versailles, however, show a movement towards the quality of spectacular display we associate with the Baroque; the garden facade faces the magnificent formal gardens by Le Nôtre in which nature itself, controlled and ordered, is pressed into the service of the King. Vast additions were made to the palace itself by Jules Hardouin Mansart (1646–1708). His most successful work was in the interior; the Galerie des Glaces has a curved ceiling covered with painted and stucco decoration, the walls glitter with mirrors. The lavishness is Baroque, but compared with Italian decoration the illusionism is restrained and the compartments on walls and ceiling remain sharply separate from one another.

The gardens were decorated with fountains and statues commissioned from leading sculptors, of whom François Girardon (1628–1715) and Antoine Coysevox (1640–1720) were the most important. Girardon's style was severely classical, based on a study of Hellenistic sculpture and of the compositions of Poussin; Coysevox seems to have repressed a natural tendency towards the Baroque in order to conform to the taste of his time; his later works are more Baroque.

In the last two decades of the century, a tendency towards the Baroque became increasingly marked. This was encouraged by the more emotionally religious atmosphere and wilder extravagance of the now declining court. The leading architect of this period was Hardouin Mansart; his forms remained classical, but he strove towards increasingly grandiose effects and a richer grouping of the masses. The church of the Invalides, Paris, (1680–91) is Baroque in its accent on the center of the facade and in the richness of the dome; inside, the inner dome opens to reveal a second painted dome lit by concealed windows—a typically Baroque effect.

In sculpture, the works of Pierre Puget (1620–94), who had worked in Italy from 1640 to 1643, showed a direct influence

from Bernini. In painting, there was a powerful Baroque movement; an interest in Venetian and Flemish color, in highly emotional effects and diagonally based compositions, replaced the stress the Academy had laid on drawing and lucidity. Charles de Lafosse (1636–1716) and Jean Jouvenet (1644–1717) produced religious and historical paintings truly Baroque in feeling; Antoine Coypel (1661–1722) based his ceiling fresco for the chapel at Versailles (1708) on Gaulli's ceiling for the Gesù. Finally, the portraits of Hyacinthe Rigaud (1659–1743), which use the Baroque accessories of column and rich curtain introduced into portrait painting by van Dyck, are brilliant in color and flamboyant in their general effect.

Flanders. In the 17th century the sourthern Netherlands remained Catholic; the art of this period has an opulent richness

The church of the Invalides, Paris, by Jules-Hardouin Mansart; 1680–91

and grandeur very different from the directness of Dutch art. After the religious strife of the 16th century, the Church was anxious that art should celebrate its power in this most northern stronghold in Europe. Another fruitful source of patronage were the archdukes and governor-generals with their court in Brussels.

In Peter Paul Rubens (1577–1640), both Church and State found an artist outstandingly gifted to satisfy their demands for large-scale decoration and glorification. Rubens' art broke decisively with the northern tradition for small-scale works; his art revealed to his contemporaries the immense possibilities of powerfully naturalistic art. The art of Rubens typifies the Baroque; in it may be found all the characteristics we associate with that style. It is full of power, massive gesture, and dynamic movement; the color is glowing and radiant, the brushwork free and expressive. It is based on an intense study of nature, and given an exuberant vitality by his feeling for the sensuous beauty of surface and texture, of flesh,

Preliminary sketch for the Madonna and Child adored by Saints in the Royal Museum of Fine Arts, Antwerp, by Rubens; oil on wood; 79×55cm (31×22in); 1627–8. Staatliche Museen, Berlin

of rich fabrics, of grass, and of water. An abundant confidence in the power of the body, a belief in energy that expresses a religious gratitude for life, is at the center of his style, manifested both in the joyful festivity of his altarpieces and in the lustrous skins of his female nudes.

Rubens spent eight years in Italy (1600–8), where he studied an immense range of Italian art. His aim, like that of Annibale Carracci, was to return to and reinterpret the monumental style of the High Renaissance. Before he returned to Antwerp, he had already produced several key works in the development of the Baroque; his portrait *The Duke of Lerma* (Prado, Madrid) introduced the Baroque equestrian portrait: the horse is shown head-on, boldly foreshortened, and apparently about to break through the picture plane. In his *Madonna adored by Saints* (Musée de Peinture et de Sculpture, Grenoble), the billowing draperies, the movement of light and air, and the ecstatic expressions of the saints anticipate effects developed by Giovanni Lanfranco and Gian Lorenzo Bernini. His interest in Venetian color became characteristic of the High Baroque.

In Antwerp, Rubens rapidly moved towards a fully developed Baroque style. By the 1620s he had made his most distinctive contribution to the Baroque—the concept of a dynamic thread of movement which runs through his compositions. The altarpiece *Madonna and Child adored by Saints* of 1628 (Royal Museum of Fine Arts, Antwerp) rejects the High Renaissance principle of symmetry and balance; instead, Rubens creates a sweeping movement which begins in the bottom right-hand corner and curves through three dimensions up to the enthroned Virgin. This movement into the composition is answered by the outward movement of St John, so that the Virgin's throne is framed by a rich oval of figures. The impression is one of unity and movement; an all-pervading rhythm binds the figures together, and they seem to blend and merge into an inextricable whole. The dominant rhythm is accentuated by the billowing draperies, dramatic gestures, and expressive brushwork.

In the 1620s, the sheer scale of Rubens' achievement was overwhelming; Rubens himself commented that he was better fitted by temperament for large undertakings than small. He did many altarpieces, 39 ceiling paintings for the Jesuit church in Antwerp, designs for tapestries, and a series of decorative works for Marie de' Medici. The latter inaugurated a new type of political allegory in which historical, mythological, and Biblical figures mix or alternate, and in which abstract ideas are made live and concrete. In the 1630s, he received important commissions from Charles I of England and Philip IV of Spain.

In the last years of Rubens' life, the power of his Baroque style gave way to gentler rhythms and a more lyrical and romantic mood. This is particularly apparent in his landscapes, inspired first of all by a characteristically northern interest in precisely observed reality. Yet Rubens also had a feeling for the grandeur and abundance of nature; his paintings show immense, fertile plains that sweep into the distance,

An Autumn Landscape with a View of the Château de Steen by Rubens; oil on wood; 131×292cm (52×115in); c1636. National Gallery, London

full of activity and detail: intense effects of light often transform them into romantic visions.

Rubens dominated Flemish painting, and most famous painters of the period were connected with his studio. Frans Snyders (1579–1657) and Jan Fyt (1611–61) specialized in still-life and animal painting. The most famous of Rubens' pupils was Anthony van Dyck (1599–1641). He was Rubens' leading assistant from 1617 to 1620, and was deeply influenced by him. Later, he spent seven years in Italy where he developed a passion for the works of Titian; his religious works show a response to the emotional pathos of Guido Reni. From 1628 to 1632 he was back in Antwerp; from 1632 to 1641 he worked in England at the court of Charles I.

By temperament, van Dyck was a very different kind of artist from Rubens; his art is characterized above all by elegance and refinement. His greatest contribution to European art was the creation of a new mood in portrait painting; his portraits of Genoese and English aristocrats gave visual form to a poetic ideal of aristocracy. In England, his success lay in his sensitivity to the poetic sensibilities of those around him. He painted Charles I several times, as warrior, in robes of state, *à la chasse*; each painting was a subtle variation on the theme of divine right, of effortless authority. His portraits of the Caroline courtiers are less sumptuous than those of the Genoese nobility; an air of dream-like unreality seems to hover over them, and they recreate the atmosphere of the masque and pastoral so fashionable at the court.

Van Dyck brought to the art of portrait painting an abundant fertility of invention, only paralleled by Titian; he created new formulae for family portraits, for double portraits, both full and half length, for equestrian portraits and for full-

Charles I by van Dyck; oil on canvas; 266×207cm (105×81in); c1635. Louvre, Paris

lengths set on terraces or within landscape frameworks.

Jacob Jordaens (1593–1678) was probably associated with Rubens' studio from 1618. His most distinctive contribution was in the field of genre painting; he specialized in painting scenes of feasts, and his compositions are crowded, full of detail and humorous incidents.

The most interesting painters outside the circle of Rubens were Adriaen Brouwer (c1605–38) and David Teniers (1610–90). Brouwer specialized in peasant paintings, and in depicting the interiors of murky taverns. Often the atmosphere is menacingly violent; Brouwer's peasants snarl and fight like animals. Teniers' genre scenes are more decorative and light-hearted.

Holland. The northern Netherlands, unlike the south, revolted against their Spanish overlords and by 1648 had won their independence. The new society was essentially middle class and predominantly Protestant; there was, therefore, little demand for vast decorative works or for altarpieces and statues. These bourgeois patrons were more attracted by small-scale works, realistic, simple, and direct in approach. The most important large-scale works were group portraits: of the civic guard companies, the regents of hospitals and guilds, or the aldermen of towns.

The full Baroque style, then, gained only a small foothold in Holland. Dutch architecture of the period was sober, classical, and restrained. The most important architect was Jacob van Campen (1595–1657); his Mauritshuis at the Hague (1633–44) is small and domestic by contemporary standards, the plain brick walls articulated by a series of correct giant pilasters and pediment. The grander Town Hall of Amsterdam (1648–55), designed as a monument to the prosperity and power of the new country, shows nonetheless the same restraint and lack of ornament.

The greatest originality of Dutch 17th-century painters lay in their realistic subject matter; for the first time, painters set out to record every aspect of the world around them. They excelled in landscape, still life, portraiture, genre scenes, animal painting, marine painting, and church interiors. Artists tended to specialize in one kind of subject matter—sometimes even more narrowly; there are specialists in moonlit scenes, snow scenes, as well as in general landscapes. The main towns tended to be centers for different kinds of painting—Haarlem for landscape, Delft for genre. The century's art was not dominated by great individuals; Rembrandt remained uncharacteristic, and did not dictate the development of painting as Rubens did in Flanders.

In the 1620s, a group of artists who had traveled in Italy, centered on Utrecht, and introduced aspects of Caravaggio's style into Dutch painting. They made popular dramatic contrasts of light and dark, and often painted nocturnal scenes with artificial light sources. They specialized in large-scale figures of musicians, drinkers, or violinists, characterized by a boisterous gaiety and a directness of appeal: these figures often reach towards the spectator through a window or door.

The Baroque spontaneity of these Utrecht paintings influenced Frans Hals (c1580–1666), particularly in a series of genre paintings from the 1620s. Hals came originally from Flanders; he worked in Haarlem throughout his life, almost exclusively as a portrait painter. His portraits are remarkable for their bold directness and informality. He excelled in capturing a fleeting expression, most often one full of vivacious energy; he is popularly best known for his paintings of smiles and laughter—witness the famous *Laughing Cavalier* of 1624 (Wallace Collection, London). *Isaac Massa*, painted in 1626, (Art Gallery of Ontario, Toronto) seems just to have turned in response to some event outside the painting. His pose is relaxed and casual; the composition is based on a pattern of diagonals. Liveliness of pose and expression were further enhanced by the virtuoso freedom of Hals' brushwork. In his lifetime, Hals was most famous for a series of group portraits, executed between 1616 and 1639, of the local militia units. Earlier group portraits tend to show rather dull rows of heads all on the same plane; Hals' are more subtly grouped, the strongly individualized figures arranged in lively and varied poses; the compositions are organized in depth, and unified by dramatic diagonals. In the second part of his career, Hals' portraits became more somber and restrained.

Landscape, still life, and genre underwent a similar stylistic development. In the early years of the century, paintings were full of brightly colored realistic details; the compositions, however, were artificial, and the artists tended to use a high viewpoint to include as many details as possible. Landscapes were full of human activity, and still lifes showed a medley of domestic articles. Around 1620, a school of landscape artists in Haarlem—most important were Jan van Goyen (1596–1656), Esaias van de Velde (c1591–1630), and Salomon van Ruysdael (c1600–70)—began to use simpler compositions and to allow nature itself to dominate man. They concentrated on the sky and stretches of water, and unified their compositions by atmosphere; often their colors were a subtle range of grays and grayish greens. For the first time unidealized, natural beauty became the subject of the landscape painter; yet these paintings do not lack poetry, which resides in the purity of perception and in the beautiful effects of atmosphere and space.

In still lifes of the 1620s and 1630s, particularly in the paintings of Pieter Claesz. (1596–1661) and Willem Claesz. Heda (1594–1680/2), there was a similar tonal treatment; simple subjects—a glass, a herring, a loaf of bread—were clearly grouped. Dutch still life had none of the florid abundance of Flemish; they depended rather on the reassuring pleasures of pure perception.

In the second half of the century, landscape painting became more grandiose and monumental; the colors became stronger, the compositions more firmly structured around a

Laughing Cavalier by Frans Hals; oil on canvas; 86×69cm (34×27in); 1624. Wallace Collection, London

ÆTA·SVÆ·26
Aº·1624·

balance of horizontals and verticals, and the mood more dramatic. The great artists of this generation were Aelbert Cuyp (1620–91) whose landscapes are characterized by a hazy golden sunlight, Philips Koninck (1619–88), who specialized in panoramic landscapes of immense spaciousness, and Jacob van Ruisdael (1628/9–82). No other Dutch painter had so true a sense of the grandeur and heroism of nature; Ruisdael's landscapes are full of massive trees, great rocks, rushing waterfalls, and desolate marshes; they are permeated by a sense of the growth and decay of nature, of the majestic movement of clouds, light, and atmosphere.

Still lifes of this period showed more luxurious objects— silver vessels, precious glasses, exotic carpets. Willem Kalf (1622–93) gave them a sense of mystery and glamor by using glowing colors against deeply shadowed backgrounds.

Genre painting reached its greatest heights with Jan Vermeer van Delft (1632–75). Most of his paintings show quiet scenes of domestic interiors or townscapes. Unlike many of his contemporaries, he had little interest in anecdote; often he showed single figures, strangely remote, absorbed on some trivial task—letter-reading, perhaps, or pouring milk. The *Young Woman with a Water Jug*, of c1665, (Metropolitan Museum, New York) has an attractive freshness and all the charm of apparent simplicity. Yet the more we study it, the more we see how carefully organized and selected the objects are, and how precisely located in space; how carefully the horizontals, verticals, rectangles and round forms are balanced. Vermeer's is, then, an art of unusual discipline and formal harmony—yet the light, in this case a cool clear daylight, makes his works intensely poetic too.

Pieter de Hooch (1629–c1685), another Delft artist, painted domestic interiors and courtyards. He was attracted by more elaborate spatial effects, and often showed vistas leading from one room into another. Jan Steen (1626–79), who worked in many different centers, painted genre scenes packed with humorous incident and full of allusions to old proverbs, emblems, and theatrical traditions; his compositions have a Baroque vitality, and are often dependent on crossing diagonals.

The greatest painter in Holland in the 17th century was Rembrandt Harmensz. van Rijn (1606–69). The son of a miller, he was born in Leiden, where he entered the university; but he left to become a painter. In 1631 or 1632, he moved to Amsterdam where he quickly achieved an international reputation and material prosperity. However, after the death of his first wife, Saskia, in 1642, he was constantly beset by financial and personal difficulties; after 1645 he lived with Hendrickje Stoffels, but both she and his children died before him.

Rembrandt drew, painted, and etched incessantly; he stretched the resources of all three media to their limits. His drawings were usually impulsive, direct studies from nature which provided the stimulus to his imagination; although he

The Presentation in the Temple by Rembrandt; oil on panel; 61×48cm (24×19in); 1631. Royal Museum of Art (Mauritshuis), The Hague

Young Woman with a Water Jug by Vermeer; oil on canvas; 46×42cm (18×17in); c1665. Metropolitan Museum, New York

used the etching needle with unprecedented spontaneity, his etchings were often as elaborately worked as his paintings.

Rembrandt's earliest paintings were small-scale, dramatic crowd scenes. In the 1630s he went through a flamboyant Baroque phase, perhaps in a deliberate attempt to emulate Rubens; his compositions were sometimes based on the latter, and his forms had a sense of weight and mass that suggest the latter's influence. His subject-pictures of this period are dramatic, full of violent and exaggerated gestures and expressions; he showed a romantic taste for exotic materials and precious metals. His self-portraits and the portraits of his family were self-confident and almost swaggering. The *Night Watch* of 1642 (Rijksmuseum, Amsterdam), which shows the parade of a militia company, sums up this Baroque phase. The leaders of the company seem to stride out of the painting; diagonal movements zigzag into depth; the lighting has a theatrical glamor.

In the 1640s, Rembrandt's style became quieter and more restrained; he rejected Baroque display in favor of a classical simplicity, and attempted to communicate a sense of inner life. He often painted scenes of the Holy Family or from the youth of Christ, tender and lyrical in feeling, and he took a greater interest in landscape.

After 1648 the depth of Rembrandt's understanding of the subtlety and complexity of human feeling, and his unique ability to communicate a sense of man's spiritual as opposed to his worldly or active life, became more highly developed. The basis of Rembrandt's art had, from the beginning, been chiaroscuro; by the late 1640s, it had become a means of creating mood and emotion and suggesting spiritual values. In the portrait of a *Woman with an Ostrich Fan* (National Gallery of Art, Washington, D.C.), it is the intangible play of light and shade that creates the quality of watchful introspection; the left-hand side of the face receives the strongest light, while deep shadows veil all but the eye on the right. The sitter seems withdrawn from the spectator, sunk in a private world of meditation; Rembrandt shows none of the Baroque artist's interest in a speaking likeness.

As a Biblical painter, Rembrandt created a new kind of art by his intense sympathy and ability to grasp the essence of a human situation. In the late period, his works became increasingly somber; often he chose tragic subjects. His *Jacob blessing the sons of Joseph* of 1656 (Gemäldegalerie Alte Meister, Kassel) shows how far he had moved from the Baroque; there is no action or external excitement. Instead Rembrandt concentrates on the delicate relationship between the figures, on expressing its significance to each participant. The intensely spiritual atmosphere is created by the glow of light that seems to emanate from the figures themselves.

England. English painting in the 17th century made little contact with either the Baroque or classical styles that had developed in Italy. The dominating influence on painters of the period was van Dyck; the best portrait-painters—there was very little painting of any other kind—who were influenced both by him and the Venetians were William Dobson, (1610–46) and Sir Peter Lely (1618–80). Dobson's portraits have a particular interest because they commemorate Charles I's court during the troubled years of the Civil War (1642–46). Although owing much to van Dyck, his mature style was more Baroque; the paint is thickly applied, the backgrounds often stormy and crowded with accessories. Dobson thrusts the sitter towards the spectator by cutting off the design below the knees. In mood, his portraits have none of van Dyck's refinement; they are heartier and more robustly English.

Sir Peter Lely, a Dutch artist, had arrived in London by 1647, possibly by 1641. His style was more heavily dependent on van Dyck than was Dobson's; particularly in his portraits of women, he moved towards a stereotype of voluptuous and languid beauty. His late works often suggest a pastoral charm and prettiness, that leads on to the Rococo.

A watered-down version of the Baroque decorative style, based on a use of illusionistic architecture, was introduced to England by the Italian Antonio Verrio (c1639–1707) and developed by Sir James Thornhill (1676–1734) in the Painted Hall at Greenwich (1708–27).

In architecture also, England was isolated from European developments. In the first half of the century, the style of the Italian Renaissance was introduced by Inigo Jones (1573–1652). The Queen's House at Greenwich, begun in 1615, and the Banqueting House, Whitehall, of 1619–22, were inspired by the style of Palladio; both are restrained and classical buildings. Sir Christopher Wren (1632–1723) was influenced by Jones' Palladianism, by the Baroque (he had met Bernini in Paris in 1665), and by recent developments in Dutch architecture. After the fire of London in 1666, Wren was commissioned to rebuild St Paul's Cathedral (1675–1712) and 51 City churches; he also worked on Chelsea and Greenwich hospitals and Hampton Court. Wren's style, predominantly classical, was tempered by Baroque elements. The massive dome of St Paul's is classical; the western facade is Baroque—most obviously in the towers with their contrasts of convex and concave.

A highly original and eccentric development of the Baroque aspects of Wren's style was produced by his pupil, Nicholas Hawksmoor (1661–1736). He was closely associated with Sir John Vanbrugh (1664–1726) whose Blenheim Palace (1705–20) has the colossal scale and theatrical self-confidence of the Baroque; all the forms are weighty, massive, and often deliberately discordant, and the detailing is original and highly personal.

HELEN LANGDON

Bibliography. Blunt, A.F. *Art and Architecture in France: 1500–1700*, Harmondsworth (1980). Gerson, H. and ter Kuile, E.H. *Art and Architecture in Belgium: 1600–1800*, Harmondsworth (1960). Kitson, M. *The Age of Baroque*, London (1966). Kubler, G.A. and Soria, M. *Art and Architecture in Spain and Portugal and their American Dominions: 1500–1800*, Harmondsworth (1959). Rosenberg, Slive, S., and ter Kuile, E.H. *Dutch Art and Architecture: 1600–1800*, Harmondsworth (1977). Sewter, A.C. *Baroque and Rococo Art*, London (1972). Tapié, V. L. (trans. Williamson, A.R.) *The Age of Grandeur, Baroque and Classicism in Europe*, London (1960). Waterhouse, E.K. *Italian Baroque Painting*, London (1962). Waterhouse, E.K. *Painting in Britain: 1530–1790*, Harmondsworth (1978). Wittkower, R. *Art and Architecture in Italy: 1600–1750*, Harmondsworth (1980). Wölfflin, H. (trans. Hottinger, M.D.) *Principles of Art History*, London (1932). Wölfflin, H. (trans. Simon, K.) *Renaissance and Baroque*, London (1964).

38

THE ROCOCO

The high altar of the abbey of Weltenburg with St George by Egid Quirin Asam
1716–36 (see page 728)

THE Rococo began as a purely decorative style in France in the early years of the 18th century. Its distinguishing features can be generalized into three headings: flatness and lack of three-dimensionality in the decoration, abundance of curved *rocaille* elements twisting into back-to-back curls, and asymmetrical design. Many forms are taken from the architectural features of the French Baroque, but these are flattened out and reduced in scale.

Because the Rococo was essentially a decorative style it produced great activity in the fields of smaller decorative objects, such as silver and porcelain. Many porcelain manufacturers were set up, often at the instigation of a monarch, for example those at Sèvres, Meissen, Nymphenburg, and Capodimonte, inspired by technical advances as well as by the decorative possibilities of the material. Furniture became less architectural and overbearing, and more useful, practical, and infinitely prettier. The great *ébenistes* (cabinet-makers) working in France during the 18th century—J.F. Oeben (*c*1720–63), Jacques Dubois (*c*1693–1763), Charles Cressent (1685–1768), and J.H. Riesener (1734–1806)—are perhaps the most consummate and representative artists of the Rococo. In England, the Rococo was never much more than a type of furniture design.

In southern Germany, the Rococo was something quite different from the new style developed in France; it culls from and develops the Baroque rather than trying to get away from it. There is little connection with French ideas—the main influence comes from the Italian Baroque, often received by way of Austria. Native Italian Rococo is also a decorative development of the Italian Baroque, used in many thousands of palaces and villas built in Italy during the 18th century. Official church and court circles encouraged the more subdued architectural style of Baroque classicism.

The French decorative style and the German decorative style are equally important aspects of the Rococo. The former, spreading throughout Europe and the rest of the world, reflected a new style of living among the rich and fashionable; the latter was more an end in itself, creating a heaven-bound world of fantasy.

The Rococo in France. The spate of royal building in France at the beginning of the 18th century coincided with a move away from the classical and academic architectural forms of the 17th century and the formalized lifestyle created by Louis

Embarkation for Cythera by Watteau; canvas; 129×191cm (51×75in); 1717. Schloss Charlottenburg, Berlin

The Chambre de l'Oeil de Boeuf, Versailles, decorated by Pierre Lepautre c1700

XIV at Versailles. The King himself began to prefer the more intimate châteaux at Marly and Trianon to the vistas of Versailles, and there was a general exodus to Paris which turned into a rout after the deaths of the Dauphin, the Dauphine, and their eldest son, between 1711 and 1713. Although the Dauphin had been the leading patron of the new relaxed spirit in art, the movement continued and a large number of private *hôtels* were built in Paris. The most important of the new patrons was Philippe d'Orléans, the King's nephew and the future Regent, and the vagaries of the French economic system created a new class of very rich bourgeoisie who, after conjugal union with the old noblesse, regarded a new *hôtel* in one of the fashionable districts of Paris as the ultimate status symbol.

The Rococo was a reaction against the pomposity of the *Grand Siècle*, just as, in France at least, Neoclassicism was partly a reaction against the frivolity of the Rococo. However, unlike the interior decorators who displayed the wealth of their patrons in as abandoned and flamboyant a way as possible, the architects of early-18th-century France had to abide by a number of unwritten rules. The parts of a house had to be closely interrelated, and the progression of public rooms had to reflect the decoration—which became steadily richer as a visitor proceeded from the entrance hall to the *salon*.

The great architectural theorist of mid-18th-century France, and the most important disseminator of French taste in architecture and decoration, was Jacques-François Blondel (1705–74). In 1743 he founded the École des Arts in Paris and his *Distribution des Maisons de Plaisance* ("The Arrangement of the Informal Residence") (1737) and Charles-Étienne Briseux's *Art de Bâtir des Maisons de Campagne* ("Art of Building Country Houses", 1743) became the standard text

books of the new style.

The first important designer of the French Rococo, Jean Bérain (1637–1711), was the main artistic force in the office of the *Menus Plaisirs* (the government department dealing with the decoration of royal buildings) at the end of the 17th century. His engraved arabesque designs, including those for chimneypieces and backgrounds to tapestries, were published in 1711 and had a widespread influence on interior design throughout Europe, even though they were no more than surface patterns applied to preexisting walls and ceilings.

Pierre Lepautre (c1648–1716), who had previously been employed in the production of engravings for architectural books, including some with designs by Bérain, was in the regular employ of the *Bâtiments du Roi* (the "Royal Works") from 1699 and seems to have encouraged a greater freedom of line in official decoration. At Marly he raised the cornice and eliminated the cove of the ceiling of the *Chambre du Roi* (he did the same at the rooms he decorated at Trianon), and his designs for chimneypieces show a new and softer outline incorporating Bérain's arabesques into the framework of the wall-panels. His simple, slender proportions contrast with Bérain's Mannerist complexities, and he makes the all-important transition from flat decoration to decoration in relief. Lepautre was given important work at Versailles, including the *Chambre de l'Oeil de Boeuf* with its gilded frieze of dancing children on the inclined band above the cornice.

Claude Audran (1658–1734), perhaps the most important decorative painter of early-18th-century France, painted arabesques at the Château Anet in 1698 and joined Bérain at Château-Neuf, Meudon, in 1699, where his work in the *Cabinet* included a chinaman and monkeys—features that later became standard elements for Rococo decoration. Au-

The Hôtel de Soubise

Hercule-Mériadec de Rohan, Prince de Soubise, married his second wife, Marie-Sophie de Courçillon, in 1732. Although only 19 years old, she had been the widow of the Duc de Pecquigny for three years. The prince's first marriage had lasted for 33 years and he was in his sixties when he married for the second time. To placate his young wife, the prince decided to redecorate his Paris town house, the Hôtel de Soubise, in the latest light and airy style, with a suite for himself on the ground floor and a separate suite for his wife on the floor above.

Hercule-Mériadec's father, François de Rohan, Prince de Soubise, bought the site in 1700 and commissioned Pierre-Alexis Delamair (1675–1745) to design an *hôtel*. Delamair's main facade, with its coupled columns and colonnaded courtyard, an updated and more elegant version of the Hôtel de Souvré by Pasquier Delisle of 1667, was a great success. However, his interior designs, with suites of rooms joined by central doors, were considered woefully old-fashioned and, at the suggestion of Hercule-Mériadec, Delamair was replaced by Gabriel-Germain Boffrand (1667–1754) in 1707.

Boffrand presumably made the house less of a 17th-century parade ground and more of an 18th-century residence. We are not sure what he accomplished by way of interior decoration in his first period of work on the Hôtel, which probably ended in the early 1720s, but the most important change was to move the central doors to the sides of the rooms. It was not until his second period of work on the Hôtel, the changes for the Princess, which began in 1732, that Boffrand created the logical terminal to his re-positioned doors along the main suite of rooms. They lead directly into the center of the oval *salon* which was started in 1732 on the site of the keep of the old Hôtel de Clison. The oval pavilion joins the major suite to the minor at right angles.

The exterior of the oval pavilion is severe and simple; the only decoration is the flurry above the central windows and the brackets supporting the balconies. There is no rustication as on the facade of the building, and the decorated Ionic and Doric pilasters of the rest of the garden front are flattened into plain strips. There is much more plain wall surface here than elsewhere on the Hôtel.

Boffrand made up for exterior simplicity with the extravagance of the interior decoration. The two oval *salons* inside the pavilion were the architectural and decorative center-pieces of his work at the Hôtel de Soubise. Although the Prince's ground-flour suite, and the Princess's suite directly above, were decorated completely by Boffrand, only the bedroom and oval *salon* from each survive as originally conceived. We must imagine the decoration slowly building up to the climax of the oval *salon*, and the monochromatic *salon* of the Prince as a prelude to the blaze of color and ornament of the Princess's *salon*.

Both *salons* are decorated with rounded spandrels between the arcades of the windows and doors. Those in the Prince's *salon* are filled with sculptural medallions and

▼ The oval *salon* of the princess in the Hôtel de Soubise, Paris, decorated by G.-G. Boffrand, *c* 1735

allegorical figures by Lambert-Sigisbert Adam (1700–59) and Jean-Baptiste Lemoyne (1704–78). Despite the fulsome Rococo frills and spills, the iconography of the figurative decoration (for example, Justice, Wisdom, Astronomy, Geometry), the subdued color scheme, and the virtual restriction of the decoration to the wall areas, all suggest some attempt at seriousness.

The spandrels in the Princess' *salon* prepare us for the lascivious abandon of the rest of the decoration. Eight canvases by Charles-Joseph Natoire (1700–77) depict the story of Psyche, based on works by Apuleius and La Fontaine. The earliest dated picture of the series is *The Nymphs offering Flowers to Psyche on the Threshold of the Palace of Love* of 1737 and the latest *Zephyr giving Shelter to Psyche* of 1739. Natoire's roseate nymphs on their blushing meringue clouds are ideally suited to the room, and demonstrate perfectly the artist at his decorative best—the undulating rhythm of the compositions in the irregularly shaped paintings echo the undulating line along the tops of the doors and windows.

Natoire's eight allegories are the culmination of French decorative painting, a rather outworn tradition by the late 1730s. Another commission roughly contemporary with that for the Hôtel de Soubise, for a series showing the *History of Clovis* for Orry, the Directeur

des Bâtiments, gave Natoire an opportunity to prove himself as an early painter of scenes from French history. It was not a success, and Natoire was evidently happier working in the spirit of the Baroque rather than the Neo-classical.

◄ The severe and simple exterior of the oval pavilion of the Hôtel de Soubise, by G.-G. Boffrand; built *c* 1732

▲ The main facade of the Hôtel de Soubise, Paris, by P.-A. Delamair; built 1700–7

Natoire's paintings are only one of the decorative elements in the Princess' *salon*; if they are meant to be the focal point, they are somewhat overwhelmed by the tumbling gilt stucco which frames the paintings, cascades down the walls, and twists and curls across the ceiling to form the central rosette. The stucco not only acts as a border to certain decorative elements, such as the paintings and looking glasses, it also joins them together with a harmonizing leitmotiv. The stucco softens the emphatic architectural features such as the recessed panels, the high, rounded arches, and the very shape of the room.

The finest surviving interior of the French Rococo, the Princess' *salon* in the Hôtel de Soubise, is the culmination of a much older tradition in which the various decorative elements of the scheme combine to create a satisfying whole. Boffrand's architectural skill combines a strong architectonic skeleton with a delightful fantasy of decoration, and provides the necessary central pivot for his commission from Hercule-Mériadec de Rohan, Prince de Soubise.

GEOFFREY ASHTON

dran's most famous works, apart from his tapestry designs, were the arabesques of *c*1700 painted for the Duchesse de Bourgogne on the ceilings of La Ménagerie at Versailles.

The Duc d'Orléans' palace, the Palais-Royal, was redecorated by Gilles-Marie Oppenord (1672–1742). He studied in Italy, unlike Bérain and Lepautre, but his decorative schemes are in the latter's new style. In the *Chambre à Coucher* of 1716, Oppenord did away with an entablature, fusing the cornice and the cove of the ceiling. In the same year, he gave a richly decorated semicircular end to Mansart's gallery of 1692 and, in 1717, designed two rooms for the Duc d'Orléans' magnificent collection of pictures. The decoration of one of these, the *Salon à l'Italienne*, was so elaborate that little space remained for even the smallest collection of pictures. The available hanging space itself was covered with an effusion of decorative panels, similar to those carved on the choir stalls of Notre Dame in Paris, *c*1711–12, by François-Antoine Vassé (1681–1736). Vassé also carved the trophies on the pillars and the reliefs on the pulpit in the new chapel at Versailles in 1708. In the choir stalls at Notre Dame, he created scenes in large, flat cartouches in the middle of highly decorated panels; his important innovation was to allow the decoration to run from the borders into the panels. Vassé took over the leadership of the new style from Lepautre, the older artist, who was working in Notre Dame at the same time.

Vassé's sculptural quality is matched by Oppenord's emphasis on movement, the result of his deep admiration for Francesco Borromini (1599–1667). In such rooms as the *Salon* of the Hotel d'Assy (1719) and the *Salon d'Angle* in the Palais-Royal, Oppenord's curves and flowing lines are more pervasive than in the earlier works of Lepautre and Bérain. Oppenord and Vassé represent the mature new style of the 1720s, but took no part in the final asymmetrical phase of the French Rococo. Free and uninhibited by the standards of the *Grand Siècle*, their decoration was architectonic and contrived compared to the later works of Pineau and Meissonnier.

Nicholas Pineau (1684–1754) worked in Russia from *c*1716 to 1727. His most remarkable work there was the *Cabinet* of Peter the Great in the palace of Peterhof (now Petrodvorets, USSR; *c*1720) where his part in introducing asymmetry into French Rococo decoration is already evident in the arrangement of the carved dragons over the doors. On his return to France, Pineau quickly adopted the spirit of the work of Oppenord and Vassé, developing his own individual style in the early 1730s. In the Hôtel de Rouilles, for instance, he gave narrow moldings instead of architraves to the doors and emphasized height by recessing the door in a thin frame which rose to the ceiling. Pineau continued to decorate until his death, but after 1735 his work lost its freshness.

Juste-Aurèle Meissonnier (1695–1750) was probably trained as a silversmith and, in 1726, became *Dessinateur de la Chambre et du Cabinet du Roi* (personal draftsman to the King), a position held at one stage by Bérain. A weather vane, designed for the Duc de Mortemart in 1724, and a candlestick designed in 1728, show the asymmetry that was to be crucial to the development of Rococo in his and Pineau's later interior designs. The Maison de Sieur Brethous at Bayonne (1733) is Meissonnier's only room-by-room design for a house. The *Salon* includes a number of new features, such as the undulating cornice supported by consoles over the chimney-piece looking-glass, the volute endings to the door-cases, and the asymmetrical door and pier panels. The wall-panels are much more asymmetrical in the *Cabinet* of M. Bielenski (1734, in Warsaw) where the cornice is broken by swirls of foliage. Meissonnier's engravings were widely influential, and when his collection of 50 *Morceaux de Fantasie* was published in 1734, the review in the *Mercure* for March 1734 called them *Rocailles et Coquillages*, the first time that the term *Rocaille* (*Rococo* in Italian) was used. All the forms were basically derived from cartouches, like those of Bernard Toro (1672–1731) who was inspired by the 17th-century Italian artist Agostino Mitelli.

Though the new style, or the *style pittoresque*, was largely ignored by France's Academy of Architecture, the *Petits Appartements du Roi* for Louis XV at Versailles were decorated in the style of Pineau. The general design was probably the work of Jacques-Ange Gabriel (1698–1782), but the influence of Pineau is seen in the relatively low ceilings, woodwork painted in pastel shades, and doors set into shallow recesses. There is great freedom in asymmetrical panel moldings and in the line of the cornice, especially in the *Cabinet de la Pendule* (1738) where scraggy birds leave the cornice and take flight across the ceiling.

The culmination of the Rococo style in France is to be found less in the work of Nicholas Pineau, however, than in the interiors created by Gabriel-Germain Boffrand (1667–1754) for the Prince de Soubise in the Hôtel de Soubise in Paris (1735–6). The most notable features of the Hôtel are the two oval *Salons*, one each for the Prince and Princess. The Prince's room has large figurative reliefs in the spandrels and trophies in the lunettes, but seems subdued when compared with the Princess's *Salon* above it. Here, however, the overall effect is richer than in any other French Rococo interior. The spandrels are filled with Charles-Joseph Natoire's paintings of the story of Psyche; open bands of scrollwork rise from the cornice, and divide the vault by joining in a central rosette.

From 1745 until her death in 1764, Mme de Pompadour was the Royal *Maîtresse en Titre* and the source of most official art patronage. She had her favorites—Boucher, for example—but her taste was catholic and she patronized whoever was available. It was probably through her influence that Rococo interiors appeared in the royal residences until well into the 1760s, despite the excited encouragement given to Neoclassical artists and architects in France from the middle of the 18th century.

The Rococo in Germany. The proliferation of building in southern Germany in the early 18th century was not due

The Amalienburg hunting box in the gardens of the palace of Nymphenburg, built by François Cuvilliés for Electress Amalie; 1734–9

wholly to the thrill of indulging in a new art form. Germany was only just recovering from the desolation of the Thirty Years War. There was no large-scale building in this part of Europe in the second half of the 17th century, and the War of the Spanish Succession (1701–14) delayed what might have been an earlier start. Though essentially an ecclesiastical movement—a northern artistic Counter-Reformation—the German Rococo was also a great and highly secular sigh of relief and reaction against the strictures of the previous 100 years. Most of the buildings constructed were either churches, or palaces belonging to high church dignitaries, but the pleasure pavilions and the elaborate pastoral garnitures of architecture-cum-decoration are equally important to the style as a whole.

However, unlike the French Rococo, which was created for a bored aristocracy or rich bourgeoisie, the German version catered for the rural proletariat as well—the simple pilgrim and the ordinary man-in-the-field who wished, now and again, to escape into never-never land. The French Rococo, essentially a linear style, is more refined and effeminate than its German counterpart, where a feeling of total conviction and commitment takes the viewer into a land of sweetness and chubby smiles.

From 1704 to 1714, the Electors Maximilian II Emanuel of Bavaria, and his brother Joseph Clemens of Cologne, members of the Wittelsbach family, were exiled in France while their territories were occupied. Maximilian II Emanuel saw that the men he later appointed as his court architects, Joseph Effner (1687–1745), and François de Cuvilliés (1695–1768)—who also happened to be the court dwarf—were instructed in the new style. The earliest surviving Rococo interiors in Germany are those created by Paris-trained craftsmen for Maximilian II Emanuel in the Pagodenburg (1716–19), a pavilion in the garden of the Schloss Nymphenburg near Munich. The most outstanding features here, however, are the stuccoed moldings which are quite unlike anything to be found in France. The work of the important Bavarian stuc-

catori, most of whom, like the Zimmermanns and the Schmutzers, came from Wessobrun in Upper Bavaria, was extremely important in the development away from the French style with its domestic scale and relatively formalized lines to the monumentality and florid exuberance of the German Rococo. It was decidedly different to that of the Italian stuccatori, although the ceiling paintings, inevitably surrounded by stucco work, owe their genesis to the distant examples of Andrea Pozzo (1642–1709) and Baciccia (Giovanni Battista Gaulli; 1639–1709) and were often painted by German or Austrian artists trained in Italy.

Maximilian II Emanuel's main architectural achievement, on his return from exile in Paris in 1714 after the end of the War of the Spanish Succession, was the construction, or rather the continuation of the building of the palaces of Nymphenburg and Schleissheim, both of which had been started before the Elector left Bavaria in 1704. The garden pavilions created at Nymphenburg are the most important features there, the most remarkable one being the small hunting box, the Amalienburg, built between 1734 and 1739 by Cuvilliés for the Electress Amalie. The large circular saloon occupying the whole of the center of the building is painted blue-white and three other shades of blue; the stucco, overlaid with silver foil, glitters with light from the window recesses and with the reflections thrown by the many mirrored surfaces. On one side of the saloon is the Electress' bedroom, painted couleur de citron (cool yellow) and the smaller blue cabinet; on the other is the hunting room, painted couleur de paille (a straw yellow) and the Pheasant Room. Beyond this is the decorative kitchen.

François de Cuvilliés was sent back to France to study architecture under Jacques François Blondel (1705–74), and was appointed court architect in 1725 along with Effner. He was the first to make use of Rococo scrolling in Germany, in his decoration of the Reiche Zimmer (1730–7) in the Munich Residenz. In April 1751 he began to construct his theater in the Residenz, finishing it for the Elector's name-day in October 1753. The slightly curved horseshoe of the auditorium is resolved into an undulating line by the curvilinear balustrades of the boxes; the lintel, above the stage boxes, dips to follow the line of the perspective scenes used on the stage. The Cuvilliés theater is a beautiful example of delicate Rococo decoration adding to the completeness of a Baroque theater: a unity of audience, decorative effect, and stage presentation. It is also a reminder of the theatrical nature of all Rococo interiors, both secular and religious.

Cuvilliés produced books of engraved Rococo ornament deriving from French prototypes, in which his fantasy exceeds even that of his executed designs for the Amalienburg, the theater, and other interiors in the Munich Residenz.

Lothar Franz von Schönborn's palace at Pommersfelden was one of the many built in Germany in the early 18th century, in optimistic emulation of Versailles. Because of the time-span occupied by construction work, these buildings

The Kaisersaal in the Residenz at Würzburg, with its ceiling painted by Giambattista Tiepolo; 1749–54

The Garden facade of Schloss Sanssouci, built by von Knobelsdorff for Frederick the Great; 1745–53

were often conceived as vast Baroque monsters and subsequently decorated in a more intimate Rococo style. This intimacy was developed in the garden pavilions built during the 18th century after the main building had been completed. Pommersfelden was, unusually, built over a very short period of time (1711–18): the design was largely the responsibility of the architect Johann Dientzenhofer (1663–1726) who concurrently built the nearby church of Banz.

The Residenz at Würzburg, also largely a Schönborn conception, is much grander and more imposing than even Pommersfelden and was begun in 1720 by the Prince-Bishop Johann Franz von Schönborn. The principal architect was Balthasar Neumann (1687–1753), but the Prince-Bishop wrote to ten architects of international repute for their ideas, including Johann Lukas von Hildebrandt (1668–1745), Robert de Cotte (1656–1735), and Boffrand; many others were involved during the 60 years spent building the palace. Little had been constructed when Johann Franz died in 1724, and nothing more was added until the election of Friedrich Karl Graf von Schönborn to the Prince-Bishopric in 1729, when Neumann began the south wing. The central pavilion of the Residenz faces a large square on the town side with extensive facades facing the gardens at the back. In the palace's Treppenhaus are the *Weisser Saal* and the *Kaisersaal*: the most grandiose secular interiors of the German Rococo. They were begun *c*1736; their roofing and vaulting was completed by 1742 and the stuccoed interior of the *Weisser Saal* finished by 1744, two years before the death of Friedrich Karl. Karl Philipp von Greiffenklau was Prince-Bishop from 1749 to 1754, and commissioned Giambattista Tiepolo (1696–1770) to paint the ceilings of the *Kaisersaal* and the Treppenhaus (1750–3).

The enormous ceiling of the Treppenhaus (105 ft by 60 ft; 32 m by 18 m) is painted with *The Four Parts of the Earth in Homage to the Bishop of Würzburg*. The cartouche-carrying figures in the four corners are the only elements in relief over the whole area, contrasting strongly with the *Kaisersaal* where the paintings are but the most important part of a decorative scheme that includes stucco, statuary, variously shaped window openings, and other architectural features. The oval shape helps to unify the many elements of the room. The two main paintings on the ceiling show *The Marriage of Frederick Barbarossa and Beatrice of Burgundy*, illustrating the power of the Church and *The Emperor Giving a Dukedom to Bishop Perold*, presumably showing the weakness of the Church. Various grisaille paintings, in elaborate Rococo cartouche frames, repeat the allegory of the main scenes, intermittently connected by a frieze of spectators, some painted, some in relief, and some cut out. The *Kaisersaal* at Würzburg is the apotheosis of the German Rococo *Gesamtkunstwerk*—the fusion of elements into a coherent and splendid whole.

In the realm of pleasure pavilions, as distinct from the more serious status-seeking world of palaces, the Amalienburg has only one rival in 18th-century Germany: the Zwinger in Dresden, built 1711–22 by Matthäus Daniel Pöppelmann (1662–1736) for Augustus the Strong of Saxony. It consists of a large garden-filled square with long galleries on two sides, one of which is a picture gallery built in the mid 19th century by Gottfried Semper (1803–79). The other two sides have wings with heavily decorated pavilions in the middle of the arc, terminating the spaces which were designed to contain temporary theater structures. Although the Zwinger is now unique, it would have been a familiar conceit when built, reminiscent of the temporary structures created for state entries, festivals, and anniversaries, one of which it replaced.

North of Dresden, in Frederick the Great's Berlin, Neoclassicism began earlier than elsewhere in Germany. This style ran parallel with the Rococo in the decoration of royal palaces

Vierzehnheiligen

On 28 June 1446, a young shepherd working for the Cistercian monastery of Langheim saw a vision of a naked child, with a red cross over his heart, surrounded by 14 small boys. It was the second of several such visions experienced by the shepherd in the same place and he was informed by the child, "We are the 14 heavenly helpers and want our chapel to be built on this spot . . ." The chapel was built, high on a ridge on the side of the valley of the River Main opposite the much older Benedictine monastery of Banz.

By the early 18th century, Vierzehnheiligen ("14 Saints") had become such a popular place of pilgrimage that the Abbot of Langheim, Stephan Mössinger, asked the Prince-Bishop of Bamberg, Friedrich Carl von Schönborn, for permission to replace the simple chapel with a splendid new church. Banz was being rebuilt (1698 onwards) by the architects Johann Leonard (1660–1707) and Johann Dientzenhofer (1663–1726). The

Abbot of Langheim no doubt wished to respond to the Benedictine challenge.

An early centralized design for Vierzehnheiligen by Gottfried Heinrich Krohne (1703–56) of 1738 was replaced, in 1742, by a more conventional plan by Balthasar Neumann (1687–1753), with a long nave flanked by three pairs of chapels, a crossing supported on pairs of columns, and a choir and transepts with polygonal ends. At the time, Neumann was working for the Prince-Bishop Friedrich Carl von Schönborn in Würzburg on various projects, including the Hofkirche in the Residenz, the Schönbornkapelle in the Cathedral, and the Käppele, a pilgrimage chapel just outside the city. When work began on the new church at Vierzehnheiligen in 1743, Krohne was the architect in charge and, taking advantage of the absence of the busy Neumann, substituted his own version of a long-naved plan. By 1744 Abbot Mössinger noticed that something was seri-

◀ The second, Grace altar in the church of Vierzehnheiligen, designed by J.J.M. Küchel; c1764

▲ The high altar of Vierzehnheiligen by J.J.M. Küchel

Above The pilgrimage church of Vierzehnheiligen seen dominating the countryside; built 1743–72

ously wrong, and Neumann was asked to provide a series of alternative designs.

Neumann's revised plans—using Krohne's foundations, which were partly dictated by the difficult lie of the land—provide one of the most ingenious arrangements of space in 18th-century architecture. His problem was to provide two important focal points: the high altar, and the independent altar of the Vierzehnheiligen in the apse. St Peter's, Rome, with its double focus of the high altar and the *baldacchino* under the crossing, was an obvious inspiration, but Neumann was unable to put his second altar under the crossing because of the inept foundations. Neumann overcame the problem by designing a series of vaults that ignored the crossing altogether: a long oval over the votive altar flanked by two more rounded ovals over the choir and vestibule. The transepts are cut off from the main body of the church by galleries, and are almost independent circular rooms. The galleries and aisles, necessary features of all German pilgrimage churches because they required processional routes, help to mask the conventional ground plan of the church which is transformed by the simple but extremely effective system of vaulting. The intersections of the oval vaults, which can be read as shallow domes, form complex arches with three-dimensional curves. The scheme of intersecting oval vaults

had been used by the Dientzenhofers across the valley at Banz, and by Neumann himself in the Hofkirche in the Würburg Residenz, but those at Vierzehnheiligen were the first to disguise the internal shape of the building.

Neumann died long before Vierzehnheiligen was completed, so he cannot have supervised the decoration. However, the architectural features closely follow his model of 1744 in the Historisches Museum in der Alten Hofhaltung, Bamberg. The church built in a glorious honey-colored stone, has a twin-tower facade harking back to medieval prototypes. The impression of height, exaggerated by the dominant geographical position of the church, is emphasized by the high, lower rusticated layer,

and by the lower windows in the upper level breaking through the zone of the pilaster bases. Johann Jakob Michael Küchel (1703–69) supervised Neumann's design and contributed the extraordinary Gnadenaltar himself. The stucco is by Franz Xavier (1705–64), Johann Michael Feichtmeyer (1709–72), and J. G. Ubelherr (1700–63), the ceiling frescoes by Giuseppe Appiani (1701–96). The church was consecrated by the Prince-Bishop of Bamberg, Adam Friedrich Graf von Seinsheim, on 14 September 1772.

GEOFFREY ASHTON

◤ The facade of Vierzehnheiligen designed by Balthasar Neumann

► The interior of Vierzehnheiligen showing both the high altar and the Gnadenaltar

The Assumption of the Virgin in the church of Rohr by
Egid Quirin Asam; 1722

until it took over completely at the end of the 18th century.
Georg Wenzeslaus von Knobelsdorff (1699–1753) not only
built the Berlin Opera House (1741–3) with its imposing
Corinthian portico raised on a podium, but also designed the
east wing of the Schloss Charlottenburg with its magnificent
and wildly Rococo *Goldenegalerie* at about the same time.
His architectural and decorative dual-personality is even more
evident at Potsdam, just outside Berlin, where his Stadtschloss
(1741–3) had a classical portico reached by flights of steps,
and the garden palace of Sanssouci (1745–53) was much less
pretentious and in the tradition of the Amalienburg.

The influence of the Italian Baroque on the architecture of
the German Rococo—especially on the architecture of
German Rococo churches—came *via* the great Austrian exponents of the Baroque, Johann Bernhard Fischer von Erlach
(1656–1723) and Johann Lukas von Hildebrandt (1668–
1745); many German designers studied and worked in Austria
if not in Italy. The main French ecclesiastical prototypes for
German Rococo art, the carved panels in the chapel at
Versailles, and the choir stalls in Notre Dame, were slight
inspiration—only a few churches were built in France during
the 18th century, all of them in a severe Baroque style redolent
of the 17th century.

German Rococo churches were designed by a surprisingly
large number of different people, but only two men, Johann
Michael Fischer and Balthasar Neumann, stand out as
architectural personalities who could use and develop the spatial experiments of the Italian Baroque. Most of the other
designers were painters, *stuccatori*, decorators, or sculptors
before they were architects: men like the Zimmermann
brothers Dominikus (1685–1766) and Johann Baptist (1680–

1758), the Schmutzers, and, perhaps most remarkably, the
Asam brothers.

Cosmas Damian Asam (1686–1739), the elder brother, was
basically a fresco painter, and Egid Quirin Asam (1692–1750)
a *stuccatore*. Exceptional for German artists of the period,
both had studied in Rome for two years—the small church of
Rohr (1717–23) was designed by Egid Quirin Asam fresh
from Italy. The church is simple, and nothing detracts from
the staggering group depicting the *Assumption of the Virgin*
beyond the high altar. Zooming through the air, propelled by
two angels and supported by only one iron prop (hidden in the
clouds), the straw and stucco Virgin looks as surprised as the
Apostles around the tomb below, from which she has just
been catapulted. Supremely theatrical and technically brilliant, the group is also deeply religious: a three-dimensional
version of a miraculous event and a miracle in itself.

The silver and gold statue of St George riding out of a
magical aura of golden light over the high altar of the Benedictine abbey of Weltenburg (1716–36) is only slightly less
theatrical, but rather more subtle in its impact. The small oval
church was designed by Cosmas Damian Asam, who also
painted the ceiling fresco which is separated from the lower
part of the church by a suspended crown. The St George side
altars, with their wealth of stucco and gilding, and the half-
light effects, were designed by his brother.

It was probably Egid Quirin's idea to build a votive church
in Munich dedicated to St John Nepomuk, now usually called
the Asamkirche. The church was squeezed between the
Asams' house and the presbytery (now destroyed), and has a
facade resting on a base of sculpted "natural" rock. The three-
story interior has the high altar at ground-floor level. A gallery
above, connecting with the house, has a statue of St John
Nepomuk silhouetted against the bright light of the window
behind. A Trinity breaks through the clouds above the statue
of the Saint and the high altar. The church is not an excuse for
yet another theatrical sideshow, but a personal expression of
piety by the artist brothers.

Johann Michael Fischer (1691–1766) built for a circle of
patrons that included Clemens August of Cologne and Herzog
Clemens Franz of Munich, both members of the ruling Wittelsbach family. His churches often feature the bowed fronts
and central planning of the buildings of his namesake Fischer
von Erlach, but they always provide a clear and decisive setting for the Rococo decorations that encrust their interiors.

The great abbey church of Ottobeuren—where Fischer
began, in 1744, to work over the plans already prepared by
Andreas Maini in 1731, by Dominikus Zimmermann in 1732,
Simpert Kraemer in 1737, and by Effner—is the culmination of the German Rococo, its largest and richest monument. The
ornament, however, is subordinate to the architectural conception. Unlike the interiors created by the Asam brothers, the
Rococo decoration enhances, but does not dominate, the

The interior of the abbey church of Ottobeuren completed by
Johann Michael Fischer; built 1736–66

organization of the space. When viewed from the entrance, Ottobeuren seems to be conceived as a long building; when seen from the crossing, it looks as though it is centrally planned—the eye is directed vertically rather than horizontally. The Rococo decoration begins about 6 ft (2 m) from the ground, thus helping the vertical emphasis, riots all over the architectural elements, and at the same time encourages the general impression of space and richness.

The enormous interior of Fischer's abbey church of Wiblingen is much plainer than Ottobeuren; color is restricted to the ceiling frescoes and to the altars. The walls and sculpted figures are white, and accentuate the overwhelming space contained by the Rococo decoration. The library, on the other hand, is highly colored, decorative and frivolous, and is one of a number of German Rococo abbey libraries built for important foundations. They seem to represent an intellectual ecstasy rather than the religious frenzy of the church interiors, and the frescoes and statuary follow strange iconographic sequences which are sometimes difficult to decipher but always amusing. Notable examples of abbey libraries include Schussenried (1754) by Dominikus Zimmermann, St Gallen (1758–67) by Peter Thumb (1681–1766), Fürstenzell (1740–8) perhaps by J.M. Fischer, and Ottobeuren with its statue of Minerva.

Vierzehnheiligen (1743–72) was built from a plan by Balthasar Neumann and is his best known ecclesiastical work. The lie of the land obliged the builder to reduce the size of the choir indicated in the plan, and Neumann had to modify his original scheme. The votive altar of the Fourteen Saints, the centerpiece of the interior of the church, had to be brought forward from the crossing into the nave, so Neumann invented an ingenious system of vaulting which ignored the crossing altogether. It consists of a large oval over the votive altar between the equal oval extending from the choir and the vestibule. The horseshoe transepts are almost autonomous rooms as a result of the large gallery that covers the areas between the walls of the church and the central ovals as far as the crossing. This spatial complexity is not obvious from inside the church: the Rococo decoration softens the transitions, and everything blends into a series of curves.

Another triumphant arrangement of space of the German Rococo, the Benedictine abbey church of Neresheim, was begun by Neumann in 1745 although the decoration as not completed until 1792. It is a large church with an enormous, flat central cupola flanked by two smaller ones, as well as obliquely placed pairs of double columns which form an undulating line down the body of the church. The parallel outside walls are masked by the diagonal emphasis of the groins which make a continual figure of eight, and by the unusual positioning of the columns. There is little decoration below the ceiling, and Neumann's juggling with space remains unsullied by subordinate hands.

Dominikus Zimmermann (1685–1766) achieved the spatial dynamism of Fischer and Neumann—though on a much more intimate scale—in his pilgrimage churches of Steinhausen, Die Wies, and Maria-Steinbach. Steinhausen (1727–35) was built in the form of an elongated double cube that has melted into an oval. The ceiling fresco by Johann Baptist Zimmermann (1680–1758), the brother of Dominikus, is framed by a varied and delightful series of stuccoed flora and fauna. Figures seated on the entablature are supported by each of the columns surrounding the nave. The areas of white are enlivened with pale oranges, greens, and pinks.

At Die Wies (built 1746–57), a pilgrimage church paid for and built by local peasants, Dominikus Zimmermann uses the same formula as he did at Steinhausen and at Günzburg in 1736. The large central oval space for the congregation is surrounded by freestanding double columns supporting the wooden vaults. Around these pillars, the pilgrimage procession could move along the walls of the church with the greatest of ease. The ceiling is again frescoed by J.B. Zimmermann, though the stucco work is rather less figurative than at Steinhausen. The church has long, irregularly shaped windows with a small *oeil-de-boeuf* window above; the shape of this opening is repeated throughout the decoration of the church.

In its own jewel-like way, Die Wies epitomizes the achievement of the German Rococo; the careful organization of available space, fused with absolute control of light sources, combines to turn the superabundant decorative elements into a cohesive whole.

GEOFFREY ASHTON

Bibliography. Hempel, E. *Baroque Art and Architecture in Central Europe*, Harmondsworth (1965). Hitchcock, H.R. *Rococo Architecture in Southern Germany*, London (1968). Kimball, S.F. *The Creation of the Rococo*, Philadelphia (1943). Kalnein, W.G. and Levey, M. *Art and Architecture of the Eighteenth Century in France*, Harmondsworth (1973). Powell, N. *From Baroque to Rococo*, London (1959). Wittkower, R. *Art and Architecture in Italy: 1600–1750*, Harmondsworth (1980).

The Apotheosis of Homer; relief design by John Flaxman, vase by Josiah Wedgwood;
jasper ware; height 47cm (19in); c1785. Castle Museum
and Art Gallery, Nottingham (see page 738)

Neoclassicism, a style that began in the 18th century and developed throughout the 19th, was particularly important in the arts of France and northern Europe, though few countries remained unaffected by its influence. The style originated from a dissatisfaction with existing artistic traditions among European artists and writers. It was felt that a reexamination of the arts of Antiquity might regenerate accepted creative standards; the movement therefore became a revival of the ideals and images of the ancients.

Neoclassicism became so popular that it influenced ceramics, furniture, and textiles as well as dictating the inspiration of painters, sculptors, and architects. It is fairly easy to recognize the works of artists or craftsmen of this period because the articles they made often display a similarity of basic construction. It was important for Neoclassical designers to work in simple forms and colors, avoiding all unnecessary complication. This applied to architecture as much as to painting and sculpture so that the arts became formally geometrical and austere, rejecting the bright colors and movement of the previous Rococo and Baroque styles.

By the end of the 18th century the aim of the Neoclassical artist was to reproduce the forms of Greek and Roman art as authentically as possible. However, it was not until the trade routes to Greece and the Middle East were freed from Turkish domination that archaeologists could find and publicize genuine antique works. Consequently there are stylistic variations within Neoclassicism itself: some artists, in reaction to the frivolous themes treated by their Rococo predecessors, felt that they should treat serious subjects; others explored the heroic literature of the remote past, using Roman and Greek antiquities as models for portraying the stories. Sometimes artists read the descriptions of lost works by ancient painters and sculptors written by such writers as Pliny.

The interest in historical accuracy distinguished Neoclassicism from the more conventional ideology of the classic revival. The latter relied on traditional styles derived from concepts of beauty and decorum established by High Renaissance artists, for example Raphael (1483–1520) and Michelangelo (1475–1564). Neoclassicism did not reject these accepted ideals but the movement was concerned to produce accurate reconstructions of antique works of art. This does not imply that the Neoclassical artist was a conscious plagiarist, but he was bound by strict rules. For example, if an artist painted a Roman soldier, he was obliged to make the armor and weapons historically correct; if he illustrated a scene from Homer's *Iliad*, he would keep exactly to the text. Some artists, John Flaxman (1755–1826) for example, even taught themselves to read Greek for illustrating Greek words and attempted to produce artificially "primitive" illustrations that approximated to 18th-century notions of painting at the time of Homer. The same kind of demand influenced the designs of everyday objects and fashions: by 1800 chairs, beds, clothes, and even ladies' hairstyles were fashionably "Greek", that is, they were based on the objects and descriptions recently discovered by archaeologists.

Eighteenth-century enthusiasm for the past first appeared in Rome where between 1700 and 1721 Pope Clement XI collected and maintained Roman antiquities. Clement's successors continued the practice—in 1734 Clement XII opened the first European public museum of antiquities. Excavations began at Herculaneum in 1738 and at Pompeii ten years later. This interest in restoring ancient ruins and art objects encouraged scholars from all over Europe to visit Italy and record their finds in large books of engravings. The first important 18th-century publication to extend the layman's knowledge of Roman art was written by a Frenchman, the Abbé Bernard de Montfaucon (1655–1741), and appeared in Paris in 1719. Entitled *L'Antiquité Expliquée et Représentée en Figures* (English translation 1721–5: *Antiquity Explained and Represented in Figures*) it became a valuable source of information for subsequent generations of writers and artists. Later books, however, became more accurate and specialized as scholars traveled further in search of the past; in 1758 Julien-David LeRoy (1724–1803) published *Les Ruines des Plus Beaux Monuments de la Grèce* ("Ruins of the Most Beautiful Monuments in Greece"), the first work to deal specifically with Greek architecture. Robert Wood's *Ruins of Palmyra* (1753) showed the architecture of the Middle East, and Stuart and Revett's *Antiquities of Athens* (1762) again dealt with the architecture of Greece. The writers were limited by the amount of material they could find, but the quality of the engraved illustrations in these books is generally superb. Their influence on later architects and designers as pattern books is inestimable.

One unique quality in these publications was the authors' tendency to romanticize the past. This appears in the texts as well as in the illustrations and is particularly noticeable in the work of the Italian engraver G.B. Piranesi (1720–78). His *Vedute di Roma* (*Views of Rome*; 1748) showed Roman ruins in a markedly dramatic manner. Piranesi transformed the crumbling edifices of Imperial Rome into sumptuous monuments. Sometimes they are set against stormy skies, and overgrown with fantastic foliage. The effect of these engravings was so startling that later travelers to Italy—Goethe among them—were disappointed on seeing the real buildings. This same romantic nostalgia and sense of drama also permeated the writings of 18th-century scholars when they described Antiquity. A sentimental dream of a vanished golden age haunted artists and writers of the 18th century. By c1760 the onus was on the artist to produce a replica of that age that was both authentic and evocative.

The most influential Neoclassical writing appeared in a pamphlet written and published by a German librarian, Johann Joachim Winckelmann (1717–68). Entitled, in English, *Reflections Concerning the Imitation of Greek Works in Painting and Sculpture* (1755), it formulated a fairly concise set of instructions for 18th-century artists to follow. Winckelmann did not assume the position of connoisseur or archaeologist, trying to interpret the past according to the information at his disposal; instead, he conceived a personal vision of

A view of the temple of Jove from G.B. Piranesi's book of prints "Views of Rome"; published in 1748

Greek society, mainly from reading Homer's *Iliad* and *Odyssey*. He wrote a vividly imaginative account of the heroism and physical beauty of the Greek people and described how the Greek artist was inspired to produce works that exemplified such perfection. Winckelmann saw the Greek cult of physical excellence as expressing the development of an inner, spiritual beauty; he asserted that the Greek sculptor had learned to portray this spiritual beauty through almost imperceptible means. Winckelmann stressed the serious nature of the artist's profession among ancient people and invited the 18th-century artist to examine the great works of Antiquity and to change his style into a similarly elevated expression of heroic sentiments.

Winckelmann himself had little first-hand knowledge of antique art, though, despite the extreme poverty of his early years, he had managed to acquire a classical education. He had first worked as a schoolmaster and then as a librarian to a rich scholar in Dresden. He was lucky enough to become a protégé of the King of Saxony, Augustus III, whose family had formed an impressive collection of works of art: it was in the Royal Collection at Dresden that Winckelmann first saw fragments of ancient statues and plaster casts of Roman copies after Greek prototypes. These included such famous images as the *Laocoön* and the *Apollo Belvedere*. From studying them Winckelmann maintained that Greek sculpture was calm and smooth, made to reject facial or bodily distortion. He argued that few modern masters had learned to recreate nature as the Greeks had done. The exceptions were Raphael (1483–1520), Michelangelo (1475–1564), Correggio (1489–1534), and Poussin (1594–1665), who were also to become models for late-18th-century artists. For Winckelmann the supreme artistic ideal was embodied in the Hellenistic figure of the *Laocoön*: it represented an unrivaled expression of stoicism. Although tormented to the point of death, the noble figure still preserved an outward calm. Winckelmann wrote:

> The outstanding character of the Greek masterpiece is thus a noble simplicity and a calm grandeur ... Such a soul is portrayed in the face of Laocoön ... We too would wish to endure misery with such fortitude.

This comment on a work of art expresses two major tendencies which eventually became fundamental to Neoclassicism: the first is the intensely subjective nature of most Neoclassical criticism; the second is the moral fervor that underlies Neoclassical creative work. Five years before Winckelmann wrote his pamphlet, in 1750, Jean-Jacques Rousseau had delivered a prize-winning essay to the Academy of Arts and Sciences at Dijon. In this work, known as *A Discourse on the Sciences and the Arts*, Rousseau had demanded a series of drastic reforms in 18th-century French art. Both Rousseau and Winckelmann regarded the lightweight content of Rococo art as positively damaging to the society that countenanced it. Like Winckelmann, Rousseau wanted to see artists exhibit subjects conveying a morally edifying purpose, but Winckelmann's pamphlet outlined the actual vocabulary of such an art: it was to be based on the pictorial language of Greece and Rome.

Winckelmann's pamphlet was instantly successful and enabled him to realize his lifelong ambition to live in Rome. Here he became librarian to a leading collector and scholar,

Cardinal Albani, and also met a fellow countryman, the painter Anton Raphael Mengs (1728–79). These three men— the scholar, the collector, and the painter—collaborated to produce the first Neoclassical painting, completed by Mengs in 1761. It was painted on the ceiling of Cardinal Albani's gallery of antique sculpture in his Roman villa (the Villa Albani). Entitled *Parnassus*, it represents Apollo with the Nine Muses and comprises so many academic references that it appears to be rather like an 18th-century art-historical compendium. The composition was copied from a fresco by Raphael in the Vatican (which also shows Apollo with the Nine Muses on Mount Parnassus), and the central figure of Apollo imitates the famous *Apollo Belvedere* so closely that few knowledgeable 18th-century spectators could have mistaken the analogy. However, this kind of artistic game of cross-reference was probably quite intentional since Winckelmann's theory of imitation was a major influence on the formation of the picture. Additionally, *Parnassus* was designed as a decoration for a room whose function was that of exhibiting antique works of art. The painter's synthesis of famous prototypes was therefore eminently suitable.

Nevertheless, Mengs' painting of *Parnassus* does share the stilted academic quality of many early Neoclassical pictures. It indicates the uneasiness felt by European painters as they attempted to meet the rules of the new style. Winckelmann's pamphlet had initiated a quest for an ideal art reached only through the imitation of ancient masterpieces not easy to fulfill in practice. This pamphlet was translated into English in 1765 and its circulation coincided with a movement towards artistic reform in several European countries. Subjects from ancient history and literature were already becoming popular among painters and sculptors. In England, after the foundation of the Royal Academy in 1768, numerous Classical subjects dominated the annual exhibition and the training program in the Academy's School. Sir Joshua Reynolds (1723–92) preached a modified version of the worship of Antiquity to Academy students in his *Fifteen Discourses* given between 1769 and 1790. Reynolds also thought that selective imitation was a beneficial foundation for 18th-century artists; however, his opinions were those of a classical revivalist who was inclined to place the Neoclassicist's direct dependence on Antiquity within the more conventional academic structure of Renaissance and 17th-century art.

Neoclassicism was probably less popular in England than in other parts of Europe, though it had a major influence on the first generations of students at the Academy. Between the mid 1760s and 1770s Benjamin West (1738–1820), an American painter who eventually succeeded Reynolds as President of the Royal Academy, produced a number of classically inspired canvases. These treated mainly scenes from Roman history and were painted in cool colors with their figures arranged in the foreground like a frieze. However, by the last decades of the 18th century Greek and Roman subject matter was becoming subordinate to a new vogue in England for contemporary histories. It was West himself who metamorphosed the

convention of the death of an antique hero into the *Death of General Wolfe* (1770; National Gallery of Canada, Ottawa), a historic scene showing a battle that had taken place in 1759. Many contemporaneous British artists who felt inclined to attempt a more doctrinaire Neoclassicism found opportunities for work in Rome, by now the European capital of the whole movement.

One of the most influential of these proto-Neoclassical painters was, in fact, British: Gavin Hamilton (1723–98), who lived in Rome from the mid 1740s until his death. Hamilton executed many paintings of subjects from Homer. Essentially transitional works, they incorporate dusky but vivid colors and show figures who employ sweeping, flamboyant gestures. Hamilton also exploited his interest in archaeological details, which was extensive because he was a dealer in antiquities as well as a painter. His work was well-known in France, mainly through the engravings of Domenico Cunego (1727–94), and it had a profound effect on masters like Jacques-Louis David. Other British artists who tried to find a market in their own country were influenced by Neoclassicism, even if they did not completely absorb the rules of the style into their work. The heroic masterpieces of James Barry (1741–1806), the rather primitive paintings of William Blake (1757–1827), and the classically garbed ladies who appear in portraits by Sir Joshua Reynolds all owe something to the intervention of fashionable Antiquity.

It was in France that Neoclassical art became the subject of acute debate. Diderot campaigned from 1761 to 1781 to improve the subjects, values, and techniques of French painting. Having mercilessly criticized the late Rococo works of the aged François Boucher (1703–70), Diderot found an artistic protégé, the painter Jean-Baptiste Greuze (1725–1805), whose moralizing family scenes seemed to promise a career devoted to the improvement of French art. Nevertheless, Diderot ruthlessly abandoned Greuze in 1769 when the artist entered his first authentic Neoclassical work as a *morceau de reception* ("presentation piece") at the French Academy. Greuze had painted a scene showing the Emperor Septimus Severus reproaching his son Caracalla for having plotted against his life. The picture combined copies after antique statues with a composition directly dependent on Poussin. It was a brave attempt to reconcile the artistic idealization described by Winckelmann with the stern and moving sentiments of an event from Roman history. However, in trying to achieve historical accuracy and convey an inspiring theme, Greuze had produced a picture which, ironically, failed to reach the standards established by the French Academy for serious history painting. *Severus and Caracalla* (1769; Louvre, Paris) is, in fact, a key work for the development of Neoclassical painting in France, but in 1769 it was criticized as lacking in proportion and failing to express the theme in sufficiently strong pictorial terms. However, in his search for a solution to this problem of uniting aesthetic theory with artistic practice Greuze was not alone. Another early Neoclassical French painter, Joseph Vien (1716–1809), attempted to combine the popular erotica of 18th-century French Rococo painting with the outward trappings of Antiquity. The result was ingenious, showing inconsequential Rococo subjects in which the figures were dressed in antique-styled drapery with matching hairstyles, and inhabited interiors decorated with archaeologically "correct" furniture and fittings.

Vien's most famous pupil was Jacques-Louis David (1748–1826) who became one of the greatest Neoclassical artists and produced outstanding works based mainly on subjects from Roman history. His severe style subordinated the superficial imitation of antique prototypes to the importance of restricted detail and emphatic action: few artists could have painted such masterpieces within such a narrow set of rules; few had so stormy a career. David's life, ruined by political involvements, ended in exile in Belgium.

After five years in Italy as a student, from 1775 to 1780, David was totally converted to the new creed of Neoclassicism. Overwhelmed by the visual impact of the Greco-Roman art he had seen in Rome and Naples, David contributed a series of stunning canvases to the annual exhibition in Paris, after his return to France. His pictures mainly represented ancient themes of stoicism, a philosophy that was to haunt David throughout his career. The first, *Belisarius Begging Alms* (1780–1; Musée des Beaux-Arts, Lille), was seen by Diderot at the Salon of 1781, a year before the writer died. It

was an allegory on the passing of human glory. The principal figure, a once-famous Roman general, now a blind beggar, is recognized by one of his former soldiers. The setting recalled the pictures of Nicolas Poussin to whom David owed much of his inspiration and who provided the 18th-century artist with an illuminating model. Diderot hailed David's painting as a new artistic achievement, and although he was not to live long enough to witness David's ultimate success, his maxim "Paint as they spoke in Sparta" could have been taken as literal instruction by the young painter. In 1784 David returned to Rome to fulfill another commission: the famous *Oath of the Horatii* (1784; Louvre, Paris), which is the most impressive Neoclassical work ever painted.

David's Neoclassical pictures often portray similar subjects: individuals who bravely accept their fate and are undefeated by circumstance. In the *Death of Socrates* (1787; Metropolitan Museum, New York) the hero takes the cup of hemlock almost casually as he continues his discourse to mourning friends. *Brutus* (1789; Louvre, Paris) portrays the consul seated beneath a statue that symbolizes the city of Rome. Behind him lictors carry into the house the bodies of Brutus' own sons, executed at the command of their father because they plotted against the state. These paintings had a profound effect on 18th-century French spectators. David's style was an essentially personal interpretation of Neoclassical artistic

Electra leading a procession to the tomb of Agamemnon, one of John Flaxman's influential illustrations for the works of Aeschylus; published in 1795

Oath of the Horatii by David

Oath of the Horatii (Louvre, Paris) depicts a stirring scene from Roman history in which patriotic duty conflicts with family ties. Rome is at war with Alba, a neighboring state; their conflict is to be resolved by three heroes from each side fighting to the death in hand-to-hand combat. Chosen by the Romans as their representative warriors, the three brothers Horatius swear on swords held by their father to defend their country at all costs. The oath is not taken lightly since the Horatii are related by marriage to their opponents, the Alban Curatii. On the right of David's picture, grief-stricken women prophesy an inevitable tragedy. After the battle in which the Horatii triumph, although only the oldest survives, Camilla, their sister, portrayed here as the girl in white, reproaches the victor for the death of her Alban lover and is herself killed by him. In one drawing, David chose to represent the death of Camilla but later decided in favor of the earlier event where three generations of the Horatius family watch the terrible vow taking place in the *atrium* of their house.

The story of the Horatii is told in the writings of Livy, Plutarch, and Dionysius of Halicarnassus; subsequently it gave the French dramatist Corneille (1606–84) the theme for one of his greatest tragedies. First performed in 1640, Corneille's *Horace* appeared on the Paris stage in 1784, the year David completed his picture. But no literary text described the Horatii's oath and David probably turned for inspiration to another picture—exhibited in 1771, by the minor artist Jean-Antoine Beaufort (1721–84)—the *Oath of Brutus* (Musée Frédéric Blandin, Nevers). David himself said of the *Horatii*: "If I owe my subject to Corneille, I owe my picture to Poussin." Having selected a constricted, heroic style for the subject, David

▲ *Death of Germanicus* by Poussin; oil on canvas; 148×198cm (58×78in); 1627. Minneapolis Institute of Arts

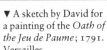

▼ A sketch by David for a painting of the *Oath of the Jeu de Paume*; 1791. Versailles

▲ *Distribution of the Eagles* by David; oil on canvas; 610×931cm (240×367in); 1810. Versailles

also achieved the diffuse lighting, monumental gestures, and smooth brushwork consonant with the 17th-century artist's own greatest pictures that represent antique heroism, notably the *Death of Germanicus* (Minneapolis Institute of Arts).

As the first distinguished Neoclassical painting, David's *Horatii* epitomizes the movement's love for precisely copied antique costume, edifying subject matter, and simple imagery. But the wiry toughness of the male figures, sharp contours, and subtle highlights—which make every detail distinct—are entirely individual, and typical of David's finest work. The hand of the elder Horatius, clenched around the swords, forms the apex of a triangle which leads the beholder's eye down through the arms of the heroes and across to the answering contrast of the desolate women.

Commissioned for Louis XVI by the *Direction des Bâtiments* and completed by David in Rome in 1784, the *Oath of the Horatii* was first shown publicly in the artist's Roman studio early in 1785. News of the picture's success soon reached Paris. From Rome, David wrote repeatedly to France

imploring a favorable place at the Salon and the sensational reception accorded to the *Oath of the Horatii* when it finally appeared there ensured David's future eminence and prosperity as the most highly acclaimed painter in France. In 1786 he painted a reduced variant for the Comte de Vaudreuil (Toledo Museum of Art). He also produced two more "oath" compositions: *Oath of the Jeu de Paume* (1791), never completed and known only from sketches, and *Distribution of the Eagles* (1810; Versailles). In both works the antique heroism of the *Horatii* is transformed into a heroic representation of contemporary history.

SARAH SYMMONS

Further reading. Friedlander, W. *From David to Delacroix*, Cambridge, Mass. (1952). Honour, H. *Neoclassicism*, Harmondsworth (1968). Levey, M. *Rococo to Revolution*, London (1966). Rosenblum, R. *Transformations in Late Eighteenth Century Art*, Princeton (1967).

▲ *Oath of the Horatii* by David; oil on canvas; 330×425cm (130×167in) Louvre, Paris

▼ From *Oath of the Horatii*, the apex of the left-hand figure composition

▼ From *Oath of the Horatii*, a woman comforts the two members of the youngest generation

rules. His pictures are simple in construction: all action is confined to the foreground and the colors he uses maintain cool, consistent tones. By means of this formal simplicity, the sentiments conveyed are made doubly arresting.

Like Rousseau, David felt that it was the artist's moral duty to paint elevated subjects and that these subjects should be rooted in ancient notions of virtue. Such notions could also be applied to the way in which the painter depicted contemporary events. In his speeches to the Convention in the earliest years of the French Revolution, David expressed the belief that works of art might become inspiring to future generations of spectators. In fact, the compelling nature of David's paintings is sometimes considered as propaganda for the Jacobin cause. However personally disastrous David's commitment to politics may have been—he was imprisoned after the downfall of Robespierre—the quality of his work became supremely expressive at the time of his most violent political activity. His talent for striking exactly the right note in a painting directly relevant to contemporary issues appears in the *Death of Marat* (1793; Musées Royaux des Beaux-Arts de Belgique, Brussels). Here David concentrated on a single figure, which occupies the whole canvas: a figure visually analogous to a piece of ancient sculpture because it forms a pale silhouette against the darkness of the background. It is, however, a portrait of the corpse of Jean-Paul Marat, an imaginatively reconstructed scene of immediately after the subject's assassination by Charlotte Corday which had taken place on 13 July 1793. For French spectators of the 1790s, this work by David formed a pictorial balance between the stark heroism of Antiquity and the sordid reality of political murder. The French poet and critic Charles Baudelaire observed in 1846 that such a perfect visual expression of pathos put David's *Death of Marat* far beyond the associations of political bias; it also puts it beyond any superficial Neoclassical displays of scholarly learning. David placed the remote source material of the Neoclassical artist within the comprehension of ordinary spectators, without compromising the original ideal.

In 1766–7 and 1791–3 Sir William Hamilton had a number of volumes of engravings published which showed the complete collection of his "Etruscan" vases. (The ambassador's collection was eventually given to the British Museum, London, where much of it can still be seen.) The decorative designs of these vases caused many scholars and artists to reconsider their original assumptions about the artistic conventions of Antiquity. The ceramic paintings were emphatically primitive, consisting mainly of elongated figures worked into flat patterns. The subsequent rage for vases and vase paintings became another facet of international Neoclassicism. From the late 1760s, Josiah Wedgwood's pottery factory in Staffordshire created an enormous international market for modified versions of antique ceramics. The most popular style invented by Wedgwood was "Jasper Ware", a combination of white motifs on a colored background, generally blue or green, which paralleled the hard-edged silhouettes painted on the sides of authentic antique vases.

It was not long before similar patterns appeared in the more elevated branches of the arts. Wedgwood's most eminent designer was the English sculptor John Flaxman (1755–1826), who exploited the commercial precedent of Wedgwood's pottery by applying comparable abstractions of figures both to his sculpture and to his graphic work. During a long study period in Rome, from 1787 to 1794, Flaxman was commissioned to draw a series of illustrations to the works of Dante, Homer, and Aeschylus. The artist intentionally designed a composition that rejected all graphic illusion and made his illustrations flat and colorless, drawn and printed in thin outlines which formed austere patterns over the white background. The success of these designs was almost unequaled in the history of illustration. They were published in new and repeated editions throughout Europe and America in the 19th century and were frequently pirated. And they exercised a unique influence as formal pattern books on several generations of 19th-century artists.

The strange forms of many works of art and design produced at the end of the 18th century were manifestations of an artistic creed of primitivism. The search for authentic, ancient images and the uncluttered truth of representation reached back to the roots of civilized society itself. Between 1803 and 1805, two young German artists, the brothers Franz and Johannes Riepenhausen, produced a series of rudimentary line drawings which they felt approximated to lost paintings from the time of Homer. In England, the poet and engraver William Blake (1757–1827) spent his life delving into ancient art forms and became convinced that a flat, linear style such as Gothic was closer to the primal ideal than the art of Classical Antiquity. In France, David's pupils denounced their master, criticizing his work for being "Rococo"; they founded a new sect, "Les Primitifs", in which they tried to unite art and life in a general effort to recreate remote Antiquity. It was in answer to the abuse of these students that David painted his most artificially "primitive" work, *The Sabine Women ending the Battle between the Romans and the Sabines* (1799; Louvre, Paris), whose composition was based on an illustration by Flaxman and an engraving from one of the "Etruscan" vases in the Hamilton collection. Nevertheless, such traditional Roman histories were no longer considered exclusively worthy of the artist's skill. Homer's works were still overwhelmingly popular as subject sources for painters and sculptors but new subjects were recommended: sources as diverse as the Bible and reconstructed verses of the Celtic bard Ossian, which were greatly admired in Europe at the end of the 18th century. This widening of Neoclassical interests appears in the work of Jean-Auguste-Dominique Ingres (1780–1867), a pupil of David, who carried Neoclassicism through to the second half of the 19th century. Ingres revered the masters of the past and copied their styles quite openly in his work. Eventually he created a unique synthetic style with adaptations after Raphael and Poussin, early Renaissance and Gothic art, Flaxman engravings, primitive vase designs, Eastern art, and Roman wall-paintings.

Like his contemporaries, Blake and Flaxman, Ingres argued that ideal art had developed from a supremacy of line over color. This accounts for much of the experimental nature of his work, when he copied subjects from Homer into undulating, flatly colored compositions, for example *Venus Wounded by Diomedes* (1805; Öffentliche Kunstsammlung, Kunstmuseum, Basel). These were condemned by French critics for their primitive qualities. The restricted character of Ingres' inspiration led him to a doctrinaire means of expressing the aims of Neoclassicism. In *The Apotheosis of Homer* (1827; Louvre, Paris) Ingres painted a ceiling panel for the Salle Clarac of the Louvre which recalled the ceiling painting by Mengs of *Parnassus* (Villa Albani, Rome): neither picture made any concessions to the spectator and both were intentionally derivative. In his version Ingres portrayed the most eminent personalities in the history of human culture, including Raphael, Mozart, Poussin, Dante, Orpheus, and Apelles. They are arranged before a Greek temple to pay homage to Homer, who is being crowned by a winged Victory. At Homer's feet are two seated female figures, personifications of the epic masterpieces, the *Iliad* and the *Odyssey*, which had provided so much inspiration for Neoclassical artists. Like Winckelmann, Ingres placed the achievement of Greek culture above even the greatest masters of succeeding civilizations.

Nevertheless, this doctrinaire ideal, which forms the basis of Ingres' paintings, also makes the artist's work uniquely progressive. Each painting by Ingres establishes its own pictorial laws, regardless of conventional perspective or anatomy. Ingres made the painted world an autonomous reality, distinct from everyday life. It was this abstraction in pictorial terms that not only divided Ingres' work from that of his master, David, but also made Ingres a source of inspiration for early-20th-century masters like Picasso. A picture like Ingres' *Antiochus and Stratonice* (1839; Musée Condé, Chantilly) becomes, therefore, an ultimate development of Neoclassical painting. The figures are perfectly static; the setting, which Ingres copied exactly from a Pompeiian interior, monumentalizes this stillness. As the most personal expression of an artistic doctrine, Ingres' picture confirms the fact that Neoclassicism was perhaps the most artificial of any European art movement.

An analogous development towards formal simplicity appears in Neoclassical architecture. European architects who began studying Greek and Roman buildings—intending to copy them for wealthy patrons—became more ambitious: the Neoclassical architect became the Neoclassical town-planner and studied the writings of the ancient Roman architect, Vitruvius. Neoclassical urban projects usually showed architectural complexes based on regular grid or semicircular systems which avoided cramped streets and small, mean dwellings.

Antiochus and Stratonice by Ingres; oil on canvas; 57×98cm (22×39in); 1839. Musée Condé, Chantilly

The work of the German Friedrich Weinbrenner (1766–1826) at Karlsruhe, or that of the English architect John Wood the Younger (1728–81) at Bath, were realizations of such ideals. The more visionary example of Neoclassical urbanization was Claude-Nicolas Ledoux's saltworks at Arc-et-Senans in central France, constructed between 1771 and 1774, and his unbuilt futuristic city project at Chaux, where Ledoux also envisaged a new social order.

Many early Neoclassical architects made journeys to view ancient ruins in the quest for new ideas. James Stuart (1713–88) who, with Nicholas Revett (1720–1804), was one of the first English explorers to reach Greece, also designed the first building to use an accurate Greek Doric order since Classical times: a garden pavilion in the shape of a temple, erected in 1758 in the gardens of Hagley Park, near Birmingham. The most popular British architect of the 1760s, Robert Adam (1728–92), spent four years in Italy and Dalmatia where he made an analysis of Diocletian's Palace at Spalato, published in 1764. Adam used ancient architectural units and decorative details as a means to create a new type of domestic architecture. The best example of his stylistic compromise between the exoticism of antique architecture and native British styles is at Osterley Park on the outskirts of London (1761–80). Here Adam inserted an exact copy of the Temple of the Sun from Palmyra on to the existing redbrick Elizabethan facade to form an unusual portico which contrasts daringly with its surroundings. But the academic nature of such an exercise was soon eclipsed by the inventions of Adam's successors.

In architecture, Neoclassicism developed a new freedom and sense of fantasy. The prophetic designs of Claude-Nicolas Ledoux were able to carry the movement beyond the doctrine of merely copying Antiquity as an end in itself. Additionally, the work of architects like Sir John Soane (1753–1837), exemplified in the new buildings for the Bank of England, London, showed a free adaptation of both Greek and Gothic forms. In public building, enormous demands were made on the architect at the end of the 18th century and the beginning of the 19th. Different types of civic building were required by rapidly expanding industrial societies. The theater, the church, the prison, the factory, and the college all offered the architect opportunities to exploit the new techniques and forms he had learned from Antiquity. The importance of ancient structures for large architectural complexes was especially important in the erection of museums in the early 19th century. The conservation of antique works of art, brought back to Europe by archaeologists, and the formation of great national collections of painting and sculpture, gave rise to much architectural debate as to the kind of building suited to house such trea-

Osterley Park, Middlesex; the portico was designed by Robert Adam and built c1762

The Glyptothek, Munich, designed by Leo von Klenze; built 1816–30

Étienne Louis Boullée's vision for a monument to Sir Isaac Newton; c1780–90. Bibliothèque Nationale, Paris

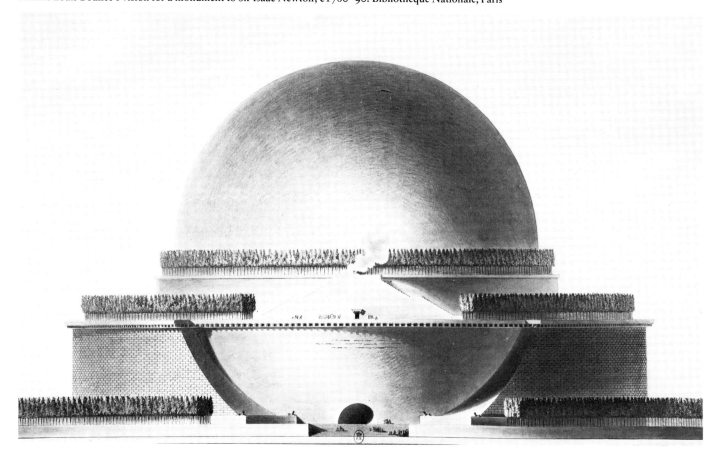

Cupid and Psyche by Antonio Canova; marble; 46×58×43cm (18×23×17in); 1787–93. Louvre, Paris

sures. In Germany the Altes Museum, built in Berlin between 1823 and 1830 by Karl Friedrich Schinkel (1781–1841), and the Munich Glyptothek, erected between 1816 and 1830 by Leo von Klenze (1784–1864), showed how simple, cubic forms and the orders of Antiquity could be adapted to plain, light interiors for the display of art objects. Later museum buildings owe much to the work of these architects. In America, the museums of Washington and Philadelphia use similar designs. The apparent modernity of much Neoclassical build-

ing developed from the exploitation of structural simplicity and lack of extraneous decoration. The epitome of the resulting futuristic vision in architecture appears in designs by Étienne Louis Boullée (1728–99). His monument to Sir Isaac Newton (plans in the Bibliothèque Nationale, Paris) formulated between 1780 and 1790, was both prophetic and impossible to build. The edifice is a perfect sphere which also incorporates a planetarium. The scale of the project is of an immensity that perhaps reflects the scope of Newton's own researches and their significance for the 18th century. Boullée's plan, with its decorative rows of tiny trees and geometrical purity, summarizes the ultimate aspirations of the Neoclassical movement.

Sculpture was probably the most expressive Neoclassical artistic medium. It was also the most historically immediate, since fragments and even whole figures of Greco-Roman statuary had survived in a state of reasonable preservation and could therefore be studied first hand. In Winckelmann's pamphlet of 1755, antique sculpture formed the principal source of knowledge for the writer's description of the art of Antiquity.

Inevitably Rome became the center of Neoclassical sculpture. The city housed the best examples of antique prototypes available for the European artist to study and the foreign patrons and scholars who visited Italian collections formed the main market for the professional sculptor. Most of these leading European sculptors spent as much time as possible in Rome. Antonio Canova (1757–1822) came to Rome from Venice in 1780 and, under the tutelage of the painter Gavin Hamilton, established himself as the most important Neoclassical sculptor. His principal rivals and colleagues were John Flaxman, who spent seven years in Rome, Thomas Banks (1735–1805), who visited Rome in the 1770s and in-

troduced doctrinaire Neoclassical sculpture into England, and the Dane, Bertel Thorvaldsen (1770–1844), who first arrived in Rome in 1797 and remained there for 41 years.

In Rome, the sculptor's studio was generally open to visitors who could see work in progress and where replicas of the most popular statues were produced by assistants. Antonio Canova ran the largest and most important studio and eventually became the most renowned sculptor of the 18th century. His work was revered on a worldwide scale; at least five European monarchs became his patrons and the Pope made him a Marchese in 1816. Canova studied Antiquity as a way of achieving his conception of perfect beauty in sculpture, which might transcend the imperfections of nature. He was never a blindly imitative artist, despite his dependence on antique prototypes, and his mature achievement preserved the doctrines of Neoclassicism without losing the originality of the artist's own vision. The dynamic qualities of Canova's style recreated the vitality of ancient notions of carving, as in *Cupid and Psyche* (1787–93; Louvre, Paris).

In 1810 the marble frieze from the Parthenon in Athens, which had been brought to England by Lord Elgin, was exhibited in London. This frieze initiated a new idea of ancient sculpture, and one opposed to the original strict rules of Neoclassicism. Some artists and scholars refused to accept the

The monument to Penelope Boothby by Thomas Banks; marble; 1793. Ashbourne Church, Derbyshire

frieze as a genuine example of Classical Greek work; for others like Canova, who visited London in 1815, the frieze was a revelation. It was realized, almost for the first time, that ancient sculpture was not exclusively designed in terms of the static, compact outlines first described by Winckelmann. The Greeks had also created vital surface textures which conjured dramatic events. European sculptors were subsequently divided in their approach to the recreation of antique ideals: those like Thorvaldsen continued to produce cool, statuesque figures, while new experiments in sculpture appeared from other Neoclassical masters.

John Flaxman was a particularly talented designer of low relief. His outline illustrations demonstrate his interest in undulating surface patterns which could also be transferred to sculpture. Flaxman's tombs formed a new achievement in shallow carving on plain marble surface, exemplified by the monument to Agnes Cromwell (1800; Chichester Cathedral). In tomb sculpture Flaxman found the greatest opportunity to exploit his lapidary skills. It was also in this medium of tomb design that many sculptors expressed the deeper concerns of the Neoclassical movement. The most impressive English Neoclassical tomb was the work of Thomas Banks, the monument to Penelope Boothby (1793; Ashbourne Church, Derbyshire), a simple marble effigy of a dead child lying on a classical sarcophagus. In Vienna, Canova's great tomb to the Austrian Archduchess Maria Christina (1798–1805; Augustinerkirche) is probably the most moving Neoclassical monu-

ment ever made. It consists of a frieze of classically draped figures, depicting all ages of man. At the time, this frieze was compared to a chorus from Sophocles. The figures seem to advance towards the blackness of an open door, set in the side of the tomb itself, which is a plain marble pyramid. Neither Banks nor Canova chose to add any supernatural images to these monuments, despite the pathos and sentiment of both works. They seem to be expressing a disillusion and doubt which was also expressed by writers and philosophers at the end of the 18th century. In this context Neoclassicism can be seen as a transitional phenomenon: contemporary uncertainties of faith and dramatic social and political changes experienced by 18th-century societies underlay much of the Neoclassical nostalgia for the simpler ideals of the pagan world. It is this sense of uncertainty and yearning for the past which, almost imperceptibly, introduces Romanticism into the heart of Neoclassical artistic inspiration.

SARAH SYMMONS

Bibliography. Arts Council of Great Britain *The Age of Neoclassicism*, London (1972). Bindman, D. (ed.) *John Flaxman R.A.*, London (1979). Honour, H. *Neoclassicism*, Harmondsworth (1967). Irwin, D. *English Neoclassical Art; Studies in Inspiration and Taste*, London (1966). Klingender, F.D. *Art and the Industrial Revolution*, London (1968). Rosenblum, R. *Transformations in Late Eighteenth Century Art*, Princeton (1969). Rykwert, J. *The First Moderns: the Architects of the Eighteenth Century*, London (1980).

40

ROMANTICISM

Liberty Guiding the People by Delacroix; oil on canvas; 260×325cm (102×128in); 1831. Louvre, Paris (see page 756)

ROMANTICISM was the principal movement involving all the arts that flourished in Europe in the first half of the 19th century. It gained its epithet because the movement was understood to stand for an emotive and intuitive outlook, as against the controlled and rational approach that was designated "classical". While modern opinions differ as to the meaning of Romantic, the history of the term's usage is clear. Deriving from the medieval chivalric tale—the *romaunt*—and used since the Renaissance to denote the fanciful or improbable, the word was first applied to a type of art in 1798 in the definition of "Romantic poetry" given by the German critic Friedrich von Schlegel (1772–1829) in *Athenaeum*, the magazine edited by himself and his brother August Wilhelm (1767–1845). It rapidly gained currency in Germany to describe the kind of literature and art supported by the Schlegels: a literature that emphasized the subjective and fantastic and took as leitmotivs the art of the Middle Ages and a fascination with wild, uncultivated nature. The Schlegels considered Romanticism to be modern in its broadest connotation, applying it to the whole of the post-classical age. In this sense the word first reached a non-German public through *De l'Allemagne* (1813) by the French writer Madame de Staël (1766–1817). As the poet Coleridge observed, this work made the British public (as well as the French) "familiar with the habit of distinguishing the productions of Antiquity by the appellation Classic, those of modern times by that of Romantic".

Romanticism was thus first seen as a revival of the fundamentally modern, spiritual, and fantastic ethos of the Middle Ages which had been subverted by the pagan throwback of the materialist Renaissance. And if such "modernity" contained an implicit censure of the present, its corollary was an ironic, anti-heroic view of the contemporary world. It was in both senses that the word became a battle cry during the 1820s—particularly in France. The movement only seriously lost impetus when the Realists began to champion a less emotively charged view of the present in the 1840s.

The attractiveness of the notion of Romanticism was greatly enhanced by the circumstances in which it arose. The mystic idealism of the original German Romantics was inspired by the transcendental philosophies being developed by their associates J.G. Fichte (1762–1814) and F.W. Schelling (1775–1854) from the *Critiques* of Immanuel Kant (1724–1804). Such a direction was more universally stimulated by political developments; the decline of the French Revolution of 1789 into the Reign of Terror and the subsequent Dictatorship of Napoleon seemed to many—especially those outside France—to give lie to the faith of the 18th-century Enlightenment in the ability of pure reason and natural sentiment to sweep away the injustices and superstitions of the past. To these intellectual and political upheavals can be added a third: the Industrial Revolution, which brought social evils that cast serious doubts upon the benefits of material progress. However, although industrialization had been gathering force in England during the late 18th century, and had been the subject of some

of Blake's most eloquent protests, it was not until the 1830s that the effects of industrial progress became a cause of widespread social concern.

While Romanticism was used by major critics— from Friedrich Schlegel to the French poet Baudelaire in the 1840s—to describe what they considered to be most significant in contemporary art, it never became an explicit movement among visual artists in the way that later tendencies, Realism for example, were to become. In painting, sculpture, and architecture we ought properly to speak of Romanticism in terms of the influence of, or analogy with, current literary and critical notions.

In this sense, however, "Romantic" does have a positive application, for we can see how intimately the predominant pictorial tendencies of the period are connected with the characteristics then currently being hailed as Romantic. Individualism and intuition were central concerns—especially for Blake and Goya. The fascination with the evocative qualities of nature gave a new impetus to landscape painting which is reflected in the work of Turner, Girtin, Palmer, Friedrich, Runge, and Corot. The enthusiasm for the Middle Ages encouraged a full-scale revival of pre-Raphaelite art by the German Nazarenes and gave a new seriousness of purpose to the Gothic revival in architecture—especially in England, where it was championed by the fanatical A.W. Pugin (1812–52). Similarly, the "Romantic irony" first formulated by Friedrich von Schlegel, which stemmed from the contradiction felt by the Romantic between his boundless idealism and the reality of his situation, seems mirrored in a new type of pictorial subversion. This is already evident in the satirical fantasy of Goya, but it was the French who took this furthest in the atmosphere of anticlimax that followed on Napoleon's final defeat in 1815. Pictures like Delacroix's nihilistic fantasy on *The Death of Sardanapalus* (1827; Louvre, Paris) appeared to flout all conventional notions of morality and pictorial propriety. It is significant that this period should also have seen the establishment of that enduring form of the mock heroic, the political cartoon, so brilliantly exploited by the English satirist James Gillray (1757–1815).

Because Romanticism was essentially a matter of outlook, we can hardly talk of it in terms of a set of formal stylistic characteristics. However, there were some predominant pictorial tendencies. While styles ranged from the extreme linearity of the Germans to the extreme painterliness of the French there was in both a peculiar intensity, a state of heightened awareness that is at times visionary and at times simply sensuous. In both, too, there is a predominant interest in color—that emotive property so scorned by Neoclassical theorists like Winckelmann (1717–68). Runge, Delacroix, and Turner all became deeply interested in color theory both for its symbolic potential and for the creation of more vibrant effects. The interest in association evident here also led to the simulation of styles from far-off times and places either for sheer effect or, in the case of the medieval revival, to censure the present. The proliferation of stylistic allusions was matched by a disre-

The Death of Sardanapalus by Delacroix; oil on canvas; 395×495cm (156×195in); 1827. Louvre, Paris

gard for traditional distinctions among the different types of art. History painting lost its former moral supremacy—frequently becoming merged with genre—and landscape was seen by many as the most important of art forms. In sculpture the animalier came into prominence. There was a similar breakdown in tradition in architecture; the informal principles of planning, unknown outside small domestic architecture since the time of the Renaissance, were reintroduced into church building and such major civic edifices as the Houses of Parliament in London (1836–65).

While "romantic" elements can be traced in certain works of art in most ages, the late 18th century saw the emergence of more tangible precursors to the historical movement. Despite the efforts of such propagandists as Winckelmann, the emulation of the "noble simplicity and calm grandeur" of Greek art

was never more than a notional ideal, and if it encouraged a move towards greater simplicity and succinctness it was never able to suppress totally more expressive tendencies. In the very city at the center of the classical revival, Rome, there flourished a circle of artists who were reinvigorating a Baroque sense of the megalomanic and bizarre, basing their awesome scenes on the exaggerations in the works of the 17th-century Neapolitan painter Salvator Rosa (1615–73) and of such surviving masters of the architectural capriccio as Giovanni Paolo Panini (1691–1765). The most notable and influential member of the Roman circle was the architect Giovanni Battista Piranesi (1720–78), a Venetian who settled in Rome in 1740 and became renowned for his etchings of Roman antiquities and for his fantasies on massive darkened interiors, the Imaginary Prisons (c1745).

Landscape Painting

One of the most striking features in the art of the late 18th and early 19th centuries was the growing importance attached to landscape painting. This reflected new attitudes to nature. Under the influence of such writers as Jean-Jacques Rousseau (1712–78) an idyllic image of the natural world had been evoked which provided a contrast to the corruptness and artificiality felt to abound in contemporary society. At the same time, developments in the natural sciences encouraged a closer study of the individual forms of nature.

Religious support was provided by the argument that God's creative spirit could be directly observed in nature. Such reasoning was used, for example, by the critic John Ruskin (1819–1900) when defending the landscapes of Turner in volume one of his *Modern Painters* (1843).

The landscape painting stimulated by such interests tended to dwell on emotive effects. These ranged from the dramatic and frightening, as in Turner's *The Shipwreck* (1805; Tate Gallery, London), to the soothing and tranquil, as in Constable's affectionate portrayal of his native scenery in *The Cornfield* (1826; National Gallery, London). Yet such works were also explorations of new means of describing natural phenomena. There were considerable naturalistic advances, particu-

▲ *The Shipwreck: Fishing Boats Endeavoring to Rescue the Crew* by Turner; oil on canvas; 172×241cm (68×95in); 1805. Tate Gallery, London

▶ Landscape in watercolor: *Tintern Abbey* by Turner; 37×27cm (15×11in); 1794. British Museum, London

▶ Divine Revelation witnessed in the landscape of Kent: *The Magic Apple Tree* by Samuel Palmer; watercolor and pen; 35×27cm (14×11in); 1830. Fitzwilliam Museum, Cambridge

◀ *The Cornfield* by John Constable; oil on canvas; 143×122cm (56×48in); 1826. National Gallery, London

larly in the field of atmospheric effects. It was during this period that the habit of making out-of-doors studies in oil and watercolor became common, although it was not until the time of the Impressionists, later in the 19th century, that it became desirable to complete landscape paintings out of doors.

While the new attitudes to landscape can be found throughout Europe and North America, they were most dominant in Britain and Germany. It is perhaps easier, however, to grasp the variety of Romantic landscape painting by considering thematic types rather than national distinctions.

In the later 18th century the painting of sensational scenes became a major interest. Part of the stimulus for this came from Edmund Burke's critical treatise *A Philosophical Inquiry into the Origin of our Ideas of the Sublime and Beautiful* (1757) which provided a striking new definition of the Sublime, seeing it as a sensation generated from feelings of repulsion and fear. Before this time, however, the French painter Claude-Joseph Vernet (1714–89) was evolving a type of stormy scene that provided contemporaries with a *frisson* of alarm. Vernet's example was followed by many other artists, including J.M.W. Turner (1775–1851) in his early years. Turner's *The Ship-wreck* described a kind of disaster that was highly common at the time. Some artists deliberately exploited the popular appeal of sensational themes. One of the most successful of these was John Martin (1789–1854), whose *The Great Day of His Wrath* (1851–4; Tate Gallery, London) was part of a three-picture spectacular based on descriptions from the Book of Revelation.

The use of landscape to convey uplifting spiritual sensations related to a more traditional conception of the Sublime than Burke's. However, nature did not have to be dramatic or overpowering to stimulate such thoughts. The visionary painter and poet Blake talked of seeing "a World in a Grain of Sand and a Heaven in a Wild Flower". Blake himself rarely practiced landscape, but he influenced a number of artists who did. Most notable among them was Samuel Palmer (1805–81) who used the gentle scenery of Kent to suggest Divine Revelation. In Germany a similar approach to landscape was explored by Philipp Otto Runge (1777–1810) and Caspar David Friedrich (1774–1840). The latter painted both dramatic and intimate scenes, using carefully constructed designs and exquisite light effects to intimate a hidden meaning in his works.

The growing interest in the Natural in the 18th century stimulated a love of irregular and unkempt effects. In England this led to the development of the informal garden and

Above: *The Great Day of His Wrath* by John Martin; oil on canvas; 197×303cm (78×119in) 1851–4. Tate Gallery, London

▲ *The Oaks* by Théodore Rousseau; oil on canvas; 64×100cm (25×39in); c1850–2. Louvre, Paris

to the search for pleasingly varied scenes in the countryside. Under the stimulus of such writers as William Gilpin (1724–1804), such views became described as "Picturesque". Around 1800 it became a habit to make "Picturesque tours" both in Britain and abroad. This fashion was encouraged by topographers who provided "Picturesque" views of famous beauty spots. Turner produced such works in his early years.

The Picturesque movement fostered the appreciation of especially scenic places. But there were those who emphasized that all nature was worthy of attention. Constable—

disdainful of topographers and the Picturesque—made a virtue of depicting the everyday appearance of his native Suffolk. Similar views were expressed by other artists throughout Europe and America, such as the Austrian Ferdinand Georg Waldmüller (1793–1865) and the American painters of the Hudson River School.

While the Romantic emphasis on heightened awareness fell increasingly out of favor after 1840, the close attention to natural description remained influential, as, for example, with the French painters of the Barbizon school.

WILLIAM VAUGHAN

Further reading. Clark, K. *Landscape into Art*, London (1978). Parris, L. *Landscape in Britain c1750–1850*, London (1973). Rosenblum, R. *Modern Painting and the Northern Romantic Tradition*, London (1975).

For the English connoisseur Horace Walpole (1717–97) these scenes with their exaggerations in scale and chiaroscuro could be summed up by the word "sublime", and his use of this was typical of contemporary reaction. For after another English connoisseur, Edmund Burke (1729–97), had published his *A Philosophical Inquiry into the Origin of our Ideas of the Sublime and Beautiful* (1757) this term had taken on a new dimension. From being seen as an extreme kind of beauty, the Sublime now came to mean exactly the opposite. For Burke explained that whereas the sense of beauty was derived from feelings of love and attraction, the sense of the Sublime derived from feelings of hatred and repulsion. It was only the fact that we were experiencing the *representation* of something horrid or overpowering rather than the thing itself that caused such feelings to be transmuted into a thrilling sensation of awe. In itself Burke's explanation was a rationalization and left the door open for the uninhibited enjoyment of the sensational by men of taste and learning.

The "sublime" effects of Piranesi were emulated by many other artists who came to Rome, notably Claude-Joseph Vernet (1714–89), who began c1760 to add wild shipwrecks and other stormy scenes to his Claudian repertoire, and Hubert Robert (1733–1808), who made paintings of evocative ruins popular in France. It was a painter trained in the French tradition, Philip Jacques de Loutherbourg (1740–1812) who conveyed such landscapes to Britain when he settled in London, after leaving Paris in 1771. De Loutherbourg's interest in dramatic effect was exploited to the full when he worked at the Drury Lane theater as a scene painter (1773–81). He subsequently set up his own miniature theater, the Eidophusikon, in which paintings were enhanced by moving parts, changing lights, and sound effects—a forerunner of the dioramas and panoramas that became so popular in the early 19th century. De Loutherbourg's illusionism gave a strong impetus to dramatic landscape painting in England, particularly affecting the young Turner.

A concern for sublime effect also developed among figure painters who came to Rome, especially after the 1770s. For these, the vast murals of Michelangelo formed the point of departure, particularly for John Henry Fuseli (1741–1825) and his associates—the Swedish sculptor Johan Tobias Sergel (1740–1814) and the Danish history painter Nicola Abraham Abildgaard (1743–1809). Among architects there was also an emulation of Piranesian grandeur, which culminated in the schemes of the French architects Étienne-Louis Boullée (1728–99) and Claude-Nicolas Ledoux (1736–1806)—schemes vast in scale and based on geometric forms of overpowering simplicity. These architects devised some of the most radical—if most impractical—ideas for buildings prior to the 20th century; the sheer daring and scope of their ambition has often led to them being accorded the paradoxical title of "Romantic Classicists". Yet is should be emphasized that such architects, like Fuseli and his circle, saw no breach between their art and the ideals of Antiquity.

If the Sublime was largely inspired by current and ancient art in Rome, England was the setting for another aesthetic revaluation, one that encouraged the informal in art. Through the writings of such amateurs as William Gilpin (1724–1804), Sir Uvedale Price (1747–1829), and Richard Payne Knight (1750–1824), the word "Picturesque" became applied to those pleasurable sensations felt before art and nature that were not powerful enough to be either beautiful or sublime, but which were nevertheless considered to be worthy of interest. Of the theorists, Gilpin had the clearest idea about what constituted the Picturesque, looking for an amalgam of the features of Dutch and Claudian landscapes and insisting in particular that there should be "variety" in the foreground—as could be provided by rocks, cottages, or some homely scene of rustics and livestock—and a tranquil distance in contrast. Other theorists were more concerned with the evocative qualities of the Picturesque rather than in formulating precise regulations. But however much views might differ, the notion stimulated a greater appreciation of the irregular and accidental.

The Picturesque made its mark first on that art most directly concerned with nature: landscape gardening. The taste for "landscaping" gardens—as opposed to imposing a formal pattern on them as in Italy and France—was an English innovation. The first to establish the practice was the architect and painter William Kent (1685–1748), whose Claudian glades can still be found at Rousham, Oxfordshire (c1730). He was soon to be followed by such consummate cosmeticians of nature as Lancelot "Capability" Brown (1715–83) and Humphry Repton (1752–1818). And while the taste for an "English Garden" spread throughout the courts of Europe—even penetrating Versailles during the reign of Louis XVI—the indigenous product moved further and further away from the measured effects of Claude. The apogee of wildness was reached in the untamed woods that surrounded the mock-Gothic abbey of Fonthill, Wiltshire (1795–1800) built for the millionaire eccentric William Beckford (1760–1844) by James Wyatt (1746–1813).

Fonthill Abbey had originally been conceived as a folly to adorn this wilderness; Beckford's decision to turn it into a dwelling represents a stage in the invasion of the principles of the Picturesque into domestic architecture. The progenitor of this taste appears to have been Horace Walpole who, in 1749, began to "Gothicize" his villa of Strawberry Hill at Twickenham and had by 1785 turned it into a confection of crockets, battlements, and irregularly placed turrets. By that time even the leading arbiter of mid-century classicism, Robert Adam (1728–92), had made essays in the "Castle style" and was concerned for the "picturesque of a composition" in such evocations of Roman Antiquity as Kedleston Hall, Derbyshire (c1765–70). The dominant personality in late Georgian architecture, John Nash (1752–1835), brought the Castle style to such small villas as Luscombe, Devon (c1800). In these, informal planning was a major feature. Similarly, it is the graceful but *irregular* sweep of the streets that provides the principal charm of Nash's layout for the area in London between Re-

Elohim Creating Adam by William Blake; color print finished in watercolor (only known copy); 43×53cm (17×21in); 1795. Tate Gallery, London

gent's Park and the Mall (1812–25). His chief rival, the more ingenious and intellectual Sir John Soane (1753–1837), was less ostentatious in the informality of his planning. Yet he had the most eclectic notion of proportion and delighted in the creation of "Gothic" lighting effects.

In painting, the Picturesque has most effect in revising the topographical view—the description of a specific landscape. The change can be seen in the medium favored by the English for such work, watercolor. A consummate recorder like Thomas Sandby (1721–98), who began his career working on a military survey, ended it painting rich and evocative scenes in Windsor Forest. But the most poignant of all such view-painters was John Robert Cozens (1752–97). The son of Alexander Cozens (c1717–86)—an artist best remembered for a system of inventing new compositions from random blots—John Robert Cozens interpreted the mountainous and hilly scenes of central and southern Italy with an almost painful sensibility—see, for example, *View from Mirabella* (1782; Victoria and Albert Museum, London). His feeling for the nuances of light was to have a great influence on a younger generation of watercolorists, particularly Thomas Girtin (1775–1802) and J.M.W. Turner (1775–1851).

In the later 18th century the word "romantic" came to be used increasingly for those effects whose poignancy was felt to transcend even the Picturesque. Thus it could be chosen by the architect William Chambers as a synonym for a kind of "enchanted" garden he supposed the Chinese to have devised. It was also used for the wistful late lakeland scenes of Thomas Gainsborough (1727–88), such as the *Rocky Landscape* (c1783; National Gallery of Scotland, Edinburgh). Finally, in a posthumous publication by Gilpin (1808), the term was firmly separated from the Picturesque when this auther supposed Arthur's Seat in Edinburgh to be romantic, but not picturesque because it was "odd, misshapen, and uncouth"—"a view with such a feature could no more be picturesque than a face with a bulbous nose can be beautiful".

While the later 18th century saw an increasing move towards the emotive and the evocative, it was not until the 1790s that these emerged anywhere as overriding principles. Although the effects of this change can be traced in all the arts it was explored most extensively in painting, considered at the time to be the most Romantic of the visual arts because it depended on evocation to suggest such intangibles as color and atmosphere. In this it contrasted strongly with the "classical" presentation of three-dimensional form by the sculptor.

Romantic painting. Before the formulation of any Romantic theory of the arts in Germany, there emerged in England and

Third of May, 1808 by Goya; oil on canvas; 266×345cm (105×136in); 1814. Prado, Madrid

in Spain two major and totally independent artists who made the Visionary a major feature of their work. In this sense, and this sense only, can we compare William Blake (1757–1827) and Francisco Goya (1746–1828). For whereas Blake considered his visions to be a form of Divine Revelation, Goya explored the darker side of his creative imagination without attempting an interpretation.

Blake's declaration "talent thinks, genius sees" drew a clear distinction between rational deduction and the insights of creative genius. All his life he fought a battle against the "law-givers", whether they were political, religious, or artistic. Believing that "one law for the Lion and Ox is oppression", he defended the need of the individual to follow his own inner convictions rather than obey the regulations of others. In artistic matters this led him to attack the academic system of education, in particular the teachings of Sir Joshua Reynolds, the first President of the Royal Academy of Arts in London, who had propounded a set of general precepts for painters in his *Fifteen Discourses* (1769–90).

The radical nature of Blake's views on individual freedom accorded with the upsurge in liberal opinions that emerged at the time of the French Revolution. During the 1780s he was an associate of such reformers as William Godwin and Mary Wollstonecraft (the proponent of women's rights) and his own prophetic books—the kernel of his artistic production—were deeply concerned with contemporary social and political problems. Casting such reforming zeal in the form of prophecies was not unusual for that time—there were many other emulators of the Old Testament seers who arose in the wake of Revolution, the millennialist Joanna Southcott for example. Blake differed from the other prophets of the age, however, in associating art with religious experience. For him even Christ was an artist, who acted "from impulse, not rules". The deliberately archaic nature of his own pictures and poems accorded with his view of them as the product of Divine Revelation: he spurned the worldliness of acquired accomplishments. In painting, this led to the rejection of oil painting in favor of a more rigorous and primitive form of tempera painting which he referred to as "fresco".

While expressing a mounting independence of thought, Blake's pictorial style was related to many of the concerns of his contemporaries. His early watercolors of historical and religious subjects, such as the scenes from *The Story of Joseph* exhibited at the Royal Academy in 1785 (Fitzwilliam Museum, Cambridge), share the sentimental Neoclassicism of his friend John Flaxman (1755–1826). Like Fuseli and other imaginative history painters of the period, Blake had a great admiration for the vigor of Michelangelo's creations. This can be felt most strongly from the series of large monoprints he made during the 1790s. Superficially, the succinctness and force of these designs have affinities with the "heroic" art of the 1790s elsewhere, as in David's *Death of Marat* (Musées Royaux des Beaux-Arts de Belgique) and the cartoons of the German J.A. Carstens (1754–98). But Blake has none of the humanism of these classical artists. Nothing could be further from Michelangelo's ennobling view of the Creation than Blake's *Elohim Creating Adam* (1795; Tate Gallery, London) where God the Father is shown as a harsh lawmaker enslaving a free spirit with the coils of mortality.

Blake's appreciation of the expressive in Michelangelo also made him an admirer of the pictorial qualities of the Gothic. His own books—printed by a method devised by himself—revived the interrelation of illustration and text to be found in the illuminated manuscript, using it to achieve a continuous association of verbal and visual meaning. While an admirer of the Grecian line in the 1790s, Blake moved during the next decade to the position of exclusive medieval revivalist, declaring Gothic form to be "living" and Grecian to be "mathematical". However, while his later work shows an increasing love of the undulating rhythms of the Gothic, he never abandoned his admiration for Michelangelo. His last undertaking, an unfinished series of designs for Dante's Divine Comedy (1824–7), shows a synthesis of the two. Such designs as the *Circle of Luxury: Paolo and Francesca* (City of Birmingham Museums and Art Gallery) have vibrant form and flickering color that provide a perfect visualization of visionary energy.

An artist so concerned with individual inspiration was hardly likely to be concerned with imprinting his style on followers. And while his designs were occasionally adopted by Fuseli (who confessed "Blake is damned good to steal from") his most gifted admirer, Samuel Palmer (1805–81), worked in landscape painting, a genre Blake rarely attempted. It was not until the end of the century that his forms began to find imitators among the Symbolists.

While Blake gradually developed from the poetic to the prophetic during the 1780s, the visionary tendencies of Goya (1746–1828) emerged in the 1790s with little prelude. Previously he had successfully pursued a professional career as a tapestry-designer for the Spanish court and as the most fashionable portrait-painter in Madrid. Nor did his excursions into the imaginative affect his worldly status; he remained in the service of the monarchy to the last decade of his life, from 1799 as first painter to the King.

The dramatic changes in Goya's art during the 1790s may have partly resulted from his sensitivity to the changing situation in Spain—the decline in government after the accession of Charles IV in 1788 and the growing threat from Revolutionary France which culminated in the invasion of 1808. Certainly Goya's portraits take on a more somber tone in the 1790s; his vast and grandiose group portrait of *The Family of Charles IV* (1800–1; Prado, Madrid) is so candid in its characterization of the ineffectual king and his rapacious wife that it seems to verge on caricature.

But a more profound cause of Goya's development was the severe illness he suffered in 1792 which enfeebled him for several years and left him permanently deaf. This traumatic experience and the resulting isolation appear to have made him more introspective. Soon after his illness he presented the Academy of Madrid with a series of vigorously handled satires on religious ceremonies and superstitions, such as *The Burial of the Sardine* (1792–3; Academy of San Fernando, Madrid) which he claimed to have painted "to make observations for which commissioned works generally give no room, and in which fantasy and invention have no limit". But it was the savage and fantastic etchings *Los Caprichos* (1796–8) that first showed his imagination in full spate. The plate *The Sleep of Reason Produces Monsters* could be taken as a leitmotiv for the whole, showing as it does Goya being prompted involuntarily into action by the creatures of the night. Here, as elsewhere in the series, he adds aquatint to the etching to combine somberness with sensitive detail.

Goya's penetrating gifts were put to a very different use in his next series, *The Disasters of War* (1810–13; first published in 1863), the outcome of his experiences of the Peninsular War (1808–12). In these, Goya bore witness to the full horror of the conflict between the occupying French forces and the populace. Moments of heroism are few: Goya is more concerned to bring himself (and us) to face the butchery and other senseless acts of inhumanity than to spread any political message. He took a similar approach when painting two large scenes for the restored regime in 1814 showing the events that had sparked off the Spanish resistance: the uprising in Madrid on 2 May 1808, and the retaliatory mass executions during the subsequent night (*Madrid, the Second of May* and *Third of May, 1808*; both in the Prado, Madrid).

In his last years, Goya continued to explore his imagination, producing another series of fantasies, *Los Proverbios* (c1815–24) and, more extraordinary still, a series of murals for his house on the outskirts of Madrid. These starkly painted *Black Paintings* (c1821–3; Prado, Madrid) show a hypnotic series of visions—two giants clubbing each other in a landscape, a witches' sabbath, a procession of leering pilgrims. The meaning of most of these can only be guessed, but even recognizable myths have been given a new twist to emphasize the passions. *Saturn Devouring one of his Children* shows the god as a fear-crazed old man, acting out of a blind instinct for self-preservation.

In 1824, Goya left Spain to end his days in voluntary exile in France, a gesture against the brutish actions of the current Spanish King, Ferdinand VII. While living in Bordeaux, he apparently had no connection with the young French Romantics in Paris, although Delacroix was later to become one of the first Frenchmen to admire *Los Caprichos*. Yet despite this, it was one of these younger artists, J.L.A.T. Géricault (1791–1824) who came closest to Goya's unflinching exploration of experience.

The Raft of the Medusa by Géricault; oil on canvas; 490×716cm (193×282in); 1819. Louvre, Paris

Both Goya and Blake's subject pictures had, to a large extent, developed out of the conventions of history painting. But even within the genre there was a gradual move towards a greater sensationalism and a more complex understanding of motivation. In England, the American-born painter Benjamin West (1738–1820) had challenged the viability of painting noble events in a generalized manner when he depicted the recent death of an English hero during the war against France in Canada—*Death of General Wolfe* (1770; National Gallery of Canada, Ottawa)—in contemporary dress. The immense success of this work was due to its skillful blending of apparent reportage with a carefully controlled design based on a religious *pietà*. It was a formula to be repeated with even greater boldness and effect by David, a great admirer of West, in such modern subjects as his *Death of Marat* (1793; Musées Royaux des Beaux-Arts de Belgique, Brussels). These topical moral exemplars reached their apogee in the vast celebrations of the Napoleonic campaigns by David's pupil A.-J. Gros (1771–1835). Gros' own hero worship of the Emperor made it possible for him to give a sense of deep conviction to his presentation of Napoleon as a man of compassion, visiting the sick in *The Pesthouse at Jaffa* (1804; Louvre, Paris), mourning the dead in *Napoleon on the Battlefield of Eylau* (1808; Louvre, Paris). Yet it also encouraged him to develop a rich

painterly manner to conjure up these scenes of far-off places with persuasive vividness: it was this quality that, to his great dismay, was to help the young Romantics bring a new immediacy into history painting.

The first to respond to such febrile emotiveness was Théodore Géricault (1791–1824). A pupil of the animal painter Carle Vernet (1758–1836) and the history painter P.-N. Guérin (1774–1883), he fused both genres in his full-scale early equestrian Salon pieces *Officers of the Imperial Guard* (1812; Louvre, Paris) and *The Wounded Cuirassier* (1814; Louvre, Paris). The first of these is full of fire and movement, but the second, painted at the moment of the defeat of the French, is heavy in color and subdued in design. Its somber mood was to remain a constant note in Géricault's later works. The general atmosphere of anticlimax heightened Géricault's personal restlessness: after abandoning a scheme to turn a modern theme, the "Race of the Riderless Horses", into a formal classical design while studying in Rome (1815), he returned to France to devote himself to the topical. Bereft of the heroic, he turned instead to the sensationalism of crime and scandal. *The Raft of the Medusa* (1819; Louvre, Paris), the vast canvas with which he sought to make his name at the Salon of 1819, was a monumentalization of ministerial incompetence. It showed the ghastly outcome of a shipwreck brought about by the folly of a captain of a government ship. The design, with its complex pyramid of rigorously studied figures and corpses, was an academic *tour de force*. Yet it moved outside the conventions of history painting by depict-

Left: Saturn Devouring one of his Children by Goya; detached fresco on canvas; 147×82cm (58×32in); 1821. Prado, Madrid

ing a scene without a hero, and by representing the whole with a lurid pallor more nauseous than cathartic.

Disappointed at the tepid reception of his work, Géricault attempted no other *grande machine* in his short life. However, he continued to explore the disconcerting sides of modern life with rare sympathy, especially in his lithographs of the workers and outcasts of London (which he visited in 1821) and in some portraits of mental patients painted for a doctor friend. In the sense that Géricault was confronting his spectator with an unfamiliar, if unwelcome, truth, he still shared the moral outlook of the classical history painter. But even this was brought into question during the 1820s by Eugène Delacroix (1798–1863).

Although often seen as Géricault's successor, Delacroix rarely concerned himself with modern France, preferring instead the exoticism and fantasy aready explored by such favored painters of Napoleon's court as A.-L. Girodet-Trioson (1767–1824) and P.-P. Prud'hon (1758–1823). Delacroix's *Massacre at Chios* (1824; Louvre, Paris), a scene from the Greek War of Independence, may have been topical but it was also exotic in its setting. The nonchalance and painterly lassitude objected to in this work were nothing compared to those in his principal contribution to the Salon of 1827, *The Death of Sardanapalus* (Louvre, Paris). This fantasia on the

The Mad Assassin by Géricault; oil on canvas; 60×50cm (24×20in); 1822/3. Museum of Fine Arts, Ghent

climax of a play by Byron shows the notorious eastern potentate watching dispassionately as his goods and struggling concubines are piled around him prior to their communal immolation. Painted in gleaming clashes of hot color, its amorality and pictorial subversiveness brought him official censure. No doubt his truly modern—if faintly ambiguous—allegory celebrating the July Revolution of 1830, *Liberty Guiding the People* (1831; Louvre, Paris) was carefully devised to keep him in favor with the new regime. Certainly the government of Louis Philippe supplied him well with official commissions, as well as enabling him to accompany a diplomatic mission to Morocco in 1832. The heightened sense of color he gained from this helped him to capture the sensuous tedium of the harem in *Women of Algiers* (1834; Louvre, Paris), a work which, as Baudelaire hinted, was all too relevant to the predicament of the Madame Bovarys of contemporary France.

Despite such innuendoes, Delacroix had reached a position of total disdain for the modern world by the mid 1830s and devoted his energies to the isolated task of becoming a great mural painter. In his decorations of ministerial buildings and churches, which culminated in the tranquil poetry of *Jacob Wrestling with the Angel* in St Sulpice, Paris (1856–61), he is as traditionalist as his arch rival, the classicist Ingres. Only in his continued exploration of the vibrancy of color did he remain a Romantic.

By the 1830s, Romantic history painting in France was popularly represented by artists like Paul Delaroche (1797–1856), who specialized in depicting such fateful and poignant scenes from the past as *The Princes in the Tower* (1831; Louvre, Paris) in minute and seemingly accurate detail. Their sensationalist style was emulated throughout Europe, notably by Gustav Wappers (1803–74) and the macabre Antoine Wiertz (1806–65) in Belgium, by Karl Friedrich Lessing (1808–80) in Germany, and—in his later years—by David Wilkie (1785–1841) and by Daniel Maclise (1806–70) in England.

Such vivid accounts of notable events are often hard to distinguish from contemporary anecdotal genre. Delacroix himself followed his friends R.P. Bonington (1801–28), Eugène Devéria (1805–65), and A.-G. Decamps (1803–60) in painting spirited, small medieval scenes, oriental subjects, and other exotica. At the same time, low-life genre painting took a more sentimental turn, following the lead of such virtuous representations of peasant life as *The Paralytic Tended by his Children* (1763; Hermitage Museum, Leningrad) by J.-B. Greuze (1725–1805). In the early 19th century, Wilkie's engaging Dutch-inspired Scottish scenes like *The Penny Wedding* (1819; Collection of H.M. Queen Elizabeth II) became highly popular, and after he abandoned the genre in the 1830s it was continued by such artists as William Mulready (1786–1863). Mulready's domestic lyricism was matched in central Europe by a type of emotive but unpretentious art referred to as *Biedermeier*—seen for example in the small interiors by the German painter G.F. Kersting (1785–

1847) and in the rosy narratives of the Viennese Moritz von Schwind (1804–71). A similar mood can also be found in the works of such French genre painters as the meticulous Louis Léopold Boilly (1761–1845).

The interest in the passions gave a new significance to animal painting. In England the 18th-century animal painter George Stubbs (1724–1806) had depicted such dramatic moments as *White Horse Frightened by a Lion* (1770; Walker Art Gallery, Liverpool). But it was James Ward (1769–1855) who reveled most fully in the untrammeled energy of purely sensual creations, turning Rubensian vigor into savage conflict in his *Bulls Fighting before St Donat's Castle* (1804; Victoria and Albert Museum, London). Such uninhibited painting was greatly admired in France in the 1820s and was imitated by Géricault and Delacroix. In England, however, it was to degenerate into the sleight-of-hand animal surrogates for mawk-

ish human emotion painted by Sir Edwin Landseer (1802–73).

In portraiture, too, there was an increasing emphasis on mood. The darkening tone of Goya's later portraits witnessed not only the artist's changing disposition but also a growing cult of melancholy. Manifestations of this in Napoleonic France can be found in Prud'hon's enchantingly soulful portrait of *The Empress Josephine* seated in a darkened forest (1805; Louvre, Paris) or in Girodet-Trioson's programmatic image of the writer Chateaubriand, unkempt and tousled, before his native Breton heath (1808; Musée de St-Mâlo). The most prestigious portrait-painter of the period was the Englishman Sir Thomas Lawrence (1769–1830), who brought a new suavity to the Augustan tradition of Gainsborough and Reynolds. His nonchalantly posed figures (for example *Charles William Bell*; 1798; Louvre, Paris) were admired not only for the brilliance of their handling, but also for epitomiz-

The Princes in the Tower by Delaroche; oil on canvas; 181×215cm (71×85in); 1831. Louvre, Paris

Rain, Steam, and Speed—the Great Western Railway by J.M.W. Turner; oil on canvas; 90×121cm (35×48in); R.A. 1844. National Gallery, London

ing the careless elegance of the English man of fashion, the dandy. However, the finest Romantic portraits were not those of the professional, but ones that penetrated to a more intimate level like the sensitive self-portrait of Samuel Palmer (c1828; Ashmolean Museum, Oxford), the candid child portraits of Runge (for example *The Hülsenbeck Children*, 1805–6; Hamburger Kunsthalle, Hamburg) or the sympathetic pathological studies of Géricault (*The Kleptomaniac*, c1822–3; Museum of Fine Arts, Ghent).

While most Romantic figure painters sympathized with the fantasy and spirituality of the Gothic, the Romantic period also was an attempt to revive more thoroughly the pictorial principles of the Middle Ages. As with Blake, it was the emulation of Grecian purity that first led to a full appreciation of the primitivism of the Gothic. In the 1790s Rome became a center for this, as reflected in the Gothic elements in the *Outlines to Homer and Dante* Flaxman designed there (1790–4). At the same time, the growing reaction to the changes that followed the French Revolution stimulated a nostalgic view of the Age of Faith and its artifacts, notably in the writings of W.H. Wackenroder (published 1797), Novalis, and Friedrich von Schlegel (published 1803–4) in Germany, and of Chateaubriand (published 1802) in France—a mood strengthened as sequestrations of church property brought to light many previously unknown works of art. In the Rhineland,

Flemish and German primitives were rediscovered and collected by the Boiseree Brothers, who were later to instigate the completion of Cologne Cathedral according to the 14th-century plans. In Paris, many Northern and Italian primitive paintings found their way into the Musée Napoleon (c1798–1815)—the vast agglomeration of booty from the Emperor's campaigns. Among the pupils of David, J.-A.-D. Ingres (1780–1867) and Fleury Richard (1777–1852) evolved a minuteness of manner from the museum's works by the van Eycks and from other Flemish paintings. Indeed, Ingres was roundly censured for his Gothicism when he exhibited his three portraits of individual members of the Rivière family (Louvre, Paris) and the hieratic *Napoleon I on the Imperial Throne* (Musée de l'Armée, Paris) at the Salon of 1806. But the style enjoyed the support of the Empress Josephine, and it was at the Imperial court that the foundations of what later became known as the *style troubadour* were laid. Ingres himself, despite his Grecian predilections, returned to medieval themes from time to time throughout his life, while the bright colors and sinuous lines of his style show an enduring debt to Gothic art.

However, it was the German Nazarenes who staged the most far-reaching revival. Originally a "Guild of St Luke", formed by six art students in Vienna in 1809 to restore the truth, purity, and character of pre-Renaissance art, the leading members of the group went to Rome in 1810 where they lived for two years in a deserted convent, hermetically sealed in a world of their own fancy and hoping to paint it into existence. Together with the earlier neo-Grecian "Primitifs" in David's studio c1800, the Nazarenes—so called on account of the medievalizing costume they adopted—represent the beginning of the familiar pattern of breakaway groups of the modern avant-garde. And, as with all such groups, success modified its radicalism. The early period was dominated by the passionately imaginative Franz Pforr (1788–1812), who painted such scenes of medieval chivalry as *Rudolph of Habsburg and the Priest* (1810; Städelsches Kunstinstitut, Frankfurt am Main) with a radical naivety. After his tragically early death, the movement turned—under the influence of his close friend Johann Friedrich Overbeck (1789–1869)—towards a simple piety, its Düreresque emphasis on character being modified into a schematized version of the early style of Raphael evident in Overbeck's major didactic statement *The Triumph of Religion in the Arts* (1830–40; Städelsches Kunstinstitut, Frankfurt am Main). In this form, Nazarene art became a model for the art of the international Catholic revival that flourished in the decades after the fall of Napoleon. In France it was emulated by such religious painters as Jean-Hippolyte Flandrin (1809–64). In England, the style of Overbeck was particularly praised by Pugin and was adapted to English tastes by the architect's protégé J.R. Herbert (1810–90). It also met with more qualified approval from the Anglo-Catholic revivalist William Dyce (1806–64), whose combination of medievalism and naturalism prefigured that of the Pre-Raphaelites.

Meanwhile the movement was also being channeled towards a more secular revival by Peter Cornelius (1783–1867), who joined them in Rome in 1812. Under the aegis of this aspirant monumental artist, the group painted a series of scenes, the *Story of Joseph* (1815–16; Nationalgallerie, East Berlin) in a room of the house of the Prussian Consul in Rome, Salomon Bartholdi. Painted in the manner of the Quattrocento and reviving the technique of pure fresco, this achievement commanded great respect in Rome. It also led to the adoption of the revivalist style as the official monument art form in Germany, particularly in Munich, whither Cornelius was summoned by Crown Prince Ludwig of Bavaria in 1820, and where he decorated the Glyptothek (decorations since destroyed) and the Ludwigskirche with a *Last Judgment* (1836–9). Although endowed with a genuine dramatic gift—which occasionally emerged, as in cartoons such as the Düreresque *Four Horsemen of the Apocalypse* (1845; Nationalgallerie, East Berlin)—in most of his work he reverted to the principles of the High Renaissance, in which the Classical was more evident than the Gothic.

Today, the revivalism of the Nazarenes seems lifeless and pedantic—it seems hard to credit the authority they exerted in their own day. This must be put down to an unquestioning faith in their thoroughness and idealism. For as one English admirer, the painter Sir Charles Eastlake (1793–1865) wrote

when dealing with the Cesa Bartholdi, "they have dignified their style by depriving the spectator of the power of criticizing the execution".

During the Romantic movement landscape painting emerged as one of the most important genres. This was partly a legacy of the veneration of the Natural inspired by the philosopher Jean-Jacques Rousseau (1712–78); but added to this was the pantheistic belief—so evident in the poetry of William Wordsworth (1770–1850)—that intimations of the Divine could be found in the workings of nature, and the observation that the moods of man could be reflected in its forms—later censured by Ruskin as the "pathetic fallacy". In landscape painting this led in two seemingly contradictory directions: the exploration of the visionary or dramatic, evident in the works of Samuel Palmer, John Martin, and Caspar David Friedrich, and a close study of the appearance of local scenes, as in the works of Constable and the French Barbizon painters.

The greatest landscape painter of the period, J.M.W. Turner (1775–1851), encompassed both within his art. A truly protean figure, his vast output ranged from the quietest and most intimate of moments to the wildest of storms. It is true, as Ruskin remarked, that Turner dwelt on these two extremes rather than on the middle ground, but there is more than exaggeration and showmanship to his work. For in his exploration of effect he moved beyond mere descriptiveness to the discovery of more vivid forms of pictorial equivalents. In his last years in particular he conveyed his atmospherics through the juxtaposition of pure colors and freedom of handling unrivaled before the advent of abstraction.

The son of a London barber, and with a poor formal education, Turner was from the start a virtuoso in painting. He was made a full member of the Royal Academy in 1802 at the youngest possible age of 27. Before then he had fully mastered the genre of topographical watercolor (which he was to practice throughout his life) and had become engaged in emulating and then intensifying the effects of the great 17th-century masters of landscape. From the breezy seascapes of the van de Veldes he developed such archetypally Romantic scenes of man pitted against the elements as the *Wreck of a Transport Ship* (1810; Gulbenkian Foundation, Lisbon) in which the feeling of a storm is conveyed through a whirling, vortex-like composition which was to become increasingly familiar in his later life. *Snowstorm: Hannibal and his Army Crossing the Alps* (1812; Tate Gallery, London) shows a masterful combination of the sublime effects of Salvator Rosa (1615–73) with the control of Nicolas Poussin (1594–1665); *Crossing the Brook* (1815; Tate Gallery, London) brought the ethereal calm of Claude to an idyllic rural scene.

Such themes had always been accompanied by an assiduous recording of nature, mostly in pencil and watercolor, but occasionally in the open-air oil sketch; it was this receptiveness that led Turner in the 1820s to develop a new approach to color after he had experienced the vividness of southern light during his first visit to Italy in 1819. The outcome of this can be seen in *Ulysses Deriding Polyphemus* (1829; National Gal-

Wreck of a Transport ship by J.M.W. Turner; oil on canvas; 173×245cm (68×96in); 1810. Gulbenkian Foundation, Lisbon

lery, London) where the Homeric hero mocks his former captor against a sunrise of strident bands of complementary colors. His new feeling for luminosity gave him a deeper appreciation of the "mystic veil" of Rembrandt's color which can be felt in such interiors as *Interior at Petworth* (c1835; Tate Gallery, London). He also took a great interest in color theory at this time, studying Goethe's *Theory of Colors* (English translation published in 1840) and experimented in color symbolism in such pictures as *Peace: Burial at Sea* (1842; Tate Gallery, London) where the unrelieved blackness of a ship's sails dominates the silvery harmonies of a nocturnal seascape. In the 1840s these developments culminated in such limpid atmospheric evocations as *Rain, Steam, and Speed—the Great Western Railway* (1844; National Gallery, London), a somewhat ambiguous celebration of the awesome achievement of the new railways. While these last works seem close to abstraction, as do his innumerable studies and preparations, the subject remained a crucial element in his art: in this fundamental relationship of pictorial effect to association and evocation, Turner was completely of his age.

While Turner abandoned all ostentatious exploitation of

scale after *Snowstorm: Hannibal and his Army Crossing the Alps*, this aspect of his art was taken to improbable lengths by John Martin (1789–1854). Scale was so much the essence of this melodramatist's craft that he would often calculate the exact height of his vast mountains to demonstrate their stupendousness. The main effect of Martin's *The Great Day of his Wrath* (1851–4; Tate Gallery, London) derives from the literalness with which he attempts to visualize the eschatological predictions of the Book of Revelation. Francis Danby (1793–1861) was his main rival in popularizing the extremist side of Romantic landscape. But Danby was too sophisticated a painter to vie with Martin's most uninhibited exaggerations, and his finest works were the small, fresh views of the neighborhood of Bristol—such as *Clifton Rocks from Rownham Fields* (c1822; City Art Gallery, Bristol)—where he lived from 1811 to 1824.

The poignancy and calculated naivety of these relates them to the near-contemporary visionary landscapes of Samuel Palmer (1805–81). Under the inspiration of Blake, Palmer studied nature "with a child's simple feeling and with the industry of humility". And during the 1820s he was able to endow his small scenes of the Kent countryside around Shoreham—where he lived from *c*1827 to 1832—with a jewel-like intensity. The clear outlines and magnified features of his rich vegetation and rounded hills, seen, for example, in *A Hilly Scene* (*c*1826–8; Tate Gallery, London) celebrate the fruitfulness and spirituality of nature. Like Blake, he spurned the illusionistic accomplishments of post-Renaissance art for the precision of the primitives, declaring "there is no aerial perspective in the valley of vision".

While at Shoreham, Palmer was a member of a group of similarly minded artists—notably John Linnell (1792–1882), Edward Calvert (1799–1883), and George Richmond (1809–96)—whose isolationism, archaism of style and costume, and title "The Ancients" have affinities with the Nazarenes.

The German medieval revival also stimulated an intensive form of local landscape, notable in the sensitive Düreresque pen drawings of the surrounds of Salzburg and Vienna by Ferdinand Olivier (1785–1841), a member of the Guild of St Luke who never undertook the journey to Rome. However, it was in the Protestant north, beyond the sphere of the revivalists, that the visionary landscape reached its apogee in Germany. The most significant practitioners were two Pomeranians, Philipp Otto Runge (1777–1810) and Caspar David Friedrich (1774–1840), both of whom came to maturity under the influence of the Romantic circle in Dresden after having studied in the Neoclassically orientated academy of Copenhagen. Runge was essentially a figure painter, who became obsessed with the notion of landscape while in Dresden (1801–3). Believing that "a work of art comes into being only at the moment when we feel ourselves united with the universe", he sought to encompass the universal in his scheme to paint four interrelated pictures of the "Times of Day". The outline plans he drew for these in 1803 are a beautiful series of arabesques interweaving *genii*, flowers, and other natural images into symmetrical patterns of growth and decay. It was his ultimate aim to paint these as large canvases which would be shown in a specially designed Gothic building to the accompaniment of poetry and music. Like Blake, Runge was inspired by Jakob Böhme, sharing the early-17th-century mystic's view of light as a spiritual source. During the last years of his life, while living with his brother in Hamburg, he made a thorough study of light effects and color, published a book on the latter, and developed a fine sensibility for both in his paintings. His early death prevented the completion of the "Times of Day" scheme and it might in any case have proved impossible to convey his ecstatic feeling before nature "when everything harmonizes in one great chord" with the clarity that he sought. Nevertheless he had great perceptive powers as a painter, as can be appreciated in his portraits of his friends and family, in particular *The Hülsenbeck Children* (1805–6; Hamburger Kunsthalle, Hamburg), which captures the elemental nature of young children without a breath of sentimentality.

The longer-lived Friedrich created a more substantial achievement. However, while deeply imbued with a sense of

The Hülsenbeck Children by Philipp Otto Runge; oil on canvas; 130×140cm (51×55in); 1805–6. Hamburger Kunsthalle, Hamburg

the spiritual in nature, he never attempted Runge's ambitious synthesis of landscape and religious ideologies. He concentrated instead on intensifying his actual experiences, advising the painter to "close your bodily eye, so that you may see your picture first before your spiritual eye. Then bring to the light of day that which you have seen in the darkness, so that it may reflect upon others from the outside inwards." The remembered nature of his images can be felt in the precision with which they are painted, but the features of the landscapes themselves are always based upon careful studies. For the most part he painted scenes that had a special meaning for him, in particular the coastlands of his native Pomerania and the high mountains of the Harz and Riesengebirge which he visited from Dresden, where he had settled in 1799. While never portraying moments of dramatic action, Friedrich was habitually a painter of extremes—barrenness, ruins, mists, and snow. Yet even in his midday scenes of verdant farmlands there is a sense of the transcendental, conveyed through his control of design and feeling for luminosity.

Friedrich's deep sense of religion led him in 1808 to fulfill a commission to paint a landscape as an altarpiece (*The Cross on the Mountains*, 1807; Gemäldegalerie Alte Meister, Dresden), a work that associated him in the popular mind with the mysticism of the Schlegel brothers and their followers. His most radical achievement, however, was his abandonment of conventional notions of landscape design in favor of simpler and more compelling arrangements. His *Monk by the Sea* (1809; Schloss Charlottenburg, Berlin) shows an individual dwarfed by the endlessness of nature, using an unbroken horizon line and suppressing all introductory coulisses to emphasize its monotonousness. In later years his style became distinctly more spontaneous under the influence of the naturalist movement. Yet he still maintained a sense of reverence for the spiritual in nature by means of such devices as the inclusion of figures in the foreground staring towards the distance (for example, *Moonrise over the Sea*, 1822; Nationalgalerie, Berlin).

A number of German painters emulated the imagery and lighting effects of Friedrich, in particular the Dresden artists E.F. Oehme (1797–1855) and C.G. Carus (1789–1869). However, they lacked his intensive sensibility and religious preoccupations. Carus' notion of landscape as "earth-life painting", expressed in his *Nine Letters on Landscape Painting* (1815–24), is closer to Goethe's scientific approach to nature. By 1830, Romantic landscape painting in Germany had moved from the fatalistic towards the playful irony of Karl Blechen (1798–1840) and the lyrical sentimentality of such Biedermeier artists as A.L. Richter (1803–84).

As we saw in the case of Turner, the exploration of the emotive in nature in no way precluded a growing keenness of observation. Yet there is an emphatic difference between the search for more vivid effects and the analysis of appearances for their own sake which is found in the works of Realists and Impressionists later in the century. It is questionable whether any of the so-called painters of nature of the early 19th century were so dispassionate in their outlook. Certainly the leading representative of this tendency, the Englishman John

Constable (1776–1837), was not. Although the formative part of his career—from his declaration in 1802 that "there is room for a natural painture" to the completion of *The Hay Wain* in 1821 (National Gallery, London)—showed a growing understanding of the effects of light and atmosphere, he never abandoned the notion of the composed *grande machine* (which *The Hay Wain* in fact is) or of what he called the "moral feeling of a landscape". Even his habit of making open-air oil sketches for his finished pictures was not new. It was a well established practice among painters active in Rome in the mid 18th century like Pierre Henri de Valenciennes (1750–1818) and Thomas Jones (1742–1803). It is true that Constable made a more frequent use of the oil sketch than either these or his contemporaries Turner and John Linnell. His cloud studies in particular show a far more analytical interest in meteorological phenomena than those of such earlier artists as Alexander Cozens, while his habit of making a full-scale compositional sketch for his large works helped to preserve in them something of the spontaneity of the original scene. But he never saw the art of landscape as a mere matter of recording appearance. Not only was he fully aware of the impossibility of imitating nature precisely, but he also remained convinced of the emotionally beneficial effects of his art. The calm lyricism of *The Hay Wain* reflected his fond memories of the countryside of his Suffolk childhood rather than the strife-ridden rural world of the 1820s, in the grips of

Monk by the Sea by Caspar David Friedrich; oil on canvas; 110×171cm (43×67in); 1809. Schloss Charlottenburg, Berlin

The Hay Wain by John Constable; oil on canvas; 130×185cm (51×73in); 1821. National Gallery, London

an economic recession. In later life, when his Wordsworthian delight in the Natural had darkened under the strain of such losses as the death of his wife (1829), he sought a catharsis for his sadness in such stormy handling as that of the sketch for *Hadleigh Castle* (1829; Tate Gallery, London).

> How for some wise purpose is every bit of sunshine clouded over in me. Can it be wondered at that I paint continual storms "Tempest o'er tempest rolled"? Still the darkness is majestic and I have not to accuse myself of ever having prostituted the moral feeling of Art ... My canvas soothes me into a forgetfulness of the scene of turmoil and folly and worse.

(Leslie, C.R. *Life of Constable*, 1843.)

Constable's most influential achievement was to bring a new freshness into *salon* painting, and he was censured, as Géricault was, for painting the apparently trivial on a monumental scale. In English watercolor painting, the local landscape was being recorded with a similar vividness and in more acceptable dimensions. The fine sensibility for light of J.R. Cozens (1752–97) was emulated both by Turner and by Thomas Girtin (1775–1802) when Dr Monro set them to copy paintings by Cozens in the 1790s. While Turner was inspired by these to a bolder exploration of atmospherics, Girtin captured more of their quiet control and poignancy, as can be seen in *The White House* (1802; Tate Gallery, London). Another master of the structured watercolor (in his early years) was John Sell Cotman (1782–1842) who in works

like *Chirk Aqueduct* (c1804; Victoria and Albert Museum, London) used flat, simple washes to bring a sense of the monumental to the chance view. But the most fashionable watercolorists were those who painted with a breezy virtuosity, such as Peter de Wint (1784–1849) and David Cox (1783–1859).

In France, the spontaneity of the English school had a great effect on the Romantics in the 1820s. Constable's *The Hay Wain* was greatly admired by Géricault when he visited England in 1821. And when the work was subsequently shown in the Salon of 1824 (where, characteristically, it was described as a "sketch") it stimulated Delacroix to rework parts of his main exhibit there, *The Massacre at Chios*. It was at this time that Delacroix became a strong admirer of English art and a close friend of the Anglo-French painter Richard Parkes Bonington (1801–28), whose brilliant watercolor effects he emulated. A Constabelian bravura can be found in the moody landscapes of Paul Huet (1803–69); but the profoundest response to the English master in French landscape came from P.E.T. Rousseau (1812–67), the leader of the group of artists that formed in the 1830s around the village of Barbizon in the forests of Fontainebleau to study a pure and unaffected nature. Rousseau, who had been greatly impressed by *The Hay Wain* when he saw it in 1833, shared Constable's poetic pantheism and love of trees. The other principle members of the group, Jean-François Millet (1814–75), Charles-François Daubigny (1817–78), and Virgilio-Narcisse Diaz de la Pena

The White House by Thomas Girtin; watercolor; 30×52cm (12×20in); 1802. Tate Gallery, London

(1808–76) had differing interests in nature and rural life but were all convinced of the need to study their subjects on the spot. There were at the same time more indigenous traditions of French naturalism, such as the Dutch-inspired renderings of the heathlands around Montmartre by Georges Michel (1763–1843): Jean-Baptiste-Camille Corot (1796–1875) brought to the naturalist movement the careful tonal control of the oil sketches of the Roman school. In later life he became popular for a feathery, silver-toned, manner of painting whose wistfulness is romantic in a more conventional sense.

If links can be forged between the naturalist movements of England and France, these are more tenuous in the case of Germany and Scandinavia. The cloud sketches made by the Norwegian painter Johan Christian Clausen Dahl (1788–1857) at Dresden in the 1820s have remarkable affinities with those of Constable. They were partly inspired by the meteorological interest of the German Romantics, and partly by the objectivity of his former master at the Copenhagen Academy, the Roman trained C.W. Eckersberg (1783–1853), who was also the instructor of the greatest Danish naturalist, Christen S. Købke (1810–48). A similar interest in freshly handled local scenes can be found throughout central Europe in the 1830s, notably in the work of Andreas Achenbach (1815–1910) in Düsseldorf, Karl Blechen (1798–1840) in Berlin, and Ferdinand Waldmüller (1793–1865) in Vienna.

The graphic arts. The early 19th century saw a great expansion in graphic illustration stimulated by a growing popular demand for books and by the introduction of cheaper and more rapid reproduction techniques—lithography and wood engraving, for example. It also saw the establishment of regular pictorial journalism, the scabrous and fantastic satires of James Gillray (1757–1815) being followed by the more innocent wit of George Cruikshank (1792–1878), who in later life turned to the exposure of such social evils as drunkenness in *The Bottle* (1847). In France the continued political upheavals provoked a more trenchant and heroic form of comment, notably in the lithographs designed by Honoré Daumier (1808–79) for *La Caricature* and *Le Charivari*. While Daumier absorbed some of the repertoire of romantic effects—such as darkened ambiences and a brilliant nervous line—his unsentimental exposure of corruption and poverty is best seen in connection with the Realist movement. Amongst other graphic artists, the imaginative side of Gillray and Goya stimulated a lively fantasy. Cruikshank's book illustrations—notably those to *Grimm's Fairy Tales* (1824) and Dickens' *Oliver Twist* (1838)—delight in bizarre characterizations and effects. But the most extreme illustrator in this direction was the French satirist Grandville (J.-I.-I. Gérard; 1803–47) who skillfully concealed his social and political attacks in an almost surrealist juxtaposition of improbabilities, *Un autre*

Monde (1844) for example. At the same time Charles Meryon (1821–68) was employing a Gothic sense of the macabre to suggest the sinister aspects of the modern city (for example, *Etchings of Paris*, 1853).

The rise of interest in medieval art also affected book production. While Blake's return to the illuminated page went unregarded, the German revival of the border design—first evident in Strixner's lithographic reproduction of Dürer's pen drawings for the prayer book for Emperor Maximilian I (1808)—led to the popularization of the expensive, sumptuously illustrated "ballad book". The finest example of this in Germany was the 1840 edition of the *Nibelungenlied*, which contained brilliant page designs by Alfred Rethel (1816–59); it was emulated in England by such works as Daniel Maclise's designs to *Lenore* (1844). While largely historical in outlook, revivalist illustration was also used to comment upon contemporary events by Alfred Rethel, especially in his *Another Dance of Death* (1849) in which the consequences of the 1848 Revolution are depicted in the format and style of a 16th-century woodcut.

Sculpture. Sculpture was less strongly affected by Romantic tendencies than painting—at the time it was considered an essentially un-Romantic art. Yet while such sculptors as Bertel Thorvaldsen (1770–1844) maintained the most unyielding of classical styles, there was a more emotive side to most Neoclassical sculpture. This is especially the case in the Gothic overtones of Flaxman and the sensual innuendos in the work of Antonio Canova (1757–1822) and such French sculptors of the Napoleonic period as Joseph Chinard (1756–1813) and Antoine Chaudet (1763–1810).

It was only in France, however, that a programmatic stand was taken against classicism in sculpture. The principal representative of this movement was Pierre-Jean David d'Angers (1788–1856), a sufficiently dedicated modernist to insist on clothing his monuments to famous men in the costume of their age (for example *Condé*, 1817; Versailles). His modeling had a fiery bravura, admirably suited to a subject like the virtuoso violinist, *Paganini* (1830; Musée des Beaux-Arts, Angers). D'Angers fully subscribed to the Romantics' adulation of genius, and traveled throughout Europe to record the physiognomies of such men as Goethe, Napoleon, and Victor Hugo, turning their features into phrenological case studies along the lines of F.J. Gall (1758–1828) and J.K. Lavater (1741–1801).

Death approaches the town, the second plate in Alfred Rethel's Another Dance of Death; 1849

The finest sculpture that can unequivocally be referred to as Romantic, however, is the work of Antoine-Louis Barye (1796–1875). A pupil of Antoine-Jean Gros (1771–1835), he brought a painterly sensibility to sculpture, preferring the textures and light effects that could be achieved in modeling and bronze. Early in his career he restricted himself to portraying animals, although he did occasionally combine figures with these in such fanciful themes as *Roger and Angelica on the Dragon* (1847; Louvre, Paris), an incident from Ariosto's *Orlando Furioso*. In the choice of subjects he usually followed Delacroix, Géricault, and Ward in depicting savage conflicts, as in his famous *Jaguar Devouring a Hare* (1850; Louvre, Paris). Despite his close association with the subjects and techniques of contemporary painting, Barye had a profound understanding of the resources of his medium and of three-dimensional design. Perhaps understandably, he never emulated the experimental nature of the models of two painters with strong interests in the tactile: Géricault and Daumier. The latter has a rival—in topic, if not in ability—in the grotesque and humorous portrait satires of the professional modeler Jean-Pierre Dantan (1800–69).

Outside France, Romanticism hardly penetrated sculpture beyond the sporadic illustration of dramatic or medieval themes. Curiously, there was no revival of the sculptural style of the Middle Ages, except where this was a matter of architectural decoration, as in the case of the carving supervised by John Thomas (1813–62) for Barry and Pugin's Houses of Parliament (1836–65) in London.

Architecture. In architecture the Gothic revival became a powerful movement, particularly in England. Already in the 18th century there had been a renewed interest in Gothic building as a result of the Picturesque movement and a growing taste for the exotic—culminating not just in such medieval fantasias as Fonthill Abbey, but also in a proliferation of such outlandish modes as the Oriental trappings with which Nash decked out the Prince Regent's seaside residence at Brighton, the Pavilion (1815–21). In subsequent decades there was a move away from such extremes to an increasing interest in the associational, in the choice of style for a building in accordance with its provenance and function.

In France, England, and Germany, Gothic became associated with national interests; it was supposed at that time that Gothic had been indigenous to each of these countries. In Germany, the Wars of Liberation (1806–14) gave an impetus to Gothic architecture as it did to medievalism in painting. However, while the leading Prussian architect K.F. Schinkel (1781–1841) designed a number of Gothic monuments, for example, the War Memorial, Berlin (1819–21) and churches, the Werderkirche in Berlin (1825) for example, the style never became widespread. The most enduring achievement of the Gothic revival in Germany was the completion of Cologne Cathedral in accordance with the original plans—an idea generated during the period of the Wars of Liberation by the Boiseree brothers and undertaken by three generations of ar-

A plaster model for part of The Departure of the Volunteers, 1792, by François Rude; 1835. Louvre, Paris

A more complex personality was François Rude (1784–1855), a devotee of the painter David, who sought to maintain the monumental in the modern age in a manner similar to Géricault. Like Géricault, his figures have a weighty reality, whether they were of Classical subjects (for example, (*Theseus*, 1806; Louvre, Paris) or modern ones (*Bust of David*, 1833–8; Louvre, Paris). His masterpiece is *The Departure of the Volunteers, 1792* on the side of the Arc de Triomphe in Paris (1835–6). Although the volunteers are shown here in antique costume, they are impelled forward by a figure of the "motherland" whose maenadic energy outstrips that of Delacroix's *Liberty Guiding the People*.

Jaguar Devouring a Hare by A.-L. Barye; bronze; 42×95cm (17×37in); 1850. Louvre, Paris

The Houses of Parliament, London, by Sir Charles Barry and A.W. Pugin; built 1836–64

chitects between 1824 and 1880. On the other hand the predominance of Romanesque buildings in southern Germany led to the forging of an alternative "national" style, the "round-arched" style, in which Romanesque elements could be blended with the forms of the early Renaissance. This style was widely used in Munich in the ambitious building program undertaken by Ludwig I of Bavaria, for example, E. Gärtner's Ludwigskirche of 1829–40. In France the medieval revival was also less original in its manifestations, but one architect, E.E. Viollet-le-Duc (1814–79) devoted the majority of his energies to restoration work, and achieved incomparable results with such famous buildings as the Sainte Chapelle and Notre Dame in Paris.

In England, where the fascination with the life of the

Middle Ages was fanned by such detailed evocations as those in Scott's "Waverley" novels, archaeological interest, evident in the publications of John Britton (1771–1857) and Thomas Rickman (1776–1841) led to a creative revival. Gothic had already become well established as a picturesque villa style by such architects as John Nash, but after an Act of Parliament in 1818 to provide new churches for England's rapidly increasing population Gothic was revived as an ecclesiastical mode. Finally, the seal was set on the success of Gothic by its adoption for the new Houses of Parliament in 1836. It is a measure of the growing respect for historical accuracy that the architect chosen for this building, Sir Charles Barry, should have called in an expert, Augustus Welby Pugin (1812–52), to design the details for him. But Pugin was a polemicist as well as an architect. A Catholic convert, he sought to demonstrate in his *Contrasts* (1836) that the abandonment of Gothic in the 16th century had been symptomatic of a social and moral decline engendered by the Reformation. In fact, most of the evils Pugin censured could be more closely associated with the Industrial Revolution, and it was as a reaction to this that the medieval world was made a paradigm by the economist Thomas Carlyle in *Past and Present* (1843), and by Disraeli's revivalist "Young England" faction in the conservative party.

Pugin's greatest ability was for decorative effect, and his buildings appear at their best in the evocative etchings he made of them in such works as *An Apology for the Revival of Christian Architecture* (1843). Nevertheless, he also insisted on the functional nature of Gothic, and during the 1840s other architects—notably Anthony Salvin (1799–1881), Sir George Gilbert Scott (1811–78), and William Butterfield (1814–1900)—concentrated on this aspect of the style. The outcome was the widespread use of Gothic in Victorian domestic and ecclesiastical architecture with a pragmatism distinct from the picturesque and associational interests of earlier generations.

The decline and legacy of Romanticism. The change in attitude to Gothic in the 1840s was part of a general reaction to the assumptions of Romanticism. In painting this can be found in the French painter Courbet's evolution from the posturings of his early self-portraits to such untheatrical portrayals of modern life as *The Stonebreakers* (1849; believed destroyed), in the English Pre-Raphaelites' alliance of revivalism with naturalism, and in the German artist Adolph von Menzel's use of the painterly manner to make dispassionate records of contemporary bourgeois life in Berlin.

While these developments effectively challenged the Romantics' claim to modernity, much of the imaginative imagery of the movement survived in the art of the later 19th century. It can be found, for example, in the wistful medievalism of Dante Gabriel Rossetti (1828–82) or in the macabre fantasy of Gustave Doré (1832–83). The movement left a more permanent legacy in its expressiveness and exploration of the irrational, which have been an inspiration to such movements as Symbolism, Expressionism, and Surrealism. The image of the artist as an independent, self-determining original, moreover, has remained a cherished ideal of the avant-garde.

WILLIAM VAUGHAN

Bibliography. Boase, T.S.R. *English Art 1800–70*, Oxford (1970). Clark, K. *The Romantic Rebellion*, London (1974). Eitner, L. *Neoclassicism and Romanticism 1750–1850* (2 vols.), New Jersey (1970). Friedländer, M. *From David to Delacroix*, Cambridge, Mass. (1952). Hitchcock, H.-R. *Architecture: Nineteenth and Twentieth Centuries*, Harmondsworth (1977). Honour, H. *Romanticism*, Harmondsworth (1979). Novotny, F. *Painting and Sculpture in Europe: 1780–1880*, Harmondsworth (1978). Rosenblum, R. *Transformations in Late Eighteenth Century Art*, Princeton (1967). Vaughan, W. *German Romantic Painting*, London (1980).

41

REALISM

The Bathers by Courbet; oil on canvas; 227×193cm (89×76in); 1853
Musée Fabre, Montpellier (see page 770)

THE word "realism", imprecise in meaning and used over the centuries for contradictory purposes, here has two roles: to indicate a period during which art tended to be factual in its representations and references and, within that period, a particular tendency (it was never a formal movement). For the latter we shall use the capital initial: "Realism". The near identity of the two terms will remind us how much the tendency and its general context have in common, though the more extreme forms of Realism proved to be intolerable to a public happy to be regaled by realistic art. And the vagueness and breadth of the basic word hints at the fact that some degree of realism—in the sense of essaying a convincing image relatable to common visual experience—has been common to many periods of art and basic to some. The breadth of our keyword comes from man's inalienable need to distinguish between fact and illusion and between fact and fiction, without denying the potency of fiction, the conscious and unconscious product of our imaginations upon our minds and actions.

Dr Johnson's commonsensical dispatch of Bishop Berkeley's proof that matter does not exist—kicking a large stone and saying to Boswell, "I refute it thus"—showed characteristic firmness but raises the question whether the stone he kicked was more material than all the stones he might have kicked but did not have within his reach. Questions of reality are not answerable merely in terms of physical presence unless we take so strict a reading of what is and what is not real that the possibility of shared experience—of communication—is removed. All artistic activity depends on a lenient attitude to such questions, whilst changes in the major modes of art often indicate shifting, corrective evaluations of them. All creativity, it can be argued, addresses itself to the sometimes painful gap between the circumstances we call real and the potentialities our minds present to us in the form of ideals.

Nineteenth-century realism comes between two periods in which the best art attended more to the ideal and the imagined. Romanticism, in the first decades of the century, was a revolt against the reins of taste and reason that had generally been obeyed by Renaissance and post-Renaissance art (see Romanticism). In its last decades, the century saw a second wave of Romanticism in the guise of Symbolism, initiated in poetry and producing an art happy to display its poetic aims (see Symbolism and Art Nouveau). In between came a period when art, in France especially, gave particular attention to recording the visible world of the present. This was something more than the recourse to data from the visible world common to most or all periods of art: it tended to an exclusion of anything not classifiable and verifiable as fact and a denial of symbolic meanings.

There are degrees of realism, of course. It is easy to present the 19th century—the century of commercial as well as political empires, of vast historical researches and archives and statistics, of amazing technical advance and industrial harvests—as the century of facts. We could also adduce the rise of the increasingly naturalistic novel, the invention of the camera and then also the invention of film, as clinching cultural evidence of this. But not only was the century equally rich in poetic invention, it was also the period when music was at last able to challenge the other arts and to some extent even achieve a dominant position. Also, it was a time when the middle classes began to look to art as an alternative to everyday life, as an escape from reality, as entertainment. Many a realist artist learnt quickly how to sweeten facts by selection, and by their employment to illustrate subject matter that would appeal to such a public. Exotic scenes, pleasing anecdotes, landscapes implying adventure or relaxation, still lifes signaling pleasure and plenty—all these could be factual and yet elicit responses going well beyond the facts. This was especially the case with representations of the naked figure, whether they were called *Samson and Delilah* or *The Turkish Bath* or, as increasingly now, *Nude Study* or *Nude*. Also, realism could almost imperceptibly be moderated in idealistic terms derived from classicism. Compositional structures, types of physical beauty, poses and groupings of a time-honored sort, can often be found beneath an apparently purely factual, observed surface. This is partly because all art demands some process of transformation, partly because some recourse to that great tradition assured public approval, and partly also because tradition was not easily shaken off.

In this context the more radical ways of Realism were shocking. They were received by most critics and by the Salon-going public as aggressive; to some extent they were meant to be aggressive: they were attacks on artistic convention, obviously, but also on proprieties that were as much social as artistic. A realist painter might show some naked figures in or near water and call the result *Bathers*; he could thus be referring to the real world and suggest ordinary pleasures, whilst also hinting at the long and primarily idealistic tradition of classical figurative art. To represent a very fleshy woman walking away from a rather nondescript patch of water, past a seated companion, both women gesticulating broadly but without clear purpose, was an affront to thoughts both of classicism and of standard sensual satisfactions; on a large scale, and painted very vigorously, it was an affront to the expectations of well-educated art lovers. Courbet's *The Bathers* (Musée Fabre, Montpellier) was the scandal of the 1853 Paris Salon. The police discussed removing it lest it give offence; the public, loving to be offended, crowded to see it; critics and caricaturists mocked it. Only lower-class females would be so ungainly and so meaningless in their gestures. With some it was the meaninglessness that weighed more heavily than the flesh—with Delacroix, for instance, who thought Courbet's handling of paint masterly: "The vulgarity of the forms would not matter; what is unbearable is the vulgarity and pointlessness of the idea; what is more, if only that idea, such as it might be, were clear!" The absence of a discussable narrative or idea short-circuited the process of appreciation and criticism instilled by the long tradition of intelligent art, and broke the network of prepared references by which works of art drew significance and thus life from

Olympia by Manet; oil on canvas; 130×190cm (51×75in); 1863. Musée du Jeu de Paume, Paris

broad sectors of inherited learning. To refute such linkages, especially when working on the scale of this picture—7 ft 5 in by 6 ft 4 in (2.27 m by 1.93 m) and thus clearly a *magnum opus*—damaged art and the whole hierarchy of civilization.

This helps us to understand also the fuss over Courbet's *A Burial at Ornans* (painted 1850, shown at the Salon in 1851; now Louvre, Paris). On the scale of the most grandiose history paintings (10 ft 4 in by 22 ft 11 in, 3.15 m by 6.68 m) it shows the anonymous folk of Ornans, a faraway country town, taking rather incomplete notice of an anonymous event. That many of them—the landscape too—might be accurate portrayals merely stressed the lack of significance: truth perhaps, but the truth of what? Ten years after Courbet painted his *Bathers*, Manet painted his version of the old Venus theme (*Olympia*, 1863; Musée du Jeu de Paume, Paris)—received from Antiquity *via* Titian's *Venus of Urbino* (1538; Uffizi, Florence) and normally welcomed by 19th-century taste in a myriad of guises as celebrations of ideal beauty and concurrently a pleasantly sensual encounter for those with a taste for it. He seems to have been surprised by the fury it aroused when he showed it in 1865, yet he had severed every possible link with that tradition except for the compositional one. The setting and the appurtenances—black servant with bouquet, black cat—were taken to indicate that the woman portrayed was a prostitute: this had indeed been

Manet's intention. Worse, he had painted her without the inviting mien and proportions that might have made the picture attractively wicked. Instead, she was shown blankly, coldly. That Titian's painting too probably represented a courtesan could not shield him: Manet had jarred a tradition close to the central concerns of art and beauty by jerking it into the present, and what echoes of the past he had preserved merely served to emphasize the loss.

When Manet was working on the picture, his mentor Baudelaire was writing that "for any 'modernity' to be worthy of one day taking its place as 'antiquity', it is necessary for the mysterious beauty which human life accidentally puts into it to be distilled from it". Manet had distilled it very thoroughly, even from his brushwork and palette which, though marvelously subtle, deprived spectators of the optical charms they expected as of right. He may thus be accounted, to some degree, as the urban counterpart to Courbet's largely and somewhat insistently country-based campaign to bring art down to earth. (Parisians at this time encouraged each other in disparaging the provinces, an attitude Courbet's friend the socialist philosopher Proudhon was working to correct.) Yet Manet's open use of traditional antetypes at this period of his career—as also in the slightly earlier *Déjeuner sur l'Herbe* (1863; Louvre, Paris), a theme from Giorgione composed à la Raphael but again shot into the present—turns his realism into a way of processing tradition, of confronting tradition without deference, not a wholehearted insistence on the present and on ordinary facts. We must also ask, however, to what extent even Courbet was able to elude the pull of time-honored artistic fictions.

When Courbet set up his own one-man show close to the entrance to the Paris World Exhibition of 1855, having refused an invitation to produce a major work for inclusion in the official exhibition because he would have had to submit it to the judgment of a jury, he wrote over his door: "Realism. G. Courbet: exhibition of forty of his paintings." In his catalog he partly rejected the term:

> The title "realist" has been imposed on me in the same way as the title "romantic" was imposed on the men of 1830 ... I have studied the art of the ancients and moderns without any dogmatic or preconceived ideas. I have not tried to imitate the former nor copy the latter ... To achieve skill through knowledge—that has been my purpose. To record the manners, ideas and aspect of the age as I myself have seen them—to be a man as well as a painter, in short to create living art—that has been my aim.

Six years later, encouraged by the success he had had outside Paris, Courbet wrote a fuller statement addressed to his students (he had opened a Courbet school, but it lasted only a few months). In it he asserted that art could not be taught, being essentially individual.

> I add that art or talent, in my opinion, can be for an artist only the means of applying his personal faculties to the ideas and things of the epoch in which he lives. Especially art in painting can consist only in the representation of objects visible and tangible to the artist ... It is a totally physical language which uses for words all visible objects; an *abstract* object, not visible, nonexistent, does not lie in painting's domain. Imagination in art consists in knowing how to find the most complete expression of an existing thing, but never to suppose or create the thing itself ... The beautiful, like the true, is a thing relative to the time in which we live and to the individual competent to conceive it.

And so on, at some length. In the year of *A Burial at Ornans* he summarized his position more briefly in a letter to a newspaper:

> I am not only a socialist but also a democrat and a republican; in brief, I support the entire revolution, and above all else I am altogether a Realist ... because to be a Realist means to be the sincere friend of actual truth.

That year, 1851, saw also another of his key works at the Salon, *The Stonebreakers* (formerly Dresden; believed destroyed), a model for other Realists—for those who sought to

The Stonebreakers by Courbet; oil on canvas; about 213×312cm (84×123in); 1849. Formerly Gemäldegalerie Alte Meister, Dresden; destroyed

use more or less naturalistic images in support of progressive social and political campaigns. Courbet stressed that the picture sprang from a chance encounter; he did not say how much it owed to reconstruction. The youth and the old man seen on the road at work on their endless labors were not caught by him as in a snapshot; he had to interrupt their work and pay them to come and pose for him in the studio, one at a time. The composition he used was decidedly classical—like, say, a section of the Parthenon frieze—with his figures in profile, parallel to the picture-plane and also to the landscape which almost closes the picture-space like a backdrop. Proudhon called it the first socialist painting and "a satire on our industrial civilization which keeps on inventing a marvelous machine to execute all sorts of labors … yet cannot liberate man from the most backbreaking toil". Courbet spoke of it as a rare "expression of misery and destitution"; his response, he said later, was that of pity. Not, therefore, that of demanding change: it was others who turned the picture into a socialist manifesto. Art is notoriously bad at making polemical pronouncements without ambiguity. Courbet seems to have been more conscious of the endlessness of the men's work and situation than of any clear sense of injustice. "In these jobs", he wrote while engaged on it, "this is how you begin and how you end".

If the picture was charged with classical dignity—much more obviously so than contemporaries were willing to recognize—it was disconcertingly realistic in its detail, in the clothing particularly. The figures were large, life-size, and so the holes in the man's socks were life-size also. Such elements in the picture, which was shown together with the *Burial*, were taken to prove that Courbet was a political extremist and a savage. He accepted the latter term at least: "In our over-civilized society I must lead the life of a savage—I must free myself from governments", and in 1853 there followed his refusal to produce a painting at the government's behest. He produced it nonetheless, for his own exhibition: *The Artist's Studio* (now Louvre, Paris), combining realism of observation with a smattering of Realism in its social implications in the context of an allegorical program.

None of this—the ideas and the actions—was entirely new: for instance, Delacroix might aptly have called his 1830 painting, *Liberty Leading the People* (Louvre, Paris), a "realistic allegory". Behind Courbet's questioning of civilization stood not only Proudhon the anarchist but also Jean-Jacques Rousseau (1712–78), that pivotal figure between the Enlightenment and Romanticism; behind his thematic choices stood the 18th century's liking for genre subjects, and 17th-century Dutch painting. In turning down the official invitation in 1853 Courbet had written to the Director of the Beaux-Arts that "I alone, of all the French artists who are my contemporaries, have had the strength to express and represent in an original way both my own personality and society itself." This was claiming too much, but it is characteristic of Realism and of him that he should need to make such claims. He had a strong urge to dominate, but there is in Realism also an essential

projection of personality, of the authentic expression of one human being's experience of human society, and this insistence is the main difference (leaving questions of quality aside) between Courbet's kind of Realism and our own century's Socialist Realism. When art abandons established themes and ceases to support agreed values, personal authenticity becomes the only available yardstick (and one very difficult to apply with certainty). The Impressionist alternative—offering objective, almost scientific truth, at the expense of a more personal delivery—remains quite ambiguous in its content, especially where values are concerned. Socialist and other totalitarian countries, on the other hand, enrolling art as a part of the system of government-controlled education and exhortation, assume or pretend to assume that themes and values are once again firm common property, so that what is called Realism immediately transforms itself into idealization. On the other hand, this individualism was clearly an inheritance from late Enlightenment sensibility and from Romanticism's in-turned focus. In this respect, Courbet and those writers who championed him were heirs of Romanticism; they could not have countenanced the objectivity of Impressionism.

Courbet's somewhat older contemporaries, Jean-François Millet (1814–75) and Honoré Daumier (1808–79), shared many of his aims and intentions. The critic Castagnary was thinking of Courbet and Millet when he wrote, in 1857, that the aspirations of the day were well expressed through rural subjects because these were timeless in their significance in a way that urban subjects could not be. Choosing peasant subjects for art could be taken to imply the rejection of more elevated subjects and thus of traditional values as upheld by the academies, but it also suggested a Rousseauistic penetration through the facades of present-day society to its timeless base. Thus Realism could be seen as an attack on civilization, and equally as a statement of civilization's true nature. This is particularly so when themes are generalized to bring out their timelessness. Behind Millet's *The Sower* (1850; Museum of Fine Arts, Boston; one of a series of paintings on the same theme), which was shown in the same Salon as Courbet's *Burial* and *Stonebreakers*, stands not only Michelangelo and ancient sculpture but also the deep sense—voiced by various writers over the centuries—of humanity's continuing priorities. Millet's epic paintings of peasants at work represent his response to the promises of 1848, but it was characteristic of him that he turned not to contemporary texts for stimulus but to the Bible and Virgil and perhaps to Homer. Far from limiting itself to verifiable facts of the time, Realism in his hands took on the form of fused archetypes.

Daumier proved that an urban setting need not exclude this kind of spiritually charged monumentality with his paintings of Paris washerwomen coming up the steps from the Seine and carrying their heavy burdens along the quay; the action is again archetypal and can be interpreted as metaphor. Daumier's paintings were little known during his lifetime; it was his caricatures (today we would call them cartoons) that

The Artist's Studio by Courbet

In 1855, Gustave Courbet (1819–77) submitted his most recent and ambitious work—a huge canvas measuring about 12 ft by 20 ft (3.6 m by 6 m)—to the committee of the Paris World Exhibition. It was rejected. His response was defiant: he mounted his own exhibition. He had a temporary building constructed next to the main Exhibition pavilion, in which he exhibited 40 of his paintings in a one-man show entitled "Realism. Gustave Courbet" which amounted to a private retrospective of his own work. It was apt that *The Artist's Studio* (now in the Louvre, Paris) should be found in this context. The painting's full title is *The Interior of my Studio, a Real Allegory Summing up Seven years of my Artistic Life*; so the picture was intended as a retrospective of sorts too, as Courbet looked back over the years that followed the Revolution of 1848.

Courbet himself, at work on a landscape painting and watched by a small peasant boy and a nude model, is the focal point of the picture. From the early 1840s, Courbet had produced a whole series of self-portraits which showed not only a certain narcissistic delight in depicting himself but also a real fascination with his own image in different roles and moods. After 1855, Courbet's interest in painting himself waned, as if he were largely satisfied with *The Studio* as a grand and final public declaration of his own role as an artist. But it is obviously a very different kind of picture from the small, often intimate nature of the self-portrait. Courbet, instead, presents us with what would at first appear to be a disparate group of people with no obvious activity linking them but the fact that they are assembled together in the studio of the artist. The individual characters seem unrelated, even lost in his or her own thoughts, almost suspended in a timeless zone. Yet their dress is contemporary and, in spite of their rather dreamy air, Courbet portrays them very much as *real* people, all firmly rooted on the ground in the frieze-like composition.

Many interpretations of *The Artist's Studio*'s allegorical meaning have been suggested, but aspects of the picture still remain mysterious. Why Courbet chose the odd selection of characters on the left is far from clear; what seems certain is that although he treated them as individuals, they were not meant to be recognized as specific contemporaries. In a letter to the Realist writer, Jules Champfleury, discussing *The Artist's Studio* in some detail, Courbet referred to them as "types": "the others, the world of trivialities: the common people, the destitute, the poor, the wealthy, the exploited, the exploiters; those who thrive on death". On the far left, for example, a Jew stands next to a self-satisfied-looking *curé*, who represents the hypocrisy of religion. A fine huntsman is seated with his dogs; a pedlar of cheap textiles is crouched before a clown and an undertaker's mute. Courbet also included a reaper, a farm laborer, a proletarian, and a poverty-stricken Irishwoman with her child, among his cross section of social types. The artist is turned towards them: they are the objects of his art and for that reason he is dependent on them.

On the other hand, he is dependent on the group gathered behind him because they sustain his existence as an artist. These are "the 'shareholders', that is my friends, the workers, the art collectors". What is more, it is possible to recognize most of them as portraits of actual people. The poet Baudelaire sits reading; the hunting features of Jeanne Duval, Courbet's black mistress, are now just visible through the layer of paint with which Courbet had covered her after the affair ended. Champfleury is seated in front of Max Buchon, Courbet's old friend, poet and activist during the 1848 Revolution and now in exile after the *coup d'état* of 1851. The bearded Socialist philospher, Proudhon, also stands at the back and, next to him, in profile, is Courbet's great friend and patron from Montpellier, Alfred Bruyas. Their social and artistic thinking, and the financial backing of wealthy collectors, had enabled Courbet to steer the path towards the new art of Realism.

Courbet represented this group as his reverent admirers, but they too were the objects of his art. Though depicted here in his Paris studio, Courbet was actually painting the picture in the Franche-Comté, his home in the provinces. This meant that his friends were not available to sit for him. For the nude, or naked "truth", he worked from a

◄ Courbet and his works were popular with illustrators from 1851 onwards—as objects of ridicule. "Quillenbois" (the Comte de Sarcus) published this caricature of *The Artist's Studio* in *L'Illustration* on 21 July 1855

▲ Courbet's self-portrait in *The Artist's Studio* is based on his *Self-Portrait in Striped Collar* of 1854; oil on canvas; 46×37cm (18×15in). Musée Fabre, Montpellier

photograph, but for the other figures Courbet largely relied on portraits he had already painted. So the visitor to Courbet's one-man show in 1855 would have noticed, for instance, his portrait *Charles Baudelaire* (*c*1847; Musée Fabre, Montpellier), which Courbet had closely followed in *The Artist's Studio*, hanging in the same exhibition. These references to earlier paintings run right through *The Artist's Studio*; they become much more explicit in the two pictures on the back wall—hazy now but intended by Courbet, at any rate at the time of his letter to Champfleury, as his own paintings *Return from the Fair* (Musée des Beaux-Arts, Besançon) and *The Bathers* (Musée Fabre, Montpellier), both of which had previously caused great controversy. And, of course, the landscape depicting the bit of the world Courbet knew and loved the best—the Valley of the Loue in his native France-Comté—takes the center of the stage.

The lack of response to his one-man show disappointed Courbet and *The Artist's Studio* was not well received. It fell between two camps. For the Establishment critics, it was yet another example of Courbet dragging Art into the gutter more provocatively than ever because of its pretensions as an allegory. And Courbet's former Realist allies felt there was no room in the new art for allegory at all, since by its nature it was ideal

▲ *The Artist's Studio* by Courbet; oil on canvas; 361×598cm (142×235in); 1854–5. Louvre, Paris

▶ *Charles Baudelaire* by Courbet; oil on canvas; 53×61cm (21×24in); *c*1847. Musée Fabre, Montpellier

rather than "real". Indeed, Baudelaire, Champfleury, and Proudhon all strongly objected to the picture in spite of their presence within it.

So *The Artist's Studio* is a painting about the way Courbet saw his own role as an artist: he is the pivotal point of the painting and the assembled company make up, as Courbet described, "all the people who serve my cause, sustain me in my ideal and support my activity . . . the whole world coming to me

to be painted". They are portrayed as real people, but at the same time they represent ideas in the artist's mind. Courbet is at once apart from society, fiercely independent in his search for an artistic "truth", and yet immersed in that society, dependent on and responsible to it.

BRIONY FER

The Sower by Millet; oil on canvas; 101×82cm (40×32in); 1850.
Museum of Fine Arts, Boston

"And they have refused that ... the ignorant fools", a lithograph
by Honoré Daumier; 1859

the world saw, and saw frequently: comments on political personalities and events and on bourgeois and working class *mores*. These were self-evidently based on contemporary fact and at times were close to objective reportage, yet Daumier fed into them his awareness of the art of the past as well as his extraordinary skills as draftsman. An early work like the *Rue Transnonain* lithograph (1834) is in the tradition of Caravaggio and Géricault while appearing to be a factual account of a scene; *Membres de la Société de Secours du Dix Décembre dans l'Exercise de leur Philantropiques Fonctions* (members, in effect, of the support group for the election of Louis-Napoleon and his elevation to Emperor "exercising their philanthropic functions" on a disbeliever), shows Daumier using Baroque stagecraft in combination with the 18th century's interest in physiognomy—studied perhaps in Goya's prints—to produce a vivid image for transcending fact. The realist's assumption that fact alone could constitute worthy art was not shared by the Realists. Daumier himself made occasional sport of the attitude later expressed particularly tellingly by Zola's character, the painter Claude Lantier, who is made to exclaim: "the day is coming when a single original carrot will be pregnant with revolution". Our Realists, and the writers around them, condemned mere realism as an expression of materialism.

The word "naturalism" was introduced into art criticism by Jules Antoine Castagnary in 1862 and came to supersede "realism" thanks to its suggestion of greater objectivity and echoes of the activities of natural scientists. Zola used the new label to indicate writing that presents man not as he might be but as he is, "natural man, man as the subject of physico-chemical laws, a being determined by the influence of his environment". Yet he gave his attention to suffering humanity, to the laboring classes and what the *Daily News* in 1881 described as "that unnecessarily faithful portrayal of offensive incidents". He claimed a dispassionate interest in human behavior and in the "interior mechanisms" that direct it, yet his concern with misery and the context of misery was neither purely objective nor sensational in purpose. His too was an art of protest; his accumulations of observed detail were corroborative evidence behind which the author could hide his face. Zola's naturalism has a conscience, and it is much the same conscience as the Realists'.

Impressionism, which Zola supported in his writings and which is often seen as corresponding to his work as a novelist, has neither the same subject matter nor the same purpose. It does not even fit the definition Zola produced (for dramatic art, to be exact, but his implied meaning was broad): "a corner of nature seen through a temperament". For some years at any rate, the Impressionists avoided letting temperament interpose itself between the scenes they chose to paint and the paintings in which they represented them. It was notoriously difficult to tell one man's work from another at the time; it can still be so today. Perhaps responding to their

Right: Nana by Manet; oil on canvas; 151×116cm (59×46in); 1877.
Hamburger Kunsthalle, Hamburg

example, Manet largely abandoned his challenging position. In 1877 he portrayed Nana, the anti-heroine of Zola's story of a prostitute's revenge on the world, but quite without the sharpness her story (in *L'Assommoir*, "The Drunkard", 1877, and *Nana*, 1880) called for: the cool aggressiveness of *Olympia* had yielded to description of a lively, almost charming sort. In the same way Manet's and the younger Impressionists' street scenes give no special significance to any part and draw no drama from it as Zola would certainly have done, and that very emptiness—what came to be thought of as the purity of their art—was what people objected to. It was shocking to find the human image accorded no more presence, physically or spiritually, in a painting than any other light-catching and light-reflecting substance such as clouds or foliage. Zola said of Manet that "he knows neither how to sing nor how to philosophize; he knows how to paint and that is all". The remarkable thing is that this (exaggerated) innocence in the artist, and this notion of a work of art as a purely visual product with conceptual content, has been mistaken as a norm by which the greater part of the public judges art to this day. Yet this concentration on pure visibility—unique in the long story of art—could achieve significance through intensity. Monet's fascination with the visible could lead him both to the extraordinary painting of his wife on her deathbed—done not as a loving memento but because he could not resist the urge to capture the "succession of appropriate color gradations which death was imposing on her immobile face"—and to those series of repeated scenes under changing conditions of light—again the immobile transformed by the mobile: Rouen Cathedral, the haystacks, the Palace of Westminster, Monet's garden at Giverny. His Impressionist colleagues by this time had found the Impressionist program too limiting pictorially and too detached from human concerns; Monet alone pushed it to the paradoxical extreme where transient phenomena, noted and translated into paint with unique acuity and persistence, turn into epic celebrations of visual experience.

In this there could be no room for social commentary, even of an oblique sort. Monet does not claim equal social status for cathedrals and haystacks, merely equal visual value. Monet was a grocer's son and some of his earlier paintings (when he was under the influence of Courbet) had shown scenes of labor and industry, but this practice did not continue and it is difficult to wring much social significance out of his, or his friends', representations of the leisure activities of average Parisians. The one Impressionist who does remind us from time to time of his social allegiances is Camille Pissarro (1830–1903), and it may be significant that he was markedly older than the others, older even than Manet to whom the Impressionists looked as a sort of father figure. Pissarro was a socialist of the anarchist persuasion. He believed that human excellence would surface to guide the world into universal brotherhood if only oppressive systems of government and economics were swept away. During his later years he contributed illustrations to anarchist journals—this was when he

was associated with the Neo-Impressionists, particularly with Signac who wrote in 1891 of using art as "testimony to the great social contest which is beginning between workers and capital". It will be recognized that art is a very contrary thing: Neo-Impressionism, the offspring of Impressionism and—like many another offspring—dissatisfied with its father, rejected his laconic ways to make art, once again, into a social weapon. In other respects, it could hardly be more different from Realism.

Degas (1834–1917) too was somewhat older than Monet, Renoir, and Sisley (who with Pissarro formed the core of the Impressionists). Moreover, he was steeped in the classical tradition and was disinclined to deny the human image its central role in art. He did produce some exquisite landscapes which few knew about, and his interest in horses as forms of energetic motion was so intense that one wonders sometimes, especially before the modeled figures that were his means of studying horses and human bodies, whether he allowed them differences of status. But then we may also ask whether he distinguished—in his paintings, pastels, drawings, and monotypes—between laundresses, middle-class women attended at their baths and dressing tables by servants, ballet dancers at rest or in motion, and naked whores unselfconsciously awaiting their everyday business. Objectivity of the coldest sort would seem to have been his only program, combined with a Monet-like appetite for working again and again from the same motif. Degas was no revolutionary in matters of politics. His contemporaries accused him of misogyny. His taste for observing as though (as he said) through a keyhole and for showing women "deprived of their airs and affectations, reduced to the level of animals cleaning themselves", may suggest a lust for truth that goes beyond objectivity and points to animosity. But we should not forget his roots in classicism. His long pursuit of the female animal should perhaps be seen as evidence of a solitary (but not entirely unique) program of reform, not social or political or sexual but artistic. As a classicist he knew the value and the staying power of an inherited repertory of proportions and positions. Once he decided to set that heritage aside he worked ceaselessly and with unequalled cunning to create an alternative repertory relying on personally observed fact. By one of those splendid coincidences, the camera was to hand and so were Japanese woodblock prints; they offered alternatives, one through the limited but objective means of the apparatus, the other through sophisticated processes of observation followed by simplification and composing. Both drew attention to the importance of the tensions the represented object makes with its surrounding spaces and objects and with the framing edge of the total image. "Everything in a painting is the interrelationship", Degas said in 1891, objecting to the superficial naturalism that strains to capture the truth of a detail but ignores the viability of the whole.

Degas was proving the efficacy—the beauty even—in art of activities such as washing, of resting after fatiguing motion, and also of the conventional movements and positions of the ballet (another repertory). His one exhibited sculpture, *The Little Dancer of 14 Years* (shown in 1881; one example in the Tate Gallery, London) was considered an affront to girlhood and to art, partly because of the real clothes in which the bronze girl had been clad; yet a few critics were well-read enough to know that this oddity was sanctioned not only by Neapolitan and Spanish traditions of sculpture but also by the ancients' habit of painting and dressing sculptures of which archaeologists were currently becoming aware. When Degas exhibited a series of pastels of women at their toilet, in 1886, the novelist J.K. Huysmans thought them so monstrous that he seemed almost to wish to enrol Degas among those who were using distressing naturalistic detail and sordid scenarios to entertain the public with shocks and horror. The pictures, he wrote, "reeked of the stumps of the maimed, the embrace of the prostitute, the sickening gait of the legless cripple". Renoir, however—certainly no misogynist in art or in life—called the series "a piece of the Parthenon", sensing perhaps the birth of a new classicism in which realism has taken on the function formerly reserved to idealism.

Rodin's incessant study of the moving figure suggests a similar desire for a new kind of figuration, but his aim was primarily to widen the potential of the human body as a vehicle of emotional expression. His early figure, *The Age of Bronze* (1875–6; Tate Gallery, London) was so lifelike that it drew the charge of being merely a cast taken from the living model (this process has proved its worth in the work of the American sculptor George Segal, 1924–). Rodin's aim was more ambitious than this scandal implied: it was the expressiveness of Michelangelo and of medieval sculpture he sought, and if he looked for foundations for this in observed nature, he also studied the work of his predecessors with the greatest attention and was willing to charge what he learnt from both sources with passionate meaning through antinaturalistic means. Very extreme poses, gravitation-defying arrangements, various forms of distortion and exaggeration—including the remarkable one of the incomplete figure—all this combined with sharp contrasts of scale and with his use of a broken, disruptive surface: Rodin was not concerned with portraying the visible world of his own time or any other. Nature and reality were merely a starting point. Degas, by contrast, accepted the datable contexts in which he found the

The Tub by Degas; pastel on cardboard; 60×83cm (24×33in); 1886. Louvre, Paris

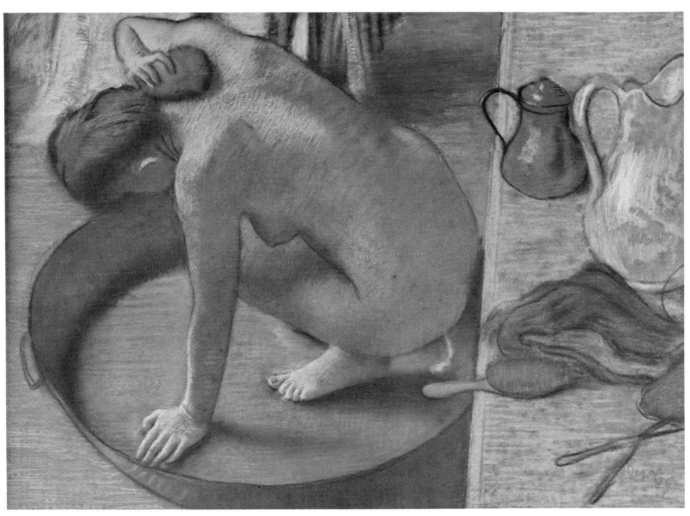

Left: The Age of Bronze by Rodin; bronze; 180×60×60cm (71×24×24in); 1875–6. Musée Rodin, Paris

Above: The Little Dancer of 14 Years by Degas; bronze with added fabric; height 90cm (39in); first exhibited in 1881. Tate Gallery, London

motif he studied; he felt no need to remove period elements and to universalize his work. Neither did he wish to be the author of an encyclopedic treatment of the human theme. The scale of his work was modest and its tone was untheatrical; behind Rodin's labors, especially that broad range of work associated with the *Gates of Hell* (begun 1880; left unfinished at his death in 1917; preliminary drawings and models in the Musée Rodin, Paris), was not only Dante but also Wagner.

Outside France realism and naturalism came and went in various guises, with and without stimuli from French examples. To repeat the point: the century was in pursuit of facts *and* of visions. In Germany the Romantic painters C.D. Friedrich (1774–1840) and P.O. Runge (1777–1810) based their essentially religious paintings on long studies of particular natural phenomena (*see* Romanticism). As a method this was not fundamentally different from many another painter's before them; it is the intensity of their pursuit of visual truth and their trusting delivery of it to our eyes—vivid and clear—that makes their relationship to reality unusual. From this, and also from a more directly naturalistic, descriptive tradition of painting, associated with pictures of specific locations—town, country, interiors—developed particularly in Copenhagen (where Friedrich and other North Germans received their training), continued a line of often modest but sprightly naturalistic painting, usually on a small scale and of unexceptional subjects, detailed enough to please a novel and travel-story reading public, and kept fresh by elements of Neoclassical tidiness. This direction was in part recharged and redirected by Courbet's example.

In 1852 Courbet showed *The Stonebreakers* and *A Burial at Ornans* in an exhibition in Frankfurt. In 1858 four paintings by him were on show at the Frankfurt Kunstverein and he was invited to visit the city. He came and enjoyed himself—painting, hunting, and feasting vigorously. In 1869 he had a room to himself in a vast exhibition in the Munich Glaspalast (*The Stonebreakers* was again shown); he was awarded a gold medal by Ludwig II and he arrived in person in October to spend a month as the hero of a growing band of German disciples. Chief among these was Wilhelm Leibl (1844–1900), for whose work Courbet expressed his lively admiration. Leibl's most famous painting, *Three Women in Church* (Hamburger Kunsthalle, Hamburg), was painted in 1878–81, some years after his personal contact with Courbet. It shows a directness that Courbet might have respected, but none of his bravura. Much of the piety inherent in it comes from a degree of self-effacement on the painter's part. This makes Courbet look the more Romantic of the two, Leibl the more naturalistic, but there is no mistaking the artfulness of Leibl's presentation or the meaning of this icon of rustic decency at a time when cities were growing fast and Germany was undergoing galloping industrialization. Other German painters took in aspects of Courbet, some more, some less blatantly and obviously, and some of these were to wield influence in their own right: Franz Lenbach (1836–1904), Hans Thoma (1839–1924), Wilhelm Trübner (1857–1917) etc. Courbet had written from Munich that "the young painters here work entirely in my manner"; Germany, and Belgium too he felt, were avid to continue his work. One aspect of this influence is associated with Dutch 17th-century painting. Courbet's enthusiasm—in Munich he painted copies of a Hals and a Rembrandt—gave additional force to a rebirth of interest in Dutch painting, and this, conversely, joined with and gave additional charge to his own influence. Another aspect is more metaphorical and suggests the impact of Courbet's romantic character and Romantic leanings. "My blood still roars through my veins to gush hotly into my paintings": the identification of a painter's personality and passing emotions with the marks he makes on the canvas, of his lifeblood with the medium itself, was not unprecedented but found particularly pointed expression in Courbet's wake. The formulation quoted here was that of Karl Schuch (1846–1903), a Viennese painter who had arrived in Munich in 1869, just in time to meet Courbet, and who was to work for a while in Leibl's studio. It encapsulates a notion that became fundamental to much German art and art criticism as well as the essential basis of Expressionism.

The German tradition of naturalism had its own achievements to offer, and at times these suggest an independent Impressionist or at least Manet-like focus on visible reality and vividness of rendering. Adolf von Menzel (1815–1905) is still not well known outside his country. His image is perhaps darkened by the series of brilliant but also essentially nationalistic history paintings celebrating the court life and the wars of Frederick the Great, excellent works that join a warm sense of period to lively stagecraft in a way that only the most sensitive of film makers have been able to match. But Menzel was also the painter of townscapes and domestic interiors that predate and in some instances outclass the best that realism and naturalism can offer elsewhere, paintings in which the value of an ordinary experience held for ever is made miraculously evident. These pictures, painted in the 1840s, were not known until the end of the century, but the predisposition to naturalism of this sort remained potent in Germany, showing itself in the readiness of painters such as Max Liebermann (1847–1935), Max Slevogt (1868–1932), and Lovis Corinth (1858–1925) to devote themselves to a German version of Impressionism, modified in Liebermann's case in terms of Millet and of Dutch painting of the Hague School—that is modified towards Realism—and in Corinth's case in terms of Romantic and Expressionist self-revelation. In the Low Countries the Hague School itself offered a sort of fusion of Romantic and Realistic ways. That is, Jozef Israëls (1824–1911), Hendrik Mesdag (1831–1915), the Maris brothers (Jacob, 1837–99; Matthys, 1839–1917; Willem, 1844–1910) and Anton Mauve (1838–88)—its leading members—did not put naturalism before their desire to comment on the world about them but showed townscape, landscape, and often scenes of work in gentle, rather melancholic terms

Three Women in Church by Wilhelm Leibl; oil on canvas; 113×77cm (44×30in); 1878–81. Hamburger Kunsthalle, Hamburg

that literally discolored their representations, tending towards rather foggy, monochrome effects. Van Gogh's early paintings of peasants at work and at home were deeply affected by the Hague School's example, and it was through Mauve that he knew of Millet whose art he drew on at many stages of his development.

England too had strong naturalist traditions, associated with Constable and Turner, and these had been charged with moral meanings in the writings of John Ruskin (1819–1900). Partly because of this, French Realism and Impressionism made little impact, even though Impressionist paintings were repeatedly shown in London in the 1870s and 1880s. Artists and public looked for significant themes and found the new French art lacking in them. In any case, if social commentary was required, England had her tradition in that genre too, stemming from Hogarth and surviving even more vividly in novels than in paintings. The Pre-Raphaelites' originality lay in combining the edifying content of serious history painting with an astonishing degree of naturalistic truth. When John Millais (1829–96) painted *Christ in the House of His Parents* (1850; Tate Gallery, London) he filled the picture with details that add up to a convincing carpenter's shop in a Middle Eastern country and light. In a sense he achieves a Millet in reverse, using the Bible as foreground, so to speak, where Millet had used it latently, and human labor as support where

Millet had made it his overt theme. Judging by the revulsion of Charles Dickens and others when *Christ in the House of His Parents* was shown, the painter had come close to being a Realist. In 1849 a critic had seen in Millais' work and in Holman Hunt's a regression to "the expression of a time when art was in a state of transition or progression rather than accomplishment": this reference to their early Italian, pre-Raphael, ways points up the contrast with Menzel whose historical paintings show a comparable fusion of natural detail and historical accuracy yet start from an assumption that painting cannot be too accomplished to capture the Rococo world of Frederick II. Rossetti's *Found*, begun c1853 and left unfinished (Delaware Art Museum, Wilmington, Delaware), was an exceptional attempt at a socially relevant subject of the sort that might warrant talk of Realism; Holman Hunt's *The Awakening Conscience* (1853; Tate Gallery, London) was another. In both, realism is directed towards symbolism, and Realism is damped down by the poetics of history painting. For Realism of a more direct, less sermonizing and archaicizing sort, yet oddly well received at a time when most honors went to much more glamorous and sentimental confections, one looked to the paintings of men such as Luke Fildes (1844–1927), Frank Holl (1845–88), and Hubert von Herkomer (1849–1914), combining Millet's emotional warmth with a reporter's insistence on informative detail. Fildes' *Applicants for Admission to a Casual Ward* (Royal Holloway College, Egham, Surrey), exhibited at the Royal Academy in 1874, was a much worked-up version of a drawing first published in the weekly *The Graphic* in 1869, almost literally a piece of reportage processed to become a genre painting on a history painting scale. (Van Gogh greatly admired printed drawings of this kind, collected them, and referred to them frequently.) Herkomer's *On Strike* (1891; Royal Academy of Arts, London), confronts a social problem even more firmly, insisting on the individuality of the persons represented and putting them before us with an immediacy reminiscent of Leibl. In other respects too, Herkomer links English Realism to Munich and the legacy Courbet left there.

During the last third of the 19th century, Munich contested Paris' domination of the Western art world. Already in 1858 an American art magazine referred to the Bavarian city as the "Art Capital" of Europe, and it is noticeable that Realist tendencies in American painting from that time on point first towards Munich and to German examples until the last years of the century, when there is a sudden swing towards Paris. Frank Duveneck (1848–1919), William Merritt Chase (1849–1916), and other subsequently influential painters studied their art in Munich in the 1870s when the memory of Courbet's visit was still fresh; what they brought back to America was a naturalism heightened by expressive brushwork and occasionally also troubled by socially disquieting subjects. Compared with this, the vivid "slice-of-life" paintings of

Found, by Dante Gabriel Rossetti; oil on canvas; 91×80cm (36×31in); begun c1853; unfinished. Delaware Art Museum, Wilmington

Right: On Strike by Hubert von Herkomer; oil on canvas; 228×126cm (90×50in); 1891. Royal Academy of Arts, London

Winslow Homer (1836–1910) are more purely naturalistic and unrhetorical. The same applies to the scientifically prepared outdoor scenes by Thomas Eakins (1844–1916); it is only when he picks on a subject that challenges the mind and stomach of the observer, as in his monumental *The Gross Clinic* (1875; Jefferson Medical College, Philadelphia) that we can speak of Realism. In 1908 a group of Philadelphia painters moved to New York and put on an exhibition of their work at the Macbeth Gallery—and found themselves dubbed the Ashcan School. Robert Henri (1865–1929) was the leader of this group. He and his friends looked to Eakins and to Duveneck, Chase and other Munich alumni as their masters; in addition Henri had studied in Paris and had acquired, and now taught, a version of Manet's style, 40 years or so after it was first fashioned. Many of their paintings dealt with the seamy side of city life, but they were not only insisting on the viability of this inelegant reality as matter for art; they were bringing forward scenes and moments which spectators could recognize as essentially American and also as of pronounced regional character, just as Courbet, Leibl, and others had done for their homelands.

National self-awareness and Realism could, in fact, be fertile bedfellows. The Swiss painter Ferdinand Hodler (1853–1918), himself of simple origins, was able to move from Realism through naturalism to a very persuasive form of Symbolism which retained elements of both; much of his work was nationalist and regional in its emphasis, yet his most mature paintings are allegories that could hold their own with the best Symbolist paintings Paris could mount, which exercized a profound influence on emergent modernism in Paris, Berlin, and Vienna, and which to this day maintain remarkable power. When the students of the St Petersburg Academy revolted against the imposition of specified subjects for their competitions, in 1863, they were demanding not merely the right to choose their own subjects but also to make subject matter more relevant nationally and socially. They were inspired partly by Nikolai Chernyshevski's influential thesis, *The Aesthetic Relations of Art to Reality* (1855), which proclaimed not only that art should concern itself with the visible world but also that artists should recognize the social role of their work. Much of the art that followed fused naturalism with historical themes chosen for their polemical value or implied social criticism. Ilya Efimovich Repin's *Bargemen* (1870–3; State Russian Museum, Leningrad) is a major contribution to the Realist tendency with its firm concentration on individual character while capturing the slavishness of the team's task. His technical means at this time were thoroughly traditional; later, after he had spent some time in Paris, his palette lightened in partial recognition of the vividness of Impressionism.

The question of what means were demanded by Realism, or indeed by naturalism, was central to some artists and of no concern to others. For some, Realism implied not only a close attention to facts and the commitment of art to a polemical purpose, but also a new attitude to the processes of art itself and to the reality of the chosen medium. Courbet's handling of paint, which many found merely clumsy, was the admiration of those who understood him to be asserting the reality of a painting *qua* painting, and of the process of painting as a process of depositing colored stuffs on a surface. When the Cubists, in 1912, wanted to dissociate themselves from Symbolism and decadence, and insisted that they were realists and pointed to Courbet as their essential forerunner, it was partly this physicality they were referring to. Out of Courbet's material bluntness and also out of the traditions of sketchy painting for study purposes, usually connected with out-of-door subjects, came the relatively systematic brushwork of Impressionism and thence the thoroughly systematic procedure of Neo-Impressionist pointillism, and this in turn served as a basis for the experiments of Delaunay, Severini, and others in the early 20th century. A concern for reality could thus lead the way to the (in common parlance) unreality of Abstract art.

NORBERT LYNTON

Bibliography. Clark, T.J. *Image of the People*, London (1973). *Courbet und Deutschland*, Cologne (1978). Farr, D. *English Art 1870–1940*, Oxford (1978). Gombrich, E.H. *Art and Illusion*, London (1960). Hamilton, G.H. *The Art and Architecture of Russia*, Harmondsworth (1954). Hamilton, G.H. *Painting and Sculpture in Europe: 1880–1940*, Harmondsworth (1967). Hanson, A.C. *Manet and the Modern Tradition*, London and New Haven (1977). Nochlin, L. *Realism*, Harmondsworth (1971). Novotny, F. *Painting and Sculpture in Europe: 1780–1880*, Harmondsworth (1960).

42

IMPRESSIONISM

Impression: Sunrise by Claude Monet; oil on canvas; 48×63cm (19×25in); 1872. Musée Marmottan, Paris (see pages 788 and 799)

I N 1874, a group of artists mounted an independently organized exhibition of paintings in Paris, in a deliberate attempt to find another outlet for their work besides the official Salon. One of the participants, Claude Monet, showed a picture with the title *Impression: Sunrise* (Musée Marmottan, Paris); several reviews of the exhibition picked on this title as reflecting the dominant characteristic of the works exhibited, and one critic, Louis Leroy, entitled his review "The Exhibition of the Impressionists". Though none of the artists wholeheartedly accepted the label—it was used to describe paintings of many varied types—the title stuck to the group, and what originated as a critical quip has become the name of one of the most significant art movements of the later 19th century.

It is impossible to find a single definition to cover the range of paintings often described as "Impressionist", but the quintessential Impressionist landscape (for example, Monet's *Sailing at Argenteuil*, 1874; private collection) has certain rec-

ognizable characteristics: it is comparatively small in scale and informal in composition, and was normally largely executed out of doors; its colors are generally bright and contrasting, its brushwork free and intuitive. It is from discussion of these factors, and from a consideration of Impressionism in its historical context, and against its intellectual and social background, that we can define the true nature and extent of the movement.

The participants in the first group exhibition of 1874 included Claude Monet (1840–1926), Camille Pissarro (1830–1903), Pierre Auguste Renoir (1841–1919), Alfred Sisley (1839–99), Edgar Degas (1834–1917), Paul Cézanne (1839–1906), and Berthe Morisot (1841–95). These seven artists, along with Édouard Manet (1832–83), are generally regarded as the principal Impressionist painters, though in their methods and techniques Degas and Manet belong less closely to the group. The links between the artists were forged in the 1860s; Monet, Renoir, Sisley, and Frédéric Bazille (1841–70)

Le Déjeuner sur l'Herbe by Manet; oil on canvas; 215×270cm (85×106in); 1863. Musée du Jeu de Paume, Paris

met in 1862 in the studio of the academic artist Charles Gleyre (1808–74); Monet had met Pissarro c1860, and Cézanne first met this group c1863. In 1863, a rallying point was provided for them by the Salon des Refusés (an officially sponsored exhibition of the paintings rejected from the official Salon in that year), and in particular by Manet's major work shown there, *Le Déjeuner sur l'Herbe* (Musée de Jeu de Paume, Paris). By the late 1860s, Manet and Degas were in close touch with the other painters; the Café Guerbois became the meeting place of the group, where they aired their opinions on art. Until 1870 they all continued to submit their work to the Salon, but, after some initial success, they were generally refused by the jury; a project of Monet and Bazille for an independent exhibition in 1867 came to nothing, but it was the germ of the exhibition of 1874.

The group was broken up in 1870 by the Franco-Prussian war; Monet and Pissarro took refuge in London, and Bazille died at the front. After the suppression of the Paris Commune in 1871, they came together again in Paris and soon decided to cease exhibiting at the Salon; only Manet continued to submit his work to it regularly, and he never participated in the sequence of group exhibitions. These exhibitions—which took place, under various names, in 1874, 1876, 1877, annually from 1879 to 1882, and in 1886—were the focus of the joint activities of the group, but their artistic aims and their ideas on exhibiting became increasingly divergent. The final show in 1886 included only Degas, Berthe Morisot, and Pissarro of the original inner circle, alongside younger artists such as Gauguin, Seurat, and Signac.

Between c1868 and c1883 various members of the group frequently also worked together, particularly in the Seine valley to the northwest of Paris, where they often simultaneously painted the same subjects, notably at Argenteuil, where Monet lived from 1872 to 1878, and at Pontoise, where Pissarro lived from 1872 to 1882. Sisley, Renoir, and Manet worked on occasion with Monet at Argenteuil; Cézanne, and later Gauguin, with Pissarro at Pontoise. It was as much through these immediate working contacts, as through their joint enterprises in Paris, that their painting acquired a certain coherence of style and purpose during the 1870s.

Some of the artists remained linked by close personal friendship, notably Monet with Renoir and Pissarro, but in artistic terms they began to go their own way increasingly after 1880. Though all retained the basic aims that had guided them in the 1870s, they increasingly followed their own preoccupations, and most of them continued to expand and develop their artistic languages until the end of their careers.

Most of the smaller landscapes exhibited by the Impressionists in the 1870s seem to have been largely or entirely executed out of doors, in front of the motifs they represent. Instead of using the studio, as most previous landscapists had, to produce large, highly finished works for exhibition from small preparatory studies, they treated their small outdoor oils as finished works in their own right, placing great importance on the spontaneity and directness of their record of nature. Good

Hoar-frost by Camille Pissarro; oil on canvas; 65×93cm (26×37in); 1873. Musée du Jeu de Paume, Paris

examples of this, all of which were shown at the first group exhibition in 1874, are Monet's *Impression: Sunrise* and *Wild Poppies* (Musée du Jeu de Paume, Paris), Renoir's *Harvesters* (Stiftung Sammlung E.G. Bührle, Zurich), and Pissarro's *Hoar-frost* (Musée du Jeu de Paume, Paris).

However, outdoor work in oils was not in itself anything new. Oil sketching of the motif had been a standard part of the training of the French landscapist since at least the later 18th century, as is shown by the small studies of Pierre Henri de Valenciennes made in the 1780s (Louvre, Paris); on occasions, Valenciennes even sketched the same subject as it appeared under several different weather conditions, as Monet, in particular, was to do later. A similar tradition existed in England by the early 19th century, as the oil sketches of John Constable show (examples in the Victoria and Albert Museum, London). However, these small oils were not meant for exhibition; they were notations of light and atmosphere for the artist to use in making the ambitious composite studio paintings he showed in public. Only gradually did artists come to place a greater value on their outdoor studies; Corot on occasion showed an outdoor study at the Salon, instead of his usual studio compositions, and Daubigny in the 1850s and 1860s began to exhibit large landscapes on which he had worked extensively out of doors, for instance *Villerville-sur-Mer* (exhibited in 1864; Hendrik Willem Mesdag Museum, The Hague). This French tradition supplies the background to the Impressionists' outdoor work. It seems most unlikely they would have known of the most thoroughgoing previous attempts to execute exhibition paintings out of doors, those of the Pre-Raphaelite group in England between 1848 and 1856, which resulted in such paintings as Ford Madox Brown's *Pretty Baa-Lambs*, 1851–2 (City of Birmingham Museums and Art Gallery).

Pissarro and Berthe Morisot in their earliest outdoor studies treated Corot as their model; Monet's immediate mentors were Eugène Boudin (1824–98) and Johan Barthold Jongkind

(1819–91), both of whom had given him advice when they were working on the coast around Le Havre. Neither of them worked exclusively out of doors, but Boudin advocated direct work from nature or painting done "when the impression was still fresh", and Jongkind regularly painted watercolors, and on occasions in the 1860s small oils, on the motif. In 1864, Monet proudly spoke of having painted "a study entirely from nature", but his submissions to the Salon in the 1860s (for example, *La Pointe de la Hève*, 1864–5; Kimbell Art Museum, Fort Worth) were with one exception studio works. His one attempt to execute a monumental canvas out of doors, *Women in the Garden* (1866–7; Musée du Jeu de Paume, Paris) had no successor, and when in 1880 he decided, for the last time, again to submit to the Salon, he sent works enlarged in the traditional way from smaller outdoor paintings. In the 1860s, the other young Impressionists also submitted large canvases to the Salon, similarly enlarged from small studies.

However, they became increasingly preoccupied with working on smaller canvases out of doors—Sisley seems to have exhibited two outdoor works at the Salon of 1870 (including *The Canal Saint-Martin*; Musée du Jeu de Paume, Paris)—and the independently organized exhibitions of the 1870s provided the ideal outlet for such paintings. It was during the 1870s, too, that Manet began, under the influence of Monet and his friends, to execute smaller oils out of doors, such as *Claude Monet on his Studio-boat* (1874; Neue Pinakothek, Munich); for his Salon-submissions, though, Manet continued to paint more ambitious studio works (for example, *The Conservatory*, 1878; Nationalgalerie, Berlin), while Degas never painted out of doors. None of the Impressionists, except Sisley, confined themselves to smaller outdoor works; in the group exhibitions, Monet also showed large decorative canvases (for example, *La Japonaise*, 1876; Museum of Fine Arts, Boston), and Renoir exhibited important figure paintings such as the *Moulin de la Galette* (1876; Musée du Jeu de Paume, Paris). Pissarro probably used his studio throughout the 1870s for his more ambitious oils (for example, *The Côte des Boeufs at the Hermitage, Pontoise*, 1877; National Gallery, London).

After 1880, several of the Impressionists came to realize increasingly the limitations of outdoor painting, both because they saw the anomaly of executing exclusively outside works which were meant to be viewed indoors, and because their experience of distinguishing the minutest changes in natural effects showed them the impossibility of making a direct and immediate record of what they saw while the effect lasted; Renoir lamented the constantly changing effects of cloud and sunshine, Monet the difficulty of finding again the same combination of weather and tide levels on the coast. Late in his life, Renoir described how in the 1880s the frustrations of outdoor working had led him to readopt Corot's methods of working from small studies in the studio to produce, for example, *Woman Arranging her Hair* (1885); Sterling and Francine Clark Art Institute, Williamstown). Pissarro rarely worked outside after 1880, partly because troubles with his

Storm on Belle-Isle by Claude Monet; oil on canvas; 65×81cm (26×32in); 1886. Musée du Jeu de Paume, Paris

eyes forced him to work in the studio or from the vantage point of a window, but principally because, he stated in 1892, it was only in the studio that he could give his canvases the "intellectual unity" he was seeking.

Monet continued to maintain the outdoor image of Impressionism, and gave his interviewers the impression that he worked exclusively outside, but his letters show that he came increasingly to use the studio for retouching his canvases. In 1886, he insisted that his latest paintings (for instance *Storm on Belle-Isle*; Musée du Jeu de Paume, Paris) needed to be worked over in the peace and quiet of his studio, and from the 1890s onwards most of his work was extensively revised indoors. In part, this was the result of the impossibility of rendering on the spot the "instantaneity" of natural effects which he declared himself to be seeking, but he, like Pissarro, came to look for a new sort of unity in his work, for "more serious qualities", he said in 1892, than could be obtained in a simple outdoor sketch. No art movement before or since Impressionism has set such store by outdoor work, but paradoxically it was through their experience of it that the Impressionists came to see that making a picture, on a two-dimensional surface, imposed demands that could not be met simply by trying to make quick sketches of transitory natural effects.

Allied to the Impressionist landscapists' outdoor work came a free, spontaneous handling of paint, used as a notation for the varied textures of nature. In part, this freedom arose simply from the demands of outdoor working, but an emphasis on the value of the individual brushstroke became a deliberate part of their aims, one that owed much to Manet. Manet inherited from this teacher Thomas Couture (1815–79) the European tradition of free, painterly handling, and even in his large exhibition paintings (for example *Le Déjeuner sur l'Herbe*, 1863; Musée du Jeu de Paume, Paris) Manet left the individual strokes of the brush as distinct elements in creating the rhythm and pattern of the work; in his smaller pictures, his bold, economical handling is very marked (for example, *Music in the Tuileries Gardens*, 1862; National Gallery, London). Delacroix, too, was an important influence on the Impressionists, for the flowing, expressive gestures of the brush in his later work.

The chief characteristic of Impressionist brushwork until *c*1877 was its flexibility. Pissarro, Sisley, and Renoir adapted their touch to convey natural textures of all sorts—compare, for example, Pissarro's *Hoar-frost*, 1873, and Sisley's *The Road to Sèvres*, 1873 (both Musée du Jeu de Paume, Paris). Monet's handling was equally varied, and in his treatment of reflections in water, in particular, he began to adopt emphatic, separate brushstrokes which create fragmented paint-surfaces quite unlike those of previous French landscape painting, as in his sketches of La Grenouillère of 1869 (for example, that in the Metropolitan Museum, New York) and in *Regatta at Argenteuil* (1872/3; Musée du Jeu de Paume, Paris).

From the later 1870s, all the Impressionist landscapists began to refine their brushwork, both to give a fuller rendering of the variety of nature, and at the same time to organize more tightly the patterns of the brush on the picture-surface. Pissarro and Cézanne came to use small parallel brushstrokes which impose a structure on the picture-surface more rigid than any found in nature (as in, for example, Pissarro's *Landscape at Chaponval*, 1880; Musée du Jeu de Paume, Paris).

From this preoccupation with surface, Pissarro in 1886 adopted the even greater systematization of the Neo-Impressionist "petit point". Cézanne's "constructive stroke" of *c*1877–83 (used in, for example, *Zola's House at Médan*, *c*1880; Burrell Collection, Glasgow) developed into the networks of colored planes of his late works (as in *Mont Sainte-Victoire*, *c*1904/6; Philadelphia Museum of Art). Sisley and especially Monet began *c*1880 to establish flowing patterns of brushstrokes across the canvas, not rigid like Pissarro's, but free and calligraphic. In works like Monet's *Storm on Belle-Isle* (1886; Musée du Jeu de Paume, Paris) the brushwork is a means of uniting color and drawing in a single stroke, a type of handling which greatly influenced Van Gogh in 1887–8. After *c*1890, though, when Monet became preoccupied with unified effects of atmosphere, he sought denser, more uniform paint-surfaces to convey his subjects (for example, *Rouen Cathedral*, 1892–4; five examples in the Musée du Jeu de Paume, Paris). In terms of handling, the most varied experiments were made by Renoir, particularly *c*1879–87, when he was deeply studying the old masters; his techniques varied between translucent glazes of color and an opaque, dense surface in which, for a time, he tried to reproduce in oils the effects of fresco

Music in the Tuileries Gardens by Manet; oil on canvas; 76×118cm (30×46in); 1862. National Gallery, London

painting (for example, *Woman Arranging her Hair*, 1885; Sterling and Francine Clark Art Institute, Williamstown).

The different directions the Impressionists took in their handling after *c*1880 were in all cases attempts to emphasize certain surface-qualities in their brushwork. But their painting retained one of the most important innovations Manet and the others had made in the 1860s: to leave the individual strokes of the brush distinct and visible on the paint-surface. This had two basic results: first, to undermine the demands for smooth finish which dominated the Neo-classical tradition in French painting, and second, to establish the appearance of spontaneity and directness as a positive aesthetic value in the final appearance of a painting.

The bulk of the Impressionists' work was executed in oils on canvas; this was the standard medium for their Salon exhibits and for the smaller landscapes they painted out of doors. However, many of the artists actively experimented in other media—an important element in their work. Pastel was Degas' principal medium from the late 1870s; he found ways of using it in superimposed layers to achieve great richness of color as in *The Tub*, *c*1885 (Hill-Stead Museum, Farmington, Conn.). In Cézanne's later work, watercolor allowed him to exploit the luminosity of the white paper—seen through layers of translucent color—a technique which seems to have influenced his handling of oil paint. Drawing was only occasionally of importance: for Cézanne, in his drawings after the works of the old masters, for Renoir, in the preparatory studies for his figure-compositions of the 1880s, for Manet and Degas, also for preparatory studies, and for Pissarro, for quick notations from nature. Of the reproductive media, etching became the most important for the Impressionists, after its revival in France *c*1850 and its popularization by the *Société des Aquafortistes* in the 1860s (to whose publications Manet and Jongkind contributed); Manet and Pissarro made most use of this graphic method of notating quick effects from nature.

Most Impressionist outdoor scenes, from the 1870s onwards, were quite unlike previous French landscape paintings in their use of color. Whereas paintings of the Barbizon school (for example, Théodore Rousseau's *The Oaks*, *c*1850–2; Louvre, Paris) were modeled by clear contrasts of dark and light tones with a restricted range of subdued color and a few small accents of stronger color, the archetypal Impressionist landscape (for example Monet's *Sailing at Argenteuil*, 1874; private collection) was predominantly modeled by contrasts and nuances of clear color which suggest the forms and space within the picture. Yellow is used for sunlit highlights in foliage, blue often for shadows; the sharper contrasts in the foreground stand out from the softer colors in the distance. It was

Left, above: The Road to Sèvres by Alfred Sisley; oil on canvas; 54×73cm (21×29in); 1873. Musée du Jeu de Paume, Paris

Left: Zola's House at Médan by Cézanne; oil on canvas; 59×72cm (23×28in); *c*1880. Burrell Collection, Glasgow

Terrace at Sainte-Adresse by Claude Monet; oil on canvas; 98×130cm (39×51in); 1867. Metropolitan Museum, New York

such an approach to color that Pissarro taught Cézanne in the early 1870s, to "replace modeling by the study of colors" and "justify this by reference to nature", in the belief that it was a more truthful way to represent the varied play of light and color out of doors.

However, this use of color evolved only gradually. Manet in the 1860s retained the traditional methods of tonal modeling, relieved only by a few colored accents, as in *Music in the Tuileries Gardens* (1862; National Gallery, London), and it was Monet who began to incorporate a wider range of color into his work, introducing into pictures such as *Terrace at Sainte-Adresse* (1867; Metropolitan Museum, New York) strong color-contrasts and some soft blue shadows. Effects such as these, though, initially appear only in some sunlit effects, and many Impressionist paintings of the early 1870s, for instance Pissarro's *Penge Station* (1871; Courtauld Institute Galleries, London), remain dominantly tonal in their structure. Throughout the 1870s, indeed, the color-range of individual paintings depended closely on the subject and type of weather shown.

Artistic precedent played some part in this development. Pre-Raphaelite painting in England shows a range of bright color, but can have had no direct influence on the Impressionists; most important for them was Delacroix, whose later work (for example, *Jacob Wrestling with the Angel*, 1856–61; St Sulpice Church, Paris) and published views on color revealed the possibilities of composing scenes in terms of dominant color contrasts. Japanese color prints, too, notably those of Ando Hiroshige (1797–1858), when discovered in Paris in the 1860s, supplied a sanction for using simple, juxtaposed planes of clear color, such as appear in Monet's *Regatta at Argenteuil* (1872/3; Musée du Jeu de Paume, Paris). But these influences, on their own, did not create Impressionist color practice. The basic stimulus was the artists' own study of

Regatta at Argenteuil by Claude Monet; oil on canvas; 48×73cm (19×29in); 1872/3. Musée du Jeu de Paume, Paris

nature; artistic precedents only helped to show them how to translate their experiences of nature into color in a fresh and direct way.

In the later 1870s, as their brushwork became more complex, the Impressionists began to introduce a greater range of small colored touches to their paint-surfaces, even in less brightly lit scenes, for instance Pissarro's *The Côte des Boeufs at the Hermitage, Pontoise* (1877; National Gallery, London). In part this was an attempt to refine their rendering of the effects of nature, but it also served to accentuate the internal color relationships on the picture-surface, and in Monet's work of the early 1880s (for example, *The Douanier's Cottage at Varengeville*, 1882; Museum of Fine Arts, Boston) sequences of small color-oppositions give the whole painting a structure of contrasts, of pinks and oranges set against greens and blues.

In some later works, from the mid 1880s onwards, Monet, Renoir, and Sisley keyed up their color still further, emphasizing broad contrasts of complementary colors over the whole picture-surface, and mixing their paints with white to heighten the overall luminosity of the scene. In Monet's and Renoir's work, this was, in part, caused by their attempts to paint the light of the Mediterranean: they had to find a way of conveying the brightness of the South with the paints at their disposal. Late in his life, Cézanne said that one of his great discoveries had been that "sunlight cannot be reproduced, but it must be represented by something else, by color". Monet and Renoir seem to have reached the same conclusion in the South (for example, in Monet's *Antibes*, 1888; Courtauld Institute Galleries, London). The effect of these adjustments is to emphasize the overall color structure of the picture, and in Monet's later work, such as the *Rouen Cathedral* series (1892–4; five examples in the Musée du Jeu de Paume, Paris), integrated color-harmonies become predominant. Renoir's later work, too, achieves a new warmth and luminosity, seen in *The Bathers* (1918–19; Musée du Jeu de Paume, Paris). This changing attitude to color was, in general terms, another symptom of the Impressionists' gradual realization of the im-

possibility of making a literal record of nature, and of the importance of composing their scenes in terms of the two dimensions of the paint surface.

During the mid 19th century, great progress was being made in the scientific study of color, pioneered in France by Eugène Chevreul (1786–1889), whose book *On the Law of the Simultaneous Contrast of Colors* appeared in 1839. This and other later treatises were a dominant influence on the Neo-Impressionists, whose systematic approach to color was enthusiastically espoused by Pissarro between 1886 and 1888. However, the Impressionists themselves, though exploring the effects of contrasts of colors, did not approach color from a theoretical basis but founded their practices on their own empirical experience of working from nature. Optical mixture, as advocated by the Neo-Impressionists, by which two colors are juxtaposed in small dots to produce a resultant color, plays no part in Impressionist painting; in Impressionist pictures, the juxtaposed touches of varied color are meant to be seen as distinct accents and are used to suggest the constant variety of natural hues and textures. Scientific color theory may have created the background of interest in the potential of color out of which the Impressionists' color evolved, but this evolution itself was in no sense theoretical or scientific.

Traditionally, Impressionist painting has been presented as wholly casual and unorganized in composition. In 1898, the Neo-Impressionist Paul Signac criticized it for its failure to organize and arrange its forms on the canvas. However, its apparent informality was part of a deliberate attempt to convey the immediacy of man's perception of the world around him. Manet, and Courbet before him, favored loosely structured groups of figures seen frontally, disposed in a shallow space across the canvas, as in Manet's *Music in the Tuileries Gardens* (1862; National Gallery, London), and both artists looked to the simple frieze-like compositions of French popular imagery and illustration for their inspiration. In the 1860s, the arrival of Japanese prints in Paris provided a fresh compositional stimulus; their high viewpoints, cut-off forms, and jumps in space suggested ways of presenting an image with great immediacy without using the traditional European device of linear perspective to define space. Monet's *Terrace at Sainte-Adresse* (1867; Metropolitan Museum, New York) is an early example of their influence, and Degas' typical compositional forms, with their strong diagonals and cut-off forms, as in *The Ballet Rehearsal* (1874; Burrell Collection, Glasgow), owe much to the lessons of Japanese art which Degas harnessed to the representation of the unexpected vistas and viewpoints characteristic of life in the modern city.

Contemporary photography has been cited as an influence on the urban scenes of Degas and the Impressionists, but for several reasons it seems unlikely that it played any great part in dictating the type of compositions they used. Its instantaneous effects were quite alien to Degas' careful planning of his

Rouen Cathedral by Claude Monet; oil on canvas; 115×65cm (45×26in); 1894. Museum Folkwang, Essen

The Ballet Rehearsal by Degas; oil on canvas; 60×100cm (24×39in); 1874. Burrell Collection, Glasgow

compositions, and the effects of studied asymmetry, which Degas favored, appear before any such devices became popular in photography: indeed, Degas probably influenced the development of photography, *not* vice versa. Those urban photographs that have been compared to such street scenes by the other Impressionists as Monet's *Boulevard des Capucines* (1873; William Rockhill Nelson Gallery, Kansas City) and Renoir's *Pont Neuf* (1872; National Gallery of Art, Washington, D.C.) are themselves dependent on a tradition of popular urban prints. It was to this tradition—not specifically to photography—that the Impressionists looked when choosing viewpoints for their canvases.

In their landscapes, the Impressionists created the compositions of their paintings by their choice of viewpoint, which dictated how the forms in front of them should relate to each other and to the edges of the canvas. Sisley, Renoir, and Pissarro in general favored a fairly clearly defined and simple perspectival structure in their work, often showing views straight down roads or paths—a type of composition which looks back to the work of Corot and Jongkind—seen in Pissarro's *Penge Station*, 1871 (Courtauld Institute Galleries, London) and in Sisley's *The Road to Sèvres*, 1873 (Musée du Jeu de Paume, Paris). However, Monet and Cézanne tended to choose compositions that lacked any direct lead-in, and concentrated on the disposition across the canvas of forms in successive planes of space. Cézanne's landscapes are generally built up of such overlapping planes, which are linked together by effects of color and brushwork on the paint-surface (for example, *Mont Sainte-Victoire*, *c*1904/6; Philadelphia Museum of Art), a type of close-knit structure which Picasso and Braque made the basis of their Cubist paintings of 1908–11. Monet in the 1870s favored simple forms, often seen frontally across water (for example, *Regatta at Argenteuil*, 1872/3; Musée du Jeu de Paume, Paris), but after 1880 he often used high viewpoints, with dramatic cut-offs and breaks of space, which, as he acknowledged, owed much to Japanese

prints. In his last canvases, the monumental *Water Lily* decorations (*c*1916–26, Orangerie des Tuileries, Paris; other canvases in Museum of Modern Art, New York, and elsewhere), the composition was reduced simply to the play of lily-pads and reflected trees and clouds over a single continuous water-surface. This created a type of surface which has seemed, in retrospect, to anticipate some of the features of American Abstract Expressionism.

In the 1860s and 1870s, besides their similarities of technique and method, the Impressionists shared another characteristic: an interest in painting quintessentially modern subjects. The tradition of modern-life painting was nothing new; it could be traced back to 18th-century Venice, 17th-century Holland, and beyond. But in a period whose official tastes were dominated by various forms of historicism, young artists felt that art was becoming alienated from the great changes they saw taking place around them, notably the rebuilding of Paris under the direction of Baron Haussmann (1809–91) and the development of industrialization and the railways. As early as the 1840s, Baudelaire had urged the artist to take up the theme of the "heroism of modern life", but it was not until the 1860s that modern urban subjects gained any wide currency.

The immediate background for many of the early themes of the Impressionist group was another essay by Baudelaire, *The Painter of Modern Life* (written 1859/60, published 1863) which concerned the watercolorist Constantin Guys. Baudelaire's concentration on fashionable Paris, and on the anonymity of the individual in crowds, was immediately echoed by Manet—who knew Baudelaire well—in *Music in the Tuileries Gardens* (1862; National Gallery, London), and by Boudin, who began to paint the *habitués* of the Paris boulevards, as they appeared in summer on the fashionable beaches of Trouville (for example, *The Empress Eugénie on the Beach of Trouville*, 1863; Burrell Collection, Glasgow). In 1868, Boudin wrote that he wanted to "find a way of making acceptable men in ulsters and women in waterproofs ... The bourgeois, walking along the jetty towards the sunset, has just as much right to be caught on canvas as the peasant." Monet and Renoir, too, soon took up the themes of urban Paris and the suburban recreations of the bourgeoisie, showing the middle-classes on parade in the city, and at leisure in the parks and the surrounding countryside—now easily accessible by train from the capital—for example, Renoir's *Le Pont des Arts* (1866/7; Norton Simon Inc. Museum of Art, Los Angeles) and *Pont Neuf* (1872; National Gallery of Art, Washington, D.C.), Monet's *Women in the Garden* (1866–7; Musée du Jeu de Paume, Paris) and *Boulevard des Capucines* (1873; William Rockhill Nelson Gallery, Kansas City). The work of Monet and his friends at Argenteuil falls into the same category, showing the boating and regattas of the outer suburbs of Paris. Manet, Monet, and Pissarro also treated the theme of the railway station and its trains in such paintings as Pissarro's *Penge Station* (1871; Courtauld Institute Galleries, London) and Monet's paintings of the Gare Saint-Lazare (examples in the Musée du Jeu de Paume, Paris, and the Art Institute of Chicago). Pissarro mainly focused on the small country towns around Paris, and the life of the peasants who worked there; often his themes echo Millet, though the utopian anarchist views Pissarro held, at least by the 1890s, were a far cry from Millet's fatalism. Only after 1895 did Pissarro undertake important urban themes, painting the port of Rouen and the boulevards and river in Paris.

Other aspects of the modern scene preoccupied Manet, Degas, and Renoir during the 1870s, such as the world of urban entertainments, from the Opéra to the working-class café. Much of Renoir's and Manet's work concentrates on individuals and their psychological situations, for example, Renoir's *La Loge* (1874; Courtauld Institute Galleries, London) and Manet's *The Conservatory* (1878; Nationalgalerie, Berlin), or at least includes a characterized principal group, as in Renoir's *Moulin de la Galette* (1876; Musée du Jeu de Paume, Paris). Degas, treating in particular the ballet, focused not on the sentiments of the participants, but on the intricate interweaving of figures in varied groupings, as in *The Ballet Rehearsal* (1874; Burrell Collection, Glasgow); only rarely, as in *L'Absinthe* (1876; Musée du Jeu de Paume, Paris) does characterization play an important part in his work.

The public world of modern Paris was not the Impressionists' only sphere; in their treatment of the female nude, in particular, a greater variety of approaches becomes apparent, as a result of their attempts to harness the theme of modern women to the old-master tradition of the female nude. Manet's *Olympia* (1863; Musée du Jeu de Paume, Paris) is a nude Venus translated into the guise of a modern courtesan, his *Le Déjeuner sur l'Herbe* (1863; Musée du Jeu de Paume, Paris) a modernization of the theme of Giorgione's *Concert Champêtre* (Louvre, Paris). Degas, in his nudes of the 1880s and later (for example, *The Tub*, c1885; Hill-Stead Museum, Farmington, Conn.), and Gauguin in his *Nude* (1880; Ny Carlsberg Glyptotek, Copenhagen), represented woman explicitly in her everyday surroundings, while Renoir, in his bather paintings of the 1880s and later, presented the nude in a more traditional way, in Arcadian settings and without modern references (for example, *The Bathers*, 1885–7; Philadelphia Museum of Art). Cézanne, too, in the monumental imaginary "Bather" compositions of his later years (those in the National Gallery, London; Philadelphia Museum of Art; Barnes Foundation, Merion, Pa., for example) avoided any modern details, while the erotic scenes in his earlier work, though often modern in their setting, are highly personal in their imagery, *A Modern Olympia* (1873; Musée du Jeu de Paume, Paris) for example.

Similarly, in their landscapes the Impressionists did not confine themselves to overtly modern themes. Much of the landscape they painted is essentially man-made (roads, fields, villages), but Monet and Cézanne, in particular, were also fascinated by nature at its most intractable (mountains and rocks), and Monet by the forces of the elements (snow and ice, sea and wind lashing broken coastlines). These interests link them to Romantic views of man's insignificance in face of the forces of nature, and are a far cry from the everyday world of their more human-scaled scenes. In his coastal scenes of the 1880s, in particular, Monet showed natural forms at their most dramatic, as in *Storm on Belle-Isle* (1886; Musée du Jeu de Paume, Paris) and increasingly planned his groups of paintings to convey an overall mood; in his exhibitions, he played off contrasting groups against each other. Moreover, he and Cézanne came to concentrate on single images in long sequences of canvases, which gave some of their subjects an almost metaphysical force, such as Cézanne's views of Mont Sainte-Victoire (for example, the one in Philadelphia Museum of Art), and Monet's of Rouen Cathedral (five in Musée du Jeu de Paume, Paris). Though Pissarro and Sisley also came to paint such series of related canvases, they remained more specific in their recording of the varied play of light and weather, while Monet used his series as the basis for elaborate and integrated color-harmonies, and Cézanne his for exploring the play of colored planes on the picture-surface.

A paradox is involved in any attempt to translate Impressionism into sculpture, because of sculpture's three-dimensionality, its materials, and its absence of color. Of the Impressionists, Degas alone, after c1880, used sculpture extensively, exploring the problems of the representation of movement by modeling in clay and wax. Auguste Rodin (1840–1917) is often associated with the movement, though the link can only be made in very general terms. Rodin, like the Impressionists, pursued a type of naturalism in his forms, and studied incessantly from nature; but in his concentration on the human form, and in the allegorical and mythological themes he favored, his concerns were far from theirs. Perhaps closest to Impressionism among sculptors was the Italian Medardo Rosso (1858–1928), in his interest in the way light dissolved the solidity of forms. His characteristic work—basically relief modeling, not sculpture in the round—allowed him to explore such effects more easily. However, in general terms, Impressionism is essentially a pictorial style, devoted to the problems of translating experiences of nature into strokes of colored paint on a two-dimensional surface, and any attempt to define Impressionist sculpture will miss the basic qualities of the style.

In the broadest sense, the Impressionists belonged to the period of Naturalism in their concern for making a record of their experiences and of the characteristic scenes of the world around them. At this level, their interests can be paralleled with contemporary developments outside the field of painting, with trends in literature, political thought, and philosophy. However, the value of such comparisons lies as much in their limitations as in their overall validity: they show both the importance of a shared intellectual background and the uniqueness of the defining characteristics of Impressionism as a pictorial style.

The modern scenes the Impressionists painted are precisely those described by Naturalist novelists and writers, such as Émile Zola, the Goncourt Brothers, and Guy de Maupassant,

Paintings of La Grenouillère

Monet's and Renoir's paintings of La Grenouillère of 1869 have acquired an almost legendary status in the history of Impressionism. Freely painted and boldly colored, they anticipate many of the central characteristics of Impressionist painting of the following decade. However, their true importance can only be assessed by seeing them in the context of the two men's work of 1869–70.

Monet spent the second half of 1869 living at St-Michel, on the edge of Bougival, a village on a loop of the River Seine downstream from Paris. Renoir, meanwhile, was living nearby, at Voisins near Louveciennes; the two men spent time working together. In a letter to Frédéric Bazille in September, Monet described his plans for the next year's Salon exhibition: "I have a dream of a painting of the bathing place of La Grenouillère, for which I have done some bad sketches (*mauvaises pochades*). Renoir also wants to paint the same subject." La Grenouillère was a pleasure spot on the Île de Croissy, an island in the Seine near Bougival.

In the event, Renoir was represented at the 1870 Salon by a figure-subject, not a view of the bathing place; but this painting, *Bather with a Griffon* (Museum of Modern Art, Sao Paulo, Brazil), shows a river bank with a tree and boat very like the setting of La Grenouillère. The landscape Monet submitted to the 1870 Salon was rejected, but it may have been his planned major painting of the place. It can probably be identified with a painting now lost, and known only from an old photograph (reproduced in Wildenstein, D., *Claude Monet, Biographie et Catalogue Raisonné*, Lausanne and Paris, vol. one, 1974, no. 136).

The paintings which have since become famous must be identified as those Monet called "bad sketches". Two paintings by each artist clearly belong to this group. Monet's canvas in the Metropolitan Museum, New York, and Renoir's in the Nationalmuseum, Stockholm, both show the floating café on the right with, in the center, the *camembert*, an islet planted with a tree. The other pair, Monet's painting in the National Gallery, London, and Renoir's in the Sammlung Oskar Reinhart "Am Römerholz", Winter-

▼ *Bathers at La Grenouillère* by Monet; oil on canvas; 73×92cm (29×36in); 1869. National Gallery, London

▲ *La Grenouillère* by Monet; oil on canvas; 75×100cm (30×39in); 1869. Metropolitan Museum, New York

▲ *La Grenouillère* by Renoir; oil on canvas; 66×81cm (26×32in); 1869. Nationalmuseum, Stockholm

◀ *Bather with a Griffon* by Renoir; oil on canvas; 184×115cm (72×45in); 1870. Museum of Modern Art, Sao Paulo

▲ *Impression: Sunrise* by Monet; oil on canvas; 48×63cm (19×25in); 1872. Musée Marmottan, Paris

exist alongside quick sketches such as his *Impression: Sunrise* (Musée Marmottan, Paris). But increasingly elements from the sketch style of the La Grenouillère paintings became an integral part of their completed landscapes—notably the shorthand treatment of forms and, in Monet's work, the broken handling of reflections in water. It was in the La Grenouillère paintings of 1869 that these elements were first fully realized.

The La Grenouillère paintings have another level of significance: in their subject matter. To a 20th-century viewer, the scenes shown have no obvious connotations, but an audience at the time would at once have recognized in La Grenouillère a celebrated meeting place of the *demi-monde*, one of the pleasure spots on the Seine where well-born young men could entertain their mistresses. The setting and clientèle of the place are vividly described in Guy de Maupassant's story *La Femme de Paul*, written about a decade after Monet and Renoir had painted the place. Thus, in their intention of exhibiting paintings of La Grenouillère at the 1870 Salon, Monet and Renoir were choosing a heavily loaded subject, one that told much about the morals of the age. In the dispassionate way in which they treated it, though, they were deliberately avoiding making any judgments about it. Renoir's *Bather*, shown at the 1870 Salon, raises just the same issue in a rather different way: her clothes and context are modern, but her pose is that of the Classical Cnidian Venus, goddess of Love. To understand the full significance of the Impressionists' landscapes it is important to study what the scenes themselves signified, as well as the ways in which the Impressionists painted them.

thur, show the view looking further to the left, with bathing huts on the left of the pictures. Monet's lost painting was more panoramic, taking in most of the views seen in both his smaller canvases.

The four surviving paintings all measure between 2 ft 8 in and 3 ft 3 in across (between 81 and 100 cm)—sizes standard at the period for easel paintings, but smaller than the usual paintings shown at the Salon exhibitions. In them, forms are treated summarily, the reflections in the water in crisp individual strokes of paint. The touch is more feathery in Renoir's paintings, broader and more slab-like in Monet's, in which the treatment of the water is particularly bold. Their handling and the disregard for detail

set them apart from both men's more finished canvases of the period (for instance Monet's *The Magpie*, private collection), and suggest that their original function was, as Monet suggested in his letter to Bazille, to be *pochades*—a term commonly used at the time to describe quickly, often boldly, executed sketches.

Thus, in the two men's work of 1869, the surviving paintings were preparatory, not final statements. However, in the early 1870s both Monet and Renoir in their landscapes concentrated more on smaller-scale, freely painted canvases. Even after 1870, more highly finished paintings, such as Monet's *Riverside Walk at Argenteuil* of 1872 (National Gallery of Art, Washington, D.C.),

JOHN HOUSE

though strictly working-class themes are rare in Impressionist painting. Both writers and painters frequented the same social circles—Zola in particular was at this time a close friend of several of the Impressionists—and they were trying, in their own media, to create works of art which would be truly characteristic of the milieu in which they lived. But in no sense is Impressionist painting literary; only very rarely, as in Manet's *Nana* (1877; Hamburger Kunsthalle, Hamburg), is there any reference to contemporary writing or any suggestion of specific narrative content in the Impressionists' work. Instead, they were seeking ways of rendering the modern world with the means at the disposal of the painter, by form and color within the confines of the canvas, just as the writers were with their available means—the development of characterization and plot possible in the novel. Scenes from novels can be used to supply background information for paintings, and paintings can be used to help visualize scenes from novels, but the Impressionists' pictures cannot be read in any sense as illustrations of the novels; the common element is the milieu shared by the painters and writers.

In the context of the conventions of the day, Impressionism appeared as a radical and revolutionary form of art, both in technique and subject matter; but this is not to say that the artists held revolutionary political views. All of them, apart from Degas and probably Cézanne, were broadly republican in their sympathies, but only Pissarro—active in anarchist circles in the 1890s—had any deep political commitment. Pissarro's treatment of themes of peasant life shows a sympathy with a simple preindustrial form of society, but the ideological content in his art is never overt, and his work, along with that of his friends, remained conspicuously unaffected by the major political upheavals of the day. Even the cataclysmic events of 1870–1 had no perceptible effect on either their subject matter or their approaches to their art; only Manet, in a few small works, made any record of the year's happenings. In general, in their treatment of themes of modern life, the Impressionists showed an awareness of the structure and social divisions of society, but recorded them in a detached, dispassionate way which deliberately avoided any ideological comment.

One strand of opinion at the time felt that the revolutionary artist should never be a political propagandist. For the anarchist theorist Peter Kropotkin (1842–1921), propaganda was the natural medium for the artistic revolutionary, but even so committed an anarchist as the Neo-Impressionist Signac declared that the task of the anarchist artist was to overthrow the artistic establishment of his day, while his political brother overthrew the State; by this criterion, he could declare Monet and Pissarro to have belonged to the anarchist cause by virtue of their art alone. But the artistic revolution achieved by the Impressionists in the 1870s and 1880s conspicuously lacked such a political dimension; the role adopted

by the artists was the traditional one of the Bohemian at odds with a materialistic society, not that of the revolutionary at war with capitalism.

Certain broad parallels can be made between Impressionism and some of the ideas of Positivist philosophy. On one level, the Impressionists' interest in showing modern man in his characteristic everyday surroundings relates to Hippolyte Taine's belief in race, environment, and point in time as the factors that determine men's destinies—a theory which became the basis of Zola's literary ideas. Equally relevant, in a different way, is the Positivists' interest in modes of perceiving the world around us, and their contribution to the psychology of perception; they used the terms "sensation" and "impression" to describe the stimulus received by the senses from the outside world, a vocabulary adopted by the Impressionists. Indeed the term "impression" itself had become a standard term in art criticism by the 1860s, being used initially to describe the effect a scene made on the viewer, and then, by transference, the quick record the painter made of this effect; it was the latter sense that Monet adopted in titling his painting *Impression: Sunrise* in 1874. But the Impressionists' basic concern was never to investigate the nature of perception as such, but to find ways of recording their sensations pictorially.

Comparisons with literary, social, and philosophical thought are necessary to understand Impressionism in its context, as an art movement that belonged to the period c1860–90. However, the nature of Impressionism itself cannot be explained in terms of any other discipline. Against a shared intellectual background, the distinguishing characteristics of Impressionism are precisely those it does not share with other activities—the pictorial qualities that make it an art form and not a theoretically based mode of expression. It was in pictorial terms that the Impressionists defined their own aims; Cézanne used to declare that his aim was to realize in paint his sensations in front of nature, and Monet wrote in 1912: "I do what I think best in order to express what I experience in front of nature ... to fix my sensations." Each artist's painting was the result of his own explorations of the problem of translating these sensations and impressions into pictorial form.

In rejecting the Salon as the principal outlet for their work, and concentrating on independently organized group exhibitions, the Impressionists initiated a total reappraisal of the relationship between the artist and his public. Instead of depending on officially sponsored exhibitions of works selected by a jury, the artist gradually came to find a wide range of outlets for his art. The foundation of the jury-free Société des Indépendants in 1884 provided the Post-Impressionists and later groups with a regular chance to exhibit, but the Impressionists themselves relied principally on a different type of outlet, smaller group exhibitions and one-man shows mounted by art dealers.

Independent art dealers had begun to play a greater part in the Paris art market in the 1850s and 1860s, and men such as Martinet, Latouche, and Martin began to patronize Manet and the Impressionists in the 1860s. However, their principal

La Loge by Renoir; oil on canvas; 80×64cm (31×25in); 1874.
Courtauld Institute Galleries, London

dealer was Paul Durand-Ruel, who met Monet and Pissarro in London in 1870–1, and thereafter bought the work of the whole group, whenever he could afford to. Durand-Ruel showed Impressionist paintings in exhibitions in London in 1870–5; in Paris, he mounted the group exhibitions of 1876 and 1882, and from 1883 onwards held a sequence of one-man and mixed shows of the Impressionists; in New York, he put on a number of larger exhibitions from 1886 which introduced Impressionism to America. His Paris one-man shows seem to have been the first systematic attempt to convert the public by exhibitions of single artists, a method that has become fundamental to the art market today. Rival dealers took up the Impressionists in the 1880s, such as Georges Petit and Boussod & Valadon (in the person of their branch manager, Théo van Gogh, Vincent's brother), but Durand-Ruel remained their primary outlet, and became a close personal friend particularly of Monet, Renoir, and Pissarro.

In the 1870s, the Impressionists had only a few regular buyers, all of whom were friends to whom the artists could turn in a crisis, and who bought what they could when they could, often at very low prices. Most belonged to the same Bohemian circles as the artists themselves: men such as the singer Faure, the painter Caillebotte, the composer Chabrier, the baker Murer, and the civil servant Chocquet. By the late 1870s, Renoir has been introduced by the publisher Charpentier into a circle of art lovers, mainly from the fashionable bourgeoisie and nouveaux riches, who effectively subsidized his more experimental work by a sequence of portrait commissions; the same group began to patronize Monet too. During the 1880s, Durand-Ruel introduced further buyers, but it was only from the late 1880s that Impressionist painting began to command a wide following and high prices; aristocratic patrons seem only to have taken them up after their success was assured. In the United States, where a large part of their work was sold after c1889, their principal buyers were the new generation of commercial and industrial magnates.

The critical response to Impressionism in France in the 1870s was generally hostile; only a few writers tried to understand its innovations; otherwise it gave the art critics a chance to flex their muscles as satirists. Reactions became more sympathetic in the 1880s, but when, in the 1890s, Impressionist paintings began to be exhibited widely abroad, the initial responses were again critical or even abusive, as the critics of each country tried to reconcile their features with the conventions of their own national schools of painting. However, in France in the 1880s and all over Europe and the United States in the 1890s, Impressionism became the dominant influence on avant-garde art, and its superficial characteristics gradually became the accepted conventions of the next generation of artists.

This is not to say that the innovations of Impressionism quickly lost their relevance: its discoveries have supplied the seeds for many later developments in painting. In retrospect, Impressionism can be seen to have undermined finally the traditional idea of the large, highly-finished exhibition picture in favor of a type of painting which was more informal, and a more immediate expression of the artist's personality. Various aspects of the Impressionists' style were taken up by later groups of artists in France; the Fauves adopted the freedom of their brushwork, and the small, loosely structured canvases they favored, while the dazzling color of Fauvism is a development from the accentuated color of later Impressionism, as transmitted by Van Gogh and the Neo-Impressionists. The Cubists adapted Cézanne's treatment of the picture-surface as a close-knit sequence of colored planes, but made of it an anti-naturalistic type of art quite opposed to Cézanne's basic aims. Impressionism's perceptual, empirical nature sets it apart from the formalist and surrealist traditions in 20th-century painting, but in general terms the concentration on the surface qualities of the painting, found particularly in Cézanne and Monet, have anticipated many of the central preoccupations of subsequent painting.

Outside France, Impressionism had a very wide, but basically fragmented, influence. Artists of many sorts harnessed various aspects of it to their own ends, and it was in general synthesized with the traditions of painting already current in each country. Impressionist color, handling, or subject matter appear widely in many contexts, but it was only rarely—for instance, in some works by Philip Wilson Steer (1860–1942) in England, Max Liebermann (1847–1935) in Germany, and Childe Hassam (1859–1935) in America—that all the French Impressionists' preoccupations appear at one and the same time. Even these painters, though, belonged more, in general, to their own national traditions than to the Impressionist camp. Impressionism itself was essentially a French phenomenon, with its concentration on freshness, informality, detachment, and modernity, and it could only appear as a coherent artistic movement in France.

JOHN HOUSE

Bibliography. Denvir, B. *Encyclopaedia of Impressionism*, London (1990). Leymarie, J. *Impressionism*, Geneva (1955). Pool, P. *Impressionism*, London (1967). Rewald, J. *The History of Impressionism*, London and New York (1973).

43

POST-IMPRESSIONISM

Sunday Afternoon on the Island of the Grande Jatte by Seurat; oil on canvas; 207×308cm (81×121in); 1883–5; completed 1886
Art Institute of Chicago (see page 806)

THE term Post-Impressionism was first used in 1910 by the English art critic Roger Fry (1866–1934). It acted as a convenient title, "Manet and the Post-Impressionists", to a rather mixed exhibition of modern French painters which Fry arranged in London. With the exception of Manet, Cézanne, and Redon, the artists represented were younger than the Impressionists and painted in styles that differed from those of Monet, Renoir, Pissarro, and Sisley. Fry had originally proposed "Expressionist" as the title for the exhibition. He wrote later: "For purposes of convenience, it was necessary to give these artists a name, and I chose, as being the vaguest and most non-committal, the name of Post-Impressionist. This merely state their position in time relatively to the Impressionist movement."

Certainly, in 1910, the term was vague and non-committal. Fry's exhibition included works by artists who would now be classed as Symbolists, Nabis, Fauvists, and Cubists. In its literal, temporal sense, Post-Impressionism implies anything produced after Impressionism—that is, after 1886, the date of the last Impressionist exhibition, or even after 1880, when already signs of personal and artistic disenchantment with the movement were apparent. The problem is to define its chronological extent: up to 1910, or 1900, or 1890?

The chronological problem is inseparable from that of constitution and membership. Which artists are Post-Impressionist, and what are the stylistic characteristics of Post-Impressionism?

In one sense, Post-Impressionism never existed; it was named posthumously. Impressionism, Fauvism, and Cubism all resulted from art critics' abuse and irony; Symbolism, Futurism, and Surrealism were all positively launched by manifesto. In 1910, Fry's fortuitous usage was wide and all-embracing in its implications. Yet it was the nature of the first Post-Impressionist exhibition to emphasize the achievements of Paul Cézanne (1839–1906), Paul Gauguin (1848–1903) and Vincent van Gogh (1853–90). And of these, Fry himself saw Cézanne not only as the most significant artist, but virtually the "onlie begetter" of the movement. He more or less ignored the contribution of Georges Seurat (1859–91) and Neo-Impressionism.

Once launched, however, the term was quickly abused by the generally hostile English critics. And it lost any critical validity it might have had. By the 1920s, both dealers and critics were using the term regularly—and indiscriminately. But a Post-Impressionist hierarchy slowly evolved and claimed its rightful place in the evolution of modern art. It was headed by a quartet of major artists, Cézanne, Gauguin, Van Gogh, and Seurat, who were seen as the essential precursors of the main 20th-century movements. To these were added (fairly often) the name of Renoir (1841–1919), in his guise of classical revivalist and constructive picture-maker, and (less frequently) the name of Toulouse-Lautrec (1864–1901). Around two of the major names were ranged their followers and associates: Émile Bernard (1868–1941) and the Pont-Aven Group (leading to the Nabis) around Gauguin, Paul Signac

(1863–1935) and the other Neo-Impressionists around Seurat. The time-span thus extended from c1880 to c1906 (the death of Cézanne and the birth of Fauvism).

More recently, a revision of the hierarchy has taken place, as well as a reduction of the time-span. In 1956, John Rewald's *Post-Impressionism* scrupulously charted the careers of Van Gogh (*ob.* 1890), Seurat (*ob.* 1891), and Gauguin (up to the end of his first visit to Tahiti in 1893). It ignored Cézanne, Renoir, and Toulouse-Lautrec, but clarified the affairs of the Pont-Aven Group and the Neo-Impressionists. In 1959, Sven Loevgren's volume, aptly entitled *The Genesis of Modernism*, confined its discussion to three artists: Seurat, Gauguin, and Van Gogh. In 1970, Mark Roskill, in his study *Van Gogh, Gauguin and the Impressionist Circle*, felt obliged to devote a chapter to Seurat, but able to exclude Cézanne from the main discussion. Emphatically, the enquiry was now concentrated on the 1880s. The same triumvirate of painters formed the chapter on Post-Impressionism in Alan Bowness's *Modern European Art* (1972), although Gauguin's career was followed through until his death in 1903.

The exclusion of Cézanne, once the very foundation of the Post-Impressionist edifice, does not imply a downgrading of his historical position. He is now in massive isolation; his style from 1880 is as isolated as that of Degas or Monet, who were also erstwhile Impressionists. And historically, the image of Cézanne's exclusion and isolation is a just one. In the 1880s, he withdrew from the Paris art scene: he did not exhibit there between 1877 and 1895 (apart from one painting, ironically now unidentifiable, at the Salon of 1882). The only place his paintings could be seen—and bought—was at the shop of the artist's colorman, Père Tanguy. Cézanne spent most of his time in the South: his acute sense of alienation was increased by the break-up of his long friendship with Zola as a result of the latter's novel, *L'Oeuvre*, published in 1886.

Cézanne summed up his position in a letter to Octave Maus, secretary of the Belgian artists' exhibiting society, "Les Vingt". He wrote on 27 November 1889:

> I must tell you with regard to this matter (of exhibiting) that the many studies I made having given only negative results, and dreading the critics who are only too justified, I had resolved to work in silence until the day when I should feel myself able to defend in theory the results of my attempts.

Cézanne's "Post-Impressionist" style, then, was achieved in deliberately chosen quarantine: it was not revealed to either painters or public until the large one-man show at the gallery of the art dealer Ambroise Vollard in 1895. Historically—in the narrow sense of participating in the art world's events—Cézanne was not part of Post-Impressionism. Ironically, the artist who had made no public contribution was claimed, posthumously, by Fry as the major progenitor of the movement. In actual fact, this period of public exposure and critical acclaim came *after* Cézanne's death in 1906. Fry's exhibition in 1910 took place when Cézanne's reputation was at its highest: not unnaturally, Fry named him the most important single figure. Few would deny Cézanne that accolade. In 1910, he was a potent, activating historical force; now, he is a massive historical monument.

To confine Post-Impressionism to three major artists and mainly to the decade of the 1880s still leaves some areas of overlap, for example, with Symbolism and Art Nouveau. Formally, in content, and critically, Gauguin, Seurat, and Van Gogh have contacts with—and indeed, made significant contributions to—Symbolism and Art Nouveau. There is a tendency to equate Post-Impressionism with form (structure, composition, purely pictorial considerations) and to leave questions of subject matter, content, and symbol to Symbolism. This seems to be a false dichotomy, and no more so than in the case of Gauguin, whose "body artistic" seems pulled apart by the battle between the Post-Impressionist formalists and the Symbolist soul-searchers. As a compromise, a chronological split might be suggested: leave Gauguin of the 1880s to Post-Impressionism, and give Gauguin of 1890 onwards to the Symbolists. In so doing, the Pont-Aven Group, its essential ideology and practice being settled by 1890, could also be confined to Post-Impressionism, while the Nabis, although clearly owing a debt to Gauguin and the Pont-Aven Group,

could be classed with the Symbolists. These divisions, while not always avoiding overlapping and cross-references, will be followed here.

In the early 1880s Impressionism had reached a crisis. There were three main reasons. First, its very perfecting of naturalistic illusionism could not be maintained forever. It was subject to internal dissolution and decline as a style; while dissension among the artists themselves was also growing. Secondly, it was subject to external pressures: younger artists in particular would critically examine its achievement. Thirdly—a phenomenon that often troubles artists in their forties and fifties—a period of self-doubt sets in, a sense of lost exuberance and dissipated experimental fervor. Thus in 1884, Degas, aged 50, wrote:

> Ah! where are the times when I thought myself strong. When I was full of logic, full of plans. I am sliding rapidly down the slope and rolling I know not where, wrapped in many bad pastels, as if they were packing paper.

Renoir spoke of this period when he was in his mid forties:

> Around 1883 I had gone absolutely to the limit of "impressionism" and I came to the conclusion that I did not know either

La Parade by Seurat; oil on canvas; 100×150cm (39×59in); 1886–8. Metropolitan Museum, New York

how to paint or how to draw. In a word, I was in an impasse.

And Pissarro, in his early fifties, also found himself in an impasse, discontented with his rough and rugged execution and his need to retouch his paintings.

Degas, with a self-sufficient fund of artistic reserves to call on, found his release in the concentrated series of female nudes that dominated his art from 1884 onwards. (For Gauguin, these nudes restored design when it was at its lowest ebb.) For his part, Renoir deliberately changed his style, using elements of ancient, Pompeian, Renaissance, and Neoclassical art to sustain his pictorial thinking. Instead of looking back to the achievements of older art, Pissarro threw in his lot with a new movement which was to be called Neo-Impressionism, the first radical alternative to Impressionism.

In November 1886, Pissarro wrote to his dealer, Paul Durand-Ruel, attempting to explain the nature of the new movement:

To seek a modern synthesis by methods based on science, that is, based on the theory of colors developed by Chevreul, on the experiments of Maxwell and the measurements of O.N. Rood; to substitute optical mixture for the mixture of pigments, which means to decompose tones into their constituent elements, because optical mixture stirs up luminosities more intense than those created by mixed pigments.

And Pissarro pointed out:

It is M. Seurat, an artist of great merit, who was the first to conceive the idea and to apply the scientific theory after having made thorough studies. With my confreres, Signac and Dubois-Pillet, I have merely followed Seurat's lead.

Pissarro was characteristically generous, as well as historically correct, in acknowledging Seurat's primacy in the forging of the new style. And it seems ironical that the first public manifestation of Neo-Impressionism took place at the last Impressionist exhibition in May 1886. In addition to works by Seurat and Pissarro, there were paintings by Pissarro's son, Lucien (1863–1944), and by Paul Signac.

One painting, however, imposed itself on the rest: Seurat's *Sunday Afternoon on the Island of the Grande Jatte* (now in the Art Institute of Chicago). For one thing it was by far the largest picture on view, 6 ft 6 in by 9 ft 10 in (2 m by 3 m). Yet it was an Impressionist subject—a casual Sunday afternoon crowd taking their ease on a pleasure-island on the Seine. It appeared also to owe something to Impressionist color and brushstroke. But on closer inspection, it was proclaiming a radical reform of Impressionist technique and vision.

Instead of a haphazard, variable brushstroke, there was a fairly uniform dot of paint (hence, "Pointillism"). Instead of mixing colors on the palette, they were juxtaposed on the canvas: optical mixture gave much greater luminosity and vibration (hence, "Divisionism"). As Signac wrote later: "The technique of the Impressionists is instinctive and instantaneous, that of the Neo-Impressionists is deliberate and constant." In 1886, the young art critic Félix Fénéon (1861–

1944) coined the term Neo-Impressionism, which has gained currency over Seurat's less felicitous "chromo-luminarism".

Simply defined, Neo-Impressionism means "New Impressionism", "Neo" in the sense of most recent or latest. Yet it also clearly implied Impressionism reshaped and reformed. And the extent of the reformation can be judged from some of the critical reactions to the *Grande Jatte* in 1886. Some critics referred to Egyptian art and Quattrocento painting, even to Kate Greenaway. Fénéon wrote:

Seurat has treated his forty or so figures in summary and hieratic style, setting them up frontally or with their backs to us or in profile, seated at right-angles, stretched out horizontally, or bolt upright: like a Puvis de Chavannes gone modern.

Yet the picture had its oddities: it is not as simple and unambiguous as it appears. There are changes in viewpoint; there is a curious diminution of figures from right to left; there are arbitrary shadows, especially the large area in the foreground. It is not just a piece of startlingly modernized classicism.

Spatial ambiguities and arbitrary elements increase in Seurat's later work. In 1886, he met Charles Henry (1859–1926), aesthetician and mathematician, and was greatly influenced by Henry's theories of the emotional character of linear directions. Another critic reported Seurat as saying:

The Panathenaea of Phidias (the Parthenon frieze) was a procession. I want to show the moderns moving about on friezes in the same way, stripped to their essentials, to place them in paintings arranged in harmonies of colors—through the direction of hues—in harmonies of lines—through their orientation—line and color fitted for each other.

La Parade (Metropolitan Museum, New York) of 1886–8, and *Le Chahut* (Kröller-Müller Museum, Otterlo) of 1889–90 demonstrate his programmatic intentions. In addition to these large "statement pictures", Seurat produced a series of landscapes of the Channel ports. *Le Pont et les Quais à Port-en-Bessin* of 1888 (Minneapolis Institute of Arts) is typical of the melancholic mood, the air of displaced reality, and the essential harmony that characterize them all. Seurat's method—as it was applied to his later work—was codified in a letter of 1890. It is worth quoting in full.

Aesthetic: Art is harmony. Harmony is the analogy of contraries, the analogy of similarities in tone (*ton*), color (*teinte*), and line considered under the aspect of the dominant one and under the influence of lighting in gay, calm, or sad combinations. The contraries are: in tone, a lighter, more luminous one in place of a darker; in color, complementaries, that is, a certain red opposed to its complementary, red-green, orange-blue, yellow-violet etc; in line, those making a right-angle. Gaiety, in tone is obtained through the use of dominant luminosity; in color, of prevailing warmth; in line, through those above the horizontal. Calmness, in tone is the equality of light and dark; in color, of warm and cool; and the horizontal for line. Sadness, in tone is prevailing dark; in color, a prevailing cool one; and in line, directions downward from the horizontal. Tech-

Le Pont et les Quais à Port-en-Bessin by Seurat; oil on canvas; 65×83cm (26×33in); 1888. Minneapolis Institute of Arts

nique: When we admit the phenomena of the duration of lumi-nous impressions on the retina, synthesis imposes itself as a result. The means for expression is the optic mixture of tones and colors (according to the placing and the way the colors are lighted, by sun, oil lamp, gas, etc), that is to say, the mixture of lights and their reactions (shadows) following the laws of con-trast, diminution, and irradiation. The frame is in harmony opposed to that of the tones, colors, and lines of the picture.

In Paris, Seurat's closest associate was Paul Signac (1863–1935), as Camille Pissarro began to turn away from Neo-Impressionism by 1888. Other important members of the Neo-Impressionist group were Charles Angrand (1854–1926), Henri-Edmond Cross (1856–1910), Maximilian Luce (1858–1941), and Albert Dubois-Pillet (1846–90).

Signac produced the occasional large figure-subject, but never as ambitiously as Seurat. He concentrated on landscape and seascape—Mediterranean as well as Normandy coast. He did, however, produce one picture that neatly brings together the various threads of Neo-Impressionism. This is *Against the Enamel of a Background Rhythmical with Beats and Angles, Tones and Colors, Portrait of M. Félix Fénéon in 1890* (Col-

lection of Mr and Mrs Samuel Josefowitz, Switzerland). The pointillist brushstroke is combined with a background based partly on the theories of Charles Henry and partly on the Japanese print. The witty, stylized, anti-naturalist, and deca-dent feeling clearly puts it into an Art Nouveau ambience.

Support from Symbolist poets (several of whom were also art critics) made Neo-Impressionism the best organized avant-garde movement in Paris from 1886 to Seurat's death in 1891. The Symbolist manifesto was launched in 1886. There was common ground in the refutation of the positivist ethic and the Impressionist slice of nature, and, more positively, in the search for the allusive sign and symbol, the emblematic pat-tern and the universal image. And politically, there was the growing attraction of anarchism. As a group the Impression-ists were apolitical. Monet had radical notions, but these never penetrated his paintings. Only Pissarro had a more active political consciousness, which crystallized into an-archist views of a nonviolent nature. These formed another bond with the younger Neo-Impressionists: Pissarro, Signac, and Luce contributed illustrations to the anarchist journals. There is less direct evidence of Seurat's anarchist involvement;

but it would seem that he shared his colleagues' opinions. It makes an unlikely Trinity—Neo-Impressionism, Symbolism, and Anarchism.

For other artists, however, acceptance of this trinity was not essential. Rather, they looked at the luminous color effects, the structured brushwork, the controlled surface, the deliberate composition. In varying degrees of intensity and duration, Gauguin, Bernard, Van Gogh, and Toulouse-Lautrec went through a Neo-Impressionist phase.

In Brussels, however, the effects of Neo-Impressionism went deeper. Seurat was invited to exhibit with Les Vingt—an avant-garde group of 20 artists founded in 1884—on several occasions, in 1887, 1889, and 1891. In 1892, a small memorial exhibition was arranged. Signac was invited in 1888 and 1890, Cross in 1889 and 1893. Belgian and Dutch artists quickly adopted the Neo-Impressionist technique. Among them were A.W. Finch (1854–1930), Georges Lemmen (1865–1916), Theo van Rysselberghe (1862–1926), Jan Toorop (1858–1928), and Henry van de Velde (1863–1957). It was van de Velde who moved from a Neo-Impressionist painting phase into his historically more significant role as Art Nouveau designer and architect.

In the 1890s, the impact of Neo-Impressionism lessened. The early death of Seurat in 1891 was a severe blow to the movement. Signac took over the leadership; he and Cross modified Seurat's "dot" into a larger, rectangular stroke. Signac's book *From Delacroix to Neo-Impressionism*, published in 1899, was an attempt to demonstrate the greater scientific truth and the more fully achieved luminosity of the movement over its two important forerunners, the painting and theory of Delacroix and the work of the Impressionists.

Signac's book influenced Matisse (1869–1954) and Derain (1880–1954), and hence Neo-Impressionism was a formative influence on Fauvism. It is reported that Braque had a reproduction of Seurat's *Le Chahut* in his studio c1907, and the example of Neo-Impressionism was not without its impact on the evolution of Cubism. Its influence, too, was felt by several early practitioners of Abstract art.

The avant-garde in the 1880s was a very small section of artists indeed. Their impact was confined to small coteries; this gave them a special, elitist feeling (deliberately cultivated) on the one hand, or, on the other, an alienated and increasingly anti-establishment stance. There was frequently a search to get at the public by unconventional, and sometimes untried means. In many ways, the 20th-century view of the alienated artist (not just the Bohemian in the attic) and the exaggerated avant-garde posture have their roots in the late 1880s. There is the manifesto. There is the astonishing increase in the number of small magazines in the mid 1880s—*La Vogue, Le Symboliste, La Revue Wagnérienne, La Revue Indépendante*. There is the importance of the café as the intellectual exchange mart for poet, critic, painter, and musician. There is the Salon des Artistes Indépendants, founded in 1884, a juryless exhibiting society, where the Neo-Impressionists regularly showed their work, and where Signac was to rule as President from

1908 to 1934. There were small group and one-man shows held in the offices of the avant-garde magazines—those held at *La Revue Indépendante*, for example—in enterprising dealers' galleries, in café and restaurant, and in the foyer of a theater, aptly called Le Théâtre Libre.

In Paris, then, there was a coming together of the arts, a sharing of premise and of premises: a physical and theoretical ambience in which Wagner, Baudelaire, Poe, Schopenhauer, Ibsen, Dostoevski, Walt Whitman, Carlyle, and Prince Kropotkin formed the ideological melting-pot. (And the 30-year-old Freud was studying with Dr Charcot 1885–6.)

Symbolist poet becomes art critic; artist writes Symbolist poetry; each is a confessed Wagnerian. Fénéon can publish Rimbaud's *Illuminations* in 1886 as well as coining the term Neo-Impressionism. Édouard Dujardin, more Wagnerian than most, applied the term "Cloisonnism" to a certain style of painting of 1888. Albert Aurier was a Symbolist poet, editor of a very small magazine, *Le Moderniste* (for which Gauguin was invited to write) and the author of the first major articles on both Van Gogh and Gauguin.

No sharply attuned artist could ignore all these proliferating manifestations of jointly engineered "modernism". A shift in sensibility, a reorientation of intellectual ideas, a readjustment of the artist's social stance took place in the 1880s. Post-Impressionism is the outward stylistic expression of this fermenting inner change.

Gauguin's response was to search for expressive signs and symbols whose synthesis would enlarge our spiritual apprehension of reality. He wished to refute the inherited European experience (which he felt had gone rotten with its over-insistence on materialistic "progress"), and to go back to primitive and non-European sources (Breton calvaries, Javanese temple sculpture, Oceanic carvings) and to live in a primitive, and preferably tropical, environment. In so doing, Gauguin would eventually refute the Impressionist view of nature.

As early as 1881, we find Gauguin asking Pissarro for the secret of Cézanne's "sensation": "Has M. Cézanne found the exact formula for a work acceptable to everyone?" And in 1885, he could write of the emotional effects of line and color and the mystical relationship of numbers. But up to 1886, Gauguin can be classed with the Impressionists. He exhibited with them in their last five shows (1879–86). He collected their work. He was particularly friendly with Pissarro. And it was the example of Pissarro and Cézanne in landscape and still-life pictures and of Degas in figure-subjects that dominated his work. Even after 1886—indeed right up to his death—Cézanne and Degas continued to act as paradigms.

Gauguin continued to paint in a modified Impressionist style during his first stay in Brittany in 1886. New signs appeared in his Martinique works of 1887: a much more audacious viewpoint in his landscapes, a greater insistence on the presence and play of figures, and a more decorative treatment. But the desired breakthrough occurred in the late summer of 1888. At Pont-Aven in Brittany, he painted the *Vision after the Sermon* or *Jacob Wrestling with the Angel* (National Gallery of Scotland, Edinburgh). He described it in a letter to Van Gogh:

I believe I have attained in these figures a great rustic and superstitious simplicity. It is all very severe ... To me in this painting the landscape and the struggle exist only in the imagination of the praying people, as a result of the sermon. That is why there is a contrast between these real people, and the struggle in this landscape which is not real and is out of proportion.

This is not merely anti-naturalist in presentation, and anti-Impressionist in technique; it is also asking painting to project inner thoughts, private dreams, and visions. It is related to a painting by Émile Bernard, *Breton Women in the Meadow* (private collection). Both artists, in their use of arbitrary, flattish color and strong outlines, were illustrating Dujardin's Cloisonnism, but their preferred nomenclature was "Synthetism".

Something of Gauguin's attempt to extend the expressive language of painting can be gauged from another letter, sent to Van Gogh in September 1888. He was describing a recently completed self-portrait, inscribed *Les Misérables* (himself and Émile Bernard) and dedicated to Van Gogh. *Les Misérables* is an allusion to Victor Hugo's novel and its tormented hero, Jean Valjean. Gauguin saw in his own head

the mask of a badly dressed and powerful ruffian like Jean Valjean who has a certain nobility and inner kindness. The hot blood pulsates through the face and the tonalities of a glowing kiln which surround the eyes indicate the fiery lava that kindles our painter's soul. The design of the eyes and nose, resembling that of flowers in a Persian rug, sums up an abstract and symbolic art. The delicate maidenly background with its child-like flowers is there to signify our artistic virginity. And this Jean Valjean whom society oppresses, an outlaw, with his love, his strength, is he not also the image of an Impressionist of today? By painting him in my own likeness, you have an image of myself as well as a portrait of all of us, poor victims of society, who retaliate only by doing good.

Gauguin had his own struggle with his own vision. The ambitious complexity of his thought is clearly shown here. Extra-pictorial considerations are brought into play—the memories of his experiences as a potter, the decorative effects of a Persian rug. The anti-naturalist stance is described as "abstract" and "symbolic". Yet he still calls himself an Impressionist. But in the late 1880s the term had not received its art-historical refinement, and was still synonymous with a rebellious, innovatory painter. When, during the Paris International Exhibition of 1889, Gauguin, Bernard, and others set up their own exhibition in the Café Volpini (note the venue), the title they used was "Impressionist and Synthetist Group".

Gauguin was the leader of the group. In Pont-Aven, he gathered young painters round him. Among them was Paul Sérusier (1863–1927). Increasingly, Gauguin moved towards an abstract use of color—color used for purely pictorial reasons, color that can have musical analogies but no longer

Night Café at Arles by Gauguin; oil on canvas; 72×92cm (28×36in); 1888. State Pushkin Museum of Fine Arts, Moscow

descriptive verisimilitude. Gauguin gave Sérusier a painting lesson: "How do you see these trees? They are yellow. Well then, put down yellow. And that shadow is rather blue. So render it with pure ultramarine. Those red leaves? Use vermilion." Sérusier took the message, as from the new Messiah, back to Paris, and the group who called themselves the "Nabis" (Prophets) took heed.

In Arles, Van Gogh welcomed Gauguin as abbot and instructor in the matter of painting from memory ("abstractions", as Van Gogh called them). The two artists endlessly discussed and dissected the various elements of painting: line and color, the role of shadow (if any), and the place of light expressed only by color. Gauguin continued his exploration of figure-subjects; his *Night Café at Arles* (State Pushkin Museum of Fine Arts, Moscow) seems to be a deliberate answer to Van Gogh's picture of the same subject.

In Brittany again in 1889, Gauguin exploited traditional Christian iconography in three paintings: the *Yellow Christ*, the *Green Christ*, and *Gethsemane*. In each Gauguin as Christ may be blasphemous, yet it also asserted his feeling of rejection by society. The *Yellow Christ* (Albright-Knox Art Gallery, Buffalo) is based on a medieval crucifix Gauguin knew in the local church, transferred to the outdoor landscape he also knew well.

He felt the need to invent new forms to contain his new content. And in so doing, he often experimented in new media—lithography, pottery, and sculpture. Take the relief sculpture, *Be in Love and You will be Happy* (Museum of Fine Arts, Boston) which he carved and polychromed in the autumn of 1889. The spatial ambiguity, the curiously indeterminate background, and the enormous differences in scale, all help—indeed, may be intended—to mystify the spectator as he tries to unravel the meaning of the injunction.

Gauguin's advance towards a private, esoteric symbolism continued in the decorations in an isolated inn at Le Pouldu that he and the Dutchman Meyer de Haan (1852–95) were largely responsible for in the winter of 1889–90. (Sérusier contributed, significantly, a motto on the ceiling from Wagner.) The iconography was strangely mixed, part de-

Vision After the Sermon

There are several titles for this picture (in the National Gallery of Scotland, Edinburgh). Gauguin called it *Apparition* and *Vision of the Sermon*. It is now generally called *Vision after the Sermon* or *Jacob Wrestling with the Angel*. The very existence of these alternative titles gives a clue to Gauguin's ambitious intentions. He explained those intentions in a letter of September 1888 to Van Gogh: "I believe I have attained in these figures a great rustic and *superstitious* simplicity. It is all very severe ... To me in this painting the landscape and the struggle exist only in the imagination of these praying people, as a result of the sermon. That is why there is a contrast between these real people and the struggle in this landscape, which is not real and is out of proportion."

This is a valuable testimony. It tells us that the Breton peasants in the foreground, with their picturesque headgear, are imagining the scene of Jacob wrestling with the angel in the upper part of the picture. They have just left church having heard the sermon given by the priest, who is seen in the lower right of the picture. He looks dangerously like Gauguin himself. These Breton peasants, in their superstitious simplicity, are his models and his victims: two years previously, he had used them in a more conventional genre scene, chatting together outdoors (*Four Breton Women*; Neue Pinakothek, Munich). Now, they are the starting point for his "abstractions", answering to his primal need: to create. For the image of Jacob wrestling with the angel is not merely a response to the Biblical story (or to a sermon), but is capable of more arcane interpretations, such as the creative artist wrestling with his idea.

In the *Vision after the Sermon*, Gauguin is manifestly renouncing his Impressionist style. He is creating a new pictorial language no longer based on perception and sensation, more on idea and symbol. The simplifications of style apparent in this picture concern line, color, and composition. The heavy enclosing contour is firm and decisive, derived from medieval enamels or stained glass—hence, the term "Cloisonnism, which Gauguin and his friends used to describe the technique. Gauguin also used the term "Synthetism" as a more comprehensive description of the style. These cloisonnist lines enclose the color, which is simplified, but not yet flat and monochromatic, especially in the modeling of the figures and the tree, where separate, distinct strokes are still visible. But the unreality of the scene is expressed most potently in the vermilion ground on which the struggle of Jacob and the Angel takes place. The two fighting figures are based on two wrestlers taken from the *Mangwa* of the Japanese artist Hokusai (1760–1849). The composi-

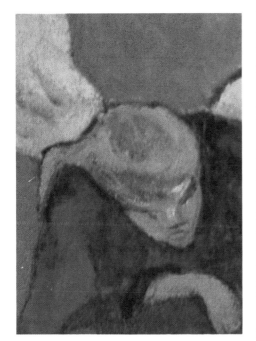

tion as a whole owes much to Degas' dance pictures, as if the foreground audience of Breton peasants are watching a stage performance. But the picture is also said to owe most to Émile Bernard's *Breton Women at a Pardon* (private collection) which the 20-year-old artist brought to Pont-Aven and from which, he claimed, Gauguin stole his ideas. Gauguin, however, was already moving towards such a simplification of means and technique: at most, Bernard's picture acted as a catalyst. There is also the story that Gauguin, together with Bernard and other friends, took the picture to the village of Nizon outside Pont-Aven to present it to the parish priest as an altarpiece for his church. The offer was refused.

Instead, the *Vision after the Sermon* has become the altarpiece of Post-Impressionism. The attempt to paint a vision contradicts the Impressionists' struggle with rendering the outward appearance of reality. So Camille Pissarro, once Gauguin's mentor, lamented not so much the vermilion ground, nor the Japanese and what he called Byzantine borrowings, but Gauguin's failure to apply his synthesis to "our modern philosophy which is absolutely social, anti-authoritarian, and anti-mystical". But the young Symbolist poet and art critic Albert Aurier saw Gauguin as "the uncontested initiator of Symbolist painting". The *Vision after the Sermon* openly renounces Impressionism; it augurs Symbolism in painting; and its pure pictorial simplifications point the way to such 20th-century manifestations as Fauvism and Expressionism.

RONALD PICKVANCE

Left: *Vision after the Sermon* by Gauguin; oil on canvas; 74×93cm (29×37in); 1888. National Gallery of Scotland, Edinburgh

Above left Jacob wrestles with the Angel, a detail from the top right-hand corner of the *Vision after the Sermon* by Gauguin

▲ *Breton Women at a Pardon* by Émile Bernard; oil on canvas; 74×92cm (29×36in); 1888. Private collection

▼ *Four Breton Women* by Gauguin; oil on canvas; 72×91cm (28×36in); 1886. Neue Pinakothek, Munich

monic, part blasphemous, part still-life, part local landscape, part philosophical. The latter may be seen in the presence of books by Carlyle and Milton in Gauguin's portrait of *Meyer de Haan* (private collection), where, additionally, the stylization and simplification of the Synthetist style are fully developed.

In the winter of 1890–1, Gauguin moved in Parisian Symbolist circles. He painted portraits of both Mallarmé and Moréas. Aurier wrote his article on him. Gauguin arranged an auction of his own work in Paris and left for Tahiti in April 1891. He had stretched pictorial language by his constant searching for new, expressive devices. He had created a lifestyle, an image of the artist, alienated, yet resilient and productive, a Messiah figure. And he had shown an ingenious inventiveness in technique and use of media. He would continue to develop these aspects in the remaining 12 years of his life. His influence grew in the 1890s: it reached flood tide in 1906 at the large retrospective exhibition at the Salon d'Automne.

Seurat and Gauguin had exhibited together at the last Impressionist exhibition in 1886. The next occasion their works appeared in the same exhibition was at Les Vingt in Brussels in 1889. They were the respective leaders of the avant-garde in Paris, whose paths never crossed after 1886. (Indeed, the only close contact before then was their mutual interest in a manuscript by a mysterious Turkish painter of the early 19th century: each of them copied it, each, however, emphasized different aspects.) And, by and large, their critical supporters seldom coincided (Fénéon alternated between warm encouragement of Gauguin the potter and sculptor, and rather spiky criticism of Gauguin the painter). But one person who knew them both, greatly admired their work, and took much from each without ever wholly subscribing to either, was Vincent van Gogh.

Van Gogh's arrival in Paris in February 1886 launched him on a two-year course in "modernism". He moved from a dark-toned, Dutch palette to a bright, high-keyed Impressionism; from there, he tried Pointillism, painting with Signac and the Pissarroes; but he met Gauguin in November 1887, grew friendly with Bernard, and moved towards a Synthetist style of his own.

On the day he left Paris for Arles in February 1888, Van Gogh visited Seurat's studio. That visit left a deep impression. He recalled Seurat's calm and ordered temperament; he recalled the impact of the large paintings he saw in the studio, *La Grande Jatte, Les Poseuses,* and *La Parade*; he noted their colour, their "stippling" (as he was wont to call Pointillism), and their grand, monumental design; he saw that Seurat was so well-organized an artist that productivity would never be a problem for him. Finally, he defined Seurat's position in the Parisian avant-garde—as leader of the "Petit Boulevard", by which Van Gogh meant the younger, unattached artists (Gauguin, Bernard, Signac, Toulouse-Lautrec) as against those of

Left: Yellow Christ by Gauguin; oil on canvas; 92×74cm (36×29in); 1889. Albright-Knox Art Gallery, Buffalo

Meyer de Haan by Gauguin; oil on canvas; 80×52cm (31×20in); 1889. Private collection

the "Grand Boulevard" (Degas, Monet, Renoir, and Sisley).

During his stay in Paris, Van Gogh had entered the fray. His brother, Theo, who ran a small gallery devoted to modern painters, bought the works of the "Grand Boulevard" artists and, less frequently, those of the "Petit Boulevard". Among the latter was Seurat's drawing *À l'Eden-Concert*, now in the Rijksmuseum Vincent van Gogh, Amsterdam. To further the cause of the "Petit Boulevard" artists, Van Gogh himself arranged exhibitions in the unlikeliest of places, for example, in a restaurant known as La Fourche. And he made exchanges of pictures with Gauguin, Bernard, and others.

Once in Arles, however, he was isolated from the exciting stimulus of the Paris art world. The stage of Synthetism he had reached there was not followed up immediately. There is a relaxation of physical stresses and artistic tensions in the series of paintings of orchards, drawbridges, and wheatfields. Not until August 1888 did he attain what might be called a truly Synthetic style. Three things happened. First he tried a simple technique, "which is perhaps not Impressionistic. I would like

Self-portrait by Vincent van Gogh; oil on canvas; 62×52cm (24×20in); 1888. William Hayes Fogg Art Museum, Cambridge, Mass.

Sunflowers by Vincent van Gogh; oil on canvas; 92×73cm (36×29in); 1888. National Gallery, London

to paint in such a way that everybody, at least if they have eyes, would see it." And of his *Sunflowers* (National Gallery, London), he wrote: "I am trying to find a special brushwork without stippling or anything else, nothing but the varied stroke." Second, he felt that Impressionism was too restricting. He wrote to Theo in September 1888:

I am returning more to what I was looking for before I came to Paris. I do not know if anyone before me has talked about suggestive color, but Delacroix and Monticelli, without talking about it, did it. But I have got back to where I was in Nuenen, when I made a vain attempt to learn music, so much did I already feel the relations between our color and Wagner's music. It is true that in Impressionism I see the resurrection of Eugène Delacroix, but the interpretations of it are so divergent and in a way so irreconcilable that it will not be Impressionism which will give us the final doctrine. That is why I myself remain among the Impressionists, because it professes nothing, and binds you to nothing, and as one of the comrades I need not declare my formula.

Third, a simplified technique and the exploitation of "suggestive" color gave rise to Symbolist, and even Expressionist interpretations. Of his painting, *The Night Café* (Yale University Art Gallery, New Haven), he wrote:

I have tried to express the terrible passions of humanity by red and green. The room is blood red and dark yellow with a green billiard table in the middle; there are four citron-yellow lamps with a glow of orange and green. Everywhere there is a clash and contrast of the most disparate reds and greens in the figures of the little sleeping hooligans, in the empty, dreary room, in violet and blue ...

As a contrast to *The Night Café*, Van Gogh painted another interior in October 1888.

It's just simply my bedroom, only here color is to do everything, and giving by its simplification a grander style to things, is to be suggestive here of *rest* or of sleep in general. In a word, looking at the picture ought to rest the brain, or rather the imagination.

Gauguin's two months' stay in Arles accentuated the process towards "abstraction". Imagination, or rather painting from the imagination, was discussed and practiced. If you have freed yourself from the demands of local, descriptive color, then you can also free yourself from dependence on nature and the model. Van Gogh could never quite make the break with nature; and however "suggestive" his color, however simplified his technique, his Symbolism was based on a continued contact with reality. He expressed his vision through portrait, still-life, and landscape, rather than through a programmatic series of allegories or a set of self-revealing myths.

In the last 18 months of Van Gogh's life, first at St-Rémy, then at Auvers-sur-Oise, painting was partly a form of therapy. Yet he remained very conscious of the stylistic implications of what he was doing, aware of his sources and of the relationship of his work to Gauguin's and Bernard's in Paris and Brittany. Moreover, his paintings could be seen in Paris. At the Salon des Indépendants in 1890, Gauguin thought one of these the most remarkable picture in the exhibition. He wrote to Van Gogh:

Among those who work from nature you are the *only one who thinks*. I have talked about it with your brother and there is one canvas that I should like to *exchange with you for anything of mine you choose*. The one I mean is a mountainous landscape; two very small travelers seem to be climbing in search of the unknown. There is in it an emotion like in Delacroix, with very suggestive colors. Here and there some red notes, like lights, and the whole in a violet harmony. It's beautiful and impressive.

(The painting in question was *Les Peyroulets: The Ravine*, now in the Kröller-Müller Museum, Otterlo.)

The notion of thought, as well as emotion, of ideas as well as passion, actually expressed *in*, as well as *through*, the paint indicates the abstract-symbolist nature of Post-Impressionist thinking in 1890. And Van Gogh himself touches the nerve center of this thought when he writes a month before his suicide of his portrait of *Dr Gachet* (private collection).

What impassions me most—much, much more than all the rest of my metier—is the portrait, the modern portrait. I seek it in color, and surely I am not the only one to seek it in this direction ... I should like to paint portraits which would appear after a century to the people living then as apparitions. By which I mean that I do not endeavour to achieve this by a photographic resemblance, but by means of our impassioned expressions—that is to say, using our knowledge of and our modern taste for color as a means of arriving at the expression and the intensification of the character.

In Aurier's article on Van Gogh (*Mercure de France*, Janu-

Les Peyroulets: the Ravine by Vincent van Gogh; oil on canvas; 28×36cm (11×14in); 1889. Kröller-Müller Museum, Otterlo

ary 1890) the intensity of expression is subsumed in an exaggeratedly Symbolist iconography. So much so that Van Gogh protested his love of reality, his dependence upon nature, as well as his debt to, and admiration for other artists—Delacroix, Monticelli, Gauguin, and surprisingly the academic painter Meissonier—a protest that warns the pigeon-holing critic against a too sweeping and too simplistic categorization. And Aurier's exaggerated claims for Van Gogh's individual achievement provoked the response: "What encourages me in my work is precisely the feeling that there are others who are doing exactly what I do."

Van Gogh was clearly thinking of Gauguin and Bernard and the Pont-Aven Group, rather than Seurat, Signac, and the Neo-Impressionists. Nonetheless, by 1890, the stylization of line and shape, the flattened and arbitrary areas of color, and the search for heightened emotional effects were common to the work of Seurat, Gauguin, and Van Gogh, however differently each expressed them. Each had built on Impressionism, but each had rejected it for its apparent lack of interest in pictorial construction and linear and coloristic expressiveness. Each had rejected its narrowness of attitude to alternative artistic sources and its failure to exploit the symbolic potential of even everyday imagery. Japanese print and popular imagery had been used by the Impressionists; but Seurat, Gauguin, and Van Gogh exploited them more fully. Egyptian, Classical, and medieval sources were consulted and absorbed into their art.

Remarkably, too, they shared a deep admiration for certain 19th-century French artists. Three in particular exercised an enormous influence upon them: Delacroix, Millet, and Puvis de Chavannes. In the early 1880s, Seurat and Van Gogh were deeply affected by the example of Millet; Gauguin was not unaware of him then, but appears to have taken a renewed interest in Millet in 1889–90, as also did Van Gogh with his series of painted copies after Millet. Delacroix was a profoundly formative influence on the young Seurat; Van Gogh discovered Delacroix in 1885, and never ceased to praise his use of "suggestive" color; Gauguin, too, expressed his high regard for Delacroix in letters, as well as in painted and drawn copies. In his simple yet subtle compositions and in his combination of antique and modern manners, Puvis de Chavannes pervades the art of the three Post-Impressionists.

Shared experiences and shared influences naturally led by 1890 to something of a shared style. Inherent in their work was the possibility of Art Nouveau. The fact that all three exhibited with Les Vingt in Brussels helped assure the early manifestation of Art Nouveau in Belgium. The emergence of the small avant-garde periodical, in Brussels as well as Paris, and the founding of Les Vingt and the Salon des Indépendants in 1884 helped nurture Post-Impressionism. And the way critics talked about art changed. In their interchange, Fénéon and Seurat, Aurier and Van Gogh, Fénéon, Aurier, and Gauguin grappled with a rapidly changing language that demanded elucidation and definition. It released some of the esoteric thought and convoluted writing that have come to be associated with "modern" art criticism. But it also released the "open", revealing letters of Van Gogh and Gauguin—revealing not only personally and psychologically, but above all in the discussion of painterly problems, technical procedures, and artistic sources. This outpouring of creative comment on the work-in-hand provides a further distinction between the letters of Degas, Monet, and Renoir and those of Gauguin and Van Gogh.

The term Post-Impressionism is sometimes applied to the work of artists whose style was created outside France: for example, James Ensor (1860–1949) in Belgium and Ferdinand Hodler (1835–1918) in Switzerland. And following Roger Fry's Post-Impressionist exhibition of 1910, we can talk of English Post-Impressionism in the work of Vanessa Bell (1879–1961), Duncan Grant (1885–1979), the Camden Town Group, founded in 1911, and the London Group, founded in 1913.

RONALD PICKVANCE

Bibliography. Denvir, B. *Post-Impressionism*, London (1992). Herbert, R. *Neo-Impressionism*, New York (1968). Loevgren, S. *The Genesis of Modernism*, Stockholm (1959). Rewald, J. *Post-Impressionism from Van Gogh to Gauguin*, New York (1956). Roskill, M. *Van Gogh, Gauguin and the Impressionist Circle*, London (1970).

44

SYMBOLISM AND ART NOUVEAU

A detail from Salome by Gustave Moreau; oil on canvas; full size 92×60cm (36×24in); 1876. Musée Gustave Moreau, Paris (see page 825)

For the historian, the Symbolist movement, like the Romantic before it and the Surrealist after it, appears as a forest of contradictory achievements. Each of these three movements stressed the importance of the individual's imaginative life. In the case of Romanticism and Symbolism, this exploration of the imagination was to occur expressly in response to sensual experience; in the case of Symbolism and Surrealism the concept of a creatively potent dream (le rêve) serves to liberate the dreamer from the constraining disciplines of creativity, for if the artist *dreamed* in front of his work, necessarily it was at once remote from the exigencies, and indeed the responsibilities, of daily life.

Seen in this context, the Symbolists appeared to embody but one phase in the development of a broader loosening of the imagination from the mundane. Romanticism, Symbolism, and Surrealism appear as three distinct but related investigations of the relation of creativity to the imagination.

For the Symbolists, *le rêve* meant an escape from the mundane and the intolerably boring world of practicality, yet the Symbolist dream had nothing to it of the Freudian dreams of sleep: the Symbolist knew nothing of his subconscious. The Symbolist dream was a waking reverie, triggered by any sensual experience that by aesthetic means could lift the mind from mundane preoccupations, to hint, suggest, and evoke experiences that were not chaotic and in need of ordering, that were not foreseen and planned, but which were unexpected, ordered by human imagination, full of emotional and sensual suggestiveness. Far from being asleep, the Symbolist was painfully alert and thoroughly awake.

It is one of the ironies of the movement that the book that effectively crystallized those tendencies which all around had been held in suspension, should be a novel in many respects thoroughly of the realist school of Émile Zola. Its author was Joris-Karl Huysmans (1848–1907) who had closely studied Zola's techniques—in the accumulation, for example, of precisely observed and explicitly described detail and of his studies of particular sentiments reacting to physical circumstance. *À Rebours* (*Against Nature*) was published by Huysmans in 1884 and heralds the elucidation of a body of Symbolist principles. It was a minutely descriptive novel, but its "hero", Duc Jean Floressas Des Esseintes, was to provide a model for many Symbolists. Sickened by the common mundanity of daily life in Paris, Des Esseintes isolated himself almost totally within his apartment; he reduced his physical activities to a remarkable degree to the predilection of sensual experience, collecting—to alleviate the threat of suffocating tedium—books, precious objects, paintings, prints, and liqueurs that provoked an inner life that for all its dependence upon senses painfully tuned, turned its aesthetic nerve toward inner experience. Huysmans' meticulous descriptions of Des Esseintes' "Aladdin's Cave" were at once influential. Ironically it was the matter-of-fact descriptive reporting that made the emulation of so other-worldly a figure possible. Huysmans' book was not suggestive; it was explicit. This made it an axial work, not fully Symbolist in itself, yet a vital force in the crystallization of a Symbolist Movement.

Des Esseintes was based partly upon contemporary men investigated by Huysmans, and he directly reflects certain emergent tendencies in Parisian painting and writing: a clear interest in the poetry of Mallarmé is evident, for example, and on Des Esseintes' walls hung works by Gustave Moreau (1826–98) and by Odilon Redon (1840–1916). In due course, Redon repaid this sign of recognition by producing a lithographic portrait of Des Esseintes as a frontispiece for a subsequent edition of the book. In it the sickly hero, all but sinking from sight in his large armchair, stares wistfully and diffidently before him, a fleeting raven-like appearance suggested by the rich blacks of Redon's print and by the lugubrious arch of Des Esseintes' nose. In his great armchair, Des Esseintes, to the promptings of precious and obscure sensual experience, would undertake journeys of the imagination. His collection was accumulated to this end: to show nothing of the mundane world shut off from him by the darkened casements of his apartment, but to replace that world by exotic scenes and terrifying visions, works not of description but of wonder and suggestion. The Symbolist work, be it poem or painting, was to be above all suggestive, precious not commonplace, to reflect and to evoke a journey of the imagination. Huysman's book had established and made explicit criteria that were already in existence but unfocused.

Very soon the apartment and the possessions of Des Esseintes were widely admired and emulated. The book had provided a detailed list of his preferences and, by example, his criteria: it was for this reason that the book became known as the breviary of the decadents. His sources, the literary and visual artists cited and discussed, were increasingly discovered, celebrated, and adopted by younger practitioners. Mallarmé, Redon, and Moreau all became part of the Symbolist movement in this way, both as precursors and contributors. Huysmans' book *À Rebours* crystallized a complex mixture of values and aims whose unifying feature relied not upon stylistic coherence but upon the varied search for art that was suggestive and an ordered imaginative assemblage of sensual experience, an art that was incomplete without the imaginative and sensitive response of its viewer or audience. In this complex body of opinion, experience, and practice, 30 years of increasingly material considerations in French art and literature met a forceful challenge and rebuttal. The Symbolists no longer wished to be explicit: they were eager not to be fully intelligible, and their works were to embody an experiment in the sensual provocation of the imagination. Des Esseintes, an ultimate armchair traveler with his own exotic tastes to which his sanctum was finely tuned and remote from daily life, provided a stimulating, influential example.

During the evolution of the Symbolist movement in art and literature in Paris, a number of creative men whose essential stance had been known for several years became increasingly influential and respected. Gustave Moreau and Stéphane Mallarmé, who experienced sudden popularity among Symbolists, both dealt with the theme of Salome's dance before Herod, and both produced creative work that was not preoccupied with mundane descriptive matters. They were richly suggestive rather than explicit, creative men, and despite the utter dissimilarity of their work from many other viewpoints, this very predilection for a suggestive art was to prove contagious. Where Des Esseintes led, many were to follow. The art work was to be closely controlled and carefully measured in terms of the clues divulged to its ultimate meaning. While it acted upon the senses of its viewer, reader, or observer, it was nevertheless complete in itself: it increasingly abandoned depiction in favor of a closer awareness of the means of the art work. Be it the dense or ravishing textures of Mallarmé's poems, or the scratched paint of Moreau's paintings, the less art was explicitly descriptive of objects, the more it focused upon suggestive aesthetic sensation, and the only means to control and articulate this was to make increasingly sensitive manipulation of the work's internal material and structure. With the abandonment of realism and its preoccupation with the description of objects came an increased awareness of the means and techniques available to the artist. As a result, the painting or poem more evidently acknowledged the rhythms of colors and lines across a flat surface, or the rhythms of lines and sounds in poetry. With Mallarmé, words no longer function as transparent and self-evident means to a descriptive end: the words in Mallarmé's poems are astutely tuned with an ear to their musical resonance as much as to their meaning. The whole point of the Symbolist's poetry may well consist in not going straight to the point for precisely this reason: the advent to meaning is made circuitous and far from readily available in order that the more physical aspects of his words'

sounds are noticed and explored. To restrain direct access to the meaning of a poem establishes a hiatus within which these more material considerations begin to be heard and to make their presence felt.

In seeking a painter whose control and awareness of his means was comparably material-oriented and inexplicit in terms of access to a specific meaning, it is possible to turn to either Moreau or to Redon, as Des Esseintes had done; yet it is possible, too, to find in an American artist who was for a period close to Mallarmé something of just such an otherworldly and evocative expertise. That was James Abbott McNeill Whistler (1843–1903), whose study of Japanese art in particular had led him by the 1860s to denounce his own early realist phase and to commit himself instead to the perfection of canvases, etchings, and lithographs according, as far as possible, to their own internal demands, and to elude the commitment to laborious description that appeared so arduous and yet so essential a feature of much 19th-century painting. Long before the Symbolists were to call the same tune, Whistler had condemned nature for her lack of taste—a viewpoint echoing Charles Baudelaire's. Beauty was the professional field of the artist, and his approach to it could scarcely be premeditated however much it demanded of lessons learnt from experience. Whistler was attracted to the Thames in the twilight, when the hubbub of diurnal activity died and the jagged edge of the materialist world was softened by crepuscular dim light. The love of twilight and the evocative mystery of shadows all found responses among Symbolists in the 1880s, which reveals the extent to which Whistler's nocturnes and his love of exotic Japanese interiors provided a

I Lock My Door Upon Myself by Fernand Khnopff; oil on canvas; 72×140cm (28×55in); 1891. Neue Pinakothek, Munich

precedent for the Symbolists, and provided, too, an honorary place for Whistler in their midst. To recall simply the musical titles that distinguished his works is to recognize Whistler's determination that the compositional arrangements of colors in his paintings should be determined not by the kaleidoscopic and accidental juxtapositions of daily life but by paintings' own demands of balance and harmony, as independent of subject matter and descriptive purpose as a sequence of notes within a passage of music. Necessarily, illusion gave way to decorative effects, and material elements—the liquidity of paint, for example, and the signs of its application to the canvas—became more emphatically evident. When such an innovative artist turned his hand to the elaboration of a decorative scheme for a room, the results, not surprisingly, were rhythmic, exotic, and brilliant: they were not at all mundane.

Whistler's *Harmony in Blue and Gold: the Peacock Room* (1876–7; Freer Gallery of Art, Washington, D.C.) comprised an event of widespread cultural significance, yet its patron was barely satisfied with it and its clearest influence was not to be felt for almost a quarter of a century. The peacock itself is exotic, but in Whistler's swirling and decorative wall decorations it takes on a glittering menace. The eyes of its tail billow across the blue walls, echoing their ultimate sources of inspiration in Oriental porcelain and Japanese prints. Indeed, the room was to house his patron's collection of blue and white china on that level the designs have an explanation that is rational enough. Yet Whistler goes well beyond so plagiaristic and self-effacing a response. In this room, the dominance of rhythmic, decorative effect over descriptive anatomical precision is so decisive as to render the peacocks no more than a theme upon which every variation is played in terms of rhythmic repetition and cumulative display. The room is like no other in the precedence it gives to decorative painting, yet conversely it is like no other in the licence permitted to the decorative motifs which, far from remaining constrained within firmly defined frames, have spread beneath Whistler's hand across walls and shutters, almost wilfully negligent of the surface beneath them. The ensemble comprises an exotic and dynamic room that is a vital forerunner of Symbolist interiors in its domination by aesthetic criteria at the expense of practical criteria: within Whistler's Peacock Room no element that is not art intrudes. Description is minimal and detail devoted to the rhythmic display of decorative motifs.

This decorative emphasis characterized in due course much Symbolist painting, and, appropriately transcribed, much Symbolist writing too. It also provided the common ground for Symbolist art, with its search for significance in the action of colors and lines, with Art Nouveau, whose attenuated and whiplash rhythms by the early 1890s had invaded every branch of design from the book page to the drawing room, from the apartment block to the jewel upon a female neck. All of these developments occurred many years after Whistler's *Peacock Room*, which cannot therefore ultimately be considered part of them. On the other hand, Whistler's importance as a pioneer in both camps can scarcely be overstressed—

particularly in view of his reputation amongst Symbolists in Paris, Brussels, and elsewhere in the late 1880s and early 1890s, in view of his involvement with Mallarmé, and, finally, in view of his own manifest willingness to express his ideas, aims, and criteria with devastating and unambiguous clarity.

In England, Whistler had been close to those Pre-Raphaelite painters who most consciously sought beauty. The exotic medievalism of D.G. Rossetti (1828–82) and Edward Burne-Jones (1833–98) to a degree complemented his own insistent Japanism. As exoticism and a wan, otherworldly renunciation of daily life's tribulations became increasingly a feature of the Symbolist in Paris and Brussels, so Rossetti and Burne-Jones, as well as Whistler, found there an appreciative and an appropriately aesthetic audience.

In Fernand Khnopff's painting *I Lock My Door Upon Myself* (1891; Neue Pinakothek, Munich), all of these influences are subtly and sensitively intertwined to produce an evocative painting of beguiling stillness and mystery. Khnopff greatly admired the medievalizing Pre-Raphaelites and was well aware of English art in the 1890s. The title of his painting is borrowed from the poem by Christina Rossetti: its appeal to the Symbolist is clear, for it suggests an inner world of emotional, spiritual, and aethetic events, cut off from communication with other human beings, a reverie akin to sleep yet stirred by sensitivity to beauty. Khnopff's model recalls the designer William Morris' wife Jane, with her powerful jaw and luminous eyes. Above her, the bust of Hypnos, the god of sleep, refers poetically to dreaming and to a life of the imagination. The reverie depicted is lavish and exotic, reflecting Burne-Jones and Rossetti on the one hand and Whistler on the other in its frieze-like composition rhythmically divided by vertical intervals. The strangely colored lilies emphasize how precious, artificial, and sensual is this locked-away interior. It is as remote in its way as that of Des Esseintes; indeed Fernand Khnopff constructed an altar in his Brussels studio surmounted by his cast of Hypnos and inscribed, "On ne a que soi" ("One has but oneself"). No more succinct definition of the Symbolist ethos could exist, if it were not for the Symbolists' simultaneous need to display their exotic sensitivity and to indicate, at least, the existence if not the meanings of their secrets.

Khnopff's theme is close to the closeted world of Des Esseintes, yet his pictorial devices are not without an English flavor. Symbolist art had become thoroughly international. Whistler and Burne-Jones were exhibited in Brussels, Paris, and Munich, as well as in London. Khnopff and many other painters contributed both to the group exhibitions of Les Vingt and La Vie Moderne in Brussels and to the Rosicrucian Salons in Paris. Many groups and journals flourished briefly, and even if they disappeared almost at once, internationalism was frequently amongst their policies. Furthermore, with the sudden flourishing of larger periodicals devoted to the latest decorative and fine art activities in many cities, influences were very directly transmitted abroad whether in terms of decorative motifs of Art Nouveau (variously renamed *Jugend-*

Part of *Harmony in Blue and Gold*: the Peacock Room by J.A.M. Whistler; 1876–7. Freer Gallery of Art, Washington, D.C.

stil and *Stilo Liberty* elsewhere) or the thematic heritage of Symbolist writing and painting. Such periodicals as *Pan* from Munich, *Ver Sacrum* from Vienna, and *The Studio* from London, assured in the 1890s a vivid awareness of artistic developments many hundreds of miles from their first development. For the first time a movement that so intimately involved both writers and visual artists was able to publish effectively work in both fields. The new-found dominance of the decorative agitation of plane surfaces with fast-moving curvilinear forms made Art Nouveau a phenomenon from Chicago to Moscow, leaving no capital untouched between them. The publication of Beardsley's work alone, by *The*

Studio in 1893, led to echoes of his distinct blending of Art Nouveau rhythms with Symbolist themes, as evident in Barcelona as in Vienna, as much in the works of Picasso (1881–1973) as in those of Gustav Klimt (1862–1918).

The new emphasis that Symbolist painting had placed upon the suggestive qualities of artists' techniques was closely explored in Paris where aspects of Post-Impressionist painting contributed to Symbolist developments. Gauguin's Pont-Aven works were particularly important in this respect. On the other hand, Brussels and Munich remained more committed to academic *trompe l'oeil* illusionism, but turned to the service of making credible the surprising events of the imagination.

The Three Brides by Jan Toorop; black chalk and pencil heightened in white and color on brown paper; 78×98cm (31×39in); 1893. Kröller-Müller Museum, Otterlo

Franz von Stuck (1863–1928), and before him the Swiss, Arnold Böcklin (1827–1901), were brilliant exponents of this approach. In Holland and in Scandinavia, the newly formed rhythmic dominance in the painting, the new quality of expressive exaggeration of line and color to provocative and suggestive effect, found a richly enthusiastic response.

In Holland, Jan Toorop (1858–1928) and Jan Thorn-Prikker (1868–1932), in particular, carried to an extreme stage the rhythmic stylization of form without ever abandoning their essential commitment to a powerful subject matter. Within the Symbolist fold, decorative elements were of use for their expressive power, for the degree to which they permitted emotion to be implied by the work. When Art Nouveau made less of this link by deleting recognizable subject matter, much of this expressive force was lost or at least endangered. As long as the link remained, however, even a brooch could impart a sense of jungle-thick associations, of poetic suggestiveness, could evoke the *femme fatale*, the oblivion of sleep, or the call to a waking imagination.

Subject matter was of paramount importance and often, for all their apparently wild and uncontrolled dreaming, the Symbolists returned both in writing and in painting to particular incidents of Classical mythology—the sphinx and the Chimaera, for example—or to biblical characters—Adam and Eve, Salome and John the Baptist—often making blatant use of such themes to their own ends, as indeed had Des Esseintes, yet often, too, employing such themes to focus attention upon a particular human dilemma, that of sin, for instance, or the balance of animal instinct against emotional experience in the act of love. Occasionally, by setting their subject beyond all reference to specific time, place, or person, Symbolist artists were able to evolve images that were effective without such inbuilt reference to the Classical or Biblical past. Such works rely upon the clear evocation of emotional associations: in other words, to be intelligible they demand a subtle emotional response from their observer to make up for specific and literary references which would otherwise have provided a context of associations. For an image to function efficiently without such props it needed to be stripped of superfluities and to be acutely sensitive to the pictorial means available: maximum use had to be made of the expressive resources of line, color, and rhythm, and their link with subject matter enforced not neglected.

Two such paintings, and entirely successful ones in this respect, are Jan Toorop's *The Three Brides* (1893; Kröller-Müller Museum, Otterlo) and *The Dance of Life* by Edvard Munch (National Gallery, Oslo). In each of them a frieze composition, roughly symmetrical, obliges a series of comparisons upon the viewer. In neither case is the setting specifically identifiable: both appear out of time and beyond place. Despite the personal preoccupations that led each of these artists to manipulate images of considerable potency and importance to themselves, they have each so efficiently charged their images with emotional implications that beyond the personal links with Munch or with Toorop there emerges a generally intelligible level of meaning. This in itself is no small achievement—Munch is further along this road than is Toorop. To abandon specific references, whether to religion or to mythology, is to place maximum reliance upon the inherent properties of the means at the artists' disposal. Toorop retains certain recognizable iconographic features, yet turns them to his own ends, while Munch has the power to evolve his own imagery entirely and without loss of intelligibility.

The two paintings have much in common despite a significant difference in size: they are both Symbolist works in their dedication to the embodiment of ideas and emotions beyond the mundane description of daily existence. Indeed Toorop's work is distinctly exotic, Munch's less so. They may be taken as examples of the internationally widespread percolation of Symbolist influences, techniques, and ideas. Without doubt Paris and Brussels were vital centers of Symbolist thought and work. Yet even there the Symbolist movement had crystallized from diverse and often long extant principles, united and brought into focus to form a body of theory and practice with a new coherence. Outside Paris and Brussels, too, elements of Symbolist thought had been long maturing. The example from

The Dance of Life by Edvard Munch; oil on canvas; 125×190cm (49×75in); 1899–1900. National Gallery, Oslo

Salome in Symbolist Art

As the dream provided a recurrent theme for Symbolist writers and painters, the imagery of dreams with its necessary commitment to fantasy and to images of emotional potency became characteristic of Symbolist work. Salome was one such image, so popular among Symbolists that for a span of ten years she appeared throughout Europe in paintings, sculptures, novels, and poems depicted as convincingly as if she stood before them in person:

> under a bluish veil which concealed her head and breasts, one could just make out the arch of her eyes, the chalcedonies in her ears, and the whiteness of her skin. A square of dove-colored silk covered her shoulders and was fastened to her loins by a jewelled girdle. Her black trousers were spangled with mandrakes, and she moved with indolent ease, her little slipper of humming-bird's down tapping the floor

The novelist Joris-Karl Huysmans follows close upon this description of Salome by Flaubert; Huysmans in turn made the Salome theme—observed in the paintings of Gustave Moreau—the center of a symbolist cult for painters and writers alike with the publication of *À Rebours* (*Against Nature*) in 1884.

▲ Salome's triumph: *The Beheading of St John the Baptist* by Pierre Puvis de Chavannes; oil on canvas; 124×166cm (49×65in); 1869. Barber Institute of Fine Arts, Birmingham

◀ *Head of a Martyr* by Odilon Redon; charcoal; 37×36cm (15×14in); 1877. Kröller-Müller Museum, Otterlo

◀ *Salome* by Lucien Lévy-Dhurmer; pastel on blue paper; 44×50cm (17×20in); 1896. Collection of Michel Perinet, Paris

▶ Aubrey Beardsley's image of Salome: *The Dancer's Reward*; pen and ink; 23×17cm (9×7in); 1893. William Hayes Fogg Art Museum, Cambridge, Mass.

◄ Gustave Moreau's influential *Salome*; oil on canvas; 92×60cm (36×24in); 1876. Musée Gustave Moreau, Paris

▲ *Salome* by Max Klinger; marble; height 88cm (35in); 1893. Museum der Bildenden Künste, Leipzig

The theme of Salome and Flaubert's description make clear the nature of the Symbolist dream: for the work of art, be it painting or writing, was to provoke by its suggestive power an image primarily sensual. The Symbolist sought to explore sensual experience through the imagination, or, in other words, by making his senses acutely aware and painfully finely tuned, he sought to escape the mundane world. There is nothing in this of the dreams that come with sleep: the Symbolist dream was delectation of actual sensual experience provoked by artificial stimulus, be it art work, incense, or eroticism. Against this background the figure of Salome has special importance: she embodies destructive female sensuality and is amongst the most hypnotic of themes for the other-worldly Symbolist, for she threatens his rarified isolation with the twitching of her hips, and challenges the solitariness of Symbolist experience with the supremacy of the flesh over intellect. In this she becomes the *femme fatale*, as dangerous to the artificially constructed and cloistered world of the Symbolists' imaginings as she was fatal to the spiritual man whose head was demanded as reward for her lascivious dance.

To the heightened sensual awareness of the Symbolists, the image of Salome provided an object both of horror and of fascination; she appealed so directly to their innate and repressed sexuality. She was a rich source of sensual speculation, inhabiting a densely jeweled and barbaric palace and proving deadly by her arbitrary destruction of a spiritually pure and aspiring male. In this context, the beheading of John the Baptist is seen as a challenge to spirituality by the demands of animal bodily instinct. Sensuality and spiritual guilt are linked. The creative work of the writer or painter is identified with the spirituality of the Baptist. His death is tantamount to the loss of artistic potency. Salome represents, for the Symbolists, the embodiment of the male's image of female sensuality, at once fascinating and deadly. The sense of failure, of submission to base and animal lust, the thralldom Salome imposes upon the male, is a theme rich in the suggestion of fading strength, of magical fascination and of lavishly beautiful failure that so excited the Symbolist imagination from Gustave Moreau to Aubrey Beardsley, and from Gustave Flaubert to Oscar Wilde.

JOHN MILNER

Further reading. Flaubert, G. (trans. Baldick, R.) "Herodias" in *Three Tales*, Harmondsworth (1970). Jullian, P. *The Symbolists*, London (1973). Huysmans, J.-K. (trans. Baldick, R.) *Against Nature*, Harmondsworth (1966). Milner, J. *Symbolists and Decadents*, London (1971). Wilde, O. (trans. Douglas, Lord A., illustrated by Aubrey Beardsley) *Salomé*, London and Boston (1894), republished in New York (1967).

The Angel of Love by Giovanni Segantini; oil on canvas;
210×144cm (83×57in); 1894–7. Galleria d'Arte Moderna, Milan

France and Belgium did much to trigger in other countries the formation of groups that were both thoroughly indigenous and at the same time substantially Symbolist in their aims and work. Edvard Munch provides an example of this: for all that his work answers many of the demands of French Symbolist theory, for all that he executed a lithographic portrait of Mallarmé and was a visitor to Paris, his paintings and prints are nevertheless an essentially Scandinavian phenomenon with as many links to Northern writers—among them Strindberg and Ibsen—as to French painters or writers. In this way, the crystallization of principles that became the Symbolist movement in Paris was enormously and internationally influential, but on two levels: it precipitated a comparable crystallization of ideas and attitudes in other countries within their own cultural contexts, and, secondly, it was influential through the impact of particular works and artists directly through exhibitions and periodicals.

Toorop's *The Three Brides* presents a dense tangle of images of which a number are distinctly Christian in origin, but he uses them to invoke a complex set of associations and not to specifically Christian ends. The rhythmic organization of the painting emphasizes its expressive role and suggests a pulsating chant which echoes to the corners of the work. The painting is substantially symmetrical: three brides face the viewer. The central figure radiates suggestions of innocence; to one side of her the Bride of Christ is received with lilies, to the other a demonic bride with horned headdress and necklace of skulls receives a mysterious libation, her stance immovably and hypnotically grim. Chanting choruses behind each of these two brides emit sounds characterized by linear patterns that are curvilinear for the blessed half of the painting, and jagged for the damned half. The central bride is depicted in her innocence caught between opposing forces. The top corners of the work reveal crucified hands and bells from which flow hair-like lines which perhaps once more indicate sound. Toorop's lines of sound flow also from smaller bells rung by

attendant females in the foreground. His imagery richly and convincingly depicts the battle of good and evil for the innocent human who hovers here between nun and *femme fatale*. Yet there is much in the painting too that is emotionally expressive through the direct action of the lines and rhythms of the painting, over and above the explicit theme depicted. Toorop's painting is Symbolist because it evades the mundane depiction of daily life and attempts to display a generalized and spiritually significant theme; it does so by suggestive and expressive means inherent in his medium and handling as well as in his subject matter.

Edvard Munch developed this further. In his *Dance of Life*, he depicted three ages of woman before a view of a beach where a dance takes place beneath liquid moonlight. The scene set is not located specifically and no attempt is made to articulate a lucid or credible transition from foreground to background. Instead of this, three contrasting figures are placed against a backdrop of the hectic dance in progress, an activity from which they are momentarily withdrawn for the observer's convenience. No specific religious imagery helps our interpretation of the scene, but the figures are characterized by their pose, expression and, above all, by the color of their clothes—white for virginity and girlhood, red for love and mature womanhood, and black for death and widowhood. The work progresses from left to right and from light to dark in a frieze beyond the call of the temporal reality Munch has characterized by the hectic dance upon the beach.

By the time that both Toorop's *The Three Brides* and Munch's *The Dance of Life* were executed, the relation of subject matter to the expressive use of line and color had been vigorously explored by many artists. The new suggestive rather than explicit credo had come as a revelation to many writers and painters, and had opened up new vistas of exploration. The basic core of principles had emerged by 1886 in Paris at precisely the moment when Impressionism began to develop in surprising directions and when followers of Impressionist techniques began both to adopt and explore Impressionist color and handling in new directions. Gauguin, Seurat, and Van Gogh all derived much from Impressionist painting, yet developed certain of its techniques further. All of them showed an acute sense of the importance of drawing, composition, and subject matter, all vital elements in the rendering of a painting expressive and suggestive and no longer apparently casual, informal, or mundane.

The search undertaken by both Van Gogh and Paul Gauguin into the emotional expressive qualities of art were of sustained intensity. They depicted the inner as much as the outer experience and the artist's awareness was as often turned to the service of his emotions as his eyes. On the other hand, it was, for Gauguin and Van Gogh, always by visual means that their pictorial compositions were to operate. That is to say, that arising immediately from the first generation of the Impressionists' followers came painters who sought to preserve the importance of handling and strong color of Impressionist painting, yet who sought also to resolve these techniques with a commitment to expressive and suggestive painting. This development was contemporary with the emergence of the Symbolist movement in art and literature, so it is not surprising that Gauguin became concerned with Symbolist artists and writers, or that Paris in the later 1880s should appear so dense a knot of conflicting groups, theories, and achievements.

It was a prolifically rich moment for French art and letters, and much of the subsequent 10 or 15 years was taken up with the elucidation and evaluation of ideas and tendencies initiated towards the end of the 1880s. Gauguin's ties with the writers Charles Morice, Albert Aurier, and Mallarmé did much to make his work a search for significance in the impressions of visual experience. By contrast with the disordered sensual impressions engendered by events in the mundane world, the Symbolist art work provided an instance of material reality minutely and meticulously controlled. Within the frame all could be, in the phrase that Matisse was to borrow from Baudelaire, "luxe, calme et volupté" (luxury, calm, and voluptuousness). Under such circumstances, the otherworldly quality of the scenes and places depicted by Munch, by Segantini, by Gauguin, or by Maurice Denis is not surprising. Indeed, under such circumstances, the inherent expressive potential of the artist's means—his colors, lines, or composition—found an ideal arena for their activity, where no intruding or banal irrelevance was able to distract the observer or interfere with his response to the suggestions of feeling that the work embodied and transmitted.

Across so subtly adjusted a pictorial surface, color and line could have maximum effect; detailed descriptive work would be more distracting than efficient as a prop to the whole. Elision of detail between the presentation of essential imagery was characteristic of much Symbolist painting, whether in the swirling mists of Carrière, the black and velvet gloom of Redon's or indeed Seurat's graphic works, or by simple omission and replacement by flat areas of scarcely modulated color, as in Gauguin's extraordinary *Symbolist Self-Portrait with Halo* (National Gallery of Art, Washington, D.C.), his head floating above a plane of yellow, apparently unattached to the hand depicted at the base of the painting, and in no specific relation to the curvilinear decorative motif of plant-like derivation that fills the lower part of the painting. In Symbolist painting of the kind evolved by Gauguin, owing still a large debt to the strength of color Impressionist painters initiated, color has forsaken the depiction of daylight, and with enamel-like density and separation of its parts has been given over to juxtapositions at once decorative and expressive. For the viewer, those relationships generate feeling: they are

April by Maurice Denis; oil on canvas; 38×61cm (15×24in); 1892. Kröller-Müller Museum, Otterlo

Symbolist Self-Portrait with Halo by Gauguin; oil on wood; 88×57cm (35×22in); 1889. National Gallery of Art, Washington, D.C.

tuned one against another to reveal abruptness or harmony; they may be shrill or leaden, evaporating or dense. The whole construction of a painting, in support of its subject matter, has become evocative and suggestive, as much concerned with feeling as with sight.

With such means at his finger tips, Gauguin was able to impress certain Symbolists enormously. Aurier in particular became a spokesman for him. Gauguin, on the other hand, even when painting far from the urbane Symbolist circles of Paris, was sending from Tahiti paintings redolent of Symbolist themes and achievements. The power of his *Nevermore* (1897; Courtauld Institute Galleries, London) owes much to lessons learnt from Symbolists as well as from Impressionists, as does the enormous painting *Where Do We Come From? What Are We? Where Are We Going?* (1897; Museum of Fine Arts, Boston), a grave and contemplative work full of personal symbols, yet made approachable and intelligible by Gauguin's unparalleled expressive mastery.

Gauguin's contribution to French Symbolist painting is in-

creasingly recognized. There were literary painters among the Symbolists, but neither Gauguin nor those who followed his lead were among them: indeed, they represented the most strictly painterly element within the movement, as sensitive to color relationships as Mallarmé was to the musical cadence of letters and words.

Such awareness of the demands of the painter's means leads to an exploration of those means. Increasingly, the flatness of the picture surface, for example, is clearly recognized and lines are read by the observer as moving across a surface and less readily as moving illusionistically into picture-space. The painting no longer resembled a window looking out upon an event or scene; increasingly the painting appeared, to use Maurice Denis' phrase, "a flat surface covered with colors in a particular sequence". Whistler's paintings had foreshadowed something of this and had also led to decorative results. With the variety of vibrant colors employed by Gauguin, his followers from Pont-Aven, and the Nabis, such decoration became vital, forceful, and expressive. Decoration and expression evolved hand-in-hand; as a result, no clear distinction remained tenable between painting and a variety of applied and decorative arts. Gauguin executed ceramic sculptures and painted ceramic pots. He produced mural decorations, as did Sérusier—that vital link between Pont-Aven and the Nabis in Paris. Among the Nabis, Bonnard and Vuillard designed posters, Bonnard executed screens, Denis became engaged in stained glass and mural painting, and Paul Ranson turned to decorative hangings and paintings that emulated them. Any consideration of the relation of Art Nouveau to Symbolist painting must take the complexity of this development into account.

Art Nouveau was not simply a fashionable style of designing all manner of objects from wallpapers to brooches or beds during the 1890s: it had, directly and actively at work within this flow of products, the Symbolist commitment to evocation and expression, and it was heir, also, to the whole range of Symbolist imagery, to the lily, the sphinx, and the vampire. It is less fruitful to think of Symbolist artists being impressed by the florid visual fireworks of Art Nouveau and incorporating them incidentally into their works, than to recognize that Symbolist painting had within its own evolution arrived at an increasingly decorative art, redolent with references, associations, and feelings. All of this by 1893 had become available to the designer, who attenuated those rhythms further with astonishing indefatigability throughout Europe. In addition to this, the Symbolist cult of the exotic, lavish, and esoteric interior led to a demand for the consciously beautiful interior for clients who wished, as the *Punch* cartoonist George du Maurier showed often enough, to be thought hypersensitive to aesthetic thrills, capable of rapture before a vase or other man-made work of beauty. For a few years the artist and designer shared a broad common ground: Beardsley (1872–98), for example, whose work in 1893 became so popular, with unprecedented ease united in his work for Wilde's *Salomé* elegance and economy in the design of a book, with the interpretation of a theme revived a decade before by Flaubert, Huysmans, and Moreau. The artist and the designer are here inseparable.

The jewelry of R.-J. Lalique (1860–1945) was pure Art Nouveau, yet his precious creature with female human head is a denizen of Symbolist writing and painting, a direct relative of the sphinx, the harpie, the vampire, and every other anthropomorphic embodiment of the glittering and menacing *femme fatale*.

Both in England and on the continent crafts developed vigorously in the 1880s. Painters, sculptors, and architects on the

one hand involved themselves increasingly with the construction and decoration of useful objects. In England, William Morris (1834–96), so closely involved in Pre-Raphaelite literary and artistic developments, argued vociferously for the reexamination of the comparative roles of artists and designers. His firm engaged the painters Ford Madox Brown (1821–93), Rossetti and Burne-Jones in design work. Morris, believing the distinction between artist and craftsman to be a modern error originating in the Renaissance, wrote convincingly—his voice was heard and respected.

As English Pre-Raphaelitism was increasingly admired in

Art Nouveau furniture: a bed designed by Émile Gallé; 1904. Musée de l'École de Nancy

continental Europe, and was reflected in the works of Khnopff, Delville, Point, Denis, Klimt, Thorn-Prikker, and many other painters, the commitment to design work was to find an increasingly sympathetic audience. The poster and the book lent themselves perhaps most readily to the painters' abilities: Bonnard, Vuillard, Toulouse-Lautrec, Georges de Feure were all active painter-designers in this field. The literary wealth of the Symbolist also led to the collaboration of pictorial artists with writers. Mallarmé had collaborated with Manet on the translation of Poe's *The Raven*. Later, Mallarmé was to admire the intimate, strange revelations of Redon's portfolios of lithographs—both for the verbal poetry of their titles, as enigmatic as his own, and also for the revelations of each page, emulating the intimacy of the book format, in preference to the public and simultaneous exposure offered by the wall of a gallery. When Georges de Feure in 1898 designed *La Porte des Rêves* ("The Door of Dreams") by Marcel Schwob, his book's physical process of opening was imbued with significance and became a gateway or door to the dreams the text contained. De Feure executed, as well as books and posters, designs for screens, chairs, and other furnishings. A prolific man, his talents scarcely distinguished between art and design: the highly suggestive imagery of his paintings was provided therefore with a direct route into his design work. As in Beardsley's work, whose style de Feure occasionally recalled, it is not a useful exercise to determine the extent to which the designer or the artist is in evidence, for there is no distinction between them, and symbolic imagery is transferred directly to Art Nouveau design.

In printed works especially, the painter's tendency to employ flattened color areas with clear and rhythmic outlines was reinforced and emphasized by the necessarily and decis-

Art Nouveau jewelry: a diadem with a siren; antique bronze, emerald, and opal. Musée des Arts Décoratifs, Paris

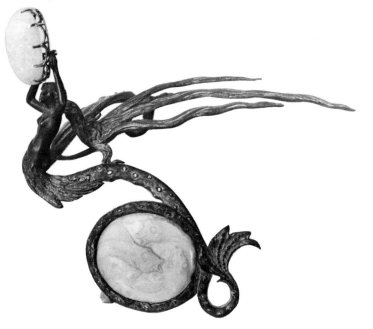

ively flat areas of the printed surface. This is particularly clear in Toulouse-Lautrec's work. The almost ever-present later 19th-century preoccupation with the Japanese wood-block print further spurred on this tendency, so that by the early 1890s a system of design began to emerge that was universally applicable. The asymmetrical compositional techniques of the pictorial artist were introduced to flat and even non-representational decorative schemes. The introspective, poetic, overtly aesthetic, and often sinister imagery of Symbolist painting and writing provided a storehouse of references to which the designer could specifically refer or to which he could hint through whatever imagery the growing rhythmic boldness of his designs might permit. Lalique incorporated a woman's head upon his dragonfly brooches and others were based upon sphinxes, sea-nymphs, or harpies. The exotic and precious mystery of such jewelry was, by implication, transferred to the wearer. As Khnopff had devised an altar surmounted by a winged head for Hypnos, the Greek god of sleep, visible in his painting *I Lock my Door upon Myself* (1891; Neue Pinakothek, Munich), so a designer informed in depth of Symbolist imagery could incorporate the images of insects into his vases, and gigantic moths, as denizens of the night, at the head and foot of his bed. Sarah Bernhardt, the tragedian and theme of so many of Alphonse Mucha's posters, designed an ink stand comprising a bronze self-portrait with bats' wings, to project her image as a *femme fatale*, the vampire so clearly identified with the destructive power of female attraction by Edvard Munch, Felicien Rops, and others.

The printed surface in particular led to the flourishing and even obsessive embellishments of Art Nouveau. Its characteristic rhythmic device of a long, slow curve suddenly completed by a swift and tighter curve in a new direction appeared universally on printed surfaces from book covers and spines, the layout of periodicals, the mass-produced poster, such ephemera as tickets and notices, printed materials and textiles made into curtains, coverings, or dresses, and in wallpapers dominating both public and private interiors. Throughout Europe, its whiplash curve penetrated to the poorest and grandest of settings. Its sources were diverse—Whistler, Morris, Japanese prints, Gauguin, Burne-Jones—yet its extraordinary popularity is undeniable. It was richly suggestive—Symbolist—recalling roots, rhythms of growth, and the heavy scent of lilies; yet it was also primarily decorative and grew in popularity as a system of stylistic distortions imparting rhythm to all it encountered. For the first time in perhaps a century, a rhythmic stylistic system had emerged that could be learnt and adapted at every level and for every detail.

This produced in the hands of its most accomplished masters a dynamic coherence, combining facility, complexity and control. Horta in Brussels and Guimard in Paris carried its swirling rhythms into every part of their buildings, at times with astonishing structural severity and at other times with an intimate facility that made clear the calligraphic resemblance of the Art Nouveau line to handwriting. Shape and rhythm took precedence over material considerations and structural clarity, in due course leading to an emphatic reaction amongst designers and architects especially to the excesses of Art Nouveau as applied to decoration. Hector Guimard had made of his Métro entrances in Paris structures that were vigorous, extraordinarily rhythmic, and strongly suggestive of insects and of butterfly wings. Yet with Guimard and with Horta, such fantasy was underpinned by vigorous discipline. Horta's buildings grew increasingly restrained and severe. Guimard's sculptural Métro entrances were reproducible and built from preconstructed sections.

The Kiss by Gustav Klimt; watercolor and gouache on paper mounted on wood; 180×180cm (71×71in); c1909. Österreichische Galerie, Vienna

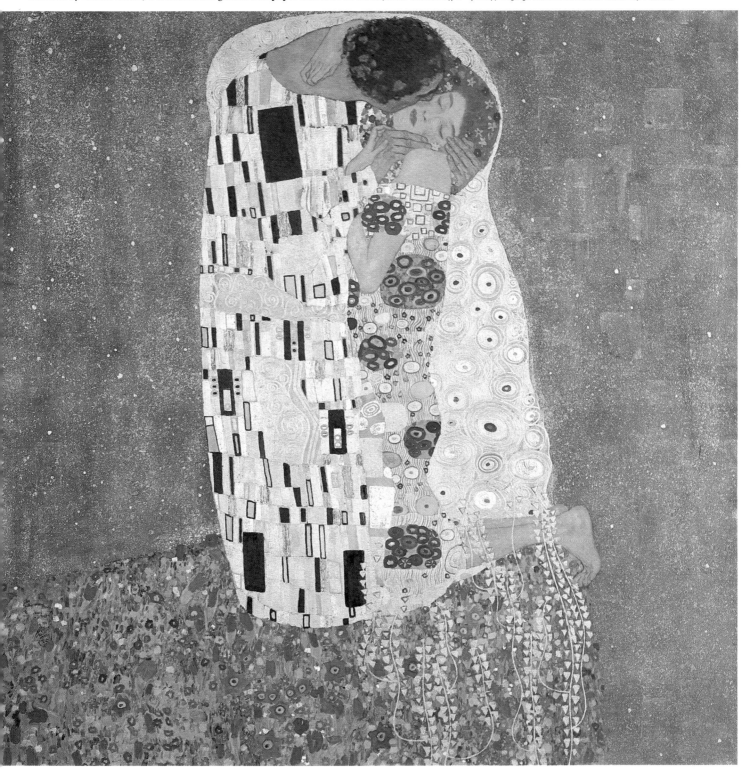

There is no clear distinction to be made between the Symbolist Movement and Art Nouveau: they were interdependent in a complex way. Symbolists numbered many writers as well as painters amongst their various groups; Art Nouveau evolved as a primarily visual phenomenon. As such, however, it owed a great deal to the suggestive and expressive sense of decoration essential to the Symbolists.

The Palais Stoclet in Brussels illustrates this complex interaction. The building itself, by Josef Hofmann, is the work of an Art Nouveau designer-architect who has abandoned all repetitive and inessential decorative detail yet retained a precise sense of rhythm and interval, a control of line and surface in his elevations that is fully informed by the rhythmic precedence of Art Nouveau at its earliest and fullest phase. Within the house, the Viennese Secessionist Gustav Klimt, a highly cultured virtuoso and an internationally aware painter, executed a mural frieze that extends around the dining room walls. The painted and appliqué frieze is perfectly poised between Symbolist painting and Art Nouveau decoration: it reveals their interdependence and the debt of each to the other. The swirling tree of life sends its spirals right around the room, a dynamic decorative motif that carries too the significance of its subject matter. In case this remained obscure, Klimt counterbalanced the tree of life motif by the figures of an embracing couple, the man dominating and all but overwhelming the woman. The theme of love, of the fall of man, of the tree of life, is explicitly revealed in brilliantly decorative terms that in their rhythm are distinctly Art Nouveau. Klimt, by means as much those of the designer as the painter, has decorated the room. Simultaneously he has characterized the man with angular forms and massive shape, and the woman by slender shape and curving forms. Decoration and depiction are at one. Such a balance did not last many years but it clearly revealed the interaction of Art Nouveau and the Symbolist movement, and Klimt was an accomplished master of both.

JOHN MILNER

Bibliography. Duncan, A. *Art Nouveau*, London (1994). Jullian, P. *The Symbolists*, London (1973). Madsen, S.T. *Sources of Art Nouveau*, New York (1975). Milner, J. *Symbolists and Decadents*, London (1971). Rheims, M. *The Age of Art Nouveau*, London (1966).

45

FAUVISM AND EXPRESSIONISM

Fishermen at Nanterre by Maurice de Vlaminck; oil on canvas; 81×100cm (32×39in); 1906. Private collection

THE term *Fauves*, meaning "wild beasts", is said to have been coined by the French critic Louis Vauxcelles. At the Paris Salon d'Automne of 1905, paintings by a number of younger artists—including Matisse, Derain, Manguin, Marquet, Vlaminck, and Rouault—were hung in the same room, paintings characterized by vivid use of color and startling abbreviations of form. In the middle of this room was displayed a small, Quattrocento-like bronze by the sculptor Albert Marque. Vauxcelles, so the story goes, was so struck by the contrast between this piece and the surrounding canvases that he exclaimed: "Ah, Donatello au milieu des fauves!" The name stuck, and the 1905 exhibition became famous as the "Fauve Salon", the room in which the paintings by Matisse and his companions were exhibited being dubbed "la cage centrale".

If this story is true, Vauxcelles can claim to have christened two of the most important movements in early-20th-century art, Fauvism and Cubism, although Fauvism can be described as a "movement" only in a limited sense. The Fauve painters, unlike, for example, the artists of the *Brücke*, did not formally constitute themselves as a society or association. They had no manifesto, no coherent aesthetic. It was, rather, an informal circle of friends, with Matisse as the acknowledged leader. The earliest members of the group—Matisse, Rouault, Manguin, Marquet, and Camoin—had been fellow students in Gustave Moreau's studio between 1891 and 1897. In 1901, Matisse met two more future Fauves, Vlaminck and Derain, who had been working together at Chatou. The following year, this loosely knit group, the composition of which was constantly changing, began exhibiting at the gallery run by the Parisian dealer, Berthe Weill. During the years 1903–7, Matisse and his friends exhibited together fairly frequently, both at the newly founded Salon d'Automne and at the older Salon des Indépendants. In April 1904, Berthe Weill showed a collection of works by Matisse, Camoin, Manguin, Marquet, and Jean Puy; in the spring of 1905, virtually all the members of Matisse's circle showed together at the Indépendants, although it was not until the autumn of that year that critics began to speak of them as a group and to recognize an underlying similarity between their works. Also at the 1905 Indépendants, Matisse showed his major figure-painting of this period, *Luxe, Calme et Volupté* (private collection), with its obvious debt to the Neo-Impressionism of Signac and Cross. Despite a certain amount of adverse criticism, this painting was immediately bought by Signac himself, evidently delighted to have gained, as he thought, another convert to the Neo-Impressionist doctrine. He did not realize how short-lived that conversion was to be.

The lack of enthusiasm which greeted the showing of *Luxe, Calme et Volupté* was, however, nothing compared to the storm that broke at the opening of the Salon d'Automne later the same year. Leo Stein, soon to become one of the artist's most important patrons, called Matisse's *Woman with the Hat* (Walter A. Haas Collection, San Francisco) "the nastiest smear of paint I had ever seen". One reviewer described the works by the Fauve group as having "nothing whatever to do with painting". Evidently, what caused greatest offence was the strident, non-naturalistic use of color which appeared to be the common characteristic of the group as a whole. Contemporary critics made little attempt to distinguish between works by different artists, although, if we look at the various paintings shown at this "Fauve Salon", the differences are often as striking as the resemblances.

Matisse had come to his heightened colorism by experimenting with the pure colors of Neo-Impressionism; Vlaminck was closer to Van Gogh than to any modern French painter; Derain showed a greater interest in the structural use of color than any of his contemporaries. Rouault, somewhat on the periphery of the Fauve group, was more interested in distortions of form than of color, and his palette remained somber, "a Fauve seen through dark glasses", in Alfred H. Barr's striking phrase. Apart from Rouault, however, the other Fauves did share a delight in pattern-making, and in the decorative effects of color. In this period up to 1907, they obviously regarded color as the painter's prime vehicle of expression.

The years 1906–7 marked the high point of Fauvism. At the Indépendants of 1906, Matisse showed his major canvas of this early period, the *Joy of Life* (Barnes Foundation, Merion, Pa). At the Salon d'Automne that year, the Fauve painters were out in force, among them two relative newcomers, Othon Friesz and Raoul Dufy, representing the "school of Le Havre". The following year, 1907, the group was further enlarged by the presence of what might be termed "passing Fauves", Le Fauconnier, Metzinger, and Braque. That autumn, Matisse sent five more paintings to the Salon d'Automne, among them two highly important works, *La Musique* (Conger Goodyear Collection, New York) and *Le Luxe I* (Musée National d'Art Moderne, Paris). By now, however, his position as leader of the avant-garde was already threatened by the rising tide of Cubism. We remember the Salon d'Automne of 1907 not so much for Matisse's contributions as for the large retrospective showing of Cézanne's work, which produced a profound impression upon the future Cubists. Many of the younger painters who, like Braque, had been temporarily seduced by the coloristic charms of Fauvism, now began to devote principal attention to form, rather than color (it is, in any case, tempting to decide that Fauvism was essentially a transitional style, since the ever-greater intensification of color could scarcely be regarded as a permanent goal for painting). And Matisse himself, despite his suspicion of the Cubists, was developing away from the apparent spontaneity of his early Fauve manner towards the more calculating structural logic characteristic of his painting during the years 1908–14.

Curiously, the Fauve painters, especially Matisse, enjoyed a far higher reputation outside France than they did at home. Before the First World War, one of the finest collections of Fauve painting in the world was in Russia, that belonging to the Moscow merchant Sergei Shchukin. The impact of the

The Pool of London by André Derain; oil on canvas; 66×99cm (26×39in); 1906. Tate Gallery, London

movement was widespread; although there were no important group exhibitions of Fauve painting outside Paris before the end of the decade, numerous foreign artists were in Paris during the crucial years 1905–7. Kandinsky, for example, would have seen both the Salon d'Automne of 1906 and the Indépendants of 1907. Paintings by Matisse were shown, albeit reluctantly, by the art dealer Paul Cassirer in Berlin in the winter of 1908–9. Also in 1909, Matisse's Notes d'un Peintre appeared in German translation in the periodical Kunst und Künstler. And in April 1911, artists including Manguin, Marquet, Derain, Puy, Braque, Friesz, van Dongen, Vlaminck, and—strangely—Picasso were shown at the XXII exhibition of the Berlin Sezession under the title "Expressionists".

Beginnings of Expressionism. The origin of the term Expressionsim is uncertain. By it, we mean a movement of revolt in art, literature, and music which reached its climax with the First World War. Today, we regard this movement as being specifically German in character. There is, however, no doubt that the term was earlier used to refer to French rather than German artists. Writing in the periodical Der Sturm in August 1911, the art historian Wilhelm Worringer alluded to contemporary French "Synthetists and Expressionists". And at the Sturm exhibition in Berlin in the spring of 1912, the organizer, Herwarth Walden, again labeled the works of the French contributors "expressionist", but not those of the "Blue Riders", Kandinsky and Franz Marc. Not until the Sonderbund exhibition in Cologne in the summer of 1912, the most important prewar manifestation of avant-garde art, was any attempt made to define the new movement. Writing in the foreword to the exhibition catalogue, Richard Reiche described Expressionism as striving "for a simplification and enhancement of forms of expression, a new rhythm and color". And not until the war years was the term used to refer to a specifically German movement in the visual arts, a movement having its own positive aims and ideals.

That the word became used in this way was due largely to two writers, the critic Paul Fechter and the playwright and essayist Hermann Bahr. In his book Expressionismus, first published in 1916, Bahr emphasized that the origins of the Expressionist movement lay in German 19th-century aesthe-

Village aux Toits Rouges by Maurice de
Vlaminck; oil on canvas; approximately
71×56cm (28×22in); Christie's, London

tics, especially the writings of Goethe, further developed in modern times by such writers as Worringer, Alois Riegl, and Theodor Lipps. He also interpreted Expressionism as a movement giving primary importance to the inner world of the emotions, by contrast to Impressionism, which remained "enslaved" to the external world of nature or of the senses. But before this, in 1914, Fechter had published a monograph, also under the title *Expressionismus*, in which he distinguished between two different kinds of Expressionism: "intensive Expressionism", which derived its inspiration from inner experience, and "extensive Expressionism", which depended upon a heightened relationship with the external world. For Fechter, the most important representative of the former "school" was Kandinsky, of the latter, Max Pechstein.

In fact, most of the artists who are today labeled Expressionists would have agreed on the importance of inner experience. Kurt Pinthus, who edited a collection of Expressionist verse published in 1920 under the title *Menschheitsdämmerung* ("Twilight of Mankind"), demanded that "in art, the process of realization must proceed from the internal to the external, not from the external to the internal; it is a question of realizing inner reality through the resources of the spirit". And as early as 1911, Kandinsky characterized the dawning 20th century as the "century of the internal", as opposed to the 19th century, the "century of the external". Art aimed to express the soul, not the skill of the artist. Fechter wrote that art "not only derives from ability, but also depends upon a certain spiritual disposition, desire, or rather, necessity". His remarks echo the composer Arnold Schoenberg's famous dictum, which became one of the slogans of Expressionism: "Art comes from necessity, not from ability". As a result of this insistence upon the artist's inner vision, coupled with a disdain for mere technical prowess, the distinctions between different art forms became blurred. Artists, writers, and composers tended to regard the differences between their respective arts as only external, and therefore unimportant. Most of the leading Expressionists experimented in a number of different media. Ernst Barlach made sculptures and graphic works and wrote plays; his prose play *Der Tote Tag* ("Dead Day") is one of the earliest examples of Expressionist theatre. Kandinsky produced paintings and graphics, poetry, criticism, and drama. Kokoschka made paintings, drawings, prints, sculptures, and wrote plays and essays. Schoenberg both composed music and painted. Artists frequently turned to their contemporaries working in different media for inspiration. Often, the results of such experiments are surprisingly similar. There is an evident relationship between Kandinsky's stage composition *Der Gelbe Klang*

Composition IV by Kandinsky; oil on canvas; 160×250cm (63×98in); 1911. Kunstsammlung Nordrhein-Westfalen, Düsseldorf

("Yellow Sound") and Schoenberg's music drama *Die Glückliche Hand* ("The Lucky Hand"). This relationship may be due in part to their common ancestry in the works of Strindberg, whose late plays, like the paintings of his contemporary Edvard Munch, exerted a decisive influence upon the early Expressionist movement.

To Fechter's "intensive Expressionism" and "extensive Expressionism" we should add a third category: political Expressionism. By 1914, the "heightened relationship with the world" Fechter describes had been largely supplanted by a heightened political consciousness, made more acute by the crisis of the First World War. In literature, what had started as a revolt against society became, in its most extreme form, a kind of anarchistic pacifism. In the visual arts, this political consciousness is reflected in the works of such artists as Barlach, Max Beckmann, and Käthe Kollwitz. Beckmann's large painting *The Night* (Kunstsammlung Nordrhein-Westfalen, Düsseldorf), or his later triptychs, are symbols of the artist's anguish in the face of war and its aftermath. The war itself also claimed a heavy toll among Expressionist artists, most significant of those killed in action being August Macke (*ob.* 1914) and Franz Marc (*ob.* 1916).

Die Brücke. In Pechstein and Kandinsky, Fechter had singled out representatives of the two most important groups of Expressionist artists: *Die Brücke* (The Bridge) and *Der Blaue Reiter* (The Blue Rider). Of these, the earlier group was the *Brücke*. It was founded in 1905 in Dresden by four friends, all students of architecture: Ernst Ludwig Kirchner (1880–1938), Erich Heckel (1883–1970), Karl Schmidt-Rottluff (1884–1976), and Fritz Bleyl. The only founder member of the group who had trained as a painter was Kirchner, having studied in Munich under Wilhelm von Debschitz and Hermann Obrist during 1903–4. His graphic work of this period is clearly influenced by *Jugendstil*, the prevalent Art Nouveau manner of turn-of-the-century Germany. In Munich, Kirchner became acquainted with the technique of Divisionism. In a letter of 1937 to Kurt Valentin, he recalled:

> An exhibition of French Neo-Impressionists gave me pause. I found the drawing weak, to be sure, but I studied the science of color based on optics in order to arrive at the opposite: not complementary colors, but to let complementaries be created by the eye, according to Goethe's theory.

Kirchner is almost certainly referring to the tenth exhibition of the Munich society Phalanx, organized by Kandinsky, at which works by Seurat, Signac, Luce, Cross, and van Rysselberghe, as well as ones by Toulouse-Lautrec and Vallotton, were to be seen.

Kirchner, who began studying in Dresden in 1901, met Bleyl the following year. At about the same time, Heckel met Schmidt-Rottluff at a performance, it is said, of Hauptmann's *The Weavers*. Both were students at the high school in Chemnitz, and both became members of a progressive literary club, immersing themselves in the writings of Ibsen, Strindberg,

The Night by Max Beckmann; oil on canvas; 133×154cm (52×61in); 1918–19. Kunstsammlung Nordrhein-Westfalen, Düsseldorf

Dostoevski, and Nietzsche. Heckel's woodcut *Two Men at Table* (an illustration of a scene from *The Idiot* by Dostoevski) reveals the importance of the influence his early literary experiences exerted upon his later pictorial work. Heckel was the most intellectual of the *Brücke* artists. Kirchner later recalled that, at their first meeting, Heckel bore down on him, quoting aloud from Nietzsche's *Thus Spake Zarathustra*. Nietzsche's ideas, like those of Dostoevski, profoundly influenced the painters of the *Brücke*, especially in their choice of subject matter.

For a time, the four artists worked together in the studio of either Kirchner or Heckel. Their first exhibition came about almost by chance. Heckel was employed in the drawing office of the architect Wilhelm Kreis, one of whose designs, for the country house of a collector, was seen by the Dresden lampfactory owner Seifert. Seifert was impressed by the design for the picture gallery of the house, which was in fact by Heckel, and had it built as a setting in which to exhibit his lamps. Heckel designed several new lamps for Seifert, and hung the walls with pictures by himself and his companions. The exhibition opened in Seifert's factory in the Löbtau quarter of Dresden in October 1906, and attracted little attention.

At about this time, the four founder members were joined by the young Max Pechstein, then a student at the Dresden Academy, the Swiss painter Cuno Amiet, and the Finnish artist Axel Gallen-Kallela. In February 1906, Schmidt-Rottluff wrote to Emil Nolde inviting him to join the group: Nolde accepted, but left the group again the following year. Also in 1906, the group was enlarged to include "passive members" who, for an annual subscription of 12 Marks, received a yearly report, and a portfolio of three or four original graphics. The painters formulated a manifesto of the group, and Kirchner cut the text in wood. It began:

> Putting our faith in a new generation of creators and art lovers, we call upon all youth to unite. And being youth, the bearers of the future, we want to wrest from the comfortably established older generation freedom to live and move. Anyone who di-

rectly and honestly reproduces that force which impels him to create belongs to us.

It is difficult to identify a coherent *Brücke* style before *c*1907, the year the group first showed at the Galerie Richter in Dresden. Moreover, the way in which that style developed is obscured by problems of chronology. Kirchner especially, in later years, misdated his own early works, probably quite consciously, putting them sometimes as much as three or four years too early. At this time, the desire of younger artists to appear more original or avant-garde than they really were often led to falsifications of this kind. Up until 1906, Kirchner was still experimenting with a divisionist technique, albeit in his own highly personal interpretation (*Lake in Dresden Park*, 1906; private collection). The early work of the other *Brücke* painters was also eclectic in manner, owing an evident debt to Post-Impressionism in general, and to Van Gogh and Munch in particular. Heckel, Kirchner, and Schmidt-Rottluff all denied such influences, claiming that the works of these artists were unknown to them during the crucial years before 1908; but Nolde put his finger on the nub when he wrote, in a letter to Hans Fehr: "They ought to call themselves Van Goghians". Even if they had not seen any of the important French Salons (and Pechstein had been in Paris in 1907–8), works by foreign artists could be seen with comparative ease in Germany. As early as 1905, the Galerie Arnold in Dresden held an exhibition of 50 paintings by Van Gogh; the following year, the *Sächsischer Kunstverein* showed 20 works by Munch, and the Galerie Arnold paintings by French Neo- and Post-Impressionist artists including Seurat, Gauguin, and Van Gogh. In May 1908, the Galerie Richter had a retrospective exhibition of 100 works by Van Gogh, and also showed Fauve paintings by van Dongen, Marquet, Vlaminck, Friesz, and others. And Kirchner's trip to Berlin in January 1909 coincided with Cassirer's exhibition of works by Matisse.

Equally difficult is the problem of knowing exactly when the *Brücke* artists first interested themselves in primitive art. Kirchner's claim that he discovered Negro sculpture and the art of the South Seas in 1904 is scarcely plausible. Certainly no trace of exotic influences can be detected in the work of any of the *Brücke* painters before 1906–7. By this date, both the Fauves and Picasso had discovered primitive art. In *Les Demoiselles d'Avignon* (1907; Museum of Modern Art, New York), Picasso explored the formal consequences of the distortions of human physiognomy characteristic of certain kinds of African sculpture. The *Brücke* artists, however, were interested in primitive art for different reasons: they admired its expressive power, often employing primitive sexual imagery in their own works. They wished their way of life to be primitive, too; they not only surrounded themselves with examples of primitive art, but decorated the walls of their studios, and even objects of everyday use, in a primitivizing manner somewhat reminiscent of Gauguin. Negro sculptures feature in studio interiors by both Kirchner and Heckel after 1907.

From 1906, members of the group worked closely together, especially during the holiday months. Each summer or autumn from 1906 to 1910, Schmidt-Rottluff and Heckel painted together at Dangast on the North Sea; in the summer of 1910, Heckel and Pechstein joined Kirchner at Moritzburg. Their favorite subject was nudes in a landscape, which they studied repeatedly; the similarity of their work during this period permits us to speak of a "group style". Different members of the group experimented extensively with graphic techniques; the woodcuts of Kirchner and Heckel, especially, are extremely powerful. The artists cut their own blocks, and allowed the grain of the wood to appear as a decorative element in the finished print, a technique also favored by Munch. Schmidt-Rottluff made both woodcuts and lithographs. The most lasting monuments to these experiments are the *Jahresmappen*, the annual portfolios produced for the "passive members" of the association. In later years, each portfolio was devoted to the work of a single artist: in 1910 Kirchner, in 1911 Heckel, in 1912 Pechstein.

In 1910, paintings by the *Brücke* artists and by Nolde were rejected by the Berlin *Sezession*. Nolde mounted a public attack on Max Liebermann, the president, and the *refusés* founded their own association, the *Neue Sezession*, under Pechstein's chairmanship. The painter Otto Müller, whom Kirchner later credited with having introduced his fellow artists to the technique of painting in tempera, joined the group. In 1911, the remaining *Brücke* artists moved to Berlin (Pechstein had been living there since 1908), and Kirchner and Pechstein opened a painting school, the MUIM institute. At about this time, the Czech painter Bohumil Kubista also joined the *Brücke*. This shift in the group's center of gravity, from Dresden to Berlin, coincided with a far greater formality, and a noticeable change of subject matter. It was now the big city that occupied most of their attention, especially the seamier side of city life, the twilight world of the drunk, the nightclub artiste, and the prostitute, seen in Kirchner's *Five Women on the Street* (1913; Museum of Modern Art, New York). In 1912, the *Brücke* participated in the second *Blaue Reiter* exhibition, returning the visit of the Munich artists to Berlin, when representatives of the *Neue Künstler-Vereinigung München*, among them Kandinsky and Jawlensky, had shown at the fourth exhibition of the *Neue Sezession*. In the same year, the group exhibited at the great *Sonderbund-ausstellung* in Cologne, where Kirchner and Heckel decorated the chapel with frescoes.

By this time, however, a rift was beginning to develop within the *Brücke*. Pechstein, who exhibited with the Berlin *Sezession* in defiance of a resolution that the group would participate collectively, or not at all, was expelled from the *Brücke*. The following year, matters came to a head when Kirchner prepared for circulation a "Chronicle of the *Brücke*", which provoked violent disagreement among the other members. In May, the group disbanded, the "passive members" being informed by a letter signed by Amiet, Heckel, Müller, and Schmidt-Rottluff. The artists themselves, however, continued to exhibit with the Berlin *Sezession*, the newly founded *Freie Sezession*, and at the private gallery owned by

Street, Berlin by Ernst Ludwig Kirchner; oil on canvas;
120×90cm (47×35in); 1913. Museum of Modern Art, New York

the dealer Fritz Gurlitt.

Today, the artists of the *Brücke* are considered part of the mainstream Expressionist movement, perhaps because of their contempt for the "comfortably established older generation" and their disdain of merely technical skill. But in other ways, it may be asked to what extent this nomenclature is convincing. Neither the savage allegories of a Beckmann, nor the apocalyptic visions of a Meidner have any place in the *Brücke's* work; and, unlike the other leading Expressionists, they confined themselves largely to painting and graphics, and made few excursions into other media. Given the literary sources upon which they drew (works by Nietzsche and Dostoevski) it seems that they might more accurately be called "Naturalists" rather than Expressionists. In his choice of subject matter, an artist like Kirchner appears more closely related to such literary Naturalists as Ibsen or the early Strindberg (Scandinavian literature had a powerful influence upon many German artists at the beginning of the century), rather than to, for example, Georg Trakl or Stefan Heym. Moreover, by comparison with the artists of the *Blaue Reiter*, the art of the *Brücke* remains essentially representational. Kirchner wrote with evident distrust about abstract painting:

There is no gradual development from increasing unintelligibility right up to the abstract image, rather ... the manner of

creation is totally different. The artist ... has to invent forms, they can only arise from his mind ... To be deciphered, these pictures require a key which only the artist or the art historian can supply ... But is this a development worth striving for? Might not art in this way cease to be art, and become merely a school discipline, like geometry and algebra?

Der Blaue Reiter. If the *Brücke* artists were Nietzscheans in their philosophical outlook, Naturalists in their choice of subject, and more interested in the practical than the theoretical, the Blue Riders were the exact opposite. Owing philosophical allegiance to Schopenhauer, rather than to Nietzsche, they manifested an evident penchant for theory, as well as a tendency towards abstraction.

The leading Blue Riders were the Russian Kandinsky and the German painter Franz Marc. Regarding the name, Kandinsky wrote: "We both loved blue: Marc—horses, myself—riders. So the name invented itself." The *Blaue Reiter* was, however, neither an exhibiting society nor a formal association. The name was originally devised as the title for an almanac or yearbook which Kandinsky and Marc were preparing for publication during the summer and autumn of 1911, a conspectus of contemporary art, which aimed to demonstrate the unity of the arts in general, and of "primitive" and "modern" art in particular. In a letter of 1930 to Paul Westheim, Kandinsky recalled:

At that time, there matured in me the desire to compile a book (a kind of almanac), to which only artists would contribute as authors. I dreamed of painters and musicians in the front rank. The harmful separation of one art from another, of "Art" from folk art or children's art, from "ethnography", the stout walls which divided what were, to my eyes, such closely related, often identical phenomena—in a word, their synthetic relations—all this gave me no peace.

The *Blaue Reiter* Almanac was eventually published in May 1912 by the firm of R. Piper and Co. in Munich, who had also produced Kandinsky's treatise *On the Spiritual in Art* (1912). It contained a number of important articles, among them Kandinsky's "On the Question of Form", Marc's "Two Pictures", and "The German 'Fauves'", August Macke's "The Masks", and Schoenberg's "The Relationship to the Text". The editors had originally wanted no less than eight articles on music, which proved ultimately impossible, but the Almanac is still remarkable for the amount of musical material it contains, including as it does articles on Skryabin and modern Russian music, as well as a musical "supplement", consisting of facsimiles of short pieces by Schoenberg and his pupils Alban Berg and Anton von Webern. Most remarkable of all, however, were the illustrations, which in the end numbered over 140. Children's drawings, Easter Island sculptures, African carvings, Alaskan textiles, Russian folk prints, Bavarian glass paintings, German Gothic sculptures, paintings by El Greco and Cézanne, Henri Rousseau and Picasso, as well as by the artists who contributed articles to the Almanac—Kandinsky, Marc, Macke, Schoenberg—were all reproduced. On the other hand, examples of what we might consider the main-

The Blue Rider — *Der Blaue Reiter*

The Blue Rider was, first and foremost, a book or almanac, *Der Blaue Reiter*. It was published in Munich in May 1912, edited by Kandinsky and Franz Marc. It included important theoretical statements by both artists. Kandinsky had also made a number of preparatory studies for the cover of the almanac, showing a rider figure with flying cloak. In the end, he abandoned this rather traditional image in favor of a far more abstract design for a three-color woodcut, based on the subject of St Martin and the Beggar.

Before the Almanac was actually published, the two editors had already organized two exhibitions to which they also gave the name *Der Blaue Reiter*. The first, which opened in Munich in December 1911, was a relatively small affair, consisting mainly of paintings by Kandinsky, Marc, and artists of their immediate circle such as August Macke and Heinrich Campendonck. The second (spring 1912) was more elaborate, though limited exclusively to graphic work. Most of the major figures of European avant-garde painting were represented, among them Picasso, Braque, Delaunay, and the artists of

the *Brücke*. These exhibitions, like the Almanac, were intended to show the diversity of contemporary trends in art.

For this reason, it would be misleading to speak of a Blue Rider "movement" or "style". There was no group, because the Blue Rider was not an exhibiting society nor an association of artists sharing an agreed program. Moreover, if we look at the works of Kandinsky, Marc, and Macke, they are stylistically very different. Kandinsky, at this date, was moving very close to pure abstraction; where his paintings still have a recognizable theme, it is usually of an apocalyptic or eschatological kind, for example, his watercolor-over-pencil study for the volume *Klänge, Judgment Day* (1912; Städtische Galerie im Lenbachhaus, Munich). Marc, by comparison, made relatively few abstract experiments. Animals played an important role in his paintings, while stylistically, his work shows the influence of Italian Futurism, especially in the translucent colored facets and strong diagonals which cut across the composition, as in *Deer in a Forest II* (1913–14; Staatliche Kunsthalle Karlsruhe). Macke's work is more

▲ A frontispiece from *Der Blaue Reiter*; a drawing by Kandinsky after a Bavarian mirror-painting; 28×21cm (11×8in); 1912. Städtische Galerie im Lenbachhaus, Munich

Below left A design for the cover of *Der Blaue*

Reiter by Kandinsky; watercolor; 28×21cm (11×8in); 1911. Städtische Galerie im Lenbachhaus, Munich

▼ A woodcut design for the cover of *Der Blaue Reiter* by Kandinsky; 22×17cm (9×7in); 1912

▲ *Deer in a Forest II*
by Franz Marc; oil
on canvas; 110×100cm
(43×39in); 1913–14.
Staatliche Kunsthalle,
Karlsruhe

Above right A work
from August Macke's
visit to North Africa in
1914: *Market in Tunis I*;
watercolor
29×23cm (11×9in).
Private collection

▶ An important
influence on the Blue
Rider painters was the
work of Robert
Delaunay; from 1913
comes his *Circular
Forms, Sun and Tower*;
oil on canvas;
110×90cm (43×35in).
Private collection

gentle and lyrical—especially the watercolors
he brought back from a trip to North Africa
which he made in spring 1914, together with
his painter friends Louis Moilliet and Paul
Klee. His paintings after 1912 also reveal the
influence of Delaunay's Orphism—a kind of
colorful, highly personal version of Parisian
Cubism which much impressed the Munich
painters. Admiration for Delaunay, an interest in naive and primitive art, and a similarity
of philosophical outlook are the most important features which unite this otherwise
rather loose-knit conjunction of personalities.

PETER VERGO

Further reading. *Abstraction: Towards a New Art,
Painting 1910–1920* London (1980). Lankheit, K.
(ed.) *The Blaue Reiter Almanac*, London and New
York (1974). Vergo, P. *The Blue Rider*, Oxford
(1977).

stream tradition in Western art, paintings by Renaissance and post-Renaissance masters, were conspicuous by their absence. The object of the often carefully-calculated juxtapositions of visual material was to demonstrate the "inner identity" between primitive forms of expression and those utilized by contemporary artists—a directness of approach, a communicative power which had, Kandinsky felt, been overlaid in Renaissance and Baroque art by representational or narrative concerns.

That the name *Der Blaue Reiter* strayed beyond the confines of the Almanac itself was due to political rather than purely artistic circumstances. Kandinsky and Marc, together with Gabriele Münter and Alfred Kubin, were members of a society called the *Neue Künstler-vereinigung München* (New Artists' Association of Munich) which had been founded in 1909 under Kandinsky's presidency. Before long, tensions began to be felt. The members coalesced into opposing groups, the conservatives led by the German painters Alexander Kanoldt and Adolf Erbslöh, the radicals by Kandinsky and Marc. As early as August 1911, Marc wrote to his friend Macke: "I can foresee clearly, with Kandinsky, that the next jury (in the late autumn) will bring about a dreadful altercation, and then, or the next time, a split, or the resignation of one or other party; and the question will be, who *stays* ..."

The split came in December that year, when Kandinsky's *Composition Five* (private collection), one of his most advanced works of this period, was rejected by the jury which had been called upon to judge works submitted for the society's third exhibition, scheduled to take place in the Thannhauser Gallery in Munich. At this declaration of war, Kandinsky and his friends resigned, and immediately started to organize a rival exhibition of their own, to which they gave the name of their still unpublished Almanac. Thanks to prodigious efforts, the "first exhibition of the editorial board of *Der Blaue Reiter*" opened concurrently with the third exhibition of the *Neue Künstler-vereinigung*, in an adjacent gallery. As foreword to the catalogue, Kandinsky wrote:

> In this little exhibition, we do not seek to propagate any *one* precise or special form. We aim to show, by means of the different forms here represented, the variety of ways in which the artist's inner wishes manifest themselves.

For the most part, it was those artists who had already collaborated in preparing the Almanac who contributed to the first exhibition, although they were not "members" of any association, but simply invited to participate by Kandinsky or Marc. The exhibition went on tour after it had closed in Munich, forming an important part of the second "Jack of Diamonds" show in Moscow in 1912, and ending up at Herwarth Walden's *Sturm* galleries in Berlin. The second exhibition (spring 1912), confined to graphic work, was far more international in character, featuring work by French and Russian, as well as by German artists; it offered a significant resumé of the latest tendencies in European art prior to the First World War.

It seems foolish to try to define the characteristics of a *Blaue Reiter* style. Not only was there no association, no manifesto, but since the aim of the exhibitions was to demonstrate the variety of forms of expression employed by contemporary artists, we are more likely to be struck by the differences than by the similarities between the works of the different contributors. At this time, Kandinsky's work was by far the most abstract, although he never entirely abandoned references to reality in his paintings before 1914. Marc also experimented with abstraction in some of his highly colorful works from immediately before the war; Macke's work was no less colorful, but mostly remained true to representational aims. Klee, who hovered on the fringes of the group, found color a struggle, displaying in his early works a far greater aptitude for line. We may, however, recognize in the works of these last three artists a common interest in the paintings and especially in the theories of Delaunay, whose essay on light was translated into German by Klee and published in Walden's periodical *Der Sturm* in 1913.

Other Expressionists. A number of other artists worked independently, often without affiliating themselves to any or-

Right, above: **The Embrace by Egon Schiele; oil on canvas; 110×170cm (43×67in); 1917. Österreichische Galerie, Vienna**

Right, below: **Reclining Woman by Egon Schiele; oil on canvas; 96×171cm (38×67in); 1917. Collection of Dr Rudolf Leopold, Vienna**

Below: **Auguste Forel by Kokoschka; oil on canvas; 71×58cm (28×23in); 1910. Städtische Kunsthalle Mannheim**

ganization. In Vienna, the young Egon Schiele (1890–1918) scandalized the bourgeoisie by the overt eroticism of his works; he was actually imprisoned for a time during 1912 for disseminating indecent drawings. The Viennese public were equally incensed by the work of Oskar Kokoschka (1886–1980), who made his début at the first *Kunstschau* exhibition, organized by Gustav Klimt (1862–1918) and former members of the Vienna Secession, in the summer of 1908. At this exhibition, Ludwig Hevesi, one of the most perceptive critics of his day, dubbed him "Oberwildling", which might be translated as "super-*Fauve*". It is, however, doubtful to what extent either artist can correctly be described as an Expressionist. It is true that Kokoschka, in his portraits, is more interested in the inner life of his sitters than in details of physiognomy, in a way reminiscent of the desire of many Expressionist writers to lay bare the "inner man", without concerning themselves about such trifles as milieu or even plot. Kokoschka wrote: "I look for the flash of the eye, the tiny shift of expression that betrays an inner movement." But as far as his dramatic works were concerned, he denied they had anything to do with that "rejection of society or plans for the improvement of the world which characterize the literary breakthrough and change in style called Expressionism". Schiele, on the other hand, despite his evident desire to shock, at times reverted to an almost mathematical manner of composing, and some of his late works, for example the *Reclining Woman* of 1917 (Collection of Dr Rudolf Leopold, Vienna), combine erotic subject matter with extreme intricacy of composition. It might be thought that an Expressionist artist should attend primarily to expressive rather than formal considerations; and yet several other so-called Expressionists, Kirchner and Feininger among them, emphasized the importance of painstaking composition, of discipline in art. Even Ludwig Meidner, whose works of the immediately prewar years in Berlin appear as if painted in an apocalyptic frenzy, wrote in his essay "An Introduction to Painting Big Cities":

We cannot record instantaneously all the accidental and disorganized aspects of our motif and still make a picture out of it. We must organize, courageously and deliberately, the optical impressions we have absorbed in the great world outside, organize them into compositions.

It will be clear by now that the term "Expressionist" is of little use, either as a declaration of intent, or as a stylistic label. Most artists have been concerned in one way or another with "expression", which is why certain historians have lumped together such diverse personalities as Bosch and Grünewald, Klee and Jackson Pollock, calling them all "Expressionists". But how much credence can be given to any definition that tries to reconcile such evident differences of artistic purpose? On the other hand, while most of the artists more usually termed Expressionists shared at least some aims and ideals, the differences are often as striking as the resemblances. Nor are comparisons between Expressionism in art and literary Expressionism, which seems in some ways a more unified phenomenon, entirely satisfactory. If Expressionism had a center, it was probably Berlin; if Expressionist artists and writers sought a focus, it was to be found in such periodicals as Walden's *Der Sturm* or Franz Pfemfert's *Die Aktion*. In the visual arts, the heyday of Expressionism was short-lived; its period of greatest influence is circumscribed by the early exhibitions of the *Neue Sezession*, the Cologne *Sonderbund-ausstellung*, and Walden's *Erster Deutscher Herbstsalon* of 1913. The War roused some Expressionists to a creative fury; but by the early 1920s Expressionism, or what remained of it, had a very different face. Artists like Beckmann, formerly hailed as Expressionists, now termed themselves "Objectivists", and Kandinsky, Feininger, and the other artists of the Bauhaus now pursued an entirely new direction.

PETER VERGO

Bibliography. Barr, A.H. *Matisse, his Art and his Public*, New York (1977). Behr, S. *Women Expressionists*, Oxford (1988). Dube, W.-D. *The Expressionists*, London (1972). Gombrich, E.H. *Kokoschka and His Time*, London (1986). Gordon, D.E. *Ernst Ludwig Kirchner*, New Haven (1968). Gordon, D.E. "The Origins of the Term 'Expressionism' ", *Journal of the Warburg and Courtauld Institutes* vol. XXIX (1966). Roethel, H.K. *The Blue Rider*, London and New York (1971). Vergo, P. *Art in Vienna 1898–1918*, London and New York (1982). Whitfield, S. *Fauvism*, London (1991).

46

CUBISM AND FUTURISM

Les Demoiselles d'Avignon by Picasso; oil on canvas; 244×234cm (96×92in); 1907
Museum of Modern Art, New York (see page 848)

The name "Cubism" originated from hostile criticisms of the angular and volumetric style of some landscapes by Braque, exhibited in 1908–9. The style was evolved simultaneously by Picasso and Braque and was rapidly adopted by other Parisian painters including Delaunay, Léger, Gris, Gleizes, Metzinger, Villon, and Duchamp—and by sculptors, including Lipchitz, Laurens, Duchamp-Villon, and Archipenko. By 1910–11 it had become the dominant avant-garde idiom in Paris and during the next two years exerted such widespread influence that it virtually transformed the face of progressive painting throughout Europe, in Russia, and to some extent in America. It became, briefly, an international modern style, its angularity in tune with the modern technological world. The extreme example of its influence was Futurism in Italy. Although the Futurists had been positively committed in their socio-political ideology, they lacked a suitably modern pictorial language until the advent of Cubist influence c1911.

As a progressive style Cubism did not outlive the First World War and in this sense its name, which more or less describes the appearance of early Cubist painting, is misleading. Its theoretical and technical propositions may now be seen as a central thread in the subsequent history of painting and sculpture. All Cubist thinking and all its innovations concerned a closer equation between art and "the real", introducing new senses, expressions, and experiences of reality into art. Although it was highly influential upon the early experimental years of Abstract art, Cubism itself was always concerned with readable images of reality.

It is no surprise, then, that the Cubists identified with the great 19th-century tradition of French Realist painting and saw Courbet, Manet, Impressionism, Cézanne, and Seurat as pioneering ancestors in a campaign against artificiality in art, against any thoughtless conservation of artistic conventions for their own sake. Between them, Realism and Impressionism had eliminated from the modern painter's concerns all those historical, literary, symbolic fields of subject matter that had underpinned the body of traditional European art. The subject was now the object seen, and the painter's interest was concentrated on radical innovations of technique in pursuit of rendering the object seen. Post-Impressionism gave a new meaning and order to these innovations, most clearly in the work of Cézanne and Seurat. In their refined sequences of color contrast and color analogy and their use of a consistent technique of regular marks, we see posed the sort of questions about painting that were to be early Cubism's main concern. Each of Cézanne's late paintings was both a full-blooded representation of external nature and an independent fabric of colors, marks, and values with its own internal logic. Braque's Fauve paintings (1905–6) already show allegiance to this attitude and in the next few years he focused increasingly on the dual nature of painting. "The new painting seeks to represent not the object, but the new unity," he wrote, "it is a lyricism achieved entirely by pure pictorial means."

Picasso was less committed to a tradition of modern French painting and brought a more aggressive objectivity to the problem of painting's duality. His early work had involved a ruthless questioning of European styles, past and present. He was closely interested in art with Symbolist leanings—the painting of Van Gogh, Gauguin, and Munch, for example—and, like many of the Cubists, in Symbolist literature. Symbolism's departure from traditions of nature-transcription and its proposal of a more oblique imagery made important contributions to Cubist thinking. The influence of writers with whom Picasso associated in the 1900s—Gertrude Stein, Alfred Jarry, and the great Cubist apologist and theoretician Guillaume Apollinaire—was to encourage a belief in change as the most vital impulse of the artist. For the Cubist this also found an echo in the wide circulation of contemporary ideas of Henri Bergson (on reality) and of Einstein (on relativity), as well as in the dramatic technological changes affecting urban experience. Absolute values were being widely questioned: Gertrude Stein compared the monotonous normality of former times with the marvelous new century in which "everything cracks, is destroyed, isolated". Picasso's appetite for radical new experiences drew strength from this mood.

By 1906–7 Picasso was looking outside Europe's heritage at the tribal masks and carvings of Africa. In this primitive art he recognized principles of image-making that had little to do either with European traditions of naturalism and classical beauty or with the illusionistic conventions by which Western artists had for centuries depicted the external world. In Picasso's own words: "a head is a matter of eyes, nose, mouth, which can be distributed in any way you like—the head remains a head." This liberated and conceptual attitude to imagery underlines all the subsequent thinking that Picasso contributed to Cubism.

In *Les Demoiselles d'Avignon* (1907; Museum of Modern Art, New York), often called the first Cubist painting, images from the external world are subjected to ruthless conceptual redistribution. The compression of space so characteristic of much post-Impressionist painting is now extreme and the surface alive with a heated exchange of angular lines, curves, and disjointed planes. Other paintings of the period by Picasso also show this vital sense of formal energy that he valued so highly in primitive art.

At this point Picasso and Braque were introduced to each other by Apollinaire and for the next five or six years they were to work in close partnership. While this partnership formed the watershed of Cubist art and thinking, Picasso and Braque did not exhibit in any of the annual Salons after 1909 or in the many group manifestations of Cubism by which the movement became publicly known.

Braque's interest in the structural properties of Cézanne's late work drew Picasso into an increasingly self-conscious and analytical investigation of painting itself, particularly in its poise between a flat internal identity and a representation of the external world. Together they sought new ways of expressing three-dimensional objects on a two-dimensional surface. Out of this radical exploration of the forms of painting many

Still Life with Violin and Pitcher by Braque; oil on canvas;
117×74cm (46×29in); 1909–10. Öffentliche Kunstsammlung,
Kunstmuseum Basel

Portrait of Vollard by Picasso; oil on canvas; 92×65cm (36×26in);
1910. State Pushkin Museum of Fine Arts, Moscow

other ideas about visual imagery were thrown up.

Landscapes painted in 1908–9, by Braque at l'Estaque, by Picasso at Horta del Ebro, are powerful arrangements of angular volumes spread across the surface. The motifs of trees and houses, while clearly identifiable, are brutally reduced to simple elements of a visual language. While the mass of the buildings is clearly represented and their relative positions in space suggested by overlap and by changes of scale, the most coherent reality to emerge is that of the painting itself. Its image is of a densely crowded relief, all of whose forms relate clearly to each other, even down to the vigorously hatched brushmarks with which the paint is applied. Braque's *Houses at l'Estaque* (1908; Kunstmuseum, Basel) is a good example.

In the years 1909 to 1911 Picasso and Braque painted mainly still lifes and figure paintings in a manner that became increasingly identifiable as a Cubist "style" and was rapidly taken up by other painters in Paris. The color scale was gradually reduced from a basically green-to-brown palette to an almost monochromatic range of warm grays: "color disturbed the space in our paintings", Braque wrote later. Drawing became progressively a linear, often rectilinear scaffolding, and paint—now very closely related to the consistent regular fabric of late Cézanne—was spread like a protective skin from edge to edge of the canvas.

The complexity of early Cubist painting is commonly explained in terms of assembling together different viewpoints of the objects depicted. Certainly it was central to the collaborative intention of Picasso and Braque to expose and reject the artifice of naturalistic illusionism, which was concerned with painting an object or objects from one fixed viewpoint at one fixed moment in time. In a painting like Braque's great *Still Life with Violin and Pitcher* (1909–10; Öffentliche Kunstsammlung, Kunstmuseum Basel), we *do* see the pitcher as if from several angles simultaneously: its inside and outside, its hard, straight silhouette, as well as the full softness of its curves. There is indeed something of a plan-section-elevation fusion of its attributes. But it is probably more rewarding to see the intention less simply or mechanically.

The Cubists intended painting to take account of the shifting, sometimes irrational and random, nature of human experience of things and places and of time and space. The major painters, at least, did not evolve *one* particular system of painting: they were neither scientific nor consistent in their approach to motifs. Systems were artificial, out of touch with the intuitive reality they wanted painting to encompass. "Cubism, which is accused of being a system, condemns all systems" (Gleizes and Metzinger, *Du Cubisme*, 1913).

The fragmentary planes in Picasso's *Portrait of Vollard*

(State Pushkin Museum of Fine Arts, Moscow), the first of his three great portraits of 1909–10, are not literally an accumulation of multi-viewpoint observations. Many of them might seem to contribute little to our knowledge of the sitter's characteristic forms. But the image as a whole appears both a stable physical presence and to be full of allusions to time, movement in space, shifts of light—indeed to all the complex, often simultaneous perceptions and circumstances that affect our experience of things. In the *Portrait of Kahnweiler* (Art Institute of Chicago) it is even clearer that early Cubism was as much intellectual and conceptual as concerned with visual analysis. Still painted from a sitter and (just) a recognizable likeness, it is a highly refined poise between the painting of a presence in space and the ordering of marks on a flat surface.

In this manipulation of marks, the spaces between and around the objects are as physically articulate as the objects themselves. (Braque wrote later: "There is in nature a tactile space, I might almost say a manual space ... This is the space that fascinated me so much—that is what early Cubist painting was, a research into space.") There was a precedent for this system of painting in Cézanne's *passage*, the means by which he held together the spatial composition of his late landscapes. But in the monochromatic context of Analytical Cubism, the homogeneity of the whole surface fabric seems more complete. Kahnweiler's presence is elusive; clues to it are scattered and compressed within a very shallow continuum of planes and tonal modulations. In this way, form-space relationships are repeatedly created without compromising the flat surface of the canvas.

A year later in Picasso's *Toreador Playing a Guitar* (National Gallery, Prague) or in Braque's *Man with Violin* (Siftung Sammlung E.G. Bührle, Zurich) of 1911, the ostensible subject matter has gone. The poise between the external reference and internal identity has tipped in favor of the internal. Without titles, we are faced with a rectangle or an oval covered in marks, lines, and tones. They have become a succession of allusive painterly events across a surface: intuitive and improvisatory in execution, seductively sensual to the eye. The painting is essentially a painting, itself part of external reality in its own right.

It was this late phase of Analytical Cubism—sometimes called "Hermetic Cubism" since visual analysis was now of marginal significance—that was so influential for Abstract art. It seemed an incentive for a type of painting—derived from the divisionist tradition of Impressionist and Post-Impressionist painting—concerned with the abstract properties of the medium at the expense of any recognizable subject matter. Many painters moved from this transitional formal stage to a point of pure abstraction, some only briefly but others as an irrevocable step.

In Paris, Robert Delaunay (1885–1941) painted the first French Abstract painting (*The Disk*, 1912; private collection)

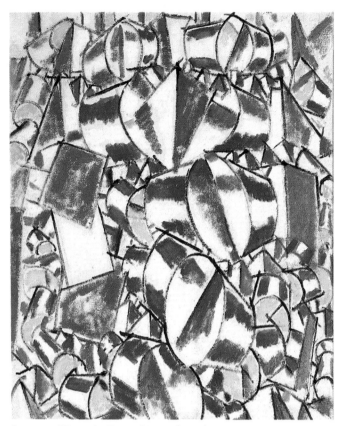

Contrast of Forms by Fernand Léger, from the series Contrasts of Forms; oil on burlap; 130×98cm (51×39in); 1913. Philadelphia Museum of Art

and in later writing made it clear that Cubism was a transition between the 19th-century and Abstract art. Others, like Picabia, flirted temporarily with abstraction. Léger recalled that he had to "go almost as far as abstraction to free myself from Cézanne's influence": see his *Contrasts of Forms* paintings of 1912–13. The Abstract tendencies in the work of Larionoff, the Italians Balla and Russolo, and the English Vorticists (Lewis and Bomberg) also derive from Analytical Cubism.

For Mondrian, who was working in Paris at the time, as for Malevich in Russia, the implications in Cubism seemed finite. He wrote later that "Cubism did not accept the logical consequences of its own discoveries: it was not developing abstraction towards its ultimate—the expression of pure reality." In fact he misinterpreted the basic intention of the Cubists. The reality that they were ultimately concerned with expressing was not the reality of abstract forms. Many of them made subsequent refutations of Abstract art's validity. ("Abstract art is just painting," Picasso said. "But what about drama?") The pioneers of abstraction saw the value of 1911 Cubism as discrediting the object in painting. The developments in Cubism after 1911 were all very consciously concerned with reinstating the reality of the object into painting.

Since 1911 both Picasso and Braque had been experimenting with various devices to emphasize the surface reality of a painting. Sand, sawdust, plaster, metal filings, even ashes had

Portrait of Kahnweiler by Picasso; oil on canvas; 110×73cm (43×29in); 1910. Art Institute of Chicago

The Impact of African Art

Among the 20th-century Parisian painters it was probably Maurice de Vlaminck (1876–1958) who first looked seriously at African art. He acquired a small collection of carved figures and masks—some bought, some given to him—*c*1904–5 and later claimed to have shown them to Derain and then to Matisse and Picasso. Others have laid claim to "the discovery", claims now impossible to prove or disprove. Matisse too started collecting African objects *c*1905; so did Picasso a year or two later. Independently and simultaneously the German *Brücke* painters (notably Ernst Kirchner) were looking at African and Oceanic carvings in Dresden's ethnographical museum.

Why African art? Why at this time? Part of the answer to these two questions lies toward the fringes of art history—the outcome of political and economic history: colonial expansion and the opening up of intercontinental trade. Just as Japanese art reached 19th-century Europe as a chance by-product of East–West trade, so the artifacts of primitive cultures were first collected in the context of colonial trading and of a generalized ethnographic curiosity. European collectors had made isolated acquisitions since the 16th century—as travelers' curios more than as art—but, reflecting the pattern of European colonization, Africa was less well represented in their collections than the South Seas.

The last 50 years of the 19th century saw the successive foundation of ethnographic museums throughout Europe and America, and large ethnographic sections in all the great Universal Exhibitions. The 1878 foundation of the Trocadéro Museum in Paris (now the Musée de l'Homme), for instance, was largely inspired by the ethnographic section of the Paris *Exposition Universelle* of the same year. When Picasso visited the Trocadéro in the late 1900s, it was an uncatalogued collection of ethnic objects, very casually displayed.

During the 20th century—largely because artists recognized primitive masks and carvings as "art"—the quasi-scientific character of these museums has been transformed and replaced by the aesthetic priorities of the art gallery. In a parallel way, many modern private patrons have collected and exhibited African art objects alongside modern paint-

▲ An Ashanti *akuaba*, carried by a pregnant woman as a charm; height 36cm (14in). Dallas Museum of Fine Arts

▼ A Bakota *mbulungulu* (guardian figure) from Zaire; wood covered with brass and copper. Friede Collection, New York

Top left A *fang* mask that once belonged to André Derain; wood whitened with kaolin; height 48cm (19in). Musée de l'Homme, Paris

▶ The lasting influence of African art on sculpture: *Appeasement* (or *Reassurance*) by Max Ernst; bronze; height 68cm (27in); 1961. Private collection

ings and sculptures. Many artists, too, have built up their own collections.

Up to a point then, African art just "became available" to the modern artist. But the motives for his interest were particular. Gauguin's attitude to Kanaka art in Tahiti had set the pattern. He asserted that primitive Oceanic cultures were superior to the debased and decadent state of the Classical-based European traditions. The avant-garde of the 1900s—conscious of being the "primitives of a new age"—sought the principles of a new and modern language for art. They,

too, questioned the sophisticated artifice of European "high art", particularly its illusionistic naturalism, its adherence to Classical ideals of beauty, and its art-for-art's sake concept of the *objet d'art*. The fact that African art was uninhibited by these concerns focused their interest. Although they

▼ *The Dancer of Avignon* by Picasso; oil on canvas; 382×256cm (150×101in); 1907. Collection of Walter P. Chrysler Jr, New York

made occasional stylistic references at first, it is in the confident scale of freedom—brilliant color and violent, apparently artless, execution—of the Fauves and Expressionists that we should look for its assimilation. "We felt no need to protect ourselves from foreign influences," Matisse wrote, "for they could only enrich us, and make us more demanding of our own means of expression."

The influence of African art is most explicit in the art of Picasso and the young Cubists, and of early-20th-century sculptors. The willful distortions of the repainted figures in Picasso's *Les Demoiselles d'Avignon* (1907; Museum of Modern Art, New York) are a clear instance; as is his *Dancer* 1907 (Collection of Walter P. Chrysler Jr)—its surfaces scored and savaged with scratches and incisions into the paint. More lastingly, the influence of African art liberated his attitude to image-making. "A head is a matter of eyes, nose, and mouth", he now told Leo Stein, "which can be distributed in any way you like; the head remains a head". Picasso penetrated the "noble savage" romanticism that had clouded most earlier thinking about primitive cultures and looked objectively at primitive imagery as a valid alternative to the European tradition—as simply another form of art. The animistic qualities of his later constructions, from 1915 onwards, also express the appeal for him of the fetish-like properties of tribal masks.

In modern sculpture, too, there are clear examples of direct stylistic influence at first (in works by Epstein, Modigliani, the *Brücke*), but the more oblique assimilation of African forms and concepts is of lasting importance, as in the works of Brancusi, Arp, Moore, Hepworth, the young Giacometti, and Ernst. The massive revival of carving was partly inspired by this source, as were a new scale of vigorous formal invention and an experimental approach to media: the incessant use of totemic and mask-like images owes everything to it.

Artists at the start of the 20th century sought new ways of image-making, new references to reality more in keeping with the radical innovations in modern consciousness. African art seemed *most* radical, offered alternative means that were *most* different from the European norms. Its formal freedoms and inventions have become deeply subsumed into modern art's imagery and its influence has also paved the way to a very open-minded attitude to the art of other cultures.

NICHOLAS WADLEY

Further reading. Goldwater, R. *Primitivism in Modern Painting*, New York (1938). Willett, F. *African Art*, London (1971).

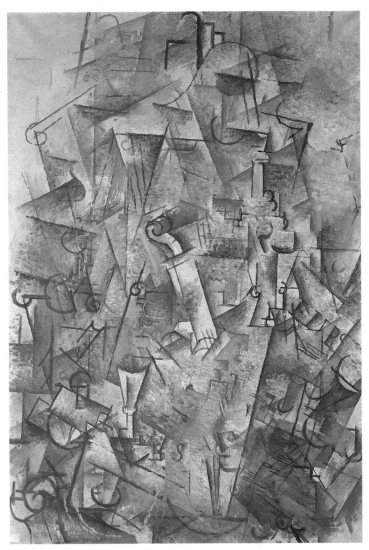

Still Life with Harp and Violin by Braque; oil on canvas;
116×81cm (46×32in); 1912. Kunstsammlung
Nordrhein-Westfalen, Düsseldorf

been mixed with pigment to exaggerate the paint's material presence on top of the canvas; the first collage (from the French *coller*, "to paste") was probably Braque's *Fruit Dish and Glass* of 1912 (Douglas Cooper Collection, France). Braque had used the wood-graining and marbling effects of commercial house-decorators (in whose trade he had served as an apprentice) and both he and Picasso had introduced letters and figures into some paintings.

The association of letters with flat surfaces is fixed and permanent. Picasso has said that he used them "to force the painted surface to measure up to something rigid"; Braque said that "these were forms which being themselves flat were not in space, therefore by contrast, their presence in the picture made it possible to distinguish between those forms which were in space and those which were not." In practice, the letters were drawn in various ways into the spirited dialogue between surface and depth: atmospheric paint was often dragged across them, compromising their flatness.

The letters can also be read as words and were a non-illusionistic, non-naturalistic way of referring to the subject or meaning of the painting. They form the title of Picasso's *Ma Jolie* (1911; Museum of Modern Art, New York) and a sort of subtitle to Braque's *Le Portugais* (1911; Öffentliche Kunstsammlung, Kunstmuseum Basel), where they are letters and figures from a poster in a painting of a café entertainer.

The pasting of papers (patterns, printed images, newsprint) and other materials or objects on to the surface dramatically achieved the same dual effect. It proposed freedom from the inhibitions of traditional paint on canvas and from the illusionistic representation of nature. These were not painted signs that coalesced to represent things: these were things themselves. Taken together, these two properties of collage emphasized the independent reality (often called the "object quality") of the work of art.

Sometimes the pasted elements were ready-made illusions. Examples are wood-grained wallpaper to represent wood as in Picasso's *Still Life with Violin and Fruit*, 1913 (Philadelphia Museum of Art). In other collages, the *collé* element represents itself: newspaper, matchboxes, a visiting card. Gris even pasted a piece of mirror in a painting called *The Washstand* (1912; private collection) and in another an engraving—by someone else—in an illusionistically drawn frame. In yet other collages, the extraneous elements are purely abstract in function like a painted area of color or tone.

A playful humor and witty allusions to the condition of painting abound in these early collages, particularly in those of Picasso and Gris. Among the newspaper headlines that Gris incorporated into paintings were "THE TRUE AND THE FALSE" and "WORKS OF ART WILL NO LONGER BE FORGED". Gris, who had hitherto been in the shadow of Picasso and Braque, emerged to make a major contribution to later Cubism, from 1912. He exerted considerable influence on other Cubist painters in Paris.

Collage also emphasized Cubism's ambition to bring art closer to everyday reality. The objects used are commonplace, often life-worn and disposable trivia. Their character is intimate, urban, or domestic, and their concerted effect is of an immediate art far from the remote "high art" of the museums. The Cubists themselves were enthusiasts for popular art and culture—they were great circus-goers, for instance, and Picasso at least was an ardent fan of American comic strips—and something of this taste emerges from the collages. This aspect of collage was fully exploited later by the Dadaists, especially by Kurt Schwitters. The abrupt posing of oblique and unexpected relationships between images that recurs in Picasso's collages was to be richly influential for Dada and Surrealism.

Cubist painting from *c*1912–13 is full of the implications of collage. Paintings like Picasso's *Violin and Guitar* (1913; Philadelphia Museum of Art) have a simple, concrete reality in stark contrast to the elusive abstraction of 1911. Braque used collage elements only in drawings, though many of these were large and some on canvas (for example, *Guitar* 1913–14; Museum of Modern Art, New York). He transcribed collage's principles directly into contemporary paintings like the 1913 *Composition with the Ace of Clubs* (Musée d'Art Moderne de la Ville de Paris). Colors, textures, and lines are arranged and "applied" to the surface.

If Analytical Cubism was a sophisticated and extreme refinement of traditional painterly techniques, Synthetic Cubism rejected outright some of its principles. The surface was now immutable and absolute. In no sense was it any longer a transparent window on to an illusion. The image's own reality was also now absolute: a part of the real world.

Gris later described Analytical art as starting from the particular (a seen motif) and moving to a generalization (the painting), whereas Synthetic art started from the generality of the surface and the artist's materials and created a particular and unique image from them. In general terms this distinction holds true for Cubism at large. The monochromatic and textural style of early Cubism was abandoned by both Picasso and Braque in favor of flat, often highly colored paintings, with unequivocally exposed surfaces. The paintings originate from ideas if not just from the materials: they were no longer based on the visual analysis of the 1908–10 still lifes.

For Picasso, this was a resumption of his natural method of working as shown in the early period. Perhaps not fortuitously, some of his early subjects reappear, as in *Harlequin*, 1915 (Museum of Modern Art, New York). In the aftermath of the invention of collages the distinct personalities of Picasso and Braque reemerged after a period of partnership in which individuality was deliberately suppressed. Picasso reverted—in paintings, drawings, collages, and constructions (of paper, wood, metal, and other materials)—to the sort of prodigal outburst of inventive energy that had characterized his earlier work. Even still-life paintings, for example *Green Still Life*, 1914 (Museum of Modern Art, New York), and *Still Life in a Landscape*, 1915 (private collection), exploit to the full the expressively disquieting and magical qualities of Cubist juxtaposition.

The close collaboration between the two major Cubists (Picasso called it a marriage; Braque compared them to two mountaineers roped together) was at an end by 1912. By 1914—not least through the outbreak of the First World War in which many Cubists served—the wider Cubist movement in Paris was also losing its collective identity.

In general, the other Cubist painters in Paris did not conduct such an intensive exploration of the mechanics of painting. Although Léger and Delaunay were led towards experimental Abstract works c1912–13, most Cubist painting was more concerned with subject matter. (It is some measure of this that collage as a medium was not taken up by anyone other than Picasso, Braque, and Gris.) The Cubist idiom pioneered by these three became the basis for explicit images of modern city life, with subjects—and sometimes technical devices—reflecting the heritage of Post-Impressionism.

On the whole, this outer Cubist movement was more concerned with "modernism" *per se*. Léger's *Nudes in a Forest* (1909–10; Kröller-Müller Museum, Otterlo) shows the

stronger allegiance to narrative, as well as a more dynamic physical energy than in Picasso's and Braque's analytical paintings. The same energy pervades his more abstract works of 1913–14 and reappears in clearly figurative images of heroic modern man by 1917, such as *The Card Players* (Kröller-Müller Museum, Otterlo). The subject matter of Delaunay's figurative paintings is almost insistently modern, for example the *Eiffel Tower* series (1910–11; examples in the Öffentliche Kunstsammlung, Kunstmuseum Basel, and the Solomon R. Guggenheim Museum, New York), the *Window on the City* series (1912; one example in the Tate Gallery, London), and *Homage to Blériot* (Musée de Peinture et de Sculpture, Grenoble).

Gleizes, Metzinger, and the Duchamp brothers were the principal movers behind collective activities—exhibitions, meetings. A Cubist section was a regular feature of annual Paris Salons from 1910. The *Section d'Or* group founded in 1911 included the Duchamps, Gleizes, Metzinger, Léger, Le Fauconnier, Gris, de la Fresnaye, Lhote, Picabia, Delaunay, Archipenko, the architect Mare, and the writers Apollinaire, Allard, Mercereau, and Salmon. It met twice weekly. In 1912 there was a *Section d'Or* exhibition in Paris: probably the most representative Cubist exhibition ever, with 30 contributors. Additionally, numerous exhibitions were sent throughout Europe, by 1914 as far afield as Moscow, New York, and Tokyo. By this means the Cubist style was disseminated among the avant-gardes of Moscow, St Petersburg, Prague, Berlin, Munich, Milan, and London. The poet Apollinaire, prominent among the writers who supported Cubism, (for example in his essays *The Cubist Painters* published in 1913) also became involved with the divergent tendencies that emerged within the movement.

Delaunay's experiments in "pure" painting, based on the simultaneous contrasts of color, were christened "Orphism" by Apollinaire. Its followers included Sonia Delaunay, Bruce, Frost, and the American "Synchromists" Russell and Macdonald-Wright. Chagall and Archipenko were also associated with Orphism as were the poets Canudo (editor of the Orphist review *Montjoie*) and Cendrars (writer of the first *simultanéiste* poem—on a scroll 6 ft, 2 m, long with type printed in various colors and sizes against an abstract design by Sonia Delaunay. Delaunay's painting was also greatly admired by the *Blaue Reiter* Expressionists in Munich (Klee, Macke, Marc). By 1913, Marcel Duchamp, close friend of Apollinaire, became increasingly involved in intellectual resolutions about art, issues largely arising out of Cubism. Virtually rejecting painting, he turned, with Picabia, into an area of activity that closely anticipated Dada.

Cubist sculpture fell into two general categories. First there were works in the traditional media of bronze or stone that interpreted painting's new attitude to image and form in three dimensions. Archipenko made the first "sculpture with a hole in it", his *Walking Woman* of 1912 (Denver Art Museum) and he and Duchamp-Villon were concerned with the form-space dialogue thrown open by early Cubist painting. Laurens and Lipchitz made still lifes and figures of austere and angular formal relationships that are close to the simple planear forms of Synthetic Cubism.

The second category—in the wake of collage—was more concerned with new materials. Picasso was the most prolific maker of multimedia constructions, often painted. Constructions like the painted wood *Still Life with Upholstery Fringe*, 1914 (Tate Gallery, London) relate to particular primitive masks (*wobe*, from the Ivory Coast) in which he was interested at the time. Generally, his three-dimensional pieces have a fetish-like, animistic quality which had lain dormant in his painting since 1908. Laurens and Archipenko also made inventive polychrome constructions, uninhibited in their freedom from conventional media. As in Synthetic Cubist painting, the particular image emerges very much from the nature of the materials themselves.

Cubism's influence on later sculpture can be related to these two areas of activity. The Constructivist tradition, stemming from Tatlin, Gabo, and Pevsner, is in direct descent from the Cubists' reductive analysis of form and their concern with interactions of form and space. For the Constructivists, a totally Abstract sculpture was the logical outcome—they viewed the decorative and animistic qualities of Cubist constructions as degenerate. Modern sculpture's general concern with space (with linearity and transparency) must also be seen in relation to Cubism.

What has become known as the "art of assemblage" is essentially derived from collage's loosening of the boundary between painting and sculpture and from its new dimension of reality of the art object. Picasso's constructed objects, of 1912 to 1915, and Duchamp's "ready-mades" from 1914, are ancestors to a new genre exploited fully by the Dadaists and Surrealists (particularly by Miró, Ernst, and Schwitters) which

Still Life with Chair Caning by Picasso; oilcloth and oil on canvas; 29×37cm (11×15in); 1912. Musée Picasso; Paris

is still very alive in Europe and America.

Apart from its transitional influence on early Abstract art, the angular style of early Cubism made a massive impact on art and design at large, from Expressionist painting to Purist art and architecture and product design. It replaced the seductive curvilinearity of Art Nouveau as a modern international language.

The wider influence of Cubism revised standards of reality in art: both with the independent reality of the art work itself, and with art's proximity to the everyday real world. Concepts of time and space in art bore more relationship to real life than they had in the static closed world of traditional art. Cubism's central historical relationship is clear, both to 19th-century Realism and to much subsequent art in a century obsessed with "the real".

Cubism also proposed a generous freedom of access for the artist, both to any materials and to any source of imagery. The free association and correspondence of images or part images and of objects or materials characteristic of much modern art originated in Cubism. Miró, Klee, or Chagall provide varied examples from the 1920s and 1930s; much American and European art of the 1950s and 1960s lies as clearly in the same tradition.

It has been thought that the freedoms proposed by Cubism have subsequently been abused: that ultimately they have spelt the death of painting. But in hindsight, considering the challenges to painting as a living medium thrown up by film, photography, and other audio and visual media of the modern world, the major painters associated with Cubism (Picasso, Braque, Léger) can be seen—like Matisse—to have sustained and revitalized the faith and the principles of great art.

Futurism. The foundation manifesto of Futurism was published by F.T. Marinetti in 1909. It was the first modern art movement to choose its own name. Sociopolitical in its impulse, Futurism was a movement embracing all the arts and in the course of the next five years, manifestos were published on subjects from *Geometrical and Mechanical Splendor* to *The Futurist Art of Noises*. In a country that stood as a symbol for the very traditions in art that were being universally overthrown by the avant-garde, the Italian Futurists were more anxious than most to disclaim the classical past. Their manifestos proclaim the glory and beauty of modern dynamism, youth, speed, originality, danger, energy, the expendable; they call for the destruction of museums, libraries, and academies, of dreams, traditions, and morals. The movement was centered on Milan, heart of the belated industrialization of modern Italy. The movement as a whole survived the First World War (which in principle it welcomed as a potential purifying force on society), but was widely discredited for its endorsement of the Italian Fascist Party c1919. In the visual arts, its significant lifespan was c1909 to 1915.

The two 1910 manifestos of Futurist painting were signed by Boccioni, Balla, Carrà, Russolo, and Severini. Their early work reflects universal trends in turn-of-the-century art: Art

A Girl Runs along the Balcony by Giacomo Balla; oil on canvas; 128×128cm (50×50in); 1912. Galleria d'Arte Moderna, Milan

Nouveau, Symbolism, and Post-Impressionism. The only native contributor to modern European art had been the sculptor Medardo Rosso, whose work (particularly its transient urban qualities) is repeatedly acclaimed in the manifestos.

By 1910 Boccioni was painting self-consciously modern images: *The Outskirts: Factories of Porta Romana* (1908–9; Collection of the Banca Commerciale, Milan), *The Modern Idol* (1910; Collection of E. Estorik, London). Paintings shown in the 1911 Milan exhibition of Futurist painting were images of the great modern metropolis, such as building sites, rioting crowds, and night clubs. The techniques were either loosely impressionist (broken brushwork to convey the shifting light, movement, and vitality of city life) or they still echoed the symbolic, languid arabesque of Art Nouveau. Boccioni's *The Laugh* (c1911; Museum of Modern Art, New York) expresses well both the manifestos' aim to "put the spectator at the center of the picture" (here he is assaulted by an array of simultaneous highly colored fragments of a night-club image) and the closeness to 19th-century urban Impressionism.

In 1911–12 Futurist painting matured under the influence of Analytical Cubism, known through periodicals and particularly from a group visit to Paris in 1911. The Futurists' palette, while still gaudy by comparison with the Cubists', was reduced and less literal, their style is more abstract, angular, and schematic. The crystalline structure of early Cubism was adapted to kinetic and environmental images of the city. The multi-viewpoint fragmentation lent itself readily to the Futurists' dynamic vision of a total and simultaneous interaction of urban sensations: see Boccioni's *States of Mind* series (1911–12; one example in the Museum of Modern Art, New York), Carrà's *Funeral of the Anarchist Galli* (1911; Museum of Modern Art, New York), and Severini's *Dynamic Hieroglyph of the Bal Tabarin* (1912; Museum of Modern Art, New York). Boccioni's *Forces of a Street* (1911; private collection) is the archetypal Futurist image of a city street at night. Headlights, street lights, and house lights are abstracted into symbolic lines of force and energy. An exhibition of these paintings was shown in Paris, 1912, which then toured Europe and was internationally very influential. Balla, whose earlier Neo-Impressionist works were influenced by chrono-photography (for example, *A Girl Runs along the Balcony*, 1912; Galleria d'Arte Moderna, Milan), moved in 1913 into uncompromisingly Abstract paintings in which Futurist dynamics were interpreted as simultaneous color contrasts.

Boccioni's *Manifesto of Futurist Sculpture*, published in 1912, was the first clear statement of Cubism's implications for sculpture. It emphasized the abolition of "closed" statues, the expression of movement and atmosphere, and the use of all available materials in any combination. His bronzes, *Unique Forms of Continuity in Space* (1913) and *Evolution of a Bottle in Space* (1912), rank among the most original and influential Futurist works. Exhibitions of his sculpture were held in Paris and elsewhere 1913–14. These and his manifesto were probably more instrumental in transmitting the radical ideas of Cubist sculpture than anything produced in Paris.

A *Manifesto of Futurist Architecture* published by Antonio sant'Elia in 1914 was equally prophetic and influential. It stressed the new needs of modern city life—functionalism and expendability. His visionary drawings of *La Città Nuova*, 1912–14 (factories, flats, generators, airship hangars, rooftop aerodromes, multi-level railway terminals) have been echoed repeatedly in the subsequent theory and practice of modern architecture.

Futurists actively participated in the political demonstrations and riots of 1914–15, and with Italy's entry into the war in 1915 Boccioni, Marinetti, Russolo and sant'Elia enlisted. Boccioni and sant'Elia were both killed in 1916.

The influence of Futurism—through exhibitions, publications, and, not least, Marinetti's propagandist lecture tours—was considerable. Its influence is clearly discernible in the later phases of Parisian Cubism—in works by Léger, Gris, Delaunay, Gleizes, and Duchamp-Villon—although there were some heated disputes between artists in Paris and Milan about who initiated Futurist ideas. Elsewhere the influences of Futurism and Cubism often acted in concert, for example on the Vorticism of Wyndham Lewis and others in England, on the city paintings of Marin, Stella, and Weber in America, on Expressionist art in Germany and Prague, on the "Cubo-Futurism" of the Russian avant-garde (Larionoff, the Burliuk brothers).

The importance of Futurist influence lay in its spirit of aggressive and anarchic modernism. It was the most succinct expression of a widely felt romantic concept of modern artists as the primitives of a new world. The Futurists' ambition to engage in all artistic media and their pioneering activities in free-form typography, a primitive *musique-concrète*, and a wide range of demonstrations, performances, and happenings, were all taken up by the Dada movement and absorbed into the mainstream of modern art.

NICHOLAS WADLEY

Bibliography. Fry, E. *Cubism*, London (1966). Golding, J. *Cubism: a History and Analysis 1907–14*, London (1968). Martin, M. *Futurist Art and Theory 1909–15*, London (1968). Rosenblum, R. *Cubism and 20th Century Art*, New York (1968). Taylor, J.C. *Futurism*, New York (1961). Wadley, N. *Cubism*, London (1972).

47

ABSTRACT ART

Improvisation 13 by Kandinsky; oil on canvas; 120×140cm (47×55in); 1910. Neue Pinakothek, Munich (see page 864)

ABSTRACT Art is the generally accepted term for certain works of 20th-century painting and sculpture which have no representational or symbolic function and yet are not simply pattern making. The adjective "abstract" is not altogether appropriate. but nor are such alternatives as "nonobjective", "nonrepresentational", and "concrete". Abstract art is not an artistic style as such, and within this general heading more explicit categories, Neo-Plasticism and Abstract Expressionism, for example, have been defined in stylistic terms.

The first completely Abstract paintings appeared in Paris and Munich in 1912, and within a year or two comparable work was being produced in Moscow, Milan, New York, London, and elsewhere. Much of this pioneering Abstract painting was experimental in character, representing a short-lived phase in the careers of such painters as Larionoff, Léger, Delaunay, Picabia, Marc, Balla, and Wyndham Lewis. For others, however, Abstract painting was a total commitment, and here four major artists must be named: the Dutchman, Piet Mondrian, working in Paris and in Holland, the Russian, Wassily Kandinsky, working in Munich, another Russian, Kasimir Malevich, working in Moscow, and the Czech, Frank Kupka, working in Paris. None of these four artists was young when they painted their first Abstract pictures; all had passed through a long period of developing their ideas in relation to the pictorial innovations of the time. Kandinsky, in his theoretical text of 1910, *Concerning the Sprititual in Art*, discerned two main ways to abstraction: the painterly way of the Impressionists and Post-Impressionists which led to Fauvism and Cubism, and the route of the Symbolist painters which led to a more religious art of "inner necessity", which, for Kandinsky, was the essential quality that made Abstract art meaningful.

It is certainly true that the general tendency in late-19th-century art can be described as an increasing abstraction of the means of painting. Impressionism was a late phase of realism, in which the artist's aim remained an objective rendering of the thing seen. But the greatest of the Impressionists, Monet and Cézanne, were equally aware of the artist's role as a picture-maker; slowly the emphasis shifted to a concern with the very nature of perception, and the problem of how those "little sensations before nature" (in Cézanne's words) can be rendered in terms of paint on canvas (*see* Impressionism). Both Monet and Cézanne were, in different ways, obsessed with the structural nature of picture-making, and the magic and mystery of creating space on a flat surface. In their hands, the whole development of painting seems to turn inwards, with momentous consequences for the 20th century.

The new generation of painters at work in Paris in the 1880s took these ideas further. Here the leaders were Seurat and Gauguin, both of whom can be seen as important precursors of Abstract art. Seurat analyzed the art of painting into its component parts—line, color, tone, composition—believing that within each division emotional moods could be expressed by formal means alone. For Seurat, descending lines, dark tones, cool colors suggested sadness and despair, whereas ascending lines, light tones, and warm colors gave a feeling of gaiety and excitement. It was widely considered that particular feelings could be associated with particular colors; it was certainly expected then that with further research this equivalence could be put on a proper scientific footing.

Gauguin, perhaps more daring and imaginative than Seurat, began in 1888 to use colors in an abstract way, advising his friends to paint a field, for example, not the way it looked, but the way they felt. His friend and associate, Vincent van Gogh, also accepted liberated color in his paintings: he remained firmly attached to a linear depiction of the object he was painting—be it landscape, still-life, or figure—but felt free to choose whatever colors seemed appropriate. The lessons of Seurat, Gauguin, and Van Gogh were perhaps too far-reaching for their younger contemporaries, though one of them, Maurice Denis, was prepared in 1890 to say: "Remember that a picture—before being a battle horse, a nude, or some anecdote—is essentially a flat surface covered with colours arranged in a certain order". It was, however, not until 15 years later, at the Salon d'Automne of 1905, that Matisse and his friends produced the restatement of these post-impressionist ideas that we know as Fauvism (*see* Fauvism and Expressionism).

Fauvism was primarily about color; the movement that followed, Cubism, was more concerned with the creation of a new kind of pictorial space, in the pursuit of which respect for appearances was slowly abandoned. A search for the permanent qualities of things led Picasso and Braque to pass from a perceptual to a conceptual vision. Pictures were constructed out of the very simple forms of very simple objects. The first marks made on the canvas were like signs that would slowly come together to represent an object: it was not an inventory of the world of appearances that the painter was presenting, but things as they exist in the mind—in Platonic terms, not the shadows in the cave but the thing itself (*see* Cubism and Futurism).

In this belief in a transcendental reality, the Cubists had something in common with the artists who represent Kandinsky's other way to abstraction—the Symbolists. Successive generations of painters in France and England had cast doubt on the need for painting to be enslaved to the pursuit of appearances, and had preferred instead to paint an imagined world. In many cases they offered this as an alternative to the materialism of the time. D.G. Rossetti and Edward Burne-Jones in England, Puvis de Chavannes, Gustave Moreau, and Odilon Redon in France had all by the 1880s made it clear that art could concern itself with the dream and the vision. Inevitably such painting presumed to appeal to some spiritual reality, considering itself superior to any art based on the pursuit of appearances alone (*see* Symbolism and Art Nouveau).

There was, furthermore, a certain widespread feeling that the values of Western society were hollow, that scientific progress was an illusion, and that the whole capitalist system which had flourished since the industrial revolution was essentially self-destructive, despite the enormous wealth and prosperity that had been created. Europeans were prepared to look outside their own society and its historical sources for inspiration in thought and art. Far from being dismissed as inherently inferior to Christianity, Eastern religions were now studied for what seemed to be their superior wisdom, and such pan-religious faiths as Theosophy became immensely attractive to thinking men. The art of the East and, more dramatically, that of black Africa and of Polynesia, seemed to have those qualities of strength and vitality that Western artists were on the point of losing. Gauguin's flight to Tahiti, and his recreation in his own paintings of a lost and paradisiacal society, exemplifies in an extreme form this loss of confidence in Western values. Art simultaneously seemed to become both less important and more important: less important because of its peripheral, elitist nature, of no direct consequence to the masses, but more important because with the decline of religion and the loss of faith in material progress art alone could aspire to contain a message for the future.

This then is the artistic and philosophic climate out of which Abstract art emerged. The four pioneers, and their associates, were all touched by these ideas, and in many cases responded directly to them. Making a viable Abstract art was seen as a heroic, even promethean activity, and immense claims were made for its implications. In the case of Mondrian they were perhaps justified, because the kind of Abstract art he produced had greater possibilities of development than that of his fellow pioneers: its influence on architecture, design, and the applied arts in general is incontrovertible.

Nevertheless, in some respects the primacy in the conception of an Abstract art must go to Wassily Kandinsky (1866–1944). He remembered seeing one of Monet's *Haystack* paintings in Moscow in the late 1890s, and, as he later wrote "deep inside me there was born the first faint doubt as to the importance of an 'object' as the necessary element in painting". It was, however, not until *c*1910 that Kandinsky's own logical development as a painter brought him to the verge of the object-less picture. He had left Russia, settling in Munich, but made long study visits to Italy, and to France where he saw and was profoundly impressed by Matisse's work at the so-called Fauve Salon of 1905. His own painting at this time was for the most part expressionist landscape, with simplified and

Landscape with Houses by Kandinsky; oil on canvas; 70×97cm (28×38in); 1909. Kunstmuseum, Düsseldorf

Yellow-Red-Blue by Kandinsky

Yellow-Red-Blue (1925; Musée National d'Art Moderne, Paris) is a large painting (4 ft 2 in by 6 ft 6¾ in, 1.27 m by 2 m) intended by the artist as a major statement. (His second book, an analysis of forms and compositional methods and their inner meaning, was published as a Bauhaus book the following year: *Point and Line to Plane*.) It is an Abstract painting. Its geometrical style, a more controlled and precise version of the free style Kandinsky had used before his return to Moscow in 1914, is typical of his work in the 1920s and can be associated with the style and aspirations of Bauhaus productions of the same period. Its title, listing the three primaries which appear in the painting accompanied by many other colors, is actually less suggestive than Kandinsky's titles often are, and again has a Bauhaus ring about it.

Everything in the painting floats: colored shapes and black signs hover in front of a luminous space. Some shapes are transparent and relate ambiguously to each other; others suggest a clear spatial sequence, especially on the left. The left group of forms is assertive, with sharp silhouettes and accents, and luminous; the right group is softer, made up of more and suaver colors and less clear forms ranging from vague veils of pink and purple to a large blue circle, all set off by the little checkerboard forms that seem to be in

motion. Generally the background is a soft yellow, but blue appears in the background on the left whereas on the right that color belongs to the circle. We sense a formal dialogue between left and right, echoed in a counterchange in the disposition and function of colors. A cloudy margin of purple adds to the sense of lightness and space. Something akin to an occluded sun at the top, left of center, shines mysteriously on both groups from, perhaps, further back.

During the years 1910–14 Kandinsky painted pictures, conventionally called Abstract, that incorporated recognizable if much simplified motifs from his previous work, combined with more purely instinctive nonrepresentational forms. Both sorts of motif would carry their sensory appeal and associational values (for example, red suggests warmth and strength) but insofar as we are able to recognize in Kandinsky's summary notations the images of horse and rider or mountain-top church or boat with rowers, we are additionally affected by the meaning such references have for us. During 1914–21 Kandinky began to use clearer forms, more consciously predetermined and tested for the response they evoke, and it was as a painter of geometrical Abstract paintings that he returned to Germany at the end of 1921. We need not assume that this development removed from his idiom all references to

specific things. The curved line on the right of *Yellow-Red-Blue*, for example, may echo the "whiplash" line favored by some *Jugendstil* designers around 1900; more specifically, it recalls the wavy line Kandinsky had come to use as a sign for horse and rider and may thus have been charged with special meaning for him in the 1920s. Yet a preparatory drawing for the painting shows a pair of similar waves, and here they suggest water to support a geometrically summarized sailing boat.

It seems that Kandinsky never drew a firm and final line between full abstraction and figuration, but was more concerned to follow whatever pictorial suggestions his subconscious and his working process produced. Indeed, he stated repeatedly that the intensely representational art of primitives and Abstract art of the sort he proposed were alternative paths towards spiritual, as opposed to material, expression. Only realism could be defined as "the antithesis of art".

In his earlier book, *Concerning the Spiritual in Art*, published in December 1911, he had quoted Delacroix to this effect, from the French painter's *Journal* entry for 22 February 1860. In 1862, a year before his death, Delacroix painted a small picture, *Hercules and Alcestis* (The Phillips Collection, Washington, D.C.), illustrating one of the labors of Hercules in profoundly poetic

Above, right: *Yellow-Red-Blue* by Wassily Kandinsky; oil on canvas; 127×200cm (50×79in); 1925. Musée National d'Art Moderne, Paris

◄ *Hercules and Alcestis* by Delacroix; 46×50cm (18×20in); 1862. The Phillips Collection, Washington, D.C.

► A detail from *Yellow-Red-Blue* by Kandinsky showing part of the right-hand group of forms

terms. His pictorial stage shows, on the left, attendants making a sacrifice on an altar, on the extreme right the mouth of Hades marked by fire, an infernal being, and serpents (which recall an earlier event in the Alcestis story), and center right, Hercules bringing Alcestis back to her grateful husband, Admetus. Delacroix has chosen the satisfying culmination of a complex narrative. Today even "educated" people looking at this painting are not likely to know the story, and in this sense it will be obscure to them, but they will respond to the longing and melancholic mood expressed by Delacroix's figures and staging, to the colors, the light and shadow, and to the soft textures. That response we can all make, and Kandinsky asks that we should make it to his painting. This, larger than the Delacroix and lighter in tone and arrangement, is remarkably similar to the Delacroix in its major dispositions. Kandinsky would claim that the Delacroix, though a most moving contribution to the continuing life of antique themes in art, makes divisive demands of the spectator, whereas his own painting, communicating through responses to form and color innate in everyone, can address itself directly to all mankind. He did not quote, but would support, another sentence from that entry in Delacroix's *Journal*: "For what is the supreme purpose of every type of art, if it is not effect?"

NORBERT LYNTON

distorted forms and liberated color. It was such a picture as the *Landscape with Houses* of 1909 (Kunstmuseum, Düsseldorf) that gave Kandinsky the necessary revelation. He tells us what happened:

> I was returning, deep in thought, from my sketching, when on opening the studio door I was suddenly confronted with a painting of unbelievable incandescent beauty. I stopped, bewildered, gazing at it. The picture had no subject, it depicted no recognizable object but was entirely composed of patches of bright color. I approached closer, and then I recognized the painting for what it really was—one of my own works, placed on its side on the easel ...
>
> One thing was now clear to me: the depiction of objects, of the objective world, had no place in my own paintings, and was indeed actually damaging to them.

The importance of such a chance event should not be exaggerated. In any case, Kandinsky's problem was how to create the object-less picture in such a way that it could be seen as something more than decoration or pattern. He decided to pursue a two-fold course: to carry on the abstracting process in his painting so that slowly all recognizable forms would disappear, and at the same time to provide a philosophical justification for such art.

The latter came first. Kandinsky wrote in the summer of 1910 at Murnau, near Munich, a long essay which he called *Über das Geistige in der Kunst (Concerning the Spiritual in Art)*. Kandinsky was no philosopher, his argument was emotional rather than rational. He was forced to postulate an artistic driving force of "inner necessity" to justify his artistic experiments, always implying that if the artist can "go beyond" the reality of external appearances he will somehow be able "to touch the beholder's soul". He was very interested in the physical and psychological effects of color—one of the painter's means of making the required direct contact.

In his paintings of 1910–14 Kandinsky moves progressively away from representation. *With the Black Arch* of 1912 (Musée National d'Art Moderne, Paris) represents the midway position. If we know that the artist has been painting pictures of armed knights on horseback locked in combat, we can immediately recognize the source of certain configurations of lines and colors. Indeed, the trained eye can distinguish the starting point of every single line and patch of color in the picture. What Kandinsky has done, however, is to use this as raw material in the development of his own pictorial language. Here this has reached the stage where he can see the picture as the meeting of three colored masses, "like the thunderous collision of worlds". Thus his art takes on a cosmic quality, reflected in the quasi-atomistic organization of the composition, and in the taste for apocalyptic subjects, prophetic of the impending 1914 war and the destruction it involved.

Kandinsky was also much concerned with a musical analogy. There is a long prehistory here: artists have frequently compared painting with music, making the obvious point that music has, for the most part, no representational function, but

that this does not mean it lacks meaning, only that it conveys a different sort of meaning. Why should painting not be a kind of visual music, the argument proceeds, rather than the visual poetry of, for example, Romantic art? Already in the 1870s Whistler had called the portrait of his mother an *Arrangement in Grey and Black*, arguing that its formal qualities made the picture a masterpiece, not the fact that it portrayed his mother. Kandinsky followed this example of using musical nomenclature by calling his major paintings "Compositions", and his less ambitious works "Improvisations" and "Impressions".

By 1914 Kandinsky had evolved a language of regular forms—circles, wedges, triangles—which he used in his pictorial compositions. Color was free, with an expressive power of its own; line had been liberated from its traditional role as contour, and was equally free; the horizon line had long since been destroyed, so that pictorial space was directly related to the surface of the picture. His paintings were increasing in size and scale, yet it might be argued that Kandinsky was still not absolutely sure about the self-sufficiency of the Abstract painting. The four Campbell panels of 1914 are each given the title of a season, as if some extra-pictorial reference was still required to explain that they were not simply decoration.

At this point the logical development of Kandinsky's art was interrupted by the outbreak of war. He left Germany, and after spending some time in Switzerland and Sweden returned in due course to Russia. After the 1917 Bolshevik Revolution, Kandinsky was for a time in a position of considerable authority, reorganizing the artistic life of the country. He had little time for painting, and when he started again it was under the influence of such younger Abstract artists as Malevich. The lyrical, soft, free-flowing forms of his prewar paintings were now hardened and geometricized. In 1921 Kandinsky left Russia forever to return to Germany.

The artistic career of Piet Mondrian (1872–1944) parallels Kandinsky's very closely, though the Abstract art that emerges is in many respects the antithesis of Kandinsky's painting—more intellectual than emotional, more geometric than organic, more classical than romantic. It is the contrast between the simplicity of the square and that of the amoeba.

Mondrian was another slow developer. He began as a naturalist painter, then flirted with Symbolism—a strong force in Dutch and Belgian art. In 1909 he passed through a spiritual crisis, and for a time he was, like Kandinsky, deeply impressed by theosophical ideas, and by the then leader of the German theosophical group, Rudolf Steiner. Mondrian was familiar with theosophical literature, with its illustrations of spiritual aura as seen by clairvoyants and of abstract pictorial symbols offered as aids to meditation. He could see that painting might have a significant role to play; his ambitious triptych, *Evolution* (1911; Haags Gemeentemuseum, The Hague) was probably conceived as a theosophical altarpiece. A figure is depicted in a state of spiritual illumination: the triadic structure, the yellow and blue coloring, the stars and passion flowers all remind us of Mondrian's close links with Symbol-

Autumn, Panel II of the four Campbell panels by Kandinsky; oil on canvas; 160×121cm (63×48in); 1914. Solomon R. Guggenheim Museum, New York

ism. The painter suggests an explanation for the strange and cryptic title in a 1914 diary entry:

> Two roads lead to the spiritual: the road of doctrinal teaching, of direct exercise [meditation, etc] and the slow but certain road of evolution. One sees in art the slow growth of spirituality, of which the artists themselves are unconscious. To approach the spiritual in art.

Thus, apparently in complete independence of Kandinsky, Mondrian too is emphasizing the need for a spiritual basis in art, associating the idea with the increasing abstraction of his own work.

The *Evolution* triptych was a dead end for Mondrian: an attempt to find the new spiritual art by a leap forward, whereas what was needed was a slow and steady progression. He had realized that he must take into account the innovations of modern painting; that the *language* of art must be completely renewed if it was to carry the message he wanted it to convey. So Mondrian went back to the works of Monet and Cézanne, and concentrated on a restricted range of subjects—a church facade, a tree, a landscape of sand dunes—exactly as Monet had done, subjecting them to the kind of searching pictorial analysis that he observed in Cézanne.

Mondrian realized that other painters, some younger than himself, were working from similar starting points; early in 1912 he left his native Holland to move to Paris, still without

any doubt the center of the artistic world. Within months he had established himself in the French capital, and had achieved a remarkably perceptive understanding of the very latest developments in painting. He realized in particular that Cubism had reached a crucial stage: Braque and Picasso had taken the analytical process to the point where the ostensible subject of the picture—a nude girl, a man with a guitar or whatever—was in danger of disappearing into the geometricized structure of the painting itself, a sort of scaffolding which was totally dominating the subject on which it was superimposed.

Neither Picasso nor Braque was willing to lose contact with the subject in their paintings, however minimal its importance had become. For them an Abstract art was simply decoration, without any deeper meaning, and to this position both Cubist painters adhered for the remainder of their long careers. They chose in 1912 to forge a new link with external reality, by introducing objects directly into their paintings—sticking a piece of newspaper on to the canvas rather than painting it, using the simulated textures of house decorators' papers (oil cloth, chaircaning, and the like) to represent at one remove the thing depicted. Thus were the *papier collé* and, by further extension, the collage and the ready-made, invented.

Some of the contemporaries of Braque and Picasso persisted in their attempt at taking Analytical Cubism up to and beyond the hermetic stage. Mondrian actually chose scaffolding on a Parisian wall as a motif, as well as continuing to paint church facades where the regular pattern of doors and windows imposed an architectural structure on his compositions. Yet all his paintings of 1912–14 are abstracted and not Abstract pictures, in the same way that Kandinsky's are: once again, if we know the artist's work, we can trace back the figurative origin of every form, however completely abstract it may appear at first sight.

Mondrian was not the only painter in Paris in 1912 whose work verged on complete abstraction. Robert Delaunay (1885–1941) sought to introduce color into Cubism, with the incitement (and perhaps at the prompting) of a friend, the poet and critic Guillaume Apollinaire (1880–1918). For several years Delaunay had been painting pictures of the Eiffel Tower seen across the rooftops of Paris from a balcony window. By 1912 the window dominated the composition, and colors were applied and divided according to the precepts of the early-19th-century color theorist, Eugène Chevreul. Delaunay used Chevreul's expression "simultaneous contrasts" to describe his own paintings in which he broke up and reassembled light itself, just as Braque and Picasso had treated the figure or the still-life object. It was perhaps inevitable that Delaunay should choose the source of all light, the sun, and its reflected counterpart, the moon, as appropriate subjects for his work, and the *First Disk* of 1912 (private collection) might be considered as a pioneer Abstract painting, except for the element of cosmic symbolism certainly present. In any case, Delaunay does not appear to have considered the window and disk paintings as completed work suitable for exhibition in

The Cardiff Team by Delaunay; oil on canvas;
196×132cm (77×52in); 1913. Van Abbemuseum, Eindhoven

Paris, and he continued to plan more complex pictures such as *The Cardiff Team* (1913; Van Abbemuseum, Eindhoven) while working on the disks.

This same consciously experimental status was given to a comparable series of paintings by Delaunay's great friend, Fernand Léger (1881–1955), the *Contrastes de Formes* of 1913 (one example in the Philadelphia Museum of Art). Although the forms themselves derive from the highly abstracted figures and landscape features of Léger's slightly earlier Cubist-influenced work, these paintings are very close to complete abstraction. But this was not in fact Léger's aim in producing them; he seems to have regarded Abstract art as something suitable for large-scale mural decoration, but essentially inferior to the subject picture. This distinction, established in 1913, persists in Léger's work in the 1920s.

Other painters in Delaunay's circle were experimenting with abstraction in 1912–13. The most important were Kupka and Picabia, and it is of these three artists that Apol-

linaire first used the term Orphism (or Orphic Cubism). Frank Kupka's work will be discussed shortly; the Abstract period of Francis Picabia (1879–1953) lasted for only a few months in 1912–13 and is, statistically, another late Cubist derivation, as canvases such as *Udnie* of 1913 (Musée National d'Art Moderne, Paris) make plain. Picabia could not see his way forward to a totally Abstract art, and began instead to experiment with collages and drawings of fantastic machines, which, like the contemporary work of Marcel Duchamp, contributed to the genesis of Dada.

Delaunay's closest associate in these years was his wife, the Ukrainian-born Sonia Terk (1885–1980), whom he married in 1910. She was perhaps more committed to Abstract art in 1912 than her husband, calling her canvases of the period "simultaneous rhythms", and producing book illustrations and cover designs of uncompromising abstraction. With the outbreak of war in 1914, however, the Delaunays fled to neutral Portugal, and both returned to figurative painting. It was not until 1930 that Robert Delaunay painted Abstract pictures again.

Two young American painters working in Paris were inspired by Delaunay's Orphism of 1912 to create their own

Synchromy to Light by Morgan Russell; oil on canvas;
33×24cm (13×9in); 1913. Los Angeles County Museum of Art,
Los Angeles

Udnie by Picabia; oil on canvas; 300×300cm (118×118in); 1913. Musée National d'Art Moderne, Paris

movement: Synchromism. They were Morgan Russell (1886–1953) and Stanton Macdonald-Wright (1890–1973). Their paintings of 1913 were, strictly speaking, abstracted rather than Abstract, except for the enormous *Synchromy in Deep Blue Violet* (Los Angeles County Museum of Art, Los Angeles) which Russell showed at the Paris Salon des Indépendants in March 1914. Macdonald-Wright was slower in reaching complete abstraction, with his Synchromies of 1915–18. He returned to the United States in 1916, and thus his are the earliest Abstract paintings executed in America. The reception both painters received in New York in 1916 was discouraging, however, and shortly afterwards they abandoned abstraction altogether, returning only much later in their careers when their work was of comparatively little con-

sequence. A third American in Paris, Patrick Henry Bruce (1880–1937), was a member of Delaunay's Orphist group in 1913–14; he too lost heart after a few years and stopped exhibiting his work, destroying much of it in a fit of depression in 1933.

All the Paris-based Abstract artists found that, after the euphoric excitement of 1912–14, they were working in an environment profoundly unsympathetic to Abstract art. Nobody knew this better than Frank Kupka (1871–1958). Czech-born, Kupka's early work is Symbolist in character: of particular interest are the paintings and drawings that show the influence of Odilon Redon. *The First Steps* of 1909 (Museum of Modern Art, New York) has sometimes been called the first Abstract painting, but it is a picture about the

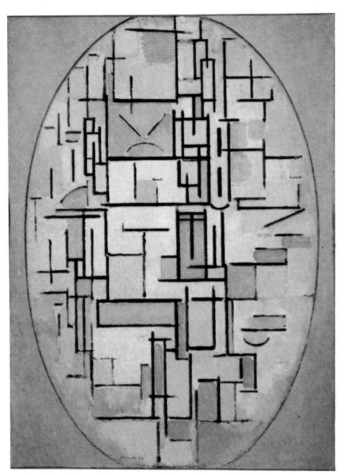

Color Planes in Oval by Piet Mondrian; oil on canvas;
107×79cm (42×31in); c1914. Museum of Modern Art, New York

origins of the universe, and is thus better described as cosmic symbolism. Another early work, *Girl with a Ball* of 1908 (Museum of Modern Art, New York), was the source of a long series of drawings and paintings in which Kupka progressively abstracted the colors and forms until he reached the two large pictures *Amorpha, Warm Chromatics* (private collection) and *Amorpha, Fugue for Two Colors* (National Gallery, Prague) which he showed at the Paris Salon d'Automne in 1912. They are perhaps the first Abstract paintings to be publicly exhibited anywhere. Kupka was simultaneously developing other series of pictures: a painting of a girl turning against the light exhibited earlier in 1912 is the prototype for the *Vertical Planes* pictures; a moonlit scene develops into the Abstract *Nocturne* of 1912 (private collection).

Musical analogies were important for Kupka, and, as we have seen, played an important role in providing a justification for the assumed pure inventions of Abstract art. He had a taste for musical titles—*Amorpha, Fugue for Two Colors, Solo of a Brown Line* (both National Gallery, Prague), for example. Another group of Kupka's paintings have such titles as *Creation, Cosmic Spring* (both National Gallery, Prague), and *A Tale of Pistils and Stamens* (National Gallery, Prague, and Musée National d'Art Moderne, Paris), and, though

Abstract up to a point, are really a curious kind of organic symbolism. The Symbolist origin of Kupka's abstraction is confirmed by the fact that he, too, like Mondrian and Kandinsky, was interested in Eastern thought and religion; indeed he sought to show the mystical way to abstraction in yet another group of paintings called *Cathedral, The Way of Silence* (or *Sphinxes*; National Gallery, Prague), and *Hindu Temple Motif* (Musée National d'Art Moderne, Paris).

A fair assessment of Kupka's contribution to Abstract art is very difficult to make. Despite the extraordinary imagination which the paintings of 1910–14 display, they seem to have been received with complete incomprehension by the Parisian public, and after 1914 Kupka was forgotten until the very last decade of his long life. During the years of obscurity he continued to work on earlier canvases, sometimes repainting them completely, so that we do not always know for certain what a picture originally looked like.

Repercussions of the new painting of Delaunay and his friends were quickly felt outside Paris, especially in Germany. It is a fact that Delaunay showed the Abstract *Disk* paintings at the Berlin Autumn Salon of 1913, but never in Paris, where he preferred to appear in public as the author of subject pictures. Delaunay's Orphism was of considerable interest to the young German painters of the Munich *Blaue Reiter* (Blue Rider) group. Through their close association with Kandinsky they were prepared to accept an Abstract art, and Delaunay's color experiments stimulated the relatively few abstractions of August Macke (1887–1914) and Franz Marc (1880–1916), quite as much as did the work of Kandinsky. Marc in particular left behind an album of studies for Abstract pictures which make it particularly regrettable that he did not survive the war. The color-square pictures of another Munich Blue Rider painter, Paul Klee (1879–1940), are virtually Abstract works, though Klee always retained a link with nature which makes it impossible to categorize him as an Abstract artist.

Further east, in Russia, a major contribution to the development of Abstract art was taking place, especially in the years after 1914, when general experiment came to an end in the West because of the First World War. Here the important figure is Kasimir Malevich (1878–1935), but two precursors must first be mentioned. One was the Lithuanian composer, Mikolojus Ciurlionis (1875–1911), a contemporary of Scriabin and subject to similar philosophical and mystical influences. Untaught, he turned to painting in 1905, seeking in such works as *Sonata of the Sea* to find a visual parallel for his musical ideas. Ciurlionis died insane in 1911; his paintings remained unexhibited, but it seems probable that Kandinsky and others knew about them and about Ciurlionis' conception of art.

The other Russian pioneer was Michail Larionoff (1881–1964), always closely associated with his wife Natalia Goncharova (1881–1962). Larionoff launched his own modern

Right: a painting in the series *A Tale of Pistils and Stamens*
by Franz Kupka; oil on canvas; 85×73cm (33×29in); 1919.
Musée National d'Art Moderne, Paris

Hindu Temple Motif by Franz Kupka; oil on canvas; 124×122cm (49×48in); 1921–3. Musée National d'Art Moderne, Paris

art movement with the *Rayonist Manifesto*, written in June 1912 and published in Moscow in 1913. Rayonist paintings, characterized by their patterns of diagonal parallel lines, were shown in Paris at Paul Guillaume's gallery early in 1914: how much earlier they were painted is still a matter of dispute, though the dates of 1909 and 1910 suggested by Larionoff for the most Abstract examples are not likely to be correct. After 1914 both Larionoff and Goncharova concentrated on designing sets and costumes for opera and ballet, in particular for Diaghilev's company, and they made no more Abstract paintings.

The dating of Malevich's first Abstract works is also uncertain, as is the exact chronology of his artistic development in the years 1913–18. Malevich's manifesto, *From Cubism to Suprematism*, was published in Moscow in 1915; he was certainly executing Abstract pictures by this date, but nothing had been exhibited. If Suprematism may be said to begin in 1913, it is with Malevich's stage designs for *Victory Over the Sun*, which have a somewhat equivocal status as Abstract art.

Malevich's own earlier paintings show him absorbing the lessons of French Symbolism and Post-Impressionism, of Fauvism and Cubism (especially the work of Picasso and Léger), and of Italian Futurism. By 1912 he was recognized as the leader of a Russian Cubist, proto-Abstract group, whose members included Ivan Puni (1894–1956), Alexander Exter (1882–1949), and Liubov Popova (1889–1924). In the *Woman at a Poster Column* of 1914 (Stedelijk Museum, Amsterdam), Malevich imposes plain, flat rectangles of color on

top of a vestigial Cubist analysis, and it is these rectangles that he isolates and uses on their own in the first Suprematist compositions.

It would nevertheless be wrong to see Malevich's Suprematism as a totally Abstract art. The Symbolist element remains, in two distinct forms. Sometimes the shapes are arranged in such a way that they recall views of buildings from the air (Malevich was deeply impressed by the first aerial photography) or the formation of aeroplanes in flight. At other times Malevich was concerned to emphasize the essentially spiritual nature of his art, as if to demonstrate that he was not just arranging regular shapes in simple compositions. Thus he demanded a transcendental significance for his paintings, as is demonstrated by the culmination of Suprematism, the *White Square on a White Background* (Museum of Modern Art, New York), or more obviously perhaps by the white cross on a white ground.

This stage, reached by Malevich in 1918, meant for him the end of art, and he stopped painting altogether. Other Russian artists who had watched his development but did not share his unorthodox Christian beliefs did not feel bound to follow his example. Alexander Rodchenko (1891–1956) declared his theoretical opposition to Malevich when he showed a *Black Circle on a Black Background* (Staatsgalerie, Stuttgart) in the 1919 Tenth State Exhibition in Moscow at which Malevich showed the *White Square*. Two years later Rodchenko showed three pure colors—three squares of red, yellow, and blue, called *The Last Painting*; this marks the end of nonobjective painting in the USSR. The political atmosphere was now hostile to any form of Abstract art and demanded a more

White Square on a White Background by Malevich; oil on canvas; 79×79cm (31×31in); 1918. Museum of Modern Art, New York

Woman at a Poster Column by Malevich; oil on canvas; 71×64cm (28×25in); 1914. Stedelijk Museum, Amsterdam

useful, practical role from the artist. Rodchenko turned from painting to typography and photomontage, as did another gifted artist of this same generation, Elizier (El) Lissitzky (1890–1941).

Contemporaneously with Malevich's Suprematism, Vladimir Tatlin (1885–1953) was exploring the formal possibilities of the Cubist relief constructions of such objects as guitars that he had seen in Picasso's studio in Paris in 1913. Using metal sheet, rods, and wire as well as wood, he made three-dimensional corner reliefs from 1915 onwards—the earliest Abstract sculptures. Despite his admiration for Malevich, Tatlin opposed his mystical conception of art, and sought a direct social and political role for the new abstraction. His own work developed towards an ideal architecture, exemplified by the projected Monument for the Third International of 1919, a glass and iron tower 1,300 ft (395 m) high. The brothers Antoine Pevsner (1886–1962) and Naum Gabo (1890–1977) also moved from figurative relief construction to

The Sculptures of Brancusi

Constantin Brancusi (1876–1957) was both a Rumanian peasant and a sophisticated intellectual, at the heart of the Parisian avant-garde during the first decades of the 20th century. His formal expression has its roots both in his native environment and in contemporary artistic concerns.

In comparison with Western Europe his early environment was primitive and superstitious. The peasants of his native Carpathian mountains retained a rich folkloric tradition of beliefs, customs, and myths from which Brancusi drew inspiration throughout his life. As he grew older his native belief in the occult evolved, under the influence of Eastern philosophy, into a personal philosophy rich in mysticism.

Working in Paris at a time when artists were seeking inspiration and confirmation in the art of less technically advanced civilizations, the dual nature of Brancusi's experience made his work fundamentally important in the evolution of modern art. For Brancusi himself, the reconciliation of peasant and intellectual milieu was central to his artistic statement; the balance and unity it implied were constant concerns.

During the early years of the 20th century there was a movement within the arts that responded to the insecurity and uncertainty of the external world by turning for inspiration to the internal. Renouncing pure representation, artists created forms which stood as symbols for inner feelings and responses. Because the experience of the artist was common to all men, such primarily individual statements would be of universal relevance. An artistic vocabulary was sought which might embody a sense of security, of permanence, vitality, and unity—all the qualities felt to be lacking in the external world.

In the relationship of man to the unknown, and in his conception of the nature of his existence, the symbol had always played a central role. The symbolic art of early and of primitive societies, living in an essentially hostile and obscure world, helped to establish a degree of equilibrium within man's alienation. Western artists, finding themselves in a society at odds with its self-created environment, and in need of a vocabulary of expressive and symbolic form, found inspiration in the arts of Africa and the East.

The influence of African negro art upon some of Brancusi's fellow artists was fundamental. For the sculptor himself, the relationship is more complex. Unusual among his

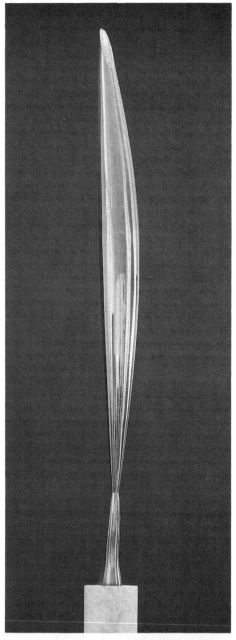

▲ *Gate of the Kiss* by Brancusi; stone; height 527cm (207in); 1937. Tirgu Jiu Public Park, Rumania

Above, right: *Bird in Space* by Brancusi; bronze; height 193cm (76in); 1941. Musée National d'Art Moderne, Paris

◄ *The Kiss* by Brancusi; stone; height 28cm (11in); 1908. Craiova Museum of Art

► *Beginning of the World* by Brancusi; bronze on metal dish; height 30cm (12in); 1924. Musée National d'Art Moderne, Paris

▲ *Endless Column* by Brancusi; iron and steel; height 29.30m (96ft); 1937. Tirgu Jui Public Park, Rumania

▼ *King of Kings* by Brancusi; oak; height 300cm (118in); early 1930s. Solomon R. Guggenheim Museum, New York

contemporaries, he carried an element of the primitive within himself. In the superstitious environment from which he came, the symbol had retained its key role in day-to-day living. *King of Kings* (early 1930s; Solomon R. Guggenheim Museum, New York) undoubtedly bears a strong resemblance to African tribal forms, but equally convincing parallels exist between its component elements and examples of traditional Rumanian wood carving. The repeated units of the motif of the *Endless Column* (1937; Tirgu Jiu Public Park, Rumania), initially thought to be an invention of Brancusi, have since been convincingly compared to carved poles from his native region. In his work, elements from Rumanian folk art were transformed into vehicles of artistic innovation.

As a heavily wooded country, Rumania's primary material for construction, decoration, and household articles was wood. While the raw material was often used in a frank and simple manner, Rumanian craftsmen were also capable of producing highly intricate and decorative designs. Brancusi believed that only the Rumanian peasant and the African tribes, which had escaped the influence of Mediterranean civilization, had preserved the art of wood carving. The role of African art in Brancusi's development was essentially that of memory trigger. By focusing attention upon the symbolic potential of form, tribal art served to confirm Brancusi's own native tradition. It also reinforced the artist's personal conviction that by working directly upon his material he could endow the final form with a profound expressive quality, or presence. In abandoning the use of scale models and technical assistants, Brancusi made sculpture once more an art of direct statement, thereby profoundly affecting the course of its development.

Brancusi's ideals of simplicity, purity, vitality, and harmony were gradually realized in the series of formal themes he explored. With their inspirational source in the natural world, the forms he chose were often symbolic of the life forces. The quality of semi-pagan, quasi-religious mystery they possess was clearly apprehended and stressed by Brancusi himself. Influenced by Buddhist and Hindu philosophy, his understanding of existence was transcendental. His simplification of form—no mere exercise in plastic design—gave expression to his conception of the metaphysical foundation of life. His desire was to express ultimate reality in essential form—the spiritual being implied in the almost totemic presence of his work.

By a process of distillation and abstraction, Brancusi moved from descriptive to symbolic object. *Beginning of the World* (1924; Musée National d'Art Moderne, Paris) is a mature statement within a series of forms which began as a representational head, and moved progressively towards the "egg" of the present work. The philosophical significance of the form, symbolic or original unity, is reflected in the title. Brancusi relies in part upon the association of an egg with life in an unborn state to reinforce the symbolism.

Throughout his life Brancusi sought to attain in his work something of the harmony and balance implicit in the concept of primal oneness. He expressed the need to create unity from the duality of man's physical and spiritual condition in the *Kiss* series, first explored 1907–8. Locked in embrace, the lovers are a monolithic form. As the series evolves, they merge and become a single being with a central unifying eye. They reach their ultimate expression in the *Gate of the Kiss* (1937; Tirgu Jiu Public Park, Rumania): set in a garden of remembrance, they symbolize the unification inherent in death.

For Brancusi, reality was not the external appearance of things, but rather their essence, which could not be expressed by imitating outward appearance. The essence of an object consists of what remains invariable in all the variants of that object, and is to be discovered by subtraction. As Brancusi eliminated dispensable and individual detail, so the permanent, essential character of his subject emerged and its ultimate form was achieved. In his *Bird in Space* sculptures, he sought to express the essence of flight in the ascending form. In their feather or flame-like shape they contain also the essential aspects of the original *Maiastra* or Firebird theme from which they evolved. Symbolic of resurrection, the Rumanian *Maiastra* legend inspired Brancusi's exploration of the potential of the bird form to express a spiritual concept. As the form evolves through the *Maiastra, Golden Bird*, and *Bird in Space* series, so the bird becomes integrated and streamlined. The progression towards spiritual awareness, and the ultimate attainment of unity, is symbolized in physical form.

Bird in Space exemplifies Brancusi's struggle with the limitations of mass and weight. He pushes his material almost to the limit of its structural capacity and exploits the ability of a highly reflective bronze surface to incorporate light and surrounding movement. He seeks to create a form as insubstantial as the concept it embodies.

LYNNE MITCHELL

Further reading. Elsen, A.E. *Origins of Modern Sculpture: Pioneers and Premises*, London (1974). Geist, S. *Brancusi: the Kiss*, New York (1978). Geist, S. *Brancusi, a Study of the Sculpture*, London (1968). Spear, A.T. *Brancusi's Birds*, New York (1969). Tucker, W. *The Language of Sculpture*, London (1974).

Suprematist Composition by Alexander Rodchenko; lino cut;
17×11cm (7×4in); 1919. Staatsgalerie, Stuttgart

Tatlin's model for a projected Monument for the Third International;
1919; a photograph in the Modern Museum
(National Museum), Stockholm

a completely Abstract art which they justified in the Realist
Manifesto published in Moscow in 1920. They demanded an
art based on space and time, and the result was the invention
of what has been called "Constructivism", an abstract three-
dimensional art which now has an international history of its
own. Gabo made the first Abstract Kinetic construction in
1920, a vertically mounted thin steel blade, driven by a motor,
which describes a simple form in space.

Both Pevsner and Gabo left Russia in 1922, the year in
which all experiment in Soviet art was suppressed in favor of
socialist realism. Pevsner settled in Paris in 1923, but Gabo
went first to Berlin, moving to Paris in 1932, on to England in
1936, and finally to the United States in 1946. During the
Berlin years he was closely associated with Lissitzky and the
Hungarian Laszlo Moholy-Nagy (1895–1946) in spreading
Constructivist ideas in Germany. These were particularly influential in the Bauhaus, the design school established by
Walter Gropius at Weimar in 1919 which moved to new

buildings at Dessau in 1925.

Another stream of Abstract art had already helped to shape
Bauhaus thinking: that associated with the Dutch movement
De Stijl. To appreciate the genesis of De Stijl we must retrace
our steps a little. When Mondrian returned to Holland from
Paris in 1914 he found himself working in isolation, and at
one moment in 1916 was almost ready to abandon Abstract
art. His discovery of the work of the Dutch mathematician
and philosopher, M.H.J. Schoenmaekers, led him to change
his mind however, because Schoenmaekers provided a spiritual justification for the kind of art Mondrian was on the
point of inventing. Using visual metaphors to express religious
ideas, Schoenmaekers propounded a system of Positive Mysticism, or Plastic Mathematics. This depends on the resolution
of fundamental contradictions—active and passive, male and
female, space and time, darkness and light—in the geometrical
form of a meeting of horizontal and vertical. These in turn
were related to cosmic forces—the vertical to rays from the

sun, and the horizontal to the earth's constant movement around the sun. The three primary colors were also given cosmic meaning: yellow is the sun's light, blue the infinite expanse of space, red the unifying color.

These ideas gave Mondrian something none of the other pioneer Abstract artists had been able to discover: a way of investing painting with a spiritual significance but without external reference. There is a symbolic meaning in the Abstract work itself which makes it more than decoration and pattern, because the spiritual is best expressed in such pure plastic terms as the primary colors, and the contrast of dark and light, of vertical and horizontal. It took Mondrian a few years before he had worked out a grammar for the new Abstract art, declared triumphantly in such pictures as the *Composition with Red, Yellow, and Blue* of 1921 (Haags Gemeentemuseum, The Hague). For the rest of his life Mondrian consistently developed the language of Neo-Plasticism, as he called it, working in Paris from 1919 to 1938, then in London until 1940, when he moved to New York where he died. In each of the three cities Mondrian's example was a talismanic one: without achieving much public success, he nevertheless had a profound effect on practicing artists who spread his ideas, often transforming them in the process.

Mondrian's first significant collaborator, in Holland during the 1914–18 war, was Theo van Doesburg (1883–1931). In October 1917 they planned and launched the review *De Stijl*. Van Doesburg was quick to see that the new Abstract art of Mondrian embodied principles that could be applied beyond painting; he used his magazine *De Stijl* as a mouthpiece and, with the help of collaborators, revolutionary theories of architecture and of every field of design were propagated. Van Doesburg's personal impact on the development of the Bauhaus is of particular importance: his activities in Weimar in 1920–1 mark a turning point that the influence of Russian Constructivism confirmed.

The expansion of Abstract art was greatly hindered by the 1914–18 war. In Paris and Munich abstraction was effectively crushed: only in neutral Holland and in revolutionary Russia could a natural development continue. Countries that came late to Abstract art—like Britain and Italy—witnessed only a brief flowering which quickly died out. In London Percy Wyndham Lewis (1882–1957) and his Vorticist associates drew and painted Abstract compositions, some of which were reproduced in the pages of their magazine, *Blast* (1914 and 1915). In Rome Giacomo Balla (1874–1958) had painted a series of "iridescent interpenetrations" in 1912–13, and in March 1915 declared himself a Futurist Abstractionist in his manifesto, *The Futurist Reconstruction of the Universe*. Planning transparent structure as symbols of a new world, Balla expressed the utopian idealism that is never far below the surface in Mondrian's writings. His own work, *Mercury Passing the Sun* of 1914 (Gianni Matteoli Collection, Milan), for example, is often not so much Abstract as cosmic symbolism.

By 1918 the theoretical and practical basis of Abstract art was complete, but it took another 40 years before Abstract art

began to win public acceptance. Between the wars the ideas were kept alive only by the determined conviction of isolated pioneers, like Mondrian in Paris and Kandinsky, who taught at the Bauhaus from 1922 until 1933, when Hitler prohibited Abstract art, and Kandinsky too moved to Paris. Small groups of younger Abstract artists formed themselves in Paris under such titles as *Cercle et Carré* ("Circle and Square", 1930) and *Abstraction-Création* (1932–34). A prominent member of both groups was the Strasbourg-born sculptor, Jean (or Hans) Arp (1887–1966), who c1930 began to make three-dimensional sculptures which he called "human concretions". Arp had experimented with Abstract collages in Switzerland during the 1914–18 war, often in collaboration with Sophie Taeuber (1889–1943); he was equally active in Surrealist circles and denied that his sculptures were Abstract. In much

Composition with Red, Yellow, and Blue by Mondrian; oil on canvas; 80×50cm (31×20in); 1921. Haags Gemeentemuseum, The Hague

the same way the work of Constantin Brancusi (1876–1957) is, strictly speaking, never Abstract, though his search for the essential form underlying appearances results in such pure shapes as *The New Born* of 1915 (Philadelphia Museum of Art). There are obvious parallels between Brancusi's artistic development and that of Mondrian, for example, but despite the metaphorical overtones Brancusi's *The New Born* remains a severely abstracted head and not Abstract art. Apart from Gabo's Constructivism, the earliest true Abstract sculptures would seem to be the quasi-architectural compositions of the Belgian Georges Vantongerloo (1886–1965) and a group of sculptures made between 1932 and 1940 by Barbara Hepworth (1903–1975) in which no figure references are apparent.

The series of white reliefs by Hepworth's husband Ben Nicholson (1894–1982), begun in 1933, marked a new beginning for Abstract painting in England. With the help of Gabo and the architect Leslie Martin, Nicholson published a book, *Circle* (1937), which served as an international survey of Constructive art, stressing the interrelationship between Abstract art and architecture. Once again, however, the natural progress of a regrouped Abstract movement in France and England was restricted by the outbreak of war, and in 1939 much activity in Europe simply came to a stop.

The final, and ultimately triumphant, stage in the development of Abstract art was centered on New York in the 1940s. Stimulated by the presence in the city of many European exiles, young American painters seized an opportunity to create a recognizably new kind of art for which the labels Abstract Expressionism and Action Painting were invented (*see* Modern American Art).

In the second half of the 20th century the existence of Abstract art is accepted: its viability is no longer disputed and dismissed as it was in the years from 1910 to 1960. It is seen to represent a new dimension in art, comparable with the invention of portraiture and landscape painting in earlier periods. Now that Abstract art manifestly exists as something more than just pattern or decoration, artists no longer feel obliged to claim a spiritual justification for their work. Nor is there any longer the feeling that to paint an Abstract picture is a sort of conversion, and that to paint anything else subsequently is a renegade step. An artist can produce Abstract work, or work with a symbolic or figurative reference as he pleases. The range of art has been substantially widened: and this in itself makes the invention of Abstract art one of the great artistic developments of our time.

ALAN BOWNESS

Bibliography. Moszynska, A. *Abstract Art*, London (1990). Seuphor, M. *Abstract Painting: Fifty Years of Accomplishment*, London and New York (1961). Seuphor, M. *Dictionary of Abstract Painting*, London and New York (1958). Tate Gallery *Towards a New Art: Essays on the Background to Abstract Art 1910–20*, London (1980).

48

DADA AND SURREALISM

Amorous Parade by Picabia; oil on canvas; 97×74cm (38×29in); 1917
Collection of M.G. Neumann, Chicago (see page 879)

ANIMATED initially by opposition to the First World War, Dada was a movement committed to the destruction of all existing values in life and art. The movement can be said to date from 1915, but it was not until early in the following spring, in Zurich, that it received its name. Confusion surrounds the actual circumstances, but according to the most probable of the rival accounts, Hugo Ball (1886–1927) and Richard Huelsenbeck (1892–1974) were leafing through a German–French dictionary when they were struck by the French word *dada*, meaning hobbyhorse. Partly because of its nonsensical sound, partly because of its associations with the freedom of childhood, they immediately adopted it. Dada flourished until *c*1922 in New York, Zurich, Berlin, Cologne, Hanover, and Paris, and was succeeded in Paris by the more philosophical, systematic, and positive movement, Surrealism. The word "surrealism" had been coined in 1917 by the poet and critic Guillaume Apollinaire (1880–1918), and was appropriated by the Surrealists because it expressed their preoccupation with a world beyond the "real" world. Under the continuous leadership of André Breton (1896–1966), Surrealism survived as a major force in European art until 1939, and during the Second World War was vital in the American avant-garde.

Dada. Dada was established first in the liberal and neutral territories of New York and Zurich, and only after the war was over in Germany and Paris. Ball, writing in Zurich in 1916, explained that Dada intended to cross "the barriers of war and nationalism". George Grosz (1893–1959) and Wieland Herzfelde (1896–), both members of the Berlin group, described the original political motive behind the formation of Dada and its anti-art aesthetic:

Dada was not a "made" movement, but an organic product originating in reaction to the head-in-the-clouds tendency of so-called holy art, whose disciples brooded over cubes and Gothic art, while the generals were painting in blood ... The shooting goes on, the profiteering goes on, hunger goes on, lying goes on; why all that art? Wasn't it the height of fraud to pretend art created spiritual values?

Among targets for Dada attack was what they considered to be the whole inhibiting and corrupting apparatus of the art world: the bourgeois who identify art with good taste and pleasant decoration, the connoisseurs with their academic prejudices, the dealers and collectors with their concern for market values. The Dadas retaliated by producing works that deliberately flouted the accepted standards of beauty and were unsaleable, either because of their subject matter and style or because of the materials and techniques used: "Let it [art] then be a monstrosity that frightens servile minds and not a sweetening to decorate the refectories of animals in human costume", wrote Tristan Tzara (1896–1963) in his *Dada Manifesto* of 1918. The rigid code of morality instilled into the individual by the combined forces of family, Church, and State was rejected; the Dadas demanded absolute personal freedom. In particular they disparaged reason and logic, which Tzara identified as "an enormous centipede stifling independence", and sought to demonstrate the primacy of the anti-rational forces. Taking negation as their starting point, the Dadas asserted that only after the *tabula rasa* could the work of reconstruction begin; in Tzara's words:

There is a great negative work of destruction to be accomplished. We must sweep and clean ... I proclaim bitter struggle with all the weapons of DADAIST DISGUST.

Reacting against traditional aesthetic standards, the Dadas rarely employed the usual media of painting, drawing, or sculpture; instead, they used assemblage techniques such as collage and photomontage. In order to tap the rich funds of the unconscious, they invited the intervention of chance and pioneered automatist techniques. They sabotaged grammar and language in their phonetic poems and in the poems they collaged together from scraps of printed material, or by reciting several poems simultaneously. They created "noise music" from cacophonous and random juxtapositions of sounds. Their typography was equally startling: different typefaces were mixed freely together, while lines of print were often organized into eccentric patterns. The Dadas also used the periodical as a weapon with which to attack the enemy or attract support: their reviews were numerous and usually ephemeral.

Group action was regarded as more important than individual work, for it undermined the status of the artist as "solitary genius" and made more impact on the public. In typical Dada soirees, against a background of jarring noises, poems were recited, dances performed in outrageous costumes, manifestoes declaimed, and individuals made provocative gestures to stir up the audience, as when in New York in 1917, Arthur Cravan (1887–?1919) arrived drunk to give a lecture on modern art and began stripping on the stage. Successful Dada soirees ended in uproar and sometimes fighting. Dada exhibitions were organized in a similar spirit.

Many of these provocative techniques were indebted to Futurism, although the Dadas rejected Futurist attitudes to contemporary society and politics. From Cubism, which they otherwise deplored as retrogressive in its concern with aesthetic problems, the Dadas inherited collage: certain *papiers collés* made in 1912–14 by Picasso anticipated the Dada disrespect for fine materials and painstaking execution. Popular art also influenced them: for instance, photographic techniques used in First World War picture postcards were acknowledged by the Berlin Dadas as the source for the photomontage technique. The most immediate precursor was, however, Marcel Duchamp (1887–1968). In 1913 he abandoned oil painting and assembled out of a stool and a bicycle wheel his first "ready-made" (*The Bicycle Wheel*; original lost, third version 1951; Museum of Modern Art, New York). The iconoclasm of both gestures is genuinely proto-Dada.

A still nameless group began to forgather in New York in 1915 in the home of the wealthy collector Walter Arensberg,

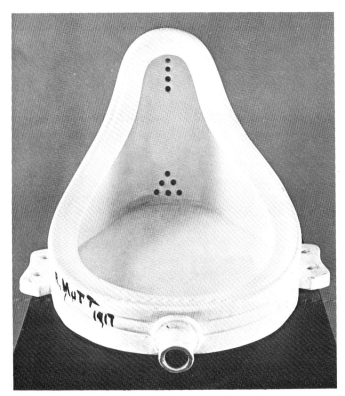

Fountain by Marcel Duchamp; sanitary ware and enamel paint; height 30cm (12in); a replica made in 1964 of the original of 1917 (now lost). Galleria Schwarz, Milan

Gift by Man Ray; a flatiron with tacks; height 17cm ($6\frac{7}{10}$in); a replica of the original of 1917 (now lost). Collection of M.G. Neumann, Chicago

and in the avant-garde gallery run by the photographer, Alfred Stieglitz (1864–1946). Duchamp and Man Ray (1890–1976) were prominent members, Francis Picabia (1879–1953) an occasional participant, while Arthur Cravan, who combined poetry with amateur boxing, created Dada legend with his scandalous behaviour and his mysterious death. Probably because of its geographical isolation from the realities of the European war, New York Dada was less political, less aggressive, less tightly knit and more frivolous than Dada elsewhere, but the anti-art views expressed in periodicals like *291*, *391*, and *New York Dada* are typical of the whole movement.

Picabia's wry drawings of people as machines perfectly reflect the mood of the New York group: in the dead-pan, informative style of technical drawings, he depicts, for instance, Stieglitz as a camera (*Portrait of Alfred Stieglitz*, in *291*, nos. 5 and 6 1915), and an American girl as an electric light bulb that flashes up the sign "Flirt-Divorce", (title page, *391*, no. VI, 1917).

Duchamp's ready-mades epitomize Dadaist irony: a snow shovel is distinguished only from other identical tools in that Duchamp chose it and entitled it *In Advance of the Broken Arm*, 1915, (original lost, reconstruction, 1945; Yale University Art Gallery, New Haven), while his notorious *Fountain* of 1917 is a urinal exhibited upside down and signed R. Mutt in ironic tribute to the manufacturer, Mott Works Company (original lost, third version, 1964; Galleria Schwarz, Milan).

Man Ray's Dada career was divided between New York and Paris where he settled in July 1921. A close friend of Duchamp's, he too created some witty and disconcerting Dada objects, such as *The Enigma of Isidore Ducasse* of 1920 (destroyed)—apparently a bulky parcel, in fact a sewing machine wrapped up in cloth and tied with string—and the ironically named *Gift* (replica in the Collection of M.G. Neumann, Chicago)—a flatiron with a row of tacks glued to the bottom, which he made soon after he moved to Paris in 1921. Man Ray frequently experimented with new techniques in order to break down the conventional barriers between "Fine Art" and modern technology; in 1917 he made his first "Aerographs", pictures executed with an airbrush, while in Paris in 1921 he made his first "Rayographs", photographs created in the darkroom without a camera. His permanent removal to Paris signaled the end of Dada in New York.

Early in February 1916, Hugo Ball, a pacifist poet and philosopher and a refugee from Germany, founded the Cabaret Voltaire in Zurich. He was joined by the Rumanians, Marcel Janco (1895–) and Tristan Tzara, the Alsatian Hans Arp (1887–1966), by Huelsenbeck, the future founder of Berlin Dada, and by the German, Hans Richter (1888–1976). The name Dada was found, and on 14 July 1916 Tzara read aloud in public the first *Dada Manifesto*. Early in 1917, Ball, "encased in a tight-fitting cylindrical pillar of shiny blue cardboard", intoned a lengthy and unintelligible phonetic poem, composed of invented words and syllables organized into rhythmic patterns. At first baffled, the audience quickly became vociferous, and thus the pattern for future Dada soirees was established. Afterwards, Ball withdrew from Dada, alarmed by its increasingly anarchic tendencies. Tzara assumed leadership, writing manifestos, masterminding events, and editing *Der Dada*, the chief Zurich review.

In contrast to the nihilistic views of Tzara and of Picabia, who visited Zurich in 1919, Arp, Janco, and Richter foresaw the creation of a new order on the ruins of the old by means of a kind of Abstract art that was dependent on the use of automatism and chance and on the exploration of the unconscious. In reliefs like *Plant Hammer* (1917; Collection of F. Arp, Paris), with their organic, biomorphic forms, Arp expressed his faith in spontaneity and instinct. He used abstract terms not in order to analyse or widen the means of art, but to purge it of "vain and dead" illusionism and "to find another order, another value for man in nature". He allowed the play of line to develop "automatically", while some of his collages were constructed "according to the laws of chance": he would scatter scraps of paper and allow the pattern formed when they settled on the ground to dictate the basic design. Richter pioneered films composed entirely of abstract elements in pursuance of the ideal of a pure new art language, and Janco incorporated the hitherto despised debris of everyday life into his reliefs.

The cover of the first issue of Der Dada, published in Berlin in 1919

With the war over, the Dadas left Zurich and the initiative passed to Germany and Paris.

In April 1918, Huelsenbeck founded the *Club Dada* in Berlin. He was the principal editor of the most important reviews, *Club Dada, Der Dada,* and *Dada Almanach,* and guided the group until it split up in 1922. The other leading members were Johannes Baader (1876–1955), George Grosz, Raoul Hausmann (1886–1971), Hannah Höch (1889–1978), and Helmut Herzfelde (1891–1968), who anglicized his name to John Heartfield in protest against German nationalism. After the War, Berlin was in a state of acute political, social, and economic crisis, and to the Berlin Dadas, some of whom joined the Communist Party, political revolution was a central issue; to Huelsenbeck, for instance, a realist art that "presents the thousandfold problems of the day" alone seemed relevant. Condemning the preoccupation with abstraction of the Dada artists in Zurich, they specialized in political and social satire. Grosz's brilliant collection of drawings and watercolors executed between 1915 and 1922, and published in 1923 as *Ecce Homo,* is a scathing comment on the hypocrisy and corruption rife in "respectable" society.

The photomontage technique—a collage of fragments of photographs, often supplemented by printed slogans—was "invented" independently by Hausmann and Heartfield in 1918, and constitutes the most significant artistic contribution of Berlin Dada. In the hands of Heartfield especially, it became the perfect vehicle for political satire. Hausmann and Höch, on the other hand, often used photomontage to suggest, as Höch says, "a new and terrifying dream world", by playing on the dichotomy between the precision of industrial or scientific photographs and the fantasy released through unexpected juxtapositions. *Tatlin at home,* (1920; Modern Museum, Nationalmuseum, Stockholm) by Hausmann is a fine example of this, while a sceptical attitude to human intellect and modern technology is suggested in his *The Spirit of our Times,* (*Mechanical Head*) of c1919 (Musée National d'Art Moderne, Paris)—a wooden hatmaker's dummy to which various objects have been attached.

"The Dada Conspiracy of the Rhineland" was founded in 1919 by Max Ernst (1891–1976) and Alfred Grünwald, alias Johannes Baargeld (1891–1927); they were joined shortly by Arp. Wayward humor and bizarre fantasy characterize their collages, constructions, and photomontages, especially those by Ernst. For instance, in his *The Hat Makes the Man,* (1920; Museum of Modern Art, New York), four "gentlemen" are assembled from illustrations of hats linked by transparent, colored cylinders; other works, like *Two Ambiguous Figures,* (1919–20; Collection of Mme M. Arp-Hegenbach, Meudon), testify to Ernst's admiration for de Chirico and Carrà.

The Cologne Dadas published their own reviews, including *Bulletin D* and *Die Schammade* (a word invented by Ernst), and in 1920 organized a typically provocative exhibition which could only be entered through a public urinal; inside, a girl in her first communion dress recited obscene verses, and Ernst exhibited an object supplied with a hatchet which the

The Worker Picture by Kurt Schwitters; collage; 125×91cm (49×36in); 1919. Modern Museum (National Museum), Stockholm

spectators were invited to, and did, destroy. On the instigation of the Parisian Dadas, Ernst moved to Paris in 1922, and Cologne Dada broke up.

In Hanover in 1918, Kurt Schwitters (1887–1948) developed his idiosyncratic brand of Dada which he called *Merz*. He rejected the political bias of Berlin Dada and, contrary to orthodox Dada, insisted that "*Merz* always strives towards art". His collages and constructions, whether miniature in scale or environmental, as in his *Merzbau* ("Merz-House"; 1918–38; Hanover; destroyed during the Second World War), were all assembled into a consciously aesthetic abstract design out of junk and rubbish. It was in his choice of materials that Schwitters came closest to the spirit of Dada. His *Merz* activities involved poetry, music, and editing a review, which he also called *Merz*. Schwitters' ultimate aim was to create the "total work of art", his *Merz-Stage*, but this project was never realized.

The Dada movement did not survive the recrimination and discord that characterized its later stages in Paris, and in retrospect, it seems inevitable that the ideological differences dividing the leading participants should have resulted in the formation of a new movement—Surrealism. During the course of 1919, Picabia, Duchamp, and Tzara arrived in Paris and were enthusiastically welcomed by Breton, Louis Aragon (1897–1983), Paul Éluard (1895–1952), and Philippe Soupault (1897–1990), the young poets associated with the ironically named new review *Littérature*. They had been introduced to Dadaist ideas in 1917 by Apollinaire (a close friend of Picabia)

and by Breton's friend Jacques Vaché (1896–1919) who, although not part of any Dada group, professed a violent anti-art aesthetic and a doctrine of provocation. Nevertheless, the sober presentation of the first numbers of *Littérature*, and the veneration accorded to certain Symbolist and post-Symbolist writers, indicate clearly enough the emotional and aesthetic gulf that really existed between Breton and his friends and the old-guard Dadas.

Meanwhile, however, the arrival of Tzara in Paris at the end of 1919 was the signal for the outbreak of typical Dada activities; for example, in May 1920, 23 manifestos were published in *Littérature*—by now committed officially to Dada—and during the *Festival Dada* of the same month, balloons bearing the names of eminent people were released, and it was announced that "all Dadas will have their hair cut on stage".

But in the following year, Breton, who was by nature too autocratic, serious-minded, and idealistic to tolerate Tzara's supremacy and buffoonery for long, began to organize rival events and to call for the development of a new positive philosophy. The mock trial of the popular writer, Maurice Barrès, which he arranged in 1921, and his proposals for an *International Congress for the Determination of Directives and the Defense of the Modern Spirit* in 1922, led to a rupture with Picabia and Tzara, and to the disengagement from Dada of the original *Littérature* group.

Despite the antagonisms of the transitional period, Surrealism inherited much from Dada that was crucial to its theoretical structure—for instance, the rejection of the Western cultural tradition and attitude to art, the pattern of political agitation and involvement in contemporary issues, the defense of the claims of the unconscious and irrational forces. Dada also bequeathed many of its techniques to Surrealism—automatism, collage, object making—and all its machinery of publicity, from pamphleteering to the organization of group events.

Dada readily accepted its own extinction: even in 1920 Huelsenbeck had written, "Dada foresees its end and laughs". Yet despite its self-mockery and its nihilistic doctrines, the impact of Dada has been anything but negative, for it has also directly marked such post-Second World War developments as Pop art, Action painting, Conceptual art, and "Happenings" (*see* European Art Since 1945). In general, it has stimulated a radical revision of artistic values.

Surrealism. Although always international in outlook, Surrealism was at first based in Paris with a subsidiary group, from 1925 onwards, in Brussels. In the 1930s a series of exhibitions held in New York, London, Tokyo, Copenhagen, Tenerife, and elsewhere, led to the formation of other groups and to the wide dissemination of Surrealist ideas.

Although painting was mentioned only in a footnote in Breton's first *Manifesto of Surrealism* of 1924, it quickly came to be recognized as a primary means of Surrealist expression, and in 1928 Breton published his crucial essay *Surrealism and*

Painting. Among the artists who belonged to the movement at one time or another were the ex-Dadas Arp, Man Ray, Picabia, and Ernst, and Masson, Miró, Tanguy, Magritte, Giacometti, Dali, Brauner, Bellmer, Dominguez, Matta, and Lam. Delvaux worked in a Surrealist manner but did not participate directly; Picasso and Duchamp were close associates; Chagall and Klee shared certain preoccupations with Surrealism.

Periodicals played a vital role in the Surrealist movement, the most important being *Littérature*, new series, 1922–4, *La Révolution Surréaliste*, 1924–9, *Le Surréalisme au service de la Révolution*, 1930–3, and *Minotaure*, 1933–9.

If the theory underlying the Surrealist attitudes to art, the artist, and artistic tradition was inherited directly from Dada, the emphasis was very different. The Dadas were satisfied to curse or poke fun at the hallowed periods of art and the Great Masters; the Surrealists, by contrast, were not only more systematic in their condemnation of the "classical" tradition, of the ideal of "truth to nature", and of any art-for-its-own-sake aesthetic (it was on the last charge that they criticized most Abstract painting), but they also sought to draw attention to the "alternative" tradition in world art which had been overlooked by art historians and connoisseurs and with which they felt in profound sympathy. Intending to effect a complete revolution in taste and to demonstrate that the "surreal" had always been an integral part of human consciousness, they freely acknowledged their numerous and varied sources. Chief among these were painters of fantasy such as Bosch (c1450–1516), Uccello (1397–1475), and Arcimboldo (1530–93), Romantic and Symbolist painters and writers such as Rimbaud, Lautréamont, Goya, Moreau, Redon, Seurat, and Gauguin, "Naive" painters such as Henri Rousseau, the art of the insane, of mediums and of children, the art of "Primitive" peoples, especially the Pacific Islanders, the Inuits, and the American Indians, and the more eccentric manifestations of popular art from picture postcards to silent comedy films. Sigmund Freud's writings, especially *The Interpretation of Dreams* (published in 1899), were also crucial to the development of Surrealism in the 1920s. The more immediate visual sources, apart from Dada, were certain Cubist works by Picasso, works by Duchamp that lie outside Dada, including the *Large Glass*, 1915–23 (Philadelphia Museum of Art), and, above all, the "Metaphysical" paintings of de Chirico.

The two years following the break with Dada, 1922–4—known as *l'époque des sommeils* ("the period of trances")—were devoted to intense experimentation with hypnosis, dream-analyses based on the work of Freud, and automatism. These activities and the theories and aims of the group were summarized in the first *Manifesto*, published in October 1924, in which Breton gave the classic definition of Surrealism:

> pure psychic automatism, by which one proposes to express . . . the actual functioning of thought. Dictated by thought, in the absence of any control exercised by reason, exempt from any aesthetic or moral concern . . . Surrealism is based on the belief in the superiority of certain forms of previously neglected as-

sociations, in the omnipotence of dreams, in the disinterested play of thought.

By inducing trance-states, the Surrealists found they could obliterate the outside world, and, unhampered by reason, inhabit a marvelous realm of heightened reality denied to the conscious mind and equivalent to the dream world. Speaking, writing, drawing, like automatons, their texts and pictures seemed to them unequaled in their imaginative freedom. These revelations of a hitherto repressed psychic life were not credited to any superhuman power, but were recognized as consistent with a truly integrated personality. From this point on, the ultimate aim of Surrealism, in the words of the *Manifesto*, was "the future resolution of these two states, dream and reality, which are seemingly so contradictory, into a kind of absolute reality, a *surreality*". The dream and the irrational impulses and images constantly experienced when awake—not the "objective", ordered world of fact—were defined as the source and proper subject matter of creative expression. Breton's definition of beauty follows directly from this: "the marvelous is always beautiful, anything marvelous is beautiful, in fact only the marvelous is beautiful".

Despite the neglect of painting in the *Manifesto*, an authentic body of Surrealist painting did, in fact, exist by 1924. In the winter of 1923–4, André Masson (1896–1987), who had recently met Breton and knew about the experiments of the *époque des sommeils*, made his first automatic drawings. Allowing his pen to travel uninhibitedly across the paper, he was able to free himself from the conventions of composition and subject matter and, in theory, to release the "marvelous" images buried in his subconscious. His automatic drawings became, in this way, a visual equivalent of the mind itself.

Ernst's paintings of 1921–4, like *Woman, Old Man, and Flowers II* (1923; Museum of Modern Art, New York) are records of his dreams and fantasies, rendered in a factual, descriptive style influenced by de Chirico. Later Surrealist painting can be seen to divide into these two basic types, defined as early as 1923–4 by Masson and Ernst: the more abstract, spontaneous, "automatic" works, and the illusionistic, carefully executed, irrational "dream-images".

Joan Miró (1893–1983) began to make the transition to Surrealism in 1923 in a series of minutely detailed paintings full of fantastic imagery, which relate stylistically to both these types. *The Hunter: Catalan Landscape* (1923–4; Museum of Modern Art, New York) is a fine example.

The emphasis on automatism in the first *Manifesto* profoundly affected Surrealist painting for the next few years. The freedom of line of Masson's drawings also dominated the fluid, organic structures of his oil paintings, which were, however, still labored in execution. In 1927, wishing to carry over automatic techniques into painting, he began a series of sand paintings—for example, *Battle of the Fishes* (1927; Collection of E.A. Bergman, Chicago)—in which the composition, texture, and hue were established by throwing handfuls of sand at a canvas pasted here and there with glue; meandering lines and color were then added "automatically".

Woman, Old Man, and Flowers II by Max Ernst; oil on canvas; 97×130cm (38×51in); 1923. Museum of Modern Art, New York

Ernst developed new automatic techniques in 1925, *frottage* (rubbing) in his drawings, and *grattage* (scraping) in his paintings. Exactly as children take rubbings from coins, Ernst took rubbings from a variety of surfaces, including wood and leaves, and then organized them into delicate and evocative images of birds, trees, flying monsters, and so on. A selection of his *frottages* were published in 1926 as *Histoire Naturelle*. His *grattage* paintings, including the series of *Doves, Hordes, Forests*, and *Shell-* or *Snow-Flowers* (1925–8), contrast greatly with his earlier illusionistic paintings. The technique involved applying several coats of color to the canvas, placing objects underneath, scraping off the raised portions, thus revealing the underlying layers of color, and then interpreting the forms which emerged—a spool, for instance, often becomes the head or eye of a bird.

In 1925 Miró's work also became more "automatic" in a number of extremely free, rapidly executed canvases, for instance, *The Birth of the World* (1925; Museum of Modern Art, New York). Although highly abstracted, these paintings, with their poetic titles, always recall the real world, however remotely.

In 1923 Yves Tanguy (1900–55) decided to become a painter when he was struck by a painting by de Chirico in a dealer's window. His earliest work often echoes de Chirico's haunting scenarios, while the spontaneity of the execution and the enigmatic, abstract or biomorphic shapes depicted show the influence of Miró and Arp.

The Surrealists' interest in collective action and their belief that art should be made by everyone found expression in the *cadavre exquis* ("exquisite corpse") game: a sentence or drawing was composed by three or four people working in rotation, who could not see the contributions of the other collaborators. The astonishing images that resulted are, arguably, the most thorough-going fulfilment of Surrealist aesthetic theory. The Surrealist ideal was *peinture-poésie* ("painting-poetry") and the close collaboration between poets and painters at this time is seen in these *cadavres exquis* and also in the vivid visual quality of Surrealist poetry, in the use

The Menaced Assassin by Magritte

The "Whodunit", the genre René Magritte so wittily exploits in *The Menaced Assassin* (1927; Museum of Modern Art, New York), is instantly familiar. But it is a popular genre, not one we expect to encounter in a painting—especially in a painting on the grand scale of this one. In its subject, the *crime passionnel*, and in its relationship to popular culture, *The Menaced Assassin* reflects two abiding preoccupations of the Surrealists: the criminal's supremely intransigent attitude to law and order, and the belief that the imaginative riches of the human psyche find uninhibited release more readily in popular than in "official" art forms. As Magritte here drew upon and modified the detective story, so slightly later Max Ernst pillaged popular 19th-century weeklies for their illustrations, which he then converted into images of unforgettable oneiric strangeness by means of collage.

As a boy, Magritte first savored the episodic *Fantômas* novels written collaboratively in the period 1912–14 by Allain and Souvestre, the silent films based on them directed by Feuillade, and the serialized thrillers which had an American detective—Nat Pinkerton or Nick Carter—as hero. (In the 1920s and 1930s, he himself tried his hand at writing *Fantômas* and Nat Pinkerton stories.) A still from one of Feuillade's *Fantômas* films may have directly influenced the composition of *The Menaced Assassin*, while the bare floorboards and blank walls, the stiffly posed figures and carefully placed furniture, and the severely frontal view of the steeply raked, stage-like space, echo settings typical of all the *Fantômas* films. The gaudy, melodramatic covers of novelettes of the *Nick Carter* type are another possible source.

The film still and the covers have a narrative context which explains the meaning of

▼ *The Menaced Assassin* by Magritte; oil on canvas; 150×193cm (59×76in); 1927. Museum of Modern Art, New York

▲ A collage scene from *La Femme 100 Têtes*, a collage novel by Max Ernst published in 1929, two years after Magritte painted *The Menaced Assassin*

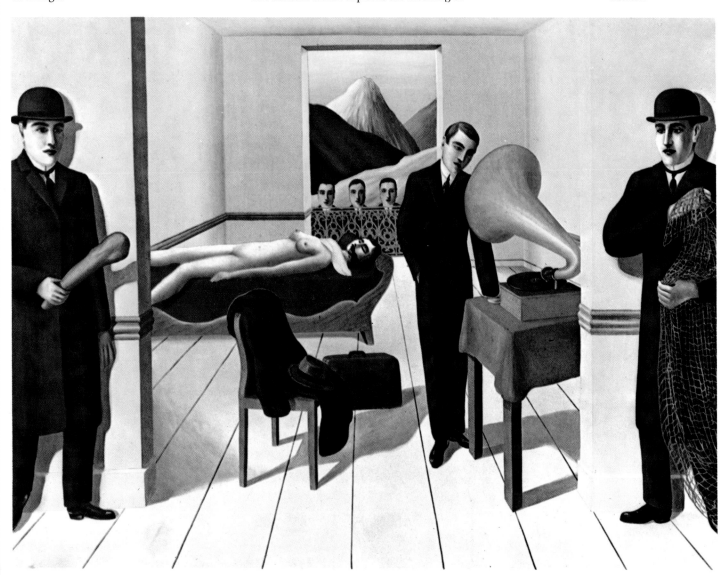

▲ The cover of issue no.35 in the French *Nick Carter* novelette series; undated

that selected, frozen moment. *The Menaced Assassin* is like a still and has a deceptively informative title. We are tricked into believing that we can "read" the painting, that despite the expected presence of red herrings the mystery of the murder can be solved. But the clues offered remain irreconcilable; the title is the principal red herring. We cannot, for instance, assume that the meditative figure apparently listening to the phonograph is the assassin: the hat and coat on the chair—if they are his—resemble the archetypal detective's uniform. We cannot assume that the bowler-hatted men are on the right side of the law: the caveman's club that one of them brandishes could have killed the girl, and the net clutched by his twin recalls the net used to bag a naked girl in another early painting. Magritte's *hommage* to the detective story takes the form of irony: his mystery endlessly eludes solution; the delicious, nagging uncertainty that makes detective fiction addictive remains perpetual. A touch of mockery may also be detected in another of his open references to the genre, *The Backfire* (1943; Collection of Émile Langui, Brussels): it is a replica of the cover of the first of the *Fantômas* novels, but the hero/villain's dagger has become a rose.

The Menaced Assassin calls to mind many other paintings by Magritte. Thus, twinned bowler-hatted figures occur in a work of the same period (*The Meaning of Night*, 1927; private collection), but they are there like somnambulists in an enchanted world. The

▲ *Golconda* by Magritte; oil on canvas; 80×100cm (31×39in); 1953. Private collection

▼ *The Heart of the Matter* by Magritte; oil on canvas; 116×81cm (46×32in); 1928. Collection of Marcel Mabille, Rhodes St Genèse, Belgium

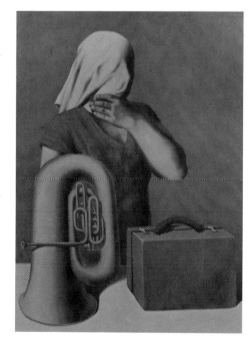

enigmatic suitcase reappears in another painting (*The Heart of the Matter*, 1928; Collection of Marcel Mabille, Rhodes St Genèse, Belgium) redolent with sinister drama, teaming up with a tuba reminiscent of the phonograph and a woman, alive but threatened. A much later painting *The Grape Harvest* (1959; private collection) isolates and develops the motif of the row of identikit men staring through the empty window. The systematic stereotyping of figures, furniture, and buildings—so noticeable in *The Menaced Assassin*—becomes the hallmark of Magritte's mature work, for example *Golconda* (1953; private collection).

Magritte's habitual style—a form of simplified realism, seemingly impersonal in its avoidance of painterly bravura—is so frank it makes us believe that the horrifying or absurd events depicted are true. It is peculiarly appropriate in *The Menaced Assassin*, for it is the style neither of the academy nor of the avant-garde, but of advertisements, signs, illustrations in children's primers: a popular style comparable to the popular imagery of the painting.

ELIZABETH COWLING

Further reading. Gablik, S. *Magritte*, London (1970). Passeron, R. *René Magritte*, Paris (1970). Scutenaire, L. *Avec Magritte*, Brussels (1977). Sylvester, D. *Magritte*, New York (1969). Waldberg, P. *René Magritte*, Brussels (1965).

The Birth of the World by Joan Miró; oil on canvas; 245×195cm (96×77in); 1925. Museum of Modern Art, New York

Lengthy Days by Yves Tanguy; oil on canvas; 92×73cm (36×29in); 1937. Musée National d'Art Moderne, Paris

of evocative, poetic titles by all the painters, in Miró's and Ernst's introduction of words or phrases into some of their pictures, and in the allusive, metaphorical approach to imagery of the painters.

About 1928–9 the illusionistic manner of de Chirico and of Ernst in the early 1920s reasserted itself, and automatism went temporarily out of favor, because, as Breton said in the *Second Surrealist Manifesto* of 1929, it could too easily degenerate into aestheticism. It was also felt that dreams and fantasies, and the Surrealist image—defined as the meeting of two different realities on a plane foreign to them both—could be rendered more directly and precisely by means of illusionistic description.

Miró now reverted to a detailed and linear manner in paintings which, while remaining extremely spontaneous in feeling, were crowded with incident. In the 1930s, his subject matter in, for example, *Man and Woman in front of a Pile of Excrement* (1936; Joan Miró Foundation, Barcelona), became increasingly dramatic, and is characterized by trauma, violence, eroticism, and savage humor.

Ernst's work also became more figurative, and in 1929 he published the first in a series of "collage-novels", *La Femme 100 Têtes* ("The 100-Headed Women"), which were entirely

created from elements cut out of popular magazines. He recomposed these originally bland images into fantastic, disturbing, or humorous scenes.

In Tanguy's work the early tendency towards biomorphism was confirmed and, indeed, all identifiable references to the outside world were eradicated. Yet his work from *c*1929 onwards became increasingly precise in detail and labored in execution, and the biomorphic forms that inhabit the seemingly endless space of his paintings became more and more tangible and three-dimensional; he seems, indeed, to give an exact and "real" transcript of the landscape of his dreams or his imagination.

In 1927, René Magritte (1898–1967), who had been one of the founder members of the Surrealist group in Brussels, moved to Paris. All his work is executed in a taut, precise "realistic" style. The bizarre happenings he depicts—for instance, a man and woman are kissing but their heads are swathed in cloths (*The Lovers*, 1928; Collection of R. Zeisler, New York)—are rendered more shocking and disturbing because the style is completely deadpan and objective. In many of his paintings he calls into question our assumptions about the nature of our universe, and suggests that the forces of unreason hold secret sway: for instance, our faith in language and the favorite axiom that "art imitates nature" are challenged in *The Treason of Images* (1929; Los Angeles County Museum of Art, Los Angeles), in which a copybook image of a pipe carries underneath it the legend *Ceci n'est pas une pipe* ("This is not a pipe").

Salvador Dali (1904–89) made his debut at the end of 1928 when the Surrealist-inspired film *Un Chien Andalou* ("An Andalusian Dog"), which he had made with his compatriot Luis Buñuel, was shown privately in Paris. The years 1928 and 1929 had been ones of considerable internal strife in the movement, occasioned partly by dissent over the vexed question of Surrealism's relationship to the Communist Party, and partly by the autocratic idealism of Breton who refused to tolerate any compromise with Surrealist principles and did not hesitate to expel backsliders. Dali was exactly the tonic that Breton and those who were still faithful to him needed, for his small-scale, minutely detailed, *trompe-l'oeil* paintings, such as *The Lugubrious Game* (1929; private collection), with their obsessive sexual content, epitomized the Surrealist mission defined by Breton, in the *Second Surrealist Manifesto*, as a "total recuperation of our psychic powers by means ... of the dizzying descent into ourselves, the systematic illumination of the hidden regions ... the perpetual excursion into the midst of the forbidden zone". Dali's theory of double images, which he called "the paranoiac-critical method", gave a Freudian extension to the concept of the Surrealist image and was influential in the 1930s, but his sympathy with Fascism and his eagerness for material success led to his eventual exclusion from the group.

In 1929, the sculptor, Alberto Giacometti (1901–66), made the transition to Surrealism, and for the next six years he worked entirely from the imagination. In cage-like structures enclosing enigmatic objects, in intestine-like plaster corridors, in constructions resembling curious board games, in insect-like figures, Giacometti exteriorized sensations of anxiety and persecution, and an unsettling ambivalence towards violence. In slightly later, more conventional sculptures of women, such as *The Invisible Object* (1934–5; Collection of A. Maeght, Paris), an apparitional presence is evoked.

The 1930s were distinguished by a new activity, object-making, which recommended itself to the Surrealists because no special technical skill was required. As early as 1924, Breton had called for the fabrication of "certain of those objects that one sees only in dreams", but it was not until 1930–1, when Giacometti began to make his object-like sculptures and Dali to construct his so-called "objects of symbolic function", that Breton's idea was realized. Conceived of as "the objectification of desire", and as a means of liberating the object from the slur of functionalism, Surrealist objects were composed from any bric-à-brac that, through some subconscious mechanism, had attracted the maker. Often extremely elaborate, sometimes involving the use of poetry (as in Breton's "poem-objects"), Surrealist objects are private fetishes. Among the most famous is the *Fur-covered Cup, Saucer, and Spoon* by Meret Oppenheim (1913–85) of 1936 (Museum of

Modern Art, New York). The cult of the object, which included collecting objects as well as making them, reached its climax in 1936 when a "Surrealist Exhibition of Objects" was organized in the Galerie Charles Ratton in Paris.

The considerable success and notoriety Surrealism, especially Surrealist painting, began to enjoy in the 1930s— thanks to the many international exhibitions—led to a certain dissipation of the rigor and daring of the "heroic" 1920s. The new recruits did not equal the first generation of painters and poets. Victor Brauner (1903–66), a Rumanian, joined the group in 1932, and in an illusionist manner developed a personal mythology in nightmarish scenes that are usually aggressively sexual and peopled with monstrous beings.

Although the German artist, Hans Bellmer (1902–75) did not move to Paris until 1937 or 1938, photographs of his *Doll* were published in *Minotaure* in 1935. Seen from provocative angles and in erotic poses, her limbs and organs grotesquely rearranged, Bellmer's "articulated minor" epitomizes the Surrealist interest in sadomasochism.

Titanic Days by Magritte; oil on canvas; 116cm×81cm (46×32in); 1928. Private collection

Oscar Dominguez (1906–57), from Tenerife, was the creator of many striking objects, and "rediscovered" in 1936 the process, used by children, and known as "decalcomania". Spreading gouache on a sheet of paper, laying another sheet on top, applying pressure, and then peeling the top sheet off, Dominguez was able to create "automatically" impressions of strange landscapes and exotic natural growths. Ernst took over the technique during the Second World War and used it to remarkable effect.

Paul Delvaux (1897–1994) worked in Belgium from 1937 onwards in a Surrealist-inspired, illusionistic manner. His pictures of desirable but unapproachable naked women and anxious, ineffectual men, suggest unconsummated erotic encounters and a sexuality so inhibited that its only outlet is in voyeurism and fantasy.

The outbreak of war in 1939 disrupted the art world in Paris and the Surrealist group split up. Many of the Surrealists took refuge in New York, and there a new group formed around Breton. In 1942 a Surrealist-oriented review, *VVV*, began publication with Breton and Ernst as editorial advisers. Of the painters who joined at this time, Roberto Matta Echaurren (1911–) and Wifredo Lam (1902–82) are the most important. After a period of sensuously lyrical abstraction when he used automatist techniques and rich and rhythmic contrasts of color and tone, Matta began to introduce first linear elements, and then science-fiction-like personages into his work, which became, as a result, more aggressive and sinister in effect.

Lam's work is characterized by a greater concern with formal structure and is deeply influenced by his admiration for Picasso and African tribal sculpture, while his imagery suggests primitive rites conducted in tropically abundant undergrowth.

Meanwhile, Surrealist automatist theory and painting significantly influenced the young American avant-garde painters: Arshile Gorky (1904–48) was actively supported by Breton, while others such as Motherwell, de Kooning, Still, Rothko, and Pollock were deeply indebted to Surrealist techniques, and particularly to the work of Miró and Masson and the Surrealist-inspired work of Picasso.

Thus, Surrealism's immediate influence was on the development of Abstract Expressionism, while its example lies more or less directly behind those artists, who since the war, have been opposed to geometrical abstraction. So, for instance, *Art Brut*, pioneered in 1948 by Dubuffet with the support of Breton, sought to direct attention towards areas of art the Surrealists had advocated in the 1920s—the art of children, of the insane, of the self-taught, and of "primitive" peoples.

The Surrealist concept of beauty has also undoubtedly affected contemporary taste, in its emphasis on the value of the fantastic and the esoteric tradition in European and non-European art. If the lofty political, social, and moral ideals of Surrealism have not been realized, the movement has, at least, helped to stimulate a broader and richer approach to culture and an alternative way of thinking and looking.

ELIZABETH COWLING

Bibliography. Ades, D. *Dada and Surrealism Reviewed*, London (1978). Breton, A. *Surrealism and Painting*, London (1972). Jean, M. *The History of Surrealist Painting*, London (1960). Motherwell, R. (ed.) *The Dada Painters and Poets: an Anthology*, New York (1951). Nadeau, M. (trans. Howard, R.) *The History of Surrealism*, London (1968). Picon, G. *Journal of Surrealism 1919–39*, Geneva (1976). Richter, H. *Dada: Art and Anti-Art*, London (1965). Rubin, W.S. *Dada and Surrealist Art*, London (1969).

49

INTERNATIONAL STYLE

The sanatorium at Paimio, Finland, designed by Alvar Aalto; 1928–33 (see page 901)

THE *International Style: Architecture Since 1922* was the title of a study by Henry-Russell Hitchcock and Philip Johnson published in New York in 1932. It was written in conjunction with an exhibition of architecture of the past decade organized by the authors at the Museum of Modern Art, New York. The book illustrated and briefly assessed buildings of many different kinds by 72 architects from 15 different countries, most weight being given to Mies van der Rohe (1886–1969) and Walter Gropius (1883–1969) from Germany, J.J.P. Oud (1890–1963) from Holland, and Le Corbusier (1887–1965) from France. It was a book written to prove a point: that a contemporary architectural style, which ignored national boundaries, had been evolved to satisfy not only functional considerations but aesthetic ones as well. The Director of the Museum of Modern Art, Alfred Barr, remarked in his preface that the authors had proved "that there exists today a modern style as original, as consistent, as logical, and as widely distributed as any in the past".

The buildings selected did have a certain stylistic unity, and Hitchcock and Johnson were able to characterize the main features of the style. The buildings were conceived in terms of volume rather than mass. They were supported by regular skeleton frames which were undisguised. They were covered with a thin surface or skin, often of smooth stucco painted white, and their windows, usually with light standardized metal frames, were an integral part of this skin. There was no surface ornament, but windows and doors were often placed according to a proportional system. Axial symmetry was avoided, and, because of the load-bearing frame, internal walls could be placed to form a free plan and external elements could be composed asymmetrically. Roofs were flat for functional and aesthetic reasons. There was a stress on the rectangle and on the horizontal. The new architecture was Gothic in ideology but Classical in feeling.

Although the International style was thus first explicitly characterized and codified by Hitchcock and Johnson, there were in fact earlier publications written by the architects who were themselves responsible for the style. These earlier works were full of idealism, exhortations, and excitement—indeed, if architects such as Le Corbusier and Walter Gropius had not been such skillful propagandists for their cause, the Museum of Modern Art would not have been attracted to their architecture and we would pay less attention to it today. Avant-garde architects in the 1920s had to fight strongly against reactionary forces to prove that their buildings would satisfy new and urgent needs.

In 1925 Walter Gropius' book *Internationale Architektur* was published as the first Bauhaus book. This too contained a selection of buildings of varying types—factories, houses, flats, offices—drawn from many different countries and designed by architects such as Frank Lloyd Wright, Le Corbusier, Oud, and Gropius himself. Gropius stated that their buildings were stylistically linked because they were all conceived logically and all used materials, space, time, and money economically. They were functional but also well pro-

portioned and above all they were in tune with the new technology which was international:

> The uniformity of the appearance of modern buildings, bred of world travel and world technology, overrides the natural frontiers which continue to restrain individuals and peoples and beats a path through all cultural regions.

Gropius' stress on the international qualities of the new architecture was to lead later to confrontation with the National Socialists.

In the following year Adolf Behne, a close colleague of Gropius in the left-wing association *Arbeitsrat für Kunst* ("Working Group for Art"), published a book called *Der Moderne Zweckbau* ("Modern Utilitarian Building"). In this the sources for the new style were seen in industrial and office buildings by men such as H.P. Berlage, Peter Behrens, F.L. Wright, Tony Garnier, and Auguste Perret. Although the practitioners of the International style rejected all the "Salon" architecture of the past, they were anxious to establish their pedigree in great and often anonymous engineering structures, such as exhibition halls and American grain silos, and in the work of those few pioneers who were active in many different countries before the First World War. The Dutchman H.P. Berlage (1856–1934) was admired for his reduction of ornament and his interest in geometry and unbroken planes. The Viennese Adolf Loos (1870–1933) was also singled out for his vehement dislike of ornament—it is interesting that his famous essay of 1908 on this subject, *Ornament and Crime*, was republished by Le Corbusier in the magazine *L'Esprit Nouveau* ("The New Spirit") in 1920. The German Peter Behrens (1868–1940), in whose office Le Corbusier, Mies van der Rohe, and Gropius all worked for a short time, showed them the importance of total design and the power of industry to create standard types and a new classicism. His monumentality was offset by the dynamic visionary drawings of *La Città Nuova* by the Italian Futurist Sant'Elia. The project for a *Cité Industrielle* (1917) by the Lyons architect Tony Garnier also impressed them, especially Le Corbusier.

Perhaps their most important source was the architecture of the American, Frank Lloyd Wright. His work was known through two volumes published in Berlin by Wasmuth in 1910 and 1911 (Frank Lloyd Wright, *Ausgeführte Bauten und Entwürfe*), and through Berlage, who had visited Wright and was a keen admirer. In Wright they found a bold use of modern materials such as concrete to create wide, horizontal cantilevers and block shapes, the repeated use of standardized elements, and above all a ready acceptance of the power of the machine to form a new style. Significantly, they chose to ignore for the most part his fondness for abstracted ornament and his insistence on unifying his houses with the landscape. International style houses are usually clearly separated from the landscape although nature is often important as a foil.

When Hitchcock and Johnson's book was published, the style had been established for about a decade. Despite the authors' claims, the International style was mainly a European

parts, looks back to Gropius and Meyer's pre-War industrial buildings, the Alfeld shoe-last factory for example, but the strong asymmetric pattern of the balconies is characteristic of the International style. These characteristics are more developed in the less awkward project of the same year for the Kappe Brothers' Machine Factory at Alfeld.

Gropius had founded the Bauhaus in 1919 and during its early years there was a great stress on the crafts, but by 1923 the problem of machine production was being tackled. At an exhibition in the summer of that year at Weimar, a prototype mass-produced house, the Haus am Horn, was erected and equipped with furniture by Marcel Breuer of simple, basic shapes. The house, designed by Georg Muche, was square and white with an almost flat roof, but it was symmetrical and rather heavy in appearance. A project by Gropius and Meyer for an International Philosophy Center at Erlangen of 1923–4 is much more advanced and forms a prototype for the Bauhaus building at Dessau itself. The Philosophy Center was to have been a large building of varying heights, flat-roofed with horizontal strips of standardized windows, and a boldly asymmetrical plan. Gropius illustrated it in his *Internationale Architektur*.

The Bauhaus moved to Dessau in 1925 and the new building—Gropius' masterpiece and one of the most famous examples of the International style—was opened in December 1926. The different functions of the school are reflected in the form and grouping of the parts of the building. The students' own rooms form a tall block, each room with its own balcony; the administrative offices are placed in a low bridge spanning a road, with the Director's office in the very center; the workshops have a skeleton frame from which is hung a large, glazed curtain wall with an industrial metal frame. The building's asymmetry and the balanced relationship of the parts are best appreciated in aerial views—in fact it was photographed from the air soon after it was built. Gropius

A competition drawing for an office tower for the Chicago Tribune, submitted by Walter Gropius and Adolf Meyer; 1922

The Bauhaus building at Dessau, designed by Walter Gropius; opened in 1926; an aerial view taken soon after the opening

style, the product of a few forceful personalities. In Germany it centered on the group of architects of *Der Ring*, founded in 1925 in Berlin. Here, immediately after the First World War, architects went through an Expressionist period, designing exciting, visionary, and utopian projects. It was only in 1922 that a stress on orthogonal structure replaced prismatic and organic forms. In Gropius' case the timber house for Adolf Sommerfeld designed with Adolf Meyer in 1920–1 is an example of this Expressionist phase, while their project of 1922 for an office tower for the *Chicago Tribune* shows that the change in style has taken place. The *Tribune* tower with its clearly exposed, regular frame, its repeated standardized

The Barcelona Pavilion

The Barcelona International Exhibition of
1929 was a large and bustling affair on the
scale set by its predecessors in Paris, London,
and Chicago. A specially built National
Palace, massive and multi-domed, dominated
the exhibition with its display of govern-
mental power and the exhibition itself included much rhetorical architecture, most of
it classical in idiom and stuffed with atten-
tion-seeking items, along its imposing avenues. The German contribution was easily
overlooked in this context. Even the words
spoken at the opening by the German com-
missioner were not designed to cause a stir:
"We want nothing more than clarity, simplicity, and integrity". The German pavilion
itself, designed by Mies van der Rohe of
Berlin (1886–1969), echoed these words.

Never has an exhibition building been less
encumbered with explicit messages and displays, and never has an architect had fuller
control over a national building and its
contents. Mies himself chose the site, backed
by the tall, plain wall of the Palace of Alfonso
XIII. He designed every part of the pavilion
and the sparse furniture it contained, and
selected the sculpture (by Georg Kolbe,
1877–1947) which stood above the inner
pool. Only the flag of the German Republic,

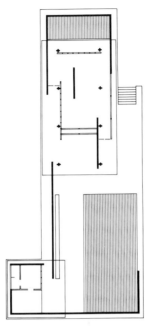

▲ The ground plan of
the German Republic's
pavilion at the Barcelona
International Exhibition
of 1929, designed by
Mies van der Rohe

▼ A view along the back
of the pavilion

Below right The
Barcelona chair,
designed by van der
Rohe; a reproduction;
Ashmolean Museum,
Oxford

planted a few feet from the southeast corner
of the pavilion, announced its origin and
purpose, the flag pole drawing a fine vertical
across the repeated horizontals of the building. The chaste and narrow steps leading up
to its podium were not designed to draw
crowds.

Architecturally, the pavilion represents an
extreme statement of modernist logic. The
elements necessary for a building (a quasi-
domestic building, but untrammeled by the
coarser needs of living—thus a distant
descendant of the primitive hut on which
Vitruvius and others since had based their
architectural theory) were clearly and dis-
cretely displayed: base, roof, supporting columns, dividing and articulating screens. The
eight cruciform columns make a legible grid
related to the rectangle of the roof slab,
leaving the screen walls to be placed according to aesthetic and functional purpose.
These could thus be non-loadbearing, of
glass—clear, etched, or colored—or of
stronger material. They are placed, nonetheless, in exclusively rectangular relationships,
in accord with the idiom followed by every
part of the building in which the human
being—the visitor, and his artistic surrogate
in the sculptured nude—alone represents organic nature. The furniture—the famous Barcelona chair and stool—serves an intermediate function with its exquisitely curved
frames, and so probably did the water in the
two pools sunk into the podium.

The logic and language of this design look
to American architectural invention of the
last years of the 19th century, particularly to
L.H. Sullivan (1856–1924) and Frank Lloyd
Wright (1869–1959), and to the aesthetics of
Dutch *De Stijl* paintings and architectural
projects which combined a system of straight
lines and right angles with this separateness,

▲ A view of the Barcelona pavilion, seen across the open pool

▶ A preliminary sketch for the Barcelona pavilion by Mies van der Rohe

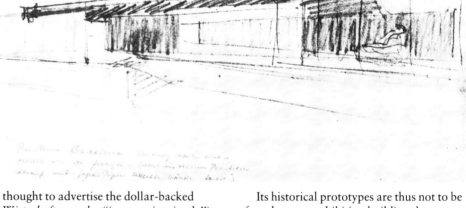

integrity of elements, allowing space and light to flow between them. These stimuli fused perfectly with the innate love of order and precision which had earlier led Mies to base himself on the Neoclassicism of *c*1800, more particularly on the work of the great German architect K.F. Schinkel (1781–1841) whose influence is seen also in the work of other German architects of the modern movement, but Mies' fusion of this tradition with the structural logic and spatial flow of the Americans and Dutch was unique.

Unique also was, and remained, Mies' sense of quality and visual splendor in materials. Here considerations of fine but minimal design met his taste for luxury. The podium of the pavilion and the walls that appear light in photographs were built of Roman travertine, the beautiful grainy stone of which, for instance, G.L. Bernini (1598–1680) built the colonnades of the piazza of St Peter's in Rome. The walls framing the inner pool were of green Tinian marble; the short freestanding wall inside the pavilion was of solid onyx. The generously proportioned, largely handmade furniture combined the finest polished steel with kid leather cushions. The columns were cased in polished chrome. The pools were lined with black glass.

This discreet luxuriousness, exercised for such a representational occasion, may be thought to advertise the dollar-backed *Wirtschaftswunder* ("economic miracle") that had followed Germany's economic collapse of 1923–4. Germany's mood was, however, more hard-headed than this would suggest, and there were many who, while admiring the succinctness of Mies' design, complained that he had not used for his walls some of the many man-made materials being developed at the time, which stood for industrial prowess as well as a modernism intent on independence of nature's ready-made materials, however exquisite. These confections would not have satisfied Mies' ambition: he seems to have recognized fully the opportunity offered by the commission to represent a Germany whose civilization, as much as economy, appeared to be resurgent after a disastrous war, and also a Berlin that appeared to have become the cultural capital of the Western world, with a building whose prime function was to exhibit classical perfection in modern terms.

Its historical prototypes are thus not to be found among exhibition buildings but among the temples and other pleasure pavilions with which gentlefolk of the 18th century and after, emulating Antiquity, articulated their extensive gardens: ideal constructions, as much for looking at as for resting in, images of taste and tranquillity. Behrens, in whose design office Mies had worked for a while, prophesied that the Barcelona Pavilion would "one day be called the most beautiful building of the century"; the architectural critic Raymond McGrath in 1932 called it an epoch-making work. Long before that, however, it had been taken down. We can know it only from visual and verbal documents.

NORBERT LYNTON

Further reading. Blaser, W. *Mies van der Rohe*, London (1965). Bonta, J.P. *An Anatomy of Architectural Interpretation: a Semiotic Review of the Criticism of Mies van der Rohe's Barcelona Pavilion*, Barcelona (1975). Johnson, P. *Mies van der Rohe*, London and New York (1978).

was probably influenced in this dynamic composition by the Russian artist El Lissitzky (1890–1941) who had come to Berlin in 1921, bringing with him Suprematist and Constructivist ideas. In his paintings called *Prouns*, described as "the interchange station between painting and architecture", Lissitzky suggested an architecture that "revolves, swims, flies". His "Skyhook" project of 1924–5 for a raised horizontal skyscraper also looks forward to the Dessau Bauhaus. Gropius ends his *Internationale Architektur* with the Lissitzkyan statement that buildings are striving to hover above the ground.

One of the major characteristics of the International style in general—one that Hitchcock and Johnson underplay—is its dependence on painting, but this is very important. At the Bauhaus, painters determined the appearance of many of the three-dimensional, "utilitarian" objects. As well as Lissitzky, the Dutch nonfigurative artist Theo van Doesburg (1883–1931) was influential there from *c*1921. Johannes Itten, Kandinsky, Klee, and—from 1923—Laszlo Moholy-Nagy were members of the staff, and from them derives the Bauhaus concern for experiment with different materials, for balanced designs, for easily understood (and therefore democratic) basic shapes and primary colors. It was largely through the painters' influence that unified interiors were produced with lights, tables, ashtrays, and floor coverings all closely relating to each other. Moholy-Nagy, who took charge of the Preliminary Course and the Metal Workshop when he arrived, was particularly influential in his research into new materials, exercises in balance and tension, and the use of kinetic and artificial lighting techniques offered by 20th-century technology. His Bauhaus book *Von Material zu Architektur* (1929) is one of the most thrilling source books of the period and suggests an architecture that would make more use of glass and artificial lighting effects than existed in any building actually built, except perhaps the Van Nelle Factory at Rotterdam which Moholy does in fact reproduce.

The influence of artists such as van Doesburg is evident in the house Gropius built for himself at Dessau which has an entrance front composed like a *De Stijl* painting. This was one of seven houses put up for members of the Bauhaus faculty and equipped with fitted cupboards, mechanized kitchens, and light, metal-tube furniture by Breuer. The Törten Estate at Dessau was completed in 1927, and in the same year Gropius was responsible for a prototype prefabricated house at the Weissenhof Siedlung at Stuttgart. The Dammerstock Siedlung at Karlsruhe followed in 1927–8, and then, from 1929 to 1931, the very large blocks of flats at Siemensstadt in Berlin. All are good examples of International style housing: by the late 1920s the style, in Germany at least, had become strongly identified with low-cost housing.

"Minimum housing" was the subject of the second congress of the association *Congrès Internationaux d'Architecture Moderne* (C.I.A.M.) held in 1929 in Frankfurt, while the famous *Deutscher Werkbund* exhibition at the Weissenhof in Stuttgart of 1927 was also devoted to low-cost housing. It was at this exhibition that the international quality of the style

became fully apparent. Thirty-one buildings by architects were erected under the supervision of Mies van der Rohe, vice-chairman of the *Werkbund*. Most of the architects were members of the Berlin *Ring*—Mies himself, Gropius, Behrens, Poelzig, Max and Bruno Taut, and Ludwig Hilbersheimer (who published his book *Internationale Neue Baukunst*, "International New Architecture", at this time). Other Germans were A.G. Schneck, R. Döcker, A. Rading, H. Scharoun, while from abroad there were J. Frank (Austria), Oud (Holland), Stam (Holland), and Le Corbusier (Switzerland/France). The *Werkbund* stipulated that the houses should be sold or let after the exhibition. Mies himself specified that the roofs should be flat and he produced an overall layout for the estate consisting of a sculptural series of interrelated blocks on the hillside.

Methods of assembly varied and individual contributions could be distinguished. Oud and Stam, for example, produced small, simple row houses, Gropius two semi-prefabricated houses, Le Corbusier three reinforced concrete houses partly raised on pilotis with novel interior spaces and roof terraces, while Mies himself designed a steel-framed block of flats. But a visual unity was achieved through the use of white render, horizontal bands of windows, and the predominant rectangularity of the buildings—characteristics which later led the National Socialists to compare the estate to a north African village. That architects from several different countries had produced works similar in style was remarked on at the time; Professor Paul Schmidtthenner, for example, wrote: "We are on the point of getting a prescription for the international style of the 20th century".

Mies van der Rohe's block had 24 flats with a variety of plans, but regular and carefully proportioned elevations. It well justified its important site at the top of the estate. The block was his first building in the International style, although earlier works pointed the way. In 1922 or 1923 he designed a

The block of flats designed by Mies van der Rohe for the Deutscher Werkbund exhibition at the Weissenhof Siedlung, Stuttgart; 1927

concrete office block with unbroken, horizontal glazed and solid bands in front of a concrete frame. Another project of 1923 for a brick villa can be compared to the nonfigurative, strictly horizontal- and vertical-based compositions of van Doesburg or Moholy-Nagy and this despite the fact that Mies wrote in the magazine G in July 1923, "We reject all aesthetic speculation, all doctrine, and all formalism". His flats in the Afrikanische Strasse in Berlin, of 1926–7, are again beautifully proportioned but much solider and heavier in appearance than the Weissenhof block.

Mies van der Rohe's best-known European work post-dates the Weissenhof. His German Pavilion for the International Exhibition at Barcelona in 1929 was a luxurious but functionless building of carefully related beautiful materials—travertine, marble, onyx, opaque and clear glass—used with startling simplicity. The flat roof slab was held above the level *podium* by slim chrome-plated pillars and the screen walls were clearly separated from these supports. The overlapping rectangles of the roof, pools, and screens and the play with opaque and translucent materials again recall Moholy's paintings. The Tugendhat House of the same date at Brno in Czechoslovakia uses similar materials and ideas. The plan of the large, open ground floor with curved and straight dividing screens resembles Kandinsky's Bauhaus paintings. The long, drawn-out base, the terraces and the low white upper story of this house tie it in more closely with the landscape than most International style houses. Before emigrating to America in 1937, Mies directed the Bauhaus, from 1930 to 1933, when it was closed by the National Socialists, and designed buildings for the silk industry in Krefeld which are his last works in the International style.

Although Mies van der Rohe and Gropius are given pride of place among the German contributors in Hitchcock and Johnson's book, other architects active in that country, especially in Berlin, made important contributions to the style. Two of Erich Mendelsohn's buildings were reproduced by Hitchcock and Johnson: the Schocken Department Store at Chemnitz (1928–30) and the German Metal Workers' Union Building in Berlin (back view, 1929–30). Mendelsohn was clearly a major figure, but his relationship to the style was suspect and he did not contribute to the *Weissenhof* exhibition. His Einstein Tower (1920–1) at Potsdam had been one of the very few Expressionist designs to be built, and something of its streamlined, Futurist quality was retained in many of his later works. But a group of villas in suburban Berlin built shortly after the Einstein Tower, in 1922–3—the house for Dr Sternfeld in Heerstrasse for example—are cubic and Wrightian and show that Mendelsohn could accept elements of the new fashion. In the Schocken Store for Stuttgart (1926–8; later demolished) Mendelsohn used repeated, flowing horizontal lines and a glazed wrap-around corner tower to which purists of the International style probably objected. The Schocken Store at Chemnitz has a gently curved facade with uninterrupted ribbon windows alternating with bands of stone facing, and the back of the Metal Workers' Building has a similar light,

banded appearance. Mendelsohn left Germany in 1933 and went to England where the De la Warr Pavilion at Bexhill-on-Sea, which he designed with Chermayeff, is a good example of his work.

Like Mendelsohn, the Luckardt brothers, who also practiced in Berlin, passed through an Expressionist phase before adopting the International style. Their houses at the Rupenhorn, Berlin (1928) are good examples of the style but are mounted on widely sweeping, wing-shaped terraces which are decidedly unclassical. Hans Scharoun also used curves and wing shapes, which make his work relate uneasily to the style. He contributed a house to the Weissenhof estate—one that has two firmly rounded corners. His hostel for the Home and Work Exhibition at Breslau (1928), although it has pilotis, ribbon windows, a flat roof, and a sense of lightness, throws off startling arc shaped extensions. One of his large blocks of flats at Siemensstadt (1930) was illustrated by Hitchcock and Johnson, but even these have balconies projecting at less than a right-angle with curved, nautical screens for privacy.

Outside Berlin, Ernst May, who was City Architect for Frankfurt from 1925 to 1930, produced the largest International style contribution to minimum housing. In the new estates around Frankfurt he successfully fused ideas learnt from the English Garden City movement with the latest mass production methods of building. He thought deeply about the needs of the inhabitants of his houses, gave them large living rooms, fitted storage space and packaged equipment. At Frankfurt he supervised a competent team of designers who left with him for Russia in 1930 in the hope of building mass housing under Communist rule.

Architects from France and Holland made major aesthetic contributions to the International style, but were perhaps less concerned with function than Germans such as May. In France the contribution came from one man, Le Corbusier, although the style was popularized—and misunderstood—by less able architects such as Mallet-Stevens. Before the First World War, Corbusier had made contact with many of the great pioneers—Behrens, Loos, Berlage—as well as with Garnier and Perret in France. He had also traveled extensively around the Mediterranean and been deeply impressed both by the simple, vernacular block houses painted in white and pastel colors and by Classical remains such as the Acropolis.

His ideas came to fruition in Paris immediately after the War. Once again, painting was a vital stimulus. In November 1918 he and an artist friend, Amédée Ozenfant (1886–1966), to whom he had been introduced by Perret, published a book about contemporary painting titled *Après le Cubisme*. With this they launched "Purism", a post-War, post-Cubist, two-man movement signifying a "recall to order" after the years of destruction. The subjects of their Purist paintings were *objet-types*, everyday café utensils, standard bottles, glasses and plates, which had evolved their shapes over a long period, through a process of natural selection. Corbusier and Ozenfant painted these objects in elevation and bird's-eye view, with contours clearly outlined and brought together like parts

The tiny Maison Ozenfant in Paris, designed by Le Corbusier; probably c1923–4

of a machine. Compositions were based on proportional systems such as the Golden Section so that chance was excluded and a mathematical, ideal harmony conveyed.

Le Corbusier, who painted under his real name C.E. Jeanneret, and Ozenfant produced these clear, concise pictures from c1919 to c1926: Le Corbusier's buildings of this period owe much to their compositions. His architectural plans from 1922 usually show a rectangular exterior frame enclosing curved and straight interior partitions which bear a startling resemblance to the profiles of bottles, bowls, and cups! His elevations often made use of a proportional system. The idea of *objet-types*, of a selective evolutionary process at work among machine-made products, was also very important for his choice of furnishings. It determined as well the sources from which Corbusier derived his architectural style—the latest ocean liners, trains, aeroplanes, industrial buildings whose forms had been evolved to suit the needs of 20th-century man.

Le Corbusier spread his ideas through the magazine *L'Esprit Nouveau* (1920–5) and several very forceful books which were largely drawn from it—*Vers une Architecture* (1923), *L'Art Décoratif d'Aujourd'hui* (1926), *Urbanisme* (1926). His writing is declamatory, urgent—in *Vers une Architecture* he writes:

> We must create the mass-production spirit.
> The spirit of constructing mass-production houses.
> The spirit of living in mass-production houses.

> ... the mass production house, healthy (and morally so too) and beautiful in the same way that the working tools and instruments which accompany our existence are beautiful.

> We claim, in the name of the steamship, of the airplane, and of the motor-car, the right to health, logic, daring, harmony, perfection.

Illustrations of grain silos, the superstructure of liners, aeroplanes, details of motor engines are juxtaposed with Classical buildings to make a startling equation between the ancient and modern worlds: "the airplane mobilized invention, intelligence, and daring: *imagination* and *cold reason*. It is the same spirit that built the Parthenon." The machine had established a new spirit and set up international standards which were exact, precise, ordered, pure. Engineers could teach architects aesthetic as well as practical lessons. In *Vers une Architecture* Corbusier's famous definition of architecture is printed below a photograph of a Canadian Pacific liner, *The Empress of Asia*: "Architecture is the masterly, correct and magnificent play of masses brought together in light."

In 1920 Corbusier designed a "mass-production" house, the Maison Citrohan. This had load-bearing lateral walls, a flat roof terrace, and a double-height living room lit by a large studio window. It resembled a Mediterranean block house but was also inspired by vernacular cafés and workshops in Paris. At the Salon d'Automne of 1922 he showed a plaster model of the house which was now partly raised on "pilotis": an invention he thought to be of great value as it freed the ground beneath the house and when carried through as a supporting frame enabled interior partitions and exterior elements, such as windows, to be composed at will.

The Citrohan house was finally built in a further revised version on a conspicuous site at the Weissenhofsiedlung. From outside, it, and the two semidetached neighboring houses which Corbusier also designed, appeared as light, white, rectangular boxes partly raised above the ground with roof decks and windows which were either of the studio type or else grouped into long narrow ribbons like those in a train carriage. The interior spaces were also influenced by liners and trains; the living rooms were large and open, whereas passageways, lavatories, and kitchens were pared down to the smallest practical dimensions. In the Citrohan house the two-story-high living room had an open mezzanine at the back forming a sleeping area and the bathroom was separated from this space by a curved partition which stopped several feet short of the ceiling. The living rooms of the two semidetached houses had movable partitions which could be closed at night to turn the space into "sleeping-cabins" connected by a corridor with dimensions based on those in *Wagon-Lits Cie Internationale* (The International Railway Sleepers Co.).

Similar characteristics are found in Corbusier's other houses of this period, most of which were built in or around Paris. Some, for artists, were on small, restricted sites; others, for wealthy but artistically minded patrons, enjoyed rural views. The Villa at Vaucresson (1922–3) is one of the earliest. It has a "nautical" facade composed according to a proportional system, large, open living areas, and a central bathroom. This is enclosed in partly curved walls, following the curve of the bath, but the other interior walls and the exterior ones, which are load bearing, form rectangles. The tiny Maison Ozenfant, usually dated 1922 but more likely to be 1923–4, is more advanced. Its interior plan resembles a Purist painting composition—the large studio space is broken into by a shelf-like open loft and a crow's-nest *bibliothèque* accessible by metal companion ways. The saw-tooth roof, now altered, resembled that of a factory, and the industrial glazing was again disposed according to a proportional system. The linked La Roche and Jeanneret houses of the same date are also on a restricted site in Auteil, Paris, but they are larger with enjoyable roof terraces and a gallery—for La Roche's Purist paintings—raised on pilotis and resembling the bridge of a ship.

Nautical elements are also important in the Villa Cook at Boulogne-sur-Seine (1926), the Villa at Garches for the Steins (1927) and in the well known Villa Savoye (1928–30). These are luxurious houses; in them Le Corbusier was able to realize fully his aesthetic ideas. All have regular reinforced concrete frames of free standing pilotis which enabled him to compose elevations and interior plans as he wished. Ribbon windows run without interruption along the framing facades; balconies or viewing terraces are punched out or slotted in creating an asymmetric balance; curved partitions, stairways, and ramps

The Villa at Garches, designed by Le Corbusier; 1927

form exciting sculptural shapes in the open, unified interior spaces.

Although these unique houses are Le Corbusier's best-known buildings in the International style, much of his time in the 1920s was taken up with—for the most part unrealized—schemes for mass housing. As well as the Citrohan house, he showed at the Salon d'Automne of 1922 his plans for *Une Ville Contemporaine de Trois Millions d'Habitants* and in the 1925 International Decorative Arts Exhibition in Paris he presented his *L'Esprit Nouveau* pavilion as an ideal living cell for machine-age man. The cell was intended as one of many which, when stacked together, would form a block of *Immeubles-villas* (villas-flats). It was equipped with standard mass-produced furniture, such as Thonet chairs and laboratory glassware. With these *objet-types* the Purists cocked a snook at the frivolous *Art Déco* in the official pavilions in the Exhibition. But the only mass housing that was actually built was an estate at Pessac near Bordeaux, financed by M. Frugès, a sugar refiner. The estate was opened in 1926, but aroused considerable controversy and remained empty for several years. The houses, basically of two different types, had flat roofs and were built of reinforced concrete painted white, brown, green, and blue. They were likened to sugar lumps and the estate was nicknamed *la ville de Maroc*.

In Holland as in France the formation of a new style of architecture depended on an aesthetic derived from avant-garde painting. Here it was produced by the *De Stijl* group, founded in 1917 and consisting of the painters Mondrian, van Doesburg, Huszar, and van der Leck with the architects Oud, Wils, and van t'Hoff. Their magazine, *De Stijl*, was launched in October of that year and continued until 1931 when van Doesburg, who was largely responsible for it, died. It explained their ideas and reproduced their work, and after the First World War was extremely influential outside Holland, especially in Germany.

Mondrian was the most important painter and, with van Doesburg, the main theorist of the group. He had been painting Abstract pictures with compositions based exclusively on the horizontal and vertical since c1914, but it was only in 1921 that his style was fully mature. Then he composed his pictures on an asymmetrically balanced grid of black horizontal and vertical lines and restricted his palette to the primary colors with gray and white. Van Doesburg produced similar, though not identical work. They thought that these basic angles and colors expressed fundamental reality, that the universe was formed from opposing forces. By painting harmonious, balanced pictures they were showing these forces in an ideal equilibrium. The balance had to be asymmetric, according to Mondrian, as symmetry marked things as being apart, separate, and therefore against the universal (*see* Abstract Art).

The architecture of the *De Stijl* group lagged behind their painting; it was only in 1923 that their ideas started to influence buildings, or rather projects for buildings because very little was actually built. But earlier work by van t'Hoff and

Oud must be mentioned. In 1916 van t'Hoff built a concrete villa at Huis-ter-Heide outside Utrecht. It has a flat roof with wide cantilevered eaves and a blocky, rectangular form which betrays the strong influence of Frank Lloyd Wright whom van t'Hoff had met in Chicago. But it is symmetrical and rather monumental, and in this way differs from later De Stijl buildings.

In the following year (1917) Oud produced a project for a terrace of holiday houses at Scheveningen which resembles Garnier's repeated housing units. Then c1919 Oud designed a project for a factory at Purmerend which again has Wrightian parts and an asymmetric central element recalling paintings of a slightly earlier date by Mondrian and van Doesburg. Another unrealized project of 1921, for the Kallenbach house in Berlin, was extremely advanced with a flat roof and planar walls, but his only executed buildings that show the influence of De Stijl theory are a temporary builder's shelter (1923) and the facade of the Rotterdam café De Unie (1925; destroyed).

Oud had been appointed City Architect for Rotterdam in 1918, and by the mid 1920s was designing low-cost housing in the International style. His work of this kind of c1925 to c1930 features prominently in Hitchcock and Johnson's book. A short street of small row houses at the Hook of Holland (1924–7) are rendered white, have horizontal windows, mass-produced metal door frames, and decidedly nautical curved elements. The Kiefhoek estate at Rotterdam (1925–9) is much larger but built in a similar style. For the Weissenhof Exhibition Oud designed a row of five houses which are again very small, but practical, with carefully worked out plans and functional, metal furniture. A single living room faces the garden in front, while services are at the back on the street. In their scale there is something traditionally Dutch about these houses.

For Oud the new aesthetic meant primarily an acceptance of the machine. He welcomed industrialized techniques and new materials. In this he opposed the ideas of the Amsterdam school of Expressionist architects, such as de Klerk, who used brick and tile, but agreed with his De Stijl colleagues van Doesburg and Mondrian. Van Doesburg used the term "the mechanical aesthetic" in a lecture he gave at Weimar and elsewhere in 1922. He considered that the machine liberated man from material concerns, led to the universal from the particular, and was thus a major unifying force. Mondrian welcomed the artificiality of modern life and preferred the city, where nature had been straightened out, to the country.

In December 1920 van Doesburg visited Berlin, where he met Gropius, and during the next two years he established contacts with other architects and artists working in Germany—Lissitzky, Hans Richter, and Feininger. His influence at the Bauhaus was considerable. Perhaps in turn influenced by the Bauhaus he became increasingly interested in applying De Stijl ideas to architecture and in October and November

1923 showed models for three De Stijl houses at Léonce Rosenberg's gallery in Paris, "L'Effort Moderne". He was helped with these by Cor van Eesteren, a fully qualified École des Beaux-Arts architect. With van Eesteren and Rietveld, who had built one of the models, van Doesburg issued a manifesto presenting his ideas; a fuller statement, signed by van Doesburg alone, was published in De Stijl in the following year.

The new architecture shown in the models—particularly the one for a private house—consisted of a balanced composition of rectangular planes linked at right angles to each other. The planes appeared to float, forming positive/negative, open and closed spaces which broke down the usual separation between inside and outside. As the planes were of unequal size, and colored with De Stijl colors, they were clearly distinguished from each other: van Doesburg stressed that this clear distinction gave movement, and with it time, a new importance. De Stijl architecture was anti-cubic, and as it consisted of "a balanced relationship of unequal parts" it "rendered front, back, right, left, top and bottom, factors of equal value".

Regrettably, van Doesburg was unable to realize these ideas in a building. By 1926, when he started to decorate the Aubette in Strasbourg, his style had changed, and he had adopted the more dynamic 45-degree angle; in 1929, when he designed his own studio at Meudon, he used a mathematically based plan relating to the most recent Concrete art. He was not invited to contribute to the Weissenhof Exhibition nor to the Decorative Arts Exhibition in Paris, although an associate, Frederick Kiesler, did show there, in the Austrian Pavilion, a "System of Tension in Free Space" which was De Stijl in conception.

But in the year following the exhibition of models at Rosenberg's gallery, one De Stijl house was built by Gerrit Rietveld, who had joined the group in 1919. This was a small house for Mde Schroeder attached to the end of a row of conventional houses in Utrecht. Although it was not freestanding and the primary colors were restricted to the supporting metal "I" beams, it resembled the models in its balance of planes and of closed and open spaces. The interior could be transformed, by means of screens, from an open to a closed plan, and it was equipped with furniture, by Rietveld, unified with the architecture by means of its color and form.

Despite the originality of this house, Rietveld, like van Doesburg, was not invited to contribute to the Weissenhof Exhibition. Nor does his work appear in Hitchcock and Johnson's book. It was probably felt that the true De Stijl architecture of c1923–4 was too anti-cubic, too asymmetric, too much lacking a regular supporting skeleton to be classed as International style. Neither did Hitchcock and Johnson wholly approve of the use of bright colors, as they thought it made "too sharp a contrast with natural surroundings". Rietveld's later work, his row houses at 5–11 Erasmuslaan, Utrecht (1930–1) and at the Wiener Werkbund Siedlung (1930–2), for example, have simple rectangular outlines, horizontal bands of windows, and white stucco, and so can be

The Villa Savoye at Poissy designed by Le Corbusier; 1929–31; above, a roof terrace; below, an interior view

Houses at the Hook of Holland designed by J.J.P. Oud; 1924–7

classed more easily than the Schroeder house as International style buildings.

Two other Dutch architects must be mentioned: Mart Stam (1899–1986) and Johannes Duiker (1890–1935). Stam is a truly international figure who worked in Holland, Germany, Switzerland, and Russia. He had met and been impressed by both Lissitzky and Mies van der Rohe in Berlin in the early 1920s; Russian and German influences can be seen in his early projects. Two designs for schools, the St Wendel Boys' Grammar School (1924) and the Thunn Boys' Grammar School (1925) were already in the International style. To the Weissenhof Siedlung he contributed a terrace of three houses composed into a rectangular block in such a way that some aesthetic choices must have been made, although Stam thought of himself as a pure functionalist. Hitchcock and Johnson remarked defensively of his Budge Home for Old People at Frankfurt (1929–30), which they illustrate, that though built by an architect who claimed "to be guided solely by considerations of economy and function, the building has real aesthetic merit as well." Stam worked at this time with May in Frankfurt and he went with May to Russia in 1930.

J. Duiker is even less well known than Stam and as undeservedly neglected. He designed at least three buildings of very high quality indeed: the Zonnestraal Sanatorium (1926–8) near Hilversum, an open-air school in Cliostraat, Amsterdam (1928–30), and the Handelsblad-Cineac (1934) in the

same city. All are astringently functional buildings: skeletal, light-weight, and tough. In them the conventional division between industrial and public or civic buildings seems to have completely disappeared.

The International style pioneered in Germany, France, and Holland had spread to a great many other countries by 1932 as Hitchcock and Johnson showed. In the USSR some of the architects who had come forward after the Revolution used the style for large-scale socialist building schemes. The group most open to Western ideas was the "Association of Contemporary Architects" (O.C.A.) founded in 1925 by M. Guinzbourg and the brothers A., V., and L. Vesnin with M. Bartch, A. Gan, I. and P. Golossov, and M. Kolly. In their magazine *Contemporary Architecture* they reproduced works by Gropius, Mies, Le Corbusier, and other Western architects: Le Corbusier seems to have been particularly admired by them. His influence can be seen, for example, in the Vesnins' project for the Lenin Library (1929), Guinzbourg's Narkomfin Flats (1928–9) and his Government Buildings for Alma-Ata, and in the many communal living projects of the late 1920s by Bartch, Vladimirov, and others. The influence was in fact a two way one; Corbusier later used some of their ideas, such as the "interior street" with communal facilities. His Centrosoyus building in Moscow—conceived in 1928 but only finished several years later with the help of N. Kolly—was the largest of his works until the Marseilles Unité was built after the Second World War; it too seems to reflect earlier O.C.A. group projects.

In Finland Alvar Aalto (1898–1976) passed through an International style period. His editorial offices for the *Turun Sanomat* (1927–9) at Turku are in the style, and so is the more photogenically impressive sanatorium at Paimio (1928–33). The clear articulation of parts in this building, the tall stack of sun-decks cantilevered from a narrow spine rising above the forest, and perhaps the sense that the style relates well to the building's purpose, make it one of the most attractive in the period.

The other Scandinavian countries had no architect with as much conviction as Aalto, but in Denmark Arne Jacobsen (1902–71) used the Style with great restraint in the Bellavista Housing Estate (1933) near Copenhagen. In Sweden Gunnar Asplund (1885–1940) introduced it with a tremendous flourish at the Stockholm Exhibition of 1930.

Several interesting International style buildings were erected in Czechoslovakia, particularly in Brno where Mies van der Rohe's Tugendhat house was built. Hitchcock and Johnson illustrate other buildings in Brno in the style by O. Eisler, B. Fuchs, and J. Kranz. In Prague, L. Kysela's Bata Shoe Store (1929), also illustrated by Hitchcock and Johnson, had remarkably advanced glazed facade: an International style version of the great Art Nouveau store fronts in Paris and Brussels. Of a later date but still in the style is the very large cruciform office block, also in Prague, of the General Pensions Institute Headquarters (1932–4), by J. Havlicek and K. Honzik.

Although Italy produced nothing as avant-garde as Futurism after the First World War, the founders of the International style, such as Gropius and Le Corbusier, greatly admired Matté-Trucco's Fiat factory (1923) with its rooftop testing

track. Their work in turn was influential for a body of young architects called the *Gruppo 7* founded in 1926. The most talented member of this group, G. Terragni, tried to give a more three-dimensional quality to his architecture than he found in that of the French and German International style architects. He also tried to link the new sense of classicism with Fascist ideology. That he was successful in both these aims can be seen in, for example, his Novecomum flats (1927) and the Casa del Fascio (1936) at Como.

In Switzerland, examples of International style architecture are surprisingly scarce, but a large estate (1930–2) at Neubühl outside Zurich by E. Roth, Haefeli, H. Schmidt, and others is clearly modeled on Ernst May's estates at Frankfurt, and two apartment houses on the Doldertal in Zurich (1933–6) for Siegfried Giedion—the secretary of C.I.A.M. and one of the principle apologists of modern architecture—are indebted to Le Corbusier. These were designed by Marcel Breuer and the Swiss architects A. and E. Roth. Their pilotis, roof terraces, and rectangular framing skins recall the Villa Cook and the Villa Savoye. Le Corbusier himself and the other major Swiss architect of this period, Hannes Meyer, found little work in Switzerland. Tragically Le Corbusier's design for the League of Nations building in Geneva (1927) was not accepted and his only building of this period in Switzerland is a very small house on Lake Léman (1925).

From America, Hitchcock and Johnson illustrated two skyscrapers—the McGraw-Hill building in New York (1931) and the Philadelphia Savings Bank in Philadelphia (1931–2) by Howe and Lescaze—a filling station, a laboratory, an experimental aluminum house and Richard Neutra's Lovell Health House, in Los Angeles (1927–9). They criticize the Lovell House for being "complicated", but Neutra's buildings and those of the other West Coast architects, Irving Gill and

The house at Utrecht designed by Gerrit Rietveld for Mde Schroeder; 1924

Houses built on the Weissenhof Siedlung at Stuttgart designed by Mart Stam; 1927

The reception desk in the sanatorium at Paimio, Finland, designed by Alvar Aalto; 1928–33

Rudolph Schindler, really have very little in common with European International style works. Gill's white, rectangular Dodge House, in Hollywood, built as early as 1916 (now demolished) was indebted to vernacular Spanish buildings in California and possibly to a knowledge of Loos' houses in Vienna. Both Schindler and Neutra had actually trained in Vienna, and after their arrival in America both worked with Wright. Wright taught them how to destroy boxy space, to admire Japanese post-and-beam building, and above all to establish a dramatic dialogue between their buildings and the landscapes in which they are sited. Schindler's Beach House at Newport Beach, California (1926), Neutra's Lovell House, and Wright's own Falling Water House at Bear Run, Pennsylvania (1935–7), in which the influence of the European masters has been detected, use steel, glass, and whitened concrete, but not in the way of the International style. Their white, rectangular, cantilevered elements form ledges, beneath which are dark and mysterious horizontals of deep shade.

Only one English building, Joseph Emberton's Royal Corinthian Yacht Club at Burnham-on-Crouch (1931), found a place in Hitchcock and Johnson's book. The style in fact came late to Britain and was only practiced in the 1930s. It

had to overcome considerable opposition which at its most extreme resembled that of the German National Socialists. In 1933 Sir Reginald Blomfield, for example, remarked that the new architecture "is essentially Continental in its origin and inspiration, and it claims as a merit that it is cosmopolitan. As an Englishman and proud of his country, I detest and despise cosmopolitanism."

Apart from the Yacht Club, one of the earliest English buildings in the International style was a house at Amersham, "High and Over" (1929–30), by Amayas Connell, a young architect with a conventional training; he had won the Rome Prize. This house has a Y-shaped plan that looks back to Arts and Crafts country houses, but it was built of white concrete and had horizontal bands of windows and a flat roof. Connell, soon joined by Basil Ward and Colin Lucas, continued to design houses which often have adventurous, picturesque plans. New Farm at Grayswood, Surrey (1932), for example, has a fan-shaped plan and International style elevations. Le Corbusier seems to have been particularly influential for their houses at Parkwood Estate, Ruislip, London (1933–5) and at 66 Frognal, Hampstead, London (1938), which again caused great opposition.

The reluctance of local councils to accept modern architecture limited the style to a middle-class market in Britain, although some low-cost housing was built: Kent House, Chalk Farm, London (1935) by Connell, Ward, and Lucas and Sassoon House, Camberwell, London (1934) by Maxwell Fry are examples. The well-known flats at Lawn Road, Hampstead (1933–4) by Wells Coates and at Highpoint, Highgate, London (1933–5) by the Tecton firm were for middle-class residents. The Lawn Road flats is a sculptural, rather Russian-looking building with cantilevered access balconies leading to minimum flats equipped with fitted furniture. Wells Coates thought modern people should travel light. He was an engineer by training and was, of all the avant-garde architects in England, the one most in tune with recent Continental ideas. At the 1933 C.I.A.M. congress he represented the newly founded English branch who called themselves the Modern Architectural Research Association (M.A.R.S.).

Highpoint One by the Tecton firm is a large double-cross shaped block, beautifully sited and justifiably admired by Le Corbusier. Tecton had been set up in 1933 by the Russian refugee Berthold Lubetkin with a group of young English architects—Drake, Skinner, Chitty, Dugdale, Harding, Samuel, and, later, Lasdun. With the help of the structural engineers Arup and Samuely the firm used reinforced concrete excitingly and sensitively: their Penguin Pool at London Zoo with its spiral ramps (1934) is well known. As with Connell, Ward, and Lucas, Le Corbusier was the Tecton firm's main inspiration; his influence can be seen not only in Highpoint One but in their Health Centre at Finsbury, London (1939) and in the houses by Lubetkin and Pilichowski in Genesta Road, London (1934), in Six Pillars, Crescent Wood Road, London (1935) by V. Harding, and in 32 Newton Road, London (1938) by Lasdun.

Hitchcock and Johnson end their book optimistically: "We

Flats at Highpoint, Highgate, London, designed by the Tecton firm; 1933–5

have an architecture still", but ironically by 1932 the International style was almost unused in its countries of origin. In Germany the National Socialists disliked the style because it was international: "The new dwelling is an instrument for the destruction of the family and the race." When they came to power, the architects who had founded the style emigrated: it did not survive transplantation. Similarly in Russia the political situation prevented International style building after *c*1932. In Holland Duiker died young (in 1935), while van Doesburg—who had anyway settled in Paris by the mid 1920s—had also died young in 1931. In France Le Corbusier abandoned the style. His Maison Suisse in Paris incorporates a random rubble wall and is raised on massive central pilotis left textured from the grain of their wooden shuttering.

The International style had been a movement of tremendous excitement and optimism, full of the belief that the new technology would enable architects to provide healthier, lighter, more functional, and enjoyable buildings than ever before, but because it *was* a style, the International style only lasted a short time. Moreover, because many of the buildings were put up cheaply and their white stucco finishes have not been well maintained, they have become shoddy. Today the optimistic belief in the machine has almost vanished. We are also more aware of the work of other architects who practiced at the same time but with very different approaches, such as Buckminster Fuller and Pierre Chareau. But International style buildings are still studied today because they were built as answers to problems that are still with us, and because, at their best, they are beautiful.

ALASTAIR GRIEVE

Bibliography. Banham, R. *Theory and Design in the First Machine Age*, London (1960). Benton, T. and C. *History of Architecture and Design 1890–1939*, Milton Keynes (1975). Conrads, U. (ed.; trans. Bullock, M.) *Programmes and Manifestoes on 20th Century Architecture*, London (1972). Hatje, G. (ed.) *Encyclopaedia of Modern Architecture*, London (1963). Hitchcock, H.-R. and Johnson, P. *The International Style: Architecture since 1922*, New York (1932), reprinted in paperback (1966). Whitford, F. *Bauhaus*, London (1984).

50
LATIN AMERICAN ART

A detail of the Prophet Ezekiel, a sculpture by O Aleijadinho, one of the 12 prophets he carved
to stand in front of the church of Bom Jesus de Matozinhos,
Congonhas do Campo, Brazil; 1800–5 (see pages 909–10)

THE term "Latin American" itself needs some explanation and qualification. It was during the Independence movements in Central and South America in the early 19th century that people were encouraged for political reasons to think of themselves as "Americans". The desire to sever connections with the old colonial powers, Spain and Portugal, effectively ruled out terms like New Spain, although linguistic and cultural links are maintained through the use of the term "Latin". For some this remains an unsatisfactorily vague term, and "Ibero-American" or "Hispano-American" are both also in common use.

The term's fundamental inadequacy, however, is that it fails to account for the original and surviving inhabitants of the continents, the Maya of the Yucatan and Guatemala, for example, or the Quechua speakers of the Andes, as well as the considerable African population of the Caribbean and parts of Central and South America. The term "American Indian" itself depends entirely on the Old World, deriving from a geographical error, and from the name of one of the earliest explorers, Amerigo Vespucci (1454–1512), who happened to be first into print with the account of his travels, *Nuevo Mundo*, in 1503. The name "America" first appears on a German map of the then known world in 1507.

Neither the political nor the cultural consciousness of the native inhabitants was extinguished overnight. Native civic and religious stone architecture ceased to be built, although ordinary dwellings in many places have remained as they always were. But mural painting in the 16th century still—occasionally and startlingly—drew on native stylistic conventions and imagery (compare the church at Ixmiquilpan, or the cloister at Cuauntinchan where the Jaguar and the Eagle assist at the Annunciation).

Native pictorial books were still produced during the 16th century (though possession of these ritual or genealogical manuscripts was punishable by the Inquisition) and even up to the 18th century, in the deliberately archaic Techiacloyan manuscripts produced to substantiate land claims. The Maya, the only people to possess hieroglyphic writing, quickly adopted the Roman script in which they continued to write their own history into the 19th century, and indeed until the present day.

It is important to raise these problems, because they help to explain why "Latin American" does not automatically correspond with any kind of cultural homogeneity, and they suggest the problems of identity experienced in the region during the post-Independence period, when Indian culture and society was rediscovered and explored as an essential element in a new national identity.

Colonial Art. In 1493 the as yet largely undiscovered territories of America were divided by papal decree along a line of latitude 370 leagues west of the Cape Verde Islands, the lands to the west of this line being given to the Spaniards, and those to the east to the Portuguese. The art that developed in the countries settled by the Spaniards differs from that of the Portuguese lands—now Brazil—for two main reasons: first, the cultures of Spain and Portugal at the time of the conquest were very different despite frequent cross-fertilization, and these differences became exaggerated in America; second, the lands given to the Spaniards included those already populated by the most sophisticated indigenous cultures—the Aztec, Maya, and Inca peoples, already skilled in techniques such as metalwork, stone-carving, and fresco painting, and quick to understand and adapt to their conquerors' artistic needs. Indigenous and *mestizo* (mixed race) craftsmen in Spanish America played an important part in the development of a style easily distinguishable from its European counterpart, although the arts of colonial Brazil always relied heavily on European sources.

Throughout the colonial period the most important function of the arts was the service of the church; of the arts architecture played a more important role than painting or sculpture. Initially, the successful conversion of the Indians depended on the rapid establishment of suitable centers for worship, and during the 16th century thousands of simple, barn-like churches were built to accommodate the neophytes. In some areas, in Mexico in particular, a new architectural form known as the open chapel developed, consisting of no more than a small, usually vaulted shelter for the altar and the officiants, which was open on one or more sides, so that the Indians gathered in the sunshine in front could hear the preaching and witness the rituals.

But once an architectural framework was established, then paintings and sculptures were needed to illustrate and reinforce the lessons and sermons of the priests. The first missionaries were well aware of the importance of replacing the iconography of the indigenous belief-systems with that of Christianity, and, to start with, the enormous demand for suitable works of art was met in two ways: first, by the importation from Europe of large numbers of religious images, hurriedly and often shoddily made specifically for the American market; and second, by the establishment in monasteries of schools in which Indian craftsmen would be instructed in the principles of European-style representational art, and in the rudiments of Christian symbolism.

In Mexico and Peru in the 16th century, for example, the monks trained the Indians to paint in fresco, because it was a cheap and effective way of simulating architectural details as well as illustrating the Christian story. These frescoes generally use European prints as sources of inspiration, and interesting examples survive in several churches and monasteries (for example, Actopan, Mexico, 1570s, and Andahuaylillas, Peru, *c*1600). In these two countries in particular the large output of Christian works of art is paralleled by the vigorous survival of many native artistic traditions. In Mexico, painted books continued to be produced long after the conquest, modified by contact with European art; in Peru, private houses were built by Inca-trained masons in the traditional style, and the mestizo Guamán Poma de Ayala illustrated his history of Peru with drawings that display a pleasing synthesis of European

A Ranch-owner and his Foreman, a lithograph from "A Journey ... through the Republic of Mexico"; 1828. Library of Congress, Washington, D.C.

forms with indigenous motifs and ideas (c1613).

Meanwhile, throughout the 16th century, artists, especially painters, emigrated to Spanish America from several European countries. From Antwerp came Simon Pereyns (fl. 1566–88) who settled in Mexico, and used northern European engravings for inspiration, as, for example, in his retable at Huejotzingo (1586), while, also in Mexico, the elegant works of Andrés de la Concha (fl. 1575–1612) and the St Cecilia Master demonstrate their Sevillian training. Several Italians settled in South America: Bernardo Bitti (1548–c1620) and Mateo Pérez de Alesio (1547–c1628) worked in Peru, and Angelino de Medoro in Columbia. In Tunja in Colombia several mansions have richly frescoed ceilings (of c1590–c1628) which betray French influence. In Quito in Ecuador the Dominican Pedro Bedón (c1556–1621) derived his Italianate style from his master Bitti, while, in contrast, the Franciscan-trained Indian craftsmen formed the basis of a strong Flemish-influenced school of painters.

From about the beginning of the 17th century the Indian and mestizo craftsmen begin to set up workshops of their own, and craftsmen's guilds were founded. In the major centers of Lima, Bogotá, and Mexico City, these guilds had a monopoly and membership was restricted to those of European blood. Working for patrons culturally orientated towards Europe, guild members received the most valuable commissions and were dependent on Europe for inspiration, while the Indians and mestizos produced works of art for an audience initially wholly ignorant of Christianity and of Christian imagery, and so could deviate more from European models.

Thus, during the 17th century and later, the distinction between art produced by and for the European elite and that produced by and for the Indians remains fairly clearly marked. Painters emerge, for example, who, while born in South America, are nevertheless always orientated towards Europe: Mexican examples include Luis Juárez (fl. 1610–33), Baltasar de Echave Ibía, and Alonso López de Herrera (1579–1648). The work of the latter shows the influence of imported paintings by Zurbarán, whose influence was also felt in Lima, in Peru. The influence of Rubens, Murillo, and Valdés Leal is evident in later-17th-century painters such as the Mexican Cristóbal de Villalpando (c1652–1714), particularly in his important allegorical works in Mexico City Cathedral. Murillo was also influential in South America, especially in the art of the mestizo Miguel de Santiago (fl. in Quito, c1625–1706) whose soft, mystical style in turn influenced Colombia's Gregorio Váquez Ceballos (1638–1711).

In Peru, Diego Quispe Tito, unusually for a mestizo (fl. in Cuzco, mid 17th century) followed Mannerist norms, using Flemish prints as sources, while the rest of the Cuzco mestizo school developed in different directions. The series of paintings The Procession of the Corpus (S. Ana, Cuzco, c1660) for example, used untraditional spatial arrangements, while also providing useful information about the role of religious images in processions. Generally speaking, in the Cuzco school, figures are rigid and full frontal, colors strong, and decorative patterns are often applied in gold leaf over the garments. In Bolivia, strong schools of painting emerge in Sucre and Potosí which draw heavily on Cuzqueñan models. Melchor Pérez de Holguín, for example (c1660–1724), successfully combined details of indigenous inspiration with a European sense of depth and contour.

But despite the obvious dependence of the metropolitan schools on European models, all colonial art differs to a greater or lesser extent from that being produced contemporaneously in Europe: intially there is a simplification of both style and subject matter, and this allows room for later expansion in new, untraditional directions. The repeated copying of imported works of art and of engravings tends towards a simplification of style. This is particularly noticeable in the cult images of the Virgin or of Christ which flourished all over Latin America—the phenomenon deserves attention. An original image, such as the 17th-century wooden crucifix known as the *Cristo de los Temblores* ("Christ of the Earthquakes") in Cuzco Cathedral, was attributed with miraculous powers, in this instance the cessation of an earthquake; it became widely renowned, and was copied by other artists so that its veneration could continue elsewhere. In many cases a cult-image in wood or stone was copied on to canvas or panel, complete with the curtains, candles, and flowers which decorated the altar. These copies then often acquire miraculous power themselves, becoming copied in turn, and at each stage they become flatter and more hieratical in style, especially when the copy involves a change in medium such as from sculpture into paint. This loss of contour is balanced by an elaboration of decorative elements, producing a style quite distinct from anything in Europe.

Subject matter becomes radically simplified in America: only the Virgin, a few favored saints, and scenes from the birth and death of Christ occur with any regularity in the early colonial years, and this is at least partly because the newly converted Indians would have been confused by too great a variety of imagery. Gradually, new elements are introduced into the traditional vocabulary: the Virgin, for instance, may forsake her accustomed blue robe in favor of a skirt made of multicolored feathers, or a fashionable riding hat, while her pose remains unchanged, easily traceable to its European prototype. And in South America in the 18th century, rows of archangels in magnificent contemporary costumes and carrying firearms decorate many of the churches: here the artists, seeking something new, invented a genre without precedent in Europe, finding inspiration in engravings in manuals of instruction for musketeers.

Throughout the colonial period the most important sculptural forms were church facades and retables, but the names of their creators are rarely preserved. In the 16th century, the plateresque style was dominant, typified by a profusion of

The Plateresque cloisters of the Acolman Convent, Mexico; 1560

fanciful decorative detail wreathing the architectural members, while niches contain relatively simple, realistic statues. In Mexico, the Acolman facade (1560) is pure plateresque, while the retable of San Francisco, Maní, Yucatán, where columns are replaced by stiff, flat caryatids while the niche statues remain three-dimensional, shows the direction of local developments. Other examples are the facades at Tlamanalco (early 1560s) which includes Aztec motifs, and at Yuririapúndaro, an interesting, less classical version of Acolman (*post* 1560).

During the 17th century, church facades become increasingly highly decorated. In Mexico, at La Soledad, Oaxaca (1689), many fine statues survive, and a comparison of the reliefs from the Augustinian churches in Mexico City (1677–92) and Oaxaca shows the continuing trends of classicism in the former, as against stylization in their animated derivatives at Oaxaca.

In South America the early church portals are generally very simple, but some fine figure-sculpture survives in Quito and Lima. In Bolivia towards the end of the 16th century, fine choirstalls were produced for Sucre Cathedral (1592–9) by Cristóbal Hidalgo, based on Flemish engravings, and a richly polychromed altar (1583) survives in La Merced, by Gómez de Hernández de Galván (fl. 1572–1602) and Andrés Hernández (fl. 1583–92).

During the 17th century, as in church facades, the architectural structure of retables becomes more decorated: twisted columns entwined with vines support friezes overflowing with grotesques, and all are richly gilded and polychromed. Church interiors, too, become increasingly ornate, especially in Quito where several were decorated throughout with red, white, and gold sculpted stucco.

During the 17th century, Peru produced a wealth of fine figure sculpture in retables, pulpits, and especially choirstalls, such as those in Lima Cathedral (1624–6), designed and executed by Pedro de Noguera (1592–1655)—architect as well as sculptor—with the help of several assistants. In Lima, as in Central America, figure-sculpture, generally polychrome, was strongly influenced by the Sevillian Martines Montañés, and even in Cuzco the work of the Indian Juan Tomás Tuyru Tupac displays Sevillian tendencies. In Quito, Manuel Chili, known as Caspicara (later 18th century) is memorable for the translucent quality of the white flesh of his long-limbed Christs.

During the 18th century the architectural structure of retables and church facades all but disappears under a riot of decorative detail. In Mexico, good examples are Zacatecas Cathedral facade, and the facade of the Sagrario, Mexico City (1749), where the fantastically sculpted pillars are scarcely distinguishable from the statues between them. In southern Peru and Bolivia, the wealth of flat decorative details of flora and fauna on church facades and retables is very distinctive; good examples are the facades at San Lorenzo, in Potosí, San Pedro in Zepita, and Puno Cathedral.

In South America, religious painting remained the dominant genre throughout the colonial period, but from the early 18th century until the Revolution it was fashionable for well-to-do Mexicans to have their portraits painted: viceroys, bishops, army generals, and bejeweled noblewomen appear in paint. The portraits of nuns are particularly interesting: often they are young girls about to enter the order, as in the painting of Sor María Ignacia de la Sangre by José de Alcibar (fl. 1715–1801) where the girl's serious face contrasts with her sumptuous robes. Miguel Cabrera (1695–1768) was the most important Mexican artist of the time, who painted both portraits and large-scale works for churches and convents.

The Spaniards were quicker to settle in America than the Portugese; only after the mid 16th century were proper towns established in Brazil; artists are rarely recorded before the end of the century. During the 17th and 18th centuries the main artistic centers were Bahia, Recife, and Rio de Janeiro on the coast, and towns in the province of Minas Gerais in the interior. Brazilian painting, always very dependent on Europe for inspiration, was specifically influenced by Holland in the 17th century and by France in the early 19th. As in Spanish

The facade of the Jesuit church of the Company of Christ, Quito, Ecuador; 18th century

America, most 17th-century painting is religious, but in the 18th century, portraits and battle scenes occur. Cult-images of Christ and the Virgin were widely venerated but they never inspired the lively local adaptations produced, for example, by the Cuzco school in Peru.

Unlike in the Spanish colonies, externally Brazilian architecture remains relatively austere, although the 18th-century facade of São Francisco, Bahia, is an exception. Lavish retables tend increasingly to be built into the overall sculptural decoration of a church interior. Examples include, in Rio, São Bento and the Carmen, on which Luiz da Fonseca Rosa, Valentím da Fonseca e Silva and others worked from the mid 18th century until 1855, and in Bahia, São Francisco, also 18th century, where the decoration is gilded throughout, and the distinctions between retable and wall are blurred.

The most important individual in the history of Brazilian colonial art is the sculptor Antonio Francisco Lisboa (1738–1814), a mulatto known as "O Aleijadinho" from Minas Gerais, whose sensitivity to the dramatic power of spatial arrangements in both his architecture and his sculpture is unmatched in Latin America. Of his huge output he is best known for the series of 12 grim Old Testament prophets that stand in front of the church of the Bom Jesus, Congonhas do Campo, overlooking the monumental staircase and the valley below (1800–5).

Post-colonial art. The struggle for independence throughout the Spanish Colonies in Central and South America from 1810 to 1820 led to a century of turbulence but not to the cultural blossoming that followed the Mexican Revolution of 1910. The church remained powerful, and although it lost its stranglehold on art, it was still responsible for a number of major mural paintings.

Throughout the 19th century, Europe remained the cultural mecca for most Latin American writers and artists. There were, however, weak and fitful signs of a search for an American art. American history was accepted as suitable subject matter for academic painters, with scenes drawn not only from incidents of the discovery of the New World, and the Conquest, but from native history. There had, broadly, been two forces working for independence: the Creole families, who, although Spanish, were barred from responsible official posts which were all reserved for Spaniards born in Spain, and who also resented the unnecessary financial drain imposed by colonial status, and the more or less landless Indians and peasants.

The first uprising in Mexico was led by the parish priest Hidalgo in 1810, who disguised his true goal of national independence as a crusade to save New Spain from the atheistic monster Bonaparte (Spain being at this period a satellite of France). He was followed by thousands of Indians, on whose behalf he called for the abolition of the tribute they had paid since the Conquest, and for land reforms. Independence was finally supported by Mexicans, afraid of suffering from any last ditch liberal reforms imposed by Spain; this set the pattern for the struggle between reactionary and liberal forces that lasted throughout the century. In art, the new power of the Creole families led to a flourishing portraiture, usually in the style of David or Ingres, although there were also numerous portraits of heroes of the liberation like Simon Bolívar and the Peruvian José de San Martín.

In the second half of the century, Indianism began to make an impact. In 1889, the Mexican national pavilion at the Paris World Fair was a "restoration of an Aztec temple ... surmounted by strange and forbidding statues of kings and divinities". The Mexican dictator Porfirio Díaz, who held power for nearly 30 years until 1910, firmly turned cultural attention back to the Old World, but towards the end of the century a number of landscape painters, notably in Lima and Mexico, began to turn their attention towards their own land and forged a distinctive style independent of Impressionism.

The Royal Academy of San Carlos was founded in Mexico City in 1785, dependent financially on the Royal Academy of Madrid and on Spain for the artistic directors of all its departments. Founded to refine the arts of Mexico, it presided over a neoclassical revival in building and painting, which formed the background to and survived independence, after which the academy was renamed the National Academy of San Carlos.

During the 19th century, painting was largely dominated by the Academy, with one or two exceptions, including the gifted and self-taught Francisco Eduardo Tresguerras (1759–1833), who was born in Guanajuato, western Mexico. An architect, mural painter, poet, and musician, he rebuilt the church of El Carmen, Celaya, Guanajuato, in neoclassical style, and decorated it with frescoes containing figure scenes and landscapes of delicate and unusual realism.

Mural painting witnessed a revival during the second half of the century, notably in the fruitful rivalry between Cordero and Clavé. Juan Cordero (1824–84) trained at the San Carlos Academy and then independently in Europe, where he painted *Columbus before the Catholic Monarchs* (1850), and the *Redeemer and the Woman taken in Adultery* (1853) which won him instant fame when exhibited in the Academy in 1854. Resenting the director of the Academy, the imported Catalan Peregrin Clavé, Cordero initiated a series of grand mural schemes to demonstrate his superiority, of which the most famous are the dome of Santa Teresa and San Fernando in Mexico City. Executed in tempera, a medium considered coarse by Clavé compared with oil paint, they are robust and highly colored, mingling smooth and solid neoclassical flesh with exuberant rococo skies. In 1872 he painted *The Triumph of Science and Labor over Ignorance and Sloth* on the staircase of the National Preparatory School (an Institute of Higher Education, formerly the Regal College of San Ildefonso) in support of a positivist as opposed to a church-dominated education program. It was destroyed in 1900, but was an important precedent for the revolutionary muralists of the 20th century. Santiago Rebull (*ob.* 1902), a "belated Ingrist", was briefly director of the Academy after the 1860 Revolution of the Zapotec Indian, Juárez. He was commissioned by the Emperor Maximilian (1864–7) to paint mural panels in Chapultepec Castle. His most famous canvas was the *Death of Marat* (1875). José María Velasco (1840–1912) was the finest plein-air landscape painter of this period, painting many scenes of the country round and south of Mexico City, including a panoramic view of the *Valley of Mexico*.

The most notable sculpture of this period is the monument in Mexico City to Cuauhtémoc, last of the Aztec kings. It was constructed between 1878 and 1887 by Francisco Jiménez (architect-engineer), Miguel Norena, who was the sculptor of the statue, and Enrique Guerra, who made the bas-reliefs round the base.

The 20th century in Latin America, as also in Europe, was marked by the reaction against academic painting. Artists turned for inspiration more and more to popular and primitive sources, and to the radical modernist movements in Europe. Because of the richness of popular and folk art in Latin America, and because of its importance for the post-revolutionary mural Renaissance in Mexico, it will be discussed here briefly as a separate theme.

Popular arts. The term "Popular arts" is used to cover a multitude of different kinds of objects and paintings, from the most naive copies of the Virgin or Christ to the noble geometrical patterns on painted pots and woven textiles, which, throughout Mexico, Peru, Bolivia, and Columbia, still belong to the long, native American tradition. The popular arts have been remarkably tenacious of ancient forms while at the same time devouring or adapting themselves to new mediums or images. They form probably the first genuine *mestizo* culture, and for this reason objects like the brightly painted tin ex-votos—offered as receipts by grateful worshipers to beneficent saints and piled high in their shrines—were admired by 20th-century artists in search of the roots of their national culture. This tradition goes back to early colonial times. Impossible to date too—though most of the surviving examples are probably of the late 19th or early 20th century—are the mural paintings that adorn the walls of countless small commercial establishments, butchers' shops, restaurants, *pulquerías* (shops selling the native drink *pulque*), vividly depicting popular sports, pastimes, and legends (subjects taken from academic official art in the 19th century), and figures in landscapes whose tentative perspective and strong sloping profiles still echo the earliest post-Conquest Indian manuscripts. Particularly popular was the *mundo al revés* ("world upside down") imagery, long familiar in Europe and America, which might show the butcher strung up like an ox, with the ox grinning beside him, cleaver in hand. Folk and popular arts are often but not necessarily anonymous: Dr Atl described the potter, Zacarias Jimón, and Jean Charlot told of the admiration the revolutionary muralists felt for the humble and inspired craftsmen like the serape weaver León Venado from Texcoco, or the master potter Amaco Galván from Tonalá.

The production of popular and satirical prints reached a peak *c*1880 with the enormously successful publisher Antonio Vanegas Arroyo, who produced penny pamphlets, corridos (rhymed ballads), children's stories, recipes, fashions, and satirical broadsheets. The most famous of his journalist-illustrators was José Guadalupe Posada (1851–1913) a self-taught *mestizo* whose engravings and woodcuts accompanied the sensational news items ("The man who eats his own children"), or anti-Díaz satires. Often using the traditional skull or skeleton *calavera* for his anti-hero, Posada cut his pictures to tell a story fast, making it graphic for a largely illiterate public. His simple, powerful images were admired by the revolutionary muralists searching for alternatives to an elitist and moribund academic art, alternatives also to European modernism.

Latin American art of the 20th century. Latin American art of this century has been dominated by Mexico, and it is there that, at least in painting, two of the most marked qualities in modern Latin American culture are most in evidence: an interest both political and cultural in the past civilizations and present life of the original inhabitants, with an attempt to revive native forms (Indianism or *indigenismo*), and an intense concern for the social role of the artist. Throughout Latin

A Mexican bark painting: an example of popular art

America, artists and intellectuals have been in the vanguard of political struggle, and, in many countries, founder and executive members of Communist and Socialist parties. Many artists believed that art should have a direct and public role; in Mexico, with State patronage now replacing the Church, and in the absence of a commercial art market, it was natural that, under favorable governments, the walls of public buildings should be their adopted sites.

The Revolution of 1910 and the following 11 years of civil war sharpened artistic ideals and fostered a cultural nationalism inevitably stronger in Mexico than elsewhere. In 1921 José Vasconcelos, Secretary of Education in the newly

A caricature by J.G. Posada of General Victoriano Huerta as a spider crushing the bones of his victims: a print from a relief zinc engraving; 22×22cm (9×9in); c1910. The University of Michigan Museum of Art, Ann Arbor, Michigan

A detail from the facade of El Teatro de los Insurgentes, Mexico City, painted by Diego Rivera in 1953, later covered with Italian mosaic: the leveler of the economy taking from the rich and giving to the poor

stabilized government, commissioned Diego Rivera (1886–1957) and subsequently a number of other young Mexican painters, to decorate the walls of the National Preparatory School. They included Ramón Alva de la Canal, Fernando Leal, Fermín Revueltas, Jean Charlot, Amado de la Cueva, Carlos Orozco Romero, Emilio García Cahero, as well as David Alfaro Siqueiros and José Clemente Orozco. Rivera began painting a humanist allegory, *Creation*, in the Auditorium; the others set up their scaffolds on the staircases and in the courtyards. They searched for formal inspiration in their own country, bypassing the years of bad academic art to look at the 16th-century frescoes in the monastery at Actopan, at *pulquería* paintings, 19th-century popular and satirical prints, more rarely the great mural feats of the Italian Renaissance. Jean Charlot (1898–1979) used Uccello (1397–1475) as his model for his Conquest scene *Massacre in the Great Temple*; Siqueiros (1898–1974) looked back to Masaccio (1401–?28) for his *Elements*. The simplified planes and expressive outlines of Rivera's *Creation*, a synthesis of Cubism and Giotto, were a strong influence. But above all, they longed "to come closer to the works of the ancient settlers of our vales" (Siqueiros); "I could tell you much concerning the progress to be made by a painter, a sculptor, an artist, if he observes, analyzes, studies, Mayan, Aztec, or Toltec art, none of which falls short of any other art in my opinion." (Rivera, 1921). Rivera even tried to rediscover the ancient native techniques of preparing and applying pigments. Orozco, however, formed a style completely distinct from Rivera's, with dark, even monochrome, paintings, heavy, bold outlines and sweeping, dramatic, expressionist forms.

The National Preparatory School offered the muralists the chance to put their ideal of working communally into practice: an ideal encouraged by their mentor Dr Atl (Gerardo Murillo), a revolutionary and landscape painter who in his brief reign as Director under Carranza in 1914 tried to turn the Academy into a "popular workshop". After years of defending their walls against hostile and sceptical students, the muralists were finally ejected in 1924. But the mural movement continued to grow in strength, and remained most concerned with the three topics, often interwoven, of Indianism, Mexican history, and Marxism. The complex phenomenon of *indigenismo* has probably been more successfully explored in Latin American literature than in painting. Too often in art it became a formal archaism, or purely decorative and symbolic, like the use of Aztec symbols in Juan O'Gorman's mosaic for the Library building of the National University in the 1940s; Orozco was the only painter to reject Indianism.

The first murals were often inconsistent and even contradictory in their attitudes to Mexican history: the Conquest, the coming of Christianity, Indian survivals, 19th-century survivals, and the recent Revolution were open to and were given different interpretations. Rivera hardened in his attitude to the Conquest, and his Cortés became an increasingly brutal figure; Orozco's remained highly ambiguous.

The three major muralists were Rivera, Orozco, and Siqueiros. Both Rivera and Orozco executed major mural schemes not only in Mexico but also in the United States, where they had a substantial influence in the 1930s and 1940s. After the National Preparatory School, Rivera's next project was the decoration of the courtyard of the Ministry of Education (1923–8), which consisted of 168 fresco panels painted on three stories and stairways, including scenes from daily life and labor, fiestas, and the Revolution. Before completing the cycle, Rivera visited Moscow, and returned with a sharper dialectical method and an even more pronounced commitment in his paintings to the class struggle, for which he begins to use a caricaturist's satirical weapons. In the *Night of the Poor*, white-clad, brown-skinned Indians contrast with the pasty capitalists of the *Night of the Rich* (1923–8; Secretariat of Public Education, Mexico City). The Agricultural School at Chapingo (1925–7) treats the subject of land reform; in the chapel, Rivera painted symbolic frescoes of fruitfulness, including one of the dead revolutionary heroes Zapata and Montanos, from whose bodies spring sunflowers. The Nation-

The Chamber of Deputies and administrative offices of Brasilia, designed by Oscar Niemeyer and built in the 1960s

al Palace frescoes (1929–35) are a massive, peopled panorama of Mexican history in dialectical form, which at least partly borrows its narrative pattern from native pictographic books. On the right is pre-Conquest America, leading across to the Conquest, Inquisition, Slavery of the Indians, colonial rule, struggle for National Independence, ending with a vision of the future triumph of Socialism over Capitalism (frequently represented by North America). He was a massively prolific painter; other works include the Palace of Cortés at Cuernavaca (1930), the *Sunday Dream in Alameda Park* (1947–8) at the Hotel del Prado in Mexico City, which includes a portrait of himself as a boy beside Posada, and a mural for the Detroit Institute of Arts, U.S.A., (1932). His murals are increasingly didactic, using a precise and brilliantly colored realism.

José Clemente Orozco (1883–1949) was an eyewitness to the violence of the Revolution and Civil War, and was incapable of Rivera's political optimism, although he believed in the mural as the "highest, the most logical, the purest and the strongest form of painting". Despising Marxism, Indianism, and the very idea of a "national" art, Orozco displays an ironic humanism in his works together with a convinced anticlericalism. Among his major works are *Prometheus* (1930), Pomona College, California, and the murals in the Palace of the Governor (1937) and the Hospicio Cabanas (1938–9) in Guadalajara. *Hidalgo*, a mural in the Palace of the Governor, is characteristically paradoxical: the powerful figure of the priest who led the uprising in 1810 lights the torch of the Revolution but brings fraternal strife rather than liberation.

David Alfaro Siqueiros (1896–1972) was the most politically active of the muralists. In 1921 he published an important manifesto: *Three Appeals of Timely Orientation to Painters and Sculptors of the New American Generation*, (Vida Americana, Barcelona). From 1923 to 1930 he worked actively as a trades-union leader. Returning from exile in 1939, he painted *Portrait of the Bourgeoisie*, with José Renau, Antonio Pujol, and Luis Arenal. In 1945 he painted *New*

A detail of a mural in the Palace of the Governor, Guadalajara, Mexico, painted by Orozco in 1937: Father Miguel Hidalgo y Costilla raises the torch of rebellion against Spain in 1810

Democracy and three panels on the theme of *Cuauhtemoc* in the Palace of Fine Arts, Mexico City. He veers in his murals between elaborate allegory and simpler, more dramatic scenes. The Auditorio Siqueiros, begun in 1964, was a specially built auditorium for the gigantic mural *The March of Humanity*. Siqueiros advocated the use of modern technology in murals, and experimented with plastic paints and spray guns. He increasingly simplified his style, using strong black outlines for his figures.

Rufino Tamayo (1899–1991) was of the same generation as the muralists, but used Indian subject matter in a more formalized, abstract style. The individuality of younger painters in Mexico makes it hard to classify in groups or movements, although there has been a notable influence of both Dada and Surrealism. Among the most interesting are Pedro Coronel (1922–), Enrique Echevarría, (1923–), José Luis Cuevas (1933–), and Alberto Gironella (1929–).

Latin America has increasingly attracted the attention of European avant-garde poets and painters. Indianism coincided with the new taste in the Old World for "primitive" art, and the New World offered a rich ground for artists in search of more expressive forms outside the outworn European classical tradition. Secondly, it attracted left-wing artists searching for a model for a public, non elitist art. Surrealism in particular found natural affinities with America. In 1940 the International Surrealist Exhibition was held in Mexico City; Rivera and his wife Frida Kahlo (1910–54), who painted intimate, imaginative, dreamlike pictures, both exhibited, together with the fine photographer Manuel Alvárez Bravo (1904–) and the Guatamalan Carlos Merida (1893–1984). Surrealist groups were established in the 1930s and 1940s in Chile ("Mandragora"), Argentina, Peru, and Martinique. Just before the Second World War, Surrealist painting in Europe received an infusion of new blood from the Americas, with Roberto Sebastian Matta Echaurren (1911–, Santiago, Chile), and Wifredo Lam (born in Sagua la Grande, Cuba, in 1902). Lam joined the Surrealists in 1939 and was the first to translate the Surrealist interest in primitivism and magic into striking totemic images with strong African affinities.

Outside Mexico, on the whole, there has been a greater internationalism in painting, sculpture, and architecture and a greater openness to abstraction, although there have also been other notable muralists, like Candido Portinari (1903–62) in Brazil, and an interesting burst of mural activity in Chile under Allende's socialist government in the early 1970s, which was influenced by Siqueiros. Pedro Figari (1861–1938) was the most influential of the Argentinian River Plate School, a painter of intimate local scenes and a fine colorist. Joaquin

Torres García (1874–1948) was born in Uruguay and spent many years in Paris; his highly individual paintings show an affinity with Joseph Cornell or Max Ernst in their taxonomic arrangement of symbols. Fernando Botero (1932–; born at Medellín, Colombia) is also a highly individual painter whose grotesque, overblown portraits are in the tradition of Grosz and Otto Dix.

In architecture, from the beginning of the 19th century there was a greater technical simplicity, and an architecture with its origins in academic models began to take the place of the exuberant traditional forms. In Brazil, where the developments in architecture have been the most interesting, there were two main trends: firstly the Portuguese background, and secondly one that became stronger after 1822, a more sophisticated French-derived neoclassicism. "A style begins to appear which reflects the rigid and severe social structure of the time, the supremacy of man, the almost Oriental segregation of woman, the exploitation of the negro and the Indian."

In this century, there has been a long and fruitful interchange with European modernism, which began with the "Modern Art Week" of 1922 in São Paulo. After the Revolution of 1930 there was a new impetus to building, and Le Corbusier came to Brazil in 1935 to advise on plans for the new Ministry of Education, and a *Cité Universitaire*. He influenced a group of architects headed by Lucio Costa—including Carlos Leao, Jorge Moreira, and Alfonso Eduardo Reidy—which was later joined by Oscar Niemeyer and Ernani Vasconcelos. With the inauguration and construction of the capital city, Brasilia, from 1960 by Lucio Costa and Oscar Niemeyer, modern architecture in Brazil has itself become a major world influence. More idiosyncratic in terms of modernism, but functionally dramatically effective, are the two major buildings in Mexico City by the architects Pedro Ramirez Vázquez and Rafael Mijares, the Museum of Anthropology and the Aztec Stadium.

DAWN ADES and VALERIE FRASER

Bibliography. Ades, D. et al. *Art in Latin America: the Modern Era, 1820–1980*, London (1989). Baddeley, O. and Fraser, V. *Drawing the Line: Art and Cultural Identity in Contemporary Latin America*, New York and London (1989). Charlot, J. *The Mexican Mural Renaissance 1920–5*, New Haven (1963). Edwards, E. *Painted Walls of Mexico*, Austin (1966). Kelemen, P. *Baroque and Rococo in Latin America*, New York (1967). Kubler, G. *Art and Architecture of Spain and Portugal and their American Dominions*, Harmondsworth (1959). Lucie-Smith, E. *Latin American Art of the 20th Century*, London (1993). Rodríguez, A. (trans. Corby, M.) *A History of Mexican Mural Painting*, London (1969). Wethey, H. *Colonial Architecture and Sculpture in Peru*, Cambridge, Mass. (1949).

51

MODERN AMERICAN ART

Cliff Dwellers by George Bellows; oil on canvas; 100×105cm (39×41in); 1913
Los Angeles County Museum of Art, Los Angeles (see page 917)

For many years, students of modern American art have too readily taken for granted the artist's isolation from Europe and have emphasized the existence of compelling native traditions of a vernacular character, in opposition to long-established visual traditions and the cultivated European sense of art. The issue is complex and a balanced view must be sought. It should take into account the special virtues of American art—its particular qualities of energy and innovativeness—as well as its persistent provincialism, at least up to 1945. At the same time, the American debt to Europe—especially the revival of the cosmopolitan spirit at the time of the Armory Show (1913)—must be given due weight, for it has become increasingly clear in recent years that modern American art of the early 20th century could not have developed in a cultural vacuum, or flourished merely on the basis of complacency. The issue of making an invidious choice and commitment between the opposing forces of European modernism and a less demanding native realism was firmly joined in the United States in the years between 1908 and 1913.

At the turn of the 20th century, the American art reflected in exhibitions and publications appeared predominantly academic. Art and literature aped the graces of the "genteel tradition", which in painting and sculpture took the form of watered-down versions of outmoded European styles: a combination of American idealism, French Impressionism, Whistlerian aesthetics, and Sargent's bravura brushwork. This painting combined a maximum of social unreality and polite genre with an enfeebled aestheticism. The city was seldom painted, landscape art focused on an idyllic nature, and historical painting and sculpture mirrored the escapist fantasies and shallow values of the Gilded Age. There was a basic assumption that culture was something derived from Europe of the grand epochs. During the last years of the 19th century, the historicist *beaux-arts* attitude, in its most derivative sense, dominated three generations who characteristically made their foreign studies in the most conservative ateliers of Munich, Düsseldorf, Paris, and London.

Around 1905, this academic calm was rudely shattered by a group of young realist painters centering around the Philadelphia artist Robert Henri (1865–1929). Rebelling against a pompous European academicism and its out-of-date mythologies, they turned for inspiration to the teeming life of the modern city, which they painted with a new energy, humor, and social conscience notably absent from the vapid academic confections of the period. As early as 1886, the literary critic William Dean Howells had predicted a specifically American and "democratic art", an art capable of dealing with the urban casualties of industrialization in a more humane spirit. Howells called for an end to the charade of the genteel tradition and demanded a more insurgent art that would "front the everyday world and catch the charm of its workworn, careworn, brave, kindly face".

The first group of American artists to advocate a new "democratic art" and to explore the everyday life of ordinary people in large cities came to be known as The Eight or, more loosely, in a reference to their humble content, as the Ashcan School. Led by Robert Henri, they shared his passionate conviction that painting must reflect the artist's involvement with life as lived, rather than with some polite, unreal pictorial surrogate. Although their paintings represented an abrupt departure from academicism, the new direction of The Eight lay more in content than in style. No more advanced than pre-Impressionist French painting, their formally unsophisticated pictures did not change the course of American art, but they did manage to discredit and break the hold of the National Academy by opening up art to contemporary life.

Henri's band of progressive artists made known their organized opposition to academic domination with a group exhibition at the Macbeth Gallery in New York in 1908. The Eight, in fact, were not entirely united in their aims, nor did they share a homogenous group style of realism. The refined post-Impressionism of Maurice Prendergast, the poetic fantasy of Arthur B. Davies, and the naturalism of Ernest Lawson were far removed from the vigorous, fresh realism of John Sloan, William Glackens, George Luks, and Everett Shinn. Nor did they ever exhibit as a group again after their first collaboration. They did, however, succeed in bringing a novel immediacy and honesty of vision into American art. Their realism, considered daring in 1908, consisted simply in painting what they saw with strict attention to the character of the actual scene.

Philadelphia was the cradle of Henri's new realism. A remarkable teacher and stimulator of ideas, he gathered Luks, Glackens, Shinn, and Sloan about him and furnished them with the intellectual drive that turned these young newspaper illustrators into artists. Henri may have been more important as a leader than he was as a painter. He urged his young men to "forget about art and paint pictures of what interests you in life." Aesthetic truth was considered part of social truth, and a fight against the tyranny of the Academy was just another aspect of the perpetual struggle of the young against old-fashioned and reactionary ideas. The brotherhood of man was Henri's ethical ideal, supported, in varying degrees, by his followers.

Although many of The Eight avowed their interest in urban "life", following Henri's dictums and reportorial instincts, they also conspicuously emulated the styles of early- mid-19th-century French realists, drawing on both Daumier's sentimental anecdotes of lower-class life and Manet's more sophisticated boulevard scenes. Despite their obvious debt to a somewhat outmoded European heritage, many of the American realists uttered pronouncements which openly scorned cultivated European style in art as effete. A tone of stridency later also marked the utterances of regionalist American scene painters of the 1930s, Grant Wood, Thomas Hart Benton, and John Steuart Curry, all of whom affected the pose of the artist-primitive—even though some had a sophisticated European training—in a defensive and provincial spirit reminiscent of some members of The Eight. Earlier, George Luks had boasted: "The world has but two artists,

Frans Hals and little old George Luks." And he would fume when people spoke of painting as an end in itself: "Art—my slats! Guts! Guts! Life! Life! I can paint with a shoestring dipped in pitch and lard."

Although he did not officially exhibit with The Eight, George Bellows (1882–1925) was associated with them as a realist, and some of his better-known themes resembled those of Luks in their celebration of manly virtue and violent physical combat. His *Cliff Dwellers* (1913; Los Angeles County Museum of Art, Los Angeles) is a powerful and richly painted evocation of life in the vital, ramshackle New York slums: it captures the essence of a street scene jammed with tenement dwellers seeking relief from their sweltering apartments. He defines his human characters as slovenly but good-natured figures with an earthy, gamin charm. Their energies spill out of the frame, matched by an appropriately loose, exuberant brushwork.

Maurice Prendergast (1859–1924), on the other hand, can only nominally be described as a realist. His *The Promenade* (1913; Whitney Museum of American Art, New York) recalls Puvis de Chavannes' idealized processions as much as it does the European Impressionists and realists. He was probably the most original painter of The Eight, despite archaisms, which derived from Bonnard, the Nabis, and the tapestry-like color surfaces of their painting. In the medium of watercolor, however, he was undoubtedly the first true American modernist, a painter who understood Cézanne's color theory and general aims before the French master was even known in the U.S.A.

The new urban realists were primarily concerned to develop a typically American subject matter. Their vision was limited, however, by a rather undemanding mood of reportage and by their ignorance of the revolution of form erupting simultaneously in Europe. Nonetheless, their interest in contemporary life did establish one of the dominant realists strains in 20th-century American art, later echoed in the work of an American scene painter of more astringency, Edward Hopper (1882–1967).

Almost simultaneously, the European modern movements of Fauvism, Cubism, and Futurism, among others, began to reach the United States. The year 1980 marked a critical moment of transition and conflict in American art. Just as The Eight established itself, Alfred Stieglitz (1864–1946), the photographer and art dealer, inaugurated his exhibitions of the radical new European moderns.

Stieglitz has a special place in the history of American art: a photographer of genius, he was the founder, the central figure, and the spokesman of the Photo-Secession, a group of pictorialist photographers who dominated artistic photography in the first two decades of this century. He also operated "291", the most progressive art gallery in pre-First World War America, The Intimate Gallery (1925–9), and An American Place (1929–46); all were devoted exclusively to artists of his circle, including Georgia O'Keeffe, Marsden Hartley, Arthur G. Dove, John Marin, Max Weber, and Charles Demuth.

The Promenade by Maurice Prendergast; oil on canvas; 76×86cm (30×34in); 1913. Whitney Museum of American Art, New York

Stieglitz was the first forceful advocate of photography as a fine art, and of the collective artistic revolution we now call Modernism. But he was also the outspoken champion of a modern aesthetic distinctly and uniquely American. So important a role did he play in introducing the American public to avant-garde European art that he can justly be compared with Gertrude Stein as one of the two crucial figures in establishing European modernism in America. Miss Stein (1874–1946) was the first to admire and buy the paintings of Cézanne, Picasso, and Matisse when those artists were either unknown or despised in Paris. In New York, Stieglitz, with similar acuteness, singled out new American talent, crusaded for rigorous critical standards in his publications, and provided a sympathetic atmosphere for innovation. His efforts infused new vitality into the fine arts and photography in America in the first two decades of the new century.

The list of Stieglitz exhibition "firsts" is still impressive: among others, he first showed in America the work of Matisse, Henri Rousseau, Cézanne, Picasso, Picabia, Brancusi, and African Negro sculpture. But Stieglitz also believed in the future of American art, and specifically in certain young modernists: he was the first to give one-man shows to Maurer, Marin, Hartley, Dove, Carles, Bluemner, Nadelman, O'Keeffe, and Macdonald-Wright. His Younger American Artists exhibition in 1910 was probably the first all-modern group show. Stieglitz liked to describe 291 as a "laboratory". Here the new American modernists could meet and, with Stieglitz as a catalyst, engage in the endless talk that is the essential accompaniment of any new movement.

Most of the artists whose works Stieglitz showed after 1908 had been living and painting in Europe, and were familiar with the work of Cézanne, Van Gogh, the Fauves, and the

Cubists. While the Henri realists were engaged by urban subject matter and used a dated pictorial style, these young artists had begun to establish direct contact with the most emancipated expressions of their time. Max Weber and Arthur Burdett Frost, Jr joined Matisse's painting class, which started in 1907, followed later by Morgan Russell and Patrick Henry Bruce. During 1900–13, nearly every significant modern American artist traveled to Europe where Paris was a mandatory stop if not their primary destination. Arthur B. Carles, Arthur G. Dove, Marsden Hartley, John Marin, Charles Sheeler, Abraham Walkowitz, and many others lived there for long or short intervals. Other Americans who directly experienced European innovation included Charles Demuth, Stanton Macdonald-Wright, Andrew Dasburg, William and Marguerite Zorach, Thomas Hart Benton, Morton Schamberg, Joseph Stella, Oscar Bluemner, and John Covert.

In Europe, the Americans felt at first hand the impact particularly of Abstract art and the influence of such new movements as Fauvism, Cubism, Futurism, *Der Blaue Reiter* (The Blue Rider), and Orphism. As they began to drift back home in the years preceding the First World War and to exhibit paintings that revealed new Continental derivations, the whole center of gravity of the new American art shifted. The insurgent realists survived, but even their forms assumed the traits of French modernism. One of the boldest experiments in Abstract art was the color painting invented by Stanton Macdonald-Wright, Morgan Russell, Patrick Henry Bruce, and Andrew Dasburg. Macdonald-Wright and Russell were living in Paris, and there they created an abstract style of their own, which they named "Synchromism". This was based on combinations of colors planned in dynamic rhythms, a style which, according to Wright, would refine art "to the point where the emotions of the spectator will be wholly aesthetic."

Although Stieglitz's gallery 291 became a focus for the new artistic forces, exercising a unique influence on the avant-garde of the day, the larger public had still been given little opportunity to see European Modernism. This opportunity was to be furnished by the famous Armory Show of 1913. The Armory Show brought modern European art to America both physically and intellectually. For the first time, Americans gained a comprehensive view of the work not only of contemporary Cubists and Fauves but also of the great high priests of modernism, Cézanne, Gauguin, and Van Gogh. The Show was predominantly French. This in itself was a revelation to native artists who were dissatisfied with old styles but unable to develop their talent along new lines. The impact of the Armory Show on the general public was mixed. Their response was more or less hostile but, nonetheless, filled with curiosity. They made fun of the more extreme paintings and sculptures, particularly Marcel Duchamp's celebrated *Nude Descending a Staircase* (Philadelphia Museum of Art) and Brancusi's suavely geometrical figure sculpture. Public conservatism reflected the enmity of die-hard traditional artists and critics. But, hostile or not, the average citizen became aware that modern art was a compelling public issue and that

its development had not stopped with Impressionism.

Generally speaking, the Armory Show opened up for American artists the exciting prospect of meeting the challenge of a new world—born of the machine age—by developing radically revised intellectual attitudes and artistic methods. The modernist painter and architect Oscar Bluemner declared: "It is a vision of things and of their relation to one another and that of ourselves to them, in which modern life and art differs from the past." Artists will have to learn "to see and to feel the world as science reveals it today. In this way originates the new vision of external objects and of imagination. There is a necessary analogy between the impressions of the artist and the scientific and philosophical evolution going on." On the other hand, the results of decades of philistinism were not to be undone overnight, and the less progressive artists with realist training were unprepared to absorb the shattering blows delivered to academicism by Matisse and Picasso. As William Glackens frankly, and ruefully, admitted some time after the show took place, "We have no innovators here. Everything worthwhile in our art is due to the influence of French art. We have not yet arrived at a National art."

The impact of European art on the American avant-garde was, however, mixed and unpredictable. Max Weber (1881–1961) absorbed and subscribed fully to Cubist principles in his early exhibitions at 291. John Marin (1870–1953), on the other hand, retained a more individual voice in such soaring transcriptions of New York City as *Lower Manhattan* (1922; Museum of Modern Art, New York), combining Cubist structure with a native expressionism and a special grace in the fluent watercolor medium. Arthur Dove (1880–1946) was one of the first artists in the world to experiment with abstraction in 1910, possibly under the influence of Kandinsky. Dove also showed himself to be an effective ironist: the influence of Picabia and Dada probably explains the wit and irreverence of his collage, *The Critic* (1925; Whitney Museum of American Art, New York)—a subject whose attributes include an evening hat and pince-nez, and also roller skates (suggesting only a fleeting perception of gallery offerings) and an attached vacuum cleaner for venting his shallow pontifications. Georgia O'Keeffe (1887–), who later married Stieglitz, became famous for her magnified details of flowers, cactuses, and aspects of the Southwest landscape, which she sublimated into a mysterious kind of organic abstraction suggesting the universe in microcosm. She was also capable of painting crisp edges and visual detail of a magical clarity, linking her art to the sharp-focus, meticulous photography of Paul Strand, Edward Weston, and, later, Charles Sheeler.

Charles Demuth (1883–1935) presents himself as an urbane and reserved modernist dandy when compared with John Marin's impetuousness. *I Saw the Figure Five in Gold* (1928; Metropolitan Museum, New York) was inspired by a poem of William Carlos Williams, and combines a spare and elegant Cubism with the kaleidoscopic effects of Futurist motion. Many of Demuth's paintings also contain allusions to

Dada. It was a period when the iconoclasm of Picabia and Duchamp offered stiff competition, as a formative influence on American avant-garde art, to the formulaic abstraction of the geometric tradition.

The spirit of Dada flourished vigorously, if briefly, in New York with the presence of Picabia, from 1913, and of Duchamp, in 1915, providing the main impetus. In a period of ferment, reform, and progress, the bloody and violent interruption of the First World War cast serious doubts on the efficacy of a machine civilization—now apparently intent on destroying itself. The Dadaist puns, social outrage, and nihilism made a case for a newly disenchanted generation, even though American disillusionment never matched the bizarre, fantastic, and savage forms of European Dada (*see* Dada and Surrealism). Man Ray (1890–1977) undoubtedly became the first and most enduring Dada convert, after making contact with Duchamp in 1915. By the following year, in *The Rope Dancer Accompanies Herself with her Shadows* (Museum of Modern Art, New York), his work reflected Duchamp's interest in movement and states of change. Painted entirely in oils, the picture is also a transposition of ideas that Man Ray had been developing in a series of colored-paper collages influenced by Cubism. From 1917 until the end of the Dada period, *c*1922, he was primarily an object-maker and an explorer of new mechanical methods of image-making, which included a new kind of lensless photography.

I Saw the Figure Five in Gold by Charles Demuth; oil on board; 91×76cm (36×30in); 1928. Metropolitan Museum, New York

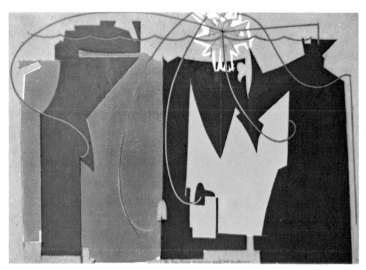

The Rope Dancer Accompanies Herself with Her Shadows by Man Ray; oil on canvas; 132×186cm (52×73in); 1916. Museum of Modern Art, New York

Picabia's and Duchamp's machinest imagery and their polemics, together with Man Ray's mechanical techniques in photography, became in the 1920s an important source of the American Precisionist movement, which included such artists as Demuth, Sheeler, O'Keeffe (briefly), Niles Spencer, and others. The Precisionists painted the American industrial landscape—factories, grain elevators, high-rise buildings, steamships—in a style that combined "immaculate" surfaces, a Cézannesque and Cubist formal vocabulary, and meticulous drawing which utilized geometric angles, curves, and clean lines.

Like painting, American sculpture passed through a vigorous experimental phase in the first two decades of the century, although the impact of European modernism was less decisive, and there were far fewer modernists. In the hands of Gaston Lachaise (1882–1935), the classic theme of the nude acquired an air of overpowering sensual glorification. With consummate craftsmanship, he fashioned figures of gargantuan voluptuousness—earthy and swelling with opulent curves that often approached a purely Abstract configuration and expression, as in *floating Figure* (1927; Museum of Modern Art, New York). French-born, Lachaise left Paris permanently for America in 1906. Among the many other European-born artists who enriched American sculpture was the Polish-born Elie Nadelman (1882–1946). He emigrated first to Paris, where he came into contact with Picasso's circle, before going to New York in 1914. His virtuoso style combines classic elegance with witty sophistication. Nadelman's simplified formal geometries have led to extravagant and unwarranted claims by some of his critical supporters who feel that the style predicted and influenced the development of European Cubism.

The realist vein of American painting was too strong to be overwhelmed by the currents of modernism. After 1920, when the first effects of the Armory Show were over, the American

The Houses of Frank Lloyd Wright

The career of Frank Lloyd Wright (1869–1959) spanned seven decades. Although he designed buildings of almost every type, his major preoccupation was the single-family house. He planned villas for the very rich, houses for the middle class, and cottages for clients who did much of the construction themselves. These evolved a new sense of domestic space, innovations of lighting and heating, and a vocabulary of functional symbols that stressed Wright's ideas about American family life.

The house that Wright designed for himself in Oak Park, Illinois (1889), was a simple, gabled structure of compact, but semi-open plan. It followed the Colonial Revival of the previous decade, as the large window and cladding of cedar shingles indicate. Yet it was more severe and abstract than any of its predecessors.

In the early years of the new century, Wright perfected what was to become known as the "Prairie" house. It usually sat on a heavy plinth, with some symmetrical elements in plan and elevation. But it reached out dramatically into the landscape with wings in several directions, its porches extending the limits of the inhabitable, protected space. All of this was capped by a massive hipped roof of low pitch and wide eaves. Captured in one complex gesture were feelings of movement, of protection, and of permanence.

The Ward W. Willits house in Highland Park, Illinois (1902–3)—Wright's first thoroughly integrated masterpiece—illustrates the "pin-wheel" plan, centered on a massive chimney with adjacent fireplaces in the living and dining rooms. Integral seating with semitransparent, spindled half-walls screened the passages from one main space to another. The dining room, with its pointed prow, was lit from above—a space almost ecclesiastical, that revealed Wright's concept of the family's evening meal as a religious ritual.

The prairie house imagery was borrowed quickly by other architects in the Chicago area, and was varied and restated by Wright himself. One of his most eloquent versions was the Frederick C. Robie house, Chicago (1907–9). The narrow Roman bricks, the copings of the long balcony, the bands of doors and casement windows, as well as the extended eaves, join in a romantic sweeping ode to the prairie—and to the street. For the Robie is a city house built on a narrow lot. We enter from behind and circulate via a stairway that forms a vertical core in tandem with the fireplaces and chimney. The living

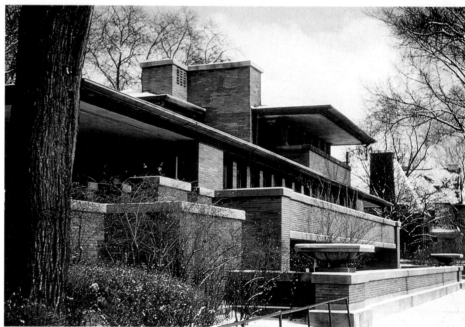

and dining rooms are on the second level, with bedrooms on the third.

Wright designed much of the Robie house's furniture, as he did for many clients throughout his career. A drawing of the interior of the Avery Coonley house in Riverside, Illinois (1907–9), for example, shows not only Wright's unusual conception of a tent-like space, but also reminds us that he was a late-19th-century architect who entered the 20th century in the spirit of the Arts and Crafts movement.

Above La Miniatura, the house in Pasadena, California, designed by Frank Lloyd Wright for Mrs George Millard; 1923

▲ A version of the prairie house, the Frederick C. Robie house by Frank Lloyd Wright; Chicago; 1907–9

▶ Fallingwater, the weekend house designed by Frank Lloyd Wright for Edgar Kaufmann Sr, near Pittsburgh, Pa; 1935–7

Wright's flight to Europe in 1909, and the interruption of life caused by the First World War, brought a disorienting hiatus. In the 1920s his practice was small and his production erratic; yet it took on national, even international, dimensions. For sites in southern California he designed several houses of concrete "textile blocks", the first and finest of which was "La Miniatura" for Mrs George Millard in Pasadena (1923). In the lush vegetation of a small ravine, Wright created a textured and shadowed sanctuary of three levels. Gone, for a while, was his obsession with the roof.

When Wright was commissioned to design a weekend cottage near Pittsburgh for Edgar Kaufmann, Sr (1935–7) he revealed affinities with the International Style—the cubic, abstract language which he had earlier helped to inspire. Built mainly of reinforced con-

crete, its superimposed, boxed balconies reach out from a vertical mass of stone quarried nearby. "Fallingwater" is one of the most famous houses in the world, owing to the dramatic photographs of these interlocking forms hovering over the falls of the Bear Run. It is a bold but private retreat, inextricably placed in a memorable site.

During the Depression years of the 1930s Wright gave attention to designs for a repeatable utopian town, "Broadacre City", and to single-family houses buildable for as little as $5,000. The latter he called "Usonian" houses, and some of them, despite their comparative modesty, were extremely elegant. The one for the Misses Goetsch and Winckler in Okemos, Michigan (1939), invites comparison with Mies van der Rohe's Barcelona Pavilion of ten years before (see The International Style). It is clear, however,

Above The Ward W. Willits house in Highland Park, Illinois; 1902–3

▲ An interior of the second house designed by Frank Lloyd Wright for Herbert Jacobs, at Middleton, Wisconsin; 1943–8

that the basic forms were already present in Wright's own work before 1910.

Throughout his domestic oeuvre, as well as in his corporate and ecclesiastical buildings, Frank Lloyd Wright's conceptual and structural innovations marked a fascinating trail. Perhaps even more interesting now than when it first appeared in the 1940s is the second house for Herbert Jacobs in Middleton, Wisconsin. Built against a berm of earth to protect it from harsh winds in the winter and to cool it in the summer, Wright's solar hemicycle embraces the low winter sun. At once a cave-like shelter and a curved pavilion opened with glass towards a sunken garden, it sums up many of the architect's favorite themes: it is protective, yet open, modern, yet respectful of the traditions of pioneer life on the mid-western plains. Despite such Americanisms, however, Wright's contributions to modern domestic architecture must be measured on an international scale. He was the most influential architect of his generation, anywhere.

ROBERT JUDSON CLARK

Further reading. Hitchcock, H.-R. *In the Nature of Materials*, New York (1942). Manson, G.C. *Frank Lloyd Wright to 1910*, New York (1958). Scully, V., Jr *Frank Lloyd Wright*, New York (1960). Smith, N.K. *Frank Lloyd Wright: a Study in Architectural Content*, Englewood Cliffs (1966).

Floating Figure by Gaston Lachaise; bronze (cast in 1935); 131×96cm (52×38in); 1927. Museum of Modern Art, New York

Scene returned vigorously both as an inspiration for artists and as a popular subject. Its most prominent figures were Edward Hopper (1882–1967) and Charles Burchfield (1893–1967). The former romanticized the unpicturesque loneliness of American town and country life, the latter dreamed up near-fantasies of similar subjects, first in his imaginative watercolors and later in dramatic oil paintings. No American realist has been able to capture the vacancy and frustration of modern urban existence with more evocative pictorial means than Hopper. *Eleven A.M.* (1926; Joseph Hirshhorn Museum, Washington, D.C.) is a haunting expression of his unique combination of bleakness of vision, austere geometric structure, and a surprising undercurrent of sexual tension.

By the mid 1920s, in reaction against international modernism, there was a wave of Nationalism: a conscious rediscovery of America—still an unexplored continent for most 20th-cen-

tury American artists. Regionalists such as Benton, Wood, and Curry returned to their native Midwest and became champions of the old-fashioned virtues of what they considered to be the heartland of America. At the same time, many Eastern painters besides Hopper and Burchfield—Reginald March and Raphael Soyer, among others—pictured the city and small town with a more drastic realism, a full acceptance of their ugly aspects, but also with a deep emotional attachment. The American Scene painters continued the interrupted tradition of 19th-century genre painting and the 20th-century realist revival of The Eight.

After the Great Depression of 1929, American Scene realism became more socially conscious. It was the prevailing style of work done under the Federal Government's W.P.A. (Works Progress Administration) program to assist artists, which operated from 1934 to 1939. Some of the more directly political artists also benefited by the Federal Art Project. Painters Philip Evergood, Ben Shahn, and Jack Levine all worked in a sharp and allusive realist style to communicate in art their strong feelings about social justice. The work of such Mexican muralists as Jose Clemente Orozco and Diego Rivera was an evident source both of imagery and design.

Ben Shahn (1898–1969) was a prolific W.P.A. muralist who combined the social themes and fervent radical political beliefs of the Mexican nationalist painters with a new cognizance of the importance of modern abstraction. His edgy, nervous line and condensed, flat space probably derived from Klee, as did his chromatic brilliance. He was also a practicing photographer, close to Walker Evans, whose documentary visual accounts of the rural South created some of the most haunting imagery of the Depression years. Shahn's *Handball* (1939; Museum of Modern Art, New York) departs from an actual photograph made by the artist, combining a sense of actuality with the elliptical formal devices of modern tradition. Shahn frequently painted in tempera to obtain effects of dry incandescence with a metallic luster. Both his medium and his pictorial effects demonstrate a magical clarity of detail that may have been a formative influence on another notable realist emerging in the 1940s—Andrew Wyeth. Wyeth (1917–) adapted Shahn's precision of flat detail and sense of human solitariness to his own quirky vision. He linked the theme of human loneliness to rural and outdoor settings, often against the background of a malign Nature. Despite a modern "psychological" note in his closely observed studies of human personality, Wyeth shows clearest affinities with the spirit of the Thirties regionalists, who turned away from the "corruption" of urban life to celebrate the homespun virtues and nostalgic myths of the farm and countryside.

Abstract art led a precarious existence during the years of the Depression when all cultural values were necessarily affected by material needs. It was not until 1937—when the Society of American Abstract Artists (A.A.A.) was founded by painters George L. K. Morris and Balcomb Greene, and sculptor Ibram Lassaw, among others—that a new chapter began. A distinguished contribution to this movement was made in

Eleven A.M. by Edward Hopper; oil on canvas; 71×91cm (28×36in); 1926. Joseph Hirshhorn Museum, Washington, D.C.

the refined Abstract painting of A. E. Gallatin, who was also known as a collector. Among its earliest supporters were Carl Holty, Charles Shaw, and Stuart Davis. Arshile Gorky, Willem de Kooning, and the sculptor David Smith established close ties with the A.A.A., but did not subscribe entirely to its more purist and Constructivist aesthetic viewpoints, or officially join the group. However, the sculptor Theodore Roszak and the painter Ad Reinhardt were early members, and their participation later provided one basis for the flowering of American art in the 1940s in the quite different form of Expressionist abstraction.

Undoubtedly the most influential Abstract painter of these transitional years was Stuart Davis (1894–1964), who courageously maintained some sense of continuity with international abstraction at a time when realism dominated the American scene and when there was considerable public hos-

tility to modernism. Davis' painting mixes Cubist structure and fragmentation with such nativist elements as a cursive script of lettering fragments taken from American signs and images—shopfronts, houses, and streets—depicted in strong, personal color combinations. Despite his dependence upon European examples, particularly upon Fernand Léger (whom he once described as "the most American painter painting today"), Davis achieved a special lightness of touch and a whimsical humor that were distinctly American.

In sculpture, Alexander Calder (1898–1976) was another American of stature, who maintained unshakable ties with European innovation. By 1923 he had produced his first motorized, freestanding sculptures in Paris, and by 1934 had made the first in a long series of suspended, air driven mobiles, with all the characteristic insouciance and lyrical invention of his maturity. During the late 1920s and 1930s Calder spent

WNYC Studio B Mural by Stuart Davis; oil on canvas;
213×336cm (84×132in); 1939. Metropolitan Museum, New York
(on loan from the Arts Commission of the City of New York)

most of his time in Paris, and there established friendly relations with Miró and Mondrian, among others. It was the
American temper of his plastic genius, his tinkering and inventive resourcefulness, that first won him recognition in the demanding international art world. He also became known as
an inspired toy-maker, for his famous miniature circus whose
expressive wire-and-wood figures of big-top performers enchanted Miró and a wide circle of artists in Paris when it was
shown there in the years 1927–30.

Calder's art bridges the period not only between early modernism and the 1930s, but between the reemergence of modernist experiment in the early 1940s and the decade of the
1960s. Until 1960 Calder seemed to be moving along established and predictable paths in his elegant and ingenious art.
However, in the last decade of his life his magnificent
"stabiles" grew to environmental scale, and today they must
rank among the most impressive monumental sculpture in
steel of the century. *La Grande Vitesse* (1969), now the pride
of Grand Rapids, Michigan, shows a characteristic enlargement of biomorphic, Miróesque forms, inevitably painted a
sizzling orange. The combination of large-scale forms in
metal, his illusionist richness and reduced means gave the
public a foretaste of the Minimalist sculpture movement of the
same period initiated by members of a younger generation of
sculptors.

From the Second World War to the present. The decades since
the beginning of the Second World War have seen prodigious
activity among painters and sculptors. The upheaval of the
war disturbed what continuity of tradition there was in
American art; the artists who have since come to the fore have
established new traditions of their own. In the first postwar
decade abstraction was the dominant style of members of the
avant-garde. But in the 1960s and the 1970s the hegemony of
abstraction, particularly of an expressionist character, was
sharply challenged by Pop Art, photographic realism, new

conceptions of art as action, performance, and idea, and by
the exploration of a variety of new technologies including
videotape and film. Like the earlier revolutionary tendencies
of 20th-century art, the succession of trends from 1940 to the
1980s—from Abstract Expressionism to environmental systems, performance, and Conceptual Art—has been motivated
by the ingrained experimentalism endemic to 20th-century
art.

The artistic energies, and in a sense, too, the social anxiety
released by the onset of the Second World War, lent special
urgency and impetus to the new American movement of Abstract Expressionism, or, to adopt Harold Rosenberg's suggestive epithet, Action Painting. The two terms cover a loose
association of artists guided by common aims who emerged in
New York at the close of the Second World War—a period
when most progressive American artists felt that the formerly
dominant school of Paris was vacant of new ideas and dying
for lack of skill. As Americans turned to Paris for direction
after the war, they found a tasteful and unchallenging type of
painting whose familiar and predictable formula usually combined Pierre Bonnard's hot palette with loose variations on the
Cubist and Orphist formal structures of Jacques Villon or
Robert Delaunay, exemplified by the innocuous, decorative
work of Lapique, Bazaine, and Manessier. The decline in
European innovation in the 1940s—except in the work of
Jean Dubuffet, Alberto Giacometti, Francis Bacon, and a few
artists of the *art informel* group—and catastrophic events on
the Continent, however, had the paradoxical effect of
stimulating an episode of experimentalism among the young
American vanguard.

For a moment it even seemed that the major impulses of
modernism had been expatriated and driven underground in
America, for the emerging progressive American artists drew
support and inspiration in their complex beginnings from the
presence in New York during the war years of a number of
Europe's leading artists and intellectuals. Léger, Tanguy,
Mondrian, Breton, Ernst, and Matta, among others, came to
New York in the early 1940s, and maintained warm, influential relationships with many of the younger Americans who
were thus able to bridge the intimidating distance between
themselves and European modernism. A number of these
European artists began to show at the Peggy Guggenheim
Gallery, Art of This Century, and it was there that the pioneer
American Abstract Expressionists—Jackson Pollock, Mark
Rothko, Clyfford Still, Hans Hofmann, Robert Motherwell,
and William Baziotes—held their first revolutionary one-man
shows between the years 1943–46.

The Surrealist group became a major catalyst in enabling
the new American generation of artists to express their sense
of crisis in pictorial form with directness and immediacy.
Robert Motherwell (1915–91) was an eloquent spokesman for
the new generation, and conveyed their concern to move to-

**Right: La Grande Vitesse by Alexander Calder; Steel; 1969;
Vandenburg Plaza, Grand Rapids, Michigan**

Cathedral   by Jackson Pollock

Painted in 1947, *Cathedral* (Dallas Museum of Fine Arts) is representative of a crucial phase in the development of the unique artistic statement of Jackson Pollock (1912–56). Together with *Full Fathom Five* (Museum of Modern Art, New York) of the same year, it marks the point at which his mastery of the poured and dripped paint technique was reaching its height. The control and precision of the mature works that followed was the result of concentrated effort and experiment, the fruits of which are already evident in the closely organized structure of *Cathedral*.

During 1947, his first year in Long Island remote from the pressures of New York, Pollock relinquished the literal imagery he had continued to explore despite increasingly unconventional working methods. In abandoning an imagery dependent for its realization upon a directly marked contour, he was able to exploit to the full the expressive potential inherent in the freedom of paint dribbled from sticks and wornout brushes, and applied direct from the tube or with a syringe.

In *Cathedral*, Pollock's abstract line, relieved of its delineating role and independent of form, is set free. Now an equal participant in the unfolding drama, it acts as an enlivening element upon the picture-plane. Wiry lines are woven into sculptural networks, independent of the background. In the dense series of planes of which the painting is constructed, webs of unmixed color are formed and spatial depth achieved. As the eye moves and is caught by the shimmer of red, yellow, or blue, so each plane advances or recedes.

The silver of aluminum paint, which was to play an even greater and more integral part in many of the later canvases, makes its first appearance here. As the light changes or the spectator moves, so its tone varies, making it an effective spatial device. It shimmers, the tone is lightened and heightened, its delicate scaffolding pushing the picture-plane forward, and so creating depth. Dull, static, and opaque, the silver recedes and assumes the unified tone of the other colors. The transient nature of line and color in motion breathes life into the painting, the structure of which constantly resolves into rhythmic accents and dissolves into a harmony of integrated color and line.

In the contrast between the strongly articulated areas of black, silver, and white, and the delicate crossing and recrossing of line, Pollock introduces a visual texture which, at times, becomes physically real on the picture surface. Always conscious of the nature of his materials, he exploits their tactile quality and creates a frontal plane constantly in motion. The texture of impasto and thick lines of paint, direct from the tube, increases the ambiguity of the painting's spatial depth.

Together with the "drip" technique, the use of silver, and, in other paintings, of enamel paint, freed Pollock's work from traditional associations within painting of weight, mass, and the physical properties of bodies. *Cathedral*'s indeterminate gravitational and spatial system is expansive and cosmic. Transcending the limits imposed by the traditional spatial boundaries of the picture frame, Pollock's forms are not confined by the dimensions and shape of the canvas. Pushing outwards, they imply an infinite extension of pictorial space.

The strong vertical emphasis, carried in two distinct movements which thrust up and outwards, may in part account for the title—uncharacteristic in Pollock's work. In the concept of a cathedral as the physical embodiment of man's faith and spiritual aspiration, and in the glorification implicit in its ascendant form, Pollock may have found an echo of the mystical nature he believed art to possess.

During the late 1930s and early 1940s, young New York artists had rejected both the narrow chauvinism of American Regionalism and the formal limitations of current Abstract art. In an alienating world, in which the individual suffered isolation and

◀ A detail from the center of *Cathedral*

▶ *Cathedral* by Jackson Pollock; mixed media on canvas; 179×89cm (70×35in); 1947. Dallas Museum of Fine Arts

dislocation, it was felt that art must be concerned with the universal, the elemental. In his personal expression of the collective experience, the artist might act as a representative individual, creating an art universal in its relevance. Unifying mankind on a fundamental level, it was to the unconscious and its exploration that artists turned for the source and medium of their communication. To express the energy of the inner forces, new means of expression, new techniques were required.

Pollock's "drip" paintings, and their method of execution, confirmed a place for him in the mythology of 20th-century art. They became a metaphor for the wild, primitive forces within modern man, unleashed upon the canvas. His approach to painting epitomizes the belief in the automatic bodily gesture: in the significance of the act itself as the medium of communication. Under the influence of Surrealist and psychoanalytic doctrine, the artistic act is acknowledged as the artist's personal mark, in the same sense that handwriting can be indicative of character. Pollock did not illustrate his feelings: he delivered them directly on to the canvas. Rejecting the conventional detached, external relationship of the artist to his painting, the canvas was for Pollock an arena in which to perform.

The immediacy of Pollock's technical approach exemplified the contemporary avant-garde emphasis upon painting as a direct statement. Preoccupied with the need to express his inner world, Pollock sought to lose the conscious self in a spontaneous dialogue between the fluency of paint, developing form, and the unconscious gesture. In the expressive application of pigment, feeling is transformed into pictorial sensation. Charged with the intensity of his emotion, Pollock's paintings communicate the sense of urgency with which he approached his medium of self expression. In each expansive stroke of *Cathedral*, each flick of the paint-laden stick, Pollock is present. The length of his arm determines the extent of the stroke, each instinctive response to the unfolding statement leaves its mark upon the whole. Each work is an autobiographical statement: Pollock *is* the painting—the painting, Pollock.

LYNNE MITCHELL

Further reading. Friedman, B.H. *Jackson Pollock: Energy Made Visible*, London (1972). O'Connor, F.V. and Thaw, E.V. *Jackson Pollock: A Catalogue Raisonné of Paintings, Drawings, and Other Works* (4 vols.), London and New Haven (1978). Robertson, B. *Jackson Pollock*, London (1968).

wards a new aesthetic that allowed the artist to express himself more freely and subjectively. As he put it: "The need is for felt experience—intense, immediate, direct, subtle, unified, warm, vivid, rhythmic." Many painters began to concentrate on the act of painting itself for its own sake, giving an almost moral urgency to their decision to paint.

Particularly influential was André Breton (1896–1966), who took his cue for an unprecedented "automatist" artistic strategy from the procedures of psychoanalysis—especially the device of exploiting free association to release personal fantasies. Breton cultivated and directly encouraged Arshile Gorky (1904–48), with whom he was in close contact; his intellectual leadership also influenced many other Americans, including David Hare, the sculptor, and Robert Motherwell. It was Motherwell who coined the phrase "plastic automatism" in place of Breton's "psychic automatism", as defined in the first *Manifesto of Surrealism*. An important distinction was thus established between the Surrealist art of subconscious imagery and the young Americans' more physical involvement with the "act of painting".

Jackson Pollock's first one-man show held in 1943 at Peggy Guggenheim's gallery became symbolic of the new wave of Abstract Expressionism in painting. Indeed, it took on something of the character of a visual manifesto for the new points of view. In the beginning, Pollock was, in fact, mistakenly identified with the artistic productions of the European Surrealists who showed in the same gallery, and his rather narrow, violent early painting reveals obvious relationships to Surrealist automatism. At the same time, Motherwell was also testing automatic painting, and Gorky worked directly under the influence of Matta's abstract Surrealism. Matta was the youngest member of the group of refugee Surrealists, who arrived in the United States during the war years. More than any of the others, he acted as a liaison between the older Surrealist generation and the emerging American avant-garde.

By 1947, most of the European Surrealists had returned to France, their influence on the wane in the face of a strongly independent American accomplishment. Pollock's breakthrough into his so-called open "drip" style or poured paintings was symbolic of the change, and helped to establish the new-found authority of the American avant-garde. His paintings were achieved by spilling liquid paint on unstretched canvases laid flat on the floor—thus taking Breton's automatism to its logical conclusion in an apotheosis of lyrical abstraction. But Pollock's paintings from 1947 until his death in 1956 became increasingly remote from their Surrealist inspiration. In the end, the actions of the artists working with the exigencies of the moment determined their outcome and visual character. Existentialist engagement with the canvas, and self-definition through the act of painting, replaced the Surrealist commitment to dreams and the unconscious. Pollock's *Number One* of 1950 (Museum of Modern Art, New York) is one of his most important large-scale "poured" paintings. The fantastic anatomies and mythic figures of his Surrealist-influenced paintings have evaporated in a powerful tension between controlled draftsmanship and a Dionysian outburst of great expressive power. The distinctions between scrolling lines of paint and phantasmagoria, and between symbolic allusions and the plastic accents dissolve into an overall rhythmic pulsation.

During the late 1940s and early 1950s, Willem de Kooning (1904–) became the acknowledged leader of American progressive painting, providing a dictionary of vital pictorial ideas and a departure for new explorations. Although Pollock's liberating energies had given him the status of a culture hero for young artists—his untimely death in 1956 expanded the legend—his direct influence was negligible until color-field painting came into vogue and the optical vibrancy of his all-over style became a focus of artistic interest. De Kooning's painterliness, with its aggressive incorporation of traditional figuration and its equally compelling Abstract invention, most decisively affected a new generation of younger artists of the 1950s. *Woman, Sag Harbor* (1964; Joseph Hirshhorn Museum, Washington, D.C.) reveals the artist in a moment of transition from figuration—reminiscent of Soutine perhaps—to an even more fragmented and aggressive painterliness, set in a tensely structured, depthless space. His characteristic pictorial formula fuses improvisational surface, gesture, and event into a new, unified structure.

If any artist deserved Harold Rosenberg's epithet of "Action Painter", it was Franz Kline (1910–62) who translated gesture into a lattice of broad black bands like the enlarged strokes of a house-painter's brush. At its best, Kline's work conveys a sense of tensely controlled excitement in the act and gesture of painting. Many of the other Action Painters in Kline's and de Kooning's tradition of excited paint marks and energetic handling were clustered together by critics as "gestural" painters, in opposition to a radically different style of color-field or chromatic abstraction which was also emerging in the 1950s, in New York. Bradley Walker Tomlin, Lee Krasner (Pollock's window), and Conrad Marca-Relli were among the more distinguished gesture painters of the older generation. Two women, Grace Hartigan and Joan Mitchell, extended the Action Painters' discoveries among the younger generation, with distinctive personalizations of idiom, either in the direction of realism, or towards an ambitious "all-over" field painting.

Hans Hofmann (1880–1966) was a special case, making his early reputation primarily as the academic teacher of many of the second-generation Abstract artists. Actually, Hofmann invented the pour and splash technique, as if anticipating Pollock, but did not push his invention into the now-familiar codified method or use it, as Pollock did, to extend the frontiers of art. Hofmann's finest paintings summarize the conflicting achievements of early-20th-century art within the context of an individual manner, combining German Expressionist exuberance, Cubist structure, and the expressive color of Matisse and Delaunay.

In a significant reaction to the gestural painters, the chromatic abstractionists—Barnett Newman, Clyfford Still, Mark

Woman, Sag Harbor by Willem de Kooning; oil on board; 203×91cm (80×36in); 1964. Joseph Hirshhorn Museum, Washington, D.C.

Sublime in art (*see* Romanticism). Although all of these artists set themselves the goal of purifying the act of painting in order to assert the Sublime, they were also in touch with the firm, concrete sensuous color of Matisse and with modern Abstract tradition: these influences clearly overweighed the elaboration of a calculated romantic atmosphere in their work.

Reinhardt's enigmatic icons are even more single-minded in their purity; they approach monochromism, providing perhaps the most extreme example of formal rigor in contemporary American painting. After a primitivist phase of making pictographs—which resemble Indian art of the Northwest Coast—Adolph Gottlieb (1903–73) turned from mythic figuration to Abstract emblems like a number of others of his contemporaries, among them William Baziotes (1912–63). Interestingly, a new generation in the 1960s took as their point of departure the more impersonal pictorial invention of Newman and Reinhardt rather than the works of Rothko or Gottlieb with their obvious evidence of a more poetic sensibility. The Minimalists of the recent past are more interested in the reductive character of color-field painting than in the romantic rhetoric of the Sublime. The new generation found themselves most in accord with Reinhardt's insistence on anonymity and the absence of emotion in his work.

There was considerable diversity among other Abstract Expressionists. Philip Guston (1913–80) brought to the New York school a searching intellect and probing brush. His loaded, slow-moving brushstroke suspends and visibly prolongs the Action Painting gesture, creating strongly felt metaphors for doubt and certainty, chaos and order, disquiet and calm. Robert Motherwell provided an interesting exception to the "either/or" pattern of gestural and non-gestural color-field painting among the Abstract Expressionists. Between 1965 and 1980 he associated himself with the field paintings of Newman and Rothko to a surprising degree, rather than with the more emotive, gestural style of Abstract Expressionism.

The postwar period produced major innovations in sculpture close in spirit to Action Painting. An idiom of fluid metal construction appeared shortly after the war as the common bond between notable sculptures of diverse character by David Smith, Ibram Lassaw, Théodore Roszak, David Hare, Herbert Ferber, Seymour Lipton, and others. Borrowing from the Surrealists their addiction to accident and the random mark, the new sculptors worked in a fluent welded steel and in metal alloys, synthesizing open linear space drawing and Constructivist formalism. Like the Abstract Expressionists, they discovered that their first ventures were subjective, fantasy-ridden, and aggressive in handling. The new sculpture, however, was not all barbed form and exasperated, strident feeling. It ranged in mood from the luminous serenity of Ibram Lassaw's delicately fused cages to the nature-derived imagery of Seymour Lipton's hybrid organic-machine forms.

The major innovator in sculpture was inarguably David Smith (1906–65), who came to steel sculpture after assimilating the work of Picasso and Gonzalez, and after working in a factory during the war years as a welder of army tanks.

Rothko, Ad Reinhardt and others—created great unvaried expanses of alternately bright and somber hue in color fields rather than stress linear detail, agitated surface, and formal diversity. Their large canvases were intended to subdue the spectator's ego and to create a sense of tranquil awe. The awesome scale of Rothko's Four Seasons Restaurant mural cycle of paintings (1958–9; now in the Tate Gallery, London), with their unrelieved color sensation of homogenous red fields, were meant to assert the boundlessness and the mystery of being, in keeping with Edmund Burke's concept of the

The Sculptures of David Smith

David Smith (1906–65) recognized no demarcation between painting and sculpture. His sculptural expression grew naturally out of his work as a painter: even after sculpture had become his central means of expression, his output of drawings and paintings continued unabated. Everything he produced was part of a cohesive statement: his activity as draftsman, never subsidiary to that of a sculptor, was merely executed in a different dimension.

By attaching materials, "found" and shaped objects, to the surface of his paintings, Smith had achieved increased textural effects and liberation from the restrictions of the two-dimensional picture-space. Gradually, as the three-dimensional nature of his work developed, the canvas became the base, and the painting was sculpture.

The calligraphy of *Australia* (1951; Collection of Professor William Rubin, New York), the integral role of color in *Zig II* (1961; Des Moines Art Center, Des Moines, Iowa), and in the deployment in *Cubi XIX* (1964; Tate Gallery, London) of form in the shallow space of a Cubist picture, all testify to Smith's exploration of sculpture as drawing and painting in three dimensions. In the monumental *Zig* series, color is essential to the realization of form. It reveals and enforces plane, line, and volume; without it the statement would be incomplete. Like intervals in a painting, the voids of the *Cubi* series can be as significant as the stainless steel volumes, which in their apparent weightlessness defy gravity. Smith's approach to gravity as a limiting concept, one that must be challenged and transcended, is characteristic. His work as a whole is the product of repeated encounters with, and liberation from, accepted boundaries and criteria.

Smith's first welded steel structures of 1932 were influenced by those of Picasso and Julio Gonzalez. During the years that followed, he explored the vocabulary of most contemporary art movements without committing himself to any one of them: he took from each only what was useful to him. Intensely individualistic, he was cosmopolitan in his taste and eclectic in his sources. He was as capable of gaining inspiration from a Sumerian cylinder seal as from a painting by Kenneth Noland (1924–). In consequence he achieved a synthesis that encompassed the Constructivist idea, elements of the Cubist tradition, and a Surrealist tendency to allow the free play of subconscious imagery. But Smith's essential source of development and invention was within his art itself. From experimentation and the spontaneous dialogue between the artist and his materials, new forms emerged and were explored.

◀ *Cubi XIX* by David Smith; stainless steel; height 287cm (113in); 1964. Tate Gallery, London

▲ *Zig II* by David Smith; polychromed steel; height 255cm (100in); 1961. Des Moines Art Center, Des Moines, Iowa

Smith's commitment to iron and steel resulted from both his early experience as a metalworker in an automobile factory, and from his search for a new and vital vocabulary. Utilizing his industrial skills and the materials and techniques symbolic of modern society, he sought to anchor his work firmly in his own time. He identified himself as a workman; his creative process was one of construction: he cut profiles, welded together a sequence of elements; he seldom carved or modeled. Delighting in the progress of industrial technology and the new techniques it offered the sculptor, Smith was a pioneer in open, freestanding metal form. The characteristics of metal offered the choice of rapid, spontaneous invention and clearly articulated structure, or solid, considered form which could assert inherent qualities of toughness and durability. By exploiting the malleability of steel, Smith drew in space the open, linear forms of *Australia*, and constructed the geometric volumes of *Cubi XIX*. Permitting greater freedom of expression, the combined strength and fragility of iron and steel was, to Smith, symbolic not only of the potential of man's industrial achievement for construction and destruction, but also of the dual forces inherent in man himself.

For Smith a machine environment was a natural one. He enjoyed the scale and power of industry, and wished ultimately to create a sculpture as large as a locomotive. In his desire to create a wholly contemporary artistic statement, he consciously duplicated industrial processes and equipment in his workshop, constantly utilized new techniques, and incorporated factory-made components and industrial found objects in his work. Regarding everything in the natural world as objects to be discovered and utilized by the artist, Smith looked upon discarded

▲ Sculpture by David Smith in the artist's garden at Bolton Landing, New York State

▶ *Australia* by David Smith; painted steel; width 280cm (110in); 1951. Collection of Professor William Rubin, New York

industrial hardware, steel offcuts, and stock components, as the equivalent in an industrialized society of the found objects that have always played a part in man's creativity. In his workshop store of metal scrap, even the stock he ordered or had made to his specification became "found" objects: searching for a particular formal configuration, he would rediscover them.

When in use, forms are seldom appreciated for anything other than their mechanical performance. When they are separated from their past use or established function and employed with other forms, a metamorphosis takes place which creates a new, purely visual, unity: yet the formal elements retain an associational charge. Although his found objects were chosen primarily for their basic geometric form, they were required to fit a particular formal relationship: Smith exploited this inherent ambiguity. In the *Agricola* (from the Latin "farmer") series, Smith utilized the forms of discarded farm

equipment. The iron wheel hub from a wagon, for example, is a circle, a sun, and is endowed with romantic association stemming from its past use.

At Bolton Landing, in the mountains above Lake George, New York State, Smith lived in a landscape filled with his accumulating work. Initially through lack of space, the placing of sculpture outdoors became an integral part of his original conception. The burnished surface of *Cubi XIX*, intended to assume sky and environmental color, makes the sculpture a living, responsive part of the natural scene. It is this quality that Smith sought to achieve in all his work.

LYNNE MITCHELL

Further reading. Gray, C. (ed.) *David Smith by David Smith*, New York (1968). Krauss, R.E. *Terminal Iron Works: the Sculpture of David Smith*, Cambridge, Mass. (1971). McCoy, G. (ed.) *David Smith*, Harmondsworth (1973).

Smith's art of the 1940s and 1950s was highly diverse and crowded with personal symbols; it varied in style from delicate linear detail to strong, rugged volumes of joined metal sheets. He alternately evoked Surrealist totems and Constructivist rationalist techniques and methods. As early as 1956, Smith began to experiment with modular sculpture and made stacks of box-like shapes which led to his most significant sculpture series during the last five years of his life, the *Cubi* series. These precarious ensembles of welded cylinders, disks, and rectangular boxes in asymmetric alignment, burnished and ground with a wire brush until their surfaces reflected light like fish scales, are among the most original and powerful plastic inventions of 20th-century American art. They directly anticipated the unadorned metal boxes, modular compositions, and geometric severity of the rising Minimalist generation of sculptors in the 1960s in the work of Don Judd, Robert Morris, and others.

Curiously, another sculptor of Smith's own generation predicted even more clearly, and directly influenced, the course of Minimalist sculpture. It was Tony Smith (1912–80), who initiated the practice of having his severe geometric forms in plywood fabricated into large-scale metal constructions in 1962, well in advance of the cult for anonymous metalwork manufacture which became the rule later in the decade.

A unique and mysterious figure in American sculpture was Joseph Cornell (1903–72) who began to make his Surrealist box constructions in the mid 1930s. His work combined the structural stringencies of Constructivism with subconscious sources of imagery in Surrealist fantasy, and embraced an entrancing assortment of romantic bric-a-brac. Jasper Johns' plaster molds in his target paintings, and Lucas Samaras' rather menacing boxes of pins, taxidermy objects, and bright-colored yarns can be considered direct descendants of Cornell's bizarre inventions. The work of Louise Nevelson (1899–1988) represents another sharp departure from the typical artistic product of the sculptor-welders of the 1950s. Her walls in wood and other constructions, large and small, invariably contain commonplace "found" objects—newel posts, discarded furniture parts, and the like—which she still assiduously collects today. The flotsam of the street is stacked and composed in rigorous Abstract compositions. She has worked successfully in recent years in large-scale fabricated metal sculpture, though here her works are perhaps less poetic than her wooden constructions but more assured and controlled in formal terms.

In the 1960s the interaction of art and technology captured the popular imagination as artists began to experiment throughout the world with such new materials as synthetics and plastics, and embarked on collaborations with scientists. The new paths had been opened by the activation of optical

Black on Maroon, one of Mark Rothko's Four Seasons Restaurant mural cycle; oil on canvas; 267×457cm (105×180in); 1959. Tate Gallery, London

Smoke by Tony Smith; steel; 7.31×10.36×14.63m (24×34×48ft); 1967–79. Corcoran Gallery of Art, Washington, D.C.

illusion and other perceptual phenomena in so-called "Op Art", which preceded the investigation of more complex industrial techniques and electric technology in art. The American pioneer in Op art was the German-born Josef Albers (1880–1976) who had created and introduced at the Bauhaus, as early as 1930, a new, dynamic perceptual element in painting with a variety of optical devices and color contrasts. Albers was among the first to discover the emotive potential of complex visual stimuli. He left Germany to teach at Black Mountain College in North Carolina in 1933, and from that date until his death he became the leading figure in a current of purist abstraction. In the 1960s his earlier color experiments were recognized for their prophecy of optical art. In the years after 1949 he painted modular nests of color squares in different dominant hues and sizes and almost identical formats. His celebrated Homage to the Square series was the first example of serial and optical art in America. Although his influence as a teacher at both Black Mountain College and Yale University was considerable—he taught, among others, Robert Rauschenberg, Kenneth Noland, and Richard Anuskiewicz—only Anuskiewicz pursued and extended his investigations of an art of activated perception within a rigorously geometric format.

While optical art did not have nearly so pervasive an influence in America as it did in Europe, a number of sculptors allied themselves with the related international interest in motion sculpture, or Kineticism—a movement that similarly expressed a sympathy for the world of modern technology.

One of its most remarkable exponents has been the New Zealand-born Len Lye (1901–). He made programmed machines constructed of exquisitely fine metal components of stainless steel; in motion, their violently activated forms move so quickly that they give the impression of dematerialized form and flickering tongues of light. The sculptor George Rickey (1907–) creates more slowly moving, stainless-steel or painted metal blades of great length, balanced precariously on a fulcrum like heroic shears, and other egg-beater forms which he calls "space churns". His refined sculptures gently swing and rotate, driven by air currents. Their burnished, highly reflective surfaces give off light in a way that denies solid form and volume and is thus related to the energy release in Len Lye's motion sculpture.

In Light art, Chryssa (1933–) was the first American to use emitted electric light and illuminated neon tubes. She combined elements of neon with fragments of lettered commercial signs taken from the urban environment. In the late 1960s, light and neon were also utilized by artists as dissimilar as Dan Flavin, Robert Morris, Bruce Nauman, and Keith Sonnier to realize a quite different goal of environmental expansiveness, and to define a specific site in purely formal terms.

By the late 1960s a more factual rather than an expressionist or romantic account of the artistic process prevailed in both painting and sculpture. As an example of the changes that occurred, the painting Lilac Frost (1977; Collection of Hanford Yang, New York) by Helen Frankenthaler (1928–) offers a mixture of gestural abstraction with color-field scale and brightness. She has, however, significantly transformed her Abstract Expressionist sources. Her richly loaded pigment surfaces are more optically active and yet less substantial in texture. The wandering edges of her forms are determined by gravity and the drying process, a method she shared with the exquisite color painter, Morris Louis (1912–62). Color, shape, and edge speak for themselves as pure physical and optical phenomena in the art of both Louis and Frankenthaler, released from romantic rhetoric about the "abstract sublime". Such paintings no longer suggest a sense of urgent moral purpose, or of difficulties overcome, as did those of the first "heroic" generation of American Abstract artists. They are openly more hedonistic and propose an impersonal approach to artistic activity, characteristic of the 1960s and 1970s. Such talented and facile successors of the Abstract Expressionists as Frankenthaler, Kenneth Noland, and Ellsworth Kelly paid the Abstract Expressionist pioneers the respect of formal emulation, at least in terms of scale, but something of the old sense of adventure and social iconoclasm was lost in the art of the new generation.

One of the most influential younger artists of the 1960s was the painter Frank Stella (1936–). Beginning with his unprecedented black-striped paintings of the period 1958–60, continuing in his vividly chromatic, grand-scale "protractor" series of segmented color shapes of the 1960s, and then in his constructed reliefs, Stella managed to reverse the customary roles of geometry and Bauhaus design in modern art. He cre-

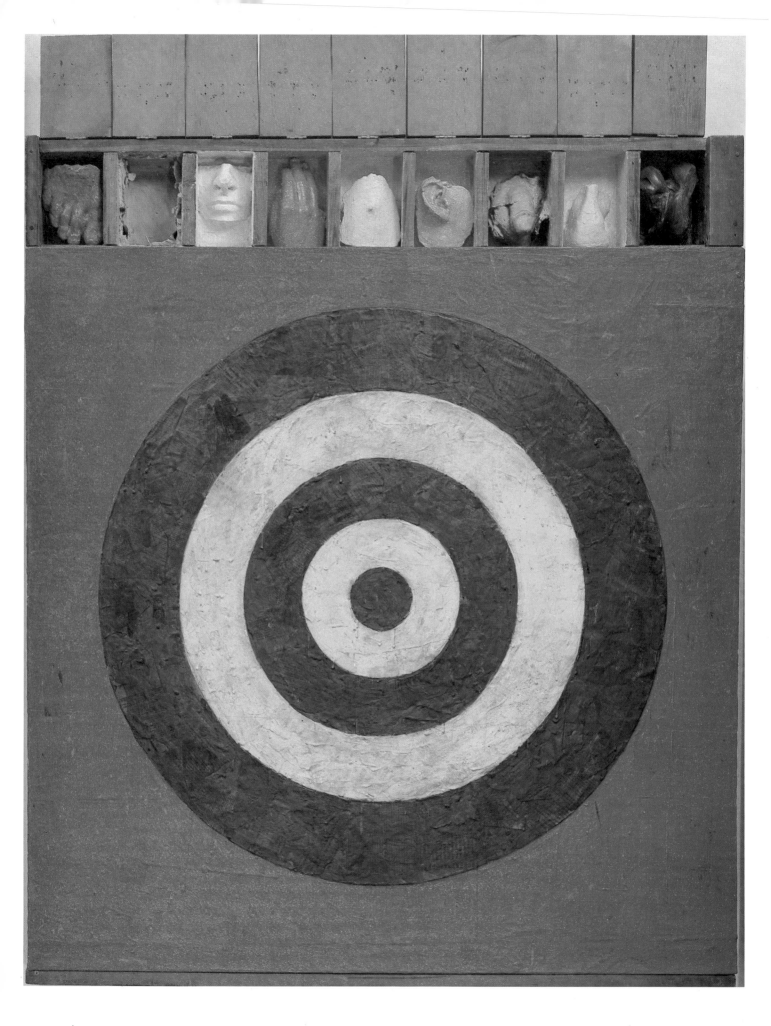

ated a new balance between the concepts of the painting as pictorial illusion and as an object—a thing of literal and denotative meaning. Surprisingly, paintings of the late 1970s—expressionist high relief—revived the emotionalism of Abstract Expressionism, despite their adherence to preordained rules and the used of standard French curves and other devices taken from the engineer's drafting board. In their different ways, Robert Ryman, Brice Marden, and Robert Mangold have respectively extended definitions of the pictorial field as a nearly blank environmental wall, and have integrated it with a physically tangible color surface, or have established a new kind of equilibrium between atmospheric color space and the sense of the painting as an architectural structure.

To an extraordinary degree, however, the last years of the 1960s saw idea rather than physical mass or visual definition become the controlling feature of art. The sculptor and painter Sol LeWitt (1928–) described the idea as "the machine that makes the work". The artist's aim, he wrote in the first published declaration on Conceptual art, is "not to instruct the viewer, but to give him information. Whether the viewer understands this information is incidental to the artist." Despite the value placed on cerebral process, the character of the end product, nevertheless, remained, in LeWitt's words, "intuitive". Although he is undoubtedly best known for his austere, Minimalist sculptures and for the invention of Conceptual art, LeWitt began in the late 1960s to design influential wall drawings, executed by other hands, projects in which the conceptual clarity of his ideas dominated. Even though the governing ideas were stringent and methodical, the results demonstrated sensibility as well as theoretical considerations.

While both Abstract and Conceptual art have continued to flourish since the first postwar explorations, many other idioms of a less narrowly formal character have also since emerged, and expanded their domain in the 1960s and 1970s. Notable among these are new forms of realism, including Pop art and Photo-Realism, autobiographical forms of Conceptual art, varieties of performance art, and an unprecedented genre of large-scale environmental sculpture.

One of the most important innovators who succeeded in wedding objective realism to Abstract form following the de Kooning generation was Jasper Johns (1930–), best known for his early paintings of targets and his paintings of the American flag. Both these series managed to raise serious questions about the nature of the art object, even as Johns elaborated his subjects in almost loving, and obviously skilled painterly terms. These paintings demonstrated that it was possible to make pictures from forms which were both complex and so familiar that they could be seen as a complete unit, without parts or a functioning relationship between the parts. Since the image in question either filled the canvas entirely or was centrally placed, no relationship between the image and

Bed by Robert Rauschenberg; combine painting; 187×79cm (74×31in); 1955. Leo Castelli Gallery, New York

Left: Target with Plaster Casts by Jasper Johns; encaustic and collage on canvas with plaster casts; 129×112×9cm (51×44×4in); 1955. Leo Castelli Gallery, New York

the field was activated. Yet Johns' targets and flags were represented as "fine art" by reason of their execution in the most palpable, sensuous paint medium imaginable.

Johns' deliberate choice of two-dimensional subjects challenged the viewer, who could not be sure whether he was looking at a picture of an object or the literal object itself—albeit an object made of paint. To achieve this effect, the forms had to be so familiar that the painter obviously could not have invented them. By this stratagem Johns restored imagery to painting without becoming a representational painter, which had been for Pollock and de Kooning almost an unresolvable dilemma. Johns was clearly aware of the paradoxes and visual puns of Duchamp's art, and of his anti-art ruses. He more than once directly paraphrased this fertile source of his own metaphysical speculations on artistic and common-day realities.

Johns and his friend Robert Rauschenberg (1925–) shocked the public of the late 1950s by presenting commonplace objects and imagery taken from popular culture as works of art. Their bold new tactics opened the door directly to Pop art. Unlike their precedessors, the work of the Pop artists was not dominated or veiled by seductive paint quality. Even more vehemently, they rejected both the notion of art as the elitist property of the Abstract Expressionists and their presumed monopoly of high culture and qualities of moral purity. Pop art scandalized the American art world by extending art into the realm of *Kitsch* and bad commercial art which the champions of "high art" had been educated to despise. One of the critical messages of Pop art was, in the words of Roy Lichtenstein (1923–), that good art could actually be made of such "despicable" and debased subject matter as the comic strip, or the billboard.

For James Rosenquist (1933–) the large billboard format inspired an original example of American Pop art. Rosenquist has a taste for the marvels of technology. His commercial icons, often painted on mural scale, as in *Flamingo Capsule* (Leo Castelli Gallery, New York), which measures 10 ft by 32 ft (3 m by 9.7 m), account for his major stature in American art. The imagery is somewhat obscure, and even invites a reading as a poetic comment on technique itself, suggesting constant change, dissolution, and metamorphosis in the brilliant, rippling reflections and changeful color surface. His large paintings are visually dazzling and subjective at a euphoric level of sensations.

An interesting aspect of Pop art, now that its offending shock has been dulled by distance in time, is its narrative method. Narration may seem at first glance a misnomer for imagery as static and repetitive as that of Pop art, but it can also offer an illuminating approach in relation to other, more recent contemporary artistic developments. In the case of the most notorious Pop artist, Andy Warhol, his alternatively bland and violent scenarios are plotless, lacking beginning, middle, or end. The familiar narrational devices of anecdotal or realistic art are also absent. Nothing actually happens in the sense of conventional story-telling. The point of his paint-

Clothespin by Claes Oldenburg; Corten steel; height 13.7m (45ft); 1977. Centre Square, Philadelphia, Pa

Left: Sixteen Jackies by Andy Warhol; acrylic and silkscreen enamel on canvas; 203×163cm (80×64in); 1965. Walker Art Center, Minneapolis

ings is, at least in part, to confront us with boredom as an issue rather than to elicit specific responses to subject matter, which an unrelenting, mechanical presentation has neutralized. No matter how gruesome Warhol's imagery—for example, in his familiar *Disaster* series of mangled bodies and crushed automobile chassis—a cool, detached stance effectively thwarts emotional involvement. Despite the iconography of blankness and impassivity, he also operated in the area of public myth and parable in the 1960s. It is impossible to forget his haunting images of Jacqueline Kennedy at the President's funeral. Warhol may, in fact, be taken as a modern history painter, because his dominant imagery and visual ironies are so intimately linked with the conditions and social meanings of contemporary mass urban culture, and with the communications media of newspapers and T.V. journalism.

Photography made itself felt in the 1960s through a new art style known as Photo-Realism. Paintings by the Photo-Real-

ists create an even more faithful simulacrum of the media world of illusion and hype than Pop art, relying on hauntingly exact duplications of actuality as viewed through the camera lens. The blatant, elephantine humor of Claes Oldenburg's Pop imagery of giant food replicas and monumental object sculptures, or Rosenquist's montages of popular culture and commercial icons were transformed by the Photo-Realists into cool, double-edged visual ironies by their precise and detailed rendering of anything from a model bathroom to the neon signs and facades of New York's Times Square.

Translating the photographic image directly on to canvas, the Photo-Realists emphasize the gleaming artificiality of contemporary life. The favorite subject matter of Ralph Goings and a number of other realists has become the motor car. They paint it today with a discerning sense of its character as a status symbol. Curiously, however, the intense emotion that so often goes into the ordinary consumer's acquisition of the

Canadian Club by Richard Estes; oil on canvas; 122×152cm (48×60in); 1974. Collection of M.G. Neumann, Chicago

automobile as a mark of social caste is contradicted by the artists' dispassionate manner of paint handling when representing this and related banal consumer objects. Through the painters' understatements, the glamorous automobile subject matter of color advertising is rigorously neutralized. This is one of the many ironies of Super-Realism, for it treats the highly charged, erotic symbolism of the American's hunger for the latest model of automobile, or for the consumer goodies of the department store and supermarket, in a banal and offhand manner. But even these images often reveal a curious complexity and incongruity in the abstract patterns of their reflective surfaces; in the canvases are mini-worlds and holes which strongly resemble contemporary painterly abstraction.

Inevitably the obsession with visual data, based on the photographic medium, opened the way for a similar transcription of the world of sight into three dimensions. The polyester humanity created by Duane Hanson appears to be simultaneously real and bizarrely unreal, and thus parallels the inanimate subject matter of related paintings by the Photo-Realists. His figures and those of John de Andrea closely resemble Madame Tussaud's waxworks with their accurate mimicry of human gesture. A fascination with duplications of human beings in convincing life-size replicas is an age-old obsession, dating back in modern times to Mary Shelley's *Frankenstein*. Today, when originals and reproductions are no longer so easily distinguishable because of the impact of the mass media, at a time when consumers are increasingly manipulated by advertising, sinister overtones can attach themselves to these counterfeit three-dimensional human lifenesses. The more exact the anatomical replicas and the clothes they wear, the more they gain a monstrous quality, reminding us of the Walt Disney World Hall of programmed, automated American Presidents, or more ominously, of the robot killer of the film *Westworld* played by Yul Brynner—the surrogate human being socially out of control.

Another fascinating development stemming from traditional realism and narrative art forms has been "Story Art". The epithet was coined to characterize an offshoot of Conceptual art which mixes its verbal and visual means but discards much of the philosophical pretensions of standard Conceptual art in favor of light-hearted autobiographical observation and fantasy. Instead of exploring theoretical ideas primarily, in order to challenge the traditional sensuous concerns of painting, narrative artists Peter Hutchinson, John Baldessari, Bill Beckley, and other have made their art a vehicle for their own wry, quixotic perceptions. An indication of their hedonistic approach is a new emphasis in the 1970s on glossy, lustrous color photography, rather than the more arid black-and-white film of the past.

John Baldessari's photograph series, *Cigar Smoke to Match Clouds that are Different* (1971) consists of two quite separate and unrelated visual events, one based on memory and the other on sight. Each contains two kinds of ephemera, in three color photographs, clouds and cigar smoke. The artist, perhaps absurdly, tries to duplicate cloud formations with a

Spiral Jetty by Robert Smithson; earthwork; 1970. Great Salt Lake, Utah

puff of cigar smoke. The cloud scene is visible in the form of a small-scale color snapshop stuck to his forehead, permitting us to judge the success or failure of his visual experiment. The work thus plays back and forth between the sense of past time and the present, raising questions about identity and the artistic process even though at first glance the idea of a comparison may seem preposterous or arbitrary.

In the late 1960s and early 1970s as the sociopolitical tensions in America eased, the *Zeitgeist* began to change, moving towards populism and away from the emotional involvements and commitments of the Vietnam War period. New kinds of academic realism emerged as dominant styles, lacking the implicit criticism of the culture which even Pop art's deadpan mode could scarcely disguise. Where the spirit of the 1960s was expansively creative and inclusive, the spirit of the art scene in the 1970s was quite the opposite. A new kind of narcissistic and "loner" mentality was evident; it permeated many other areas of American culture. It was reflected particularly in solitary video and performance art events. Analogies can be drawn with the popularity of contemporary forms of meditation, withdrawal, and self-realization. There was an evident impulse to seek detachment from shared social experience, a turning away from public issues; this produced artists who prefer to work away from the crowd. Much of the art of the early 1980s is of a private rather than a public nature, and the phenomenon is particularly apparent in the emphasis on artistic biography in video art.

The lively "Happenings" of the 1960s, involving masses of enthusiastic participants, have now been succeeded by solitary, static, and often voyeuristic performances of which Vito Acconci's "Body Art" is a representative example. Innumerable artists have retreated from conceiving and executing the large-scale, bold paintings and sculptures of the 1960s in favor of a more controlled, even portable microcosm. One of the most unusual has been Joel Schapiro, who makes tiny sculptures that, in effect, miniaturize the universe—obsessive expressions just large enough to be seen and handled.

On the other hand, in formalist sculpture there is still a trend toward a more public confrontation and orientation, with the proliferation of large-scale steel works by such fine artists as Mark di Suvero, Claes Oldenburg, Louise Nevelson, and Tony Smith. A surprising number of contemporary monumental sculpture productions have been government-sponsored commissions. For the most part, they are generally amplifications of ideas and styles staked out in the 1960s, and have little relationship to the introspective object-making of many of the most promising young artists. However, there are moments when the artist's private and public faces do merge. The great Japanese-American sculptor, Isamu Noguchi (1904–88), is a case in point. In the 1940s Noguchi was best known for his private Surrealist-inspired sculptures and for his public stage sets which he designed for the dance company of Martha Graham. In the 1980s, he continued to synthesize his private, imaginative world with a more conventional, externalized symbolism in the form of public monuments; two of these are the *Landscape in Time* in Seattle, Washington, and the Dodge Fountain and Plaza in Detroit.

The public environment has also lent itself to such private and fanciful constructions as Robert Smithson's earthworks, *Spiral Jetty* in the Great Salt Lake, and to Christo's 23-mile (37km) long strip of cloth, moving like a river of light in the California landscape, his *Running Fence*, which was erected for a week in 1977 and then dismantled. At a time of material glut and ecological danger to the environment, earthworks and environmental art remind us of man's indissoluble bonds with nature.

While the forms of art change continuously, it seems clear that one aspect of the dialogue in the American visual arts remains constant: the debate between the artist's private imaginative needs and public communication.

SAM HUNTER

From the 1970s onwards many American artists began to see themselves as "postmodernist". Drawing on feminism, Pop art and Conceptualism, as well as the ideas of the French theorists Jacques Derrida and Jean Baudrillard, they wanted to move beyond Modernism and develop an art appropriate to the values and demands of the late 20th century. Complex, many-sided and sometimes contradictory, postmodernism encouraged a wide range of responses.

In architecture, Charles Jencks (1939–) and Robert Venturi (1925–) led the attack on Modernism. Rejecting the severity of functionalism, they argued in favor of ornament, rich decoration and color, and also encouraged the confident exploitation ("quotation") of both contemporary vernacular and traditional (usually classical) styles. Two of the most exuberant examples of American postmodernist architecture are the Piazza d'Italia, New Orleans (1975–80), by Charles Moore (1925–); and the Public Services Building, Portland, Oregon (1978–82), by Michael Graves (1934–).

In painting, there was a renewed interest—after the puritanical austerities of Conceptualism and Abstraction—in the painterly tradition: in decoration, figurative painting, expressive brushwork, and symbol, allegory and narrative. Central themes now included feminism, gay rights, ecology, consumerism, and, above all, the nature and limits of art itself.

The Pattern and Decoration movement, which emerged in New York in the mid 1970s, was inspired by craft traditions, by Islamic, Oriental and Native American art, as well as by Matisse and Bloomsbury. Artists such as Robert Kushner (1949–) and Miriam Schapiro (1923–) created rich visual effects in a variety of media. The desire was to provide a democratic, non-sexist alternative to the Western (male) tradition of "high art"; feminist artists played a major role in the movement.

Graffiti (or Ghetto) art, striving to be the art of the poor and the culturally dispossessed, was inspired by the street graffiti of New York (though Surrealism and the *art brut* of Dubuffet also played a part). It too emerged in the mid 1970s, though its two best-known practitioners—Keith Haring (1958–90) and Jean-Michel Basquiat (1960–88)—worked in the 1980s, when the style was being promoted by fashionable galleries.

An exhibition at the Whitney Museum in New York in 1978 gave its name—New Image Painting—to the work of several leading artists of the 1970s and 1980s, Susan Rothenberg (1945–) and Jennifer Bartlett (1941–) among them. New Image painting, which took many forms, is broadly characterized by a confident return to figurative painting and also by a postmodernist attitude (largely ironic) to style. In the absence of any radically new style, artists during the 1980s "appropriated" Surrealism and Superrealism, Pop, kitsch and commercial art, Abstraction, cartoons and comic strip, naive and native art, Baroque, and Purism (to name only a few sources). European Neo-Expressionism helped to create the raw, intense canvases of Julian Schnabel (1951–), and, in a more subtle way, the erotic fantasies of Eric Fischl (1948–). The Neo-classical academicism of Milet Andrejevic (1925–) set Poussin-like allegories in Central Park.

Whether this still evolving postmodernism has created an art appropriate to its age, heralding a profound change in sensibility, is as yet unclear. What is clear, however, is that American art in the last three decades of the 20th century has lost none of its vitality and bravura.

CHRIS MURRAY

Bibliography. Baigell, M. *Dictionary of American Art*, New York (1979). Brown, M.W. *The Modern Spirit: American Painting 1908–1935*, London (1977). Gablik, S. *Has Modernism Failed?*, New York (1984). Greenberg, C. *Art and Culture: Critical Essays*, Boston (1961). Hoffman, K. *Explorations: The Visual Arts Since 1945*, New York (1991). Hunter, S. and Jacobus, J. *American Art of the Twentieth Century: Painting, Sculpture, Architecture*, New York (1973). McCoubrey, J.W. *American Art 1700–1960: Sources and Documents*, Englewood Cliffs (1965). McCoy, G. *Archives of American Art: a Directory of Resources*, New York (1972). Rose, B. *American Art since 1900: a Critical History*, New York (1975). Rose, B. (ed.) *Reading in American Art*, New York (1975). Sandler, I. *The Triumph of American Painting: a History of Abstract Expressionism*, New York (1970).

52

POSTWAR EUROPEAN ART

Upright Motive no.1 (The Glenkiln Cross) by Henry Moore; bronze
height 333cm (131in); 1955–6. Tate Gallery, London (see page 944)

WE owe one of the first comprehensive definitions of modern art to Hitler's government in Germany, when they collected all that is now admired as the best and most revealing expression of its time under the heading of "degenerate art". In so doing they also did the best they could have done to ensure its postwar survival, for modern art, proscribed by tyranny, became an apt symbol of freedom. Apt to the historical situation, too, was the adoption of conspicuously modern art in the U.S.A.—the bastion of freedom. The power that had escaped from Europe was beamed back across the Atlantic, magnified by American sense of scale and supported by that specially American alliance between wealth and avant-gardism. In the symbolism of German regeneration and American free wealth, modern art found a new importance and, from being a poor survivor in 1945, grew to a powerful estate in the West in less than two decades.

In 1945 this development could not have been confidently foreseen. There were those who, in spite of its validation by Nazi persecution, associated modern art with the castastrophe of the Second World War. Postwar art was pulled in contrary directions by conflicting hopes and fears in the uneasy peace after the Nuremburg trials and the Yalta Conference. An unprecedented need for inward expression found the available visual forms inadequate. For those artists with historical consciousness, there were broadly three tendencies to which they could feel attached: Surrealism, Constructivism-abstraction, and a loose complex of metamorphic styles associated with the school of Paris. Surrealism should have been well equipped to deal in the psychopathology of the aftermath of war, given its interest in extreme situations and its connections with Freudian theories of the subconscious. But although its leaders had survived the war and had many years to live, Surrealism was compromised socially and politically; similarly, its reliance on specific kinds of imagery made its continuance after the war unlikely (*see* Dada and Surrealism).

Compared with Surrealism, abstraction had had an unremarked existence in the years just before the war. Its early idealistic force had faded. The Russian nonfigurative movement and the Bauhaus in Germany had lost political credence in the late 1920s; both were to be extinguished in the early 1930s. The Dutch group *De Stijl* broke up from internal causes in 1931. These movements were reborn in Paris in the looser, less fiercely ideological groupings of *Cercle et Carré* (1930) and *Abstraction-Création* (1932) which served as rallying points for artists of different nationalities with tendencies to geometric abstraction. In spite of the urgent need for actual constructive and environmental harmony, manifest in Europe after 1945, the Constructivist and Abstract stance had little appeal in the early postwar years. It may be inferred that the need for psychic expressionism was even more urgent.

Between the extremes of Surrealism and Constructivism is a wide space in which a varied morphology of art had developed by 1939. Metamorphism—the presentation of something belonging to one form-family in the guise of another—was the device that united diverse artists of the school of Paris.

Strangely, it was in Britain that metamorphism, though never formulated as such, was most important after 1945. A type of vitalistic, animistic nature-worship already marked two leading English artists, Henry Moore and Graham Sutherland, before the war. The English sculptors whose angst-ridden work had such success in the 1950s, such as Lynn Chadwick (1914–), Kenneth Armitage (1916–), and Elisabeth Frink (1930–93) achieved their ends by metamorphic fusion of crystalline, crustacean, or anthropoid forms together in the bonding medium of rough, rebarbative materials. Francis Bacon's greater renown was equally based on metamorphism, never greater than in his *Three Studies for Figures at the Base of a Crucifixion* of 1944 (Tate Gallery, London), the painting that established his reputation and mature style. The metamorphism of Henry Moore has survived the main change in his work, from form elicited from materials by carving, to biomorphs abstractly conceived and built up. The vigor of this vitalistic morphology in postwar Britain muffled the appearance of informal abstraction here as the dominant modern art of the West.

The art that came rapidly to dominate the exhibitions and art magazines of the postwar period did not adopt any one of the three tendencies described. This painting, just described as "informal abstraction", had various other names which betrayed different critical attitudes as well as wide variations within the art itself. The nomenclature stressed its capacity for poetry ("lyrical abstraction"), its inner motivation ("psychic improvisation" or *art autre*), or its procedures (*tachisme* or "gestural painting"). Action Painting and Abstract Expressionism were terms coined to describe the American counterpart, with which European informal abstraction must inevitably be measured. The meteoric rise of informal abstraction may well seem baffling, but it met an urgent need in Western postwar society. What seemed to underlie informal abstraction was freedom, or at least spontaneity. Representational forms came under attack through disillusion with all received symbolism, but also because representation limits spontaneity. The conceptual basis of geometric or ordered abstraction did so equally. Informal abstraction allowed the artist, as never before, to "speak" directly through manipulation of his materials. Hence the term Abstract *Expressionism*. But such freedom raised more acutely than ever the problems of ensuring authenticity and avoiding empty contrivance and rhetoric.

In retrospect, the most important source of informal abstraction seems to have been Surrealism. The Surrealists had sought authenticity through the idea of psychic automatism—trying to yield as far as possible to the promptings of the unconscious—and through the exploitation of chance. With the European Surrealists, conscious control, leading to the development of images, soon intervened in this process. The younger Americans tried to push automatism further and

Composition, 1954 by Hans Hartung; oil on canvas; 130×97cm (51×38in). Musée National d'Art Moderne, Paris

finally, prompted by the needs of their generation and by contingent history, into the elimination of images. Thus Surrealist ideas received a powerful new expression in the paintings of Arshile Gorky (1904–48) and above all Jackson Pollock (1912–56), which was quickly relayed to Europe. Once the impulse was generated, other sources were to hand. Kandinsky's paintings before 1914, taken together with his writings, provided a theoretical and spiritual justification for free abstraction. The very late works of Monet, with his rejection of boundaries, offered a historical antecedent for informal art. As time went on, it became fashionable to ransack the art of the past in search of validation, aided by a burgeoning art-publishing industry. One class of material was specially relevant to the emerging character of informal abstraction in Europe: anything that had a strong element of handwriting or which depended on calligraphic, ideogrammatic signs.

The order of precedence (in date or merit) between American and European Abstract Expressionism is a sensitive area for historians. Hans Hartung (1904–89) practiced gestural or calligraphic abstraction from 1935. The artist who has been called "the primitive of *art informel*", Wols (1913–51), showed pure psychic improvisations in Paris in December 1945. The Venice Biennale of 1948, when the new American painting had hardly begun to reach Europe, already showed the tendency firmly established. The revelation of the Americans did not, in reality, swing European painting behind their kind of informal abstraction. The European version remained far more diffuse. The postwar scene could embrace a consciously French group round Alfred Manessier (1911–) and Jean Bazaine (1904–75) who were not gestural painters but who aimed to extract evocative sensations from late Impressionism, Orphism, or the late Braque. On the other hand, it could include the CoBrA group of artists from *C*openhagen, *B*russels, and *A*msterdam, with Karel Appel (1921–) and Asger

Le Bâteau by Nicolas de Staël; oil on canvas; 46×61cm (18×24in); 1954. Scottish National Gallery of Modern Art, Edinburgh

Jorn (1914–73) among them, whose methods were more gestural, and also brash, iconoclastic, and expressionist. Within the developed and near-universal Western style of informal abstraction—it still dominated the international *Documenta* exhibition at Kassel in 1959—there were national variants and individual eddies. In Paris, Nicolas de Staël (1914–1955) and Serge Poliakoff (1906–69) represented a controlled, nongestural abstraction using planes and slabs of color which, in de Staël's case, had an intensely material aspect, and which he began to match up with external appearances to produce a semi-figurative painting. His delight in the material splendor of paint as he applied it links him loosely with the so-called *matière* painters (those using highly tangible and textural surfaces, often built up in relief) of which the best known is the Spaniard Antoni Tapies (1923–). Tapies prepared canvases with sand, plaster, or other materials to receive traces of his activity which, given the revelation of aerial photography, could often appear like the traces of natural or human activity on the surface of the earth itself.

In Britain, Abstract Expressionism was grafted on to the still strong tradition of metamorphic imagery and nature-worship, and was no more than one factor in the development of the St Ives school around Roger Hilton (1911–75) and Peter Lanyon (1918–64) who were also influenced by the constructive and lyrical abstraction of Ben Nicholson (1894–1982). In Italy, abstraction allowed an untraditional expressionism to enter the work of Emilio Vedova (1915–) and others. Alberto Burri (1915–), linked with the *matière* painters, used stitched sacking, iron, and burnt materials to extend the expressive powers of abstraction, discharging thereby the horrors of wartime experiences as a medical orderly. Many other examples of manipulation of materials formed a subculture within informal abstraction. Their existence side by side with ideogrammatic abstraction pointed to a dilemma: should art move towards a closer identity with the physical world and human interaction with it, or should it move towards a language of *signs* capable of an abstract life? And should "Abstract" painting present itself as a material presence, or a disembodied principle? The dangers of this impasse are aptly illustrated by the frozen gestural abstractions of the prominent Parisian, Georges Mathieu (1921–).

Europe was slower than America to find a way out of the impasse of Abstract Expressionism. The material of reaction was present within American abstraction itself, especially in the work of Barnett Newman (1905–70), as early as 1948. British art, by the mid 1950s, was in an intermediate position. British artists born in the 1920s and 1930s began to look to the U.S.A. rather than follow the traditional alignment to France, and some were quick to see the implication of Newman and of younger Americans such as Kenneth Noland (1924–). Through easy travel and American-orientated international art magazines, British artists joined in the American critical dialogue which at this time—the late 1950s and early 1960s—was assuming a strongly reactive character, testing artists' new formulations as responses (often negative) to what

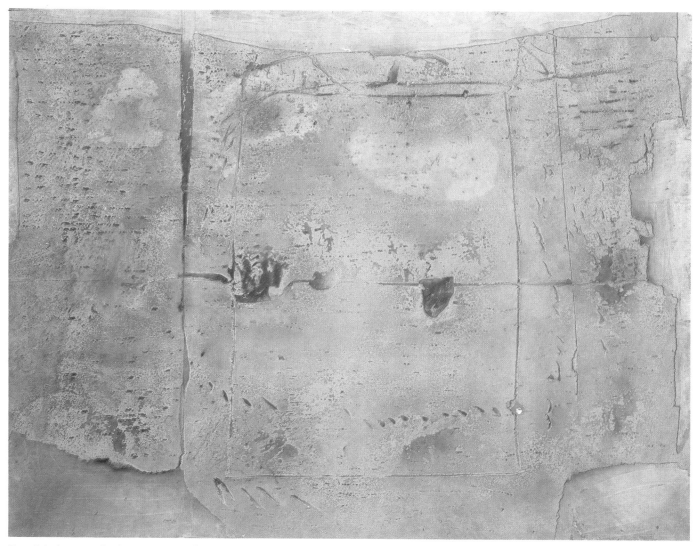

Great Painting, 1958 by Antoni Tapies; oil and sand on canvas; 200×260cm (79×102in). Solomon R. Guggenheim Museum, New York

had gone before. The underlying reaction was the one that replaced Abstract Expressionism with a less personalized medium. A clue to the character of the new phenomenon is the term "Post-Painterly abstraction" coined in America in 1964. While yielding nothing to Abstract Expressionism in size or ambition, the artists grouped under this term repressed "handwriting" in favor of flat areas and hard edges, avoiding spatial illusionism and detailed tonal contrasts. The atmosphere of this art was attractive to young British artists, who had their own "cool" reaction to assert against the metamorphism or the lyricism of their seniors.

One way in which the reaction was expressed was in the large size of the paintings of the young British artists, brought out at an exhibition of historic moment (although little appreciated at the time), Situation, at the RBA Galleries, London, in 1960. The title drew attention to the problems of presenting large-scale work but has also come to infer a certain kind of painting. Part of the exhibition was still gestural in character, but the work of Robyn Denny (1931–), William

Turnbull (1922–), and others could not have been further from the ideogrammatic, quasi-symbolic basis of much gestural painting. Their paintings denied the possibility of direct psychic interpretation, offering a self-referential aesthetic system in which the work itself is *fact* and what is required from the spectator is primarily adaptation to this fact. The large size, the straight edges and unbroken planes, the strict subordination of parts to whole which insists on the work as a *total* fact, make it quite difficult for spectators to empathize with the artist, to put themselves in that *situation*. To do so requires that innate coolness with regard to art and life which is fundamentally the content of this post-gestural abstraction. A similar trend in British sculpture was even more striking because of the postwar fame that British Metamorphic and Expressionist sculpture had enjoyed. Anthony Caro (1924–) was an early and essential link in applying to sculpture some lessons of American Post-Painterly abstraction. Caro's rejection of the pedestal went further than ever before in using the ground plane to extend sculpture almost to room size. His use

of prefabricated steel sections instead of wrought metal, equals, in sculpture, the rejection of gestural painting. The elaborate spatial extension of Caro's large works is intended to baffle compositional analysis: he insists, like the Americans, that he does not "compose".

Post-Painterly and situationist abstraction was an Anglo-American, rather than international, reaction to Abstract Expressionism. In mainland Europe, reaction or opposition to informal or gestural abstraction either used systems that were already available, such as Constructivism, or expressed itself in a revival of Dada individualism or dissidence. Or it took elements from both.

As an available system, Constructivism was to provide a good antidote to the personality cult and romantic aspirations of gestural abstraction. It had played such a role before when the hard-core Constructivists in Russia won an ideological victory over Malevich and Kandinsky, c1921, or when Gabo and Pevsner denounced Futurism. In spite of the factions within Constructivism and the erosion of its original sociopolitical meaning, its spokesmen consistently opposed "the tyranny of the subjective" and also lyricism or drama. Constructivism proposed instead a preconceived, objectively planned self-referential art, beautifully made with the best available technology. Yet in the postwar world, the successors to Constructivism have branched out in directions that seem dramatic and personal, and instead of adopting a constant standard of visual value have directed attention to relativity, illusion, and instability.

Some of the surviving members of the prewar *Abstraction-Création* movement were grouped together after 1947 in a loose association known as the *Salon des Réalités Nouvelles*, a significant change of name which asserted the "reality" of Constructivism over the new trend to psychic improvisation. Among the artists was one of particular energy and ambition, Victor Vasarely (1908–), who had been a member of *Abstraction-Création* before the war. His fellow Hungarian, Nicolas Schöffer (1912–), came to Constructivism after 1950 and imbued it with still more dramatic and visionary qualities. Both men promoted tendencies which differed radically from pure Constructivism, although their own statements incorporate at least one essential Constructivist idea: they both anticipate an art of mass spectacle and multiple production, ever more integrated with the technological architecture that was supposed to reconstruct the inadequate social framework of our time. Vasarely coined the term "planetary folklore" to denote an aspiring global and popular technology. He himself remained mainly in the production of traditional "art works"—paintings, prints, and reliefs—although in an increasingly impersonal and mechanical mode. Starting from

old *Abstraction-Création* principles, he developed by the early 1960s a repetitive method using various modules on a grid system—inviting analogies with architecture—later using color and luminosity to create strident three-dimensional illusions. Schöffer's work is confined to three-dimensional structures and, being dependent on elaborate realization in practice, is much less familiar. Schöffer is one of the first, and certainly the most elaborate, of the postwar Kinetic artists, that is, those using actual and not merely implied movement. His works are open structures—scaffoldings—always based on right-angled members, within which greater and lesser parts move mechanically in constantly changing counterpoint. The extent and complexity is multiplied by mirror surfaces and by lights, which also move and change, so that we seem to witness a world of infinite flux and infinite possibility of development. The aim, according to Schöffer, is not to bring to birth a finite work of art but to "create creation".

The ramifications of Constructivism—like Kinetic, Optical, or Systemic art—have been far more prominent in the postwar period than its original principles, such as its transcendental claim to universal harmony and its scientific idealism. Although Constructivism stood for an alliance between art and science, the *kinetic* tendency, which accustomed artists and public to introduce and accept moving sculptures and reliefs, encouraged a kind of surreal mechanics having little to do with contemporary technology, even in a symbolic connection. The slowly moving wooden components of Pol Bury (1922–) for example, conceal their source of energy and suggest hidden animal or insect life rather than mechanical power. Jean Tinguely (1925–) has earned great attention for his large, rattling or self-destructive pseudo-machines which are only nominally Kinetic, having nothing to do with the Constructivist tradition, but a great deal to do with the Neo-Dada revival.

Artists of Constructivist and Kineticist inclination did retain from their own tradition an aptitude for group activity. The German *Gruppe Zero* founded in 1957 by Otto Piene (1928–) and Heinz Mack (1931–), with Gunther Uecker (1930–) soon turned away from any constructivist discipline. The French *Groupe de Recherche d'Art Visuel*, existing from 1960 to 1969, included in its members Vasarely's son Yvaral (1934–) and was to some extent based on Vasarely's ideas. Although apparently more properly Constructivist in the Russian tradition, it too deviated in embracing instability and showing no interest in architectural scale. Its aims, as defined in 1962, were to demystify art and make it more available, but also included a program for disrupting habitual visual responses and eliminating intrinsic stable values—one paradox among many in the artistic programs of the 1960s. Its methods rested on dividing up a visual field on a rhythmical or pulsating system, in order to manifest patterns of energy. This can be and was done on a flat surface, but is greatly enhanced if other planes are added by relief, or by using transparent materials, to enable one to be played against the other. Movement, whether by motorizing the components or by using pro-

Left, above: Baby is Three by Robyn Denny; oil on canvas; 213×366cm (84×144in); 1960. Tate Gallery, London

Left, below: Early One Morning by Anthony Caro; acrylic sculpture on metal supports; 290×620×335cm (114×244×132in); 1962. Tate Gallery, London

grammed light, emphasized the Kinetic effect in a dramatic way. Where they did not use actual movement, the *Groupe de Recherche d'Art Visuel* remained in the camp of "Op art", a journalistic term (conveniently pairable with "Pop art", its opposite pole) coined to describe the creation of energy by purely optical means.

In its purer forms, when it was not invaded by Neo-Dadaism, Constructivism and its legitimate offshoots offered a central alternative to subjectivism in the mid 20th century. Yet its scientific idealism has been undermined by the subjectivity of science itself, and by the increasing human dissatisfaction with Western technology and disillusion with the planned environment. Constructivism is well fitted to express the fundamental dialectical, existential problems of human personality and society, but these must be translated into the formal language of 20th-century abstraction. It has remained an art for artists, constantly disappointing the hopes of its founders that, through the prevalence of manufactured shapes in society, Constructivism would acquire a universally understood vocabulary. Such hopes continue to be undermined by the obsti-

Diego Seated by Giacometti; oil on canvas; 32×20cm (13×8in); 1948. Sainsbury Centre for Visual Arts, University of East Anglia, Norwich

nate desire of the majority of people to see art in their own human image.

The prevailing existential philosophy of the postwar period emphasized humanity's singular plight, our isolation from organic or inorganic nature, the fear of aimlessness in human life. Although existentialism's effect on art was ambivalent, it certainly did nothing to encourage optimistic or transcendental ideas in Abstract art. On the other hand, those few artists who, against the whole trend of gestural or post-gestural abstraction, held out for the human image, are readily seen in terms of existentialism. Alberto Giacometti (1901–66), as a friend of the existential philosopher Sartre, easily assumed the role of typical existentialist artist. Giacometti was a living link between prewar Surrealism, in which he was distinguished, and the postwar world of self-assertion against clouded vision and amorphous fears. In his paintings of people, nearly always portraits of single, immobile persons, space is shown as a tangible property, actively weighing on them, and they in turn as opposing it with unconscious, essential dignity. His sculptures take this further in their elongation and emaciation. By placing small figures on large bases, Giacometti emphasized their reduction and defined the space that imprisoned them. In groups of figures, the hostility of space was doubled by their own inability to communicate with each other. As a type, the Survivor claimed great importance in the postwar period and was of existential interest. Giacometti's persons are survivors and also, like survivors from a major disaster, are at the same time new creatures existing uncertainly in an unfamiliar world.

The figures of Francis Bacon (1909–92) are not so much survivors as victims. As a British artist Bacon sensed, and used, the metamorphism of Henry Moore (1898–1986), Graham Sutherland (1903–80), and others in the early 1940s. But his interest in extreme situations has more in common with the Surrealist group to which Giacometti also belonged, or with the imagery of the Surrealist films of Luis Buñuel. Like Giacometti's, Bacon's figures are often small in relation to the space they occupy, and are oppressed by it. But instead of confronting it with immobile dignity they are actively victimized or are diverting themselves as best they can, often sexually. They are then unconscious victims on whom the painter has projected his own fears of boredom and the void. They are also doubly imprisoned, not just by their environment but also by the flesh they inhabit, on which Bacon (possibly following Buñuel) has always insisted. The mobility of Bacon distinguishes him from Giacometti's iconic world. He is interested in the early efforts to record evolving movements, such as the photographs of Edward Muybridge, and one purpose of his deformations is to set bodies in motion, a familiar aim from the Futurists through to Picasso.

It is possible to see Neo-Dada as the dominant mode of the

Right: Lying Figure with Hypodermic Syringe by Francis Bacon; oil on canvas; 197×144cm (78×57in); 1963. University Art Museum, Berkeley

1960s in Europe, as informal abstraction had been of the 1950s. But it was not a "style", any more than original Dada had been. If there was one favored stylistic device, it was *assemblage*: a bringing together of elements of painting and sculpture with collage, relief, and found objects. Through the use of objects, *assemblage* and Neo-Dada maintained some hold on the real. Indeed realism, as proclaimed in Pierre Restany's *Nouveau Réalisme* manifesto published in 1960, was one of the main planks of the Neo-Dada platform. Restany's conception of "modern nature" as an integration of

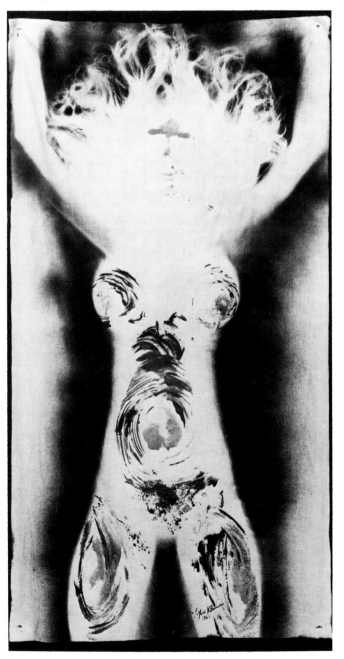

Shroud (Suaire). ANT-SU 2 by Yves Klein; mixed media and techniques; 138×75cm (54×30in); 1962. Modern Museum (National Museum), Stockholm

technology and everyday life within the medium of mass communication, was similar to the one that inspired early Pop art in Britain. But Neo-Dada, by renouncing the traditional activities of paintings and sculpture, was bound to take a different course.

The first signs of Neo-Dada overlapped with some of the latest manifestations of the old Surrealism. The American, Robert Rauschenberg (1925–), showed at the same exhibition as the veteran Surrealist Meret Oppenheim in Paris in 1959. Rauschenberg and Jasper Johns (1930–) had already introduced Neo-Dada ideas in the mid 1950s by incorporating real objects in their work. In Europe, a very conspicuous avant-gardist, Yves Klein (1928–62), acted as a catalyst of Neo-Dada. Klein's "exhibition" of a bare white gallery in 1958 followed a series of all-one-color canvases. The other manifestation which brought him notoriety was his painting (before an audience) with the human body—applying paint to nude models who then pressed themselves against his canvas. These actions make him an antecedent of the Performance art movement.

Klein attracted the enthusiastic collaboration of Jean Tinguely, a Kinetic Constructivist, who turned his machine art into a series of Neo-Dada manifestations. César (1921–) used scrap metal components to create *assemblage* sculptures in the mid 1950s, but these had an informal character and conveyed an effect of expressionist anxiety common to much sculpture of the 1950s. In 1960, adhering to Restany's new realism, he exhibited his *Compressions*, block sculptures made by reducing colorful motor bodies in powerful hydraulic presses. These marvelous works were multiple analogues of industrial society: the results of controlled violence producing stereotypes in which may be traced the attractive colors and brightwork of yesterday's status objects. Violence is never far away in Neo-Dada. Another new realist, Arman (1928–), made *assemblages* which were not so much assembled as dismembered objects, such as sliced-up musical instruments, and others which he called *Colères*. Both César and the much older Italian artist of different background, Lucio Fontana (1899–1968), used slicing and stabbing (of metal or canvas) as a demonstrative technique which both records the action and changes the material as the stroke of a brush could never do.

One senior and important French painter had anticipated aspects of Neo-Dada while informal abstraction was still in the ascendant—even before it had fairly begun. Jean Dubuffet (1901–85) held the first exhibition of his characteristic paintings in Paris in 1945—thickly painted pictures in a deliberately clumsy technique which was the very opposite of the "fine painting" to which even modernists in Paris subscribed. Equally shocking were his subjects, ordinary ones like people in a car, represented apparently without art as a child or someone who "can't draw" might represent them. This was a new primitivism as shocking as the cult of African art had been at the beginning of the century, perhaps more so because it uncovered primitive sources right there within society. Primitivism of a certain kind is the most consistent principle in

Dubuffet's subsequent very diverse work and constitutes his personal variety of realism. The provocatively named *Corps de Dames* ("bodies of ladies") showed the female body plastered shapelessly as if on a wall, seeming to invite comparison with the most moronic sexist graffiti. In other works, such as the *Texturologies*, Dubuffet displays a kind of *nostalgie de la boue* by reveling in mud colors and gritty textures. That he made works of ravishing beauty on these principles reveals Dubuffet as an immensely sophisticated operator in the best French tradition of modernism, and has tended to reduce his credibility today when the cumulative American example has

undermined the concept of sophisticated taste in European art. Dubuffet was perhaps already responsive to this current when in 1964 he gave up his diverse experiments in favor of a unified, more insistently visible style with heavy black lines enclosing white spaces or primary colors. Dubuffet's own work has been underpinned throughout by his advocacy of the primitive art of his time, namely the products of people without art conditioning or, sometimes, education, and of psychotics. Dubuffet coined the term *Art Brut* ("raw art") to describe this category and has founded a private museum devoted to it.

The Yellow Buick by César; crushed automobile; 149×79×62cm (59×31×24in); 1961. Museum of Modern Art, New York

Dustbin no. 1 by Arman; 66×40×10cm (26×16×4in). Kaiser Wilhelm Museum, Krefeld

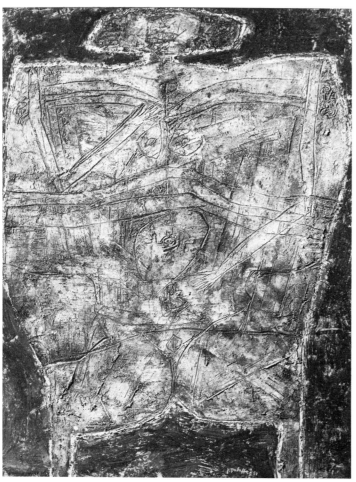

Blood and Fire, one of the series Corps de Dames by Jean Dubuffet;
oil on canvas; 117×89cm (46×35in); 1950.
Pierre Matisse Gallery, New York

The parallel with *Art Brut* must have been obvious to the critic Reyner Banham when he applied the term "brutalism" to tendencies in Britain in 1955, in architecture and, in a small way, sculpture and painting. The anodyne background of European informal abstraction and English lyricism was then provoking thoughts of a return to realism. The thickly impasted paint of Frank Auerbach (1931–) or Leon Kossoff (1926–) gave their images a grave clumsiness that was anti-art in that context. A more radical reconsideration of contemporary reality, more like that of the French new realism, was emerging in the work of Eduardo Paolozzi (1924–) and Richard Hamilton (1922–) who proposed close study of the visual material of contemporary machine and media culture. Paolozzi's bronzecast sculptures made little use of this material up to 1962, except that, like César's, they incorporated small scrap components. They combine the "survivor" imagery of the postwar period with a ponderous roughness recalling Dubuffet. From 1962 Paolozzi found ways of incorporating into his work elements of the huge collection of source material he was amassing to illustrate the Americanized popular culture and simple technology of the 1940s and 1950s. At the same time his own procedures became technically more sophisticated with use of large aluminum castings. Richard Hamilton, not a sculptor, had nothing in common with brutalism, but is a spare and fastidious artist in the manner of Duchamp, whose interpreter he became. His sources lay in the up-to-date world of packaging and advertising. His critique of consumerism was carried out in an oblique manner employing collage and a delicate, English-style line-and-wash way of representing his selected emotive images. Using a spatial ambiguity derived from Surrealism, his early works explore the sexual and social ambivalence of consumerism from the standpoint of an ironic man of the left.

In employing visual traces of contemporary life, Hamilton and Paolozzi were renewing the practice of early modern art and their importance in the 1950s was to provide a link between the established tendencies—Surrealism, abstraction and metamorphism—and nascent Pop art. Pop art as usually defined had to wait for the media-orientated, hedonistic and youthful climate of culture in Britain—in a word, the Pop culture of the 1960s—to become fully established. At the same time, it played a part in preparing its own ground. Pop art is at least as important as a liberating force as for its original products. David Hockney (1937–) seemed iconoclastic in his work in 1961 and 1962 because of its large size, its primitivist drawing recalling Dubuffet, its frank treatment of homosexual themes. *The First Marriage* (1962; Tate Gallery, London) shows Hockney indulging his own highly selective interest in particular images, appealing to the freedom already granted to painters by abstraction in order to treat the rest of the canvas as undefined space. Hockney's trajectory through the world of high camp fashion and popular acclaim in the 1960s was reflected in his painting, which became a perfect visual expression for a subculture with an overwhelming but implicit sense of style. The cool surfaces, parallel planes, and impersonally schematic details provide a faithful reflection of the guarded relationships where reaction and alienation seem to tremble beneath the surface. It has been said that in Pop art style is itself the subject. In later Hockney, style is subsumed in a knowing rejection of styles, leaving only traces of his comprehensive knowledge of modernism, from Bonnard to Post-Painterly abstraction.

The Neo-Dada tendency in the 1960s was most effective in throwing art open—some would say far too open—and in creating the belief that in art "anything goes". Although consistently ignored in Britain and America, Neo-Dada was pervasive, and really subsumes the Pop movement. The freedom of art to use *any* material, any object, any theme, in any combination, was only kept in check by the limits of the imagination which proved all too finite. The succeeding stages, Conceptualism and Process art, which dominated the 1970s, both exploited this freedom and reacted against it; in either case they were born of Neo-Dada, and could not have originated from Pop art alone.

Right: $he by Richard Hamilton; oil and other media on board;
122×81cm (48×32in); 1958–61. Tate Gallery, London

The First Marriage by David Hockney

The Pop art phenomenon in Britain in the late 1950s and early 1960s can be summarized simply as a new approach to figuration, when much progressive art was Abstract. Most Pop artists drew on new sources for the imagery in their work, but what characterized David Hockney (1937–) and set him apart from mainstream Pop was his preference for traditional subjects.

In the year he painted *The First Marriage*, 1962, he wrote in the catalog to the group exhibition at the Grabowski Gallery, London "Image in Progress":

> I paint what I like, when I like and where I like with occasional nostalgic journeys. When asked to write on "the strange possibilities of inspiration" it did occur to me that my own sources of inspiration were wide—but acceptable. In fact, I am sure my own sources are classic, or even epic themes. Landscapes of foreign lands, beautiful people, love, propaganda, and major incidents (of my own life). These seem to me to be reasonably traditional.

Two years later in another catalog statement ("The New Generation: 1964") Hockney wrote about two distinct groups of his paintings: those that start from or are about "technical devices" and those that are "dramas, usually with two figures".

The First Marriage incorporates a number of Hockney's themes and at the same time epitomizes his working process at the time. Like so many of his paintings *The First Marriage* was inspired by a personal experience. While staying in Berlin in August 1962, Hockney and his friend Jeff Goodman visited the Pergamon Museum in East Berlin. They became separated and when Hockney next saw his friend he was standing next to an Egyptian sculpture of a seated woman. From Hockney's viewpoint they were both seen in profile, apparently looking at the same thing which was hidden from Hockney's view. "From a distance they looked like a couple, posing as it were, for a wedding photograph", he wrote in a letter to the Tate Gallery. He was simply amused at first, but later in his West Berlin hotel he made two or three drawings of the scene from memory and started the painting on his return to London in September.

The painting has an alternative title, *A Marriage of Styles*, because of the heavily stylized figure juxtaposed with a real human being, although both figures are stylized in the painting itself, the Egyptian sculpture more obviously so. Hockney described how he enjoyed elaborating the scene in the

◀ *The Marriage* by David Hockney; an etching; 31×40cm (12×16in); 1962. Victoria and Albert Museum, London

▼ *The Second Marriage* by David Hockney; oil on canvas; 198×229cm (78×90in); 1963. National Gallery of Victoria, Melbourne

painting:

> the husband stands politely, and the sculpture is made to look like his wife who is a bit tired and therefore sitting down ... I loved the idea of playing with the word "marriage". The setting is vague but the Gothic window in the bottom left-hand corner was, I remember, added for its ecclesiastical connections with marriage.

Elsewhere he suggested that the ambiguous setting looked like a desert island with a palm tree and white sand. However, the sand was only put there to give the figures something to stand on, and the rest of the setting left "slightly out of focus". An etching *The Marriage* (1962) is a simplified version of *The First Marriage* but with the image reversed.

Hockney did not pay much attention to the Egyptian sculpture at the time. He has described it as made of wood. But not only are seated figures in wood, especially ones of this size, exceedingly rare in Egyptian sculpture, single seated women in any media are probably even rarer. If one existed in the Berlin museum it would be very famous. So what *did* Hockney glimpse momentarily?

If we look for a similar seated woman and recall that he saw her in profile we must conclude that it was almost certainly part of a group. One prominent group in the Ägyptisches Museum in East Berlin fits the bill. It depicts Ptahmay flanked by two women seated on a flat bench with two tiny children standing between them. From a distance Hockney would have seen only the nearest figure of the woman in profile, noting her

▼ *The First Marriage* by David Hockney; oil on canvas; 183×215cm (72×85in); 1962. Tate Gallery, London

long wig and flower-petal fillet (headband), rounded breasts beneath her gown, and her left hand on her knee.

Hockney never paints from nature, and only occasionally from memory. Generally he does a great deal of drawing before he starts a painting and then develops the ideas but without much reference to the drawings. In the early 1960s he displayed a magpie-like tendency to pick up images from surprising and paradoxical sources and build them into the paintings. The stylization of objects—whether drawn from memory or nature or copied from illustrations—was partly a conscious naivety and partly a search for the cliché or recognizable image. For example, in *Rocky Mountains and Tired Indians* (1965; Scottish National Gallery of Modern art, Edinburgh)—also a "drama" with two

figures, the woman seated—the mountains are painted as if in a geological diagram of rock strata, the Indians themselves from magazine illustrations, and an eagle from a photograph of a wooden totem pole, yet all are painted illusionistically.

Hockney regularly makes series of paintings on the same themes, and even occasionally refers back to earlier paintings. *The First Marriage* was originally called *The Marriage*. He changed the title when he painted *The Second Marriage* based on the same idea in 1963. *The Second Marriage* (National Gallery of Victoria, Melbourne) is more complex, illusionistically painted on a shaped canvas to exaggerate perspective effects, whereas the earlier painting was flat and hierarchical, like Egyptian painting.

CHRISTOPHER JOHNSTONE

Peter Getting out of Nick's Pool by David Hockney; acrylic on canvas; 214×214cm (84×84in); 1966. Walker Art Gallery, Liverpool

An immense change occurred in the community of modern art *c*1965. Its origins are very complex, lying both within the history of modern art (the influence of Marcel Duchamp was crucial) and in the social and political currents of the 1950s and 1960s. Unlike Pop, Conceptualism was common to Western Europe as well as to America, evidence that a more far-reaching critique of Western culture was involved. One of the earliest Conceptual art "acts", John Latham's literal distillation of a copy of Clement Greenberg's *Art and Culture* in

1966, indicates the direction of the Conceptualists' criticism. It is also an analog of an overriding tendency towards "the dematerialization of the art object" as Lucy Lippard has called it. It was a perfect Neo-Dada act (the book was ritually chewed by a group of like-thinking people) but the subsequent exhibition, of documents, bottles of chemicals, etc, the whole constituting a "work", was typical of the more labored concern of Conceptualism with presenting the evidence of the artist's procedures.

The beginning of Conceptualism took place in the mid 1960s, but there had been earlier pointers. Yves Klein "exhibited" an empty gallery in Paris in 1958, and had himself photographed jumping from a window in 1960. Piero Manzoni (1933–63) had produced a signed edition of a line of measured length rolled in a small drum, in 1959. These "conceptual" acts were done in the context of Neo-Dada as already described, and do not pretend to the elaborate theoretical or practical development of later Conceptual art. But the fame enjoyed since 1958 by Christo (Christo Javacheff, 1935–) rests on exteriorizing on a vast scale a small private concept: the way a wrapped object acquires a sense of mystery and disquieting ambiguity. Christo has put the concept to the test in projects to wrap public buildings and even stretches of coastline. The plans, drawings, preparations, and, when actually done, the doing of these things constitute their real interest and are minutely recorded.

An artist who came to embody the spirit of advanced art in the early 1970s, Joseph Beuys (1921–86), took his departure from the Neo-Dada technique of *assemblage* and the transformation of found objects. From 1966 he developed the performance, with himself as sole actor, as his principle medium. It is impossible to sum up the long performances of Beuys, which employed a mixture of body symbolism and fetishistic props significant to his beliefs. In the 1970s Beuys more and more transferred his performances to the plane of verbal discourse, and his main effort to promoting a form of millenarian politics of self-regulation. Beuys' success exemplifies the search within the modern art public—mainly young and disillusioned by the 1960s—for spiritual enlightenment or, more truly, any form of mystical or personal magnetism. Many characteristic elements of the Conceptual art era can be seen together in Beuys. His adoption of himself, his appearance, and clothes as both principal means and subject, is the natural conclusion of the tendency for medium, "style", and subject matter to come together and be identical. This aspect of Beuys shows the first of three main strands in Conceptualism—of the artist in his person, of the image, and of the word.

When the artist in person is the agent of Conceptualism, it may result in "body art" in which the artist submits himself to various ordeals either in public view, or recorded photographically. Stuart Brisley (1931–) has taken the personal ordeal (immersion in water) to an extreme point, but not with the sadism shown by members of the "Direct Art Institute" founded in Vienna in 1966. Or it may result in the simple assertion of artisthood—as in the case of Keith Arnatt (1930–) who exhibited his wall inscription *Keith Arnatt is an Artist* in 1972. Such acts had a place in Dada and Neo-Dada, but were now accompanied by elaborate linguistic explanations. The "living sculptures", Gilbert and George, are the most noted examples by far of "the artist as concept". By adopting a pose with nostalgic music-hall overtones, and ironically rejecting involvement in art discourse, they have baffled criticism but have nevertheless been accepted into current orthodoxy. Their work includes actual performances or appearances, and

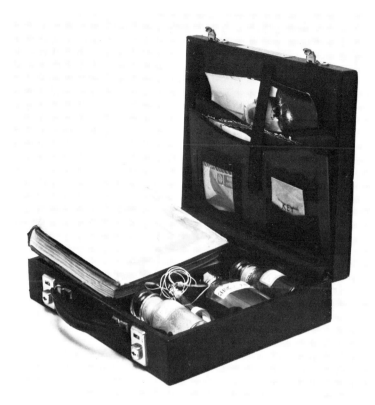

Art and Culture by John Latham; assemblage of book, labeled vials filled with powders and liquids, letters, and photostats in a leather case; 8×28×25cm (3×11×10in); 1966–9. Museum of Modern Art, New York

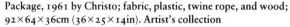

Package, 1961 by Christo; fabric, plastic, twine rope, and wood; 92×64×36cm (36×25×14in). Artist's collection

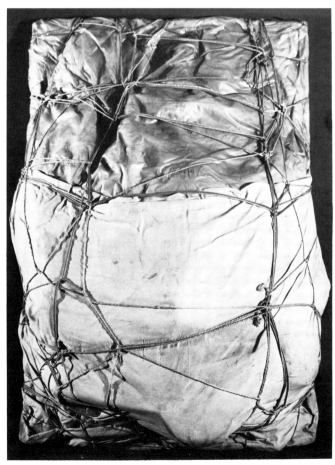

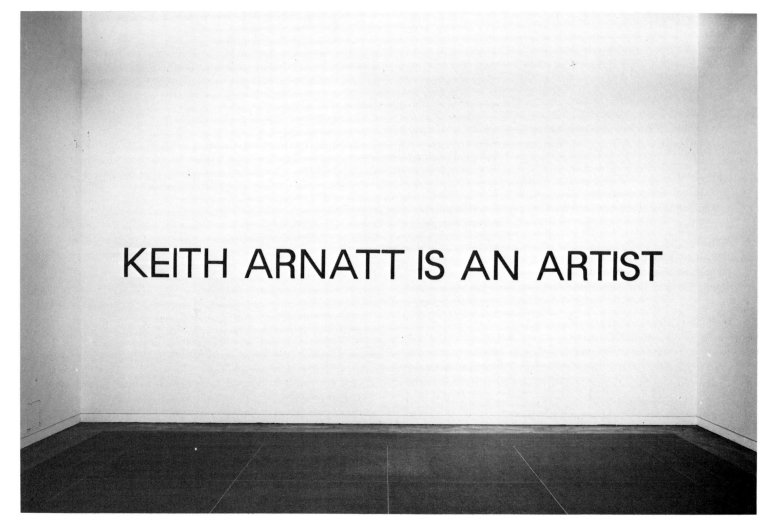

photographic and video record. The careful control and management of the artist's projected personality is also seen in artists who do not directly appear in their work. Richard Long, for example, does not permit any personal data or discussion of his work to appear at his exhibitions, and does not give interviews. Other artists exercise detailed supervision, if they can, over what is written about them.

The work of Richard Long (1945–) shares in the Conceptualism of artist and of image, in so far as the word Conceptualism fits him at all. Long does not appear in his work, but his inferred passage through a landscape creates it. He is a traveler on foot to remote and beautiful places, where he makes some small intervention or trace in the landscape which is recorded photographically. Sometimes this image—usually beautiful—is withheld and the record of his passage, on a map, is presented instead. Back in the urban and fashionable galleries, he brings stones or sticks with which he makes shapes of symbolic resonance, echoing primeval signs and traces he may have seen on his travels. The difference between Long and the romantic English landscapists of the past is not deep, and is contained in his contemporary belief in semiotics—a belief in a valid system of sign language replacing representation. There is also a strong element of Duchampian arrogation in Long as in others of his generation, as he reserves the right to elect objects to art status—for example, a photograph framed and inscribed, as opposed to the same photograph in a book, is more than merely an original photographic print as opposed to a reproduction.

Works of imagist Conceptual art have been the most numerous, but seldom in so pure a form as Long's photographs. Much of it has dealt in images repeated in series with small variations. The concepts behind it have often involved a program of periodic observations or interventions. John Hilliard (1945–) in Britain and Jan Dibbets (1941–) in Holland attempt to chart a progressive distortion in perception by focusing on the means of perception in series of parallel photographs. Along with imagist Conceptual artists must be considered a few who use abstract configurations for Conceptual purposes. Daniel Buren (1938–) and three other French artists founded a group in 1966, each of whom adopted a minimal Abstract form for their work henceforward—in Buren's case vertical stripes of a set width. A "piece" of Buren hung in a gallery would therefore appear to be like a Minimalist painting. But Buren, who became a politicized person in the wake of the Parisian events of 1968, has refused to let this happen, but has consistently tried to install his stripes in contexts where they could function as irritant and as critique of the art system. This has led Buren into several confrontations, as when his immense striped banner was removed from the

well of the Guggenheim Museum in New York in 1971 at the insistence of other participating artists.

Although Buren is cited here, he has been a savage critic of "Conceptual" art. His own form of art is wholly visual; he expresses himself with Gallic clarity and is specially intolerant of those Conceptual artists who take words as their medium. The Art and Language group, who have comprised ten or more members in the period since 1966, are the most rigorous in this respect. Their work has no visual "product". Their subject is the meaning of art and it could be claimed that they are the most authentic of Conceptual artists because they deal with the fundamental concept of art itself. Their discourse is so dense and so hampered by the necessity to qualify words, especially "ordinary" words, as to be partly unintelligible even to specialists. This is no by-product of their aims, however, but central to them as it assists the disorientation they seek, and the subversion of the whole critical and historical apparatus that sustains art in its present state. The obscurity of art language may be accounted for by the explanation recently offered by Marcuse for the obscurity of Adorno: that ordinary use of language is so impregnated by the concepts of the ruling order that it has to be subverted. It is no surprise that at least one member of Art and Language has recently adopted a much more direct political form of expression.

The interaction of political and social dissidence with art since 1965 has been complex and pervasive. The ability of Conceptualism to present raw data in an acceptable "artistic" form made it the perfect vehicle for a political art. Hans Haacke (1936–) has made the attack on art institutions from within, always implicit in modern art, quite explicit with his published statements about, for example, the detailed financial backing of the Guggenheim Museum in New York. For him, museums are political institutions irrespective of the stance they take. Other artists have used the museum as a theater for manifesting contradictions and abuses in the society outside its walls, as in Victor Burgin's (1941–) commentary in 11 photographic panels, *Britain 1976*, where social-realist photographs are overprinted with "up-market" advertising copy. Notably, Burgin has moved to this simple and direct form of expression from an earlier involvement with linguistic and perception theories which led him to question the necessity of any form of art object.

To "question" the meaning of art: this has been, together with the preoccupation with "process", a constant activity of artists since 1965. They have followed out these preoccupations in many more ways than can be described here. One form of reaction from conventional painting and sculpture took art into the realm of performance, where "process" and result are one and the same. The Neo-Dada revival and the increasing politicization of art both tended to encourage performance, which seemed to promise more direct contact with, and participation by, a nonspecialist public. But although it attracted more artists in the late 1970s than before, Performance art has occupied until now a very marginal position, despite the crucial importance for the future of opening new

Left, above: *Keith Arnatt is an Artist*, a wall inscription by Keith Arnatt exhibited in 1972 in the Tate Gallery, London

Left, below: *119 Stones* by Richard Long; approx. 15×700×587cm (6×276×231in); 1976. Tate Gallery, London

channels to a democratic audience. As a "questioning" form of activity, Performance art shared in producing increasing public mystification and disorientation from the 1960s onwards. Why have so many socially conscious artists accepted and shared in this obscuration, while sometimes claiming to oppose it? One answer may be that they are not interested in making art easy for its traditional, bourgeois audience, and that for them the possibility of direct interaction with a mass public has not yet dawned.

Performance art may be regarded as Conceptualism enacted physically. Minimalism, the production of ultra-simple, often massive regular structures and paintings, may be considered an objectified form of Conceptualism. It represented the ultimate renunciation of aesthetic, relational qualities, and was executed from a preordained conceptual plan with no room for intuitive variations. By remaining so emphatically within the parameters of paint and canvas, or of fabricated objects, while many artists were giving them up, Minimal artists turned this deeply skeptical, questioning activity against their predecessors, the critics, and themselves. As compared with the sprawling, anarchic nature of the Performance art movement, Minimalism inspired a disciplined group of mainly American artists, who imposed their severe orthodoxy on the art establishment for a decade after 1965. Yet almost at the same time, a dialectic opposite emerged in early examples of Superrealist (Hyperrealist or Photorealist) art. Like Minimalism, Superrealism is seen in its most radical development only in America. Its exponents all employ exact imitation of external appearance, but there are many variants according to the type of subject and the degree of implied comment or interpretation the artist permits him/herself to apply to it.

On a superficial view, Superrealism might seem to imply an end to the "questioning" and a revived belief in the end-product rather than the process. It has been widely received, and perhaps practiced, in that light. Further reflection shows that Superrealism offers no answers to the important questions about art, any more than photography does; moreover, interest in how it is done—process again—outweighs interest in what is done. Only here and there does Superrealism seem to inherit the role of 19th-century realism in focusing concern about the human condition.

The late 1970s was, reputedly, a period of uncertainty and retrenchment in art. As a reflector of social and political attitudes, art could not fail to show such a result. If Conceptualism lost ground, it was not lost to any one succeeding orthodoxy. New forms of figuration began to dispute with a revived formalism for the right to express the democratic humanism that is widely acknowledged to be the matter and *raison d'être* of art.

DOUGLAS HALL

One of the most dynamic of the new forms of figuration was Neo-Expressionism, which emerged in Germany and Italy in the mid 1970s. Rejecting both Abstraction and Conceptualism, artists such as Georg Baselitz (1938–) and Anselm Kiefer (1945–) in Germany, and Francesco Clemente (1952–) and Sandro Chia (1946–) in Italy, began to explore the potential of gestural brushwork, bold colors and distorted forms. But they also shared a postmodernist self-consciousness in the use of symbols and in allusions to traditional art and Pop culture, and to history and myth. This allowed German artists—Kiefer in particular—to create works that dealt directly with the traumas of Germany's recent history: Neo-Expressionism brought back to art a political, social and historical dimension.

This was also true of the postmodernist "appropriation" of academic Neo-classicism. The Russians Vitaly Komar (1943–) and Alexander Melamid (1945–), who work together, combined Pop and Neo-classicism to satirize Soviet politics, while the Italian Carlo Maria Mariani (1931–) used Neo-classicism to question the nature of art.

In Britain, as elsewhere, pluralism flourished throughout the 1970s and 1980s. In sculpture, for example, while Caro and Long were still pursuing their own distinctive idioms, Anish Kapoor (1954–) was creating abstracts partly indebted to Indian art; Tony Cragg (1949–) was piecing together sculptures from bits of discarded industrial materials; and Anthony Gormley (1950–) was making casts of his own body. The figurative tradition in painting, which Freud, Auerbach, Hockney, Kitaj and others had kept alive, was given new expression in Scotland. John Bellany (1942–), for example, developed an Expressionist style influenced by German artists such as Max Beckmann. Steven Campbell (1953–) and Adrian Wiszniewski (1958–), on the other hand, explored figurative styles that, with an emphasis on Surrealistic narrative, marked a return to the Romanticism that is an enduring feature of British art.

During the 1970s and 1980s, as the influence of New York declined, European artists became more confident, particularly in exploring their own national and regional cultural traditions. Nevertheless, for some observers the pluralist arts of the period were a sign of a *fin de siècle* decadence, of a moral and creative bankruptcy. For others, they were not merely a spirited defense of democratic humanism, but were the expression of a bold search for new values in a period of crisis and change.

CHRIS MURRAY

Bibliography. Burnham, J. *The Structure of Art*, London and New York (1971). Compton, M. *Art Since 1945*, Milton Keynes (1976). Godfrey, T. *The New Image: Painting in the 1980s*, London (1987). Goldberg, R. *Performance*, London (1979). Haftmann, W. *Painting in the 20th Century* (2 vols.), London (1965). Henri, A. *Environments and Happenings*, London (1974). Hill, A. (ed.) *Data: Directions in Art, Theory, and Aesthetics*, London (1968). Lippard, L. (ed.) *Six Years: the Dematerialization of the Object*, London (1973). Lucie-Smith, E. *Art Today*, Oxford (1977). Lynton, N. *The Story of Modern Art*, Oxford (1980). Nairne, S. *State of the Art: Ideas and Images in the 1980s*, London (1986). Popper, F. *Art, Action, and Participation*, London (1975). Richardson, T. and Stangos, N. (eds.) *Concepts of Modern Art*, Harmondsworth (1974).

53

AUSTRALIAN ART

The Selector's Hut: Whelan on the Log by Arthur Streeton; oil on canvas; 77×51cm (30×20in)
1890. Australian National Gallery, Canberra (see page 965)

WHEN the first British colony in Australia was established on Sydney Cove in 1788 the continent was still called New Holland. The elegant neoclassical name Australia—a Latin form for what had long been vaguely referred to as the South Land—did not gain currency until the early 19th century, though one of the earliest high-style European objects which can be claimed for Australian art is a small medallion commissioned in 1789 from the Wedgwood pottery factory, bearing a graceful neoclassical allegory of the new colony. The medallion's title was *Hope encouraging Art and Labour under the influence of Peace, to pursue the employments necessary to give security and happiness to an infant settlement.* It was made of clay shipped from Sydney to Etruria in Staffordshire, and was commissioned by an influential and energetic scientific amateur, Sir Joseph Banks.

Sir Joseph Banks's particular interest was botany. He had imposed himself and a party of naturalists on to a scientific voyage in the South Pacific under the command of Captain James Cook, and in 1770 during that voyage a landing was made at what they enthusiastically named Botany Bay (opposite present-day Sydney Airport). Natural-history artists were among Banks's chief protégés, and natural-history drawings are the most characteristic art form in the earliest years of the colony. The finest are the 2,000 botanical studies made by Ferdinand Bauer (1760–1826), who spent 1801–5 in Australia with Matthew Flinders' expedition. William Westall (1781–1850), of the same expedition, was also the first to paint artistically significant Australian landscapes. Because of the extreme peculiarity of Australia's native flora and fauna, natural history has remained a continuing theme in Australian art.

More interesting has been the outbreak of Australian flora and fauna in decorative arts, design, graphic arts, and popular arts as patriotic emblems at moments of heightened national consciousness. The 1850s goldrush influx coincided with the intricacies of Rococo-revival design, Gothic-revival architecture, and Pre-Raphaelite minuteness in painting; the delicate intricacy of tree-ferns, grass-trees, cabbage-palms, and lyrebirds became preferred decorative-arts emblems. The boom period of the 1880s and the centenary celebrations in 1888 coincided with William Morris's aestheticism, and so the larger-scaled, compact waratah blossomed in architectural stone-carving and stained-glass windows. The federation of the six colonies in 1901 coincided with the mannered linearity of Art Nouveau, which gave the elongated eucalyptus leaf and cascading yellow wattle-blossom their opportunity. The 1970 Bicentenary celebrations for Captain Cook, and preparations

Raby, a Farm Belonging to Alexander Riley, Esq. by Joseph Lycett; watercolor; 21×28cm (8×11in); c1820. Australian National Gallery, Canberra

for the 1988 Bicentennial of first settlement, have drawn upon Pop art and a heightened appreciation of kitsch to reintroduce most previous emblems plus the Koala bear and such man-made artifacts as the Sydney Harbor Bridge and the Sydney Opera House for use in jewelry and clothing. The best animal (and figure) painter of the 19th century was William Strutt (1825–1915), who spent 11 years in Australia and New Zealand from 1850 but his magnum opus, executed in 1864, is history painting—a vast canvas of terrified Australian and European animals and humans fleeing the midsummer bushfires of "Black Thursday, February 6th, 1851."

Botany was often central to landscape painting. William Westall's canvases, worked up in England from his field sketches, set a pattern for a theatrical foreground parade of clearly identifiable curious plants for which the landscape is little more than a perfunctory background. The botanical-parade formula is still found in major landscape paintings by John Glover (1767–1849) and Conrad Martens (1801–78), who settled in Australia in 1831 and 1835 respectively, and by Eugene von Guérard (1811–1901) who arrived in 1852. John Glover, the first artist of consequence to settle permanently, placed the predominant eucalyptus tree at center stage, accurately observed and also identified as a prime emblem of a foreign land. Earlier landscapes than Glover's, for example

the watercolors of Joseph Lycett (c1774–post 1824), painted c1820, had already begun to place illustration of colonial life in the foreground but this human-interest tradition nevertheless continued to provide specifically rendered botanical backgrounds. Augustus Earle (1793–1838), who spent three years in Australia and New Zealand in the mid 1820s, painted a few landscape canvases of this kind, though he was primarily a portraitist. S.T. Gill (1818–80), chiefly an illustrator in watercolor and lithography of the life of squatters and gold-diggers, was also fascinated by the inland deserts and demonstrated a special sensitivity to their delicate vegetation.

If the first European visitors were most interested in botany they were also interested in the native Aborigines. One of the earliest and most tender images is a book-illustration of 1793, *A family of New South Wales*, engraved in London by William Blake from a colonial officer's amateur drawing. Blake presented the naked family as innocent, graceful inhabitants of a natural paradise. By the 1820s the characteristic locally produced images also included detribalized degradation. And by the 1830s in Tasmania, when it was believed that that colony's distinct race was possibly on the point of extinction, there was a sudden rush of ethnographic documentation mingled with sentimental regret. John Glover, whose own farm in northern Tasmania had recently ceased to be an

Ferntree Gully in the Dandenong Ranges by Eugene von Guérard; oil on canvas; 92×138cm (36×54in); 1857. Australian National Gallery, Canberra

The Golden Fleece: Shearing at Newstead by Tom Roberts; oil on canvas; 104×159cm (41×63in); 1894. Art Gallery of New South Wales, Sydney

Aboriginal hunting ground, painted several reminiscences of those who had "led a gay happy life ... before being disturbed by the white people."

Less sensitive to the Tasmanian Aborigines is Benjamin Duterrau's (1767–1851) large composition of 1840, *The Conciliation* (Tasmanian Museum and Art Gallery, Hobart), the first grand-manner history painting in Australian art. Although Duterrau's admiration is directed chiefly towards the white conciliator, George Augustus Robinson, who had gone among the remnants of the "savages" and persuaded them to accept resettlement, the Aborigines are given dignity, humanity, and individuality. The painting speaks very strongly to late-20th-century Australians about the largely dispossessed Aborigines. The finest 19th-century Australian artist, the romantic landscape painter Eugene von Guérard, in the 1850s executed a number of tranquil arcadian scenes inhabited by Aborigines. In other landscapes without figures, Australian native animals, kangaroos grazing within the chance shelter of a natural stone circle, are threatened by a European fox. Thus the cloistered sanctuary of *Ferntree Gully in the Dandenong Ranges* (1857; Australian National Gallery, Canberra) may not be a permanent sanctuary for the two beautiful lyrebirds it shelters. The romantic qualities of exotic botany and zoology are presented with patently honest accuracy of detail, but a narrative of past and future, decay and regeneration is also implied by juxtapositions of erect live and fallen dead veg-

etation, forest giants and minute herbage, cool shadow and hot sunshine. The cycle of nature is symbolized by such details and is reinforced by the strong surging circular movement of the composition. The painting was perceived as a masterpiece when first exhibited in Melbourne in 1857 and became the focus of an unsuccessful campaign to make it the beginning of a National Gallery for the colony of Victoria.

Melbourne was then the largest and wealthiest Australian city and for the rest of the century the most significant art was to be found there. Louis Buvelot (1814–88), a Swiss painter who settled in Melbourne in 1865, quickly found favor for his assertively commonplace landscapes of outer-suburban countryside and riverbanks frequented by big-city excursionists. Buvelot suppressed the natural variety of vegetation and focused almost exclusively on old, twisted eucalyptus trees. They are ubiquitous throughout Australia and thus to feature them so obsessively was to give Australians the pleasure of recognizing that affectionately familiar everyday objects could be elevated into art.

In 1885 the painter Tom Roberts (1856–1931) returned to Melbourne from studying in London. A group which formed around him produced for the first time a genuinely collective movement in Australian art; naturalistic landscape painting *en plein air* became an article of faith, and their outdoor painting camps were later remembered with the romantic haze attached to having been young artists in a city where aesthetic decoration and young artists were in fashion. In 1889 Tom Roberts, Arthur Streeton (1867–1943), Charles Conder (1868–1909), Frederick McCubbin (1855–1917), and others held a provocatively aesthetic exhibition of unusually small, sketchy landscape "Impressions". Whistler's English Impressionism, not the French, was the principal influence.

McCubbin's painting *The Lost Child* (1886; National Gallery of Victoria, Melbourne) is filled with loving observation of the rich diversity of subtle color and texture, and appreciation of the peculiar delicacy and fineness of forms to be found in native Australian vegetation. A year later Tom Roberts was perhaps the first to paint naturalistic naked Europeans, as bathers, amongst Australian trees. In the 1890s bushrangers (bandits) from the recent past would appear in landscape paintings by Tom Roberts as a realistic kind of nature spirit; at the same moment Classical Greek figures appeared in Symbolist paintings titled *The Spirit of the Plains* (by Sydney Long, 1871–1955) or *The Hot Wind* (by Charles Conder) which depicted a drought spirit. In the 1940s Nolan's Ned Kelly paintings and in the 1950s Tucker's explorers revived the same impulse towards providing mythology figures for the Australian landscape.

If Symbolist ideas sometimes account for the figures in landscape paintings, the land itself began to be charged with a new symbolism of heat, drought, and implacable sunlight. In 1888, after several decades of good seasons, long droughts became a new fact in Australian life. Streeton's painting *The Selector's Hut: Whelan on the Log* (1890; Australian National Gallery, Canberra) is realist in its sympathy for an Australian worker, aesthetic in its Japanese-style placement of a single slender eucalypt off-center above a low horizon, but more significantly, in its assertively yellow landscape and blue sky it helped launch a standard symbolic color for Australian landscape painting. Symbolist yellow grasslands displaced the Dutch green woodlands of Glover and Buvelot and would in turn be displaced in the 1940s by Surrealist red deserts.

Tom Roberts, the most accomplished figure painter of the movement, was the most successful of the many who began, around the centennial year of 1888, to elevate depiction of national life from illustration to heroic museum-scale painting. *The Golden Fleece: Shearing at Newstead* (1894; Art Gallery of New South Wales, Sydney) clearly indicates by its Greek-myth title that Australia's economic basis, the wool industry, is being ennobled. The subject, shearing, was the climactic moment in the creation of Australia's wealth. And the composition, academically compiled from many studies, sets the firmly structured figure-group in a woolshed whose rude architecture evokes the nave of a church, thus converting the activity of shearing into a kind of sacrament.

In Sydney W.C. Piguenit (1836–1914) evolved a late Romanticism. Deriving largely from Turner's art and his own upbringing in the dampness of southern Tasmania, Piguenit's art from the 1870s maintained an obsessive preference for low clouds, water and mud as fit subjects for the liquid medium of paint. Disastrous floods on the plains of New South Wales in the 1890s became the subject of Piguenit's finest paintings.

Many artists chose not to produce the "Australian" art which, from the 1880s onwards, was always in demand by Australian society. Instead they preferred to express their own individuality by becoming, for varying periods, expatriates in Paris or London where they joined the fringes of the artistic mainstream. In general they were finer practitioners of their craft than those who remained in Australia, but their art requires less explanation than that of the stay-at-homes. Among the expatriates the sculptor Bertram Mackennal (1863–1931) made a distinguished contribution to the late-19th-century revival of Mannerist marble and bronze. George W. Lambert (1873–1930), who departed in 1901 for 20 years in London, painted neo-Baroque portraits and groups in emulation of Brangwyn and Velazquez. John Russell (1859–1930) in Paris in the 1880s gained a true understanding of French Impressionism, and left many attractive landscapes of Italy, the Côte d'Azur, and Belle-Île. E. Phillips Fox (1865–1915), during his second period in Europe from 1902, became an Impressionist painter of sunlit gardens and beautiful women relaxing. The work of Rupert Bunny (1864–1947) in France passed through three phases: Symbolist figure and landscape compositions in the 1890s; luxurious *douceur de la vie* compositions in the 1900s; and, after the First World War, high-color decorative figure compositions and landscapes influenced by the Russian Ballet and by Bonnard respectively. The few years Hugh Ramsay (1877–1906) spent in Paris before his early death in Melbourne saw some splendid portraits, dispassionate yet psychologically penetrating. Ramsay and Max Meldrum (1875–1955), who spent the first dozen years of the new century in France, were two of many who followed Whistler's cult of Velazquez in their figure painting.

It is difficult to assess the conservative Australian painters in

The Lacquer Room by Grace Cossington Smith; oil on paperboard; 74×91cm (29×36in); c1935–6. Art Gallery of New South Wales, Sydney

The Aeroplane by Margaret Preston; colored woodcut on silver paper; 25×19cm (10×7in); c1932. Australian National Gallery, Canberra

relation to those from other countries during this internationalist, old-master oriented period. However, the high quality of Bunny's, Ramsay's, and Meldrum's work perhaps suggests that Australians, then especially deprived of museum art, were likely to be especially stimulated by it when at last they reached Europe, and were determined to make the most of it while they were there.

By 1915, in the wake of Roger Fry's Post-Impressionist exhibitions in London, painters in Sydney were experimenting with heightened color and nondescriptive autonomous brushwork in emulation of Cézanne and Vincent van Gogh. In 1919 Roy de Maistre (1894–1968) and Roland Wakelin (1887–1971) shared an exhibition of small stylized landscapes organized in terms of color scales and bearing such titles as *Synchromy in Orange Major*. Roy de Maistre eventually developed, in England, a Cubist style as a vehicle for his rather literary preoccupation with the interlace of human relations as well as music. Wakelin remained a warmly romantic landscape and figure painter, and in Melbourne Arnold Shore (1897–1963) and William Frater (1890–1974) became similarly Cézannesque.

Grace Cossington Smith (1892–1984) was more individual. Occasional paintings of high moments in national life—troops embarking in the First World War, church thanksgiving in the Second World War—provoke the realization that all her paintings fix lyrical moments of heightened consciousness in an everyday world. She suddenly sees the exhaustion of pumpkin leaves drooping in heat, the rhythmic order in a grouping of trees, or in a chance arrangement of chairs, the persistent flood of light from outdoors through corridors and mirrored rooms. Such ecstatic delight in grasping order implies a special awareness of potential disorder and chaos. That was Cézanne's greatest quality and Cossington Smith is remarkable for a rare sympathy with the master's content when many of his admirers merely followed his style.

Margaret Preston (1875–1963), a more decorative Post-Impressionist and more assertively modern, was less consistently successful, but at moments could equal anything in Australian art. Around 1927 some Cubist angularity entered her still-life paintings of modern household equipment and of such geometric (hence modernist) Australian flowers as the banksia. Around 1942 her oil paintings began to emulate the earth colors and the simple outlined style of Australian Aboriginal ocher paintings on eucalyptus bark. These were not only still lifes and landscapes, but also wartime military subjects. She was one of many prolific modernist woodcut and linocut printmakers, and her woodcut *The Aeroplane* is an earlier essay at honoring Aboriginal art by introducing its primitivism (the concentric rings of sound at the aeroplane's propellers) to the world of self-conscious modernism.

In 1932 in Sydney, Dorrit Black's Modern Art Center, followed by Grace Crowley's and Rah Fizelle's school, introduced an academic Cubist style to Australia. Out of this circle there later developed the major Constructivist Abstract painters Ralph Balson (1890–1964) and Frank Hinder (1906–92) and the sculptor Margel Hinder (1906–). Their principal works of that kind belong to the 1940s and 1950s and like most such abstraction theirs aimed at metaphors of scientific truths and spiritual states of universal order. Also in 1932, but in Melbourne, a reality-based modernism stressed firm, solid, pictorial construction but soon took on board Romantic and Surrealist attitudes. Peter Purves Smith (1912–49) and Russell Drysdale (1912–81) were the outstanding products of that school. Ian Fairweather, (1891–1974), an English Post-Impressionist painter who had migrated between Shanghai, Bali, Melbourne, and other parts of the east, moved towards abstraction in the 1950s after he settled in Queensland. His *Mangrove* (1961–2; Art Gallery of South Australia, Adelaide) has some basis in the mudflats near Brisbane, but it is more a symbolic Tree of Man, paying homage to the linear delicacy and grace of Aboriginal art, the will towards order of Chinese ideogrammatic writing, the layered space of Cézanne.

The early phases of Australia's modernism are closely related to English modernism. Henceforth Australian art would no longer develop in phase with British art.

The war years 1939–45 saw an extraordinary outbreak of collective artistic energy, chiefly in Melbourne, fuelled by the artists' enforced isolation from Europe as well as by social disruption. Realist artists of social conscience, for example

Death of Constable Scanlon from the first series of Ned Kelly paintings by Sidney Nolan; enamel on composition board; 90×121cm (35×48in); 1946. Australian National Gallery, Canberra

William Dobell (1899–1970) and Noel Counihan (1913–86), painted working men as heroes at their difficult labour or memories of general hardship in the 1930s economic depression. Refugee artists from Hitler's Europe imagined the hardships in the Polish ghettoes they had escaped (for example, Josl Bergner, 1920–). The vivid street life of slum children was pointed out (by Danila Vassilieff, 1897–1958, for example). However, the three outstanding painters of the time, Tucker, Nolan, and Boyd, were individualists.

Albert Tucker (1914–) responded to a specific experience of military work in 1942: drawing mutilations in a military hospital for the purposes of plastic surgery. The following year he began his series *Images of Modern Evil*, an expression of the night-time hysteria of Melbourne's cinema and street life. Tucker in 1947 escaped Australia for 13 years in Europe and New York. Direct confrontation with Europe often makes those from transplanted European cultures intensely aware of their own non-European character and in Rome in 1955 Tucker began to paint explorers from Australian history, their features ambiguously treated as an Australian desert landscape.

Barry Humphries in the Character of Mrs Everage by John Brack; oil on canvas; 97×130cm (38×51in); 1969. Art Gallery of N.S. Wales, Sydney

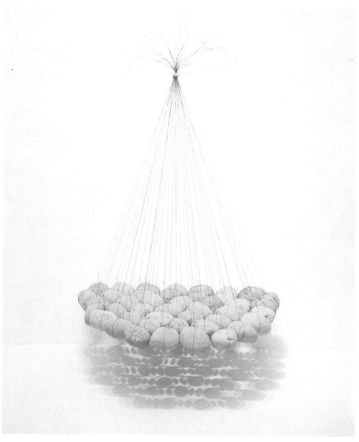

An untitled work by Ken Unsworth; stones, steel wire; 215×104×105cm (85×41×41in); 1975. Australian National Gallery, Canberra

Sidney Nolan (1917–92) explored the high-spirited inventiveness of Klee, Picasso, Matisse, and the sense of wonder and transformation in Rimbaud's poetry. A poet himself, Nolan constantly renewed direct experience of the senses by endless travel; he painted quickly, celebrating the wonder of fresh, innocent experience in bright enamel paint wafted magically into an image. From the 1960s, a more tragic dimension entered his art in darker oil paintings.

If all Nolan's art is about the miracle of transformation—paint into image, perception into form—much of it is about Australian landscape and its inhabitants. He observes the appearance of the land and its light with great accuracy, especially relishing so flat a land's dramatic, horizontal, flaring confrontation with the sky. And he populates it with figures, faces, and animals that have a sense of belonging there. His Ned Kelly paintings of 1946–7 are incidentally concerned with a particular narrative about a particular antiestablishment Irish bushranger who was hanged in Melbourne in 1880 and became an ambiguous folk-hero. They are more concerned with how an outlaw might love the bush, feel at home in it, and bestow upon it the gift of poetry, myth, or legend.

Arthur Boyd (1920–) loved Old Master artists and traditional culture more than modernism and his paintings are usually concerned with private fears and obsessions. A close associate, John Perceval (1923–) used related imagery for war-time subjects but then turned, as did Boyd, more to landscape. Perceval's landscape was usually friendly, worked with, untidy; Boyd's though sometimes similar often introduced his personal symbolism.

The outstanding sculptures associated with the Melbourne

Landscape by Fred Williams; oil on canvas; 92×198cm (36×78in); 1969. Art Gallery of New South Wales, Sydney

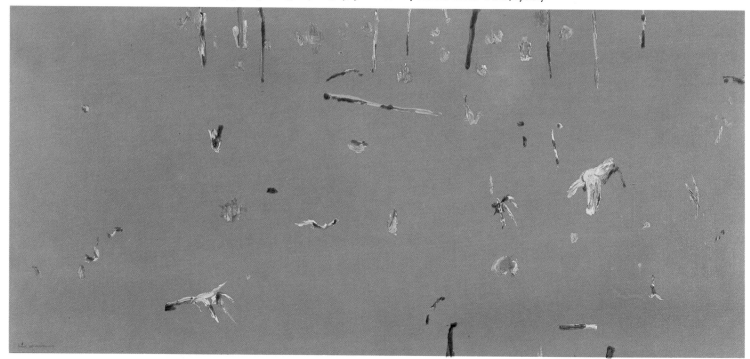

Constructive Painting by Ralph Balson; oil on cardboard; 63×79cm (25×31in); 1951. Australian National Gallery, Canberra

expressionists were the stone carvings of Danila Vassilieff, late works which summed up his admiration for the direct spontaneity of primitive, naive, and child art.

In the 1950s Australia began to receive a steady stream of exhibitions of contemporary European and American art. In general the 1950s were dominated by French art, post-Cubist angularity and intense, saturated color. However, Lloyd Rees (1895–1988), admired as a pen-and-ink and pencil draftsman from the 1920s, developed a later style of high-keyed radiant skies and water. It was a response to the specific charms of Sydney, a harbor city of winding waterways, wayward hills and intense, expansive light. Similar subject matter in more characteristic 1950s style is found in the shifting, Cézann-esque water-views by John Passmore (1904–84).

Abstract art now flourished for the first time—the constructivist art of Ralph Balson, Grace Crowley (1890–1979), and the Hinders, already mentioned—and it too was French in its ordering of color-planes in space. The constructivist painters were closely associated with the sculptor Robert Klippel (1920–). His career began with Surrealist carvings and con-

structions, but by 1952 he was exhibiting Abstract constructions of color-planes on rods. Klippel's innumerable collages and drawings, his ideas for sculpture, his constantly developing personal vocabulary of form, are, like his sculptures, among the finest and most vital works in Australian art.

In the early 1950s the work of the isolated Melbourne stylist, the painter John Brack (1920–), had something of the period style of austere French angularity, but it is transcended in an inventive series of speculations on the artificiality of art: the still life, the nude model, the studio, the posed portrait as conventions; the paint surface, the color-relationship as exercises in taste. For such serious mannerism the best subjects are those that are already works of artifice or skill: window reflections superimposed on an interior, acrobats precariously balanced, competitive ballroom dancers. His portrait of the actor Barry Humphries in female travesty is an admiring homage to perfectionist characterization by means of carefully studied 1969 petit-bourgeoise dress in Melbourne. The subject has as many levels of artifice as the virtuoso play of line, form, and color; it is stretched to the limits of taste.

Fred Williams (1927–82) also emerged from the French 1950s in Melbourne but after an early preference for figure painting in which he relished the expressive presence of Daumier, he settled chiefly for landscape. His apparently highly abstracted landscapes embody very exact observation of color, light, and the characteristic forms that occur in the spacious flatness of Australia. Ambiguously, they can be read both as intimist closeups or as bird's-eye views. As with McCubbin in the 19th century, a superficially monochrome world is seen to be filled with varied and subtle colors, and Williams's great body of black-and-white landscape etchings also underlines the subtle tonal values of the land. But Williams's triumph is to have combined the subtlety of tone and color and the delicacy of small accents and incidents with the grandeur, firmness, and weight of land itself: his forms hold their place on the surface of the canvas as no others in Australian landscape art; they have self-possession and stability as well as energy. Previous Australian landscape painters had seen the land in many different and illuminating ways: Williams was the first not only to see it but also to grasp it.

Abstract Expressionism first came to Australia as French *Tachisme* in the late 1950s. Tony Tuckson (1921–73) was unusual in equating his earlier Abstract Expressionist paintings not with landscape but with the humanity of graphism, of communication through writing or through Aboriginal symbols. Even more unusual, he occasionally adumbrated the human face. The artist himself was a presence in Tuckson's work.

An early reaction against Abstract Expressionism was that of the Imitation Realists, a group consisting of Mike Brown (1938–), Ross Crothall (1934–) and Colin Lanceley (1938–) which in 1962 dragged real life back into art by means of poetic Dadaist rehabilitation of neglected, outcast materials (found objects, junk) and an embrace of outcast styles (child art, naive art, commercial art, Realism). Pop art, a more specific celebration of large-scale advertising and media images, was a style of some influence on Richard Larter (1929–) but otherwise had little influence in Australia. It was American-style color abstraction which in the late 1960s largely swept Abstract Expressionism aside.

Among these Conceptual abstractionists appeared the beginnings of the strong move into photographic media which characterized the 1970s. Photography had been confined chiefly to photojournalism in the mid 20th century, but later revived its traditional concerns for beauty and strangeness at the same time as painters and sculptors began to make use of photography as the prime medium for Conceptual art and as a documentary medium for ephemeral landscape sculptures, body sculptures, and performance art. Of all works of landscape art the best known to the general Australian public is the mile of coast at Little Bay, Sydney, wrapped in 1969 by Christo (1935–), a visiting artist from New York. Since it existed for only six weeks it is known chiefly from its photographs.

Performance art was as strong in the mid 1970s as landscape and ecology sculpture. Ken Unsworth (1931–) makes sculptures that are metaphors of bodily experiences of heaviness, suspension, and compression at their most extreme limits: the sculptures are alternatives to the performances in which his own body is the principal art material. Mike Parr (1945–) and Stelarc (1946–) are other performance artists whose work is strongly individual and obsessive.

Printmaking since the mid 1970s has been most interesting in the form of screenprint posters made outside the traditional art world by collectives of political, feminist, and other social activists. Craftwork of all kinds has also flourished, not only ceramics, though the ceramic tradition was strongest, both in the pure Far Eastern manner and in the rougher, more sculptural manner of Californian funk art.

Painting participated during the revivals of realism and expressionism in the 1970s. The realist Ivan Durrant (1947–) showed an individual, tender concern for animals; the expressionist Peter Booth (1940–) made public his personal nightmares.

If Australian art has had any new characteristics in the 1980s they are partly due to more than 10 years of jet travel. Australia no longer seems physically isolated from its cultural sources on the other side of the world, nor from the alternatives available to the north, in China and Japan. Nor is the third cultural stream, from the Australian aboriginal, so psychologically distant as before. Long-term expatriation by Australian artists is no longer common. Since the visit of Christo to Australia in 1969 there has been a steady stream of European, American, and Japanese artist-visitors. And Australian Aboriginal art and artists, though preserving a tribal base, have become a part of the big-city art world. The result is a more relaxed individualism. Earlier there were mass movements, alternately nationalist and internationalist. Now Australian artists have begun to take an interest in the history of Australian art, and therefore to exert pressure for its inclusion, for the first time, in international surveys of art.

DANIEL THOMAS

Bibliography. Burn, I. et al. *The Necessity of Australian Art*, Sydney (1988). McCulloch, A. and S. *Encyclopedia of Australian Art*, Sydney and London (1964; revised 1994).

54

SOUTH AFRICAN ART

Pondo Woman by Irma Stern; oil on canvas; 86×72cm (34×28in); 1929. Pretoria Art Museum (see page 974)

Every society has a cultural background rooted in the past, but in few are origins and recent history divided by such a yawning, silent chasm as in South Africa. The earliest of what are considered as South Africa's "Old Masters" were heirs of Western culture and many were active well into the 20th century. Yet the real dawn of South African art took place in a Paleolithic era (*c*30,000–10,000 BC) and preceded the coming of Europeans by many thousands of years. That art is a remarkable heritage of paintings and engravings, on the surfaces of rocks and in natural shelters. There is no certainty as to the identity of the hunting, food-gathering peoples who produced the images; they are generally assumed to have been the ancestors of the nomadic San tribes—the so-called Bushmen—whose surviving members live today in the Kalahari Desert.

The primary subject matter of South Africa's lithic art is the animal. Figures of men occur, but they are probably of more recent origin and are usually conventionalized, whereas the animals are more commonly depicted as perceptual likenesses—in outline, monochrome, or polychrome. Those images were the first local documents of man's encounter with primeval nature. Although rock art continued in southern Africa

after the subcontinent was settled from the West, it belongs in spirit to another time frame and gives expression to a state of mind Europeans had long forgotten.

South Africa's modern cultural era began during the 17th century, when the Cape was colonized by representatives of the Dutch East India Company of Holland. The indigenous Khoi-San peoples—the Bushmen and the Hottentots—retreated as settlers drove ever deeper into the interior. Ancestral shrines and shelters were barely noticed by the European pioneers. The first colonists came from a European society that was experiencing a golden age of cultural achievement, but they themselves were yeomen, mariners, and farmers, too preoccupied with survival to give attention to the fine arts.

It was in the field of architecture that the colonists made the first artistic response to both the very different climate and topography and to the much-altered way of life encountered at the Cape. The whitewalled, thatched, gabled "Cape Dutch" homesteads of the 18th century share esteem with the refined proportions of contemporaneous public buildings and townhouses, as examples of one of the world's most attractive styles of colonial architecture.

The beginnings of sculpture in South Africa were intimately

An example of rock painting, from a farm in the Orange Free State

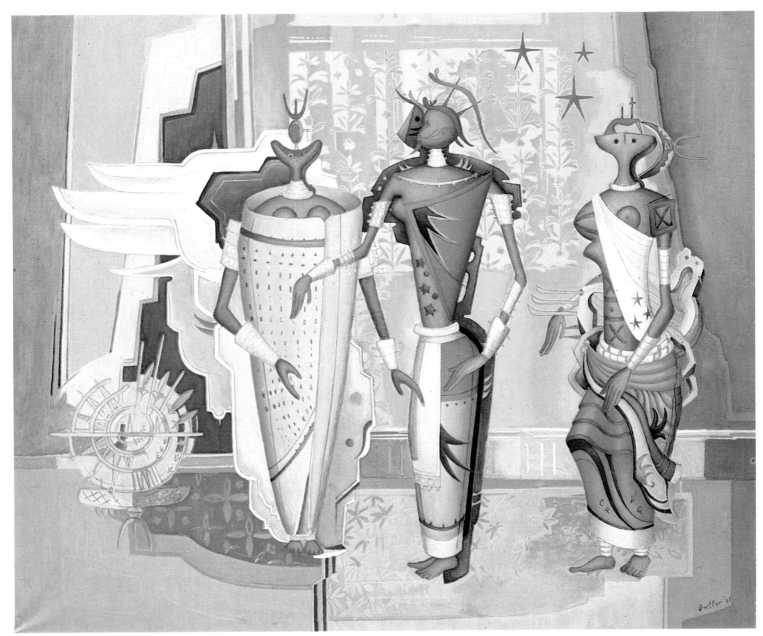

Hieratic Women by Alexis Preller; oil on canvas; 85×101cm (33×40in); 1955. Johannesburg Art Gallery

associated with Cape Dutch architecture. For unlike the tribes of West and Central Africa, the black peoples who had migrated into the subcontinent from the northeast had no tradition of sculptural expression. There were thus no indigenous precedents. The individual regarded as South Africa's first sculptor, Anton Anreith (1754–1821), was born and trained in Germany and executed the bulk of his oeuvre in embellishing Cape Town buildings. Anreith settled in the Cape in 1777. Almost 100 years were to elapse before the commencement of any organized artistic activity in South Africa.

It was only in the latter half of the 19th century that circumstances of life in the Cape Colony and in the interior became at all conducive to professional artistic practice and public exhibition. There was now a greater sense of permanence among the white community, though it was nonetheless an archetypal colonial society. Indeed, most of the early professional artists were settlers, primarily from England and the Netherlands, who had acquired their training and their viewpoints in the European communities from which they stem-

med. South African art of the period was thus essentially provincial and derivative in character. Painting tended to reflect—in somewhat jaded, academic terms—the awe with which the majestic landscape was regarded. Few painters were able to come to terms with South Africa's bright light and spacious atmosphere, and fewer still seemed to be aware of the innovations of the modern movements in Europe.

Following the declaration of Union in 1910 the country's development was accelerated: towns and cities expanded, industrialization commenced. But South Africa was still far from being an urbanized society, and its art reflected the condition. In continuing the dominance of landscape themes in easel painting three figures stood out: Hugo Naudé (1869–1941), Pieter Wenning (1873–1921), and Jacob Hendrik Pierneef (1886–1957). All foreswore the previous dependence on academic realism.

However, it was not only how they were expressed but also the perceptions being given visual form that altered as the 20th century proceeded. The most notable changes concerned

Symbols of Life by Walter Battiss; oil on canvas; 122×122cm (48×48in); 1967. Pretoria Art Museum

attitudes to man and to the African identity. The first significant interest in human subject matter was manifested fairly early in this century by the realist sculptor Anton van Wouw (1862–1945). He won initial acclaim for his interpretation of themes and figures venerated by the Boers. But he was also the first artist to create percipient portraits of black models and to portray black figures engaging in traditional pursuits and practices.

The first painters to be more concerned with people than with scenery were also the first to introduce European subjectivism into local art, during the 1930s. Two of them, Irma Stern (1894–1966) and Maggie Laubser (1886–1973), had been directly influenced by German Expressionism, but they differed considerably in their individual application of the features they adopted. Laubser created a highly personal, folkloric world, inhabited by colored fishermen and peasants. Stern was fascinated by the sensuous beauty of unspoilt Africa and the vital splendor of its tribal figures. The themes of both were mainly African, but their styles were European.

Although the creation of artistic objects, for whatever purpose, occupied a very minor role in black South African culture, there was one form of artistry unique to local tribes, a

Above: Confrontation by Edoardo Villa; steel; height 423cm (167in); 1978. Collection of the artist

Right: Seated Couple by Cecil Skotnes; engraved woodpanel; 70×51cm (28×20in); 1965. Egon Guenther Gallery, Johannesburg

tradition that excelled among the 'Ndebele peoples of the Transvaal: the embellishing of walls of adobe houses with colorful painted decoration. The decoration was and is executed by the women of the tribe, a characteristic which unites it with the total pattern of South African artistic activity, in which women have played a larger role than in any other known society.

The first evidence of a conscious artistic encounter between the post-Renaissance West and the heritage of ancient Africa appeared during the 1940s. It stemmed, on the one hand, from the fascination exerted by the 'Ndebele murals on the imagination of the Pretorian artist Alexis Preller (1911–75); on the other, from a long-delayed communion with the spirit of the ancient artists of the rocks. Although the original colonists had taken little note of South Africa's treasury of rock art, it aroused the curiosity of later archaeologists. It was appreciated mainly for its archaeological significance, until it attracted the attention first of the landscapist Pierneef and later, and more lastingly, of the imaginative Walter Battiss (1906–82). Battiss was immensely impressed by the aesthetic quality inherent in the works. Not only did he energetically record and publicize the art, he also identified himself with the "ancient men" of Africa and adopted many of their formal devices into his own contemporary style of painting. Preller found greater affinity with the mystique of Africa than with its forms, but jointly the two artists introduced a new perception of the continental past into the art of present-day South Africa.

The postwar rush to close the gap that still divided South African art from the modern Western movements coincided with a surge of industrialization, urbanization, and technological advancement in the 1950s. The development was coupled with acute awareness of the "winds of change" sweeping through Africa—and with a need among all South Africans, particularly whites, to establish an identity within the complex ethos of the continent. "Africanism" became a dominant theme of local art. For the first time also there was evidence of emergent artistic interest among the urban black community.

A central figure in the encouragement of black artistic aspiration was the Johannesburg artist Cecil Skotnes (1926–). He also epitomized a new phase in the South African collective consciousness, giving expression in his colored engraved woodpanels to his awareness of the country's duel heritage of African and Western culture. Skotnes was a member, in the 1960s, of the small Amadlozi Group, which became the first professional artistic fellowship to number a black artist among its members, the sculptor Sydney Kumalo (1935–). Before long other promising black newcomers had begun to draw attention. Paradoxically, however, this "African" art developed solely in response to Western urban inspiration. The other sculptor in the Amadlozi Group was the Italian immigrant Edoardo Villa (1920–). To his embodiment in bronze and steel of the elusive spirit of the land, he later added a further dimension of the South African experience: the encounter with contemporary technology. Villa's interpretations of African technological man brought the art of the 1960s to a climax.

The burning issue of the 1970s was the relationship of man to man. Humanism dominated; "relevance" became the primary requirement; "Protest Art" became the vehicle of many younger artists, black and white.

ESMÉ BERMAN

Resistance or Protest art also dominated the 1980s, the central concern being what form resistance should take. Some argued for an art that explicitly opposed apartheid and asserted a black South African identity. Others argued that when art becomes propaganda it loses its profounder significance, and that the cause of a democratic humanism was best served by allowing artists complete freedom, especially from political dictates.

The range and quality of the artistic response to the situation is illustrated by the works of (among others) Johannes Maswanganyi (1948–), Johannes Chauke (c1930–), Shelley Sachs (1950–), Chabani Cyril Manganyi (1959–) Dumile (1939–), Freddie Ramabulana (1930–), and William Kentridge (1955–). The work of such artists, whether expressing a rural or an increasingly urban imagination, often draws strongly on craft traditions.

With the dismantling of apartheid in the early 1990s there was a profound shift in emphasis from resistance to integration. The challenge now, as in many African countries, is how artists living through a period of profound social and cultural change are to fashion a national identity that draws on both African and European traditions.

CHRIS MURRAY

Bibliography. Berman, E, *Art and Artists in South Africa*, Cape Town (1983). Fransen, H. *Three Centuries of South African Art*, Johannesburg (1982). Manaka, M. *Echoes of African Art: A Century of Art in South Africa*, Johannesburg (1987). Nettleton, A. and Hammond-Tooke, D. *African Art in South Africa*, Johannesburg (1989). Williamson, S. *Resistance Art in South Africa*, London (1989).

INDEX